世界交通运输工程技术论坛（WTC2021）论文集

（中册）

世界交通运输大会执委会 编

人民交通出版社股份有限公司
北京

内 容 提 要

本书为世界交通运输工程技术论坛（WTC2021）论文集，是由中国公路学会、世界交通运输大会执委会精选的378篇论文汇编而成。此论文集重点收录了交通运输工程领域的前沿研究及创新成果，分为公路工程、桥梁工程、隧道工程、交通工程、运输规划、水上运输、轨道交通、航空运输、交叉学科9个方向。

本书可供从事交通运输工程等领域的人员参考，也可供院校相关师生学习。

图书在版编目（CIP）数据

世界交通运输工程技术论坛（WTC2021）论文集：上中下册／世界交通运输大会执委会编．— 北京：人民交通出版社股份有限公司，2021.6

ISBN 978-7-114-17355-4

Ⅰ．①世… Ⅱ．①世… Ⅲ．①交通工程—文集 Ⅳ．①U491-53

中国版本图书馆CIP数据核字（2021）第095758号

Shijie Jiaotong Yunshu Gongcheng Jishu Luntan(WTC2021)Lunwenji(Zhongce)

书　　　名：	世界交通运输工程技术论坛（WTC2021）论文集（中册）
著　作　者：	世界交通运输大会执委会
责任编辑：	韩亚楠　郭晓旭
责任校对：	赵媛媛　卢　弦
责任印制：	张　凯
出版发行：	人民交通出版社股份有限公司
地　　　址：	(100011)北京市朝阳区安定门外外馆斜街3号
网　　　址：	http://www.ccpcl.com.cn
销售电话：	(010)59757973
总　经　销：	人民交通出版社股份有限公司发行部
经　　　销：	各地新华书店
印　　　刷：	北京交通印务有限公司
开　　　本：	880×1230　1/16
印　　　张：	163
字　　　数：	4900千
版　　　次：	2021年6月　第1版
印　　　次：	2021年6月　第1次印刷
书　　　号：	ISBN 978-7-114-17355-4
定　　　价：	600.00元（含上、中、下册）

（有印刷、装订质量问题的图书由本公司负责调换）

世界交通运输大会执委会学部委员会

编委会

主　　席　　沙爱民　张占民
副 主 席　　龙奋杰　陈春阳　安　实　顾祥林
　　　　　　王云鹏　刘　攀　赵　鹏　何　川
　　　　　　杜修力　严　伟　王小勇　谈传生
　　　　　　吴超仲　周建庭　巨荣云

编辑委员会

主　　任　　刘文杰
委　　员　　汪海年　陈艾荣　陈建勋　陈　峻
　　　　　　姚恩建　葛颖恩　张卫华　曹先彬
　　　　　　王兴举　等

本 册 目 录

第三篇 隧道工程

软弱围岩隧道锁脚锚管力学特性现场模拟试验
………………………………………………………… 石 州 罗彦斌 陈建勋 刘伟伟 李 尧(1125)
浅埋超大跨小净距隧道合理净距优化研究 ………………………… 宋泽光 陈建勋 罗彦斌(1131)
基于模糊主成分分析的隧道原位扩挖爆破参数优化 ………… 常宏涛 任 锐 王亚琼 李嘉琦(1139)
Cloud-computing- and Big-data-based Integrated Information Platform for TBM
　　Construction—massive Data Collection, Management and Mining
　　………………………… Liujie Jing　Lianhui Jia　Jianbin Li　Shoutian Xu　Xiangxiang Wang(1146)
考虑空气层的寒区隧道防冻隔温层表面铺设研究 ………………… 肖 镇 李邦兴 姚孟其(1159)
寒区运营隧道冻害风险评估体系 ………………………………………………………… 肖 镇(1163)
隧道群连接段光照环境研究 …………………………………………………………… 李洪祥(1168)
基于图像处理的隧道火灾烟雾识别算法研究 …… 陶 杰 朱熙豪 郑于海 刘海萍 汪内利(1173)
某山区国道千枚岩隧道群病害处治及关键技术分析 ……… 陈祥斌 康孝先 周子豪 陈俞嘉(1181)

第四篇 交通工程

全国联网收费形势下高速公路稽核工作建议 ………………………………………… 宗 原(1189)
Real-time Traffic Signal Control of Logistics Park Based on Web Crawler Technology
　　………………………………………………… Jie Li　Ruimin Li　Yufei Yue　Zheng Li(1192)
基于冲突分析技术的公交专用道设置安全影响研究 ………………………… 侯宁昊 张 晖(1203)
The Evaluation on Anti-Interference Reliability of Highway Network and Calculation
　　Examples during the COVID-19 Outbreak
　　………………………… Wen Deng　Leihong Dong　Jinsong Ye　Guorui Li　Mingyue Yan(1208)
基于非线性综合法的单交叉口交通状态评价方法 ………………………… 徐 琰 张伟斌(1215)
城际交通综合感知的多群组结构方程模型 ………………………………… 王建军 张宇辉(1225)
基于家庭结构变化的家庭成员出行方式选择研究 ………………………… 李芷倩 张 敏(1234)
基于MNL模型的中小城市学生通学方式影响因素研究 ……………… 张祎薇 潘卫龙(1237)
基于二项Logit模型的西安市P&R换乘行为的影响因素分析
　　……………………………………………… 张 鹏 翁婷婷 赵宇飞 李佳晨 赵家充(1242)
基于SERVQUAL模型的高速铁路车站旅客满意度调查分析
　　……………………………………………… 罗江莲 吴 娟 梁同天 徐志中 栾鹏博(1246)
城市干道车辆的初始车道选择、换道时机及协作换道的实证研究 ……… 章宇凯 祁宏生(1250)
基于零膨胀模型的机动车-电动车事故频次研究 … 秦 丹 魏 雯 杜雨萌 董傲然 朱 彤(1258)
Trajectory-data-based Velocity Prediction of Vehicles Across Intersection
　　………………………………………………………… Xu Liu　Zeyu Shi　Yangzhou Chen(1267)

基于神经网络的交叉口通行时间预测 ·· 袁新利 师泽宇 陈阳舟(1276)
How Much Extra Cost Can be Induced by a Freeway Toll Plaza: a Quantifying Approach
　　Based on Data-mining ·············· Shanshan Wei　Shichao Chen　Jin Ran　Lin Wang(1281)
交叉口自行车事故严重程度的差异性分析 ··· 刘　婷　杜志刚(1289)
小城镇城区公交系统优化策略——以浙江天台为例
　　··· 刘歆余　丁　剑　倪丽莉　韩　斌　严　馨(1296)
Macroscopic Traffic Emission Analysis of Xi'an City using MOVES Model
　　·············· Tianqi Wang　Lan Yang　Fei Hui　Mengjie Han　He Sheng(1302)
基于长短时记忆神经网络的城市主干道流量预测 ·· 胡煦生(1312)
Big Data Applications in Rail from Academic to Commercial View
　　·············· Rui Xue　Zhiqiang Ma　Xiaoning Ma　Dongsheng Yang　Siqi Sun(1319)
浅谈交通强国背景下中小城市如何构建综合立体交通网——以淮安市金湖县为例
　　··· 钱　芳　邹俊杰　莫明龙(1329)
基于多源数据的区域综合交通OD分布研究 ·· 周　涛　白　桦　潘卫鹏(1333)

旧城更新背景下城市交通综合改善策略研究——以武汉市归元片为例
　　··· 马成喜　黄兰莉　邓　帅　王　韩　常四铁(1337)
面向跨江融合发展地区的过江通道交通疏解体系研究——以南京为例
　　··· 陈　昊　汤伟健　罗中萍(1345)
考虑客流特征的常规公交与地铁竞合关系甄别及并行线路优化策略——南京案例
　　··· 刘锡泽　陈学武　孙　健　雷　达　程剑珂(1350)
深圳市地面公交运速提升实践 ··· 张　彬　颜建新(1360)
美丽乡村建设背景下乡村驿站布局与发展研究——以南京市江宁区为例
　　··· 徐新星　李竹薇　申梦婷　曾竹喧　卢佳诚(1368)
城市常规公交网络连通性能分析与改善策略——苏州案例
　　··· 齐　超　陈学武　周　航　王　瑄(1373)
地铁瓶颈区段定制公交线路设计方法 ··············· 郑姝婕　陈学武　李少彬　华明壮(1382)
基于共享单车轨迹的社区微循环公交布设方法——南京案例
　　··· 程剑珂　陈学武　刘锡泽　华明壮(1392)
基于群体关注度的步行过街设施适老性评价方法 ········ 王　迪　翁剑成　王　鑫　孔　宁(1400)
城市片区智能停车管理规划研究及应用 ················ 徐　辉　梁天明　张鹏鹏(1404)
超高层城市综合体停车泊位指标研究——以南京金鹰世界项目为例
　　··· 杨　斌　祁　健　罗中萍　崔竞誉　宁　丹(1408)
基于大数据的智慧停车管理系统设计 ··············· 周晓阳　邓高峰　刘一濠　姜　亮(1413)
Research on Parking Route Optimization Based on Improved Dijkstra Algorithm
　　··· Wenya Liu　Yergneng Xu(1420)
基于场所特性的非机动车道宽度标准精细化研究 ······· 吴俊获　姚　霏　常四铁　焦文敏(1430)
基于轨道交通换乘的公共自行车站点选址研究 ········· 潘卫龙　张祎薇　韩永贵(1434)
基于SWOT模型的温州机场发展策略研究 ··· 励　瑾　钟　罡(1439)
智能网联车换道决策建模研究综述 ················ 罗开杰　何赏璐　叶　茂(1444)
交旅融合背景下农村公路旅游指引标志分级设置方法研究
　　··· 罗中萍　王卫军　余　豪　于思源　金江凯(1451)
武汉市城市道路修建性详细规划编制标准研究 ········ 焦文敏　刘　凯　常四铁　王岳丽(1456)

城市副中心核心区交通品质提升研究及应用 ………………………………… 谭振霞 潘晓玮(1460)
基于移位左转的直行非机动车道优化设计方法 ………………………………… 杨 杰 邵海鹏(1466)
一级公路平面交叉口合理间距值分析 ………………… 史伟伟 武方涛 郝鑫桐 张祎薇 潘卫龙(1477)
阜新市某主干道交通优化设计 ……………………………………… 邹利刚 陈宽民 杨 杰(1481)
城市道路交通设计评价体系与方法研究 ………………………… 汪 涛 马 岳 江泽浩 孙 伟(1489)
中小型高速铁路枢纽配套交通设施综合评估研究 ……………………………… 郑明伟 蔡逸峰(1496)
An Improved Multi-valued Cellular Automaton Approach for Non-motorized Traffic
　　Flow Considering Counterflow ……………… Yifan Dong　Haipeng Shao　Miaoran Zhang(1504)
Research of Car-following Models Based on Deep Learning in Different Traffic Scenarios
　　……………………………………………………… Xing Guo　Cheng Wei　Wenwei Wang(1514)
基于交通波参数的排队长度估计方法 ………………………………… 白孜帅 张伟斌 张峻屹(1522)
Time-space Trajectory Similarity-based Performance Evaluation of Signal Coordination
　　Via Smartphones ……………………………………… Zhenlong Li　Jingsi Zhang　Lei Yang(1530)
普通信号交叉口行人早开先退相位设置研究 …………………………… 宋 杰 王永岗 郑少娅(1543)
流量不对称干线信号协调相位设计研究 ……………… 李丙烨 张 敏 向宇杰 彭恩鹏 李超同(1550)
基于通行需求的绿灯时间计算模型 ………………………… 董栩鑫 张伟斌 张峻屹 姜 影(1556)
Simulation Analysis of Applicable Conditions of Two-Way Left-Turn Lane under
　　the Condition of Multi Factor Combination
　　………………………………………… Junjie Cai　Binghong Pan　Zhenjiang Xie　Lin Zong(1561)
基于虚幻4引擎的道路交通场景逼真化建模 …………………………………… 雷凯婷 杜志刚(1572)
快速路高峰期激励诱导出行——以苏州为例 …………………… 赵 坡 施庆华 王 翔 吴 戈(1577)
基于公交专用道复用的疫情期间应急运输车辆管控模式研究
　　……………………………………………………………… 蒋 瑶 赵 智 李泓辰 王江锋(1582)
疫情持续期间城市公共交通的设施改善及运营优化研究 ……………………………… 张焕炯(1587)
中小城市公交优先发展策略研究——以浙江省天台县为例
　　……………………………………………… 陈坤杰 杜 璇 朱雨晴 朱力颖 刘歆余(1591)
Electric Bus Scheduling Optimization Based on Charging Strategy
　　………………………… Guo Linfeng　Xue Yongzhe　Liang Jingxin　Ji Hao　Han Yan(1596)
城市机动化与公共交通运输需求关联分析研究
　　……………………………………………………………………… 秦选龙 杨 琦 魏 娜(1605)
基于RBF神经网络PID的四轮转向汽车循迹控制仿真研究
　　……………………………………………………… 刘 强 杨蔡进 张卫华 张众华(1611)
无人驾驶货车编队控制方法综述 ………… 鲁果亚 吴问涛 孙怡平 董海霞 文子卿 晏 秋(1618)
A Model with Time Windows for Share-A-Ride Problems
　　…………………………………………… Min Zhang　Jing Xue　Kaijun Zhou　Shuguang Hou(1626)
V2X与边缘计算相结合的交叉口高精度地图信息服务系统架构及其应用
　　……………………………………………… 周 轶 魏俊生 安 康 韩 慧 刘靖馨(1635)
借非机动车道右转交通组织在城市道路交叉口中的实践与探索
　　……………………………………………………… 廖诗琪 谢和杰 尤 彬 刘长清(1641)
对"超级高速公路"的几点深度思考 …………………………………………………… 张焕炯(1646)
中国国际航空航天博览会交通运输保障方案研究 …………………………………… 陈 叶 周 越(1649)

Literature Review of HOV Lane and HSR Control on Freeway ………… Yao Xu　Huachun Tan(1654)
Intelligent Scheduling Algorithm of Bus Priority Control Strategy in the Internet of
　　Vehicles Environment ………………… Yao Jiang　Zhi Zhao　Hongchen Li　Jiangfeng Wang(1662)
进口单独放行交叉口非机动车组织仿真分析 ………… 杨　震　马健霄　王宝杰　董可可(1675)
城市轨道交通地下行人设施评价方法 ………… 郝鑫桐　杨　帅　武方涛　史伟伟　黄　旭(1682)
城市相邻景区内部路径优化分析及交通组织优化——以西安市大唐不夜城为例 ……… 陈桂珍(1688)
基于区块链的超限超载运输治理应用研究 ………………… 张　炜　施　展　赵彩娥(1692)
基于科学知识图谱的汽车智能化发展研究 ………… 张奕骏　张　晖　肖逸影　张　琦(1698)
台辉高速公路铁路并行段铁路行驶眩光对高速行车安全影响分析及解决对策研究
　　…………………………………………………… 刘　昊　钱　威　明小梅　陈　杰(1703)
京港澳高速公路河南省路网段运营风险评估与事故预防措施研究
　　…………………………………………… 赵建有　张振东　李　斌　董贝贝　刘清云(1708)
基于博弈论的高速公路合流区汇入决策分析 …… 景云超　朱　彤　王兴隆　李　青　朱秭硕(1713)
礼让行人背景下无信号控制人行横道交通冲突研究 ………… 郑少娅　王永岗　宋　杰(1717)
基于动态PET算法的互通立交合流区交通冲突研究 ………… 宋　杰　王永岗　郑少娅(1723)
基于天气状况和光照条件共同影响的交叉口多车事故影响因素分析
　　…………………… 吴建清　吕　琛　江健宏　皮任东　宋修广　张　朔　何海东　王　冰(1729)
Injury Severity Analysis of Electric Bicycles-Involved-Crashes during Peak Traffic Periods
　　……………………………………………………………… Zishuo Zhu　Tong Zhu　Pei Xie(1738)
分心行为对驾驶员视觉的影响研究 …………………………………………… 米　奇　吉　柯(1745)
交叉口未按规定让行的车辆驾驶行为研究 ………………… 陶　锋　邵海鹏　苏松茂(1752)
Research on Management of Traffic Anomie Behavior Based on Theory of Reasoned Action
　　………………………………………… Guohua Liang　Chenchen Dong　Yanwen Han(1758)
三对应原理之实施8——三三归一续消除 …………………………………………… 黄剑飞(1765)
低速提示音对电动汽车车内噪声影响的测试分析 ………… 马　可　陈　煜　匡成效　仄伟杰(1768)
基于用户调研的换电式出租车满意度与技术需求分析 ………… 李晓菲　李　成　吴忠宜(1774)
基于景观格局的生态旅游公路最优路径模型 …………………………… 陈帅铭　邵海鹏(1779)
跨海大桥建设期应急管理标准体系构建
　　…………………………………… 王　冀　吴忠广　张　宇　孙晓军　潘　硕　陈巍峰(1786)
基于驾驶安全舒适性的公路隧道分类研究 …………………………… 胡江碧　王　旭(1789)
Accessibility of Integrated Transportation Systems Against Debris Flow Hazards
　　………………………………………………………………… Junhao Jiang　Liu Hong(1796)

第三篇 隧道工程

软弱围岩隧道锁脚锚管力学特性现场模拟试验

石 州 罗彦斌 陈建勋 刘伟伟 李 尧

(长安大学公路学院)

摘 要 锁脚锚管在软弱围岩隧道安全施工方面应用广泛,其力学作用机理及合理支护参数的研究对维持结构安全稳定意义重大。本试验根据自主研发设计的隧道钢架——锁脚锚管相互作用模拟试验装置,分析了不同打设角度下锁脚锚管的弯曲应变,研究了锁脚锚管的内力分布及荷载响应情况,并结合不同打设角度下锁脚锚管端部位移和试验前后锚杆的变形情况,揭示了锁脚锚管的力学作用机理,并提出了锁脚锚杆的合理打设长度和角度。现场试验结果表明:锁脚锚管主要靠管口附近部位抵抗弯矩,且锁脚锚管在端部竖向荷载作用下主要依靠其竖向抗弯刚度提供承载力;对于同一端部竖向荷载,锚管端部竖向位移随着打设角度的增大而减小,建议锁脚锚管的合理打设角度和长度分别取为45°和2.5m;孔口围岩的塑性变形和剥离破坏集中在锚管下方部位,主要由锚管的竖向挤压变形引起。

关键词 隧道工程 软弱围岩 锁脚锚管 现场试验 力学特性

0 引 言

锁脚锚管作为软弱围岩隧道建设中的一种常用支护手段,在控制隧道变形沉降和提高结构稳定性方面发挥了重要作用,其结构简单、操作方便、经济适用,因此被广泛应用于以分部开挖法施工的软弱围岩隧道工程建设中[1-2]。其结构力学承载特性及合理支护参数的选取已经成为国内外隧道研究人员普遍关注和重点研究的问题[3]。

近些年来,国内外专家学者和工程技术人员,通过理论分析[4]、数值模拟[5]和工程实践[6-8]等方法对锁脚锚管展开了一系列研究。尽管锁脚锚管在软弱围岩隧道变形控制和大变形灾害处治中应用广泛,但目前对于锁脚锚管的作用机理和受力特性的研究仍不够全面和深入,尤其对于锁脚锚管在围岩荷载作用下的受力判别以及应变和位移的分布变化规律等方面缺乏系统地研究,大多相关研究是采用数值模拟或者通过监测隧道变形而间接反映锁脚锚管的作用效果[7-8],缺乏对其更为直接、有针对性的试验研究,并且对于软弱围岩条件下锁脚锚管的合理打设角度、长度等力学参数缺乏符合工程实际的定量化分析研究。同时,由于隧道中锁脚锚管属于隐蔽型的支护措施,结构受力复杂,操作空间狭小,现有的结构受力测试方法和传感器无法直接应用于锁脚锚管的现场测试。因此,需要寻求一种能够模拟隧道中锁脚锚管实际传力机制和准确测量锚管力学及变形特性的试验方法,对复杂环境条件下锁脚锚管的内力分布规律及结构变形特性进行研究。

本文借鉴传感器外贴、导线内引的思路,提出采用非电量电测法对锁脚锚管的受力变形进行测量,设计出一套可以模拟隧道中钢架对锁脚锚管竖向作用力的试验装置对锁脚锚管进行了现场模拟试验。通过分析不同打设角度下锁脚锚管的弯曲应变,揭示了锁脚锚管的内力和变形分布及荷载响应情况,并结合不同打设角度下锁脚锚管端部位移和试验前后的变形情况,对锁脚锚管的力学作用机理和结构承载特性进行了系统全面地研究。

1 锁脚锚杆模拟试验设计

本试验选取与隧道围岩土质相同的黄土边坡来模拟隧道围岩,通过加载装置在锁脚锚管端部加载模拟钢架对锁脚锚管的竖向作用,采用在锁脚锚管管壁外粘贴箔式电阻应变片、导线内引的方式测量管身应变。为研究锁脚锚管在不同打设角度下的力学特性,本现场试验锁脚锚管的打设角度分别为0°、30°、

45°和60°。

1.1 试验锚管设计

本试验采用与剪子岔2号隧道中相同规格的无缝钢管制作试验锚管。试验锚管相关物理力学参数如表1所示。选用量程为±20000με的BE120-5AA电阻应变片进行锚管应变监测。试验锚管测点布置如图1所示,每个断面上测点布置图如图2所示。

锁脚锚管物理力学参数 表1

内径(mm)	长度(m)	外径(mm)	弹性模量(GPa)	屈服强度(MPa)	变形系数(m^{-1})
43	2.5	51	200	205	2.776

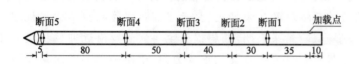

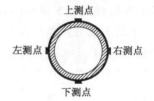

图1 锚管测点布置图(尺寸单位:mm)　　　　图2 各断面测点布置图

为降低钻孔对锚管截面强度的影响,锚管测点截面圆周上、下孔与左、右孔2对钻孔交错布置,试验锚管具体处理流程如图3所示。

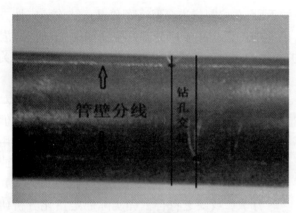

a) 管壁钻孔

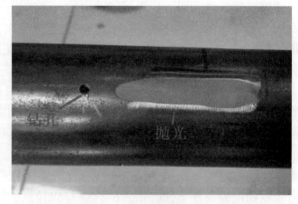

b) 测点抛光

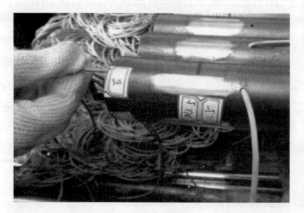

c) 导线穿引

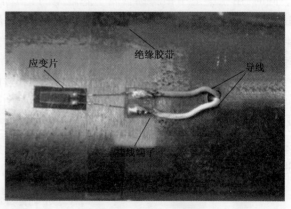

d) 应变片粘贴及导线连接

图 3

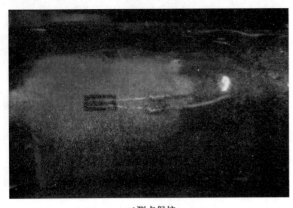

e)测点保护

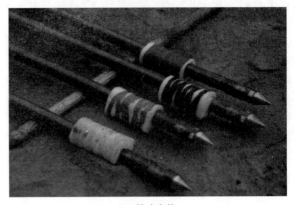

f)锚头安装

图 3　试验锚管设计安装

为抵消沿锚管长度方向土体温度不同而产生的误差,本次试验取与锚管相同的钢管制作了温度补偿块,利用机床从钢管上切割宽度为 2cm、$L=2.5m$ 的板条,将贴好应变片的温度补偿块放置在 $L=2.5m$,$\phi 26mm$,壁厚为 2mm 的镀锌管内,具体如图 4 和图 5 所示。

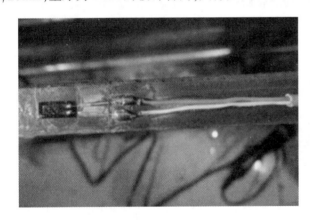

图 4　温度补偿块应变片粘贴

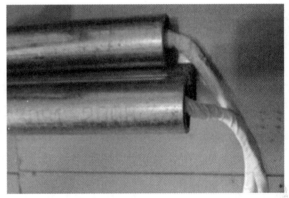

图 5　温度补偿块保护

1.2　现场试验

隧址区位于陕北黄土高原南部,地貌以黄土台塬、黄土梁峁—沟壑为主。试验以与隧道围岩土质相同的边坡模拟围岩,试验区域的土层为上更新统马兰组黄土(Q^{3col}),湿陷性不明显,自然边坡整体稳定性好,土体呈硬塑状。现场对试验边坡黄土取样并进行室内实验测定,土样的工程性质指标如表 2 所示。

围岩土体工程指标参数　　表 2

指标	重度 γ(kN/m³)	弹性模量 E(MPa)	黏聚力 c(kPa)	内摩擦角 ϕ(°)
参数	16.7	31	35	22

现场试验时通过自主研发的加载装置和反力装置在锁脚锚管端部竖向加载模拟钢架对锁脚锚管的竖向作用,通过锚管端部施加荷载的层级变化来模拟锁脚锚管在不同埋深及不同荷载条件下的力学承载机制,如图 6 所示。锚管端部位移采用 SW-40 型手持式激光测距仪并结合白纸描点测量,如图 7 所示。

图6 加载装置及反力装置安装

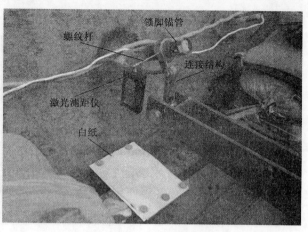

图7 端部位移测量仪器布置

2 锁脚锚模拟试验结果分析

2.1 锁脚锚管各断面弯曲应变的分布变化规律

锁脚锚管各断面测点应变实际上是拉(压)弯组合应变,其分布变化规律主要从两个方面进行分析,即各级荷载作用下锁脚锚管应变沿锚管长度的分布规律和锁脚锚管各方位应变随端部荷载的变化规律。同时根据隧道工程中锁脚锚管以竖向变形为主的承载作用机制,本文中仅对锁脚锚管横截面上下部应力应变分布规律进行重点分析研究。根据材料力学及锚杆轴力分析可知,各断面的上下弯曲应变可由下式计算得到:

$$\varepsilon_{M上下} = \varepsilon_{M上} = \frac{\varepsilon_上 - \varepsilon_下}{2} \tag{1}$$

下面根据各测点应变对弯曲应变进行计算,并对其分布规律进行分析。

2.1.1 各级荷载下弯曲应变沿锚管长度的分布规律

图8为不同打设角度下锁脚锚管各断面上下弯曲应变沿锚管长度的分布情况。

由图8可知:①打设角度一定时,各级荷载作用下锁脚锚管上下弯曲应变随着锚管长度的增加而迅速衰减直至趋于零,说明锚管主要为其加载点附近的部分管段承受弯矩;②当荷载相同时,对于同一断面,其上下弯曲应变值随着打设角度的增大而减小,其原因是随着打设角度的增大,竖向荷载在锚管端部的横向分力随之减小,这一分布规律表明增大锁脚锚管的打设角度有助于减小其管身的竖向弯矩;③锁脚锚管端部荷载的传递长度因锚管打设角度而异,此处用上下弯曲应变第一零点长度来衡量(某一荷载作用下弯曲应变为零对应的断面的最小锚管长度),打设角度分别为0°、30°、45°和60°时,荷载为8.64kN对应弯曲应变第一零点长度分别为1.50m、1.15m、1.65m和1.40m,容易得知,当锁脚锚管的打设角度为45°时,端部荷载的传递长度最大,此时锁脚锚管的竖向承载力发挥的最极致。

2.1.2 各个断面的弯曲应变随端部荷载的变化规律

图9为不同打设角度下锁脚锚管各断面上下弯曲应变随端部竖向荷载的分布情况。

由图9可知:①任意打设角度下,锁脚锚管各个断面的上下弯曲应变在数值上与端部荷载基本呈正相关;②同一打设角度时,各断面上下弯曲应变值随着断面距离加载点的距离增大而减小,说明锁脚锚管能有效将其承受的端部竖向荷载沿其长度方向逐渐向围岩深部传递;③断面1和断面2的上下弯曲应变远远大于其他第三个断面的弯曲应变,说明锁脚锚管主要靠加载端部附近部分承受弯矩;④在相同的端部荷载下,锁脚锚管同一断面处的上下弯曲应变随着打设角度的增大而减小,说明增大锁脚锚管的打设角度有助于改善锁脚锚管的弯矩受力状态。

2.2 锁脚锚管端部位移随端部荷载的变化规律

不同端部荷载作用下锚管端部竖向位移如图10所示。

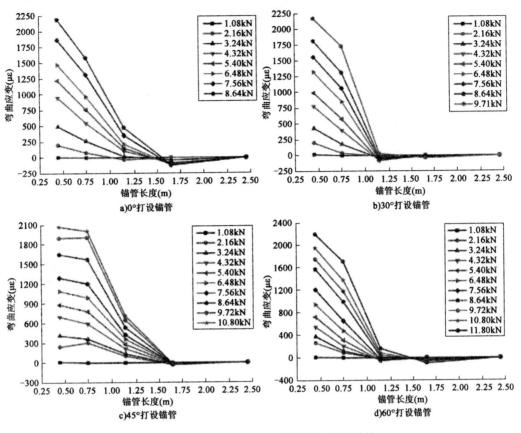

图8 锁脚锚管上下弯曲应变沿锚管长度分布曲线

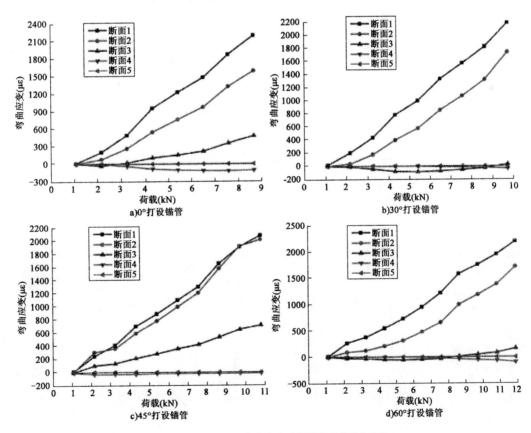

图9 锁脚锚管上下弯曲应变随端部荷载的变化曲线

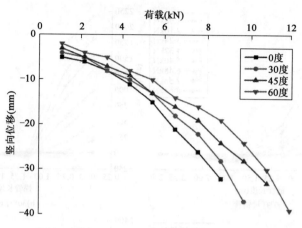

图10 锁脚锚管端部竖向位移随荷载的变化曲线

对于各端部荷载作用下锚管端部竖向位移,由图10可知:①对于不同打设角度下的锁脚锚管,各锚管端部竖向位移随着荷载的走势基本一致。在加载前期,锚管端部竖向位移增速都较为缓慢,随着荷载的逐渐增大,竖向位移增速相应增大,说明随着端部荷载的持续施加,锚管的某些断面测点的应变达到了钢材的屈服应变从而使其变形速率逐渐增大;②相同荷载作用下锚管的端部竖向位移随着打设角度的增大而减小,说明在端部竖向荷载作用下,增大锁脚锚管的打设角度有利于控制其端部竖向位移。

2.3 试验前后锁脚锚管与围岩变形对比分析

为了更好地研究锁脚锚管整体的变形破坏特点,以下对锁脚锚管的变形情况和围岩的破坏情况进行分析研究。图11为不同打设角度下锁脚锚管试验前后的变形对比图。图12为围岩孔口附近试验前后的变形破坏对比图。

a)试验前锁脚锚管

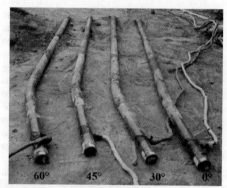
b)试验后锁脚锚管

图11 试验前后锚杆对比图

a)试验前钻孔围岩

b)试验后钻孔围岩

图12 试验前后围岩对比

由图 11 可知,锁脚锚管的变形主要在靠近加载点的一定管身范围内发生弯折变形。经测量,折弯点均位于距锚管端部 55cm 左右的位置,说明锁脚锚管主要靠其孔口附近部分承受荷载。

由图 12 可知,孔口附近均发生了不同程度的围岩剥离破坏,且破坏区域主要集中在钻孔的下部,说明孔口附近围岩主要是在锁脚锚管的竖向挤压下产生了塑性变形和剥离破坏,施工时应注意保护孔口附近围岩并采取适当的补强措施。

3 结 语

本文根据现场模拟试验对锁脚锚管的力学作用机理和结构承载特性进行了系统全面地分析研究,主要结论如下:

(1) 在端部竖向荷载作用下,锁脚锚管的弯曲应变随着锚管长度增加而迅速衰减,锁脚锚管主要靠管口附近部位抵抗弯矩。在端部竖向荷载作用下锁脚锚管主要依靠其竖向抗弯刚度提供承载力。

(2) 锚管端部竖向位移和水平位移均随端部荷载的增加而增大。对于同一端部荷载,竖向位移随着打设角度的增大而减小,结合工程经济性及可操作性可得锁脚锚管的合理打设角度宜取为 45°。

(3) 锁脚锚管的变形破坏主要为集中在孔口附近的弯折破坏,锁脚锚管主要依靠其抗弯刚度提供承载力。孔口围岩的塑性变形和剥离破坏集中在锚管下方部位,主要由锚管的竖向挤压变形引起。

参考文献

[1] 陈建勋.软弱地层隧道初期支护技术—钢架喷网锁脚锚杆组合结构[M].北京:科学出版社,2011.
[2] 陈建勋,王超,罗彦斌,等.高含水量土质隧道不设系统锚杆的试验研究[J].岩土工程学报,2010,32(5):815-819.
[3] 梁辉如,王永东,燕新,等.锁脚锚管—钢拱架在软岩隧道中的力学稳定性研究.[J] 北京交通大学学报,2020,44(4):34-41.
[4] 罗彦斌,陈建勋.软弱围岩隧道锁脚锚杆受力特性及其力学计算模型[J].岩土工程学报,2013,35(8):1519-1525.
[5] 邓国华,邵生俊,陶虎,等.锁脚锚管对土质隧道围岩变形和支护内力的影响研究[J].土木工程学报,2010,43(1):108-113.
[6] 谭忠盛,杨旸,陈伟,等.中老铁路高地应力软岩隧道大变形控制技术研究[J].铁道学报,2020,42(12):171-178.
[7] 黄彬.大断面黄土隧道土石分界段施工技术[J].现代隧道技术,2013,50(1):139-142.
[8] 赖金星,樊浩博,来弘鹏,等.软弱黄土隧道变形规律现场测试与分析[J].岩土力学,2015,36(7):2003-2012.

浅埋超大跨小净距隧道合理净距优化研究

宋泽光 陈建勋 罗彦斌

(长安大学公路学院)

摘 要 合理净距的选择一直是小净距隧道设计与施工过程中的重点与难点,在确保小净距隧道建设的安全性和线路选择方面起着至关重要的作用。为探究浅埋超大跨小净距隧道合理净距的选择问题,本文以山东滨莱高速公路改扩建工程佛羊岭、樵岭前和乐疃三座不同净距的隧道为依托,通过现场试验和数值模拟的方法对不同净距条件下围岩与支护体系的变形与受力情况进行了研究。研究结果表明:小净距隧道先后行洞在施工过程存在明显的相互扰动,并且随着相邻隧道间距的增大,相互扰动在逐渐减小。Flac3D 数值模拟结果表明,不同净距下大跨度小净距隧道先后行洞在施工过程中的相互扰动规律与现场监测结果一致。$1D$ 是先行洞与后行洞产生相互扰动的临界值。

关键词　小净距隧道　合理净距　数值模拟　滨莱高速　特性曲线

0　引　言

近年来,随着经济的快速发展,交通运输需求日益增大,越来越多的高等级公路穿越崇山峻岭,中小跨度隧道已无法满足当下需求,因此大跨度双洞八车道公路隧道成为了建设的重点。山区高等级公路双洞隧道由于地形限制、线路规划、环境保护等原因,隧道选线时常采用小净距隧道方案。

龚建伍等[1]通过建立不同跨度小净距隧道有限元分析模型,对三车道与两车道公路隧道施工过程中的力学特性与围岩稳定性进行对比分析,研究结果表明随着隧道跨度的增大围岩应力状态逐渐变差,且净距越小,差别越大。王辉等[2],通过精确罚函数法以及 Nelder-Mead 优化算法相结合的有限元优化分析计算程序,对建立的参数化模型进行计算。研究结果表明,扁平率为 0.61,开挖间距为 8.5 m 是拟建工程的最优设计方案。陈秋南等[3]基于 Flac3D 数值模拟软件研究大跨度小净距隧道不同施工工法与扁平率对最小合理净距的影响,研究结果表明双侧壁导坑法较适合扁平率为 1.13 的小净隧道施工,最小合理净距为 24m. 杨小礼等[4]结合三座相邻隧道的实际工程,建立隧道荷载结构模型,研究结果表明隧道间的相互作用力随隧道间距增大而增大。

可见,对于大跨度小净距隧道的净距优化问题,过去主要使用数值模拟[5,6]的方法进行研究。此外,隧道跨度多为三车道及以下,对四车道超大跨小净距隧道的研究极为罕见。因此,对于超大跨小净距隧道的净距优化问题,需要结合实际工程进一步研究。

本文依托山东滨莱高速公路改扩建工程中佛羊岭、樵岭前和乐疃三座不同净距的隧道进行现场测试,对不同净距隧道地表沉降、拱顶沉降和净空收敛变化规律进行对比分析。并由于现场实际条件的限制,利用 Flac3D 数值模拟软件,分析 6 种($0.25D/0.5D/0.75D/1D/1.25D/1.5D$,$D$ 代表隧道开挖跨度,下同)净距下先后行洞分部开挖过程中围岩变形情况。

1　工程背景与量测方案

1.1　工程概况

为了对相似地质条件下不同净距隧道分部开挖过程中变形情况进行对比,选择了滨莱高速公路隧道群进行现场试验。本文以佛阳岭隧道,樵岭前隧道,乐疃隧道三座隧道洞口浅埋段为例,分析不同净距下隧道变形情况,隧道分布及洞口情况如图 1 所示,左洞为先行洞,右洞为后行洞。

图 1　滨莱高速公路隧道整体布置图

基金项目:国家自然科学基金资助项目(51978065;41831286)。

1.2 监测方案

根据公路隧道施工设计规范[7]的基本要求，针对小净距隧道的结构特点，施工工法及地质情况，监测内容主要包括地表沉降、拱顶沉降和净空收敛。在三座隧道洞口处各布置一个断面进行地表沉降监测，每组埋设 13 个地表观测点(1~13)代表性监测断面地表沉降测点如图 2 所示。隧道设计断面尺寸与支护参数如图 3 与表 1 所示。

图 2　地表沉降监测点布置图

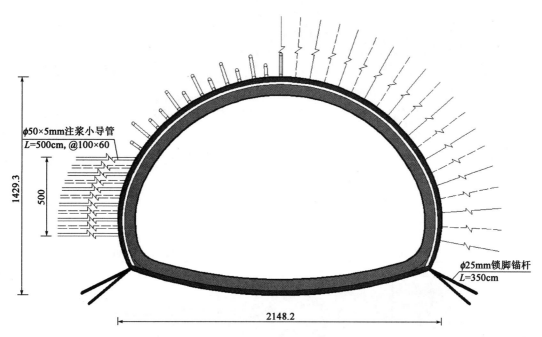

图 3　隧道洞口段支护参数

隧道洞口段支护体系　　　　　　　　　　　　　　表 1

项　目	主要内容
超前支护	$\phi50\times5$mm 双排超前小导管；第一排：$L=3$m，$\alpha=8°\sim12°$，环向间距 40 cm，搭接长度 1.2m；第二排：$L=4.5$m，$\alpha=3°\sim6°$；环向间距 = 40cm，搭接长度 1.5m
初期支护	喷射 C25 混凝土 30cm；$\phi25$ 中空注浆锚杆 $L=500$cm，间距：100cm(环)×60cm(纵)；$\phi8$mm 钢筋网 20cm×20cm(双层)；H200×200mm 型钢架，纵向间距 60cm；预留变形量 18cm
二次衬砌	C30 模筑钢筋混凝土 70cm；400g/m² 无纺布；1.5mm 厚 EVA 防水板

2 围岩变形监测结果与分析

2.1 地表沉降

地表沉降时态曲线如图4所示。

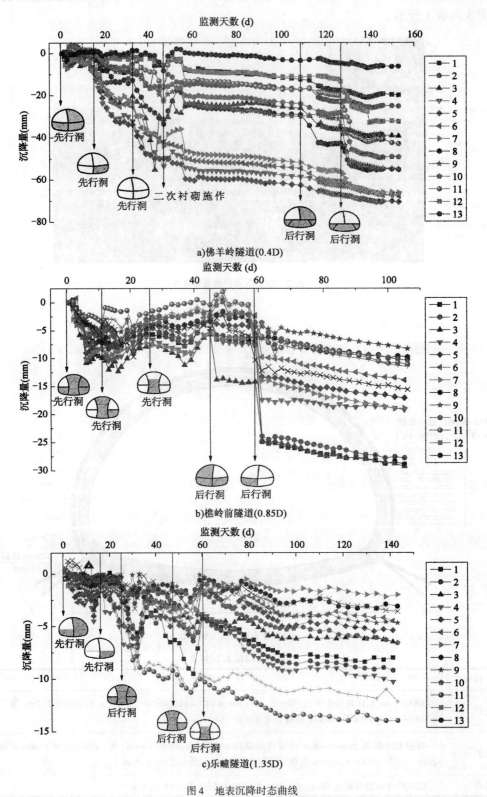

图4 地表沉降时态曲线

由于佛羊岭隧道净距极小,因而为确保施工过程的安全与结构的稳定,后行洞在先行洞二次衬砌施作完毕以后才进行挖掘,其余两座隧道则在二次衬砌施作过程中进行挖掘。由图4可知,先行洞与后行洞开挖过程中,各测点沉降值均产生不同程度的波动。如图4b)所示,樵岭前隧道后行洞开挖过程中,先行洞上方对应点的地表沉降值产生突变,说明后行洞的开挖对先行洞处的围岩产生了明显的扰动。而如图4c)所示,乐疃隧道先后行洞开挖过程中,各点沉降值波动幅度较小,未产生明显的突变现象,且稳定后的最终沉降量远远小于另外两座隧道,说明当相邻隧道间净距较大时,先后行洞开挖过程中的相互扰动明显减弱。

2.2 拱顶沉降与净空收敛

选取围岩条件与埋深相似的樵岭前隧道 ZK108+220 断面与乐疃隧道 ZK105+957 断面进行研究。拱顶沉降时态曲线如图5所示。净空收敛时态曲线如图6所示。

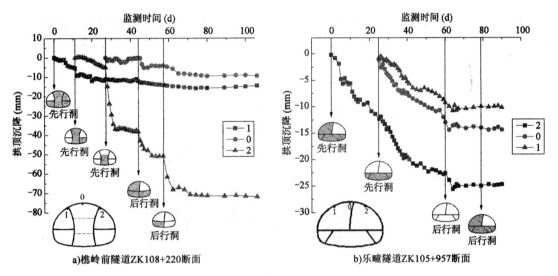

图 5　拱顶沉降时态曲线

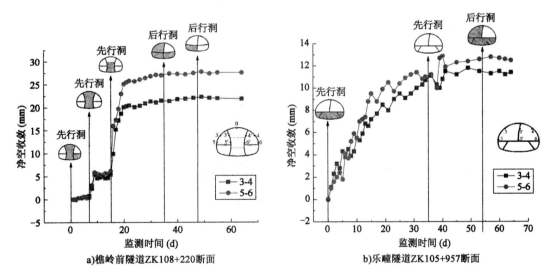

图 6　净空收敛时态曲线

由图5a)可知,中间导洞0号测点处的拱顶沉降值明显小于左右两侧导洞1号与2号测点,且远离后行洞的1号测点处的拱顶沉降值受到后行洞开挖的扰动很小。然而靠近后行洞的2号测点处的拱顶沉降值在后行洞先导与后导开挖后由 -38.3mm 增长到 -50.9mm 与 -72.5mm,后行洞开挖导致的沉降量占总沉降量的47.2%。由此可知,当相邻隧道间净距较小时,后行洞的开挖对先行洞靠近后行洞一侧的边墙扰动较大,更进一步说明了中夹岩墙在施工过程中受到了明显的扰动。由图5b)可知,当隧道净距达到1.35D时,后行洞开挖过程中先行洞各测点拱顶沉降保持稳定,说明此时后行洞开挖对先行洞没有产生扰动。

从图6中可以看出,同一断面净空收敛的最终稳定值远小于拱顶沉降,拱脚(5-6)处的收敛值略大于拱腰处(3-4),且无论净距大小,后行洞施工过程中先行洞净空收敛均保持稳定。这一现象说明超大跨小净距隧道施工过程中围岩主要产生竖向变形,且后行洞的开挖对先行洞净空收敛不产生影响。

3 数值模拟

3.1 隧道开挖模拟

3.1.1 数值计算模型

根据现场试验断面情况建立Flac3D计算分析模型,如图7所示。隧道开挖断面宽度21.48m,洞高14.29m。根据圣维南原理,模型的左右边界均取距离隧道边墙70m,下边界距离隧道70m,隧道埋深27m,沿隧道轴向长度60m。

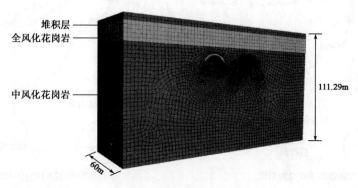

图7 三维计算模型

3.1.2 隧道开挖计算方案

左右洞均采用上台阶CD法施工,施工工法与顺序如图8所示,左洞开挖完毕后再开挖右洞,单次开挖进尺为2m,各部分开挖面之间相距20m。

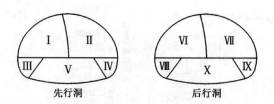

图8 上台阶CD施工步骤

3.1.3 材料计算参数

围岩计算参数选取情况如表2所示。

地层参数 表2

材料	密度 ρ(kg/m³)	弹性模量 E(GPa)	泊松比 ν	黏聚力 c(kPa)	内摩擦角 φ(°)
堆积层	1750	0.015	0.42	20	16.5
全风化花岗岩	2060	0.7	0.45	35	18
中风化花岗岩	2250	1.2	0.39	62	23

左洞位置不变,改变右洞水平位置,分别模拟了 0.25D、0.5D、0.75D、1D、1.25D、1.5D,共 6 种不同净距。

3.2 变形特性分析

3.2.1 地表沉降

沿两隧道中心向两侧每 6m 布置一个地表沉降监测点,根据隧道净距的大小分别布置了 18~23 个监测点,隧道开挖完成后不同净距条件下各点地表沉降最终值分布如图 9 所示。

由图 9 可知,当隧道间净距为 0.25D 时地表沉降曲线总体呈"V"字形,与单洞隧道开挖后地表沉降曲线形状相同,说明当隧道间净距很小且未对中夹岩墙进行加固的情况下,中夹岩墙已经完全失去承载作用。随着隧道间净距从 0.25D 增加至 1.5D 的过程中,地表沉降曲线逐渐由"V"字形转变为"W"字形,中夹岩墙中心处的沉降值由 55.41mm 减小到 10.04mm。如图中虚线所示,先行洞开挖完毕以后,先行洞中心对应的地表沉降监测点下沉了 20.75mm。不同净距下,后行洞开挖对该点产生的扰动不同。当净距为 0.25D 与 1D 时,后行洞开挖过程中产生的沉降分别占总沉降的 53.31% 与 10.51%。说明随着净距的增大,后行洞开挖对先行洞周边围岩以及中夹岩墙产生的扰动逐渐减小。

3.2.2 拱顶沉降与净空收敛

随着施工的进行,6 种不同净距下先行洞拱顶沉降及左右边墙水平向位移时态曲线如图 10 与图 11 所示。

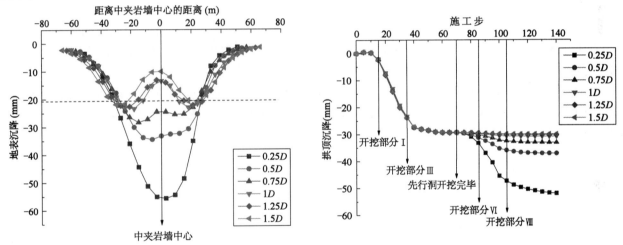

图 9 不同净距地表沉降分布

图 10 先行洞拱顶沉降时态曲线

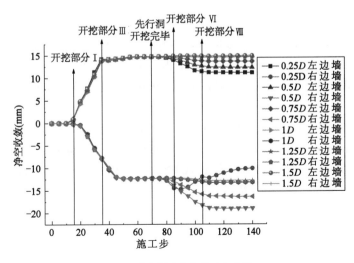

图 11 先行洞净空收敛时态曲线

由图 10 可知,隧道分部开挖过程中,拱顶沉降产生不同程度的波动,其中上半断面开挖过程中变形尤为明显。由于先行洞开挖完毕后,后行洞才开始挖掘,因此 6 种净距下,先行洞施工过程中拱顶沉降时态曲线完全一致。随着后行洞的开挖,先行洞拱顶沉降产生了不同程度的增长。当净距为 $0.25D$ 与 $0.5D$ 时,后行洞开挖过程中产生的沉降占先行洞开挖过程中产生沉降的 77.68% 与 26.16%,说明当隧道间净距较小时,后行洞的开挖会对先行洞产生剧烈的扰动。当净距增加到 $1D$ 及其以上时,后行洞的开挖对先行洞拱顶沉降的影响基本消失。

从图 11 中可以看出,在施工过程中先行洞净空收敛与拱顶沉降呈现出相似的规律,在后行洞施工过程中先行洞左右边墙变形产生明显改变("+"为向右变形,"-"为向左变形)。当净距为 $0.5D$ 与 $0.75D$ 时,后行洞开挖过程中先行洞左右边墙均向左侧变形,因此在现场试验中发现后行洞开挖过程中先行洞的净空收敛总量并未发生改变。当净距为 $0.25D$ 时,后行洞施工过程中右边墙的变形方向与其余净距情况下相反,这是由于净距过小而导致在后行洞施工过程中,后行洞左边墙向右变形的同时带动先行洞右边墙同向移动导致的。这样的情况同样说明,当净距过小时,后行洞的开挖会对先行洞及中夹岩墙产生明显的扰动。

4 结　语

本文依托山东滨莱高速公路改扩建工程佛羊岭、樵岭前和乐疃三座不同净距的隧道工程,基于现场实测,针对浅埋大跨度小净距隧道在施工过程中先行洞与后行洞的相互影响与净距大小的关系进行分析讨论。并采用 FLAC3D 数值模拟软件,对合理净距的选择提供了更加完善的依据,得到以下研究成果:

(1)根据现场地表沉降监测数据可知,小净距隧道先后行洞在施工过程存在明显的相互扰动,并且随着相邻隧道间距的增大,相互扰动在逐渐减小。当净距达到 $1.35D$ 左右时,相互扰动基本消失。而当相邻隧道间距较小时对中夹岩墙存在强烈的扰动。

(2)通过 Flac3D 数值模拟进行研究,变形结果表示不同净距下大跨度小净距隧道先后行洞在施工过程中的相互扰动规律与现场监测结果一致。综合变形分析可知,$1D$ 是先行洞与后行洞产生相互扰动的临界值。

参考文献

[1] 龚建伍,雷学文.大断面小净距隧道围岩稳定性数值分析[J].岩土力学,2010,31(2):412-417.

[2] 王辉,陈卫忠,陈培帅,等.浅埋大跨小净距隧道断面形态及合理间距的优化研究[J].岩土力学,2011,32(2):641-642.

[3] 陈秋南,赵磊军,谢小鱼,等.浅埋偏压大跨花岗岩残积土小净距隧道合理间距研究[J].中南大学学报(自然科学版),2015,46(9):3475-3480.

[4] Yang X L, Jin Q Y, Ma J Q. Pressure from surrounding rock of three shallow tunnels with large section and small spacing [J]. Journal of Central South University, 2012, 19(8):2380-2385.

[5] Chehade F H, Shahrour I. Numerical analysis of the interaction between twin-tunnels: Influence of the relative position and construction procedure [J]. Tunnelling and Underground Space Technology, 2008, 32(2):210-214.

[6] Wang H N, Gao X, Wu L, et al. Analytical study on interaction between existing and new tunnels parallel excavated in semi-infinite viscoelastic ground [J]. Computers and Geotechnics, 2020, 120.

[7] 中华人民共和国交通运输部.公路隧道设计规划　第一册　土建工程:JTG 3370.1—2018[S].北京:人民交通出版社股份有限公司,2019.

基于模糊主成分分析的隧道原位扩挖爆破参数优化

常宏涛 任 锐 王亚琼 李嘉琦

(长安大学陕西省公路桥梁与隧道重点实验室)

摘 要 针对原位扩挖隧道光面爆破参数不明造成爆破超挖及对新建衬砌影响大的问题。本文依托芋家垭隧道,基于模糊主成分分析方法并结合现场开挖爆破试验,对不同爆破参数组合方案下隧道爆破效果进行了定量评价。研究结果表明:采用周边孔最小抵抗线65cm,周边孔间距55cm,线装药密度0.25 kg·m^{-1}的爆破组合方案可取得最优的爆破效果。原有的4个评价指标可简化为2个主成分指标,其方差占比分别为68%,18%。优化后,总装药量减少33.9%,平均超欠挖量减少61.9%,测点最大振速减小44.5%,石渣大块率减小至4.7%,周边眼半孔率增大至91.2%。研究成果可为类似原位钻爆扩挖隧道施工爆破方案优化提供一定的参考。

关键词 隧道工程 爆破参数优化 模糊主成分分析法 爆破效果评价 现场测试

0 引 言

随着我国交通事业的大力发展,在新建隧道数量不断增多的同时,一些老旧隧道也出现了不同程度的病害。部分病害隧道需要进行原位扩挖,而原位扩挖爆破参数的选取及优化对施工的安全性不言而喻,然而爆破参数的选取受多方面因素的影响[1-5]。为了合理选择爆破参数,国内外众多学者已进行了大量研究。如袁红所等[6]对掏槽眼设计参数进行优化研究,并利用低密度、低爆速乳化炸药解决V级围岩爆破施工效果不稳定的问题;龚敏等[7]依托重庆市某隧道,根据不同种建筑物的爆破振速限值,建立了炸药量与隧道空间的函数关系式;杨庆等[8]以地铁隧道下穿建筑物为工程背景,对爆破网络进行了优化,减少了爆破次数;石洪超[9]从炸药破岩机理以及应力波传播规律方面对爆破参数进行优化。上述研究主要集中在隧道爆破振动对隧道围岩、支护结构以及临近隧道等构筑物的稳定性影响,对爆破参数优化缺乏定量分析[10-11]。而对原位扩挖隧道进行系统性爆破参数优化研究,尤其是定量评价爆破效果对选择合理的隧道爆破施工方案具有重要的现实意义。

本文依托芋家垭隧道原位扩挖工程,通过对扩挖过程中新建及既有衬砌爆破开挖效果观测及振动监测,提出利用模糊主成分分析方法对爆破方案进行综合评价,并据此对施工爆破参数进行优化。研究成果对原位扩挖隧道施工爆破控制和效果优化具有实际应用价值。

1 模糊主成分分析法原理

隧道原位扩挖过程中光面爆破参数的不同组合构成不同的爆破方案,模糊分析法是利用模糊数学原理建立爆破参数与各爆破效果评价指标之间的对应关系。隧道爆破效果最佳评价指标为:开挖面的超欠挖量、石渣块度大小、爆破振动速度、周边半孔率;而光面爆破参数主要包括:装药不耦合系数、周边眼间距、最小抵抗线、炮眼密集系数、线装药密度等。

爆破效果评价指标具有不同的物理量纲,采用相对隶属度概念将所有评价指标进行归一化及标准化处理。假设组合方案共有 n 个,评价指标 m 个,其构成 $\boldsymbol{C} = (c_{ij})_{n \times m}$ 的初始数据矩阵。

$$\boldsymbol{C} = \begin{bmatrix} c_{11} & c_{12} & \cdots & c_{1m} \\ c_{21} & c_{22} & \cdots & c_{2m} \\ \vdots & \vdots & \ddots & \vdots \\ c_{n1} & c_{n2} & \cdots & c_{nm} \end{bmatrix} \quad (1)$$

式中：c_{ij}——i 方案中 j 指标的值，$1 \leq i \leq n, 1 \leq j \leq m$。

m 个评价指标具有不同的量纲，对初始数据进行归一化处理，将所有指标转化为 $[0,1]$ 区间上的数值，应用相对隶属度原则，将各指标无量纲化。

对于正向指标，其计算式为：

$$x_{ij} = \frac{c_{ij} - \min\limits_{1 \leq i \leq n} c_{ij}}{\max\limits_{1 \leq i \leq n} c_{ij} - \min\limits_{1 \leq i \leq n} c_{ij}} \quad (i = 1, 2, \cdots, n; j = 1, 2, \cdots, m) \tag{2}$$

对于逆向指标，其计算式为：

$$x_{ij} = \frac{\max\limits_{1 \leq i \leq n} c_{ij} - c_{ij}}{\max\limits_{1 \leq i \leq n} c_{ij} - \min\limits_{1 \leq i \leq n} c_{ij}} \quad (i = 1, 2, \cdots, n; j = 1, 2, \cdots, m) \tag{3}$$

式中：x_{ij}——i 方案中 j 指标的无量纲值。

由此可得到 m 个评价指标的相对隶属度矩阵为：

$$X = \begin{bmatrix} x_{11} & x_{12} & \cdots & x_{1m} \\ x_{21} & x_{22} & \cdots & x_{2m} \\ \vdots & \vdots & \ddots & \vdots \\ x_{n1} & x_{n2} & \cdots & x_{nm} \end{bmatrix} \tag{4}$$

将相对隶属度矩阵 X 进行标准化处理：

$$z_{ij} = \frac{x_{ij} - \bar{x}_j}{\bar{s}_j} \quad (i = 1, 2, \cdots, n; j = 1, 2, \cdots, m)$$

$$\bar{x}_j = \frac{1}{n} \sum_{i=1}^{n} x_{ij} \tag{5}$$

$$\bar{s}_j = \sqrt{\frac{1}{n-1} \left[\sum_{i=1}^{n} (x_{ij} - \bar{x}_j)^2 \right]}$$

式中：z_{ij}——x_{ij} 标准化后的值；

$\bar{x}_j$——第 j 个指标的均值；

$\bar{s}_j$——第 j 个指标的标准差。

由此可得标准化后的指标矩阵 Z：

$$Z = \begin{bmatrix} z_{11} & z_{12} & \cdots & z_{1m} \\ z_{21} & z_{22} & \cdots & z_{2m} \\ \vdots & \vdots & \ddots & \vdots \\ z_{n1} & z_{n2} & \cdots & z_{nm} \end{bmatrix} \tag{6}$$

标准化后的指标矩阵中各向量满足 $E(Z_j) = 0, D(Z_j) = 1$，则标准化后的相关系数矩阵为：

$$r_{kl} = \frac{1}{n}(z_{ji} \times z_{ij}) \quad (i = 1, 2, \cdots, m; j = 1, 2, \cdots, m)$$

$$R = \begin{bmatrix} r_{11} & r_{12} & \cdots & r_{1m} \\ r_{21} & r_{22} & \cdots & r_{2m} \\ \vdots & \vdots & \ddots & \vdots \\ r_{m1} & r_{m2} & \cdots & r_{mm} \end{bmatrix} \tag{7}$$

式中：r_{kl}——第 k 个指标与第 l 个指标的相关度。

求解相关系数矩阵中的特征值，若 R 有 q 个大于 0 的特征值，$\lambda_1 \geq \lambda_2 \geq \cdots \geq \lambda_q > 0$，特征值对应的规范特征向量为 A，则 q 个主成分矩阵 Y：

$$Y = A^T Z \tag{8}$$

易知主成分之间协方差：

$$\text{cov}(y_a, y_b) = \begin{cases} 0 & a \neq b \\ \lambda_a & a = b \end{cases} \quad (9)$$

选取特征值大于1的成分作为主成分指标。各主成分指标之间互不相关，且第 a 主成分指标的特征值即为该指标的方差，某主成分指标方差对总方差的贡献率为：

$$\omega_a = \frac{\lambda_a}{\sum\limits_{\lambda=1}^{q} \lambda_a} \quad (10)$$

指标贡献率反映了该指标携带原始数据信息的百分比，此时爆破方案的综合评价函数为：

$$f = \sum_{a=1}^{q} \omega_a y_a = \omega_1 y_1 + \omega_2 y_2 + \cdots + \omega_q y_q \quad (11)$$

根据综合评判函数的数据即可优选合理的隧道原位扩挖光面爆破方案。

2 工程应用

2.1 工程概况

芊家垭隧道位于陕西省略阳县，隧道起讫桩号为 K101+850~K102+368，长度为518m，于1999年6月15日建成通车。2015年7月14日，芊家垭隧道发生混凝土局部崩裂坍落，根据检测统计，隧道存在衬砌坍落、衬砌强度不足、衬砌裂缝与渗水等病害问题。因此，决定采取拆除既有衬砌并进行扩挖，新建衬砌保障隧道安全运营。

2.2 原设计爆破施工方案

芊家垭隧道原位扩挖爆破施工采用上下台阶纵向光面爆破法，掘进工作面包括既有混凝土衬砌结构和外侧围岩。掘进工作面布置周边孔位和辅助孔位如图1所示。设计炮孔深度为2.2m，考虑到炮孔底部爆破不完全，实际进尺深度2.0m，炮孔直径为42mm，乳化炸药径向不耦合系数约为1.30。原设计爆破施工参数如表1所示。

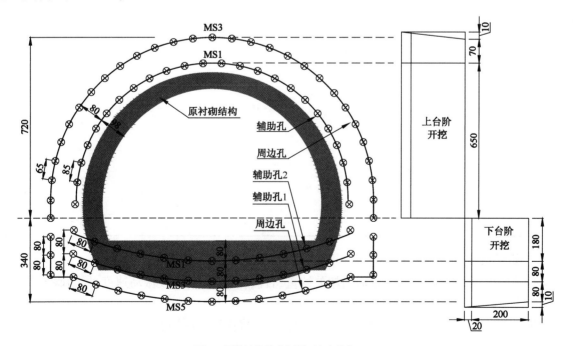

图1 原设计炮孔布置图(尺寸单位:cm)

原设计爆破施工参数 表1

台阶	炮孔类别	雷管段别	孔距(m)	排距(m)	炮孔深度(m)	炮孔数量(个)	装药量 单孔药量(kg)	装药量 总药量(kg)	装药密度(kg·m⁻¹)	炮泥长度(m)
上台阶	周边孔	MS3	0.65	0.80	2.0	29	0.60	17.4	0.30	0.40
上台阶	辅助孔	MS1	0.85	0.98	2.0	24	2.10	50.4	0.90	0.40
下台阶	周边孔	MS5	0.80	0.80	2.0	19	0.90	17.1	0.60	0.40
下台阶	辅助孔1	MS3	0.80	0.80	2.0	13	1.80	23.4	0.90	040
下台阶	辅助孔2	MS1	0.80	0.80	2.0	13	2.10	27.3	0.60	0.40
	总计					98	—	135.6		—

2.3 原位扩挖爆破参数优化设计

本文通过调整周边孔间距 E、周边孔最小抵抗线 W、线装药密度 q_1 三个主要爆破参数进行爆破效果优化研究,且针对的是隧道上台阶原位扩挖爆破参数。

由于现场施工条件限制,炮眼调整工作烦琐,为了便于合理确定各爆破参数取值。选定周边眼最小抵抗线 W 为65cm,周边孔间距 E 及线装药密度 q_1 在合理的取值范围内分别选出4个代表值,由此包括原设计在内,共有17种工况及现场试验,不同爆破参数组合如表2所示。

不同爆破参数组合工况 表2

试验序号	周边孔最小抵抗线 W(cm)	周边孔间距 E(cm)	线装药密度 q_1(kg·m⁻¹)
1-1	80	65	0.30
2-1	65	45	0.20
2-2	65	45	0.25
2-3	65	45	0.30
2-4	65	45	0.35
3-1	65	50	0.20
3-2	65	50	0.25
3-3	65	50	0.30
3-4	65	50	0.35
4-1	65	55	0.20
4-2	65	55	0.25
4-3	65	55	0.30
4-4	65	55	0.35
5-1	65	60	0.20
5-2	65	60	0.25
5-3	65	60	0.30
5-4	65	60	0.35

2.4 爆破效果评价指标

本文爆破效果评价指标选取:开挖面的超欠挖量、石渣块度大小、爆破振动速度、周边眼半孔率四个指标。

周边眼半孔率,每次爆破后对残留炮孔数量进行统计,多次统计取均值作为统计结果。

$$周边眼半孔率(\%) = \frac{周边眼残留数量}{周边眼总数量} \times 100\%$$

开挖面的超欠挖量采用 HPSD-2F 隧道激光断面仪检测进行检测。

$$\text{平均超欠挖量} = \frac{\text{超挖面积}}{\text{爆破设计开挖断面周长(不含隧底)}}$$

爆破石渣块度大小,选定直径大于 500 mm 的石渣为大块石渣,爆破后对石渣进行粗略的筛分统计。

$$\text{石渣大块率}(\geq 500\text{mm}) = \frac{\text{石渣质量(直径} \geq 500\text{mm})}{\text{爆破石渣总质量}} \times 100\%$$

爆破振动速度,采用 TC-4850 型爆破测振仪对爆破前方设置的 3 个测点进行振速测定,如图 2 所示,选取峰值振速作为评价指标。

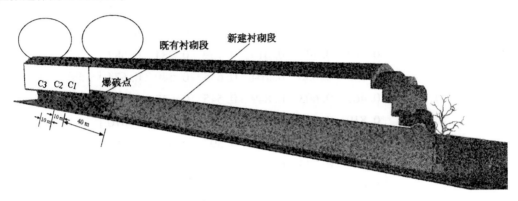

图 2 爆破振动监测示意图

3 模糊主成分分析

对芋家垭隧道原位扩挖光面爆破方案的效果指标进行数据采集,可得出 17 组数据结果,如表 3 所示。

光面爆破效果统计表   表3

工况	试验序号	总装药量(kg)	周边眼半孔率(%)	平均超欠挖量(cm)	石渣大块率 ≥500mm(%)	最大振速(cm·s⁻¹)		
						C1	C2	C3
1	1-1	67.8	58.6%	11.8	15.3%	2.92	1.62	0.95
2	2-1	48.0	78.6%	8.3	10.6%	2.02	1.28	0.91
	2-2	52.2	76.2%	7.5	8.4%	2.06	1.11	0.87
	2-3	56.4	71.4%	8.6	8.9%	1.93	1.37	1.12
	2-4	60.6	69.0%	9.7	7.6%	2.23	1.40	1.10
3	3-1	46.4	78.9%	7.1	9.2%	1.68	1.19	0.82
	3-2	50.2	84.2%	6.4	8.8%	1.82	1.22	0.93
	3-3	54.0	76.3%	7.2	7.2%	1.97	1.34	0.89
	3-4	57.8	73.7%	7.4	6.3%	2.13	1.29	1.20
4	4-1	44.8	85.3%	6.0	7.6%	1.75	1.16	0.80
	4-2	48.2	91.2%	4.5	4.7%	1.62	1.14	0.85
	4-3	51.6	82.3%	6.5	6.5%	1.89	1.18	0.93
	4-4	55.0	79.4%	7.1	6.0%	1.78	1.32	0.82
5	5-1	44.0	78.1%	7.8	8.7%	1.88	1.25	0.74
	5-2	47.2	71.9%	8.9	8.5%	1.47	1.20	0.79
	5-3	50.4	81.3%	6.3	7.9%	2.02	1.23	0.87
	5-4	53.6	81.8%	5.8	5.6%	1.95	1.36	0.96

由表 3 中的数据,利用式及通过 matlab 计算可得相对隶属度矩阵 X,由式(5)~(7)可得相关性矩阵参数,并对其进行显著性检验如表 4 所示,为确保统计数据可以进行主成分分析,采用 KMO 检验法进行检验,如式(13)所示。计算可得 KMO = 0.732,适合进行主成分分析。

$$X = \begin{bmatrix} 0.000 & 0.000 & 0.000 & 0.000 & 0.000 & 0.543 \\ 0.613 & 0.479 & 0.443 & 0.621 & 0.667 & 0.630 \\ 0.540 & 0.589 & 0.651 & 0.593 & 1.000 & 0.717 \\ 0.393 & 0.438 & 0.604 & 0.683 & 0.490 & 0.174 \\ 0.319 & 0.288 & 0.726 & 0.476 & 0.431 & 0.217 \\ 0.623 & 0.644 & 0.575 & 0.855 & 0.843 & 0.826 \\ 0.785 & 0.740 & 0.613 & 0.759 & 0.784 & 0.587 \\ 0.543 & 0.630 & 0.764 & 0.655 & 0.549 & 0.674 \\ 0.463 & 0.603 & 0.849 & 0.545 & 0.647 & 0.000 \\ 0.819 & 0.795 & 0.726 & 0.807 & 0.902 & 0.870 \\ 1.000 & 1.000 & 1.000 & 0.897 & 0.941 & 0.761 \\ 0.727 & 0.726 & 0.830 & 0.710 & 0.863 & 0.587 \\ 0.638 & 0.644 & 0.877 & 0.786 & 0.588 & 0.826 \\ 0.598 & 0.548 & 0.623 & 0.717 & 0.725 & 1.000 \\ 0.408 & 0.397 & 0.642 & 1.000 & 0.824 & 0.891 \\ 0.696 & 0.753 & 0.698 & 0.621 & 0.765 & 0.717 \\ 0.712 & 0.822 & 0.915 & 0.669 & 0.510 & 0.522 \end{bmatrix} \quad (12)$$

相关性矩阵　　　　　　表4

	项目	周边眼半孔率	超欠挖量	石渣大块率	C1 爆破振动速度	C2 爆破振动速度	C3 爆破振动速度
相关性	周边眼半孔率	1.000	0.959	0.697	0.711	0.760	0.394
	超欠挖量	0.959	1.000	0.790	0.671	0.719	0.274
	石渣大块率	0.697	0.790	1.000	0.647	0.547	-0.019
	C1 爆破振动速度	0.711	0.671	0.647	1.000	0.780	0.447
	C2 爆破振动速度	0.760	0.719	0.547	0.780	1.000	0.439
	C3 爆破振动速度	0.394	0.274	-0.019	0.447	.439	1.000
显著性	周边眼半孔率		0.000	0.001	0.001	0.000	0.059
	超欠挖量	0.000		0.000	0.002	0.001	0.143
	石渣大块率	0.001	0.000		0.003	0.011	0.471
	C1 爆破振动速度	0.001	0.002	0.003		0.000	0.036
	C2 爆破振动速度	0.000	0.001	0.011	0.000		0.039
	C3 爆破振动速度	0.059	0.143	0.471	0.036	0.039	

$$\text{KMO} = \frac{\sum\sum_{i \neq j} r_{ij}^2}{\sum\sum_{i \neq j} r_{ij}^2 + \sum\sum_{i \neq j} r_{ij \cdot 1,2,\cdots}^2} \quad (13)$$

由表 4 可以粗略地看出,前 5 个指标相关性很强,可以归纳出一个主成分因子,最后一个指标可以归纳出一个主成分因子。

利用式(8)~式(10)进行主成分分析,可得各成分对总方差的贡献率,如表 5 所示。

总方差解释表 表5

成分	初始特征值			提取载荷平方和	
	特征值	方差百分比	累积贡献率	特征值	方差百分比
1	4.080	68.002	68.002	4.080	68.002
2	1.074	17.902	85.904	1.074	17.902
3	0.400	6.671	92.575		
4	0.284	4.732	97.307		
5	0.136	2.271	99.578		
6	0.025	0.422	100.000		

由此可以得到主成分方差贡献率 $\omega = [0.68002, 0.17902]$。主成分指标 a_1 及 a_2 的成分矩阵和成分得分系数矩阵数值，如表6所示。

主成分得分系数表 表6

参数	成分矩阵		成分得分系数矩阵	
	a_1	a_2	a_1	a_2
周边眼半孔率 z_1	0.940	-0.044	0.230	-0.041
超欠挖量 z_2	0.927	-0.201	0.227	-0.187
石渣大块率 z_3	0.785	-0.513	0.193	-0.477
C1 爆破振动速度 z_4	0.870	0.123	0.213	0.115
C2 爆破振动速度 z_5	0.872	0.161	0.214	0.150
C3 爆破振动速度 z_6	0.449	0.853	0.110	0.794

由表6得主成分 a_1 及 a_2 的评判函数及综合评判函数为：

$$\begin{cases} f_1 = 0.230 \times z_1 + 0.227 \times z_2 + 0.193 \times z_3 + 0.213 \times z_4 + 0.214 \times z_5 + 0.110 \times z_6 \\ f_2 = -0.041 \times z_1 - 0.187 \times z_2 - 0.477 \times z_3 + 0.115 \times z_4 + 0.150 \times z_5 + 0.794 \times z_6 \end{cases} \quad (14)$$

由式(11)可以得到各方案的综合评判数值矩阵：

$$\boldsymbol{F} = \begin{bmatrix} -1.9465 \\ -0.1279 \\ 0.2196 \\ -0.7249 \\ -1.0009 \\ 0.4707 \\ 0.3240 \\ -0.0506 \\ -0.6740 \\ 0.7582 \\ 1.0590 \\ 0.3419 \\ 0.3028 \\ 0.3609 \\ 0.3588 \\ 0.2736 \\ 0.0555 \end{bmatrix} \quad (15)$$

根据综合评判数据越大越优的原则，最差的工况1-1，最好的为工况4-2，即选取周边孔最小抵抗线 W

为65cm，周边眼间距E为55cm，线装药密度q_1为$0.25\text{kg}\cdot\text{m}^{-1}$时最优。结合现场施工的实际情况判断，4-2方案与现场最优方案一致。

利用模糊主成分分析法将原有的4个评价指标简化为2个主成分指标，使综合评判系数计算只需考虑2个主成分指标的变化，提高了现场爆破施工的效率。

4 结　语

(1) 隧道原位扩挖爆破参数优化为非线性规划数学问题，传统的理论方法求解过程较为复杂。本文利用模糊主成分分析法对爆破参数进行优化，模化原理综合考虑不同量纲评价指标的相互作用，为复杂评价系统决策问题提供了新途径，具有较高的工程适用性。

(2) 建立基于模糊主成分分析的方法，并针对芋家垭隧道进行实际应用，对比优化前后爆破效果评价指标，C1点爆破振速峰值下降了44.5%，线装药密度从$0.3\text{kg}\cdot\text{m}^{-1}$减小至$0.25\text{kg}\cdot\text{m}^{-1}$，对比分析优化后既减少了炸药使用量又减少了对新建衬砌和既有衬砌的扰动。

(3) 本文中爆破参数组合方案受工程实际制约未设计更多的爆破方案，主成分分析相关性未特别显著，在日后的工作中从工程实践和数学理论角度出发对模糊主成分分析方法进一步优化。

参考文献

[1] 张维明,肖柳,卜俊锐,等.月亮山隧道爆破减震试验研究[J].爆破,2016,33(2):23-27.

[2] 龚敏,陈哲,吴昊骏,等.掏槽药量与起爆时差的关系对隧道爆破合成振速的影响[J].应用基础与工程科学学报,2016(6):1110-1124.

[3] 张新彬,刘新荣,范兵旗,等.复杂立交隧道爆破开挖参数设计及动力响应分析[J].地下空间与工程学报 2017(s2):736-740.

[4] 李得,杨溢,李睿,等.多级复式楔形掏槽在大断面隧洞掘进中的应用研究[J].爆破,2017,34(1):52-56.

[5] 程跃辉,江鸿,陈伟.隧道下穿匝道爆破振动控制技术及效果分析[J].爆破,2017,34(3):63-67.

[6] 袁红所,张家铭,贺立新,等.复杂地质条件下隧道爆破方案优化设计[J].爆破,2016,33(1):50-54.

[7] 龚敏,赵振振,吴昊骏,等.针对建构筑物不同振速要求的隧道爆破药量计算方法[J].煤炭学报,2016,41(7):1747-1754.

[8] 杨庆,王海亮,王军涛.城市硬岩隧道下穿砖木结构建筑爆破控制技术[J].现代隧道技术,2014,51(1):199-202.

[9] 石洪超.层状围岩小净距隧道掘进爆破振动效应及围岩稳定性研究[D].成都:西南交通大学,2017.

[10] 费鸿禄,曾翔宇,杨智广.隧道掘进爆破振动对地表影响的小波包分析[J].爆炸与冲击,2017,37(1):77-83.

[11] 周仕仁,周建敏,王洪华,等.地铁隧道爆破参数优化及其振动效应研究[J].爆破,2018,35(02):85-89.

Cloud-computing- and Big-data-based Integrated Information Platform for TBM Construction—massive Data Collection, Management and Mining

Liujie Jing[1]　Lianhui Jia[1]　Jianbin Li[2]　Shoutian Xu[1]　Xiangxiang Wang[1]

(1. China Railway Engineering Equipment Co., Ltd.; 2. China Railway Hi-Tech Industry Co., Ltd.)

Abstract　Fast and comprehensive acquisition of hard rock tunnel boring machine (TBM) construction data benefits field management, and the knowledge and rules built from data mining can provide guidance for TBM design, selection and operating. To address the problems of "lack of data, platform and analysis" existing in the TBM industry, this paper, based on cloud computing, big data technology and the concept of "born by digital, born in format, born to the cloud", presents an integrated information platform which provides multiple functions including data collection, storage, analysis and mining. The platform not only provides basic information services for project participants, but also gives a massive data analysis and mining platform for basic research of TBM. It has the following characteristics: (i) collection of real-time rock mass information via an anchor drilling rig monitoring system and a rock muck intelligent recognition system; (ii) building of a big data repository for multisource TBM construction information based on data standardization and association rules; (iii) building of a private cloud computing platform based on OpenStack technology; and (iv) deployment of an algorithm component in an SaaS layer to carry out TBM big-data mining. Finally, a case study of platform development and application is carried out on Yinsong TBM project in Jilin, China.

Keywords Tunnel boring machine Cloud computing Big data Integrated information platform Data mining

0 Introduction

With such advantages as high tunnelling efficiency, safety and environmental compatibility, the tunnel boring machine (TBM) has become a preferred construction method for long tunnel (Barla et al., 2000; Hasanpour et al., 2011). However, the TBM suffers from poor adaptability to geological changes, resulting in frequent equipment failures, accidents and geological disasters during construction (Barton 1996; Zhao et al., 2007; Ramoni 2010).

Facts show that the above accidents are closely related to basic research of TBM, and the mechanism of geological disaster and of rock breaking by TBM cutters and the characteristics of rock mass-TBM interaction are still unknown. Researchers tend to address the above problems via numerical simulation, disc cutter cutting tests and case analysis. Numerical simulation is normally performed to investigate the normal force of cutter during rock cutting, determine the generation and expansion of rock cracks, and evaluate the squeeze pressure and deformation borne by the shield or segment adjacent to the rock wall under excavation unloading (Hasanpour 2014; Zhao et al., 2012; Cho et al., 2013). Cutting tests are conducted to investigate the relationship between the cutter force and penetration when cutting various types of rock or to design and optimize the cutter spacing with an objective of minimizing the specific energy of rock breaking (Rostami 1997; Ma et al., 2016; Geng et al., 2016). The extensive experience and lessons accumulated from the recorded field construction data are used to predict TBM performance and address adverse geology (Bruland 1998; Gong 2006).

As TBM construction is affected by various factors relating to human, machine and geology, the tunnelling process is extremely complicated, and construction management is challenging. Fast and comprehensive acquisition of TBM construction data can improve field management, and such data is also worth of further mining. This paper focuses on how to identify knowledge and relations from construction data to guide TBM selection, design or construction. However, the TBM industry has not paid enough attention to construction data for a long time and established unified data standards and storage methods or effective data management platform. As a result, the data of completed TBM projects are owned by different project participants, which creates technical barriers for data sharing. Even if these problems can be tackled, due to fragmentation across varied formats and standards, the acquired data is incomplete with a low value density and is unsuitable for in-depth analysis and rule mining (Kocha et al., 2017; Xue et al., 2018; Han et al., 2017).

To address the common problems of "lack of data, platform and analysis" existing in the TBM industry, in this paper, the concept of "born by digital, born in format, born to the cloud" is proposed and followed to build an integrated information platform. An anchor drilling rig monitoring system and a rock muck intelligent recognition system are employed to collect digital rock mass parameters in a real-time manner. Based on data standardization and association rules, a MongoDB-based big data warehouse for multisource TBM construction data is established. A private cloud computing platform is created, and an algorithm component is deployed at the SaaS layer to perform big-data mining. Finally, an integrated information platform is created for collection, storage, analysis and mining of TBM construction data. This platform provides basic information services for project participants and also presents a massive data and mining platform for TBM basic research to obtain knowledge and rules.

1 Background

1.1 TBM Database and Information Platform

Many studies on TBM are based on construction data. According to existing TBM project databases, Bruland (1998) developed and improved a TBM performance prediction model and a cutter life prediction model. Barton (2000) created a TBM rock mass quality evaluation system designated as QTBM. Rostami (2016) investigated TBM selection, utilization and construction management optimization. Hassanpour et al., (2011) investigated and proposed the classification of rock mass boreability and developed a tunnelling performance prediction model.

The main challenges to build a TBM project database are as follows: (1) data generated from TBM construction is various; (2) the design information, management information and construction data are frequently scattered and uncorrelated because TBM construction involves multiple project participants; (3) statistical analysis of field data is time- and energy-consuming; and (4) data formats for different projects are varied, and no suitable tool or platform exists for data storage and management (Liu et al.,2016).

With the development of Building Information Model (BIM) technology and Industry Foundation Classes (IFC) standard, information management platforms for different construction areas are emerging (Meschke et al., 2011; Guglielmetti et al.,2008; Hegemann et al.,2013). Some platforms also arise in the TBM industry, which can integrate information of design, construction and management and provide functions such as remote monitoring and construction management, but they focus on ensuring safe TBM construction and improving field management and control. As in-depth data mining is not performed, the characteristic behavior cannot be acquired to facilitate scientific decision making. The above information platforms cannot assist in improving TBM design, evaluating rock conditions or equipment operational states, or optimizing TBM operational parameters. Therefore, it is necessary to develop a construction data platform that can solve the problems associated with lack of data, platform and analysis.

1.2 Comparison Between TBM Construction Data and Big Data

Big data involves analysis and verification of objective rules based on a full set of data, which can describe the current status, predict future situations and be service-oriented. Big data analysis is not determined by the scale of data set, and the data association, value and mining challenges are also important factors to evaluate big data. Its four main characteristics are summarized as follows: volume, variety, velocity and veracity (Hilbert 2016).

TBM construction data have following characteristics: (1) spatial feature: TBM construction data vary with the geological conditions at different tunnel sections; (2) real-time feature: TBM parameters constitute real-time feedback of geological information, and adjustment of TBM operating parameters causes real-time response of TBM parameters; (3) multisource heterogeneity: geological parameters, TBM parameters, process parameters, construction images and videos are various, and structured data and nonstructured data differ significantly; and (4) massiveness: a single TBM generates billions of data records each year, and with the increase in the number of TBM projects, the total amount of information is expanding rapidly.

The comparison in Fig. 1 shows that TBM construction data have basic features of big data. Solving the challenge of TBM data collection, storage and mining by means of big data concepts and methods is the key to build an integrated information platform.

1.3 Cloud Computing

Cloud computing, a key technology for big data, supports integration of an enormous computing resource pool and flexibly allocates virtual resources according to the customer computing load to meet user requirements. Cloud computing technology is divided into multiple layers (Mell et al., 2011). For TBM construction data platform presented in this paper, infrastructure as a service (IaaS) provides network communication, data storage and computing resources; platform as a service (PaaS) provides shared access and big data environment; and software as a service (SaaS) provides various applications such as basic information services and data mining. Layered services provide support for different requirements of TBM construction big data, as shown in Fig. 2.

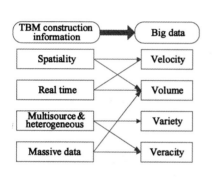

Fig. 1 Comparison between TBM construction data and big data

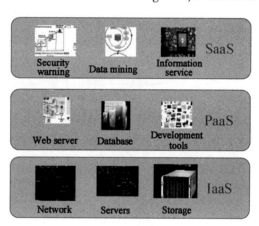

Fig. 2 Cloud computing service models arranged as layers

2 Methodology

2.1 Technological Framework of The Integrated Information Platform for TBM Construction

The integrated information platform manages TBM construction data according to the concept of "born by digital, born in format, born to the cloud", which effectively solves problems such as challenges associated with data collection, inconsistent data formatting, data dispersion and lack of analysis. The born-by-digital component implements digital collection and transmission of multisource information by means of Internet of Things (IoT) technology. The born-in-format component creates data standards and association rules to solve the problem of TBM big data storage and management. The born-to-the-cloud component provides layered services via cloud computing platforms. The technological framework of the information platform is shown in Fig. 3.

2.2 Digital Collection of Multisource TBM Construction Information

2.2.1 TBM Parameters

About 300 sensors are installed in a single TBM to monitor different function systems. An analog signal generated by a sensor is converted to a digital signal with physical meaning via a programmable logic controller (PLC). TBM construction technicians and operators manage and optimize TBM progress according to these parameters. In addition, parameters of TBM auxiliary function systems such as guide system, environment sensing system, and water circulation system are integrated into a host computer, as shown in Fig. 4.

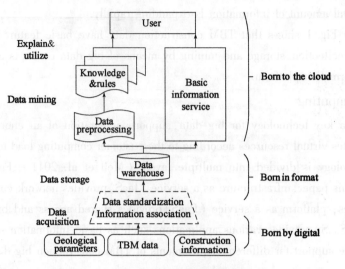

Fig. 3　Technical framework of an integrated platform for TBM construction data

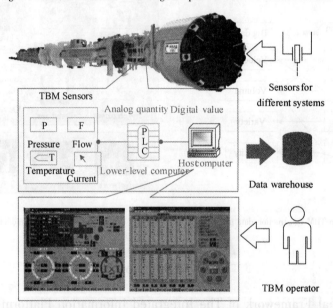

Fig. 4　TBM data acquisition system

2.2.2　Geological and Rock Mass Parameters

Geological and rock mass parameters provide important evidence for TBM selection, design and construction. However, restricted by limited survey time, cost and technology, the geological and rock mass parameters provided in the survey report are inconsistent with the information obtained after excavation. During TBM construction, the acquisition of rock mass parameters via manual sampling and geological mapping sketches requires long time and high cost. Moreover, it is challenging to reach the similar scale required by equipment parameters, which is also the bottleneck that constrains TBM big data mining in later stages.

To address the above problems, a TBM anchor drilling rig monitoring system and a rock muck intelligent recognition system are developed to characterize rock mass strength and integrity in a real-time manner during construction and facilitate the creation of a rock mass parameter database.

(1) Rock mass strength

Anchor bolt support is an indispensable procedure for open TBM. On the basis of research findings of Yue

(2014) and Kahramana et al., (2003), the TBM anchor drilling rig monitoring system can monitor boring process parameters. The rock mass strength of this tunnel section is estimated on the basis of correlation between drilling speed and rock mass strength, as shown in Fig. 5 and Fig. 6.

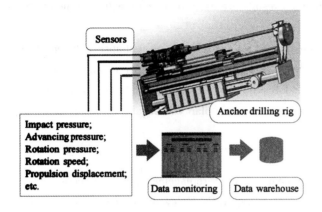

Fig. 5 Monitoring system with drilling for anchor drilling rig

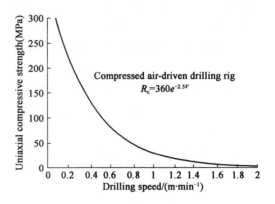

Fig. 6 Rock uniaxial compressive strength versus drilling speed for compressed-air-driven drilling rig (Yue 2014)

(2) Rock mass integrity

Mucks are generated due to the interaction between cutter head and rock mass of the tunnel face. Their **geometrical shape and particle size distribution** reflect the integrity of rock mass under excavation. A high-frame-rate industrial camera is installed above the TBM muck conveyor to automatically photograph mucks. An **intelligent algorithm** is developed to automatically recognize and divide muck edge, acquire geometrical shape **and particle size distribution** pattern and determine rock mass integrity on the basis of a muck pattern database, **as shown in Fig. 7**.

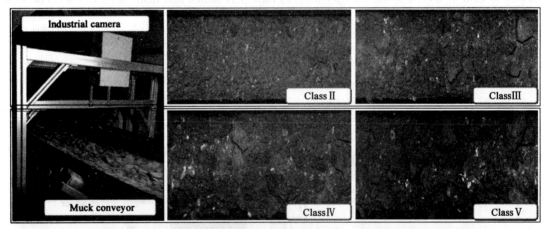

a) Muck image collection system and muck images of various rock mass integrity classes

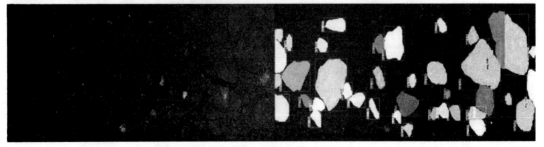

b) Muck image and segmentation diagram by intelligent algorithm (particle size>25 mm)

Fig.7

(3) Real-time data collected via the above two methods are subjected to machine learning or statistical model calculation to obtain rock mass strength and integrity parameters which are then transmitted to the host computer and collected simultaneously with equipment parameters. In addition to digital collection methods, conventional sampling methods are also necessary. The obtained results are used to compare with and modify the rock mass parameters collected by the digital method.

(4) When a TBM encounters adverse geological condition, accidents such as collapse-induced TBM jamming and water inrush may occur, which pose a severe threat to safe TBM operation. An advance detector is employed to predict geological conditions, and the interpreted results are uploaded quickly to an information platform via data interface and reminds the contractor to prepare a response plan via visualized images and texts and information to prevent disaster.

2.2.3 Other Construction Data

TBM construction information, such as repair and maintenance, cutter replacement, material consumption and strata consolidation, is recorded by field staff or exported from other APPs. Relevant information is uploaded to the database on the basis of predefined rules. In addition, information files in any format and related to TBM construction are uploaded to a database in the central server via a client to achieve complete information collection.

2.3 TBM Data Transmission

A data collection terminal is installed at the TBM main control room. First, construction data are cached in the terminal, which is then connected to the data centre under TCP/IP protocol for real-time transmission. The data transmission system exhibits low coupling and allows parallel transmission and receipt of data for multiple projects by defining standard protocol and interface, which ensures system extensibility for TBM cluster construction, as shown in Fig. 8. A server connected to the big data centre ensures reliable data storage and efficient access to data by means of technologies such as data persistence and distributed Redis cache to support big data management.

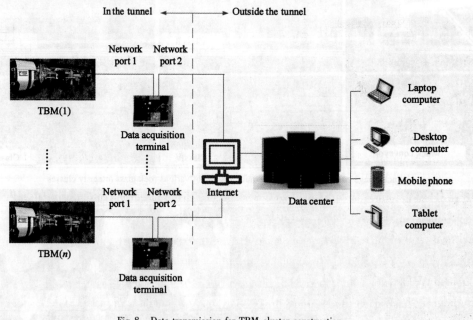

Fig. 8 Data transmission for TBM cluster construction

2.4 TBM Construction Data Standardization and Association Rules

Construction data of different projects vary significantly. To facilitate data searching, data calling and comparative analysis in the later stages, TBM data should be standardized and correlated before they are stored in the database. The basic principles are as follows: (1) all TBM information must follow the principles of time-space uniqueness, time and tunnel chainage correspond to each other, and the time stamp is the unique identifier of TBM data; (2) data shall have a unified physical meaning, naming convention, format and storage address; and (3) all data of a project are correlated by means of project number, time stamp, tunnel chainage and address. Therefore, before data collection and storage, a data mapping table should be created based on the above rules to define data storage method. Manually recorded data and uploaded files must follow predefined rules in the information platform, and only specific types of data and default format files are accepted.

2.5 Storage of TBM Big Data

Utilization cost increases sharply when traditional relational databases such as SQL-Server or MySQL are processing massive data, and such databases are improper for storing nonstructured data. The MongoDB database, which is based on distributed file storage, supports network access and cloud computing extension, exhibits advantages such as high parallelism, high throughput and extendibility, and is suitable for storage of various types of data. Therefore, MongoDB is selected as the database for massive TBM construction information. Moreover, the MongoDB database storage enables data partition and redundant backups to improve data safety. Considering the need for fast reading and calculation of big data, database read splitting is enabled, which significantly improves efficiency of data computing. The database storage hierarchy is shown in Fig. 9.

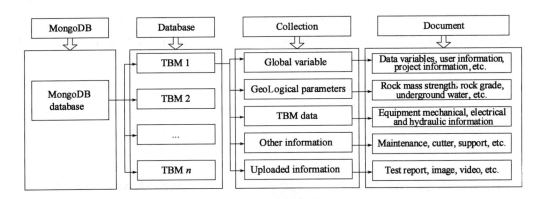

Fig. 9　TBM construction data storage hierarchy in MongoDB database

2.6 Cloud-Computing-Based Integrated Information Platform for TBM Construction

A single TBM can generate billions of data records each year. As conventional data platforms cannot support computing and analysis of such dataset sizes within an acceptable time, new models must be developed to process massive and diversified data with a high growth rate. In this study, a private cloud computing platform is built on the basis of OpenStack technology and can achieve big-data storage, management, analysis and visual demonstration of construction data by means of Hadoop cluster and subsystems, as shown in Fig. 10. The main planning goals of the platform are to: (1) implement standardized collection and cloud management of massive TBM construction data; (2) provide basic information services for project participants via web page; and (3) provide a platform and tools to support big data mining of massive TBM construction information.

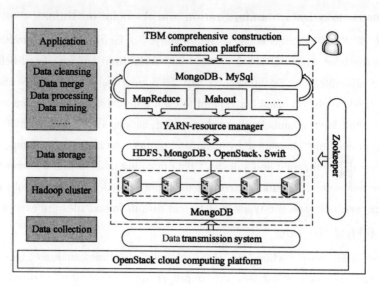

Fig. 10 Overall architecture of the information platform

3 Case Study

3.1 Overview of The TBM Project

Yinsong Water Supply Project, located in Jilin Province, China, supplies water for domestic and industrial use from Songhua River to the cities in the central region of Jilin Province. The diversion tunnel with a total length of 263.4 km consists of 3 sections excavated by TBM and 1 section formed by using the drilling and blasting method. The tunnel of TBM 3 lot, which has an excavated length of 22.9 km and a diameter of 8.03 m, mainly passes through limestone and granite and had been completed in March 2018.

3.2 Basic Services of The Integrated Information Platform for TBM Construction

The basic services provided by the integrated information platform include the following:

(1) Information sharing. Administrators assign different levels of platform access rights according to the user's identity information, and then the user can log in the platform freely and share project information.

(2) Real-time monitoring. The platform manages all TBM projects via a directory tree, and the user can select a TBM project to monitor its operational state and main parameters in a real-time manner, as shown in Fig. 11.

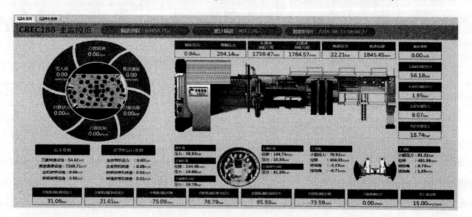

Fig. 11 Monitoring of main TBM parameters of Songhua River Water Supply Project (in China)

(3) Geological information query and safety warning. The user can obtain TBM tunnelling location and tunnel geological and rock parameters in a real-time manner to facilitate construction management. In addition, this system can be set in advance to accommodate adverse geological condition as risk points (based on survey

reports). When TBM approaches the risk point, the platform automatically generates a safety warning and leverages an expert knowledge base to notify the project participants to prepare a construction plan, as shown in Fig. 12.

(4) Equipment parameter query and fault warning. The user can customize tunnelling time and chainage on the basis of the requirements to screen the data and accurately query equipment operational parameters and health tendency. Furthermore, important equipment parameters are selected to set alarm threshold values so that maintenance personnel can be promptly notified to monitor operational state to reduce failure rate.

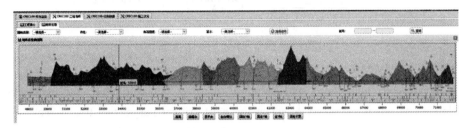

Fig. 12 Geological information system for Songhua River Water Supply Project (in China)

(5) Statistical analysis. The platform supports automatic statistical analysis of information such as construction progress, utilization rate and downtime. The on-site workers can log into the system to fill in daily report, upload progress images and record material consumption. A report including the above information can be automatically generated to improve standardized management of project information.

3.3 Mining of Massive TBM Construction Data

Massive TBM construction data go far beyond improving construction management. The knowledge base and rule base extracted from data mining have wide applications, such as providing evidence for main parameter design for new TBM machines, guiding TBM operator for safe and efficient excavation, estimating construction period and cost, and evaluating the life of critical components in aging machines for maintenance or remanufacturing. Therefore, the integrated information platform provides both basic information services for project participants and an effective platform for storage, analysis, and mining of massive TBM construction data to maximize data value.

3.3.1 Data Pre-Processing

The basic characteristics of big data are high data volume and low value density. Therefore, the primary task of big data mining is data pre-processing which is detailed as follows.

(1) Data screening. Based on the requirements of data mining, specific screening conditions are defined to extract data from massive original data that meets the conditions.

(2) Data pre-processing. TBM operational data not only contains 0-value data generated by equipment failure, but also include those data related to equipment faults or abnormal construction. According to professional knowledge and experience, requirements are defined to remove the above abnormal data and reduce data set size.

(3) Data processing. Each normal tunnelling cycle includes an initial rising section and a stable tunnelling section. Each increase of the cutter head tunnelling speed from 0 at the initial rising section to a stable value is treated as a small-scale tunnelling test. Data at the stable tunnelling section are employed for machine learning. Based on professional knowledge and data variation patterns, a corresponding algorithm is designed to implement automatic recognition and segmentation of tunnelling models. Moreover, as different types of data have different dimensions and sparsity, new characteristic data is acquired through normalization, averaging and multiparameter integration.

(4) After data pre-processing, massive construction data are processed and saved as databases at different hierarchies and in different categories for data engineers to use. The basic steps for data pre-processing are shown in

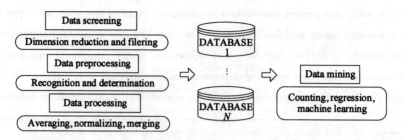

Fig. 13 Data pre-processing procedure

3.3.2 Correlation Analysis

Data mining focuses on interactions and response patterns between TBM and rock mass and TBM parameters. Correlation analysis is necessary to select the most critical parameters that reflect these interactions and patterns from more than 100 construction parameters. The information platform database takes MongoDB and Hadoop Distributed File System (HDFS) as the database and deploys the correlation analysis algorithm component in combined with the distributed computing framework MapReduce, ensuring fast identification of correlations between each pair of parameters. In addition, the information platform allows the user to drag the parameters to be selected on a web page and generate scatter plots via a visualization plugin, which facilitates an intuitive determination of the correlation and relationship category, as shown in Fig. 14.

Correlation analysis of TBM construction data from Yinsong Water Supply Project has shown certain correlation rules for main parameters under various surrounding rock types, providing a basis for parameter selection, establishment and optimization of rock-machine interaction models and rock mass state perception models, as shown in Fig. 15.

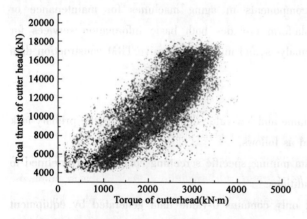

Fig. 14 Visualization of a scatter plot of the total thrust and torque of a cutter head

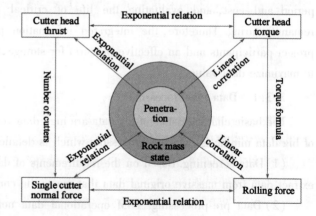

Fig. 15 Interactions among the main TBM control parameters

3.3.3 Machine Learning

The neural network and support vector machine approaches represent a type of supervised machine learning. Learning samples are selected from the database that correspond to the rock-machine parameters collected by the information platform. TBM and rock mass parameters are mutually used as an input and output to train the model to study the mutual feedback relationship. As the size of the data sample becomes larger, the accuracy of the supervised learning model can be improved continuously.

Cluster analysis is a type of unsupervised machine learning, which is commonly used in sample classification. The clustering algorithm is deployed in the platform, and important TBM parameters are selected as clustering indexes to classify rock mass state. Fig. 16 shows TBM parameter clustering results of a section in

Yinsong Water Supply Project. Comparisons demonstrate that when the normalized value of the thrust and the field penetration index (FPI, the ratio of the normal force per cutter to the cutter head penetration) are used as clustering indexes to classify rock mass grade (4 grades, where field wall rock belongs to classes II - V, missing class I), the results are substantially consistent with the actual measurements.

3.3.4 Online Verification and Upgrade of The Forecast Model

TBM performance forecast is important for estimating construction period and cost and remains a hot topic concerning TBM. Various forecast models obtained from previous research and machine learning are deployed in the information platform. The accuracy and applicability of the models are verified via real-time data to select the best ones. Furthermore, new sample data provide support for model iterative upgrades to ensure that the model accuracy improves continuously.

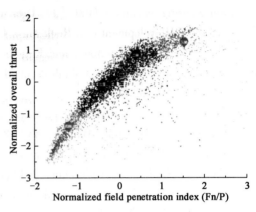

Fig. 16 TBM thrust force and FPI cluster analysis

4 Conclusions

An integrated information platform for TBM construction is a useful project information exchange platform that provides basic information services for TBM project participants. Based on cloud computing technology and big data methods, this platform effectively enables massive TBM construction data collection, storage and mining to extract the potential value of TBM data. The main contributions of this study are as follows: (i) The concept of "born by digital, born in format, born to the cloud" (or 3B concept) for TBM couction data is proposed, which provides a methodology to address challenges associated with data collection, inconsistent data format, scattered data and lack of analysis; (ii) Based on IoT technology, an anchor drilling monitoring system and a rock muck intelligent recognition system are employed to collect rock mass parameters in a real-time manner, which facilitates collection of digital rock mass information; (iii) On the basis of cloud computing technology and big data methods, a technology framework of an integrated information platform for TBM construction is developed and improved to conduct exploratory work for TBM big-data, including data pre-processing, correlation analysis, machine learning, model verification and upgrading.

With the further development and application of an integrated information platform for TBM construction, we plan to investigate the rule of interaction between TBM and rock mass in the future. On this basis, automatic sensing and recognition of equipment state and rock mass condition will be achieved, and related knowledge bases and rule bases will be built to provide a scientific basis for intelligent design, construction decision-making and optimization.

References

[1] Barla G, Pelizza S. TBM tunnelling in difficult ground conditions[A]. In: Geo Eng2000-An International Conference on Geotechnical & Geological Engineering[C], Melbourne, Australia, 2000, 20.

[2] Barton N, Rock mass characterization and seismic measurements to assist in the design and execution of TBM projects[A]. In: Paper Presented at the Proceedings of 1996 Taiwan Rock Engineering Symposium [C]. National Taiwan University Centre for Education, Taipei, 1996.

[3] Barton N, TBM Tunneling in Jointed and Fault Rock. Balkema, Rotterdam, 2000.

[4] Bruland A, Hard rock tunnel boring [D]. Trondheim: Norwegian University of Science and Technology, 1998.

[5] Cho J W, Jeon S, Jeong H Y, et al., Evaluation of cutting efficiency during TBM disc cutter excavation within a Korean granitic rock using linear-cutting-machine testing and photogrammetric measurement, Tunn [J]. Undergr. Space Technol, 2013, 35, 37-54.

[6] Geng Q, Wei, Z, Meng H, An experimental research on the rock cutting process of the gage cutters for rock tunnel boring machine (TBM)[J]. Tunn Undergr Space Technol. 2016, 52, 182-191.

[7] Gong Q M. Development of a Rock Mass Characteristics Model for TBM Penetration Rate Prediction[D]. School of Civil and Environmental Engineering, Nanyang Technical University, 2006.

[8] Guglielmetti V, Grasso P, Mahtab A, et al, Mechanised Tunneling in Urban Areas[M]. Taylor & Francis Group, London, 2008.

[9] Han M D, Cai Z X. Dynamic numerical simulation of cutter head loads in TBM tunneling, Tunn [J]. Undergr Space Technol, 2017, 70, 286-298.

[10] Hasanpour J, Rostami J, Zhao J. A new hard rock TBM performance prediction model for project planning. Tunn[J]. Undergr Space Technol, 2011, 26, 595-603.

[11] Hasanpour R. Advance numerical simulation of tunneling by using a double shield TBM, Comput [J]. Geotech., 2014, 57, 37-52.

[12] Hegemann F. Manickam P, Lehner K. Hybrid Ground Data Model for Interacting Simulations in Mechanized Tunneling J[J]. Comput. Civ. Eng, 2013, 27, 708-718.

[13] Hilbert M. Big Data for Development: A Review of Promises and Challenges [J]. Development Policy Review, 2016, 34, 135-174.

[14] Kahramana S, Bilginb N. Feridunoglu C. Dominant rock properties affecting the penetration rate of percussive drills, Int. J. Rock Mech. & Min. Sci., 2003, 40, 711-723.

[15] Kocha C, Vonthronb A, König M. A tunnel information modelling framework to support management, simulations and visualisations in mechanised tunnelling projects[J]. Automat. Constr., 2017, 83, 78-90.

[16] Liu Q S, Huang X, Gong, Q M, et al. Application and development of hard rock TBM and its prospect in China, Tunn[J]. Undergr Space Technol, 2016, 57, 33-46.

[17] Ma H S, Gong Q M, Wang J, Study on the influence of confining stress on TBM performance in granite rock by linear cutting test Tunn[J]. Undergr Space Technol, 2016, 57, 145-150.

[18] Meschke G, Nagel F, Stascheit J, Computational Simulation of Mechanised Tunneling as Part of an Integrated Decision Support Platform[J]. Geomech, 2011, 11, 519-528.

[19] Ramoni M. On the feasibility of TBM drives in squeezing ground and the risk of shield jamming[D]. ETH Zurich, 2010.

[20] Rostami J. Development of a force estimation model for rock fragmentation with disc cutters through the theoreticalmodeling and physical measurement of crushed zone pressure[D]. Golden: Colorado School of Mines, 1997.

[21] Rostami J. Performance prediction of hard rock Tunnel Boring Machines (TBMs) in difficult ground, Tunn [J]. Undergr Space Technol, 2016, 57, 173-182.

[22] Xue Y D, Zhao F, Zhao H X, et al., A new method for selecting hard rock TBM tunnelling parameters using optimum energy: A case study[J]. Undergr. Space Technol, 2018, 78, 64-75.

[23] Yue Z Q. Tunneling process monitoring for refining and upgrading rock mass quality classification methods [J]. Rock Mech Eng, 2014, 33, 1977-1996.

[24] Zhao J, Gong Q M, Eisensten Z. Tunnelling through a frequently changing and mixed ground: a case history in Singapore[J]. Undergr Space Technol, 2007, 22, 388-400.

[25] Zhao K, Janutolo M, Barla G. A completely 3D model for the simulation of mechanized tunnel excavation [J]. Rock Mech Rock Eng., 2012, 45, 475-497.

考虑空气层的寒区隧道防冻隔温层表面铺设研究

肖 镇 李邦兴 姚孟其

(长安大学公路学院)

摘 要 在隧道内铺设防冻隔温层可有效地减轻甚至消除冻害带来的不利影响。防冻隔温层铺设于隧道二次衬砌表面时,存在于防冻隔温层与纤维增强板之间的密闭空气层可减弱隧道内冷空气与围岩之间的热量交换,但在既有研究中都忽略了空气层对防冻隔温层的效果影响。本文通过现场调研、数值模拟手段,结合实测数据对考虑空气层的防冻隔温层隔温效果进行分析,旨在揭示空气层对寒区隧道温度场分布规律的影响,并对考虑空气层作用下的防冻隔温层厚度设计进行了优化研究,以期为寒区隧道工程设计中防冻隔温层厚度的取值提供参考。

关键词 隧道工程 寒冷地区 防冻隔温层 温度场

0 引 言

近年来,我国在西部高海拔和北部高纬度地区修建了大量的寒区隧道工程[1]。由于对寒区隧道工程特性认识不足,许多刚开通运营的隧道在当年寒季就出现渗漏水、路面结冰、洞顶和边墙挂冰等隧道病害[2]。更有甚者因形成冰塞而报废,造成了巨大的经济损失。已建兴安岭隧道、岭顶隧道、东北嫩林线的西罗奇2号隧道、新疆217国道天山段铁力买提隧道等均在运营中发生过严重的冻害事故,损失严重。

高海拔、高纬度寒冷地区隧道,运营阶段发生冻害现象后,比较常用的处置方法是疏通隧道排水渠道,同时,在隧道二次衬砌表面铺设防冻隔温层来减小隧道内冷空气对隧道温度场的影响[3]。谭贤君[4]研究将6cm厚的保温材料直接铺设在二衬表面工况,进行数值模拟得到了不同风速影响下和不同纵向长度防冻隔温层表面铺设对隧道围岩温度场的影响;范东方、夏才初[3,5]等人通过对不同类型冻土防冻隔温层表面铺设、夹层铺设和离壁式铺设下的围岩温度场进行了模拟,认为多年冻土隧道优先推荐防冻隔温层表面铺设法。郝飞[6]通过对保温层铺设在二次衬砌表面时进行数值模拟,简化认为保温层直接与隧道内冷空气接触,分析了隧道温度场的分布规律;姚红志[7]简化保温材料表面铺设模型,同样假定保温材料直接与隧道内冷空气接触,研究了保温材料的保温隔热效果。

通过对以上研究的梳理可知,在进行防冻隔温层表面铺设厚度设计或者研究防冻隔温层对隧道温度场的影响时,一般都忽略了防火板(或纤维增强板)的影响,认为保温板直接与隧道内冷空气进行热传递,简化处理后进行数值模拟得到相应的温度场分布结果。但是通过调研发现,防冻隔温层表面铺设法在实际工程应用中,由于轻钢龙骨的存在,保温层与防火板之间势必会存在着一定厚度的密闭空气层,空隙宽度甚至可以达到2~3cm。由于空气的导热系数为0.023W/(m·K)左右,其保温隔热作用不可忽视。鉴于此,本文通过现场调研、数值模拟手段,结合实测数据对考虑空气层的防冻隔温层隔温效果进行分析,旨在揭示空气层对寒区隧道温度场分布规律的影响,并对考虑空气层作用下的防冻隔温层厚度设计进行了优化研究,以期为寒区隧道工程设计中防冻隔温层厚度的取值提供参考意见。

1 保温层表面铺设数值模拟计算

1.1 依托工程概况

某寒冷地区隧道位于青海境内,隧址区属中高山剥蚀地貌,海拔为3700~3960m,隧道全长2315m。隧址区属高原大陆性气候中冷温性干旱草原类型,冻结期为当年的10月到次年的4月。最冷月份1月最低气温为-29℃,月平均气温为-16.1℃,最热月7月平均气温16.1℃;最大冻结深度为2.11m,隧道采用防冻隔温层表面铺设法,厚度设计为5cm。

1.2 保温层表面铺设数值模拟

采用大型有限元分析软件Ansys对隧道防冻隔温层表面铺设模拟分析,研究以下两种工况:工况一为忽略保温层与防火板之间空气层影响,认为隧道内冷空气直接通过保温层与衬砌和围岩发生热量交换;工况二考虑保温层与防火板之间空气层的影响。两种工况均采用平面四节点二维热实体单元PLANE55单元来模拟隧道温度场。在进行数值模拟计算之前,作出的假设条件为:①忽略围岩、初期支护、二次衬砌和保温板各接触界面的接触热阻;②衬砌结构混凝土和隧道围岩为均匀的、各向同性;③假设各种材料的热物性参数不随温度的变化而变化,均为常数。

1.2.1 建立计算模型

选取依托工程典型断面为计算断面,建立有限元模型,模型外边界选取长度为30m的正方形,左、右边界距隧道中心点的距离均为15m,模型下边界距隧道底部中心的距离为10m。模型左、右边界采用绝热边界条件,隧道内边界与隧道内部空气相通。得到计算模型如图1所示,两种工况的局部示意图如图2所示。各材料的热物理参数,如表1所示。

各材料热物理参数 表1

材　料	导热系数[W/(m·K)]	比热容[J/(kg·℃)]	密度(kg/m³)
保温板	0.024	2040	80
混凝土	2.56	1390	2480
围岩	3.5	2000	2700
空气	0.023	1004	1.29

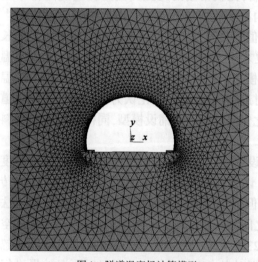

图1 隧道温度场计算模型

1.2.2 工况分析

建立计算模型时,两种计算工况以防冻隔温层相同厚度为计算基准,防冻隔温层厚度取为5cm。其中,工况一铺设5cm防冻隔温层,计算隧道内冷空气直接通过防冻隔温层与隧道衬砌、围岩发生热量交换;工况二在铺设5cm防冻隔温层基础上,在防火板与防冻隔温层之间存在有2cm厚密闭空气层。对比分析与工况一、二隧道衬砌、围岩温度场分布差异。

1.2.3 计算结果分析

以最冷月平均气温-16.1℃作为温度荷载施加到计算模型,计算时间为30d,子步长为2d,两种工况计算结果如图3所示。结合现场测点监测结果,得到不同工况下各监测点温度折线图,如图4所示。

从两种工况的计算结果和监测点温度折线图来看,工况一隧道的衬砌结构部位出现了负温,而工况二隧道衬砌结构基本无负温区域出现,也就是说,在不考虑防冻隔温层与防火板之间的空气层时,隧道衬砌结构在冷空气影响下会出现负温;考虑防冻隔温层与防火板之间的空气层时,隧道衬砌结构温度场负温区域将会大幅度减少;对比工况一与现场实测结果,发现不考虑空气层下进行数值模拟得到的衬砌部位温度值比实测结果偏低;实际现场监测结果显示,在隧道二次衬砌表面铺设5cm厚的防冻隔温层,二次衬砌表面温度为正温。因此,有必要考虑空气层的影响而进行防冻隔温层厚度计算优化。

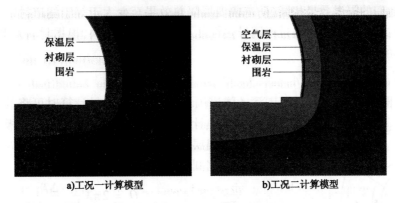

图 2　两种工况计算模型局部示意图

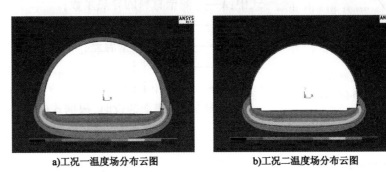

图 3　计算结果温度场分布云图

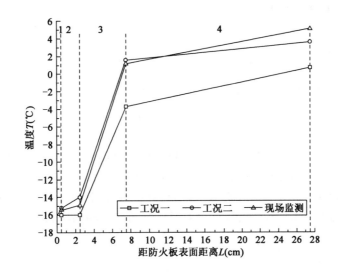

图 4　不同工况下监测点温度折线图

注:图中 1 代表防火板;2 代表空气层;3 代表防冻隔温层;4 代表距衬砌表面 20cm。

2　保温层表面铺设厚度优化

通过以上分析结果,发现存在于防冻隔温层与防火板之间的空气层对隧道衬砌温度场分布有一定的影响。在进行防冻隔温层厚度计算时,应将空气层考虑在内。鉴于此,在之前研究的基础上,进行考虑空气层的防冻隔温层等效厚度法解析计算,来进行防冻隔温层厚度设计优化。

2.1　等效厚度法

等效厚度法应用于隧道防冻隔温层厚度设计:防冻隔温层与隧道(衬砌和围岩组合体)的导热性能

存在差异,为保证他们的隔温效果相同(防冻隔温层隔热效果至少大于等于隧道衬砌和围岩的组合体),可令其热流量相同,即同一热流量通过不同导热性能、不同厚度的材料,根据材料两侧的温差相等,即可以解出这两种材料的等效厚度[8]。

2.2 保温层厚度计算优化

隧道整体为长圆管状,隧道冻结范围深入隧道围岩,在进行热流量计算时可将其视为圆筒。在进行圆筒传热计算时,考虑防冻隔温层与防火板之间空气层的影响进行保温层厚度设计优化,其计算模型如图5所示。

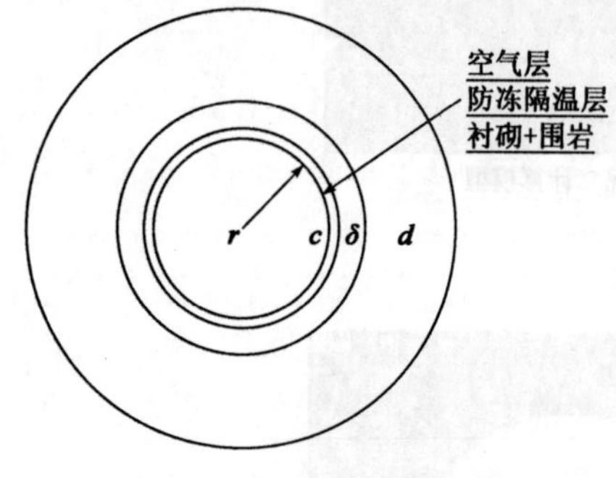

根据圆筒传热计算公式:

$$Q = 2\pi\lambda \frac{\Delta T}{\ln r_2 - \ln r_1} L \tag{1}$$

式中:λ——筒壁材料的导热系数;
L——圆筒长度;
ΔT——圆筒内、外壁温差;
r_1——圆筒内半径;
r_2——圆筒外半径。

图5 等效厚度法计算模型示意图
r-隧道当量半径;c-空气层厚度;δ-防冻隔温层厚度;d-衬砌+围岩冻结深度

防冻隔温层表面铺设时,根据式(1),由计算模型得:

$$2\pi(\lambda_1 + \lambda_2)\frac{\Delta T}{\ln(r+c+\delta) - \ln(c+\delta)}L = 2\pi\lambda_3 \frac{\Delta T}{\ln(r+c+\delta+d) - \ln(r+c+\delta)}L \tag{2}$$

式中:λ_1——空气层的导热系数;
λ_2——保温层的导热系数;
λ_3——衬砌+围岩的导热系数。

由式(2)得:

$$(\lambda_1 + \lambda_2)\ln\frac{r+d}{r} = \lambda_3 \ln\frac{r}{c+\delta} \tag{3}$$

由式(3)可解出防冻隔温层表面铺设优化计算厚度δ。

3 结 语

本文通过对保温层和防火板间的空气层考虑与否两种工况,对寒区隧道温度场进行了数值模拟,结合现场隧道各测点温度测试数据,对比分析两种工况,发现不考虑空气层影响时,隧道衬砌部位将会出现负温区域,而考虑空气层作用以及现场实测结果表明二次衬砌部位几乎未出现负温区域。此外,在考虑保温层与防火板间空气层的影响条件下,应用等效厚度法对防冻隔温层表面铺设保温层厚度计算进行了优化研究。

参考文献

[1] Wang T, Zhou G, Wang J, et al. Stochastic analysis for the uncertain temperature field of tunnel in cold regions[J]. Tunnelling& Underground Space Technology Incorporating Trenchless Technology Research, 2016,59:7-15.

[2] Yan Q, Li B, Zhang Y, et al. Numerical Investigation of Heat-Insulating Layers in a Cold Region Tunnel, Taking into Account Airflow and Heat Transfer[J]. Applied Sciences,2017,7(7):679.

[3] 夏才初,范东方,韩常领.寒区隧道不同类型冻土段隔热(保温)层铺设厚度计算方法[J].中国公路学报,2013,26(5):131-139.

[4] 谭贤君,陈卫忠,于洪丹,等.考虑通风影响的寒区隧道围岩温度场及防寒保温材料敷设长度研究[J].岩石力学与工程学报,2013,32(7):1400-1409.

[5] 范东方,夏才初,韩常领.不同类型冻土中隧道隔热保温层铺设方式的选择[J].地下空间与工程学

[6] 郝飞,孙全胜.寒区公路隧道温度场及保温层的研究[J].现代隧道技术,2012,49(1):39-43.
[7] 姚红志,张晓旭,董长松,等.多年冻土区公路隧道保温隔热层铺设方式及材料性能对比分析[J].中国公路学报,2015,28(12):106-113.
[8] 陈建勋,罗彦斌.寒冷地区隧道防冻隔温层厚度计算方法[J].交通运输工程学报,2007,7(2):76-79.

寒区运营隧道冻害风险评估体系

肖 镇

(长安大学公路学院)

摘 要 冻害作为寒区运营隧道的重大安全隐患,易造成衬砌挂冰、路面结冰等严重灾害,但对相关的风险辨识预警理论尚缺乏系统的研究。文章通过调研统计与理论分析,将冻害致险因子划分为外部因素与内部因素两类,基于寒区运营隧道中冻害的发生与致险因子的关系,采用层次分析法计算各致险因子的常权重值,且考虑到不同寒区隧道之间地质条件、气象条件、施工质量等的差异,在常权重基础上提出了变权重算法。针对寒区运营隧道安全事故系统演化规律,确定致险因子评估取值范围,并给出了冻害风险评估等级划分标准。结合工程实例,验证了文章所建立的寒区运营隧道冻害风险评估体系的合理性。以期在寒区隧道设计、建设、运营等环节中为减小甚至消除各冻害风险因子的不利影响提供参考。

关键词 寒区隧道 冻害 致险因子 权重风险评估

0 引 言

近年来,我国在西部高海拔和北部高纬度地区修建了大量的寒区隧道工程[1]。由于对寒区隧道工程特性认识不足,许多隧道在运营当年冷季就出现路面结冰、衬砌挂冰、消防管道结冰等隧道病害[2],严重威胁隧道内行车安全,更有甚者因形成冰塞而报废,造成了巨大的经济损失。

国内外相关学者从20世纪末开始尝试将风险评估理论应用于工程领域:Einstein[3]首次将风险理论应用于岩土工程领域;Sturk et al.[4]将风险决策分析方法应用于大型地下工程;国际隧道协会颁布的Guidelines for Tunneling Risk Management为隧道设计与建设环节风险管理提供了参考标准[5-6]。Brown E T[7]通过使用贝叶斯网络和决策分析技术在不确定条件下进行推理来增加现有概率分析方法,并且在项目的各个阶段进一步地完善分析;Phoon K K,Ching J[8]在Reliability-Based Design in Geotechnical Engineering Computations and Applications的基础上,通过解释计算过程,并且通过实例来辨析各分析方法的优缺点,由此向广大相关工程人员或科研人员展示可靠性理论与风险方法学;国内针对隧道建设阶段隧道风险评估进行了一系列的研究[9-11],但很少有针对运营阶段的隧道进行风险评估研究,尤其是寒区隧道冻害的风险评估[5,12]。

本文在调研总结与理论分析的基础上选取冻害风险致险因子并计算致险因子权重;在层次分析法常权重基础上考虑不同工程工况的区别,引入变权理论进行计算[13];确定致险因子的评估取值范围,结合寒区运营隧道中冻害事故的发生概率和损失大小划分冻害风险等级;建立冻害风险评估体系,结合实际工程应用案例验证该风险评估体系的可行性和合理性。以期在隧道设计、建设、运营等环节中为减小甚至消除各风险因子带来不利影响提供参考。

1 选取冻害致险因子

建立寒区隧道冻害风险评估体系的第一步即调研分析与确定导致冻害现象产生的致险因子,以冻害对寒区运营隧道产生不利影响为主要原则,由此选出符合实际情况的致险因子(又称第二类风险源)。在确定冻害风险评估体系致险因子时,需要选取致险因子的合理数量,选取的原则是这些致险因子能够较为全面综合地反映主要矛盾,为此忽略次要矛盾(即次要致险因子)带来的影响。结合现场调研最终遴选出风流起始端隧道洞口平均风速、最冷月平均气温、冻结深度、施工质量四个外部因子,另取地下水赋存、地下水渗入和围岩完整性三个内部因子,共七个因素作为致险因子[14-23]。

2 致险因子权重

通过采取指标模糊量化方法(调研统计和分析总结)得到各冻害风险致险因子和各致险因子权重,以作为目标(多指标)、多方案优化决策的系统方法。但由于不同隧道的地质条件、气象条件等千差万别,所以应该采取措施来弥补层次分析法中场权重的不足,变权重计算具有动态评估的优点,能较为理想地应用于不同工程工况,因此采用变权重计算来确定致险因子的权重。

2.1 层次分析法计算常权重

建立层次分析模型后,构造成对比较矩阵(判断矩阵),求解此成对比较矩阵的最大特征值 λ_{max} 以及其所对应的特征向量,满足一致性检验后,即得到权重向量。本文将冻害对寒区运营隧道风险评估体系分为三个层次:其中评估体系为 A 层次(最高层),外部因素和内部因素为 B 层次(中间层),上述所选定的七个致险因子为 C 层次(最低层),如表 1 所示。

评估体系层次结构表　　　　　表1

		风流流入端隧道洞口平均风速 C_1
		最冷月平均气温 C_2
	外部因素 B_1	冻结深度 C_3
		施工质量 C_4
寒区隧道冻害风险评估体系 A		地下水赋存 C_5
	内部因素 B_2	地下水渗入 C_6
		围岩完整性 C_7

综合分析外部因素与内部因素对寒区隧道运营安全的影响程度,实地调研后统计分析冻害发生概率和可能造成的损失,得出外部因素的影响大于内部因素的结论,前者在形成隧道冻害现象所产生的影响大于后者。建立由最高层(A 层次)到中间层(B 层次)的成对比较矩阵:

$$P_{A-B} = \begin{bmatrix} 1 & 2 \\ 1/2 & 1 \end{bmatrix} \quad (1)$$

计算得到权重向量 $\overrightarrow{\omega_{A-B}} = [0.86, 0.14]$,满足一致性检验。同理,分别对比分析风流流入端隧道洞口风速 C_1、最冷月平均气温 C_2、冻结深度 C_3、施工质量 C_4 四种外部因素和地下水赋存 C_5、地下水渗入 C_6、围岩完整性 C_7 三种内部因素对冻害发生的影响程度,得到在外部因素中,风流流入端隧道洞口风速 C_1、最冷月平均气温 C_2 和冻结深度 C_3 影响较大,施工质量 C_4 次之;在内部因素中,地下水赋存 C_5 比地下水渗入 C_6 影响小。构造 B_1-C 的成对比较矩阵和 B_2-C 的成对比较矩阵:

$$P_{B_1-C} = \begin{bmatrix} 1 & 1/5 & 1/4 & 1/3 \\ 5 & 1 & 5/4 & 5/3 \\ 4 & 4/5 & 1 & 4/3 \\ 3 & 3/5 & 3/4 & 1 \end{bmatrix} \quad (2)$$

$$P_{B_2-C} = \begin{bmatrix} 1 & 1/3 & 1/5 \\ 3 & 1 & 3/5 \\ 5 & 5/3 & 1 \end{bmatrix} \quad (3)$$

由式(2)计算可得权重向量 $\overrightarrow{\omega_{B_1-C}} = [0.08, 0.38, 0.31, 0.23]$,$\lambda_{max} = 4$,CI = 0,其随机一致性比率 RI = 0,矩

阵的检验系数 CR=0<0.1,可满足一致性的检验。由式(3)可得权重向量 $\overrightarrow{\omega_{B_2-C}}=[0.11,0.33,0.56]$,$\lambda_{max}=3$,CI=0,其随机一致性比率 RI=0,矩阵的检验系数 CR=0<0.1,可满足一致性的检验。由此得到致险因子 $C_1\sim C_7$ 权重值分别为 0.07、0.32、0.26、0.20、0.02、0.05、0.08。

2.2 变权理论计算变权重

为了体现对致险因子重要性的偏好以及满足对状态均衡偏好的要求,采用变权重计算来弥补层次分析法中常权重的不足[24],得到变权公式:

$$\omega_i(x_1,\cdots,x_m)=\frac{\omega_i^{(0)}x_i^{\alpha-1}}{\sum_{k=1}^m \omega_k^{(0)}x_k^{\alpha-1}} \quad (4)$$

式中:ω_i——第 i 个致险因子的变权重;

$\omega_i^{(0)}$——第 i 个致险因子的常权重;

x_i——第 i 个致险因子的评估分值;

α——均衡函数,本文取 $\alpha=0.5$。

3 建立风险评估体系

在遴选分析致险因子和确定权重计算方法后,需建立寒区运营隧道冻害风险评估表,以便计算冻害风险。参考 Guidelines for Tunnelling Risk Management,完成寒区隧道冻害风险评估体系。

3.1 冻害风险评估表建立

风险评估表中每个等级取 10 分,确定每一个致险因子等级取值区间,参照现行风险评估指南《公路桥梁和隧道工程设计安全风险评估》[25],建立寒区运营隧道中冻害风险评估表(表2)。实际工程总风险值,根据表2评定各项指标分值后,根据式(5)和式(6)计算确定:

$$R=\sum_{i=1}^n \omega_i \cdot R_i \quad (5)$$

$$\omega_i=\frac{\omega_i^{(0)}R_i^{\alpha-1}}{\sum_{k=1}^m \omega_k^{(0)}R_k^{\alpha-1}} \quad (6)$$

式中:R——总的评估值;

n——评估指标个数;

ω_i——第 i 项指标的变权重;

R_i——第 i 项指标的评估分值;

$\omega_i^{(0)}$——第 i 个致险因子的常权重。

3.2 评估风险等级划分标准

在指标常权重计算中已考虑了各指标引发事故的概率和可能导致的损失大小,因此根据寒区运营隧道冻害风险评估表(表2)评定各项指标分值后,计算得到的总评估值涵括了风险概率和损失,即总风险。参考《公路桥梁和隧道工程设计安全风险评估指南》,同时为使工程评估计算简便,将各评估指标基本分值中最大值的 60%、45% 和 30% 分别定为极高风险、高度风险和中度风险的下限,确定寒区运营隧道冻害风险评估等级划分表(表3)。

寒区运营隧道冻害风险评估表　　　　表2

评估指标	常权重	影响程度分类	基本分值
风流流入端隧道洞口平均风速	0.07	洞口平均风速 $v\geq 12$m/s	21~30
		6m/s< 洞口平均风速 $v<12$m/s	11~20
		洞口平均风速 $v\leq 6$m/s	0~10

续上表

评估指标	常权重	影响程度分类	基本分值
最冷月平均气温	0.32	最冷月平均气温 $t \leq -25℃$	21~30
		$-10℃ <$ 最冷月平均气温 $< -25℃$	11~20
		最冷月平均气温 $\geq -10℃$	0~10
冻结深度	0.26	冻结深度 $h \geq 2.9m$	21~30
		$1.3m <$ 冻结深度 $h < 2.9m$	11~20
		冻结深度 $h \leq 1.3m$	0~10
施工质量	0.20	施工质量不符合规范要求	21~30
		施工质量基本满足规范要求	11~20
		施工质量按规范要求执行	0~10
地下水赋存	0.05	含水隧道,有地下水补给	21~30
		含水隧道,无地下水补给	11~20
		含少量水隧道,无补给	0~10
地下水渗入	0.08	渗水、涌水	21~30
		少量渗水、滴水	11~20
		无地下水渗入	0~10
围岩完整性	0.02	围岩完整性指数 $K_v \leq 0.15$	21~30
		$0.15 <$ 围岩完整性指数 $K_v < 0.55$	11~20
		围岩完整性指数 $K_v \geq 0.55$	0~10

寒区运营隧道冻害风险评估等级划分表　　　　　表3

风险等级	风险评估值
极高风险Ⅳ	$R \geq 18$
高度风险Ⅲ	$13 \leq R < 18$
中度风险Ⅱ	$9 \leq R < 13$
低度风险Ⅰ	$R < 9$

3.3 工程应用

在河卡山隧道通车运营前,本文研究小组按调研所得气象资料和地质勘察资料,结合施工情况,对河卡山隧道进行冻害风险评估。根据调研资料,河卡山隧道在未铺设保温板的情况下有发生冻害的风险。在铺设完成4.5cm厚的保温板后,结合隧道设计中所采取的防排水措施,大大降低了运营中隧道发生冻害的风险。用本文提出的风险体系进行冻害风险评估,计算得到风险值 $R = 7.67$,对照表3风险等级划分标准可确定风险等级为Ⅰ级,属低度风险。

按照常权重计算方法将会得到此寒区隧道冻害运营风险值 $R = 13.30$,对照表3风险等级划分标准可确定风险等级为Ⅲ级,属高度风险。但在实际运营期间隧道内并未出现拱顶、边墙渗漏水结冰以及路面冻结等冻害现象,对照表3风险等级划分标准判定为Ⅰ级风险更合理,更符合工程实际,验证了权重计算方法和评估体系的合理性。

4　结　语

(1)通过调研统计、理论分析后选定风流起始端隧道洞口平均风速、隧址区最冷月平均气温、冻结深度、施工质量四个外部因素,以及地下水赋存、地下水渗入隧道情况和围岩完整性三个内部因素,共七个因素作为寒区隧道冻害的主要致险因子。

(2)本文在常权重基础上进一步用变权理论来弥补层次分析法中常权重理论的不足,满足了对致险因子重要性以及对状态均衡偏好的要求,可较好地实现评估体系在不同地质条件、气象条件隧道工程中的应用。

(3)建立寒区运营隧道冻害风险评估表和确定风险等级划分标准,最终建立了寒区运营隧道冻害风险评估体系,并结合工程实例验证了评估体系的合理性和可行性。

参考文献

[1] Wang T, Zhou G, Wang J, et al. Stochastic analysis for the uncertain temperature field of tunnel in cold regions[J]. Tunnelling& Underground Space Technology Incorporating Trenchless Technology Research, 2016, 59:7-15.

[2] Yan Q, Li B, Zhang Y, et al. Numerical Investigation of Heat-Insulating Layers in a Cold Region Tunnel, Taking into Account Airflow and Heat Transfer[J]. Applied Sciences, 2017, 7(7):679.

[3] Einstein H H. Risk and risk analysis in rock engineering[J]. Tunnelling& Underground Space Technology, 1996, 11(2):141-155.

[4] Sturk R, Olsson L, Johansson J (1996) Risk and decision analysis for large underground projects, as applied to the Stockholm ring road tunnels. Tunn UndergrSp Tech 11:157-164.

[5] 周国恩. 基于ANP与模糊理论的寒区隧道冻害风险评估与管理研究[J]. 现代隧道技术, 2013, 50(1):60-66.

[6] Eskesen S D, Tengborg P, Kampmann J, et al. Guidelines for tunnelling risk management: International Tunnelling Association, Working Group No. 2 ☆[J]. Tunnelling& Underground Space Technology, 2004, 19(3):217-237.

[7] Brown E T. Risk assessment and management in underground rock engineering—an overview[J]. Journal of Rock Mechanics and Geotechnical Engineering, 2012, 4(3):193-204.

[8] Phoon K K, Ching J. Risk and Reliability in Geotechnical Engineering[J]. Open Access Publications from Tilburg University, 2014, 10(3):209-218.

[9] Wu M, Zhang Q, Wu S. Risk Assessment of Operation Period Structural Stability for Long and Large Immersed Tube Tunnel [J]. Procedia Engineering, 2016, 166:266-278.

[10] 李永宽, 张顶立, 房倩. 海底隧道建设全过程风险评估分析[J]. 现代隧道技术, 2015, 52(03):47-54.

[11] Xu CB, Tian HN, Zhou N. Risk source identification and risk assessment analysis for AoFengmountain tunnel entrance section. [J]Journal of Highway and Transportation Research and Development 2012; 29(10):96-101.

[12] 蔚立元, 李术才, 梁巍, 等. 隧道建设运营中的各种灾害及研究方向[C]//全国地下工程超前地质预报与灾害治理学术及技术研讨会论文集(Ⅲ). 2009.

[13] 薛亚东, 李硕标, 丁文强, 等. 隐伏溶洞对隧道施工安全影响的风险评估体系[J]. 现代隧道技术, 2015, 54(4).

[14] Martinelli F, Cara S, Domenichini L. Rail Tunnel Risk Analysis: A Tool to Improve Rail Tunnel Design [J]. Transportation Research Record Journal of the Transportation Research Board, 2008, 2043(2043):41-48.

[15] Tan X, Chen W, Yang D, et al. Study on the influence of airflow on the temperature of the surrounding rock in a cold region tunnel and its application to insulation layer design [J]. Applied Thermal Engineering, 2014, 67(1-2):320-334.

[16] 徐鑫. 考虑通风条件下寒区隧道围岩及衬砌温度场变化规律研究[D]. 西安: 西安科技大学, 2015.

[17] 罗彦斌. 寒区隧道冻害等级划分及防治技术研究[D]. 北京: 北京交通大学, 2010.

[18] 罗彦斌, 陈建勋, 王梦恕. 隧道冻害等级的划分[J]. 北京工业大学学报, 2010, 36(4):458-462.

[19] Feng Q, Jiang B S, Zhang Q, et al. Reliability research on the 5-cm-thick insulation layer used in the

[20] 崔凌秋,吕康成,王潮海,等.寒冷地区隧道渗漏与冻害综合防治技术探讨[J].现代隧道技术,2005,42(5):22-25.
[21] 田俊峰,杨更社,刘慧.寒区岩石隧道冻害机理及防治研究[J].地下空间与工程学报,2007,3(z2):1484-1489.
[22] 张镇国,伍毅敏,张庆宁.经时视角下山岭隧道水害冻害若干问题的实证研究[J].铁道科学与工程学报,2016,13(06):1129-1134.
[23] 邓刚.高海拔寒区隧道防冻害设计问题[D].西安:西南交通大学,2012.
[24] Wang P Z. A factor spaces approach to knowledge representation[M]. Elsevier North-Holland, Inc. 1990.
[25] 张喜刚.公路桥梁和隧道工程设计安全风险评估[M].北京:人民交通出版社,2010.

隧道群连接段光照环境研究

李洪祥

（长安大学公路学院）

摘要 为研究隧道群连接段光照环境变化规律，采用Ecotect Analysis软件建立隧道群仿真模型，以视点照度为光照环境强弱的评价指标，在检验模型可靠的基础上分析连接段长度对视觉环境的影响，结果表明：当连接段长度小于60m时，下游隧道入口照明应适当折减，此时连接段长度与连接段内视点照度最大值呈对数函数关系。最后借助模型仿真75m长连接段内视点照度变化趋势。

关键词 隧道安全 光照环境 模型仿真 隧道群连接段 视点照度

0 引言

驾驶员获取外界信息最重要的方式是视觉[1]，但其在隧道群路段尤其是连接段行驶时要在短时间内经历多次光暗环境变换，这会对生理和心理产生极大影响[2]，因此我们有必要明确隧道群连接段外界光照环境的是如何变化的。

叶飞[3]对隧道群光环境、交通事故分布等进行分析发现，驾驶员瞳孔面积与环境光照度比值的对数和环境光照度的对数之间具有线性关系。杜志刚[4]基于实测数据得出，隧道出入口段驾驶员瞳孔面积与面积变化临界速度之间的关系，且隧道长度与明暗适应时间呈正相关。唐鹏飞[5]将驾驶员在逐渐接近隧道的过程中的光暗感受分为4级，并确定了不同感受级别的亮度阈值。胡江碧[6,7]以驶入隧道过程中看到目标时车辆与目标之间的距离作为评价指标，得出不同设计速度所对应的亮度折减系数阈值。Buchner[8]指出驾驶员判识距离随道路环境照度降低而增大。Adrian W[9]从驾驶员接近隧道时的适应过程中生理与心理方面考虑，讲述了推导隧道入口区域亮度的方法。Verwey W. B[10]等指出驾驶员在逐渐接近隧道的过程中，眨眼频率降低，扫视幅度逐渐减小，且不同的隧道之间有较大区别。因此当前研究多数是从人的主观感受出发分析驾驶员的视觉特性，且主要集中于隧道出入口段，对隧道群连接段真实光照环境的研究涉及较少。

本文通过Ecotect Analysis建立隧道群物理模型，以实测西汉高速公路隧道入口段照度数据检测模型可靠性，选择2000lux、3000lux、4000lux三个视点照度水平为高、中、低光照强度的代表，对隧道群连接段进行光环境仿真。这对明确隧道群路段交通事故产生机理，改善连接段驾驶员视觉环境具有重要的意义。

1 数据采集与模型建立

视点照度是指驾驶员瞳孔处光照度,即射入瞳孔内的光线在瞳孔处所形成的光照强度,其能够真实反映外界明暗变化,以此为切入点开展连接段光照环境研究最为有效。

1.1 公路隧道入口段驾驶员视点照度实测方案

1.1.1 试验仪器和设备

(1)试验车。以小型汽车的代表大众 Passat 作为试验车辆。

(2)照度计。当照度计光度头受光方向摆放的与驾驶员视线注视方向一致时,光度头表面照度与人眼瞳孔处照度完全相同。所以采用台湾泰仕 TES1339 专业级照度计检测视点照度值,该照度计每 0.2s 测一个照度数据。

(3)行车记录仪、笔记本电脑。

1.1.2 试验人员与实验步骤

选择不同驾龄、年龄男驾驶员 3 人、女驾驶员 2 人,保持匀速行驶排队依次进入隧道,开启行车记录仪,后座人员将照度计按上述方法摆放,以记录视点照度值。

1.2 模型建立

(1)利用 AutoCAD 构建隧道口断面三维模型,净宽 10.25m,高 8.00m。在视图选项中选择与 Ecotect 相应的坐标轴方向,将结构图进行三维旋转得到所需的断面图。

(2)将上述断面图导入 Ecotect 软件中,通过连线、画面等步骤后在模型底部添加一个平面当作隧道中路面模型,取隧道长度为 200m,如图 1 所示。

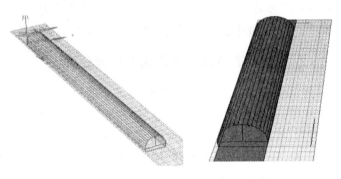

图 1 隧道模型示意图

(3)按照现行《公路隧道照明设计细则》要求,采用对称布设的方法在模型内部添加照明灯具,灯具布设从洞口断面以内 10m 处开始,设置在距地面 5m 的两侧侧壁拱腰处,使用复制功能,建立由两个隧道构成的隧道群模型。

(4)模型构建完成后对不同构件的参数进行设置,如将隧道表面材质设置为墙体(透光系数为 0),在分析网格管理器中设置网格参数,综合仿真时间及结果精度的基础上选择 y 方向分析网格数为 18,z 方向为 16。

(5)因为真实情况下驾驶员只能注视到前方的东西,只有前方光线能射入眼睛内部,因此需在分析网格后设置 0.5m×1.8m 挡板,材质设置为墙体。

(6)在计算向导中进行各参数设置,其中对于不同的视点照度条件下的仿真分析,仅需改变其中的照度数值。

1.3 模型检验

选取右侧行车道中心线、1.6m 高度处的照度值作为视点照度,当行车速度为 70km/h 时,0.2s 行驶的距离为 3.9m,因此以 4m 的长度调整分析网格位置并记录数据,选取实测西汉高速隧道入口处的视点照度数据与软件仿真数据对比,检验实测数据和模拟数据的一致性部分如表1所示。

实测数据与模拟数据 表1

与洞口断面的距离(m)	实测数据(lux)	模拟数据(lux)
−28	1381.5	1345
−24	1305	1318.6
−20	1287.1	1284
−16	1260	1245.4
−12	1238	1236.5
−8	1213	1215.4
−4	1186	1189
0	607	632.6
4	108.2	98.8
8	98.9	100.3
12	92.4	93
16	91.2	90

此时通过spss进行两配对样本非参数检验,显著性分析结果如表2所示。

spss显著性检验结果 表2

	Wilcoxon符号平均秩检验	样本符号检验
显著性	0.962	1.000

由表2可知,Wilcoxon检验的显著性为0.962,样本符号检验显著性为1,故仿真数据与实测结果无显著性差异,认为Ecotect软件所建立的隧道群光环境仿真物理模型具有较高的可靠性。

2 隧道群路段视点照度规律分析

我国不同地方年阳光辐射总量相差较大,综合所测的视点照度值和全国不同省市年辐射量,将不同地区视点照度大致分为三个水平,第一个水平为西藏、新疆和甘肃部分地区,以4000lux作为高光照强度下代表值;第二个水平即为山西、陕西、宁夏、重庆部分地区,以3000lux作为中等光照强度代表值,第三个水平即为黑、吉、辽、京、津、冀、鲁等年辐射总量较低的地区,选取2000lux作为低光照强度条件代表值。

2.1 连接段长度对视点照度的影响

模拟连接段长度从10m变化到100m时视点照度最大值的变化如图2所示,分析连接段长度对外界视觉环境的影响。

由图2可知,当连接段长度大于60m时,视点照度最大值能够达到并维持在与普通路段接近的恒定值;当连接段长度小于60m时,视点照度最大值均小于相应的环境照度,即连接段光照强度无法完全增长到正常路段的光照强度,此时若下游隧道进口段的照明灯具仍然按照单一隧道进口的照明方案布设,可能会出现照明过度的问题。

采用SPSS对连接段长度为0~60m时连接段长度与视点照度最大值二者的关系进行回归分析拟合,如表3所示。

连接段长度与视点照度最大值回归分析表 表3

函数模型	2000lux		3000lux		4000lux	
	F	Sig	F	Sig	F	Sig
线性	5.554	.065	6.322	.054	5.810	.061
对数	1474.277	.000	405.584	.000	1499.346	.000

续上表

函数模型	2000lux		3000lux		4000lux	
	F	Sig	F	Sig	F	Sig
逆函数	144.565	.000	84.641	.000	132.043	.000
二次	10.970	.024	14.013	.016	11.543	.022
三次	29.724	.010	49.916	.005	27.725	.011
幂	247.370	.000	259.631	.000	247.886	.000
指数	3.144	.136	3.18	.135	3.147	.136

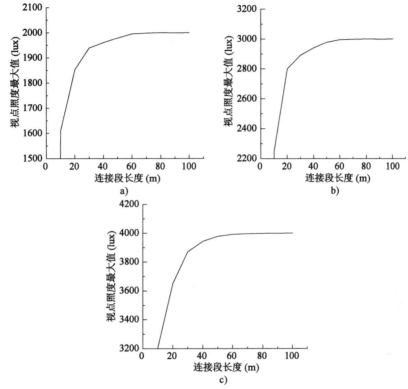

图 2　视点照度最大值随连接段长度变化趋势

由表 3 可知,当连接段长度小于 60m 时,三种照度水平下对数函数模型最为显著,视点照度最大值与连接段长度之间符合对数函数关系,分别为:

$$Y = 1265.197 + 183.957 \ln X \tag{1}$$

$$Y = 1877.196 + 275.493 \ln X \tag{2}$$

$$Y = 2526.026 + 368.037 \ln X \tag{3}$$

式中:Y——视点照度最大值(lux),$Y \geq 0$;

X——连接段长度(m),$X > 0$。

因此当两隧道连接段长度小于 60m 时,第二条的可根据连接段长度计算出对应的视点照度最大值,与实际环境光照度对比后进行适当的照明折减;当连接段长度大于 60m 时,可认为两隧道之间照明没有影响,可独立设置照明灯具。且由上式可以看出,外界光照环境越大,随着连接段长度的增加,视点照度最大值增长越快。

2.2　连接段视点照度变化

选择 75m 的连接段长度,以前一隧道出口断面为起始点 0,以下一隧道入口断面为终点,模拟连接段视点照度变化趋势,由于三种光照度水平下变化规律相似,因此只列出其中一种,如图 3 所示。

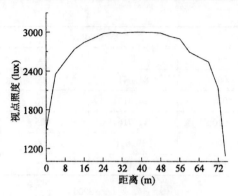

图3 连接段视点照度变化趋势

从图3可以看出,前一隧道出口至隧道外16m左右,视点照度上升速度较快,16m以后有较小幅度的增加,30m后逐渐稳定在环境光照强度周围很小的范围内浮动。在距下一隧道前近30m时,视点照度呈下降趋势,初期下降较缓,直至入口断面前12m,曲线下降斜率增大,即视点照度急剧下降。

3 结 语

本文借助Ecotect Analysis仿真软件构造隧道群物理模型,分析了隧道群光照环境变化,具体结论如下:

(1)当连接段长度小于60m时,连接段内光照环境无法完全增长到正常路段行驶时的强度,连接段长度X与连接段内视点照度最大值Y呈对数函数关系,在2000lux、3000lux、4000lux视点照度水平下,函数关系式分别为:

$$Y = 1265.197 + 183.957 \ln X$$
$$Y = 1877.196 + 275.493 \ln X$$
$$Y = 2526.026 + 368.037 \ln X$$

此时下游隧道入口段应根据计算所得视点照度与普通路段对比后进行适当的照明折减。

(2)在75m长连接段内,视点照度呈现前16m急剧增大,16m至30m缓慢增加,30m后逐渐稳定,在45m至60m缓慢减小,60m后急剧降低的变化趋势。

但现在由于道路线形越来越复杂,曲线形的隧道越来越多,而本文所构建的为直线型隧道群物理模型,曲线形隧道视觉特性的分析还有待进一步研究。

参考文献

[1] 方鼎.汽车驾驶人动态视认性的实验研究[D].西安:长安大学,2005.
[2] 方守恩,邬洪波,廖军洪,等.山区高速公路隧道群路段安全评价[J].同济大学学报:自然科学版,2013,41(5):693-699.
[3] 叶飞.高速公路隧道群路段驾驶人视觉明暗适应变化规律研究[D].西安:长安大学,2014.
[4] 杜志刚,黄发明,严新平,等.基于瞳孔面积变动的公路隧道明暗适应时间[J].公路交通科技,2013,30(05):98-102.
[5] 唐鹏飞.基于驾驶人视点照度的公路隧道入口遮阳棚设计方法[D].西安:长安大学,2018.
[6] 胡江碧,马文倩.基于驾驶视认需求的隧道入口段光环境研究[J].上海交通大学学报,2015,49(04):464-469.
[7] 胡江碧,李然,马勇.高速公路隧道入口段照明安全阈值评价方法[J].中国公路学报,2014,27(03):92-99.
[8] Buchner A, Branddt M, Bell R, et al. Car backlight position and fog density bias observer-car distance estimates and time-to-collision judgments[J]. Human Factors,2006,48(2):300-317.
[9] Adrian W. Investigations on the required luminance in tunnel entrances[J]. Lighting Research and Technology,1982,14(3):151-159.
[10] Verwey W B. Effects of tunnel entrances on driver's physiological condition and performance[J]. Report TM,1995.

基于图像处理的隧道火灾烟雾识别算法研究

陶 杰　朱熙豪　郑于海　刘海萍　汪内利

(浙江省机电设计研究院有限公司)

摘 要　为解决隧道预防早期火灾蔓延,急需准确快速的烟雾检测算法。面向视频图像的烟雾检测算法有效克服了传统烟雾探测器的不足。本文构建运动差异深度矩阵进行背景建模,利用火焰烟雾的运动特性提取运动目标,通过腐蚀、膨胀得到火焰烟雾疑似区域。然后提取出火焰与烟雾独有特征,运用遗传算法优化后的BP神经网络建立烟雾火焰识别模型。将提取出的火焰与烟雾特征作为输入量,利用遗传-BP神经网络进行识别。并选取大量不同环境的视频进行实验测试,其中烟雾检测成功率为91.61%,火焰检测成功率为93.45%,烟雾火焰检测并行处理综合识别率达到97.55%。证实了该算法能够可靠的排除隧道运动车辆、灯光等干扰,能有效地检测出火焰和烟雾并报警,能够应用于实际场景的火灾烟雾检测。

关键词　隧道工程　火灾识别　BP神经网络　遗传算法　目标提取

0 引 言

随着我国隧道建设的快速发展,隧道火灾也日益增加。火灾会导致整条线路交通的瘫痪,特别是对于各类长距离隧道,一旦发生交通火灾事故,其后果不堪设想。近年来,随着计算机视觉图像处理快速发展,基于视频图像的火灾烟雾检测成为可能。同传统火灾烟雾检测装置相比具备监测范围广、准确率高等优点。因此,利用计算机视觉图像处理技术对隧道进行火灾烟雾实时检测尤其重要。

1 现状分析

交通隧道火灾一般是由隧道内通行的车辆或电路短路引起的,且隧道火灾发生位置具有随机性,并受隧道纵向风的影响,火势蔓延速度快,救援难度大、经济损失高。

传统火灾烟雾实时检测实质是利用传感器感知温度、烟雾、光照强度等,再通过特定的阈值转换为报警信号。由于隧道中的跨度空间大,因此需要铺设大量的传感器。同时,鉴于传感器的准确度和灵敏度有限,且易受隧道自身环境和通行车辆的干扰,往往当隧道中火灾已经发生到一定程度才报警,已经很难满足当前隧道运营和安全保障的需求。

国内外针对计算机视觉图像处理的火灾烟雾实时检测已经开展了广泛研究。其研究方向主要集中于提取出火焰及烟雾区域,通过对火焰、烟雾的形状颜色和运动数据等进行识别。目前在抗干扰和识别精度方面仍有一定的缺陷。本文针对目前隧道火灾烟雾检测现状,通过隧道内已有摄像机获取视频图像,应用计算机图像处理技术处理视频图像数据,能够准确的地取出火焰及烟雾区域,而且检测速度快。

2 系统的构成

本系统主要由视频监控系统、算法识别系统组成。视频监控系统的作用是观察隧道内的实时情况,并通过光纤通信系统将视频画面传输至服务器,可以将本系统通过展示大屏进行展示。视频监控系统组成结构图如图1所示。

算法识别系统是将视频画面通过图像处理算法对隧道内是否出现火灾烟雾进行识别。系统设计框架图如图2所示。

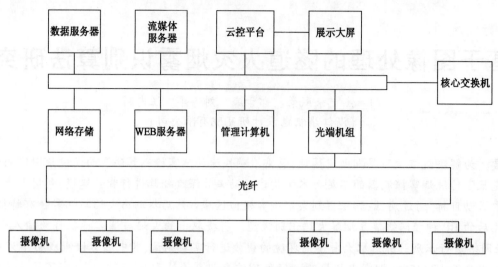

图 1 视频监控系统组成结构图

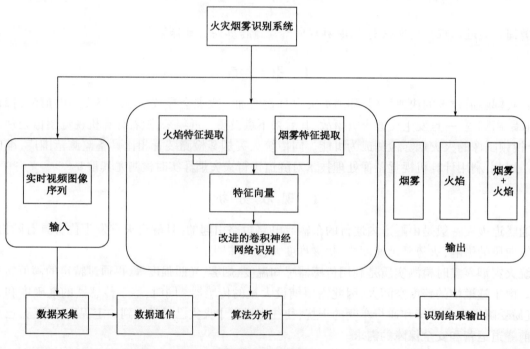

图 2 系统设计框架图

本系统主要直接利用隧道已有的监控系统,加载火灾烟雾图像处理模块即可实现火灾烟雾检测。适用隧道恶劣环境,可以辅助传统火灾烟雾探测器综合判据识别火灾。可以有效利用已有资源、增大检测距离、提升检测效率,并能具备实时报警、在线定位、历史数据分析等能力。

3 火灾烟雾检测的实现

3.1 目标检测

火焰与烟雾的目标检测是本系统的基础,并且火焰与烟雾都具备运动属性,火灾烟雾在温度差和压力差的作用下,不断向上方和周围扩散,时刻处于运动状态。并利用该特性可以排除一些与烟雾火焰颜色相近的静止物体,如隧道的墙壁、灯具等。由于背景差分法计算速度快、提取运动目标区域完整等特点,是进行目标检测的较好选择。

3.1.1 构建运动差异深度矩阵进行背景建模

为了得到差异图,需要对视频流中的两帧图像做差值,其优点就是不积累背景、更新速度快、算法简单、计算量小。将得到的差异图进行图像处理技术中常用的二值化处理。通过二值化处理的图像可以使图像中数据量大幅度降低。

$$d_{ij}(x,y)\begin{cases}1 & |f_1(x,y,t_i)-f_2(x,y,t_j)|>T \\ 0 & \text{else}\end{cases} \quad (1)$$

上式中 f_2 为图像参考帧,T 为阈值。

$$D(x,y,t_{k-1})=\begin{cases}D(x,y,t_{k-1})+1 & d_{ij}(x,y)=0\cap D(x,y,t_{k-1})<\lambda \\ 0 & \text{else}\end{cases} \quad (2)$$

式中:λ——深度值,如果 $D=\lambda$,则可以认为在 λ 帧内,像素变化较小,可以将此像素动态更新至模型中。

$$B(x,y,t_k)=\alpha f(x,y,t_k)+(1-\alpha)B(x,y,t_{k-1}) \quad (3)$$

式中:α——更新速度,取值不大于1;

B——k 时刻的背景模型。

3.1.2 最大类间方差法提取运动目标

为了准确提取出运动目标,本文利用最大类间方差法对当前帧与背景模型做差值,以类间的方差作为判别依据,求出最佳的灰度值作为阈值。

$$B_d(x,y,t_k)=|f(x,y,t_k)-B(x,y,t_k)| \quad (4)$$

提取出运动目标后,仍存在噪声的干扰。因此,本文对提取出的运动目标采用中值滤波进行去噪处理,再通过膨胀腐蚀得到较完整的运动区域。其效果如图3所示。

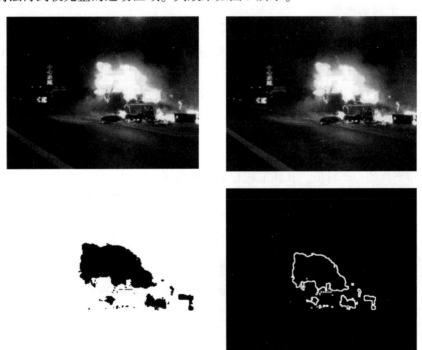

图3 提取效果图

由图3可见,对火焰效果提取较好,已较好除去周边噪声,并且细小之处的火焰细节也得到了保留。

3.2 特征提取

3.2.1 烟雾特征提取

烟雾是火灾初期的一个最重要的特征,具有颜色、形状变化和扩散等特征。对灯光非常敏感,其形状也常随空气的流动而改变。单纯利用颜色和形状特征实现对烟雾的检测是不可靠的。本文增加烟雾纹理、模糊性、动态性等特征对火灾烟雾进行判别。

1) 烟雾的纹理特征

在隧道中,常用纹理特征来区分火灾烟雾和干扰物。LBP 是一种能有效反映中心像素点与周边像素点差异情况的纹理描述算子,且对光照具有很好的鲁棒性。计算公式如下所示:

$$\mathrm{LBP}_{P,R} = \sum_{P=0}^{P=1} s(g_p - g_c) 2^p, s(x) = \begin{cases} 1, x \geq 0 \\ 0, x < 0 \end{cases} \quad (5)$$

式中:P——邻域中像素数目;

R——邻域像素距中心像素点的距离;

g_c——中心像素点灰度值;

g_p——邻域像素点灰度值。

采用 LBP 算子计算得到其二进制 LBP 编码,采用旋转不变模式和等价模式对每层的 LBP 编码进行降维,统计每种 LBP 编码的数量并将其作为一个特征值。

2) 烟雾的形态特征

在隧道中,火灾发生早期,火灾烟雾边缘不断变化并呈现出无规则的轮廓,而其他干扰物形状相对较规则。在图像中,圆形度可以表征物体轮廓的复杂度,因此,可以用圆形度区分烟雾和干扰。圆形度的计算公式如下:

$$k = \frac{s}{s_1} \quad (6)$$

式中:s——疑似烟雾区域的面积;

s_1——周长为 l 的圆的面积;

l——疑似烟雾区域轮廓长度。

视频图像中烟雾的圆形度值多数小于 0.6,视频图像中车辆的圆形度值多数在 0.8 以上。

3) 烟雾的模糊性特征

在隧道中,火灾烟雾会使背景图像呈现模糊性,仍可以观察到背景图像。利用图像平均梯度作为区分烟雾和干扰的一个特征。获取流程如图 4 所示。

4) 烟雾的动态特征

在隧道中,火灾烟雾扩散时其浓度和面积时刻发生变化,因此,烟雾像素占比面积的动态变化特征可以作为区分烟雾和干扰的一个特征。其获取流程如图 5 所示。

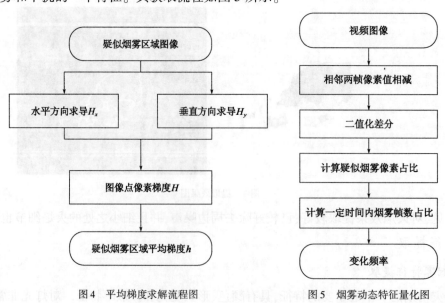

图 4 平均梯度求解流程图　　图 5 烟雾动态特征量化图

3.2.2 火焰特征提取

隧道灯光、汽车灯光等都会对火焰识别结果产生影响。因而需要寻找火焰独有特征作为判别依据。

1) 火焰的颜色特征

火焰具有其独特的是颜色特征，火焰的颜色在 RGB 等颜色空间中有其特定分布范围，而且外焰与内焰的颜色表现出深浅程度不同。

2) 火焰区域面积变化值

火灾发生过程中，火焰区域不断变化，而干扰物的面积变化值几乎为零。

3) 火灾图像致密度

同上文烟雾致密度算法一致。

4) 火灾图像质心点偏移距离

火灾发生的过程中，不同帧之间的火焰区域的位置会产生一定量的移动，其移动速度一般不可能像行驶的车辆车灯一样发生跳跃性突变。

3.3 神经网络选取与建立

3.3.1 BP 神经网络

火焰与烟雾的识别用单一的特征是很难实现高准确率的识别，由于实际环境下的隧道干扰较多，需要采用多特征综合起来进行检测。本文采用 BP 神经网络作为隧道火灾识别的神经网络模型对提取的火焰烟雾特征进行融合，以此最终判定火灾的存在。满足隧道环境中对目标实时检测的要求。

3.3.2 遗传-BP 神经网络

BP 网络具有很强的分类能力，可以将捕获到的火焰烟雾特征与火灾发生概率之间构建非线性映射关系，从而实现对火焰烟雾的识别检测。为得到更好的网络初始权值和阈值，需要优化 BP 神经网络，就是利用遗传算法改造 BP 神经网络。遗传算法优化 BP 神经网络流程如图 6 所示。

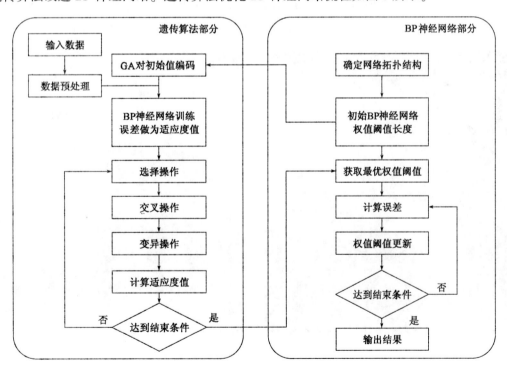

图 6　遗传算法优化 BP 神经网络流程图

遗传-BP 神经网络包括如下 5 个步骤：

1) 种群初始化

种群由多个个体组成，个体包含了神经网络全部权值和阈值，多个个体构成一个结构、权值、阈值确定的神经网络,因而需要先对种群进行初始化。

2)染色体适应度计算

首先是产生初始化权值,初始化权值即用染色体代表,并对染色体适应度进行计算:

$$F = \frac{1}{2}\sum_{k=1}^{q}\sum_{i=1}^{m}[y_i(k) - \bar{y}_i(k)]^2 \tag{7}$$

式中: q——样本个数;

m——输出神经元的个数;

$y_i(k)$、$\bar{y}_i(k)$——训练样本 k 在第 i 个输出节点的实际输出和期望输出。

3)选择染色体

染色体通过适应度计算后,从中选取适应度高的个体并逐步淘汰劣者。然后遗传到下一代,再次进行优胜劣汰,直至满足要求。

4)交叉与变异

交叉是为提高网络的收敛速度,对中间代中的染色体间进行两点交叉。变异则是为搜索到更优的解,对中间代个体独立进行变异产生新的一代群体。

5)赋予 BP 神经网络新的权值

通过遗传算法迭代计算,当满足终止条件后选择最优的染色体作为 BP 神经网络的初始权值向量 ω_{ij},如果不满足则重新从计算染色体适应度开始。

3.3.3 识别效果

建立好遗传-BP 神经网络后,通过对火焰和烟雾独有特征的数据进行人工标签,划分为训练数据集、验证数据集和测试数据集。

将上述三类数据集引入正样本和负样本进行对模型的训练学习,可以有效降低和避免一部分误识别的概率。正样本即为正常烟雾火焰数据,负样本即为形似烟雾火焰的干扰物。使用训练数据集对遗传-BP 神经网络模型进行训练至模型满足验证数据集对模型的评估其火灾识别效果如图 7 所示。

图 7 火灾识别效果展示图

4 试验分析与评估

4.1 试验视频库建立

为了验证算法的准确性和实时性,本文建立了烟雾样本、火灾样本和干扰样本视频库,视频 1 为隧道中正常视频,无烟雾无火焰;视频 2 为隧道中全火焰无烟雾视频;视频 3 和视频 4 为隧道中烟雾火灾视频,照明为 LED 灯;视频 5 为隧道中烟雾火灾视频,有疑似烟雾、火焰颜色的车辆干扰,有行人干扰等;视频 6 为隧道中烟雾火灾视频,照明为高压钠灯;视频 7 为隧道出入口烟雾火灾视频;视频 8 为隧道中全烟雾无火焰视频。

4.2 试验检测结果

用试验视频库里的测试样本测试烟雾和火焰识别模型的有效性,各视频相互之间构成对照试验组。烟雾识别检测结果如表 1 所示。

烟雾识别统计　　表 1

视频序列	烟雾帧数	非烟雾帧数	传统 BP 神经网络识别率	遗传算法优化后的 BP 网络识别率
视频 1	0	3700	91.54%	93.58%
视频 2	0	3700	90.69%	91.35%
视频 3	758	2942	90.32%	91.32%
视频 4	956	2744	90.25%	91.22%
视频 5	1125	2575	83.65%	88.12%
视频 6	1756	1944	88.24%	89.24%
视频 7	2630	1070	89.85%	90.29%
视频 8	3700	0	91.95%	93.92%

由上表可见遗传算法优化后的 BP 网络识别率较为改善,在正常运营中的隧道中,识别率较高,并且与隧道内照明质量也有略微影响。在设立大量人为干扰的视频 6 中,识别率大幅度下降,但是仍然保持了一定的水平,具备实用性。

火焰识别检测结果如表 2 所示。

火焰识别统计　　表 2

视频序列	火焰帧数	非火焰帧数	传统 BP 神经网络识别率	遗传算法优化后的 BP 网络识别率
视频 1	0	3700	93.11%	95.85%
视频 2	3700	0	93.15%	94.61%
视频 3	2642	1058	93.42%	95.52%
视频 4	2144	1556	93.20%	95.55%
视频 5	625	3075	88.22%	91.05%
视频 6	244	3456	90.54%	92.24%
视频 7	1170	2530	91.15%	93.81%
视频 8	0	3700	93.95%	95.84%

由上表可见火焰的识别率较烟雾的识别率更高,相对而言火焰的特征更明显,更容易识别。在面对人为干扰的情况下保持了较高的识别率。

遗传算法优化的 BP 神经网络算法性能如表 3 所示。

算法性能　　表 3

试验总帧数	平均每帧处理时间	烟雾平均识别率	火焰平均识别率	并行处理综合识别率	并行处理综合误检率	并行处理综合误检率
18500 帧	37ms	91.61%	93.45%	97.55%	1.21%	1.24%

本文提出的算法每帧视频的平均处理时间约为 37ms,具有较强的实时性,具有一定的抗干扰能力。烟雾和火焰检测成功率均高于 90%,由于在火灾检测中只需要检测出烟雾与火焰一个信号即可认定发生火灾,因而烟雾火焰检测并行处理综合识别率达到 97.55%,可以实际应用于高速公路隧道视频火灾

的检测。其准确率和鲁棒性还需要保持摄像机正常的使用,保证画面清晰。

5 结 语

由于公路隧道极易发生事故并诱发火灾,由于隧道复杂的环境,传统的火灾探测技术难以实现准确的实时检测。本文根据隧道实际情况,利用现有高速公路隧道现在摄像机,采用视频处理方法展开了对高速公路隧道火灾检测技术的研究。该检测方法由烟雾检测和火焰检测组成,首先利用背景差分法提取隧道内的运动前景目标,然后提取烟雾火焰独有特征,利用遗传算法优化的BP神经网络对这些特征进行综合判断实现对隧道火灾烟雾进行判别。通过大量试验仿真验证了遗传-BP神经网络算法的有效性,体现了检测效果优于传统BP网络。但是该算法仍有局限性,只能有限提高原有BP神经网络的检测精度,其检测精度的核心仍然基于BP神经网络的性能。尤其对一些少量的负样本的学习问题,优化后的网络识别检测能力不能得到明显提高。后期将继续对识别检测能力进行研究优化。

参考文献

[1] 陈长友,杨健晟.面向视频图像的烟雾检测算法综述[J/OL].激光与光电子学进展:1-16[2021-01-28].

[2] Sergio Saponara, Abdussalam Elhanashi, Alessio Gagliardi. Real-time 视频 fire/smoke detection based on CNN in antifire surveillance systems[J]. Journal of Real-Time Image Processing,2020(prepublish).

[3] 陈磊,邹北骥.基于动态阈值对称差分和背景差法的运动对象检测算法[J].计算机应用研究,2008(02):488-490+494.

[4] 齐丽娜,张博,王战凯.最大类间方差法在图像处理中的应用[J].无线电工程,2006(07):25-26+44.

[5] 李亮,罗毅.帧间差分法在视频监控中的应用研究[J].四川理工学院学报(自然科学版),2015,28(06):58-62.

[6] 曹毅超,吴泽鹏,周宇飞,等.基于循环神经网络的森林火灾识别研究[J].林业与环境科学,2020,36(05):34-40.

[7] 任嘉锋,熊卫华,吴之昊,等.基于改进YOLOv3的火灾检测与识别[J].计算机系统应用,2019,28(12):171-176.

[8] 冯路佳,王慧琴,王可,等.基于目标区域的卷积神经网络火灾烟雾识别[J].激光与光电子学进展,2020,57(16):83-91.

[9] 刘春艳,凌建春,寇林元,等.GA-BP神经网络与BP神经网络性能比较[J].中国卫生统计,2013,30(02):173-176+181.

[10] Wang Shi-Jie, Weng Zhi-Dan, Jin Bo et al. Multi-objective genetic algorithm optimization of linear proportional solenoid actuator[J]. Journal of the Brazilian Society of Mechanical Sciences and Engineering,2021,43(2).

[11] 武钦芳,吴张倩,苏兆品,等.遗传算法优化时间卷积网络的手机来源识别[J/OL].计算机工程与应用:1-10[2021-01-28].

[12] Ma L, Wu K, Zhu L. Fire smoke detection in 视频 images using Kalman filter and Gaussian mixture color model[C]//2010 International Conference on Artificial Intelligence and Computational Intelligence. IEEE,2010,1:484-487.

[13] Luo Y, Zhao L, Liu P, et al. Fire smoke detection algorithm based on motion characteristic and convolutional neural networks[J]. Multimedia Tools and Applications,2018,77(12):15075-15092.

[14] Umar M M, Silva L C D, Bakar M S A, et al. State of the art of smoke and fire detection using image processing[J]. International Journal of Signal and Imaging Systems Engineering,2017,10(1-2):22-30.

某山区国道千枚岩隧道群病害处治及关键技术分析

陈祥斌[1]　康孝先[1,2]　周子豪[1]　陈俞嘉[1]

(1. 西南科技大学；2. 四川省绵阳市交通运输局)

摘　要　千枚岩是具有千枚状构造的低级变质岩石。千枚岩的遇水泥化、粉尘化是隧道施工中各种病害的根源，也导致了建成隧道的后期维修养护困难。本文结合某山区国道千枚岩隧道群的病害处治，介绍了千枚岩隧道的主要病害，对比分析了衬砌加固方案的优缺点，并结合现场实际情况，为同类隧道病害处治提供参考。

关键词　千枚岩隧道　病害处治　衬砌裂缝　渗漏水

0　引　言

千枚岩是一种浅变质的软岩[1]，具有千枚状构造，属于区域变质浅变质带岩之一。在工程上，千枚岩具有两个典型的特征，一是遇水泥化，二是脱水粉尘化，导致在千枚岩隧道施工过程中出现断面缩小、衬砌裂损、拱架扭曲等变形破坏病害，而且在隧道施工期间围岩及结构的稳定较差，增加了施工的难度。

本文结合某山区国道千枚岩隧道群的病害处治，介绍了千枚岩隧道的主要病害，对比分析了衬砌加固方案的优缺点，并结合现场实际情况，可为同类隧道病害处治提供参考。

1　隧道群概况

该项目工程区域位于四川绵阳市境内，隧道群顺序编号为1~7号，防水等级为Ⅱ级，主体结构设计基准期100年。工程区域岩体为千枚岩，千枚状、块状、薄层状构造，岩芯多为碎块状。其中1号隧道设计为单洞双向行车特长隧道，设计隧道纵面为单向上坡，坡度为1.876%，隧道最大埋深约730m；2号隧道设计为单洞双向行车长隧道，设计隧道纵面为人字坡，坡度为0.814%接-3.000%；3号隧道设计为单洞双向行车隧道，设计隧道纵面位于-2.936%下坡段；4号隧道设计为单洞双向行车长隧道，设计隧道纵面位于-2.852%下坡段；5号隧道设计为单洞双向行车隧道，设计隧道纵面位于1.212%上坡段；6号隧道设计为单洞双向行车隧道，设计隧道纵面位于1.212%上坡段；7号隧道设计为单洞双向行车隧道，隧道总长340m。设计隧道纵面位于-0.404%下坡段。

2　主要病害

1号隧道存在的主要病害为隧道衬砌开裂和渗漏水，该隧道主要病害为隧道衬砌渗漏水并伴有开裂现象。在对隧道进行实体检测过程中发现隧道衬砌结构局部存在脱空、不密实、空洞现象，同时在衬砌结构混凝土强度检测中发现，局部段落混凝土抗压强度略低于设计值[2]。

2号隧道通过外观检查发现，该隧道的主要问题为局部段落衬砌混凝土渗漏水较为严重。实体检测发现隧道衬砌混凝土存在19处欠厚段落，累计长度达290m，22处衬砌及围岩不密实现象，累计长94m，整体看，隧道衬砌结构存在一定的缺陷，对病害的产生有一定的助推作用[3]。

3号隧道的专项检查发现，该隧道衬砌结构的技术状况较为完好，未发现明显的衬砌开裂、破损现象。

4号隧道现场外观检测过程中发现，目前该隧道存在的主要病害有3处，K9+150~K9+200范围内左右两侧边墙及拱腰斜向裂缝较为密集,该裂缝多为深度贯穿裂缝,对结构整体性和稳定性影响较大;K9+600~K9+610范围内左右两侧边墙存在环向裂缝;K9+660~K9+760为该隧道病害最为严重段落,衬砌严重开裂,左右两侧边墙、拱顶等均存在密集的网状裂缝,并伴有渗漏水现象发生。

5号隧道进口洞门结构基本完好,未发现明显缺损等病害,但现场外观检测过程中发现该隧道衬砌多处存在严重的渗漏水,二衬混凝土有多处剥落现象,且有进一步加重的趋势,严重威胁洞内行车安全。拱顶混凝土掉块如图1所示,部分阶段衬砌开裂展开图如图2所示。

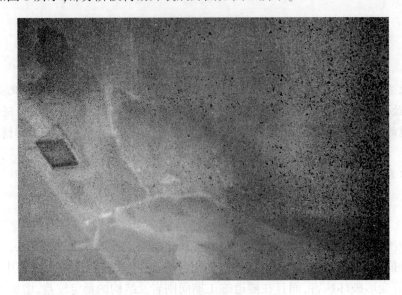

图1 拱顶混凝土剥落图

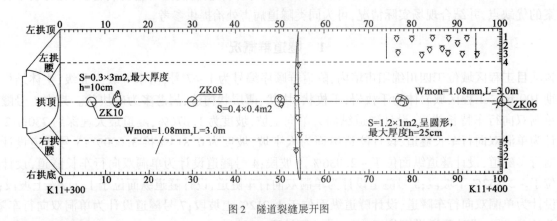

图2 隧道裂缝展开图

6号隧道的专项检查发现,大马庄隧道结构衬砌共计发现5处开裂现象。体检测发现衬砌结构的厚度、断面净空均较好,存在的主要问题为局部衬砌混凝土强度不足,抵抗围岩变形能力削弱,在后期运营中易产生结构开裂等病害。

7号隧道的外观检查发现,该隧道衬砌共计发现2处开裂。

3 处治措施

本隧道群病害整治措施土建部分主要有隧道洞门病害处治、全环套衬加固、拱边墙套衬加固、轻型钢轨套拱加固、二衬裂缝修复、衬砌背后空洞注浆等措施。

对隧道衬砌裂损的处治主要是分为两大类:对隧道围岩进行加固稳定、加固补强衬砌本身。

3.1 加固围岩类

目前对隧道围岩的加固主要有三种方法[5],分别是深孔压浆法、深锚杆加固法、支挡加固等。

(1)深孔压浆法

在衬砌表面上采用风钻打出 4~6m 深的均匀孔,再对衬砌周边的破碎围岩进行压浆处理,起到加固围岩的作用,可以有效地控制了衬砌与围岩的共同受力,使其更加的稳定。同时由于降低了地下水对衬砌的渗透性能,使得衬砌的防水作用也得到了提高。

(2)深锚杆加固法

相对于围岩较好的隧道,可以在衬砌表面上采用风钻打出 4~6m 深的均匀孔,再对衬砌围岩进行压浆处理,再进行金属锚杆的打入。采用深锚杆加固法能有效地提高其衬砌的承载能力和控制其变形,更加有效地控制了衬砌与围岩的共同受力,使其更加的稳定。

3.2 衬砌加固措施

针对不同的衬砌损伤情况,可采取不同的衬砌加固方式。

(1)喷锚加固裂损衬砌[6]

如今喷锚加固常用的方式有如下几种:

①素喷,不需加设钢筋网来喷射混凝土。主要是对于围岩压力小,结构基本上较稳定,衬砌的裂纹较少且衬砌变形不大的情况下采用这种方法。

②锚网喷,即在进行网喷过程中加设锚杆。对于围岩呈大块状或较稳定的地段可以采用锚网喷,也可以单独适用于加固墙中部和拱腰处的张裂型裂纹。

③喷射钢纤维混凝土,即把钢纤维加入喷射的混凝土中。其抗渗性、抗裂性、抗震性、抗腐蚀性都比较好的。因此,对于隧道的抗震加固、抢险以及衬砌裂损漏水的综合整治上,常常把喷射钢纤维混凝土与早强混凝土配合使用。

(2)钢筋混凝土套拱

现今通常是采用钢筋混凝土套拱来对原衬砌进行加固补强[7]。这种方式主要适用于在隧道拱部的衬砌严重开裂,拱顶出现压劈掉块现象,拱腰部出现纵裂错台,但边墙是基本上完好,且具有相应的承载能力及一定的整体性的情况。

(3)嵌补衬砌

对于隧道衬砌具有一定的整体性,而衬砌裂缝在快速的发展且有规律可循,则可以考虑在全环或局部上进行钢拱支撑的加设。加设钢拱支撑优点是能够与原衬砌形成一个共同受力的整体。如图 3 所示。

(4)更换衬砌

在衬砌发生严重的变形或其大部分断面侵入建筑限界,而必须拆除旧衬砌,导致限界扩大的情况下可采用这种方法[8]。它与衬砌混凝土共同受力,增加了其承载能力。如图 4 所示。

3.3 衬砌病害处治措施

3.3.1 全环套衬加固

针对实际隧道情况结合上述技术[10],对 3 号隧洞、4 号隧道、5 号隧道、6 号隧道需要进行全环套衬加固,全环套衬加固段落针对既有结构存在结构性贯穿裂缝,结构损伤严重,电缆沟倾斜等病害。

①在墙拱凿槽,槽宽 20cm,嵌入 I22b 工字钢拱架,拱架纵向间距 50cm,每段裂缝处治段落两端分别延长 5m,也凿槽嵌 I22b 拱架,纵向间距为 100cm。

②根据检测报告,套拱厚度最小 13cm,因此拱墙部位混凝土采用喷钢纤维砼,钢纤维掺量 77kg/m³。

③未开槽处混凝土应进行凿毛处理,每平方米 120~150 个小坑。

④每榀拱架拱脚深入二衬仰拱内,使基础稳固,并在每榀拱架拱脚处设置两根锁脚锚管,锁脚锚管采用 $\phi 42 \times 3.5$m 钢花管,$L = 5$m。

⑤对于所有拱墙裂缝采用钻孔注环氧树脂浆液灌缝充填修补,对于由于挤压脱落部位,可采用环氧树脂砂浆填平[9]。

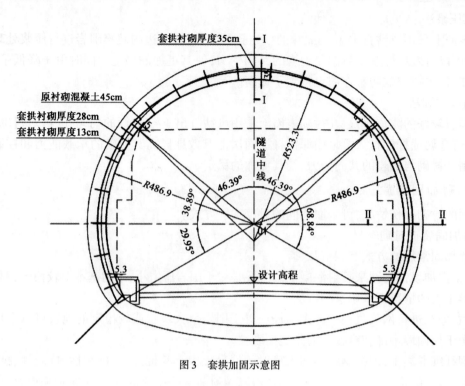

图 3 套拱加固示意图

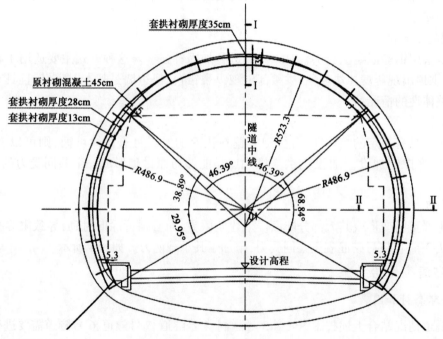

图 4 衬砌加固示意图

3.3.2 拱边墙套衬加固

拱边墙套衬加固段落针对既有结构存在结构性贯穿裂缝,结构损伤较严重等病害。主要是针对1号隧道、2号隧道、3号隧道、6号隧道、7号隧道。

①在墙拱凿槽,槽宽20cm,嵌入I22b工字钢拱架,拱架纵向间距50cm。每段裂缝处治段落两端分别延长5m,也凿槽嵌I22b拱架,纵向间距为100cm。

②根据检测报告,套拱厚度小13cm,因此拱墙部位混凝土采用喷钢纤维混凝土,钢纤维掺量77kg/m³。

③未开槽处混凝土应进行凿毛处理,每平方米 120~150 个小坑。

④每榀拱架拱脚深入二衬仰拱内,使基础稳固,并在每榀拱架拱脚处设置两根锁脚锚管。锁脚锚管采用 $\phi 42 \times 3.5m$ 钢花管,$L=5m$。

⑤对于所有拱墙裂缝采用钻孔注环氧树脂浆液灌缝充填修补,对于由于挤压脱落部位,可采用环氧树脂砂浆填平。

4 结 语

在今后的施工中需要加强对千枚岩的研究,寻找新的更有效的施工技术,制订安全、合理、可行的隧道病害处治方案。采取新措施加强施工质量控制和运营期间的管理和养护。

参考文献

[1] 周艺,何川,邹育麟,等.破碎千枚岩隧道施工工法比选试验研究[J].岩石力学与工程学报,2013,32(03):537-548.

[2] 中华人民共和国交通运输部.公路隧道养护技术规范:JTG H12—2015[S].北京:人民交通出版社股份有限公司,2015.

[3] 王春景.运营公路隧道结构病害安全性评估及综合处治技术研究[D].长沙:中南大学,2010.

[4] 王学武,冯学钢,姜云,等.西南某高速公路隧道病害成因分析及处治设计[J].西南公路,2007(03):30-33.

[5] 李世强.重庆涪丰石高速方斗山隧道病害处治方案研究[D].西安:长安大学,2018.

[6] 刘海京,郑佳艳,邹宗良,秦之富.某运营高速公路隧道衬砌坍塌病害检测及快速处治[J].公路交通技术,2010(05):103-106.

[7] 周武召,陈棚.奉溪高速喜口池隧道病害分析及处治方案研究[J].公路交通技术,2019,35(01):123-128.

[8] 肖博,秦峰.隧道路面病害检测及处治设计[J].公路交通技术,2012(03):105-109.

[9] 罗亨俊,刘黎,周绍文.公路隧道常见病害的成因与处治[J].公路交通科技(应用技术版),2014,10(01):66-68.

[10] 黄瑞,胡晓勇.公路隧道衬砌病害原因分析及处治方法的探讨[J].公路交通科技(应用技术版),2016,12(05):30-32.

第四篇 交通工程

全国联网收费形势下高速公路稽核工作建议

宗 原

(湖北楚天智能交通股份有限公司)

摘 要 根据国家正式颁布的《深化收费公路制度改革取消高速公路省界收费站实施方案》文件，全国高速公路并网运行。在新政策带来的巨大变革下，也随之出现了一些亟待解决的问题。其中稽核工作难度的增加，对高速公路运营单位、从业人员也是一个全新的挑战。为此，如何创新稽核方式成为高速公路行业最为关注的问题之一。本文将从数据分析、形势影响、方式方法、稽核建议等层面来探讨新形势下开展稽核工作的方向，为不断提升稽核工作能力提供一些实用思路。

关键词 高速公路 逃费 分析 稽核 追缴

0 引 言

随着国家经济的高速发展，机动车拥有量和高速公路车流量急剧增加，使得交通需求与交通供给的矛盾日益突出，取消高速公路省界收费站，使高速公路收费行业产生了巨大变革，如全国联网收费、货车车型收费、实际路径收费、绿通预约机制、ETC信息录入不准等，这些都对我们的稽核工作提出了更高的要求。笔者从工作实际的角度出发，对现阶段高速公路逃费形势、稽核方法进行分析研究，总结出一些相关工作建议，供读者参考。

1 数据分析

根据2019年湖北大广北高速公路稽核情况分析，9个收费站(含黄冈北省界站)，共计追缴通行费37.28万元，追缴车次6352次。其中黄冈北省界站追缴次数和追缴金额占比分别为42.19%、75.98%。

基于以上数据，假设一个省400个收费站，且以每10个收费站一年追缴车次6500次、金额40万元计算，全省一年至少应追缴车次26万次、金额1600万元。

以上仅仅是数据估算，实际上全国各省(区、市)逃费案例层出不穷，金额之大是令人咋舌。江苏省撤站后首例暴力闯卡逃费案，车辆遮挡号牌，从出口强行撞断栏杆逃逸，逃费金额近3万元。2019年四川省首例假冒水产品逃费刑事案件，车主罗某因犯诈骗罪被判处有期徒刑三年，缓刑五年，处罚金5000元，并退还通行费54600元。这些只是冰山一角，随着省界收费站的"撤除"，此类现象愈演愈烈，冰山之下到底还有多少逃费行为是我们看不见的？

2 形势影响

2.1 一站到底、一逃到底

省界收费站"撤除"后，全国一张网，无论从哪里上高速公路，都只需要在出口收费站缴纳一次通行费即可，通行费被最大化，因此单次缴费金额也将远远高于以前，车辆逃费将获得更大的利益，在利益的驱使下，逃费动机也被最大化。

2.2 ETC推广、标准不一

自ETC推广以来，办理ETC的用户不断增加，ETC发行方在对车型信息录入时，可能因为各种因素错误录入，导致出现大量"大车小标""客货混标""标签拆卸""一车多签"等用户，因系统原因，无法输入实际金额,即使在补费时,部分用户对高速公路行业出现此类问题表示无法理解。

2.3 系统影响、查询困难

当车辆通行费额存在不同的多义性路径时,利用各种方式屏蔽通行介质,导致路段门架无法进行识别计费,达到节约时间成本和经济成本的目的。有的车辆即使已经存在逃费事实,也会有难以取证而无法足额收取通行费的情况发生。

3 方式方法

为不断提高稽核工作的方式方法,进行有针对性的稽核,首先必须对各类逃费方式有一定的了解,虽然在新形势下稽核工作还存在一定盲区,但我们仍然可以借鉴以往的稽核手段,对逃费车辆进行一定程度上的打击。

3.1 逃费方式

3.1.1 大车小标

"大车小标"是目前最常见的逃费方式之一,主要是因为货车按车型收费后,由于办理 ETC 时大多货车牵引车只有车头,部分 ETC 发行方根据标准便按照普通 3 型货车录入,而运输货物要行驶高速公路时,牵引车就会链接上挂车,变成了 6 型车,这类 ETC 逃费情况较为普遍。

如果走混合车道或人工车道,细心的收费员在车辆感应扣费后,通过观察系统界面显示的车型,还是比较容易发现"大车小标"的问题。但如果走 ETC 专用车道,即使事后也不太容易发现,而且大多数时候连司机都不知道自己已经造成了逃费的事实。

3.1.2 假冒逃费

利用国家相关减免政策,将车辆伪装成免费车辆,如假冒绿通车,假冒救灾车,假冒军警车等,此类车辆大多通过现场仔细查验和过往经验较容易被发现。自国家相关减免政策出台以来,假冒逃费现象一直层出不穷,这里不做过多赘述。

3.1.3 挂车逃费

此种逃费形式主要为牵引货车,因牵引货车基本办的都是牵引车头 3 型的 OBU 信息。当牵引货车进入离目的地最近的服务区后,将牵引的车厢放在服务区,然后驾驶牵引车头在目的地收费站下高速公路后再领卡上路,再到服务区前面一个收费站下站绕行到服务区,拉上车厢后到相邻的收费站下,从而缩短了 6 型车的缴费距离。

3.1.4 屏蔽逃费

此种逃费方式主要为车辆上站领 CPC 卡后利用某些工具非法屏蔽、损坏、丢弃 CPC 卡,使门架无法对 CPC 卡进行计费标记,出口无法正常读取卡内入口信息,从而谎报入口信息以达到逃费的目的。虽然通过卡号或车牌号可以查询到入口站信息,但如果该车将通行卡丢弃,再遮挡或更换车牌,就很难准确查到其通行信息了。

3.1.5 留卡逃费

此种逃费方式为车辆入站时有 ETC 设备,但领 CPC 卡留置或出站时谎称卡丢失,收费员按无卡程序操作后,驾驶员就留置了通行卡一张,返回时正常领卡,在出口就用留置的通行卡在通行卡入口信息最近的站点下站,如此循环留置通行卡。

3.1.6 倒卡逃费

此种逃费方式主要为同一货运公司的车辆,车辆颜色、车型都一样,然后车主购买假牌照使每辆车都用两套相同车牌照。在行驶高速公路时,两辆车分头对发,在中途互换通行卡,并换上与通行卡读取信息中对应的车牌号,然后分别从对方入口较近的收费站下高速公路,以达到逃缴通行费的目的。

3.1.7 U形、J形逃费

此种逃费方式是利用高速公路与相邻高速公路互通设计与管理的盲区，通过改变行驶方向和路线，从而达到少缴费或逃缴通行费的目的。

3.1.8 跟车逃费

此种逃费方式主要是紧随前ETC扣费车的尾部，利用栏杆机的"防砸"功能紧随前车冲岗出站或者利用前车ETC已感应扣款，突然从旁边车道插入占用前车抬杆空隙冲岗出站。

3.2 稽核方法

3.2.1 数据稽核

通过后台导出数据，使用Excel表格的功能，进行大数据筛查，可以准确地查找到同车牌不同车型、特情、卡号、时间异常等信息的可疑车辆，再通过视频稽核等手段锁定逃费车辆，对证据确凿的逃费车辆进行追缴。

3.2.2 实时稽核

通过现场发现的特情车辆，实时对其进行后台查询，再从出入口等各类信息的比对可第一时间发现异常，根据异常情况详细调查，对存在逃费事实的车辆进行追缴。

3.2.3 对内稽核

通过日常稽核工作，实时监控真实反映车道情况，最大程度上杜绝从业人员违规操作、收受好处等跨红线行为，从而有效将内部影响降至最低。

3.3 稽核重点

3.3.1 异常信息

对征费过程的异常数据、特殊操作，要敢于怀疑，重点以不合常理的行驶时长、门架路径、重量减少、特殊计费模式等作为突破点，进行排查。通行异常的车辆采用"在线服务计费"和"最小费额"进行计费，特殊计费模式的出现就是疑点。

3.3.2 分析印证

要充分利用大数据，发挥好稽核业务平台、门架监测系统和门架路径拟合等软件的运用，多系统综合分析，相互印证。

3.3.3 跨省联动

充分利用全国高速公路投诉咨询电话，致电咨询相关所站的联系方式，跨省查询相关车辆信息，有效解决跨省查无对证的短板。

4 稽核建议

在新形势下，除开传统的稽核方式，我们可以将稽核的重心适当做一下调整，尝试一些新的稽核方式来有效遏制逃费行为。

4.1 强化服务区、停车区的联勤联动

从各类逃费行为来看，在服务区、停车区的逃费行为较为隐蔽，自由度较高，适当增加巡查力度，从而对逃费司机形成一定的威慑作用，再加强与服务区、停车区工作人员的联动，确保稽核巡查的连贯性、持续性。

4.2 强化入口信息核实、操作规范。

大部分逃费行为都是从入口开始实施，入口信息不实或操作不规范，将分在出口造成大量特情车辆，特情车辆增加容易对后台信息造成混淆，不利于数据稽核工作的开展。

4.3 强化宣传、收集案例、宣讲法律。

将各类案例或相关法律事件收集，通过宣传期刊的形式，利用服务区、停车区巡查等地发放给司机，

增加司机的法律意识，减少逃费者的侥幸心理。

4.4 培养稽核人才，打造专业稽核队伍。

从稽核的基础知识、操作规范、对内对外稽核等多方面，培养一批具有创新精神和创新能力、一专多能的稽核业务人才；通过提高片区稽核频次、定期组织经验交流会等方式，发挥专职稽核人员优势，深化专项稽核力度，全面打造一支专业的稽核队伍，适应稽核新形势的需要。

4.5 收集车辆信息数据，建立车型数据库。

根据车牌号与车型关系的唯一性，把车辆的车型信息收集起来，建立一牌号一车型对应的数据库，进行车型预分类。在车辆通过出口的时候，若车型库中保存的该车车型和本次收费员输入的车型不一致，则产生报警。

4.6 明确法律依据，完善稽查合法性。

当前高速公路从业人员对客户进行追缴、补缴通行费时，也存在在何种情况不可以追缴，何种情况可以追缴的疑虑。所以不断完善相关法律制度也是遏制逃费行为的有效手段之一。

5 结 语

全国各省（区、市）的数据目前还无法对接，如此庞大的数据信息的储存、调出等问题该如何解决？5G时代的到来，是否可以将横贯在我们与稽核工作之上的鸿沟轻松瓦解？

从我国第一条高速公路建成，到现在全国一张网的智能高速公路系统，偷逃通行费、强行闯关、跟车冲岗等行为也随着技术的发展层出不穷，问题的根源到底在什么地方？是因为软硬件不够完善、从业人员疏忽大意，还是司机法律意识淡薄、违法成本太低？

由于笔者对新收费系统还在摸索、学习阶段，对问题的理解深度还有所欠缺，观点上可能有失偏颇，甚至存在一些错误，还望读者朋友能够海涵！

参考文献

[1] 江苏交通控股有限公司营运安全事业部稽查管理中心.苏鲁破获撤站后首例暴力闯卡逃费案[J].中国公路,2019,(14):46-47.

[2] 四川高速公路建设开发集团稽查监控中心.四川首例假冒水产品逃费刑事案件宣判[J].中国公路,2019,(22):40.

Real-time Traffic Signal Control of Logistics Park Based on Web Crawler Technology

Jie Li[1]　Ruimin Li[1]　Yufei Yue[2]　Zheng Li[3]

(1. College of Civil Engineering, Hunan University;
2. Department of Civil Engineering, Hong Kong University of Science and Technology;
3. Department of Traffic Engineering, Tongji University)

Abstract　Against the background of actively promoting the construction of the "Global 123 Fast Cargo Flow Circle", realizing the goal of forming a multimodal transportation system with high efficiency and economy, urban transportation interconnection and sharing. This study adopts AutoNavi open API to obtain real-time traffic data. The traffic state of the road network was estimated after analysis and processing. According to the road network traffic state, a predesigned and optimized signal control scheme could be selected. Python could be used to call the Vissim interface to evaluate the effectiveness of the signal control plan. A simulation test was carried out for a certain peak period. The results show that the signal management strategy proposed in this study achieves real-time dynamic adjustment, reducing vehicle delays by 69% and parking time by 78%, achieving the goal of improving road traffic efficiency.

Keywords Real-time control   Traffic big data   Web Crawler   Traffic simulation

0 Introduction

Building a country with a strong transportation network is a major strategic decision by the 19th National Congress of the Communist Party of China. The construction of a robust transportation system is one of the necessary guarantees for national development, of which urban road traffic is an important part. Many problems are waited to be improved and resolved in urban roads, such as complex traffic composition, uneven traffic flow, and low capacity in some sections. This paper studies the road signal control based on real-time traffic big data based on the logistics park's road network.

The earliest traffic signal appeared in 1868 in the mechanical wrench type signal machine in London, England, which was only used at night ZHU et al.,2003. Unlike today's three-color signal lights, it used gas lightings and only had red and green. In 1968, the British Institute of Transportation and Road Research successfully developed the TRANSYT system LI et al.,2009. In 1973, the SCOOT (Split, Cycle, Offset Optimization Technique) system was developed based on this system and was widely used. After years of development and improvement, they are still the mainstream control system. Hansen, BG et al. connected the adaptive signal control system SCOOT with the CORSIM traffic simulation model Hansen et al.,2000. Ghassan Abu-Lebdeh and Rahim F. Benekohal Abu-Lebdeh et al.,2000 suggested to adopt genetic algorithms for traffic signal control and queue management of oversaturated two-way arterials. Luyanda et al. proposed an ACS-lite algorithmic architecture that is applying adaptive control system technology to closed-loop traffic signal control systems Luyanda et al.,2003. Niittymaki, J and Turunen, E used similarity logic reasoning to study traffic signal control Niittymaki et al.,2003. The SMOOTH signal control system, in light of the traffic characteristics of Shenzhen SONG et al.,2007, applies different signal schemes, focusing on alleviating traffic congestion during peak hours, and focusing on better traffic capacity during off-peak hours. There are also many studies on real-time traffic signal control from 2008 to 2020. A hybrid strategy for real-time traffic signal control of urban road networks was proposed Kouvelas et al.,2011 to be used within TUC to drop the requirement for a prespecified fixed signal plan. Coll, P., Factorovich, P. et al. Coll et al.,2013 presented an adaptive system based on a linear programming model for the signal-control problem, whose objective was to minimize the queues' total length of vehicles waiting at each intersection. In the field of real-time adaptive traffic signal control, Yin, B., Dridi, M. et al. Yin et al.,2015 proposed algorithm called forward search algorithm based on dynamic programming. Besides, deep policy-gradient and value-function-based reinforcement learning were used in traffic light control as well Mousavi et al.,2017. In 2019, Shu Aibing, Xu Xindong et al. SHU et al., 2019 proposed a dynamic green wave signal control system and method for urban traffic arterial lines based on real-time traffic flow data, which can carry out real-time dynamic control of road signal timing and greatly improve the intelligent control level of coordinated arterial lines. Seyit Alperen Celtek et al. Celtek et al.,2020 worked on studying real-time traffic signal control with swarm optimization methods.

To sum up, the signal control system of urban traffic has been gradually developed and improved, most of the existing urban traffic signal control systems can only provide regular traffic coordination signal schemes, such as morning peak, evening peak, or other fixed periods. However, the current signal control system is still limited by the following factors: ①The cost of data acquisition is high, while its accuracy is low. It faces the defects of difficulties in maintaining the acquisition equipment and complicated data processing process; ②It lacks the evaluation of the signal control scheme's effectiveness. Most of the current signal control systems directly apply the generated signal control scheme to the actual road network, which lacks real-time evaluation of the generation scheme, increasing operational risks.

1 Traffic Research and analysis

For quantitative evaluation of the signal control scheme, this paper establishes a simulation model of the road network around the logistics park based on the micro-simulation software, Vissim 4.3. After comprehensively considering the scale of the logistics park and the traffic characteristics nearby, the road network nearby the Tongchao Taoyang Logistics Park in Changsha was selected as the research object.

1.1 Network Data Crawling

In thearea of big data, the collection of information is an important task. Collecting information on human is inefficient and cumbersome and increase the cost of collection. However, web crawlers can automatically collect and sort information on the Internet. Therefore, this paper applies an Internet open-source data crawler to obtain on-site traffic characteristics.

API will make data acquisition more direct and effective. In this paper, the network's real-time traffic characteristics are obtained by accessing the API interface provided by the AutoNavi Map through Python, as shown in Tab.1. Up to now, the AutoNavi Map has an immense amount of high-precision data with the largest total mileage and data accuracy as fine as 10cm. Although the data can only be updated every two minutes due to technical limitations, but it is enough for this project.

The values of road conditions in Tab.1 are 0 (unknown), 1 (unblocked), 2 (slow), 3 (congestion), 4 (severe congestion), describing the traffic condition of the road section atthis moment; the angle is the driving direction of the vehicle; the speed is the average of the speeds of all vehicles on the road at this moment, and the unit is km/h.

Example of open-source data on traffic situation of AutoNavi Map　　　Tab.1

Time	Road	Road conditions	Angle	Speed
2020-04-10,08:01:25	Huanbao east road	2	11	25
2020-04-10,08:01:34	Huanbao east road	1	191	45

1.2 Data Processing

According to the data crawled, this paper further processes and analyzes the data to obtain the estimated value of road traffic volume and the average speed of the road network.

From Table 1, the AutoNavi Map data is the overall road congestion evaluation. The smaller the value is, the smoother the road is (except for unknown road conditions), in line with the level division of *Code for Design of Urban Road Engineering* (CJJ37). Therefore, this paper applies the CJJ37 to convert the index of AutoNavi Map to estimate the road flow. The four road conditions correspond to the first, second, third, and fourth service levels, and the saturation (V/C) corresponding to the discrete value of each road condition is obtained.

The relationship between saturation and maximum service traffic volume and capacity is as follows:

$$\frac{V}{C} = \frac{MSF_d}{C_R} \quad (1)$$

Where: C_R —— the capacity value of a lane corresponding to the design speed (pcu/h/ln);

MSF_d —— the maximum service traffic volume of each lane under actual roads and traffic conditions (pcu/h/ln).

Relating the relationship described in the above formula and the design capacity when the design speed is

60km/h, the road condition index can be converted into an estimate of the road section's maximum service traffic volume. Since MSF_d is the maximum service traffic volume, the actual traffic volume must be less than or equal to the value of MSF_d. In order to prevent the obtained flow value from exceeding the actual road flow value, this paper multiplies the estimated value of the maximum service traffic volume by the discount coefficient 0.8 to obtain the final flow estimation value, and the flow estimation value is input into the simulation model for simulation(Tab. 2).

Capacity of one lane of a basic section of the expressway Tab. 2

Design speed(km/h)	100	80	60
Basic capacity(pcu/h)	2200	2100	1800
Design capacity(pcu/h)	2000	1750	1400

The speed data obtained by the network data crawler is the average speed of a road section in one direction. Since the traffic simulation model established in this paper is based on a partial road network composed of multiple roads, the data is converted into the average road network speed based on the road flow's estimated value.

$$\bar{v} = \frac{\sum Q_i v_i}{\sum Q_i} \quad (2)$$

This paper mainly aims at optimizing the design of traffic signal timing during peak hours, so the road network speed and flow data from April 10 to April 17, 2020, is calculated from 7:30—9:30.

2 Model Establishment and Calibration

It takes incredible money and effort to evaluate the design scheme directly in the actual project. Therefore, traffic simulation technology is widely adopted. Vissim, a microscopic traffic simulation software system developed by the German PTV company, is currently one of the most adopted software in the transportation industry. Vissim can analyze the traffic operation under many conditions such as lane type, traffic composition, traffic signal control, and stop control.

2.1 Road Network Building

The research object is a comprehensive logistics park integrating parking logistics, and the geographical position is superior with apparent advantages in transportation, location and environment. Comprehensively considering the driving route of large trucks and *the Technical standards of traffic impact analysis of construction projects*(CJJ/T 141—2010) *Institute et al.*, 2010, the modeling scope as shown in Fig. 1 is determined, and various necessary parameters in the model are set according to the results of field investigation.

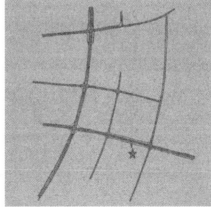

Fig. 1 Road network establishment range

2.2 The Output of Evaluation Results

In order to obtain the evaluation output data, the corresponding evaluation type must be activated first. This paper's main evaluation contents include Node evaluation, Data collection, Network performance, Travel time, and Delay.

2.3 Parameter Calibration

The parameters of the simulation model directly affect the simulation results. Therefore, the parameters' calibration can make it more realistic and effective for the traffic system operation, traffic flow characteristics and driver's behavior.

The road network model is established through Vissim, and the parameters are set based on the actual survey data. In order to make the simulation model as close to the actual traffic characteristics as possible, this study takes the average speed of the road network as the optimization index to calibrate the simulation model's main parameters. Five parameters to be calibrated, which significantly impact the average speed of the road network, are obtained by using a one-variable multi-factor analysis of variance. They are Desired Speed, Observed Vehicles, Average Standstill Distance, Additive Part of Safety Distance, and Multiple Part of Safety Distance.

At present, the methods commonly used in simulation model parameter calibration include sampling algorithms and heuristics algorithms, such as Latin hypercube sampling, genetic algorithm, particle swarm algorithm, simulated annealing algorithm, etc. Byungkyu et al., 2006; Hou et al., 2018; Wang et al., 2019 After comparing the calibration performance of each parameter calibration algorithm to the simulation model used in this research, it is found that the parameter calibration efficiency and calibration accuracy of the particle swarm algorithm is better than other parameter calibration algorithms, so this paper uses the particle swarm algorithm to perform parameter calibration on the simulation model after the input flow and signal control scheme.

3 Signal Control Scheme Design

According to the survey, the general route for vehicle travel in the logistics park is shown in Fig. 2. It passes through three intersections: ①the intersection of Huobi East Road and Xing'an Road; ②the intersection of Xinxing Road and Xing'an Road; ③the intersection of Huanggu Road and Xing'an Road.

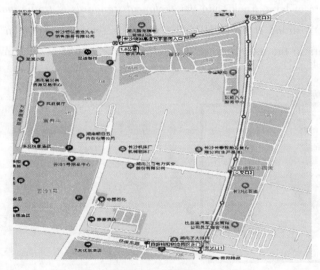

Fig. 2 Truck route

3.1 Signal Timing Scheme Design

This paper's signal control scheme design mainly applies VRIGEN *XIONG*, 2016, professional software for the optimal design of intersection signals. It adopts standard lane codes, which are practical and straightforward. The duration of each phase and the green light time of each lane can be obtained from the plan, providing a feasible plan for the setting of signal lights and effectively improving the intersection's traffic capacity. Take the intersection of Huanbao East Road and Xing'an Road as an example to design the intersection signal control (Fig. 3). The road traffic volume determined by the selected plan is input into the original model. The signal timing of the original model uses the data obtained from the investigation. The traffic flow diagram of the intersection is obtained through simulation.

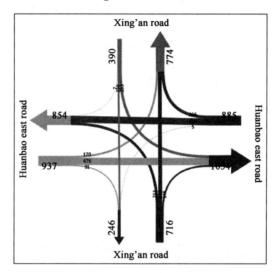

Fig. 3 Traffic flow diagram (Take the intersection of Environmental Protection East Road and Xing'an Road as an example)

Since the right turn is not controlled, the eight traffic flows that need to be designed for signal control should be analyzed. The conflicting relationship between them can be obtained. The conflict matrix is a symmetric matrix.

The clear time can be obtained directly through VRIGEN. Calculating it with EXCEL for accuracy:

$$T_{clear} = \max\{(T_{exit} - T_{enter})\} \tag{3}$$

Where: T_{clear} —— clear time;

T_{exit} ——The time when the last phase of the traffic flow leaves the conflict zone is calculated as (4)

T_{enter} ——The time when the traffic head of the next phase reaches the conflict zone, as (5)

$$T_{exit} = \frac{L_{exit} + L_0}{V_{exit}} \tag{4}$$

Where: L_{exit} —— The distance of the previous phase of the traffic flow from the conflict zone;

L_0 ——The length of the car;

V_{exit} ——The speed at which the traffic flow of the previous phase leaves the conflict zone.

$$\begin{cases} T_{enter} = T_{react} + \sqrt{\dfrac{2 L_{enter}}{a}} \text{ (Shorter } L_{enter} \text{ for motor vehicles)} \\ T_{enter} = T_{react} + \dfrac{v_{exit}}{a} + \left(\dfrac{L_{enter}}{v_{exit}} - \dfrac{v_{exit}}{2a}\right) \text{ (Longer } L_{enter} \text{ for motor vehicles)} \end{cases} \tag{5}$$

Where: L_{enter} ——the distance of the next phase of the traffic flow into the conflict zone;

V_{enter} ——the speed at which the next phase of traffic flow enters the conflict zone;

T_{react}——response time for the next traffic flow (start delay);

a——starting acceleration of the next traffic flow.

L_{enter} and L_{exit} in (3)(4)(5) can be obtained through the distance measurement function of the Baidu map.

After calculation, all clear time is 0s. In view of a large number of trucks on this section and the large traffic volume, the clear time is set to 2s for traffic safety. With the intersection input parameters into VRIGEN, a lot of phase design plans can be obtained. Choosing the most suitable plan for the intersection based on experience, and the paper has the minimum period and the Webster period calculation result of the plan. The calculation formula of the signal period is as (6):

$$\begin{cases} T_{L_i} = T_{clear_i} + \lambda_1 + T_{yellow} - \lambda_2 \\ T_{Cmin} = \dfrac{\sum T_{L_i}}{1 - \sum_i q_i/s_i} \\ T_{Cw} = \dfrac{5 + 1.5 \sum T_{L_i}}{1 - \sum q_i/s_i} \end{cases} \quad (6)$$

Where: T_{L_i}——signal loss time;

T_{clear_i}—— clear time;

λ_1—— start delay time;

λ_2—— yellow light use time;

T_{Cmin}—— minimum period;

T_{Cw}—— Webster cycle;

q_i/s_i——flow rate ratio.

Finally, it comes out. Set in VISSIM4.3 according to the phase loop diagram. The other two intersections adopt the same method for phase optimization design.

3.2 Optimization

Generally speaking, two methods are used to design coordinated timing schemes: the method of minimizing performance indicators (such as delay, queue length, etc.) and the method of maximizing green wave bandwidth. Thispaper tends to realize green wave transportation because of its convenience for subsequent optimization, such as linkage with logistics parks and other roads.

Adopting the MAXBAND model *Cho et al.*, 2019. Its principle is mainly to establish the relationship between parameters based on the geometric relationship diagram of each intersection's time distance and to maximize the two-way green wave bandwidth as the optimization goal to establish the model. The model green wave time-distance effect diagram is shown in Fig. 4. According to the principle of maximum green wave bandwidth and the principle of two-way priority, the model's objective function is $F = max(b = \bar{b})$. According to the geometric relationship in Fig. 4, we can get:

$$\begin{cases} \omega_i + b \leq 1 - r_i \\ \bar{\omega}_i + \bar{b} \leq 1 - \bar{r}_i \end{cases} \quad (7)$$

$$\begin{cases} \varphi_{i,i-1} + 0.5\, r_i + \omega_i = 0.5\, r_{i-1} + \omega_{i-1} + t_{i-1,i} \\ \bar{\varphi}_{i,i-1} + 0.5\, \bar{r}_i + \bar{\omega}_i = 0.5\, \bar{r}_{i-1} + \bar{\omega}_{i-1} + \bar{t}_{i-1,i} \end{cases} \quad (8)$$

$$\varphi_{i,i-1} + \bar{\varphi}_{i,i-1} + \Delta_{i-1} - \Delta_i = \lambda C \quad (9)$$

$I(i)$ is intersection, i takes values from 1 to n, ω_i and $\bar{\omega}_i$ are the differences between the end (start) time of the red light signal and the edge time of the green band; b and $\bar{b}$ indicate two-way green wave belt models respectively; r_i and $\bar{r}_i$ indicate the red light time for the downlink and uplink respectively; $\varphi_{i,i-1}$ and $\bar{\varphi}_{i,i-1}$ represent the time difference between the midpoints of two-way red lights at two intersections; $t_{i-1,i}$ and $\bar{t}_{i-1,i}$ indicate the ratio of the running time of the downward and upward vehicles respectively; Δ_i indicates the time difference between the middle point of adjacent r_i and $\bar{r}_i$.

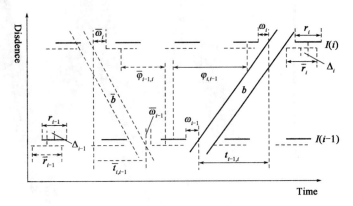

Fig. 4 Green wave time-distance rendering

In summary, the basic expression of the model is as follows:

$$F = \max b \tag{10}$$

$$\begin{cases} b = \bar{b} \\ \omega_i + b \leq 1 - r_i; \bar{\omega}_i + \bar{b} \leq 1 - \bar{r}_i \quad (i = 1, 2, \cdots, n) \\ 0.5(r_i + \bar{r}_i) + \omega_i + \bar{\omega}_i + \Delta_{i-1} - \Delta_i = 0.5(r_{i-1} + \bar{r}_{i-1}) + \\ \omega_{i-1} + \bar{\omega}_{i-1} + t_{i-1,i} + t_{i,i-1} + \lambda C \quad (i = 2, 3, \cdots, n) \\ b; \bar{b}; \omega_i; \bar{\omega}_i \geq 0 \quad i = 1, 2, \cdots, n \\ \lambda \in Z \end{cases} \tag{11}$$

The final green wave design diagram is shown in Fig. 5, and other schemes of flow combination based on data are also designed and calculated according to this principle. Modeling and simulation are carried out according to different schemes with the output results compared. Adopting average vehicle delays, vehicle stops and vehicle stop time as indicators for comparison, it can be found that the optimized design scheme has greatly improved various indicators compared with the original scheme, indicating that the realization of green wave-traffic has alleviated road traffic problems. There is a significant improvement.

3.3 Evaluation of optimization

The selection of evaluation indicators is based on simple, intuitive and effective criteria, combined with the evaluation content given by VISSIM. This paper selects four parameters: delay d, stopping time t, stopping times and traffic flow to compare the optimization scheme with the original plan was compared and evaluated.

The travel time section, set up on the road section required by the simulation model established by VISSIM, monitors the vehicles passing the start and endpoints and outputs once every 5 minutes for a total of 1 hour of simulation, providing the travel time, delay and other data during the driving process and output the results.

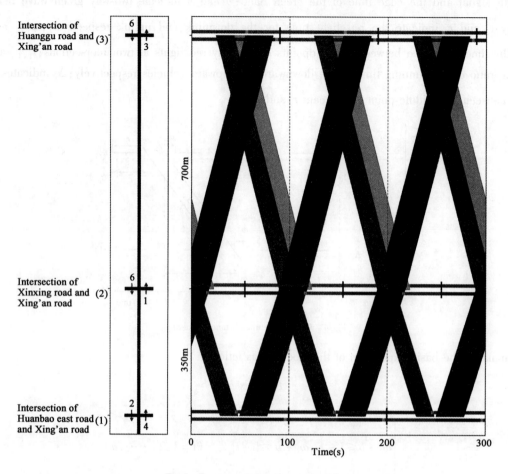

Fig. 5 Two-way priority green wave graph

The control group is the signal timing scheme being used for the trunk line and the signal timing scheme to achieve "green wave" linkage after optimization. The realization of the "green wave" plays an important role in alleviating urban road traffic congestion. Through the charts, it can be found that delays have dropped by about 69%, and the number of stops has fallen similarly, and the stop time has been reduced more significantly, reaching 78%. Obviously, due to the reduction of delays and parking, the number of vehicles passing through the same time will increase. Still, overall the number of vehicles passing through the main line under green wave traffic is about 2.3 times that of the original plan(Fig. 6).

4 Conclusions

In this paper, the possible traffic congestion near the logistics park in the urban area is studied based on the real-time data of Internet maps. This data collection method can not only obtain the traffic data of the research road network at any time, but more importantly, the data collection process is cheap and fast, which provides stable and accurate data support for the design and evaluation of signal control schemes. The adoption of Vissim to model and implement parameter calibration ensures that the difference between the simulated traffic flow and the actual traffic flow is within the specified range, i.e., the model conforms to the actual situation and can be used for simulation analysis. Based on the evaluation system of urban traffic congestion at home and abroad, four indicators are selected to evaluate the optimized design plan, including delay, parking times, parking time and traffic flow.

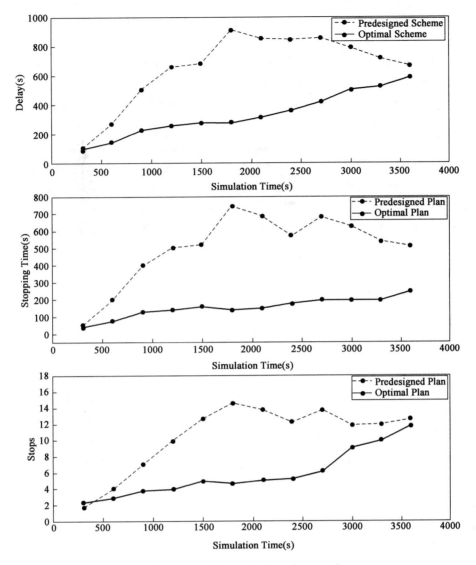

Fig. 6 Comparison of the results of signal timing schemes

The research found that, to facilitate transportation, the straight-line distance is only 1.1km between the logistics park and Ring Expressway in Changsha. However, it faces serious traffic congestion because it is built near the urban secondary arterial road and the traffic volume is relatively large, especially during peak hours. Therefore, after phase optimization and green wave linkage on intersections' signal timing, the effect will be extremely significant. It can increase the passing rate of vehicles, reduce delays, and alleviate traffic congestion. By crawling the traffic in real-time, the corresponding signal timing optimization plan can also be obtained in time to improve the road network's efficiency.

5 Acknowledgements

This research has been made possible by grants from Changsha Science and Technology Commission under project kq1801010, Department of Communications of Henan Province under number 2020G11, the National Science Foundation of China (NSFC) under project 51878264, National Key Technology Support Program under number 2015BAJ03B01.

References

[1] Zhu Y, Lu H P. Development trend of urban traffic control system[J]. Integrated transportation, 2003(12):48-50.

[2] Li Q G, Xia Q G, et al. Status and development of the urban traffic signal control system[J]. Science Technology and Engineering 2009,9(24), 7436-7442,7448.

[3] Hansen B G, Martin P T, et al. Scoot real-time adaptive control in a corsim simulation environment[J]. Advanced traffic management systems and automated highway systems 2000: Highway operations, capacity, and traffic control,2000, 27-31.

[4] Abu-Lebdeh G, Benekohal R F, et al. Genetic algorithms for traffic signal control and queue management of oversaturated two-way arterials[J]. Advanced traffic management systems and automated highway systems 2000: Highway operations, capacity, and traffic control, 2000,61-67.

[5] Luyanda F, Gettman D et al. Acs-lite algorithmic architecture - applying adaptive control system technology to closed-loop traffic signal control systems[J]. Freeways, high-occupancy vehicle systems, and traffic signal systems 2003: Highway operations, capacity, and traffic control,2003:175-184.

[6] Niittymaki J,Turunen E Traffic signal control on similarity logic reasoning[J]. Fuzzy Sets And Systems 2003,133(1), 109-131.

[7] Song H,Zheng G, X, et al. Shenzhen intelligent traffic signal control system[J]. Public Safety in China: Intelligent Transportation,2007, 000(008), 45-49.

[8] Kouvelas A, Aboudolas K, et al. A hybrid strategy for real-time traffic signal control of urban road networks[J]. IEEE Transactions on Intelligent Transportation Systems. 2011,3(12), 884-894.

[9] Coll P Factorovich P, et al. A linear programming approach for adaptive synchronization of traffic signals [J]. International Transactions In Operational Research. 2013,5(20), 667-679.

[10] Yin B Dridi M, et al. Forward search algorithm based on dynamic programming for real-time adaptive traffic signal control[J]. IET Intelligent Transport Systems. 2015,7(9), 754-764.

[11] Mousavi S S, Schukat M. et al. Traffic light control using deep policy-gradient and value-function-based reinforcement learning[J]. IET Intelligent Transport Systems. 2017,7(11), 417-423.

[12] Shu A B, Wang T T,et al. Automatic calculation system of trunk line green wave coordinated control parameters based on traverssaal pruning algorithm [J]. Computer applications and software, 2019, 4(36):251-254,267.

[13] Celtek S A, Durdu A, Alt MEM. Real-time traffic signal control with swarm optimization methods, Meas J Int Meas Confed,2020(166):108206.

[14] Institute Standard-Urban Construction. Technical standards for traffic impact assessment of construction projects. CJJ/T 141—2010[S], B65, 60. (in Chinese).

[15] Byungkyu P, Hongtu Q. Microscopic simulation model calibration and validation for freeway work zone network - a case study of vissim[J]. IEEE Intelligent Transportation Systems Conference, 2006:1471-1476.

[16] Hou Z H, Lee J. Multi-thread optimization for the calibration of microscopic traffic simulation model[J]. Transportation Research Record 2018,2672(20): 98-109.

[17] Wang B, Gu J. Calibration Method for Microscopic Simulation Model of Urban Expressway Using Internet Traffic Operation Data[J]. IOP Conf Ser Mater Sci Eng,2019:688(2).

[18] Xiong J J. Traffic analysis at the intersection of Chengnan road and Furong road in Changsha city based on VRIGEN[J]. Urbanism and Architecture,2016(6): 393-395.

[19] Cho H-J, Huang T-J,et al. Path-based maxband with green-split variables and traffic dispersion[J]. Transportmetrica B: Transport Dynamics,2019 7(1), 726-740.

基于冲突分析技术的公交专用道设置安全影响研究

侯宁昊[1,2] 张晖[1,2]

(1. 武汉理工大学智能交通系统研究中心；
2. 武汉理工大学水路公路交通安全控制与装备教育部工程研究中心)

摘要 公交专用道的设置目的在于保证公交车在出行高峰时段的流畅通行,以实现城市交通中的"公交优先"。可是在日常,公交专用道的设置会对主干道上的车辆进出造成阻碍。本文以微观交通仿真软件为工具,以安全替代模型为方法,研究在现有的公交专用道设置条件下,交通组织方式对道路交通冲突的影响情况,并提出安全性较高的交通组织方案。以武汉市友谊大道武汉理工大学4号校门部分路段为例,研究现有交通组织方案与改善方案下的车辆冲突变化情况。研究结果表明,在改善后的交通组织方案下,冲突区域内的冲突数量显著减少,冲突时间有所增加,道路交通安全状况得到改善。

关键词 交通仿真 车辆冲突 交通安全 安全替代模型

0 引言

传统道路交通安全评价方法主要基于事故统计模型。交通事故是一种小概率随机事件,建立科学可靠的事故统计模型需要事故数据积累。事故统计模型是一种事后的被动评价机制,难以实现主动安全防控策略,因此,以交通冲突为对象的交通安全评估方法被提出。朱顺应等[1]对研究人员应用交通冲突对交通安全进行交通安全评价的方法进行了总结,认为交通冲突的数量、类型及各项参数可应用于交通安全分析。

交通仿真作为一种交通安全研究方式,相较于实车实验具有成本低、易控制、数据采集便捷等特点,周嗣恩、叶红波、Ghanim、孙林、Srie 等[2-6]利用 VISSIM 进行交通仿真,并运用 (Suragate Safety Assessment Model,安全间接分析模型) SSAM,分析道路交叉口的冲突情况。

将交通仿真与冲突分析进行结合,采集车辆轨迹数据,并以此对车辆冲突进行分析,以此判别道路交通安全水平。Wu 等[7]用 VISSIM 软件仿真信号交叉口行人与车辆之间的冲突,以确定信号交叉口行人与车辆冲突的最佳后侵犯时间和时间碰撞参数。王晨等[8]提出了基于微观交通仿真和极值理论的交叉口安全评价方法。Kim 等[9]评估了 SSAM 是否可以用于评估高速公路路段的安全冲突数量及类型。

因此,本文提出设置公交专用道缓冲带,使进出校门车辆能够借用公交专用道进行转向以实现进出校门,同时避免转向跨越车道的行为发生。研究以微观交通仿真获得的数据和 SSAM 冲突评价结果为依据,检验交通组织改进方案的改善效果。

1 道路冲突分析技术原理

1.1 冲突的概念及分类

交通冲突是指在可观测的情况下,两个或两个以上的道路使用者在时间和空间上相互逼近,如果不采取相应的措施,将会发生碰撞产生危险的现象。

根据发生冲突的两辆车的车头朝向,冲突可以分为追尾冲突、变道冲突以及交叉冲突。

基金项目:国家重点研发计划课题(2019YFB1600803),新能源汽车运行安全风险评估预警技术及系统研发,2019.12-2022.11。

根据冲突的形成过程及机理,可将冲突分为基于点的冲突和基于线的冲突两种类型,如图1所示。

1.2 SSAM模型

SSAM模型是由美国Turner-Fairbank Highway Research Center提出的一种基于网格的冲突识别分析模型。SSAM模型原理示意图如图2所示。

图1　冲突点与冲突线示意图

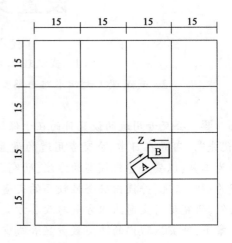

图2　SSAM模型冲突分析示意图(尺寸单位:m)

SSAM主要的分析指标有TTC(time to collision,冲突期间观察到的最小冲突时间值)、PET(post-encroachment time,冲突期间观察到的最小的后侵犯时间)、MaxS(maximum speed,冲突期间两辆车的最大加速度)、DeltaS(difference in vehicle speeds,在tMinTTC观察到的车辆速度差)、MaxD(maximum deceleration of second vehicle,第二辆车的最大减速度)。

2　交通仿真数据采集及处理

2.1　道路线形信息获取

友谊大道是武汉市武昌区的一条主干道,武汉理工大学余家头校区4号门位于该道路上。将友谊大道与武汉理工大学余家头校区校内交通一路交界处作为研究路段,如图3a)所示。研究路段的横断面设置为双向六车道,每条车道的宽度为3.75m,双向最外侧车道均为公交专用道,其公交专用道时段为7:00—9:00与16:00—19:00两个时段。研究路段车道设置如图3b)所示。

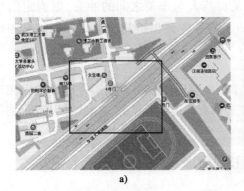

图3　研究路段示意图

2.2　路段车流量数据获取及处理

在横跨友谊大道的理工二桥上架设摄像机,将镜头对准道路,记录友谊大道上车流的行驶情况。摄像机拍摄画面如图3b)所示。采集2019年12月27日周五早7:45—8:35这50min的视频数据,后期经过统计,道路车流量数据见表1。取进出学校车辆数最多的30min车流数据作为研究对象,将30min数据翻倍获得 1h 数据,统计进入学校的车辆占友谊大道上通行的小汽车数量的比例,经计算,该比例为 12.7%(表 2)。

友谊大道车流量数据(单位:辆) 表1

序 号	时 间 段	小 汽 车	公 交 车	进入学校的车辆数	从学校出来的车辆数
1	7:45—7:50	129	8	12	17
2	7:50—7:55	33	9	16	9
3	7:55—8:00	159	6	18	12
4	8:00—8:05	144	5	18	25
5	8:05—8:10	157	6	19	12
6	8:10—8:15	159	9	20	9
7	8:15—8:20	133	1	22	7
8	8:20—8:25	134	8	15	15
9	8:25—8:30	133	14	15	9
10	8:30—8:35	123	11	8	8
合计		1304	77	163	123

进出学校车辆数最多的 30min 车流量数据(单位:辆) 表2

序 号	时 间 段	小 汽 车	公 交 车	进入学校的车辆数	离开学校的车辆数
1	8:00—8:05	144	5	18	25
2	8:05—8:10	157	6	19	12
3	8:10—8:15	159	9	20	9
4	8:15—8:20	133	1	22	7
5	8:20—8:25	134	8	15	15
6	8:25—8:30	133	14	15	9
合计		860	43	109	77
1h 数据		1720	86	218	154
比例		100%	—	12.7%	—

3 基于 VISSIM 软件和 SSAM 的冲突仿真分析

3.1 VISSIM 路网模型搭建

3.1.1 路网搭建及路径决策

依照 VISSIM 软件自带路网[图 4a)],绘制路网,如图 4b)所示。

在路网中对行驶的交通流设置两种交通组织方式,如图 5 所示。图 5a)所展示的方案 1 就是现实多数车辆所采取的进出校门的方式,即单次跨越 1 条车道进入 4 号门。而图 5b)所展示的是本文所提出的改善方案。方案 2 提出的改进在于设置公交专用道缓冲带,使得社会车辆以"右进右出"的方式进出某个开口时,可以暂时借用公交专用道,使得整个车辆行驶路线更加流畅,驾驶员寻找时机进行右转的机会更多。

3.1.2 车辆输入设置

路网输入的车流量数据按照表 2 所列的数据设置,由校内进入友谊大道的车辆全部为小汽车,每小时车流量为 154 辆;友谊大道公交专用道行驶的公交车每小时车流量为 86 辆;友谊大道上通行的小汽车的车流量为每小时 1720 辆,其中有 12.7% 的车辆会右转进入武汉理工大学余家头校区 4 号门,剩余的 87.3% 的车辆会继续沿着友谊大道直行。

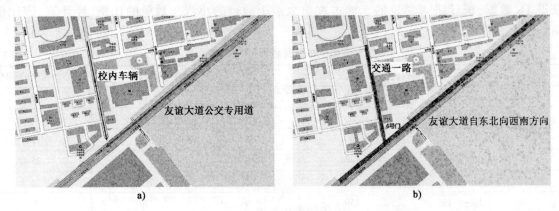

图 4 VISSIM 路网示意图

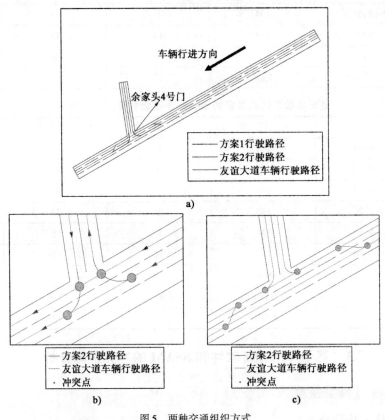

图 5 两种交通组织方式

3.1.3 交通区域交通组织方案

在同一个道路条件下,在仿真中设置两种不同的交通流组织方案,对比仿真动画及仿真运行结果。两种方案车辆进出余家头4号门的行驶轨迹示意图如图5a)所示。

方案1所表述的交通组织方案(图5b)是车辆在余家头4号门附近区域进行右转,跨过公交专用道,进入4号门,车辆如此行驶会产生1个分流冲突点以及1个交叉冲突点。

方案2所表述的交通组织方案(图5c)是车辆首先右转进入公交专用道缓冲带(允许社会车辆暂时进入公交专用道的一片区域),然后在缓冲带上右转进入4号门。出校门时同理。这样的交通组织方案会产生2个分流冲突点和1个合流冲突点。

3.2 VISSIM 仿真运行与轨迹文件输出

将仿真运行时间设置为3600s,在评价选项中设置输出SSAM文件,如图6所示。仿真运行效果如图7所示。将导出的trj文件导入SSAM软件,得到初步的冲突分析数据。

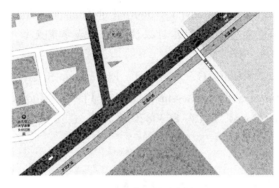

图6 VISSIM软件输出SSAM文件设置

图7 仿真运行示意图

3.3 冲突数据分析

从交叉、追尾、车道变换的分类冲突入手,统计各仿真指标,见表3。

两个方案的冲突指标 表3

冲突类型	数量(起/h)		TTC平均值(s)		相对速度DeltaS (m/s)		冲突加速度MaxD (m/s²)		最大速度MaxS (m/s)	
	方案1	方案2	方案1	方案2	方案1	方案2	方案1	方案2	方案1	方案2
追尾	49	32	1.210	1.325	5.040	4.712	-3.598	-3.317	6.736	6.797
车道变换	4	0	1.025	—	6.580	—	-3.010	—	7.220	—
交叉	0	0								

从表3可以得到如下结论:

(1)两个方案追尾冲突的数量较多,所占比例较大,分别为92.45%和100%。

(2)交通组织方案改善以后,冲突数量明显减少,追尾和车道变换冲突分别减少了34.69%和100%。追尾冲突的平均TTC增加了9.5%,相对速度减小了6.51%,说明通行能力提高后车辆运行状况得到改善,安全性能有一定的提升。

4 结 语

本文通过VISSIM微观交通仿真软件对武汉市友谊大道于园林路至铁机路之间的部分路段进行了建模,以视频的方式采集了友谊大道高峰时间段的车流量及车型占比,研究对比了直接跨越公交专用道右转以及设置公交专用道两种车辆通行方案。经过对两种方案下车辆冲突数据进行分析可知,设置公交专用道缓冲带可有效缓解社会车辆与公交车之间的变道冲突。

在未来的研究里,可针对公交专用道缓冲带的设置长度展开研究。为保证仿真结果的精度,可对仿真中控制车辆驾驶行为的模型进行参数标定。

参考文献

[1] 朱顺应,蒋若曦,王红,等.机动车交通冲突技术研究综述[J].中国公路学报,2020,33(02):15-33.

[2] 周嗣恩,李克平,孙剑,等.道路交叉口冲突仿真分析[J].中国安全科学学报,2009,19(5):32-37.

[3] 叶红波,廖彩凤.基于SSAM的平面交叉口交通安全评价[J].城市道桥与防洪,2016(4):5-8.

[4] Ghanim M. S., Shaaban K. A Case Study for Surrogate Safety Assessment Model in Predicting Real-Life

Conflicts[J]. Arabian Journal for Science and Engineering, 2019, 44(5): 4225-4231.

[5] 孙林. 基于交通冲突技术的城市交叉口交通安全评价方法研究[D]. 西安: 长安大学, 2015.

[6] Kusumastutie N. S., Rusmandani P. A brief review: traffic conflict techniques and the challenges of the studies in Indonesia[J]. MATEC Web of Conferences, 2019, 270(2): 3004.

[7] Wu J., Radwan E., Abou-Senna H. Determination if VISSIM and SSAM could estimate pedestrian-vehicle conflicts at signalized intersections[J]. Journal of Transportation Safety & Security, 2018.

[8] 王晨, 夏井新, 陆振波, 等. 基于微观仿真与极值理论的城市交叉口安全评价方法[J]. 中国公路学报, 2018, 31(4): 288-295, 303.

[9] Min K. K., Mitsuru S., Schultz G. G. et al. Evaluating Safety Impacts of Access Management Alternatives with the Surrogate Safety Assessment Model[J]. Transportation Research Record Journal of the Transportation Research Board, 2018: 863082010.

The Evaluation on Anti-Interference Reliability of Highway Network and Calculation Examples during the COVID-19 Outbreak

Wen Deng[1]   Leihong Dong[1]   Jinsong Ye[2]   Guorui Li[1]   Mingyue Yan[1]

(1. Highway Monitoring & Response Center, MOT;
2. China Academy of Transportation Sciences)

Abstract   The indices of highway network reliability commonly describe the dynamic characteristic of network performance and probability of road-use efficiency. Indices system which measures the validity reliability, invulnerability reliability and self-healing reliability has been preliminarily built. However, anti-interference performance indices which describe the reliability of highway network performance when emergency occurs are deficient. This paper focused on the enclosed highway network, and defined a new parameter which indicates the anti-interference reliability of network, as well as the particular travel costs. This paper also proposed the algorithm of the new parameters and evaluated the network recovery from the COVID-19 outbreak.

Keywords   Network performance   Anti-interference reliability   Game theory   Reliability evaluation   COVID-19

0 Introduction

The national economy and social development were severely affected by outbreak of the COVID-19 in 2020. Transportation industry also went through the process from decline to recovery. Taking highway transport as an example, the volume of freight transport in the first quarter is 5.29 billion ton, only accounting for 77.8 percent of the previous year's volume. There are 1.37 billion highway passenger trips in the first quarter, only accounting for 40.6 percent of the previous year's passenger volume. The freeway traffic volume fell to a record low on February 16th this year (5.42 million vehicles), 78.61 percent less than the last year. The freight traffic volume reduced by more than 82 percent (0.99 million vehicles). In order to accelerate the work resumption, the government has adopted a series of measures, such as toll-free policy and emergency vehicles traffic priority policy. As a result, the highway network reliability has been gradually enhanced. The freeway traffic volume is 46.2 million on April 30th, which is the highest this year, and the freight traffic volume increased to 9.21 million vehicles. The recovery of highway network reliability supported the national economy and social development.

At the present, the studies on highway network performance reliability mostly focus on the open network and free flow. The indices of network reliability at normal conditions include travel time reliability, capacity reliability and unblocked reliability. The indices of network reliability at emergencies include connectivity reliability, like invulnerability and self-healing, and recovery time reliability. However, connectivity reliability and recovery time reliability cannot cure actively in case of emergency. There must be a two-player non-cooperative game between interference factors and anti-interference circumstances as well as the process of which trip costs drop and reliabilities restore. In this circumstance, establishing anti-interference reliability of a network is important for network performance reliability evaluation.

1 Methods Comparison

The network reliability reflects the ability to complete the particular functions at the specific conditions and time. The degree of reliability measures the probability of network reliability. Network performance is susceptible to travel demand, interference factors, variable control measures and different link capacity, which is time-varying and unstable.

There are five evaluation methods to measure the probability of network performance reliability, including Terminal Reliability Estimation Methods, Game Theory, Monte Carlo Simulation, Absorbing Markov Chains, and Micro-simulation. Bell (1999) first applied the game theoretical approach to the study of network performance reliability and the assessment of travel time reliability.

1.1 The Game Theory Approach

According to the network game theory (Bell, 1999), there is assumed to be a two-player, non-cooperative, zero sum game between network users and "evil entities". Network users seek a path to minimize the expected travel cost on one hand and "evil entities" impose link costs on the user so as to maximize the expected travel cost on the other. The users guess what link costs will be imposed and the evil entities guess which path will be chosen. A network is reliable if the expected trip costs are acceptable even when users are extremely pessimistic about the state of the network. The mixed strategy Nash equilibrium offers a useful measure of network reliability by yielding the expected costs.

In the case of emergencies like COVID-19 outbreak, toll-free policy might make the trip expense costs not so important while travel purpose and demand are more essential. However, the contraction between network users and "evil entities" still exists, namely the non-cooperative, zero sum game considering other travel inference factors. Accordingly, applying game theory approach to the study of network anti-interference reliability is appropriate.

1.2 Travel Cost under Interference

Travel costs mainly consist of time cost, risk cost and responsibility cost under the influence of COVID-19. The interference factors for travel cost include epidemic prevention, traffic control, traffic interruption and so on. In the early days of the outbreak, a great number of highway checkpoints were set up and many roads were closed. There were up to twenty thousand checkpoints nationwide. Checkpoints were established on almost all the freeway provincial boundaries and one third of toll stations. Health check led to long-time and long-distance congestion, which brought risk to public travel and clustering transmission. Epidemic prevention and control in some degree affected the network performance and resulted in dramatic decrease of reliability for parts of network.

1.2.1 Definition of Interference Index

Anti-interference performance describes the external interference on the network reliability in case of emergency, from the perspective of robustness. Even though game theory can work for the assessment of reliability, the application conditions should be identified first. Interference indices are defined are shown in Tab. 1.

Interference Indices Tab. 1

Travel Cost	First-grade Interference Index	Second-grade Interference Index
Travel Mode Cost	Travel Mode	Self-Driving, Taxi, Truck, Coach Bus, Other Modes
Travel Purpose Cost	Travel Purpose	First-Grade Essential Travel, Second-Grade Essential Travel, Third-Grade Essential Travel, Fourth-Grade Essential Travel
Travel Distance Cost	Travel Distance Of One Single Trip	Within Province < 200 km, 200km ≤ Within Province < 500km, Inter-Province < 500km, 500km ≤ Inter-Province < 1000km, Inter-Province > 1000km
Travel Time Cost	Travel Time Of One Single Trip	0~3h, 3~6h, 6~10h, >10h
Travel Expense Cost	Travel Expense Of One Single Trip	Highway Toll Policy-Toll, Highway Toll Policy-Toll Free, Highway Toll Policy-Toll Discount
Travel Risk Cost	Emergency Classification (Like Public Health Emergency)	Extraordinary Major (Grade I) Emergency, Major (Grade II) Emergency, Less Major (Grade III) Emergency, General (Grade IV) Emergency
		Number of Confirmed Cases, Number of New Cases
	Emergency Impact Degree (Like Public Health Emergency)	Number of Closed Highway Entrance and Exit (Toll Gate)
		Number of Check Points
		Number of Blocked Links
		Number of Toll Stations where Queue Length More than 500m, Number of Toll Stations where Queue Length More than 200m
		Number of Links where Queue Length More than 3000m, Number of Links where Queue Length More than 1000m

1.2.2 The Particular Travel Cost

There are a great many interference factors influencing travel costs, including travel mode, travel distance, travel time, travel expense and travel risk. Consequently, highway travel cost could be defined as the sum of interference which the individuals or groups are imposed to achieve the travel purpose.

Let

C_R: actual travel cost;

C_t: travel time cost;

C_e: travel expense cost;

C_d: travel risk cost;

C_m: travel mode cost;

C_s: travel distance cost;

C_p: travel purpose cost;

$\beta_t, \beta_e, \beta_d, \beta_m, \beta_s, \beta_p$: weights of six travel costs respectively.

Note that

$\beta_t \in [0, 0.7), \beta_e \in [0, 0.5), \beta_d \in [0, 1), \beta_m \in [0, 0.4], \beta_s \in [0, 0.3], \beta_p \in [0, 0.3]$

Hence

$$C_R = \beta_t C_t + \beta_e C_e + \beta_d C_d + \beta_m C_m + \beta_s C_s + \beta_p C_p \tag{1}$$

In the case of emergencies like COVID-19 outbreak, most of the highway trips have rigid demands. The particular travel costs are more affected by the epidemic prevention and control measures, purpose and expenses than the travel modes, distance and time. As a result, during COVID-19 outbreak, travel risk, purpose and expense are converted into corresponding costs, which compose the particular travel cost.

Let

C_{Rt}: the particular travel cost;

C_e: travel expense cost;

C_d: travel risk cost;

C_p: travel purpose cost;

$\beta_e, \beta_d, \beta_p$: weights of three travel costs respectively.

Note that

$\beta_d + \beta_p + \beta_e = 1, \beta_d \in [0.5, 1), \beta_p \in (0, 0.5], \beta_e \in [0, 0.3)$

Hence

$$C_{Rt} = \beta_d C_d + \beta_p C_p + \beta_e C_e \tag{2}$$

The value of β_e, β_d and β_p vary with epidemic prevention and control measures.

The travel expense costs depend on the toll policy. Travel expense is zero when toll free.

2 Definition and Algorithm of Anti-interference Reliability Indices

2.1 Definition and Calculation

Anti-interference reliability takes the travel costs under interference as the measurement of reliability to evaluate network or link performance, in order to improve the movement and lower the probability of congestion of network.

Anti-interference reliability is defined as the probability of which within a certain period of time, network performance could meet the primary traffic demand under the influence of the particular interference factors.

Let

R_a: anti-interference reliability;

C_R: actual travel cost;

α: threshold value of cost;

C_0: travel cost under ideal conditions;

Then

$$R_a = P\{C_R \leq \alpha C_0\} \tag{3}$$

2.2 Classification of Anti-interference Reliability

From (1) and (3), we can see that anti-interference reliability varies with different interference factors and travel costs. The value of reliability depends on the measurement of probability. Four classes of anti-interference reliability are defined as follows (see Tab. 2).

Classification of Anti-interference Reliability   Tab. 2

Classification	Value Ranges	Anti-Interference Ability	Descriptions
Grade IV	[0, 0.2)	Weak	The interference impact is very strong. The network capacity and efficiency decrease gravely
Grade III	[0.2, 0.5)	Medium	The interference impact is strong. The network capacity and efficiency decrease dramatically
Grade II	[0.5, 0.7)	Stronger	The interference impact is moderate. The network capacity and efficiency decrease slightly
Grade I	[0.7, 1]	Very Strong	The interference impact is small. The network capacity and efficiency are basically normal

3 Evaluation of Network Reliability in Case of COVID-19 Outbreak

The COVID-19 outbreak this year is one of the most wide-spread, influential and long-lasting emergencies in China. The outbreak started during the spring rush, namely the peak period of the whole year. Till January 29th, 31 provinces have activated the first level public health event responses, which had a huge impact on the highway travel mode, distance, time, expense, risk and so forth. Anti-interference reliability (2)(3) are adopted to evaluate and analyse the network performance reliability during the outbreak. The process is as follows.

3.1 R_a Declined To Grade IV

Early on in the outbreak, during the Spring Festival holiday, most of the highway trips were essential. Travel time and travel distance impacted slightly on the trips. Consequently, the interference factors of reliability are proposed to be the emergency level, emergency impact degree, travel mode and travel expense.

Let

$$C_{Rt} = \varphi C_0 \tag{4}$$

Note that φ is the value coefficient of the actual travel cost, which refers to the multiple of ideal travel cost, positively correlated with emergency level, impact degree and travel purpose.

Hence

$$R_a = P\{C_{Rt} \leq \alpha C_0\} = P\{\varphi C_0 \leq \alpha C_0\} = P\{\varphi \leq \alpha\} \tag{5}$$

According to the variation trend of outbreak, φ is approximately considered to be normally distributed.

Let

$\varphi(t)$: the distribution function of φ and the variable of which is time;

μ: the mean value of $\varphi(t)$;

σ^2: the variance of $\varphi(t)$.

Hence

$$\varphi(t) \sim N(\mu, \sigma^2) \tag{6}$$

As Fig. 1 shows, R_a refers to the proportion of shaded area to the whole area. Thus the value of R_a could be measured as the approximate shaded area ratio. From Fig. 1, we can get that:

$$\varphi(t_0) = \varphi(t'_0) = \alpha, \varphi(\frac{t'_0 + t_0}{2})$$

$$= \varphi(\mu) = \varphi(t)_{max} = \frac{1}{\sqrt{2\pi}\sigma} \quad (7)$$

Hence

$$R_a = P\{\varphi(t) \leq \alpha\} \approx \frac{\alpha t_0}{\frac{t'_0 + t_0}{2} \times \varphi(t)_{max}}$$

$$\approx 2 \times \left(\frac{\alpha}{\varphi(t)_{max}}\right)^2 \quad (8)$$

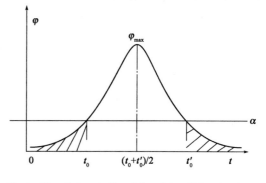

Fig. 1 Normal Quantie Plot of Actual Cost Value Coefficient

Particularly from January 20th to February 16th, the actual travel cost increased greatly and high to around 4 times of the ideal travel costs. Therefore, $\varphi(t)_{max} \in (3.8, 4]$. The anti-interference reliability could be measured as follows.

$$R_a = P\{C_{Rt} \leq \alpha C_0\} \approx 2 \times \left(\frac{\alpha}{\varphi(t)_{max}}\right)^2 \in [0.18, 0.20) \quad (9)$$

Where $\alpha = 1.2$.

According to the value of R_a, the anti-interference reliability grade was IV. In this circumstance, the anti-interference ability of network was poor and network efficiency dropped a lot. Consequently, traffic volume decreased dramatically, from 33.25 million vehicles per day before the outbreak to the lowest point of 5.42 million vehicles on February 16th. Especially for the week after resuming tolling from February 9th to 16th, the daily average traffic volume was less than 6 million vehicles, only 20% of the historical standard.

3.2 Effects of Anti-Interference Measures

It is assumed that anti-interference reliability R_a varies with interference factors and the specific trips. The government has implemented a series of policies and measures, such as toll-free policy and emergency vehicles traffic priority policy, which had a positive impact on the network performance. The network reliability got back to normal slowly.

From February 17th to May 5th, all the toll roads nationwide were free of charge. As a result, network traffic volume gradually went up. Till February 20th, traffic volume has been 13.59 million vehicles, about 60% of the historical standard. The traffic volume has risen by 27.84% on average during these four days. The toll-free policy has provided strong support for the transport during outbreak, work resumption and economic stability. The anti-interference reliability at this stage could be measured as follows.

$$R_a = P\{C_{Rt} \leq \alpha C_0\} \approx 2 \times \left(\frac{\alpha}{\varphi(t)_{max}}\right)^2 \in [0.32, 0.60] \quad (10)$$

Where $\alpha = 1.2$, $\varphi(t)_{max} \in [2.2, 3]$. Actual travel costs dropped because of toll-free policy and the maximum travel cost could be 2.2 to 3 times of ideal travel cost. The anti-interference reliability grade was III or II.

After February 21st, all the low risk areas cancelled the traffic restrictions, while the medium and high risk areas optimized the traffic control measures. On March 5th, the freeway traffic volume has been 26.54 million vehicles, surpassing which of last year. Since then, the freeway traffic grew rapidly. On March 26th, the traffic volume has been 33.93 million vehicles, increasing by 26.28% year-on-year.

Due to toll-free policy, the traffic on ordinary roads only returned to 80% of the previous year. The average daily traffic volume is 7,420 vehicles, falling 15.77% from the previous year. Traffic congestion eased greatly. The average daily amount of toll stations of which waiting line was more than 500 meters long was only 105, decreasing by 76.16% from the previous year. The average moving speed went up by 54.31% and the amount of congested links dropped by 32.24%. It seemed that anti-interference reliability returned to level I.

$$R_a = P\{C_{Rt} \leqslant \alpha C_0\} \approx 2 \times \left(\frac{\alpha}{\varphi(t)_{max}}\right)^2 \in [0.72, 0.89] \quad (11)$$

Where $\alpha = 1.2, \varphi(t)_{max} \in [1.8, 2]$. The actual travel cost returned to normal level. The maximum travel cost was about 1.8 to 2 times of ideal travel cost.

3.3 Network Self-Healing Ability

Anti-interference reliability R_a is closely related to the recovery time of network self-healing ability. As Fig. 2 shows, in the early days of the outbreak, public health emergency level, checkpoints setting and the toll gates closing had a strong impact on the network. The network traffic volume decreased and the particular travel cost increased day by day. Due to the positive stimulation of toll-free policy, along with the revocation of checkpoints and toll gates control, traffic volume and the particular travel cost recovered to the normal level. The self-healing ability of network reliability gradually reflected.

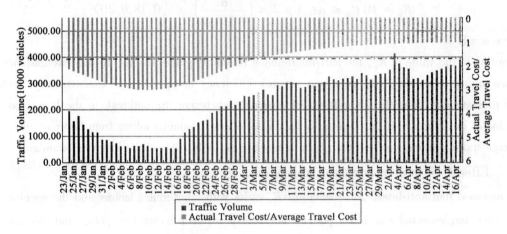

Fig. 2 Traffic Volume and Travel Cost

3.4 Recovery of Network Reliability

Toll-free policy and order restoration measures accelerated the network reliability recovery. Since March this year, freeway traffic volume, especially truck traffic volume, stayed high, which implied that the stage of work resumption started. The daily average volume of March was up to 7.41 million vehicles, an increase of 1.26 million vehicles from the previous year. The growth of truck volume was significantly faster than that of cars and the proportion of trucks grew by 3%. Meanwhile, the passenger number of railway and civil aviation was only 35% to 45% of the historical standards. It illustrated the significance of highway network reliability recovery.

4 Conclusions

In the case of emergency, the studies on the anti-interference factors for network performance reliability are required. Taking the enclosed highway network as applicable scenario, this paper defined the network anti-interference reliability and the particular travel cost. The corresponding algorithm was also proposed. The formulas of the particular travel cost C_{Rt}, the actual travel cost C_R and the anti-interference reliability R_a were built. According to the numerical examples, it is concluded that the network anti-interference reliability was grade IV early on in the outbreak, and the anti-interference reliability had its own recovery cycle. This paper has provided a new evaluation measure for the network performance reliability analysis in the circumstance of emergency.

5 Acknowledgements

The work described in this paper was supported by a grant from the Open Foundation of Key Laboratory of Transport Industry of Big Data Application Technologies for Comprehensive Transport.

References

[1] GAO Ai-xia, CHEN Yan-yan. Study on the Index System of Highway Network Reliability[J]. Journal of Beijing People's Police College, 2008(11), 22-25.

[2] CHEN Jian-jun, YU lei, CHEN Xu-mei. General Description of Evaluation Techniques of Highway Network Reliability[J]. Urban Transport of China, 2008(6), 67-70.

[3] Bell M. G. H. A Game Theory Approach to Measuring the Performance Reliability of Transport Networks[J]. Transportation Research Part B, 2000(34), 533-545.

[4] KANG Xi-ru. CHEN Yan-yan. Relationship between Accident Deposing Time and Network Recovery Reliability[J]. Journal of Transportation Systems Engineering and Information Technology,2009(9), 124-129.

[5] Bell M. G. H. Chris Cassir. Estimation of Travel Time Reliability Using Stochastic User Equilibrium Assignment Sensitivity[J]. Transportation Planning, 2000:69-84.

[6] Chen A, Yang H, Lo H K, et al. Capacity Reliability of A Road Network: An Assessment Methodology and Numerical Results[J]. Transportation Research Part B, 2002, 36(3):225-252.

[7] Anthony Chen, Hai Yang, Hong K. Lo, et al. A Capacity Related Reliability for Transportation Networks[J]. Journal of Advanced Transportation,1999,33(2). 183-200.

[8] Yasunori Iida. Basic Concepts and Future Directions of Road Network Reliability Analysis[J]. Journal of Advanced Transportation,1999,33(2). 125-134.

[9] Zhen-Ping Du, Alan Nicholson. Degradable Transportation Systems: Sensitivity and Reliability Analysis[J]. Transportation Research Part B:Methodological,1997,31(3). 225-237.

[10] CHEN Yan-yan, LIANG Ying, DU Hua-bing. The Application of Reliability in the Road Network Performance Evaluation[J]. China Civil Engineering Journal, 2003(1). 36-40.

基于非线性综合法的单交叉口交通状态评价方法

徐 琰 张伟斌

(南京理工大学电子工程与光电技术学院)

摘 要 近些年交通拥堵已成为一个社会问题,道路拥挤使得行车速度下降,出行成本增加,同时油耗以及尾气排放造成环境污染,因此解决交通拥堵问题刻不容缓。对道路拥堵状态准确判断和评价是进行有效城市交通管理的基础,从而可以根据具体情况采取合理的交通信号控制策略。本文设计基于非线性综合法的交通评价方法,首先将平均延误和停车率处理形成二范数形式的指标,与通行能力结合得到一个综合指标,再根据已有的配时方案,选取可变时长的历史样本数据计算得到拥堵指数。最后对所得到的拥堵指数进行K均值聚类,并对聚类情况采用多总体假设检验分析验证分类区间指数的差异性。结果表明,本研究所提出的方法合理有效。

关键词 评价方法 拥堵指数 聚类分析 假设检验

基金项目:国家自然科学基金项目(71971116)。

0 引言

随着国民经济的快速发展,我国机动车保有量持续大幅度增长。城市交通设施规划和建设跟不上交通需求的变化,城市交通的供需矛盾尖锐。交通拥挤严重影响着城市的可持续发展和居民日常工作,已成为社会共同关注的焦点和急需解决的重要问题。随着大数据、人工智能、检测技术等新兴技术的发展[1],交通控制技术也在不断进步,成为处理城市交通拥挤问题的有效方法之一。进行科学的管理与控制,特别需要对交通信号控制的实施和效果进行有效的评价,即对交叉口交通状态进行评价。

对交通状态准确评价才能进行相应的控制和调节,国内外不少学术机构研究了交通状况的评价指标及指标系统等内容[2]。国外发达国家20世纪五十年代开始对拥堵指标展开了一系列研究,Meyer、Michael、Byme等建立了一些主要城市区域的拥堵指标,但不能对发生在不同地点或时间的拥堵进行比较;Lindley、Schrank、Marlon等根据道路路段以及城市区域的不同特点,对拥堵指数中的参数进行设计;Francois和Willis、Schwartz、Lomax等建议对拥堵进行量化,提出了许多量化的性能指标[3];还有较为常用的公路通行能力手册(HCM)指标、排队论指标和基于出行时间的指标等[4];我国公安部发布了《城市交通管理评价指标体系》,使用的是主干线上机动车的平均行程速度反映其交通状态;北京市市政设计研究院综合延误指标、排队长度、损失时间和驾驶员感受等,对路口交通运行状况进行评级;有关道路交通状况评价指标系统的研究[5-6],在单个交通参数指标选取上比较成熟,而且基本形成了指标系统。

道路交通状态反映交通流运行特性,具备客观性、多样性、动态性、相对性和统一性。对交通状态的评价是交通管控的决策依据,运用交通流理论、概率论、数理统计等理论知识对系统进行分析,判断城市道路状态处于哪个层面。一般验证交通状态划分的合理性可以采取仿真验证的方法,本文基于概率统计方法,对聚类结果进行假设检验分析[7],从单样本到配对样本,再到多总体检验,根据样本对所提出的假设作出接受或者拒绝的决策。假设检验是作出这一决策的依据,该方法使得对于交通状态的评价更具备理论性[8]。

1 评价指标分析

1.1 数据获取

交通流检测(图1)一般分为直接检测法和间接检测法。直接检测法是通过监控摄像机采取图像信息,再根据图像处理的算法提取出图像所包含的交通信息,或者通过工作人员巡逻或是路人观察;间接检测法需要在道路下布设检测线圈,由线圈采集交通流等参数。

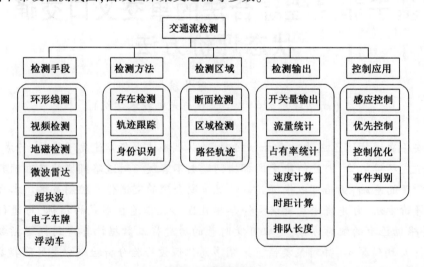

图1 交通流检测

本文数据采用视频检测方式,对交通流量以及占有率信息进行收集和分析。视频检测系统主要由摄像机、视频检测器主机、管理服务器、客户终端操作系统等构成。它利用在视频图像范围内设置检测区,采用车辆图像动态跟踪技术,动态图像背景自适应技术等多项计算机视频处理技术,对摄像机采集的视频图像进行计算机模式识别,从而统计分析出交通信息数据。

1.2 指标选取

常用的交通状况评价参数包括:饱和度、平均延误、平均排队长度、速度、密度等[9]。国内外对交通状况评价的研究具备一定的理论基础和依据。一般来说,对交通状态进行评价是一种直观的感受,容易受时间、环境等因素的影响。

本文认为对单交叉口的交通状态进行评价,延误与停车情况可以较好反映该路口特征。由于已有配时方案,可选用通行能力作为指标之一,以下是对所选取指标的介绍。

1.2.1 通行能力

车道组的通行能力是指一小时内该车道组通过的最大车流量。

$$\text{CAP}_i = S_i \frac{\theta_{ci}}{c} = S_i \lambda_i \tag{1}$$

式中:CAP_i——第i个车道组的通行能力,pcu/h;

S_i——第i个车道组的饱和流量,pcu/绿灯小时。

1.2.2 平均延误

延误是评价交叉口服务水平的核心指标,也是评价信号控制效果的主要指标之一。

$$d = \frac{c(1-\lambda)^2}{2(1-y)} \tag{2}$$

式中:c——信号周期,s;

λ——绿信比;

y——流量比。

1.2.3 停车率

由于信号控制的原因,车辆通过交叉口时可能因为红灯需要停车等待。停车率是指车辆通过交叉口时总的停车次数与车辆数的比值,是反映车辆通行顺畅程度的指标之一。

$$h_i = 0.9 \times \frac{1-\lambda_i}{1-y_i} \tag{3}$$

式中:λ_i——第i个相位的绿信比;

y_i——第i个车道组的流量比。

1.3 模型构造

传统交通状态评价方法有单指标法以及多指标求和法。单指标是只使用一项指标来评价交通状态,较为片面;多指标指将多项指标进行组合处理。本文采取多指标非线性组合的方法对单交叉口状态进行评价各指标最大最小值见表1。

将通行能力、平均延误和停车率作归一化处理,采用极值法实现指标的归一化。

各指标最大最小值 表1

	vol	c	d	h
min	0	0	26	0.6
max	2000	800	134	3.3

$$\bar{y} = \frac{y - y_{\min}}{y_{\max} - y_{\min}} \tag{4}$$

重新定义后的各指标:

$$c = \frac{\text{res}\_c - c_{\min}}{c_{\max} - c_{\min}} \tag{5}$$

$$d = \frac{\text{res\_}d - c_{\min}}{c_{\max} - c_{\min}} \tag{6}$$

$$h = \frac{\text{res\_}h - c_{\min}}{c_{\max} - c_{\min}} \tag{7}$$

$$\text{TCI} = \frac{\sqrt{d^2 + h^2}}{c} \tag{8}$$

式中：TCI——交通拥堵指数；

   d——平均延误，s；

   h——停车率；

   c——通行能力，pcu/h。

2 数据与相关方法描述

2.1 配时方法

韦伯斯特(Webster)以对交叉口车辆延误的估计为基础，通过对周期长度的优化计算，确定相应的一系列配时参数[10,11]。包括有关原理、步骤和算法在内的韦伯斯特法是交叉口信号配时计算的经典方法。

最佳周期计算公式：

$$C_0 = \frac{1.5L + 5}{1 - Y} \tag{9}$$

式中：C_0——最佳周期长度，s；

   L——总损失时间；

   Y——交叉口交通流量比；

这样总损失时间为：

$$L = nl + AR \tag{10}$$

式中：l——相位信号的损失时间；

   n——信号的相位数；

   AR——一周期中的全红时间。

2.2 配时方案

本次调研区域的特点是流量适中，但极易造成拥堵。非机动车与行人冲突，非机动车与非机动车的冲突以及非机动车与机动车的冲突时常发生。对于该区域发生拥堵的情况采用如表2所示信号控制配时方案[12]。

配 时 结 果   表2

相 位	时长(s)	绿 信 比
方案一 0—4点,23—24点,周期:45		
A	10	0.22
B	10	0.22
C	25	0.56
D	0	0
方案二 5—6点,19—22点,周期:70		
A	20	0.28
B	20	0.28
C	30	0.44

续上表

相 位	时长(s)	绿信比
D	0	0
方案三 7—8点,周期:118		
A	26	0.25
B	26	0.25
C	40	0.34
D	18	0.16
方案四 9—11点,周期:106		
A	20	0.19
B	18	0.17
C	45	0.42
D	23	0.22
方案五 12—14点,周期:93		
A	20	0.19
B	18	0.17
C	45	0.42
D	23	0.22
方案六 15—18点,周期:115		
A	26	0.26
B	26	0.26
C	25	0.30
D	20	0.18

2.3 流量数据以及指数计算

根据视频检测可以得知交通流量信息,本文选用2019年11月14日到21日以及2020年11月21日到29日的流量数据(表3)。

2019年11月14日到21日C相位流量情况 表3

2019年	11/14	11/15	11/16	11/17	11/18	11/19	11/20	11/21
00:00-01:00	326	335	456	440	363	359	336	335
01:00-02:00	265	244	357	313	250	295	200	205
02:00-03:00	160	176	253	268	185	183	164	180
03:00-04:00	117	98	191	171	120	137	137	101
04:00-05:00	140	134	168	184	142	133	138	115
05:00-06:00	140	121	149	172	153	121	100	104
06:00-07:00	374	385	380	381	291	368	348	374
07:00-08:00	773	641	731	778	1489	1073	718	1194
08:00-09:00	1301	1291	1172	1276	2156	1682	1200	1624
09:00-10:00	1279	1302	1437	1453	1475	1233	1330	1525
10:00-11:00	1224	1279	1518	1476	1245	1128	1207	1369
11:00-12:00	1155	1154	1405	1373	1184	1069	1231	1239
12:00-13:00	869	972	1092	1160	1004	828	965	964
13:00-14:00	907	976	1195	1297	1039	812	987	1025
14:00-15:00	1025	1156	1396	1340	1251	987	1067	1183

续上表

2019 年	11/14	11/15	11/16	11/17	11/18	11/19	11/20	11/21
15:00-16:00	1002	1114	1434	1406	1213	961	1170	1139
16:00-17:00	1144	1330	1566	1556	1276	1084	1244	1323
17:00-18:00	1241	1320	1247	1073	1085	1203	1356	1367
18:00-19:00	632	720	708	678	648	724	720	744
19:00-20:00	915	963	972	1028	870	884	997	911
20:00-21:00	845	861	842	880	791	769	907	761
21:00-22:00	885	945	842	819	823	860	1006	792
22:00-23:00	648	694	612	592	555	556	621	617
23:00-24:00	455	609	549	454	450	451	454	513

根据配时以及流量信息得出的拥堵指数见表4。

拥 堵 指 数 表4

2019 年	11/14	11/15	11/16	11/17	11/18	11/19	11/20	11/21
00:00-01:00	0.142	0.141	0.137	0.137	0.140	0.140	0.141	0.141
01:00-02:00	0.144	0.145	0.140	0.142	0.144	0.143	0.146	0.146
02:00-03:00	0.148	0.147	0.144	0.144	0.147	0.147	0.147	0.147
03:00-04:00	0.149	0.150	0.147	0.147	0.149	0.148	0.148	0.150
04:00-05:00	0.148	0.149	0.147	0.147	0.148	0.149	0.148	0.149
05:00-06:00	0.121	0.122	0.120	0.119	0.120	0.122	0.124	0.124
06:00-07:00	0.105	0.105	0.105	0.105	0.111	0.106	0.107	0.105
07:00-08:00	0.236	0.176	0.215	0.239	1.107	0.437	0.209	0.561
08:00-09:00	0.705	0.690	0.536	0.668	5.274	2.012	0.568	1.643
09:00-10:00	0.364	0.386	0.552	0.577	0.614	0.324	0.415	0.711
10:00-11:00	0.316	0.364	0.696	0.615	0.334	0.248	0.303	0.459
11:00-12:00	0.266	0.265	0.505	0.464	0.286	0.214	0.322	0.329
12:00-13:00	0.076	0.097	0.134	0.162	0.105	0.071	0.095	0.095
13:00-14:00	0.082	0.098	0.178	0.238	0.115	0.069	0.100	0.111
14:00-15:00	0.111	0.160	0.317	0.269	0.209	0.100	0.125	0.172
15:00-16:00	0.498	0.617	1.212	1.135	0.749	0.462	0.688	0.647
16:00-17:00	0.654	0.956	1.714	1.665	0.852	0.582	0.798	0.942
17:00-18:00	0.793	0.936	0.803	0.570	0.583	0.734	1.013	1.0378
18:00-19:00	0.246	0.292	0.286	0.269	0.254	0.295	0.292	0.306
19:00-20:00	0.121	0.132	0.134	0.150	0.113	0.115	0.141	0.120
20:00-21:00	0.109	0.111	0.109	0.114	0.103	0.101	0.119	0.100
21:00-22:00	0.115	0.127	0.109	0.106	0.106	0.111	0.143	0.103
22:00-23:00	0.096	0.097	0.096	0.096	0.097	0.097	0.096	0.096
23:00-24:00	0.137	0.131	0.133	0.137	0.137	0.137	0.137	0.099

将数据进行处理,可得图2。将2020/11/21—2020/11/29数据做同样处理,可得到图3。

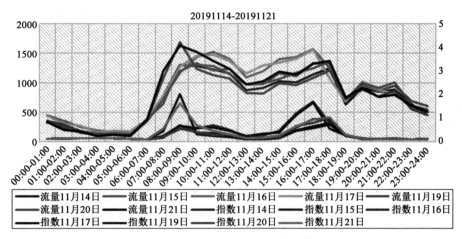

图2 2019/11/14—2019/11/21 流量与指数对比图

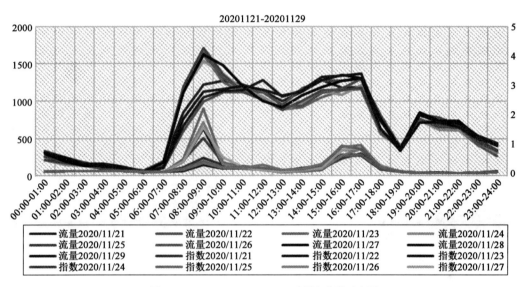

图3 2020/11/21—2020/11/29 流量与指数对比图

根据上述图示,时段划分如表5所示。

时 段 划 分　　　　　　　　　　　　　　　　　表5

时　段	时　间
平峰	00:00-7:00、10:00-16:00、19:00-24:00
早高峰	7:00-10:00
晚高峰	16:00-19:00

3 验证与结果分析

3.1 拥堵指数聚类

聚类分析研究已有数十年的历史,是数据挖掘、模式识别等研究方向的重要研究内容之一,在识别数据的内在结构方面具有重要的作用[13-14]。迄今为止,很多聚类任务都选择 K 均值聚类算法,它能够对大型数据集进行高效分类(图4~图9),计算复杂性为 $O(tKmn)$。

本文将交通拥堵指数分成多类进行观察,可知不同簇之间存在着明显的界限。对聚类情况进行整合分析并进行,合并处理综合对比选取 $k=4$ 的聚类结果(表6)。

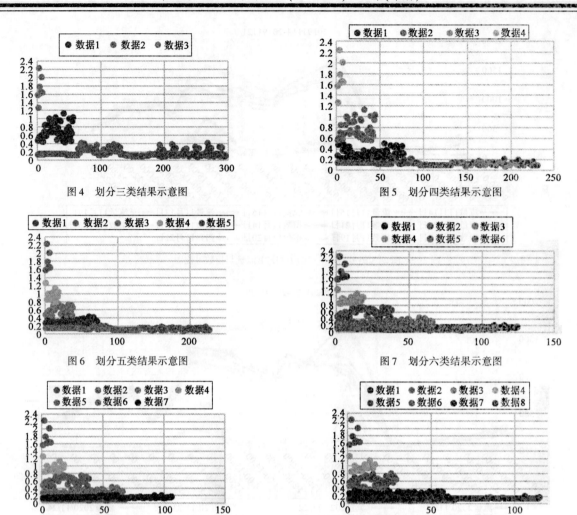

图 4 划分三类结果示意图

图 5 划分四类结果示意图

图 6 划分五类结果示意图

图 7 划分六类结果示意图

图 8 划分七类结果示意图

图 9 划分八类结果示意图

聚类划分对比结果　　　　表 6

k	A	B	C	D	E
3	(0,0.4)	(0.4,0.9)	(0.9,2)	(2,+∞)	
4	(0,0.2)	(0.2,0.5)	(0.5,1.4)	(1.4,2)	(2,+∞)

3.2 实例验证分析

假设检验是根据一定的假设条件,由样本推断总体的一种方法[15]。它的基本思想是小概率反证法思想,小概率思想认为,小概率事件在一次试验中基本上不可能发生。在这个方法下,我们首先对总体做出一个假设,假设大概率会成立。如果在一次试验中,试验结果和原假设相背离,也就是小概率事件发生,那就有理由怀疑原假设的真实性,从而拒绝这一假设[16]。

3.2.1 明确问题

问题:时段划分下的指数是否有差异,如果有差异则可以划成阈值。

零假设:多个研究样本来自的总体不存在显著性差异。

备选假设:多个研究样本来自的总体存在显著性差异。

3.2.2 选取样本

中心极限定理:合理足够多的样本可以代表总体。

样本数据:红谷中大道南斯友好路口_进口道车道流量(2019/11/14—2019/11/21、2020/11/21—2020/11/29)。

3.2.3 确定判断标准

用于作出决策的标准5%,在假设检验里叫作"显著水平"(图10)。

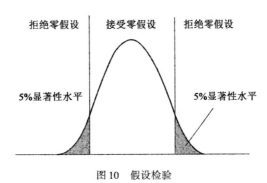

图10 假设检验

3.2.4 做出结论

将样本证据计算出的值与判断标准α作比较,如果$p<=\alpha$,拒绝零假设,备选假设成立;如果$p>\alpha$,那么零假设成立。

多样本假设检验是对多个研究样本的差异性进行检验的假设检验方法,通过比较多个研究样本总体数据分布的特征差异性,来判断不同时段交通拥堵指数之间的异同[17-18]。本文采用Kruskal-Wallis检验对多个样本进行假设检验,该检验也称为H检验,是一种非参数检验,不需要知道原始数据的分布和总体参数[19-20]。

(1)检验假设。H_0:总体分布相同即多个研究样本来自的总体不存在显著性差异;H_3:总体分布不相同即多个研究样本来自的总体存在显著性差异。

(2)编秩。按绝对值大小差值为0舍去不计,秩次相等取平均秩次。

(3)求秩和并计算检验统计量。

$$H = \left[\frac{32}{n_T(n_T+1)}\sum_{i=1}^{k}\frac{R_i^2}{n_i}\right] - 3(n_T+1) \tag{11}$$

式中:k——总体的个数;

n_i——样本i中的观测值个数;

n_T——代表所有样本的观测值总数;

R_i——样本i的秩和。

如果样本中存在结值(数据相同秩值的个数),则校正系数C为:

$$C = 1 - \frac{\sum(\tau_j^3 - \tau_j)}{n^3 - n} \tag{12}$$

其中τ_j表示第j个结值的个数。调整后的H_c统计量为

$$H_c = \frac{H}{C} \tag{13}$$

交通指数如表7所示。

样本时段交通指数　　　　表7

2020年	08:00-09:00	11:00-12:00	16:00-17:00	22:00-23:00
11/21	0.595	0.255	0.708	0.097
11/22	0.369	0.245	0.899	0.100
11/23	1.575	0.209	0.681	0.103
11/24	1.265	0.207	0.745	0.101
11/25	2.235	0.188	0.699	0.010

续上表

2020年	08:00-09:00	11:00-12:00	16:00-17:00	22:00-23:00
11/26	1.787	0.253	0.891	0.101
11/27	1.627	0.179	0.914	0.098
11/28	0.485	0.267	0.910	0.098
11/29	0.421	0.366	1.033	0.099

由表7可知,总体 $k=4$, $n_1=n_2=n_3=9$,当 $x^2>7.815$ 时,则拒绝 H_0。样本存在结值,所以

$$H_c = \frac{H}{C} = \frac{\left[\frac{12}{n_T(n_T+1)}\sum_{i=1}^{k}\frac{R_i^2}{n_i}\right]-3(n_T+1)}{1-\frac{\sum(r_j^3-\tau_j)}{n^3-n}} = 29.602 \tag{14}$$

通过查卡方检验表可知,自由度为 $k-1=3$,显著性水平为0.05时,卡方值为7.815。计算得检验统计量 H 等于29.602,远大于卡方值,所以拒绝原假设,认为这4组数据是有显著差异的。

3 结　语

对于交通拥挤的评价模型大多沿用HCM美国道路通行能力手册,且指标较为单一化。本文根据实际已有数据,选取符合单交叉口信号控制方案的评价指标并将其进行整合处理,克服单指标的片面性。提出的模型能够对单点配时情况做有效的评价,对单交叉口的交通状态也能合理反映。不同于仿真检验,本文对于K-means交通状态聚类结果运用统计概率的方法,从理论上对所得成果进行验证。基于不同时段,采用多总体的假设检验理论表明聚类结果是有意义的,有着显著差异性。本文研究尚存在不足之处,例如仅对于指数结果进行一维聚类,在后续研究中需要对多种数据多维分析,以取得更好的状态划分结果。

参考文献

[1] 陈浩然. 基于多源数据的交通特性信息估计[D]. 山东大学, 2016.
[2] 谢丹丹. 交通状态分类方法研究与设计[D]: 杭州: 浙江工业大学计算机科学与技术学院, 2014.
[3] Agureev I, Elagin M, Pyshnyi V, et al. Methodology of Substantiation of the City Transport System Structure and Integration of Intelligent Elements into it. Transportation Research Procedia 2017. (20): 8-13.
[4] Khalighi F, Christofa E. Emission-based Signal Timing Optimization for Isolated Intersections[J]. Transportation Research Record Journal of the Transportation Research Board, 2015, 2487(2487): 1-14.
[5] 祝付玲. 城市道路交通拥堵评价指标体系研究[D]. 南京: 东南大学, 2006.
[6] 基于大数据的单点交通信号配时优化策略研究[J]. 罗云辉, 李林, 靳文舟. 公路与汽运. 2017(04).
[7] 林璐, 陈健, 曲大义, 等. 基于K均值聚类算法的交通状态判别方法研究[J]. 青岛理工大学学报, 2019, 040(004):109-114.
[8] 邴其春. 城市快速路交通状态评估与预测关键技术研究[D]. 长春: 吉林大学, 2016.
[9] Ramadhani F, Bakar KA, Hussain M A, et al. Optimization with Traffic-Based Control for Designing Standalone Streetlight System: A Case Study. Renewable Energy, 2017, (105): 149-159.
[10] 排阵式交叉口延误及最佳周期模型[J]. 赵靖, 郑喆, 韩印. 中国公路学报. 2019(03).
[11] Kentaro Wada, Koki Satsukawa, Mike Smith, et al. Network Throughput Under Dynamic User Equilibrium: Queue Spillback, Paradox and Traffic Control[J]. Transportation Research Part B. 2018.
[12] 朱海峰, 刘畅, 温熙华, 等. 均衡流量和饱和度的交通瓶颈控制[J]. 控制理论与应用. 2019(05).
[13] 周志华. 机器学习[M]. 北京: 清华大学出版社, 2016.1.
[14] 杨俊闯, 赵超. K-Means聚类算法研究综述[J]. 计算机工程与应用, 2019, 055(023):7-14,63.
[15] 吴海燕, 赵茜琳. 假设检验与P值的再认识[J]. 统计学与应用, 2020, 9(4):8.
[16] 徐红霞, 范国良. 假设检验中单边检验和双边检验的区别解析[J]. 数学学习与研究, 2020(01):7-7.

[17] 牛凯,陈悦.假设检验中T检验原理与对比应用[J].产业与科技论坛,2019,018(004):50-51.
[18] 傅莺莺,田振坤,李裕梅.方差分析的回归解读与假设检验[J].统计与决策,2019,035(008):77-80.
[19] 魏立力.假设检验与置信区间的对偶关系[J].高师理科学刊,2018,038(004):51-53.
[20] 魏立力,张定强.确定假设检验拒绝域的证据原理[J].数学的实践与认识,2018(16).

城际交通综合感知的多群组结构方程模型

王建军　张宇辉

(长安大学运输工程学院)

摘　要　为分析城际出行中旅客的经济消耗和时间成本的关联性,及其对交通综合感知的影响,并进一步探讨所述因素在使用4种城际交通方式群体中的差异,本文先整体构建了结构方程模型,标定了城际出行中各潜变量间的路径系数,整体分析4种交通方式的一般特性。然后,以不同交通方式为依据,将多群组结构方程模型引入到交通选择行为差异分析中,进行了多群组研究。结果表明:在城际出行中,经济消耗和时间成本呈显著的正向关联(0.47),其均对旅客的综合交通服务感知存在显著的负向影响,且经济消耗(-0.16)的影响远低于时间成本(-0.65);不同交通方式分群下,除飞机和高速铁路及动车外,其余交通方式潜变量之间的关联性和影响力均存在显著性差异。

关键词　交通工程　城际交通　交通综合感知　多群组结构方程模型　潜变量

0　引　言

交通综合感知是旅客获得出行体验的直观反映,主观反映着不同交通方式的服务质量,进一步影响着旅客的出行选择行为和选择意向,对不同交通方式的配合与衔接有着重要意义,对综合交通系统的有效构建有着重要的参考价值。进一步地,结合城际出行旅客的交通感知,在城际出行时间、费用因素的影响下比较其在不同交通方式之间的差异,可以精细化把握不同交通方式的优缺点,提高不同交通方式和综合交通系统的服务水平。

由于交通综合感知反映的是交通出行者或参与者的生理及心理,具有较强的主观性。因此,对交通综合感知尚无统一的研究方法和明确的框架体系。但是,国内外学者使用不同方法对其也进行了部分研究。Kita等[1]运行大数据技术,以区域路网的道路运行情况来模拟交通场景,并以效用值来评价了服务水平感知。Das等[2]利用连续间隔尺度的方法来衡量用户的感知,该方法为以动态间隔划分方式取代了传统固定的等级划分方式。郑玲钰等[3]从用户感知的角度构造了城市道路服务水平评价的白化聚类函数,其结果能很好地与出行者的主观评分匹配。乔相荣等[4]以城市轨道交通接驳过程中给出行者带来的约束感知,利用Rasch模型对城市轨道交通的接驳服务进行了评价。

从本质上来说,影响城际交通综合感知的一个重要影响因素在于交通方式的选择,而在众多影响出行方式选择的因素中,时间和经济因素尤其受到了重视,JosephS.Desalvo[5]静态分析比较了成本最小化模型和边际时间价值模型,认为出行费用的最小化是出行者考虑交通方式选择的重要条件。Ennio Cascetta[6]以高速铁路的产生和发展为基础,将车辆晚点的时间因素纳入出行选择考虑条件,建立了Logit模型,分析了旅客城际出行选择行为。华诗雨[7]研究了公路、铁路、飞机3种城际交通方式,发现人们对选择高速铁路最为关心的因素是票价,并且出行方式的票价对于出行费用有较高的敏感度。魏薇[8]以Logit模型为基础,以杭州至绍兴的城际轨道交通为实例,发现时间和费用在旅客出行中是最为敏感的因素。

基金项目:城建专项资金支持项目(SZJJ2019-22)。

结构方程(Structural Equation Modeling,简称SEM)是一种可以用于交通选择行为分析的非集计模型,即从微观个体出发探讨宏观规律。鉴于交通行为问题的复杂性,国内外学者已经开始将结构方程模型应用于交通行为中,进一步将出行者的主观变量纳入到了行为选择研究中。Christian A. K. 等[9]以环境友好型出行选择行为为基础,研究了行为意向和规范、外部环境和习惯等因素,发现出行习惯和意向对出行行为的影响力最大。Zeid 等[10]将出行者的主观幸福感作为方式选择行为的影响因素。进一步地,李巧茹[11]等构建 SEM-Logit 模型,选取了包含易用性、有用性、愉快性、情绪 4 个维度来表征出行的主观幸福感,发现其对旅客出行选择行为存在显著的影响。胡骥[12]等将方便性、安全性、便捷性等变量引入出行行为选择模型中,提高了模型分析的准确性和解释力。

但是,对交通感知的研究多局限在道路服务水平或某一交通方式,未将旅客的时间、经济等客观因素与获得的交通感知主观变量结合考虑,鲜有对不同交通方式群体的差异分析。因此,本文构建城际旅客交通综合感知的多群组结构方程模型,定量研究各因素对交通综合感知的影响,进一步探讨不同群组差异。

1 城际出行的构成

城际出行一般涉及 3 个阶段:①出发城市的市内出行;②出发城市到终点城市间的出行;③终点城市的市内出行。其全过程如图 1 所示。

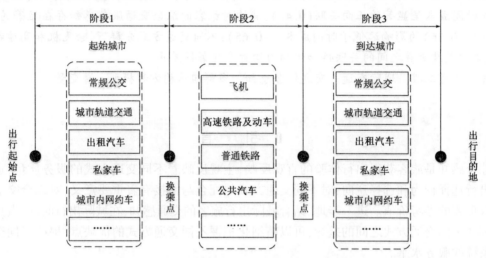

图 1 城际旅客出行全过程解析

作为城际出行核心的第 2 阶段,其交通方式的异同不仅影响自身的时间和经济消耗,而且影响着第 1、3 阶段到达换乘点的方式及离开换乘点的方式,以及 1、3 阶段的时间成本和经济消耗。本文选取第 2 阶段比较典型且覆盖旅客人数较多的 4 种交通方式作为研究对象,即飞机、高速铁路及动车、普通铁路和公共汽车,其时间成本、经济消耗和到达(离开)换乘点的方式不尽相同。

2 城际交通综合感知模型

2.1 基础理论

结构方程模型(Structural Equation Modeling,简称 SEM)是一种被广泛应用于心理学、经济学、社会学等学科,结合了路径分析和因子分析的多元统计方法。

2.1.1 模型中的变量

潜变量:难以直接观测或描述的变量。潜变量又可分为内生潜变量和外生潜变量,前者可以作为因变量受其他潜变量的影响;后者作为自变量影响着其他潜变量。

测量变量:可以直接观测的变量,其用来反映对应的潜变量。因此,信号交号可进一步分为内生测量变量和外生测量变量。

2.1.2 模型结构

测量模型:用于说明观测变量对潜变量的反映情况;
结构模型:用于说明潜变量间的因果关系[13]。
构建整体模型时应当先构建测量模型,再进一步构建结构模型。

2.2 潜变量的选取

结合本文将要开展的研究,将经济消耗(COMO)、时间成本(TICO)和旅客一次出行的交通综合服务感知(TCP)设为3个潜变量,各变量的含义与其测量变量的选取见表1。其问卷均采用李克特5级量表形式,按"非常满意"赋值为5分,"满意"为4分,"一般"为3分,"不满意"为2分,"非常不满意"为1分。

潜变量与测量变量   表1

潜 变 量	潜变量定义	测量变量	变量编号
经济消耗	旅客一次城际出行的总体经济消耗	阶段1 从出行起始点到达换乘点费用	COMO1
		阶段2 不同交通方式的费用	COMO2
		阶段3 离开换乘点到达出行目的地的费用	COMO3
时间成本	旅客一次城际出行的总体时间消耗	阶段1 从出行起始点到达换乘点的时间	TICO1
		阶段2 不同交通方式的乘坐时间	TICO2
		阶段3 离开换乘点到达出行目的地的时间	TICO3
旅客一次出行的综合服务感知	旅客根据自身情况对本次出行做出的直观评价	总体满意度	TCP1
		总体舒适度	TCP2
		总体准时度	TCP3
		总体轻松度	TCP4

2.3 模型假设

选取经济消耗、时间成本和交通综合感知作为模型的潜变量,提出以下3个模型假设,并构建城际交通综合感知模型框架,如图2所示。

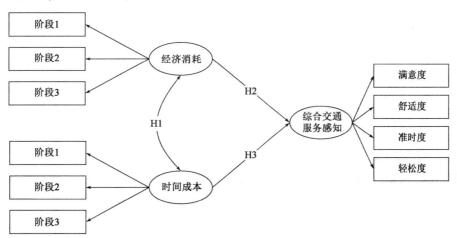

图2 模型框架

H1:城际出行的经济消耗与时间成本有正相关关系;
H2:城际出行的经济消耗对交通综合感知有负向影响;
H3:城际出行的时间成本对交通综合感知有负向影响。

2.4 数学模型

2.4.1 测量模型

测量模型包含2个方程式,式(1)用于说明经济消耗和时间成本2个外生潜变量与外生测量变量之

间的关系,即:

$$X = \Lambda_x \xi + \delta \tag{1}$$

式中:X——6个外生测量变量构成的向量;

Λ_x——X对ξ的因子载荷矩阵;

ξ——2个外生潜变量构成的向量;

δ——X的测量误差构成的向量。

式(2)表示交通综合感知——内生潜变量与其内生观测变量的关系,即

$$Y = \Lambda_y \eta + \varepsilon \tag{2}$$

式中:Y——4个内生测量变量构成的向量;

Λ_y——Y对η的因子载荷矩阵;

η——内生潜变量构成的向量;

ε——Y的测量误差构成的向量。

2.4.2 结构模型

结构模型用于说明内生潜变量——交通综合感知与经济消耗、时间成本2个外生潜变量之间的因果关系,计算公式为:

$$\eta = B\eta + \Gamma\xi + \zeta \tag{3}$$

式中:B——内生潜变量构成的结构系数矩阵;

Γ——2个外生潜变量对内生潜变量的结构系数矩阵;

ξ——2个外生潜变量构成的向量;

ζ——误差向量。

2.5 模型求解与检验

运用AMOS软件进行求解,选取适当的拟合参数——卡方值与自由度比(χ^2/df)、近似误差均方根(RMSEA)、拟合优度指数(GFI)、调整拟合优度指数(AGFI)、规范拟合指数(NFI)、比较拟合指数(CFI)、增值拟合指数(IFI)等来检验模型的拟合度。模型拟合度越好代表模型可用性越高,参数估计越准确。表2列出了以上指标的检验标准。

模型拟合指数标准　　　　表2

检验指标	χ^2/df	RMSEA	GFI	AGFI	NFI	CFI	IFI
标准值	1~3	<0.08	>0.90	>0.90	>0.90	>0.90	>0.90

2.6 模型修正

根据Tanaka,Maruyama[14]的研究,当模型样本数大于200时,会造成卡方值的膨胀,直接导致χ^2/df的增大,致使配适度下降。AMOS软件根据Kenneth A. Bollen和Robert A. Stine[15]提供的卡方值测试的方法,来矫正模型标准误差以及影响模型配适度的统计量。

2.7 基于不同交通方式的多群组分析

多群组结构方程模型是用来研究已得到验证的模型在不同特征群体中是否同样适用。因此,本文对不同交通方式的使用群体进行多群组分析,以验证此前得到的城际交通综合感知模型在飞机、高速铁路及动车、普通铁路和公共汽车4种交通方式使用群体之间是否有显著差异。

基本步骤为:先设定测量模型系数相等的限制性模型,再设定2条影响路径系数相等的限制性模型,将其与测量模型系数限定相等模型进行比较;在此基础上,再设定关联路径系数相等,将其与路径系数限定相等模型进行比较。其过程如图3所示。如果卡方差值达到显著,说明4类群体的路径影响有显著差异。再对每一条路径进行T检验,找出有差异性的具体路径。

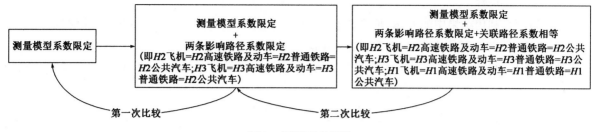

图 3　多群组比较过程

注：图中 $H1$ 表示时间成本和时间成本的关联系数；$H2$、$H3$ 分别表示经济消耗和时间成本对交通综合感知的影响系数

3　实证分析

以西安市主城区居民为研究对象，于 2019 年 5 月在西安市咸阳国际机场、西安北站、西安站及西安汽车站等主要城际交通客运集散点，对旅客通过现场和网络等形式进行调查，回收问卷 1122 份，剔除无效样本 45 份。调查统计结果见表 3。

调查统计结果　　　　　表 3

属性	类别	样本数	比例(%)	属性	类别	样本数	比例(%)
性别	男	532	49.4	个人月收入（元）	0~3000	566	52.6
	女	545	50.6		3000~4000	174	16.2
年龄	0~19 岁	65	6.0		4000~5000	111	10.3
	20~29 岁	589	54.7		5000~6000	103	9.6
	30~39 岁	149	13.8		6000~7000	52	4.8
	40~49 岁	157	14.6		7000 以上	71	6.6
	50~59 岁	105	9.7	家庭居住区位	市中心	362	33.6
	60 及 60 岁以上	12	1.1		近郊区	438	40.7
职业	企业单位人员	217	20.1		远郊区	277	25.7
	机关事业单位人员	164	15.2	城际交通方式	飞机	260	24.1
	学生	468	43.5		高速铁路及动车	356	33.1
	农民	60	5.6		普通铁路	279	25.9
	个体户	56	5.2		公共汽车	182	16.9
	其他	112	10.4				

3.1　模型检验与修正

对于有效样本利用 AMOS 软件进行模型求解，初步得到模型适配度结果见表 4。

模型适配度　　　　　表 4

检验指标	χ^2/df	RMSEA	GFI	AGFI	NFI	CFI	IFI
标准值	1~3	<0.08	>0.90	>0.90	>0.90	>0.90	>0.90
初步试验实验值	16.169	0.119	0.914	0.852	0.864	0.871	0.872
修正后实验值	1.070	0.010	0.990	0.970	0.990	1.000	1.000

观察表 4 可知，除 GFI 指数达到标准值外，其余指标均未达标，初步的模型适配度并不理想，用 Bollen-Stine 方法对模型加以修正才获得了良好的适配结果。

3.2 模型求解

模型求解后,利用结果中的C.R.值和P值来对模型路径系数进行显著性分析并对模型进行假设检验,即:当C.R.值的绝对值小于1.96时,即表示假设检验的置信度$P>0.05$,应拒绝原假设;当C.R.的绝对值大于1.96时,即表示假设检验的置信度$P<0.05$,应接受原假设[16]。模型求解和假设检验结果见表5。

路径系数及假设检验结果   表5

参数路径	非标准化估计				标准化估计	验证结果
	Estimate	S.E.	C.R.	P	Estimate	
COMO↔TICO	0.68	0.08	8.88	***	0.47	H1 成立
COMO→TCSA	-0.07	0.02	-3.77	***	-0.16	H2 成立
TICO→TCSA	-0.50	0.05	-10.96	***	-0.65	H3 成立

注:Estimate 表示路径系数的估计值;S.E. 表示路径系数的标准误差项;*** 表示$P<0.001$。

3.3 模型结果初步解释

整理模型计算结果如图4所示。图4中标注出了标准化路径系数的估计值,其值基本表明测量变量能很好地反映其潜变量的信息且潜变量间存在作用关系。

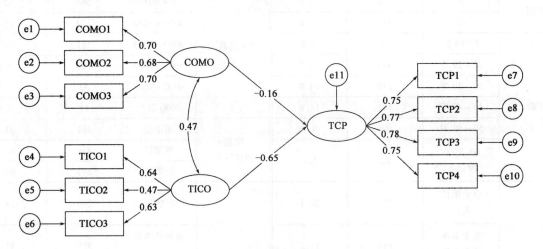

图4 实证分析结果

COMO1(从出行起始点到达换乘点费用)和COMO3(离开换乘点到达出行目的地的费用)对于经济消耗的反映相当,其负荷系数均为0.70,而COMO2(城际出行费用)对于经济消耗的反映略低,其负荷系数为0.68。TICO1(从出行起始点到达换乘点的时间)、TICO3(离开换乘点到达出行目的地的时间)对于时间成本的反映效果基本相当,其负荷系数分别为0.64和0.63,而TICO2(城际出行时间)对于时间成本的反映较低,仅为0.47。对于旅客的交通综合服务感知来说,TCP1(满意度)、TCP4(轻松度)对其反映效果相当,负荷系数均为0.75,且略低于TCP2(舒适度)的0.77、TCP3(准时度)的0.78。

COMO 和 TICO 有显著的正相关关系,其相关系数为0.47,而COMO 和 TICO 对 TCP 有显著的负向影响,其中COMO对于TCP的负向影响系数为-0.16,远低于TICO对TCP的影响系数(-0.65)。

3.4 多群组结构方程模型研究

3.4.1 样本分群求解

用AMOS软件对样本按照不同的交通方式即飞机、高速铁路及动车、普通铁路、公共汽车进行分群,构建多群组结构方程模型,并初步求解,多群级模型路径系数见表6。

多群组模型路径系数 表6

不同群组	参数路径			非标准化估计				标准化估计
				Estimate	S.E.	C.R.	P	Estimate
飞机	COMO	↔	TICO	0.29	0.12	2.52	*	0.27
	COMO	→	TCSA	-0.07	0.05	-1.37	0.17	-0.13
	TICO	→	TCSA	-0.29	0.08	-3.72	***	-0.34
高速铁路及动车	COMO	↔	TICO	0.52	0.10	5.17	***	0.71
	COMO	→	TCSA	-0.17	0.06	-2.75	**	-0.33
	TICO	→	TCSA	-0.46	0.12	-3.82	***	-0.49
普通铁路	COMO	↔	TICO	0.77	0.14	5.34	***	0.60
	COMO	→	TCSA	0.16	0.05	3.11	**	0.37
	TICO	→	TCSA	-0.52	0.08	-6.62	***	-0.89
公共汽车	COMO	↔	TICO	1.28	0.23	5.54	***	0.65
	COMO	→	TCSA	-0.11	0.05	-2.29	*	-0.29
	TICO	→	TCSA	-0.20	0.09	-2.22	*	-0.30

注：* 表示 $P<0.05$；** 表示 $P<0.01$；*** 表示 $P<0.001$。

3.4.2 多群组模型的差异化分析

多群组模型初步求解后,为比较 4 种交通方式综合感知的差异性,对不同群组的部分路径系数进行相等限定,并进行 2 次比较,其结果见表 7。当 $P<0.05$ 时,认为多群组的限制性模型存在显著性差异[17]。

卡方差检验结果 表7

比较次序	参数路径			ΔDF	Δχ^2	P
1	COMO	→	TCSA	6	65.886	***
	TICO	→	TCSA			
2	COMO	↔	TICO	9	26.681	***

注：*** 表示 $P<0.001$。

由表 7 可知,4 种城际交通方式的路径影响存在显著性差异。对每一条路径进行 T 检验,结果见表 8。当 T 检验数值的绝对值大于 1.96 时,认为两条路径存在显著性差异。

结构路径系数差异矩阵 表8

城际交通方式	参数路径	飞机	高速铁路及动车	普通铁路	公共汽车
飞机	COMO→TCSA	—	—	—	—
	TICO→TCSA	—	—	—	—
	COMO→TICO	—	—	—	—
高速铁路及动车	COMO→TCSA	-1.24	—	—	—
	TICO→TCSA	-1.22	—	—	—
	COMO→TICO	1.47	—	—	—
普通铁路	COMO→TCSA	3.20	4.11	—	—
	TICO→TCSA	-2.14	-0.42	—	—
	COMO→TICO	-5.81	1.43	—	—
公共汽车	COMO→TCSA	-0.61	0.70	-3.83	—
	TICO→TCSA	0.70	1.71	2.65	—
	COMO→TICO	3.82	3.03	1.89	—

3.4.3 差异结果解释

整理求解结果如图5所示。

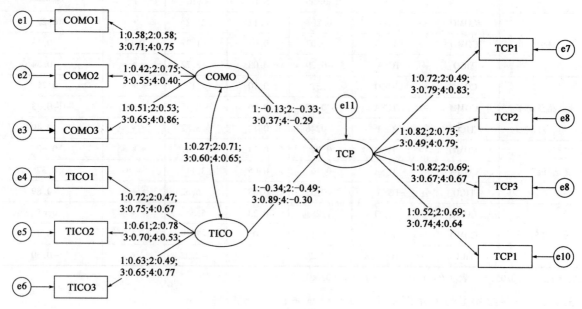

图5 多群组模型实证分析结果

注：各路径上1代表飞机群组；2代表高速铁路及动车群组；3代表普通铁路群组；4代表公共汽车群组

下面结合表8的差异系数矩阵进行解释。

(1)飞机群组。

与其他群组相比，飞机群组的COMO对TCP的影响不显著，与高速铁路及动车群组相比无显著性差异。与普通铁路群组相比，结构路径系数均存在显著性差异：普通铁路群组的COMO对TCP呈显著的正向影响；TICO的负向影响远高于飞机群组；COMO与TICO的相关性也高于飞机群组。与公共汽车群组相比：飞机群组的时间消耗对于TCP的影响较高。

(2)高速铁路及动车群组。

高速铁路及动车群组与各个群组之间的差异不大。与普通铁路群组相比，在COMO对TCP的影响方面，高速铁路及动车群组呈显著的负向影响，而普通铁路群组呈显著的正向影响。与公共汽车群组相比，在COMO与TICO的正向关联方面，高速铁路及动车群组略高于公共汽车群组。

(3)普通铁路群组。

普通铁路群组是4个群组中唯一COMO对TCP有显著正向影响的群组。与公共汽车群组相比，除COMO对TCP的影响外，还体现在TICO的影响方面，公共汽车群组的负向影响远低于普通铁路群组。

(4)公共汽车群组。

公共汽车群组的TICO和COMO对TCP的负向影响基本相当，而其他3个群组的(正)负向影响都有较大差异，且TICO的影响较高。

4 结 语

本文构建了城际交通综合感知多群组结构方程模型，以西安市区主要城际交通客运集散点出行调查数据进行了实证分析，得到以下结论：

(1)经过修正后，所构建的以经济消耗、时间成本和交通综合感知为潜变量的多群组结构方程模型各项检验指标良好、拟合优度较高，可以用来分析影响城际旅客出行交通综合感知的时间成本和经济消耗因素。

(2)总体而言，一次城际出行活动中，经济消耗和时间成本呈显著的正相关关系，经济消耗和时间成本对交通综合感知均有显著的负向影响。但是,经济消耗对于交通综合感知的负向影响远低于时间成本。进一步地,到达换乘点和离开换乘点的费用和时间对于整体经济消耗和时间成本的反映程度均高于城际出行。

(3)分群组而言,除飞机和高速铁路及动车群组模型之间无显著性差异外,其余3个群组模型的结构路径系数均存在显著性的差异。各群组的经济消耗对于综合交通服务感知的影响差异较大,时间成本则全部呈显著的负向影响,时间成本和经济消耗的关联性也略有差异。

本文对不同城际交通方式的经济消耗和时间成本对与旅客出行的综合交通感知进行了分析,把主要客观因素和旅客的部分主观因素结合在一起,对提高不同城际交通运输体系的服务水平有一定的意义,对于综合交通运输体系的优化、改善有一定参考价值。后续,可以进一步利用其他方法、模型进行更加细致的调查,分析其产生差异的深层原因,对于不同的城际交通方式提出更加具体的改善措施。

参考文献

[1] KITH H,KOUC'HI A. A utility-based evaluation method on the perceived quality of traffic service[J]. Procedia-Social and Behavioral Sciences,2011,16(1):820-831.

[2] DAS S,PANDIT D. Determination of level-of-service scale values for quantitative bus transit service attributes based on user perception[J]. Transportmetrica A:Transport Science,2015,11(1):1-21.

[3] 郑玲钎,赵益,王忠宇,等.基于用户感知的城市道路交通服务水平评价方法[J].同济大学学报自然科学版,2016,44(5),753-757.

[4] 乔相荣,姜珊,巩舜妹,等.考虑出行者感知的城市轨道交通接驳服务评价[J].城市轨道交通研究,2020,23(08):40-43.

[5] Joseph S. Desalvo,lvlobinul Huq. Income,Residential Location,and Mode Choice[J]. Journal of Urban Economics,1996,84-99.

[6] Cascetta E,Papola A,Pagliara F,et al. Analysis of mobility impacts of the high speed Rome – Naples rail link using withinday dynamic mode service choice models[J]. Journal of Transport Geography,2011,19(4):635-643.

[7] 华诗雨.不同认知条件下旅客出行方式选择行为研究[D].北京:北京交通大学,2016.

[8] 魏薇.基于城际旅客出行行为的客流敏感性分析[D].西安:长安大学,2015.

[9] Christian A. Kloclrner,Anke Blobaum. A comprehensive action detsrminarion model:Toward a broader understanding of ecological behavior using the example of travel mode choice[J]. Journal of Environmental Psvchology,2010,30(4):574-586.

[10] Abou Zeid M. Measuring and modeling activity and travel well-being[D]. Massachusetts Ave:Massachusetts Institute of Technology,2009.

[11] 李巧茹,陈克,陈亮,等.主观幸福感视角下的交通出行决策[J].科学技术与工程,2020,20(19):7916-7921.

[12] 胡骥,姚鸣,刘艳,等.基于SEM-MNL模型的运输通道出行方式选择行为研究[J].铁道工程学报,2017,34(04):80-85.

[13] 吴明隆.结构方程模型——AMOS的操作与应用[M].重庆:重庆大学出版社,2010.

[14] Tanaka,Maruyama,et al. Some Clarifications and Recommendations on Fit Indices[J]. Newsom 2 USP 655 SEM Winter 2012,1-4.

[15] Kenneth A. Bollen,Robert A. Stine. Bootstrapping Goodness-of-Fit Measures in Structural Equation Models[J]. Sociological Methods Research,1992(21):205-229.

[16] Ahern A A. Tapley N. The use of stated preference techniques to modal choices on interurban trips in Ireland[J]. Transportation Research Part A:Policy &Practice,2018,42(1):15-27.

[17] Chia-huei Wu,Grace Yao. Analysis of factorial invariance across gender in the Taiwan version of the Satisfaction with Life Scale[J]. Personality and Individual Differences,2006(40):1259-1268.

基于家庭结构变化的家庭成员出行方式选择研究

李芷倩 张 敏

(长安大学运输工程学院)

摘 要 为剖析家庭结构变化下各家庭属性对家庭成员出行行为选择的影响,基于非集计理论,构建家庭成员出行方式选择模型。根据255份有未婚子女的家庭出行行为调查问卷,标定MNL模型参数,获取影响家庭成员出行选择的主要家庭属性因素,并进行分析。结果表明,在家庭结构变化前后,家庭年收入对家庭成员出行方式选择多样性均有非常显著的影响;家庭结构的变化会加大家庭人数对出行方式多样性的影响程度,减小家庭拥有的交通工具种类和数量对出行方式多样性的影响程度;家庭结构变化后,子女与父母的居住模式对家庭间活动出行方式选择的影响非常显著。

关键词 出行方式选择 MNL模型 非集计理论 家庭结构变化

0 引 言

随着社会经济发展和城市化水平的提高,我国的家庭规模变得越来越小,传统的大家庭逐渐分成由一对夫妇和他们的子女组成的小家庭。家庭结构变化通常伴随着子女结婚而发生。家庭结构变化引发的不仅仅是家庭中部分个体出行行为的改变,而是整个家庭出行行为的改变,即所有家庭成员的出行行为特性发生变化。因此家庭结构的变化,最直观的表现是子女与父母之间的小家庭居住模式明显变化,并间接渗入家庭全体成员日常出行交通方式选择特性,包括家庭结构变化前后的交通方式选择多样性、小家庭之间联系时交通方式选择等多个维度,进而重塑家庭结构变化下家庭日常活动的出行行为模式。

近年来,基于家庭属性的出行行为特性逐渐受到国内外学者的关注,相关研究已有很多。Chatman等的研究认为,幼年家庭成员对成年家庭成员的出行行为具有显著性影响。Tricia Kenny等发现,随着家庭规模的扩大,出行总量呈现递增态势,但受家庭内部决策的相互作用,人均出行次数有所降低。何保红等以迁居家庭为研究对象,分别从个体和家庭2个层面分析迁居前后出行行为的调整变化。骆晨等针对大学生群体,研究了家庭结构、家庭关系对大学生出行行为的影响。

但在现有研究中,忽略了家庭结构变化对家庭成员出行行为产生的影响。实际出行中的个人偏好很大程度受家庭属性影响,而家庭结构是家庭属性的重要体现,影响着家庭各类活动中的出行行为选择。本文以家庭中未婚子女为研究对象,根据SP调查得到的问卷统计数据,引入MNL模型,重点剖析家庭结构变化下的家庭成员出行方式选择特性及相关影响因素。

1 非集计模型构建

1.1 家庭结构概述

家庭结构是指家庭中成员的构成及其相互作用、相互影响的状态,以及由这种状态形成的相对稳定的联系模式。家庭结构包括2个基本方面:家庭人口要素,即家庭由多少人组成、家庭规模大小;家庭模式要素,即家庭成员之间怎样相互联系,以及因联系方式不同而形成的不同的家庭模式。

家庭结构主要表现为家庭代际层次的模式,可分为:①核心家庭,指家庭由两代人构成,由父母与未婚子女组成的家庭;②主干家庭,指由每代不超过一对夫妻的两代或两代以上无断代构成的家庭,由(外)祖父母、父母与未婚子女构成的家庭;③联合家庭,指任何一代中包含两对以上夫妻构成的家庭,由

(外)祖父母、父母、未婚子女以及任何一代的兄弟姐妹构成的家庭;④其他家庭,指除以上3种类型外的家庭,如单亲家庭、隔代家庭等。

1.2 模型选择

非集计模型通过引入出行者的特征变量,精准刻画出行选择影响因素。故构建家庭结构变化前后的家庭成员出行方式选择非集计模型,分析家庭成员在家庭结构变化下的出行方式选择多样性的影响因素,以及家庭成员之间的居住模式对出行方式选择的影响因素。家庭属性为 i 的家庭成员选择出行方式 j 的效用 U_{ij} 为:

$$U_{ij} = V_{ij} + \varepsilon_{ij} \tag{1}$$

式中:V_{ij}——效用函数的固定项;

ε_{ij}——效用函数的概率项。

假设各交通出行方式中 V_{ij} 与影响因素 X_{ijk} 之间呈线性关系,即:

$$V_{ij} = \sum_{k=1}^{K} \theta_k X_{ijk} \tag{2}$$

式中:k——特征变量的个数;

θ_k——第 k 个变量对应的参数;

X_{ijk}——家庭属性 i 的家庭成员选择出行方式 j 的第 k 个变量。

设定一个方案为参照方案,令其系数 $\theta_1 = 0$,那么家庭成员 i 选择出行方式 j 的概率为:

$$P_{ij} = \frac{\exp(V_{ij})}{\sum_{i=1}^{J} \exp(V_{ij})} \tag{3}$$

式中:J——选择出行方式的总数量。

2 数据采集与处理

2.1 数据采集与分析

本文中用于研究的相关数据来源于出行方式选择调查问卷,包括3个主要部分,一是个人属性信息,主要包括性别、年龄、职业;二是家庭属性信息,主要包括家庭人数、家庭结构、家庭年收入、家庭拥有的各类交通工具数量;三是出行属性信息,主要是家庭成员经常使用的出行方式,以及家庭结构变化后两个小家庭间出行活动经常使用的出行方式,包括航空、铁路、公路、小汽车、公共交通、摩托车与电动车、自行车、步行8类。

剔除无家庭结构变化意愿的40份样本,最终应用215份有家庭结构变化意愿的家庭出行行为信息。其中,家庭属性统计结果如下:74%家庭中的未婚子女为学生,年龄段主要集中在18~25岁,家庭人数在3~5人的家庭占86%,家庭年收入在5万~20万元的家庭占58%。

考虑到家庭结构变化后,小家庭间活动的出行方式选择最能反映家庭成员间的交互关系,本文将选取这两类数据,对成员分别在家庭外活动和家庭间活动的互动关系进行分析解读。

为清晰地对比家庭结构变化前后成员居住模式的变化,以家庭结构变化前后未婚子女所在的家庭为单位分别进行统计,依据两个小家庭成员的居住位置来确定成员居住关系,以行政区划为分类标准,最终将家庭成员居住模式划分为5类,见表1。

家庭结构变化后成员居住调整模式 表1

家庭成员居住模式	特征描述	所占比例(%)
父母与子女在同个县(或区)	子女在结婚后形成的新小家庭与父母所在的原家庭位于同一个县或同一个区,两者之间出行距离短	37
父母与子女在同个市的不同县(或区)	子女在结婚后形成的新小家庭与父母所在的原家庭位于同一个市的不同县或不同区,两者之间出行距离较短	19

续上表

家庭成员居住模式	特征描述	所占比例(%)
父母与子女在同省的不同市	子女在结婚后形成的新小家庭与父母所在的原家庭位于同一个省的不同市,两者之间出行距离较长	25
父母与子女在国内不同省	子女在结婚后形成的新小家庭与父母所在的原家庭位于国内不同省份,两者之间出行距离长	8
其他	子女在结婚后形成的新小家庭与父母所在的原家庭的居住模式不同于以上4种,如两者有一方在国外	11

2.2 模型参数标定

根据MNL模型的参数估计方法,本文采用R studio软件对模型进行参数标定。将航空作为参考类别,选择家庭居住模式为自变量,成员在两个小家庭间活动的出行方式为因变量,参数标定结果见表2。其中,B为变量系数,S.E.为标准差,Sig.为统计量的显著性水平。显著性水平Sig. < 0.05,说明该变量对出行方式的选择有影响,应纳入家庭结构变化后成员在家庭间活动中的出行方式选择模型中,反之则予以剔除。

家庭居住调整模式系数标定结果　　表2

出行方式	指标	B	S.E.	Sig.
铁路	截距	6.405	1.783	0.000
	家庭居住模式	-1.292	0.402	0.001
公路	截距	6.870	1.833	0.000
	家庭居住模式	-1.957	0.462	0.000
小汽车	截距	7.374	1.773	0.000
	家庭居住模式	-1.420	0.398	0.000
公共交通	截距	5.816	1.856	0.002
	家庭居住模式	-1.608	0.457	0.000
摩托车与电动车	截距	7.597	1.860	0.000
	家庭居住模式	-2.508	0.540	0.000
步行	截距	5.214	1.930	0.001
	家庭居住模式	-1.616	0.506	0.001

由表2可知,家庭居住模式对上述所有交通方式的影响显著性非常大:当父母与子女在同个县城(或区)时,家庭成员更倾向于使用摩托车、电动车等方式进行两个小家庭之间的来往出行,随着距离增加,则更倾向于选择公路等出行方式。

3 结果分析

3.1 模型检验

模型检验结果见表3。模型的整体卡方检验概率P值(即Prob > chi2)都小于0.05,表明上述模型拟合的结果均较好。

模型检验结果　　表3

模型	Log-Likelihood	LR chi2	显著性
家庭居住模式与出行方式选择的关系模型	-318.92	55.803	0.000

3.2 家庭结构变化对家庭成员出行方式选择的影响

家庭结构主要由家庭年收入、家庭代际数、家庭人数组成,而家庭结构变化也会影响家庭拥有的交通工具种类、数量发生变化，从而影响家庭成员出行方式选择的多样性。

此外，家庭结构变化后家庭成员居住模式对出行方式选择的影响非常显著。由表2可知，随着两者出行距离的增长，即两者分别所在的行政区划等级每增加1个单位，选择铁路、公路、小汽车、公共交通摩托车与电动车、步行的概率分别增加0.275、0.141、0.242、0.2、0.081、0.199个单位。

4 结 语

本文从家庭结构变化的角度出发，基于多元 Logit 模型，分析家庭结构变化对家庭出行方式多样性的影响，以及家庭成员居住模式对出行方式选择的影响，得到以下结论：家庭结构的变化会加大家庭人数对出行方式多样性的影响程度，减小家庭拥有的交通工具种类和数量对出行方式多样性的影响程度；家庭结构变化后，子女与父母的居住模式对家庭间活动出行方式选择的影响非常显著，直接影响到所选择的交通出行方式，距离越远，家庭成员选择采用航空出行的概率更高。研究成果有助于更好了解家庭结构变化前后各成员出行选择特性，从而更有利于采取相应的城市交通管理对策和措施。

参考文献

[1] Daniel G. Chatman. The Influence of Workplace Land Use and Commute Mode Choice on Mileage Traveled for Personal Commercial Purposes[C]. TRB2003 Annua Meeting CD-ROM. 2002.

[2] Kenny Tricia, N. F. Gray, A preliminary survey of household and personal carbon dioxide emissions in Ireland[J]. Environment International. 2009,262-263.

[3] 何保红,何彦,刘阳,等.迁居对家庭日常活动——出行行为交互机理的影响[J].交通运输系统工程与信息,2017,17(2):240-246.

[4] 骆晨,李想,钟林峰,等.基于家庭属性差异的大学生出行方式选择行为研究[J].交通运输系统工程与信息,2020,20(3):227-232.

[5] 林强.基于家庭结构的学生家长出行方式选择研究[D].西安:长安大学,2017.

[6] AREBA E M, EISENBERG M E, MCMORRIS B J. Relationships between family structure, adolescent health status and substance use: Does ethnicity matter? [J]. Journal of Community Psychology,2018,46(1):44-57.

[7] 刘建荣,郝小妮.考虑环保意识的低碳出行行为研究[J].交通运输系统工程与信息,2019,19(1):26-32.

基于MNL模型的中小城市学生通学方式影响因素研究

张祎薇　潘卫龙

（长安大学）

摘　要　学生通学出行是居民出行的重要组成部分，因其引起的城市交通拥堵现象愈发严重。本文旨在通过对学生通学行为的影响因素进行研究，了解学生的通学特性。本文根据海宁市出行调查数据，通过建立MNL模型，总结出8项显著影响学生通学方式的因素。选取2个显著影响变量进行敏感性分析，由此得出结论：若降低20%的学生接送率或改变学生家庭的小汽车拥有量至平均0.6辆，可以分别降低10%和12%的小汽车选择概率，促使其转向选择绿色交通方式出行，从而有效优化学生的通学结构。

关键词　学生出行　通学方式选择　MNL模型　中小城市

0 引言

学生通学作为居民日常出行中的重要组成部分,其行为往往比自主出行的群体更加复杂,它是家庭偏好与时空约束共同影响下的结果。现有研究案例中多为大型城市(如深圳、武汉),较少关注中小城市的学生通学情况,因此本研究是十分必要的。

在针对学生通学行为的相关研究中,国外学者 C. D van Goeverden 和 E. de Boer 在研究学生出行行为时除学生的家庭和个人属性之外,还考虑了不同类型的学校与学生出行方式选择的关系。国内学者刘涟涟得出学校与居住区的空间布局、步行环境质量等是影响学生难以选择步行、自行车或公交进行通学的主要原因。王侠[5]等通过对西安市某些家庭的活动日志进行数据整理,提出了诸如实施弹性放学时间等改进措施。在居民出行行为模型的选择上,所使用的模型经历了由集计模型向非集计模型转变的过程,包括 BL 模型、NL 模型、MNL 模型等。

本文在借鉴各学者学术研究成果的基础上,进一步总结分析各影响因素与学生出行行为的关系,建立 MNL 模型分析中小城市学生通学出行方式选择行为,探讨学生出行所受的影响因素,为其他有相似特征的中小城市学生家庭提供出行参考。

1 学生通学出行调查

本文采用经过些许改动的家庭访问法进行 RP 调查,对海宁市部分有中小学生的家庭分发问卷进行学生通学出行相关信息调查。调查时间选在 2013 年 1 月 11 日(周五),具有一般性。调查共向海宁城区的海宁一中、南苑中学、紫微小学、实验小学等学校共发放 5000 份调查问卷,选用有效数据共 2715 份。调查结果基本翔实可信,调查对象精准,可作为本文的主要数据来源。由于调查时间较早,为使研究更符合现状,补充了 2018 年的小范围抽样调查数据,以提高本文的研究结果准确性和适用性。

2 学生通学方式模型建立

2.1 建立学生通学方式模型

BL 模型、MNL 模型和 NL 模型都是基于非集计模型中的 Logit 模型发展而来的,其中 MNL 模型适用于选择方案的集合中有 3 个及以上的模型,可为每位出行者提供多种选择方案。

MNL 模型的一般式为:

$$P_{in} = \frac{e^{V_{in}}}{\sum_{j \in A_n} e^{V_{jn}}} = \frac{1}{\sum_{j \in A_n} e^{V_{jn} - V_{in}}}, (i \in A_n) \tag{1}$$

令学生个人属性表示为 S,学生出行属性表示为 C,学生家庭属性表示为 H。假设第 i 个出行者选择第 j 种交通出行方式,则此时,该情况下的效用函数为 U_j^i,效用函数的固定项为 V_j^i,效用函数的随机项为 ε_j^i。学生通学出行方式选择效用函数公式为:

$$U_j^i = V_j^i(S + C + H) + \varepsilon_j^i \tag{2}$$

由此可得出,计算出行者 i 选择出行方案 j 的概率 P_{ij} 的公式为:

$$P_{ij} = \frac{\exp(b, V_{i,q})}{\sum_{i=1}^{j} \exp(b, V_{j,q})} \tag{3}$$

2.2 学生通学方式模型的影响因素选定

选取显著影响因素并对其进行量化赋值后,各因素和变量的赋值结果见表1。

模型内各变量赋值说明表　　　　　　　　　　　　　　　　　　　　　　　　表1

属性	影响因素		变量赋值
学生出行属性	出发时间 A	6:40 之前	1
		6:40—7:20	2
		7:20 之后	3
	出行时长 B	0~10min	1
		10~20min	2
		20min 以上	3
学生个人属性	性别 D	男性	1
		女性	2
	年龄 E	7~12 岁	1
		12~15 岁	2
		15~18 岁	3
	公交 IC 卡 F	有	1
		无	0
	有人接送 G	有	1
		无	0
	家庭类型 I	一般家庭	1
		单亲家庭	2
		其他家庭	3
	家庭拥有小汽车数 L	0~3 辆	

2.3 学生通学方式模型的参数标定

对于学生通学出行方式的选择模型,其参数标定需要经历初始标定和最终标定两次计算。模型的最终标定结果见表2。

学生通学出行交通方式的选择模型参数标定结果　　　　　　　　　　　　　　　表2

出行方式		B	显著性	出行方式		B	显著性
小汽车	截距	1.494	0.058	自行车	截距	-1.825	0.096
	D1	0.057	0.640		D1	0.669	0.000
	E1	-0.787	0.007		E1	-2.663	0.000
	E2	-0.985	0.001		E2	-0.502	0.130
	G0	-0.085	0.037		G0	3.407	0.000
	F0	0.017	0.894		F0	0.479	0.001
	A1	0.081	0.768		A1	1.527	0.001
	A2	0.359	0.019		A2	0.563	0.152
	B1	0.122	0.580		B1	-0.545	0.048
	B2	0.308	0.165		B2	0.092	0.725
	L0	-0.891	0.019		L0	0.089	0.923
	L1	0.459	0.046		L1	0.326	0.723
	L2	0.052	0.940		L2	-0.325	0.730
	I1	0.529	0.020		I1	-0.097	0.617
	I2	0.379	0.900		I2	-0.124	0.659

续上表

出行方式		B	显著性	出行方式		B	显著性
公交车	截距	-0.007	0.994	步行	截距	-0.1	0.917
	D1	0.326	0.081		D1	0.032	0.827
	E1	-0.594	0.174		E1	-1.213	0.000
	E2	-1.333	0.000		E2	-0.791	0.012
	G0	2.8	0.000		G0	3.196	0.000
	F0	-3.951	0.000		F0	0.71	0.000
	A1	1.637	0.000		A1	-0.459	0.171
	A2	0.515	0.043		A2	-0.74	0.000
	B1	-1.901	0.001		B1	-0.328	0.194
	B2	-0.634	0.008		B2	-0.318	0.207
	L0	-0.485	0.589		L0	0.192	0.816
	L1	-0.548	0.540		L1	0.304	0.712
	L2	-0.219	0.811		L2	0.165	0.845
	I1	0.191	0.399		I1	0.227	0.182
	I2	0.856	0.005		I2	0.107	0.689

根据模型似然比检验和拟合优度值检验结果可知,模型中所有变量均为显著影响因素,模型拟合程度较好,结果可信。

根据模型结果,不同交通方式其显著变量和影响关系不同。以小汽车出行和公交车出行为例,在小汽车出行中,幼龄的学生与其有更显著的负相关关系,即对于小学生和初中生而言,年龄越小选择小汽车出行的可能性越大,年龄增加其选择小汽车出行的概率降低。在公交车出行的模型中,有无家长接送和学生有无公交IC卡是最显著的影响因素,前者与公交出行正相关,即家长不接送学生的概率越高,学生选择公交的概率越大;后者与公交出行负相关,即学生没有公交卡的概率越高,不选择坐公交的概率越大。

3 学生通学方式影响因素敏感性分析

3.1 学生接送比例变化敏感性分析

有无家长接送是影响学生通学出行方式选择的一项重要因素。在现状中,有无接送学生的比例各占50%,将接送比(有接送人的学生与全体学生人数的占比)分别调整至70%、30%,研究其分担率的变化,结果见表3。

学生接送情况的敏感性分析　　　　表3

接送比	出行方式					
	小汽车	电动车	摩托车	公交车	自行车	步行
现状(50%)	34.62%	11.26%	4.07%	9.75%	18.48%	21.82%
接送比(30%)	24.46%	8.87%	2.02%	10.43%	26.27%	27.95%
接送比(70%)	38.86%	14.41%	7.06%	9.23%	11.88%	18.56%

由表3可知,选择小汽车出行的学生比例随接送比的增加而增加,反之亦然。但是,对于公交出行而言,学生接送比例的变化对其均无较明显的影响趋势,随着学生接送比例的增加或减少,自行车和步行的分担率也会相应地减少或增加。

3.2 学生家庭小汽车拥有量变化敏感性分析

小汽车对城市交通的拥堵影响较为严重,故本研究对改善交通拥堵有重要意义。本次统计中,学生家庭小汽车拥有量的平均值为 0.90 辆,对此值作调整,结果见表 4。

学生家庭小汽车拥有量的敏感性分析 表 4

小汽车拥有量(辆/家)	出行方式					
	小汽车	电动车	摩托车	公交车	自行车	步行
现状(0.90)	34.62%	11.26%	4.07%	9.75%	18.48%	21.82%
拥有量(1.20)	40.77%	11.13	4.67%	10.37%	15.62%	17.44%
拥有量(0.60)	22.83%	14.17%	6.62%	14.96%	17.91%	23.51%

由表 4 可知,当学生家庭的平均小汽车拥有量上升时,小汽车的分担率呈明显上升的趋势,同时自行车和步行的分担率则相应下降;而当学生家庭的平均小汽车拥有量下降时,原本选择小汽车出行的学生则转而选择电动车、摩托车和公交车出行。

4 结 语

(1)影响学生出行行为的因素共分为个人、家庭、出行本身 3 个方面。根据本次研究,影响学生出行最显著的还是出行因素其本身,其次,学生是否接送、家庭现有小汽车数、家庭类型也会在不同程度上影响学生选择通学的方式。

(2)通过改变学生的接送比例,能明显发现:降低 20% 的接送比例,可以较为明显得降低学生选择小汽车出行的概率,概率降低约 10%,从而转向选择公交车、自行车和步行,有利于优化学生出行结构;在提高 20% 的接送比例时,选择小汽车、电动车、摩托车出行的概率均提高了 3%~4%。目前每家平均拥有 0.9 辆小汽车,当家庭拥有的小汽车数降低至 0.6 时,可明显降低小汽车出行的分担率,该分担率降低约 12%,从而促使学生及其家庭选择公共交通或绿色慢行交通,缓解城市道路的交通拥挤状况。

(3)根据建模结果,未能得出学生家庭收入、家长职业与学生通学方式选择的关系,无法排除受受出行调查信采集信息不完整的影响,还需进一步进行建模与分析。

参考文献

[1] 崔真榕.家庭视角下深圳市小学生的通学出行特征及其影响因素研究[D].哈尔滨:哈尔滨工业大学,2020.

[2] 何峻岭,李建忠.武汉市中小学生上下学交通特征及改善建议[J].城市交通,2007,5(5):87-91.

[3] C. DVAN GOEVERDEN, E. DE BOER. School Travel Behavior in the Netherlands and Flanders[J]. Transport Policy 2013(26):73-78.

[4] 刘涟涟.中学生通学出行选择的环境影响因素分析[A].中国城市规划学会、杭州市人民政府.共享与品质——2018 中国城市规划年会论文集(06 城市交通规划)[C].中国城市规划学会、杭州市人民政府:中国城市规划学会,2018(11).

[5] 王侠,陈晓键.西安城市小学通学出行的时空特征与制约分析[J].城市规划,2018,42(11):142-150.

[6] MA L, XIONG H, WANG Z. Impact of Weather Conditions on Middle School Students' Commute Mode Choices: Empirical Findings from Beijing, China[J]. Transportation Research Part D: Transport and Environment, 2019(68):39-51.

[7] 武文,帅斌,殷焕焕,等.基于 BL 模型的居民小汽车出行行为研究[J].交通运输工程与信息学报,2012,10(03):71-75.

[8] 马书红,付建川,姚志刚.基于家庭属性和 Nested Logit 模型的学生出行选择特性分析[J].重庆交通大学学报(自然科学版),2015,34(04):122-127.

[9] 李金海,陈永胜,唐珍珍,等.基于 Multinomial Logit 模型的校车通学影响因素研究[J].道路交通与安全,2015,15(04):32-37.

[10] 咸达.基于 MNL 的中小学生通学方式选择及校车使用意愿研究[D].大连:大连理工大学,2018.

基于二项 Logit 模型的西安市 P&R 换乘行为的影响因素分析

张 鹏 翁婷婷 赵宇飞 李佳晨 赵家充

(西安建筑科技大学)

摘 要 随着城镇化的不断推进,我国城市人口快速增长,给城市交通带来了空前的压力。文中通过实地调查和问卷调查,分析了西安市地铁 P&R(Park and Ride)模式的现状,确定了影响居民选择 P&R 出行的影响因素;在二项 Logit 模型基础上,建立了不同收费和距离情况下停车换乘出行的选择模型,提出合理的 P&R 建设建议,加强 P&R 设施的换乘接驳作用。

关键词 P&R 换乘出行 停车收费 轨道交通 二项 Logit 模型

0 引 言

随着我国城镇化的推进,城市人口数量快速增长,给城市交通带来了巨大压力,以轨道交通为代表的集约型交通方式快速发展。当轨道交通发展到一定规模,伴随着城市机动车数量的迅速增长,城市中心停车问题愈加严重,甚至影响到了动态交通的质量和城市的高效运行。这些城市逐渐发现 P&R 模式能够有效减轻城市中心交通压力,减少城市中心私家车出行数量和停车需求,提高轨道交通利用率。为了促进出行者采用 P&R 模式,有必要对现状进行调查,挖掘影响公众选择 P&R 模式出行因素,以此为基础积极采取诱导措施,提高 P&R 模式出行比例。

在 P&R 方式选择方面,Clayton W[1]研究了个人特征如性别、年龄和收入等与选择 P&R 出行的关系。曹弋[2]通过四项 Logit 模型,确定了停车费用与选择 P&R 出行比例之间的关系曲线。刘涛[3]提出了 P&R 停车场规划思路和方法,并给出了同心圆城市的换乘停车场规划方案。李语萱[4]研究了长沙轨道交通 4 号线光达站,论述并分析了 P&R 出行方式的必要性,设计了光达站的停车换乘系统。喻军皓[5]根据上海市 P&R 停车场的现状,分析了影响 P&R 停车场运营的因素,提出了上海市 P&R 停车换乘规划方案和发展策略。

尽管国内外在 P&R 方面进行了一定研究,但主要侧重在公交换乘和宏观层面的 P&R 设施规划,很少以地铁 P&R 为核心开展研究,另外也忽视了换乘步行距离和收费政策的导向作用。鉴于此,本研究以问卷调查和实地调查为基础,从宏观的城市圈层和微观的具体站点周边,定量研究西安市停车费用对居民出行方式选择的影响,进而得到具有引导意义的地铁站周边停车场布置和收费策略,以充分发挥 P&R 停车出行方式的优势及换乘接驳作用,缓解主城区交通压力。

1 西安市 P&R 现状

1.1 停车设施现状

截至 2017 年,西安市汽车保有量 343 万辆,位列全国第八,年均增长率 14%。西安市三环内面积为 360km^2,共有各类停车场 14000 个,停车位 108 万个。由此可见,西安市停车资源紧张,同时新增汽车也在不断加重主城区停车压力。

目前西安市轨道交通 1、2、3 和 4 号线已开通运营,运营里程达 161.46km,为西安市居民出行带来了极大的便利。最大限度利用轨道交通也是缓解交通拥堵和停车问题的可行解决方案。

1.2 停车收费现状

根据标准规定,收费类区划分为4类,分别是道路路边特定区、明城墙以内、明城墙以外至二环路以内、二环路以外的城市建成区[6]。最高小时收费是道路特定区高峰时段停车,达到8元/h,这不仅会给出行者带来经济负担,同时也造成了公共集约型交通的浪费。

2 问卷调查

2.1 问卷设计

通过对现有的文献分析,以个人特征(性别、年龄、学历、职业)、出行者行为特征(对电子地图的看法、使用电子地图的频率、开车出行频率等)、P&R特征(是否了解P&R、换乘花费时间、停车场到地铁站的步行距离)等设计问卷。

2.2 问卷结果

问卷采取网络问卷和现场问卷结合方式,其中现场问卷根据所处城市圈层,将后卫寨、朝阳门等作为调查站点。问卷问题采取SP调查[7]和RP调查结合的方式。排除无开车出行经历者后,RP调查共回收219份有效问卷,涉及的调查对象均为有开车出行经历的西安市民。

3 问卷分析

3.1 模型选择

对出行者选择P&R方式出行的意向进行调查。以是否采用P&R方式出行为因变量,运用二元Logit回归模型对调查数据进行处理,分析各因素对P&R方式出行意向的影响程度,确定主要影响因素及其阈值。

3.2 变量筛选

将问卷中所有单选题归类为分类变量和连续变量,针对不同的变量类型,选用不同的筛选方法。此外将选择P&R出行的频率问题简化为是否选择P&R出行模式,选择"从不"一项者变量值修改为0,其余选项均修改为1,然后进行统计。

3.2.1 Pearson卡方独立性检验

Pearson卡方独立性检验适用于非连续变量,将各个分类变量分别与是否选择停车换乘这一变量做交叉表卡方检验,将SPSS输出所有结果进行整合如下,结果见表1。

Pearson卡方独立性检验　　　　　表1

属　性	pearson卡方	自　由　度	渐近Sig.(双侧)
性别	7.231a	1	0.007
年龄	3.124a	4	0.537
学历	3.898a	4	0.420
职业	2.428a	6	0.876
导航的优点	1.237a	3	0.744
P&R的了解程度	9.117a	1	0.003
影响停车时长的因素	1.048a	3	0.790
选择停车换乘的情况	7.123a	4	0.130

注:Sig.≤0.05,选入模型变量。

由表1可知,将性别和P&R了解程度选入模型变量。

3.2.2 特征因素共线性诊断

Pearson相关系数用来验证自变量与自变量之间的相关程度,要求这些自变量为连续型变量,才可得出理想效果。根据上文归类得出的连续型变量,对这些变量通过SPSS软件,两两一组进行双变量相关性诊断。

由结果知,停车场到地铁站的步行距离和可接受的泊车费用这两变量有强相关性,因此在构建模型时,不选入模型因变量。

通过以上两步检验,对变量进行筛选,选择年龄、关于P&R了解程度、开车出行频率、使用导航频率、换乘花费时间这5个变量进行Logit回归。

3.3 建立二项Logit模型

本研究中选择方式为两种:方案1选择停车换乘和方案2不选择停车换乘,以此为基础建立出行者停车换乘选择行为的二元Logit模型,模型显示了不同因素影响出行方式的选择程度和这些因素之间的联系。

选择停车换乘的概率:

$$P_{1n} = \text{prob}(V_{1n} > V_{2n}) = \frac{\exp(V_{1n})}{\exp(V_{1n}) + \exp(V_{2n})} \quad (1)$$

不选择停车换乘的概率:

$$P_{2n} = 1 - P_{1n} = \frac{\exp(V_{2n})}{\exp(V_{1n}) + \exp(V_{2n})} \quad (2)$$

得到Logit模型的效用函数为:

$$\text{Logit } P(Y=1) = \theta_0 + \theta_1 * X_1 + \theta_2 * X_2 + \theta_3 * X_3 + \theta_4 * X_4 + \theta_5 * X_5 \quad (3)$$

式中: θ_0 ——常数;
θ_1、θ_2、θ_3、θ_4、θ_5 ——自变量系数;
X_1 ——年龄;
X_2 ——关于P&R了解程度;
X_3 ——开车出行频率;
X_4 ——使用导航频率;
X_5 ——换乘花费时间;
$P(Y=1)$ ——选择P&R的概率。

3.4 模型结果

由输出的Logit回归分析结果可知,各变量在95%的置信区间上,说明这些变量与Y之间相关性显著,均可纳入最后的方程中。

由此得到Logit出行方式选择模型如下:

$$\begin{aligned}\text{Logit} P(Y=1) &= -2.22 + 0.919X_1 + 0.843X_2 - 0.801X_{31} - 0.547X_{32} \\ &- 0.29X_{33} + 0.452X_{41} + 1.508X_{42} + 0.31X_{43} + 0.629X_{51} + 0.855X_{52} + 1.304X_{53}\end{aligned} \quad (4)$$

3.5 模型检验

本模型Hosmer and Lemeshow检验结果为0.794,不显著,说明该模型的拟合较好。模型Cox&Snell R2和Nagelkerke R2分别为0.589和0.552,准确性在可接受范围内。Hit Ratio值是实际选择结果与模型预测的结果是否一致的指标,该模型值为72.1%,表示结果良好。

4 关于P&R出行模式比率的情景假设研究

由以上研究得到的二元Logit模型概率方程,通过改变自变量的取值,将会影响因变量概率的取值。

为提高居民选择P&R出行模式的比例,需从这些因素入手。我们认为,缩短地铁站与停车场之间的距离,规划换乘最优路径,增加地铁站周边停车设施容量,可以显著缩短停车换乘时间,进而增加居民选择P&R出行方式的比例。为验证这一猜想,采用弹性分析法分析停车场与地铁站步行距离对P&R方式出行的影响。

根据弹性值的定义,将自变量定义为停车场与地铁站间的距离,因变量定义为选择P&R出行方式的概率,则有:

$$P_i = f(C_i) \tag{5}$$

设当停车费用变化ΔC_i时,选择P&R出行方式概率的变化量为ΔP_i,则:

$$\Delta P_i = f(C_i + \Delta C_i) - f(C_i) \tag{6}$$

非集计模型中解释变量并非唯一的,需设定其他解释变量的值。此处采用平均值法进行设定,该方法是将研究对象全体的平均值带入求解点弹性,之后通过非集计模型求解不同收费情况下选择P&R方式出行的概率,求解结果见表2。

不同情况下对P&R方式选择概率 表2

停车场与地铁站距离(m)	选择P&R出行方式概率(%)	不选择P&R出行方式概率(%)	转移比例(%)
200	63.6	36.4	36.4
500	51.2	48.8	12.4
1000	25.6	74.4	25.6
1500	15.2	84.8	10.4

5 结 语

结合上述研究,本文认为要提高西安市私家车出行者选择地铁P&R模式的意愿和比例,可以从以下几个方面进行改善:

(1)根据停车场与换乘站点距离制定阶梯收费策略。距地铁站较远处的停车场,可适当降低收费;距地铁站近的停车场,可适当提高收费。兼顾时间敏感型和费用敏感型出行者,提高P&R出行比例。

(2)P&R设施应与轨道交通紧密衔接。P&R设施与站点之间的步行时间是影响停车换乘选择的重要因素。政府在设计P&R设施时应做好布局规划,尽量缩短步行时间,减少绕行,最大限度为换乘者提供便利。

(3)加强P&R方式宣传推广。调查显示,还有大部分出行者不了解P&R这一出行理念,因此,建议应加强对P&R出行理念的引导和推广。可从P&R出行的优势、环保需要和增强社会责任感等多角度展开宣传。

参考文献

[1] CLAYTON W, PARKHURST G, RICCI M, et al. Where to Park? A Behavioural Comparison of Bus-based Park and Ride and City Centre Car Park Usage in Bath, UK[J]. Journal of Transport Geography, 2014 (36), 124-133.

[2] 曹弋,杨忠振,左忠义.基于地铁停车换乘的区域差异性停车收费策略[J].交通运输系统工程与信息,2017,17(3):12-18.

[3] 刘涛.轨道交通小汽车停车换乘(P+R)规划与布局研究[J].城市建筑,2019,16(26):89-90.

[4] 李语萱.长沙城市轨道交通停车换乘(P+R)设施规划研究——以光达站为例[J].城市建设理论研究(电子版),2018(30):76-77.

[5] 喻军皓.上海市P+R停车场库发展策略研究[A].中国城市规划学会城市交通规划学术委员会.创新驱动与智慧发展——2018年中国城市交通规划年会论文集[C].中国城市规划学会城市交通规划学术委员会:中国城市规划设计研究院城市交通专业研究院,2018:(15).

[6] 西安市人民政府办公厅关于印发西安市城市道路和停车场机动车停车服务收费标准的通知[J].西安市人民政府公报,2019(03):3-4.

[7] 吴焕,彭湖,陈梓星,等.基于SP调查的出行时间价值估计及出行者属性影响分析[J].交通与运输,2019,35(06):9-12.

基于SERVQUAL模型的高速铁路车站旅客满意度调查分析

罗江莲 吴娟 梁同天 徐志中 栾鹏博

(西南交通大学希望学院)

摘 要 随着我国高速铁路的发展，高速铁路客运服务已成为我国铁路客运服务发展的主要方向，其客运服务的质量测评和控制是高速铁路客运服务研究和发展的主要内容。为了准确了解旅客对铁路旅客运输企业的满意度，在结合旅客心理马斯洛需求理论基础上，运用SERVQUAL模型进行影响旅客满意度的指标体系建立，并通过指标设立调查问卷，对旅客展开调查和结果分析，用对比旅客期望值和感知值的方式来衡量旅客满意度，并以此提出整改建议，达到提升铁路客运服务质量的目的。

关键词 出行行为 满意度 SERVQUAL模型 客运服务

0 引 言

2008年8月，我国第一条长120km的京津城际高速铁路开通运营，标志着我国高速铁路建设进入了新的里程。至2020年"十三五"结束之际，全国高速铁路运营里程已增加到3.79万km，我国高速铁路网络已实现大部分相邻大中城市间1～4小时交通圈、城市群内0.5～2小时交通圈，为旅客出行提供了安全可靠、优质高效、舒适便捷的旅客运输服务。

随着人们生活水平提升，对铁路出行的需求已由基本的位移需求上升到高品质的位移需求。2020年是"十三五"收官之年，在这5年里，铁路高质量服务可以说是冲破重重阻碍，甚至经历疫情的残酷考验，顺利稳步前进。在此背景下，本文通过对旅客心理需求的分析，建立相关指标对高速铁路车站客运服务进行调查，并通过建立SERVQUAL模型，从旅客角度反映了高速铁路车站客运服务质量存在的一些问题，最后提出解决方法。

1 高速铁路的优势和旅客满意度

高速铁路作为当前旅客主要的出行方式之一，带给旅客的优势是显而易见的，选择高速铁路列车出行的旅客是日益递增，这对高速铁路运输企业的客运服务质量提出了新的挑战。旅客最终选择哪一种交通方式？哪一种交通运输方式体验性最好？选择高速铁路列车出行，其出行过程的满意度如何？无论旅客选择什么样的出行方式，旅客始终会对运输企业能提供的优质服务作出满意度的分析、判断。高速铁路车站作为旅客整个旅行的起点和终点，乘客对车站的服务满意度将是对选择高速铁路列车出行的主要体验之一，因此高速铁路车站旅客满意度是运输企业不得不重视的环节。

满意度是旅客的重要心理评价，反映了旅客对于客运服务质量的感知和认可，体现了旅客心理需求。结合马斯洛需求层次理论进行进一步分析，将旅客对高速铁路车站的心理需求具体分为安全心理、可靠心理、方便心理、经济心理、舒适心理及归属感心理5点，这5点内容将是后续模型的指标建立的依据。

2 SERVQUAL模型建立与问卷设计

SERVQUAL模型是衡量旅客对服务质量感知的标准。SERVQUAL模型评价方法建立在旅客感知的基础之上，即以旅客的主观认识来衡量服务质量。服务质量(SQ) = 服务感知(P)-服务期望(E)。当$P > E$时，旅客对服务的感知超过了对服务的期望，旅客能够感知到高质量的服务；当$P = E$时，旅客对服务的感知等于对服务的期望，旅客感到服务质量尚可；当$P < E$时，旅客对服务的感知低于对服务的期

望,旅客感到服务质量低下。

通过对 SERVQUAL 模型分析,将高速铁路车站客运服务质量分为服务期望与服务感知,然后再细化为安全性、可靠、经济、舒适、归属感五个方面。

结合 SERVQUAL 原始量表,形成本文需要分析的车站客运服务具体 SERVQUAL 量表。通过调查问卷的方式,让用户对每个问题的期望值、实际感知值进行评分,并由其确立相关的 20 个具体因素来说明。最后通过问卷调查、旅客打分和综合计算得出服务质量的分数。表 1 是车站客运服务 SERVQUAL 量表。

车站客运服务 SERVQUAL 量表 表 1

维 度	指标及其序号
安全性	(1)车站整体治安怎样; (2)进/出站次序维护怎样; (3)车站环境卫生怎样; (4)车站防疫防控措施执行怎样; (5)车站小卖部餐饮和食品卫生安全怎样
可靠性	(6)是否正点发车; (7)是否正点到达; (8)是否能准时地提供所承诺的服务(及时报站、晚点通知等); (9)员工是否具有帮助旅客的主动性
经济性	(10)票价是否合理; (11)小商品价格是否合理; (12)餐饮价格是否合理
舒适性	(13)车站的服务设施是否现代化; (14)服务设施具有吸引力、乘客对服务设施的关注; (15)员工有整洁的服装和外套; (16)车站的设施与他们所提供的服务是否相匹配
归属感	(17)车站能否针对乘客提供个性化的服务; (18)遇到困难时是否能及时主动提供帮助; (19)员工是否了解乘客的需求; (20)员工是否全程微笑服务

旅客期望和感知一共设置 20 个指标问题。问卷采用 10 分制,10 分表示完全满意,1 分表示完全不满意。把这两部分中得到的调查结果进行比较,SERVQUAL 分数 = 实际感知分数 - 期望分数,因此得到 5 个维度的每个"差距分值",差距越小,服务质量评价就越高。消费者的感知离期望的距离越大,服务质量的评价越低。通过查阅文献,确定安全性、可靠性、经济性、舒适性、归属感的权重分别为 0.35、0.25、0.15、0.15、0.1。

3 计算及结果分析

本次调查共发放问卷 AB 卷 200 份,回收有效问卷 AB 卷 187 份。1 套 AB 卷代表 1 份问卷,每位被调查者填写 AB 问卷,A 卷代表期望值调查,B 卷代表感知值调查,根据有效回收进行期望值和感知值数据汇总。

期望值和感知值计算公式分别如下:

$$期望值 = \sum_{i=1}^{n} E_i \qquad (1)$$

$$感知值 = \sum_{i=1}^{n} P_i \qquad (2)$$

单项指标的感知服务质量计算公式如下:

$$SQ_1 = \sum_{i=1}^{n} (P_i - E_i) \qquad (3)$$

加权平均后的维度感知服务质量计算公式为：

$$SQ_2 = \sum_{j=1}^{m} \omega_j \sum_{i=1}^{n} (P_i - E_i) \tag{4}$$

单个旅客平均的 SERVQUAL 分数计算公式为：

$$SQ_3 = \frac{1}{n} \sum_{j=1}^{m} \omega_j \sum_{i=1}^{n} (P_i - E_i) \tag{5}$$

以上各式中：E_i——第 i 个因素在乘客期望方面的分数；

P_i——第 i 个因素在乘客感知方面的分数；

n——回收有效问卷数份数；

m——5 个维度；

ω——权重；

SQ——感知服务质量。

由式(1)～式(3)，可计算得出客运服务质量 5 个维度(20 个指标)的客运服务各项数值,见表 2。

调查值统计　　　　　　　表2

质量维度	指标序号	期望值	感知值	指标 SQ	合计
安全性	1	1813	1801	-12	-43
	2	1781	1764	-17	
	3	1801	1798	-3	
	4	1610	1599	-11	
可靠性	5	1832	1827	-5	-124
	6	1809	1800	-9	
	7	1566	1530	-36	
	8	1498	1484	-14	
	9	1384	1324	-60	
经济性	10	1421	1380	-41	-230
	11	1444	1367	-77	
	12	1460	1348	-112	
舒适性	13	1533	1528	-5	-120
	14	1357	1301	-56	
	15	1540	1510	-30	
	16	1404	1375	-29	
归属感	17	1722	1530	-192	-332
	18	1706	1640	-66	
	19	1825	1801	-24	
	20	1704	1654	-50	

由式(4)可计算得出加权平均后的维度感知服务质量各项数值,见表 3。

维度感知服务质量　　　　　　　表3

维度	安全性	可靠性	经济性	舒适性	归属感
权重分配	0.35	0.25	0.15	0.15	0.1
维度感知服务质量 SQ	-15.05	-31	-34.5	-18	-33.2

由式(5)可最终求得该车站客运服务质量整体客运服务质量平均 SERVQUAL 分值为 -0.035。

4 结果分析

客运服务质量满意度调查的最终目的,是要不断提升客运服务质量,满足旅客需求,提高旅客满意度。从以上数据可以看出,每个服务质量指标均为负数,说明旅客期望值均偏高,对运输企业的期望值高于感知值。但是各项数值差别不大,最小的差异为-3,说明了有些指标是已经接近了旅客期望值,旅客满意度较高。从以上调查中可以看出,旅客满意度依次为安全性、舒适性、可靠性、经济性、归属感。此调查数据说明旅客是以安全为首要考虑因素,对高速铁路安全性比较满意。在该维度中,指标绝对值较高的是进出站次序维护,说明在旅客聚集并集体流动的进出站环节,旅客期望能有更好的次序控制和服务体验。关于高速铁路舒适性,说明了旅客对于车站各类设施设备均有较大的认可。在可靠性维度中,差异较大的指标是员工是否具有帮助旅客的主动性,说明旅客对车站员工的积极性有更高的期望。在经济性维度中,3个指标均有一定差异,且对餐饮价格的差异性较大,说明部分旅客对于高速铁路票价还是有降低的意愿。归属感差异较大,主要体现在车站针对乘客提供个性化的服务上,这说明旅客对于车站的各种个性化服务存在较高的期待。

5 结　语

本文通过SERVQUAL模型,建立20个指标进行了调查分析,旨在得出旅客对车站客运服务的满意度。从上述计算得出的车站客运服务质量整体客运服务质量平均SERVQUAL分值为-0.035可以看出,旅客对高速铁路车站的平均满意度较高。但是从SERVQUAL量表指标各项分析,又可以看到影响满意度的具体各项指标存在的问题。下面就几项差距较大的指标进行总结,并给出相应建议:

(1)提升安全性,加强车站安全管理。加强各环节旅客的安全监督,尤其在在进出站环节,可加强员工对旅客的语音引导,起到安抚和维持次序作用;加强通道引导与站台秩序维护,以保证旅客能按时、准点进站乘车。

(2)要加强员工素质培训,提升员工帮助旅客的主动性。培训员工能急乘客所急、想乘客所想,真正做到把旅客当作自己家人一样,全心全意为旅客服务。

(3)在经济性方面,主要是小商品和餐饮价格上,建议多品种营销,配备不同的消费产品,以适应各类不同需求的人群。

(4)在车站设施设备现代化方面,建议尽可能设置实用功能的设施设备。车站是旅客集散的地方,旅客的主要目的是乘坐列车,因此车站应设置一些现代化设施设备,作为旅客在各流动环节中的必要性准备,例如进站安检及实名自动化系统以提高旅客进站速度,进出站自动检票设备加快旅客检票速度等。在非必要环节,例如候车过程中的附加服务体验等,需要根据实际情况选择合适的功能区域酌情设置。

6 不足之处

由于开展调查是在疫情防控期间,问卷调查的开展具有很大的难度,因此本文的样本数量不够,所调查的数据能反映目标车站存在的一些问题,但不能代表其他车站客运服务存在的所有问题。此外,本人及团队能力有限,虽有不断学习交通运输领域知识,但在本次文章写作中,所选取的分析方法在运用上存在深度不够的问题,在后续的研究分析中,作者将进一步努力学习,运用更科学的方法分析问题,用更实际数据说话,以达到所分析研究的内容能具体落实到实践的作用。

参考文献

[1] 蔡文振.高速铁路车站旅客满意度研究[D].杭州:浙江工业大学,2017.
[2] 丁小芳.基于旅客满意度的客运站服务质量优化研究[D].北京:中国铁道科学研究院,2020.
[3] 贾俊芳.高速铁路客运服务[M].北京:中国铁道出版社,2017.

城市干道车辆的初始车道选择、换道时机及协作换道的实证研究

章宇凯　祁宏生

（浙江大学建筑工程学院智能交通研究所）

摘　要　自动驾驶汽车通过车联网获取的道路车流信息进行决策，缺乏对驾驶员在城市干道行驶全过程中驾驶意图的理解，容易造成交通事故。为此，本文通过对NGSIM数据集进行分析，对驾驶员行驶全过程中驾驶行为进行实证研究。通过数据处理，提取了4个交叉口5600条高精度车辆轨迹数据。分析结果表明，车辆的初始车道选择与目标车道有关。直行、左转及右转车辆中强关联车辆占比分别为37.1%、66.7%和89.0%。同时通过多项式回归，建立了车辆换道概率与所处位置的关系式，MAE和RMSE均在0.03以内。定义礼貌系数函数，对驾驶员风格进行区分，将驾驶员风格分为礼貌型、中立型和粗鲁型3类，研究表明越靠近渠化路段，中立型驾驶员占比越高。研究成果为定量分析驾驶员的换道习惯提供了参考，有助于提高自动驾驶车辆对人类驾驶习惯的理解。

关键词　交通工程　初始车道选择　换道时机　多项式回归　自动驾驶

0　引　言

随着智能交通技术的不断发展，车联网的有关理论也日益成熟。车联网主要基于车载自组织网络，其主要功能是实现车辆与移动用户以及车辆与车辆之间的高效率通信[1]。自动驾驶车辆通过车联网能获取道路上的海量信息，实现不同级别的自动驾驶。

当自动驾驶车辆能准确理解人类驾驶车辆的行驶意图时，自动驾驶车辆会更加安全高效。但如果自动驾驶车辆缺乏合理的预测模型，反而事故率会更高[2]。目前，自动驾驶车辆在高速公路上的表现较出色，而在城市干道上却差强人意。相较于公路路段，城市干道的几何结构更复杂。城市道路由交叉口、普通路段以及渠化路段组成，在渠化路段内车辆无法变道[3]。

换道（Lane Changing，简称LC）是车辆在行驶过程中必不可少的一个驾驶行为。Gipps[4]在1986年提出了第一个换道模型，他将车辆换道行为分为产生需求、探测条件、换道实施3个过程。在Gipps模型基础上，Yang[5]提出了MITSIM（Microscopic Traffic Simulator）模型，将换道行为分为自由换道和强制换道两种。Hidas[6]建立了SITRAS仿真系统，并引入了协同换道的概念。

传统的交通换道模型没有考虑到在真实环境下驾驶员感知和决策的不一致性和不确定性。为此，学者们将模糊逻辑的相关理念运用到换道模型中。模糊逻辑在建模过程中引入可量化的不确定性，以反映驾驶员对真实环境的主观感知[7]。Moridpour[8]利用模糊逻辑对不同车型的换道过程进行建模，更好地模仿了驾驶员地实际操作过程。在这类基于模糊逻辑的模型中，其难点是对于模糊规则的抽象和隶属度函数的确定[9]。

从已有的研究成果来看，大部分的换道模型针对的是车辆在高速公路行驶时的换道行为，没有考虑复杂城市路段下的情况，这对自动驾驶车辆理解驾驶员的驾驶行为帮助有限。为此，本文通过对NGSIM数据集的分析[10]，对城市干道转向车辆的初始车道选择、换道时机及协作换道进行实证研究，为自动驾驶车辆理解驾驶员行驶全过程的驾驶行为提供依据。

基金项目：国家重点研发计划（2019YFB1600300）；浙江省公益技术研究计划（LGF18E080003）。

1 初始车道选择行为

交叉口和渠化路段是城市干道的重要组成部分,现有的多数换道模型研究只关注车辆在基本路段的换道行为,而忽视了车辆在交叉口的车道选择行为。本节将针对转向车辆(包括左转、直行和右转)从当前渠化路段驶入相交普通路段的车道选择行为进行分析。如图1所示,图1中的车辆在转向时可选择车道1~3中的任意一个车道驶入。

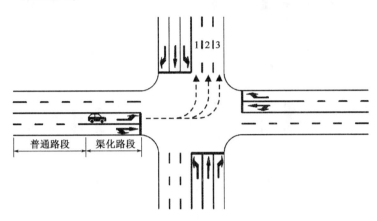

图1 车辆初始车道选择行为示意图

1.1 数据提取

本节将对NGSIM数据集中的"Lankershim"部分进行分析。Lankershim是位于美国加利弗尼亚州洛杉矶的一条主干道,路段中车道数划分较多,路况较复杂,共包含4个信号灯控制交叉口,适合用于分析城市中车辆的换道行为,该道路的具体几何特征如图2所示。

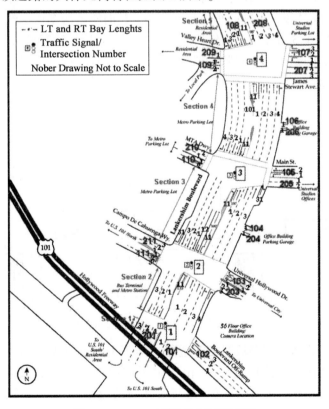

图2 Lankershim大道的节点位置和编号

通过对数据集的筛选,共选出5600条处于从渠化路段驶入普通路段的有效数据。由汇总后的数据可知,各进口道的左转或右转车辆进入普通路段时,多数车辆会选择转弯半径较小的行驶轨迹,驶入离当前所处车道距离较近的目标车道。具体数据分布如图3所示。

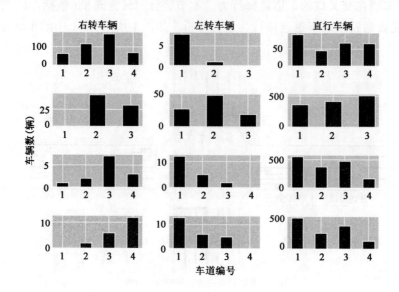

图3 转向车辆初始车道选择分布图(第1~4行对应图2中第1~4个交叉口)

1.2 数据分析

为进一步分析各进口道的转向车辆在进入相交路段时的车道选择行为,本节将分析车辆进入相交路段时的车道选择与下个路口行驶方向的关联性,并将该关联性分为强关联、弱关联和无关联3个等级。强关联指转弯车辆进入相交路段时选择的车道与下个路口转向所需的车道一致(1号车道为左转所需车道,2号车道为直行所需车道,3号车道为右转所需车道);弱关联指是转弯车辆进入相交路段时选择的车道与下个路口转向所需的车道相邻;无关联指转弯车辆进入本路段时选择的车道与下个路口转向所需的车道间隔一个车道及以上。3个等级的具体示例如图4所示,在图中车辆从左下位置出发,目的地为右上位置。

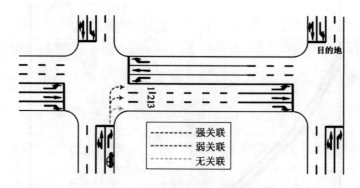

图4 强关联、弱关联和无关联定义示意图

由分析结果可知,车辆进入相交路段时的车道选择与下个路口行驶方向具有较强的关联性,无关联车辆几乎为0。当车辆在下个路口直行时,由于主干道中直行车道数较多,直行车辆有充足的机会变道,故弱关联车辆占比多于强关联车辆,这与实际交通流中的情况相符合。具体数据分布如图5所示。

图 5　车辆车道选择关联度分布图

2　换道时机

当车辆驶入干道后,驾驶员根据自己的需求变更车道,并决定换道时机。根据不同的需求,驾驶员变更车道的动机可分为两类。第一类是目标驱动的变道行为,即驾驶员当前所行驶的车道并不是目标车道,为了抵达目的地,驾驶员需要变更车道至目标车道;第二类是效率驱动的变道行为,即驾驶员变道的目的是达到更高的速度或进入一个交通流密度较低的车道[11]。

2.1　数据提取

本节选取 NGSIM 数据集中"Lankershim"部分中"Section 3"(自北向南路段)的交通流数据进行实证研究,具体路段如图 6 所示。该路段长度约为 180m,其中渠化路段长度约为 20m。

由研究结果可知,在采样区间内该路段所有车辆累计发生 1629 次换道行为,不同转向车辆换道时机的时空分布图如图 7～图 9 所示。图 7～图 9 中,颜色较浅的区域表示在该时刻该位置的换道车辆较少,颜色较深的区域表示换道车辆较多。可以看出,车辆在刚驶入普通路段以及接近渠化路段时换道频率较高。同时,相较于直行车辆,左、右转车辆会更多地选择在渠化路段路口处进行换道。

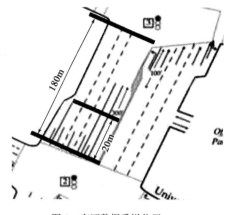

图 6　实证数据采样位置

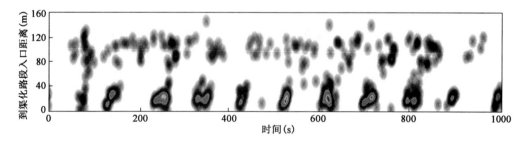

图 7　全部交通流中换道车辆时空分布图

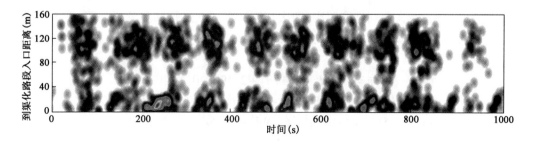

图 8　左、右转交通流中换道车辆时空分布图

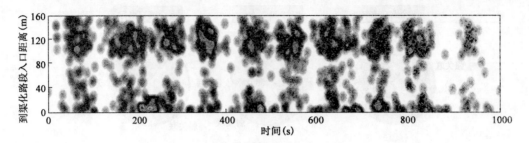

图9 直行交通流中换道车辆时空分布图

2.2 数据分析

图10所示为换道车辆在不同道路位置(不包含渠化路段)的分布。其中,横轴表示换道发生时所在的道路位置(例如驶入道路长度的10%,在横轴上表示为0.1)。折线变化趋势可以反映驾驶员在城市干道中对于换道位置选择的驾驶习惯。

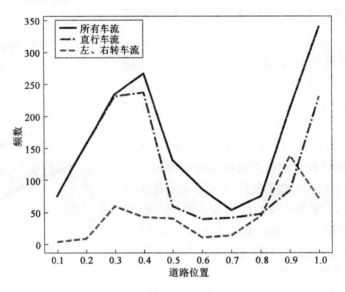

图10 车辆换道位置分布图

为了建立车辆换道概率与所在道路位置的模型,分别对直行车流和左、右转车流进行多项式回归分析。多项式回归方法的表达式为:

$$y = \sum_{i=0}^{n} a_i x^i \tag{1}$$

式中:y——预测值;
a_i——参数值;
x——输入值;
n——回归式的最高次幂。

为了更好地拟合数据,本文分别选取三次、四次和五次多项式进行回归分析。图11为多项式回归分析图。其中,直行车流的多项式回归后的表达式为式(2)~式(4),左、右转车流的多项式回归后的表达式为式(5)~式(7):

$$p = 3.29d^3 - 5.17d^2 + 2.19d - 0.11 \tag{2}$$

$$p = -2.31d^4 + 8.36d^3 - 8.88d^2 + 3.20d - 0.19 \tag{3}$$

$$p = -5.51d^5 + 12.85d^4 - 6.89d^3 - 2.06d^2 + 1.90d - 0.11 \tag{4}$$

$$p = 1.28d^3 - 1.87d^2 + 0.9d - 0.16 \tag{5}$$

$$p = -8.73d^4 + 20.5d^3 - 15.94d^2 + 4.74d - 0.36 \tag{6}$$

$$p = -57.69d^5 + 149.92d^4 - 139.12d^3 + 55.46d^2 - 8.86d + 0.46 \qquad (7)$$

式中：p——换道概率；

d——车辆位置。

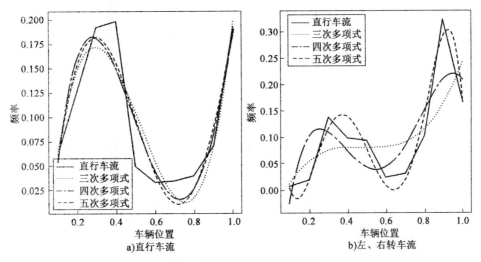

图 11　不同次数下的多项式回归

选取平均绝对误差和均方根误差作为衡量多项式回归精度的评价指标。表 1 列举了不同多项式的拟合精度。由表 1 可知，对于左、右转车流，五次多项式的拟合精度要明显优于三次和四次，精度提升约 60%。

多项式拟合精度表　　　　　　　　　　　　　　　　　　　　　　　表 1

多 项 式	直 行 车 流			左、右转车流		
	三次	四次	五次	三次	四次	五次
平均绝对误差	0.021	0.020	0.020	0.050	0.049	0.018
均方根误差	0.027	0.025	0.025	0.066	0.056	0.023

由图 11 可得，直行车道与左、右转车道上车辆的换道位置分布具有差异性，主要体现在提前变道的驾驶员比例。造成该现象可能的原因是道路上的多数驾驶员对当前交叉口的车道划分并不熟悉，尤其是对于左、右转车辆，无法提前得知左、右转车道的具体位置和数量，故多数驾驶员会选择在渠化路段入口处变道，少部分熟悉交叉口车道分布的驾驶员会选择提前变道。

3　协作换道

协作换道指当后车驾驶员发现相邻车道上车辆有换道意图时，选择降低速度并增大与前车间的空隙，协助换道车辆完成换道。当自动驾驶车辆作为后车时，出于安全考虑，自动驾驶车辆内置的决策系统会选择减速避让。但当驾驶员驾驶车辆作为后车时，由于驾驶员之间的驾驶风格不同，部分驾驶员不会选择减速避让。

本节使用 NGSIM 数据集进行分析，数据采样位置与本文第 2 节一致，随机选取 765 条滞后车辆（滞后车辆的定义如图 12 所示）的行驶轨迹。图 13 所示为换道车辆进行换道时滞后车辆的位置分布图。如图 13 所示，不同车道上不同风格驾驶员的分布特性不同。

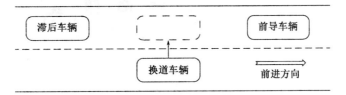

图 12　滞后车辆定义图

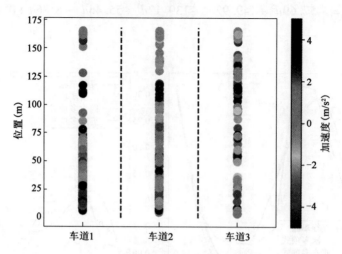

图 13 滞后车辆位置及加速度分布图

不同性格的驾驶员,在发现相邻车辆有换道意图后,会采取不同的回应方式。根据不同的驾驶行为,可以将滞后车辆的驾驶员分为 3 类:①粗鲁型,驾驶员加速不让换道;②中立型,不加速也不减速;③礼貌型,减速提供换道机会。具体评价指标可用礼貌系数表示,礼貌系数为负表示粗鲁型,为零表示中立型,为正表示礼貌型,且数值越高代表越礼貌程度越高。礼貌系数的表达式为:

$$\omega = \frac{-a_1}{\sqrt{(x_c - x_1)^2 + (y_c - y_1)^2}} \tag{8}$$

式中:ω——礼貌系数;

　　　a_1——滞后车辆的加速度;

　　　x_c——换道车辆的相对纵坐标;

　　　y_c——换道车辆的相对横坐标;

　　　x_1——滞后车辆的相对纵坐标;

　　　y_1——滞后车辆的相对横坐标。

图 14 所示为驾驶员礼貌系数的分布。可以看出,驾驶员的礼貌系数较多分布在 0 附近,礼貌系数为 $-0.4 \sim 0.4$ 的驾驶员占比为 80.4%,说明绝大多数的驾驶员在邻近车辆换道时,不会大幅改变自身的加速度,处于近似于中立型的状态;而礼貌系数为 $-1.2 \sim -0.8$ 和 $0.8 \sim 1.2$ 的驾驶员占比仅为 2.2%,说明极少驾驶员会极端粗鲁或礼貌。

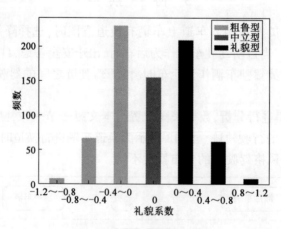

图 14 驾驶员礼貌系数分布图

图 15 所示为不同风格驾驶员在不同车道不同位置的分布,图中纵轴表示频数,横轴表示车辆位置(定义与图 9 一致)。如图 15 所示,在最靠近道路中线的车道 1 中,粗鲁型和礼貌型驾驶员集中出现在道

路长度的前40%,;中立型则分布得较平均。相较于车道1,在车道2和车道3中,礼貌型和粗鲁型没有明显的集中分布,但中立型均集中出现在道路的尾端(接近渠化路段入口处)。总体上,越靠近渠化路段入口,中立型驾驶员的比例越高。

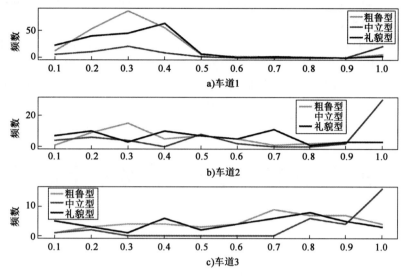

图15 不同风格驾驶员在不同车道不同位置的分布图

4 结 语

(1)本文结合高精度的车辆轨迹数据,分别从初始车道选择、换道时机以及协作换道3个方面对城市干道中驾驶员的驾驶行为进行研究。研究表明,车辆在当前交叉口的初始车道选择与在下个交叉口的前进方向有较强的关联性。车辆驶入普通路段后,其换道意愿与其所在道路位置存在联系。不同风格的驾驶员在不同车道的分布不同。

(2)在原始数据样本中,包含车辆所在车道编号,故能进行换道的实证研究,所得数据能真实反映驾驶员在城市干道驾驶的驾驶习惯。研究成果能提高自动驾驶车辆对人类驾驶行为的理解,帮助其在城市道路中做出更安全的全过程行驶轨迹规划。

(3)在未来的研究中,将考虑把更多的因素与驾驶员的这3类驾驶行为关联起来,如车辆速度、路段长度及车辆类型等,并采取更复杂的分析方式,建立一个更加精准的模型。

参考文献

[1] Li F,Wang Y. Routing in vehicular ad hoc networks:A survey [J]. IEEE Vehicular Technology Magazine,2007,2(2):12-22.

[2] Althoff M,Stursberg O,Buss M. Model-Based Probabilistic Collision Detection in Autonomous Driving [J]. IEEE transactions on intelligent transportation systems,2009,10(2):299-310.

[3] Long J C,Gao Z Y,Zhao X M,et al. Urban Traffic Jam Simulation Based on the Cell Transmission Model [J]. Networks & Spatial Economics,2011,11(1):43-64.

[4] Gipps P G. A Model for the Structure Of Lane-Changing Decisions [J]. Transportation Research Part B-Methodological,1986,20(5):403-414.

[5] Yang Q,Koutsopoulos H N. A microscopic traffic simulator for evaluation of dynamic traffic management systems [J]. Transportation Research Part C-Emerging Technologies,1996,4(3):113-129.

[6] Hidas P. Modelling lane changing and merging in microscopic traffic simulation [J]. Transportation Research Part C-Emerging Technologies,2002,10(5-6):351-371.

[7] Wu J P,Brackstone M,McDonald M. Fuzzy sets and systems for a motorway microscopic simulation model

[J]. Fuzzy sets and systems,2000,116(1):65-76.
[8] Moridpour S,Sarvi M,Rose G,et al. Lane-Changing Decision Model for Heavy Vehicle Drivers[J]. Journal of Intelligent Transportation Systems,2012,16(1):24-35.
[9] Moridpour S,Sarvi M,Rose G. Lane changing models:a critical review[J]. Transportation Letters-the International Journal Of Transportation Research,2010,2(3):157-173.
[10] Alexiadis V,Colyar J,Halkias J,et al. The next generation simulation program[J]. Ite Journal-Institute Of Transportation Engineers,2004,74(8):22-26.
[11] Qi H S,Wang D H,Chen P,et al. Location-Dependent Lane-Changing Behavior for Arterial Road Traffic[J]. Networks & Spatial Economics,2014,14(1):67-89.

基于零膨胀模型的机动车-电动车事故频次研究

秦 丹 魏 雯 杜雨萌 董傲然 朱 彤
（长安大学运输工程学院）

摘 要 为了探究显著影响机动车-电动车碰撞事故频次的关键因素，本文以国内某市2005—2017年的交通事故数据为依据，从交通特征、道路情况、环境状况3个方面选取了12个自变量，利用零膨胀负二项回归(ZINB)模型研究不同自变量与机动车-电动车碰撞事故发生频次之间的关系，并通过弹性分析来确定显著自变量对事故发生频次的影响程度大小。研究表明：ZINB模型能够对机动车-电动车碰撞事故数据中零频次过多的现象进行良好解释，模型的拟合效果良好；早高峰时段、事故发生地点、护栏、潮湿路面、雨天、能见度为101~200m 6个变量是影响机动车-电动车碰撞事故是否发生的显著因素；事故发生日期、晚高峰时段、事故发生地点、秋季、交通信号控制、护栏、水泥路面、弯道、阴天、雨天、能见度为101~200m、夜间有路灯、夜间无路灯、黎明或黄昏等14个变量对机动车-电动车碰撞事故发生频次有着显著影响。研究结果可为交通管理部门制定相应的事故预防政策和道路交通安全保护措施提供理论依据。

关键词 交通安全 电动车事故频次预测 零膨胀负二项回归模型 电动自行车 弹性分析

0 引 言

据2018年世界卫生组织（WHO）发布的《全球道路交通安全现状报告》显示，2017年全世界约有135万人死于交通事故，另有5000万人因交通事故受伤或致残，道路交通伤害已成为全球人口死亡的重要原因之一。我国的交通安全状况也十分严峻，《中国统计年鉴2019》显示，2018年我国共发生244937起交通事故，造成63194人死亡，258532人受伤，其中电动自行车（以下简称电动车）等非机动车类型的交通事故死亡人数占事故死亡总人数的6.5%。电动车以其便捷、环保等特性受到广泛欢迎，通常被用于日常的上下班通勤，是城市居民短距离出行的首选交通方式之一。2013—2017年，我国电动车的社会保有量从1.8亿辆增加到2.5亿辆，平均每年增加9.7%。电动车驾驶员作为交通中的弱势道路使用者，近年来其在事故中的死亡（重伤）率逐年攀升。因此，为了提高电动车的道路安全，有必要对影响机动车-电动车碰撞事故的因素进行研究，并提出合理的机动车-电动车事故频次预测模型，以便采取相应措施来降低机动车-电动车碰撞事故的发生频率。

近年来，国外学者对电动车碰撞事故频次展开了研究并取得了一定的研究成果。Wang等利用随机参数负二项模型研究了不同类型的交叉路口对自行车撞车频次的影响，结果表明通常在分支更多的复杂

基金项目：国家重点研发计划（2019YFE0108000）。

交叉路口更容易发生自行车撞车事故。Wei等利用广义线性回归方法及负二项模型对加拿大地区的自行车碰撞数据进行研究,发现交叉口数量、交通信号数量、公交车站数量等与自行车碰撞频次呈正相关。Cai等利用零膨胀负二项回归模型和负二项回归模型进行对比研究,发现主干道的交通流量与自行车碰撞频次之间存在正相关关系,到城市的距离与自行车碰撞频次呈负相关,且零膨胀负二项回归模型具有更好的拟合效果。Thomas等对道路设计和交通特性与电动车碰撞频次之间的关系进行了建模,研究表明较窄的车道和肩宽宽度、较大的水平曲率度和较大垂直坡度会增加撞车的可能性。

国内学者对电动车碰撞事故频次也展开了相关研究。Chen等运用泊松对数正态随机效应模型研究了北京市的土地利用及道路设计因素与自行车-汽车碰撞事故之间的关系,结果表明自行车-汽车碰撞事故多发于人口密集、道路交叉口密集、停车场较多的发达地区。李莉等的研究发现电动车碰撞事故多发于交叉口处和车辆转弯时。由于缺乏可靠的数据,国内对机动车-电动车碰撞事故频次的研究较少,且很少有研究考虑交通事故数据的频次特征,即忽略了交通事故数据中零频次过多的问题。

交通事故频次数据为计数型的数据,主要采用统计模型进行研究,常用的回归模型为泊松回归、负二项回归、广义泊松回归等。但是,上述回归模型不能用于分析零观测值过多的事故数据,为此学者们提出了零膨胀泊松(ZIP)回归模型、零膨胀负二项(ZINB)回归模型等适用于数据中零观测值过多的情形的统计模型,能解释数据中零值过多的现象,同时使模型的估计结果更为有效和无偏,参数估计的结果也更加可靠。

为了研究影响电动车与机动车碰撞事故发生频次的潜在因素,本文采用泊松回归模型、负二项回归模型、零膨胀泊松及零膨胀负二项回归模型对机动车-电动车碰撞事故数据进行对比分析,从事故特征、道路情况以及环境状况3个方面选取12个自变量展开研究。根据模型的拟合优度检验结果选择最佳的分析模型,并结合弹性分析来分析各自变量对机动车-电动车碰撞事故发生频次的影响程度大小。研究结果可以为交通管理部门制定减少机动车与电动车事故发生频次、提高电动车驾驶员的道路交通安全水平奠定理论基础。

1 数据来源与变量选择

1.1 路段单元划分

路段单元划分是进行交通事故频次预测的前提条件和基础工作。通过路段单元划分,可以得到交通事故预测模型的基础样本数据,并提高模型的适用性和拟合效果。对于划分得到的特定路段单元,交通事故的影响因素之间具有相对的一致性,便于对这些影响因素进行统一描述和赋值。目前通用的路段单元划分方法主要有定长法和不定长法两种。

定长法是指以标准的路段长度作为划分单元。定长法不考虑道路交通事故的分布和其他相关因素的影响,具有操作简单、便于划分的优点,在难以获得有关影响因素的数据(例如曲率、坡度)的情况下通常被采用。

不定长法以路段的基本属性为依据,属性主要包括路段限速、道路几何线形指标、交通量,其中道路几何线形指标包括曲度、纵坡坡度、路肩宽度等。不定长法划分出的路段道路属性相同,便于处理和建模;但以单一的道路属性划分路段,无法考虑各种线形组合和相关因素对交通安全的影响。

本文的数据来源为国内某城市2005—2017年的交通事故数据。由于城市道路路况复杂,各道路的路段限速、道路几何线形指标、交通量均不相同,采用不定长法并不合理。加之数据的缺失,这些道路属性的数据也难以获得。因此本文将采用定长法进行路段划分,以100m作为固定长度,最终得到14229个定长路段用于研究。

1.2 自变量选取

道路交通系统由人、车、道路和环境等因素组成,选取自变量时需要综合各方面的影响。此外,事故特征包括事故发生时的日期、时段、地点及季节,这些因素都有可能对事故频率有着潜在影响。因此,本文从事故特征、道路情况、环境状况3个方面选取12个可能影响机动车-电动车碰撞事故频次的潜在自变量。各自变量的定义见表1。

自变量选取及赋值 表1

	名 称	符 号	变 量 赋 值
事故特征	事故发生日期	x_1	0——周内*,1——周末
	事故发生时段	x_2	1——平峰时段*,2——早高峰时段,3——晚高峰时段
	事故发生地点	x_3	0——普通路段*,1——交叉口
	事故发生季节	x_4	1——春*,2——夏,3——秋,4——冬
道路情况	交通信号控制	x_5	0——有*,1——无
	防护设施类型	x_6	1——无*,2——行道树,3——绿化带,4——护栏,5——其他
	路表情况	x_7	1——干燥*,2——潮湿,3——其他
	路面结构	x_8	1——沥青路面*,2——水泥路面,3——其他
	道路线型	x_9	1——平直*,2——弯道,3——坡道,4——其他
环境状况	天气情况	x_{10}	1——晴天*,2——阴天,3——雨天
	能见度	x_{11}	1——≤50m*,2——51~100m,3——101~200m,4——>200m
	照明条件	x_{12}	1——白天*,2——夜间有路灯,3——夜间无路灯,4——黎明或黄昏

注:"*"表示参照类别。

1.3 事故总体频次分布规律

按照机动车-电动车碰撞事故的发生频次对数据进行描述性统计,结果见表2与图1。

机动车-电动车碰撞事故频次分布 表2

事 故 频 次	样 本 数 量	频率(%)	累计频率(%)
0	13089	91.98	91.98
1	991	6.96	98.94
2	91	0.64	99.58
3	26	0.18	99.76
4	11	0.08	99.84
5	7	0.05	99.89
6	5	0.04	99.93
7	3	0.02	99.95
8	3	0.02	99.97
9	1	0.01	99.98
14	1	0.01	99.99
20	1	0.01	100.00
合计	14229	100.00	100.00

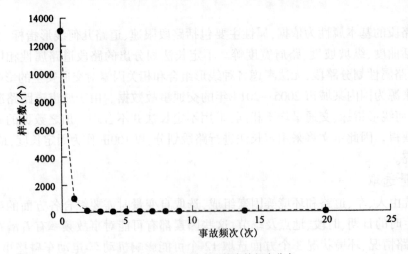

图1 机动车-电动车碰撞事故频次分布

由表 2 和图 1 可知,机动车-电动车碰撞事故频次为 0 的事故数有 13089 起,占比为 91.98%,而其他频次的数据之和约占 8%,由此可知机动车-电动车碰撞事故数据具有零膨胀的特点。

2 研究方法

2.1 泊松回归模型

若个体数量 y_i 为服从参数为 m_i 的泊松分布,则其概率分布函数为:

$$P(y_i \mid x_i) = (1 - \omega_i) \frac{e^{-\mu_i}\mu_i^{y_i}}{y_i!} \quad (y_i > 0) \tag{1}$$

泊松回归模型的条件均值等于条件方差,即:

$$E(y_i) = Var(y_i) = \mu_i \tag{2}$$

故泊松回归模型的应用需满足两个条件:①事件的发生相互独立;②等方差性。

2.2 负二项回归模型

当每起交通事故之间的差异不能由协变量完全解释时,可通过对泊松回归模型进行改进,得到负二项回归模型的概率分布函数:

$$p(y_i \mid x_i) = (1 - \omega_i) \frac{\Gamma(y_i + \alpha^{-1})}{y_i!\Gamma(\alpha^{-1})} \left(\frac{\alpha^{-1}}{\mu_i + \alpha^{-1}}\right)^{\alpha^{-1}} \left(\frac{\mu_i}{\mu_i + \alpha^{-1}}\right)^{\alpha^{-1}} \quad (y_i > 0) \tag{3}$$

式中:y_i——个体 i 的数量;
Γ——伽马分布;
ω——零膨胀参数;
α——散度参数;
μ——负二项分布的均值。

模型的期望和方差分别为:

$$E(y_i) = \mu_i \tag{4}$$

$$Var(y_i) = \mu_i[1 + \alpha\mu_i] \tag{5}$$

可以看出,该模型中的方差大于均值。因此,负二项回归模型能够解决个体协变量间未观察到的异质性造成的过度离散,是泊松回归模型的有效扩展。当 α 趋近于 0 时,其极限分布即为泊松回归模型。

2.3 零膨胀泊松回归模型

零膨胀泊松回归模型由一个离散零分布和泊松分布和组成,其概率分布函数为:

$$\begin{cases} P(y_i = 0) = \omega_i + (1 - \omega_i) \frac{e^{-\mu_i}\mu_i^{y_i}}{y_i!} \\ P(y_i \mid x_i) = (1 - \omega_i) \frac{e^{-\mu_i}\mu_i^{y_i}}{y_i!} \quad (y_i > 0) \end{cases} \tag{6}$$

式中:y_i——个体 i 的数量;
ω——零膨胀参数;
μ——泊松分布的均值。

ZINB 模型的期望和方差分别为:

$$E(y_i) = \mu_i(1 - \omega_i) \tag{7}$$

$$Var(y_i) = \mu_i(1-\omega_i)[1+\omega_i\mu_i] \tag{8}$$

由以下两式可知,由于过多零产生的过离散问题导致 ZIP 模型的方差大于期望,这体现了零膨胀数据的特征。通常 ZIP 模型选择 logit 函数作为连接函数,其表达式如下:

$$\text{logit} = \omega_i = \Lambda(v'_i\gamma) = \frac{\exp(v'_i\gamma)}{1+\exp(v'_i\gamma)} \tag{9}$$

$$\ln\left(\frac{\omega_i}{1-\omega_i}\right) = v'_i\gamma \tag{10}$$

式中:v'_i——$1 \times q$ 零膨胀自变量向量;
　　　γ——$q \times 1$ 参数向量。

2.4　零膨胀负二项回归模型

零膨胀模型是离散零分布和普通计数分布的混合,零膨胀负二项(zero-inflated negative binomial, ZINB)回归模型由一个离散零分布和负二项分布和组成,具体表达式为:

$$\begin{cases} p(y_i = 0) = \omega_i + (1-\omega_i)(1+\alpha\mu_i)^{-\alpha^{-1}} \\ p(y_i | x_i) = (1-\omega_i)\frac{\Gamma(y_i+\alpha^{-1})}{y_i!\Gamma(\alpha^{-1})}\left(\frac{\alpha^{-1}}{\mu_i+\alpha^{-1}}\right)^{\alpha^{-1}}\left(\frac{\mu_i}{\mu_i+\alpha^{-1}}\right)^{\alpha^{-1}} \quad (y_i > 0) \end{cases} \tag{11}$$

式中:y_i——个体 i 的数量;
　　　Γ——伽马分布;
　　　ω_i——零膨胀参数;
　　　α——散度参数;
　　　μ_i——负二项分布的均值。

ZINB 模型的期望和方差分别为:

$$E(y_i) = \mu_i(1-\omega_i) \tag{12}$$

$$Var(y_i) = \mu_i(1-\omega_i)[1+(\omega_i+\alpha)\mu_i] \tag{13}$$

ZINB 模型也选择 logit 函数作为连接函数,同 ZIP 模型一致,此处不再赘述。

2.5　模型检验

2.5.1　Vuong 检验

当两模型为非嵌套模型时,通常采用 Vuong 检验来选择最优模型。Vuong 的原假设为:

$$H_0: E(m_i) = 0 \tag{14}$$

其中 $m_i = \ln\left[\frac{p_1(y_i|x_i)}{p_2(y_i|x_i)}\right]$,$p_j(y_i|x_i)$ 为第 j 个模型($j=1,2$)中随机变量在 $Y=y_i$ 时模型的预测概率,则模型 1 相对于模型 2 的 Vuong 检验统计量为:

$$V = \frac{\sqrt{N}\overline{m}}{S_m} \tag{15}$$

式中:$\overline{m}$、S_m——m_i 的均值、标准差;
　　　N——总例数。

统计量 V 近似服从标准正态分布,若 $V \geq 1.96$,则认为模型 1 优于模型 2;若 $|V| \leq 1.96$,则模型 2 优于模型 1;若 $|V| \leq 1.96$,则不能表明模型的优劣。

2.5.2　拟合优度检验——AIC 和 BIC 准则

通常采用赤池信息准则(AIC)、贝叶斯信息准则(BIC)等指标来评价模型的拟合优度,各指标的计算方法如下:

$$AIC = -2\ln(L) + 2K \tag{16}$$

$$BIC = -2\ln(L) + \ln(N) \cdot K \tag{17}$$

式中：$\ln(L)$——对数似然函数的收敛值；

K——自由参数个数；

N——样本量。

指标 AIC 和 BIC 的值越小，模型的拟合效果越好。

2.6 弹性分析

利用弹性分析来研究各自变量对机动车-电动车事故发生频次的影响程度大小，表达式为：

$$E_{x_{ij}}^{\mu_i} = \frac{\partial \mu_i}{\partial x_{ij}} \cdot \frac{x_{ij}}{\mu_i} \tag{18}$$

式中：$E_{x_{ij}}^{\mu_i}$——第 i 种变量组合第 j 个自变量的弹性系数。

为了计算方便，对于离散型变量，第 j 个自变量的弹性系数可以近似为：

$$E_j = \frac{\exp(\beta_j) - 1}{\exp(\beta_j)} \tag{19}$$

式中：β_j——第 j 个自变量的回归系数。

弹性系数越大，自变量对因变量的影响程度越大。

3 结果与讨论

3.1 模型比较分析

本研究分别运用泊松(Poisson)回归模型、负二项(NB)回归模型、零膨胀泊松(ZIP)回归模型、零膨胀负二项(ZINB)回归模型对机动车-电动车事故发生频次数据进行分析，通过对比模型的拟合优度及检验结果来确定最佳的研究模型，对比结果见表3。

四种模型的拟合结果比较　　　表3

指标	Poisson	NB	ZIP	ZINB
AIC	9175.233	8695.919	8768.601	8665.542
BIC	9386.998	9115.247	9192.131	9096.636
$\ln(L)$	-4559.616	-4318.959	-4328.301	-4275.771
Vuong	—	—	4.93	4.85

由表4的结果可知，ZIP 和 ZINB 模型的 Vuong 检验值分别为 4.93 和 4.85，明显大于 1.96，且对应的 P 值均小于 0.001，由此可知零膨胀模型要明显优于泊松回归模型和负二项回归模型。此外，ZINB 模型的 AIC 及 BIC 的值在所研究的回归模型中均为最小，表明 ZINB 模型的拟合效果最好。

3.2 事故频次影响因素分析

根据上述模型对比分析的结果，本文将利用 ZINB 模型来探究影响机动车与电动车事故发生频次的因素，保留显著的自变量，模型的参数结果见表4。同时，通过计算显著变量的弹性系数值来定量分析各显著变量对事故发生频次的影响程度大小，弹性结果详见表5。

ZINB 模型的分析结果　　　表4

负二项回归部分				
变量	符号	系数	标准差	P 值
事故发生日期	x_1	-0.495	0.101	0.000
晚高峰时段	x_{2_3}	0.344	0.130	0.008
事故发生地点	x_3	0.525	0.134	0.000
秋季	x_{4_3}	-0.329	0.125	0.009

续上表

		负二项回归部分		
变量	符号	系数	标准差	P值
交通信号控制	x_5	0.467	0.109	0.000
护栏	x_{6_4}	-0.815	0.167	0.000
水泥路面	x_{8_2}	-0.610	0.180	0.001
弯道	x_{9_2}	-1.010	0.187	0.000
阴天	x_{10_2}	-0.793	0.143	0.000
雨天	x_{10_3}	1.207	0.253	0.000
能见度为101~200m	x_{11_3}	-0.366	0.160	0.023
夜间有路灯	x_{12_2}	-0.374	0.121	0.002
夜间无路灯	x_{12_3}	1.510	0.161	0.000
黎明或黄昏	x_{12_4}	1.214	0.226	0.000
常数	_cons	-0.821	0.241	0.001
		零膨胀部分		
变量	符号	系数	标准误差	P值
早高峰时段	x_{2_2}	-1.471	0.548	0.007
事故发生地点	x_3	-1.443	0.587	0.014
护栏	x_{6_4}	1.541	0.771	0.046
潮湿路面	x_{7_2}	-1.621	0.492	0.001
雨天	x_{10_3}	-2.228	0.801	0.005
能见度为101~200m	x_{11_3}	0.999	0.479	0.037
常数	_cons	1.312	0.472	0.006
Model goodness-of fit statistics				
Number of observations		14229		
Nonzero observations		1140		
Zero observations		13089		
Likelihood ratio (LR) chi-square		381.19		
Prob > chi-square		0.0000		
Log likelihood		-4275.771		

弹性分析结果　　表5

变量	符号	弹性系数(%)
事故发生日期	x_1	-4.4
晚高峰时段	x_{2_3}	2.2
事故发生地点	x_3	1.2
秋季	x_{4_3}	-1.4
交通信号控制	x_5	5.2
护栏	x_{6_4}	-3.8
水泥路面	x_{8_2}	-6.9
弯道	x_{9_2}	-7.0
阴天	x_{10_2}	-6.7
雨天	x_{10_3}	5.8

续上表

变　量	符　号	弹性系数(%)
能见度为101~200m	x_{11_3}	-0.8
夜间有路灯	x_{12_2}	-2.0
夜间无路灯	x_{12_3}	1.3
黎明或黄昏	x_{12_4}	10.9

由表5可知,事故特征、道路情况、环境状况均对机动车-电动车事故的发生有显著影响。由于零膨胀负二项回归模型由零膨胀部分和负二项分布部分组成,因此,接下来将分别从上述两方面来分析显著自变量对事故发生频率的影响情况。

(1)零膨胀部分。早高峰时段、事故发生地点、护栏、潮湿路面、雨天、能见度为101~200m 6个变量是影响机动车-电动车碰撞事故是否发生的重要因素。早高峰时段的回归系数为负且显著,表明相比于平峰时段,早高峰时段会减小"零事件"的发生,即会增加发生事故的风险,这主要是由于早高峰时段的车流量密集,交通流量大的地方更容易发生事故,发生事故的可能性更高。事故发生地点的回归系数为-1.443,由于在大多数交叉口,机动车右转时不受信号控制,因此,在交叉口处右转的机动车与电动车发生碰撞事故的可能性更大,有必要在交叉口处增设"机非"分隔设施,隔离电动车与机动车辆来减少事故的发生。护栏的回归系数为1.541,表明与没有路侧防护设施相比,当路侧有护栏时,会增加"零事件"的发生概率,即发生事故的风险较低,护栏可以有效隔离机动车道和非机动车道,故可显著降低二者发生碰撞事故的概率。潮湿路面的回归系数为-1.621,表明在潮湿路面上机动车与电动车发生碰撞事故的可能性较大,这可能是因为当路面潮湿时,车辆与路面之间的附着系数较低,车辆的制动距离较长,进而更容易发生事故。雨天的回归系数为-2.228,表明雨天机动车与电动车发生碰撞事故的风险较高,因为驾驶员的视野受雨天的干扰且雨天车辆与路面的附着系数较低,故雨天增加了事故的发生可能性。能见度为101~200m的回归系数为0.999,表明在该能见度条件下,发生碰撞事故的可能性较小。

(2)负二项回归部分。事故发生日期、晚高峰时段、事故发生地点、秋季、交通信号控制、护栏、水泥路面、弯道、阴天、雨天、能见度为101~200m、夜间有路灯、夜间无路灯、黎明或黄昏14个变量对机动车-电动车碰撞事故发生起数有显著影响。下面将结合负二项回归结果和弹性分析结果分析各因素对事故发生频次的影响情况。

3.2.1　事故特征

事故发生日期对电动车事故的发生频次有着显著影响,回归系数为-0.495,表明周末机动车与电动车发生碰撞事故的频次显著低于周一至周五,由弹性分析的结果可知,周末会使电动车事故频次降低4.4%,可能是因为周末居民的出行量较工作日小,周一至周五由于交通出行密集,车流量越大,则越容易发生碰撞事故。晚高峰时段显著且回归系数为0.344,相比于平峰时段,晚高峰时段车流量大,发生碰撞事故的风险较大,机动车与电动车事故频次增加了2.2%,这与Chiou等的研究结果一致。事故发生地点不仅影响机动车-电动车碰撞事故是否发生,还影响着事故发生的频次,其回归系数为0.525,表明与普通路段相比,在交叉口发生事故的频次更大,由于交叉口的车辆和人流密集,发生碰撞的风险也越高;弹性分析的结果表明可知,交叉口使机动车-电动车的发生频次增加了1.2%。季节对于电动车碰撞事故频次也有着显著影响,秋季的回归系数为-0.329,说明在秋季,电动车碰撞事故的发生频次更低,对应概率减小了1.4%。

3.2.2　道路情况

交通控制信号显著影响着机动车-电动车事故的发生频次,其回归系数为0.467,说明在没有交通控制信号的道路上电动车事故的发生频次更高。由表6可知,没有交通信号的道路会使事故频次增加5.2%,这可能是因为当道路上有交通控制信号,如信号灯、标志标线、交警时,驾驶员和电动车驾驶员更容易遵守交通规则,进而降低了机动车-电动车碰撞事故的发生频率。护栏的回归系数为-0.815,由弹性分析的结果可知，护栏将使电动车事故频次减少3.8%，同零膨胀部分的分析一致，护栏可以有效低隔离机动车和电动车，故可以减少事故发生的频次。因此可以通过安装明显的交通控制信号设施和护栏等措施来减少事故的发生。水泥路面显著且回归系数为负，与沥青路面相比，水泥路面导致电动车事故频次减少6.9%。弯道的回归系数为－1.010，根据表6，与平直路段相比，在弯道发生机动车-电动车碰撞事故频次减少7.0%，影响最大，可能是由于弯道处驾驶员较为谨慎，车速较低，因此事故发生的可能性也较低。

3.2.3 环境因素

阴天的回归系数为－0.793，表明在该天气条件下的机动车-电动车碰撞事故频次较低，对应的事故频次减少了6.7%。而雨天的回归系数为1.207，同零膨胀部分的分析一致，雨天使电动车碰撞事故发生频次增加了5.8%。能见度为101～200m的回归系数为－0.366，表明与能见度小于50m的环境相比，能见度为101～200m将减少机动车-电动车碰撞事故频次，弹性分析的结果表明，在该能见度条件下，电动车事故频次将减少0.8%，这可能是因为能见度越好，驾驶员的视线越开阔，发生事故时给驾驶员留有足够的反应时间，因此事故的发生频次也较低。当夜间有路灯时，机动车-电动车碰撞事故频次将减少2.0%。而在夜间无路灯以及黎明或黄昏的环境条件下时，回归系数分别为1.510和1.214，表明上述环境条件会使机动车-电动车碰撞事故频次显著增加，其对应的事故频次将增加1.3%和10.9%。这主要是由于在夜间无灯光、黎明和黄昏的环境下光线昏暗，车辆与周围环境的对比度较小，驾驶员视野较差，因此电动车碰撞事故的发生频次更高，有必要采取相关措施（如安装路灯等）改善夜间的照明条件。

4 结 语

基于国内某城市2005—2017年的交通事故数据，本文以发生在机动车和电动自行车之间的交通事故为研究对象，从事故特征、道路情况、环境因素3个方面选取了12个自变量，构建了零膨胀负二项回归模型来研究不同自变量与机动车-电动车碰撞事故频次之间的关系，并通过弹性分析来确定显著变量对电动车事故频次的影响大小。本文的主要结论如下：

（1）零膨胀负二项回归模型和零膨胀泊松回归模型相比于泊松回归模型及负二项回归模型，能更好地处理零值过多的数据，且零膨胀负二项回归模型比零膨胀泊松回归模型的拟合优度更好。

（2）零膨胀负二项回归模型的结果表明：早高峰时段、事故发生地点、护栏、潮湿路面、雨天、能见度为101～200m 6个变量是机动车-电动车事故是否发生的影响因素。而事故发生日期、晚高峰时段、事故发生地点、秋季、交通信号控制、护栏、水泥路面、弯道、阴天、雨天、能见度为101～200m、夜间有路灯、夜间无路灯、黎明或黄昏14个变量对机动车-电动车碰撞事故频次有着显著影响。

（3）电动自行车与机动车发生碰撞事故时，电动车驾驶员作为弱势道路使用者其在事故中更容易遭受重伤或死亡，因此有必要采取措施减少此类事故的发生。根据本文的研究结果，提出以下改进措施。首先，由于交叉口处的事故发生频率较高，为此应在交叉口处增设"机非"分隔设施，隔离电动车与机动车辆。其次，道路情况和环境因素对电动车事故的频次有着显著影响，有必要改善交通基础设施，如安装明显的交通控制信号设施、安装护栏以及改善夜间照明条件等。

（4）机动车-电动车碰撞事故的发生及其频次大小除了与交通事故特征、道路情况、环境因素有关，还受到驾驶员属性的影响，后续可从该方面继续深入研究。

参考文献

[1] World Health Organization. Global status report on road safety 2018[R]. World Health Organization,2018.

[2] 国家统计局. 中国统计年鉴[M]. 北京：中国统计出版社，2019.

[3] Quan Yuan, Haiquan Yang, Jing Huang, et al. What factors impact injury severity of vehicle to electric bike crashes in China？[J]. Advances in Mechanical Engineering,2017,9(8):49-56.

[4] Linjun L, Chen W, Tao W. Improving E-Bike Safety on Urban Highways in China[J]. Discrete Dynamics in Nature and Society,2015:1-8.

[5] Jie Wang, Helai Huang, Qiang Zeng. The effect of zonal factors in estimating crash risks by transportation modes: Motor vehicle, bicycle and pedestrian[J]. Accident Analysis and Prevention, 2017(98):223-231.

[6] Wei F, Lovegrove G. An empirical tool to evaluate the safety of cyclists: Community based, macro-level collision prediction models using negative binomial regression[J]. Accident Analysis and Prevention, 2013,61(dec.):129-137.

[7] Cai Q, Lee J, Eluru N, et al. Macro-level pedestrian and bicycle crash analysis: Incorporating spatial spillover effects in dual state count models[J]. Accident Analysis and Prevention, 2016, 93 (Aug.): 14-22.

[8] Flask T, Schneider W H, Lord D. A segment level analysis of multi-vehicle motorcycle crashes in Ohio using Bayesian multi-level mixed effects models[J]. Safety ence, 2014, (66)47-53.

[9] Peng Chen, Feiyang Sun, Zhenbo Wang, et al. Built environment effects on bike crash frequency and risk in Beijing[J]. Journal of safety research, 2018, (64):135-143.

[10] 李莉,杨济匡,Otte Dietmar. 长沙地区电动自行车碰撞事故研究[C]. Infats International Forum of Automotive Traffic Safety.

[11] Ezra Hauer, Jake Kononov, Bryan Allery, et al. Screening the Road Network for Sites with Promise[C]. Transportation Research Record, 2002, 1784(1):27-32.

[12] Bo Yu, Yuren Chen, Ruiyun Wang, et al. Safety reliability evaluation when vehicles turn right from urban major roads onto minor ones based on driver's visual perception[J]. Accident Analysis & Prevention 2016, (95):487-494.

[13] Zhang H, Li S, Wu C, et al. Predicting Crash Frequency for Urban Expressway considering Collision Types Using Real-Time Traffic Data[J]. Journal of advanced transportation, 2020(9):1-8.

[14] Chiou Y C, Sheng Y C, Fu C. Freeway crash frequency modeling under time-of-day distribution[J]. Transportation Research Procedia, 2017, (25):664-676.

[15] Anarkooli A J, Hosseinpour M, Kardar A. Investigation of factors affecting the injury severity of single-vehicle rollover crashes: A random-effects generalized ordered probit model[J]. Accident; analysis and prevention, 2017, 106(sep.):399-410.

Trajectory-data-based Velocity Prediction of Vehicles Across Intersection

Xu Liu[1] Zeyu Shi[1] Yangzhou Chen[2]

(1. College of Metropolitan Transportation, Beijing University of Technology Beijing Key Laboratory of Transportation Engineering;

2. College of Artificial Intelligence and Automation, Beijing University of Technology Beijing Key Laboratory of Transportation Engineering)

Abstract The velocity of vehicles across a intersection can reflect the traffic state at the intersection. The accurate velocity predictions are of great significance to drivers' path planning. In order to acquire the forecasted velocity across intersection, this paper proposes a prediction method of velocity across intersection, based on trajectory data. The method firstly divides the intersection area according to the basic assumption from the Cell Transmission Model (CTM). Then to extract the trajectory route of the vehicle across intersection, the collected video data is processed. The processed trajectory data from video is combined with GPS data to form trajectory data set. Finally the neural network is used to predict the velocity of the vehicle across the intersection. In order to verify the good generalization of the results, the actual data are used to verify the prediction model. The results show that the prediction error of the algorithm is about 12%. Such results illustrate the algorithm has good generalization and adaptability.

Keywords Intelligent transportation system　Traffic data processing　Trajectory data　Neural network　Velocity prediction

0　Introduction

The increasing traffic congestion shows that the velocity of road construction has been unable to meet the growth rate of traffic demand. The development of intelligent transportation system(ITS) brings us new ideas to solve congestion. The advanced traveler information system(ATIS), as a subsystem of ITS, needs to obtain the future traffic status. The velocity of vehicles, as the core element of the traffic state, has gradually become the focus of the current traffic forecast. Scholars at home and abroad have also carried out a series of studies on this issue, and made some progress. At present, these forecasting methods can be divided into two categories: theoretical model-based forecasting methods and data-based forecasting methods.

In the method of traffic prediction based on theoretical model(Papageorgiou. 1990), proposed METANET model based on Automatic Control theory and the model can make a good forecast of traffic flow(Daganzo. 1994) proposed CTM model and the model is widely used. The model divides the road into cells and assumes that the flow of each cell is related to the flow of the cells before and after it. The model uses cell flow relationship to predict traffic flow The prediction method based on theoretical model has good explanatory ability but the prediction accuracy is poor.

In the method of traffic prediction based on data drive (Cetin and Comer. 1965) used ARIMA (Autoregressive Integrated Moving Average) model based on statistical theory to predict traffic velocity and found that ARIMA model was able to forecast traffic velocity with stable changes better. Due to the randomness and non-linearity of traffic velocity, researchers also used Kalman filter method to predict traffic flow(Ojeda and Kibangou. 2013, Yuhan. 2016) uses Deep Belief Network (DBN) to predict traffic velocity in short time, (Cui and Ke. 2017) use Bi-directional LSTM (Bi-directional LSTM) to predict traffic velocity in a wide range of expressways. (Yu and Wu. 2017)converted the road network velocity distribution map into time-series grayscale image, and combined with CNN and LSTM model to make velocity prediction. The method of vehicle velocity prediction based on data drive is poor in interpretation and lack of theoretical basis and the methods are mostly used for the vehicle velocity prediction of expressways and urban expressways without considering the situation of urban intersections, which have a great influence on the traffic state of the road network.

This paper presents a method to predict thevelocity of vehicles across the intersection based on trajectory data. According to the basic assumptions of the Cell Transmission Model (CTM), this method processes the video data and obtains the trajectory training data set used to construct the model. A prediction model based on Back Propagation Neural Network (BPNN)was established by using the training set. BPNN was chosen because of its excellent nonlinear mapping ability, self-learning and self-adaptation ability, and low time complexity. Finally, the test validation set is used to validate the model. The results show that the model has good accuracy and generalization.

1　Models and Methods

This section describes the model and methodology.

1.1 Intersection cell division

The basic assumptions of the model are derived from the basic assumptions of CTM model. According to the basic assumptions, the intersection area is divided into the entry cell, the exit cell and the inner cell. According to the basic assumptions and basic laws of the intersection, the input vector and the output vector of the model are determined.

The model has the following basic assumptions:

(1) Cell as the basic unit of traffic dispersion

(2) Cellular length is subject to Courent-Friedrich-Lewy's (CFL) condition.

(3) The traffic flow through the cell follows the FIFO principle.

(4) Vehicle velocity and traffic density were taken as model variables.

(5) The traffic density within the cell is equal.

(6) It conforms to the relationship between traffic flow and density. The basic schematic diagram is shown in the fig. 1.

According to the basic hypothesis, the intersection area is divided into four entry cells, four exit cells and one inner cell. The length range of the entry cell should meet:

$$\max_{s}\{v_f(j)\}\Delta t \leqslant \Delta l_i \leqslant \Delta L_i \qquad j \in s \tag{1}$$

In the formula, s represents a group of vehicles entering the entry cell; ΔL_i represents the maximum queue length of the entry cell; Δt represents the sampling period; $v_f(j)$ represents the free flow velocity of vehicles.

The length range of exit cell should meet:

$$\max_{r}\{v_f(j)\}\Delta t \leqslant \Delta l_o \leqslant \Delta L_o \qquad j \in r \tag{2}$$

In the formula, r represents the collection of vehicles entering the exit cell o; ΔL_o is the distance between the intersection and the adjacent intersection in the same direction.

The area of each cell is shown in the fig. 2.

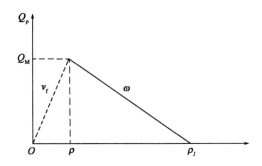
Fig. 1 Basic triangular diagram

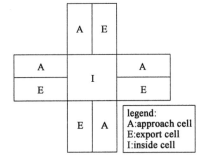
Fig. 2 Schematic diagram of cell division

By combining the basic hypothesis with the state of the signal lamp. We can express the input vector about the entry cell as: $[v_i(k), \rho_{i+}(k), \rho_{i-}(i), R_\alpha, R_\beta, R_\chi, R_\delta, \lambda]^T$. In the formula, $v_i(k)$ represents the velocity of entering the cell i at k time; $\rho_{i+}(k)$ represents the density of a cell on a cell at k time; $\rho_{i-}(i)$ represents the density of the cell next to the cell at the k time; $R_\alpha, R_\beta, R_\chi, R_\delta$ Represents the maximum absorptive capacity of the downstream cell respectively; λ is the state variable of the signal lamp. the green light turns on When $\lambda = 1$; the red light turns on when $\lambda = 0$; when the intersection is without sign $\lambda = 1$.

1.2 Video data processing

The video data in this paper comes from High Point Camera, which is mainly collected at the intersection of Xi'an (Fig. 3). Directly collected video data can be converted into traffic data through two steps: vehicle trajectory extraction and traffic densitycollection. Traffic data is used as input to train the model in the training set of video. The collected traffic data is used for verification in the video verification set.

Fig. 3   Vehicle detection

(1) Vehicle trajectory extraction.

Vehicle trajectory extraction refers to the extraction of routes passed by vehicles at different positions in different times. Vehicle trajectory extraction has two steps:

①Vehicle is recognized and tracked;②Extract the pixel coordinates of the center of mass of the vehicle.

The algorithm of vehicle position acquisition includes four parts: vehicle detection, fusion segmentation, vehicle tracking and position output. In the algorithm of vehicle position acquisition, the background difference method andbinarization processing are firstly adopted, and the vehicle is separated from the background by morphological operation "open". Then the vehicle is separated by the method of fusion segmentation and vehicle tracking, and then the pixel coordinates of the vehicle can be obtained. The flow of the whole algorithm is shown in the fig. 4.

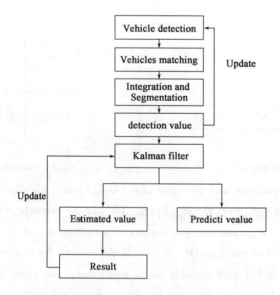

Fig. 4   Algorithm flow chart

In this algorithm, the prior information of Kalman filter is used to obtain the vehicle position. Kalman filter has the advantage of fast operationvelocity. The state update equation of Kalman filter is described as:

$$X(t) = A(t)X(t-1) + B(t)U(t) + \omega(t) \tag{3}$$

In the formula, $X(t)$ is the position vector estimated for the vehicle at the t time; $U(t)$ is the velocity vector of the object at t time; $A(t)$ and $B(t)$ are the estimated parameters at t time; $\omega(t)$ is the noise vector estimated at t time.

The observation equation of Kalman filter is:

$$Y(t) = D(t)X(t) + \nu(t) \quad (4)$$

In the formula, $Y(t)$ is the position vector observed by the vehicle at the t time; $D(t)$ is the parameter vector observed at the t time; $\nu(t)$ is the noise vector observed at t time.

The prior information provided by Kalman filter is used as the reference for fusion and se-gmentation. Fusion occurs when the two vehicle centers approximate a predicted value, that is, the midpoint of the two centers of mass is output as the observed value; When the center of mass of t-he vehicle approaches two predicted values, the segmentation is carried out, and the two predicted values are taken as the observed values of the vehicle. Kalman filter state update is the process of updating Kalman filter parameters according to the errors between Kalman filter observations. The result of this algorithm is essentially an estimate of Kalman filter.

(2) Vehiclevelocity acquisition。

The video data contains a lot of traffic information, but there is novelocity information directly corresponding to the vehicle. The velocity can be solved based on the trajectory information of the vehicle. The basic principle is to extract the trajectory of the vehicle in a certain period of time, so as to calculate the velocity of the vehicle (Fig. 5). The basic process is as follows:

Fig. 5 Trajectory diagram

①Input the video data, use the vehicle detection algorithm mentioned above to obtain the image of the target vehicle in a frame of image, and obtain the coordinates of the midpoint of the vehicle's center of massA_1 (x_1, y_1) in the image coordinate system.

②The vehicle tracking method is adopted to match and track the detected target vehicle, and the position information of the target vehicle near the intersection after a certain time interval and the coordinate$A_2(x_2, y_2)$ of it's centroid midpoint in the image coordinate system are obtained.

③According to the coordinates of the target vehicle in the obtained two frames of images, the coordinate system is used to solve, and the two coordinates $A_1(x_1, y_1)$, $A_2(x_2, y_2)$ of the target vehicle in the actual road plane are obtained, and then the actual displacement of the vehicle is solved according to the displacement formula:

$$\Delta d = |A_1(x_1, y_1) - A_2(x_2, y_2)| = \sqrt{(x_1 - x_2)^2 + (y_1 - y_2)^2} \quad (5)$$

④The running time of the vehicle can be easily known according to the set time interval, and the actual runningvelocity of the vehicle can be calculated according to the velocity-displacement formula:

$$v = \frac{\Delta d}{\Delta t} \tag{6}$$

In the formula, Δd is the distance traveled by the vehicle; Δt is the time taken for the vehicle to travel this distance.

(3) Traffic density data collection。

The calculation method for obtaining traffic density data is as follows:

$$\rho_\theta(k) = \frac{n_\theta(k)}{m_\theta \Delta l_\theta} \tag{7}$$

In the formula, $\rho_\theta(k)$ represents the density of cell θ at the moment k; $n_\theta(k)$ represents the number of vehicles of cell θ at the moment k; m_θ represents the number of vehicles of cell θ; Δl_θ represents the length of cell.

By setting up virtual detection area in the image, the cumulative traffic volume in a cycle is collected. In the collection process, in order to avoid repeated counting of vehicles, the vehicle tracks of two adjacent images should be compared. When the position of the vehicle changes, the vehicle is considered to have passed through the monitoring area; otherwise, the vehicle is still in the stop state. After the identification is completed, the number of vehicles passing the detection section within a period is calculated as the cumulative traffic volume of the period.

1.3 Intersection velocity prediction

Neural network model has been widely used in the field of traffic parameter prediction, and the black box model of neural network is more suitable for the change of traffic parameters under complex traffic conditions, and can achieve more accurate results of prediction. The principle and model of BP neural network are as follows:

BP neural network is composed of input layer, hidden layer and output layer. Its operation process includes two stages: the first stage is the forward propagation of signals, from the input layer through the hidden layer and finally to the output layer; The second stage is the back propagation of error, from the output layer to the hidden layer, and finally to the input layer, adjust the weight and bias of the hidden layer to the output layer, and the weight and bias of the input layer to the hidden layer. An important feature of BP neural network is the back propagation of error. BP neural network adopts the design of multi-layer perceptron to solve the problem of linear inseparability which cannot be solved well by single layer perceptron. The formula of forward transmission process of BP neural network is as follows:

$$y_j = f(\sum_{i=1}^{m} w_{ij} x_i + b_j) \tag{8}$$

In the formula, y_j represents the output value of the node; w_{ij} represents the weight between the node i and j; b_j represents the threshold value of the node j; f is the activation function.

The formula of reverse transfer process of error is:

$$E_k = \frac{1}{2} \sum_{j=1}^{m} (y_j^{k'} - y_j^k)^2 \tag{9}$$

In the formula, E_k represents the error between the output value and the real value; $y_j^{k'}$ is the output value of the neural network training; y_j^k is the real value of the training set.

The error of BP neural network reduces the error between the actual output and the expected output by continuously adjusting the weight and threshold of the network along the fastest decreasing direction of the sum of squares of relative errors.

The calibrated traffic data set is composed of a training set and a verification set. An important role of BP neural network is to predict, so build the neural network velocity model. The function of this model is to predict the velocity of vehicles after passing the intersection.

The mapping relationship between input and output of neural network is:
$$v_i(k+1) = f(v_i(k), \rho_{i+}(k), \rho_{i-}(i), R_\alpha, R_\beta, R_\chi, R_\delta, \lambda) \tag{10}$$
In the formula, $v_i(k+1)$ is the velocity at which the vehicle pass the cell at the intersection at the moment $k+1$; $v_i(k)$ is the velocity at which the vehicle enter the intersection at the current moment; $\rho_{i+}(k)$ represents the density of a cell on a cell at k time. $\rho_{i-}(i)$ represents the density of the cell next to the cell at the k time; $R_\alpha, R_\beta, R_\chi, R_\delta$ Represents the maximum absorptive capacity of the downstream cell respectively; λ is the state variable of the signal lamp. When $\lambda = 1$, the green light turns on; when $\lambda = 0$, the red light turns on; when the intersection is without sign, then, $\lambda = 1$.

The network structure of the constructed BP neural network is shown in the Fig. 6: the network contains an input layer, an output layer and two hidden layers. The number of neurons in the input layer is 8, the number of neurons in the hidden layer is 100, and the number of neurons in the output layer is 1.

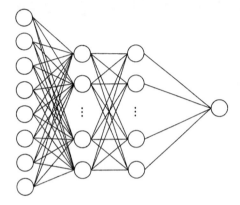

Fig. 6 Schematic diagram of neural network model

In the neural network structure, Sigmoid function is used as the activation function for neurons in the hiddenlayer. ReLU function is used as the activation function for neurons in the output layer. Mean Square Error (MSE) is used as the loss function. and adaptive learning rate algorithm is used for learning. Where, the expressions of Sigmoid function and RELU function are:

The sigmoid function:
$$S(x) = \frac{1}{1 + e^{-x}} \tag{11}$$

RELU function:
$$RELU(x) = \max(0, x) \tag{12}$$
These two functions are nonlinear functions, which can better fit the relationship between the data.

2 Experimental Results and Analytical Verification

In order to validate the presented method based on video trajectory prediction intersectionvelocity, the effect of study selected Jin Ye road and Zhang Ba Qi road intersection of video data, the intersection of two-way six lanes and four lanes signal intersection, according to the above the cell transmission model (CTM) of the intersection area is divided into nine yuan cell, the intersection of the video data for five consecutive days high video data, video data of time for the morning at 9 to 11 in the morning, this time is the flat peak stage on the road, traffic and velocity in a relatively stable state. The signal cycle of a road intersection is 87 seconds, in which the east-west green light time is 57 seconds and the north-south green light time is 30 seconds (Fig. 7).

In this experiment, 5min is taken as a prediction period to predict the velocity of vehicles passing the intersection after 5min. In the experiment, the trajectories of vehicles are divided into straight going, left turning and right turning. All trajectories of vehicles turning right and those going straight and left turning are taken within the green light period.

Fig. 7　Cell division diagram

The collected sample data are divided into training set and verification set, among which there are 100 training data and 50 verification data samples. With training set first samples for training the BP neural network, with validation after each training sample into its error and, if the output layer is not expected output, then turn to back propagation, according to the prediction error adjust the network weights and threshold, falling until when the training error and the validation error is increased, and generate network termination training.

By comparing and verifying the predicted value predicted by the model with the real value are shown in Fig. 8.

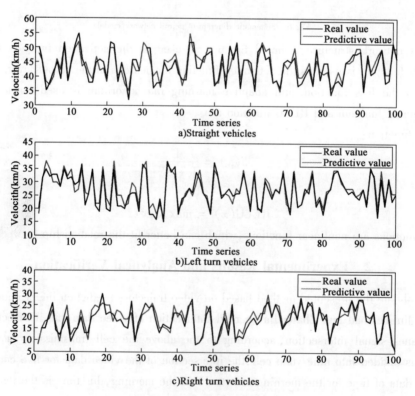

Fig. 8　Data validation results

By figure can be seen, the first figure is the averagevelocity of vehicles go straight through the intersection of forecast, through the intersection of the vehicle velocity faster, vehicle velocity and the real and estimated values of the change trend and the change law is consistent, smaller error between the predicted values and real values, this is because the green case straight vehicles affected by other directions of traffic is small, after calculation, the maximum error is 15.69%, the average error is 10.75%; The second picture is on the average velocity of vehicles left by intersection, the intersection when the vehicle is relatively stable, the velocity of the vehicle velocity and the real and estimated values of the change trend and the change law is consistent, smaller error between the predicted values and real values, this is because in the case of green left vehicles affected by other directions of traffic is small, after calculation, the maximum error is 19.05%, the average error is 12.26%; The third picture is on the average velocity of vehicle right through the intersection of the forecast, through the intersection of the vehicle velocity slower, vehicle velocity and the real and estimated values of the change trend and the change rule is the same, but the error between predictive value and true value is bigger, this is because the right turn vehicles are under the influence of the traffic, the traffic situation was complex, after calculation, the maximum error is 27.78%, the average error of 15.76%.

In general, the error between the predicted value and the real value obtained by the model is small, and the predicted result is relatively accurate. Compared with the predicted value driven by the traditional pure data model, the accuracy is not only improved, but also supported by the traffic flow theory, making the result more persuasive.

3 Conclusion

This paper presents a method to predict the velocity of the vehicles across the intersection based on trajectory data. For modeling, the traffic characteristics and the data-driven technology are combined in this paper. The results show that the model has high precision and strong generalization, and is suitable for short-term prediction.

Future work is to carry out research on data fusion to further improve the accuracy and robustness of prediction. At the same time, the future work will study how to predict the traffic state by predicting the velocity and provide a more reasonable path for drivers according to the traffic state of the road.

4 Acknowledgements

Deep appreciation and respect for the anonymous reviewers for their careful reading the manuscript, comments and suggestions. Deep appreciation and respect for the support by National Natural Science Foundation of China (61573030) and National Key R&D Program of China (2017YFC0803906, 2017YFC0803900).

References

[1] CaoJie, Shen Juner, Zhang Hong. Optimized BP Neural Network Short-term Traffic Flow Prediction Method [J]. Sensors and Microsystems. 2020,339(05):64-66,70.

[2] Cetin M, Comert G. Short-Term Traffic Flow Prediction with Regime Switching Models[J]. Transportation Research Record Journal of the Transportation Research Board,2006,1965(1):23-31.

[3] Cui Ke, Y Wang. Deep stacked bidirectional and unidirectional LSTM recurrent neural network for network-wide traffic speed prediction [C]. Processings of the 6th International Workshop on Urban Computing,2017.

[4] Daganzo C F. The cell transmission model: A dynamic representation of highway traffic consistent with the hydrodynamic theory[J]. Transportation Research Part B:Methodological,1994,28(4):269-287.

[5] Daganzo C F. The cell transmission model, part II: Network traffic [J]. Transportation Research Part B Methodological,2008,29(2):79-93.

[6] Daganzo, Laval Carlos F. Lane-changing in traffic streams. Transportation Research Part B:Methodological 2006.

[7] Glasl H. Schreiber D., Viertl N. Video based Traffic Congestion Prediction on an Embedded System[C]// International IEEE Conference on Intelligent Transportation Systems. IEEE,2008.

[8] Jenelius E., Koutsopoulos H N. Travel time estimation for urban road networks using low frequency probe vehicle data[J]. Transportation Research Part B Methodological,2013,53(jul.):64-81.

[9] Jia Y, Wu J, Du Y. Traffic speed prediction using deep learning method[C]. 2016 IEEE 19th International Conference on Intelligent Transportation Systems (ITSC). IEEE,2016.

[10] Lighthill M J., Whitham G B. On kinetic waves, II. A theory of traffic flow on long crowded roads. Proc Royal Society A 1955.

[11] Lo H K. Szeto W Y. A cell-based dynamic traffic assignment model: Formulation and properties[J]. Mathematical & Computer Modelling,2002,35(7-8):849-865.

[12] Ojeda LL, Kibangou A Y, Wit C C D. Adaptive Kalman Filtering for Multi-Step ahead Traffic Flow Prediction[C]. American Control Conference (ACC),IEEE,2013.

[13] Papageorgiou M. BlossevilleJM., Hadj-SalemH. Modellingandreal-timecontroloftraffic flow on PartA: General,1990,24(5):345-359.

[14] Porfyri K N. Delis A I. Nikolos I K. Calibration and validation of a macroscopic multi-lane traffic flow model using a differential evolution algorithm[C]. Annual Meeting of the Transportation Research Board (TRB). 2017.

[15] Qi Dehu, Kang Jichang. Design of BP Neural Network [J]. Computer Engineering and Design,1998(02):48-50.

[16] Richards P I. Shock Waves on the Highway[J]. Operations Research,1956,4(1):42-51.

[17] Sun X. Munoz L., Horowitz R. Highway traffic state estimation using improved mixture Kalman filters for effective ramp metering control[C]. Decision and Control,2003. Proceedings. 42nd IEEE Conference on. IEEE,2004.

[18] Yu B. Yin H., Zhu Z. Spatio-Temporal Graph Convolutional Networks: A Deep Learning Framework for Traffic Forecasting[J]. 2017.

[19] Yu H, Wu Z, Wang S, et al. Spatiotemporal RecurrentConvolutionalNetworks for Traffic Prediction in Transportation Networks[J]. Sensors,2017,17(7):1501.

[20] Zhao Xiajun. Timing Analysis of Urban Road Traffic Congestion Based on GPS Trajectory Data [J]. Hunan Communications Science and Technology,2018(3):210-215.

基于神经网络的交叉口通行时间预测

袁新利[1]　师泽宇[1]　陈阳舟[2]

(1.北京工业大学城市建设学部;2.北京工业大学信息学部)

摘　要　本文提出了一种基于GPS数据神经网络模型来预测车辆通过交叉口时间的方法,并应用了反向传播神经网络(BPNN)。BPNN的训练集由GPS数据组成。为了验证该预测方法的泛化能力,使用了新的实际数据构建数据集作为验证集,试验结果表明该方法具有较高的预测准确率和良好的泛化性能。

关键词　智能交通系统　通行时间预测　神经网络　出行策略

0　引　言

交叉口作为城市交通网络的重要组成部分,连接了多条道路,交叉口的通行时间影响了整个网络的通行效率,因此研究交叉口通行时间预测具有重要的意义。

目前关于通行时间预测的研究多数属于历史数据驱动模型,其中,Brennan 等[1]提取车辆轨迹行驶时间数据,通过对基本变量和噪声的线性计算得到实际的旅行时间。Wang 等[2]对快速路通行时间进行预测,精度虽高,但不适用于城市道路。Yu 等[3]提出了一种基于时空卷积神经网络的交通预测深度学习框架,但不利于大规模的交通网络。Shi 等[4]利用神经网络预测交通密度,但不能直观反映出车辆通行时间。Ma 等[5,6,7]基于 CNN 的交通预测模型通过将交通数据转换成图像,提取交通特征,进行交通预测,但没有反映历史数据和预测信息间的依赖关系。Zang 等[8]以城市典型路段为研究对象,基于车牌识别的路段行程时间的预测,并用卡尔曼滤波算法提高了预测的收敛速度与精度,但是泛化能力比较低。少数预测模型加入了空间信息,如 Liu 等[9]使用卷积神经网络,在原有的时序模型中加入了空间信息。Wu 等[10]使用长短时记忆网络模型,并利用空间特性进行预测。但是存在冗余信息导致预测效率低下。

本文提出一种基于 GPS 数据的车辆通过交叉口时间预测方法,并基于 BPNN 进行数据集的训练,利用测试验证集来验证模型。结果表明,该模型具有较好的准确性和泛化性。

1　GPS 数据结构及处理

GPS 数据具有较高的时间精度和空间精度,能够更加准确的测量汽车的活动空间,因此我们选择 GPS 数据来构建训练集与验证集。

1.1　GPS 数据结构

GPS 数据的每一条都记录了一辆车的时空信息。GPS 数据部分示意样本图如图 1 所示。

	A	B	C	D	E	F	G	H
1	REC_CARID	REC_TIME	REC_LONGITUDE	REC_LATITUDE	REC_SPEED	REC_DIRECTION	REC_CARSTATUS	DBTIME
2	AT0212	2016/9/9 0:00	117.189263	31.845477	64	176	4	0
3	A84305	2016/9/9 0:00	117.183292	31.844513	40	160	3	0
4	A81924	2016/9/9 0:00	117.210063	31.843022	0	262	3	0
5	AT1495	2016/9/9 0:00	117.193062	31.842065	16	90	3	0
6	AT2579	2016/9/9 0:00	117.193975	31.845837	0	118	3	0
7	A81021	2016/9/9 0:00	117.198067	31.837735	20	190	4	0
8	A81021	2016/9/9 0:00	117.198067	31.837735	20	190	4	0
9	AT1582	2016/9/9 0:00	117.207517	31.837163	0	174	3	0
10	A84881	2016/9/9 0:00	117.202492	31.842465	53	268	4	0

图 1　GPS 数据部分样本图

1.2　GPS 数据处理

车辆在运行过程会有很多因素导致产生数据偏差。因此,为了排除数据本身给通行时间预测带来的误差,需要对数据进行处理。

1.2.1　研究交叉口选择

将 GPS 数据与街道地图的底图添加到 ArcGIS 软件中,进行数据与路网的匹配,如图 2 所示。为了保证研究路口的便捷性,选取蓝色框内的交叉口作为研究对象。

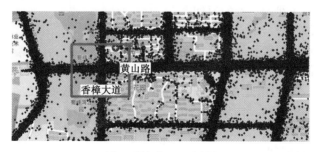

图 2　研究交叉口示意图

基金项目:国家重点研发计划项目(2017YFC0803906,2017YFC0803900);国家自然科学基金项目(61573030);北京市交通工程重点实验室开发课题。

1.2.2 浮动车GPS数据筛选处理

所选区域数据采集量约130万条。根据后续的研究,需要对数据进行筛选,筛选过程包括以下几个部分:

（1）为了减少数据干扰,需要将矩形框外的数据去除。先确定矩形框的经度和纬度,再把数据保存在csv文件中,使用条件函数筛选出矩形框中的数据。

（2）针对部分数据点在道路边缘外侧的问题,先将道路边缘向外扩展1m,确定新边缘的经纬度范围;再将新范围区和数据加到ArcGIS中,筛选出研究范围内的数据,如图3所示。

（3）根据研究,先根据车辆的编号筛选出每辆车的整个行程数据点,再确定交叉口进出口道停车线的经纬度,筛选出每一辆车经过进出口道停车线的数据。

图3 交叉口数据散点图

1.2.3 浮动车GPS数据插值处理

由于浮动车GPS数据是有时间间隔的点数据,存在一部分车辆在交叉口进出口道停车线处没有数据点,需要进行插值处理。先需要筛选出每辆车的数据形成轨迹数据,再依据时间在交叉口进口前后各取一个距交叉口进口道停车线最近的GPS定位数据。

把车辆在交叉口的运动看成匀加减速运动,依据运动学规律可以得出车辆在进出口停车线处的速度和时间,具体过程如下:

$$a = \frac{v_2 - v_1}{t_2 - t_1} \tag{1}$$

$$\begin{cases} s_1 = v_1(t_{in} - t_1) + \frac{1}{2}a(t_{in} - t_1)^2 \\ t_{in} > t_1 \end{cases} \tag{2}$$

由式(1)和式(2)得 t_{in}:

$$t_{in} = t_1 + \frac{\sqrt{2as_1 + v_1^2} - v_1}{a} \tag{3}$$

车辆经过交叉口进口道停车线处的速度为:

$$v_{in} = v_1 + at_{in} \tag{4}$$

式中:a——车辆经过进口道的加速度;

v_1——车辆在进口道停车线前一点的速度;

v_2——车辆在进口道停车线后一点的速度;

t_1——车辆在进口道停车线前一点的时间;

t_2——车辆在进口道停车线后一点的时间;

s_1——进口道前一点车辆位置到停车线的距离;

t_{in}——车辆在进口道停车线处的时间。

车辆在出口处的时间 t_{out} 也可由此方法得出。根据车辆的GPS数据,按照时间的顺序,可得出每辆车在交叉口的行程时间,计算公式为:

$$\Delta t = t_{out} - t_{in} \tag{5}$$

式中:t_{out}——车辆在出口处的时间;

Δt——车辆通过交叉口的行程时间。

1.3 车辆交叉口行为分析

先确定车道线的经纬度,利用车辆在进入交叉口前的经纬度确定车辆所在的车道 d 取值范围[1,2,3,4],

取 1 表示里侧车道,取 2 和 3 表示中间车道,取 4 表示外侧车道;再确定车辆所在车道的交通信号灯状态 λ,λ 为 0 时表示禁止通行,λ 为 1 时表示可以通行。对于单向四车道道路,左转、直行和右转有专属车道,可根据所在车道位置判断车辆转向行为,对于单向两车道道路,车辆右转和直行要加入速度变量来加以分析。车辆在外侧车道上,当交通状态为 λ 为 0 时,速度为 0 表示车辆处于直行状态,速度不为 0 表示车辆处于右转状态。

1.4 数据集构建

由处理好的数据来构测试集和验证集。测试集输入数据包括车辆在交叉口进口道停车线处的速度 v_i、进入交叉口前的时间 t_i、键入交叉口前车辆所在车道 d、车辆所在车道的交通信号灯状态 λ,输出数据为 Δt_i。

选取的激活函数为 sigmoid。BPNN 的 4 个输入特征具有不同物理意义和不同的量纲,因此需要归一化使所有分量都在一个区间内变化,从而使网络训练一开始就给各输入分量以同等重要的地位。归一化公式如下:

$$\bar{x}_i = \frac{x_i - x_{\min}}{x_{\max} - x_{\min}} \tag{6}$$

式中:$\bar{x}_i$——归一化后的数值;

x_i——输入或输出的数据;

$x_{\min}$——数据变化范围的最小值;

$x_{\max}$——数据变化范围的最大值。

2 神经网络预测

BPNN 是一种误差反向传播训练的多层神经网络模型,其学习思想为信号的前向传播和误差的反向回馈,其学习过程为:输入信号的正向传递计算输出值和误差的反向传递调整输入层到隐含层再到输出层之间的权值和偏置,通过反复训练来提高模型预测的精度。

BP 算法以目标的负梯度方向对参数进行调整,并通过不断交替此过程,来调整网络中的权值和偏置。

将训练集输入 BPNN,并用不同时间段的 GPS 数据作为验证集。该模型的作用是预测车辆通过交叉口的时间。构建的神经网络输入输出之间的映射关系为:

$$\Delta t_i(k+1) = f(v_i(k), t_i(k), d_i(k), \lambda) \tag{7}$$

式中:$\Delta t_i(k+1)$——第 i 辆车在 $k+1$ 时刻车辆通过交叉口的时间;

$v_i(k)$——第 i 辆车在 k 时刻的时间点;

$d_i(k)$——第 i 辆车在 k 时刻车辆所在的车道编号;

λ——交通信号灯的状态变量。

构建的 BPNN 包含一个输入层、两个隐含层和一个输入层,其中输入层的神经元个数为 4,两个隐含层神经元的个数均为 32,输出层神经元的个数为 1,结构图如图 4 所示。

在 BPNN 结构中均采用 sigmoid 函数作为激活函数,均方误差(MSE)作为损耗函数,并采用自适应学习率算法进行学习。

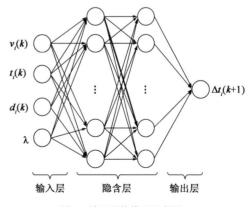

图 4 神经网络模型示意图

3 方法验证与讨论

为了验证车辆通过交叉口时间的预测效果,研究选图2所示蓝色框中交叉口的GPS数据。东西方向为向四车道,南北方向为单向双车道。GPS数据为连续9天的数据,道路信号周期为102s,其中东西方向绿灯时间70s,南北方向绿灯时间32s。

本次实验以2min为一个周期,预测2min后车辆通过交叉口的时间。选取2016年6月22—30日的数据作为训练数据,其中训练数据样本8000个,并随机选取100个2016年7月11日的数据进行验证。

将BPNN预测得到的通过交叉口的时间和车辆通过交叉口的真实时间进行对比验证,如图5所示。

图5a)所示为车辆直行通过交叉口时间的预测情况,在绿灯情况下直行车辆受到其他方向通行车辆的影响较小,其均方误差为0.31;图5b)所示是对车辆左转通过交叉口时间的预测情况,车辆在左转时受到其他方向车辆的干扰,尤其是双向两车道的路段,其均方误差为0.82;图5c)所示是对车辆右转通过交叉口时间的预测,但预测值和真实值之间的误差较大,因为右转车辆受到交通因素的影响大,交通通行情况复杂,其均方误差为0.72。

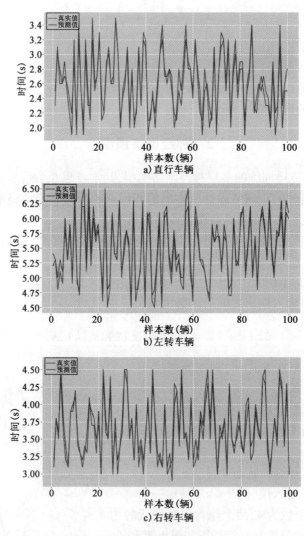

图5 数据验证结果

结果表明,此BPNN得到的通过交叉口时间的预测值和期望值之间的误差较小。对已有的GPS数据进行合理、有效的处理,能够预测出相对准确的车辆通过交叉口的时间,与传统的基于纯数据模型驱动得到的预测值相比,提高了精度和泛化能力。

4 结 语

本文主要利用 GPS 数据和信号灯配时数据,对其进行处理得到车辆进入交叉口时的速度、时间、车辆所在车道以及车辆所在车道对应的交通信号灯状态。构建了 BPNN 用于预测车辆通过交叉口的时间,车辆直行、左转和右转的均方误差分别为 0.31、0.82 和 0.72,能够满足出行诱导中对于车辆在交叉口通行时间预测的根本需求。结果表明,该模型具有较高的精度和适当的泛化性,尤其适用于短期预测。

未来的工作是在 GPS 数据的基础上加入视频数据,利用融合数据提高预测得准确性和泛化能力。此外,提高长期预测的准确性和整个路网的通行时间预测准确性也是未来要考虑的工作。

参考文献

[1] Brennan T M, Gurriell R A, Bechtel A J, et al. Visualizing and evaluating interdependent regional traffic congestion and system resiliency, a case study using big data from probe vehicles[J]. Journal of Big Data Analytics in Transportation, 2019, 1(1):25-36.

[2] 王莹. 基于动态图混杂自动机的城市快速路网交通密度估计[D]. 北京:北京工业大学, 2017.

[3] Yu B, Yin H, Zhu Z. Spatio-temporal graph convolutional networks: A deep learning framework for traffic forecasting[J]. arXiv preprint arXiv:1709.04875, 2017.

[4] Shi Z, Chen Y, Ma P F. Video data based Traffic State Prediction at Intersection[C]. 2020 IEEE 23rd International Conference on Intelligent Transportation Systems (ITSC). IEEE, 2020:1-6.

[5] Ma X, Dai Z, He Z, et al. Learning traffic as images: a deep convolutional neural network for large-scale transportation network speed prediction[J]. Sensors, 2017, 17(4):818.

[6] Ke J, Zheng H, Yang H, et al. Short-term forecasting of passenger demand under on-demand ride services: A spatio-temporal deep learning approach[J]. Transportation Research Part C: Emerging Technologies, 2017(85):591-608.

[7] Wang J, Gu Q, Wu J, et al. Traffic speed prediction and congestion source exploration: A deep learning method[C]. 2016 IEEE 16th international conference on data mining (ICDM). IEEE, 2016:499-508.

[8] 张金金. 城市道路交通行程时间预测算法研究及软件实现[D]. 北京:北方工业大学, 2014.

[9] Liu Y, Zheng H, Feng X, et al. Short-term traffic flow prediction with Conv-LSTM[C]. 2017 9th International Conference on Wireless Communications and Signal Processing (WCSP). IEEE, 2017:1-6.

[10] Wu Y, Tan H. Short-term traffic flow forecasting with spatial-temporal correlation in a hybrid deep learning framework[J]. arXiv preprint arXiv:1612.01022, 2016.

How Much Extra Cost Can be Induced by a Freeway Toll Plaza: a Quantifying Approach Based on Data-mining

Shanshan Wei[1]　Shichao Chen[2]　Jin Ran[1]　Lin Wang[1]

(1. Shandong Transportation Research Institute;
2. Shandong Provincial Urban Construction Design Institute)

Abstract　The presence of a toll plaza has a significant impact on travel time, energy consumption and environmental pollution. This work aims to develop a data-mining approach to accurately quantifying how much the extra cost can be induced by a toll booth. The trajectory data is used to estimate the extra cost as it provides the instantaneous speed and acceleration information for the vehicles moving toward a toll plaza. The quantifying approach proposed in this paper contains the following steps. Firstly, an appropriate process is performed to improve the trajectory data. Secondly, the dynamic time warping method is adopted with the vehicle trajectory data to identify whether the vehicle usesthe service of manual toll collection (MTC) or electronic toll collection (ETC). Thirdly, a microscopic model based on the estimation of vehicle specific power is chosen to estimate the amount of pollutants emitted and the fuel consumption is estimated by the carbon balance method based on the generated carbon. Finally, the extra cost in terms of the monetary value is derived from the estimated fuel cost, pollution abatement and time value. Taking the taxi trajectory data over the three toll plazas in Beijing for demonstration, we have applied the proposed method to estimate the impacts of the toll plazas. The obtained results indicate that the MTC lanes of the three toll plazas can result in a total annual loss of 39.58 Million RMB yuan approximately, while only 18.46 Million RMB yuan of annual loss can be expected for the ETC lanes.

Keywords Freeway toll plaza   Data-mining approach   Environmental impact   Traffic emission   Fuel consumption

0 Introduction

The conventional toll plazas require vehicles to stop in order to complete the toll collection. It is obvious that the approaching vehicles have to slow down, stop and accelerate again during the toll collection, resulting in extra fuel consumption and corresponding tailpipe emission. Partly for this reason, the electronic toll collection (ETC), also called the automatic non-stop charging system, has been received popularity and deployed in many toll plazas in recent years. However, not all toll booths have been facilitated due to the consideration that not all vehicles are amounted with the on-board ETC device. Even for the ETC system, the approaching vehicles are also needed to slow down to a certain speed limit in order to complete the transaction robustly with the constraint communication capability. This also implies it is inevitable to produce extra exhaust and consume more energy (Weng et al., 2015). Nevertheless, the travel time associated is also increased. This paper wants to evaluate how much a freeway toll plaza cost mainly from environmental aspect.

Scientifically evaluating the environmental impacts of freeway toll plazas is critical to provide important guidance for the improvement of the freeway toll plaza design in the future. Many previous studies have focused on evaluation indicators and computational models, most of which use field tests or simulation methods (Koupal et al., 2002). However, due to enormous efforts required, the field tests are often restricted to a small number of vehicles under study and, consequently, the results are less representative, even though the measured emission and fuel consumption have better accuracy. On the other hand, the data obtained from simulation models are likely to be affected the model adopted and the calibration associated. In addition, the setting of the plaza warning sign will have a certain impact on the driver's behaviour, but previous studies are rarely considered.

With the beginning of the big data era, how to take advantage of massive data to evaluate the environmental impact becomes a hot topic in the transportation research. Therefore, this paper attempts to formulate an approach to quantifying the environmental impact for a freeway toll plaza in a timely and multi-scale fashion with less efforts associated to the evaluation compared to the field test methods (Tseng et al., 2014).

This paper is structured as follows: the next section describes the frame work of the proposed quantifying approach. Section2 presents the data extraction and pre-processing process. Section 3 and 4 introduce emissions and fuel consumption models and the use of the data from three toll plazas in Beijing as a case to quantify the environmental impact of toll plaza using the methodology developed in this paper. This paper is concluded with section 5.

1 Data Extraction and Processing

1.1 Data Extraction

In order to capture the vehicle operation in the actual driving state before and after passing through the toll plaza, this paper adopts the GPS data for the taxis in Beijing as an example for demonstration purpose. The data used ranges from August 13, 2015 to August 31, 2015, and from September 19, 2017 to September 23, 2017, including working days and weekends for the toll plazas of Beijing Airport Expressway NorthLine, Bailu and Xihongmen. We are aware that the amount of pollutants emitted and fuel consumed can vary for different types of cars even with the same number of seats, but the taxis type involved in this paper are constrained to be the Elantra vehicle produced in Beijing as this is the main type of taxis allowed by Beijing Municipal Commission of Transport.

According to the traffic regulation issued by traffic managementdepartment, a set of signs to warn there is a toll plaza ahead should be placed on the main line before the toll plaza by 2 km, 1 km and 500 m, respectively (Zhou, 2007). Obviously, those signs can trigger the driving behavior change in order to safely passing through a toll plaza. Therefore, we have extracted the GPS data recording the vehicular trajectory starting at 2km before the toll plaza and ending at 2km after the plaza where all vehicles have reached to the normal speed to run on the mainline. Fig. 1 schematically illustrates the process of vehicles passing through a toll plaza. Although the first warning sign is located 2km in front of the toll plaza, none of vehicles begins to decelerate at this point as it is too far to initiate a deceleration but lane-changing. As shown in Fig. 1, vehicles typically begin to slow down after they moving over section of length at speed which is as high as that over the freeway mainline. The road sectionindicates the range within which vehicles start to decelerate until a full stop. Therefore, we call the point as the deceleration point for convenience. After the toll is collected, vehicles start to accelerate over link and reach to speed afterwards. The running speed over the distance of link is the same as, which can be regarded as the comfortable speed for the mainline. We name the point as the uniform point in this paper. The summation of and is the distance that vehicles are affected by a toll plaza. Clearly, and depend on not only type of vehicles but also driving behaviour.

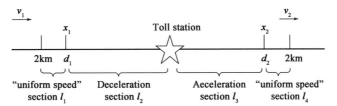

Fig. 1 Vehicle passing through the toll plaza

Tab. 1 shows the raw data format, including that information such as car ID, update time, longitude, latitude, and speed, for a taxi passing through a toll plaza. In total, more than 1.8 million data of 9090 vehicles were extracted.

The raw data format   Tab. 1

Car-ID	Update-time	Longtitude	Latitude	Speed(km/h)
京 B N3935	15:03:32	116.574013	40.121067	82
京 B N3935	15:03:43	116.571419	40.122055	76
京 B N3935	15:03:59	116.563583	40.122566	69
京 B N3935	15:04:16	116.561707	40.122494	19
京 B N3935	15:04:28	116.561501	40.122575	0
……	……	……	……	……

1.2 Data Processing

Due to communication and other reasons, there are data duplication, too few data records, errors and other problems in the originaldata. Firstly, exclude abnormal data. Then, the trajectory data should be separated for two modes of toll collection: MTC and ETC. According to the different characteristics of the vehicle speed and acceleration change during the MTC and ETC charging process, the clustering method of Dynamic Time Warping (DTW) can be used to distinguish the data of the two charging methods. The time of the first data record of each vehicle extracted is taken as the starting time, and the speed and acceleration change of the vehicle before and after passing through the toll plaza in the two charging modes is shown in Fig. 2. Finally, the higher resolution data is obtained by interpolating the data of sampling frequency of $0.1 \sim 0.03$ Hz, so as to estimate the emission and fuel consumption more accurately. To this end, the Cubic spline interpolation technique has been adopted for the raw data of the two modes of toll collection separately and the interpolated results are shown in Fig. 3.

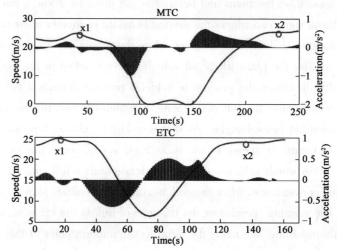

Fig. 2 Speed and acceleration changes of MTC and ETC

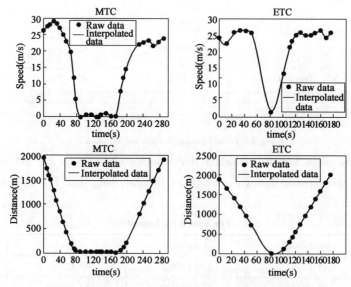

Fig. 3 Interpolation of MTC and ETC data

2 Emission and Fuel Consumption Models

2.1 Emission Model Data Processing

There are various models to estimate the pollutants emitted from vehicles (Demir et al., 2011). As the speed and acceleration information can be derived from the GPS recording, we have adopted a microscopic model based on the estimation of the specific power. The theoretical calculation of vehicle specific power (VSP) will not be described in this paper. all taxis in Beijing have been restricted to be Elantra type, due to the fact that all taxi companies are managed by Beijing Municipal Commission of Transport. Also, such type of taxi meets the emission standard issued by local government. To simplify the calibration process, we have adopted the calibrated results presented in (Wu et al.,2015) for the same type of taxi. Equation 1 shows the calibrated form of VPS.

In order to calculate the VSP value of the measured data per second, it is necessary to calculate the acceleration value of the vehicle per second. In this paper, equation (2) is used to calculate the acceleration.

$$VSP = 0.105802 \times v + 0.00135375 \times v^2 + 0.00033311 \times v^3 + v \times a \tag{1}$$

$$a_i = (v_{i+1} - v_i)/3.6 \tag{2}$$

Where, VSP is the instantaneous power of a unit mass motor vehicle; v is the instantaneous speed of the vehicle, (m/s); a is the acceleration of the vehicle, (m/s^2); α_i is the instantaneous acceleration of the vehicle at time i, (m/s^2); v_{i+1} is the speed of the vehicle at time $i+1$, (m/s); v_i is the speed of the vehicle at time i, (m/s).

Since the calculated VSP is relatively discrete and the emission rates corresponding to adjacent VSPs within fluctuate little, the VSP can be segmented by clustering method and the reference emission rate under different VSP intervals can be obtained (Wu et al., 2015). According to the base emission rate in VSP bins, the corresponding vehicle exhaust emissions per second can be obtained, and then the total emissions of the vehicle in the intervals and are obtained easily by summing all values during the interval.

2.2 FuelConsumption Calculation

The total amount of carbon element in the vehicle exhaust is equal to the content of carbon element in the fuel consumption (Fang, 2003; Zhang et al., 2005). Therefore, the carbon balance method can be used to calculate the fuel consumption of each vehicle passing through the toll plaza. The specific formula of the carbon balance method is shown in equation (3) (Wu et al.,2015). The length of the and sections passed by each vehicle is different, so the fuel consumption is calculated separately for each vehicle. The specific formula is shown in equation (4).

$$FC = (0.866 \times M_{HC} + 0.4286 \times M_{CO} + 0.2727 \times M_{CO_2}) \times 0.156 \tag{3}$$

$$FC_i = FC/100 \times (d_{1i} + d_{2i}) \tag{4}$$

Where, FC is the fuel consumption of vehicles of 100 kilometres, (L); M_{CO_2} is the CO$_2$ emissions per unit of mileage, (g/km); M_{HC} is the HC emissions per unit of mileage, (g/Km); M_{CO} is the CO emissions per unit of mileage, (g/km); FC_i is the fuel consumption of vehicle i passing through section, l_2 and l_3, d_{1i} is the distance of the vehicle i passing through the section l_2, (km); d_{2i} is the distance of the vehicle i passing through the section l_3, (km).

2.3 TravelTime Calculation

The travel time of the MTC vehicle passing through the toll plaza is the total time of the vehicle from the point x_1 to point x_2, including the deceleration time, the acceleration time, the queuing time, and the time to make a payment. The travel time of the ETC vehicle passing through the toll plaza is the total time of the vehicle from the point x_1 to x_2, including the deceleration time and the acceleration time. The time of the vehicle at points x_1 and x_2 has been given in the raw data, and the travel time can be calculated directly by using equations (5) and (6).

$$T_M = T_{x_2} - T_{x_1} \tag{5}$$

$$T_E = T'_{x_2} - T'_{x_1} \tag{6}$$

Where T_M is the travel time of the MTC vehicle passing through the toll plaza; T_E is the travel time of the ETC vehicle passing through the toll plaza; T_{x_1} is the time of MTC vehicle at point x_1; T_{x_2} is the time of MTC vehicle at point x_2; T'_{x_1} is the time of ETC vehicle at point x_1; T'_{x_2} is the time of ETC vehicle at point x_2.

2.4 Calculation of the Three Major Indicators

In order to estimate extra amount of fuel, pollutants and travel time induced by the presence of a toll plaza, it is necessary to obtain the amount of fuel, pollutants and travel time cost by the vehicle from point x_1 to point x_2 without impact of the toll plaza. For simplicity, the following assumptions are made.

- The starting speed at location x_1 is the average speed of road section l_1, while the vehicle reaches location x_2 at the speed same as that of section l_4.
- The acceleration of vehicle from x_1 to x_2 is constant.
- There are no queues or other incidents to impede the vehicle moving; that is free flow state is assumed here.
- The calculation formula of acceleration is shown in equation (7). The travel time of the vehicle from x_1 to x_2 without presence of a toll plaza can be calculated as equation (8).

$$a' = (\bar{v}_2^2 - \bar{v}_1^2)/(2 \times (d_1 + d_2)) \tag{7}$$

$$T' = (\bar{v}_2 - \bar{v}_1)/a' \tag{8}$$

Where, a' is the acceleration of vehicle from x_1 to x_2 without the toll plaza, (m/s^2); $\bar{v}_1$ is the average speed at x_1 point, (m/s); $\bar{v}_2$ is the average speed at x_2 point, (m/s); T' is the travel time of the vehicle from x_1 to x_2.

The VSP and fuel consumption of vehicle are still calculated according to the formulas (3) and formulas (7) mentioned above when the vehicle from point x_1 to point x_2 is not affected by a toll plaza. The calculation method of the three indicators is shown in equations (9) ~ (11).

$$\Delta F = FC_i - FC'_i \tag{9}$$

$$\Delta S = S_i - S'_i \tag{10}$$

$$\Delta T = T_i - T'_i \tag{11}$$

Where, FC_i is the fuel consumption of the vehicle i from x_1 to x_2 passing through the toll plaza; FC'_i is the fuel consumption of the vehicle i from x_1 to x_2 in a free flow. S_i is the emission of the vehicle i from x_1 to x_2 passing through the toll plaza. S'_i is the emission of the vehicle i from x_1 to x_2 in a free flow; T_i is the travel time of the vehicle i from x_1 to x_2 passing through the toll plaza; T'_i is the travel time of the vehicle i from x_1 to x_2 in a free flow. ΔF, ΔS and ΔT are the increased consumption, increased emission and increased travel time of the vehicle i from x_1 to x_2 passing through the toll plaza.

3 Case Study

3.1 Estimated Amount of Vehicle Emission

The emitted four pollutants, carbon dioxide, carbon monoxide, hydrocarbons, nitrogen oxides calculations, were estimated by using the VSP-based emission model for the MTC and ETC lanes of the three toll plazas based on the trajectory data. Tab. 2 lists the estimated amounts of the pollutants when a vehicle moves the same distance with and without being affected by a toll plaza per trip. The obtained results show that when the vehicle passing through the toll plaza from point x_1 to point x_2, its exhaust emissions will be increased as compared to that without the presence of the toll plaza. 66g, 26mg, 19mg is the average increase in CO_2 and CO, HC, and NO_x of three plazas for the MTC lanes, while CO_2 and CO, HC, and NO_x increase much less if the ETC lane is used.

The estimated amount of the pollutants, fuel consumption and travel times when a vehicle moves from x_1 to x_2 per trip Tab. 2

	Toll Plaza	Toll Type	CO_2 and CO(g)	HC (mg)	NO_x (mg)	Fuel (ml)	Travel Time (s)
The presence of the toll plaza	Airport Express North Line	MTC	607.62	140.96	72.20	270.34	190
		ETC	546.06	128.30	68.43	232.67	154
	Bailu	MTC	567.78	131.54	66.85	241.93	187
		ETC	544.97	125.78	66.37	232.21	157
	Xihongmen	MTC	576.09	129.22	63.15	245.45	192
		ETC	553.08	121.57	59.37	235.65	149
The absence of the toll plaza	Airport Express North Line	Free Flow	519.87	115.74	56.33	221.48	116
	Bailu	Free Flow	515.38	109.71	50.62	219.54	114
	Xihongmen	Free Flow	518.74	98.90	37.81	220.95	115
Average increase ($\Delta S, \Delta F$)		MTC	65.83	25.79	19.15	31.92	75
		ETC	30.04	17.10	16.47	12.85	38

3.2 TheEstimated Fuel Consumption

Based on the estimated amount of carbon, the consumed fuel has been estimated by using the carbon balance method for the MTC and ETC lanes of the three toll plazas. Tab. 2 shows the estimated fuel consumption when a toll plaza is presented and not. The results show that the presence of a toll plaza can attribute an increase in fuel consumption by 31.92 ml on average for the MTC lane and 12.85 ml on average for the ETC lane.

This result is consistent with the results of the literature Evaluation of the influence of toll systems on energy consumption and CO_2 emissions: A case study of a Spanish highway (P J, 2011), that the presence of a toll plaza can attribute a significant increase in not only emission but also fuel consumption, but the paper uses different fuel consumption calculation methods and considered of four categories of vehicles: cars, vans, buses and articulated trucks.

3.3 TheEstimated Travel Times

Tab. 2 lists the travel time estimated for the MTC and ETC modes of the three toll plazas. When a toll plaza exists, an average increase of 75s and 38s in travel time can be expected for the MTC lanes and ETC lanes, respectively, for a trip. When using the MTC lane, there is a need to stop to fulfill the toll transaction and even queue for the toll, resulting in a greater increase in the travel time than that using the ETC lane.

3.4 The EconomicLoss

We have estimated the environmental impact with the presence of a toll plaza in terms of the monetization value. At present, the average fuel cost in Beijing is about 7.36 RMB Yuan/L. Supposing the average air pollutant treatment cost is 8.98 RMB Yuan/kg according to the data in Environment Statistical Yearbook 2008 published by Ministry of Environmental Protection of the People's Republic of China (China, 2009). Additionally, calculate the loss value of travel time according to Beijing average hourly wage of 20 RMB yuan per hour. The monetary cost due to extra fuel, emission and travel time induced by the presence of a toll plaza is estimated to be1.24 RMB yuan for a vehicle passing through a MTC lane of a toll plaza once. On the other hand, although the ETC can reduce the extra cost to some degree, it still cost 0.58 approximately RMB yuan for a vehicle passing through the ETC once.

Further, the annual loss can be estimated based on the daily average flow through a toll plaza. Based on the data provided from the toll plaza, the average daily traffic volumes of three toll plazas have been obtained and the annual economic loss derived and listed in Tab. 3.

Tab. 3 Economic loss if all vehicles passing the MTC/ETC lanes per year

Toll Type	Toll Plaza	Economic losses (Million RMB)
MTC	Airport Express North Line	4.49
MTC	Bailu	14.79
MTC	Xihongmen	20.30
ETC	Airport Express North Line	2.10
ETC	Bailu	6.90
ETC	Xihongmen	9.46

3.5 Comparison of MTC and ETC

Fig. 4 shows the result of the vehicle passing through ETC lane and the MTC lane per trip. The vehicles using the ETC service can save 19.07ml of oil, 36g of exhaust emissions, and 37s of travel time on average, equivalent to a gain of 0.66 RMB Yuan approximately. This shows that the ETC charging method has achieved a certain effect and is an effective way for energy saving and emission reduction.

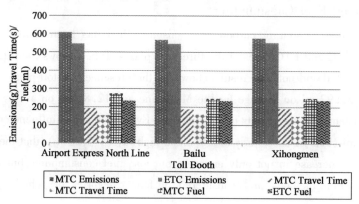

Fig. 4 The comparison of MTC and ETC

Domestic scholars have evaluated the energy conservation and emission reduction effects of ETC toll stations. The comparison of relevant results shows that, the results are not much different from those obtained by the traditional field measurement method, although the models and operating conditions are different (Wang, 2019). The fuel consumption saving of ETC channel obtained by the method in this paper is lower than that obtained by the actual measurement method, because the assumed operating state in this paper is more ideal and other reasons.

4 Conclusions

This study aims to develop a method to quantify the impact of a toll plaza based on the massive trajectory data with assistance of the microscopic emission model and the fuel consumption model. As individual trajectory data is employed, the estimation on the extra emission, fuel consumption and travel time induced by the presence of a toll plaza can be made more accurately and timely. For demonstration purpose, we have employed the trajectory data produced by the Elantra taxi through the three toll plazas in Beijing to estimate extra amount of fuel consumption, vehicle emissions and travel time. Furthermore, the economic loss is estimated for a year based on the toll plaza data with two types of vehicles. Finally, a comparison is made for the two modes, MTC and ETC, in terms of emission, fuel consumption and travel time. The main findings can be summarized as follows:

(1) As compared to the absence of the toll plaza, the MTC mode demands extra fuel consumption by 14%,

exhaust emissions by 13% and travel time by 65% while the ETC mode fuel consumption by 6%, exhaust emissions by 6% and travel time by 33%.

(2) In total, the MTC lanes of the three toll plazas can induce an economic loss of 39.58 Million RMB yuan approximately pre year, while only 18.46 Million RMB yuan of annual loss can be expected for the ETC lanes.

5 Acknowledgements

This work is supported by Shandong provincial key R & D Program "public welfare science and technology research project" (2019GSF109057).

References

[1] Weng J. C., R. Wang, M. Wang, J. Rong. Fuel Consumption and Vehicle Emission Models for Evaluating Environmental Impacts of the ETC System, Sustainability, 2015, 7(7): 8934-8949.

[2] Koupal J., H. Michaels, M. Cumberworth, et al. EPA's Plan for MOVES: A Comprehensive Mobile Source Emissions Model. Proceedings of the 12th CRC On-Road Vehicle Emissions Workshop, San Diego, CA, USA, 15-17.

[3] Tseng P. H., D. Y. Lin, S. Chien. Investigating the impact of highway electronic toll collection to the external cost: A case study in Taiwan. Technological Forecasting & Social Change, 2014, 86(340): 265-272.

[4] Zhou W. W. Technical Manual for Setting Road Traffic Marking Line [M]. Intellectual Property Press, 2007.

[5] Demir E., T. Bektas, G. Laporte. A Comparative Analysis of Several Vehicle Emission Models for Road Freight Transportation. Transportation Research Part D, 2011, 16(5): 347-357.

[6] Wu Y. P., X. H. Zhao, J. Rong, et al. Potential of Eco-driving in Reducing Fuel Consumption and Emissions Based on a Driving Simulator. Journal of Beijing University of Technology, 2015(8): 1212-1218.

[7] P. J. Pe'rez-Marti'nez *, D. Ming, G. Dell'Asin, et al. Evaluation of the influence of toll systems on energy consumption and CO2 emissions: A case study of a Spanish highway. Journal of King Saud University-Science, 2011(23), 301-310.

[8] Fang M. A. Fuel Consumption Measurement for Motor Vehicle Based on Carbon Balance Method. Automotive Engineering, 2003, 25(3): 295-294.

[9] Zhang X. M., Y. S. Ge, Y. Zhang, et al. Research on Fuel Consumption Measurement using Carbon Balance Method. Vehicle Engine, 2005(3): 56-58.

[10] Ministry of Environmental Protection of the People's Republic of China. Environment Statistical Yearbook 2008: Exhaust Gas. Ministry of Environmental Protection of the People's Republic of China: Beijing, China, 2009.

[11] Wang Ji long. Analysis on the Effect of Energy Saving and Emission Reduction Using ETC in China's Highway. Energy Conservation & Environmental Protection. 2020(10).

交叉口自行车事故严重程度的差异性分析

刘 婷 杜志刚

(武汉理工大学交通学院)

摘 要 为了分析交叉口自行车事故严重程度的差异性,以2018年英国的道路交通事故为样本。

从样本数据中根据条件筛选出处于交叉口与有自行车参与的数据样本,对数据样本中不必要的因素进行挑选,留下有效影响因素。以筛选出的12种因素为自变量,借助SAS对样本数据进行分析,运用累积Logit模型来分析自行车事故致命、严重、轻微3种等级的自行车交通事故的分布概率。最后,基于本文的研究结果,针对不同的交叉口情况给出了对策与建议,减少了交叉口自行车事故,提高了自行车出行的安全度。

关键词 数据分析 差异性分析 累积Logit模型 自行车事故

0 引 言

近年来随着绿色出行、节约能源思想的盛行,人们开始寻找节能、方便的出行方式代替小汽车出行,于是自行车依靠其经济、无需驾驶证等优势使得很多人选择其作为日常出行方式[1]。但由于法律法规与管理规划方式的落后,自行车的交通事故频发,特别是交通组织复杂的交叉口自行车事故率更高[2]。因此如何利用庞大的交通事故数据库,分析其潜在的规律,从而提出合适的方式来降低交叉口的自行车事故率显得尤为重要。

国内外学者分别从不同方面对自行车的交通事故进行过分析。欧盟试验汽车委员会[3]进行研究得出:两轮车间的道路交通事故骑行人死亡率为15.8%,比行人死亡率少22%。郭磊[4]对碰撞事故建立了多刚体碰撞模型,研究了事故中骑行人员的动力伤害。刘尧[5]对非机动车的交通事故的伤害特征、车辆的参数等进行了研究分析。聂进[6]根据已有自行车事故数据,运用多体动力学模型进行了事故重建。王涛等[7]研究得出在事故中自行车骑车人侧面是最容易发生碰撞的位置。James Mooradian等[8]针对交叉口,对数据进行现场采集,通过得到的基本数据建立了分布模型。王涛[9]等对已有事故数据中的伤人事故进行了方差分析。通过以上研究可知现有研究方法都存在片面性,评价方法基本都从单一方面出发。

本文以已有的交通事故数据为基础进行交通事故的特征分析、结合实例对交叉口自行车事故严重程度建模并进行求解并给出预防事故的建议。以2018年英国的道路交通事故作为样本,从中筛选出12种因素作为自变量,借助SAS软件对数据进行分析,运用累积Logit模型来分析自行车事故各等级的自行车事故的分布概率,对减少交叉口自行车事故具有一定意义。

1 研究技术

1.1 技术路线

本研究技术路线如图1所示,首先介绍论文的研究背景,然后对数据进行整理分析,根据整理结果完成数学建模,最后进行总结。

1.2 Logit模型

将自行车事故分为3个等级:致死、严重、轻微。将交叉口自行车事故严重程度设为因变量Y,对事故严重程度的影响因素设为自变量$X=(x_1,x_2,\cdots,x_3)$。设一个连续因变量Y',两个分界点n_1,n_2,连续因变量Y'可以根据分界点n_1,n_2设置为分段函数:

$$\begin{cases} Y=1, 若 Y' \leq n_1 \\ Y=2, 若 n_1 \leq Y' \leq n_2 \\ Y=3, 若 Y' \geq n_2 \end{cases} \quad (1)$$

$$Y' = \sum_{n=1}^{n}\beta_n X_n + q \quad (2)$$

式中:β——回归系数;

$\sum_{n=1}^{n}\beta_n X_n$——线性函数;

q——误差项;q服从Logit函数,则$Y>i(i=1,2,3)$的概率为:

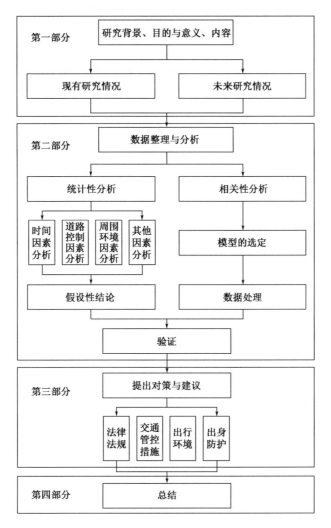

图1 技术路线图

$$P(Y > i) = P(Y' > n_i) = P\left(q > n_i - \sum_{n=1}^{n}\beta_n X_n\right) = 1 - \frac{1}{1 + e^{[-(n_i - X\beta)]}} = \frac{e^{(X\beta - n_i)}}{1 + e^{(X\beta - n_i)}} \quad (3)$$

于是3种不同严重程度的自行车交通事故发生的概率可由此预测出来：

$$\begin{cases} P(Y = 1) = P(Y' \leq n_1) = \dfrac{1}{1 + e^{(X\beta - n_1)}} \\ P(Y = 2) = P(n_1 < Y' \leq n_2) = \dfrac{1}{1 + e^{(X\beta - n_2)}} - \dfrac{1}{1 + e^{(X\beta - n_1)}} \\ P(Y = 3) = P(Y > n_2) = 1 - \dfrac{1}{1 + e^{(X\beta - n_2)}} \end{cases} \quad (4)$$

在此模型中，优势比 OR 为：

$$\text{OR}_i = e^{(-\beta_i)} \quad (5)$$

当 β_i 为 0 时，OR_i 为 1，则 x_i 对此种事故的严重程度的概率没有影响；当 $\beta_i > 0$ 时，$\text{OR}_i > 1$，则此种事故的严重程度的概率随 x_i 的变化而增长；当 $\beta_i < 0$ 时，$\text{OR}_i < 1$，则此种事故的严重程度的概率随 X_i 的变化而减小。

2 建模与结果

2.1 数据预处理

把数据中涉及其他车辆的数据剔除，留下自行车交通事故的数据。事故数据中把事故的严重程度作为因变量,选取时间因素、道路控制因素、周围环境因素以及其他因素4类因素、共12个变量作为自变量。对自变量和因变量进行代码取值如表1和表2所示。

因变量取值

表1

因变量Y	标签	变量名	代码
交叉口自行车交通事故严重程度	致死	Accident_Severity	1
	严重		2
	轻微		3

自变量取值

表2

自变量类别	自变量X	标签	变量名	代码
时间因素	日期	周日	Day_of_Week	1
		周一		2
		周二		3
		周三		4
		周四		5
		周五		6
		周六		7
道路控制	速度限制	最高速度20km/h	Speed_limit	20
		最高速度30km/h		30
		最高速度40km/h		40
		最高速度50km/h		50
		最高速度60km/h		60
	交汇点控制方式	授权人员	Junction_Control	1
		自动交通信号		2
		停止标志		3
		让路标志		4
	过街人工控制方式	50m内无人员	Crossing-Human_Control	0
		学校交叉巡逻		1
		其他授权人员		2
	过街物理控制方式	无物理控制	Physical_Facilities	0
		斑马线		1
		交叉行人道		4
		交通信号		5
		天桥或地下通道		7
		中央避难所		8
环境	照明条件	日光	Light	1
		灯光亮		4
		灯光未亮		5
		无照明设施		6
	气候条件	晴朗	Weather	1
		下雨		2
		下雪		3
		雾或霾		4

续上表

自变量类别	自变量 X	标 签	变 量 名	代 码
环境	路面状况	干燥	Road_Surface	1
		潮湿		2
		积雪		3
		霜冻或冰		4
		积水		5
	城乡因素	城市	Urban_or_Rural_Area	1
		农村		2
其他	道路类型	单向街道	Road_Type	1
		双车道		2
		单车道		3
	交汇点	微型环形交叉口	Junction_Detail	1
		T形交叉口		2
		十字路口		3
		多条道路交叉口		4

根据因变量和自变量的取值，采用 SAS 软件，用 Logit 模型建立交叉口的自行车交通事故的严重程度预测模型进行分析。

2.2 运行结果

数据集为 WORK.SHUJU；响应变量为 Accident_Severity；相应水平数为 3；模型为累积 Logit 模型；优化方法为 Fisher 评分法。结果输出如表 3 ~ 表 7 所示。

响 应 概 况　　　　表 3

有 序 值	Accident_Severity	总 频 数
1	3	381
2	2	94
3	1	2

比例优比假设的评分检验　　　　表 4

卡 方	自 由 度	Pr > 卡方
6.0041	12	0.9159

最大似然估计分析　　　　表 5

参 数	估 计	标准误差	Wald 卡方	Pr > 卡方
Road_Surface	0.0635	1.8746	1.4768	0.2243
Area	0.4674	2.0029	10.2726	0.0014
Number_of_Vehicles	0.5046	0.2214	5.1962	0.0226
Day_of_Week	0.0558	0.0613	0.8277	0.3629
Road_Type	-0.0639	0.0655	0.9501	0.3297
Speed_limit	-0.0233	0.0388	0.3615	0.5476
Junction_Detail	-0.0878	0.0696	1.5921	0.2070
Junction_Control	-0.2740	0.1456	3.5415	0.0599
Crossing_Human_Contr	-0.0649	0.2525	0.0660	0.7973
Physical_Facilities	-0.1306	0.0574	5.1690	0.0230

续上表

参　数	估　计	标准误差	Wald 卡方	Pr > 卡方
Light	0.0219	0.0754	0.0846	0.7711
Weather	0.00973	0.2653	0.0013	0.9707

优 比 估 计　　　　　　　　　　　　　　　　　　　　　表6

参　数	效　应	点　估　计	95% Wald 置信限
Number_of_Vehicles	1.656	1.073	2.556
Day_of_Week	1.057	0.938	1.192
Road_Type	0.938	0.825	1.067
Speed_limit	0.977	0.906	1.054
Junction_Detail	0.916	0.799	1.050
Junction_Control	0.760	0.572	1.011
Crossing_Human_Contr	0.937	0.571	1.537
Physical_Facilities	0.878	0.784	0.982
Light	1.022	0.882	1.185
Weather	1.010	0.600	1.698
Road_Surface	1.066	0.563	2.019
Area	1.596	0.184	13.822

预测概率和观测响应的关联　　　　　　　　　　　　　表7

一致部分所占百分比	63.3	Somers D	0.281
不一致部分所占百分比	35.2	Gamma	0.285
结值百分比	1.5	Tau-a	0.091

2.3　结果分析

从表7可以看出对于使用此模型进行交叉口自行车事故严重程度的预测,一致部分所占百分比为63.3%,高于不一致部分(35.2%)。这表明本研究的结果是可靠的。

表5显示了最大似然估计分析的运行结果,从表中可以看出所选择的所有自变量都对自行车事故的严重程度有显性影响。参与的车辆数量、日期、照明条件、气候条件、路面状况、城乡因素6种因素对交叉口的交通事故的严重程度的影响为显性因素,Wald卡方越大表示该自变量对因变量的影响程度越大。事故参与的车辆数的Wald卡方中最大为0.5046,此自变量对自行车事故严重程度的正影响是最大的;其次为城乡因素,城乡因素为0/1分类,Wald卡方值为0.4674,故城市地区为显性正相关;路面状况的Wald卡方为0.0635;是否工作日的Wald卡方为0.0558,对自行车事故的严重情况的显性正影响为第四;照明条件的Wald卡方为0.0219,排第五;最后一种因素是气候条件,其Wald卡方为0.00973。

这说明参与的车辆数越多越有可能造成严重的事故,这是因为参与的车辆数越多,骑行者的心理压力就越大,采取正确的应急措施也就越难;与农村相比城市更可能发生严重的事故,这是由于城市的车辆、人口密度更大;与干燥的路面相比,潮湿的路面状况更容易造成死亡交通事故,可能由于潮湿的路面状况制动效率低下;相比工作日,民众于周末出行,造成出行密度增加,容易发生自行车交通事故;与黑暗的情况下相比,照明条件较好时,骑行者会放松警惕;恶劣的天气条件下自行车的交通事故会更严重,这种天气条件下路面状况不好,道路积雪、潮湿,导致车辆在道路上滑行。

道路种类、速度限制、交汇点形式、交汇点控制方式、过街人工控制方式、过街物理控制方式6种对因变量自行车交通事故的严重程度有显性负相关。Wald 最大的一项为交叉口控制方式,Wald 值为0.2740;其次为交叉口的物理控制方式,其 Wald 为 0.1306;交汇点细节的 Wald 为 0.0878;第四为过街控制方式,Wald 为 0.0649;然后是道路种类,其 Wald 值为 0.0639,最后一项为速度限制,Wald 为 0.0233。

交叉口控制方式、交汇点和过街控制方式可归因于这些方式能否引起道路参与者的注意,从而采取措施规避危险;由于道路种类的不同道路上一系列参数都会不同;速度限制主要是车辆之间的速度差,道路上车辆之间速度均衡,速度差不大,则安全系数会更高。

3 结　　语

对交叉口自行车事故严重程度的因素进行分析和预测,结果表明:事故参与的车辆数、城乡因素、是否工作日、交汇点控制方式、过街的物理控制方式、交汇点形式、过街人工控制方式、道路种类8个因素与不同交叉口自行车事故严重程度显著相关。此外,通过分析不难发现:

(1)通过 SAS 分析软件及累积 Logit 模型,对交叉口自行车事故严重程度进行预测,结果表明该方法是有效可靠的。

(2)参与的车辆数量、日期、照明条件、气候条件、路面状况、城乡因素6种因素对交叉口交通事故严重程度的影响为显性正相关。其中,参与的车辆数对研究对象的影响最大,需要引起注意。

(3)道路种类、速度限制、交汇点形式、交汇点控制方式、过街人工控制方式、过街物理控制方式6种对因变量自行车交通事故的严重程度成显性负相关,其中交汇点控制方式对研究对象的影响最大,因此交汇点控制方式是减小事故严重程度的较好途径。

本文仅讨论了累积 Logit 模型预测下的结果,对于其他模型预测下的情况是否更加准确并未展开研究,还需进一步讨论。

参考文献

[1] 曲彩悦.基于贝叶斯网络模型的两轮车骑车人损伤风险研究[D].湖南:湖南大学,2014.
[2] 齐龙,韩奇.基于 PC-Crash 的混合交通环境下电动自行车事故仿真研究[J].交通工程,2018,134:179-184.
[3] Yang Li, Wei (David) Fan. Modelling Severity of Pedestrian-Injury in Pedestrian-vehicle Crashes with Latent Class Clustering and Partial Proportional Odds Model: A Case Study of North Carolina[J]. Accident Analysis and Prevention, 2019, 131:284-296.
[4] 郭磊.自行车碰撞事故的动力学响应仿真[J].系统仿真学报,2010,19(14):3331-3338.
[5] 聂进,杨济匡.基于汽车——自行车碰撞事故重建的骑车人动力学响应和损伤研究[J].汽车工程,2015,37(2):160-167.
[6] 刘尧.交通事故中电动自行车驾驶者人身伤害影响因素分析[D].北京:清华大学,2017.
[7] 王涛,黎文皓,李文勇.电动自行车交通事故严重程度影响因素分析[J].广西大学学报(自然科学版),2017,42(6):2080-2088.
[8] James Mooradian, John N Ivan, Nalini Ravishanker, et al. Accident Analysis and Prevention[J]. Analysis of driver and passenger crash injury severity using partial proportional odds models, 2013, 53:53-58.
[9] 王涛.电动自行车风险驾驶行为及事故机理研究[D].南京:东南大学,2017.

小城镇城区公交系统优化策略——
以浙江天台为例

刘歆余　丁　剑　倪丽莉　韩　斌　严　馨

（浙江数智交院科技股份有限公司）

摘　要　公交优先是落实交通强国战略,解决城市交通问题的根本策略。在大数据时代,小城镇城区公共交通的系统优化策略得到了有力的分析支撑。本文以浙江省天台县为例,统筹考虑小城镇公共交通发展策略,对供需两个角度的多源数据分析,从路网、站点和排班三方面着手,优化城区公共交通系统。研究表明,经过多源数据针对性分析和系统优化后的天台县城区公交服务水平提升明显。研究成果也为国内小城镇公共交通系统优化提供了有益借鉴。

关键词　小城镇　公共交通　多源数据　系统优化　天台

0　引　言

在城乡一体化发展进程中,小城镇空间分异特征明显。物质空间分异主要呈现"点轴模式"的分异特征,体现在相邻大城市通勤出现、旅游新业态发展、新经济下工业园区不断整合提升、区域交通枢纽系统不断强化延伸等方面;社会空间分异则一般呈现非均衡分异特征,表现在小城镇片区划分重构、人口老龄化、集体搬迁安置等方面。因此,小城镇公交服务应顺应小城镇空间分异发展趋势,突出对大都市通勤、旅游交通、城内职住、老龄化出行等特点的多方需求。然而,目前小城镇公交服务市场普遍较为原始,仅由几条常规公交路线作支撑,路线设置数字赋能程度低、现代化水平滞后,公交系统规模较小、层次结构单一、服务灵活性较差,缺乏对于数据的综合分析利用和基于系统组合的公共交通优化方法,严重影响了居民对公交出行的依赖性。

本文针对目前小城镇公交发展现状和研究情况,提出了一种基于多源数据视角的小城镇公交线网优化方法,并以浙江省天台县为例,对该方法进行详细说明,为相关研究提供思路。

1　多源数据思维下的基数要素剖析

1.1　小城镇外部环境分析

1.1.1　社会经济发展

随着新型城镇化进程深入,打造宜居宜业的现代化小城镇,提升其居住功能和人口承载能力至关重要,而公共交通的发展远不能满足小城镇社会经济发展的客观需求。

1.1.2　土地利用特征

小城镇城区公交路线的走向充分受土地利用特征影响,集中式布局的小城镇公交线网布局往往由中心向四周延伸,组团式发展的通常受道路资源制约,分布分散。

1.1.3　居民出行意愿

小城镇居民出行向出行费用低、出行距离短、出行时耗短,选择电动车、自行车、步行等个体交通出行方式占比较高,私家车出行上升明显。小城镇居民出行的主要目的包括工作、购物、就医、上学、探亲访友、游玩、办事等,其中工作、上学较为固定,购物、游玩、就医,甚至跨区域通勤等需求逐渐升高。

1.2 公交内部要素分析

1.2.1 公交线网

小城镇城区公交线网布设可能存在线路重复系数、非直线系数较大,路网密度较低、公交站点覆盖率偏低等问题,严重降低了公交吸引力。

1.2.2 公交运营情况

综合比较总体客流、单线客流、车均客流情况,综合分析需求与车辆配置、发现间隔之间的匹配程度,查找并改善配车盲点,从而提高公交服务效果。

2 美好生活图景构建

2.1 发展策略

综合分析公共交通的供求关系,以多层次、灵活优质的线网匹配供给,力争实现高水平供需平衡。
(1)形成便捷多元的公共交通体系;
(2)推进公交枢纽场站建设;
(3)搭建智慧高效的公共交通管理平台;
(4)改善公交服务水平。

2.2 技术路线

根据上述分析结论,在多源数据条件下剖析公交系统供需两端发展水平,并根据宏观发展策略,采用弹性优化供给的具体策略,促进公交系统的高水平供需平衡。主要分析思路和评测数据来源如图1所示。

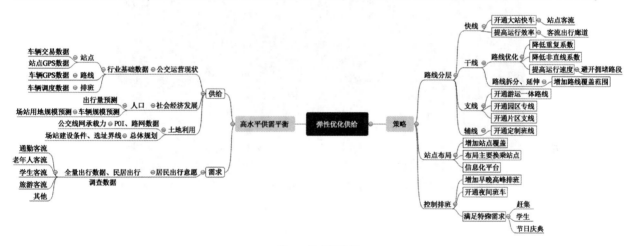

图1 技术路线图

2.3 具体操作

2.3.1 路线分层

公交路线的调整综合考虑居民公交乘坐习惯以及动态出行需求,规避现状公交线路运行缺陷,构建多层次的公交线路系统,详见表1。

路线分类表 表1

类别	主要特征
快线	沿主要客流走廊布置,快速连接主要客流点,可根据需求对高峰期、通勤期差别化处理
主干线	途经主要交通廊道,作为快线的补充,也承担片区间的联系
支线	作为补充,通达城区各点,也可作为片区内的主要联系
特色线路	提高小城镇公交吸引新的增长点,根据小城镇不同特色,综合开发夜间、集市、学生、游运一体、工业等特色班线或定制公交路线,满足小城镇发展特色需求

2.3.2 站点布局

站点的选择应充分分析不同分类的现状站点客流、站点覆盖率和承载力,通过活跃空间分布、出行不便OD分布、站点可达时圈分布等进行筛选,同时综合比较居民出行动态需求,配合新业态的出现和调整,提出需要加强或削减的点域。

2.3.3 排班控制

在现状基础上,检测班次到站稳定度(早晚高峰)、候车人数、等车时间、站点服务时长等具体情况,综合考虑通行成本和乘客舒适度等因素,动态调整调整发车班次和间距,提高公交运行经济效率。

3 浙江省天台县的公交实践

3.1 规划概况

天台县位于浙江省东中部,城区人口约23万人,是践行"快交通、慢旅游"交旅融合发展的生态旅游城市。

3.2 发展需求

从POI数据来看,主城区路网充分体现了东西干路支撑的框架,客流廊道主要包括济公大道、春晓路、唐兴大道、玉龙路、人民路、赤城路等,如图2所示。

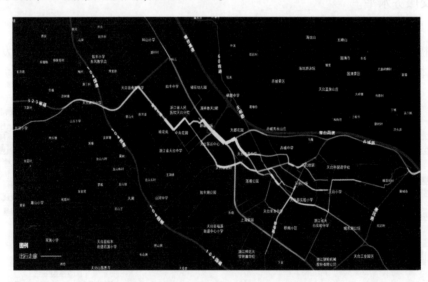

图2 天台县全方式出行客流廊道图

3.3 公交发展现状

目前城区目前天台县城区共布设公交线路11条(1条环线),线路分布如图3所示。

3.4 存在问题

根据现场调研和数据数据分析,天台县城区公交目前存在以下几点主要问题:
(1)公交体统缺乏整体规划,线路设置功能不明确;
(2)线网布设空间分布不均匀;
(3)线路重复较多,非直线系数大;
(4)站点设置不合理,基础设施建设缓慢;
(5)公交线路满载率低,日均客流差异较大。

3.5 对策建议

3.5.1 合理优化站点布局

通过场站规模预测,规划构建形成"两主四辅多点"的公交场站布局结构。结合动静态数据分析,对中间站进行充分分析,筛选出行不便 OD 分布[采用公交出行(包括换乘)步行>0.5km 或步行>5min 图4、图5]。规划新增中间站点 16 个,删减过近或重复站点 15 个,提高公交整体运行效率。

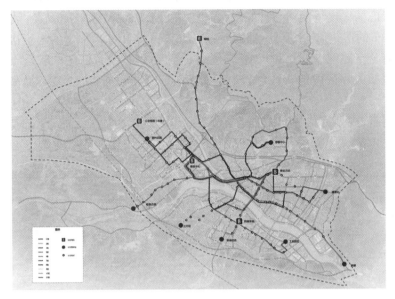

图3　天台县现状城区公交线网图

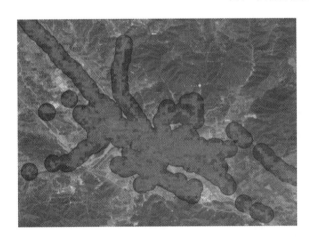
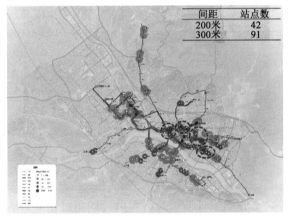

图4　天台县城区公交站点覆盖及5min步行导航覆盖情况

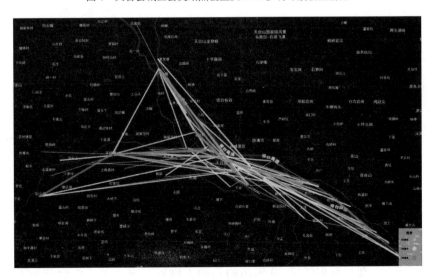

图5　出行不便OD分布图

3.5.2 分层联动公交线路

规划将天台县城区公交线路分层分级,构建结果清晰的"快干支辅"四级线网。

(1)快线:综合考虑居民出行期望、路网客流强度、城区未来发展等多项因素,呈现"X"形交通走廊,其中两条快线以大站车的形式(未来客流、路况等条件允许可设 BRT),加密发车班次,保障通行效率。

(2)干线:对原有公交路网进行总和归纳,共规划 5 条主线,作为片区间的联系。

(3)支线:主要包括大片区内的支线以及特色线路,为精准服务特色需求,提高特色线路的服务针对性。

(4)辅线:根据需求,规划定制若干辅助路线,定期发车,提高整体公交服务水平。

路线按层级进行选线,最终选择了一组方案进行重点优化,优化方案见表2。

表2 天台县路线优化方案

线路编号	线路性质	采用策略
1	新、老城主干线	延长至高速铁路站、大站车
2	新、老城主干线	局部延长、改线,减少绕行
15	新、老城主干线、中农批专线	新增,定时延长
13	新、老城次干线	新增,贯穿工人东路
1	新、老城次干线	新增,增补栖霞路、百花路
1	三片区主干线	保持不变
17	三片区次干线	新增,沿外围避开拥堵
3(10)	三片区小环线	改线、减少绕行
9	老、南城次干线	局部改线
5	游运一体	延长
7	游运一体	改线
6	游运一体、工业园区专线	延长、减少绕行
8	游运一体	延长、减少绕行
12	游运一体	延长、改线

从全方式出行期望与公交出行期望对比来看,公交出行方式在19~21片区、9~17片区和17~20片区等连接没有与全出行期望曲线较好地吻合,如图6所示。

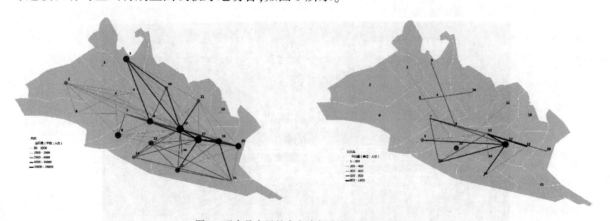

图6 天台县全目的全方式与公交出行期望线图

3.5.3 设置集约换乘大站

为方便居民公交换乘,在原有枢纽站、首末站的基础上设置换乘大站。综合选取6个中间站作为换乘大站,缩短换乘空间和时间,提高公交整体服务水平,如图7所示。

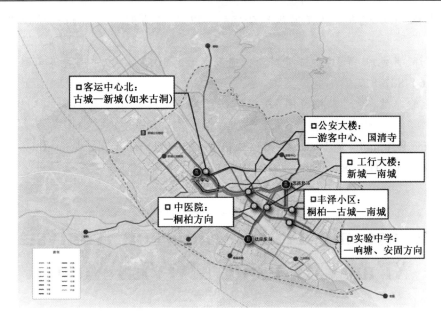

图 7　换乘大站布局图

3.6　评价反馈

根据方案调整情况进行模拟对比,结果见表 3。总体来说,新方案在各方面较现状基础上有较大的提升,实际情况还需依赖实施效力和具体影响。

天台县路线优化对比表　　　　表 3

指　标		规范值/推荐值	现状方案	调整方案	规划目标
	公交分担率(%)	—	6	10	12
中心城区公交线网和站点	线网密度(km/km²)	3~4	2.17	2.6	3.0
	线路重复系数	1.25~2.5	1.97	1.7	1.6
	非直线系数	≤1.4	1.76	1.4	1.4
	500m 站点覆盖率(%)	≥90	75	85	≥90
场站设施	公交场站面积(万 m²)		8.1	9.8	13.7
公交车辆	万人拥有量(中心城区)(标台/万人)	6.7~8.3	5.1	6.2	7
运营服务	平均运行速度(km/h)		17.2	≥20	≥22
	平均换乘系数(次)		1.6	<1.5	<1.3

4　结　语

本文在对当前小城镇交通发展趋势进行研究的基础上,建立了多源数据与公共交通系统耦合关系,提出了基于多源数据分析的小城镇城区公共交通系统优化方法。利用此方法对浙江省天台县城区公共交通进行了实证研究。研究结论表明,从供需两端的多源数据综合分析小城镇公共交通系统存在的具体问题,通过针对性策略优化后,对案例的公交系统进行模拟推演,计算得出的各项服务水平指标有明显提升。该方法对提高小城镇城区公交系统的科学管理水平和服务效率有借鉴意义。鉴于研究案例的分析评估仅依靠数据模拟得到,且未考虑公交发展对小城镇的反向影响,有待在今后的研究中进行完善。

参考文献

[1] 陈艳艳,郝世洋,王振报,等.小城市近期公交线网优化调整技术[J].交通科技与经济,2016,18(6):1-15.

[2] 李永前,杨忠振. 中小城市公共交通规划研究——以 A 县为例[J]. 贵州大学学报,2018,35(4):122-124.

[3] 刘吉祥,周江评,肖龙珠,等. 建成环境对步行通勤通学的影响——以中国香港为例[J]. 地理科学进展,2019,38(6):807-817.

[4] 杨林川,崔叙,喻冰洁,等."末梢时间"对保障房居民公共交通出行的影响[J]. 规划师,2020(4):50-57.

[5] Márquez L,Pico R,Cantillo V. Understanding Captive User Behavior in the Competition between BRT and Motorcycle Taxis[J]. Transport Policy,2018,10(3):1-9.

Macroscopic Traffic Emission Analysis of Xi'an City using MOVES Model

Tianqi Wang　Lan Yang　Fei Hui　Mengjie Han　He Sheng

(College of Information Engineering,Chang'an University)

Abstract　Based on the driving data of 370 taxis on a certain working day in 2014, this paper analyzes and studies the pollutant emissions of Xi'an in different periods of a day. Firstly, by analyzing the characteristics of taxi speed in different periods of a day, the traffic status of this period is judged. Secondly, the corresponding VSP value is calculated according to the taxi GPS data in this paper, and get the VSP distribution. Finally, the localization parameters and VSP distribution are substituted into the moves model to calculate the CO, CO_2, HC, NO_X emissions in different time periods, as well as the total emissions of taxi pollutants in Xi'an in 2014. The results indicate that:①The driving speed range of taxis is mainly [20~45]km/h. ②The simulated emission of pollutants from taxis is higher in the daytime than that at night, and reaches the highest level in the early peak period.

Keywords　Traffic big data　MOVES model　Pollutant emission

0　Introduction

With fast growth of traffic demand, China's auto population has increased rapidly in the past two decades, and the number of registered cars in China has increased from 11 million in 1996 to 205 million in 2018 (Mao S Y 2019). Motor vehicle emissions are a major source of urban air pollutions and global atmospheric conditions, and transportation accounted for 23% of global carbon dioxide emission (Anenberg, S. C 2017). Increased "personal-vehicle" traffic causes recurrent congestion and environmental degradation. According to the fifth assessment report of IPCC, the annual average growth rate of global anthropogenic greenhouse gas emissions has reached 2% from 2000 to 2010, 0.7% higher than the same period of 1970-2000(Li, Y 2017). Vehicle emissions mainly include nitrogen oxides (NO_X), carbon dioxide (CO), carbon dioxide (CO_2), hydrocarbons (HC) and particulate matter (PM)(Jielun Liu 2019).

In 2017, light vehicles accounted for 67% of total carbon dioxide (CO),58% of totalhydrocarbon (THC) and 20% of total nitrogen oxide (NO_X)(MEE 2018). Urban traffic efficiency is crucial in large cities, and one of the main participants in daily traffic activities in urban areas is a taxi, for example, there are about 15000 taxis in Madrid, Spain (Billhardt, H 2019). Compared with other light vehicles, it has higher mileage and longer operation time per day. The annual vehicle mileage of a taxi is extremely high, which is ten times of personal light vehicle (Bishop, G. A 2016). Stead, D et al. (1999) found that according to the original data of the 1989 national travel survey, the CO_2, CO, and NO_X emissions of taxis are higher than those of private cars in the UK. Wang et al. (2015) found that according to the emission per kilometer of passengers, the emission of the taxi is greater than five times that of the Beijing bus. Many researchers at home and abroad have researched the emission of taxi pollutants in various cities. An Shi et al. (2011) has developed three kinds of air pollution emission models, and concludes that reducing the number of empty kilometers of the taxi can contribute to environmental protection. Liqiang He et al. (2019) used PEMS to test gasoline and dual fuel taxis in 7 cities. The results showed that taxis with high mileage (> 300000km) far exceeded the corresponding emission limits of NO_X, THC and CO. Ruimin Li et al (2019) analyzed direct and indirect emissions. In this study, license plate recognition was used to assess the road emissions and fuel consumption of vehicles in the process of taxi vacancy and travel in Nanning, China. The results showed that in the case of taxi vacancy, the reduction of total emissions and fuel consumption was higher than that of total driving distance. Basing on the research on the connection between traffic emission calculation model and traffic planning model. Zhao Xiaohua et al (2015) analyzed the impact of taxi driving behavior on fuel consumption. Acceleration condition has a major contribution to the total fuel consumption of vehicles under low service, and ecological driving behavior has a significant potential for energy saving under acceleration condition. During working hours (10:00-16:00) in Barcelona, Spain, Moreno et al (2019) investigated the air quality in taxis. Most taxi drivers chose to drive with their windows open to keep the carbon dioxide and other organic compounds at a low concentration but exposed them to traffic-related air pollutants outside.

This paper is organized as follows: We obtains the GPS data of taxi in Xi'an City in 2014, and use them to calculate the proportion of different speed segments of taxi and the vehicle speed time curve. Then we calculate the distribution of taxi VSP according to the driving data, and localize the MOVES model to compute the emission pollutants HC, CO, NO_X and CO_2 of taxi. We analyze the pollution Emissions of taxi based on time and distance.

1 Data Source and Preprocessing

Due to special driving characteristics of taxis, some information can't truly reflect the road traffic conditions. According to the running state of the vehicle, the vehicle data in the flameout state is filtered out, the running state of the vehicle (empty vehicle and passenger-carrying) is filtered out, and then the abnormal data and repeated data with very small running speed are screened out.

The track of 379 taxis covers most areas and many kinds of roads in Xi'an city. The vehicle thermal map and track map are obtained by matching them with the map. Fig. 1 is the thermal diagram of taxi driving, and Fig. 2 is the driving track diagram of a taxi. As shown in Fig. 1, the taxi driving track is mainly distributed within the second ring road. In the northwest and southeast regions, the taxi driving path is less than other regions, and the number of passengers who choose the taxi to arrive at the northwest and southeast regions is less. As shown in Fig. 2, the vehicle driving track is concentrated on the third ring road of Xi'an City, and fewer vehicle tracks are drivingoutside the third ring road of Xi'an city. Generally, a taxi runs in a fixed range of activities.

2 MOVES Emission Model and VSP Model

2.1 Motor Vehicle Emission Simulator(MOVES)

MOVES allows users to import data for specific need to calculate emissions (EPA. 2014).

Given the predicted time, place, vehicle type and emission process in MOVES, the pollutant emission can be calculated according to the following foursteps(Koupal J et al. 2008):

Fig. 1 Thermal diagram of vehicle driving Fig. 2 Vehicle track map

(1) Calculate all driving characteristic information of vehicles, i.e. driving characteristic information based on different emission processes, such as emission source operation time (SHO), several vehicles started, emission source stop time (SHP) and emission source time (SH).

(2) Distribute all vehicle operational information to emission sources and operational condition intervals, and each interval corresponding to different emission process is unique.

(3) Calculate the emission rate. The emission rate represents the emission characteristics of the emission source based on the given emission process, emission source range and operation condition range, but at the same time, the emission rate will also be affected by additional factors, such as fuel and temperature.

(4) Add all emissions distributed in the emission source and operating condition range (from the second step). The mathematical expression is as follows:

$$TE_{process\ source\ type} = (\sum ER_{process\ bin} \times AC_{bin}) \times AJ_{process} \tag{1}$$

Where TE is the sum emission; the process is the emission process. The source type is the emission source type. Bin is the emission source and operating range. ER is the emission rate. AC is the driving characteristic, and AJ is the adjustment factor.

OpModeID represents the operation mode. Based on VSP, speed and acceleration, there are 23 operation modes for driving exhaust process, which is defined in Tab. 1 (Wu, Y et al. 2014).

Defintion of operating mode in MOVES　　Tab. 1

OpMode 0	Deceleration/Banking	OpMode 1	Idle		
OpMode	<25mph	OpMode	25–50mph	OpMode	>50mph
11	VSP<0	21	VSP<0		
12	0≤VSP<3	22	0≤VSP<3		
13	3≤VSP<6	23	3≤VSP<6		
14	6≤VSP<9	24	6≤VSP<9	33	VSP<6
15	9≤VSP<12	25	9≤VSP<12	35	6≤VSP<12
16	VSP≥12	27	12≤VSP<18	37	12≤VSP<18
		28	18≤VSP<24	38	18≤VSP<24
		29	24≤VSP<30	39	24≤VSP<30
		30	VSP≥30	40	VSP≥30

2.2 Vehicle Specific Power (VSP)

In the field of micro transportation, the concept of vehicle-specific power appeared, which Jiménez-Palacios (1999) of MIT proposed originally. Vehicle specific power (VSP) is defined as the traction power of vehicle per unit mass. VSP has a strong correlation with vehicle fuel consumption, so VSP has served as the main variable of emission estimation, and it has been used in many kinds of research on emission modeling.

$$VSP = \frac{Av}{Mass} + \frac{Bv^2}{Mass} + \frac{Cv^3}{Mass} + [a + g * \sin\theta] \quad (2)$$

Among them, A is coefficient rolling resistance (kW-s/m). B is rotary resistance $kW - s^2/m^2$. C is coefficient aerodynamic resistance ($kW - s^3/m^3$). v is speed (m/s). a is acceleration (m/s^2), and θ is road slope(%).

For light vehicle activity data, by using typical parameters of specific vehicle type, after simplifying Eq. (2) in existing research, VSP can be calculated according to vehicle speed V and acceleration a, as shown in Eq. (3).

$$VSP = v \times [1.1 * a + 9.81 * \text{grade}(\%) + 0.132] + 0.000302 * v^3 \quad (3)$$

Where v is the vehicle speed (m/s); a is the acceleration (m/s^2); grade represents the grade of road slope, because Xi'an is a plain city, this paper assumes that the parameter is 0.

In the analysis of the VSP interval, VSP is classified by an equivalent VSP interval of 1kW/ton, as shown in Eq. (2). This method can effectively reduce aggregation error and calculation complexity. VSP distribution is calculated by estimating the number of VSP values in each bin and calculating the proportion.

$$\forall VSP \in [n, n+1), VSP \text{ Bin} = \#n, n \text{ is inter} \quad (4)$$

We use VSP to establish the relationship between traffic data and emissions. Calculate VSP with Eq. (1) and VSP distribution of Eq. (2), and draw the VSP distribution diagram as illustrated in Fig. 3.

Depending on the calculated data, we can find that most of the VSP values are between -20 and 20kw/ton, and the proportion of VSP in the positive range is slightly larger than that in the negative range. VSP = 0 has the most distribution, and VSP is on the brink of the normal distribution.

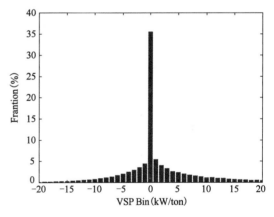

Fig. 3 Taxi VSP distribution in Xi'an in 2014

3 Traffic Pollutant Emission Analysis

3.1 MOVES Localization

The operation specification is established by the navigation panel on the left side of the MOVES user interface in Fig. 4, which includes simulation time and scale, the type of vehicle, road, fuel, and pollutant, etc. The details panel in Fig. 4 shows the data information of specific parameters selected by the user. According to the different simulation scales selected by users on the navigation panel, there are three different data managers for road sources: Data Importer, Country Data Manager and Project Data Manager. Huang Guantao analyzed the sensitivity of various input parameters of vehicle emission factors. The results showed that some parameters had a great influence on the emission factors, such as average speed of vehicle, fuel information, meteorological information, vehicle age, etc.

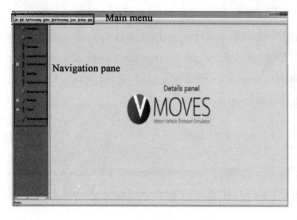

Fig. 4 MOVES main interface

China's vehicle emissions started later than the US, so the simulation year was advanced four years to reduce the error. The simulated vehicles are taxis, and the simulated pollutants are CO, CO_2, NO_X, HC. Divide the speed of GPS data into 16 speed ranges of MOVES. The taxi service life in Xi'an is 8 years, and input the vehicle age distribution according to the normal distribution. The main fuel oil of taxis in Xi'an is CNG, input it mixed with gasoline. The temperature and humidity of the working day with valid data shall be adopted, and the forecast scale is medium. The road types include urban closed road and Urban Non-closed road. MOVES analog input parameters are shown in Tab. 2.

Input parameters in MOVES Tab. 2

Parameter Name	Specific Description
Simulation Date	9-Apr – 10
Day、Hour	Weekday、0:00 – 4:00
Passenger Car	Light-Duty Vehicles
Fuel Type	CNG, Gasoline And Mixture
Meteorological Parameters	Humidity 20% - 61%
	Temperature 59-77
I/M	Default
Vehicle Age	1-8 Years Old
Road Type	Urban Closed Road
	Urban Non-Closed Road
Simulated Pollutants	CO、CO_2、NO_X、HC

The input data, calculation process and output data of MOVES are all stored in the MySQL database. Users can input data flexibly, and the calculation results of the model can also be output to excel format, which is convenient for users to process the data later.

3.2 Taxi Traffic Status Analysis

According to the data, the daily and hourly driving speeds of taxis can be obtained, Fig. 5 shows the proportion of taxi speed. To study the distribution of taxi speed, picture the proportion of different driving speed ranges in the total driving speed range as shown in Fig. 5, referring to Zhao Xiajun's urban road network traffic congestion degree division. When the vehicle speed is in the 0 ~ 10km/h, it means that the traffic flow is almost stagnant, the queue is long, the vehicle speed is extremely low, and the road bearing condition is saturated or supersaturated. The vehicle speed in the 0 ~ 10km/h accounts for 10%, indicates that the traffic congestion in Xi'an. When the vehicle running speed is in the 10 ~ 20km/h, it means that the vehicle running speed is greatly reduced, the delay is relatively large, the frequency of vehicle queuing is high, and the road load condition tends to be saturated. The speed shows that traffic congestion in Xi'an accounts for 18%. When the vehicle speed is in the 20 ~ 30km/h, it means that the vehicle will reduce when it is running smoothly, there is a certain delay, queuing phenomenon occasionally occurs, and the frequency is not high. In the above speed range, Xi'an's traffic is relatively congested, accounting for 19%. At this point, vehicle is relatively free to drive, and there is no abnormal queuing phenomenon on the main road. When the vehicle speed is in the 30 ~ 40km/h, it means that the traffic is smooth, accounting for 22%. The proportion of vehicle speed in 40 ~ 100km/h is at least 25%, which indicates that the vehicle holding in Xi'an city is high, there are few open road sections that can be driven in Xi'an City, and the most likely driving speed is in the high-speed area in the time period of low traffic flow, such as at night.

According to GPS data, draw the trend curve of taxi speed. Fig. 6 shows the trend curve of taxi speed in the day. As shown in Fig. 4, the driving speed range of the vehicle is approximately 20 ~ 30km/h, and the driving speed of the vehicle at night is less than that in the daytime. According to the trend curve of vehicle speed, the vehicle speed at 8:00, 13:00 and 18:00 is significantly lower than that in the previous period.

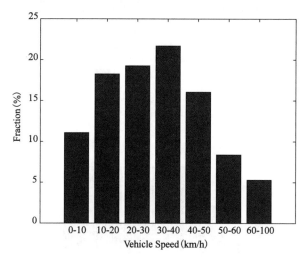

Fig. 5 Speed proportion

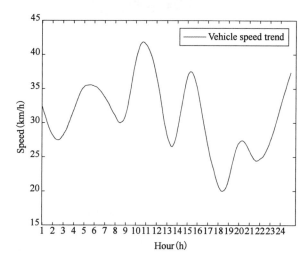

Fig. 6 Vehicle speed trend

3.3 Emission Analysis Based on Time

According to the calculation of taxi pollutant emission based on MOVES, Fig. 7 shows the emission results of 379 taxis per hour for CO, CO_2, HC, and NO_X. The abscissa is the period of taxi operation, and the ordinate is the pollutant emission. The CO_2, CO, HC, NO_X emission range is 0 ~ 303.2g/h, 113.7 ~ 2615.1g/h, 0 ~ 189.5g/h, 0 ~ 303.2g/h respectively. CO emission range is higher than other emissions.

As shown in Fig. 7a), in the early peak period of 7:00-9:00, more vehicles lead to road congestion. The CO_2 emission caused by the continuous start and stop of vehicles reaches the maximum within the day in the 75.8 ~ 303.2g/h. At the evening peak of 17:00 - 19:00, the CO_2 emission is in the range of 151.6 ~ 189.5g/h, which is slightly higher than that in the normal period. From 21:00 to 6:00, the demand of passengers for taxis is less than that of other periods, and the number of taxis driven in this period is less than that of other periods. In other periods, the CO_2 emission range is 113.7 ~ 151.6g/h.

As shown in Fig. 7b), the CO emission in the early peak period of 7:00 - 9:00 is in the range of 1288.6 ~ 2274g/h, reaching the highest emission in one day. The CO emission in the late peak period of 17:00 - 19:00 is in the range of 1749.4 ~ 2234.1g/h, which is slightly higher than that in the normal period. The CO emission in the taxi is in the range of 113.7 ~ 985.4g/h is less than that in the other periods.

As shown in Fig. 7c), the HC emission results are as follows: from 7:00 to 9:00 the HC emission is in 75.8 ~ 189.5g/h for frequent starting and stopping of road congestion vehicles. HC emission from 17:00-18:00 is 113.7g/h, and the HC emission of taxis is at least 0 ~ 37.9g/h from 21:00-6:00. The emission in other time intervals is 37.9 ~ 75.8g/h.

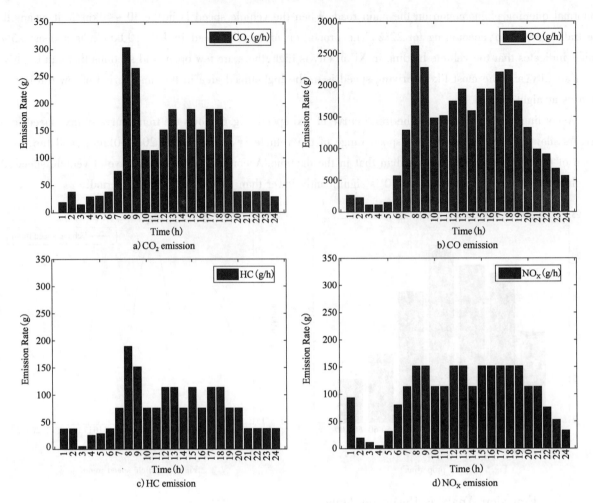

Fig. 7　379 taxis emission per hour

As shown in Fig. 7d), the NO_X emission results are 151.6g/h in the morning peak, evening peak and noon period. NO_X emission is 0 g/h in the period from 23:00 to 6:00, and the emission is 75.8 ~ 113.7g/h in other periods.

Fig. 8 shows pollutant emission of 379 taxis per kilometer in different periods. The abscissa is the taxi operation period, and the ordinate is the pollutant emission per kilometer. The emission range of CO_2 per kilometer is 0 ~ 12g/km, and the emission range of CO per kilometer is 0 ~ 100g/km. The emission range of HC per kilometer is 0 ~ 7g/km, and the emission range of NO_X per kilometer is 0 ~ 8g/km. CO emission per kilometer is higher than fresh emissions.

As shown in Fig. 8a), the CO_2 emission per unit distance shows that the average CO_2 emission per unit distance of a taxi is nearly 12g/km in the early peak period from 8:00 to 9:00. CO_2 emission per unit distance is higher than that in other periods, indicating that the congestion degree in this period is more serious. Similarly, the traffic flow on the road is large from 13:00 to 15:00, and the CO_2 emission per unit distance is 7 ~ 8g/km. The unit distance emission of CO_2 is about 6 g/km at 17:00 - 19:00, and the unit distance emission of CO_2 is 0g/km at 24:00 - 5:00. The unit distance emission of CO_2 is 2 ~ 4g/km at other time.

As shown in Fig. 8b), the emission per unit distance of CO is nearly 100g when the vehicle is driven for 1km from 8:00 to 9:00. The emission per unit distance of CO in the number of operating vehicles from 12:00 to 13:00 reaches 90g/km, and the emission per unit distance of CO in other periods is in the range of 60 ~ 70g/km.

As shown in Fig. 8(c), the emission results of HC per unit distance can be obtained. In the early peak period, the average HC pollution emission of taxis is 6 ~ 7.5g/km. The congestion degree of this section is more acute than that of other periods. In the same way, the traffic flow is heavy at 12:00-13:00 road and the emission per unit distance of CO_2 is 5 ~ 5.5g/km. At 17:00 - 19:00 the unit distance emission of CO_2 is about 3.5g/km. The unit distance emission of CO_2 is 0g/km in the period of 3:00 - 5:00, and the unit distance emission of CO_2 in other periods is 3 ~ 4.5g/km.

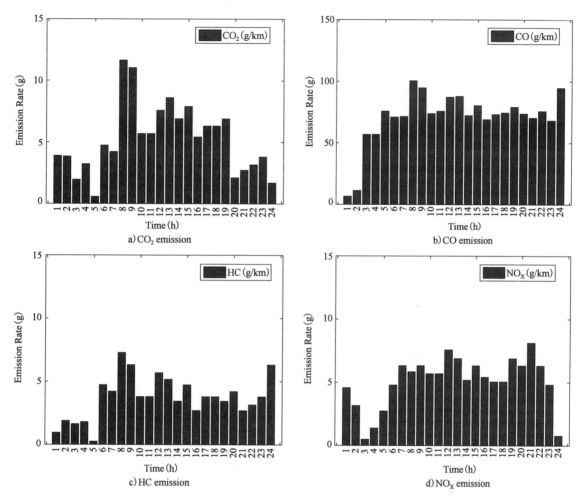

Fig. 8 379 taxis emission per kilometer

As shown in Fig. 8d), the emission results of NO_X per unit distance can be obtained. At 12:00 and 21:00, a taxi driving 1km generates 7.5g/km and 8.5g/km NO_X respectively. During the period of 23:00-6:00, the emission per unit distance of a taxi is 0g/km, and the emission per unit distance of CO_2 in other periods is 5 ~ 6g/km.

During the early peak period of 7:00 - 9:00, the unit distance emissions of CO_2, CO and HC achieved the highest level. At 24:00 - 5:00, the emissions of CO_2 and NO_X were 0 g/km, and the emissions of HC were 0 g/km at 3:00 - 5:00.

There are differences in the hourly activity and emissions of taxis. Fig. 9 indicates the proportion of CO, CO_2, HC, and NO_X in the total emissions of 24h. As shown in Fig. 9, the highest emission ratios of CO, HC, NO_X and CO_2 are 8.6% and 7.8%, 11.1% and 8.8%, 7.14% and 7.14%, 12.3% and 10.7% at 8:00 and 9:00 respectively. In this period of time, the demand for taxis is large and the traffic flow on the road is slow, which leads to the increase of pollutant emissions due to congestion. The proportion of pollutant emissions remains at 10:00 - 20:00. In a stable state, it fluctuates between 4% and 8%. The emission ratio of 21:00 - 2:00 and 6:00

is about 2%. From 2:00 to 5:00, there is a small amount of taxi activity. At this time, the proportion of emissions is close to 0%, and the demand for taxi is the lowest in this period. The activity and emission of vehicles in the daytime are far more than that at night, and the emissionof vehicles in the early peak period is higher than that in other daytime periods. The activity and emission of vehicles at night are relatively low, and the activity and emission of vehicles in the early morning are close to none.

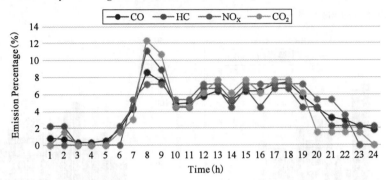

Fig. 9　Percentage of hourly emission rate

3.4　Emission Analysis Based on Distance

Fig. 10 presents the results of different driving mileage and corresponding pollutant emissions of 379 taxis. The abscissa is the driving mileage of taxis, and the interval is 158～11370km. The ordinate is the pollutant emissions within the driving mileage period, and the interval is 113.7～3260g, in which CO emissions account for the largest pollutant emissions, attended by CO_2 emissions. The longer the driving distance is, the more pollutants will be discharged. When the driving distance is greater than 1000km, pollutant emissions increase with the driving distance.

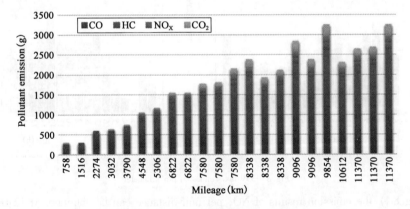

Fig. 10　Pollutant emission of the taxi based on different mileage

4　Conclusion

In this paper, the distribution of VSP is mainly in -20 to 20kW/ton, of which 0 kw/ton is the highest.

The driving speed range of taxis is mainly 20～45km/h. The simulated emissions of pollutants from taxis are higher in the daytime than that at night because of more traffic dynamics during the day. Traffic congestion has a significant impact on pollutant emissions. During the early peak and late peak, the traffic speed has a minimum value and the pollutant emission reaches the maximum. CO emission per unit distance is higher than other emissions. The pollutant emission increases with the increase in driving distance.

5　Acknowledgements

This research was funded by Natural Science Foundation of China (Grant No. 61703053), China

Postdoctoral Science Foundation Funded Project (Grant No. 2017M623091), National key research and development program (Grant No. 2018YFB0105104), National Science Foundation of Shaanxi Province, China (Grant No. 2018JQ6035).

References

[1] An, S., X. Hu and J. Wang. (2011). "Urban taxis and air pollution: a case study in Harbin, China." Journal of Transport Geography., 19(4), 960-967.

[2] Anenberg, S. C., Miller, J., Minjares, R., et al. (2017). "Impacts and mitigation of excess dieselrelated NOX emissions in 11 major vehicle markets." Nature., 545 (7655), 467-471.

[3] Billhardt, H., et al. (2019). "Taxi dispatching strategies with compensations." Expert Systems with Applications., 122, 173-182.

[4] Bishop, G. A., Stedman, D. H., Burgard, D. A., et al. (2016). "High-mileage light-duty fleet vehicle emissions: their potentially overlooked importance." Environ. Sci. Technol., 50 (10), 5405 – 5411.

[5] CAOYang., et al. (2017). "A study on localization of project-level parameters of MOVES Model in shenzhen." Traffic information and safety., 2(35), 100-108.

[6] He, L. (2019). "Real-world gaseous emissions of high-mileage taxi fleets in China." Sci Total Environ., 659, 267-274.

[7] HuangGuantao. Micro level traffic emission assessment based on moves [D]. Beijing: Beijing Jiaotong University, 2011.

[8] Jielun Liu., et al. (2019). "Spatial-temporal inference of urban traffic emissions based on taxi trajectories and multi-source urban data." Transportation Research Part C., 106, 145-165.

[9] José Luis Jiménez-Palacios. (1999). "Understanding and Quantifying Motor Vehicle Emissions with Vehicle Specific Power and TILDAS Remote Sensing." Massachusetts Institute of Technology., Cambridge.

[10] Karen M. Sentoff., ea al. (2015). "Implications of driving style and road grade for accurate vehicle activity data and emissions estimates." Transportation Research Part D., 35, 175-188.

[11] Koupal J, Cumberworth M, Harvey Michaels, et al. (2008). "Design and implementation of MOVES: EPA's new generation mobile source emission model."

[12] Li, Y., et al. (2017). "Re-estimating CO_2 emission factors for gasoline passenger cars adding driving behaviour characteristics——A case study of Beijing." Energy Policy., 102, 353-361.

[13] Lu, H., G. Song and L. Yu. (2016). "The "acceleration cliff": An investigation of the possible error source of the VSP distributions generated by Wiedemann car-following model." Transportation Research Part D: Transport and Environment., 65, 161-177.

[14] Mao S Y. (2019). "National Bureau of Statistics of China." <http://www.stats.gov.cn/>.

[15] Ministry of Ecology and Environment (MEE) of the People's Republic of China, 2018. China vehicle environmental management annual report.

[16] Moreno, T., et al. (2019). "Vehicle interior air quality conditions when travelling by taxi." Environmental Research., 172, 529-542.

[17] Ruimin Li, T., et al. (2019). "Effect of taxis on emissions and fuel consumption in a city based on license plate recognition data: A case study in Nanning, China." Journal of Cleaner Production., 215, 913-925.

[18] Stead, D. (1999). "Relationships between transport emissions and travel patterns in Britain." Transport Pol., 6, 247-258.

[19] U. S. Environmental Protection Agency. (2014). MOVES2014 Software Design Reference Manual, EPA-420-B-14-056 December 2014.

[20] U. S. Environmental Protection Agency. (2014). MOVES2014 User Interface Manual, EPA-420-B-14-057

July 2014.

[21] Wang, Z., Chen, F., Fujiyama, T. (2015). "Carbon emission from urban passenger transportation in Beijing." Transportation Research Part D:Transport and Environment.,41,217-227.

[22] Wu, Y., G. Song and L. Yu. (2014). "Sensitive analysis of emission rates in MOVES for developing site-specific emission database." Transportation Research Part D:Transport and Environment.,32,193-206.

[23] Zhang xiaoguang., et al. (2015). "statistical yearbook of Shaanxi Province-2015." China statistics press.

[24] ZHAO Xiao-hua., et al. (2015). "The Effect and Potential Study of Eco-driving on Taxi Fuel Consumption." Journal of Transportation Systems Engineering and Information Technology.,15(04), 85-91.

[25] Zhao XJ., et al. (2018). "Time series analysis of urban road congestion based on GPS track data." Hunan communication science and technology.,44(03).

基于长短时记忆神经网络的城市主干道流量预测

胡煦生

(长安大学运输工程学院)

摘 要 随着大数据技术的发展，大数据技术越来越多地被应用到高速公路短时交通流量预测中，神经网络模型对于处理交通大数据越来越显示出它的优越性。传统高速公路短时交通流预测模型，仅考虑单一位置的流量，面对复杂的路网环境时，预测效果往往效果不佳。除此之外，交通的时空特征往往被忽略。本文将时空特征融入长短时记忆(LSTM)神经网络模型中，试验结果验证了在加入了时空特征后，LSTM 模型的预测精度有了较大幅度的提升，平均绝对百分比误差、均方误差和平均绝对误差均有显著下降，该模型具有较好的扩展潜力。

关键词 短时交通流预测　LSTM 神经网络　时空特征　城市主干道

0 引 言

随着大数据时代的到来，巨大的公路总里程也给运营管理者带来了挑战。公路性能监测系统每天可以收集海量的交通参数数据，而这些数据中蕴含着丰富的信息，但由于噪声数据多、整合多源数据分析困难等原因，并没有得到有效的利用。高效利用这些信息可以为运营管理者的决策提供信息支撑。

交通流的短时预测一直都是道路运营管理者关注的热点，准确的预测道路交通参数对与智能交通的发展至关重要。在以往的城市主干道交通流量预测中，对于交通量的空间分布特征往往考虑不充分，因此，本文综合考虑时空关系，利用神经网络模型城市主干道流量进行短时交通量预测，验证考虑时空特征对短时交通流预测模型精度的影响。

1 相关工作

短时交通流预测问题一直是近年来科研研究的热点问题。短时交通流的预测模型主要包括基于线性理论的预测模型、非线性理论的预测模型、神经网络模型和组合模型等[1]。线性理论模型包括回归分析模型、历史平均模型和时间序列模型等。这类模型的优点是计算过程简单，需要的数据量小且具有较高的精度，缺点是不能很好地处理数据中的趋势和季节性问题。文献[2]提出了一种季节性 ARIMA 模型，在单点的短期交通流预测方面，最邻近非参数回归模型在单点的短期交通流预测比季节性 ARIMA 具有更优的预测结果。在历史数据有限的情况下,季节 ARIMA 模型仍然可以表现出相对精确的预测结果[3],该模型适用于没有庞大历史数据库情况下的短时交通流预测。除了技术较为成熟的 ARIMA 模型,文献[4]提出了 SUTSE 多元短期交通状况预测模型。该模型同样是时间序列模型,且与传统的时间序列模型相比,其不仅具有计算更加简洁、简单和高效的特点,而且具有较高的计算精度。然而,随着研究的进一步深入,线性模型不能很好地处理非线性因素的影响这一缺点也逐渐暴露出来,因此,非线性模型的研究逐渐获得了更多研究者的青睐。文献[5]建立了一个以神经网络模型为基础的数据聚合模型,提出将平滑移动模型、指数平滑模型和整合移动平均自回归模型的预测结果作为神经网络模型的输入的思路,很好地处理了模型线性和非线性部分,预测结果表明数据聚合模型的精度比任意单一模型的预测精度都要高。然而,由于文献中的时间粒度为 1h,该模型在更短时间粒度情况下的交通量预测适用性还有待进一步研究。

随着计算机科学与大数据技术的发展,处理大量的数据与缩小时间粒度越来越容易,新兴的数学理论被应用到传统的预测模型中,以得到更好的预测效果。文献[6]提出了一种基于小波去噪、模糊分类和模式识别的高速公路交通量短期预测的 ARTMAP 神经网络模型。在该模型中,时空特征的影响同时被考虑进预测模型。文献[7]提出一种高精度、高扩展性的多元时空回归模型,能够良好地预测城市地区 1h 内的以 5min 为粒度的交通量。除此之外,文献[8]提出了一种基于谱分析的日内交通流实时预测模型。该模型的时间粒度为 15min,在此条件下认为基于谱分析的实时交通流预测模型的预测精度可以与基于时间序列及神经网络预测模型的精度相媲美。文献[9]通过拓展随机细胞传输模型(SCTM)分析了不确定截面时空相关性和供给函数,建立了一种短期交通状态预测架构。该架构适用于存在事故或处于极端天气状态下的交通流量的预测,但由于该方法中的滞后效应导致无法捕捉由 SCTM 产生的移动瓶颈效应。文献[10]说明了交通流在自由流状态、交通事故、交通状态恢复和交通拥堵之间的过渡会导致明显的非线性特征,而深度学模型能够很好地解决该问题。近几年,随着神经网络的发展,能够处理时间序列问题的神经网络架构被广泛地应用到交通参数预测中。文献[11]提出了一种新的用于路段速度预测长短时记忆神经网络模型(LSTM),该模型能够处理学习具有长时间相关性的时间序列,自动确定最优时滞。文献[12]同样证明了 LSTM 在与其他短时交通流预测方法的对比中表现出来的优良的精度和泛化能力。单一的 LSTM 仅考虑数据的时间维度变化,而准确的时空关系表达对于模型的充分整合与应用至关重要[13]。文献[14]结合道路网在时间域和空间域的相互作用,建立了级联 LSTM 网络并证明了该方法的有效性。

受制于计算机的硬件限制及神经网络模型较长的训练时间,虽然以往的短时交通流预测模型易筋经具有较高的精度,但在模型的计算速度上并不一定能做到实时预测。然而随着大数据技术的快速发展与广泛应用,实时交通流预测的目标逐渐被实现。文献[15]提出了一种基于大数据技术和 KNN 模型的短时交通流预测方法,与传统的时间序列模型相比,该方法的效率提升了 77%,预测精度也有明显提升,并且具有很好的水平扩展性。

2 基于 LSTM 循环神经网络的短时交通流预测

LSTM 是一种基于循环神经网络(RNN)的架构,是一种特别的 RNN 类型,其特殊之处在于可以学习模型需要的长期依赖特征信息。在本节中主要介绍的是关于 RNN 和 LSTM 神经网络模型的基本原理以及本研究构建的基于 LSTM 的预测模型。

2.1 LSTM 循环神经网络基础

2.1.1 循环神经网络

RNN 在处理序列数据方面具有良好的效果,相比于不基于序列的神经网络,它更容易扩展到更长的序列,同时,它还能处理可变序列。RNN 的基本计算式如公式(1)所示。该计算式代表的含义为 t 时刻的系统状态与 $t-1$ 时刻的系统状态有关,参数 θ 为状态 s^{t-1} 向 s^t 映射时需要标定的参数。RNN 的计算图如图 1 所示。

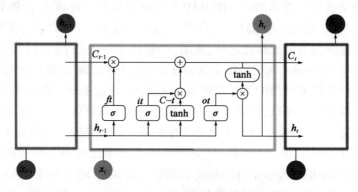

$$s^{(t)} = f(s^{t-1}; \theta) \tag{1}$$

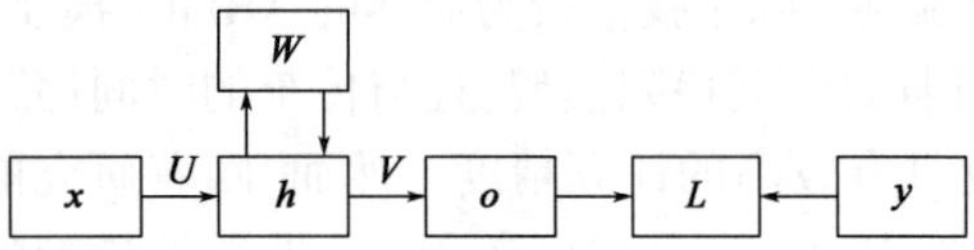

图1 RNN 计算图

图1中,x 为输入模型的输入序列,权重矩阵 U 将初始的序列参数化并连接到隐含层,隐含层通过 W 进行参数化并连接到循环层,参数 V 将隐含层参数化,并通过激活函数连接到输出 o。输出 o 与目标 y 在损失函数 L 的作用下进行循环迭代,以得到损失最小时的输出。RNN 模型虽然在处理时间序列问题上具有先天的优势,但是,在长时间的循环之后,会产生梯度消失或者梯度爆炸的问题,而 LSTM 的出现正好解决了这一问题。

2.1.2 LSTM 神经网络

LSTM 神经网络同样具有与 RNN 相似的链式结构,但相较于 RNN 的结构要复杂得多,该链式结构又由多个单元组成,对于处理长期依赖的问题又有很大的帮助。一个基本的 LSTM 记忆单元主要包含遗忘门、输入门和输出门,如图2所示。

图2 LSTM 结构示意图

如图2所示,单元上部的水平信息链将上游的信息经过微小的线性变化传递到下游,保持了信息的真实性。结构中的遗忘门控制着保留至此刻单元状态的信息量,输入门控制着此刻输入中保留至此刻单元状态的信息量,输出门此刻单元状态的输出量。

式(2)为遗忘门的计算方法,sigmoid 函数控制着遗忘门的开关。式(3)为输入门的计算方法,同样由 sigmoid 激活。式(4)表的是当前状态的候选值,遗忘门和输入门输出结果,作为当前状态的影响因素,在考虑当前状态候选值之后,通过式(5)确定当前状态的长期值,这一值将被输入下一记忆单元。而当前时刻的输出值则是通过式(6)进行激活,并通过式(7)选择过滤需要的信息作为最终的输出。

$$f_t = \text{sigmoid}(W_f \cdot [h_{t-1}, x_t] + b_f) \tag{2}$$

$$i_t = \text{sigmoid}(W_i \cdot [h_{t-1}, x_t] + b_i) \tag{3}$$

$$\widetilde{C}_t = \tanh(W_C \cdot [h_{t-1}, x_t] + b_c) \tag{4}$$

$$C_t = f_t \cdot C_{t-1} + i_t \cdot \widetilde{C}_t \tag{5}$$

$$o_t = \text{sigmoid}(W_0 \cdot [h_{t-1}, x_t] + b_0) \tag{6}$$

$$h_t = o_t \cdot \tanh(C_t) \tag{7}$$

式中:f_t、i_t 和 o_t——t 时刻遗忘门、输入门和输出门选择后的结果;

$\widetilde{C}_t$、C_t——t 时刻状态的候选值、长期值;

h_t、h_{t-1}——t 时刻 $t-1$ 时刻记忆单元输出;

sigmoid、tanh——激活函数;

W_f——遗忘门权值向量;

b_f——遗忘门限的阈值;

W_i——输入门限的权值向量;

W_c——可添加状态的权值向量；

W_0——输出单位状态的权值向量；

b_i——输入门限的权值向量；

b_c——可添加状态的权值向量；

b_0——输出单位的权值向量。

3 实验验证与分析

本研究采用的数据集为美国加利福尼亚州 PeMS 公开交通数据集[16]，对提出的模型参数进行确定以及预测效果进行评价。评价指标包括平均绝对百分比误差（MAPE）、均方误差（RMSE）、平均绝对误差（MAE）。

3.1 交通流数据预处理

数据的质量对于模型的训练过程至关重要，因此需要对数据进行预处理。预处理的内容包括数据聚合、数据清洗以及数据的归一化处理。

3.1.1 数据介绍

本文以美国加利福尼亚州萨克拉门托市为研究范围，选择 I 5、I 80、CA99 和 US 50 公路为研究对象，分别获取了这 4 条公路进入市区和出市区方向的交通量数据。数据集的采样点 A~F6 个点的位置如图 3 所示。其中，每个点位的观测数据是分方向的，如 A 点有两组数据，分别为郊区—城区方向的交通量数据和城区—郊区方向的交通量数据，其他点位亦是如此。

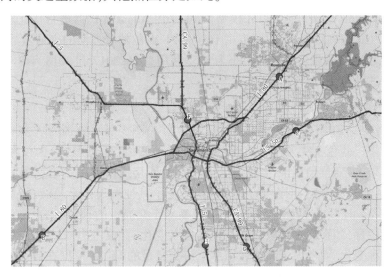

图 3 调查点示意图

数据集包含的主要字段见表 1。获取的数据集为美国佛罗里达州 12 个交通观测站的数据。数据的时间跨度为 2016 年 1 月 1 日至 2019 年 12 月 31 日。观测站统计的交通量为自然量，时间粒度为 5min。每个观测站仅观测单向各个车道的交通量数据。

数据集字段说明　　　　表1

字段名称	单　位	字段说明
时段	5min	数据集时间跨度为 2016 年 1 月 1 日至 2019 年 12 月 3 日，以 5min 为间隔
车道 n 流量	辆	第 n 个车道数的流量
车道总流量	辆	断面总流量（单向）
车道数	个	断面的车道数（单向）
观测样本百分比	%	实际观测量占比，若该值小于 100%，则说明该时段交通量中有部分量值为估算结果

3.1.2 数据处理

原始数据集的时间粒度为 5min,而本文中研究的时间粒度为 1h,因此,需要将原始数据以 1h 为时间间隔进行聚合。在聚合之后,由于交通管制、特殊事件等原因,会存在个别时段道路流量为 0 的情况,这部分数据可视为错误数据。由于这类数据会对模型的训练和预测结果产生较大的影响,因此,采用均值替换的方法消除这类错误数据的影响。

由于不同点位的交通量差距有所不同,因此,需要将数据进行标准化处理,消除不同数量级数据对预测结果的影响。本文采用 min-max 标准化方法,计算公式如下:

$$x^* = \frac{x - \min}{x_{\max} - x_{\min}} \tag{8}$$

式中: x^*——标准化处理后的值;

x——标准化处理前的值;

$x_{\min}$、$x_{\max}$——数据中的最大值和最小值。

3.2 模型建立与预测

3.2.1 考虑时空特征的 LSTM

如图 5 所示的 A~F 6 个点,控制着进出城市的绝大多数的交通量。因此,从 A 点处进出城市的交通量,与其他点位的交通量具有密切的关系。因此,在预测 A 点处的交通量时,B~F 点单向的交通量也将作为特征输入模型中。

3.2.2 模型参数设定

在本研究中,利用 Keras 框架进行 LSTM 模型预测,采用 Adam 优化器进行优化求解。预测时间间隔为 1h,时间步长设定为 3,即利用前 3h 的城市主干道 A~F 点位的分方向的交通量数据,预测第 4 个小时的 A 点或其他点位的单向交通量。批处理大小为 72。利用 2016、2017 和 2018 年 3 年的数据进行模型训练,用 2019 年的数据进行验证。

3.2.3 预测结果分析

选取 2019 年 8 月 15—21 日的预测结果进行展示。图 4、图 5 所示分别为 A 点市区方向交通量和郊区方向交通量预测结果。蓝色实线为实际交通量,单变量预测值(绿色虚线)为仅考虑 A 点交通量时间序列特征时的预测结果,多变量预测值(红色虚线)为考虑了其他城市主干道交通量的预测结果。从图中可以看出,无论是 A 点交通量时间序列的模型还是考虑了其他城市主干道交通量的模型,预测结果都与实际交通量较为相符。这反映了 LSTM 神经网络模型对于交通量的预测具有较好的性能。但是,在一些交通量急剧变化的位置,如在高峰时段交通量呈锯齿状变化时,仅考虑 A 点交通量时间序列特征的模型不能很好地适应这种变化,而考虑了其他城市主干道交通量的 LSTM 模型在流量的高峰时段更加接近实际值,更能适应高峰时段的剧烈波动。

根据 4 个模型的拟合结果,利用测试集对模型进行评价。各个模型中评价指标 RMSE、MAE 和 MAP 的结果见表 2。

模 型 对 比 结 果　　表2

位　　置	影 响 因 素	RMSE	MAE(%)	MAPE(%)
A 点(市区方向)	仅 A 点流量	363.260	276.472	10.3%
	考虑其他点位流量	229.246	165.664	6.1%
A 点(郊区方向)	仅 A 点流量	417.248	315.454	15.2%
	考虑其他点位流量	280.039	212.084	8.8%

从表 2 从可以看出,当仅考虑 A 点交通量时间序列特征时,即利用 A 点前 3 个时刻的交通量预测第 4 个时刻的交通量时,市区方向和郊区方向的 MAPE 分别达到了 10.3% 和 15.2%,RMSE 分别为 363.260 和 417.248,MAE 分别为 276.472 和 315.454。在此基础上,当仅加入空间特征时,MAPE 下降至 6.1% 和

8.8%,除此之外,RMSE 和 MAE 也有显著下降。因此,考虑了其他城市主干道交通量的 LSTM 模型具有更高的预测精度。

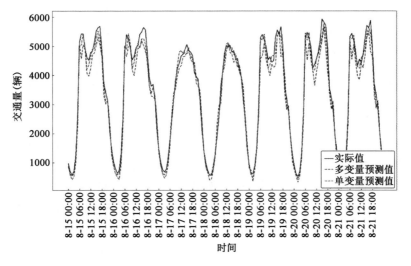

图 4　模型预测效果(A 点市区方向)

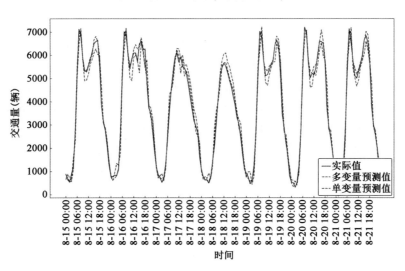

图 5　模型预测效果(A 点郊区方向)

在考虑其他城市主干道交通量的情况下,预测了 B~F 点的交通量,预测结果见表 3。结果显示,对比不同的点位,该方法都显示出了较好的预测性能,所有点位的平均 MAPE 为 10.3%。但对于个别点位(如 E 点),MAPE 具有较大的误差,达到了 17.8%,考虑为其他支路分流带来的影响。

城市主干道交通量预测结果　　　　　　　　　　　表 3

位置		RMSE	MAE(%)	MAPE(%)
市区方向	A	229.246	165.664	6.1%
	B	173.926	131.335	9.2%
	C	297.373	200.631	12.1%
	D	116.901	89.464	7.4%
	E	314.802	236.147	17.8%
	F	258.214	196.989	8.1%
郊区方向	A	280.039	212.084	8.8%
	B	206.398	151.929	7.5%

续上表

位　　置		RMSE	MAE(%)	MAPE(%)
郊区方向	C	296.832	200.790	12.0%
	D	178.751	132.839	10.2%
	E	125.046	102.312	9.2%
	F	252.167	185.166	15.7%

4 结　语

本研究在大数据处理与分析理念的基础上,利用LSTM神经网络模型,结合城市主干道的路段交通量观测数据,分析了交通量的时间序列特征、城市交通的分布特征,构建了考虑其他城市主干道交通量的LSTM模型。实验结果验证了相对于单纯的LSTM模型,在考虑其他城市主干道流量后,即考虑时空特征的条件下,LSTM模型具有更高的预测精度。本文所构建的基于LSTM的模型在考虑空间特征时还可以进行更深一步的研究与优化。本文中目前所考虑的空间特征维度较低,模型中缺少对交通环境因素等的分析,且模型中参数都是人工调试的。在后续的工作中,将更好地将环境因素纳入模型中,并实现模型参数的自动优化。

参考文献

[1] 刘静,关伟. 交通流预测方法综述[J]. 公路交通科技,2004,21(3):82-85.
[2] Smith B L,Williams B M,Oswald R K. Comparison of Parametric and Nonparametric Models for Traffic Flow Forecasting [J]. Transportation Research Part C:Emerging Technologies,2002,10(4):303-321.
[3] Kumar S V,Vanajakshi L. Short-term traffic flow prediction using seasonal ARIMA model with limited input data[J]. European Transport Research Review,2015,7(3):21.
[4] Ghosh B,Basu B,O'Mahony M. Multivariate short-term traffic flow forecasting using time-series analysis [J]. IEEE transactions on intelligent transportation systems,2009,10(2):246-254.
[5] Tan M C,Wong S C,Xu J M,et al. An Aggregation Approach to Short-term Traffic Flow Prediction [J]. IEEE Transactions on Intelligent Transportation Systems,2009,10(1):60-69.
[6] Boto-Giralda D,Díaz-Pernas F J,González-Ortega D,et al. Wavelet - based denoising for traffic volume time series forecasting with self-organizing neural networks[J]. Computer-Aided Civil and Infrastructure Engineering,2010,25(7):530-545.
[7] Min W,Wynter L. Real-time road traffic prediction with spatio-temporal correlations[J]. Transportation Research Part C:Emerging Technologies,2011,19(4):606-616.
[8] Tchrakian T T,Basu B,O'Mahony M. Real-time traffic flow forecasting using spectral analysis[J]. IEEE Transactions on Intelligent Transportation Systems,2011,13(2):519-526.
[9] Pan T L,Sumalee A,Zhong R X,et al. Short-term traffic state prediction based on temporal – spatial correlation[J]. IEEE Transactions on Intelligent Transportation Systems,2013,14(3):1242-1254.
[10] Polson N G,Sokolov V O. Deep learning for short-term traffic flow prediction[J]. Transportation Research Part C:Emerging Technologies,2017(79):1-17.
[11] Ma X,Tao Z,Wang Y,et al. Long short-term memory neural network for traffic speed prediction using remote microwave sensor data[J]. Transportation Research Part C:Emerging Technologies,2015,(54):187-197.
[12] Tian Y,Pan L. Predicting short-term traffic flow by long short-term memory recurrent neural network[C]. 2015 IEEE international conference on smart city/SocialCom/SustainCom (SmartCity). IEEE,2015:153-158.

[13] Vlahogianni E I, Karlaftis M G, Golias J C. Short-term traffic forecasting: Where we are and where we're going[J]. Transportation Research Part C: Emerging Technologies, 2014, 43: 3-19.
[14] Zhao Z, Chen W, Wu X, et al. LSTM network: a deep learning approach for short-term traffic forecast[J]. IET Intelligent Transport Systems, 2017, 11(2): 68-75.
[15] 汪雪非, 丁维龙. 面向高速公路大数据的短时流量预测方法[J]. 计算机应用, 2019, 39(1): 87-92.
[16] California Department of Transportation, Caltrans Performance Measurement System (PeMS). Available online: http://pems.dot.ca.gov/ (accessed on January 27, 2021).

Big Data Applications in Rail from Academic to Commercial View

Rui Xue   Zhiqiang Ma   Xiaoning Ma   Dongsheng Yang   Siqi Sun

(China Academy of Railway Sciences Corporation Limited)

Abstract Reflecting big data concepts, technologies, and methods in the rail sector, big data applications in China rail play a highly important role in national economic and social development. Thus, research into the rail sector is needed now more than ever, as the rail industry is entering the digital era, and the demand for improved rail transportation becomes more apparent. From comprehensive views, this study aims to better understand big data applications in rail. Based on those views, this research proposes a novel analytical framework and then uses the subsequent comparative analysis to verify it. The results show that: ① operation and equipment are two leading areas with big data applications from both academia and industry; ② trending technologies such as edgy deep learning models have been incorporated into big data applications in rail.

Keywords   Big data applications   Rail   Analytical framework   Comparative analysis

0 Introduction

A massive amount of data, regarding passenger travel, freight logistics, safety monitoring, engineering construction, and others, have been generated and accumulated in rail transportation. Other than 5V features, namely, volume, variety, velocity, veracity, and value (Wamba et al., 2015), big data in rail can be characterized by its importance in industrial applications. Big data applications in China rail play a highly important role in national economic and social development, which reflects big data concepts, technologies, and methods in the rail sector. Therefore, big data applications have been topics of big interest from both academia and industry.

There are several surveys in the literature related to big data applications in the rail context. Some studies reviewed data applications in a specific aspect of rail transportation. A few take a broad perspective of rail as a whole and cross-maps with big data applications in the rail sector (Ghofrani et al., 2018). However, there is still a lack of commercial view to look into big data applications with available insights, when previous studies tend to focus on pure literature analysis. Though somehow reflecting big data applications (BDA), studies are often viewed as presentations of scientific advances, due to novelty demand. Thus, it is inevitable to review big data applications in rail from both academic and commercial views for a comprehensive understanding. To fill the gap in research, this paper proposes a novel analytical framework based on data collected from academia and industry. This framework is then applied to the subsequent comparative analysis to research top relevant cases, evolutions, and challenges of big data applications in rail.

The contribution of this study is twofold. Firstly, we define the innovative framework to analyse big data applications in academia and industry. The subsequent analysis of literature review and practical case studies verifies this framework. Secondly, we apply a comparative analysis between academic and industrial data, which is seldom mentioned in previous work. This study finally comes with insightful findings, supporting future work of big data in rail.

The rest of the paper is organized as follows. The second part defines the research methodology, including material collection, descriptive statistics, and subsequent analytical framework. In the third part, we apply comparative analysis regarding top relevant cases, evolution study, and challenges of BDA from academia and industry. Then follows the final part with a conclusion and future directions.

1 Research Methodology

Inspired by content analysis (Mayring, 2014), generally, this study follows the four-step iterative process, from a to d, as below:

(1) Material collection which defines how data is collected and pre-processed.
(2) Descriptive analysis which overviews the general distribution of data.
(3) Framework in which dimensions are formed to cluster major aspects and topics of data.
(4) Comparative analysis that compares data from academic research and in the wild.

In this section, we will discuss step a, b, and c, and leave step d to the following section.

1.1 Material collection

To address this question, we collect two parts of data from academic research and real industrial practices, respectively.

Regarding the academic aspect, we use IEEE Xplore as the source for data collection. IEEE Xplore is a digital research database with web access to more than 5 million documents from publications in computer science, electrical engineering, electronics, and allied fields. It contains journal articles, conference proceedings, technical standards, and related materials published mainly by the Institute of Electrical and Electronics Engineers (IEEE) and other partner publishers (Wilde, 2016). To retrieve relevant data, any combination of two-word sets with the logic word "AND" is used. The keyword combination for academic dataset are shown in Tab. 1.

Keyword Combination for Academic Dataset   Tab. 1

Word set	Word set 1	Word set 2
Keywords	big data data mining intelligent (intelligence) machine learning predictive analytics artificial intelligence	rail railway(s) railway engineering railway system(s) railway operation(s) railway maintenance railway safety

Other than the logic word "AND", the search for a combination of each from word set 1 and 2 also allows the following rules:

(1) Stems, as unique word forms, are applied to avoid inflected variants, such as single or plural forms, upper case or lower case, etc.
(2) Searching is conducted in title, abstract, keywords, and keywords plus.
(3) Only journal and conference proceeding papers are considered.

(4) Year range of publication is from 2000 to 2020.

(5) Only papers in English are collected.

After reducing the duplicates, the final dataset contains 275 papers as our analysis targets in academic research, excluding papers withthe only review, purely mathematics modelling, and simulated small dataset.

To accelerate big data applications in rail, China Rail published the implementation plan in 2017, which includes 16 key directions with 211 applications in total regarding passenger and freight transportation, safety and risk assessment, engineering management, equipment status, asset management, etc. In this study, we conducted questionnaires and interviews on big data applications in rail from 2017 to 2020. Feedbacks on implementation, expected results and challenges are collected from departments in China Rail and China Academy of Railway Sciences. The survey dataset includes 202 big data applications, with 192 existing items in the plan and 10 new ones.

Data is pre-processed and labelled as follows. Items in this dataset are marked with "completed", "partially completed" and "in plan". Completed applications refer to projectsthat have been formally launched. Then, partially completed ones point to those in design, development or trial deployment. Finally, applications in plan represent items just on calendar. Another attribute is regarding expected results of big data applications in rail. Items are classified with "improvement" or "exploration", the former defines big data applications as developed ones on the current version, while the latter imply novel applications in the rail sector. Besides, applications are also labelled with "internal", "cross-domain" and "cross-industry", which outlines the scope of data resources.

1.2 Descriptive analysis

Inspired by (Gautam, 2017), two measures, publication year and citation number, are considered. Other than those, we also apply analysis in paper type. Thus, descriptive analysis is given from aspects regarding publication year, paper type, and frequency of citation. As shown in Fig. 1a), the number of publications increases in 2009 and 2016.

The number of articles published after 2014 and 2016 has shown significant growth, especially in 2016—2020. With increasing by multiples each year, the amount of published papers in recent years indicates that big data applications in rail, as hot topics, have been attracting attention from the academic community. In terms of the research type, it can tell from Fig. 1b) and Fig. 1c) that more publications focus on conferences rather than journals over the years. This might be related to the fact that research on rail applications often comes from practices, with peer discussions and communication required. Thus, conferences, as preferred choices, become big interests to researchers in this area. In addition, Fig. 1d) implies that papers that have been cited quite often only account for a tiny part of studies, while most of the works are cited one or two times. It seems there is still a lack of research with huge impacts in the community.

Based on the attributes of survey data, the descriptive analysis will be given regarding implementation, expected results, and scope of big data applications in rail. It can be seen from Fig. 2a) that fully completed big data applications in rail practices only occupies 25% in the survey, while the partially completed cases account for 35%. This suggests that big data applications in the rail sector still have a way to go when the largest proportion of them is still in plan, as shown in Fig. 2a). Fig. 2b) states the basis of big data applications in rail, most of which are upgrades or improvements on existing ones, and a few are innovative explorations. Moreover, Fig. 2c) defines the scope of data resources in railway big data applications. 45% of big data applications under this investigation are within one professional domain, and 30% of them require the collaboration of multiple domains in rail. A few big data applications demand data from other industries, such as meteorology, geography, etc.

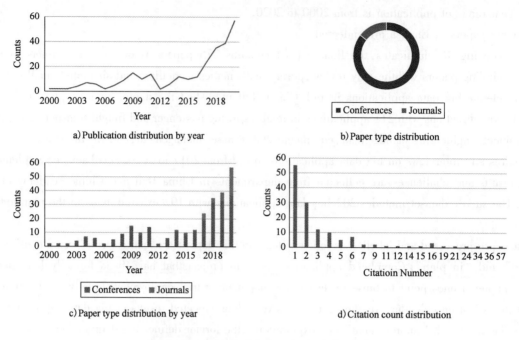

Fig. 1 Descriptive Analysis from Academic Research

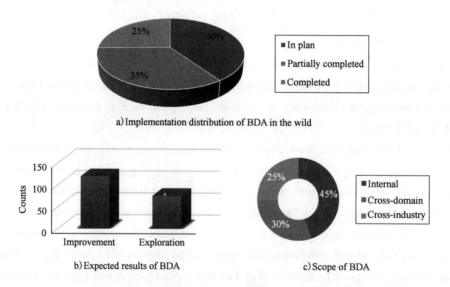

Fig. 2 Descriptive Analysis from Practical Survey

1.3 Analytical framework

Based on previous work (Ghofrani et al., 2018) and the classification of rail practices, we propose an analytical framework coping with big data applications in rail, shown in Fig. 3. This framework includes two layers, the upper of which consists of four main areas, while the lower one details specific subjects. The four main components on the 1st layer are operation, engineering, equipment, and others, respectively. Specifically, rail operation covers subjects such as passenger, freight, safety, and dispatching. Engineering in this framework is defined to a narrow scope, construction management. Besides, equipment refers to fault diagnosis, maintenance, and device monitoring. Finally, others may contain commonly seen big data applications in other areas instead of the previous three domains, including but not limited to asset management, strategy and policy, budget and investment, and human resources. The subsequent analysis and discussion will follow this framework.

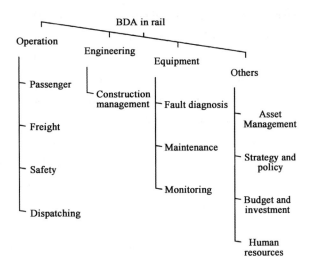

Fig. 3 Analytical Framework

2 Comparative Analysis

This section will compare and analyse academic research and field survey data from three aspects. The first one is the top relevant BDA in rail. By reviewing and comparing areas and subjects related to BDA in academic research and the wild, we explore the key developments and the differences between academics and practices. The second aspect is to study evolutions of railway big data applications. It is expected to observe the year-on-year changes in publication numbers and keywords. What's more, the implementation of BDA in various areas will be checked, and expected results will be analysed, providing references for future BDA plans. The third aspect is to sort out the challenges of big data application in rail, and clarify barriers in academia and industry.

2.1 Top relevant BDA in rail

This subsection reviews the most significant big data applications in rail from both academic and practical aspects. Based on the framework mentioned above, we focus on the following four dominant areas in rail. Top relevant applications from life and the most frequently cited work will be reviewed with details.

2.1.1 Operation

According to academics, big data applications in rail operations cover various topics, ranging from train delay analysis to demand forecasting. With most of the research being conducted in this subject related to safety and passenger flow, big data analytics helps to monitor operations and thus prevent accidents or manage massive passengers, allowing improved decision-making in real-time rail operations. A topic with high priority and concern in rail operations is safety, occupying 18 of 179 papers published from 2000 to 2020. This topic has been spurring interest from researchers, and in recent years there has been a significant increase in the number of relevant studies, covering topics such as safety monitoring and accident analysis. For example, (Hemmati et al., 2017) proposed a framework to combine specification mining, model-based testing, and analytics to help with monitoring and verification of safety-critical systems. (Sabnis et al., 2019) defined a system that can automate the monitoring of railway crossings. The object detected will be sent as an alert to the nearby stations and transferred to the operator as well, effectively reducing the rail collisions at crossings. (Mabrouk, 2016) suggested a method based on machine learning to assist investigators experts in their crucial task of analysis and assessment of the rail safety in France. (Alawad et al., 2020) explored the employment of the decision tree (DT) method in safety classification and the analysis of accidents at railway stations to predict the traits of passengers affected by accidents.

Another dominant topic relates to the passenger, specifically, passenger flow. 11 of 179 studies focus on this subject, involving various scenarios and different methods. (Xu et al., 2018) established a comprehensive forecasting model based on time series analysis with the combination of the long-term trend factor, the seasonal factor and the weather factor. (Gao et al.,2020) proposed improved measures for the shortest path fare scheme of urban rail transit based on passenger flow. (Liang et al.,2020) predicted short-term passenger flow in urban rail transit through a VMD-LSTM combination model, and an example was then used to verify this model. Besides, an artificial neural network method was applied regarding this subject at the early stage (Zheng et al.,2011).

Big data applications from rail practices mostly cover topics of passenger, freight, safety and dispatching. From the passenger aspect, an E-ticketing risk assessment and control system has been established since 2017, and big data techniques have been applied to identify malicious ticket swiping. The passenger service voice platform was fully upgraded in November 2018. And then in 2019 and 2020, business data and knowledge can be shared with various passenger service centres. Automatic circulation was established to handle passenger requests on time, improving work efficiency and passenger satisfaction. Regarding freight, the E-commerce system website (95306) has been published and improved. Besides, information interaction systems and digital ports were developed. In terms of safety, the main applications include safety pattern analysis, safety evaluation, risk assessment, and risk alert. Big data applications, such as time series analysis and text mining, have been deployed to gradually achieve overall safety monitoring, scientific safety evaluation, and accurate warning in advance.

2.1.2 Engineering

The literature in engineering is distributed quite balanced in time, mainly focusing on the economic analysis and assessment, or detection methods in specific scenarios. For example, (Lv et al., 2011) defined a technical-economic indexes simulation model as an accurate and efficient management method in rail construction. (Wang et al,2019) proposed a method for detecting temporary building demolition based on remote sensing images to automatically monitor whether the adjacent buildings in each area are demolished on time.

Big data applications in rail engineering practices focus on subjects of project progress, quality and safety, with digital techniques regarding design, construction and implementation. Big data models and algorithms have been developed in key areas, carrying out in-depth data mining and correlation analysis, to improve project management and support decision making. For instance, relying on railway engineering management platform, the quality trend analysis of the engineering raw materials and semi-finished products has been established. Besides, a measurement system of tunnel safety has been developed with rock deformation analysis. Moreover, the application of an electronic construction log has been carried out. And more big data applications have been in progress based on the combination of Building Information Modelling (BIM) and Geographic Information System (GIS).

2.1.3 Equipment

From the reviewed articles, conspicuously, the fault or defect detection/diagnosis and maintenance are the most dominant subjects, accounting for 26 of 79, and 8 of 79, respectively. The research on the two topics booms after 2013. With continuous updates, there are quite a number of studies with new technologies in machine learning and deep learning, regarding fault or defect detection. For example, (Guo et al.,2018) described a fault detection method based on stacked autoencoders (SAE), which can be easily trained and has great expressive power. (Pahwa et al., 2019) developed a multi-phase deep learning based technique to perform accurate fault detection of rail-valves. a two-step method was applied in this model, resulting in pixel-wise accurate segmentation. In maintenance-related research, the involved data types have expanded from mainly time series data to text data. For instance, (Núñez et al., 2014) discussed the applicability of Big Data techniques to facilitate maintenance decisions regarding railway tracks through condition-monitoring data. While (Zeng et al., 2020) developed an information mining system for railway traction power supply equipment maintenance based on a large number of texts.

Equipment in rail practices includes fixed equipment and mobile equipment covering various domains such as track, signal and communication, power supply, vehicles, etc. Although in multiple domains, big data applications in equipment are concentrating on data collection and correlation, status analysis and evaluation, quality evaluation, Prognostics and Health Management (PHM), correlation analysis, risk assessment, etc.

Taken signal and communication as an example, data from vital areas, such as interlocking, train control, track circuit, Centralized Traffic Control (CTC), power supply and so on, are collected. A comprehensive quality evaluation from multiple dimensions has been built, with quality trend analysis. E-records for signal and communication equipment have been available to check and manage the entire life cycle. Based on the historical overhaul and maintenance records, analysis and evaluation of equipment are offered. Correlation analysis of onboard and ground, real-time and historical, static and dynamic data assure equipment in signal and communication operate healthy and well.

2.1.4 Others

Other than operation, engineering and equipment, big data applications from academic research have come a few in very recent years, mainly on subjects such as asset management or land use. As shown, (Mcmahon et al., 2020) discussed requirements and challenges for big data analytics applications to railway asset management. (Duan et al., 2020) established the evaluation indicator of the coordinated relationship between rail transit station operating efficiency and land use, and a data envelopment analysis (DEA) model was used to evaluate the coupling degree between them.

Compared with academic research, big applications from rail practices copewith a large scope rather than subjects of asset management and land use. In terms of asset management, a targeted information system has been in service with functions covering assets in demand, plan, procurement, supply, warehousing, accounting and scrapping. Regarding economy and policy, the relationship between passenger station traffic and the local economy has been studied with data of Gross Domestic Product (GDP), population, and geography. Considering budget management and the human resources area, big data applications have been in development as well. A well-built budget management system has been in use with multiple indicators as measurements, such as the management project quota system (MPQS), to support and guide business activities. Besides, digital employee profiles have been built from 2019 to 2020. Based on these, big data models have been applied to improve the efficiency of human resource management.

2.2 BDA evolution in rail

It is necessary to observe how big data applications in rail change with time in both academic research and real practices. Analysis on evolution may reflect developments and explore the trend in rail. This subsection studies big data applications distributed by year under each area, keyword shifts with time, and implementation of main areas, better viewing the status quo of big data applications in rail.

Although differences in the data collecting period, this study still compares data of academia and industry. The reason is that the literature data was scattered in the early stage, and enriched in the past 3 ~ 4 years, consistent with the industrial data distribution. Fig. 4a) shows the changes in the number of articles published each year under four different areas. It can be observed that operation and equipment are the two dominant areas of research. The number of studies is roughly similar in the early days, but the amount of research in operation and equipment has been growing fast in recent years, widening the gap with other areas. Keyword trend with time in Fig. 4b) implies that among the series of data-driven cases, machine learning algorithms, especially deep learning models, are considered one of the most promising ones to tackle big data issues in rail.

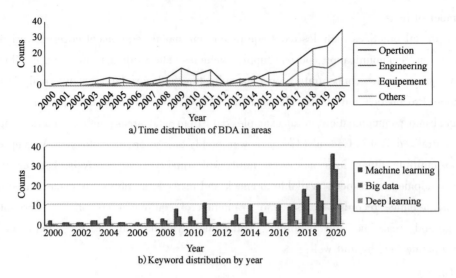

Fig. 4 Evolution Analysis from Academia

Regarding industrial evolution, implementation of big data applications in rail, as shown in Fig. 5a), implies that completed cases in the equipment and operation areas occupy higher proportions. This result presents a similar trend to the one in academic research. Besides, it can tell from Fig. 5b) that compared to explorations, big data applications based on current work are more likely to be finished.

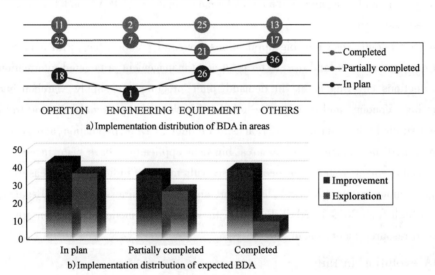

Fig. 5 Evolution Analysis from Industry

2.3 Challenges of BDA in rail

Not surprisingly, it can be observed that academic research and rail practices share some challenges. This subsection will outlinethe challenges of rail big data applications in detail.

2.3.1 Data collection

One challenge comes from data collection. Big data applications sometimes require data from multiple systems in various domains or even different industries. This demand brings difficulties when encountering data with diverse dimensions, isolated data, and sensitive data. Another concern in data collection is data quality. Data might be ambiguous with definition, or partly missing. What is worse, the same data collected from different systems is not matched or looks irrelevant. These can cause huge troubles in big data applications. Thus, data collection and cleaning might be time andlabour-consuming in practices, always asking for better solutions.

2.3.2 Data application

Another compelling challenge is in current rail big data applications, most of which apply descriptive statistics rather than analysis of correlation or predictionon a deeper level. The fact that instead of knowledge-driven, data-driven cases dominate application in rail could be the reason. To give insights into big data applications in rail, it demands that data combined with knowledge is used in future cases to carry out in-depth analysis. For instance, the knowledge graph of equipment with typical failures can be established with the corresponding solution samples. Moreover, it is demanding to relate big data applications in rail with standards, regulations and policies, to guide future developments in the rail sector.

3 Conclusion and Future Directions

This research proposes an overview analytical framework to examine 275 articles from academia and 202 applications from industry, allowing a comprehensive picture of where and how big data applications have been distributed in rail. The subsequent comparative analysis is offered to discuss top relevant cases, evolution trends, and challenges of rail big data applications. Despite the consistent developments, there are still many issues to be considered in terms of research and practices.

In this study, we review works of big data applications in rail from both academic and practical aspects. Future work could follow in two directions, one of which is extending literature sources to enrich analysis from the academic side, and the other is applying performance measurement models, such as Data Envelopment Analysis (DEA) (Bowlin and William, 1998), to validate big data applications in rail. The fact remains that further research intothe rail is needed now more than ever, as the rail industry is entering the digital era, and the demand for better rail transportation becomes more apparent.

4 Acknowledgements

This research is supported by Research Program of Institute of Computing Technology in China Academy of Railway Sciences Corporation Limited under official grant number DZYF20-32.

References

[1] A. Núñez, J. Hendriks, Z. Li, B. De Schutter & R. Dollevoet. Facilitating maintenance decisions on the Dutch railways using big data: The ABA case study[J]. 2014 IEEE International Conference on Big Data (Big Data), Washington, DC, 2014:48-53.

[2] Bowlin & William F. Measuring performance: An introduction to data envelopment analysis (DEA)[J]. The Journal of Cost Analysis 15.2, 1998:3-27.

[3] D. Liang, J. Xu, S. Li & C. Sun. Short-term passenger flow prediction of rail transit based on VMD-LSTM neural network combination model[J]. 2020 Chinese Control And Decision Conference (CCDC), Hefei, China, 2020:5131-5136.

[4] D. Zheng & Y. Wang. Application of an artificial neural network on railway passenger flow prediction[J]. Proceedings of 2011 International Conference on Electronic & Mechanical Engineering and Information Technology, Harbin, 2011:149-152.

[5] Ghofrani, F., He, Q., Goverde, R. M., & Liu, X. Recent applications of big data analytics in railway transportation systems: A survey[J]. Transportation Research Part C: Emerging Technologies, 2018(90): 226-246.

[6] Gautam, P. An overview of the Web of Science record of scientific publications (2004—2013) from Nepal: focus on disciplinary diversity and international collaboration [J]. Scientometrics, 2017, 113 (3),

1245-1267.
[7] H. Alawad, S. Kaewunruen & M. An. Learning From Accidents: Machine Learning for Safety at Railway Stations, IEEE Access, 2020(8):633-648.
[8] H. Gao, S. Liu, G. Cao, P. Zhao, J. Zhang & P. Zhang. Big Data Analysis of Beijing Urban Rail Transit Fares Based on Passenger Flow, IEEE Access, 2020(8):80049-80062.
[9] H. H. Mabrouk. Machine learning from experience feedback on accidents in transport[J]. 2016 7th International Conference on Sciences of Electronics, Technologies of Information and Telecommunications (SETIT), Hammamet, 2016:246-251.
[10] H. Hemmati, S. S. Arefin & T. R. Siddiqui. Analytics-based safety monitoring and verification[J]. 2017 IEEE International Conference on Systems, Man, and Cybernetics (SMC), Banff, AB, 2017:3608-3613.
[11] J. Zeng, D. Feng, S. Lin & Q. Chen. Research on Framework and Key Technologies of Text Mining for Operation and Maintenance of Traction Power Supply Equipment[J]. 2020 11th International Conference on Prognostics and System Health Management (PHM-2020 Jinan), Jinan, China, 2020:215-220.
[12] Lv Jun-chao, Mo Jun-wen & Zhao Yan-long. Research on simulating technical-economic indexes of railway construction project on Intelligence Agent[J]. 2011 2nd International Conference on Artificial Intelligence, Management Science and Electronic Commerce (AIMSEC), Dengleng, 2011:3280-3283.
[13] Mayring, P. Qualitative content analysis: theoretical foundation, basic procedures and software solution. Social Science Open Access Repository SSOAR, 2014.
[14] O. V. Sabnis & L. R., A novel object detection system for improving safety at unmanned railway crossings [J]. 2019 Fifth International Conference on Science Technology Engineering and Mathematics (ICONSTEM), Chennai, India, 2019:149-152.
[15] P. Mcmahon, T. Zhang & R. Dwight. Requirements for Big Data Adoption for Railway Asset Management, IEEE Access, 2020(8):15543-15564.
[16] R. S. Pahwa, et al. FaultNet: Faulty Rail-Valves Detection using Deep Learning and Computer Vision[J]. 2019 IEEE Intelligent Transportation Systems Conference (ITSC), Auckland, New Zealand, 2019: 559-566.
[17] Wilde, M. Ieee xplore digital library[J]. The Charleston Advisor, 2016, 17(4):24-30.
[18] Wamba, S. F., Akter, S., Edwards, A., Chopin, G., & Gnanzou, D. How 'big data' can make big impact: Findings from a systematic review and a longitudinal case study[J]. International Journal of Production Economics, 2015(165):234-246.
[19] W. Yangping, R. Xinlei, Z. Zhengping & G. Decheng. Research on Temporary Building Monitoring of Railway Construction Based on Remote Sensing Image[J]. 2019 IEEE Intl Conf on Dependable, Autonomic and Secure Computing, Intl Conf on Pervasive Intelligence and Computing, Intl Conf on Cloud and Big Data Computing, Intl Conf on Cyber Science and Technology Congress (DASC/PiCom/CBDCom/CyberSciTech), Fukuoka, Japan, 2019:135-141.
[20] X. Xu, Y. Dou, Z. Zhou, T. Liao, Y. Lu & Y. Tan. Railway passenger flow forecasting based on time series analysis with big data[J]. 2018 Chinese Control And Decision Conference (CCDC), Shenyang, 2018: 3584-3590.
[21] Y. Duan, X. Fan, J. Liu and Q. Hou. Operating Efficiency-Based Data Mining on Intensive Land Use in Smart City, IEEE Access, 2020(8):17253-17262.
[22] Z. Guo, H. Ye, W. Dong, X. Yan & Y. Ji. A Fault Detection Method for Railway Point Machine Operations Based On Stacked Autoencoders[J]. 2018 24th International Conference on Automation and Computing (ICAC), Newcastle upon Tyne, United Kingdom, 2018:1-6.

浅谈交通强国背景下中小城市如何构建综合立体交通网——以淮安市金湖县为例

钱 芳 邹俊杰 莫明龙

（华设设计集团股份有限公司）

摘 要 党的十九大明确提出建设交通强国的宏伟目标，吹响了交通强国建设的号角，为交通发展奠定了总基调。本文基于交通强国建设背景，以高质量发展为总思路，重点探讨中小城市综合立体交通网的构建思路与方法，并以淮安市金湖县为例，从现状评价、趋势研判、目标定位、布局方案等多方面进行研究与论证，为同类城市的综合立体交通规划提供一定的借鉴意义。

关键词 交通强国 中小城市 综合立体交通 网络布局规划 高质量发展

0 引 言

党的十九大以来，习近平总书记深刻把握新时代我国发展的阶段性特征，对交通事业发展作出一系列重要论述，提出了建设交通强国的时代课题。2019年9月，中共中央、国务院印发《交通强国建设纲要》（以下简称《纲要》），提出建成"人民满意、保障有力、世界前列"的交通强国总目标，构建现代化综合交通体系，打造"全国123出行交通圈"和"全球123快货物流圈"。《纲要》开启了交通强国建设的新篇章。

目前国内已有的研究主要侧重于传统的综合交通运输系统本身，对交通强国背景下综合立体交通尤其是中小城市综合立体交通的研究较少。石钦文等人提出综合交通体系应注重与经济发展、社会发展、人口分布、环境保护、资源节约5大方面的协调[1]。高家驹指出综合交通运输应根据不同运输方式的技术特点，进行有机结合，分工协作，形成布局合理、连接贯通的综合交通运输体系[2]。丁金学、樊一江认为应基于综合交通网络发展基础、未来运输需求特征，从多元化、功能化、专业化分工角度，以功能分工为依据，重构现代化综合交通运输网络框架体系[3]。新时代背景下，如何实现各种交通运输方式的深度融合和系统集成，促进交通高质量、一体化发展，是各地区现阶段积极探索的重要方向。本文基于交通强国建设背景，重点研究中小城市如何构建综合立体交通网规划，并以金湖县为例，对研究思路与基础设施方案进行实证分析。

1 中小城市综合立体交通网规划研究思路

2019年，长江三角洲区域一体化正式上升为国家战略，国务院印发《长江三角洲区域一体化发展规划纲要》，提出"长三角区域实现基础设施互联互通，轨道上的长三角基本建成，省际公路通达能力进一步提升，世界级机场群体系基本形成，港口群联动协作成效显著"。区域交通格局的重大变化，要求大中小城市必须积极谋划构建与其相符的综合立体交通网体系，主动融入长三角，衔接区域大通道。对于中小城市而言，其综合立体交通网的构建，需重点把握以下两方面：一是统筹布局规划，中小城市应统筹上位规划的重要交通廊道与枢纽的布局，强化各方式的衔接，以综合立体的思维构建"宜公则公、宜铁则铁、宜水则水、宜空则空"的综合立体交通网；二是协调国土空间，中小城市应落实好上位规划确定的重大交通基础设施在区域内的空间布局，处理好与城镇、农业、生态空间的关系，实现交通高质量发展。

中小城市在开展综合立体交通网规划中，应坚持"服务大局、人民满意、统筹协调、创新驱动、远近结合"的原则，从现状评价、形势与需求、规划目标、综合交通网布局方案、保障措施等方面进行一一展开。

1.1 现状评价

通过资料收集、现场踏勘调研等方式,充分掌握城市与交通的发展现状,重点从2个层次进行现状评价。首先,从城镇体系、产业布局、镇村布局等多角度出发,评价现状综合交通网络与经济社会发展的适应性;其次,采用定量与定性相结合的方法深入剖析现状综合交通供给与交通服务存在的问题,其中交通供给主要考虑与对外通道的衔接、路网的规模与结构以及各方式之间的衔接等,交通服务主要考虑客货运服务、智慧交通、行业治理等。

1.2 形势与需求

全面把握规划目标年经济社会发展态势,综合考虑国家重大战略、省市重大政策、交通行业发展趋势、城市发展定位、城镇空间格局等因素,精准分析中小城市综合立体交通发展面临的机遇、挑战和发展要求。同时,深入分析未来交通运输量、结构变化趋势和客货运输需求特征,差别化引导中小城市形成合理的综合立体交通网络。

1.3 目标

结合城市的区位特色、发展定位等,提出综合立体交通网的规划目标,重点围绕安全、便捷、高效、绿色、经济等方面进行总目标及具体目标的设置。

1.4 综合交通网布局方案

围绕规划目标,从基础设施布局、客货运服务、智慧绿色平安交通等方面提出规划方案。中小城市在规划方案上重点考虑3个层面:一是落实国家、省市等提出的重大基础设施,明确在其境内的落地方案,做好用地预控,处理好与"三区三线"的关系;二是注重对外衔接,做好与省际、市际、县际交通设施的衔接;三是以服务民生为原则,侧重考虑城乡交通基础设施,包括城乡交通基础设施、城乡客运、城乡物流等。

1.5 保障措施

以保障规划顺利实施为目的,重点从资金、组织、体制、土地等方面提出保障措施。

2 金湖县综合立体交通现状评价

金湖县位于苏皖两省交界之处,南京都市圈边缘,处于宁连通道和京沪辅助通道之间,是宁淮同城化发展的关键节点城市。

近年来,金湖县综合交通发展迅速,交通基础设施得到了长足的发展,公路骨架网络基本形成,铁路网、水运网正在逐步完善,但对比"人民满意、保障有力、世界前列的交通强国"这一目标,仍然存在3个方面的问题。首先,融入区域通道能力不足。交通地位逐渐边缘化,与两侧连宁通道和京沪辅助通道衔接仅依靠一条国道,衔接数量与方式单一,区域融入能力明显不足;其次,现状与长三角城市联系以公路为主,缺少铁路等高品质、高舒适性的交通方式,导致在私家车的冲击下,营业性公路运输量逐年下降;最后,从路网布局上分析,东南部乡镇高等级公路覆盖率偏低;从路网规模与结构上分析,通过与苏南同类型城市对比发现,低等级公路占比近苏南城市的2倍,路网结构有待进一步优化;从出行时效上分析,受水网密布影响,乡镇上高速、乡镇与乡镇之间的出行时效偏低。因此,上述存在的问题难以支撑金湖县"长三角南京都市圈北部产业高端、绿色引领、全域旅游、统筹发展示范城市"的城市发展定位。

金湖县与淮安市各区县公路基本情况如图1所示。

3 金湖县综合立体交通形势分析

3.1 国家顶层战略为金湖的交通发展创造了机遇

2020年4月,国家发展和改革委员会、交通运输部印发《长江三角洲地区交通运输更高质量一体化发展规划》,要求紧扣"一体化"和"高质量"两个关键,以服务人民为中心,以互联互通为目标,以改革创新为动力,以打造"轨道上的长三角"为重点,坚持优化提升、适度超前的原则。长三角一体化要求金湖应以更高站位、更宽视野,构建高质量的现代综合立体交通网络,深度融入长三角一体化进程。

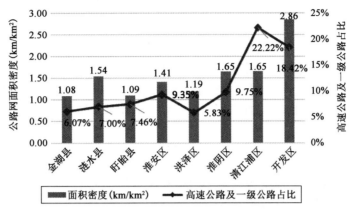

图1 金湖县与淮安市各区县公路基本情况

3.2 宁淮同城化进程加快,为金湖交通发展指引了新方向

2017年,《宁淮挂钩深度合作规划(2017—2030年)》(以下简称《规划》)获江苏省发展和改革委员会正式批复实施。《规划》要求宁淮合作实现基础设施、产业发展、技术创新、文化建设、公共服务、生态环境的协同发展。2019年,宁淮特别合作区正式挂牌成立,加快推进宁淮同城化进程。此外,国家级新区江北新区作为南京建设的新龙头,对苏北及中部地区发展发挥重要作用,进一步促进了宁淮同城化的发展。随着南京都市圈经济日渐升温,都市圈内关联度不断增强,区域交通需求逐渐网络化,商务、公务出行成为主导。宁淮通道交通需求日益旺盛,日均交通量已突破6万pcu,增长率达11.85%。

金湖地处淮安市南部,是宁淮两市联系的关键节点。宁淮同城化的稳步推进要求金湖实现多样化交通设施对接,依托城际铁路与高速公路等重大交通基础设施,深度融入宁淮通道,支撑宁淮同城化发展。

3.3 全域旅游发展赋予金湖交通新使命

金湖县境内白马湖、宝应湖、高邮湖三湖环绕,淮河入江水道自西向东穿城而过,拥有国家4A级旅游景区——荷花荡以及华东首个大型森林综合体——水上森林,是中华始祖尧帝生息的原乡故里。自2013年以来,金湖县全域旅游快速发展,旅游人数与旅游产业快速发展,以苏北水乡自然环境为基础,借助尧帝故里等文化优势,成功打造了"尧帝故里,荷都金湖"名片。

随着人民收入的不断提高,人民对旅游交通的品质要求逐步提高。金湖县应以获批首批国家全域旅游示范区创建单位为契机,提供高品质交通服务,丰富旅游内涵,提升旅游体验感,打造生态旅游示范县。

3.4 环境资源约束对金湖交通发展提出了新要求

2019年5月,中共中央、国务院发布《关于建立国土空间规划体系并监督实施的若干意见》(以下简称《意见》)。《意见》明确要求划定生态保护红线、永久基本农田、城镇开发边界等空间管控边界以及各类海域保护线,强化底线约束,为可持续发展预留空间。

金湖县作为国家生态示范县,始终把"生态优先"贯穿于经济社会建设的各个方面和全过程,以"生态+"模式刷新金湖高质量发展底色。在国土空间规划的新形势下,环境资源的约束要求金湖县必须强化生态约束底线,统筹考虑交通规划、城市发展与生态的关系,处理好重大交通基础设施与三区三线的关系,实现交通高质量发展。

3.5 科技创新快速发展引领交通进入新时代

伴随着科技创新的快速发展,新业态、新产品不断涌现,智慧交通推升新高度,引领金湖县交通发展进入新时代。金湖县应积极推进"交通强国"战略部署,强化新技术、新理念在交通中的应用,打造融合高效的智慧交通基础设施,助力信息基础设施建设,完善行业创新基础设施。

4 金湖县综合立体交通网规划方案

4.1 发展定位

以习近平新时代中国特色社会主义思想为指导,深入贯彻党的十九大精神,牢固树立新发展理念,落实高质量发展要求,以为交通强国和"强富美高"新金湖建设提供支撑和保障为目标,以满足金湖县经济社会发展和人民美好生活需要为导向,以深化交通运输行业供给侧结构性改革为出发点,提出金湖县综合立体交通发展的战略定位:宁淮交通协同引领区、全域旅游交通示范县。

4.2 综合交通网络布局方案建议

4.2.1 基础设施布局方案

(1)落实重大交通基础设施。深度融入连宁通道和京沪辅助通道,构建西接东连的东西向通道,新增盐蚌高速公路、沿淮城际铁路、420省道和331省道,提升改造闵铜线并积极纳入干线公路网,提升金宝线等级,沟通皖北地区;强化南北,发挥金湖在宁淮同城化中的作用,新增金天仪高速公路、白马湖景区连接线等重要干线公路,加快宁淮城际铁路建设。

(2)谋划城乡综合交通发展。以服务民生为目的,基于农村居民点分布,完善以县道网为骨架的农村公路网,实现乡镇至乡镇通达二级公路,乡镇至主要农村居民点通达三级公路,规划形成22条主要农村公路。以提高城乡居民出行水平为目的,规划形成"1＋5＋N"的客运枢纽体系,其中"1"是指金湖综合客运枢纽,"5"是指5个乡镇客运站,"N"是指利用城乡客运节点。以促进城乡物流水平为目的,在既有的"1＋3"物流园区基础上,规划新增24个镇村级物流配送节点,其中5个为乡镇综合服务站,主要依托乡镇客运站提供物流服务,19个为村级物流配送节点,以村委会、小超市等载体满足农村物流需求。

4.2.2 打造旅游交通示范县

金湖县全域旅游发展迅速,县域内分布有水上森林公园、荷花荡旅游景区、马草滩湿地公园以及白马湖景区等著名景点。旅游的发展要求必须构建"快达慢游"的旅游交通体系,以交通丰富旅游的内涵。依托公路网体系,新增4条重要景区连接线,规划形成"一环二轴一圈"的旅游公路网络,全长300km,主要利用沿河的堤顶路、共闵线、涂闵线、白马湖景区连接线等道路,在道路空间满足的情况下,两侧增加慢行道,空间局促情况下可单侧或利用绿化带新增慢行道,慢行道宽度宜不低于3m。依托丰富的水网体系,规划形成"一环一射"的旅游航道网,打造精品水上旅游环线。旅游航道总里程达73km,其中,"一环"是指三河湾旅游航道,"一射"是指三河湾—高邮湖旅游航道,并新建8处旅游码头。

4.2.3 提升运输服务质量

(1)优化客运服务品质。构建以城际铁路为骨架、市域(郊)铁路为延伸、个性化公交为补充的多模式公共客运体系。通过宁淮城际、沿淮城际铁路直达长三角城市核心及枢纽,服务金湖县的对外客运;通过淮安市域(郊)铁路满足金湖县直达淮安市区的交通需求;提供个性化的公交模式,衔接各乡镇以及重要社区单元,服务末梢节点。加快公路客运转型发展,推动公路客运从"站到站"模式向"点到点"和"门到门"定制模式转变;推广"互联网＋定制客运",开通网络平台,统一线上平台、线上预约、线上调度、线上结算,加速定制客运发展;推进区域客运同城化,开通省际、市际公交,提高对桐城镇、观音镇等的辐射服务。

(2)提升货运服务效率。完善城乡高效配送网络,优化县级物流中心、乡镇农村配送站、农村货运网点三级农村物流节点体系,重点建设乡镇农村物流服务站;培育农村物流经营主体,发挥龙头企业对物流资源的整合作用,引导和支持物流企业同行联手;提升邮政服务水平,加强邮政基础网络建设,优化多层次网络布局,提升骨干运输网、重点枢纽承载能力,提升网络覆盖度和稳定性;强化邮政普遍服务,推进快递普惠发展,形成以邮政普遍服务为基础,以电商快递服务为重要内容的邮政公共服务体系。

5 结 语

综合立体交通规划是面向2035年的长远规划,是交通强国战略实施的新起点。在国家、省市开展综合立体交通规划的背景下,本文以建设交通强国为目标,开展了中小城市如何构建综合立体交通的研究,并以金湖县为例进行实证研究,对其他中小城市综合立体交通网的规划具有一定的参考价值。

参考文献

[1] 石钦文,徐利民,胡思继.可持续发展综合交通运输系统规划理论研究[J].综合运输,2006(6):5-8.
[2] 高家驹.综合运输概论[M].北京:中国铁道出版社,1993.
[3] 丁金学,樊一江.现代综合交通运输网络框架体系研究[J].综合运输,2018,9(40):66-68.
[4] 庞清阁,姜彩良,石宝林.关于新时代我国综合交通运输发展的若干思考[J].交通运输研究,2019,5(4):20-25.
[5] 刘振国,常馨玉,贺明光,等.国土空间新形势下综合交通规划的问题与对策[J].交通运输研究,2019,5(4):64-68.

基于多源数据的区域综合交通OD分布研究

周 涛[1] 白 桦[1] 潘卫鹏[2]

(1.华设设计集团股份有限公司;2.南京理工大学)

摘 要 为了构建区域综合交通运输一张网,需要全面分析现状综合交通OD出行的特点,洞察各交通运输结构,指导区域出行政策制定。研究主要根据交通行业数据、调查数据等,利用OD提取算法获取各方式的OD出行,结合多源数据融合算法获取综合交通客货运输特征。本文构建了综合交通OD运输矩阵的实现方案,量化分析了江苏省综合交通及各交通方式的出行特征、出行结构及出行通道等,研究为地区精准地改善运输服务水平提供了量化的参考依据。

关键词 综合交通 行业数据 OD提取 多源数据融合

0 引 言

区域综合交通运输一张网涉及多种交通方式,如何将不同交通数据进行统一管理和分析,探究综合交通运输OD规律一直是区域交通研究的重点和难点问题[1]。现状的研究成果主要包含两类:一是传统方法下的OD获得及需求预测技术,其中包括传统的OD获得方法、OD反推方法等;二是大数据[2]在目前OD获取及需求预测技术中应用,主要包括利用GPS数据、手机信令数据[3]等获得OD的技术,而关于大数据在需求预测中的应用案例较少,尚停留在理论发展阶段。冯立光[4]分析了区域公路网OD调查工作的基础理论;柏强[5]提出了基于出行路径的大区域公路OD合成方法——"路径覆盖法";裴玉龙等[6]对黑龙江省交通分析模型和路网规划理论研究进行了论证;李昕等[7]研究了项目建设对通道内公路、铁路运量分担所产生的影响。如今国内外交通大数据主要用于单个城市或单种数据类型,针对多数据源和区域综合交通的研究较少。

本文以江苏省为例,通过交通大数据融合手段,收集各种交通方式数据,利用大数据技术手段和多源数据融合技术刻画新时期的交通OD特征,描述出行规律,为相关规划提供坚实的数据支撑。

1 各方式数据结构及OD提取技术

1.1 公路数据结构及OD提取

1.1.1 高速公路

通过高速公路联网运营管理中心搜集各高速公路收费站联网数据,联网收费数据表字段,共34个字段属性,属性如图1所示。主要利用SQL语句和大数据分析平台进行数据清洗、数据修复、数据校核、参数标定和字典匹配,然后利用大数据处理平台,按照时间、收费站进口、收费站出口、车辆类型进行OD提取,获得不同车型的OD矩阵数据。根据pcu折算系数,客车平均载客人数和货车自重等参数,可分别得到不同节点OD的车辆矩阵、pcu矩阵、客运人数矩阵和货运吨数矩阵。

EXP_KEYCOL	EXP_	EXP_ENTRY_STATIOI	EXP_ENTRY_TIME	EXP_E	EXP_EXIT_STATION	EXP_EXIT_TIME	EXP_VEHICLE	EXF	EX	EXP_DIS	EXP	EXP_	EXP_(	EXP_TOT
15505020110120180704002352000133850	3202	1010002	2018/7/4 0:05:29	3202	1550502	2018/7/4 0:23:52	苏M682CE蓝	1	0	30.41	0	0.00	0.00	0.00
00501050110220180704002923000114010	3201	50202	2018/7/4 0:08:05	3201	50105	2018/7/4 0:29:23	沪B67921黄	4	0	32.21	0	0.00	0.00	0.00
02000020110120180704002059000023700	3201	2130001	2018/7/4 0:14:51	3201	200002	2018/7/4 0:20:59	苏AE3X70蓝	2	0	0.00	0	0.00	0.00	0.00
02000020110120180704002151000023710	3201	2130001	2018/7/4 0:16:36	3201	200002	2018/7/4 0:21:51	苏EB525E蓝	1	0	0.00	0	0.00	0.00	0.00
00505010110120180704001835000276090	3201	50503	2018/7/4 0:09:35	3201	50501	2018/7/4 0:18:35	苏A7G5V5蓝	1	0	18.40	0	0.00	0.00	0.00
00505010110120180704002016000276100	3201	50503	2018/7/4 0:12:22	3201	50501	2018/7/4 0:20:16	苏A0D9N6蓝	1	0	18.40	0	0.00	0.00	0.00
00501010110520180704001621000377720	3201	50102	2018/7/4 0:04:44	3201	50101	2018/7/4 0:16:21	沪A22V28蓝	1	0	18.74	0	0.00	0.00	0.00
19500020110220180704002509000062150	3202	1950002	2018/7/4 0:25:09	3202	1950002	2018/7/4 0:25:09	皖S06271黄	4	0	0.00	0	0.00	0.00	0.00
00501020110220180704001847000044530	3201	50101	2018/7/4 0:07:59	3201	50102	2018/7/4 0:18:47	浙D067KM蓝	1	0	18.74	0	0.00	0.00	0.00

图1 高速公路主要字段原始字段结构

1.1.2 国省干道

交通调查点数据为微波监测器检测的断面数据,每5min上传一条数据,共约50个字段。交通调查点数据中,包含设备编号、设备位置、车道编码、不同车型车辆数,车速、车头时距等重要参数,对分析不同车辆类型的车流量具有重要意义。主要利用Oricle中SQL语句和大数据处理平台进行统计,获取各断面的流量,并结合交通模型进行OD反推获取国省干线的OD分布。利用统计数据和部分收费站数据对国省干线OD进行校核,通过高速公路和国省干线"串并连"的方法,剔除重复计算数据即可得到全省公路客货运数据。

1.2 铁路数据结构及OD提取

铁路票务信息系统数据库获取铁路票务数据为省内火车站客流量信息,包括上车车站名称、车次、运行区间;下车车站名称、座位类别(无座、硬座、硬卧、软卧)乘客量、不同车次乘客小计、车站客流量小计、站点分席客流量、站点合计客流量等信息。结合铁路票数数据的存储数据特征,利用Python对上车站名、下车站名及对应客流量进行数据统计,获取省内站点间客流量OD、省内站与邻省(安徽省、浙江省)城市间客流量OD、省内站与全国其他省(自治区、直辖市)间客流量OD的三列阵。其Python语句如图2所示。

```
    if "小计" in str(rtable.cell(1,k).value).replace(' ',''):
        t.append(k)
    k = k + 1
while(True):
    i = i + 1
    if i == 0:
        j = 0
        while (True):
            if "分席" in str(rtable.cell(i, j).value):
                a = a + 1
                print('')
                break
            elif len("".join(rtable.cell(i, j).value.split())) != 0:
                wtable.write(a, b, str("".join(rtable.cell(i, j).value.split())))
                b = b + 1
                print("".join(rtable.cell(i, j).value.split()), end=' ')
            j = j + 1
    if str(rtable.cell(i,0).value) =="合计":
        break
    if hasNumbers(str(rtable.cell(i,1).value)) or "".join(rtable.cell(i, 1).value.split()) == '':
        continue
    else:
        # print(str(rtable.cell(i,1).value))


        if i==1:
            continue
        b = 1
        wtable.write(a, 0,str("".join(rtable.cell(i, 1).value.split())))
        print ("".join(rtable.cell(i, 1).value.split()), end=' ')
        for w in t:
            if ((type(rtable.cell(i, w).value))==type("abc")):
                if len("".join(rtable.cell(i, w).value).split()) == 0:
                    wtable.write(a, b, 0)
                else:
                    wtable.write(a, b,"".join(rtable.cell(i, w).value.split()))
                print("".join(rtable.cell(i, w).value.split()), end=' ')
```

按"小计"关键词客流量提取

图2 Python处理OD算法语句

1.3 水运数据结构及OD提取

本次获取2018年7月约25万条江苏省船闸过闸货运数据,主要包括船舶过闸名称、船舶类型、上下行、起讫点、货种、货运量等信息,见表1。利用Python或大数据处理平台进行出行起终点OD统计获取水运 OD 及载重。

表1 船闸数据信息

字段含义	船闸	航向	船名	单放	船头	船籍	船类	总吨
字段含义	载重吨	总长度	总宽	型深	起点	终点	空载	货种
字段含义	实载	箱数	免费	ETC申报	过闸时间			

AIS 数据主要是运行在长江、海域等范围的船舶 GPS 数据,其空间分布于江、海范围。江苏一个月包含约 700 万条 AIS 数据,包括 46000 条船的船名、经度、纬度、船舶类、船长、船宽、估计到达时间最大吃水、目的地、航速等信息,如图3所示。利用轨迹 OD 数据校核船闸统计的 OD 分布矩阵,形成完整的内河水运 OD 出行分布。

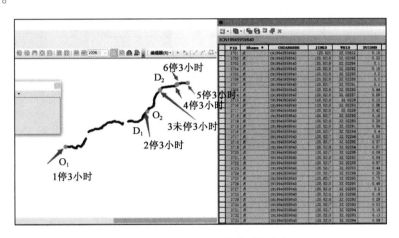

图3　船舶行驶轨迹及疑似停泊点分布

2　综合交通客货运输 OD 的构建

2.1　多源数据融合技术

针对不同数据源,需要设计对应的数据层数据融合,获得全省性区域客货运输强度指标融合。在多源数据融合[8]算法设计上,不仅需要对数据在空间上和时间上进行分类,而且需要对数据进行两两对比与校核,对错误数据进行剔除,对无效属性进行删除,对不完整的数据上进行修复处理,最后才能进行扩样和融合。数据融合主要是数据源层面和交通特征层面的融合[9]。数据源层面的融合是同一交通方式不同数据源分类融合得到同交通方式的数据,交通特征层面的融合是针对同交通方式的 OD 融合,从而得到该交通方式唯一的 OD 及特征;针对各种交通方式进行融合,获得全省客货运输 OD 及特征。全省客货运输 OD 融合技术流程如图4所示。

本次数据主要采用行业收费统计数据,数据精确度高和有效性高,通过修复后行业数据形成的 OD 具有较好的数据质量。数据融合在区域 OD 层面主要采用加权算法进行,区域间 OD 为不同交通方式 OD 之和。此次融合是基于小区 OD 层面融合,将各交通方式的 OD 的单位、时间进行统一,然后分为小区的客货运 OD 进行融合,所形成的客货 OD 对约为 5625 个,将数据统一到以区县 OD 对为基础,时间为年平均日,将客运单位统一归并到人,货运单位统一归并到吨,完成单位归一化处理。主要融合算法公式如下:

$$区域 OD = \sum 各交通方式 OD \times 标准化权重 \tag{1}$$

2.2　综合交通客货运输 OD

完成数据校核后,将所有的 OD 对按照出行起终点、载货货种、载客人数、客车车辆数、货车车辆数等信息进行汇总,形成 OD 对出行属性表,见表2。结合起终点的地理空间位置、人口、经济等形成完整的区县全方式客货出行属性三列阵,在此基础上形成全省客货运输 OD 矩阵。

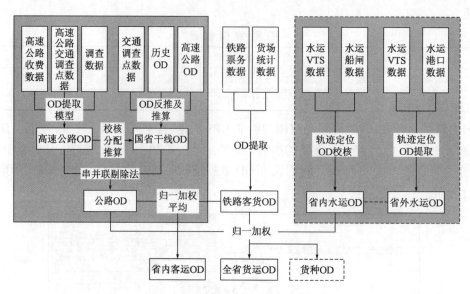

图 4 全省客货运输 OD 融合技术流程图

全省客货运输全方式出行属性表　　　　表 2

行业数据					问卷数据		社会经济数据		多种交通方式 OD		
OD 起点区县	OD 终点区县	车型	车辆数（辆）	标准车数（pcu）	出行目的	人数（人）	起点城市 CDP（亿元）	起点城市人口（万人）	铁路	水运	航空
南京市市区	浦口区	小型客车	117	117	公务出差	377	6180	603	……	……	……
南京市市区	六合区	中型客车	22	44	上班上学	510	6180	603	……	……	……
……	……	……	……	……	……	……	……	……	……	……	……
浙江省	山东省	小型客车	151	151	公务出差	302	12556	5657	……	……	……

3　江苏省综合交通运输特征分析

从全省行业数据得到的客运 OD 分布来看，江苏区域客运运输量约为 27 亿人次/年，呈现以南京、苏沪为核心的放射状。从客运联系强度来看，沪宁通道沿线城市联系最紧密，苏南客运联系明显高于苏北、

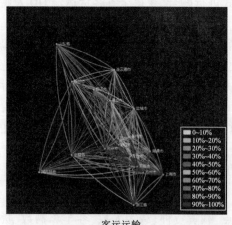

客运运输

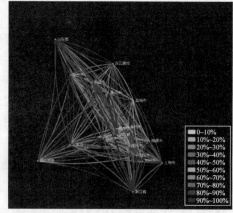

货运运输

图 5　全省客运运输与货运运输特征分布

苏中;从客运走廊来看,客流走廊集中在沪宁通道沿线五市。从省外客运来看,最强联系为苏州与上海,浙江与苏州、南京,安徽与南京之间。从全省客运内外结构看,省内:省外约为4.1:1,其中铁路客运以对外为主,公路以省内出行为主;省外占比最大的城市为徐州、苏州和南京,占比约为35.6%,28.7%和22.9%。

全省货运总量约32亿t/年,纯省内货运量约15.5亿t/年,对外15亿t/年,其中过境1.7亿t/年,内:对外:过境 =48:47:5,主要的货运通道为京沪通道。从全省货运OD分布来看,全省货运在省交界地区与省外城市联系紧密,其中苏州市、徐州市和南京市货运总量最大,约3.1亿t/年、2.9亿t/年和2.6亿t/年,形成了以南京、苏锡和徐连为节点的货运中心。

4 结　语

本文详细分析了行业数据的结构,建立了行业数据的清洗、修复和OD提取的完整路径,并建立了综合交通OD融合的方法。文中各交通方式数据处理、信息提取、多源异构数据融合分析、数据整合与归并处理,以及对多源数据获取客货运输OD矩阵和相关性分析所采取的数据分析、专业技术体系、多源异构数据融合中的算法及手段能为其他课题提供一定的参考。通过交通大数据融合手段,研究客货运输规律,分析客货运输OD特征,能为区域综合交通规划统筹协调区域各种运输需求提供一定的实证参考,同时为地区精准地改善运输服务水平提供决策的方向和重点。受限于数据采集的年限,本文暂时只形成了完整的2018年客货运输OD;未来应结合每年的数据,进行数据源和全省客货运输OD更新。

参考文献

[1] 邓润飞,周涛.基于多元数据融合的过江OD调查技术——以江苏省过江OD调查为例[J].中国公路,2019,553(1):118-120.
[2] 刘博恺.交通OD调查与交通大数据应用[J].中国公路,2016(1):144.
[3] 张晓春,于壮,段冰若,等.面向城市交通规划的多源手机信令数据相关性研究[J].交通运输系统工程与信息,2019,19(04):239-245.
[4] 冯立光.区域公路网OD调查中若干技术问题研究[D].西安:长安大学,2004.
[5] 柏强.大区域公路OD集成技术研究[D].西安:长安大学,2006.
[6] 裴玉龙,盖春英.关于黑龙江省公路交通OD调查资料开发利用问题的探讨[J].东北公路,2002(03):90-92.
[7] 李昕,辛勇,郑晓阳.公路建设项目考虑铁路转移交通量预测的OD处理方法[J].中外公路,2005(04):195-198.
[8] 苏跃江,温惠英,韦清波,等.多源数据融合驱动的居民出行特征分析方法[J].交通运输系统工程与信息,2020,20(05):56-63.
[9] 赵明,张健钦,卢剑.基于云计算的城市交通大数据分析平台[J].地理空间信息,2020,18(02):16-20,6.

旧城更新背景下城市交通综合改善策略研究
——以武汉市归元片为例

马成喜　黄兰莉　邓　帅　王　韡　常四铁

(武汉市规划研究院)

摘　要　随着我国城市发展由"增量扩张"时代走向"存量治理"时代,城乡规划也从以新城建设为主转向了以旧城更新为主的"新常态"。如何依据老旧城区的特性,量体裁衣,制定旧城交通综合改造的策略,成为当下重要的议题。本文以武汉市归元片为例,分析了老旧城区人口、用地特性,多层次、多角度探讨了老旧城区交通改造的策略,并从交通系统、慢行系统、公共交通系统等多方面提出老旧城区的改造措施。

关键词　旧城更新　综合交通改造　交通规划　交通策略

0　引　言

老旧城区是城市随着人类社会发展所保留下来的最具历史沉淀的空间区域,但同时也是空间环境最差、交通矛盾最突出的区域。改革开放以来,我国经历了历史上速度最快、规模最大的城镇化进程[1],城市的高速发展,导致老旧城区的基础设施已无法满足城市人民日益增长的美好生活需要,交通拥堵、停车难等问题接踵而来,老旧城区如何改造升级成为当下迫在眉睫的议题。

以往的老城改造中,往往是通过新建各类交通设施[2],注重交通设施的量变,落脚点着重于机动车的出行,而忽略老城的人群特征与需求、空间格局与发展。老城区交通改造需要以"绣花"功夫,在保障出行基本要求"量"的同时,更应格外注重老城区人本化、品质化方面"质"的提升。

1　旧城区现状认知

1.1　旧城区人口与用地特征

1.1.1　人口密度高、老龄化趋势明显

旧城区人口具有高密度、老龄化的趋势。以武汉市归元片为例,人口密度达3.5万人/km^2,高于武汉主城区1.8万人/km^{2}的人口密度,其中65岁以上占比为9.3%(表1)。根据《人口老龄化及其社会经济后果》的划分标准,当老年人口数量占总人口比例超过7%时,意味着该国家或地区进入老龄化。人群的老龄化,对街道的慢行环境、公共交通出行、街道品质提出了更高的要求[3]。因此,旧城人口虽然集中,但是由于区域街道空间环境品质等系列原因,城市空间活力反而并不高。

归元片现状人口结构表　　表1

年龄(岁)	占比(%)
0~5	3.66
6~14	23.43
15~29	15.22
30~64	48.37
65及以上	9.32
总计	100

1.1.2　用地聚集程度高,用地限制多

旧城区往往是城市文化的起源地。从历史上看,归元片区是武汉发源地之一,拥有荆楚文化、知音文化等多处文化遗迹[4],现状用地格局沿袭历史痕迹,用地开发建设受多方因素掣肘。大量学校、居住、中小商业用地聚集,用地利用程度高、存量用地少,对交通系统的布局提出了更高的要求。

1.2　旧城区交通特征

1.2.1　交通环境差、品质低,出行舒适度不高

旧城区区域内部现状路网等级低且不成系统,路网密度仅为5.2km/km^2,基础设施不足,街道慢行空间缺失,街道品质差,街道交往空间不足(图1、图2)。

1.2.2　交通设施供给不足,供需矛盾突出

旧城区存在大量未配建停车设施的老旧社区。随着机动化进程加快,社区内部停车供给严重不足,同时区域内部受用地制约,停车供给能力有限。社区停车供需的严重失衡,导致大量汽车外溢于路上,进

一步压榨了有限的道路资源。同时区域内公共交通发展不完善，设施布局缺口大、接驳体系效率低，难以满足区内公共交通便捷出行要求。

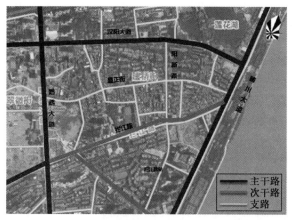

图1　区域现状路网图

图2　现状显正街—北城巷路口

2　交通改善目标与策略

2.1　交通改善目标

区内交通融合城市发展要求，打造"绿色生态、安全共享、舒适有序、便捷高效"的交通出行环境，解决旧城区交通问题，提升区域街道品质，激发旧城区活力。

2.2　交通改善策略

2.2.1　加强公共交通供给、优化接驳体系、构建多层级公交体系

为了应对远期大量客流的快速通行，应充分发挥轨道资源优势，优化轨道交通的接驳体系，建立"轨道＋公交＋旅游电车"＋慢行的多层级公共交通出行体系（图3），缓解路网交通压力[5]。

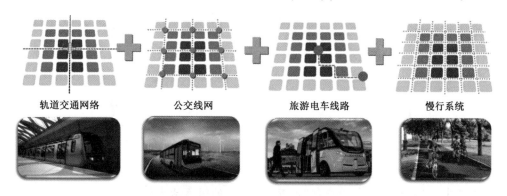

图3　多层次公共交通出行系统

2.2.2　综合交通人性化，平衡多模式交通，鼓励慢行交通

规划思路由"车本位"思想向"人本位"思想转变（图4），基于人而非车的出行需求分配街道空间，在街道的断面设计上保障慢行空间与街道活动空间，平衡多模式交通，鼓励绿色交通[6]。

2.2.3　同步区域发展，形成近远结合的道路建设方案

旧城区改造涉及的小区单位多，协调难度大、改造周期长，需因地制宜采取灵活的方式，如采取路网远近结合建设策略（图5）"统一规划、分步实施"，逐步形成区域内畅通、便捷的路网系统。

2.2.4　差异化车位供给，以满足基本停车为主，出行车位以配建为主

大量的老旧社区未配有停车位，停车位缺口大。因此提出改善现有停车供给模式，规划公共停车场主要满足老旧社区、公共服务设施的基本停车需求；购物（图6）。办公等出行车位以配建为主[7]。

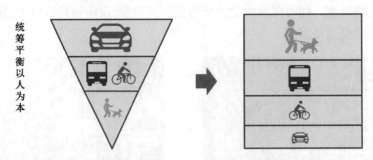

图 4　以人为本的路权转变模式图

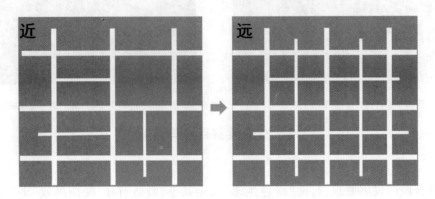

图 5　路网远近结合建设策略示意图

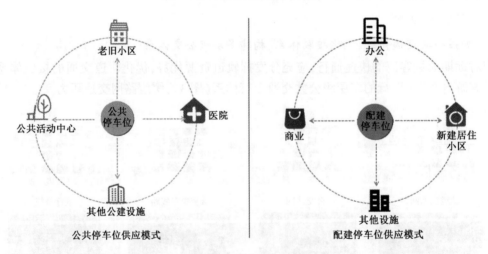

图 6　停车位供应模式图

2.2.5　构建中心"无车区",打造内部"公交+慢行"的绿色活力街区

中心"无车区"指在区域外围构建复合型交通保护环境,通过建设交通换乘枢纽、设置大型停车场以供私人小汽车交通停车换乘,衔接区域对外交通需求[8],保护内部交通。区域内部构建以"公交 + 慢行"为主的出行体系,实现交通宁静化、环境低碳化、街道活力化(图7)。

3　交通改善方案

3.1　路网系统

3.1.1　打通对外联系通道,缓解旧城交通

突破现有空间格局,规划通过打通区域内部支路,加强区域内部与外围区域的交通联系,缓解鹦鹉大道、晴川大道等外围干道的交通压力(图8),由"田字形"路网格局(图9)转变为"井字形"路网格局(图10)。

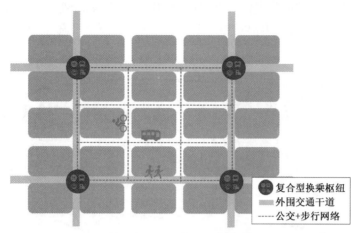

图7 中心区"无车区"交通模式图

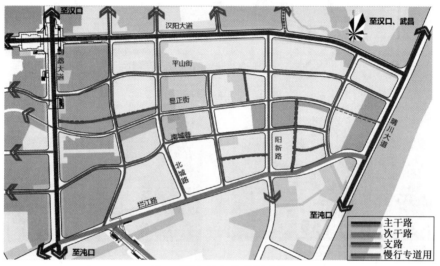

图8 规划"井字形"路网系统

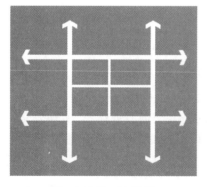

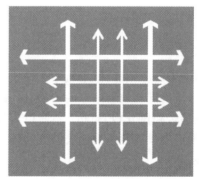

图9 "田字形"路网格局　　　　图10 "井字形"路网格局

3.1.2 践行"小街区、密路网"理念,提升区域交通微循环效率

完善内部微循环路网的建设,通过新建城市支路以及改造公共通道,实现"小街区、密路网"的空间格局。通过加密路网,实现城市空间的重塑,强化城市各个单元的联系,提升区域整体出行效率。

3.1.3 远近结合,分步实施

根据区域远期用地布局、开发建设情况、总体规划路网布局情况以及区域的交通需求,规划布局"主、次、支"相结合的完整路网系统。同时考虑本次保留的老旧建筑,制订路网近期改造与建设计划(图11)。

将区内东西向大走廊——显正街打造成为一条串联归元禅寺、汉阳树、长江之心、汉阳江滩的慢行活

力廊道。因近期显正街仍承担着第五医院、消防站、群建路小学等单位机动车出行的功能,将显正街近期弹性控制为"共享街道"(图12),远期路网建设成熟后控制为慢行专用道(图13)。

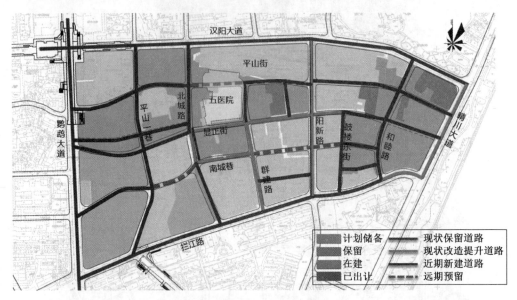

图11 近期路网建设计划图

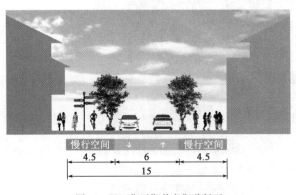

图12 显正街近期共享街道断面

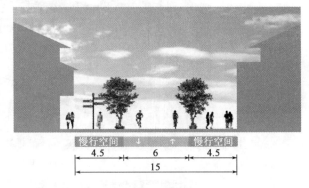

图13 显正街远期慢行专用道断面

3.2 公共交通

区域周边轨道交通资源较好,但单轨站点设于区域边界,区内服务能力不足。因此,需加强区域内公共交通供给,强化区域内部与轨道站点的衔接,提升轨道交通的服务便捷性,实现公交优先的发展目标。

规划在区域内结合路网建设,打造"环轴相交"的公共交通服务体系,实现公交站点300m服务半径对区域的全覆盖,形成更具有竞争力的公共交通体系(图14),提升公共交通服务水平。

3.3 慢行交通

平衡路权,所有道路均按照慢行系统中一级慢行道与二级慢行道的划分设置独立非机动车道,保障慢行的独立性、舒适性与安全性(图15)。提升区内规划慢行路网密度至13.4km/km²,同时结合街道的设施带设置自行车停放区,实现非机动车与公交良好的换乘衔接,从而消除非机动车乱停现象。

慢行系统分级标准见表2。

慢行系统分级标准　　　　　表2

慢行分级	宽度	建设要求
一级	自行车道≥2.5m;步行道≥3.5m	机动车、非机动车共面,物理隔离
二级	自行车道≥1.5m;步行道≥3m	机动车、非机动车共面,划线或道钉隔离

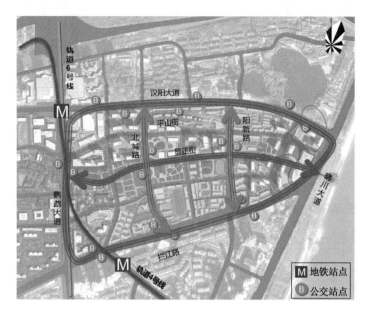

图 14　公共交通系统覆范围

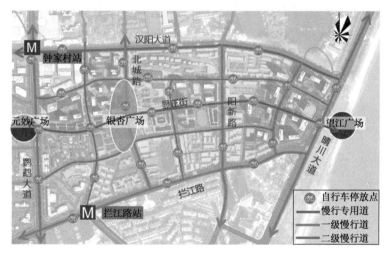

图 15　慢行系统布局图

按照街道全要素、精细化设计要求,重点打造慢行空间,对人行道与行道树设施带、绿化带、建筑前区空间进行一体化设计(图16),保障行人宽敞、舒适、连续的通行空间。

3.4　静态交通

公共停车布局兼顾区域重点共建地块和保留社区的停车需求以及外围车流截留的要求,限制小汽车进入中心区,实现中心"无车区",以鼓励绿色交通出行。如图17所示,停车场P2、P5主要服务于核心区公服设施以及停车矛盾突出的老旧社区,停车场P1、P3、P4、P6对进入本区域的车流进行停车截留,降低区域内部交通压力。同时为实现土地资源高效集约利用,5处公共停车场与绿化、商业等用地进行复合建设。

4　结　语

本文以武汉市归元片交通综合改造为例,分析旧城区的特性,研究提出了适用于旧城区的交通发展策略,如"打造多层公交体系"、构建"中心无车区""人本化交通"等,对归元片区拟定了一系列的改造交通措施,以改善交通供需矛盾、缓解交通压力、提升交通出行效率与品质、增强旧城街道空间活力。未来将通过跟踪归元片区的规划实施效果,进行规划后评估,以验证并进一步完善本次研究提出的旧城区交通改善策略。

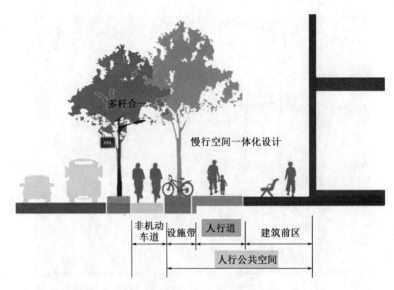

图 16　慢行空间设计示意图

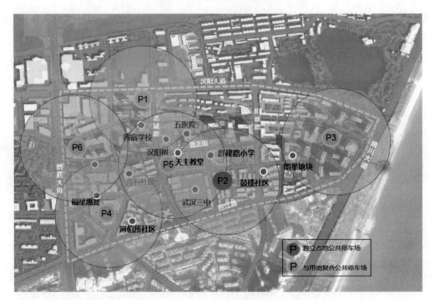

图 17　公共停车场优化布局

参考文献

[1] 方创琳.改革开放40年:中国城镇化与城市群之变[J].中国经济报告,2018,000(012):91-96.

[2] 钱林波.中心区道路交通系统改善规划评价指标与方法研究——以南京中心区为例[J].城市道桥与防洪,2000(01):7-10,2.

[3] 邹芳,邓帅.旧城慢行复兴策略研究——以构建武昌古城老年友好型慢行交通系统为例[C].2019年中国城市交通规划年会.

[4] 张帆.基于文化要素演绎的武汉市归元片旧城更新[C].2019中国城市规划年会.

[5] 杨明,过秀成,於昊,等.老城区交通特征、问题解析与改善对策初探[J].现代城市研究,2012(04):84-88.

[6] 戴光远,王昊,邓惠章,等.历史城区慢行交通改善提升研究——以苏州古城为例[C].2019中国城市规划年会.

[7] 陈蔚.交通需求管理导向下建筑物停车配建标准研究[J].城市建筑,2016,000(026):373.

[8] 雷熙文,聂华波.中小城市的"无车区"绿色交通规划研究[J].交通工程,2019(3).

面向跨江融合发展地区的过江通道交通疏解体系研究——以南京为例

陈 昊　汤伟健　罗中萍

(华设设计集团股份有限公司)

摘　要　为构建一种适合跨江发展城市的多层次过江交通疏解路网体系,本文提出了涵盖面—线—点三个层次的规划模型。面层从宏观层面确定过江通道功能体系。线层从中观层面,结合过江通道功能定位与相互之间的叠加影响,从整体的角度统筹城市路网疏解线资源对应过江通道的分配,定性地提出过江通道与城市骨架路网的衔接设计要求。点层从微观层面,定量细化各过江通道与城市骨架路网衔接节点的疏解要求,并结合实际建设条件中可能出现的问题向线层进行反馈优化方案,实现动态调整达到最优的效果。以南京为实例,对未来过江通道的疏解体系进行规划。结果表明,本规划模型很好地结合了定量和定性布局优点,可操作性强,可为交通管理部门及后续建设提出前瞻性指导意见。

关键词　过江通道　疏解体系　层次构建法

0　引　言

在区域一体化、城市群发展趋势以及"拥江发展"深入实施的背景下,跨江融合发展地区的道路过江通道交通总量呈现出逐年增加的趋势,城市发展进程中江南江北联动发展对过江通道的持续推进工作提出新的要求。在大规模的过江通道建设进程中,过江通道与城市道路网络及区域公路网络的衔接,以及在有限的城市路网资源中对过江交通进行疏解已经成为过江交通发展必须解决的难题。

本文通过提出面向过江通道交通疏解的路网衔接技术,从满足功能需求及统筹路网影响两个角度,提出过江通道交通疏解的总体思路和衔接要求,对于解决过江通道的交通疏解难题,推进跨江融合发展具有重要意义。

1　构建过江通道三层疏解体系

影响过江通道疏解方案的因素有很多,包括过江通道布局、接线布局、交通量等。为了提高过江通道布局分析的系统性和有效性,本文提出层次构建法,包括"面—线—点"三层疏解体系(图1),分别为过江通道及接线总体布局体系、疏解线体系和疏解点体系,旨在均衡交通需求分布,降低对城市路网过度冲击。

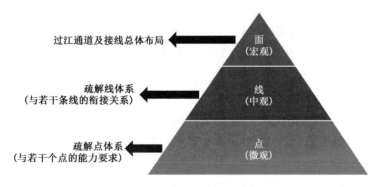

图1　"面—线—点"三层疏解体系

1.1 过江通道布局及接线体系

过江通道布局及接线体系从面的角度研究江南江北的交通联系,从规划的角度确定各过江通道的功能定位,进而明确接线道路的整体布局。该层论证的方案主要依托于上位规划,重点分析过江通道与其接线的功能、技术标准是否匹配。

1.2 过江通道疏解线体系

过江交通疏解线定义为能够疏解大规模过江需求的骨架道路,一般为城市快速路及主干道等。影响过江通道疏解线体系的因素主要有过江通道的功能、相邻间距、接线的道路功能等级等,不同过江通道功能及接线的差异会导致疏解线体系上存在差异。

研究过江通道疏解线布局需要考虑过江通道及两岸疏解路网总体布局,确保过江的交通流能够得到均衡疏解。对于定位为主要承担城市交通功能的过江通道,其疏解线应选择沿江方向主要快速路与交通性主干道。对于定位为区域功能的过江通道,其疏解线选择沿江方向主要干线公路与高速公路,同时由于公路通道服务范围更广,疏解截面分布范围更宽。

当存在多条过江通道疏解线时,会存在多条通道疏解交通叠加问题,具体表现为:一方面过江通道流量向城市路网两侧方向疏解,由内到外疏解强度逐渐变弱;另一方面相邻过江通道向疏解线疏解流量会叠加,可能导致某一条疏解线能力无法承载。为解决此类问题,一般对叠加影响较深的过江通道与疏解线的节点进行处理,主要有不衔接、往影响弱的方向衔接以及采用弱衔接形式3种处理方式(图2)。

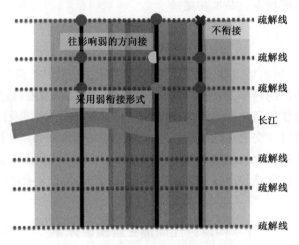

图2 多条通道疏解交通叠加解决思路

1.3 过江通道疏解点体系

过江通道点层疏解点体系主要包含"交通疏解点"和"沿线利用点"2个层次。其中,交通疏解点定义为过江通道与沿线两岸疏解线的衔接节点,对应"线"层确定的疏解线与过江通道相交节点,疏解过江通道主要流量,一般为过江通道与快速路、交通性主干路以及公路的衔接节点。沿线利用点定义为过江通道与沿线主次干路的衔接节点,作为交通疏解点的补充,辅助疏解过江通道流量,并服务通道沿线利用,一般为平面交叉口或者简易互通。两者的具体定义如图3所示。

2 南京长江干线过江通道疏解体系研究

2.1 疏解体系层次构建法在南京的适用性分析

目前南京市已布局6座道路过江通道,"拥江发展"和江北新区快速发展带来跨江联动需求高强度增长,导致衔接道路常态化拥堵。根据规划,长江南京区段将共建设15条道路过江通道,满足发展需要。应用本文提出的层次构建法,构建多层次过江交通疏解路网体系,均衡交通需求分布,降低对城市路网过度冲击。

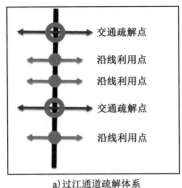 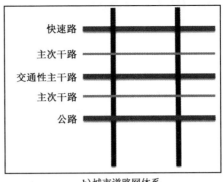

a) 过江通道疏解体系　　　　　　b) 城市道路网体系

图3　节点疏解体系层次图

2.2　构建过江通道疏解体系面层

南京长江干线过江通道布局及接线已在规划中相对明确,共布局15条过江通道,呈现出3类特征:绕城公路以内的和燕路至长江隧道区段内的过江通道以城市功能为主,绕城公路—绕越高速之间的长江五桥和仙新路、和燕路过江通道兼具城市、区域功能,绕越高速以外的过江通道以区域功能为主(图4)。

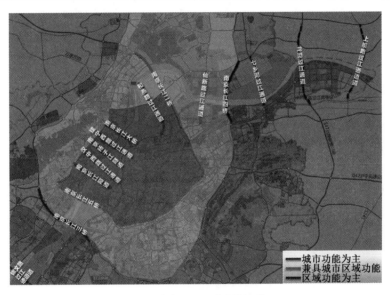

图4　南京过江通道功能情况

其中,对新建且以城市功能为主的仙新路过江通道、和燕路过江通道、建宁西路以及汉中西路过江通道进行研究。

2.3　构建过江通道疏解体系线层

利用本文提出的层次构建法,梳理江南江北城市路网中可以利用的疏解线,对各过江通道疏解交通的相互叠加影响进行分析,从功能需求、疏解道路运行效率、工程难度3个方面统筹分布各过江通道的疏解线(图5)。

2.3.1　可利用疏解道路梳理

城市过江通道,尤其是二桥至三桥间的通道疏解截面选择沿江方向主要快速路与交通性主干道。江南主要有扬子江大道、江东路、内环西线、栖霞大道、G312,江北主要有S356、浦滨路、浦乌路、浦仪公路、江北大道、浦珠北路、浦六路。

公路通道疏解线选择沿江方向主要干线公路与高速公路,由于公路通道服务范围更广,因此疏解截面分布范围更宽。江南主要有S338、G312、沪宁高速公路、S122、S338、G205、宁马高速公路等,江北主要有 S356、宁盐高速公路、G328、沪陕高速公路、G346、宁洛高速公路等。

图 5　线层构建结果方案图

2.3.2　线层构建结果

（1）仙新路过江通道在江南主要疏解线为栖霞大道与 G312，江北主要疏解线为滨江大道与浦仪公路。

（2）和燕路过江通道在江南主要疏解线为栖霞大道与玄武大道，江北主要疏解线为浦仪公路、滨江大道、江北大道、浦六路。

（3）建宁西路过江通道在江南主要疏解线为扬子江大道与内环西线辅道，江北主要疏解线为滨江大道与浦滨路。

（4）汉中西路过江通道在江南主要疏解线为江东中路与内环西线辅道，江北主要疏解线为浦滨路与江北大道辅道。

2.4　构建过江通道疏解体系点层

根据线层确定的各过江通道疏解线确定交通疏解点，结合疏解需求确定交通疏解点的疏解能力与转向量要求，提出沿线利用点疏解能力要求（图 6）。

（1）仙新路过江通道：仙新路过江通道高峰小时流量为 8692pcu/h，根据各交通疏解点的转向能力，栖霞大道、G312、S356、浦仪公路均为强衔接点。

（2）和燕路过江通道：和燕路过江通道高峰小时流量为 8587pcu/h，根据各交通疏解点的转向能力，栖霞大道、玄武大道、浦仪公路，滨江大道、江北大道、浦六路、宁连高速公路均为强衔接点。

（3）建宁西路过江通道：建宁西路过江通道高峰小时流量为 8465pcu/h，根据各交通疏解点的转向能力，扬子江大道为强衔接点、内环西线辅道为弱衔接点、横江大道为强衔接点、浦滨路为弱衔接点。

（4）汉中西路过江通道：汉中西路过江通道高峰小时流量为 9801pcu/h，根据各交通疏解点的转向能力，江东中路强衔接点、内环西线辅道为弱衔接点、浦滨路位强衔接点、江北大道辅道为弱衔接点。

图 6　点层构建结果方案图

3　实验分析

按照本文提出的层次构建法,构建南京长江干线过江通道疏解体系,借助 Trans CAD 软件进行相关检验。江南江北疏解线交通需求分布相对均衡,基本实现目标;交通疏解路网早高峰饱和度虽然较高,对于早高峰的过江交通疏解基本可满足(图 7)。

图 7　交通模型分配结果

4 结语

本方法主要研究如何将城市路网中有限的、具有较大疏解能力的骨架道路资源分配给各条过江通道，避免多条过江通道将交通量集中在某一条疏解道路上，造成疏解道路无法承载，引起交通疏解系统出现紊乱的状况。

具体研究方法主要是从满足过江通道功能定位和统筹各过江通道交通疏解的相互影响两个角度，确定各过江通道与主要疏解道路是否衔接、如何衔接的问题，研究过程中既要考虑单条过江通道的疏解要求，也要考虑尽可能减少多条过江通道在城市路网中的高强度叠加影响，从而实现交通疏解系统最优。

参考文献

[1] 吴嘉杨,胡岩.南京枢纽新建过江通道对枢纽运输布局的影响[J].高速铁路技术,2020(S1):11-14+51.
[2] 高建杰.城市过江通道交通流速度和密度关系研究[J].河北工业科技,2018:104-108.
[3] 刘艳平,王伟.过江通道与城市路网衔接规划研究[J].交通企业管理,2018,033(005):65-67.
[4] 陈锐.基于城市交通需求管理的过江交通问题分析——以重庆主城为例[J].现代商贸工业,2017(26):180-182.
[5] 郑世琦.城市过江通道施工期影响区域交通组织方法研究[D].成都:西南交通大学,2016.

考虑客流特征的常规公交与地铁竞合关系甄别及并行线路优化策略——南京案例

刘锡泽[1,2,3]　陈学武[1,2,3]　孙　健[4]　雷　达[3]　程剑珂[3]

(1.东南大学江苏省城市智能交通重点实验室；
2.东南大学现代城市交通技术江苏高效协同创新中心；
3.东南大学交通学院；
4.南京公共交通(集团)有限公司)

摘　要　已有常规公交与地铁竞合关系研究多是从出行距离或二者的空间关系角度考虑。本文通过对南京市奥南地区公交线路及客流数据进行处理分析，考虑公交线路客流OD、老年乘客比例和乘车距离等特征，分析常规公交与地铁的竞合关系，针对空间关系上的并行线路提出了相应的优化策略和实际案例分析。研究结果可为提出有效可行的公交线路调整策略提供参考，从而更好地响应和服务不同乘客群体，尤其是老龄乘客的出行需求。

关键词　城市公共交通设施规划　竞合关系　客流分析　常规公交　地铁

0 引　言

随着新建地铁线路的不断开通，地铁成网运营给常规公交运营服务同时带来了机遇和挑战。为形成"地铁到站，公交到家"优势互补的大交通格局，需要充分发挥常规公交的灵活性，甄别出常规公交和地铁竞合关系，按需调整公交线路的布局与走向。

在常规公交和地铁竞合关系分析方面学术界已有大量研究，贺建炜等[1]通过分析出行时耗和出行费用，提出了常规公交和地铁在出行距离上的竞争关系。朱飘等[2]基于广义费用的效用函数构建了常规公

基金项目：国家自然科学基础联合基金项目(U20A20330)。

交和地铁并线竞争模型,判断地铁优势出行距离,通过长沙轨道交通2号线的数据证明轨道交通适用于3~9km距离的出行。陈雪珍[3]通过分析常规公交与地铁线路走向和客流分布等情况来分析两者作用关系,对公交线路定性调整以及通过双层模型的构建迭代出新增接驳公交专线,以南昌市轨道2号线为例进行定性调整。王玉萍[4]运用需求交叉弹性理论分析了常规公交与轨道交通的竞争或替代关系,建立基于广义费用的Logit模型,考虑出行时耗与出行费用得到了不同交通方式分担比例曲线。陈贵凤[5]用生态位、耗散结构等理论分析常规公交与地铁的竞合关系,研究了两种方式的竞争区与合作区,并从合作角度提出了以地铁线路为核心的常规公交线网调整方法。总体来说,目前研究常规公交与地铁竞合关系多是基于出行距离或空间关系,结合客流数据分析的研究较少,且大部分是提出对线路进行区域化大调整,而在实践中大范围调整线路十分困难,也可能达不到应有的效果。

地铁以运量大、速度快、准点率高等优势在其影响范围内会吸引大部分客流,常规公交在这种情况下处于劣势,但是常规公交线路有其自身独特的历史延续性和灵活特征,在部分竞争中占据优势。常规公交线路与地铁线路的竞争与合作关系不是可以通过简单的空间关系来甄别的,在以需求为导向的线网调整策略下,需要考虑到客流分布和乘客类型等客流特征,而不是依据规则简单地"一刀切"。

当前城市公交的发展已经从"增量"在向"提质"方向转变,提高公交服务质量要求出行服务的提供者根据不同乘客群体的出行内在需求提供多样化针对性服务。目前,我国已逐步进入老龄化社会,许多城市推出了老年乘客可享受的优惠票价政策,在常规公交出行中老年人占比较高。为体现公交服务的人文关怀和社会公平,需要在线路调整时充分考虑中老年乘客出行特征,更好地服务乘客出行。基于此,本文提出考虑公交线路客流OD量、老年乘客比例及乘车距离等特征的常规公交与地铁竞合关系的甄别方法及优化策略,为常规公交线路规划和运营实践提供一定的借鉴参考。

1 研究范围与数据处理

1.1 研究范围

本文研究范围是南京市奥南地区。根据《南京城市轨道交通第二期建设规划调整方案(2016—2021年)》及目前建设进度,地铁7号线和2号线西延线将于2021年建成通车,预计将对奥南地区的公交线网产生重大影响。图1所示为奥南地区地铁和常规公交线路图。

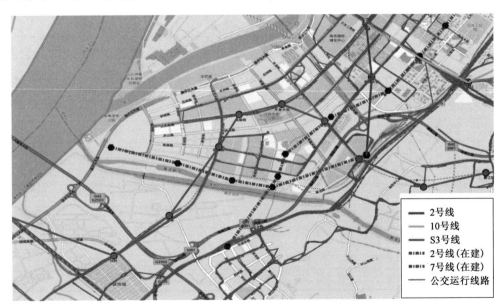

图1 奥南地区地铁和常规公交线路图

途径奥南地区的公交线路包括41路、85路、169路、170路等11条线路,受影响的公交日均客流量达到21662人次。

1.2 数据来源

本文使用的数据来源于南京公交集团提供的2020年7月份线路AVL数据、车辆运行GPS数据、线路站点经纬度数据和IC刷卡数据,各数据字段及示例数据见表1~表3、图2。

线路AVL数据字段及示例数据　　　　　　　　　　　　　　表1

字　段	示　例
线路编号	10
线路名称	1路
车辆编号	JN1-4191
站点序号	1
站点编号	10101
站点名称	夫子庙总站
进站/出站时间	2020-7-1 6:36:02
数据类型	进站
行车方向	下行

线路GPS数据示例　　　　　　　　　　　　　　　　　　　表2

车辆编号	采集时间	经度(°)	纬度(°)	行驶速度(km/h)	行驶方向
JN1-4170	2020-7-1 16:22	118.8091	32.08486	39.632	235
JN1-4170	2020-7-1 16:22	118.8081	32.08426	40.706	230
JN1-4170	2020-7-1 16:22	118.8066	32.08277	38.651	215
JN1-4170	2020-7-1 16:22	118.8058	32.08191	40.947	214
JN1-4170	2020-7-1 16:23	118.8049	32.08088	0	233
JN1-4170	2020-7-1 16:23	118.8049	32.08084	9.2414	207
JN1-4170	2020-7-1 16:23	118.8046	32.08056	0	219

IC刷卡数据字段及示例数据　　　　　　　　　　　　　　　表3

字　段	示　例
线路编码	810
线路名称	81路
车辆编号	JN2-4441
卡号	973077875295
卡号类型	DESFire卡
卡种	半价老人卡
交易流水号	285421
消费时间	2020-7-1 21:29:10
消费金额	0
上车站点编号	810008
上车站点名称	石门坎(五洲装饰广场)
换乘信息	公交转公交

1.3 数据处理

1.3.1 公交车辆运行轨迹提取

公交车辆运行轨迹提取根据公交集团提供的线路AVL数据、车辆运行GPS数据提取以及经人工核查的线路站点信息，流程如图 3 所示。首先需要筛选对应线路的 AVL 数据，选择其中任一车辆，根据 AVL 数据中行车方向和对应线路站点数据（用于数据纠错）识别一次完整的车辆运行行程。之后在 AVL 数据里提出车辆到达首末站的时间，用于确定截取 GPS 数据的大致范围，然后结合首末站点经纬度调整 GPS 数据截取范围并导出数据。最后将 GPS 数据导入 ArcGIS 软件进行可视化处理。

{'station_name': '林场', 'lat': '32.163676', 'lng': '118.67149', 'line_info': [{'line_name': '地铁3号线', 'head_station': '林场', 'tail_station': '秣周东路'}]}
{'station_name': '泰冯路', 'lat': '32.1534385595357', 'lng': '118.718928640367', 'line_info': [{'line_name': '地铁3号线', 'head_station': '林场', 'tail_station': '秣周东路'}]}
{'station_name': '南京站', 'lat': '32.0893228763272', 'lng': '118.796511208837', 'line_info': [{'line_name': '地铁3号线', 'head_station': '林场', 'tail_station': '秣周东路'}]}
{'station_name': '南京林业大学·新庄', 'lat': '32.076495', 'lng': '118.810508', 'line_info': [{'line_name': '地铁3号线', 'head_station': '林场', 'tail_station': '秣周东路'}]}
{'station_name': '鸡鸣寺', 'lat': '32.056989', 'lng': '118.7982', 'line_info': [{'line_name': '地铁3号线', 'head_station': '林场', 'tail_station': '秣周东路'}]}
{'station_name': '浮桥', 'lat': '32.048843', 'lng': '118.796235', 'line_info': [{'line_name': '地铁3号线', 'head_station': '林场', 'tail_station': '秣周东路'}]}
{'station_name': '大行宫', 'lat': '32.0417338325841', 'lng': '118.794785144794', 'line_info': [{'line_name': '地铁3号线', 'head_station': '林场', 'tail_station': '秣周东路'}]}
{'station_name': '常府街', 'lat': '32.033554', 'lng': '118.792599', 'line_info': [{'line_name': '地铁3号线', 'head_station': '林场', 'tail_station': '秣周东路'}]}
{'station_name': '夫子庙', 'lat': '32.023544', 'lng': '118.790915', 'line_info': [{'line_name': '地铁3号线', 'head_station': '林场', 'tail_station': '秣周东路'}]}
{'station_name': '武定门', 'lat': '32.013625', 'lng': '118.794612', 'line_info': [{'line_name': '地铁3号线', 'head_station': '林场', 'tail_station': '秣周东路'}]}
{'station_name': '雨花门', 'lat': '32.0038479923455', 'lng': '118.792459530188', 'line_info': [{'line_name': '地铁3号线', 'head_station': '林场', 'tail_station': '秣周东路'}]}
{'station_name': '卡子门', 'lat': '31.9950360885289', 'lng': '118.795517963835', 'line_info': [{'line_name': '地铁3号线', 'head_station': '林场', 'tail_station': '秣周东路'}]}
{'station_name': '大明路', 'lat': '31.985866108068', 'lng': '118.799990022442', 'line_info': [{'line_name': '地铁3号线', 'head_station': '林场', 'tail_station': '秣周东路'}]}
{'station_name': '明发广场', 'lat': '31.977154', 'lng': '118.800402', 'line_info': [{'line_name': '地铁3号线', 'head_station': '林场', 'tail_station': '秣周东路'}]}
{'station_name': '南京南站', 'lat': '31.9687477081467', 'lng': '118.797951256789', 'line_info': [{'line_name': '地铁3号线', 'head_station': '林场', 'tail_station': '秣周东路'}]}
{'station_name': '宏运大道', 'lat': '31.9590138698802', 'lng': '118.804066669483', 'line_info': [{'line_name': '地铁3号线', 'head_station': '林场', 'tail_station': '秣周东路'}]}
{'station_name': '胜太西路', 'lat': '31.943629108068', 'lng': '118.807392679134', 'line_info': [{'line_name': '地铁3号线', 'head_station': '林场', 'tail_station': '秣周东路'}]}
{'station_name': '天元西路', 'lat': '31.928788549428', 'lng': '118.808492305904', 'line_info': [{'line_name': '地铁3号线', 'head_station': '林场', 'tail_station': '秣周东路'}]}
{'station_name': '九龙湖', 'lat': '31.916124', 'lng': '118.821489', 'line_info': [{'line_name': '地铁3号线', 'head_station': '林场', 'tail_station': '秣周东路'}]}
{'station_name': '诚信大道', 'lat': '31.907544', 'lng': '118.829909', 'line_info': [{'line_name': '地铁3号线', 'head_station': '林场', 'tail_station': '秣周东路'}]}
{'station_name': '东大九龙湖校区', 'lat': '31.8961472352396', 'lng': '118.830515175394', 'line_info': [{'line_name': '地铁3号线', 'head_station': '林场', 'tail_station': '秣周东

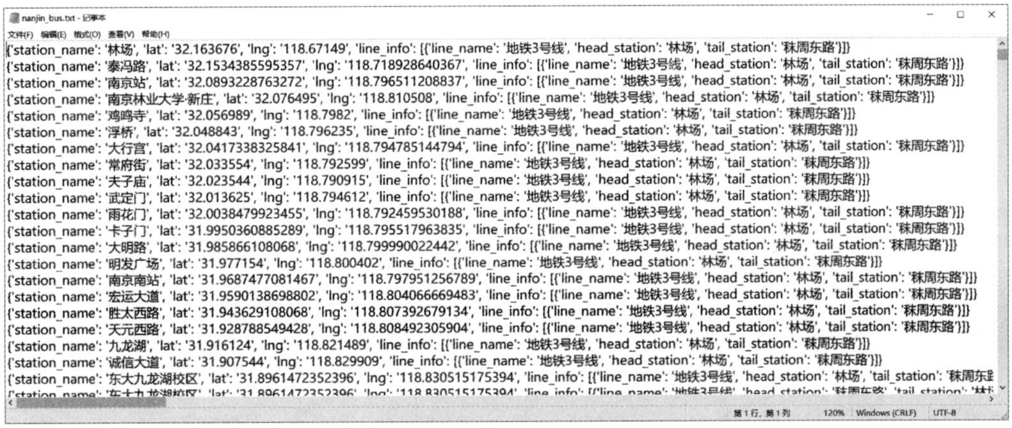

图 2 线路站点经纬度数据示例

1.3.2 乘客出行 OD 推导

由于南京市常规公交没有下车刷卡数据，故需要识别乘客出行链，从而反推出乘客下车站点位置，其流程如图 4 所示[6]。实现乘客出行 OD 推导需要用到 IC 刷卡数据、线路 AVL 数据和线路站点数据。南京公交集团提供的 IC 刷卡数据上车站点存在部分缺失，需要根据线路 AVL 数据通过比对车辆编号和运行时间进行补全。$D = 500\text{m}$ 乘客出行 OD 推导主要是依据相邻两次出行空间和时间关系，将符合条件的下次出行地点匹配为上次出行的终点，实现对下车站点的推导。由于 IC 刷卡数据没有经纬度等信息，需要根据线路站点数据进行匹配得到完整出行 OD 信息，结果如图 5 所示。

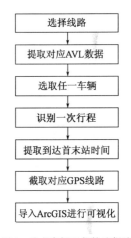

图 3 公交车辆运行轨迹提取

根据 IC 刷卡数据反推常规公交客流 OD 所用到的出行链法首先由 Barry 等[7]学者提出，该方法主要有以下两个关键假设：

（1）本次出行的下车站点与下一个行程的上车站点接近且这两次出行间的换乘时间较短；

（2）大多数乘客一天内的最后一次出行的到达站点与他们当日首次出行时的上车站点相同或十分接近。

上述两个假设对应了出行链法执行过程中的两个可控参数：允许换乘距离 D 和允许换乘时间 T。这两个参数通过从时空层面验证推导过程，以排除不符合上述假设的下车站点推算结果。本研究中允许换乘距离与允许换乘时间分别取 $D = 500\text{m}$，$T = 60\text{min}$。

图 6 所示为基于出行链法推导常规公交客流 OD 的基本思路：一名乘客在某日内首先从线路 1 的 B1 站点上车。IC 刷卡数据显示该乘客下一次出行由线路 2 的 B2 站点上车。在允许的换乘距离与时间内，线路 1 中离 B2 站点最近的站点为 A1，则将 A1 作为该乘客第一次出行的估计下车站点，同时由 AVL 数据或其他乘客在 A1 站点的上车时间，得到或估计得到该乘客首次出行的下车时间。该乘客的第三次出行由线路 3 的 B3 站点上车，线路 2 中在允许换乘距离与时间内离 B3 最近的站点为 B3 站点本身，将其标记为 A2/B3，表示该名乘客在此站点为同站换乘，并未步行至其他站点。由于第三次出行为该名乘客当日最后一次出行，将允许换乘距离内线路 3 中离该乘客当日首次出行的上车站点 B1 最近的站点 A3 作为第三次出行的估计下车站点。

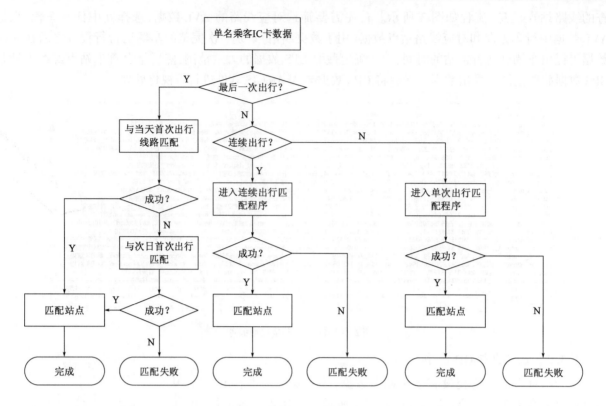

图4　乘客出行 OD 推导流程

	A	B	C	D	E	F	G	H	I	J	K	L	M	N	O	P	Q	R	S	T
1	column1	线路名称	车辆编号	卡号	卡号类型	卡种	交易流水	消费时间	消费	上车站点	上车站点	换乘信息	boarding_	boarding_	alighting_	alighting_	alighting_	alighting_	transfer_distance	
2	429566	304路	JN4-6522	0	DESFire卡	不记名卡	186273	37:39.0	1.6	3040103	鸡鸣寺	无换乘	118.7903	32.06142	大行宫北	45:07.0	118.7902	32.04783	0.021469	
3	181801	160路	JN3-0705	0	DESFire卡	不记名卡	116700	21:45.0	1.6	1600104	随家仓	无换乘	118.7694	32.05289	脑科医院	23:10.0	118.7654	32.05284	0.179482	
4	240224	179路	JN2-1080	0	DESFire卡	不记名卡	228606	27:43.0	1.6	1790004	东郊小镇	无换乘	118.9447	32.06122	文荟路	38:37.0	118.9173	32.05553	0.143281	
5	523454	33路	JN4-3906	0	DESFire卡	不记名卡	178112	47:17.0	1.6	330006	紫荆花路	无换乘	118.7882	31.99331	NULL	NULL	NULL	NULL	NULL	
6	882646	5路	JN2-9118	0	DESFire卡	不记名卡	223721	47:27.0	0	50006	百水芊城	公交转公	118.9017	32.05116	钟灵街	53:53.0	118.8654	32.04216	0.104628	
7	482014	318路	JN1-1279	0	DESFire卡	不记名卡	194216	55:37.0	1.6	3180003	省人民医	无换乘	118.7611	32.0494	西康路	59:44.0	118.7589	32.05832	0.115177	
8	724905	51路	JN2-8879	0	DESFire卡	不记名卡	309761	04:40.0	1.6	510108	永丰大道	无换乘	118.8654	32.01447	玄武军休	17:30.0	118.846	32.02876	0.017029	
9	1244495	84路	JN4-6389	0	DESFire卡	不记名卡	319008	35:41.0	0	840103	胜利村路	公交转公	118.8291	32.03107	长巷	36:23.0	118.8291	32.03107	0.03298	
10	398036	29路	JN2-9903	0	DESFire卡	不记名卡	187094	41:21.0	1.6	290004	西桐桥	无换乘	118.8445	32.00192	海福巷西	51:37.0	118.837	32.0215	0.045426	
11	151026	142路	JN2-0960	0	DESFire卡	不记名卡	307516	53:06.0	1.6	1420105	常府街	无换乘	118.7937	32.03528	五棵松	26:21.0	118.878	32.04962	0.000164	
12	241473	179路	JN2-8890	0	DESFire卡	不记名卡	300534	33:19.0	0	1790106	五棵松	公交转公	118.8781	32.04947	钟山学院	35:01.0	118.8839	32.05133	0.104232	
13	562797	37路	JN2-1026	0	DESFire卡	不记名卡	308798	57:13.0	1.6	370018	内桥	无换乘	118.7814	32.03264	NULL	NULL	NULL	NULL	NULL	
14	56299	115路	JN2-1034	0	DESFire卡	不记名卡	225946	58:17.0	1.6	1150115	富丽山庄	无换乘	118.8293	32.03118	后标营路	59:53.0	118.8338	32.03106	0.203102	
15	1003141	643路	YD-0602	0	DESFire卡	不记名卡	315614	01:50.0	1.6	6430109	盘金华府	无换乘	118.7288	32.20492	南钢六村	02:49.0	118.7299	32.20662	0.2124	
16	726496	51路	JN2-8874	0	DESFire卡	不记名卡	298409	07:49.0	0	510014	玄武军休	公交转公	118.846	32.02876	南理工科	15:06.0	118.8592	32.02303	0.220111	
17	715467	512路	YP-7456	0	DESFire卡	不记名卡	15548	23:04.0	2	5120017	浦珠南路	无换乘	118.6462	32.07875	天浦路·新	25:31.0	118.6478	32.07352	0.237313	
18	469011	312路	JN2-1066	0	DESFire卡	不记名卡	167543	38:02.0	1.6	3120102	润发路北	无换乘	118.874	32.00196	NULL	NULL	NULL	NULL	NULL	
19	469012	312路	JN2-1066	0	DESFire卡	不记名卡	167544	38:04.0	1.6	3120102	润发路北	无换乘	118.874	32.00196	NULL	NULL	NULL	NULL	NULL	
20	374946	26路	JN4-4339	0	DESFire卡	不记名卡	339907	48:00.0	1.6	260107	羊皮巷	无换乘	118.782	32.03682	NULL	NULL	NULL	NULL	NULL	

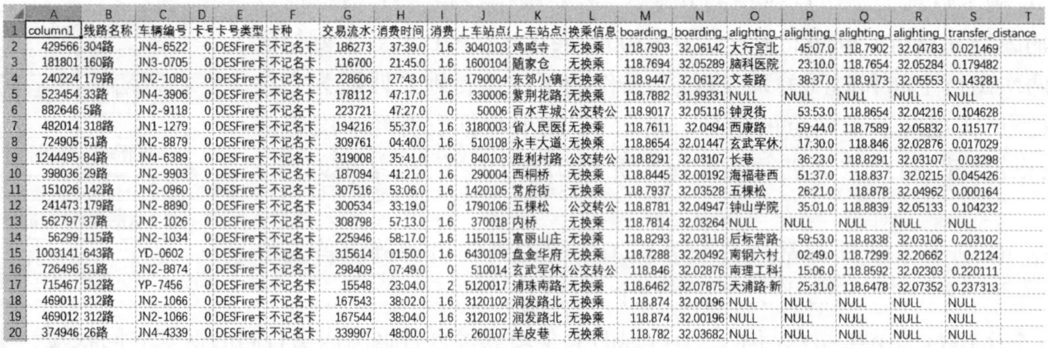

图5　乘客出行 OD 推导结果

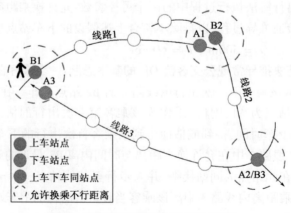

图6　出行链法推导客流 OD 的基本思路

1.3.3 客流特征提取

本文将线路每个 OD 点对的客流量、老年卡比例和乘车距离作为客流特征进行统计。通过使用 SQL Server 对乘客出行 OD 推导结果进行处理，得到每一个 OD 点对间的客流量和老年卡数量，求和即可得到线路总客流量及老年卡比例。之后通过图 7 所示的流程计算每个 OD 点对的乘车距离，得到线路的乘车距离分布情况。最后把得到的数据导入 ArcGIS 软件可得到公交线路站点 OD 分布期望线，从而对结果进行可视化分析。

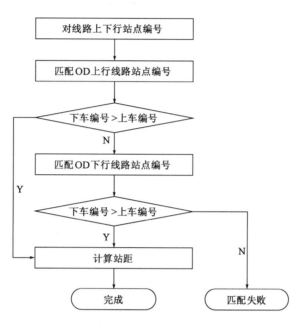

图 7　乘车距离计算流程图

2　常规公交与地铁竞合关系分析

2.1　常规公交与地铁线路的空间关系

根据地铁线路与常规公交站点布设和线路走向在空间上的关系，可将地铁线路与常规公交线路的空间关系分为三类：并行关系、相交关系和无关系，具体见表 4。

常规公交与地铁空间关系　　表 4

线路空间关系	线路空间特征	示　意　图	客　流　关　系
并行关系	常规公交线路与轨道交通并行一定距离		常规公交线路与地铁线路并行部分存在明显竞争，客流会向地铁转移

续上表

线路空间关系	线路空间特征	示意图	客流关系
相交关系	常规公交线路首末站处在地铁直接吸引范围外,公交线路穿过地铁线路		常规公交线路与地铁线路相交处如有站点,则形成接驳关系,增加公交线路客流
	常规公交线路首末站之一处于地铁直接吸引范围内		
	常规公交线路首末站均处于地铁直接吸引范围内,但主体线路在吸引范围外		常规公交线路与地铁形成接驳关系,短距离出行客流较大,中长距离出行客流较少
无关系	常规公交线路首末站在地铁直接吸引范围外,且与地铁线路无交点		常规公交线路覆盖地铁无法到达区域,与地铁基本无竞争

注: ▬▬ 为轨道交通线路, ○—○ 为地面公交线路, ┄┄┄ 为轨道交通直接吸引范围。

2.2 考虑客流特征的竞合关系甄别

为观察地铁对老年人出行的吸引强度,本文对比了南京市 11 路公交在地铁 4 号线建成前后客流量的刷卡数据。如图 8 所示,11 路公交大部分走向与地铁 4 号线重合。南京市地铁 4 号线于 2017 年 1 月正式运营,本文对比的分别是 2016 年 7 月和 2020 年 7 月的公交刷卡数据,结果如图 9 所示可以看到,在 4 号线开通之后,11 路总体客流下降 60.6%,而老年人群客流下降 38.9%,说明老年乘客对常规公交的依赖性较强。考虑到老年乘客信息获取相对不便,对公交线网进行优化的时候更应该慎重考虑调整方案,以满足老年乘客的乘车需求。

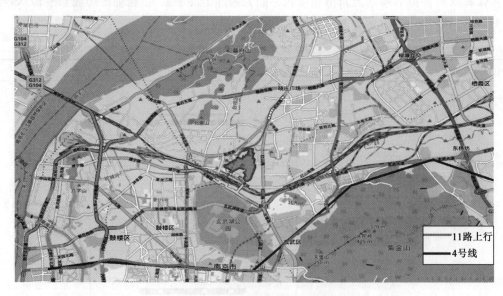

图 8 公交 11 路与地铁 4 号线走向示意图

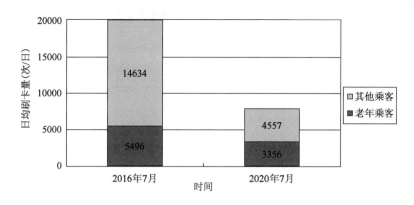

图9 公交11路在地铁4号线建成前后客流对比

考虑到客流特征,本文将常规公交与地铁的合作关系分为直接合作和间接合作,将竞争关系分为强竞争和弱竞争,见表5。对于通过与地铁接驳完成合作的线路,也就是与地铁相交的线路,无论是直接合作还是间接合作,都是促进交通运行效率的方式,无须调整。而对于竞争类型的线路,即与地铁线路重合超过一定区间的线路,需要考虑老年乘客这种对常规公交依赖性较强的乘客类型,不能仅从空间角度判别,还需要结合客流特征进一步分析,识别真正的强竞争关系,避免"一刀切"带来的负优化。

常规公交线路与地铁线路的竞争合作关系   表5

关系	分类	定义
合作	直接合作	一条公交线路与一条地铁线路直接接驳完成出行活动
	间接合作	一条公交线路与一条地铁线路通过网络内其他线路接驳完成出行活动
竞争	强竞争	地铁线路对走廊内客流吸引力较强,对公交线路客流的影响较大
	弱竞争	因老年乘客或中短乘距的乘客比例较大,常规公交在客流走廊内有客流基础,地铁线路对走廊内客流吸引力较弱,对公交线路客流的影响较小

3 常规公交与地铁并行线路优化策略及案例分析

随着轨道线路开通与网络化发展,常规公交与地铁并行的线路无论是从客流转移角度还是成本角度,需要优化调整。为构建共生共长的"大公交"网络布局,实现社会效益最大化,常规公交线网优化主要分为以下两个目标:

(1)两网融合,实现良性竞争。明确地铁线路与不同层次的常规公交线路在交通走廊及换乘节点处的空间关系与竞合关系,以空间关系、竞合关系以及共生发展关系为依据,以缓解竞争、加强合作为主要目标,实现功能补充、并行优化与接驳强化。

(2)线网覆盖,保证基本服务。中心城区是基础设施集中布设的区域,通常可以实现公交网络和站点的高覆盖。外围地区受制于落后的土地开发,其公共交通设施的配置相对落后,新建用地容易成为公共交通服务的盲区,尤其是延伸至外围地区的新地铁线路,具有引导新区发展的功能,地面公交线路与地铁网络之间的接驳需要加强。常规公交作为"门到门"的交通方式,必须要保证线网覆盖程度,提供面向大众的基础服务。

常规公交线路与地铁并行超过一定长度之后需要考虑调整,对于常规公交线路与地铁并行区间的长度,不同城市不尽相同,具体情况见表6。

不同城市对轨道交通沿线公交线路调整的规定 表6

地点	规定
德国部分城市	一般不得超过 3~4 个地铁站点服务半径的距离
泰国曼谷	对与地铁蓝线重复 10 站以上的公交线路进行优化调整。可保留部分起到分流作用的线路,但与并行长度不宜超过 4km
北京	取消与地铁重合 6km 以上的公交线路
上海	调整与地铁线路重复 5km 以上且重复长度占线路总长 50% 的线路
广州	调整与地铁线路重合超过 3 个地铁站的公交线路
深圳	调整与地铁线路重合超过 5 个地铁站的公交线路

综合以上城市经验,结合南京市实际情况,本文选取超过 3 个地铁站点与公交线路重合作为并线判断标准,在此基础上,判断老年卡刷卡比例是否高于 50%,对于老年卡刷卡比例过高的线路需要慎重考虑调整问题。

对于并行线路,考虑线路客流特征,有以下几种优化策略(表7)。

并行线路优化策略 表7

策略	适用条件
全线保留或增撤站点	对于已有或新建地铁线路沿线常规公交线路,若老年乘客比例较大或历史客流较大,则考虑保留原有线路以满足乘客群体需求,并适应线路的历史延续性
调整走向	对于常规公交客流大部分被地铁吸引的线路,如果长距离客流较多可以考虑调整线路走向,偏离地铁线路,构建新的站点覆盖新的客流区域
拆分线路	对于两端客流较多长距离客流较少的常规公交线路可以考虑将线路拆分,如果有条件可以考虑将两端线路改成微循环线路,接驳地铁客流
缩减线路	当部分常规公交线路可以被地铁线路取代时,可以考虑缩减线路长度,降低运行成本

本文选取奥南地区 169 路和 170 路对并行线路进行案例分析。

公交 169 路北起宜悦街,南至岱山南路·岱山中路,共 23 站,是一条连接奥南地区和西善桥地区的线路,其乘客出行 OD 分布如图 10 所示。公交 170 路北起清江南路,南至元前路总站,共 31 站,途经多处学校及住宅区,其乘客出行 OD 分布如图 11 所示。由于西善桥地区存在西善花苑小学、力行小学等学校和恒永西苑、平治东苑等多个住宅区,大部分客流是从 2 号线、7 号线和 S3 号线换乘的油坊桥站到达西善桥站附近地区,从油坊桥到岱山北路西站和西善花苑小学的客流强度尤为突出,在 7 号线和 2 号线西延开通之后,169 路恰好与前者跨秦淮新河客流通道重合,170 路位于 2 号线和 7 号线中间,与地铁线路走向基本相同,故二者在空间上均为与地铁存在竞争关系。

根据 OD 推导数据计算得到的公交 169 路与 170 路乘车距离如图 12 所示。可以看出,公交 169 路乘坐 8 站及以上的乘客占比 41.4%,公交 170 路乘坐 8 站及以上的乘客占比 45.4%,二者长距离出行客流均较多,从乘车距离上看潜在转移的客流较多,与地铁线路属于竞争关系。

根据线路刷卡数据计算可得出,169 路老年乘客平均比例为 35.8%,乘坐少于等于 4 站的老年乘客占比 38.8%,乘坐少于等于 3 站的老年乘客占比为 38.4%,老年卡比例较低;而 170 路老年乘客平均比例为 50.5%,乘坐少于等于 4 站的乘客中 59.9% 为老年乘客,乘坐少于等于 3 站的乘客老年人的比例更是达到了 75.4%。考虑到线路的历史延续性以及乘客人群的特殊性,在地铁 2 号线西延及 7 号线开通之后,非老年卡长距离客流大部分预期将向地铁转移,地铁线路与公交 169 路形成强竞争关系,与公交 170 路则为弱竞争关系,因此建议公交 169 路在地铁线路开通后根据客流 OD 分布进行拆分,作为地铁接驳线为西善桥地区和奥南地区的住宅区及学校提供出行服务,而公交 170 路由于老年乘客比例较大不建议做较大改动。

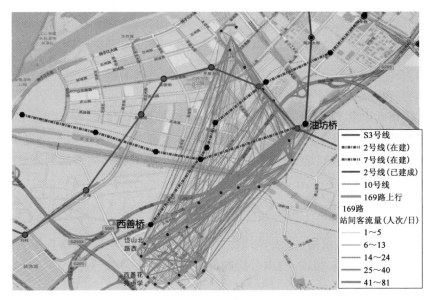

图 10　公交 169 路乘客出行 OD 示意图

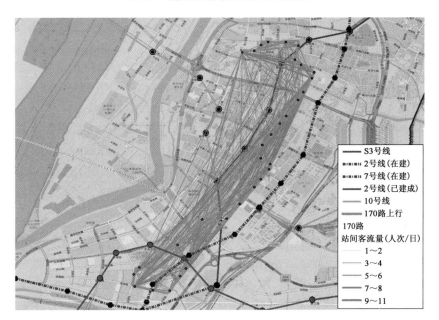

图 11　公交 170 路乘客出行 OD 示意图

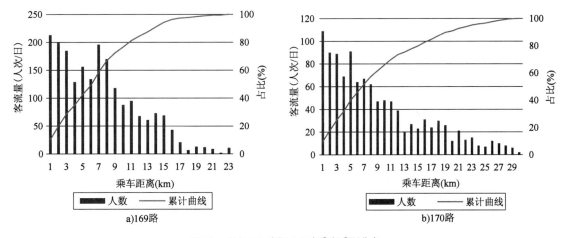

a) 169 路　　　　　　　　　　　　　b) 170 路

图 12　公交 169 路与 170 路乘客乘距分布

4 结语

本文通过对南京市奥南地区公交线路数据进行处理,分析常规公交与地铁竞合关系,将竞争关系分为强竞争和弱竞争,合作关系分为直接合作和间接合作。在此基础上提出了对于常规公交线网作优化调整的目标,而后针对并行线路提出了相应的优化策略和案例分析。

本文从工程实践角度出发,考虑对老年群体的人文关怀,根据客流特征以及实际步行距离,更真实地反映出常规公交与地铁线路的竞合关系,为公交企业提出有效可行的线路调整策略提供参考。下一步研究将强化乘客出行 OD 的推导算法,增加识别准确度,并将深入研究线路调整的网络效应,根据客流特征提出更完善的优化调整策略。

5 致谢

本文的完成来源于南京公共交通(集团)有限公司、东南大学"产学研"战略合作项目,在项目推进及数据提供方面得到南京公共交通(集团)有限公司的大力支持,在此深表感谢。

参考文献

[1] 贺建炜,彭金栓.城市轨道交通与常规公交竞争与合作分析[J].智能城市,2016,2(06):94-95.
[2] 朱飘,龙科军.轨道交通与常规公交竞合关系一体化研究[J].交通科学与工程,2019,35(01):94-100.
[3] 陈雪珍.基于双层规划的城市轨道交通接驳公交线路研究[D].南昌:华东交通大学,2016.
[4] 王玉萍.常规公交与轨道交通之间的竞争与合作[D].西安:长安大学,2004.
[5] 陈贵凤.轨道交通与常规公交的竞争与合作[D].南京:河海大学,2008.
[6] 陈学武,李海波,侯现耀.城市公交 IC 卡数据分析方法及应用[M].北京:科学出版社,2014.
[7] Barry J, Newhouser R, Rahbee A, et al. Origin and Destination Estimation in New York City with Automated Fare System Data[J]. Transportation Research Record,2002(1817):183-187.

深圳市地面公交运速提升实践

张　彬　颜建新

(深圳市综合交通设计研究院有限公司)

摘要　针对深圳市公交专用道规模已接近道路容量极限,公交运营提速进入瓶颈期等问题,通过全方位分析道路路段、交叉口、公交停靠站点等公交运营关键环节,从增加供应、提升效率、外部保障 3 个层面着手,系统性提出公交提速策略及措施,充分保障有限道路资源及管理手段向高效交通方式倾斜,助力公交运营提速及公交都市建设。

关键词　公交专用道　公交运营提速　精细化设计　创新专用道形式

0 引言

深圳市机动车保有量已突破 350 万辆,机动车密度达 533 辆/km,居国内城市首位。随着机动车保有量的持续扩大,道路交通拥堵日益显著。贯彻公交优先发展战略,强化公交路权保障,提升公交运营速度,是显著提高公交系统吸引力和竞争力,抑制个体交通快速增长的关键。

地面公交运行速度的提升,不仅体现在乘客步行到站的便捷度及车辆行驶速度的提高,更需要"公交专用路权保障—交叉口通行优先—公交停靠站进出顺畅"整个公交运营环境的全面提升,从而保障公交乘客在出行链各环节的出行时效。

本文主要围绕公交专用道、公交停靠站及道路交叉口等公交运营速度提升的关键因素,综合应用大数据挖掘与分析,制定有针对性的提速策略及精细化实施方案,从而有效提升公交出行的服务品质。

1 公交提速的内涵及国内外研究现状

1.1 公交提速的内涵

公交乘客全过程出行链如图1所示。公交提速在广义上为公交乘客全过程出行链的速度提升,既包括对路外步行、候车等环节的提速,也包括路内公交车辆运营等环节的提速。据不完全统计,在深圳的早晚高峰通勤出行中,地面公交乘客的平均路外步行和等候时长约占整个出行时间的44%左右,全过程出行链提速的意义可见一斑。考虑到公交乘客全过程出行链提速涉及的内容更加系统和广泛,受篇幅所限无法细致研究,本文重点关注路内公交车辆运营环节的瓶颈识别和提速策略。

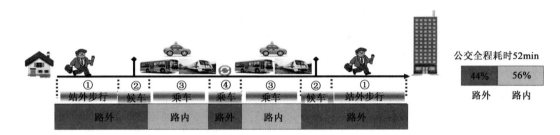

图1 公交乘客全过程出行链

根据实践经验,公交车辆运营提速是当前社会各界和政府部门的主要关注点,其中施划公交专用道是重要举措,已成为各大城市实施公交优先的首选。但从全过程出行链的角度来看,在公交车辆运行的整个过程中,除路段公交路权保障之外,公交站点瓶颈、交叉口瓶颈的存在,也是造成路内公交车辆运行效率低下的关键要素。

1.2 国内外研究现状

在公交车辆运营提速方面,国内外学者主要针对公交专用道布设方法和公交信号优先策略开展研究。张卫华、黄艳君、胡刚总结了我国城市公交专用道存在着城市道路建设缺乏对公交专用道的考虑、标志标线不统一、设置路段选择上存在一定的盲目性等问题,从路段客流量、路段公交车流量、路段饱和度、道路状况4个方面提出了设置公交专用道路段应具备的基本条件。Qiu F、Li W、Zhang J等在利用仿真和分析模型定量化对比分析了两车道路段中有无间歇式公交专用道对交通参数的影响,确定了间歇式公交专用道策略实施的交通量条件。卢小林提出基于公交走廊的专用道选址和公交线网同步调整的组合优化设计思路,并构建了双层优化模型,分析结果表明组合优化方案能够更好地发挥公交走廊的网络效益。邹智军以巴黎香榭丽舍大街为例,提出了一种在线的、基于规则的、反应式的交通走廊公交信号优先算法。Estrada M、Mensión J、Aymamí J M等基于公交车在站点的实时追踪数据,以减少车头时距变化对线路运行的影响为目标,建立了动态的公交控制策略。

2 深圳公交提速现状及问题

2.1 公交提速工作

2.1.1 公交专用道建设

深圳市于2010年构建了完善的公交专用道规划建设年度工作机制,大力推进公交专用道建设。截至2019年底,公交专用道里程已达1016车道公里,公交专用道的线网设置率15.3%,基本成规模化、网络化运行;同时,在超过100个交叉口设置了公交专用进口道,在深南大道人民南路口等13个T型信号交叉口通过渠化设置公交优先车道,在6个交叉口设置RFID公交优先。

深圳市公交专用道分布及发展进程示意图如图 2 所示。

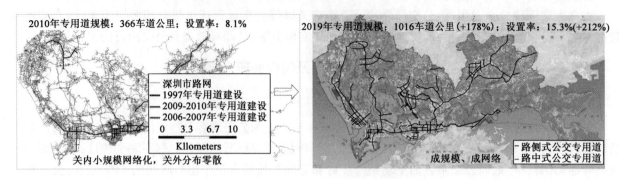

图 2　深圳市公交专用道分布及发展进程示意图

2.1.2　公交停靠站公交列车化改善

持续滚动推进公交"四站"设施升级改造工作,其中,2018 年全市共改造无设施站 26 座,迁移、改造公交停靠站 361 座,维护"四站"设施 17599 座次,显著提升了公交停靠站服务水平。同时,通过设置分站、线路调整优化等措施改善公交列车化严重的站点,降低公交运行延误。

2.1.3　管理措施及政策

出台《深圳市公交专用道设置标准及建设指引》,规定深圳市公交专用道的设置标准及设计要求;在 19 路、202 路、29 路等 24 条线路上完成 134 套公交专用道视频抓拍系统的安装,覆盖深南大道、107 国道、龙岗大道等 74% 左右的公交专用道,为强化公交专用道监管提供了支撑。

2.2　提速效果分析

(1)社会车辆平均车速稳中有降,但公交整体运行速度上升且趋稳。图 3 所示为近年来公交运行速度和道路交通平均速度变化情况。在城市交通拥堵有所加剧的背景下,设置公交专用道的客流走廊公交运行速度稳定,交通拥堵对地面公交平均车速的影响相对较小,基本维持在 20km/h 左右。

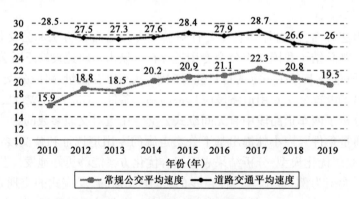

图 3　近年来公交运行速度和道路交通平均速度变化情况(单位:km/h)

(2)客流通道保障力度大,公交出行竞争力显著提高。在专用道上运行的公交线路共 810 条,占线路总规模的 86.8%。其中,公交客流 1.5 万人次/h 以上的客流走廊 90% 已覆盖公交专用道(图 4),高峰期有 190 万公交乘客受益,占全市高峰期公交乘客总量的 70%。

(3)公交运行效率得到较大提高,有效节约了政府财政补贴。据测算,随着高峰期公交行程车速提升,既有公交运力单位运输效率较 2010 年提升了 21.3%,在车辆配置不变的情况下,相当于增加运力 3088 辆,高峰小时增加运力 18.5 万人次。

2.3　问题及成因分析

受道路资源、前期设计、交通管理等因素影响,深圳市公交专用道规模已接近极限,公交运营提速已进入瓶颈期,主要体现在以下方面:

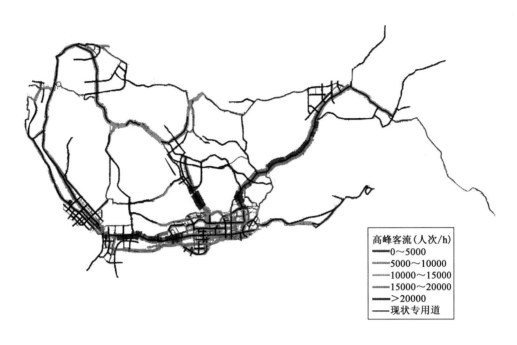

图 4　现状公交专用道覆盖公交客流示意图

（1）部分走廊关键区段及关键节点缺乏公交路权保障。受道路条件制约、交通管理措施（如潮汐车道、快慢车分离等）影响，现状超过10%的主要客流走廊尚未设置专用道，公交行驶中需要多次变道或避让，无法发挥整体优势。

（2）部分公交站点服务能力不足，导致公交列车化及公交进出站延误现象突出。现状深圳78.3%的公交停靠站为直线式站点，且有534个站点停靠线路超过15条，占全市站点总数的6.1%，导致部分站点停靠容量供需失衡，公交列车化现象突出，公交进站排队延误时间增加。

（3）部分公交专用道设计不合理，与通道公交需求匹配性不足影响使用效果。如部分路段社会车辆接近饱和，而公交专用道利用率不高，社会舆论压力较大；公交专用道标志标线施划不规范，影响使用效果；部分客流通道非传统高峰时段缺少公交路权保障等。

（4）公交专用道在交叉口、沿线地块出入口等处缺乏精细化设计，车流交织严重影响公交车辆在专用道上的连续性运行。

（5）公交专用道监管执法力度有待加强，部分区域、部分路段的社会车辆违法占道情况突出，严重干扰公交运行。

3　公交提速发展趋势研判

3.1　趋势分析

公交优先战略已上升至国家战略层面，有必要持续贯彻相关公交优先发展要求，强化公交路权保障，提高公交运行速度，打通公交运行瓶颈，大力提升公交相对小汽车的比较优势，夯实公交都市创建成果，努力创建社会主义现代化国家的城市范例。

（1）交通运输部等十二部门联合制定的《绿色出行行动计划（2019—2022年）》提出坚持公共交通优先发展，大力提升公共交通服务品质，提高公交运行速度；深圳市作为交通运输部授予的"国家公交都市建设示范城市"，公交提速工程是其"亮点工程"，按年度重点工作持续推进。

（2）大部制改革后，深圳公交提速工程效果显著，但现状公交相对小汽车仍缺乏速度竞争力，巩固并提升公交专用网效用需继续跟进。根据调查，在深圳轨道交通新线路投入运营的情况下，近两年公共交通分担率并未实现增长。且受轨道交通及其他重大交通工程施工占道影响,公交运行速度下降,公交客流持续下降。

(3)外部形势发生显著变化,小汽车调控政策逐步放宽、轨道交通即将以更大规模网络化运营、常规公交线路面临大幅调整,应按需对存量公交专用网实施评估优化。

(4)随着车路协同、5G等新一代信息技术的应用,市民对快速、准点、可靠的公交品质服务需求越来越迫切,打通运行瓶颈,提升公交运速已迫在眉睫。

3.2 提速方向

在经历了快速发展期之后,深圳市公交专用道的规划建设受交通运行态势、道路交通条件、轨道交通建设等因素影响,发展规模已逼近临界状态,边际效应愈发明显。

事实证明,施划公交专用道是提高公交车速成效明显、实施难度相对较低的手段,但不是唯一手段。现阶段应认清外部环境的变化趋势,从路段及交叉口通行、站点停靠,以及公交场站进出等多个环节着手,采取"组合拳"合破解公交运行各环节的"肠梗堵"。

4 公交提速的目标与指引

4.1 总体目标

公交优先的本质是公交优先小汽车发展,可与小汽车竞争。因此,深圳市公交提速工作的总体目标是按照公交1.5战略,推进公交专用道网络化、系统化发展,提高公交相对小汽车的吸引力与竞争力,以期优化城市交通出行结构,支撑城市交通可持续运行。

4.2 具体指标

近期高峰期公交行程车速与小汽车平均行程车速比高于1∶1.2,主要客流走廊达到1∶1,中远期高峰期主要客流走廊公交车速度应高于小汽车速度。

4.3 相关设置标准指引

4.3.1 公交专用道设置标准

根据《深圳市公交专用道设置标准及设计指引(试行)》,路段公交专用道和交叉口公交专用道的设置条件,均要求综合考虑道路条件、公交车流、公交客流和公交分担率等作为路权分配依据。

(1)路段专用道。一般单向3车道及以上路段公交车流量大于60标台/h,或单向2车道路段公交车流量大于120标台/h的道路,可考虑设置公交专用道,现状需求不足但近期潜在需求大的也可提前施划,见表1。

路段公交专用道设置标准 表1

主要类型	道路条件	高峰小时交通需求				备注
		公交车辆(标台/h)	公交客流(人次/h)	公交分担率(%)	饱和度	
1	单向机动车道(含辅道)为3车道及以上	单向≥90	—	—	单向≥0.7	单向宜设置1条公交专用道
		60≤单向<90	—	单向≥50	单向≥0.7	
2	单向机动车道(含辅道)为2车道	单向≥120	单向≥4000	—	单向≥0.7	

(2)交叉口公交专用进口道。基于交叉口所在路段车道数、交叉口进口道车道数及交叉口进口道公交车流量作为路权分配依据,同一方向原则上不设置两条及以上的公交专用进口道,见表2。

交叉口公交专用道设置标准　　　　表 2

主要类型	道路条件			高峰小时交通需求		备注
	路段单向机动车道数	交叉口直行进口道数	交叉口左转进口道数	交叉口直行公交车流量（标车/h）	交叉口左转公交车流量（标车/h）	
1	≥2	≥2	—	≥90	—	宜设置1条直行公交专用进口道
2	≥2	—	≥2	—	≥80	宜设置1条左转公交专用进口道
3	≥4	≥2	≥2	≥90	≥80	宜设置1条直行公交专用进口道,1条左转公交专用的进口道

4.3.2 公交列车化站点改善指引

根据调查及实践经验,公交站点公交列车化问题主要由公交站点停靠泊位容量不足、停靠线路过多、站点客流量过大导致车辆停靠时间过长以及社会车辆占用公交站点上下客等因素产生。针对上述问题,总结出公交列车化公交站点改善思路包括以下4个方面:

(1)增加站点泊位。针对现状停靠泊位仅1~2个的站点,通过增加站点泊位提升站点停靠能力,但站点泊位不超过3个,以此提升站点停靠压力。

(2)港湾式改造。在站点停靠泊位不变的情况下,有条件的情况下将直线式进行港湾式改造,可有效提高站点停靠能力。

(3)实施分站停靠。针对停靠线路过多问题,在既有站点停靠能力不变的情况下,通过对线路实行分站停靠,能够分流站点停靠需求,进而降低站点停靠压力。

(4)停靠线路调整。结合线路站点客流特征,对途经站点的线路进行跳站调整,减少站点停靠线路规模,降低站点停靠压力。

(5)加强停靠管理。针对社会车辆占用站点停靠候客降低站点停靠能力的问题,通过严厉查处违停行为,净化站点停靠车流,保障站点的停靠能力。

5 公交提速策略及措施

根据公交提速目标,主要围绕路段、路口、公交站点等关键环节,从增加供应、提升效率、外部保障3个方面,提出公交提速具体策略及措施,通过保障有限道路资源向高效交通方式倾斜,注重既有公交提速工程效率,提升强化外部保障,旗帜鲜明地支持公交优先。

5.1 "增加供应":增加公交路权资源供给

加强公交优先路权的成网联通性,基于不同公交需求设置各种路权优化保障形式,进一步打通公交运行瓶颈,减少公交运行延误。其中,当公交需求满足公交专用道设置条件时应做到以下几点:

(1)继续推动公交运行瓶颈路段打通(图5),持续将不连续的公交专用网连接成网。因地制宜、灵活选择适宜的路权保障形式,打通客流走廊公交专用通道瓶颈,持续扩大公交专用道网络覆盖,从公交路权"点、线"的保障拓展到公交路权"面"的保障。

(2)跨关、跨区大客流通道实施路中式专用道,升级公交路权保障力度。借鉴新彩通道路中式公交专用道实践经验,选择坂银通道、龙岗大道等通道试点路中式公交专用道。

(3)改造关键瓶颈路口,设置公交专用进口道,保障关键节点公交优先,如图6所示。

(4)针对公交需求不满足公交专用道设置条件,可考虑结合道路条件,设置合乘车道(HOV、HOT)等新形式保障公交路权。

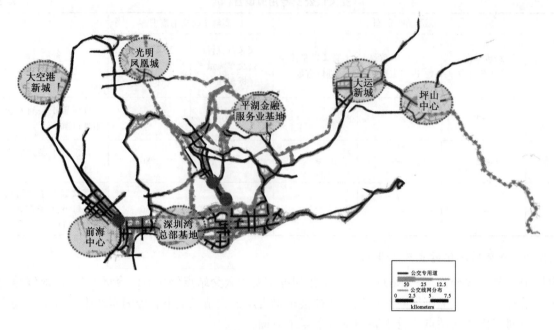

图5 需打通的公交提速主要瓶颈分布示意图

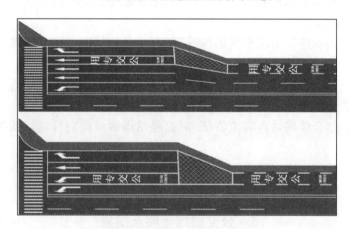

图6 公交专用进口道设置示意图

5.2 "提升效率"：精细化交通设计及组织

应更加注重对既有公交提速工程效果检讨评估，通过精细化交通设计继续挖潜既有公交提速工程实施潜力，包括以下几点：

（1）优化专用道标志标线，提高其可视性与警示性。如在既有专用道标线基础上，增设反光道钉，规范公交专用道标志牌的设置，提高标志标线的可视性与警示性（图7）。

（2）加强公交专用道与沿线设施衔接的精细化设计。重点对路段专用道与交叉口公交专用进口道、公交专用道与公交停靠站、沿线交叉口、地块出入口之间进行精细化设计。

（3）优化公交专用道管理时段，匹配高峰通行需求。结合公交专用道所在道路交通运行情况及公交客流时段分布特征，合理确定专用道通行时段，最大限度发挥

图7 优化专用道标志标线示意图

专用道的功能。

(4)持续公交站点拥堵治理,避免站点公交列车化。如对站点实施港湾式改造,并合理增加站点泊位规模,提高站点停靠能力(图8)。

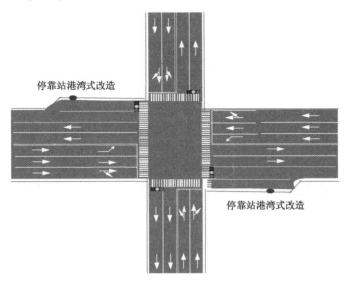

图8　公交站点拥堵治理(停靠站港湾式改造)示意图

(5)通过标志标线设计确保公交车辆出站优先通行。在公交站点出口道处设置公交出站优先通道(设置停车让行标线及禁停网格线),要求社会车辆通过前提前放缓速度、停车让行,严禁停留在黄色标志线内,使公交车辆优先出站,减少公交车辆出站延误。

其次,把公交优先理念贯彻到交通组织中,在交通组织中创造条件实施公交路权优先保障。如:探索实施单向路公交双向通行,解决市民乘车不便的问题;T型路口主方向采取公交专用道直通式设计形式;针对左转公交流量大路口,研究实施最外侧公交左转专用道;基于潮汐性客流特征,探索实施潮汐公交车道等。

几种常见的创新公交专用道设置形式如图9所示。

a)单向路公交双向通行

b)吉华路-湖南路交叉口设置最右侧左转

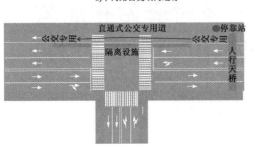

c)T型路口主方向采取公交专用道直通式设计

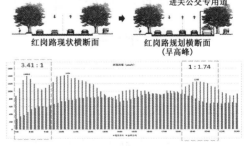

d)红岗路可实施潮汐公交车道

图9　创新公交专用道设置形式示意图

5.3 "外部保障":强化公交路权配套保障

既要在硬件层面上大力提升公交运行速度,同时要强化外部配套保障,通过"组合拳"的方式大力提升公交运行提速效果,包括完善监控设施布设,加大交通违规查处力度;建立多部门联合、高效的公交提速工作机制,推进公交提速工程有效落实;加强公交专用道等公交提速工程的宣传工作;针对道路资源紧约束公交关键运营瓶颈路段,可研究对私家车实施需求管理;推动公交路权保障立法工作,夯实公交优先战略。

6 结 语

针对深圳市公交专用道扩容已近极限、公交运行速度难以得到本质提升的问题,本文提出全面提升"公交专用路权保障—交叉口通行优先—公交站台进出顺畅"等全过程公交运行环境,并从增加供应、提升效率、外部保障3个层面着手,提出了实施性较强的公交提速策略及具体措施,充分保障有限道路资源及管理手段向高效交通方式倾斜,支持深圳市公交都市建设。本文对于资源紧约束条件下大中城市公交系统全面提速具有较强的指导意义。

参考文献

[1] 吴娇蓉,王宇沁,魏明,等.路侧公交专用道设置长度对公交线路运行可靠性的影响[J].吉林大学学报(工学版),2017,47(01):82-91.

[2] 高嵩,李玲琦,邹芳.武汉市公交专用道系统设置标准及实施评估[J].交通与运输(学术版),2017(01):138-141.

[3] 马美娜.随机均衡配流下的公交专用道布局优化研究[D].广州:华南理工大学,2018.

[4] Paul Anderson, Carlos F. Daganzo. Effect of transit signal priority on bus service reliability [J]. Transportation Research Part B,2020:132.

[5] Zhuang Dai, Xiaoyue Cathy Liu, Zhuo Chen, Renyong Guo, Xiaolei Ma. A predictive headway-based bus-holding strategy with dynamic control point selection:A cooperative game theory approach [J]. Transportation Research Part B,2019:125.

[6] 葛宏伟,罗俊,张彬,等.公交路内换乘枢纽规划设置方法研究[J].华东交通大学学报,2017,34(06):53-59.

[7] 张冬奇.重庆市主城区公交专用道规划研究[D].重庆:重庆交通大学,2017.

[8] 武艺.客流走廊地面公交运行瓶颈识别与组织优化[D].南京:东南大学,2018.

[9] 深圳市综合交通设计研究院有限公司.深圳市公交专用道规划建设2020年度技术咨询服务[R].深圳:深圳市交通运输委员会,2020.

美丽乡村建设背景下乡村驿站布局与发展研究——以南京市江宁区为例

徐新星 李竹薇 申梦婷 曾竹喧 卢佳诚
(华设设计集团股份有限公司)

摘 要 打造以乡村驿站为代表的乡村综合服务设施是国家促进交旅融合发展、建设"四好农村路"、推动美丽乡村建设的要求。为加快推进乡村驿站的发展,本文在分析日本乡村驿站和我国溧阳乡村驿站的布局模式的基础上,总结了相关经验,研究提出了乡村驿站的功能分类、布局方法和设施配置要求等,并以江宁区为例,应用了乡村驿站布局与发展研究成果,为乡村驿站的发展提出了相应的对策。本研究可以促进乡村综合服务设施有序发展,有力支撑地方美丽乡村建设。

关键词　乡村建设　驿站布局　案例分析法　乡村驿站　江宁区

0　引　言

随着全域旅游概念的提出、交旅融合的发展,乡村驿站的需求大幅提升,一系列国家政策文件提出鼓励在农村公路路侧设置驿站,完善驿站配套服务体系。在乡村驿站的研究方面,游小妹分析总结了日本川场广场田园驿站布局和功能设置的经验,但未能结合我国实际情况进行应用。陈琳等分析了日本乡村驿站的建立、运营特征及功能分类等,同样未能详细说明如何在国内实际应用。李迎丹等提出了乡村休闲驿站的设计原则和展现理念,认为需要从空间层次结构的角度对乡村驿站进行设计,但侧重于设计,对乡村驿站的布局及发展研究较少。综上,国内真正关于乡村驿站布局规划和发展方面的研究甚少,而全国各地陆续开展乡村驿站的探索和建设,尚存在驿站布局规划不够系统、未将公路设施与景区及区域发展有机结合、已建成驿站易识别程度和服务功能不足等问题。本文着重对乡村驿站的布局规划和运营发展进行系统研究,同时将研究结果应用于具体实践中,取得了良好的效果,对国内乡村驿站的建设具有十分重要的意义。

1　乡村驿站的概念

1.1　乡村驿站的定义

乡村驿站是给除高速公路之外的一般道路使用者提供舒适安全的休息环境而设置的道路服务设施,也是为了带动沿线地区经济发展、彰显沿线各地区的特色而建立的多功能复合服务设施,其基本理念是成为所在地区特色展示、生产和生活化的重要节点。

1.2　乡村驿站的功能

乡村驿站的基本功能有:①休息,全天提供一定数量的免费停车场、卫生间等;②信息传播功能,提供具备服务电话、信息传送等一系列功能的设施,提供交通、旅游、物产、紧急医疗等有效信息;③商业,开展餐饮、购物等形式的商业活动,以带动沿线经济发展。

除基本功能外,乡村驿站还具有以下复合功能:①窗口功能,作为带动城市资金、人才和信息进入乡村的窗口,推动城乡交流与协调发展;②枢纽功能,作为乡村经济社会发展的节点,促进资金的内部循环,给乡村带来新的经济增长和就业机会;③平台功能,成为乡村小型生活平台,为村民提供购物、医疗、乘车等服务。

2　乡村驿站典型案例分析

2.1　日本乡村驿站

日本乡村驿站的建设起源于20世纪90年代,从最开始的单功能休憩设施,逐渐发展为为村民提供医疗急救、教育培训、文化活动、收寄快递等多种形式公共服务的复合多功能综合服务站。

截至2020年,日本全国有乡村驿站达1180处,如图1所示。由图可知,日本乡村驿站都是分布在距离大都市圈较远的地区。如在关东地区,乡村驿站多分布在外围地区的长野县和群马县,充分说明乡村驿站的分布与当地的经济发展状况以及周边城市的发展及其布局状况相关。

日本通过乡村驿站的布局建设,引领乡村经济重构,促进城乡交流,在一定程度上解决了过疏化和老龄化引起的乡村人才缺失问题,破解了乡村发展困局。同时,乡村驿站不断强化乡村生活空间建设,逐渐成为提供村民日常生活服务的平台。日本乡村驿站体系性强,可操作性强,具有较强的借鉴意义。

2.2　溧阳乡村驿站

溧阳乡村驿站是服务于"溧阳一号公路"的配套设施,主要满足乡村公路、慢行交通等各类游客的休息、咨询、餐饮、停车等多项服务需要。溧阳驿站充分融合了当地人文景观、自然景观、生态环境资源及农业生产活动,综合考虑区域交通综合网络格局、各乡镇发展思路和生态保护要求,形成了三级驿站布局规划。各级驿站在建设与用地规模、停车设施等方面作出差异化规定,并对其发展策略加以规划引导。在全域旅游的背景下,溧阳通过配套驿站来凸显整体旅游价值,提升了旅游全过程服务。

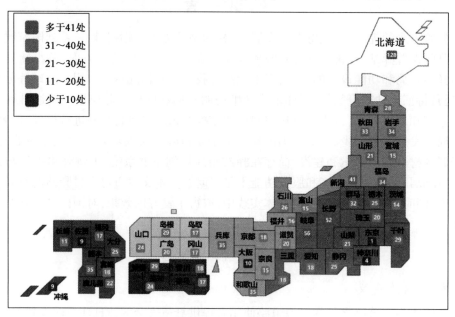

图1 日本乡村驿站布局图

资料来源:http://www.mlit.go.jp/road/Michi-no-Eki/list.html。

2.3 经验总结

日本乡村驿站是根据不同地域发展面向旅游和产业的多功能驿站,溧阳乡村驿站主要服务于"溧阳一号公路"的观光游客,以旅游功能为主。两者都根据区域的经济情况、村庄分布、服务需求等因素对驿站进行分级布局,根据驿站特色,提供饮食、文化、住宿、停车、购物等多种类型的服务,提升驿站吸引力。

3 乡村驿站功能及布局方法研究

3.1 乡村驿站功能分类

根据驿站的服务对象与要求、设置地点等因素,将驿站分为3个等级:一级驿站结合旅游景区、大型村庄等进行布局,承担综合服务、管理、交通换乘、休憩等功能,是驿站体系中的服务核心;二级驿站结合村庄、观光农业园、农家乐等重要乡村节点布置,承担售卖、租赁、停车、游憩等功能;三级驿站主要为使用者提供休闲场所,结合乡村景观灵活设置。

3.2 乡村驿站布局方法

通过对道路沿线的村庄分布、交通条件、生态环境等要素进行探勘、分析、评估,综合分析后确定需要乡村驿站的位置,优先利用现状资源,可与公交场站、社区中心、养护道班等进行合并布置。根据住房和城乡建设部发布的《绿道规划设计导则》,结合案例经验借鉴,针对不同等级驿站,提出合适的布局间距要求,见表1。

三级乡村驿站布局间距一览表　　表1

基本项目	一级驿站	二级驿站	三级驿站
间距(km)	15~20	5~10	3~5

3.3 乡村驿站设施配置

乡村驿站主要包含管理服务、商业、游憩健身、科普教育、安全保障、环境卫生和停车等几大类设施，各级驿站需配备的设施见表2。乡村驿站的功能配置要讲究整体性，不同级别乡村驿站的配置布设要功能互补，以资源最小化实现服务最大化。

三级驿站设施表　　　　表2

设施类型	基本项目	一级驿站	二级驿站	三级驿站
管理服务设施	管理中心	●	○	—
	游客服务中心	●	●	—
配套商业设施	售卖点	●	○	○
	餐饮点	●	○	○
	自行车租赁点	●	○	○
游憩健身设施	活动场地	●	●	●
	休憩点	●	●	●
	眺望观景点	○	○	○
科普教育设施	解说	●	○	○
	展示	●	○	○
安全保障设施	治安消防点	●	○	—
	医疗急救点	●	●	—
	安全防护设施	●	●	●
	无障碍设施	●	●	●
环境卫生设施	厕所	●	●	●
	垃圾箱	●	●	●
停车设施	公共停车场	●	○	○
	出租汽车停靠点	●	○	—
	公交站点	●	○	—

注：● 必须设置；○ 可以设置；— 不作要求。

4 实践案例——江宁区乡村驿站布局与发展研究

4.1 现状分析

作为首批国家全域旅游示范区创建单位，江宁区全域旅游发展迅速，打造了三大示范片区，通过"最美农村路"建设，串联起316个特色田园乡村。经实地调研，江宁全区已建乡村驿站14处，集中于西部片区旅游道路上，布局密度约为2.03km/处，沿线串起了大塘金、谷里花卉谷、石塘人家、黄龙岘等美丽乡村，可向游客提供餐饮、住宿等短途游配套服务，为江宁打造环绕越休闲旅游产业带提供重要硬件及服务支撑(图2)。

4.2 布局规划

以"落实规划，总体控制""因地制宜，特色鲜明""分区落实，协同运营"为原则，在江宁区构建三级乡村驿站体系，至2025年，全域规划乡村驿站80个，其中一级驿站10个，二级驿站15个，三级驿站55个。

一级驿站(10个)：结合江宁区全域旅游规划中重要旅游景点的游客服务中心进行布置，主要功能设施包括管理服务、配套商业、游憩、环境卫生、停车设施和安全保障等。

二级驿站(15个)：结合农业观光园、农家乐等农村旅游节点，沿县道布局，主要功能设施包括管理服务、游憩、停车和安全保障等。

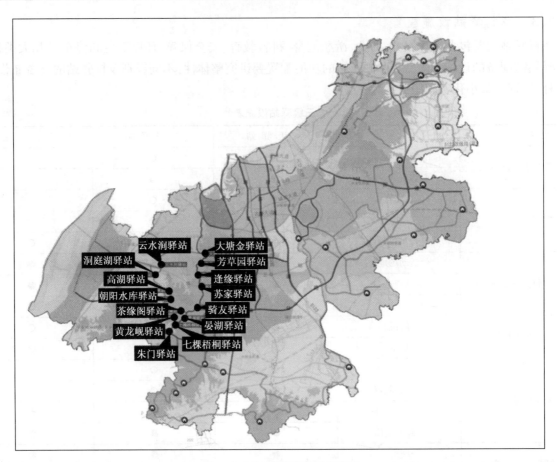

图 2　江宁区乡村驿站布局现状图

三级驿站(55 个)：依托农村自然景点于村庄，结合乡村道布局，主要功能设施包括休憩、公厕、停车。

4.3　发展策略

将乡村驿站与农村产业相结合，支持乡村振兴发展。结合日本乡村驿站和溧阳乡村驿站的建设经验，在尊重和保护好乡村生活的前提下，有效利用诸如黄龙岘茶叶等乡村特色资源，打造个性化驿站，发展乡村特色经济，形成特色农业品牌化路线。依托牛首山文化旅游区、明文化村等特色文化节点，面向观光游客，挖掘村庄文化深度，打造特色文化产业，打响驿站文化品牌，充分发挥驿站文化传播作用。

探索"乡村驿站+"的特色运营模式，提供品质生活服务。将驿站与读书、党建、邮政、运输、公路管养等相结合，打造农村公路综合服务体。深入开发村庄旅游资源，在锁石生态旅游村、钱家渡等富含旅游资源的村庄打造"乡村驿站+旅游"服务模式。结合江宁农村物流品牌，通过战略联盟、资本合作等方式加强与邮政、快递企业的深度合作，拓展邮件快递中转分拨、运输配送等服务功能，打造"乡村驿站+邮政快递"服务模式。在江宁区"宁径织美"四好农村路建设成果下，充分利用农村客运班线网络和运力资源，开通乡村驿站客运班线，打造"乡村驿站+运输"服务模式。

5　结　语

乡村驿站既是农村道路服务载体，也是乡村经济发展的重要平台。本文通过分析日本乡村驿站和溧阳乡村驿站的典型案例，总结乡村驿站布局经验，提出乡村驿站的功能分类、布局方法和设施配置要求等，并以南京市江宁区为例，提出江宁区三级驿站布局规划方案和乡村驿站的经营发展策略，研究成果有利于推动江宁区"宁径织美"四好农村路品牌打造和美丽乡村的建设，可为其他地区乡村驿站的建设提供参考，对乡村驿站的发展具有重要意义。

参考文献

[1] 游小妹.日本驿站布局和功能设置的成功经验与借鉴——以日本川场田园广场驿站为例[J].旅游纵览(下半月),2018(18):171-173.
[2] 陈林,刘云刚.日本的乡村驿站建设经验及其借鉴[J].国际城市规划,2018,33(02):128-134.
[3] 李迎丹,宁书一.乡村休闲驿站设计[J].大众文艺,2019(08):114-115.

城市常规公交网络连通性能分析与改善策略——苏州案例

齐 超[1,2,3] 陈学武[1,2,3] 周 航[4] 王 瑄[5]

(1.东南大学江苏省城市智能交通重点实验室;
2.东南大学现代城市交通技术江苏高校协同创新中心;
3.东南大学交通学院;4.杭州市规划设计研究院;5.东南大学苏州联合研究生院)

摘 要 常规公交作为城市公共交通的重要组成部分,其网络连通性能直接影响着居民公共交通出行的便捷性。本文在总结已有研究的基础上,提出连通性分析方法,以苏州为例对其常规公交网络连通性加以分析,识别存在的问题,并提出相应的改善策略。本文提出的连通性分析方法计算便捷、所需数据易获取且以居民实际出行需求为导向,因而通用性强,分析结果能够有效指导城市公共交通网络改善与优化。

关键词 城市公共交通设施规划 网络连通性 静态网络模型 常规公交 考虑服务水平的连通率

0 引 言

常规公交是城市公共交通的重要组成部分,其布局的合理性直接影响着公共交通的运输效率和吸引力。连通性是网络中的重要概念,它表示能否从网络中的一个节点到达另外一个节点,对应在公交网络中,可以认为是一个站点到另一个站点之间是否连通,或者是一条线路到另一条线路之间是否连通。

关于交通网络连通性问题,最初的研究开始于道路网络连通性,学者们提出了一系列计算方法。然而,城市公交网络虽布设于地理空间上的城市道路网络,但是在地理空间上相交(经过同一路段或同一交叉口)的两条公交线路,放在公交网络中看不一定是相交的,这是因为乘客只有在公交站点才能完成换乘,所以只有当两条公交线路有共同的停靠站点时,才将其视为相交。这一特性使得道路网连通性分析指标无法真实反映城市公交网络的连通性,必须采用其他方法。目前学术界已有以下一些研究:

(1)基于复杂网络。陈燕提出了公交线网加权连通度的概念,采用节点处的用地类型来表征节点的重要度,通过节点的重要度来确定点对重要度,从而建立了比较矩阵。T.Anrtal等提出利用网络全局效率描述反映网络的连通性能。

(2)基于谷歌公共交通数据(GTFS)数据。Yuval Hadas等将连通性度量与GTFS相结合,引入了运输网络覆盖和可达程度、交叉口覆盖、站点换乘能力和路线重复4个指标。Sarker基于GTFS数据通过量化测量公交站点和线路等不同层面的连通性,并通过图论方法将各层面的量化测量值进行整合,用于评价一个大规模多模式的公交网络。Yuval Hadas等扩展了传递惩罚的概念以及连通性属性的定义,提出了一种基于时间属性值和传递属性质量的二维连通性度量方法,从而提出不同换乘模式下的连通情况。

基金项目:国家自然科学基金项目(51338003)。

(3)组合连通性。Badredine Boulmakoul 等提出组合连通性的概念,使用 Q 分析来分析系统的结构。Lina Fu 等从广义出行时间的角度出发提出了站点级和网络层的连通性,在网络层方面提出了面积连通性和人口连通性。

总体来说,目前关于网络连通性的分析指标一部分是基于复杂网络提出的,仅仅考察了网络中节点以及边之间的数量关系,更加适用于道路网的连通性分析。一部分指标是基于 GTFS 数据提出的,在计算过程中需要大量流量、速度、时间、距离、人口、面积等资料,往往只是局限于小范围的连通性分析。还有一部分指标是从多个维度提出的组合连通性分析指标,这些指标求解通常过于烦琐,计算的时间和空间复杂度高。

本文在借鉴现有研究的基础上,首先选择方便计算且能从整体上反映公交网络连通性的指标,其次提出一套分析城市常规公交网络连通性的方法,并运用于苏州常规公交网络连通性分析,通过分析发现公交网络连通性方面存在的问题,进而提出相应的改善策略。

1 连通性分析指标选取与计算方法

1.1 连通性分析指标选取

总结现有研究,本文从网络连通便捷性、节点间连通资源是否重复、居民出行效率 3 个角度提出公交网络连通性分析指标,见表 1。

连通性分析指标　　　　　　　　　　　　　表1

角度	指标	含义	功能价值
网络连通便捷性	考虑服务水平的连通率	对网络中的所有节点对,能直达的比例、一次换乘内能连通的比例、两次换乘内能连通的比例。计算公式如下:$$p_i = \frac{n_i}{T}$$其中,p_i 表示 i 次换乘内到达的比例,n_i 表示 i 次换乘内可到达的节点对个数,T 表示节点对总个数	直达比例越高表明网络连通性能越好。而两次换乘一般是居民出行可接受的上限,若两次换乘内能连通的比例依然很低,表明公交网络连通性很差
网络连通便捷性	连通曲折率	和非直线系数含义相近,可近似用以下公式求得:$$q = \frac{n \times l}{s} \times 100\%$$其中,q 表示连通曲折率,n 表示两点间站点数,l 表示平均站距,s 表示两点间直线距离	反映当前公交网络站点间的连通是否存在绕行的问题
节点间连通资源是否重复	连通重复率	两点间所有最短路径(换乘次数最少)的数目	反映两点间居民通常会选择的出行路线数目,需结合居民出行需求,若需求不大,重复率过高可能造成资源的浪费
居民出行效率	换乘次数	从一个站点出发到达另一个站点所需的换乘次数。每个站点平均换乘次数的计算公式如下:$$t_i = \frac{\sum_{j=1}^{k} h_{ij} - 1}{n}$$其中,t_i 表示站点 i 的平均换乘次数,h_{ij} 表示节点 i 与 j 之间的换乘次数,n 表示站点 i 可以连通的站点总数,k 表示公交网络中的站点总数	平均换乘次数小于 1 的站点一般而言能够十分便捷地前往全网其他站点,连通性好

续上表

角 度	指 标	含 义	功 能 价 值
居民出行效率	网络全局效率[1]	网络中两个节点之间的效率是指节点间最短路径长度的倒数。网络全局效率的计算公式如下：$$E(G)=\frac{2}{N(N-1)}\sum_{i\neq j}\varepsilon_{ij}=\frac{2}{N(N-1)}\sum_{i\neq j}\frac{1}{d_{ij}}$$其中，ε_{ij}表述节点i与j之间的效率值，d_{ij}表述节点i与j之间的最短距离，N表示节点总数	为了解决可能出现的两个节点由于不连通、最短路长度为无穷大的问题，通过对最短路长度取倒数，将无穷大转换为0，方便求取平均值

为方便工程实践运用，反映居民公共交通出行所关注的问题，甄别常规公交网络布设中存在的不足，本文以居民实际出行需求为导向，在选取分析指标时充分考虑了如下原则。

(1) 含义明确，易于反映问题进而指导公交网络优化：指标实际含义需要十分明确，易于理解，且能够十分直观地反映出当前公交网络中所存在的问题。

(2) 计算便捷：所选用的分析指标需要方便计算。

(3) 数据易于获取：需要选取通过易于获取的数据就能对连通性作出较为完整准确评价的指标。

(4) 有评价标准：评价标准决定了评价的客观性和真实性，但由于目前诸多分析指标难以有一个绝对的评价标准，此时则要求指标需要具备可比性，即可以通过不同研究对象之间相类比进行相对性分析，从而反映出研究对象之间的差异性。

基于以上分析，本文选取考虑服务水平的连通率指标以及考虑居民出行效率的换乘次数指标作为常规公交网络连通性分析的主、辅指标。

1.2 连通性分析指标计算方法

图1所示为本文选取的连通性分析主、辅指标的计算流程。

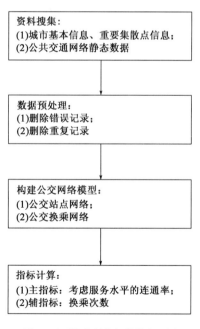

图1 连通性分析指标计算流程图

1.2.1 资料搜集

搜集的资料主要包括城市基本信息、城市重要枢纽和其他重要集散点(重点中小学、三甲医院、商圈、景区等)的基本信息以及城市的公共交通网络静态数据(公交线路信息表、公交线路站点信息表、地铁线路信息)。

1.2.2 数据预处理

所获取的公交线路和站点信息数据通常包含了错误记录和重复记录,因此需要进行数据预处理从而得到正确的线路站点信息表,见表2。

预处理后的线路站点信息表(节选)　　　　　表2

线路名称	线路方向	站点名称	站点序号	站点经度(°)	站点纬度(°)
1	上行	公交1路新村首末站	1	120.6323	31.2571
1	下行	枫津路石湖路南	2	120.6322	31.2535
1	上行	枫津路	3	120.6310	31.2511
1	上行	吴中汽车站南	4	120.6274	31.2511
1	下行	石湖东路	5	120.6255	31.2536
1	上行	吴中商城	6	120.6255	31.2582
1	下行	东吴塔	7	120.6247	31.2673
1	上行	吴中区人民医院	8	120.6243	31.2706
1	上行	南门二村	9	120.6237	31.2756
1	下行	团结桥	10	120.6232	31.2783
1	下行	团结桥北	11	120.6220	31.2841
1	上行	人民桥南	12	120.6216	31.2873
1	下行	南门	13	120.6210	31.2929
1	上行	工人文化宫	14	120.6200	31.2978
1	下行	三元坊	15	120.6198	31.2986
1	上行	苏州图书馆	16	120.6194	31.3011
1	下行	饮马桥	17	120.6188	31.3057
1	下行	乐桥北	18	120.6180	31.3100
1	上行	察院场观前街西	19	120.6170	31.3141
1	上行	接驾桥	20	120.6164	31.3180

1.2.3 构建公交网络模型

本文引入两类常用的公交网络模型:

(1)公交站点网络。公交站点网络中的节点为公交站点,连边规则为:若有一条公交线路通过这两个站点且这两个站点相邻,那么这两个节点连边。图2所示为1个简单的公交网络,共有3条线路,18个站点,以此网络所建立的公交站点网络邻接矩阵如图3所示。公交站点网络模型只可表征乘客从起点站到终点站依次经过了哪些站点。

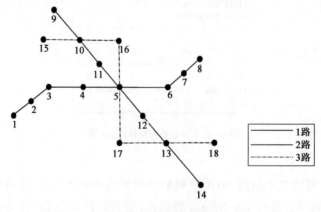

图2　公交线网图

i\j	1	2	3	4	5	6	7	8	9	10	11	12	13	14	15	16	17	18
1	0	1	0	0	0	0	0	0	0	0	0	0	0	0	0	0	0	0
2	1	0	1	0	0	0	0	0	0	0	0	0	0	0	0	0	0	0
3	0	1	0	1	0	0	0	0	0	0	0	0	0	0	0	0	0	0
4	0	0	1	0	1	0	0	0	0	0	0	0	0	0	0	0	0	0
5	0	0	0	1	0	1	0	0	0	0	0	0	0	0	0	0	0	0
6	0	0	0	0	1	0	1	0	0	0	0	0	0	0	0	0	0	0
7	0	0	0	0	0	1	0	1	0	0	0	0	0	0	0	0	0	0
8	0	0	0	0	0	0	1	0	1	0	0	0	0	0	0	0	0	0
9	0	0	0	0	0	0	0	1	0	1	0	0	0	0	0	0	0	0
10	0	0	0	0	0	0	0	0	1	0	1	0	0	0	0	0	0	0
11	0	0	0	0	0	0	0	0	0	1	0	1	0	0	0	0	0	0
12	0	0	0	0	0	0	0	0	0	0	1	0	1	0	0	0	0	0
13	0	0	0	0	0	0	0	0	0	0	0	1	0	1	0	0	0	1
14	0	0	0	0	0	0	0	0	0	0	0	0	1	0	1	0	0	0
15	0	0	0	0	0	0	0	0	0	0	0	0	0	1	0	1	0	0
16	0	0	0	0	0	0	0	0	0	0	0	0	0	0	1	0	1	0
17	0	0	0	0	0	0	0	0	0	0	0	0	0	0	0	1	0	0
18	0	0	0	0	0	0	0	0	0	0	0	0	1	0	0	0	0	0

图 3 站点网络邻接矩阵示意图

(2)公交换乘网络。公交换乘网络以公交站为节点,连边规则为:若有一条公交线路经过两个公交站点,则这两个点连边。在公交换乘网络中,每条公交线路上的所有公交站点两两互相连接。在公交换乘网络中,两节点间的距离就是乘客这次出行所乘坐的公交线路条数。仍以图 2 所示的公交线网图为例,建立换乘网络,其邻接矩阵如图 4 所示。

i\j	1	2	3	4	5	6	7	8	9	10	11	12	13	14	15	16	17	18
1	0	1	1	1	1	1	1	1	0	0	0	0	0	0	0	0	0	0
2	1	0	1	1	1	1	1	1	0	0	0	0	0	0	0	0	0	0
3	1	1	0	1	1	1	1	1	0	0	0	0	0	0	0	0	0	0
4	1	1	1	0	1	1	1	1	0	0	0	0	0	0	0	0	0	0
5	1	1	1	1	0	1	1	1	1	1	1	1	1	1	1	1	1	0
6	1	1	1	1	1	0	1	1	1	1	1	1	1	1	1	1	1	0
7	1	1	1	1	1	1	0	1	1	1	1	1	1	1	1	1	1	0
8	1	1	1	1	1	1	1	0	1	1	1	1	1	1	1	1	1	0
9	0	0	0	0	1	1	1	1	0	1	1	1	1	1	1	1	1	0
10	0	0	0	0	1	1	1	1	1	0	1	1	1	1	1	1	1	0
11	0	0	0	0	1	1	1	1	1	1	0	1	1	1	1	1	1	0
12	0	0	0	0	1	1	1	1	1	1	1	0	1	1	1	1	1	0
13	0	0	0	0	1	1	1	1	1	1	1	1	0	1	1	1	1	1
14	0	0	0	0	1	1	1	1	1	1	1	1	1	0	1	1	1	0
15	0	0	0	0	1	1	1	1	1	1	1	1	1	1	0	1	1	0
16	0	0	0	0	1	1	1	1	1	1	1	1	1	1	1	0	1	0
17	0	0	0	0	1	1	1	1	1	1	1	1	1	1	1	1	0	0
18	0	0	0	0	0	0	0	0	0	0	0	0	1	0	0	0	0	0

图 4 换乘网络邻接矩阵示意图

利用 MATLAB 软件编程可以得到上述公交站点网络模型和公交换乘网络模型。为了更符合实际,除了考虑公交网络自身的连接,对于有地铁等大运量轨道交通的城市,假设离地铁站 200m 的公交站点可以换乘地铁,因而对换乘网络邻接矩阵进一步做以下处理:

①计算所有公交站点和所有地铁站点间的距离;
②计算可以通过地铁直达的公交站点对;
③得到考虑通过地铁直达的公交站点对的换乘网络邻接矩阵。

1.2.4 指标计算

(1)主指标:考虑服务水平的连通率。利用 Pajek 软件求取换乘网络的最短路矩阵并统计矩阵中 1、2、3 分别出现的频率。其中 1 出现的频率代表直达比例,1 和 2 出现的频率代表一次换乘内到达的比例,1、2 和 3 出现的频率代表两次换乘内到达的比例。

(4)辅指标:换乘次数。利用 Pajek 软件求取换乘网络的最短路矩阵,利用表 1 中所列公式直接计算得到每个站点的平均换乘次数。

2 公交网络连通性能分析方法

当对一个大规模的公交网络连通性作分析时,仅仅从全网出发分析难以反映出局部区域连通性情况,特别是区域内部与区域之间的连通性,不容易把握连通性薄弱之处。因此为更加真实客观细致地反映城市公交网络连通性并考虑计算的便捷性以及居民生活中的实际出行需求,本文提出从全网连通性、行政区内及行政区间连通性、重要集散点连通性等角度出发的常规公交网络连通性分析方法。

2.1 全网连通性分析

全网连通性分析的目的主要是为从整体上把握城市公交网络的连通性能,发现全网中连通性明显较为薄弱的站点及区域,其计算流程如图5所示。

2.1.1 计算全网各个站点的连通性

基于全网公共交通静态数据建立换乘网络模型,利用 Pajek 软件计算得到该换乘网络的最短路矩阵,而后即可求得每个站点考虑服务水平的连通率与平均换乘次数。

2.1.2 可视化处理

将上述得到的连通性计算结果导入 ArcGIS 作可视化处理,便于直观发现网络连通性明显较为薄弱的站点及区域,甄别公交网络布设存在的问题,从全网层面提出公交线网优化的方向及策略。

2.1.3 分析各行政区连通性

从全网连通性数据中分别筛选各行政区范围内的站点得到各个行政区在全网层面的连通性,从而更加具体地反映各行政区的差异性,便于进一步发现公交网络布设的长处与不足。为了将居民出行需求考虑在内,统计每个站点周边的 POI 点,从而根据各站点处 POI 点集中程度反映居民活动强度,进而分析连通性能否满足居民实际出行需求。

2.2 行政区内及行政区间连通性分析

行政区内及行政区间连通性分析的目的主要是为分析行政区内部公交站点间的连通情况以及各个行政区之间的连通情况,便于从局部把握公交网络的连通性能,其计算流程如图6所示。

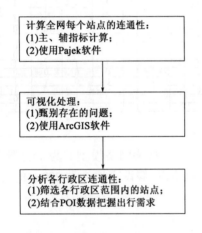
图5 全网连通性分析流程图

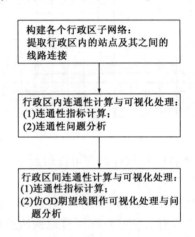
图6 行政区内及行政区间连通性分析流程图

2.2.1 构建各个行政区子网络

从全网中提取各个行政区内的站点及其之间的线路连接,构造各个行政区子网络模型。

2.2.2 行政区内连通性计算与可视化处理

对每个行政区采用与全网连通性分析相同的方法利用 Pajek 软件求解各个行政区内部的连通性指标,利用 ArcGIS 作可视化处理,从而聚焦于各行政区内部,甄别其公交网络布设存在的问题,提出相应的优化方向与策略。

2.2.3 行政区间连通性计算与可视化处理

同理,可聚焦于行政区之间的连通性,通过仿照 OD 期望线图绘制行政区间连通率图以及换乘次数图,从而直观反映行政区间的公交网络连通薄弱之处,提出相应改善策略。

2.3 重要集散点连通性分析

上述两个分析角度均是从宏观层面出发,分析区域的公交网络连通性。而居民日常出行活动往往会集中于交通枢纽、重点中小学、三甲医院、大型商圈等重要集散点处,因此为从中微观层面反映居民日常生活情景与出行需求,提出重要集散点连通性分析角度,其计算流程如图7所示。

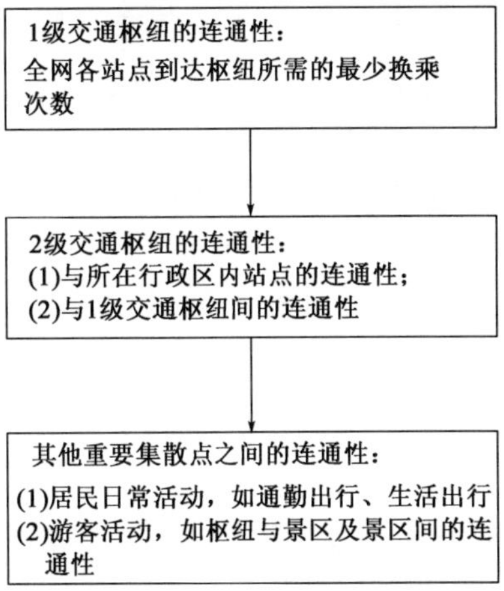

2.3.1 1级交通枢纽的连通性

1级交通枢纽主要指担负全市对外交通的大型公路、铁路、航空枢纽,这些枢纽服务对象是全体市民,居民前往其他城市通常需要先到达这些枢纽,而后乘坐长途客车、火车、航班到达目的地。因此这些1级交通枢纽与全网公交站点特别是土地开发强度大、人口集聚站点的连通性极为重要,有较高研究价值。由于居民从某个站点出发,只要到达枢纽周边任意一个公交站即可,因此计算全网其他站点到达每个枢纽周边站点所需的最少换乘次数作为1级交通枢纽的连通性,依据计算结果可作相应的优化改善。

2.3.2 2级交通枢纽的连通性

相较于1级交通枢纽,2级交通枢纽的规模、服务能力、运输班次都较小,其所服务的群体主要是区内居民,满足区内居民的市内出行及部分对外出行需求。因此重点分析2级枢纽与其所在行政区内公交站点的连通性。同时2级交通枢纽运营线路有限,乘客会有前往1级交通枢纽换乘的需求,因此还需要分析2级交通枢纽与1级交通枢纽之间的连通性。

图7 重要集散点连通性分析流程图

2.3.3 其他重要集散点之间的连通性

对于当地居民日常活动,主要以居民区与重点中小学之间的连通性作为通勤出行的代表,居民区与大型商圈、三甲医院之间的连通性作为生活出行的代表。

对于游客活动,主要分析从枢纽前往景区以及从一个景区到达另一个景区之间的连通性。

3 苏州实例分析

本文研究范围是苏州市辖区,不含其代管的昆山等县级市。所使用的数据资料主要为苏州公交线路信息、公交线路站点信息。基于上文提出的公交网络连通性分析方法,对苏州常规公交网络连通性分析如下。

3.1 全网连通性分析

苏州市全网连通率呈现出中间高、四周低的特点,即连通率最高的区域主要位于姑苏区,以该区域为中心向外连通率逐渐降低,外围区域尤其是离主城区较远的吴江区,连通率很差,两次换乘内到达的比例依然不高。苏州市全网平均换乘次数为2.39次,计算各个行政区的平均换乘次数见表3,可以发现,相城区平均换乘次数要高于同属城市副中心的吴中区。

各行政区所有站点平均换乘次数表 表3

行政区	平均换乘次数
姑苏区	1.86
相城区	2.42
吴中区	2.27
虎丘区	2.14
吴江区	2.88
工业园区	2.15

3.2 行政区间连通性分析

姑苏区以及虎丘区与其他行政区之间的直达率更高一些,平均换乘次数基本上在2次以内。工业园区与其他行政区连通性不差,但在直达率方面并不是很好。吴江区在区间连通方面依旧非常差。吴江区与每个区之间均存在有无法连通的站点对,平均换乘次数基本在3次以上。城市副中心吴中区与苏州的两个新区虎丘区与工业园区连通性较好,但与同属城市副中心的相城区之间连通性不佳。

3.3 重要集散点连通性分析

由于篇幅所限,此处仅以苏州北站为例。全网站点可直达苏州北站比例为5.53%,可通过一次换乘内到达的比例为44.98%,可通过两次内换乘到达的比例为81.44%,有8个(0.16%)站点无法到达苏州北站,平均换乘次数为1.69次。由于苏州北站附近只有2个公交站点且公交线路少,使得目前其与其他站点间的连通性较差。此外,苏州北站与2级交通枢纽——苏州新区站之间虽然有直达公交车服务,但由于距离远、站点多,直达公交的行驶时间超过了地铁换乘公交甚至公交换乘公交所需要的总时间。

3.4 公交网络连通性改善策略

从分析结果可知,目前苏州公交网络连通性方面尚存在一些值得关注的地方,例如:工业园区与其他行政区的直达率不高,需要依靠在关键节点进行换乘实现连通;相城区与其他行政区之间直达率明显偏低;苏州新区站与苏州北站间直达公交行驶时间过长;吴江区离主城区较远,连通性很差。因此提出如下改善公交网络连通性的策略,并以一些案例加以说明。

3.4.1 优化关键节点

对于经过线路数较多的关键节点,如果实际运营情况不佳,造成车辆延误过大或是换乘不便,则对于公交网络连通性仍然会产生较大影响。

以南浜站为例,该站位于金山南路,周边有休闲娱乐区和众多居民区,客流主要以休闲娱乐和通勤出行为主,客流强度较大,公交线路较多。南溪站所处的金山南路未设置公交专用车道和公交专用进口道。公交站台设置属于虚拟港湾式,由于两侧用地较为充足,可改造为港湾式停靠站,同时在高峰时期应将最右侧车道设置为公交专用车道,在交叉口开辟公交专用进口道,提高公交运行效率。

3.4.2 优化既有公交线路

通过对既有线路作适当调整使其经过更多周边土地利用强度高的站点,可以提高直达率,满足更多居民出行需求。此种优化方法主要针对目前公交直达率比较低但土地开发强度又比较大而需求高的区域,例如相城区。

以5路公交车为例,5路公交车主要经过相城区、姑苏区、吴中区,可到达观前街商圈,对于连接相城区与吴中区也有一定积极意义。取5路最北端线路(图8),蓝线为当前的行驶线路,若改为按红色线路行驶,并停靠既有华元路澄和路西站以及嘉元路相城大道西站,其连通率变化情况见表4。通过改线,两个站点的连通率均得到提升,更好地能满足了沿线居民及行政单位工作人员的出行需求。

图8 5路公交车线路图(部分)

改线前后站点连通率对比表 表4

站 点	华元路澄和路西站			嘉元路相城大道西站		
	直达比例(%)	一次换乘内达比例(%)	两次换乘内达比例(%)	直达比例(%)	一次换乘内达比例(%)	两次换乘内达比例(%)
改进前	1.76	27.11	72.96	0.59	13.64	62.14
改进后	2.50	37.64	78.36	1.33	28.01	74.59

3.4.3 开辟直达线路和设置大站快线

两个重要集散点之间应开辟直达线路,若客流强度很大,出行需求高,还应在不同时段设置大站快线方便居民更快到达目的地。

如图9所示,813路公交车是连接苏州北站与苏州新区站的一条直达公交线路,但目前由于停站达26站,出行时间达1h以上,平峰时期发车频率为28min,高峰时期发车频率为13min,发车频率较低,且乘客普遍反映该线路发车不准时,候车时间长,连通性依然很差,出行十分不便。因此应当在高峰时期开辟大站快线,根据沿线土地利用以及乘客需求设置少量站点,一方面提高两个枢纽之间连通效率,另一方面也满足该线路沿线居民出行需求。

图9　813路公交车线路图

4 结　语

本文基于既有研究,选取了考虑服务水平的连通率与换乘次数作为公交网络连通性分析的指标,并提出了一套从全网、行政区内及行政区间、重要集散点等角度出发的公交网络连通性分析方法,最后以苏州市为例,发现了其公交网络连通性方面存在的问题,给出了优化关键节点、优化既有公交线路、开辟直达线路和设置大站快线3种改善策略。

本文从工程实践角度出发,具有应用需求导向的研究思路,创新地将城市常规公交网络连通性分析指标计算理论知识与探索连通性改善需求点的实际应用场景紧密结合,既适用于较大城市连通性分析,也适用于局部小范围的分析。下一步研究可结合 OD 数据更好地把握出行需求,并从管理运营角度考量,从动态层面对于网络连通性作深入研究。

参考文献

[1] 李川. 基于复杂网络的城市公共交通网络连通性研究[D]. 成都:西南交通大学,2014.
[2] 陈燕. 中等城市常规公交线网连通度计算方法[J]. 交通科技与经济,2007(05):82-83.
[3] Antal T, Krapivsky P L. Weight-driven growing networks [J]. PHYSICAL REVIEW E, 2005, 71 (02610322).

[4] Hadas Y, Rossi R, Gastaldi M, et al. Public Transport Systems' Connectivity: Spatiotemporal Analysis and Failure Detection[J]. Transportation Research Procedia, 2014(3):309-318.

[5] 王成. 基于出行阻抗的公交网络连通性度量与优化[D]. 哈尔滨:哈尔滨工业大学, 2017.

[6] Hadas Y, Ranjitkar P. Modeling public-transit connectivity with spatial quality-of-transfer measurements[J]. JOURNAL OF TRANSPORT GEOGRAPHY, 2012(22):137-147.

[7] Boulmakoul B, Besri Z, Karim L, et al. Combinatorial connectivity and spectral graph analytics for urban public transportation system[J]. Transportation Research Procedia, 2017(27):1154-1162.

[8] Fu L, Handley J C. Measuring realistic transit network connectivity: a view with travel time reliability[C]. IEEE International Conference on Intelligent Transportation Systems-ITSC. 2015:2800-2805.

地铁瓶颈区段定制公交线路设计方法

郑妹婕[1,2,3]　陈学武[1,2,3]　李少彬[4]　华明壮[1,2,3]

(1. 东南大学江苏省城市智能交通重点实验室；
2. 东南大学现代城市交通技术江苏高校协同创新中心；
3. 东南大学交通学院；
4. 南京公共交通(集团)有限公司)

摘　要　为了缓解地铁瓶颈区段的客流压力，提高公共交通整体满意度，并解决现有定制公交设计流程中需求获取不全面等问题，提出了基于需求聚类的地铁瓶颈区段定制公交线路设计方法。首先，提出了改进的DBSCAN(Density-Based Spatial Clustering of Applications with Noise)算法，聚类地铁瓶颈区段地铁刷卡数据，获取潜在定制公交出行需求。然后，以共享单车订单数据和公共自行车刷卡数据聚类为补充，获取定制公交潜在站点。之后，通过一个双层规划模型确定线路中站点及站点经停顺序。最后，以南京市为例进行了案例研究。根据意向调查确定合理的聚类参数后，共聚类得到22个簇，整理得8条定制公交线路，经估计可疏解地铁瓶颈区段约6.2%的客流。

关键词　城市公共交通设施规划　线路设计　聚类　定制公交　地铁瓶颈

0　引　言

目前地铁凭借其速度快、容量大、准点、可靠等优势，成为城市居民首选的公共交通工具。然而，随着我国地铁网络化进程的不断加快，地铁客流不断增长，一些城市地铁线路的部分区段出现了服务能力瓶颈，迫切需要服务品质较高的地面公交进行分流，以缓解供求矛盾，提高乘客对公共交通的整体满意度。近年来，一种名为定制公交的新型地面公交服务模式在我国兴起[1]，它为特定的客户尤其是通勤者提供了较高品质的公交服务，具有灵活、个性化、门到门服务的优势，受到广泛关注。常规地面公交难以满足地铁乘客的需求，如何进行合理的定制公交线路设计，从而有效缓解地铁瓶颈区段的压力，是本文着力探讨的问题。

定制公交自20世纪70年代起在一些欧美发达国家和地区逐渐形成，主要提供中心城区和郊区之间早晚高峰的通勤服务。随后国内外学者对定制公交的服务和需求特征、设计方法和实施效果等进行了一系列研究。目前，定制公交的服务设计主要以线上出行需求调查为基础。通过线上调查搜集潜在用户的需求，汇总相似需求，从而生成备选线路，供用户选择。这样的方法存在以下问题：①线上调查搜集到的出行数据仅仅来自于参与调查的一小部分通勤者，不能全面反映实际需求情况，且对运营商来说过于被动；②线上调查很难及时检测到出行模式的变化。

基金项目：国家自然科学基金联合基金项目(U20A20330)。

研究表明,利用大量乘客的实际出行数据能够揭示真实的公共交通出行需求[2]。Yan 等[3]利用出租汽车轨迹数据,采用聚类方法提取乘客相似的出行模式,作为定制公交线路设计的需求来源,方案取得了良好效果。Li 等[4]建立了一个三阶段的模型,从公交数据中提取定制公交线路,该模型包括行程构建、OD 区域划分以及线路提取。Guo 等[5]利用北京市的公交数据设计定制公交线路,并得出定制公交适宜长距离出行(8km 以上)的结论。以上研究都支持了本文利用地铁数据提取定制公交需求的可能性。但在以上研究的聚类方法中,并未考虑从某方式转移到定制公交的概率,因此本研究将转移概率设置为聚类的一个参数,并通过人工调查设置了合理参数值。关于如何利用定制公交转移地铁客流,Hao 等[6]开展了一定研究,但在其研究中,所有线路只有一个起点站和一个终点站,并且所有站点都在地铁站附近,并不符合定制公交门到门的出行特征,因此本研究还利用了地铁周边的共享自行车数据捕捉地铁乘客最真实的出行起讫点,完善站点设置。

本文设计了一种基于需求聚类的地铁瓶颈区段定制公交线路设计方法,利用地铁瓶颈区段乘客实际出行数据进行定制公交需求时空聚类,作为定制公交线路设计的基础,然后补充地铁周边的共享自行车(共享单车和公共自行车)数据,完善线路设计方法,并从企业运营利润最大化的角度采用了一个双层规划模型实现了线路站点选择及站点经停顺序确定。最后以南京市为例,进行了案例研究。

1 基于需求聚类的地铁瓶颈区段定制公交线路设计方法

1.1 设计流程

本研究提出了一种基于需求聚类的定制公交服务设计方法,流程如图 1 所示。

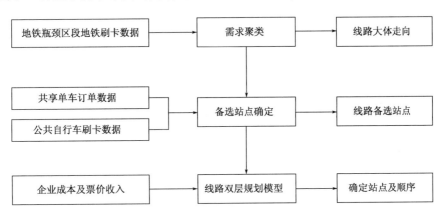

图 1 基于需求聚类的定制公交线路设计方法

首先需要利用地铁刷卡数据,进行地铁瓶颈区段的出行需求聚类。本节基于改进的 DBSCAN 算法,对地铁瓶颈区段的乘客进行出行需求聚类,以精准地把握乘客的出行规律。在获取地铁乘客的出行聚类结果后,便可以得到线路的大体走向。然而,由于聚类结果是通过地铁刷卡数据得到的,只能得出乘客乘坐地铁的起终站点,并不能得到乘客出行的起终点。因此,在出行聚类后,需要提取聚类结果的起终地铁站点附近的共享单车和公共自行车的数据,来探究乘坐地铁的乘客出行的初始起点和最终目的地,作为定制公交线路备选站点。确定备选站点后,再利用双层规划模型,在充分考虑企业运营成本与票价收入的情况下,得到最佳线路设计方案,从而设计出门到门的便捷的定制公交线路,实现企业营收最大化。

1.2 地铁出行需求聚类

1.2.1 改进的 DBSCAN 算法

聚类是按照某种特定标准,将相似的对象划分到同一个"簇"中,簇内所有样本的重心称为"聚类中心"。有学者依据 K-means 聚类算法对定制公交平台的 OD 数据进行过聚类[7]。而基于密度的聚类 DBCSN(Density-Based Spatial Clustering of Applications with Noise)方法,将分布稠密的样本划分到同一个簇,有着不受异常值的干扰,可发现任意形状的簇,能排除分散样本的优势。

利用 DBSCAN 聚类方法，可以对乘客出行的起点或终点进行聚类，聚类中心代表了需求量大的出行源点。本文对 DBSCAN 进行改进，能够对乘客的出行起点、出行终点和出行时间 3 个参数同时聚类，提取这 3 个参数都接近的乘客出行数据作为同一个簇，每一个簇代表了一群有着相似出行需求的乘客，认为他们有乘坐同一线路的定制公交的可能性。

算法原理具体如下。

首先，任意一个出行数据 T_i，由三个要素组成：①出行起点 o_{T_i}；②出行终点 d_{T_i}；③出发时间 t_{T_i}。

传统的 DBSCAN 有邻域的概念，这里沿用并加以改进：假定空间半径为 r、时间半径为 t，若某出行数据 T_j 同时满足以下 3 个条件，则认为它处在出行数据 T_i 的邻域内：

（1）T_j 的起点 o_{T_j} 距 T_i 的起点 o_{T_i} 的空间距离小于 r；

（2）T_j 的终点 d_{T_j} 距 T_i 的终点 d_{T_i} 的空间距离小于 r；

（3）T_j 的出发时间 t_{T_j} 距 T_i 的出发时间 t_{T_i} 的时间差小于 t。

T_i 的邻域内的所有数据的集合记为 $N_{r,t}(T_i)$，根据 DBSCAN 算法的规定，要能构成一个簇，该簇中至少要有 M 个数据，即：

$$|N_{r,t}(T_i)| \geq M \tag{1}$$

假如满足上述条件，则 T_i 被视为一个核心对象，加上其邻域内所有数据，则构成了一个簇。若这些数据中也有满足核心对象条件的数据，它们邻域内的数据也属于这个簇。

1.2.2 聚类参数确定

由于聚类的目的是得到可能乘坐定制公交的地铁客流簇，所以可根据实际意义来标定聚类参数，空间半径 r 取乘客可接受的步行到定制公交站点的距离，时间半径 t 取乘客可接受的等车时间。密度阈值 M 应该使得所得到的簇中，可能乘坐定制公交的乘客数量至少满足发出一辆定制公交，即：

$$M \geq N/p \tag{2}$$

式中：p——地铁乘客向定制公交的转移概率；

N——要发出一辆定制公交，所需的最小实际载客量。

本文结合了意向调查，确定了空间半径 r、时间半径 t、地铁乘客向定制公交的转移概率 p 的取值，具体见 3.2 节。

1.3 备选站点确定

定制公交的线路不同于常规公交，其停靠站一般只位于起讫点区域内，离用户的居住地和工作区很近，可以提供门到门的服务，且定制公交在起终点区域间的公交线路可随路况变更。根据这样的线路特点，设计了如图 2 所示的备选站点集确定方法。

应用改进的 DBSCAN 聚类算法，可以将出行需求相似的地铁乘客划分到同一个簇中，认为其有乘坐同一线路定制公交的可能性，因此可将地铁乘客簇对应的地铁站，作为定制公交线路固定的起、终点停靠站，如图 2 中方形符号所示。但聚类地铁数据只能得出 1~2 个起、终点站，且地铁站的服务半径较大，不能体现定制公交门到门的服务特征。因此论文利用共享单车和公共自行车（共享自行车）数据来细化定制公交的站点设计。提取还车地点在线路固定起点站（地铁站）附近 500 m 内的共享自行车数据，视作接驳地铁的出行，对其骑行起点（图 2 中黑点）经纬度进行传统的 DBSCAN 密度聚类，将聚类中心视为地铁乘客的真实出发点，并设为定制公交线路起点区域的备选停靠站（图 2 左侧三角形符号）。同理，可以确定终点区域的备选停靠站（图 2 右侧三角形符号）。由此，可以得到定制公交备选站点集。

1.4 线路设计双层规划模型

在获取备选站点后，需要在备选站点中选择合适的站点并确定站点顺序以完成定制公交线路的具体设计。本文从企业运营收入最大化的角度出发，将该问题简化为一个双层规划模型。

上层：根据客流量从备选站点集中挑选站点，作为起、终点区域的停靠站，使得企业运营收入最大化。

下层：在上层确定的站点中，规划路径，使车辆经过所有的站点一次，路径总长度最短。如果加上车辆需回到起始点的限制,这相当于运筹学中经典的旅行商问题(TSP)。

图2 定制公交备选站点确定方法示意图

注:■ 定制公交固定起终站点,由地铁出行聚类得到;△ 定制公交备选站点,由接驳地铁的自行车骑行源点聚类得到;. 接驳地铁的自行车骑行源点。

模型的假设如下:

(1)地铁出行聚类得到的是固定的起、终点站,由接驳地铁的共享自行车数据出行源点聚类得到的是备选站点集。认为定制公交站点只从固定站点和备选站点集中产生。

(2)任意相邻两站点的路径长度以两点间的直线距离代替。

(3)车辆在站点停靠时间为定值。

(4)不同站点上下车的乘客采取统一票价。

模型的具体表达如下:

(1)上层模型。

决策变量:

$$y_k = \begin{cases} 1 & 将备选站点 k 选作正式站点 \\ 0 & 不将备选站点 k 作为正式站点 \end{cases}$$

目标函数:

考虑企业的运营收入最大化,公式如下:

$$\max B = B_1 - C_1 - C_2 \tag{3}$$

$$B_1 = \sum_k y_k \times n_k \times \rho \tag{4}$$

$$C_1 = \sum_k y_k \times n_k / N_0 \times \rho_1 \tag{5}$$

$$C_2 = (d/v + S \times t_{\text{stop}}) \times \rho_2 \tag{6}$$

式中:B_1——票价收入;

n_k——第 n 个站点的上车人数;

ρ——乘客票价;

C_1——发车成本;

N_0——车辆额定载客数;

ρ_1——单位发车成本;

C_2——运营成本;

d——线路长度;

v——定制公交运行速度;

S——线路站点数量;

t_{stop}——车辆停靠时间;

ρ_2——车辆小时运营成本。

约束条件:

停靠站点数量应不超过上限 $S_{\max}$:

$$S = \sum_k y_k \leq S_{\max} \tag{7}$$

线路长度约束应在线路长度下限 $l_{\min}$ 和线路长度上限 $l_{\max}$ 之间:

$$l_{\min} \leq d \leq l_{\max} \tag{8}$$

(2)下层模型:经典 TSP 问题。

决策变量:

$$x_{ij} = \begin{cases} 1 & \text{从站点 } S_i \text{ 直接前往站点 } S_j \\ 0 & \text{不从站点 } S_i \text{ 直接前往站点 } S_j \end{cases}$$

目标函数:

定制公交停靠所有站点后,回到起始站点,总行驶距离最短:

$$\min d = \sum_{i=1}^{n} \sum_{j=1}^{n} d_{ij} x_{ij} \tag{9}$$

约束条件:

下列公式为 TSP 问题约束条件的经典表达方式。

$$\begin{cases} \sum_{i=1}^{n} x_{ij} = 1 & (j = 1, 2, \cdots, n) \\ \sum_{j=1}^{n} x_{ij} = 1 & (i = 1, 2, \cdots, n) \\ u_i - u_j + n x_{ij} \leq n - 1 \\ i, j = 1, 2, \cdots, n, i \neq j \\ x_{ij} = 1, 0, u_i, u_j \text{ 为连续变量} \end{cases} \tag{10}$$

2 求解流程或算法

2.1 地铁出行需求聚类算法

地铁出行需求聚类算法见表 1。

地铁出行需求聚类算法 表 1

输入:地铁出行样本数据集 $T = (T1, T2, \ldots, Tm)$,邻域参数 (r, t, M)

1:首先将数据集 T 中的所有样本标记为未处理状态
2:for(数据集 T 中每个样本)do
3: if(某样本 T_i 已经归入某个簇或标记为噪声点)then
4:    continue;
5: else
6:    根据邻域参数 (r, t, M) 计算得到 T_i 的邻域子样本集 $N_{r,t}(T_i)$
7:    if $|N_{r,t}(T_i)| \geq M$ then
8:      标记 T_i 为核心点,并建立新簇 CL,并将 T_i 邻域内所有点加入 CL
9:      for ($N_{r,t}(T_i)$ 中所有尚未被标记的样本 T_j) do
10:       检查其邻域子样本集 $N_{r,t}(T_j)$,若 $|N_{r,t}(T_j)| \geq M$,则将 $N_{r,t}(T_j)$ 中未归入任何一个簇的样本加入 CL;
11:     end forV
12:    else
13:     标记对象 T_i 为边界点或噪声点;
14:    end if
15: end if
16:end for

输出:簇划分结果。

2.2 站点集确定及线路规划模型求解

备选站点集的确定采用传统 DBSCAN 算法,上文已对改进后的 DBSCAN 的原理和算法进行了描述,这里不再赘述。线路规划模型分为两层,上层模型的目标是挑选合适的站点以实现企业营收最大化,由于每条线路的站点总数较少,目标函数相对简单,这里采用枚举法求解。下层模型是一个 TSP 问题,采用贪婪算法进行求解,可以提高求解速度。定制公交线路设计的整体流程如图3所示。

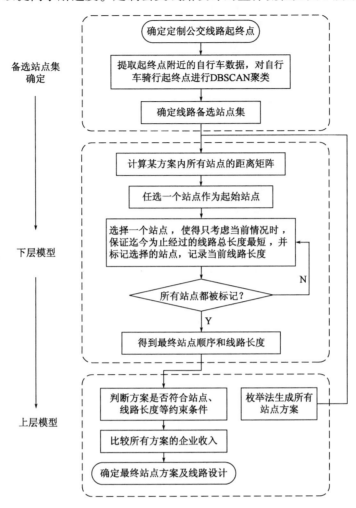

图3 定制公交线路设计整体流程

3 案例研究

3.1 南京市地铁服务能力瓶颈区段概况

根据已有研究[8],南京市早高峰时段(7:00—9:00)的地铁服务能力瓶颈区段为1号线新模范马路至新街口以及2号线明故宫至新街口区段(图4),为单向瓶颈,含8个站点,总长度6.5 km,平均断面饱和度为1.1。

提取2017年2月20—24日早高峰时段经过地铁服务能力瓶颈区段的刷卡数据,数据包括刷卡日期、进出站时间、进出站站点编号等字段。分析瓶颈区段的客流特征,得到乘车距离在5~15km的乘客占总体的63.2%,说明瓶颈区段的乘客主要为中短距离出行,符合定制公交的服务范围。

3.2 南京市地铁乘客向定制公交的转移意向调查

作者于2018年4月工作日早高峰时段在南京市地铁瓶颈区段内开展了定制公交出行意愿的调查。调查显示,乘客可接受的最佳定制公交步行到站距离为360 m,最佳等车时间为4 min(240 s),站点数量最多为6个。根据调查结果得到表2所列不同时间差、票价、定制公交总停站次数下,地铁乘客向定制公交的转移概率。"时间差"表示同一行程,定制公交与地铁的出行时间之差,负数表示比地铁慢。较常见的一种情况是,定制公交比地铁慢15min,票价8元,停站4次,对应的转移概率为28.1%。

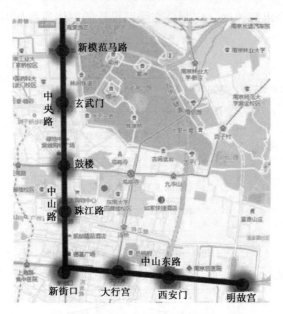

图4　南京市早高峰地铁服务能力瓶颈区段

地铁乘客向定制公交转移概率　　　　　表2

时间差(min)	票价(元)	总停站次数(次)	转移概率(%)
−20	8	2	25.7
−20	8	4	21.0
−20	8	6	17.0
−20	10	2	19.6
−20	10	4	15.8
−20	10	6	12.7
−15	8	2	33.6
−15	**8**	**4**	**28.1**
−15	8	6	23.2
−15	10	2	26.4
−15	10	4	21.6
−15	10	6	17.6

3.3　南京市地铁服务能力瓶颈区段出行需求聚类

3.3.1　聚类指标

选取2017年2月22号(周三)早高峰时段瓶颈区段的地铁刷卡数据,共104823条,使用改进的DBSCAN算法进行出行需求聚类。聚类的指标取值见表3。其中,空间半径、时间半径及转移概率都是通过3.2节中意向调查确定的。

聚类指标取值　　　　　表3

指　标	取　值
空间半径 r(可接受的步行到站距离)	360 m
时间半径 t(可接受的等车时间)	240 s
转移概率 p	28.1%
定制公交最小载客数 N	21人
密度阈值 M(簇内最低样本个数)	100

3.3.2 聚类结果

聚类后共得到23个簇,经整理后,构成8条定制公交线路,具体信息见表4和图5。

地铁乘客聚类结果　　　　　表4

线 路	起 点	终 点	簇 序 号	地铁用户数量(人)
1	柳州东路	珠江路/鼓楼	5	192
			11	267
			23	150
2	柳州东路	新模范马路	18	170
3	柳州东路	新街口/大行宫	1	986
			8	800
4	马群	大行宫/新街口	3	1 018
			9	155
			17	207
			21	118
5	迈皋桥	鼓楼/珠江路/新街口	2	3 421
			10	196
			4	1 996
			19	137
			6	1 103
			20	192
6	双龙大道	新街口	14	231
7	天润城	新街口	13	190
8	油坊桥	新街口	12	236

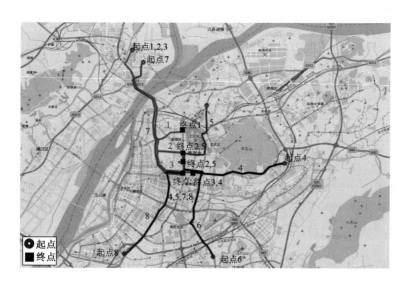

图5　地铁聚类结果线路图

假设簇内的地铁用户均有28.1%的概率乘坐定制公交,那么定制公交约能分担1952人/h的地铁客流量。经统计,当天早高峰时段瓶颈区段的单向客流量约为31447人/h,那么定制公交分担的客流占比为6.2%,可在一定程度上缓解瓶颈区段的压力。

3.4 备选站点确定

在各条线路中,马群站—新街口/大行宫(以下简称马群线)包含的地铁用户数量最大,其潜在定制公交用户也最多,下面选择马群线作为案例进行具体的线路设计。

提取还车地点在起点(马群站)附近500m范围内的早高峰时段的共享单车订单数据和公共自行车刷卡数据,共518条,它们的借车地点的位置分布如图6红色圆点所示。

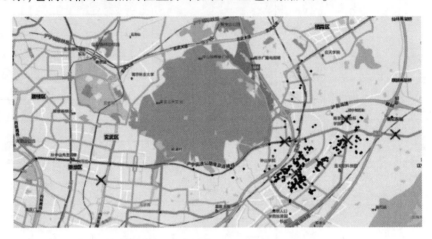

图6 马群地铁站附近自行车起点分布

对数据的借车地点的位置进行传统的DBSCAN聚类,聚类指标为360m,主要的聚类中心如图6红色"×"符号所示。

最终提取聚类中心共5个,加上固定的起终点站,共8个站点,站点信息(上车人数按照28.1%的转移概率估计)见表5。

站点信息 表5

编号	经度(°)	纬度(°)	站点	潜在上车人数(人)
0	118.7789	32.0424	新街口	0
1	118.7896	32.0431	大行宫	0
2	118.8896	32.0518	马群	288
3	118.8958	32.0379	备选站点1	88
4	118.9084	32.0423	备选站点2	21
5	118.8901	32.0520	备选站点3	4
6	118.9225	32.0524	备选站点4	19
7	118.9468	32.0548	备选站点5	2

3.5 线路设计

对线路双层规划模型中的参数进行赋值:车辆额定载客量 $N_0 = 30$ 人/车,票价 ρ 为8元/人,单位发车成本 ρ_1 为160元/车,运行速度 v 取25 km/h,车辆停靠时间 t_{stop} 取40s,车辆小时运营成本 ρ_2 为300元/h。站点数量上限 S_{max} 为6个,线路长度上下限 l_{max} 和 l_{min} 分别为50km和10km(在TSP问题中为环路,故取值较大)。

经过模型运算,共得到了满足约束条件的组合方案共27个,其中企业收入最大的5个方案见表6。

前五位路线方案 表6

方案编号	最优路径	停靠站点	线路长度(环路)(km)	企业收入(元)
19	6,4,3,2,1,0	3,4,6	32.4	707.0
23	4,3,5,2,1,0	3,4,5	29.2	705.4

续上表

方案编号	最优路径	停靠站点	线路长度(环路)(km)	企业收入(元)
16	4,3,2,1,0	3,4	29.2	698.4
24	3,5,2,1,0	3,5	26.4	686.7
31	3,2,1,0	3	26.4	679.8

由表可知,方案19为最优选择。根据备选站点3,4,6周围用地性质,将其分别命名为润康苑站、金桂园站和东方红郡站,与马群站一同作为定制公交线路起点区域站点。最终得到马群线定制公交的站点及线路图如图7所示。线路总长度约为18km,含起点区域站点4个,终点区域站点2个。

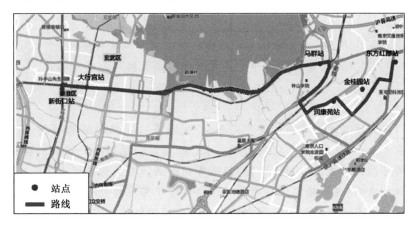

图7 马群线定制公交线路图

4 结　语

本文通过改进的DBSCAN算法实现了地铁瓶颈区段相似出行需求聚类,基于需求聚类结果,融合接驳地铁的共享自行车数据提出了定制公交备选站点识别流程,并通过线路双层规划模型实现了企业营收最大化情况下的线路设计,最后以南京市为例进行了案例研究。文中所提出的定制公交设计方法同时考虑了时空特征,能够主动识别乘客需求,诱导乘客选择公共交通,弥补了线上调查数据不足不全的缺陷,且经算例证明能够在一定程度上缓解地铁压力,但在如何实现乘客和运营商利益的平衡方面仍需进行深入研究。

参考文献

[1] LIU T, CEDER A. Analysis of a new public-transport-service concept: Customized bus in China[J]. Transport Policy, 2015(39):63-76.

[2] MA X, WU Y J, WANG Y et. al. Mining smart card data for transit riders' travel patterns[J]. Transportation Research Part C Emerging Technologies, 2013(36): 1-12.

[3] YAN L, CHOW C Y, LEE V C S et. al. T2CBS: Mining taxi trajectories for customized bus systems[C]// 2016: 441-446.

[4] LI J, LV Y, MA J, et al. Methodology for Extracting Potential Customized Bus Routes Based on Bus Smart Card Data[J]. ENERGIES, 2018, 11(9).

[5] GUO R, GUAN W, HUANG A, et al. Exploring Potential Travel Demand of Customized Bus Using Smartcard Data[C]//2019 IEEE Intelligent Transportation Systems Conference, ITSC 2019, 2019: 2645-2650.

[6] HAO T, ZHANG Q, GAO P, et. al. An Overflowing Passengers Transfer Model for Metro Congestion Relieving Using Customized Bus[C]//2019 IEEE Intelligent Transportation Systems Conference, ITSC 2019, 2019: 92-97.

[7] 雷永巍;林培群;姚凯斌.互联网定制公交的网络调度模型及其求解算法[J].交通运输系统工程与信息,2017,17(01):157-163.
[8] 王海啸.地铁服务能力瓶颈区段客流特性分析及调控策略研究[D].南京:东南大学,2017.

基于共享单车轨迹的社区微循环公交布设方法——南京案例

程剑珂[1,2,3]　陈学武[1,2,3]　刘锡泽[3]　华明壮[3]

(1. 东南大学江苏省城市智能交通重点实验室；
2. 东南大学现代城市交通技术江苏高效协同创新中心；
3. 东南大学交通学院)

摘　要　随着国内大城市地铁线网的逐步完善,公交服务的定位面临着转型,传统的常规公交已经逐渐满足不了居民多元化、便捷化、品质化的出行要求。而社区微循环公交以其机动灵活的特点,可弥补地铁和常规公交线网可达性较差、无法提供门到门服务的缺点。本文首先提出了一套基于共享单车轨迹的短距出行需求提取方法,挖掘出给定区域内微循环公交潜在客流的分布情况及客流OD,为布设微循环公交线路提供数据支撑。本文通过挖掘短距出行需求确定了微循环公交布设区域,确定了微循环公交站点,然后建立以乘客总出行时间最小化的数学模型选取了最优线路。本文为南京市微循环公交线路布设提出一套系统的理论方法,并通过实例验证该方法是可行的,具有可操作性,以期为南京公交服务转型面临的问题提供一定的参考。

关键词　微循环公交　共享单车轨迹　数据挖掘　交通小区划分　深度优先搜索

0 引　言

微循环公交是城市公交体系中的一个概念,它是一种能满足微观层面短途乘坐需求的公共交通形式。当前随着国内部分城市的地铁逐步成网,地面公交服务的定位也面临着转型,社区微循环公交以其路程短、站点少、速度快、客流集中的特点,势必成为公交未来的发展方向。

对于微循环公交线路布设,国内外有许多类似的研究,主要集中在通过公交IC卡或轨道交通刷卡数据获取微循环公交潜在乘客需求,构建双层规划模型求解最优线路[1,2]。然而,这些研究未能考虑常规公交和轨道交通客流数据并不能很好地反映居民在社区范围内的短距出行需求,导致线路布设结果并不符合实际需求。而共享单车作为目前大城市交通系统中乘客短距出行的重要交通方式,其出行轨迹数据能够更加准确地反映短距出行的需求。国内外已有相关研究提出,可以通过共享单车或公共自行车轨迹数据挖掘居民在社区范围的短距出行需求或出行特征[3,4]。

本文结合现有研究成果,提出了基于共享单车轨迹的社区微循环公交线路布设方法,具体思路如下：

(1)通过共享单车订单数据获取用户骑行轨迹,挖掘区域内短距出行需求；
(2)结合共享单车出行需求和区域用地性质分析,确定微循环公交的布设区域；
(3)根据站点选取原则及最佳站距确定微循环公交线路候选站点；
(4)考虑实际条件约束,使用深度优先搜索确定出备选路线并以乘客出行成本最小为目标函数确定出微循环公交最优行驶路线；
(5)结合南京实际案例说明该策略的具体操作步骤。

基金项目：国家自然科学基金联合基金项目(U20A20330)。

1 短距出行需求分析

1.1 共享单车轨迹概念

本文考虑从共享单车订单数据获取用户骑行轨迹,将用户骑行轨迹视作真实的出行轨迹,进而挖掘出区域内的短距出行需求。共享单车订单数据字段见表1。采用2019年5月13—19日一周内南京市共享单车订单数据,部分订单数据示例如图1所示。

共享单车订单数据字段　　　　　　　　表1

字　段	示　例
订单编号	14343637
车辆编号	didibike1153273458113216233
车辆所属公司	didibike
骑行开始时间	5/17/2019 10:00:16
骑行结束时间	5/17/2019 10:06:45
借车点经纬度	118.79564813,32.02617477
还车点经纬度	118.7952026,32.02467072

图1　共享单车订单数据示例

1.2 交通小区划分

由于共享单车系统比较复杂,且订单数据量较大,难以直接应用。本文考虑将研究区域内的共享单车汇总到虚拟站点,并基于共享单车虚拟站点划分交通小区,计算交通小区之间的出行OD[5]。交通小区划分的步骤如图2所示。

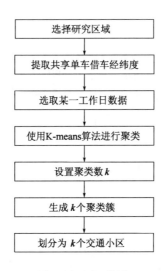

图2　交通小区划分

1.3 订单数据匹配

划分交通小区后,将共享单车订单数据中的起终点匹配到对应的交通小区中,从而获得交通小区之间的出行 OD,如图 3 所示。

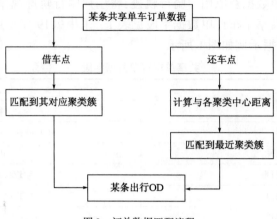

图 3　订单数据匹配流程

2　社区微循环公交线路布设方法

公交线路的生成涉及研究范围内的道路通行条件、客流分布等客观因素,线路的走向、站点的分布及运营排班等线路自身属性,本文所建立的社区微循环公交线路布设方法如图 4 所示。

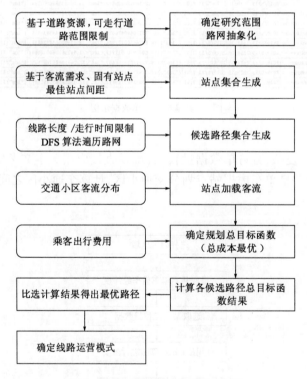

图 4　微循环公交线路布设方法流程图

2.1　布设区域

2.1.1　共享单车出行量

图 5 所示为南京市共享单车出行的空间分布热力图。其中,秦淮区部分区域的共享单车使用尤为密集,说明该区域居民短距出行需求量较大,比较适合微循环公交的开展。

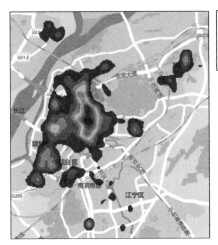

图 5 共享单车出行的空间分布

2.1.2 用地属性分析

区域用地性质影响公交线路的布设,本文结合南京 POI(Point-of-Interest)数据,对选定区域内的用地性质进行分析,并通过调用百度 API 获取各用地之间的空间阻抗,如图 6 所示。

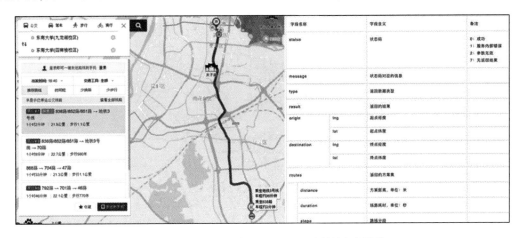

图 6 百度地图 API 路径规划及 Json 文件的字段说明

2.2 站点选址

2.2.1 站点位置选取原则

微循环公交车站的位置直接关系到乘客的可达性,因此十分关键。不合理的站位会导致乘客步行时间增加,出行满意度降低。本文主要采用以下两种方法选取微循环公交站点的位置[6]:①基于客流高密度起终点确定站点位置;②固有站点的使用。

2.2.2 最佳站距确定

合适的站距对公交公司和出行者的影响意义重大,站距过小会导致车辆行程延误增加,站距过大则可能导致居民的出行需求不能很好地被覆盖。本文借鉴 Lesley 等人提出的公交站点间距优化方法[7-8],计算微循环公交最佳平均站点间距,计算公式如下:

$$d = \sqrt{\frac{VV_w(V_a + V_b + 2abT_s)S}{2ab(V - 4V_w)}} \tag{1}$$

式中:d——公交站点间距,m;

V_w——乘客步行速度,m/s;

S——乘坐距离,m;
V——公交运行速度,m/s;
T_S——公交中途站停靠时间,包括上下客时间和开关门时间;
a、b——公交的加速度、减速度。

2.3 线路布设

2.3.1 抽象化路网

对研究区域内的路网和微循环公交站点进行抽象化处理,选取微循环公交车辆可走行的道路作为站点间的邻接道路,获得简化后的路网及站点,并确定各站点经纬度坐标。

2.3.2 模型计算

使用深度优先搜索(DFS)算法对给定路网下所有路径进行遍历搜索,确定出微循环公交线路的备选路径。

2.3.3 目标函数值计算

本文仅考虑最小化乘客出行的时间费用。乘客出行时间费用 C_P 可分为乘客步行时间费用和乘车时间费用:

$$C_P = \sum_{q \in Q}\sum_{k \in K} C_A(q,k) X[q,k] + \sum_{q \in Q}\sum_{od \in OD} C_B(q,od) X[q,od] \tag{2}$$

式中: q——划分小区编号集;
Q——小区集合;
K——公交站点集合;
$C_A(q,k)$——小区居民步行至公交站点的步行费用;
$X[q,k]$——若小区居民步行至公交站点的步行费用;
OD——出行总集合;
$C_B(q,od)$——小区始发出行的乘客时间费用;
$X[q,od]$——若出行起点为小区 q,取值为1,反之取0。

3 实例分析

3.1 研究区域概况

本文选取的研究区域位于南京市秦淮区西部,其范围为:北起白下路,南至军师巷,西起鼎新路,东至长白街,如图7所示。

图7 研究区域内住宅小区分布

调用百度地图 API 计算各住宅小区到地铁站的步行距离,部分数据示例见表2。可以看出,部分住宅小区对于轨道交通站点的步行可达性仍较低,存在接驳地铁的短距出行需求。再通过对共享单车订单数据的分析进行验证,以三山街、夫子庙和张府园地铁站为出行端点(100m 缓冲区内)的共享单车日均使用量分别为 633、584 和 1706 次,接驳客流特征十分明显。因此在该区域内开行微循环公交,不仅能满足社区内短距离出行需要,还能起到接驳地铁的作用。

表 2 部分 POI 数据示例

小区名称	地点	经度(°)	纬度(°)	到地铁站步行距离(km)		
				三山街	夫子庙	张府园
文思小区	建康路 205 号	118.7906	32.0275	0.51	0.83	1.39
琵琶小区	琵琶巷 24~36 号	118.7851	32.01917	1.37	2.26	1.92
金陵闸小区	长白街 7~9 号	118.7892	32.02308	1.03	1.35	1.68
桃叶渡小区	贡院街 43 号	118.7884	32.02529	0.67	1.28	1.51

3.2 确定短距出行需求

使用 K-means 聚类算法对研究区域内共享单车经纬度字段进行聚类分析,取聚类数 $k=5,10,15,20,25,30,35,40\cdots$,各聚类数所对应聚类结果的轮廓系数如图 8 所示。

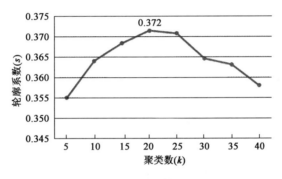

图 8 K-means 算法的轮廓系数

由图 8 可知,当聚类数为 20 时,轮廓系数最大,因此该案例中最佳聚类数为 20。设置聚类数后,通过 K-means 聚类算法生成 20 个聚类簇,计算各聚类簇之间的 OD 量,如图 9 所示。

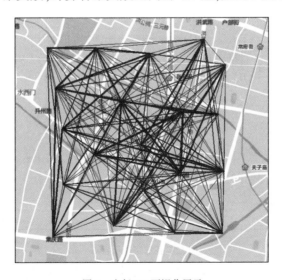

图 9 出行 OD 可视化展示

3.3 确定微循环公交站点

南京市微循环公交平均运行速度取 5m/s,最大运行速度 V 取 10m/s,乘客步行速度 V_w 取 1.2 m/s,T_s

取30 s,a取1 m/s^2,b取1.5 m/s^2,南京市居民平均乘车距离约为1600 m[9],计算得到南京微循环公交平均站点间距$d=376$ m。

根据研究区域内客流集散点及固有公交站点的实际情况,并考虑站点与交叉口的最小距离,确定出研究区域内微循环公交线路的站点,共计14个。根据交通运输相关标准,社区微循环公交站点服务半径为300 m,从而得到该微循环公交线路服务范围,如图10所示。

3.4 确定微循环公交线路走向

对研究区域内的路网及站点进行抽象化处理,简化后如图11所示。

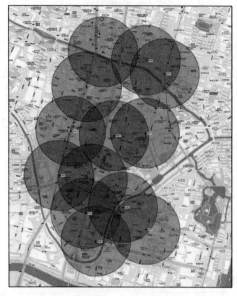

图10 微循环公交站点及其服务范围

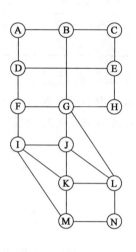

图11 抽象化路网示意图

本文根据实际情况,选取站点F作为线路的首末站,线路模式为环线双向通行。通过模型计算,并考虑实际道路,确定出3条备选路径,如图12所示。

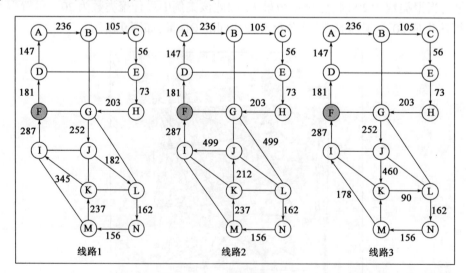

图12 备选路径示意图

计算各备选路径的目标函数值,结果见表3。可以看出,线路1为最优路径。为保证该环形微循环公交线路灵活性,确定其线路模式为双向环线运行。其中内环(顺时针)线路总长约为5.43 km,站点数为14个,平均站距为388 m,与2.2.2中计算的最佳站距376 m非常吻合,如图13a)所示;外环(逆时针)线路总长约为5.52 km,站点数为13个,平均站距为425 m,如图13b)所示。

备选线路及目标函数值　　　　　　　表3

线　路	服务路径	行驶时间(min)	目标函数值(min)
1	F—D—A—B—C—E—H—G—J—L—N—M—K—I—F	43.7	24826
2	F—D—A—B—C—E—H—G—L—N—M—K—J—I—F	50.9	30082
3	F—D—A—B—C—E—H—G—J—K—L—M—N—M—I—F	43.1	26472

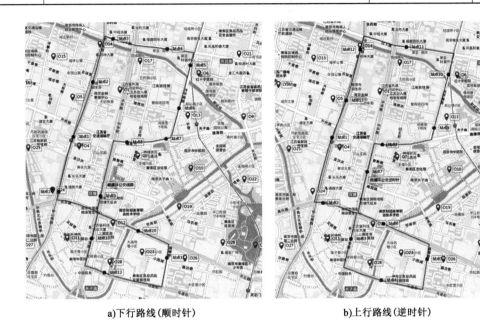

a)下行路线(顺时针)　　　　　　　　b)上行路线(逆时针)

图13　微循环公交线路布设图

4　结　语

为解决常规公交和轨道交通客流数据对于微循环公交潜在客流需求预测的不足，本文提出了基于共享单车轨迹的社区微循环公交布设方法：首先通过对共享单车轨迹的分析与处理，挖掘出区域内的短距出行需求；其次根据挖掘出的短距出行需求和其他一些因素，建立了一套的社区微循环公交线路布设方法，并结合南京实际案例说明了方法的可行性和可操作性，为南京市微循环公交线路的布设提供了一定的参考。

由于篇幅有限，本文只选取了共享单车部分骑行热点区域进行研究，且对于短距出行需求和特征的分析主要基于的是共享单车订单数据。后续可以结合更多数据来源，如网约车数据、公共自行车数据等，为南京市更多区域规划微循环公交的开行方案。

参考文献

[1] 李歌.基于大数据的区域微循环公交线路布设研究[D].西安:长安大学,2019.
[2] Li R,Li G. Research on Bus Route Layout of Regional Microcirculation Based on Large Data[C]// CICTP2020,2020:2838-2850.
[3] 胡才益.基于移动互联和公交运行数据的公交运行评价研究[D].北京:清华大学,2018.
[4] Levy N,Golani C,Ben-Elia E. An exploratory study of spatial patterns of cycling in Tel Aviv using passively generated bike-sharing data[J]. Journal of Transport Geography,2019(76):325-334.
[5] 华明壮.基于订单数据挖掘的共享单车调度需求分析方法研究[D].南京:东南大学,2018.
[6] 宋超群.城市微循环公交线路设计方法研究[D].南京:东南大学,2017.
[7] Lesley L. Optimum bus-stop spacing[J]. Traffic Engineering & Control,1976,17(Analytic).
[8] 李迎晨.城市微循环公交需求特性实证分析及线路布设方法研究[D].西安:长安大学,2019.
[9] 郭四玲,韦艳芳,时伟,等.公交车停靠时间的统计分析[J].广西师范大学学报(自然科学版),2006(02):5-9.

基于群体关注度的步行过街设施适老性评价方法

王迪[1] 翁剑成[1] 王鑫[2] 孔宁[1]

(1. 北京工业大学交通工程北京市重点实验室；
2. 中国建筑设计研究院有限公司)

摘　要　人口老龄化已成为普遍趋势，老年人过街事故率、受伤比例逐年攀升。为科学有效开展步行过街设施适老性评价，降低老年人过街事故率，提升过街交通设施的适老化水平，本文从安全、便捷、舒适3个维度进行评价指标初选，设计了评价指标重要性调查问卷，开展了针对老年群体的问卷调查。引入因子分析法遴选出能表征老年群体主观想法的评价指标。通过设定分级评分标准，构建包含20项指标的基于群体关注度的步行过街设施适老性评价体系，并提出综合评价方法。本文所提出的指标体系，充分体现了老年群体关注的关键因素和要点问题，评价方法易于理解和操作，可为步行过街设施适老化改造、城市高质量发展提供依据和参考。

关键词　交通工程　设施评价　因子分析法　适老性　步行过街设施

0 引　言

依据联合国教科文组织的标准，我国在21世纪初已步入老龄化社会，成为世界上老年人口最多、增长速度最快的国家[1]。随着老年人口比例显著增加，因交通事故受伤、死亡的老年人数也逐年增加，其中因乱穿越马路、闯红灯等违章行为导致的超过80%[2]。

为适应我国老龄化现状，保障老年人出行安全，近年来国内外专家学者在城市适老化建设、老年群体出行研究等领域开展了大量研究工作，积累了丰富的研究成果。夏晓敬等对北京市老年人进行出行调查，得出其活动频率、空间和时间分布特征及主要出行方式[3]。杨博结合人机工程学和老年心理特性，运用Logit模型分析各影响因素对老年群体早高峰公交出行困难的显著性[4]。

在适老性评价指标方面，2007年世界卫生组织发布《全球老年友好城市:指南》，评价指标包括建筑与室外、住区、交通、社会参与、就业机会、社会尊重、信息交流、健康服务8个方面[5]。Green G通过对欧洲健康城市网络城市成员问卷调研发现，老年友好型城市关键建设要素为群体生活环境、室外公共设施与社会参与度3点[6]。董赵伟分析老年群体行为特征，得到室外空间适老性指标集，分类得出1个目标层、3个准则层和8个指标层因子[8]。刘智睿等选取南京市5个不同特征的居住社区样本，建立居住社区公共设施适老性评价体系，指标包括1大类、3中类和13小类。何卫兵提出"建设新一代适老性智慧城市"，适老性城市建设就是要建设绿色、便利、安心、安全的城市，并提出适老性交通系统、公服设施等建设要求[9]。目前国内外对适老化研究主要集中在适老化住宅、社区护理设施等方面，对过街设施适老化研究缺乏关注。

本文着眼于当下适老化研究的空白点——步行过街设施适老化评价研究，采用专家咨询、文献研究等方法确定初选指标，研究过程基于老年群体关注度，通过问卷调研及实地走访等全面深入了解老年人过街需求，并运用因子分析法对调研数据进行分析研究，构建包含3个维度、20个评价指标的评价指标体系以及充分尊重老年群体主观意见、易于操作的评价方法，也为步行过街设施适老化设计提供依据。

1 基于群体关注度的评价指标体系

1.1 初选评价指标

本文构建的评价体系主要用于指导步行过街设施适老环境建设,故选取评价指标侧重于指导规划与设计。指标筛选应遵循系统性、代表性、可操作性原则,依据政策标准、文献资料和调研数据,初步形成3个一级指标、20个二级指标(表1)。

步行过街设施适老性初选评价指标　　　　表1

一级指标	初选二级指标
安全性	安全岛
	机非分离措施
	防滑设施
	路面铺装质量
	台阶和坡道坡度
	栏杆及扶手
便捷性	衔接人行道情况
	过街设施宽度
	爬升/下降高度
	绿灯时长冗余度
	无障碍过街设施
	标识系统完善度
	过街延误时长
	过街绕行距离
舒适性	被侵占情况
	卫生清洁程度
	遮阴挡雨设施
	温湿度及通风
	照明情况
	噪声情况

1.2 问卷调研

本次调查共发放250份问卷,回收有效问卷230份,有效率92%,主要请被访老年人对步行过街设施的需求指标进行重要性打分。

调查对象为北京市城区内老年人,地点分别选在北京市各区,包括:两个生活着较多老年人的街道;两个有较多日常出行频次较高老年人的公园;入户深访行动不便的老年人。此外,发放问卷时对受访者进行简单访谈,确保调查结果有效性。

调查结果从性别上看,男性占45.7%,女性占54.3%;年龄上看,80岁以上老年人占8%,75~79岁老年人占7%,70~74岁老年人占15%,65~69岁老年人占26%,60~64岁老年人占44%。

1.3 信效度分析

本文使用 SPSS Statistics 26 数据统计软件,对有效问卷数据进行信度分析,得到3个一级指标的克隆巴赫系数 α 分别为0.986、0.988、0.986,均在0.8以上,表明该量表的信度非常好。

本文采用结构效度进行效度分析,得出 KMO 值是0.937,Bartlett 球形度检验显著性为0.000,达到显著水平,相关矩阵间有公因子存在,表示有效问卷量表效度良好,适合进行因子分析。

1.4 因子分析

经SPSS因子分析,总方差解释表中有3个公因子特征值大于1,分别为10.431、1.059、1.029,累计贡献率为62.596%,因此判定20个初选指标可提取3个公因子。再根据旋转后的成分矩阵,从旋转后的载荷量表来看,3个公因子中,任一因子内都至少有一个变量的载荷量大于0.5,表示从20个变量中提取的3个公因子均有效。

取初始特征值为1来分析指标变量共同性,根据分析结果,针对调查问卷中的20个变量,所有变量的共同性均大于0.50,说明这20个变量均具有足够的重要性,考虑全部保留。

1.5 评价指标体系及重要度权重

根据某个指标因子贡献量占所有因子总贡献量的比例,来确定该项指标权重值,了解各变量重要度。各指标因子贡献量计算公式如下:

$$\omega_i = \frac{\sum_{j=1}^{m}\beta_{ji}e_j}{\sum_{i=1}^{p}\sum_{j=1}^{m}e_j}(i=1,2,\cdots,p,j=1,2,\cdots,m)$$

式中:β——因子得分系数(各因子对公因子贡献量);

e——公因子方差贡献率(公因子对所有调查样本的方差代表)。

根据以上公式可得出过街设施适老化评价指标权重值,见表2。

评价指标及权重 表2

一级指标	二级指标	指标权重
安全性	安全岛	0.087
	机非分离措施	0.089
	防滑设施	0.044
	路面铺装质量	0.065
	台阶和坡道坡度	0.063
	栏杆及扶手	0.021
便捷性	衔接人行道情况	0.062
	过街设施宽度	0.041
	爬升/下降高度	0.066
	绿灯时长冗余度	0.064
	无障碍过街设施	0.070
	标识系统完善度	0.069
	过街延误时长	0.037
	过街绕行距离	0.015
舒适性	被侵占情况	0.038
	卫生清洁程度	0.041
	遮阴挡雨设施	0.024
	照明情况	0.048
	温湿度及通风	0.042
	噪声情况	0.015

2 步行过街设施的适老性评价方法

2.1 评价目的与程序

评价工作分为评价准备、现场评价、结果分析与反馈3个阶段。首先,成立专家组,人数不少于5人,对评价专家进行培训,拟订评价计划。被评价区域管理部门全面收集相关资料,供评价专家查阅。然后,专家组听取相关管理部门汇报、审阅评价材料、开展重点区域现场查勘、质询,确定评价得分。最后,评价专家根据评价情况进行打分并编写评价报告。

2.2 指标评分标准

设定"很好""较好""一般""较差""很差"的5分制评分方式,分别对应5分、4分、3分、2分、1分,根据评估专家现场勘察、被评价设施管理方会议答辩、资料查阅情况,采用专家打分法;每位专家根据本评价体系打分,去掉最高分和最低分,其余专家评价得分的算术平均值为该步行过街设施某指标的评价得分,如专家评分意见差异较大,进行评价小组讨论。

2.3 步行过街设施适老性评价方法

步行过街设施适老化各评价指标权重 $w_i = (\omega_{101}, \omega_{102}, \cdots, \omega_{306})(i = 1, 2, \cdots, 20)$,具体数值见表2。根据各项指标得分 F_i,加权得到步行过街设施适老化评价的总得分 W,计算方法如下:

$$W = \sum_{i=1}^{20} \omega_i \cdot F_i$$

参考相关规范、文献及老年群体访谈内容,本文推荐的步行过街设施适老性评分标准表见表3。

步行过街设施适老性评价分级标准 表3

评分等级	评价分数(分)				
设施适老性	很好	较好	一般	较差	很差
得分	≥90	75~90	60~75	30~60	<30

3 结 语

本文根据老年群体关注度,构建步行过街设施评价指标体系,并在此基础上构建基于群体关注度的步行过街设施适老性评价体系。从安全性、便捷性、舒适性3个维度较为全面地构建了步行过街设施适老化评价体系,指标体系和权重在一定程度上反映了老年人关切的关键因素和要点问题,评价方法易于理解和操作,便于快速开展和较为全面地了解个别城市和地区步行过街设施适老化建设情况,同时也可为步行过街设施适老化改造提供依据和参考。

由于本次研究调研样本规模有限,集中在一线城市,同时未对中小城市老年人过街设施的适老化开展针对性研究,故后续应进一步扩大调研样本数量,根据城市等级、不同等级城市老年人出行特点对评价指标进行优化,同时结合专家评价法和层次分析法对评价体系进行完善。

参考文献

[1] 宋世斌.中国老龄化的世纪之困[M].北京:经济管理出版社,2010.
[2] 梁慧丽.老年群体出行特征及相应交通政策研究[D].上海:上海交通大学,2015.
[3] 夏晓敬,关宏志.北京市老年人出行调查与分析[J].城市交通,2013,11(5):44-52.
[4] 杨博.老年人公交出行问题分析及对策研究[D].哈尔滨:哈尔滨工业大学,2013.
[5] Global Age——Friendly Cities:A Guide[R].UN:Word Health Organization,2007.
[6] Green G. Age-Friendly Cities of Europe[J]. Journal of Urban Health,2013,90(1):116-128.
[7] 董赵伟.寒地城市室外休闲体育空间适老性评价体系与应用研究[D].哈尔滨:哈尔滨工业大学,2014.
[8] 刘智睿,曹姝君,尹秋怡,等.基于可达性的居住区周边适老性公共服务设施配套研究——以南京市鼓楼区为例[C].2017中国城市规划年会,2017.
[9] 何卫兵.建设"适老性"的新一代智慧城市[J].中华建设,2019(3).

城市片区智能停车管理规划研究及应用

徐 辉 梁天明 张鹏鹏

(悉地(苏州)勘察设计顾问有限公司)

摘 要 目前城市经济发展迅速,特别是城区中心位置,机动化需求高,存在停车供需不足问题,甚至有部分区域停车布置不合理,导致停车空间资源浪费。本文针对路内外智能停车方案进行研究,基于现状停车用地等情况提出路内外停车布局及优化方案。同时,结合优化方案进行停车诱导点位布局,并提出智能停车收费方案。

关键词 智能停车 停车布局 停车诱导 停车收费

0 引 言

"停车难"已成为目前城市急需解决的交通问题之一,机动化发展带来了经济的发展,同时给城市动静交通带来诸多矛盾,停车难、交通拥堵等越发严重。此外,随着城市快速发展,原有的停车配建指标已不足以支撑现有停车需求,供给与需求严重不匹配,导致机动车乱停现象凸显,加剧城市交通拥堵。如今,智能停车系统的普及和应用一定程度上缓解了停车难问题,但其管理经验不足,缺乏智能停车收费管理体系[1~3]。因此,需要采取智能化的手段,对城市中心片区的停车进行统筹规划与管理,以改善城市停车难问题。

我国许多城市在智能停车管理方面进行创新探索[4~6],结合各个城市的现状对停车进行管理及应用,但国内对智能停车规划与管理的普适性经验甚少。本文结合国内对标城市的停车管理与智能化,梳理出我国在智能停车管理的原则和思路。

1 智能停车管理原则和思路

1.1 智能停车管理原则

智能停车管理应以"供给要适度、需求要调控、动态要平衡、智能要集约"为考虑基础,建立起停车资源分布均匀、交通分布均匀、停车供给与需求平衡的停车目标,打造智能停车规划管理的示范区域。

1.2 智能停车管理思路

(1)疏堵结合。充分挖掘停车资源,增加停车设施供给缓解局部供需矛盾、引导小汽车向道路外围疏散。

(2)建管并举。差别化价格杠杆、违停处罚力度,提升管理水平,加强泊位利用效率。

(3)集智齐下。停车设施集约化,采用立体停车管理模式,纵向要空间,并结合国内外先进的智能管理模式,提升运营效率。

2 智能停车管理关键问题

2.1 路外停车优化改善

利用周边公园、绿化等进行停车设施改造,或新建停车设施,弥补路内停车位取消产生的影响,通过现状停车场的改造,挖掘停车潜力,补充现状停车缺口。需要充分考虑现有用地设施,并与规划用地结合,预留必要的停车设施点位,根据不同区位和周边用地性质规划预留好停车模式。停车设施应当具有适当的规模,一般应控制在 300 个车位以内,服务半径约为 300m 以内。

通过路外停车场卡口,设置必要的外围停车交通诱导标识及智能停车位计数,并且将停车数据通过后端平台进行收集和统一发布。

2.2 路内停车优化改善

目前我国城市的路内停车占用道路资源,特别是非机动车空间和人行空间,严重影响道路交通安全和通行。针对两块板或一块板道路设置路内停车,机动车与非机动车存在严重的交织,甚至导致非机动车无路可走的现象,迫使其走向机动车道,严重时,对城市道路通行效率造成极大影响,排队拥堵严重。

结合相关规范和优化研究,路内停车需结合城市道路规划宽度综合考虑,通常情况下人行道宽度至少要 4.5m,才能在人行道设置停车;非机动车道宽度至少 6m,才能在非机动车道内设置停车位。

对于现状的停车改造部分,设置智能计时装置以及智能缴费设备,减少人员管理;对于规划预留停车部分,预留好智能设置管线,减少工程二次开挖造成的浪费。

2.3 停车诱导布局

停车诱导布局要结合用地规划,疏密有致,中心城区内尽可能保证停车全覆盖,并结合智能系统综合布置,构建结构清晰、功能全面的智能化停车系统。

根据停车诱导系统分级原则,一般分为三级诱导标志。一级诱导标志通常设置于城市的主要干道,并且距离交叉口渐变段以外的路段设置较为合理,并尽可能避开与现状交安设施。二级诱导标志通常设置于城市的城市次要通道,已规划的停车场路线为基准,在一级诱导标志的基础上,向下游 3 个路口左右设置二级停车诱导标志,也需设置与交叉口渐变段外侧的路段上。三级诱导标志通常设置与停车场的出入口道路上,并距停车场出入口上游约 10m,并且无设施遮挡。

2.4 智能停车收费

智能停车收费需要划分停车收费区域,并且根据不同的停车需求,设置不同的收费标准。同时,根据不同的停车场类型,设置不通的停车收费模式。结合现有的城市收费管理规定和停车供需矛盾制定分区域、分类别以及分时段的不同收费标准,做到因地制宜、差别化停车管理措施。同时结合停车功能,在重要商业区设置反向寻车系统,让顾客智能便捷、快速地找到自己的车辆。

3 项目实例

3.1 项目概况

越溪城市副中心片区+国际教育园(南区)位于苏州市吴中区西南片区,片区主要以居住、商业和教育用地为主,现状配建停车和公共停车设施不足,导致部分停车溢出,停车矛盾突出。

片区路内停车主要集中在西北方位,共涉及 14 个路段。停车位置基本位于非机动车道上,且超过 90% 的停车位位于支路两侧,如图 1 所示。

现状路外公共停车场总数为 14 个,大部分采用地面停车形式,路外公共停车总泊位约 1115 个,如图 2 所示。

3.2 路外停车优化方案

片区已确定新建 5 处路外停车场,新建停车场主要集中在滨溪路以西,吴中大道以南范围内。同时,结合绿地、空地规划新增 4 处路外公共停车场。

根据控规要求,吴中商务中心南侧停车场地块为商业商务用地。现状作为临时停车场使用。随着地块开发逐步落实完善,建议结合吴中商务中心南侧用地,可考虑建设地下停车库(图 3)。

西交利物浦附属学校门口停车场主要用于接送学生临时停车且不收费,现状车辆均经吴中大道出入口进出。为减小上下学期间接送学生车辆对吴中大道主线交通影响,建议在吴中大道辅道增设 1 个出入口,接送学生车辆经北侧出入口进,经南侧新增出入口出,同时加强进出车辆管理(图 4)。

图 1　片区路内外停车现状

图 2　片区路外停车场布局

图 3　吴中商务停车场优化方案

图 4　学校门口停车场优化方案

3.3　路内停车优化方案

考虑近期新增停车场情况,建议远期保留 7 处路内停车,取消 7 处路内停车,如图 5 所示。

3.4　停车诱导方案

根据周边用地情况和停车需求,近期实施 2 个一级诱导屏,3 个二级诱导屏,19 个三级诱导屏,建议停车诱导系统预留远期扩容接口,如图 6 所示。

3.5　智能停车收费方案

智能停车收费包括路内智能停车收费和路外智能停车收费。路外停车主要通过车辆入场自动识别车牌号,出场通过扫描二维码进行支付停车费,实现无感停车。路内停车通过地磁感应进行停车收费,车主可通过 App 进行车位查找、车位导航、停车申请和充值缴费等。

考虑到停车效率、需求等因素,建议 SM 广场停车场和文溪路南-塔韵路西停车场采用智能停车收费系统。

考虑到以吴山街(吴中大道—溪翔路)路段两侧行政办公居多,为提高停车周转率,建议目前将吴山街(吴中大道—溪翔路)路段作为智能停车收费示范路段。

图 5 路内停车布局

图 6 停车诱导布局

优化后的智能停车收费系统布局如图 7 所示。

参照苏州市工业园区现行收费标准,结合越溪城市副中心交通发展情况及居民消费水平,通过类比拟定区域公共停车泊位收费标准,见表 1。

拟定路内外停车收费标准　　　　表 1

停车场类型	收费时段	收费标准
路外公共停车场	7:00—20:00	3h 内免费,超过 3h 每 0.5h 收费 2 元,不足 0.5h 按 0.5h 计算,24h 后重新计算
路内公共停车	7:00—20:00	2h 内免费,超过 2h 每 0.5h 收费 2 元,不足 0.5h 按 0.5h 计算,24h 后重新计算

图7 智能停车收费系统布局

4 结 语

本文根据智能停车管理原则和思路,提出智能停车管理关于路外停车优化改善、路内停车优化改善、停车诱导布局和智能停车收费等方面的问题,并通过项目实例提出路内外停车优化方案、停车诱导布局方案和智能停车收费方案。从路内外停车布局入手,保证公共停车设施供给动态平衡,再通过停车诱导和智能停车收费保证停车便利。

参考文献

[1] 李扬威,等.城市智能停车管理系统研究[J].交通信息与安全,2014(04).
[2] 段里仁,等.停车管理的基本理念与国际经验[J].综合运输,2012(02).
[3] 万剑.面向城市治理的智能停车规划及建设政策思考[J].智能城市,2018(07).
[4] 王远回.东莞市中心区停车改善规划研究[J].运输管理,2014(03).
[5] 巫志浩.广州市中心商业区停车策略研究[D].广州:华南理工大学,2011.
[6] 沈莉.常州市主城区小汽车停车优化策略研究[D].苏州:苏州科技大学,2016.

超高层城市综合体停车泊位指标研究
——以南京金鹰世界项目为例

杨 斌 祁 健 罗中萍 崔竞誉 宁 丹
(华设设计集团股份有限公司)

摘 要 建筑物停车设施配建标准大多未考虑超高层城市综合体的特殊性,测算的机动车停车泊位规模偏大,造成停车资源浪费,给周边路网带来不利影响。本文提出了按照道路环境容量约束测算、按照业态实际需求测算和类比测算等方法测算停车配建指标。以南京市建邺区金鹰世界项目为例,研究项目地块机动车停车配建指标,在满足超高层城市综合体停车需求的同时,降低对周边路网影响。

关键词 城市交通 停车泊位指标 停车需求分析 超高层建筑 城市综合体

0 引言

超高层城市综合体体量巨大,集多种功能为一体,具有很强的集聚效应,其吸引的机动车停车需求也给周边路网带来了更大的压力和负荷。目前北京、上海、南京等城市已实施的停车配建标准缺少针对超高层建筑物的停车配建指标,测算的超高层综合体机动车停车设施规模往往偏大,过高的停车供给将引发项目周边地区交通量的急剧增长,造成交通环境的恶化。目前我国对超高层建筑机动车停车指标的研究有一定基础,徐雷[1]从效率与经济双重角度出发,以避免道路拥堵与控制地下空间层数为目标,提出综合停车配建指标优化方法;董静[2]选取天津滨海新区核心区建筑进行停车调查,得到各业态停车特征,并以天津周大福金融中心项目为例,测算超高层城市综合体停车规模;朱震军[3]认为公共交通可达性水平及服务能力、超高层建筑总面积、综合体停车共享效果是影响超高层建筑停车配建指标的主要因素;《西安市建设项目停车位配建标准(市政办函〔2018〕252号)》以建筑高度、业态类型为分类,规定了超高层建筑的停车位配建标准。综合来看,国内现有研究缺少对超高层建筑停车配指标的系统分析。因此,迫切需要研究超高层城市综合体停车泊位指标计算方法,提高指标科学性、实用性,促进城市经济和交通的可持续发展。

1 超高层城市综合体机动车停车泊位配建指标优化目标

1.1 满足周边路网条件约束

超高层城市综合体建筑用地开发强度高,对人流、车流有强大的吸引力,高峰时期进出车辆将对周边道路网络及交叉口造成较大压力。为避免车辆拥堵引发周边交通秩序混乱,需要控制停车配建指标,以静制动,抑制小汽车出行需求,满足周边路网承载能力约束。

1.2 提高停车资源利用率

超高层城市综合体各类业态的交通出行时间特征差异较大,简单叠加将造成停车资源的浪费,应采取共享式停车理念,共享停车、错时利用,提高停车资源利用率。

2 超高层城市综合体机动车停车泊位配建指标测算方法

2.1 按照周边道路环境容量约束测算

根据交通调查,确定高峰期周边道路的背景交通量。通过计算道路剩余容量,测算道路环境约束下所允许的最大停车配建数量,降低新增交通流对道路影响。计算公式如下:

$$P = \sum_{i=1}^{n} S_i / \alpha \tag{1}$$

$$S_i = (0, C_i - V_i)_{\max} \tag{2}$$

式中:P——道路环境容量限制下的停车配建总量;

α——高峰期进出车辆占总泊位的比例;

S_i——高峰期周边第 i 条道路容量允许限制约束下的交通量;

C_i——D级服务水平下第 i 条道路的通行能力;

V_i——高峰期第 i 条道路的背景交通量。

2.2 按照不同业态实际需求测算

城市综合体停车泊位分为基本车位和出行车位。基本车位是为满足车辆长时间停车的相对固定的停车位,出行车位是为满足车辆临时停放的停车位,二者叠加后得到总停车需求。

基本车位的计算公式为:

$$P_a = \sum_{i=1}^{n} S_i \times \beta_i \times \frac{\tau_i}{n_i} \qquad (3)$$

式中：P_a——基本车位数；

S_i——第 i 个业态建筑面积；

β_i——第 i 个业态单位面积职工人数；

τ_i——第 i 个业态职工机动车出行分担率；

n_i——第 i 个业态小汽车出行平均合乘系数。

出行车位的计算公式为：

$$P_b = \sum_{i=1}^{n} S_i \times \eta_i \times \frac{\omega_i}{n_i} \times \frac{T}{60} \qquad (4)$$

式中：P_b——出行车位数；

S_i——第 i 个业态建筑面积；

η_i——第 i 个业态高峰期客流生成率；

ω_i——第 i 个业态客流机动车出行分担率；

T——第 i 个业态小汽车平均停车时间。

2.3 按照其他超高层建筑配建类比测算

分析其他超高层城市综合体的项目区位、经营业态、外部交通、内部停车等条件，参考不同超高层建筑的停车配建指标，综合多方面因素，类比测算配建泊位数。

3 案例分析

3.1 金鹰世界项目基本情况

金鹰世界项目位于南京市建邺区应天大街—江东中路交叉口东北角，是河西地区重要的商业办公设施。项目建筑高度368m，占地约为5.0万 m^2，总建筑面积约为91.6万 m^2，主要业态为办公、商业和酒店，经济技术指标见表1。

主要经营业态技术指标（单位：m^2） 表1

主要经济技术指标		备 注
建设用地面积	50064.75	/
总建筑面积	916314.30	/
其中	经营性业态	638104.24	/
	商业	227978.41	/
	酒店	76183.05	469 间客房
	办公	328011.78	/
	电影院	5931.00	1200 个座位
	非经营性业态	278210.06	/

以金鹰世界项目为研究对象，用不同方法测算停车泊位指标，确定最优停车泊位数。

3.2 根据停车配建标准测算

根据《南京市建筑物停车设施设置标准与准则（2015）》，共需配建4352个机动车停车泊位，具体配建要求见表2。

标准机动车位配建要求 表2

建筑类型	建设指标		配建指标	单　位	停车位(个)
	面积(m²)	备注			
商业	227978.41	/	0.7	车位/100m²建筑面积	1596
办公	328011.78	/	0.7	车位/100m²建筑面积	2297
电影院	5931.00	1200个座位	3.0	车位/100个座位	36
酒店	76183.05	469间客房	0.5	车位/客房	235
酒店配套	26840.56	/	0.7	车位/100m²建筑面积	188
合计					4352

3.3　根据周边道路容量约束条件测算

金鹰世界紧邻应天大街—江东中路快速路互通,交通区位特殊,需考虑诱增交通流对周边道路的影响。以D级服务水平为标准,分析高峰小时周边道路通行能力及背景交通量,测算最大允许新增交通量。经计算,考虑周边道路容量约束时,允许设置的停车泊位数量为3042个(表3)。

道路环境容量限制下的机动车停车泊位 表3

路段名称	方　向	背景交通量(pcu/h)	通行能力(pcu/h)	剩余容量(pcu/h)	允许设置的停车泊位数量(个)
江东中路(辅道)	南向北	4245	4100	0	0
	北向南	4218	4100	0	0
应天大街(辅道)	东向西	2276	2810	534	801
	西向东	2453	2810	357	535
云锦路	南向北	1443	1590	147	220
	北向南	1183	1590	407	611
所街	东向西	507	720	213	320
	西向东	350	720	370	555
合计					3042

3.4　根据金鹰世界城市综合体经营经验测算

基本车位服务人群包括商业职工、酒店职工、酒店住客和办公职工。目前商业、酒店已对外开放,可根据现状统计得到车位需求为50个;办公业态尚未开放,参考周边其他综合体办公业态交通生成率,按办公业态每6名/100m²名职工、小汽车出行分担率10%、合乘系数1.1,计算办公业态职工的基本车位需求为1790个。计算得到基地工作日的基本车位需求约1840个,预计周末基本车位需求约为工作日的30%,即587个。

出行车位服务人群为商业、酒店配套、电影院的顾客,这三类人群的高峰停车期为周末下午。根据需求预测结果,推算金鹰世界城市综合体出行车位需求,计算结果见表4。

出行车位指标 表4

类别	高峰小时客流生成率	单位	访客人数	小汽车出行比例	合乘系数	平均停车时长(min)	出行车位需求(个)
商业	10	人次/100m²建筑面积	22798	15%	1.1	90	2073
酒店配套	10		2685	15%		90	245
电影院	0.8	人次/座位	960	15%		120	66
合计							2384

经计算,可得基地周末的出行车位需求约为2384个,预测工作日出行车位需求约为周末的50%,即1192个。目前商业、酒店、电影院业态已全部开放,根据现状闸机记录数据统计实际停车需求,基地2019年11月17日(周日)最大停车数约为2357辆;2019年11月18日(周一)最大停车数约为1179辆。出行车位需求计算结果符合实际情况。

叠加基本车位和出行车位,基地工作日小汽车泊位总需求为3019个,基地工作日小汽车泊位总需求为2944个。

3.5 根据南京和国内其他超高层城市综合体建筑的停车配建类比测算

国内其他超高层建筑停车配建情况见表5,类似项目实际停车配建比约为0.3~0.35个/100m^2建筑面积。

国内其他超高层建筑停车配建情况　　表5

项目名称	建筑面积(m^2)	配建泊位数	配建比(个/100m^2建筑面积)
上海环球金融中心	381600	1100	0.29
上海金茂大厦	290000	993	0.34
深圳京基100	602401	2100	0.35
南京中心新百	178700	318	0.18

参考国内其他超高层综合体停车配建相关经验,建议金鹰世界总体配建比取0.35个/100m^2建筑面积,计算得到泊位建议值为3206个。

3.6 停车设施指标分析汇总

综合多方面因素,以满足实际经营需求、积极引导绿色出行、限制过多机动化出行为原则,建议标准机动车停车位数量控制在3206个。

4 结　语

本文明确了超高层城市综合体机动车停车配建指标优化的目标,提出指标可采用路网交通条件约束、业态实际需求和类比参考等方法进行计算。计算超高层城市综合体停车配建泊位时,应避免机械套用相关标准,需根据综合体的城市区位、经营业态、外部交通条件等特点具体分析,避免供需不均。由于国内超高层城市综合体调研数据相对较少,本文存在一定局限性,未来需要采集更多已运营的超高层综合体停车数据,以更好地指导停车配建指标。

参考文献

[1] 徐雷,刘冰,金涛.城市CBD的整体停车配建规模优化对策——以西咸新区沣东商务区为例[C]//中国城市规划学会城市交通规划学术委员会.品质交通与协同共治——2019年中国城市交通规划年会论文集.2019:2398-2410.

[2] 董静,阴炳成,刘建朱,等.基于共享停车理念的城市综合体停车配建研究——以天津周大福金融中心项目为例[C]//中国城市规划学会城市交通规划学术委员会.创新驱动与智慧发展——2018年中国城市交通规划年会论文集.2018:3613-3623.

[3] 朱震军,曾隽,张生瑞,等.超高层建筑停车配建指标计算方法研究——以西安市为例[J].交通信息与安全,2016,34(3):50-56.

基于大数据的智慧停车管理系统设计

周晓阳　邓高峰　刘一濠　姜　亮

（威海市安通停车服务有限公司）

摘　要　随着城市机动车保有量急剧增加，城市重点停车区域供需矛盾突出，依托大数据构建智慧停车管理系统是解决城市中心城区停车难问题的关键一步。本文通过对中心城区停车资源的数据整合、处理，挖掘传统商业模式中停车管理平台受硬件厂家牵制的问题，应对停车场管理方和用户日新月异的需求变化，提出加强路内和路外停车场规划布局、建设停车诱导系统、推进停车场智能化建设等解决对策，为进一步完善智慧停车服务，提高现有停车资源利用率，推动智慧城市建设提供数据支持。

关键词　智慧停车管理系统　大数据　数据监管平台　停车诱导系统

0　引　言

随着社会经济的快速发展，城市机动车保有量急剧增加，城市停车矛盾日趋严重，特别是中心城区"停车难"问题日益凸显，制约了城市可持续发展。近年来，智慧停车管理平台纷纷出现，实现了对单个停车场的资源管理，但较少实现城市级停车资源的动态监管，因此有必要挖掘并整合城市停车资源，构建基于大数据的智慧停车管理平台。

目前国内停车管理系统正处于迅速发展的初级阶段，国内诸多大城市陆续构建了较为成熟的智能停车管理系统。海信城市智慧停车管理系统面向政府、运营管理公司及出行用户，构建了运行监管、停车运营、决策分析、停车诱导、智能运维、出行服务等应用系统。为解决"停车难"问题，杭州推出"城市大脑停车系统"，将全市各停车场库接入该系统，围绕停车服务、缴费服务、停车管理、大数据分析、数据运营"五位一体"核心功能，通过停车系统建设，辅以配套标准、制度和规范，有效缓解了停车难问题。中建电子城市级智慧停车平台以"互联网+"停车平台为核心，结合移动互联网、物联网、云计算和大数据技术，将多个停车场统一管理，实现了车位预定、停车导航、车位导航（室内）、反向寻车（室内）、在线支付、错时停车、车位共享等功能，提高了停车设施利用率、停车服务质量和智能化管理水平。北京市第一套智能停车诱导系统于2001年12月20日在王府井全面开放投入使用。该系统主要由停车终端设备、控制中心、网络通信、停车信息室外显系统组成。该系统应用了移动互联网和云计算等新兴技术，建设全方位的智能停车诱导系统，实现了以互联网、诱导显示屏、广播、手机、车载导航等全方位的多层面、实时发布手段。

综上所述，国内停车管理系统研究多侧重于运营管理公司和用户两个层面，存在功能不完善、应用不够广泛、科学管理有待进一步提高等问题，需要以实现停车场的高度自动化管理为目标，建立城市级智慧停车管理平台架构，基于动态实时停车数据挖掘，反馈用户的停车需求，综合研判区域内停车管理的薄弱环节。本研究可为构建适应城市发展、车辆发展及配套设施技术发展的智慧停车管理系统变化奠定基础。

1　智慧停车管理系统总体架构

停车场管理方通过智慧停车管理系统可实现运营管理服务，并对停车场进行远程监管。通过平台与线下智能设备的通信，进行数据的实时交互传输，及时汇聚分析，实现停车系统云管理、车场数据云存储、财务报表云统计，有效减少管理层级，提高管理人员的工作效率。

1.1　子系统组成

智慧停车管理系统涵盖了约20个子系统，如停车监管系统、单个停车场的智慧停车管理系统、事故停车场管理系统、收费终端服务以及设备服务系统等,如图1所示。停车监管系统分为城市停车监管系统、企业停车运营监管、停车场运营监管和设备运行监控。智慧停车管理系统实现了对道路停车、封闭停车的管理,同时实现了对商户和会员的管理功能。系统考虑了欠费追缴、不同类型车辆管理等功能。优化移动办公端、用户移动端等功能,将面向管理人员的欠费追缴、包月车的录入等功能迁移到移动办公端,缩短对紧急情况的反应时间。将面向用户服务的收费、预约停车场,反向寻车等功能迁移到用户移动端,方便使用。

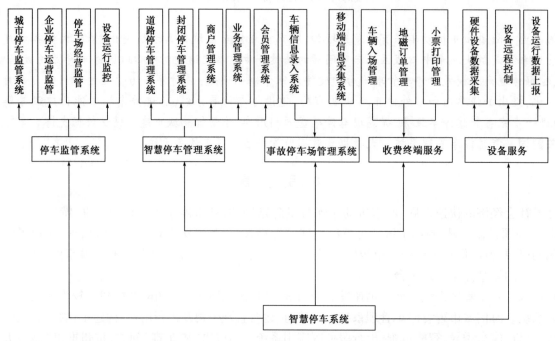

图1 智慧停车子系统

1.2 系统基础架构

威海智慧停车管理系统的开发采用前后分离的模式,前端使用 vue,子服务使用 springboot,后端服务是基于分布式的服务架构服务组件。系统解决了以往系统架构耦合度高、不可割裂、不方便扩展等问题,可以对系统进行更精细的拆分,实现各服务的独立运行,保证系统长期、稳定运行。

威海智慧停车管理系统架构如图2所示,此架构的优势在于:

(1)业务清晰、代码量少,易于开发和维护。

(2)实现系统可持续性,启动快,系统可控。比如系统内部的图片服务,同时运行有多个存储节点,在保证数据备份的同时,可保持各节点的数据一致性。

(3)局部修改容易部署。以往的开发工作中单个应用只要有修改,就需要重新部署整个应用。而在平台的架构中,想要修改某个单独服务只需重新部署该服务即可。

(4)技术栈不受限。可以结合项目业务需求及团队的习惯,部分服务使用 Java 开发,部分服务使用其他语言开发。

(5)按需收缩。可根据需求实现细粒度的扩展。

1.3 停车流程设计

分别介绍停车场管理系统中停车(路内停车、路外停车)业务流程、收费员操作流程。

1.3.1 停车业务流程

停车业务分为路内停车和路外停车。路内停车业务流程如图3所示。用户进入路内停车场后,泊位内部的地磁感应装置检测到车辆入场信息,预先生成车辆入场停车订单,随后收费员进行拍照并上传车牌号,系统在后台完成订单和车牌号的关联。用户出场时,地磁自动检测泊位车辆离场,由系统自动计算出相关费用,打印小票作为收费凭证,系统接收到车辆出场信息,修改订单状态,完成出场流程。

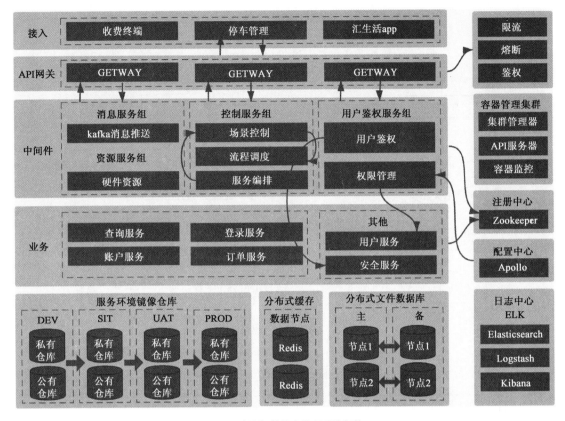

图 2　威海智慧停车管理系统架构

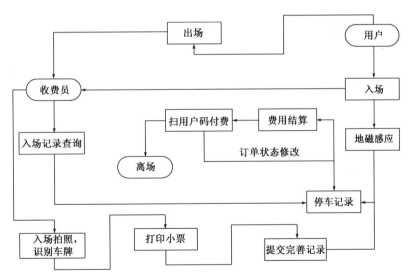

图 3　路内停车流程图

路外封闭停车场实现了预交费功能,减轻了闸口的压力,提高了闸口的出行速度。用户在车场内部可提前缴清停车费用;出场时系统可自主判断当前车辆状态,未欠费状态可正常出行。如若超出缴费后的免费时长并重新计费。用户在道闸处扫码(微信、支付宝)缴费后依然可以正常离场。缴费流程如图 4 所示。

封闭停车场无牌车入场,需要用户在进入车场时扫码入场。用户扫码后会生成入场临时车牌号,并关联扫码时产生的凭证,确认用户入场。同时检测车道是否有车,系统判断并告知该无牌车是否可以入场。车辆出场时,用户扫码查询费用,付款后即可正常离场,具体流程如图 5 所示。

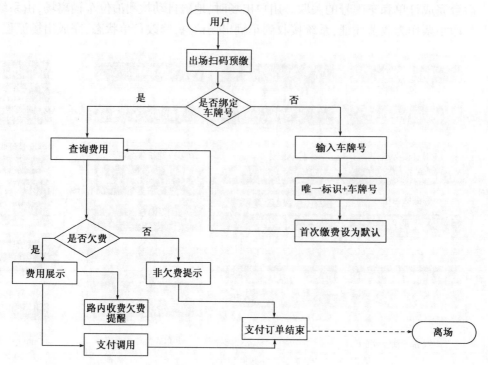

图 4 路外车场用户缴费流程

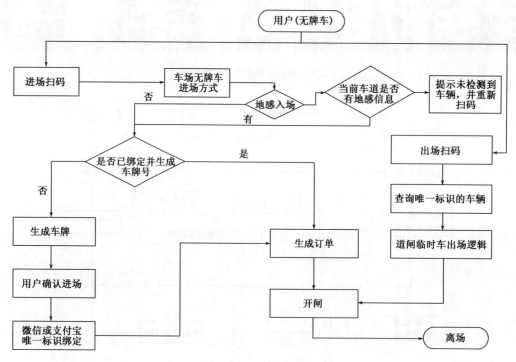

图 5 无牌车出入场流程

1.3.2 收费员操作流程

收费员在收费设备登录其系统分配的账号后可以看到其本人管理的车场,且可以在设备上进行上班签到及下班签退,进行签到操作后才可对车场进行泊位管理及收费。

收费员登录收费设备,签到并选择所负责的车场,查看当前的泊位状态,可以看到当前车位是否有车的状态、操作泊位,查询当前欠费情况。用户出示付款码,收费员调用扫码收费并打印出场小票。停车用户以小票为凭证,正常离场,操作流程如图6所示。

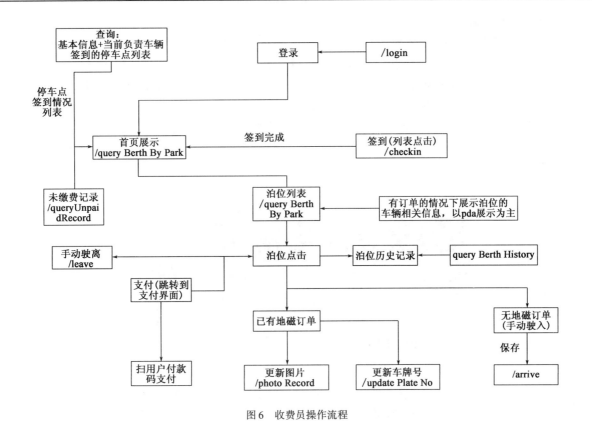

图 6 收费员操作流程

2 智慧停车管理系统设计

2.1 数据采集模块

智慧停车管理系统中涉及政府、企业管理者和用户三方。不同的用户具有不同的管理、服务需求,基于需求响应的管理和服务需要对停车数据采集、分析。海量数据采集和挖掘可以助力智慧城市建设。智慧停车管理平台汇总了所有停车场的数据,并对其进行整理和分析。

2.1.1 路内泊位信息采集

在路内停车泊位方面,通过地磁技术和视频相结合的技术手段,将路内停车泊位的停车动态数据采集到统一平台。针对路内的停车数据采集,根据地磁+网关+转发器的硬件架构模式,实现地磁感应车辆信息入场,完成入场订单生成,并由收费员进行车牌的录入绑定相关泊位信息,实现通过泊位地磁模式感应车辆出入场。最后,在车辆出场时实现自动计费及结算,以此完成泊位相关信息的采集及车辆信息的生成。

2.1.2 路外泊位信息采集

路外收费主要依靠道闸设备完成对进出场车牌的识别,并实现同时利用地感模块检测实际车辆信息,在车辆入场及出场时动态计算当前车场泊位剩余及利用情况。对于路外停车场,需根据智慧停车管理系统要求,改造停车场出入口硬件,并将改造后的数据对接到统一平台。

2.2 智慧停车平台特色

2.2.1 用户画像

在大数据环境下,利用海量的互联网流量进行用户画像,能够对人们的消费、出行、生活、金融等各个领域进行刻画。智慧停车管理平台从数据采集层、数据挖掘层、个性化服务层等方面搭建个性化服务框架,根据采集用户消费行为、使用习惯等数据,通过系统分析,构建精确的用户画像,帮助企业运营人员了解到更加详细、更加丰满的用户形象,为后期的针对性营销提供帮助。

2.2.2 人工智能

智慧停车管理平台采用高清视频采集技术和智能车牌识别算法,可以精准识别出入车辆的车牌(图7),实现自动审核,缓解高峰期时停车场的拥堵情况。通过红外线检测或地面磁感应来启动车牌识别一体机采集出入口车辆图像,设计并运用 AI 实现车牌识别技术完成云端车牌识别,再将大数据与 AI 技术相结合,提高车牌识别的准确率。通过大数据强大的分析功能,实现智能化停车出入管理,助力城市静态交通资源优化配置。系统后台目前已经通过对 10 万张不同车牌图片的学习,完成了系统内图片 cnn 卷积神经网络的优化,改进滤波阈值。同时,语义学习、情感预测、人物画像具象等功能都将由人工智能不断自主学习,完善算法。

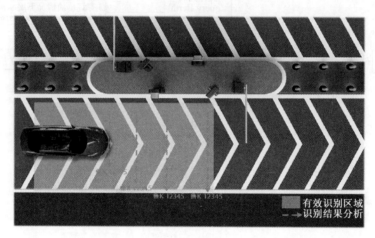

图7 车牌识别

2.2.3 电子支付

智能缴费将移动终端(App、小程序、扫码缴费)发来的离场消息上传给数据管理平台,平台对车辆信息进行查询后,分析和计算所需的数据并返回给移动终端停车时间和金额后,由用户进行缴费,支付完成后平台实时更新车辆信息作为车辆离场依据。

智慧停车管理平台的智能缴费系统不管是对管理系统还是车主,都使得停车收费更便捷,满足车主快生活的停车服务,降低停车场人工成本,使面向对象更加多元化,同时具有相对高的稳定性和安全性,保证了停车场的正常运行,目前已经被广泛使用。

2.2.4 远程管理

智慧停车管理平台通过对硬件的整合,开发了智能网关,并实现了数据的双向同步,同时支持单车场超过 10 万的并发量。智慧停车网关服务界面如图 8 所示。

未来的停车管理系统有望实现无道闸控制系统。该系统的视频采集识别一体机将智能区分进入道闸区域的人、物和汽车等,实现车辆进出停车场无须停车,停车费会在车辆驶出时自动从车主绑定账户中扣除。同时,将平台数据共享,对接市政服务和交通管理系统,实现城市停车资源的统一规划和管理的进程,提高车辆管理和出行效率,真正实现无人值守的全智能化。

2.2.5 停车场路径诱导平台

停车场路径诱导平台可按照出行目的地附近停车场的距离远近、车位空余程度、价格高低属性等方式,在移动端为用户推荐目标停车场,并进行车场定位信息诱导。用户可以在手机实时查看距离最近的停车场。选定目标停车场后,用户可实现车位预定并查看当前车场泊位情况,例如总位数、剩余泊位数、是否可包月等,并直接调用导航实现路径规划,驶入停车场后触发室内导航。停车 App 界面如图 9 所示。

基于现有业务系统的综合及多类型数据的沉淀,可完成数据的挖掘分析和业务流程优化,通过对数据的管理提高服务质量。

图 8　智慧停车网关服务界面

图 9　停车 App 界面

3　结　　语

本文建立基于大数据的城市智慧停车系统。通过构建停车监管系统,不仅可以有效整合城市停车信息,合理调度已有的城市停车资源,还可以更便捷地管理车辆,大量节省人力物力,从而降低停车场车位闲置率,提高停车场的收益。用户可以通过本系统实时查询自己所在位置的周边停车场信息,通过路内、路外智能缴费、导航服务,实现用户无感停车,提高了用户的服务水平,减少了无效寻泊产生的尾气排放,为用户节约了油耗,提升了出行效率。

参考文献

[1] 张哲.智能泊车管理系统的设计与实现[D].西安:长安大学,2010.

[2] Jae Kyu Suhr, Ho Gi Jung. Sensor Fusion-Based Vacant Parking Slot Detection and Tracking. IEEE transactions on intelligent transportation systems, 2014.
[3] 胡雅菲.大数据背景下移动互联网用户画像技术应用浅析[J].信息通信,2020(12):175-177.
[4] 刘源,张玉栋,康雷,等.人工智能技术在智慧停车领域的实践[J].人工智能,2019(01):82-89.
[5] 田永胜,奚西.浅析停车场人工智能化收费管理系统的可行性[J].城市建设理论研究(电子版),2019(10):178.
[6] 陈香.AI技术在智能停车管理系统中的应用[J].价值工程,2019,38(34):193-194.

Research on Parking Route Optimization Based on Improved Dijkstra Algorithm

Wenya Liu   Yongneng Xu

(Nanjing University of Science and Technology)

Abstract: At present, most researches on parking in cities focus on the recommendation of off-site parking lots. For the research after vehicles enter the parking lot, due to the low degree of application of existing information technology, the effective information of parking spaces is not fully known, and the parking lot does not provide it. Corresponding vehicle guidance and parking space recommendation services have prevented the driver from driving the vehicle to the ideal parking space quickly and efficiently. In order to solve the above problems, this paper selects the vehicle parking service in underground parking lots as the research object, combined with the functional requirements of the parking lot, based on the improved Dijkstra algorithm to study the guidance path of the optimal parking space. The performance verification of the search area and time was carried out in the MATLAB environment, and finally the specific data of an underground parking lot at a certain time was used to derive and analyze the optimal parking space guidance path. The results show that the improved algorithm has faster convergence speed and higher efficiency, can effectively solve the rare problem of parking in the field, achieves good application effects, and has good practicability.

Keywords: Dijkstra algorithm   Route optimization   Vehicle guidance   Optimal parking space   Parking service

0 Introduction

Nowadays, the number of cars in cities has increased greatly, and the order and efficiency of driver parking affect the development of urban traffic. According to the data released by the National Development and Reform Commission, the average ratio of parking spaces to cars in large cities in my country is about 4:5, and that in small and medium-sized cities is about 1:2. Compared with 1.3:1 in other developed countries, the ratio of parking spaces in Chinese cities is about 4:5. The proportion is seriously unbalanced, which is more prominent in large cities [1]. Therefore, it is necessary to study the parking needs of users in urban parking lots.

In terms of theoretical research, a large number of studies on parking lot models and vehicle guidance related algorithms have been carried out abroad, including optimal parking lot algorithm models [2-4], optimal parking spaces [5,6], and optimal paths [7,8] and many more. On the basis of analyzing the static and dynamic problems of graphics, Sunita [9] dynamically processed the static Dijkstra algorithm. The retrospective data structure can gradually identify the affected vertex set, and proposed adapting dynamic graphics and retrospective priority queues in time. And the dynamic Dijkstra algorithm optimized on the memory. Burak Kizilkaya [10] proposed a hierarchical method of parking lot monitoring system based on Binary Search Tree (BST), which enables users to easily reach free parking spaces and search for empty spaces with higher time efficiency. Jyothish [11] proposed to use the Internet of Things technology to detect the available parking spaces in the parking lot, which saves the user's time and eases the tension of people looking for parking spaces. Faiz Ibrahim Shaikh [12,13] used a clustering-based algorithm to understand the parking space status of the network from infrared sensors, and developed a cluster-based allocation method and implementation of automatic billing for the problem of parking by drivers during peak hours in the city center. Android application and guide the vehicle to the nearest free parking space. Scholars from Anna University in India consider using Bluetooth technology for vehicle parking management services [14]. The paper proposes to transmit parking information to the driver's on-board control unit, so as to meet the driver's needs for searching and booking parking spaces. The parking management service mainly includes three parts: wireless data communication, center management and parking facilities.

In summary, the existing system uses a query table method for parking space query guidance, and does not quickly search for path nodes based on in-site information. Vehicles that enter the venue continuously do not adopt corresponding guidance strategies, and it is easy to cause local vehicle congestion in the venue during peak periods, and there is no optimal parking space selection based on the driver's preference. In order to make the relevant information collected in the parking lot be able to provide convenient vehicle guidance services for the driver's parking needs, this chapter proposes an optimal parking space path planning model. On the basis of this model, the area division method, route search strategy, and optimal parking space route optimization are established to improve the efficiency of vehicle guidance route search, staggered guidance of vehicles, avoid regional congestion in the field, and improve driver'sparking experience.

1 Problem Description and Model

1.1 On-site Parking Process

The traditional independent search for parking spaces takes a long time and is not purposeful, resulting in a large amount of useless traffic, which increases the traffic pressure on vehicles in the peak period. In order to effectively solve the problem of parking difficulties in the parking lot, the paper studies and designs the parking process with vehicle parking route planning service, as shown in Fig. 1.

When the driver enters the parking lot, the system will search for the route according to the vacant parking space of the current parking lot, and combine the parking space situation and the driver's personal preference to calculate a parking space that best meets the requirements. The specific location of the parking space is prompted by the LED display screen, mobile phone client, etc., to guide the driver to quickly find an effective parking space to park.

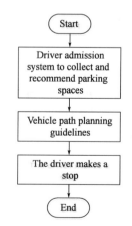

Fig. 1 A flowchart of a vehicle guiding the driver to stop

1.2 Model Building

1.2.1 Parking Lot Road Network Model

This paper analyzes the parking situation of an underground parking lot. The parking lot has a total of 1000 parking spaces. According to the situation of the internal road network of the underground parking lot, mathematical modeling is carried out, and the road junctions in the parking lot, the berths, the entrance and exit of the parking lot, and the elevator are simplified into nodes. As shown in Fig. 2, the abstract of the underground parking lot road network is established. There are adjacency matrix, adjacency table and other methods in the road network data storage structure. This article uses the adjacency matrix method in order to be convenient and easy to program. The adjacency matrix is defined as follows:

$$D_{ij} = \begin{cases} 0/\infty \\ \omega_{ij} \end{cases} \quad (1)$$

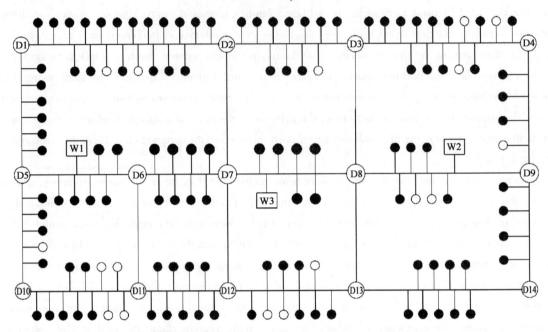

Fig. 2　Abstract map of underground parking lot road network

Among them, when i and j are not adjacent, when i and j are adjacent, it is the weight.

After the completion of the underground parking lot, the length of each road, the entrance of the site to each parking space, and the distance from the parking space to the elevator are all determined, and will not change with changes in the environment of the site. Suppose that $PathLife[\omega]$ is the inherent attribute of the parking space arriving at the elevator, and the weight information of each parking space is different.

$$PathLife[\omega] = \min[Q(x), e(\omega)] \quad \omega = 1,2,3,\cdots,n \quad (2)$$

Among them, $[Q(x), e(\omega)]$ represents the weight of the distance between parking space $Q(x)$ and elevator $e(\omega)$ in the route search.

1.2.2　Optimal Parking Space Decision Model

Comprehensively consider the three driver preference indicators of the time for vehicles to enter the effective parking space, the difficulty of parking the vehicle and the distance to the elevator entrance, and establish the optimal parking space decision model.

Assuming that there are m effective parking spaces at a certain moment in the underground parking lot, that is, there are m alternatives, then set $C = \{c_i | i = 1,2,3\cdots,q\}$ is used to represent the effective parking space set; for each effective parking space there are n decision attributes, then set $G = \{g_j | j = 1,2,3\cdots,p\}$ is used to represent the parking space attributes set. Use a_{ij} to represent the value of the j parking space attribute g_j of the scheme c_i, and then the decision matrix $A = (a_{ij})_{q \times p} (i = 1,2,3\cdots,q; j = 1,2,3\cdots,p)$ is expressed as.

$$A = (a_{ij})_{q \times p} = \begin{bmatrix} a_{11} & a_{12} & \cdots & a_{1p} \\ a_{21} & a_{22} & \cdots & a_{2p} \\ \cdots & \cdots & \cdots & \cdots \\ a_{q1} & a_{q2} & \cdots & a_{qp} \end{bmatrix} \quad (3)$$

As the physical quantities that affect the decision attributes of the optimal parking spaces are different, the above-mentioned optimal decision-making model needs to be standardized to reduce the impact of the different physical quantities of the various indicators in the parking space on the parking decision and improve the reliability of the parking decision, as shown in the following formula.

$$r_{ij} = \frac{a_{ij}}{\max\limits_{1 \leq i \leq q} a_{ij}}, \max\limits_{1 \leq i \leq q} a_{ij} \neq 0, i \in I1 \text{ (is the benefit index)} \tag{4}$$

$$r_{ij} = \frac{\min\limits_{1 \leq i \leq q} a_{ij}}{a_{ij}} \quad a_{ij} \neq 0, i \in I_2 \text{ (is the benefit index)} \tag{5}$$

Among them, $R = (r_{ij})_{q \times p} = \begin{bmatrix} r_{11} & r_{12} & \cdots & r_{1p} \\ r_{21} & r_{22} & \cdots & r_{2p} \\ \cdots & \cdots & \cdots & \cdots \\ r_{q1} & r_{q2} & \cdots & r_{qp} \end{bmatrix}$ is the standardized matrix transformed by the linear proportional transformation method of the decision matrix $A = (a_{ij})_{q \times p}$, r_{ij} is the normalized value of each decision attribute, and a_{ij} is the index value in the scheme.

1.2.3 Fuzzy Complementary Judgment Matrix Model

The broken matrix refers to the matrix composed of the corresponding judgment values obtained by comparing each evaluation factor according to the selected fuzzy scale value. It is denoted as $E = (e_{ij})_{n \times n}$. Any element in the fuzzy judgment matrix has $e_{ij} + e_{ji} = 1, e_{ii} = 0.5, e_{ij} \geq 0, i \in \{1, 2, \cdots, n\}, j \in \{1, 2, \cdots, n\}$, then this matrix is called fuzzy Complementary judgment matrix. Normally, the scale method of 0.1~0.9 is often used for the quantitative scale of fuzzy scale. For the evaluation factors e_i and e_j, the judgment scale of the judgment value e_{ij} corresponds to different attributes, as shown in Table 1.

Fuzzy model 0.1~0.9 scale   Tab. 1

Scaling	Definition	Description
0.5	Equally important	
0.6	Slightly important	
0.7	Obviously important	Compare element i with element j
0.8	Much more important	
0.9	Extremely important	
0.1	Extremely important	
0.2	Much more important	
0.3	Obviously important	Compare element j with element i
0.4	Slightly important	
Complementarity	Should meet $e_{ji} = 1 - e_{ij}$	

1.2.4 Comprehensive Evaluation Model for Effective Parking Spaces

$$Z_i(f) = \text{WGA}_f(r_{i1}, r_{i2}, \cdots, r_{in}) = \sum_{j=1}^{n} \gamma_j f_j \tag{6}$$

$$f_i = \frac{1}{n} \left(\sum_{j=1}^{n} e_{ij} + 1 - \frac{n}{2} \right) \quad i = \{1, 2, 3, \cdots, n\} \tag{7}$$

n is the number of evaluation factors.

According to the $Z_i(f)$ ($i = 1, 2 \cdots, n$) size relationship, further sorting to determine the candidate parking space, the larger the $Z_i(f)$, the better the parking space plan.

2 Path Optimization Based on Improved Dijkstra Algorithm

This paper considers the use of sector to restrict the search. In the parking lot, the information is updated quickly. The system needs a fast search response. In order to further reduce the search for useless nodes throughout the path planning process, improve the efficiency of the search, and reduce the search area, we propose a sector optimization method, which is approximately expressed as The source node is a layered arc with the center of the circle, as shown in Fig. 3.

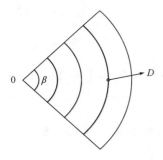

Fig. 3　Sector search area of Dijkstra algorithm

Comprehensively improve the Dijkstra algorithm, this paper introduces the constraint function as shown in the following formula. The search direction is carried out from the positive and negative directions.

$$Q(n)_{min} = q(n) + \alpha(n) \tag{8}$$

In the formula, $q(n)$ represents the weight of the optimal path from the start node or the target node to the end area node, and represents the number of nodes in the restricted search area.

2.1　Improve Dijkstra Algorithm Optimization Process

According to the division standard of the area division method, the parking space node and the road intersection node are uniformly defined as road nodes, and the two-way Dijkstra fan algorithm is applied to the road guidance in the parking lot. The idea is as follows:

(1) Determine the source node y and target node m in the road network, the source node coordinate of the system data storage is $y_i = (yX_i, yY_i)$, the target area node coordinate is $m_i = (mX_i, mY)$, and the road node coordinate of each parking space is $d_i = (dX_i, dY_i)$, according to the Euclidean distance formula.

$$\text{dist}(X, Y) = \sqrt{(x_1 - x_2)^2 + (y_1 - y_2)^2} \tag{9}$$

Calculate the distance between the road node of the parking space in the target area and the source node of the vehicle entrance, and filter the maximum value $n \text{ dist}_{max}$ of the parking node in the target area from the source node in the calculation result.

$$n \text{ dist}_{max} = \max\{|y_i, m_i|\}$$

n order to determine the angle of the sector search, it is solved by establishing a mathematical model. As shown in Fig. 4, a point n_u, the source node y and the road node D_i in the target area are randomly selected to form a triangle in the target area.

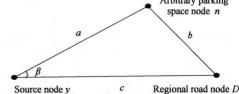

Fig. 4　Mathematical model of sector angle solution

(2) Initialize the set Everlasting, Unmarked, Outarea, Interim, E1, E2, L, and classify the nodes in the established road network model graph G. Everlasting means permanently marked nodes, Unmarked means unmarked nodes, Outarea means nodes outside the restricted area, Interim Represents temporary nodes. E1 and E2 represent the nodes that are scattered throughout the forward and reverse search process. L is used to store the nodes in the two-way search termination area.

(3) Search from the starting node, find the node that is directly connected to the source node y in Unmarked, remove it from Unmarked and put it into Interim, if it is not connected and is not within the optimization range, store Outarea, and then the edge weight constructed according to the real-time collection of the system is set as the weight from the source node to the node.

(4) Search from the target node, find the node in Unmarked that is directly connected to the target node m with an edge, remove it from Unmarked and put it into Interim.

(5) When the set of E1 and E2 meets $L = E1 \cap E2 \neq \emptyset$, stop the search and judgment, otherwise repeat (3) and (4).

(6) Find t in L, calculate the smallest $ym = yt + tm$ value, determine the description of the optimal path between the source node and the target node according to the set of midpoints of E1 and E2, and end the algorithm.

The algorithm flow is shown in Fig. 5.

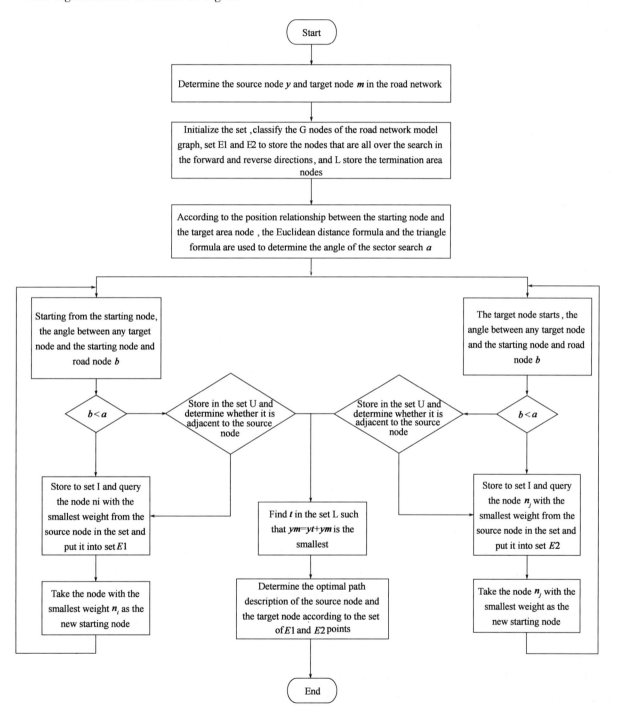

Fig. 5　Bi-directional Dijkstra sector optimization algorithm flow chart

2.2 Algorithm Validity Verification

In order to verify the superiority of the two-way sector Dijkstra algorithm in the corresponding performance, the same road edge weight information is used in the simulation environment, several starting nodes and target nodes are selected, and the search area and calculation time of the improved algorithm are compared with the traditional algorithm.

In the algorithm search area verification, assuming that the distance between the starting node and the target node is $L = (L = 2R, 0 \leqslant L \leqslant 100)$, the fan limiting angle is 2α, and the maximum angle $|2\alpha| = \frac{\pi}{2}$ is selected, the search range of the traditional Dijkstra algorithm is.

$$S_{\text{Dijkstra}} = \pi \left(\frac{L}{2}\right)^2 \tag{10}$$

The search range of the improved Dijkstra algorithm is:

$$S_{\text{sector}} = \frac{R}{2} \cdot |2\alpha| \cdot R = |\alpha| R^2 \tag{11}$$

According to the above formulas, the relationship between the effective search area of the two algorithms and the Euclidean distance between the beginning and end nodes is shown in Fig. 6.

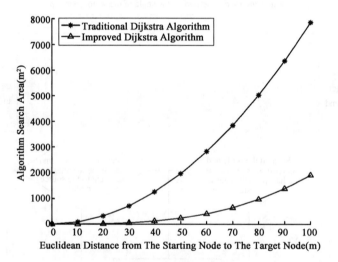

Fig. 6 Comparison diagram of search area area

From the above figure, it can be seen that as the distance between the starting node and the target node increases in the actual road network, the performance of the effective area searched by the improved Dijkstra algorithm is significantly improved, and the useless areas all over are greatly reduced.

On the basis of the same road network search node, the calculation time is compared under the condition of the same starting node and target node, and the comparison chart of Euclidean distance and algorithm running time is drawn as shown in Fig. 7.

It can be seen from the figure that the running time of the improved path planning algorithm is significantly reduced. As the straight-line distance between the starting node and the target node increases, the query time of the improved algorithm is significantly lower than that of the traditional Dijkstra algorithm. Therefore, the improved algorithm can effectively improve the path planning search time.

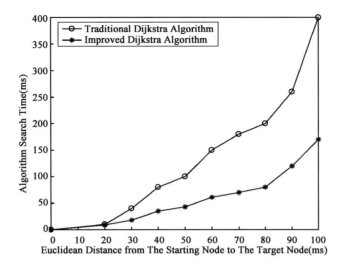

Fig. 7 The comparison curve of the average running time of the traditional Dijkstra algorithm and the improved algorithm

3 Case Study

3.1 Simulation Case

3.1.1 The influencing factors are determined

From the factors influencing parking spaces above, it is known that this article selects driving time, walking distance and parking difficulty as the influencing factors that affect the optimal parking space path planning.

3.1.2 Obtain information on vehicles and parking spaces in the venue

The vehicle guidance and path planning system platform built in the previous article is used to detect real-time vehicle and parking information, and the parking management platform determines that the mobile vehicles are distributed in the D1-D2 section, D3-D4 section, D5-D6 section, D7-D8 Section, D4-D9, D10-D11, D8-D13, D13-D14; the effective parking spaces are A1, B2, C3, E4, E5, G6, H7, H8, H9, K10, K11, K12.

3.1.3 Decision attribute weight calculation

In the vehicle guidance service platform, MATLAB is called to use the improved Dijkstra path planning algorithm to solve the adjacency matrix, so as to obtain the driving path information in the parking space attributes. Taking K10 parking space as an example, the solution is calculated and the driving path of K10 parking space is D1- D5-D10-D11-D12, after reaching the parking space in the area, the indicator light shows open parking, and the remaining effective parking paths are no longer shown one by one.

3.1.4 Calculate the comprehensive attribute value of the effective parking space

According to the classification of the effective parking space index attributes, the three parking space attributes in this paper are all cost-type indicators, and the formula is used for standardization, so as to obtain the standardized matrix γ_{ij} as shown in the table.

Attribute table of normalized matrix of effective parking spaces of underground parking lot Tab. 2

Effective parking space	Shortest driving time	Shortest walking distance	Parking difficulty
A1	0.388	0.387	0.429
B2	0.311	0.414	0.5
C3	0.284	0.462	0.429
E4	0.633	0.48	0.429
E5	0.633	0.545	0.429

contnuie

Effective parking space	Shortest driving time	Shortest walking distance	Parking difficulty
G6	0.333	1	0.333
H7	1	0.667	0.6
H8	0.526	0.462	0.5
H9	0.526	0.6	0.6
K10	0.421	0.522	0.429
K11	0.421	0.462	1
K12	0.421	0.414	0.429

In this case, suppose that a driver's preference for the shortest time, shortest walking distance, and parking difficulty is very, general, and more concerned, construct a fuzzy complementary matrix, and calculate the respective weight vector $f = (1/2, 1/5, 3/10)$. According to the obtained effective parking space index weight vector, the comprehensive attribute value of each effective parking space plan is calculated as follows:

$$z_i(f) = \begin{pmatrix} 0.4001, 0.3883, 0.3631, 0, 5412, 0.5542, 0.4664, \\ 0.8134, 0.5054, 0.563, 0.4436, 0.6029, 0.422 \end{pmatrix}$$

Comparing the comprehensive attribute values of the effective parking spaces according to the judgment criteria shows that the H7 parking space in the H area has the largest comprehensive attribute value, which is the optimal parking space at the current moment.

3.2 Result Analysis

(1) The optimal path for the vehicle to guide the optimal parking space is given. The information given in the calculated effective parking space attribute table shows that the path of the optimal parking space H7 at this time is: S-D1-D5-D10-H7. The vehicle guidance service platform releases route information for the driver through the terminal. Complete vehicle guidance.

(2) Vehicle guidance optimal parking path optimization effectiveness analysis In order to verify the effectiveness of the optimal parking path, the vehicle and parking information at the time are also selected, and the traditional shortest path algorithm is used to calculate this using MATLAB based on the road attribute information in the venue. The effective parking space of the shortest path at time is B2, so the driving distance and time of the optimized parking space after comparison are shown in Tab. 3.

Attribute table of normalized matrix of effective parking spaces of underground parking lot Tab. 3

Parking space B2 obtained by traditional shortest path planning		Optimal parking space path optimization to obtain parking space H7	
Distance from parking space to entrance(m)	Driving time	Distance from parking space to entrance(m)	Driving time
36(S-D1-D2-A2)	61S	40(S-D1-D5-D10-H7)	19S

From the table, it can be seen that the traditional shortest path planning guidance obtained by the traditional shortest path planning guidance in the same field environment is 36m. Because the road section is in local congestion at this time, the driving time of the driver is 61s, and the optimal parking path optimization guidance calculation The driving distance of parking space H7 is slightly higher than that of A2, and the driving time is 19s. From the verification and analysis of the above calculation examples, it can be seen that the parking space derived from the pre-optimized parking space can better meet the actual needs of the driver. Moreover, it can be seen from the comparison data of the traditional path planning parking space and the improved data that although the improved method The path length is longer than the traditional method, but this method avoids the different flow of vehicles in various areas, and the delay time between each other is small, so that the driver can quickly complete the parking in the field and consume less time.

4 Conclusions

Conclusion This chapter clarified the practicality of the vehicle guidance system for the driver by analyzing the parking process of the vehicle with or without the vehicle guidance system in the venue. At the same time, according to the factors influencing the choice of parking space, it is proposed that the existing vehicle guidance system does not fully consider the driver's preference attributes and Real-time changes in the information in the field may cause local path congestion and low path planning efficiency. In response to the above problems, firstly, the model was abstracted and established for the parking lot, the road edge rights of the road network model of the parking lot were constructed, and the parking space area was divided; secondly, the three main indicators that affect the driver's parking choice preference in the parking lot were considered Established the optimal parking space selection model, and at the same time made the decision-making derivation of the optimal parking space, and proposed a vehicle-guided optimal parking space path optimization algorithm. The effectiveness of the algorithm in the search area and time was verified in a simulation environment. Finally, a concrete example was calculated. The attributes of each parking space, the optimal parking space is selected, and the optimal path is planned. The analysis proves that compared with the traditional method, the driver can guide the driver to park quickly and effectively.

5 Acknowledgements

This research was supported by the National Key R&D Program (2017YFB1001801), the Jiangsu Graduate Research and Practice Research Innovation Program (KYCX20_0381), the Central University Basic Research Fund (30917012102), the Jiangsu Natural Science Foundation of China (BK20171426) and supported by "the Fundamental Research Funds for the Central Universities" No. 30920010012. We would like to thank the reviewers for their valuable suggestions and comments.

References

[1] Cheng Jie Ling, Ou Lijun, Xue Junzhi. Analysis on the status quo of domestic urban parking and information solutions[J]. Information and Communication,2018(02):114-115.

[2] Huang Runfei. Research and implementation of indoor navigation model of underground parking lot based on Bluetooth low energy [D]. Kunming: Yunnan Normal University,2017.

[3] Zhang Yujie, Tian Shuo. Application of Dijkstra optimization algorithm in parking space guidance system [J]. Computer Measurement and Control,2014,22(1):191-193.

[4] Li Wei, Yu Sen, Wang Wei. Parking lot guidance algorithm based on the shortest path in time[J]. Automation Instrumentation,2015,(08):23-25.

[5] Guo Zhanhong. Research on Vehicle Guidance and Path Planning of Underground Parking Lots[D]. Lanzhou: Lanzhou Jiaotong University,2020.

[6] Dong, Guo, Juan, et al. A vehicle path planning method based on a dynamic traffic network that considers fuel consumption and emissions [J]. The Science of the total environment,2019,140(1):935-943.

[7] Peng Yue. Parking guidance path based on Dijkstra algorithm[J]. China New Communications,2019,21 (22):74-75.

[8] Cai Jia. Parking space guidance system based on Dijkstra algorithm[J]. Electronic Technology and Software Engineering,2014.

[9] Sunita, Grag. Dynamizing Dijkstra: A solution to dynamic shortest path problem through retroactive priority

queue[J]. Journal of King Saud University Computer & Information Sciences,2018:S1319157817303828.
[10] Kizilkaya B,Caglar M,Al-Turjman F,et al. Binary search tree based hierarchical placement algorithm for IoT based smart parking applications[J]. Internet of Things,2019(5):71-83.
[11] Jyothish J,Mamatha,Gorur S,et al. Booking Based Smart Parking Management System[J]. Smart Secure System-IoT and Analytics Perspective,2017(12):312-319.
[12] Ibrahim S,Nirnay J,Pradeep B,et al. Smart parking system based on embedded system and sensor network[J]. International Journal of Computer Applications,2016,140(12):45-51.
[13] Ya'Acob N,Azize A M,Alam N M R N Z. Parking system using Geographic Information System(GIS)[C]//IEEE Conference on Systems,Malaysia,2016:16-18.
[14] Suryanarayana D V,Mariappan V,Narayanasamy P. Location Dependent Parking Service Through Bluetooth[J]. Academic Open Internet Journal,2005,15.

基于场所特性的非机动车道宽度标准精细化研究

吴俊荻　姚　霏　常四铁　焦文敏
(武汉市规划研究院)

摘　要　非机动车道宽度是非机动车系统中最基本的空间几何特性,既影响骑行服务水平,也与其他交通活动密切相关。为改善国内现行非机动车道宽度标准存在的问题,提出更适合实际使用的非机动车道宽度要求,首先根据非机动车道所处的空间位置和隔离程度,对其进行了分类,重点研究了路内、路外6种非机动车道,以及交叉口、公交站处的特殊路段非机动车道。在国内外设计标准对比的基础上,对各类非机动车道的适用条件、有效宽度影响因素、宽度标准和设置要求进行了差别化的分析和整理,为国内非机动车道宽度标准的优化提供思路和方向。

关键词　城市交通　非机动车道　标准研究　宽度　几何特征

0　引　言

2020年1月,住房和城乡建设部提出了《关于开展人行道净化和自行车专用道建设工作的意见》,要求"构建连续、通畅、安全的自行车专用网络",并强调了"科学规划、统筹建设、强化管理"三方面的要求,体现了全国层面对非机动车交通的重视。而非机动车道的宽度是整个骑行空间的基础,是满足骑行需求、保证骑行安全、适应骑行环境的重要条件。

我国目前没有针对非机动车基础设施的专项规范,其他规范中涉及非机动车道宽度的相应条款仍有完善空间,主要问题在于宽度标准过于单一,缺少与骑行流量、骑行速度及其他交通设施的关联,与实际运行时的需求有差异。为找到更合理的非机动车道宽度计算方法,国内学者通过机非冲突分析,明确了非机动车道宽度与非机动车流量和隔离程度的相关关系,但其结论偏理论化,在规划设计工作中较难应用。

欧美一些国家和地区的非机动车道设计日益精细化,不仅考虑了非机动车独立骑行的要求,而且关注周围环境的综合影响、骑行与其他交通活动的协调。以英国为例,其自行车基础设施设计标准提出了影响非机动车服务水平的三要素"人、场所和交通特性",从而对非机动车道的有效宽度进行了详细的界定。

综合国外经验和国内现实问题,对非机动车道设计有较大影响的主要有两类场所特性,一是与其他交通方式的空间关系,二是隔离的程度。根据这两类特性,可将非机动车道分为路内、路外两大类,以及设施隔离、划线隔离、共享车道三小类。此外,考虑交叉口及特殊路段的非机动车道,对其不同场所特征下的自行车道适用条件、有效宽度影响因素和宽度要求总结如下。

1 路内非机动车道

1.1 车道场所分类及适用条件

路内非机动车道一般是沿着车行道布置的,重点需考虑非机动车与机动车的关系。国内要求在主干道及车速40km/h以上道路设置机非隔离设施,但缺少与机动车流量的相关要求,也没有明确共享型非机动车道的适用条件。参考英国的自行车道国标和伦敦地方标准,考虑道路的类型、车速、流量、大型车辆比例等,对路内非机动车隔离方式选择标准总结见表1。

英国路内非机动车道隔离方式选择标准　　　　表1

隔离方式	骑行组织特点	适用交通条件	街道类型	机动车速（km/h）	机动车流量（辆/h）	大型车辆比例（%）
路内隔离	独立、安全、舒适,对路边交通活动影响大	过境交通为主、路边活动较少	主干道、区域连通道	>48		
路内划线	受相邻车道影响大,可借机动车道超车	交通功能较强,但车速、大型车辆比例、流量不过高	区域连通道、市中心街道	>36	<1000	<5
共享车道	与公交专用道等共享	道路较窄、交通功能较低	城市次干道、社区街道	<36	<2000（辆/天）	

1.2 有效宽度影响分析

有隔离的非机动车道是相对独立的骑行空间,其宽度的设计首先应考虑与非机动车流量相匹配;其次,要考虑隔离设施的垂直高度对路侧安全空间的影响。研究表明,路侧空间的物体对骑行者的影响,与其高度和连续程度呈正比。

路侧划线非机动车道受相邻车道的交通影响较大,但在需要时可以借用机动车道超车,因此,其宽度标准主要应考虑机动车、非机动车安全间距,对于非机动车流量的敏感度要求较低。

对于共享非机动车道,为保证骑行者与其他交通混合使用时的安全,其宽度应考虑足够的超车空间,或完全不设置超车空间。研究表明,当超车空间不确定时,其他车辆如果超车,则很容易给骑行者带来危险。

1.3 宽度标准及设置要求

1.3.1 路内有隔离非机动车道

当单车道高峰小时非机动车流量在200辆以下时,单向有隔离非机动车道可以考虑最低1.5m的宽度;高于此流量值时,宜按最低2.5m的标准宽度设置,见表2。

英国和荷兰有隔离自行车道最小宽度推荐值　　　　表2

自行车交通量水平	英　国		荷　兰	
	单车道高峰小时（辆/h）	单向宽度（m）	单车道高峰小时（辆/h）	单向宽度（m）
非常低/低	<100/100~200	1.5	<150	1.5
中等	200~800	2.2	>150	2.5
高/非常高	800~1200/>1200	2.5		

同时,为尽量增加有效宽度,应适当降低非机动车道路面与人行道路缘石之间的高差,最多可以减少至5cm;当有高于60cm且连续布置的垂直立面时,则需考虑1m的安全间距。

1.3.2 路内划线隔离非机动车道

由于不设置隔离设施的机动车、非机动车非安全间距(1.0m)比一般高度隔离设施的路侧安全间距(0.25~0.75m)大,因此,路内划线隔离非机动车道最小宽度要求,反而比有隔离设施的非机动车道最小宽度要求大,推荐值为2m。同时,为了保证非机动车超车时的安全,与非机动车道相邻的车道宽度不应小于3.2m。

1.3.3 共享非机动车道

基于共享车道超车宽度的要求,建议有超车空间的共享车道宽度应在4.5m以上,完全不设置超车空间的共享车道可采用3.0~3.2m,但此类较窄的共享车道,只能应用在公交车流量非常低(公交流量小于20辆/h,或公交、出租汽车总流量小于100辆/h)的情况下。

2 路外非机动车道

路外非机动车道包括穿越公园绿地、滨水空间或其他公共空间的骑行通道,一般会与人行道平行或者合并布置,需重点考虑非机动车与人行的关系。国内非机动车道标准没有对路外非机动车道的隔离方式选择提出明确要求。

2.1 车道场所分类及适用条件

参考伦敦标准,考虑人行和自行车流量两大主要因素,对路外非机动车道分类标准总结见表3。

路外非机动车道隔离方式选择标准　　　　表3

与行人隔离程度	主要应用场景	隔离方式	自行车流量(车/h)	人行流量(人/h)
完全隔离	—	硬质设施、植物	较高(>300)	较高(>200)
轻度隔离	公园绿道	划线、颜色区分、低路缘石	一般(150~300)	较低(<200)
完全共享	滨河慢行道	无	较低(<150)	任何流量

其中,轻度隔离的自行车道,会因为行人难以遵守界限,产生碰撞风险。因此,轻度隔离的自行车道仅适用于步行流量很低、自行车流量又较大的慢行空间设计中。

2.2 有效宽度影响分析及宽度标准建议

2.2.1 一般影响因素

当自行车道位于路外空间时,受其他交通因素影响较小,其宽度标准主要与自行车流量变化相关。

其中与人行完全隔离的自行车专用道和路内隔离非机动车道的设计原则类似,可按双向有隔离非机动车道的宽度标准设置;轻度隔离自行车专用道的宽度,与完全隔离非机动车道类似,可适度减少隔离设施对路侧安全间距的影响;人行、自行车完全共享的慢行道宽度,则需结合自行车与人行可能出现的关系,如并行、超越、相遇等,来综合确定断面宽度。

2.2.2 生态影响因素

与路内非机动车道宽度要求不同的是,由于路外自行车道大部分位于公园、绿地、滨水等自然空间内,即使为满足一定的交通功能,也不应过分地使自然空间城市化。因此,路外自行车道的宽度标准只有推荐值,没有最小值的要求,宽度设置应以满足骑行流量的最小宽度为宜。

综合以上因素,以英国自行车道设计标准为参考,路外自行车道宽度推荐值见表4。

路外自行车道宽度推荐值　　　　表4

自行车交通水平	单车道高峰小时(辆/h)	完全分隔宽度(m)	轻度隔离宽度(m)	完全共享宽度(m)
非常低/低	<100/100~200	2.0	3.0(自行车道:1.2~1.5)	2.2
中等	200~800	3.0	4.5(自行车道:2.5~2.8)	3.0
高/非常高	800~1200/>1200	4.0	5.9(自行车道:2.5~3.5)	4.5

3 交叉口及特殊路段的非机动车道

非机动车道的特殊路段主要包括交叉口衔接处以及与路边交通活动冲突的位置,如公交停靠站、路边停车带等。

3.1 交叉口的非机动车道衔接段

交叉口非机动车道的设计重点是保证连续性。当非机动车道穿越无信号灯控制的交叉口,应采取虚线等方式延续标准路段非机动车道的空间,宽度尽量与标准路段保持一致,最小不应低于1.5m;当非机动车道在有信号灯控制的交叉口时,则需在机动车停止线前设置非机动车前置候车区,非机动车停止线与机动车停止线之间最小间距5m。

3.2 公交停靠站处的非机动车道

非机动车道在公交依靠站处的设计,主要考虑非机动车道的连续性和公交上下客的行人安全性。而结合非机动车道的建设形式,主要有三种协调方式。具体协调方式、设计重点及宽度要求见表5。

公交停靠站处非机动车道设计重点及宽度要求　　　　表5

公交停靠站处非机动车道类型	适用条件	设计重点	非机动车道宽	其他宽度要求
非机动车后绕公交停靠站	非机动车和公交流量较大的路段	保证人行穿越非机动车道的安全,非机动车道的路面应作抬高处理与人行道同平面	延续标准路段宽度	公交站牌人行等候区至少宽2.5m
非机动车道抬升	非机动车和公交流量较小的路段	保证充足人行道空间,减少候车人群与非机动车的冲突	至少1.5~2.0m	除公交站牌外人行道至少宽2.0~3.0m
非机动车借用机动车道	非机动车与公交共享车道,且共享车道大于4.5m时	减小非机动车与其他机动车的冲突,采取取消车道中心线等稳静化措施,降低车速	—	—

3.3 路边停车

路边停车一般布置于中低等级、到发交通较多的生活型道路上。根据目的不同,路边停车可分为路边固定停车位和路边临时停车(上落客、装卸货)两大类。路边停车与非机动车道的协调,关键在于保证非机动车道的连续性,同时避免开关车门对非机动车行驶的影响。

针对有隔离的非机动车道,停车区最好布置于非机动车道和机动车道之间,且两者之间至少设置0.5m的缓冲隔离区。

对于划线隔离的非机动车道,可借用机动车道,采用虚线的方式外绕停车带。这种方式同样需要保证非机动车道和停车带之间的缓冲区,宽度要求为0.5m,且应采取交通稳静化措施提醒机动车减速。

4 结 语

综上所述,对以上三类自行车道宽度标准主要影响因素总结如下:

(1)路内非机动车道重点考虑机动车与非机动车流量特征,同时需考虑机动车速度、隔离设施高度对侧向空间的影响。

(2)路外非机动车道重点考虑非机动车与人行流量特征,同时应避免对自然空间过度城市化。

(3)对于特殊路段的非机动车道,要重点考虑保证非机动车道连续性,同时减少其他交通活动(公交停靠、停车)对非机动车的影响。

以上研究主要以文献整理、对比研究和案例分析的方法为主。实现我国非机动车宽度标准的精细化,还需要结合非机动车道的实际运行情况,对比服务水平变化,建立长期优化非机动车道相关标准的动态机制。

参考文献

[1] 胡雁宾,刘君.关于城市道路非机动车道宽度值的研究[J].道路交通管理,2019(10):34-35.
[2] 程国柱,王婉琦,徐慧智.城市道路机非冲突分析与自行车道宽度计算方法[J].哈尔滨工业大学学报,2019,51(9):130-136.
[3] London Cycling Design Standards [S]. London:Mayor of London,2014.
[4] Design Manual for Bicycle Traffic [M]. 2th ed. Dutch:CROW,2016.
[5] Cycle Infrastructure Design [S]. U.K:Department of Transport,2020.
[6] The merits of segregated and non-segregated traffic-free paths:a literature-based review [R]. London:Phil Jones Associates,2011.

基于轨道交通换乘的公共自行车站点选址研究

潘卫龙[1]　张祎薇[1]　韩永贵[2]

(1.长安大学运输工程学院;2.商河县交通运输局)

摘　要　合理布设轨道交通换乘公共自行车的站点,有助于实现换乘过程的流畅衔接,充分发挥公共自行车的灵活优势,使城市有限的交通空间得到有效地利用,提高城市出行效率。本文分析与轨道交通换乘的公共自行车选址方案评价指标,基于模型方法的优缺点分析,分别使用熵权法和灰色关联度法、熵权法赋值权重的灰色关联度模型进行方案评价,并对评价结果对比分析,实现评分排序 $r_1=0.775>r_2=0.734>r_3=0.495>r_4=0.376$,以实例验证本文模型设计的科学性和可行性。

关键词　站点选址　方案比选　熵权　灰色关联度　轨道交通　公共自行车

0　引　言

目前,国内外对轨道交通换乘公共自行车站点选址方法进行了大量研究,如陈凯缓[1]在对公共自行车换乘的站点选址评价体系的研究中,提出了改进模糊综合评价法来规划选址方案;何流、陈大伟、李旭宏[2]等人从成本目标函数出发,建立组合的双层规划模型来得到最优站点布局方案;LinJR[3]等人考虑成本和服务水平等因素建立公共自行车站点位置—规模模型,研究站点的数量和位置、规模、自行车道的建设以及用户路径的选择等内容。基于当前学者的研究结果发现,传统的站点选址定性分析依靠规划人员工程经验,简单易操作,但定性判断受到各种影响因素的主导,结果精度难以把握;站点选址的定量分析大多通过各种模型算法和计算机等新型技术方法确定规划方案,结果精确度较高,但在一定程度上忽略人为感受且操作烦琐,难以在实际规划工作中推广[4]。在定性定量的站点方案比选研究中,学者多采用层次分析法或改进赋权重的模糊评价方法来确定最优选址方案,比选方法相对匮乏。因此本文提出使用熵权法、灰色关联度法和熵权法赋值权重的灰色关联度模型方法进行选址方案比选,在既有的研究基础上补充轨道交通与公共自行车换乘站点选址方法。

1　自行车换乘站点选址评价指标

本文所选取的公共自行站点评价指标,主要包括便利度、衔接度、适应性、建设运营成本。

1.1　便利度

换乘的便利度和换乘距离有很大关系,换乘距离越短,换乘越便利。通过实地勘察以及下式,可以得到公共自行车的服务站点与最近的地铁出口的平均距离[5]：

$$B = \frac{\sum_{i=1}^{N} A_i L_i}{\sum_{i=1}^{N} A_i} \tag{1}$$

式中：B——站点与轨道交通出入口平均距离；

　　A_i——站点容量规模；

　　L_i——与邻近轨道交通出入口距离。

1.2 衔接度

衔接度与公共自行车站点到轨道交通站口这段空间的道路状况和交通环境有很大关系。道路宽敞、交通顺畅、出行的冲突点少，换乘衔接就会流畅安全、效率高，出行者更愿意选择在这类地点换乘公共自行车[7]。

1.3 适应性

适应性是指公共自行车站点宏观上应与城市未来的发展规划相适应，微观上应该与出行需求方向上适应，使用专家评议法对它进行量化，演变成适应程度[7]。

1.4 建设运营成本

公共自行车站点的建设运营需要考虑开发土地产生的费用成本以及未来运营维护成本[6]：

$$F_0 = \sum SU \frac{\theta(1+\theta)^A}{(1+\theta)^A - 1} \tag{2}$$

式中：S——站点面积；

　　U——土地价格；

　　θ——贴现率，取 0.1；

　　A——站点的服务年限；

　　F_0——站点的土地成本。

$$F_1 = \sum (C_B + W C_W^3) U \frac{\theta(1+\theta)^A}{(1+\theta)^A - 1} \tag{3}$$

$$F_2 = 0.1 F_1 \tag{4}$$

式中：C_B——站点的固定成本；

　　C_W——其他费用；

　　W——费用系数；

　　F_1——站点的设施建设成本；

　　F_2——站点的运营维护成本。

2 综合评价方法的基本原理

2.1 熵权法

熵权法基于指标变异程度所反映的信息量来确定权重，其最大优点是客观赋权，忽略指标主观影响，相比于 AHP（层次分析法）更客观。但由于不考虑指标本身的实际意义，所得出的结果可能与实际相差甚远。

（1）多方案多因素的决策矩阵如下：

$$\boldsymbol{M} = \begin{pmatrix} \chi_{11} & \cdots & \chi_{1n} \\ \vdots & \vdots & \vdots \\ \chi_{m1} & \cdots & \chi_{mn} \end{pmatrix} \tag{5}$$

(2)对决策矩阵归一化处理,计算贡献度 P_i 及贡献总量 E_j。

$$p_{ij} = \frac{X}{\sum_{i=1}^{m} X_{ij}} \tag{6}$$

$$E_j = -K \sum_{i=1}^{m} P_{ij} \ln(P_{ij}) \tag{7}$$

其中,常数 $K = 1/\ln m$,这里可以定义 d_j 为在第 j 影响因素下各个方案贡献度的同一程度,$d_j = 1 - E$。

(3)确定各属性权重 W 及权重矩阵 $\boldsymbol{B}$:

$$w_j = \frac{d_j}{\sum_{j=1}^{n} d_j} \tag{8}$$

$$\boldsymbol{B} = \begin{bmatrix} w_1 & 0 & \cdots & 0 \\ \vdots & w_2 & \vdots & \vdots \\ 0 & \vdots & w_3 & \cdots \\ 0 & 0 & \cdots & w_4 \end{bmatrix} \tag{9}$$

(4)计算综合得分:

$$Z_i = \sum_{i=1}^{n} \chi_{ij} w_{ij} \tag{10}$$

2.2 灰色关联度法

灰色关联度法和模糊评价法都是考虑多种影响因素的评价方法。其中,模糊评价法不能直接用于评价,需要将相关元素进行特征化处理,这样很容易使信息失真,极大影响评价结果的准确性。而灰色关联度法则相对于模糊评价法在这一方面有所改善,能够提供更加准确、全面的评价结果。

(1)确定决策矩阵。假设 A 是备选方案的集合 $A = \{a_1, a_2, \cdots, a_m\}$,$V$ 是决策矩阵的集合 $V = \{v_1, v_2, \cdots, v_m\}$,记方案 a_i 对指标 v_j 的属性值为 $X_{ij} = (i = 1, 2, \cdots, m; j = 1, 2, \cdots, n)$,则称矩阵 $\boldsymbol{X} = (x_{ij})_{mn}$ 为方案集合对指标集合 V 的决策矩阵。

(2)对归一化处理决策矩阵。在指标体系中,存在效益型指标和成本型指标,要分别采用不同的方法归一化。

①效益型指标 X_{ij} 的量化函数如下:

$$X_{ij} = \frac{x_{ij} - \min(x_j)}{\max(x_j) - \min(x_{ij})} \tag{11}$$

②成本型指标 X_{ij} 的量化函数如下:

$$X_{ij} = \frac{\max(x_j) - x_{ij}}{\max(x_i) - \min(x_{ij})} \tag{12}$$

(3)计算多目标灰色关联度判断矩阵。假设公共自行车站点选址方案为 u_i,在空间 V 中方案 u_i 考虑因素 v_j 时,与相对最佳方案 u_0 的相关性大小采用下式进行度量:

$$r_{ij} = \frac{\min\limits_{i}\min\limits_{j} |x_0(j) - x_j(j)| + \rho \max\limits_{i}\max\limits_{j} |x_0(j) - x_j(j)|}{|x_0(j) - x_i(j)| + \rho \max\limits_{i}\max\limits_{j} |x_0(j) - x_i(j)|} \tag{13}$$

式中:ρ——分辨系数,在 $(0, 1)$ 内取值,通常取 0.5;

r_{ij}——空间 V 中 v_j 方向上方案点 u_i 与相对最佳方案点 u_0 的关联度。

于是,站点选址方案的多目标灰色关联度判断矩阵 $\boldsymbol{R}$ 为:

$$\boldsymbol{R} = (r_{ij})_{nm} = \begin{bmatrix} r_{11} & r_{12} & \cdots & r_{1m} \\ r_{21} & r_{22} & \cdots & r_{2m} \\ \vdots & \vdots & \vdots & \vdots \\ r_{n1} & r_{n2} & \cdots & r_{nm} \end{bmatrix} \tag{14}$$

(4)计算关联度。关联度可按下式计算：

$$r_i = \frac{1}{n}\sum_{i=1}^{r_2} r_{ij} \tag{15}$$

2.3 优化评价模型方法

结合熵权法与灰色关联度的优点，利用熵权法求得的权重和灰色关联度法求得的灰色关联度矩阵计算加权关联度。

$m×n$ 个关联度系数构成规划方案多目标决策的灰色关联度矩阵 $\boldsymbol{R}$ 为：

$$\boldsymbol{R} = \begin{bmatrix} r_{11} & r_{12} & \cdots & r_{1n} \\ r_{21} & r_{22} & \cdots & r_{2n} \\ \vdots & \vdots & \vdots & \vdots \\ r_{m1} & r_{m2} & \cdots & r_{mn} \end{bmatrix} \tag{16}$$

而由熵权法求得 n 个评价指标体系相对于总目标的权值向量为 $\boldsymbol{W} = (w_1, w_2, \cdots, w_n)$，则各规划方案 u_i 与相对最优方案 u_0 的加权关联度 r_i 组成关联度 $\boldsymbol{R}'$：

$$\boldsymbol{R}' = \boldsymbol{R}\boldsymbol{W} = (r_1, r_2, \cdots, r_m) \tag{17}$$

上式中，r_i 越大，说明规划方案越接近最优方案。故当 $r_i = \max(r_1, r_2, r_3, r_4)$ 时，方案 r_i 为规划方案中的最优方案。

3 案例分析

3.1 大珠山站公共自行车站点备选规划方案

经过现场勘察，考虑留存的公共自行车用地、各种土地利用开发和周边道路环境等因素，在地铁站出口附近的 A、B、C、D、E 站点分别设置待选服务点。备选停车站点的位置如图 1 所示，站点方案评价指标基础数据见表 1。

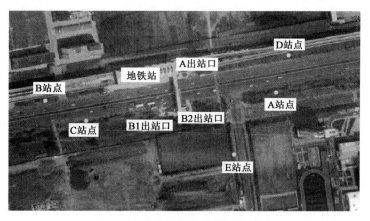

图 1 备选停车站点的位置图

备选停车场方案评价指标基础数据 表 1

类 型	站 点				
	A	B	C	D	E
用地性质	学校	商业	住宅	商业	住宅
规划面积（m²）	220	240	260	110	240
站点规模（辆）	140	150	160	70	150
距离（m）	161	225	111	127	146
土地价格（元）	9000	12000	11000	12000	11000

青岛大珠山地铁站周围用地包括居民区、学校、商业区、工业区、科研、旅游用地等。综合考虑各交通小区出行特点,规划4种公共自行车站点方案,达到最优的换乘效果。换乘自行车站点分布方案见表2。

换乘自行车站点分布方案　　　　表2

方案	站点				
	A	B	C	D	E
方案一	✓			✓	
方案二	✓	✓			
方案三			✓	✓	
方案四				✓	✓

根据定量计算与定性分析结果,初步方案的指标值见表3。

公共自行车服务点布设的影响因素的量化　　　　表3

指标	方案			
	方案一	方案二	方案三	方案四
便利度	144.38	193.621	115.87	139.96
衔接度	0.9	0.8	0.8	0.7
适应性	0.8	0.7	0.9	0.8
建设运营成本(万元)	33.04	48.63	41.85	39.65

3.2 选址方案评价

3.2.1 熵权法评价

熵权评价法中,各个指标所赋予的意义和量化单位不一样,要对其进行规范化处理。本文采用公式(11)、式(12)对矩阵数据规范化处理。

归一化处理后得到初始矩阵:

$$\begin{bmatrix} 0.633312 & 1 & 0.5 & 1 \\ 0 & 0.5 & 0 & 0 \\ 1 & 0.5 & 1 & 0.434894 \\ 0.690161 & 0 & 0.5 & 0.57601 \end{bmatrix}$$

用熵权法确定各个指标权重:$W = (0.2929120220753106, 0.2341212828267062, 0.2341212828267062, 0.238845541227127712)$

综合评分 $Z = (0.788036, 0.128233, 0.725561, 0.434855)$

方案排序:$Z_1 > Z_3 > Z_4 > Z_2$。

3.2.2 灰色关联度法评价

利用灰色关联度法得到灰色关联度矩阵:

$$R = \begin{bmatrix} 0.334099 & 1 & 0.996914 & 0.666323 \\ 0.334831 & 0.996914 & 0.991813 & 0.670936 \\ 0.333678 & 0.996914 & 1 & 0.668922 \\ 0.334034 & 0.991813 & 0.996914 & 0.668271 \end{bmatrix}$$

关联度计算:$r = (0.769227219, 0.375, 0.742359211, 0.49796785)$

方案排序:$r_1 > r_3 > r_4 > r_2$。

3.2.3 优化模型评价与结果分析

使用熵权法对灰色关联度矩阵进行权重赋值,构造加权判断矩阵。

$$R' = RWT = (0.775156272, 0.376077449, 0.734498154, 0.494706359)$$
$$R'_{max} = \max(r'_1, r'_2, r'_3, r'_4) = 0.775156272$$

方案排序：$r'_1 > r'_3 > r'_4 > r'_2$。

利用软件 python 求解可得到以上结果。可以看出，不同模型对方案的评分进行排序相同，即：方案一、方案三、方案四、方案二。熵权法所求的方案间评分差距比较明显，改进的模型方法与灰色关联度法求得结果相似，原因是新模型方法基于灰色关联度矩阵求得结果，但3种模型求解的结果排序是一致的，一定程度上验证了模型设计的准确性。综合考虑各种影响因素指标，选址方案一可以最大限度发挥站点换乘效用，满足居民换乘公共自行车的需求。

4 结 语

(1) 本文首先对自行车站点选址的研究现状进行分析，发现定性定量站点选址规划方法比较匮乏，提出了熵权法、灰色关联度法、基于熵权法赋值权重的灰色关联度选址方案比选方法。

(2) 本文以便利度、衔接性、适应性、建设运营成本构建了换乘公共自行车站点选址评价指标体系，但指标选取比较简单，后续可进一步完善站点选址评价指标。

(3) 本文以青岛市大珠山地铁站为例，建立熵权法赋值权重的灰色关联度评价模型，使用python求解结果，验证了方法的科学性和可行性，为实际工程确定选址规划方案提供了更多选择可能。

参考文献

[1] 陈凯媛. 自行车与城市轨道交通换乘研究[D]. 西安：西安建筑科技大学, 2011.
[2] 何流, 陈大伟, 李旭宏, 等. 城市公共自行车租赁点布局优化模型[J]. 武汉理工大学学报(交通科学与工程版), 2012(01): 129-133.
[3] Lin JR, Yang TH, Chang Y C. A hub location inventory model for bicycle sharing system design: Formulation and solution[J]. Computers & Industrial Engineering, 2013, 65(1): 77-86.
[4] 蒋聪之. 基于轨道交通接驳的公共自行车租赁点规划方法研究[D]. 南京：东南大学, 2015.
[5] 庄轲, 黄田芳. 基于集对分析的轨道交通站自行车换乘停车设施选址研究[J]. 交通节能与环保, 2019, 15(06): 119-123.
[6] 王秋平, 雒妮. 自行车与公共交通换乘停车设施的选址[J]. 交通科技与经济, 2013, 15(06): 14-17.
[7] 高媛. 基于需求预测的轨道交通与公共自行车换乘选址研究[D]. 西安：长安大学, 2017.

基于SWOT模型的温州机场发展策略研究

励 瑾 钟 罡

(南京航空航天大学民航学院)

摘 要 随着民航运输业的快速发展，民航机场在综合交通运输体系中的作用与地位日益凸显。在当前推进"四型机场"建设与新冠肺炎疫情影响的机遇与挑战并存的大背景下，研究民航机场未来的发展策略具有必要性和现实意义。本文以温州机场为研究对象，以SWOT模型为研究方法，通过分析疫情背景下温州机场发展存在的优势、劣势，面临的机遇和威胁，结合温州机场现阶段的发展情况，针对性地提出策略和建议。主要策略包括结合地域优势，明确机场定位；明确发展目标，努力建设成为"四型机场"；把握发展机遇，做好国内国际双循环，适当引进人才，抓准时机融入长三角地区经济社会大发展。

关键词 航空运输 发展策略 SWOT模型 温州机场 长三角地区

基金项目：国家自然科学基金项目(52002177)；南京航空航天大学引进人才科研启动基金项目(YAH19110)。

0 引言

随着综合交通运输枢纽体系的建设发展,建设成人民满意、保障有力、世界前列的交通强国是目前交通建设的主要目标。民航机场作为综合交通运输体系中重要的组成部分,对区域经济的发展具有举足轻重的作用。目前,我国正在深入推进"四型机场"建设(平安机场、绿色机场、智慧机场、人文机场),以更好地实现交通强国的目标。基于目前"四型机场"的建设导向和深入影响,本文以温州机场作为研究对象,采用SWOT模型全方位分析当前温州机场的发展情况,为温州机场未来能更好地融入长三角民航发展提供策略建议。

1 温州机场基本信息

温州龙湾国际机场位于浙江省南部,濒临东海,能够直接辐射周边300多千米范围,具有发展航空运输业得天独厚的区位优势。温州龙湾国际机场现有候机楼总面积12.95万 m^2,能够满足年旅客吞吐量1500万人次的大容量要求。

近年来,温州机场发展势头强劲。2017年11月17日,浙江省机场集团有限公司成立,标志着浙江省民航发展踏上新征程,开启新时代。经过不断的扩建扩容,2018年,温州机场年旅客吞吐量突破千万人次,真正达到了千万级国际性机场的水平。2020年,温州机场为迎合更高容量的需求,总投资约200亿元,规划进行新一轮的改扩建。经过多年的努力,温州机场航班放行正常率现已高于70%,延误率低于30%。随着"四型机场"建设行动纲要的发布,温州机场将计划通过打造"四型机场",推进机场治理现代化。

未来,温州机场发展将持续推进空铁联运和空地联运,实现综合交通运输体系融合发展。温州机场将不断完善机场集疏运体系,重点依托市域铁路S1、S2线及谋划建设的甬台温高速铁路、温福高速铁路,大力发展空铁联运,提升航空综合配套服务能力,建成集空港、轻轨、高速铁路、高速公路等一体的温州大都市区东部综合交通枢纽。

2 基于SWOT模型的温州机场发展现状分析

SWOT分析法是一种有效的战略分析方法,通过研究事物内部的优势(Strengths)和劣势(Weaknesses),结合外部的机遇(Opportunities)和威胁(Threats),系统、全面地进行分析以作出有效的决策,实现效益的最大化。如今它不仅被广泛应用于交通运输规划的研究中,还被广泛应用于评判事物是否具有强大的生命力和远大的发展前景。前人多采用SWOT模型,在机场建设和物流方面综合分析得出了具体的发展策略。因而在研究温州机场发展策略时,运用SWOT分析法能够系统全面地整合温州机场的自身特点,发挥温州机场优势,把握机遇迎接挑战,加快建设成为"四型机场"。

2.1 S——优势

2.1.1 地理位置优越

温州地处中国华东地区、浙江东南部、瓯江下游南岸,东濒东海、南毗福建,是长江三角洲中心区27城之一。温州独特的地理位置凸显了温州机场在浙南闽北大都市经济圈的核心地位。得益于优越的地理位置,温州机场腹地广阔,辐射温州、台州、丽水和宁德4个地区共计约16万 km^2、2000多万人口。同时,通过区域性综合运输枢纽建设,温州将进入上海"4h"经济圈范围,成为连接长三角和珠三角的重要通道和战略要地。因此,深入挖掘温州机场在长三角机场群中的比较优势,因地制宜制定发展策略,对于成为长三角地区重要的现代航空区域枢纽,助力温州打造全国性综合交通枢纽城市具有重要意义。

2.1.2 民营经济发达

温州是中国改革开放先行地、民营经济发祥地。改革开放以来,温州始终是观察中国民营经济发展的一个窗口。截至2017年,民营经济对全市生产总值贡献率超过80%;民营经济税收收入占82.4%。

目前,工业经济作为民营经济的主战场,温州紧紧抓住工业经济高质量发展的关键命题,做大做强制造业。温州企业家们质量为先、精益求精的工匠精神再加上温州本地传承已久的重商文化,成为温州接轨上海融入长三角的独特优势。疫情期间,依托强大的民营资源,企业家们通过航空运输将世界各地温商们捐赠的防疫物资输送到国内,维系省市救援物资的运输和供给。近年来,在发达的民营经济驱动下,企业和个人投资通用航空积极性高涨,市场潜力巨大。目前,温州的通用航空产业布局总用地面积达$13.33km^2$,正在全力打造涉及基础、制造、培训、运营、维护等通航全产业链,温州的航空产业将更上一层楼。

2.2 W——劣势

2.2.1 现代化的管理体系不够完善

由于机场应急预案体系不完善以及监测预警能力滞后,温州机场在面对复杂多变、来势汹汹的突发事件时,不能高效整合现有资源,妥善处理突发事件,严重阻碍了机场的健康发展。自2013年以来,由于天气原因,温州机场曾多次发生大面积航班延误情况,大量旅客滞留,旅客情绪激动,现场秩序混乱。又例如在此次疫情中,暴露温州机场国际航空物流体系不完善、抗风险能力弱、基础设施建设不足等方面的短板,特别是应对突发性安全事件的应急避险能力的不足。因此,为实现"四型机场"建设目标,温州机场在健全管理体系方面仍需努力。

2.2.2 人才缺乏

温州每万人口中大学文化程度人口是浙江的66.6%、全国的73.9%。高达45.5%比例的外来人口中初中及以下文化水平的占88.1%(表1)。外来涌进人口多数为低素质的廉价劳动力,高学历人才还相对缺乏。温州市曾经长期粗放型的发展方式使得产业转型滞后,资金人才外流,导致企业空心化严重,社会发展弱化。温州机场属于华东片区,与宁波、杭州、南京等长三角主要大城市在人才引进方面竞争激烈(表2)。温州能提供的发展机会少,平台小,房价高,基础设施建设差,缺乏有吸引力的人才引进政策,在杭甬两地大力推行的高待遇人才计划前黯然失色。这些因素都导致人才引进困难、留住困难。目前,民航人才匮乏依旧是温州机场加速转型发展的巨大难题。

全国、全省及温州各种受教育程度人口占比(单位:%) 表1

文化程度	全 国	全 省	温 州
具有大学(指大专以上)文化程度	8.7	10.3	7.1
具有高中(含中专)文化程度	13.7	14.9	12.6
具有初中文化程度	37.9	40.4	36.7
具有小学文化程度	26.2	31.7	29.4

杭州、南京、苏州、宁波、温州人才引进资助金额比较 表2

城市	相关人才引进资助金额政策
杭州	年薪资助引进的高端外国专家,资助区间分为:30万(含)~50万元、50万(含)~80万元、80万(含)万元以上,并分别按合同中规定年薪的40%、50%、60%的标准给予资助。以项目资金资助的方式资助引进的国外智力项目,重点项目资助30万元,普通项目资助10万元
南京	江苏省一次性资助不低于100万元的创业创新资金用于资助新引进人才;南京市海外高层次留学人员科研、创业项目资金为20万~50万元;南京市高端人才团队引进资助,每个入选团队给予300万元人才经费资助和1000万元项目经费资助
苏州	江苏省一次性资助不低于100万元的创业创新资金用于资助新引进人才;入选江苏"外专百人计划"专家根据服务时限和工作内容,每人可获得10万~50万元不等的省级专项项目经费支持
宁波	高端创业创新团队资助最高可获2000万元;一次性给予100万元的创新创业经费资助列入市计划的海外人才
温州	引进领军型创新创业团队,给予200万~1000万元科技项目资助,引进"海外工程师"10万~30万元资助;引进培养在温州市工作或创业的A、B、C、D、E类人才,分别给予不少于1200万元、800万元、400万元、200万元、100万元的资助

2.3 O——机遇

2.3.1 地区综合运输体系融合发展

温州目前正在加快综合交通枢纽的建设。在城市内部：加快建设机场综合交通中心和机场第二跑道；力争到2025年建成瑞平苍（南连）高速公路、温义（宣）高速公路、文青高速公路、泰苍高速公路以及普通国省道。通用航空基地也已开工建设。今年，温州市将实现引入或培育4~5家通用航空运营企业，完成温州机场通用航空跑道及其配套设施的建设并投入运营，示范性地利用国际运输机场发展通用机场；启动温州港总体规划修编，优化港区功能定位和布局，统筹有序推进港口、航道、集疏运通道建设，提升陆海双向辐射能力。在城市外部：为支撑区域国际航空枢纽建设，开通沿海高速铁路，建设甬台温高速铁路、温福高速铁路、温武吉铁路，推进甬台温铁路、温福铁路达速，加快形成"521"高速铁路时空圈，提升空港的区域服务能力；综合交通运输体系的融合发展有利于温州机场融入长三角世界级机场群协同发展，成为长三角南部交通门户枢纽、国家重大发展战略的区域性支点。

2.3.2 国家政策支持

早在20世纪80年代末，温州市政府就打算建机场，并且在当年中国民航局拨款2000万元用于温州机场建设。2017年发布的《浙江省民用机场发展"十三五"规划》提出，民航发展将成为浙江完善综合交通体系的新亮点，通过杭州萧山、宁波栎社、温州龙湾3000万级机场和综合交通枢纽，努力构建通达全国、连接全球的航空运输网络，形成"空中1h交通圈"。2018年，温州机场年旅客吞吐量突破千万人次，真正达到了千万级国际性机场的水平。2019年1月，温州市通过了《中共温州市委关于深入贯彻落实省委"四大"建设决策部署加快打造全国性综合交通枢纽的决定》，根据其描绘的蓝图，温州将打造全国重要的区域性国际枢纽机场和华东地区重要的通用航空基地，探索开通至长三角核心城市的"空中巴士"，增强机场国际通达性。2019年全国"两会"上建议，长三角三省一市联合打造"四条走廊"，其中一条就是包含上海在内，由连云港、温州等江浙沿海城市组成的"临海临港战略性新兴产业走廊"。2020年，中国民用航局印发《推进四型机场建设行动纲要》，该文件提出，到2035年将实现标杆机场引领世界机场发展，全面建成安全高效、绿色环保、智慧便捷、和谐美好的"四型机场"。上述国家政策是温州机场发展的重要导向和有力支撑。

2.4 T——威胁

2.4.1 疫情影响

2020年的新冠肺炎疫情使得需求和生产骤降，投资、消费、出口均受明显冲击，短期失业上升和物价上涨。对于行业而言，新冠肺炎疫情对餐饮、旅游、电影、交通运输、教育培训等行业冲击最大。由于防控工作的需要，温州机场缩减了大量的航班，从2019年的日均120~130架次降为航班起降日均70架次左右，并且飞往湖北的航班全部停飞。从非航收入上看，机场内店铺关店、退租，导致机场收入骤减。而在机场成本方面，防护设备物资的投入又进一步加大了成本压力，温州机场收入大幅缩水。此外，因为防疫要求限制流动，人员物资不能及时到位会影响温州机场的建设进度。在如今的后疫情时代，虽然温州机场的每日航班量已恢复到疫情前的90%，但疫情对于温州机场造成的损失依旧不可估量。因此，今后温州机场应消除长期以来重客轻货的观念，一方面要提升综合性机场货运设施能力，另一方面要全面提升航空货运设施使用效能，实现客货并举。

2.4.2 外部运输方式的竞争

在高速铁路方面，杭温高速铁路是长三角高速铁路圈的重要组成部分。预期2021年竣工通车后，从永嘉（温州北）到杭州东的快速列车运行约65min。建设杭温高速铁路，聚焦于省内1h交通圈以及周边的快速流动，有利于进一步发挥浙江的区位优势，连接长三角城市群和海峡西岸经济区，打通苏沪浙闽高速铁路快速通道。此外，温州市交通运输局还规划引入沿海高速铁路（温福高速铁路、温甬高速铁路），形成多向辐射的高速铁路网络，强化与国家运输大通道的衔接，使温州成为联系长三角、海峡西岸经济区甚至珠江三角洲经济区的重要平台。在公路方面，温州已经成为全国45个公路主枢纽城市之一，公路运输四通八达,104 国道和 330 国道贯穿南北,并与周边城市的高速公路网络无缝对接,大大强化了温州区域中心城市的辐射能力。与飞机相比,高速铁路耗时不太长、准点率高且票价相对低廉,所以高速铁路将会分流沿线大量航空旅客客流。高速铁路开通后,航空公司平均下调了 10% 的票价来应对需求减少的冲击。而与高速铁路相比,航空运输聚焦于省际或者国际的快速交通,大多是长途运输和出国出境人们的选择,价格高但普适性低。

3 温州机场发展策略建议

针对温州机场发展之势和加快融入长三角地区的定位要求,根据上述关于温州机场的 SWOT 分析,提出以下几点建议。

3.1 找准发展定位

温州机场定位为区域枢纽机场、长三角世界级机场群重要机场、大型国际机场、通用航空基地机场。为此首先要加快基础设施建设,特别是加快 T3 航站楼和跑道建设,从千万级机场向三千万级机场跃进。其次要利用丰富的民营资源和独特的温州文化,加强与长三角地区主要机场的交流合作,但同时要注重与长三角其他机场展开错位竞争。此外,加快温州航空物流园区建设,承担好建设浙南闽北赣东的区域性航空物流枢纽重要责任。

3.2 明确"四型机场"建设目标

"四型机场"建设是温州机场未来发展的总体目标,温州机场需要以此为导向开展具体建设工作。在建设"平安机场"方面,要加强对突发事件的应急管理,完善好应急管理组织机构和应急预案体系,提高监测预警能力。在建设"绿色机场"方面,加强机场环境绿化,强化内部环境卫生整治,加强机场老旧建筑改造,为旅客提供洁净舒适的出行场区环境和候机环境。在建设"智慧机场"方面,建立噪声监控系统,注意居民区的隔离和降噪;大力推进智慧服务项目,优化无纸化乘机流程,争取机场自助值机旅客占比达到 70% 以上,大幅提高出行效率。在建设"人文机场"方面,打造区域文化的展示窗口,在 T2 航站楼开发温州城市文化景观带,用影像、造型、实物等多种素材展现温州城市文化;大力引进经营温州特产、特色小吃的商家,强化地方特色。

3.3 把握后疫情时代发展契机

在后疫情时代,温州机场发展更要紧抓机遇,勇于变革,积极创新。一是把握住"四型发展"这个根本目标,提高在安全管理、保障能力、运行效率、服务品质和管理水平等方面的服务质量。二是聚焦国内市场。今后一段时间,由于国内外市场结构将深刻改变,航空公司和国际枢纽机场将会把重心转向"扩大国内航空需求"上来。因此,温州机场要迎合国内市场需求,同时也要兼顾国外市场,充分利用国内国际两个市场、两种资源的优势,以国内循环为主体,国内国际双循环相互促进,推动民航业高质量发展。三是筑牢安全基石。加快推进机场安全管理体系建设落地,切实推进新术应用,全面提升温州机场运行安全保障能力,实现安全生产零事故和零事故征候,使温州机场安全管理水平走在全国同类机场前列。

3.4 建立人才管理机制

国家实施"人才强国"战略,把人才作为推进事业发展的关键因素。温州当地缺乏有影响力的大学、研究院所等,人才短缺,难以为温州机场的发展提供持续的动力。为此,要建立合理的人才引进机制,提供相应的人才引进政策,吸引国内外民航领域的高科技人才扎根温州,为温州的民航事业贡献力量。其次,要建立合理的人才考核激励机制,为优秀的民航人才打通晋升通道,落实必要的待遇保障,进一步推动人才吸引,形成人才管理的良性循环。

4 结　语

本文根据温州机场发展的实际情况,采用 SWOT 分析法,围绕如何加快温州机场融入长三角地区,具体分析了温州机场现阶段的优势和劣势,也描述了面临的机遇和挑战,最后提出了加快温州机场融入长三角地区的对策和建议。总体来说,温州机场发展要因地制宜,扬长避短,充分发挥自身优势,结合时代背景把握好"四型机场"的发展目标,抓住后疫情时代的发展契机,加速融入长三角地区,促进温州与长三角地区的协同发展。

参考文献

[1] 关于印发《中国民航四型机场建设行动纲要(2020—2035年)》的通知.[DB/OL]. http://www.caac.gov.cn/XXGK/XXGK/ZCFB/202001/t20200110_200302.html,2020-01-03.

[2] 本刊编辑部.五座机场同月晋级 国内千万级机场大扩容[J].空运商务,2018(12):24-29.

[3] 温州龙湾国际机场.[DB/OL],http://www.wzair.cn,2020.

[4] 苏友灿.艰苦创业,闯出广阔新天地[N].温州日报,2019-08-12(008).

[5] Weihrich Heinz. The SWOT Matrix-a Tool for Situation Analysis[J]. Long Range Planning,1982,115(2).

[6] 王新安,李晓燕,王曦.基于SWOT模型的西咸新区空港新城发展战略探析[J].西安财经学院学报,2014,27(01):82-86.

[7] 孔令伟,柯昌波,付军明,金锋.基于SWOT分析的湖北国际物流核心枢纽综合交通发展策略研究[J].交通工程,2019,19(03):63-65,71.

[8] 邱献红.基于SWOT分析的郑州航空港经济综合试验区航空物流发展研究[J].市场论坛2019(06):16-18.

[9] 夏晶莹.温州机场如何炼成千万级[DB/OL]. http://www.wenzhou.gov.cn/art/2019/1/14/art_1217832_29406238.html,2019-01-14.

[10] 吕淼.探温州,四十年的坚与守[J].浙江经济,2017(18):30-32.

[11] 郭建东.温州发展通用航空产业的思考与建议[J].党政视野,2015(05):14-17.

[12] 戴文斌.地方民航机场突发事件的应急管理[D].长春:长春工业大学,2018.

[13] 冒一峰.中国民航迎来后疫情时代发展机遇[N].中国民航报,2020-06-18(001).

[14] 余薇.长三角地区人才政策比较研究[J].绍兴文理学院学报(自然科学),2013,33(04):33-39.

[15] 秦虹光,蒋勇.温州高质量推进综合交通发展[N].中国交通报,2019-02-15(008).

[16] 叶胜春.温州发展空港物流园区的几点思考[J].党政视野,2016(1):15-18.

[17] 温州市人民代表大会常务委员会关于打造全国性综合交通枢纽工作进展情况报告的审议意见[N].温州日报,2019-09-16(005).

[18] 罗志恒.新冠疫情对经济、资本市场和国家治理的影响及应对[J].金融经济,2020(02):8-15.

[19] 黄伟.机场对新冠肺炎疫情的应对[N].中国航空报,2020-03-17(007).

[20] 夏晶莹.温州将打造"智慧机场".[DB/OL]. http://www.wenzhou.gov.cn/art/2020/1/17/art_1217829_41737248.html,2020-01-17.

[21] 刘春晨."后疫情时代"中小机场的新机与新局[N].中国航空报,2020-07-31(007).

智能网联车换道决策建模研究综述

罗开杰 何赏璐 叶茂

(南京理工大学)

摘 要 换道决策是智能网联车辆运动规划的重要一环。为进一步明确智能网联车换道决策模型

基金项目:江苏省自然科学基金—青年基金项目(项目号BK20180486);中国博士后科学基金第64批面上资助(项目号2018M642257);中央高校基本科研业务费专项资金资助(项目号30920021140)。

的可行研究方法和未来研究方向,本文首先分别对人工驾驶车和智能网联车的换道决策模型研究进行了综述,并提炼出常用模型。其次,本文对比分析了人工驾驶车和智能网联车在换道决策建模上的差异。进而,总结出智能网联车换道决策模型未来研究的5个潜在方向,包括未来混合车流环境数据的需求、混合环境下的建模、模型安全性与计算效率的平衡、建模方法的创新、模型兼顾换道的类型、模型面向城市道路环境的适应性。研究成果有助于未来智能网联车横向运动行为的研究发展。

关键词 智能网联交通系统设施规划 换道决策 研究综述 智能网联车

0 引 言

智能网联车(Connected and Automated Vehicle,CAV)是具备通信和一定自动驾驶功能的智能化汽车。随着人们在出行上对于交通便利、舒适、方便、高效、环境友好的需求不断提升,车辆的智能网联化成为趋势,尤其是智能网联车运动行为的研究已经成为学界和业界的热点方向。总体来说,智能网联车的运动也可细分为横向运动和纵向运动,其中,纵向的跟驰行为已受到了广泛的关注和探索。本文主要从横向的换道行为切入。

从运动过程的角度,换道模型可分为两类:换道决策模型和换道执行模型。对于人工驾驶车辆(Human-driven Vehicle,HV)的换道决策模型,已有广泛的研究,并且已有学者对相关研究开展了综述,如 Z. Zheng 从换道行为的角度出发,综述了换道决策模型和换道影响模型;S. Maerivoet 等从元胞自动机角度出发,综述了基于元胞自动机的换道决策模型;M. Rahman 等和陆建等从换道决策模型的用途方面进行了综述。然而,专门针对 CAV 环境下的换道决策模型综述数量较少。本文从新的角度对 HV 换道决策进行了综述,并以此为鉴,对 CAV 的换道决策建模进行综述,进而对比展望,以期为未来高自动化等级的 CAV 研发提供一定的借鉴。

1 人工驾驶车辆换道决策模型

1.1 既有研究工作总结

HV 换道决策模型的研究相对较早且较为成熟。与以往研究综述相比,本文在梳理了46篇相关文献后,从时间、建模方法、适用场景等角度进行了归纳。其中,部分代表性方法的文献见表1。从表1中可以看出,建模方法由规则模型逐渐向人工智能模型转变;其次,近期的研究会细化换道分类并深化特定换道类型;再次,近70%的模型都需要简化假设,剩余30%中以人工智能模型为主;此外,超过半数文献的主要应用场景为高速公路,其中,可接受间距或加速度是换道决策模型中主要关键因素;约23%的文献考虑了协同/竞争,其中有接近50%考虑到了拥堵;最后,HV 换道决策模型应用于10余个仿真平台,然而人工智能模型较少应用于仿真平台。

1.2 模型比较

所梳理的研究文献大致包括4种类型的换道模型,即规则模型、人工智能模型、离散选择模型和激励模型。本文对这4类模型的基本方法、考虑因素、驾驶员可变性、应用场景、优缺点进行了总结,见表2。

2 智能网联车辆换道决策模型

2.1 既有研究工作总结

借鉴 HV 换道决策模型的研究归纳方法,本文进一步梳理了 CAV 换道决策建模相关的21篇文献。其中,部分代表性建模方法见表3。从表3中可以看出,人工智能模型在 CAV 换道建模中也具有较大比例,但近年来规则模型数量也有所增加。截止目前,高速公路仍是主要的研究应用场景;CAV 换道决策建模的主要考虑因素是车辆的动力学特征,其中,有50%的模型明确考虑了周围车辆的影响,这间接体现了协同/竞争与拥堵因素的影响;此外,近75%的文献的自动化等级为完全自动驾驶;仅1/3的模型进行了实例测试;约30%的文献明确考虑了换道类型,仅14%的文献考虑了 HV 与 CAV 混合环境。

表1 既有部分研究工作汇总表（HV）

文献	发表时间（年）	建模方法	换道类型	简化假设	应用道路	关键因素	其他因素	协同/竞争	考虑拥堵	仿真平台
P. G. Gipps	1986	逻辑结构+数学表达（规则）	—	√	城市道路	最大安全速度	距换道点距离/紧急性/特殊用途车道/重型车辆/前车影响	×	×	MULTSIM
K. I. Ahmed	1999	决策树+概率换道模型（离散选择）	强制/任意	√	高速公路	可接受间距	跨越车道数/距换道点距离/完成合流的延迟/车辆类型	×	√	MITSIM
P. Hidas	2005	逻辑结构+数学表达（规则）	自由/被迫/协同	√	高速公路/城市道路	最小可接受空间间距	车道减少/距换道点距离/排队优势/速度优势	√	√	ARTEMiS
Y. Pei	2006	博弈论+纳什均衡（规则）	被迫	√	城市道路	延迟与求解时间/空间角度	速度/密度高斯分布	√	√	×
T. Toledo 等	2007	短期目标/短期规划+数学表达（规则）	强制/任意	√	高速公路	可接受间距/加速度	因果关系/驾驶员特性/状态依赖	×	√	MITSIMLab
M. Fellendorf 等	2010	逻辑结构+数学表达（规则）	强制/任意	√	高速公路/城市道路	可接受间距	与换道点距离/紧急停车点距离	√	√	VISSIM
D. Sun 和 L. Elefteriadou	2011	焦点小组+同卷量表（离散选择）	强制/任意	√	城市道路	驾驶员特性/换道概率	车辆类型/合流车辆限驰或被跟驰/排队优势/路面状态异常行为	√	√	CORSIM
W. J. Schakel 等	2012	包含松弛和同步的换道模型LMRS（激励模型）	自由/协同/同步	√	高速公路	路径激励/速度激励/车道偏好激励	可接受车头时距减速度	√	√	×

续上表

文献	发表时间(年)	建模方法	换道类型	简化假设	应用道路	关键因素	其他因素	协同/竞争	考虑拥堵	仿真平台
J. Erdmann	2014	逻辑结构+数学表达(规则)	强制/任意	√	城市道路	速度/距离	换道置特点	√	×	SUMO
J. Schlechtriemen 等	2015	随机森林+高斯混合回归(人工智能)	向左换道/向右换道	√	高速公路	与车道线距离/横向速度/	—	×	×	×
J. Nie 等	2016	支持向量机(人工智能)	任意	√	高速公路	相对纵向速度/车间距	—	×	×	×
X. Wan 等	2017	序列决策制定模型(规则)	强制	×	高速公路	车间距/与辅道尽头距离/碰撞最小距离	间距位置/间距差/车型路径规划/驾驶员特性随机项	×	×	×
X. Wang 等	2018	隐马尔可夫模型(人工智能)	强制	×	城市主干道	可用间距/临界间距	与离开点的距离/与队的距离	×	×	×
D. Xie 等	2020	深度信任网络DBN+受限波尔兹曼机RBMs(人工智能)	—	×	高速公路	速度/相对速度/车头间距	—	×	×	×

模型分类比较 表2

模型分类	基本方法	考虑因素	驾驶员可变性	应用场景	优点	缺点
规则模型	基于固定序列的逻辑结构+数学表达	固定的换道目标和换道优势	不考虑对于可接受间距的可变性	基于驾驶员视角且目标车辆的换道原因需要首先被评估时	建模简单/应用场景广泛/决策过程简单/变量少/仿真平台易用	参数校准难/二元决策/使用初级变量/依赖简化假设/环境适应性差
离散选择模型	使用Logit或概率的效用模型	每个阶段可选项的效用值或概率值	考虑驾驶员对时间和决策变量的异质性	在面临二元或多元决策且每一个决策都可以形成Logit或概率模型时	基于概率决策/考虑因素多元	需解概率函数/普适性差/应用道路单一/忽略协同与竞争
人工智能模型	数据驱动的状态转换模型	模糊规则/车辆近期历史数据/不精确感知/决策偏见	通过数据训练捕捉可变性	有大量数据,面临不确定性,无须解释因果关系时	考虑不确定性/方法众多/易于校准/适应性强	未知困难/数据要求高/解释性差
激励模型	基于换道的期望	最大化收益/换道期望水平	通过礼貌因子(MOBIL)或决策变量(LMRS)捕捉可变性	所有考虑因素可以转化到少量效用值或期望值上时	参数少/结构灵活/具有现实性/考虑了驾驶员的异质性	依赖简化假设/在拥堵中的拟合尚不明确/应用道路单一/推广难度大

2.2 与HV换道决策模型的比较

HV和CAV因驾驶特性、驾驶环境等差异,在建模的特点上也存在着诸多不同。综合上述既有研究成果,本文从建模、应用场景、换道类型等方面对CAV和HV的换道建模研究进行了对比:对于建模方法,相较于HV,CAV换道决策建模对规则模型的使用频率更高。对于应用的具体道路,CAV换道决策模型目前更少关注城市道路。对于建模考虑因素,CAV换道决策模型更注重对车辆动力学参数的分析和考虑周边车辆影响,同时弱化各影响因素的主次关系。对于测试试验,虽然CAV较HV增加了感知/通信/定位等功能,但从其实践应用的分布来看,CAV换道决策建模仍需更多实例测试以验证其可靠性;CAV换道决策建模过程中的简化假设要远少于HV;HV模型无须考虑混合环境,CAV模型需要并且已经部分考虑了混合车流环境,但相关研究还需深化。对于换道类型,CAV建模过程较少考虑换道类型,但在一些文献的展望中表示决策过程中考虑换道类型,可以提升模型准确性。

3 结　语

本文认为可从数据、混合环境、安全性与计算效率、新的建模方法、换道类型、应用道路这6个角度开展CAV换道决策模型的后续研究。

(1)数据。①CAV换道决策模型具有数据的依赖性,而现存数据集存在不足(如存在噪声、路段长度过小、缺少驾驶员特征信息等)。因此,需要更大范围的微观轨迹数据集,数据应当包含高解析度的车辆信息和驾驶员特征信息。②需要混合环境数据集。现在的数据集都是较为纯净的人工车辆环境,从中获取的人类驾驶员的换道决策是否为最优决策仍旧存疑,且CAV的驾驶特性区别于HV的驾驶特性。

(2)混合环境。由本文2.1节可知,现存的研究中只有少数研究考虑到混合环境这一因素。混合环境下,HV和CAV的换道决策会互相影响,不同CAV渗透率下的混合环境换道决策模型研究是值得引起关注的。

表3 既有部分研究工作汇总表（CAV）

文献	发表时间(年)	建模方法	换道类型	应用道路	考虑因素	自动化等级	模型应用	混合环境
R. Schubert 等	2010	贝叶斯网络 BN（人工智能）	—	公路	车辆的位置和方向/周围移动目标/车道标线/速度/偏航率/车道曲率、宽度、变形	ADAS	人机界面 HMI	—
S. Ulbrich 等	2013	信号处理网络+部分可观测马尔可夫决策过程 POMDP（人工智能）	—	城市道路	目标车辆与周围对象的相对距离/相对速度/碰撞事件	完全自动驾驶	仿真	×
Y. Du 等	2014	混合逻辑动态系统 MLD（离散选择）	×	高速公路	行程时间/安全/行为约束纵向位置/速度/所在车道	完全或高水平自动驾驶系统	仿真 + IBM CPLEX 求解器	×
H. Tehrani 等	2015	基于离散网格的多类别驾驶场景分类法+机器学习（离散选择+人工智能）	×	公路	周围车辆速度，横向和纵向距离/道路曲率/车辆动力学/时间和距离约束	ADAS	应用于仿真平台 PreScan	√
D. Wang 等	2016	换道可行性准则+模型预测优化控制方法 MPC（规则）	×	—	位置/速度/纵向加速度	ADAS	数值模拟	×
Y. Zhang 等	2020	基于卷积神经网络 CNN + 全连接神经网络 FCNN 的驾驶风格感知换道决策模型 DSA-DLC（人工智能）	√	公路	相对位置/速度/加速度/车头时距	完全自动驾驶	数值模拟	×
Y. Yu 等	2020	动态多人博弈（规则）	×	高速公路	位置/速度/加速度/进攻性	自适应巡航控制	仿真+数值模拟	√

（3）安全性与计算效率。首先，从上述研究中可知，简化假设常存在于建模过程中，这将严重影响驾驶安全。其次，CAV换道决策模型在动态且不确定环境下，求解需有时效性。因而 CAV 换道决策建模时，尤其需要应用于实践时，应当注意模型安全性与计算效率的平衡。

（4）新的建模方法。由上可知，HV 和 CAV 换道决策建模在方法上有较多相似之处，而4类模型都有其特定的应用场景以及难以克服的缺点，这些局限性也会延续到 CAV 换道决策建模过程中。伴随着车辆智能网联化功能的发展，创新换道决策建模方法成为可能。

（5）换道类型。协同换道更易在 CAV 环境中实现，尤其是 CAV 之间的协同换道。考虑到未来不同自动化等级的 CAV 以及 HV 车辆的混合行驶，细化换道类型可能有助于提高换道决策的准确性。

（6）应用道路。城市道路是拥堵、事故发生的聚集地，CAV 技术被认为使未来解决交通效率、安全和环保的重要措施。因此，研究将城市道路作为应用道路的 CAV 换道决策模型势在必行。

参考文献

[1] 李克强,戴一凡,李升波,等.智能网联汽车(ICV)技术的发展现状及趋势[J].汽车安全与节能学报,2017,8(1):1-14.

[2] 李立,徐志刚,赵祥模,等.智能网联汽车运动规划方法研究综述[J].中国公路学报,2019,32(6):20-33.

[3] Zheng Z. Recent Developments and Research Needs in Modeling Lane Changing[J]. Transportation Research Part B:Methodological,2014(60):16-32.

[4] Maerivoet S,Moor B D. Cellular Automata Models of Road Traffic[J]. Physics Reports,2005,419(1):1-64.

[5] Rahman M,Chowdhury M. Review of Microscopic Lane-Changing Models and Future Research Opportunities[J]. IEEE Transactions on Intelligent Transportation Sysiems,2013,14(4):15.

[6] Gipps P G. A Model for the Structure of Lane-changing Decision[J]. Transportation Research Part B Methodological,1986,20(5):403-414.

[7] Ahmed K I. Modeling Drivers' Acceleration and Lane Changing Behavior[D]. Cambridge:Massachusetts Institute of Technology,1999.

[8] Hidas P. Modelling Vehicle Interactions in Microscopic Simulation of Merging and Weaving[J]. Transportation Research Part C,2005,13(1):37-62.

[9] Yu L P,Hui Z X. The Control Mechanism of Lane Changing in Jam Condition[C/OL]//2006 6th World Congress on Intelligent Control and Automation. Dalian,China:IEEE,2006:8655-8658.

[10] Toledo T,Koutsopoulos H N,Ben-akiva M E. Integrated Driving Behavior Modeling[J]. Transportation Research Part C:Emerging Technologies,2007,15(2):96-112.

[11] Fellendorf M,Vortisch P. Microscopic traffic flow simulator VISSIM[M]. Fundamentals of traffic simulation. Springer,New York,NY,2010:63-93.

[12] Sun D,Elefteriadou L. Lane-changing Behavior on Urban Streets:A Focus Group-based Study[J]. Applied Ergonomics,2011,42(5):682-691.

[13] Schakel W J,Knoop V L,Van Arem B. Integrated Lane Change Model with Relaxation and Synchronization[J]. Transportation Research Record:Journal of the Transportation Research Board,2012,2316(1):47-57.

[14] Erdmann J. Lane-changing model in SUMO[J]. Proceedings of the SUMO 2014 modeling mobility with open data,2014(24):77-88.

[15] Schlechtriemen J,Wirthmueller F,Wedel A,et al. When Will It Change the Lane? A Probabilistic Regression Approach for Rarely Occurring Events[C/OL]//2015 IEEE Intelligent Vehicles Symposium (IV). Seoul,South Korea:IEEE,2015:1373-1379.

[16] Jianqiang N, Jian Zhang, Wan X, et al. Modeling of Decision-Making Behavior for Discretionary Lane-Changing Execution[C/OL]//2016 IEEE 19th International Conference on Intelligent Transportation Systems (ITSC). Rio de Janeiro, Brazil: IEEE, 2016: 707-712.

[17] Wan X, Jin P J, Gu H, et al. Modeling Freeway Merging in a Weaving Section as a Sequential Decision-Making Process[J]. Journal of Transportation Engineering, Part A: Systems, 2017, 143(5): 05017002.

[18] Wang X, Zhang Y, Jiao J. A State Dependent Mandatory Lane-Changing Model for Urban Arterials with Hidden Markov Model Method[J]. International Journal of Transportation Science and Technology, 2018, 8(2): 219-230.

[19] Xie D F, Fang Z Z, Jia B, et al. A Data-Driven Lane-Changing Model Based on Deep Learning[J]. Transportation Research Part C: Emerging Technologies, 2019(106): 41-60.

[20] Schubert R, Wanielik G. Empirical Evaluation of a Unified Bayesian Object and Situation Assessment Approach for Lane Change Assistance[C/OL]//2011 14th International IEEE Conference on Intelligent Transportation Systems (ITSC). Washington, DC, USA: IEEE, 2011: 1471-1476.

[21] Schubert R, Schulze K, Wanielik G. Situation Assessment for Automatic Lane-Change Maneuvers[J]. IEEE Transactions on Intelligent Transportation Systems, 2010, 11(3): 607-616.

[22] Uibrich S, Maurer M. Probabilistic online POMDP Decision Making for Lane Changes in Fully Automated Driving[C]//16th International IEEE Conference on Intelligent Transportation Systems (ITSC 2013). Hague, Netherlands: IEEE, 2013: 2063-2067.

[23] Du Y, Wang Y, Chan C-Y. Autonomous Lane-Change Controller via Mixed Logical Dynamical[C/OL]//17th International IEEE Conference on Intelligent Transportation Systems (ITSC). Qingdao, China: IEEE, 2014: 1154-1159.

[24] Tehrani H, Huy DO Q, Egawa M, et al. General Behavior and Motion Model for Automated Lane Change[C/OL]//2015 IEEE Intelligent Vehicles Symposium (IV). Seoul: IEEE, 2015: 1154-1159.

[25] Wang D, Hu M, Wang Y, et al. Model Predictive Control-Based Cooperative Lane Change Strategy for Improving Traffic Flow[J]. Advances in Mechanical Engineering, 2016, 8(2): 1-17.

[26] Zhang Y, Xu Q, Wang J, et al. A Learning-Based Discretionary Lane-Change Decision-Making Model with Driving Style Awareness[J/OL]. ArXiv: 2010.09533 [Cs], 2020.

[27] Yu Y, Liu S, Jin P J, et al. Multi-Player Dynamic Game-Based Automatic Lane-Changing Decision Model under Mixed Autonomous Vehicle and Human-Driven Vehicle Environment[J]. Transportation Research Record: Journal of the Transportation Research Board, 2020, 2674(11): 165-183.

交旅融合背景下农村公路旅游指引标志分级设置方法研究

罗中萍 王卫军 余豪 于思源 金江凯

(华设设计集团股份有限公司)

摘 要 为解决农村公路旅游指引标志设置中普遍存在的区域统筹不平衡、版面设计不完善、指引内容不清晰等问题,本文在旅游风景区分级的基础上,结合农村公路旅游出行特点,研究制定农村公路旅游指引标志分级设置方法,并对不同等级指引标志的版面设计提出了相关要求;最后以南京市江宁区为例,根据其境内旅游景区的分布和农村公路建设情况,对其旅游指引标志的设置和设计进行了具体研究,为农村公路旅游指引标志设置提供了案例参考。

关键词 农村公路 旅游交通 指路标志 江宁区

0 引言

随着美丽乡村建设与交旅融合战略的不断推进,我国旅游产业结构已发生显著变化,相较完善的干线公路旅游指引体系,当前农村公路旅游交通指引标志工程普遍存在统筹不科学、设计不完善、内容不合理等问题,导致出行者难以及时、准确、连续地获得指引信息,严重制约了乡村振兴与交旅融合战略的实施。

目前,国内外对旅游交通标志的研究大多集中在高等级道路和城市内部道路的指引标志上。例如,Neill等提出了驾驶员对交通标志理解率会随时间的变化而变化,并给出了改进方案;刘明林等讨论了入市口、城市内部、景区周边三级交通指引标志系统设置的范围和原则;唐海波提出了旅游标志设置要点,并结合广州市实际情况进行了优化研究;梁科科等从郊区自驾游出行者的需求出发,确定各景区指引范围和各道路节点指引容量。但是,对农村公路旅游交通指引标志的研究还相对较少,对不同类型的指引标志设置还缺乏系统考虑。因此,本文以南京市江宁区为例,通过实地调研,开展农村公路旅游交通指引标志设置方法研究,形成等级匹配、衔接顺畅的农村公路旅游指引标志体系,为江宁区乃至全国农村公路旅游指引标志的设置提供依据和参考。

1 农村公路旅游指路标志存在问题分析

当前农村公路旅游指引标志体系不够完善,缺乏系统考虑,给乡村旅游产业的发展带来了不利影响。各地的农村公路旅游指引标志存在以下共性问题:

(1)农村公路旅游指路标志体系整体发展不平衡,基层部门普遍存在农村公路就是服务本地人的片面思维,导致很多路段指路标志难以满足宏观的诱导需求。

(2)农村公路在实际设置中存在缺乏系统考虑、设置分散、设计不完善、内容不合理、旅游信息过于集中等问题,导致出行者难以获取有效信息。

(3)农村公路交叉口指路标志的设置位置、版面形式、大小和内容的设计方法较为单一、分类不足,导致出行者难以获取及时、准确、连贯的指引信息。

2 旅游指路标志分级设置方法研究

2.1 旅游景区分级

根据旅游资源要素价值、旅游景观市场价值和旅游交通需求指标,将旅游景区划分为一级、二级和三级旅游景区。其中,已评定等级的旅游景区依据其评级归类,未评级的旅游景区根据年接待游客人数、年接待旅游车辆数等因素进行分级。若同一景区有多重等级时,选取高等级进行划定。定级旅游景区、未定级旅游景区分级标准见表1、表2。

定级旅游景区分级标准　　　　　　　　　　　　　　　　　　　表1

一级景区	二级景区	三级景区
国家级旅游度假区	3A级旅游景区	2A级旅游景区
5A、4A级旅游景区	四星级乡村旅游区	三星级乡村旅游区
五星级乡村旅游区	省级工业旅游区	省级特色田园乡村
—	省级房车露营地及自驾游基地	传统旅游特征区

未定级旅游景区分级标准 表2

评价因素	一级景区	二级景区	三级景区
年接待游客数(人次)	100万	50万	20万
年接待旅游车辆数(车次)	10万	5万	2万

2.2 标志分级设置

2.2.1 一级旅游指引标志

一级旅游指引标志是指设置在农村公路与高等级公路(国道、省道、旅游干线等)相交处一定距离范围内的旅游指引标志。一级、二级旅游景区旅游指引标志应包含景区方向标志、旅游景区距离标志、旅游景区方向距离标志3种,三级景区旅游指引标志可根据需求选择设置上述3类指引标志。一般情况下,在通往景区的农村公路与最近高等级道路交叉口处设置旅游景区方向距离标志(旅游景区距离标志),具体设置在交叉口两侧若干距离处。其中,一级景区的指引标志服务范围不超过5km,二级景区不超过3km,三级景区视情况设置。一级旅游指引标志样式如图1所示。

图1 一级旅游指引标志样式

2.2.2 二级旅游指引标志

二级旅游指引标志指设置在旅游支线、县乡道与同类型道路或村道相交处的旅游指引标志。一般情况下,二级旅游指引标志的设置应与道路指路标志相结合,且服务范围不得超过2km。二级旅游指引标志样式如图2所示。

图2 二级旅游指引标志样式

2.2.3 三级旅游指引标志

三级旅游指引标志指设置在村道上或距离景区最近农村公路交叉口处的旅游指引标志。一般情况下,三级旅游指引标志尽量结合现有交通设施进行设置,且服务半径不得超过1km。三级旅游指引标志样式如图3所示。

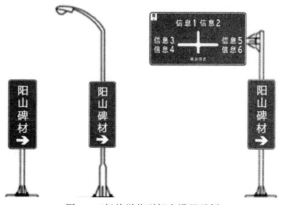

图3 三级旅游指引标志设置示例

3 旅游指引标志具体设置方法——以江宁区为例

3.1 基本情况概述

近年来,江宁区旅游业发展迅速,截至2019年底,江宁区共有1个国家级旅游度假区、1个市级旅游度假区,10个国家级景区,24个省级星级乡村旅游示范村,旅游产业已成为江宁区最具特色的产业之一。目前,全区农村公路已基本实现交通标志全覆盖,但旅游指引标志的设置尚存在一定不足,表现为旅游景区指引标识主要布局在干线公路上、农村公路上的旅游指引标志布局欠缺且不规范,层次性和连续性较差,不能很好地满足游客出行需求。

3.2 景区等级划分

根据定级景区与未定级景区分级原则,江宁区共划分一级景区7个,二级景区26个,三级景区若干,并结合景区特色进行专属图标设计。江宁区旅游景区分级见表3。

江宁区旅游景区分级　　　　表3

一级标准	一级景区	二级标准	二级景区	三级标准	三级景区
国家级旅游度假区	汤山温泉旅游度假区	3A级旅游景区	方山旅游度假区、南山湖旅游度假区等	2A级旅游景区	唐明文化旅游区、雁南飞景区等
5A、4A级旅游景区	阳山碑材、紫清湖、牛首山	四星级乡村旅游区	锁石村、汤山七坊、汤山翠谷现代农业园、汤家家温泉村等	三星级乡村旅游区	豪翔农庄、朱门农家、金和园旅游盆景基地、三界稻花村等
五星级乡村旅游区	大塘金香草谷、石塘人家、黄龙岘茶文化村	省级工业旅游区	海欣丽宁服饰公司、海龙红木艺术馆、禄口皮草小镇等	省级特色田园乡村	观音殿、哪吒河、徐家院、佘村等
—	—	省级房车露营地及自驾基地	华宁温泉房车露营地、大塘金香草谷、云水涧露营地等	传统旅游特征区	东晋博物馆、汤山猿人洞景区、上国安寺等

3.3 指引标志设置

3.3.1 一级景区指路标志分级设置方法——以黄龙岘金陵茶文化旅游村为例

黄龙岘金陵茶文化旅游村为一级景区。从235国道和207县道交叉口到黄龙岘金陵茶文化旅游村入口距离为4.9km,途中有交叉口(路侧搭接道口)21处,交叉口(路侧搭接道口)间离在100~500m。依据2.2节的分级设置方法,共设有一级指引标识3个、二级指引标识4个、三级指引标识1个,具体设置位置如图4所示。

3.3.2 二级景区指路标志分级设置方法——以南山湖旅游度假区为例

南山湖旅游度假区为二级景区。从235国道和188乡道交叉口到南山湖旅游度假区入口距离为2.7km,途中有交叉口(路侧搭接道口)9处,交叉口(路侧搭接道口)间距在80~500m。依据2.2节的分级设置方法,共设有一级指引标识3个、二级指引标识4个、三级指引标识1个,具体设置位置如图5所示。

3.3.3 三级景区指路标志分级设置方法——以上国安寺为例

上国安寺为三级景区。从235国道和02CT交叉口到上国安寺入口距离为2.2km,途中有交叉口(路侧搭接道口)9处,交叉口(路侧搭接道口)间距在50~300米。依据2.2节的分级设置方法,共设有一级指引标识1个、二级指引标识2个、三级指引标识1个,具体设置位置如图6所示。

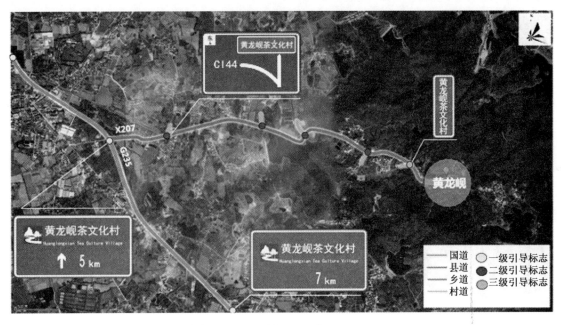

图 4 黄龙岘金陵茶文化旅游村旅游引导标志分级设置策略

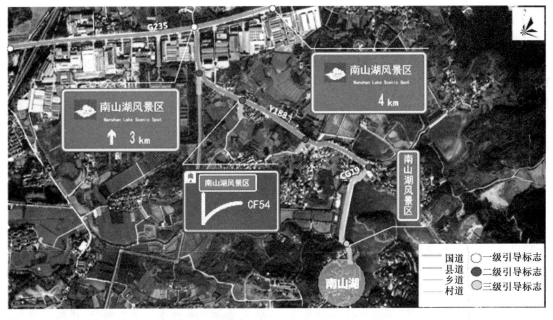

图 5 南山湖旅游度假区旅游引导标志分级设置策略

4 结 语

针对农村公路旅游交通指引标志存在的区域统筹不平衡、版面设计不完善、指引内容不清晰等痛点，本文提出了农村公路旅游指引标志设置原则，构建以高速公路、国省干线、县乡村道为主体的旅游交通三级指引标志分级设置方法，制订了基于景区分级设置的最优指引标志设置方案。本文以江宁区为例，针对 3 种等级的旅游景区，分别制订了详细的标志分级设置方案，弥补了农村公路旅游指引标志设置的空白，满足了多样化、差异化的旅游需求，为全国农村公路旅游指引标志设置提供了一种新思路。后期进行指引标志设置方案评价时，可从标志的识认性、与其他标志的兼容性、版面设计的规范性、方案的经济性等多个维度进行综合评估。

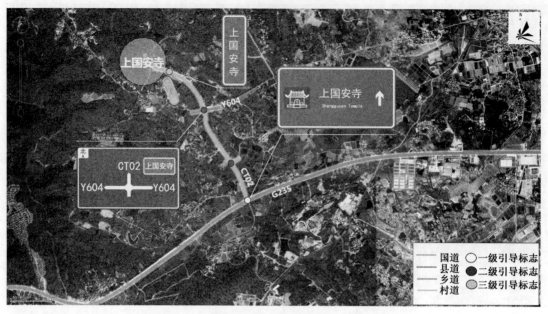

图6 上国安寺旅游引导标志分级设置策略

参考文献

[1] Neill J M, Hurwitz D S, Olsen M J. Alternative Information Signs: Evaluation of Driver Comprehension and Visual Attention[J]. Journal of Transportation Engineering, 2016, 142(1): 04015036.

[2] 刘明林, 申婵. 天津市旅游景区(点)道路交通指引标志设置研究[J]. 华东公路, 2017(05): 114-115.

[3] 唐海波. 广州市珠江两岸旅游景点标志优化研究[J]. 黑龙江交通科技, 2018, 41(08): 207-209.

[4] 梁科科, 关宏志, 韩艳, 等. 郊区自驾游旅游交通指引标志设置研究[J]. 城市交通, 2014, 12(01): 48-54, 47.

[5] 杨敏云. 建设农村公路指路体系工程的分析思考[J]. 江西建材, 2015(01): 159.

[6] 符海荣. 农村公路指路标志设置方法研究[J]. 四川水泥, 2015(05): 243.

[7] 江苏省质量技术监督局. 乡村旅游区等级划分与评定: DB32/T 1666—2016[S]. 苏州: 江苏省质量和标准化研究院, 2016.

[8] 全国旅游标准化技术委员会. 旅游度假区等级划分: GB/T 26358—2010[S]. 北京: 中国标准出版社, 2011.

[9] 中华人民共和国交通运输部. 公路工程技术标准 JTG B01—2014[S]. 北京: 人民交通出版社股份有限公司, 2015.

[10] 全国交通工程设施(公路)标准化技术委员会. 道路交通标志和标线 第2部分: 道路交通标志: GB 5768.2—2009[S]. 北京: 中国标准出版社, 2009.

武汉市城市道路修建性详细规划编制标准研究

焦文敏 刘凯 常四铁 王岳丽

(武汉市规划研究院)

摘 要 为适应城市高质量精细化发展需要,全面提升居民出行环境品质,结合武汉市近些年在道路工程规划、建设、管理等方面的经验及问题,从规划目标、规划范围、规划要素、编制重点等方面开展城市道路修建性详细规划编制标准研究,为促进武汉市城市道路建设的人本化、品质化、精细化转型升级提供技术标准。

关键词 城市道路 修建性详细规划 编制标准

0 引 言

城市道路修建性详细规划(以下简称道路修规)是武汉市城市道路建设前期设计的重要环节,对于规划意图的充分落实、空间资源的统筹利用具有积极作用。随着城市发展由高速度、粗放型向高质量、精细化的转变,武汉市在城市发展观念、建设理念上进行了思路调整,将道路品质提升作为打造宜居城市的重要抓手之一,相继开展了东湖绿道、中山大道、沿江大道等一系列人本化改造实践,积极探索城市道路高品质建设的实施路径。通过制定新时期道路修规的精细化编制标准,为全面提升居民出行环境品质提供技术支撑。

1 武汉市道路修规现状问题

"十一五"以来,武汉市城市道路建设取得了巨大成就,为国家中心城市的建设夯实了基础,但是,机动车爆发式增长带来的交通拥堵、环境污染等问题也给居民生活出行带来了压力和挑战,传统的道路修规存在着路权划分重车行轻慢行等问题,已经无法适应武汉市从功能构建向品质发展的转型要求。

1.1 路权划分重车行轻慢行

城市道路的根本目的是实现人和物的移动。传统的道路规划设计更多关注以小汽车为主的机动车通行能力及行驶速度的最大化,路权划分上首要保证机动车的通行空间,导致行人、非机动车、公交等道路其他服务对象的出行环境不佳,出行效率低下,舒适度不高。

1.2 街道空间整体性不强

完整街道界面由传统的道路红线空间、沿街建筑退让及建筑立面共同构成。传统道路规划仅限于道路红线内,道路红线内慢行空间与建筑前区空间存在统筹利用不足、建设风格及建设标准不一致等问题,街道空间的整体性较差。

1.3 规划要求的刚性和弹性不明确

道路工程在纵向技术流程上存在规划、设计、建设等诸多环节,在横向管理上涉及建设、交管、园林、城管等众多部门职责。因各环节、各部门职责缺少清晰界定,当前道路修规经常出现技术对接复杂、方案落地不彻底、部门协调难等问题,最终导致规划方案"走样"。

2 国内外研究现状

自21世纪以来,世界各地相继开展了街道设计导则的编制工作,重新定义了街道设计的内涵和重点,总体上朝着以人为本、慢行友好的方向发展。例如英国伦敦以分工权属为纲组织导则,规范街道的全周期管理流程、标准化设计材料和施工做法,确保规划设计意图的全面实现;美国纽约利用工具箱的方式详细说明街道改造措施的设计要点及可持续发展指引,通过形象的图示及充实的附录为规划设计、行政审批人员提供便利;阿联酋阿布扎比在革新传统道路分级的基础上,对街道断面进行模块化设计,同时强化街道的后建设阶段即街道的运营维护要求。这些导则在发展目标与理念、服务功能与对象、设计范围与内容等多个方面对街道设计进行了变革,有效指导了街道空间的人性化改造实践。

由于部分街道设计导则以理念输出和设计指引为主,约束性和法定性不强,不利于相关要求在后续的建设实施阶段的落实,因此,许多城市正在着手将街道设计导则提出的概念与要求转化为法定的地方规章或设计标准。武汉市基于前期编制完成的《武汉市街道全要素规划设计导则》,在申报街道全要素规划设计地方标准的同时,充分利用本市城市道路编制修建性详细规划的优势,作为落实全要素理念的有效实施路径。

3 研究目标

3.1 落实全要素规划要求

《武汉市街道全要素规划设计导则》将街道空间规划设计划分为慢行空间、车行空间、交叉口空间、活动空间、绿化空间及街道设施6个大类、40个小类要素,并分别提出了设置要求及设计指引。本次研究将道路修规作为街道建设改造的有力抓手,对全要素要求进行深化和具化。

3.2 精准服务规划审批

道路工程设计实施阶段因资金、用地、环保等不可预见因素,工程实施方案相对规划方案经常出现变化,规划阶段无法也不宜"包揽"解决所有问题。为提高规划审批效率与管理弹性,道路修规精细化既要更好地落实规划愿景,也要更好地适应"放管服"改革要求。

3.3 强化空间资源统筹

道路不仅承担着交通运输功能,还兼有市政廊道及活动空间功能,涉及的要素繁多且复杂。道路修规作为建设项目最前期的技术文件,需要统筹好各个交通方式之间的空间资源分配,协调好道路红线内外空间的关系,处理好地面交通与地下设施的关系,衔接好近期建设与远期预留改造的要求。

4 道路修规编制要求

4.1 规划要素

道路修规在武汉城建项目周期中起着落实规划愿景、确定总体方案、指导工程建设的重要作用,为实现本次研究的规划目标,通过剖析城市道路规划建设管理全生命周期过程中存在的痛点与难点,按照全流程、全空间、全要素的原则,将道路修规的基础规划要素划分为标准类、空间类以及设施类,见表1。

道路修规基础规划要素　　　　　表1

标 准 类	空 间 类	设 施 类
街道功能 道路等级 设计车速 排水分区 排水体制 排水标准	建筑前区 慢行道 车行道 分隔带/绿化带 设施带 交叉口 道路红线	公交站点 出租汽车停靠点 地下管线 箱柜集并 多杆合一

4.2 编制重点

4.2.1 拓展编制范围

为了实现街道空间的整体塑造,道路修规编制范围由传统的两根道路红线拓展至两侧建筑边到建筑边(或围墙),同时包含道路用地以及建筑前区。本次研究根据两侧用地改造情况的不同对建筑前区提出了不同的规划要求:当道路沿线用地属于静区用地时,规划结合现状建筑轮廓划定建筑前区边界,并与路内空间进行一体化设计;当道路沿线用地属于动区用地时,结合道路等级及街道功能明确建筑前区的竖向、铺装、景观等要求,需要建筑前区补充道路空间的,一并纳入后续的地块出让或方案审批予以落实。

4.2.2 突出以人为本

慢行交通是居民出行过程中不可或缺的组成部分,路权划分上应充分保证其通行空间。本次研究除了关注标准路段慢行交通的空间分配,对于人行天桥、公交站点、交叉口等非标准路段也进行了重点考虑,以保障道路全线慢行道的通行空间。

此外,城市道路的无障碍水平也是体现人文关怀、衡量城市文明程度的重要指标,能否满足特殊群体(残疾人、老年人等行动不便者)的出行要求是检验城市道路是否合格的实践标准之一。为了保障特殊群体平等参与社会生活的权利,本次研究还通过细化路缘石坡道建设要求、地块出入口慢行抬高等手段实现城市道路的无障碍化,如图1、图2所示。

图1　缘石坡道规划示意图

图2　地块出入口慢行抬高规划示意图

4.2.3　明晰刚性、弹性要求

由于传统的道路修规没有对规划要素的控制要求进行明确区分,导致下步设计和实施阶段对规划意图的理解出现分歧。研究结合当前审批"放管服"改革的要求,按照指导性和控制性细化每个规划要素的控制要求。以人行天桥为例,道路修规会对人行天桥的位置、宽度、梯坡道设置、无障碍电梯设置、桥下最小净空等控制要求进行表达(图3),并按照控制性和指导性区分,其中下步设计应严格落实的包括:过街设施的设置(有无)、坡道的设置、无障碍设施的设置、天桥桥下最小净空、地面道路慢行道最小净宽、慢行道连续性等要求;下步设计可调整的包括:过街设施的位置、宽度、坡道坡度,可结合后续市城建局等部门的审查意见相应调整。

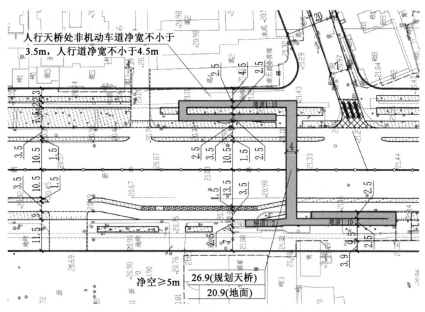
图3　人行天桥表达示意图(尺寸单位:m)

5　结　　语

规范化、高标准的道路修规,将促进道路交通、市政、景观功能的全面提升。研究在借鉴国内外先进城市道路精细化改造实践经验的基础上,通过对前期开展的三阳路、新华路等精细化修规编制的探索和总结,梳理和深化了道路修规的编制要素和控制要求,为全要素从理念到落地提供了统一技术标准。

虽然本次研究从街道整体性塑造的角度提出了交通与用地融合的要求，期望道路慢行空间与地块建筑前区在建设标准、绿化景观、风貌特色等多个方面进行统一，但后续还需要从实施机制方面展开深入研究，以确保完整街道理念的落地。

参考文献

[1] 上海市规划和国土资源管理局,上海市交通委员会,上海市城市规划设计研究院.上海市街道设计导则[M].上海:同济大学出版社,2016.

[2] 姜洋,王悦,解建华等.回归以人为本的街道:世界城市街道设计导则最新发展动态及对中国城市的启示[J].国际城市规划,2012,27(05):65-72.

[3] Transport for London, Streetscape Guidance 2009: A Guide to Better London Streets[R]. London: Transport for London, 2009.

[4] New York City Department of Transportation. Street Design Manual[R]. New York: New York City Department of Transportation, 2009.

[5] Abu Dhabi Urban Planning Council. Abu Dhabi Urban Street Design Manual[R]. Abu Dhabi: Abu Dhabi Urban Planning Council, 2009.

[6] 李雯,兰潇.城市最具潜力的公共空间再开发——世界典型街道设计手册综述[J].城市交通,2014,12(02):10-17.

[7] 武汉市自然资源和规划局.武汉市街道全要素规划设计导则[R].武汉:武汉市自然资源和规划局,2019.

[8] 广州市住房和城乡建设委员会,广州市城市规划勘测设计研究院.广州市城市道路全要素设计手册[M].广州:中国建筑工业出版社,2017.

城市副中心核心区交通品质提升研究及应用

谭振霞　潘晓玮

（悉地（苏州）勘察设计顾问有限公司）

摘要　城市交通的问题越发复杂,常发性的交通拥堵、交通事故、慢行不友好、设施不完善等,给交通出行以及城市环境品质均带来负面影响。本文从交叉口精准设计、公交站优化、慢行环境提升、交通设施提升4个维度给出相关研究策略,并以城市副中心的核心区为案例进行深入剖析,验证方法可行性。本研究能为交通品质提升提供重要的技术参考。

关键词　交通品质　精准设计　公共交通　慢行环境

0 引　言

交通是城市发展的命脉,交通品质的好坏对一个城市的整体面貌起着至关重要的作用。目前各城市副中心发展迅速,随着地块不断开发、交通需求不断提高,交通问题越发凸显,如交通拥堵、交通安全得不到保障、道路出现破损、慢行空间不友好等,交通品质逐渐下降,这与城市副中心综合环境提升相违背。

近些年,许多城市开始对道路交通进行整治,在一定程度上提升了道路交通的通行效率,但以交通效率为第一要素考虑不是很周全,进而衍生很多其他交通问题。而交通品质提升不仅仅注重效率提升,更多的是一种综合品质的提升,对道路空间与时间资料的综合利用,以及对环境的提升等。因此,交通品质提升不仅让城市交通更安全、畅通和友好,同时也可增强城市副中心在城市中的综合竞争力。

总结下来,目前城市核心区道路交通品质存在问题有以下4个:

(1)道路交通为多头管理和养护,缺乏统一的规划与设计;
(2)道路品质与城市发展阶段不相匹配;
(3)道路安全设施不足,交通事故凸显;
(4)道路交通设施技术较为传统,设施及信息冗余较多。

1 交通品质提升策略

1.1 提升目标

通过对城市道路交通品质提升,来改善城市副中心核心区整体交通安全,最终达到提升核心区整体的出行环境。

1.2 交叉口精准设计

1.2.1 交叉口空间资源优化

通过交叉口空间资源的精细化设计,充分提高交叉口的通行效率,提高交叉口的通行能力,消除节点瓶颈。

1.2.2 交叉口时间优化设计

(1)单点信号控制。根据交叉口的流量以及流量的变化特征,进行单点交叉口信号控制方案优化,包括如下内容:交叉口信号相位、相序优化;信号周期、绿信比优化;多时段信号控制方案优化;行人过街信号控制方案优化。同时从时空结合的角度,对道路空间资源与时间资源进行合理的组合,采取信号控制组合方案,即对车道功能布置与绿灯时间分配的有效结合,以实现提高通行能力、减小车辆延误的目的。

(2)绿波协调控制。根据道路网络和交通流运行特征,对干线交叉口群进行信号协调控制方案的优化设计,包括如下内容:信号协调控制范围分析;交叉口共同周期优化。

1.3 公交站点优化技术

1.3.1 公交停靠站间距

根据不同区域,设置不同公交停靠站间距。在许多城市轨道逐渐成网的背景下,公交停靠站应加大覆盖服务面积,以300m半径计算,不应小于城市用地面积的80%;以500m半径计算,不应小于95%。

1.3.2 交叉口换乘距离的要求

公交在交叉口的换乘距离要求为:同向换乘距离应不大于50m,异向换乘距离不应大于150m。在道路平面交叉口和立体交叉口上设置的车站,任何方向换乘不得大于250m。

1.3.3 港湾式公交停靠站设置策略

"Z"形路段公交停靠站。公交停靠站"Z"形布置,"尾尾相接",并且设置为港湾式,消除公交停靠站处的双重瓶颈。

"Z"形路段行人过街。行人过街横道设置在公交停靠站的尾部,保证行人过街视距不受公交停靠的影响,行人过街横道设置为"Z"形,即在中分带设置与对向来车方向形成锐角的迂回区,保证行人过街安全。

"Z"形公交停靠站设计模式如图1所示。

公交停靠站"尾尾相接",减速段开始前预留标准路段长度约10m,保证可设置行人过街横道;行人过街横道应在标准段处设置,中间若是中分带,可利用中分带宽度设置二次过街待行区,若为双黄线,可利用设置隔离栏增设处至少1.5m宽的二次过街待行区,确保行人过街安全。

1.4 慢行品质提升

1.4.1 慢行空间品质提升

慢行空间环境提升主要从慢行连通性、空间尺度、平整度以及环境友好等方面进行研究。首先是慢行连通性,特别是行人空间的连通性,在路网层面、铺装色彩等方面要连续和统一;空间尺度层面主要研究慢行宽度与需求关系,商务区与住宅区等人行道宽度需要保证3.5m以上的慢行宽度等;平整度层面需要报名非机动车道骑行环境,特别是在人非共板的区域,纵坡的平顺性是关键;环境友好层面需要慢行周边的空间友好,包括慢行区域的口袋公园等,打造高水平的交通性与生活性兼顾的慢行空间环境。

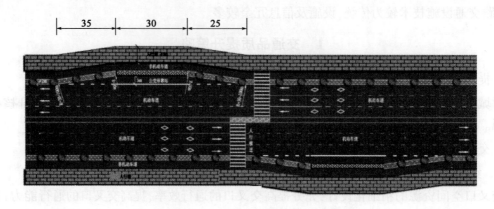

图1 "Z"形公交停靠站设计模式(尺寸单位:cm)

1.4.2 行人过街与掉头等一体化设计

支路缺乏、路网连通性差,是导致机动车掉头的首要原因。机动车掉头增加了车流与人流交织。将机动车掉头与公交停靠站和人行过街设施结合的一体化设计,通过在路段和交叉口的信号协调与空间优化,可有效减少机动车与人流的交织,提高通行效率和交通安全。

1.5 交通设施提升

交通设施包括交通语言设计、交通安全设施设计等。交通语言重点需要对不合理的标识以及信息冗余的标识进行整治提升,保证交通语言的视任性和正确性;交通安全设施是提升道路安全重要的因素,包括必要的隔离设施、交叉口安全视距三角形等。

2 案例分析

2.1 工程概括

案例位于苏州市相城区中央商贸区,研究区域北起水厂街,南到阳澄湖路,西至广济北路,东至元和塘,道路面积约160万 m^2。由于中心商贸区周边商业地产的开发,吸引了部分外来交通,加之来自区域及周边住宅及大型商圈的交通影响,中心商贸区内交通组成日益复杂,公共交通出行量剧增。为了满足商贸区周边道路通行需求,提高交通运行环境及提升道路交通品质,解决公共交通出行问题,拟对区域内公交站点进行优化和完善、交叉口进行渠化设计,同时结合现状提出合理的断头路畅通建议等。

2.2 问题诊断

2.2.1 交叉口问题

道路交叉口出现常发性交通拥堵、路口未渠化、交叉口过大等情况;路段开口不合理、不规范;部分路面损坏较为严重;慢行出现环境不友好等。通过现状调研,交叉口渠化共计6个,主要集中在春申湖路和阳澄湖路上;路段开口问题共计9处,主要集中在御窑路、沈思港路和玉成路等;路面损坏共计4处,主要集中在文灵路、人民路和御窑路上。现状节点问题分布如图2所示。

2.2.2 公交问题

根据调查,现状研究范围内共40对公交站点,其中28对存在问题,现状5对公交站点位于黄蠡路及在建御窑路上,不列入本次改造范围,另外现状7对公交站点已经建设完善,无须改造。对现状的28对公交站点进行细分,得出未进行港湾式渠化的公交站共4对,候车亭未完善的共19对,临时路边设置的站台共 5 对,如图 3 所示。

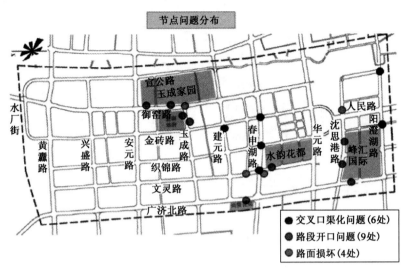

图 2　现状节点问题分布图

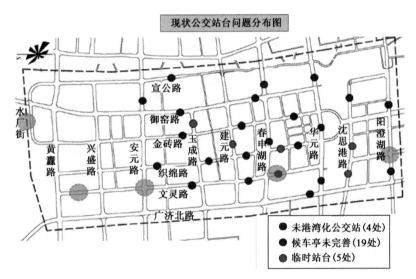

图 3　现状存在问题公交站台分布图

2.2.3　慢行问题

慢行问题主要集中在人行道路面损坏以及人行道铺装与周边环境的不协调等。通过对研究范围内调研可知,现状慢行问题主要有 8 处,现状人行道损坏共 7 处,主要分布在御窑路和文灵路上;人行道铺装问题 1 处,位于文灵路上,如图 4 所示。

2.2.4　交通设施问题

通过对现状研究范围内的交通安全设施调查,交通安全设施主要存在 24 处问题,其中指路标志缺失共计 9 个点位、禁令标志缺失共计 6 处、指路标志信息不合理共计 6 处、道路标线不合理共计 2 处、路口信号灯缺失共计 1 处,如图 5 所示。

2.3　改善方案

针对现状存在的交通问题,利用改善策略从以下 5 个方面对道路交通环境进行改善。①交叉口优化设计:增加交叉口通行能力,改善交叉口运行环境;②公交港湾式渠化:公交站点移位及港湾,减少对道路交通影响;③慢行交通设计:人行道铺装改造;④交安设施设计:完善道路交通标志标线等。

图4 现状慢行问题分布图

图5 现状设施问题分布图

2.3.1 交叉口优化方案

对春申湖路沿线主要交叉口进行渠化设计。本文选取相城区春申湖路—织锦路为例，交叉口渠化方案为：压缩分隔带宽度，渠化后交叉口车道布置为4进3出，进口道车道宽3.25m，出口道车道宽3.5m；交叉口进口道展宽段长度不小于70m，渐变段为30m；公交站结合交叉口渠化一体设计，站台位于交叉口出口道时，距交叉口不小于50m。给出交叉口的改善方案如图6所示。

2.3.2 公交改善方案

本文选取阳澄湖路公交站为例。压缩非机动车道、侧分带及车行道宽度，分隔带不小于2m，车道宽为3.25m，设计方案为：人行道不改造；侧分带由2.5m改造为2m；非机动车道由5m改为3m；车行道15m调整为17.5m，如图7所示。

2.3.3 慢行提升方案

慢行改善方案主要是针对人行道破损的修复，对人行道铺装进行详细设计。区域内人行道主要采用混凝土预制砖及花岗岩路面砖；现状水泥混凝土路面砖铺装样式应与周边路面保持一致；对区域内7处人行道损坏路面进行修复；对1处出入口附近人行道铺装与周边环境不协调进行改造。

2.3.4 交通安全设施提升

以兴旺路与御窑路交叉口为例，对交叉口标志标线进行详细设计，设计方案如下：兴旺路路口采用右进右出交通组织，增加导流标线，禁令、诱导等标志，规范路口车辆行驶轨迹。详细设计如图8所示。

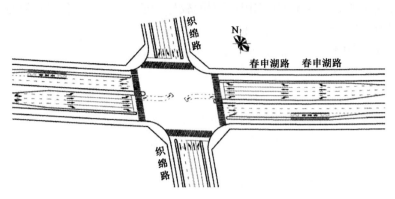

图 6 织锦路~春申湖路交叉口改善方案图

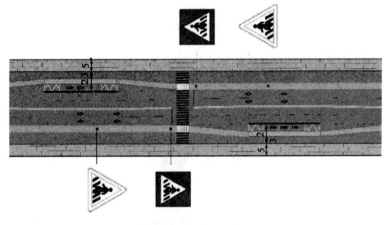

图 7 阳澄湖路公交港湾式改造图

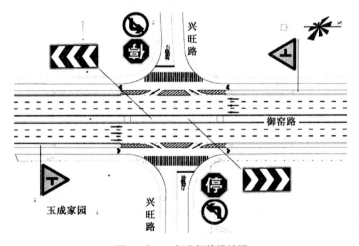

图 8 交叉口标志标线设计图

2.4 效果评价

目前现场已实施完成,核心区内交通通行能力提高约 28.5%,交通安全事故数量相比以往下降 22%。增加了交通安全设施和警示标识后,部分道路的通行速度也有较大提升,整体交通品质和慢行舒适度大大提高。

3 结 语

城市副中心核心区交通比较复杂,交通品质提升需要考虑众多方面。本文重点从 4 个维度对其方法论进行阐述,并在苏州市相城区的案例应用中得到的较好的验证,目前案例已改造完成,通行效率、交通安全和慢行环境等均得到了较大幅度的提升。

交通品质提升策略适用性较好,能提升核心区综合环境面貌,其方法论也能为规划设计师和交通学者提供参考,具有一定的借鉴意义。

参考文献

[1] 杨晓光.城市道路交通设计指南[M].北京:人民交通出版社,2003.

[2] 裘玉龙,孙明哲,董向辉.城市主干路交叉口信号协调控制系统设计研究[J].交通运输工程与信息学报,2004(2):41-46.

[3] 中华人民共和国住房和城乡建设部.城市道路公共交通站、场、厂工程设计规范:CJJ/T 15—2011[S].北京:中国建筑工业出版社,2012.

[4] 中华人民共和国住房和城乡建设部.城市道路交叉口设计规程:CJJ 152—2010[S].北京:中国建筑工业出版社,2011.

[5] 中华人民共和国住房和城乡建设部.城市道路交叉口规划规范:GB 50647—2011[S].北京:中国计划出版社,2012.

基于移位左转的直行非机动车道优化设计方法

杨 杰 邵海鹏

(长安大学运输工程学院)

摘 要 为了提升移位左转交叉口的通行效率,消除主信号处直行非机动车与本方向右转机动车、对向左转机动车之间的冲突,本文提出一种改进的直行非机动车道设置方法。建立优化后的移位左转交叉口各空间参数的计算模型,并分析主、预信号的协调控制关系,考虑相位相序、周期时长及绿灯时长等约束条件,建立信号控制的线性规划优化模型。以最大通过交通量和车均延误为评价指标,借助在济源市收集的数据,使用VISSIM仿真软件验证了本优化设计方法的效果。研究结果表明:该设计方法能够在确保非机动车通行安全的基础上,有效提升机动车通行效率,在高峰时段,优化后的交叉口车均延误相比常规交叉口和传统移位左转设计分别降低28.1%和15.7%。

关键词 交通工程 交通设计 线性规划 移位左转交叉口 直行非机动车

0 引 言

城市道路网络由城市道路和交叉口共同组成,其中交叉口是城市路网的瓶颈节点[1]。非常规交叉口设计正获得越来越多的关注,如"U"形回转、串联交叉口、移位左转等[2]。其中,移位左转能够有效解决交叉口左转和直行流量都很大情况下的冲突问题[3]。

移位左转交叉口最早于1987年由Mier[4]提出。Jagannathan[5]从通行效率方面对比分析了移位左转交叉口与传统交叉口。Zhao[6]等人对移位左转车道进行了综合优化。Chang[7]研究了移位左转交叉口的车辆移动特性。Wu[8]分析建立了左转车延误计算模型。Zhao[9]等人对左转非机动车道进行了优化设计,消除了主信号处左转非机动车和直行机动车的冲突。Chang[10]等人建立了具有普遍适应性的连续流交叉口信号配时优化模型及最优相位差模型。

以Zhao[9]提出的左转非机动车道设计方案为左转非机动车的研究假设,本文不再考虑左转非机动车的通行情况,而提出一种直行非机动车过街优化设计方法,以消除直行非机动车与本方向右转机动车、对向左转机动车的冲突。

1 交通组织优化设计

1.1 常规设计与交通冲突分析

常见的移位左转交叉口设计如图 1 所示。

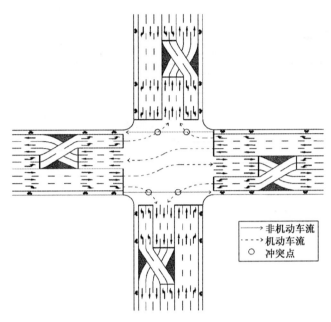

图 1　常规移位左转交叉口示意图

1.2 空间优化设计

1.2.1 路径优化

改进的移位左转交叉口示意图如图 2 所示。

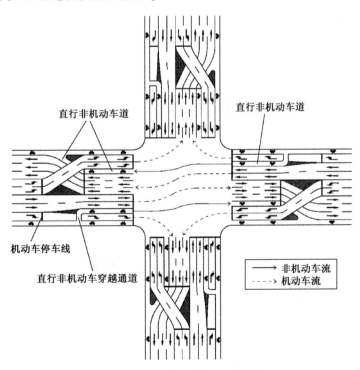

图 2　改进的移位左转交叉口示意图

改善之前直行非机动车会造成4个冲突点,优化后,4个冲突点全部消除。

1.2.2 设计参数

根据图3和图4确定空间参数。

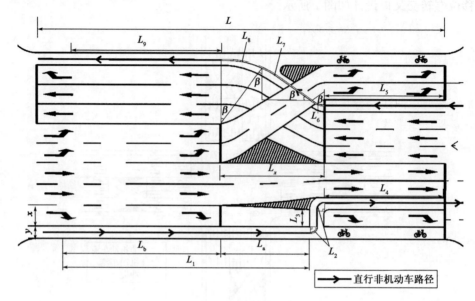

图3 交叉口西进口道参数计算示意图

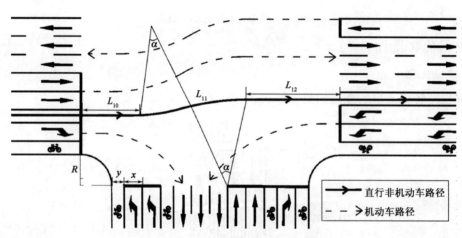

图4 交叉口内部参数计算示意图

(1) 储存段长度 L_1:

$$L_1 = L_a + L_b$$
$$L_1 = \left[\left(\frac{7}{2}x + y\right)\sin\beta + 3x - \frac{y}{2}\right] + \frac{Q_1 k h_s}{mn} \tag{1}$$

式中:L_a——右转机动车预停车线与直行非机动车穿越通道之间的距离,m;

L_b——移位左转机动车储存段长度,m;

x——储存段机动车道宽度,m;

y——非机动车道宽度,m;

β——移位左转机动车转弯角度;

Q_1——移位左转机动车交通量,pcu/h;

k——移位左转车辆到达的不均匀系数;

h_s——移位左转车辆排队车头间距,m/pcu;

m——移位左转弯车道数;

n——单位小时周期个数。

(2) 穿越通道长度:

$$\left. \begin{array}{l} L_2 = \dfrac{\pi y}{2} \\ L_3 = x - \dfrac{y}{3} \end{array} \right\} \tag{2}$$

式中:L_2——穿越通道曲线部分长度,m;

L_3——穿越通道直线段部分长度,m。

(3) 移位左转车道长度 L_5:

$$L_4 = L_5 = \frac{3600 Q_1 h_s}{mns} \tag{3}$$

式中:L_4——非机动车二次等待区长度,m;

L_5——移位左转机动车道长度,m;

s——移位左转车道饱和流率。

(4) 离开交叉口变道段长度:

$$\left. \begin{array}{l} L_6 = \dfrac{\pi(x+y)\beta}{360} \\ L_7 = 3x + \dfrac{y}{2} \\ L_8 = \dfrac{\pi(6x+y)\beta}{360} \end{array} \right\} \tag{4}$$

式中:L_6、L_8——直行非机动车离开交叉口变道段曲线部分长度,m;

L_7——直行非机动车离开交叉口变道段直线部分长度,m。

(5) 驶离路段长度 L_9:

$$L_9 = L_b = \frac{Q_1 k h_s}{mn} \tag{5}$$

式中:L_9——直行非机动车驶离路段长度,m。

(6) 路段长度 L:

$$L \geqslant L_1 + L_4 + y \tag{6}$$

式中:L——两交叉口之间路段长度,m。

(7) 交叉口内部路径长度:

$$\left. \begin{array}{l} L_{10} = R + x + y \\ L_{11} = \dfrac{\alpha \sqrt{\left(R + 2x + \dfrac{3y}{2}\right)^2 + \left(x - \dfrac{y}{3}\right)^2}}{180} \\ L_{12} = R + 2x + \dfrac{4y}{3} \end{array} \right\} \tag{7}$$

式中:L_{10}、L_{12}——直行非机动车在交叉口内部行驶路径的直线段长度,m;

L_{11}——直行非机动车在交叉口内部行驶路径的曲线段长度,m;

R——交叉口转弯半径,m;

α——直行非机动车在交叉口内部变道的转弯角度。

2 信号控制优化设计

2.1 相位相序设定

主、预信号设置如图 5 所示。

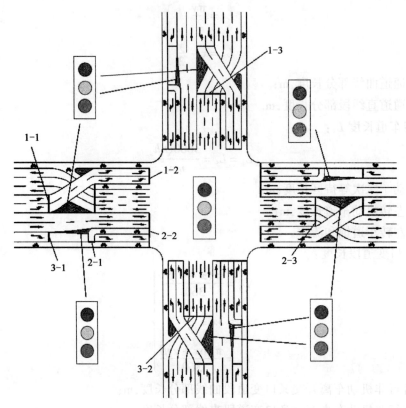

图 5 交叉口主、预信号设置示意图

如图 6 所示,本文设置两个主信号相位 EW 和 SN,分别控制东西方向车流和南北方向车流。

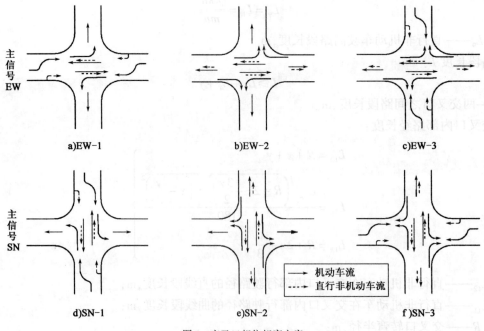

图 6 交叉口相位相序方案

优化的信号配时方案设计如图7所示。其中,g_1为第一主相位 EW 的绿灯时间,s;g_2为第二主相位 SN 的绿灯时间,s;g_{11}为东西方向预信号机动车左转、非机动车移位直行相位绿灯时间,s;g_{12}为东西方向预信号机动车直行、非机动车直行相位绿灯时间,s;g_{21}为南北方向预信号机动车左转、非机动车移位直行相位绿灯时间,s;g_{22}为南北方向预信号机动车直行、非机动车直行相位绿灯时间,s;Δt_1 为 g_{12} 与 g_{11} 的时间差,s;Δt_2 为 g_{22} 与 g_{21} 的时间差。

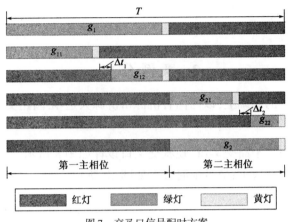

图7 交叉口信号配时方案

2.2 目标函数

以移位左转交叉口机动车通过量最大为优化目标,如下式所示:

$$Q = \max \sum_{i=1}^{4} \sum_{j=1}^{3} \lambda q_{ij}$$

式中:Q——交叉口机动车通过量,pcu/h-1;

λ——交叉口流量系数;

q_{ij}——i 进口道 j 流向的机动车流量,pcu·h,$i=1,2,3,4$ 分别代表东、西、南、北4个方向进口道,$j=1,2,3$ 代表左转、直行、右转3个流向。

2.3 约束条件

(1)一般约束。信号控制优化设计的一般约束条件如下所示:

$$\left.\begin{array}{l} T = g_1 + g_2 + L_z \\ g_{1\min} \leqslant g_1 \leqslant g_{1\max} \\ g_{2\min} \leqslant g_2 \leqslant g_{2\max} \\ L_z = \sum_{i=1}^{2} l_i \end{array}\right\} \qquad (8)$$

式中: T——信号周期时长,s;

$g_{1\min}$、$g_{2\min}$——两个主相位的最短绿灯时间,s,即满足行人过街的最短时间需求;

$g_{1\max}$、$g_{2\max}$——两个主相位的最长绿灯时间,s;

L_z——周期总损失时间,s;

l_i——主相位的损失时间,$i=1,2$。

(2)主、预信号关系约束。以东西方向通行为例,须满足直行车辆通过停车线 2-3 之前,左转车辆顺利通过移位通道变道处;第一主相位 EW 的绿灯时间须不小于本相位直行、左转和右转车辆清空时间的最大值,即:

$$g_{12} - g_{11} \geqslant \frac{L_6 + L_7 + L_8}{2v_1} = \frac{\pi(7x+2y)\beta + 1080x + 180y}{720v_1}$$

$$g_1 \geq \max\left(\frac{3600Q_l}{mns}, \frac{3600Q_s}{mns_{es}}, \frac{3600Q_r}{mns_{er}}\right) \tag{9}$$

式中：v_l——直行机动车平均车速，km/h；
Q_s——直行机动车交通量，pcu/h；
Q_r——右转机动车交通量，pcu/h；
s_{es}——直行车道饱和流率；
s_{er}——右转车道饱和流率。

3 案例分析

在符合设置移位左转条件的基础上，以河南省济源市济源大道-沁园路交叉口为例进行研究。

3.1 交叉口概况

该交叉口为城市快速路与主干路交叉口，现状交叉口设计如图8所示。
交叉口高峰时期流量如图9所示；信号配时方案如图10所示。

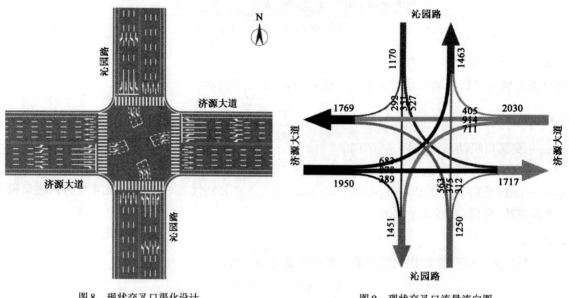

图8 现状交叉口渠化设计　　图9 现状交叉口流量流向图

3.2 优化设计

传统移位左转交叉口设计如图11a)所示；优化的直行非机动车道设计如图11b)所示。
计算图11b)的各项空间尺寸参数结果见表1，信号配时方案如图12所示。

3.3 效用分析

对现状交叉口设计方案（方案一）、传统移位左转设计（方案二）和本文提出的优化移位左转设计（方案三）进行对比。

采用VISSIM软件进行仿真，设置左转车道饱和流率为1440pcu/h，直行车道饱和流率为1500 pcu/h，右转车道饱和流率为1350 pcu/h，此时仿真结果和实际调查数据基本一致，仿真参数标定达到精度要求。根据实地调查和分析，确定交叉口4个方向的直行非机动车流量分别为：东进口693辆/h，西进口638辆/h，南进口571辆/h，北进口556辆/h。保持现状输入机动车交通量和仿真参数不变，分别采用不同的方案，除以机动车通过量为评价指标外，增加车均延误这一指标，提高结果可信度。仿真结果如图13和图14所示。

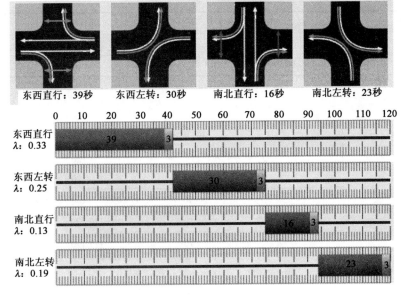

图10　现状交叉口配时方案设计

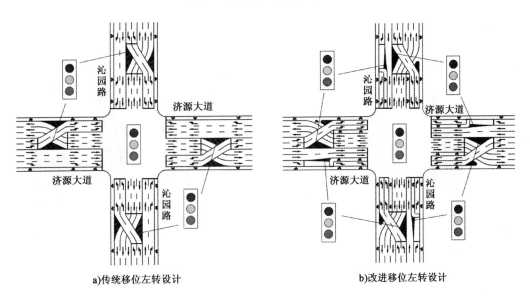

a) 传统移位左转设计　　　　　　　　b) 改进移位左转设计

图11　移位左转交叉口设计示意图

改进后的移位左转交叉口空间尺寸参数　　　　　　　　　　　表1

设计参数（东西方向，m）	数　值	设计参数（南北方向，m）	数　值
L_1	183.3	L_1	149.2
L_2	3.9	L_2	3.9
L_3	2.7	L_3	2.7
L_4	232.3	L_4	181.7
L_5	232.3	L_5	181.7
L_6	1.6	L_6	3.3
L_7	12.5	L_7	12.5
L_8	6.5	L_8	13.1
L_9	157.9	L_9	123.5
L_{10}	16.3	L_{10}	16.3

续上表

设计参数(东西方向,m)	数 值	设计参数(南北方向,m)	数 值
L_{11}	3.6	L_{11}	7.1
L_{12}	20.8	L_{12}	20.8

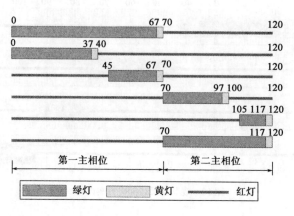

图 12 改进后的移位左转交叉口信号配时方案(单位:s)

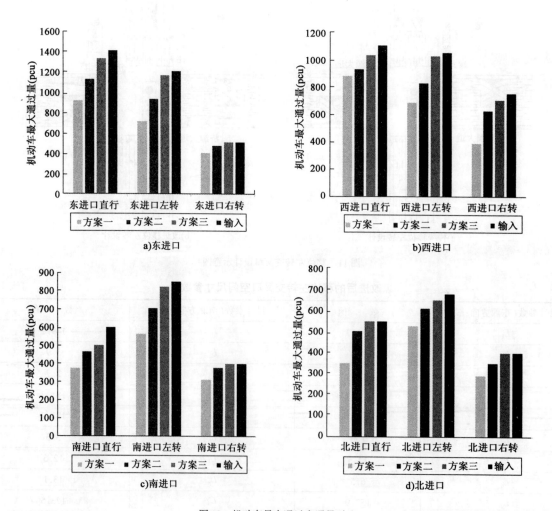

图 13 机动车最大通过交通量对比

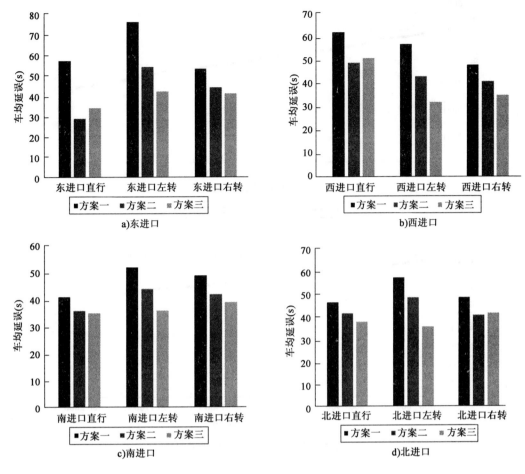

图 14 车均延误对比

在相同车辆输入情况下,方案一大都比现状最大通过量更大,方案三相较方案一、二,均有明显提升。在车均延误方面,方案三相比较方案一和方案二分别降低28.1%和15.7%。

3.4 敏感性分析

选取交叉口直行非机动车平均流量为不确定性因素,划定其变动范围为500～2000辆/h,100辆/h为单位增加幅度,以本方向右转机动车平均通过量和对向左转机动车平均通过量为经济效益指标对比方案二和方案三,结果如图15所示。

可以看出,随着直行非机动车流量的增加,方案二的经济效益指标不断降低,方案三则保持最大通过量不变。非机动车流量每增加100辆/h,方案三相比方案二经济效益指标平均增加14辆/h和15辆/h。

4 结 语

(1)本文回顾了移位左转交叉口的研究现状,提出了优化设计的直行非机动车道路径,消除了主信号处直行非机动车与对向左转机动车、本向右转机动车之间的冲突。

(2)本文分析了优化后的移位左转交叉口的各项空间参数和主、预信号关系等,建立了相应的计算模型。

(3)本设计未考虑平峰、低峰时段,在实际应用中,需要根据交通需求的变化对模型作出相应的调整,有待进一步研究。

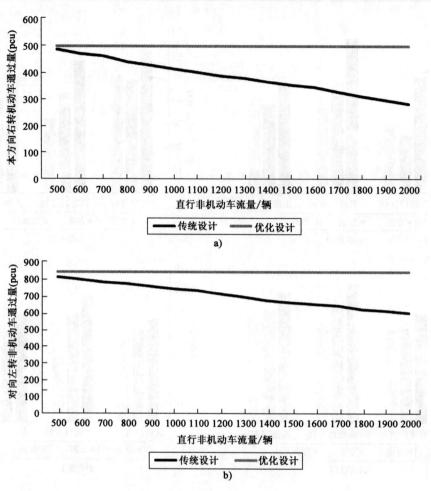

图 15 左转非机动车流量影响分析

参考文献

［1］ 高苏. 移位左转交叉口交通组织优化方法研究［D］. 哈尔滨：哈尔滨工业大学，2019.
［2］ 安实，宋浪，王健，等. 非常规交叉口设计研究现状与展望［J］. 交通运输工程学报，2020，20（04）：1-20.
［3］ 马景峰，王永岗，丁天，等. 基于移位左转的交叉口改善方法［A］. 中国科学技术协会、交通运输部、中国工程院. 2018 世界交通运输大会论文集［C］. 中国科学技术协会、交通运输部、中国工程院：中国公路学会，2018：10.
［4］ Mier F D, Romo B H. Continuous flow intersection：US，US 5049000A［P］. 1991.
［5］ Ramanujan Jagannathan, Joe G. Bared. Design and Performance Analysis of Pedestrian Crossing Facilities for Continuous Flow Intersections［J］. Transportation Research Record, 2005, 1939（1）：133-144.
［6］ Jing Zhao, Wanjing Ma, K. Larry Head, et al. Optimal operation of displaced left-turn intersections：A lane-based approach［J］. Transportation Research Part C, 2015（61）：29-48.
［7］ Chang Y, Deng X. StudyOn Four-Leg Intersection Continuous Flow Intersection Optimal Timing Modeling［J］. Transportation Research Board Annual Meeting, 2015.
［8］ Jiaming Wu, Pan Liu, Zong Z. Tian, et al. Operational analysis of the contraflow left-turn lane design at signalized intersections in China. 2016（69）：228-241.
［9］ 赵靖，徐海军，高幸，等. 连续流交叉口左转非机动车优化设计方法［J］. 交通运输系统工程与信息，2018，18（06）：178-186.
［10］ 常云涛，王奕彤. 连续流交叉口信号配时优化模型［J］. 公路交通科技，2018，35（04）：93-101.

一级公路平面交叉口合理间距值分析

史伟伟　武方涛　郝鑫桐　张祎薇　潘卫龙

(长安大学运输工程学院)

摘　要　一级公路具有运输能力强、通行能力大等优点,而发挥这些优势的关键点就在于平面交叉口的合理设计。我国相关规范中按照公路的等级简单规定了平面交叉口的最小间距,但这一间距的取值没有考虑交叉口的设计速度和交叉口几何特征的影响。本文通过借鉴国内外对一级公路平面交叉口的研究理论和结果,建立关于功能区理论的安全间距计算模型,然后通过对上下游功能区与交织路段长度的分析与计算得出一级公路设计速度分别为60km/h、80km/h、100km/h时,分别对应于双向四车道和双向六车道的平面交叉口合理间距推荐值大小。本文的研究结论对我国一级公路的规划与设计具有一定的指导和借鉴意义,尤其对改善一级公路平面交叉口间距较小的路段有一定的现实意义。

关键词　平面交叉口　合理间距　功能区理论　设计速度

0　引　言

由于我国在一级公路平面交叉口合理间距值方面缺乏较好的设计规范和准则以及一些技术人员在设计上的失误,导致一级公路特有的功能得不到充分的发挥。因此研究一级公路平面交叉口的合理间距值是非常有必要的。我国很多道路工程方面的学者对其进行了深入的研究和探讨。过秀成[1]通过分析停车视距、交通事故发生率、右转车辆冲突与交叉口间距的关系,得出了一级公路平面交叉口最小间距;吴艳[2]分别对集散公路和地方公路的平面交叉口间距的组成进行分析,得出了有无信号灯控制的交叉口间距值。国外学者Douglas主要针对通行效率对交叉口的间距进行了探讨;Hillary也研究了信号交叉口的间距问题,最后得到了车辆在交叉口不产生延误的合理间距为1320ft(约合402.3m)。

而《公路工程技术标准》(JTG B01—2014)对一级公路平面交叉口最小间距有如下规定:干线一级公路平面交叉口最小间距一般为2000m,极限最小值为1000m;作为集散功能的一级公路最小间距为500m。本文主要以一级公路主路优先的平面交叉口为研究对象,重点从交通安全方面的角度着手,以保证交叉口功能区范围为目的建立安全间距模型,并对该模型进行深入研究和探讨,最后利用模型得出一级公路平面交叉口合理间距的推荐值。

1　定　义

本文主要研究一级公路平面交叉口的合理间距值,这一间距必须满足车辆安全行驶、交通流不产生紊乱、服务水平较高等要求,具体而言这一间距值指的是车辆从一个平面交叉口驶出开始到刚刚驶入下一个平面交叉口时间内正常驶过的全部路程。一级公路平面交叉口间距设置的合理性在一定程度上对发挥一级公路特定的路网功能和技术经济优势有重要的影响。

2　建立平面交叉口安全间距模型

本文通过研究交叉口上下游功能区和交织段的长度,最后确定了一级公路平面交叉口的合理间距值。车辆在路过交叉口时,驾驶员要经过很多复杂的操作,当车流从上一个交叉口驶出后,会进入交织区完成车道变换工作,最后驶入下一个交叉口上游功能区中。具体而言,这一间距的组成如图1所示。

一级公路平面交叉口间距D的计算模型为:

$$D = D_{下游} + L + D_{上游} \qquad (1)$$

式中：$D_{下游}$——交叉口 1 下游功能区长度；一级公路平面交叉口间距；
　　　L——交织路段长度；
　　　$D_{上游}$——交叉口 2 上游功能区长度。

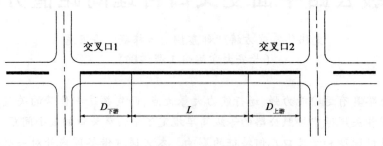

图 1　一级公路平面交叉口间距组成示意图

3　利用模型计算交叉口合理间距值

3.1　上游功能区长度

交叉口上游功能区的范围如图 2 所示。

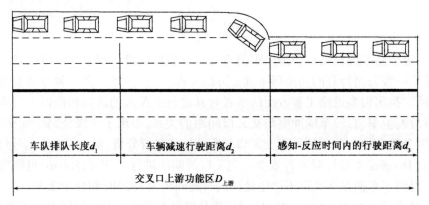

图 2　交叉口上游功能区范围示意图

驾驶员靠近交叉口时一般会有标志牌提醒其注意前方路段，驾驶员在看到并做出反应这段时间内行驶的距离就是感知-反应时间内的行驶距离d_3；驾驶员通过反应作出判断后准备减速，在这一过程中行驶的距离就是车辆减速行驶距离d_2；驾驶员在靠近交叉口时会进行排队等待，这一距离为车队排队长度d_1。很显然，$D_{上游} = d_3 + d_2 + d_1$。

其中在感知-反应时间内的行驶距离d_3为：

$$d_3 = \frac{vt}{3.6} \tag{2}$$

式中：v——车辆行驶速度，km/h；
　　　t——感知-反应时间，具体数值受驾驶员对道路情况掌握程度的影响，计算时取为 2.8s。

而车辆减速行驶距离d_2，虽然对于主路优先的交叉口通常不需要进行展宽设计，但是考虑到行车安全与实际交通流现状，这一段距离在计算时也是必不可少的。其计算公式为：

$$d_2 = \frac{1}{3.6}(t_1 + t_2)v_0 + \frac{v_0^2}{25.92a} \tag{3}$$

式中：v_0——车辆开始采取制动措施时的速度，km/h；
　　　a——车辆减速度，计算时取为 2.5m/s²；
　　　t_1——车辆制动滞后时间，计算时取为 0.6s；
　　　t_2——车辆制动增长时间，计算时取为 0.9s。

而对于车队排队长度d_1,由于本文研究的是基于主路优先下的一级公路交叉口,主路车辆在路过交叉口时根本不需要进行排队等候,因此这一距离最终取为0。从而上游功能区的长度为$D_{上游} = d_3 + d_2$。通过计算得到不同设计速度下的上游功能区长度值见表1。

上游功能区长度值　　　　表1

设计速度(km/h)	60	80	100
上游功能区长度(m)	127.2	191.3	273.8

3.2 交织区合理长度

3.2.1 建立模型

针对本文研究的基于主路优先的平面交叉口,假设车辆驶出功能区后直接进入最外侧车道,驾驶员看到出口标志牌后通过变换车道进入最内侧车道,从左侧驶出交叉口。根据这种假设来建立交织区间距计算模型,如图3所示。

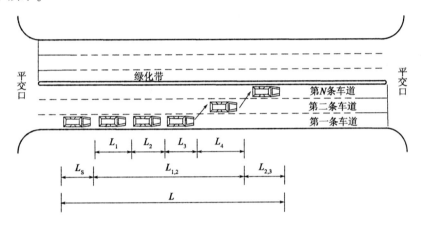

图3　交织区间距计算模型示意图

注:L_1为车辆在可插入间隙时间内行驶的距离,m;L_2为车辆在调整车速时间内行驶的距离,m;L_3为驾驶员判断并确定可插入间隙时行驶的距离,m;L_4车辆变换车道横移时行驶的距离 m。

如图3所示,车道从内到外依次为第N条车道、第二条车道、第一条车道,则一级公路相邻平面交叉口交织区合理长度计算模型为:

$$L = L_S + \sum_{i=1}^{n-1} L_{i,i+1} \tag{4}$$

式中,L_S——驾驶员判断标志牌时间内行驶的距离,m;
$L_{i,i+1}$——车辆变换一个车道所行驶的距离,m。

3.2.2 利用模型进行计算

(1)驾驶员判断标志牌时间内行驶的距离L_S。根据实际情况,这一距离应包含阅读距离和决策距离,其中阅读距离的计算公式为:

$$L_{S_1} = \frac{V}{3.6}t_1 \tag{5}$$

式中:t_1——驾驶员读完标志牌所需要的时间,通常取为1.5s。

决策距离的计算公式为:

$$L_{S_2} = \frac{V}{3.6}t_2 \tag{6}$$

式中:t_2——驾驶员的决策时间,一般取值为2.5s。

综上,驾驶员判断标志牌时间内行驶的距离 $L_S = L_{S_1} + L_{S_2}$。

(2)车辆在可插入间隙时间内行驶的距离 L_1。L_1 可由下式计算:

$$L_1 = \frac{V}{3.6} t_W \tag{7}$$

式中:t_W——驾驶员等候可插入间隙的平均用时量。t_W 可按下式计算:

$$t_W = \frac{(\lambda h_t + 1) e^{\lambda(t-h_t)} - \lambda t - 1}{\lambda e^{\lambda(t-h_t)}} [1 - e^{-\lambda(t-h_t)}] \tag{8}$$

式中:t——车辆间隙时间的最大值,取 4.0s;
λ——车道上在单位时间内平均到达的车辆数;
h_t——车道上车辆行驶的最小车头时距,计算时取 1.3s。

(3)车辆在调整车速时间内行驶的距离 L_2。L_2 可按下式计算:

$$L_2 = \frac{V}{3.6} \cdot \frac{0.76 V t_W}{V - 0.76 V} = 0.879 V t_W \tag{9}$$

(4)驾驶员确定可插入间隙时行驶的距离 L_3。L_3 可按下式计算:

$$L_3 = \frac{V}{3.6} \cdot t_3 = 0.694 V \tag{10}$$

式中:t_3——驾驶员的反应时间,取 2.5s。

(5)车辆变换车道横移时行驶的距离 L_4。L_4 可按下式计算:

$$L_4 = \frac{V}{3.6} \cdot t_4 = 0.833 V \tag{11}$$

式中:t_4——横移时间值,取 3s。

3.3 下游功能区长度

为了安全考虑,本文以停车视距作为下游功能区的长度值。停车视距主要由反应距离和制动距离两部分组成,具体计算公式为:

$$D_{下游} = \frac{Vt}{3.6} + \frac{V^2}{254(\varphi + i)} \tag{12}$$

式中:V——车辆的运行速度(当设计速度为 80~100km/h 时,取为设计速度的 85%;当设计速度为 60km/h 时,取为设计速度的 90%);
t——驾驶员的反应时间,与前文一致取 2.5s;
φ——路面纵向摩阻系数;
i——道路纵坡度。

通过计算,得到交叉口下游功能区的长度值,见表 2。

下游功能区长度值　　　　　　　　　　　　　　　　表 2

设计车速(km/h)	60	80	100
下游功能区长度(m)	75	110	160

4 结 果

本文通过分析一级公路平面交叉口之间路段的交通流特性,包括车辆的车道变换、加速、制动等行为,同时考虑路段通行能力和路段行车安全系数,针对基于主路优先的一级公路平面交叉口进行研究,建立了平面交叉口安全间距模型、交叉口上游功能区的组成模型和交织段间距计算模型,然后对模型进行深入分析和探讨,利用一系列公式最终得出关于一级公路平面交叉口的合理间距推荐值,见表 3。

一级公路平面交叉口合理间距值　　　　　　　　　　表3

设计速度(km/h)	60	80	100
双向四车道(m)	505.4	703.5	959
双向六车道(m)	—	1103.5	1509

5 结　语

　　本文研究的结论对于我国一级公路平面交叉口处的规划设计有一定的参考价值和意义,尤其对于那些平面交叉口间距较小路段的设计有较强的现实意义和价值。但在利用公式计算时,很多参数都是使用了固定值,比如驾驶员反应时间、道路纵向摩阻系数等,而在实际情况中,不同道路的参数并不相同,而且由于实际条件有限,本文对驾驶员的驾驶行为并没有进行大量的调查与分析,这样计算出的间距值难免会存在一定的误差。另外本文主要针对基于主路优先的平面交叉口,对具有其他特征的交叉口并没有做研究,研究范围比较小,从而得到的结果实用性不是很强。关于道路工程的各种设计并没有绝对解,因为影响设计的很多因素不确定,只能寻求最适合实际条件的最优解,因此本文研究所得到的结论还需进一步探析和修正。

参考文献

[1] 过秀成.一级公路最小接入间距研究[J].公路,2007(12):12-16.
[2] 吴艳.公路交叉口合理间距研究[J].山西建筑,2010,(13):261-262.
[3] 张志清,贾岩,周宇亮.穿村镇公路交叉口合理间距探讨[J].公路,2011,(05):119-123.
[4] 中华人民共和国交通运输部.公路工程技术标准:JTG B01—2014.[S].北京:人民交通出版社股份有限公司,2015.
[5] 雷晓晖.山区高速公路互通式立交最小间距的探讨和研究[D].重庆:重庆交通大学,2011.
[6] 刘国培.城市道路设计[M].北京:人民交通出版社,1993.
[7] Transportation Research Institute Oregon State University. Functional Intersection Area [R]. Oregon Department of Transportation,1996.
[8] Giguere R K. Signalized Intersection Spacing:Driveway and street Intersection spacing[J]. National Research Council,Transportation Research Board,1996:13-16.
[9] Drakopoulos A,Vergou G. Evaluation of the Converging Chevron Pavement Marking Pattern at One Wisconsin Location[J]. Field Tests,2003.

阜新市某主干道交通优化设计

邹利刚　陈宽民　杨杰

(长安大学运输工程学院)

　　摘　要　交通作为联系城市与城市、城市内部各地区等的纽带和支撑经济发展的支柱,其作用尤为重要。伴随着社会经济的不断发展,城市交通问题也逐渐显现,特别是中小城市内部的交通组织情况,存在混乱、不合理等现象,甚至阻碍城市的进一步发展。本文以辽宁省阜新市某主干道为例,调查分析城市道路交通现状,诊断交通组织存在问题,探究改善的可能性,提出两种优化设计方案,并通过VISSIM仿真等对比分析,最终确定最优优化方案,以期提高该路段的通行效率,进而完善城市道路的功能。该路段的交通组织优化设计研究可以为城市同类型道路的完善提供参考和模板,具有一定的现实意义。

　　关键词　交通工程　城市道路　优化设计　仿真分析

0 引言

随着各种交通方式的日趋完善,交通设计不够人性化、交通管理不够科学等问题日益凸显[1]。因此,需要在综合分析现存交通道路的基础上提出综合性的改进方案,进而缓解或解决交通问题。本文结合前人研究结论,将其整合进行实际应用,主要借鉴卢凯(2010)提出的多交叉口组合关联公式[2],利用黄慧琼(2020)绿波带共同周期和相位差以及算法的思想[3]确定落地方法。本文中部分数据的选取以2018年中华人民共和国住房和城乡建设部发布的《城市综合交通体系规划标准》(GB/T 51328—2018)作为依据[4]。

本文以阜新市解放大街为例,通过调查该路段的交通现状,分析存在的问题,探究这些问题存在的可能原因,提出能够有效改进交通组织的合理方案。通过对该路段的交通组织优化设计的研究,在改善道路交通状况的同时,为今后解决同类问题提供一定的参考。

1 研究区域现状调查

阜新市解放大街段处于阜新市城市中心区域,无论节假日还是平日都会产生大量人流、车流。它是此区域交通运行的瓶颈,因此需要对路段现有配备信号灯的3个交叉口进行详细调查、分析并解决问题。采取分类调查、实地调查等方法,尽量还原该研究路段的现实全貌。人工标记交叉口由北向南分别为C、E、H。

1.1 交叉口渠化调查

1.1.1 解放大街与经纬路交叉口(C)

交叉口内部长约16m,宽约10m,经纬路中央为单黄实线,解放大街是双黄实线,机动车道宽3.5m,非机动车道宽1m,无中央分隔带。

解放大街与经纬路交叉口CAD图如图1所示。

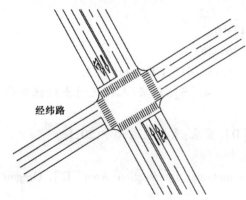

图1 解放大街与经纬路交叉口CAD图

1.1.2 解放大街与新华路交叉口(E)

解放大街与新华路交叉口东西向宽度约16m,南北向宽度约20m,占地面积约为320m²,机动车道宽3.5m,非机动车道宽1m,无中央分隔带。

解放大街与新华路交叉口CAD图如图2所示。

1.1.3 解放大街与滨河路交叉口(H)

解放大街与滨河路交叉口东西向长约20m,南北向长约18m,占地面积约为360m²,机动车道宽3.5m,非机动车道宽1m,无中央分隔带。

解放大街与滨河路交叉口CAD图如图3所示。

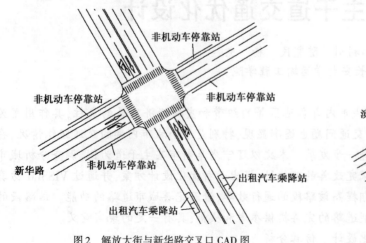

图2 解放大街与新华路交叉口CAD图

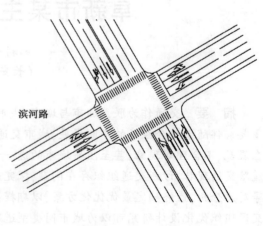

图3 解放大街与滨河路交叉口CAD图

1.2 交叉口流量和信号灯参数调查

本文调查了 3 个交叉口早、晚高峰各 0.5h 的流量,取平均值使用。表 1 中对客车、货车流量进行当量换算为标准小汽车流量。

1.2.1 交叉口流向流量调查

交叉口流向流量调查结果见表 1。

交叉口流向流量表(单位:pcu)　　　　　　　　　　表 1

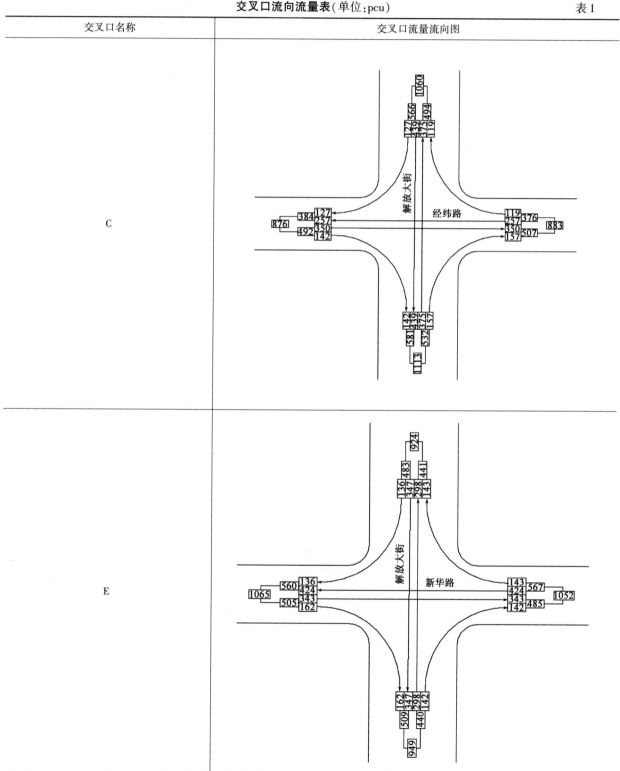

交叉口名称	交叉口流量流向图
C	
E	

续上表

交叉口名称	交叉口流量流向图
H	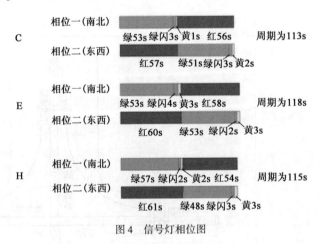

1.2.2 交叉口信号灯调查

3个交叉口信号灯均采用定时式控制系统,采用双相位,调查红灯、绿灯、绿闪以及黄灯时长等参数,信号灯相位图如图4所示。

图4 信号灯相位图

2 研究区域交叉口的问题诊断

通过实地调查分析,得出现状交叉口存在以下几点问题:

(1)研究区域标志标线模糊,识别不清晰,甚至在一些位置标线存在歧义。

(2)交叉口的信号机周期等参数的调配不分理,难以实现对交通的有效管控,达到安全畅通、最大化利用现有交通设施的目的。

(3)一个交叉口的信号灯应当包含交叉口的行人过街信号灯。在实际调查过程中,发现某些交叉口的交通信号灯周期等参数不够合理、行人过街信号灯损坏或者配时不合理。

(4)交叉口邻近区域停车位设置不合理,距离交叉口过近,影响交叉口车辆变道进入交叉口。

3 研究路段交通优化设计方案

3.1 基础设施问题解决方法

首先明确区域。重新规划机动车非机动车停车区域,根据实际情况增设机动车停车位,标志尽量设置在视线盲区之外,应设置禁止左转标志杆,增强其醒目性;细化交通渠化标线,避免出现禁左交叉口出现误入,车道划分线、转向线重新上色,使其清晰明了;所有路段、交叉口实施慢行交通一体化,设置机动车与非机动车分隔带,同时设置非机动车与行人分隔带,如图5、图6所示。

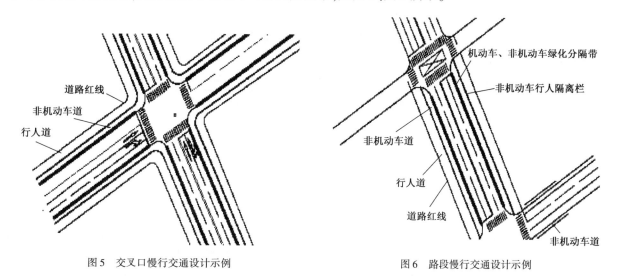

图5 交叉口慢行交通设计示例　　　　图6 路段慢行交通设计示例

3.2 交通信号灯优化方案

3.2.1 方案一

方案一包含交通渠化及绿波和红波交通设计。

1)确定公共周期

绿波和红波交通设计即干线协调控制,选取其中最大的周期作为协调控制的公共周期,对应信号交叉口是关键交叉口[5]。将不同方向车流量转化为直行当量,根据文献参考设置直行当量系数为1.0,右转直行当量系数为1.32,左转直行当量系数为1.05,接着计算系数之和及平均单车道直行当量。

最佳信号周期可按下式计算:

$$C = \frac{1.5 \times L_i + 5}{1 - Y_i} \quad (1)$$

式中:C——交叉口 i 的周期时长,s;

L_i——交叉口 i 的总损失时间,s;

Y_i——交叉口 i 的总流量比。

分别计算三个交叉口的最佳周期,取启动损失时间为3s,经调查各个信号相位的全红时间均为0。以C交叉口为例,设南北相位为相位一,较大流量为 q_1;东西相位为相位二,较大流量为 q_2,则有:

$$q_1 = \max\{北进口,南进口\} = \max\{878,769\} = 878$$
$$q_2 = \max\{西进口,东进口\} = \max\{563,512\} = 563$$

已知标准车行道的直行饱和流率值为 $S_T = 1650 \text{pcu/h}$,则各相位流率比为:

$$y_1 = \frac{q_1}{S_T} = \frac{878}{1650} = 0.532$$

$$y_2 = \frac{q_2}{S_T} = \frac{563}{1650} = 0.341$$

$$Y = y_1 + y_2 = 0.532 + 0.341 = 0.873 < 0.9$$

总损失时间 $L =$ 启动损失 + 全红时间 $= 3 + 3 = 6s$

故由公式可得，$C_1 = \frac{1.5 \times 6 + 5}{1 - 0.873} = 110s$

再分别计算其他两个交叉口的信号周期，可得 E、H 交叉口的最佳信号周期分别为 104s、98s。综上，取 $T = 110s$ 作为干线协调控制的公共周期。

2）确定干线交叉口协调控制时空图（绿波）

解放大街处设置有限速 50km/h 标志，考虑到南下人流繁杂，同时为方便计算，取车流平均行驶速度为 36km/h。交叉口间距和行驶所需时间见表 2。

交叉口间距及行驶时间表　　　　　表 2

交叉口	间距(m)	行驶所需时间(s)（取约数）	备注
南下起点-C	260	26	
C-E	183	19	
E-H	347	35	

各交叉口主次道路时间分配比例见表 3。

各交叉口主次道路时间分配比例　　　　　表 3

交叉口	主次干道流量比例	近似比	主次道路时间分配比例	主要道路绿红相时间比
C	1668:1084	6:4	60:40	66:44
E	1426:1378	5:5	50:50	55:55
H	1572:1044	6:4	60:40	66:44

根据表 2、表 3 数据绘制绿波干线协调控制时空图，如图 7 所示。

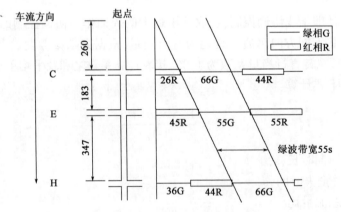

图 7　绿波协调控制时空图（单位：m）

根据时空图可知，三个交叉口组成的干线协调控制系统绿波带宽为 55s，绿波带速与之前的取值一致。

3）确定干线交叉口协调控制时空图（红波）

设置红波交通，即将每个交叉口都看作一个截流系统，不断限制车辆的连续通行，以此达到红波设计的目的。取红波带三个交叉口的公共周期为 110s，为方便后期计算，假设限制车流平均行驶速度仍为 36km/h。交叉口间距及行驶所需时间见表 4。

交叉口间距及行驶时间表 表4

交 叉 口	间距(m)	行驶时间(s)(取约数)	备 注
北上起点-H	450	45	
H-E	347	35	
E-C	183	19	

各交叉口主次道路时间分配比例见表5。

各交叉口主次道路时间分配比例 表5

交 叉 口	主次干道流量比例	近 似 比	主次道路时间分配比例	主要道路绿红相时间比
C	1668:1084	6:4	60:40	66:44
E	1426:1378	5:5	50:50	55:55
H	1572:1044	6:4	60:40	66:44

根据研究绘制的红波协调控制时空图,如图8所示。可以看出,红波带宽为44s,红波带速与之前的取值一致,为36km/h。由此可得,绿波红波设计示意图如图9所示。

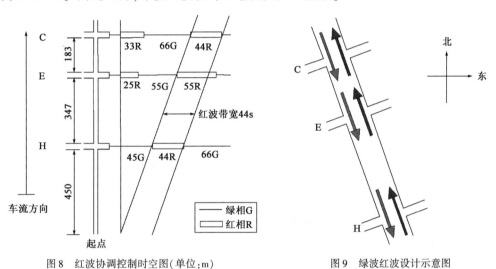

图8 红波协调控制时空图(单位:m)　　　　图9 绿波红波设计示意图

3.2.2 方案二

方案二对每个交叉口利用Webster法进行单点信号优化设计,采用最优的信号配时方案,从而实现整条交通干道的信号优化设计。分别计算三个信号交叉口的最佳配时,最佳信号配时相位图如图10所示。

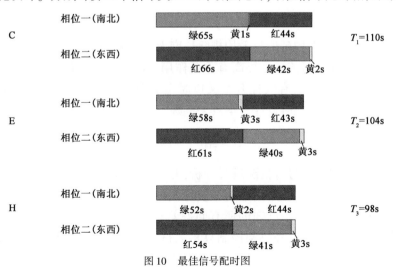

图10 最佳信号配时图

4 方案比选

对两种方案使用 VISSIM 进行仿真评价,可对各种条件下的交通运行状况进行仿真模拟[6]。通过对车辆数据及信号配时信息的录入,设置 8 个延误监测区域,每个交叉口设置 4 个排队长度检测器,主要从延误、人均延误时间、排队长度、最大排队长度等仿真效果进行评价(图 11)仿真时长设置为 1h,仿真 20 次,多次取平均值。

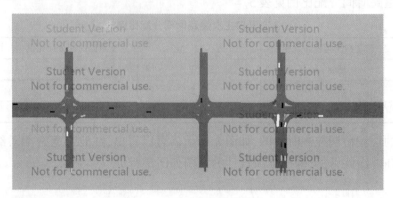

图 11 仿真图

通过仿真得到了现状、绿波交通(方案一)、单点优化(方案二)下的延误和排队长度数据(图 12)。经比较可知,两种优化方案均降低了整体的延误与排队长度,方案一人均延误降低了 21%,方案二降低了 15%;平均排队长度降幅较低,方案一降低了 15%,方案二降低了 5%,因此可看出方案一优于方案二,体现出了绿波协调系统在交通管控中发挥的巨大作用。

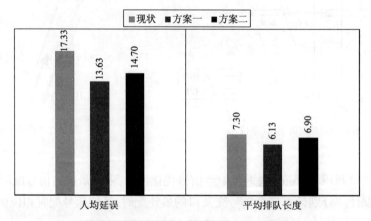

图 12 人均延误与平均排队长度优化前后对照图

方案一所形成的绿波带,使人均延误与平均排队长度大大降低,提高了研究区域整体的通行能力,对阜新市解放大街主干道的整体运行流畅度提高有重要作用。此方案可对信号时间进行精细化调配和相位相序调整、缩短慢行过街距离以及有效提升交叉口时空资源,从而有效减少停车次数,保证车流连续性,提高整体的运行速度。交叉口配时设计方案效果良好。

5 结 语

本文对三个交叉口的流量和信号灯情况进行分析,并提出两种不同的交通组织优化设计方案,同时对两种方案进行仿真评价,从而确定方案一——绿波协调控制为最优方案。本文提出了包含交通渠化、红绿波协调控制设计的措施,保证调查已知的所有问题都能得到解决。鉴于精力有限,调查数据存在一定的误差,因此方案一中的干线信号协调控制只是大概的绿波控制,并不是纯粹意义上的完全协调控制。

参考文献

[1] 周跃辉. 如何理解"我国经济已由高速增长阶段转向高质量发展阶段"[N]. 学习时报,2018-01-31(001).
[2] 卢凯. 交通信号协调控制基础理论与关键技术研究[D]. 广州:华南理工大学,2010.
[3] 黄慧琼,欧方前. 干线绿波协调控制优化研究[J]. 广西科技大学学报,2020,31(03):91-98.
[4] 祖永昶,王波,顾金刚,等. 国家标准《城市道路交通组织设计规范》(GB/T 36670—2018)解读[J]. 交通运输研究,2018,4(05):12-19.
[5] 祖永昶,顾金刚,钱晨,等. 国家标准《城市道路交通组织设计规范》(GB/T 36670—2018)解读[J]. 标准科学,2018(12):163-167.
[6] AGPTV. VISSIM 4.30 user manual. Planung transport verkehr AG[R]. Karlsruhe:PTV Corporation,2007.
[7] 杨琪,王炜. 路段通行能力的动态微观仿真研究[J]. 东南大学学报,1998(03):63-69.

城市道路交通设计评价体系与方法研究

汪 涛[1] 马 岳[2] 江泽浩[3] 孙 伟[2]

(1. 上海交通大学船舶海洋与建筑工程学院;
2. 同济大学道路与交通工程教育部重点实验室;
3. 华中科技大学土木与水利工程学院工程管理系)

摘 要 城市道路交通设计评价可为设计、规划、决策、管理人员及道路交通使用者进行方案优选、了解与评估方案效果提供依据。本文首先对城市道路交通设计评价的基础问题进行分析,包括评价主体、目的、原则、步骤与方法等;其次,参考相关行业成熟的设计评价目标与指标体系,提出城市道路交通设计评价的总目标、子目标、准则层与具体单项指标;最后,分析不同建设类型与阶段的评价特征及其指标筛选,并为具有倾向性目标或全面均衡目标的交通设计评价给出综合评价集结模型。

关键词 交通工程 评价体系 综合评价 交通设计 方案比选

0 引 言

城市道路交通设计的方案评价、优化、比选、决策及其实施效果评价,对设计人员、决策与管理人员、道路交通使用者等都至关重要。因此,需对城市道路交通设计进行科学可靠的评价,为设计人员及相关政府部门的决策提供依据。

总体上,城市道路交通设计评价流程包括明确评价前提、分析评价系统、收集数据与资料、建立评价指标体系、量化评价指标、选取评价方法、综合评价7个步骤。其中,前3项属于原理性、基础性内容,这里不进行赘述。本文仅对后几项,即与交通设计评价指标、综合评价方法相关的国内外研究进行综述。

在交通设计评价指标方面,评价指标及数据的来源主要有3类:可以基于交通仿真,如采用 VISSIM 平台进行微观仿真,输出路段延误、尾气排放量和耗油量等指标值,或采用 TransModeler 平台进行微观仿真,获取交通流参数指标和延误、停车及排队指标;可以基于驾驶模拟,如利用驾驶模拟实验,获取设计方案的美学指标;也可以基于实际观察,如通过现场采集的数据对通行能力、服务水平相关指标进行获取[4]。此外,还可以结合上述3类数据来源,共同为交通设计评价提供评价指标选择及其原始数据。

在交通设计综合评价方法方面,随着交通设计目标的多样化,交通设计评价转向多目标综合评价,如采用逼近于理想解法(TOPSIS)和熵值法建立多目标综合评价模型;使用层次分析法对各分指标赋予权重,最终形成状态向量等。

还有一些研究针对于某些专题交通设计进行评价,比如对老城区采用道路网络密度、公交站点覆盖率、自行车网络密度、步行网络密度4个指标评价其交通健康状态;以及对低碳交通、生态交通、交通安全等专题的评价。总体来说,现有研究仍缺少对城市道路交通设计评价整体流程框架和全面指标体系的研究与梳理。

本文首先对城市道路交通设计这个评价对象进行解析,接着对评价的基础要点、内容和过程进行分析,进而建立评价体系基本框架,然后对评价子目标与若干重要评价准则进行研究分析,最后提出综合评价与决策理论与方法。

1 评价基础问题

首先对城市道路交通设计评价的基础问题进行解析,即评价主体、评价目的与原则、评价步骤与方法。

1.1 评价主体

根据道路交通设计的工作与流程特点,其相关的评价主体可以分为3类,包括政府部门人员、规划设计人员与社会公众,见表1。本文从综合各评价主体的需求出发,对道路交通设计的评价体系与方法进行整体研究。

评价主体分类及其评价目的与需求　　　　表1

评价主体	评价目的/需求	信息特点
政府部门 (规划、建设、管理)	现状设计问题发现/上位规划落实; 方案比较与决策; 实施后评估	总体全面、重点突出
设计人员 (城市规划、交通工程)	设计的问题与原因剖析; 上位规划落实; 方案评价分析、筛选、对比、推荐; 实施后跟踪评价及总结反馈	详细具体、科学系统
社会公众 (使用者)	方案比选; 实施前后对比评估	直观简洁、通俗易懂

1.2 评价目的与原则

对城市道路交通设计进行评价与分析,是实现交通设计方案决策科学化和提高道路交通运行与服务水平的需要。具体而言,道路交通设计的评价目的表现在:判断交通设计是否实现设计目标,是否符合上位规划的要求,是否实现道路的目标功能和性能并在相关约束条件之内;为设计人员对方案的制定、分析、优化、比选提供支持;为政府部门提供决策依据;为实施前后的对比评估提供科学的支持,进而发现问题、总结经验。

道路交通设计不同评价主体的评价目的、需求各有侧重。城市道路交通设计具有多目标、多要素、多用户、多阶段等特征,因此,对其进行评价的原则主要考虑以下几点:

(1)系统性。城市道路交通系统是开放的复杂系统,交通设计亦是多目标的优化集成。需从全局出发,从技术、经济、社会等不同评价角度来选取指标,系统地对其进行评价。

(2)实用性。城市道路交通设计的评价主要面向现实需求,服务于规划、设计、建设与管理,因此,必须有良好的实用性和可操作性,确保评价工作的正常进行。

(3)定量与定性结合。城市道路交通设计在很大程度上具有创造性和社会性,涉及的评价指标类型多样,对可量化的指标进行定量分析,对于有些难以量化的内容,应采用定性指标进行分析。

(4)充分考虑对象特点。城市道路交通设计对象有不同类别,按建设类型可分为新建型和改建/治理型,按阶段可分为事前方案评价和事后现实评价,采用的评价指标与方法应分别考虑。

1.3 评价步骤与方法

科学合理的评价步骤是城市道路交通设计评价的保障。如图1所示,城市道路交通设计评价流程包括以下步骤：

（1）明确评价前提。首先需要明确评价目的，确定评价主体是城市道路的决策管理者、设计者还是使用者，抑或是多者兼之。其次要明确评价对象的范围和阶段，给定评价的原则。

（2）分析评价系统。城市道路交通设计评价受到多设计要素、多阶段、多交通流用户以及复杂运行管理环境的影响，因此需要对影响城市道路交通设计的诸多因素进行系统分类。

（3）收集数据与资料。在明确各种前提后，对评价数据与资料的收集至关重要，数据与资料来源于人工调研、智能交通采集系统、交通仿真软件、历史数据、文档资料，甚至交通参与者等。

（4）建立评价指标体系。城市道路交通设计评价涉及面较多，其综合评价体系一般具有多层次关系结构，指标需能够覆盖城市道路交通设计的各个方面，要能够系统地体现设计的效益。

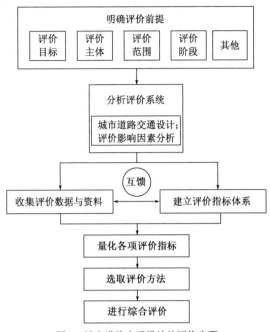

图 1　城市道路交通设计的评价步骤

（5）量化各项评价指标。在评价指标体系的基础上，确定评价函数，对指标进行量化处理。定量指标可直接获取或通过数理方法获得，如通行能力、用地面积等；而定性指标无法通过直接计算得到，如交通语言的识认性、交通与景观的协调性等；需邀请专业人士进行模糊定量。

（6）选取评价方法。为了进行系统性的评价，为决策者、管理者、设计者提供可靠的评价结论，需要深入解析各指标间的相互关系，并建立综合评价计算方法。

（7）进行综合评价。选定科学合理的评价方法，基于多个设计评价因素或指标建立综合评价模型，对城市道路交通设计整体情况进行综合评价，从而指导决策、设计和管理。

在对城市道路交通设计的评价中，可能用到的评价方法主要分为 4 类：第一类是常规的综合评价方法，包括总分评定法、指数综合法等；第二类是数理解析方法，包括技术经济分析法、层次分析法等；第三类是以统计为主的方法，包括各种多元统计方法；第四类方法是重现决策支持的方法，计算机系统仿真技术是其中的有效方法。而交通数据的获取方法和评价过程的实施统称为评价手段。城市道路交通设计评价相关数据获取方法包括：基于传统方式的数据获取、基于信息化智能化的多源数据获取、计算机仿真、驾驶模拟器等。

2　评价指标体系框架

交通设计的评价是一个较新的研究范畴，因此本文在借鉴相关行业设计的评价目标与指标体系基础上，结合道路交通设计的特征，建立道路交通设计的评价目标体系。

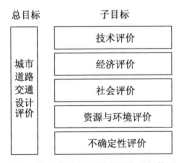

图 2　城市道路交通设计评价目标体系

2.1　评价目标的确定

借鉴相关行业设计评价目标与指标体系，城市道路交通设计评价的总目标分解为技术评价、经济评价、社会评价、资源与环境评价、不确定性评价 5 个方面的子目标，如图 2 所示。

2.2　准则层的确立

确立合适的准则层是指标层指标分类的前提，本文对城市道路交通设计评价准则层采用层次分析思想，为每个子目标选取合适的评价准则。

(1)技术评价从交通功能、性能等技术角度进行,其准则层包括功能性指标、效率性指标、匹配性指标、平顺性指标和安全性指标。

(2)经济评价从资金投入、财务分析、经济分析、费用效果等经济角度进行,其准则层包括投资估算指标、财务分析指标、经济分析指标、费用效果分析指标。

(3)社会评价从社会公众参与、利益相关者分析等社会角度进行,其准则层包括社会影响指标、社会互适性指标和社会风险指标。

(4)资源与环境评价从资源消耗、环境影响角度进行,其准则层包括土地资源指标、能源消耗指标、环境污染指标。

(5)不确定性评价从不确定因素分析角度进行,其准则层为敏感性指标。

这些因素构成评价体系的准则层。各类文献分别从不同角度对这些因素的部分内容进行过研究,针对道路交通设计不同的评价目的或对象,可选择若干准则层进行评价。

2.3 评价指标体系的建立

城市道路交通设计评价应用目标层次分析来选取指标。顶层为总目标,即城市道路交通设计评价,第二层为技术、经济、社会、资源与环境、不确定性等子目标,中间为若干准则层,最后一层为指标层,可定量或定性分析。指标体系总体结构见表2。

城市道路交通设计评价指标体系总体结构及分类别综合评价指标筛选 表2

总目标	子目标	准则层	单项指标层	新建型 事前	新建型 事后	改建型 事前	改建型 事后	度量
道路交通设计评价	技术评价	功能性	功能定位合理性;路网衔接合理性	●	●			模糊定量
			交通组织合理性;路权合理性;公交优先性;慢行友好性	●	●	●	●	模糊定量
		效率性	通行能力;延误	●	●	●	●	定量
			行程车速	●	●	●	●	定量
			停车次数;最大排队长度			●	●	定量
		匹配性	机动车交通设施匹配度;公共交通设施匹配度	●		●		定量
			行人与自行车交通设施匹配度		●		●	定量
		平顺性	机动车轨迹平顺性;行人与自行车轨迹平顺性	●	●			定量
			机动车速度变化程度;机动车加速度变化程度		●		●	定量
		安全性	视距安全性;绿灯间隔时间安全性;最短绿灯时间安全性	●	●	●	●	定量
			渠化、公交、进出口、过街、停车及交通语言等设计安全性	●		●		模糊定量
			附属设施安全性	●	●	●	●	模糊定量
			交通冲突指标;交通事故率		●		●	定量
	经济评价	投资估算	投资估算;运营维护成本	●	●	●	●	定量
			拆迁费用			●	●	定量
		财务分析	财务盈利能力;偿债能力;财务生存能力	●		●		定量
		经济分析	投资收益率;投资回收期;经济净现值;经济内部收益率	●		●		定量
		费用效果	直接和间接效益;效果费用比	●	●	●	●	定量

续上表

总目标	子目标	准则层	单项指标层	新建型 事前	新建型 事后	改建型 事前	改建型 事后	度量
道路交通设计评价	社会评价	社会影响	对居民生活的影响;对居民就业的影响;对不同利益相关者的影响;对弱势群体的影响	●	●	●	●	模糊定量
		社会互适	不同利益相关者的态度;当地社会组织的态度;当地社会环境条件;后勤保障	●	●	●	●	模糊定量
		社会风险	动迁居民安置问题;弱势群体支持问题;受损补偿问题	●	●	●	●	模糊定量
	资源与环境评价	土地资源	道路占地面积	●	●	●	●	定量
			单位机动车宽度通行能力	●	●			定量
			单位面积通过车公里数;单位面积通过人公里数		●		●	定量
			车均占地面积;人均占地面积				●	定量
		能源环境	燃油消耗量;环境污染量	●	●	●	●	定量
	不确定性评价(敏感性)		敏感度系数;临界点	●		●		定量

3 综合评价与决策

道路交通设计综合评价按阶段不同可分为事前评价与事后评价,两者在研究对象、环境性质、作用与用途、主要原则、对象的处理等各方面的特征均有所不同。从环境来看,交通设计事后评价的环境是已经发生的,相关评价信息或数据现实存在;而事前评价的环境是将来的、未发生的,其状态具有不确定性,需要相对较多的专家意见加入。从原则来看,交通设计事后评价是对现实对象进行真实的、确定的评价,客观公正是其关键原则。而事前评价的用途是方案选优,评价过程中具有一定的不确定性和预测性,所以可预测性原则是事前评价的关键原则。从对象处理和作用、用途来看,交通设计事后评价的是现实对象,不可去除,且需进行排序比较。事前评价可以预先淘汰明显不合理或不可行的设计方案,再对剩余的备选方案进行综合评价,选出最优方案[26]。

3.1 综合评价指标的筛选

道路交通设计评价的指标较多,在面向具体某类设计评价问题时,应从评价主体的角度出发,根据评价目标及评价对象的特征,进行指标筛选,合理组成评价指标集。

本文采用专家调研法,评价类别按建设类型不同分为新建型和改建/治理型两种,评价对象按阶段不同分为事前评价和事后评价两类。就相应的备选指标征询专家意见,经三轮咨询后,筛选出具体的分类别综合评价指标,详见表2。

3.2 指标权重的确定

在道路交通设计综合评价中,对于5个评价子目标的权重,可采用基于"功能驱动"原理的"指标偏好型"主观赋权法,评价主体或决策者直接对各子目标的重要性程度进行比较以获取权重系数。对于权重系数的定量计算,可采用集值迭代法、排序积分法和特征值法等。而对于各个子目标不同准则层及单项指标层内部的权重确定,可通过熵权法、标准离差法等客观赋权法,或在条件允许时通过主客观组合赋权法进行。

3.2.1 集值迭代法

设道路交通设计评价的子目标指标集为 $X = \{x_1, x_2, x_3, x_4, x_5\}$,选取 M 位熟悉评价问题的专家。总体而言,专家人数越多,权重结果越准确。一般情况下,10~16人左右的专家评审可以取得较为理想的精准度,当条件限制时,人数最少不应小于5人。让每一位专家分别从以上5个指标中选出重要的$s(1 \leq s < 5)$个指标,则第k位专家选取的结果是指标集X的一个子集:

$$X^{(k)} = \{x_1^{(k)}, x_2^{(k)}, \cdots, x_5^{(k)}\} \quad (k=1,2,\cdots,M) \tag{1}$$

作函数:

$$u_k(x_j) = \begin{cases} 1 & (x_j \in X^{(k)}) \\ 0 & (x_j \notin X^{(k)}) \end{cases} \tag{2}$$

记:

$$g(x_j) = \sum_{k=1}^{M} u_k(x_j) \quad (j=1,2,\cdots,5) \tag{3}$$

将$g(x_j)$归一化后,比值$g(x_j) / \sum_{k=1}^{5} g(x_k)$就是与指标$x_j$相对应的权重系数$w_j$,即:

$$w_j = \frac{g(x_j)}{\sum_{k=1}^{5} g(x_k)} \quad (j=1,2,\cdots,5) \tag{4}$$

3.2.2 排序积分法

选取M位专家,分别让每一位专家对全部指标x_1、x_2、x_3、x_4、x_5进行重要性排序,按先后顺序赋予重要度值5、4、3、2、1,然后把每项指标中所有专家提出的重要度值累加,形成总重要度值集。将其归一化后,即可将比值作为对应指标的权重系数。

3.2.3 排序特征值法

专家对5个评价子目标的重要性程度(比例标度)做两两比较判断,获得矩阵A,再求与特征值相对应的特征向量$w = \{w_1, w_2, w_3, w_4, w_5\}^T$,将其归一化即为评价指标的权重系数。

3.3 综合评价集结模型

将道路交通设计的5个评价子目标值整合为一个综合评价值,需要根据评价的需求及被评价对象的特点,来选择合适的集结模型。

在道路交通设计评价过程中,各子目标的权重系数都是对设计评价指标某种性能或性质的反映,考虑到贴近指标综合的本质含义并易于解释,优先选用基于指标性能(性质)的集结方式,主要包括线性加权综合法、非线性加权综合法。

3.3.1 线性加权综合法

线性加权综合法,又称加法合成法,是指应用线性模型来进行综合评价。其计算公式如下:

$$y = \sum_{j=1}^{5} w_j x_j \tag{5}$$

式中:y——综合评价值;

w_j——评价指标x_j相应的权重系数。

采用线性加权综合评价的情况下,各个评价指标之间可以互相补偿,比如匹配性指标比较低时,可通过效率性指标的提升来提高综合评价值。另外,权重系数的影响相对其他方法更显著,具有"一俊遮百丑"的特征。因此,线性加权综合评价较适用于具有倾向性目标的交通设计评价情况。

3.3.2 非线性加权综合法

非线性加权综合法,又称乘法合成法,是指应用非线性模型来进行综合评价。其计算公式如下:

$$y = \prod_{j=1}^{5} x_j^{w_j} \tag{6}$$

式中:w_j——权重系数,要求$x_j \geq 1$。

非线性加权综合评价适用于各指标间有较强关联的场合,越小的评价指标数值对综合评价值的影响越大。非线性加权综合法对指标值变动的反映比线性加权综合法更敏感,更有助于体现备选方案之间的差异。非线性加权综合评价类似"木桶原理",即木桶容量取决于长度最短的那块木板,进行交通设计过程性的评价优化,可促使设计方案更综合、更平衡。因此,非线性加权综合评价适用于具有全面均衡目标的交通设计评价情况。

4 结 语

本文分析道路交通设计评价的基础要点,包括被评价对象的解析、评价主体与评价目的、原则、内容、步骤和方法,进而建立评价指标体系基本框架及备选指标库。评价子目标分为技术、经济、社会、资源与环境、不确定性评价,并对每个子目标的准则层及重要评价指标进行了分析,进而对道路交通设计综合评价与决策进行了研究。

研究结论包括不同建设类型与建设阶段下的评价指标体系,以及不同交通设计评价情况下的指标权重与综合评价集结模型的选择。本研究结论可为相关规划、设计、建设与管理人员比选交通设计方案或评估交通设计效果提供科学参考。但是,本文对评价信息采集与处理分析方法没有着重分析,后续研究可对此进行详细补充。

参考文献

[1] 许新. 城市干道路段行人地面过街交通设计多目标评价方法[D]. 南京:东南大学,2015.
[2] 耿彦斌,李海峰,柴大胜. 基于 Trans Modeler 的城市快速路交通设计方案的微观仿真评价[J]. 道路交通与安全,2009,9(01):27-31,40.
[3] 叶飞,李文辉,韩鑫,等. 基于动静结合的公路隧道洞口设计综合评价体系研究[J]. 中国公路学报,2021:1-14.
[4] 张开碧,罗蓉. 平面交叉口交通设计评价系统的研究与设计[J]. 重庆邮电大学学报(自然科学版),2009,21(01):119-122.
[5] 《中国公路学报》编辑部. 中国交通工程学术研究综述·2016[J]. 中国公路学报,2016,29(06):1-161.
[6] 刘伟杰,城市道路平面交叉口交通设计评价技术研究[R]. 上海:上海市城市建设设计研究院,2001.
[7] 唐建强. 道路平面交叉口交通设计评价指标体系研究[J]. 山西建筑,2013,39(23):10-12.
[8] 田仪顺,李莲莲. 综合交通规划设计方案评价探析[J]. 交通科技,2013(05):127-130.
[9] 汪春. 老城区健康道路交通规划设计与评价——以合肥市老城区为例[D]. 南京:东南大学,2015.
[10] 郭胜. 城市交通系统碳排放评估体系与评价方法研究[D]. 合肥:合肥工业大学,2014.
[11] 王家祺. 深圳市生态交通系统评价研究[D]. 神州:福建农林大学,2014.
[12] 王东明. 高速公路交通安全设计与评价研究[J]. 交通标准化,2012(08):123-125.
[13] 郭显惠. 高速公路交通安全设计与评价研究[D]. 西安:长安大学,2011.
[14] 苏为华. 多指标综合评价理论与方法问题研究[D]. 厦门:厦门大学. 2000.
[15] 叶义成,柯丽华. 系统综合评价技术及其应用[M]. 北京:冶金工业出版社. 2006.
[16] Choulakian V.. Robust Q-mode principal component analysis in L1[J]. Computational statistics & data analysis. 2001, 37(2): 135-150.
[17] 汪应洛. 系统工程理、方法和应用[M]. 北京:高等教育出版社,1992.
[18] 荆琳. 关于快速公交系统(BRT)评价体系研究[D]. 西安:长安大学. 2005.
[19] 周华金. 城市设计评价建构[C]. 第八届城市发展与规划大会论文集. 2013.
[20] 陈剑锋. 基于突变级数法的建筑设计方案优选[J]. 邵阳学院学报:自然科学版. 2014(3):41-45.
[21] 杨晓光,赵靖,马万经,等. 信号控制交叉口通行能力计算方法研究综述[J]. 中国公路学报. 2014, 27(5): 148-157.
[22] 高克跃. 城市道路平面交叉口视距控制与计算[J]. 城市交通. 2013(3):15-20.
[23] 项乔君,陆键,高海龙. 基于交通冲突技术的公路平交路口交通安全评价方法[J]. 公路交通科

技, 2004, 21(11): 55-58.
[24] Felipe E, Navin F. Automobiles on horizontal curves: experiments and observations[J]. Transportation Research Record: Journal of the Transportation Research Board, 1998(1628): 50-56.
[25] 任博芳. 系统综合评价的方法及应用研究[D]. 北京:华北电力大学, 2010.

中小型高速铁路枢纽配套交通设施综合评估研究

郑明伟　蔡逸峰

(同济大学建筑设计研究院(集团)有限公司)

摘　要　国家新一轮铁路建设给高速铁路枢纽带来发展契机,但多数城市规划对高速铁路枢纽的研究不足,特别是对中小型高速铁路枢纽的重视不够。本文通过对上海周边26座中小型高速铁路枢纽进行现场调研和客流分析,发现了枢纽配套交通设施设计中存在规模控制不当、人行广场"大而无用"、换乘距离较远等问题,提出了应通过立体、紧凑布局手段,实现将换乘时间控制在3mins以内,对应换乘距离控制在150~200m的目标。此外,本文还通过回归分析发现了铁路高峰小时发送量、配套设施规模与旅客换乘时间呈现出一定的正相关性,提出应注意控制因客流规模增加、设施规模扩大,导致换乘时间变长的问题,希望可对类似枢纽配套交通设施的综合评估提供借鉴和参考。

关键词　中小型高速铁路枢纽　综合评估　回归分析　设施规模　换乘时间

0　引　言

"十三五"期间,我国铁路投资规模达3.5万亿元,新增铁路营业里程2.9万km,其中高速铁路里程增加约1.1万km,高速铁路已覆盖80%以上的城区人口数量大于100万人的城市。这意味着许多城市的高铁站将从无到有,或由一个变多个,新建的高速铁路枢纽将对配套交通设施的整合程度提出更高要求。

经济发达地区已建高速铁路枢纽存在大量改建需求。我国第一批高速铁路枢纽运行至今已有10年左右时间,由于当时建设经验不足,枢纽辐射能力不强、配套交通集成度较低等问题逐渐显露,急需按照城市最新发展要求,从功能定位、规模预测、设施布局、建筑设计、交通组织等方面进行系统分析,对这些枢纽的铁路站房、集输运系统进行改造,以提升枢纽服务等级。

《关于推进高铁站周边区域合理开发建设的指导意见》要求推进高速铁路车站周边区域合理开发建设,强调提升综合配套保障能力,要求强化城市内外交通衔接,加强新建高速铁路车站城市公共交通配套线路和换乘设施建设,实现与城市建成区、城市其他重要综合交通枢纽之间的快速连接、便捷直达[1]。在这方面,国内真正成功的案例不多,而国外经验存在"水土不服",急需探索出一条指导枢纽"高质量建设、一体化融合"的路子来。

中小型高速铁路枢纽是我国铁路建设的重要组成部分,其影响人数的总量从某种意义上来讲要比大型枢纽更多,影响范围也更广。不同的地理环境、线路的设置高程、车站客流性质等因素对于这些枢纽设计都有很大的影响[2]。这些枢纽的客运规模、出行结构、集散方式、交通组织等交通特征与上海虹桥、南京南站等大型枢纽有明显区别,不能简单复制所谓成功经验,需要有针对性地进行系统研究。

1　研究对象和调研要点

1.1　研究对象

《铁路旅客车站设计规范》(TB 10100—2018)对高速铁路与城际铁路客站规模划分的依据是高峰小

时发送量。本研究的中小型高速铁路客运枢纽即是指高峰小时发送量小于5000人次的铁路客站,重点研究其交通组织设计、配套交通设施规模、换乘时间控制等方面的问题。值得注意的是,中小型高速铁路枢纽与中小型城市的高速铁路客站不是一个概念[3],大城市、特大城市、超大城市的辅站也可能是中小型高速铁路枢纽,如上海安亭北站、苏州园区站等。

我国高速铁路车站基本情况见表1。

我国高速铁路车站规模及高峰小时发送量 表1

车 站 规 模	高峰小时发送量 PH(人)	车 站 规 模	高峰小时发送量 PH(人)
特大型	PH≥10000	中型	1000≤PH<5000
大型	5000≤PH<10000	小型	PH<1000

笔者于2019年5—7月对长三角范围的京沪高速铁路、沪宁城际、沪昆高速铁路、杭黄高速铁路、杭甬高速铁路等6条高速铁路线上的26座车站进行了现场调研,归纳总结各类交通设施规模、枢纽总规模与铁路旅客流量及换乘时间的关系,评价站前广场交通设施用地布局的经济性和换乘时间的经济性,具体调研车站及编号如图1所示。

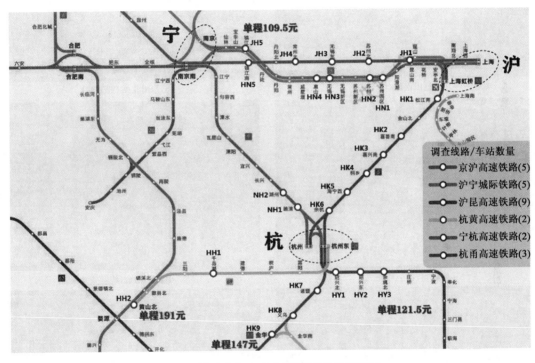

图1 调研车站分布(有字母标注的为调研车站)

1.2 现状总结

调研发现,线下式、线侧式铁路站房是中小型高速铁路枢纽铁路站房的主要形式,而线上式铁路站房本质上是大型线侧平式站房的延伸和扩展,主要适用于大型、特大型的站房。26座车站中有9座为线下式站房,其进出站道路均采用地面形式,并设有与地下场站设施沟通的上、下坡道,如昆山南站、苏州北站等;15座为线侧式站房,其中有5座的进站系统采用高架形式,分别是苏州园区站、镇江站、绍兴东站、诸暨站和黄山北站,其余车站的进出站道路为采用地面形式;苏州站、无锡站2站为线上式站房,现状客流已达到或接近大型车站规模。具有代表性的车站枢纽设施布局如图2所示。

调研车站的枢纽设施布局既存在一些共性问题,又体现出差异特征,同时部分车站已经开始或计划进行改扩建。

(1)共性需求和问题。社会车停车场、出租汽车、公交(巴士)场站、非机动车停车场、站前人行广场这五类配套是所有调研高速铁路枢纽都具备的设施类型。站区内部都有一套相对独立的道路交通系统,这套系统通常采用单行交通组织方式,以便集散枢纽客流;枢纽外围通常与国省干道、主干路、快速路等干线道路衔接,实现枢纽交通的快速转换和过境交通的分流。调研中发现部分站前道路过境与到发交通、客运与货运交通混杂的问题,如昆山南站、义乌站、无锡站、镇江站、黄山北站等;部分车站站前车道边交通组织欠合理,如绍兴北站送客车道边"反向",导致右侧开门下客后需要面对右侧车道上速度较快的来车,存在一定的安全隐患。再如苏州北站的落客车道之间采用物理隔离,本意是严格限制即停即走、禁止随意变道超车,但单条落车车道宽度设计不合理,使得部分"等不及"的车辆仍然可以变道超车通过,人车冲突时有发生,导致通行效率和安全性均不高;部分车站人行广场尺度过大、景观枯燥、功能单一,如惠山站、湖州站、无锡东站等。此外,车站站前旅客换乘路径上风雨连廊不连续的问题在所有调研车站中普遍存在,旅客换乘舒适度欠佳。

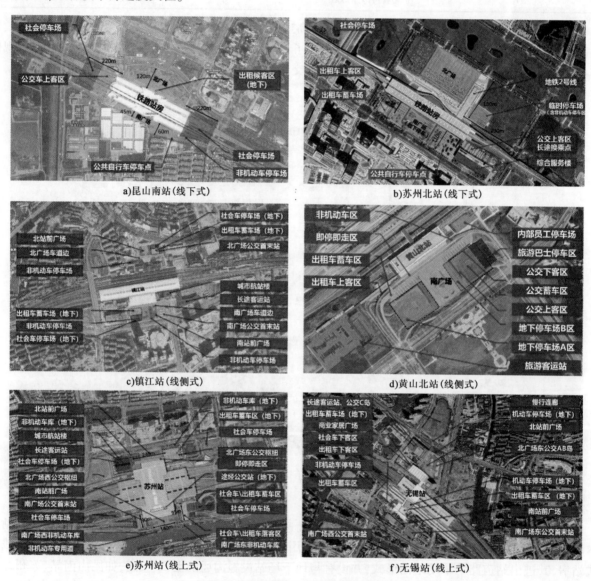

图2 高速铁路枢纽配套设施现状布局

(2)差异需求和特征。不同高速铁路站服务客流的属性存在一定差异,导致枢纽配套交通设施的类型不尽相同。如千岛湖站主要服务旅游客流,该站并无"常规公交"设施配套,取而代之的是酒店穿梭巴士和高速铁路专线巴士,更加贴合旅客对出行品质和时效性的需求;黄山北站在社会停车场中特别划定了分时租赁和租车区域,为旅客个性化出行选择;作为地铁线路的过渡,常州北站、金华站、绍兴北站将中运量 BRT 引入枢纽;苏州站、苏州北站、无锡站、无锡东站、松江南站、余杭站 6 座调研车站已经配置的大运量轨道交通线路,以服务现状大客流和远期铁路运量增长带来的客流;无锡东站、常州北站、黄山北站、余姚北站、苏州北站、惠山站、义乌站、镇江南站、德清站、镇江站、绍兴东站、苏州站、湖州站、无锡站、金华站15座高速铁路站在枢纽区域内整合了长途客运功能。值得注意的是,高速铁路与公路客运存在互补和竞争关系,随着高速铁路和城际轨道交通的逐步完善,长途客运规模将进一步缩减。

(3) 改建需求和方向。尽管本次调研的大多数高速铁路车站都是10年内建成的,由于当时高速铁路车站建设对客流发展估计不足、交通组织方案欠合理,部分枢纽已经开始实施改扩建,如常州北站、镇江南站、苏州北站、金华站、义乌站、黄山北站、绍兴北站、湖州站、松江南站10座车站刚完成或拟进行改造,改造车站数量约占调研车站总数的38%。一方面,枢纽配套设施的完善是一个动态发展过程,如常州地铁一号线引入常州北站,调研时发现北广场正在施工,后于2019年9月21日开通运营,轨道交通的引入可优化枢纽集散交通结构,较大幅度提升公共交通分担率,缓解旅客对小汽车的过度依赖;另一方面,部分车站周边将依托高速铁路车站进行TOD整体开发,建设交通枢纽综合体,如绍兴北站等。

2 交通设施规模分析

本次研究发现,具有蓄车和上下客功能的公交场站,每条线路占地面积的均值为1000m²,若单条线路的占地面积仅有400~500m²,则该场站仅具备上下客功能,蓄车场布置在远端;社会停车场的容量均值约1000个,小汽车泊位车均占地面积约32m²(地下车位约40m²/个);出租汽车蓄车场容量均值约124个,车均占地面积约25m²,需求较小的可考虑采用"通道式"蓄车;人行广场占地面积均值约3万m²,长、宽尺寸约200m×150m。上述4类场站设施的建筑面积分布规律如图3~图6所示。

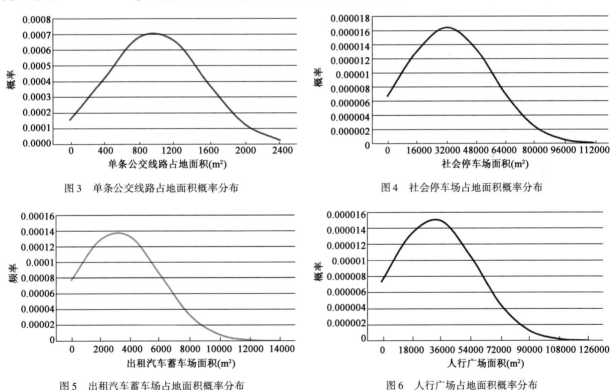

图3 单条公交线路占地面积概率分布　　图4 社会停车场占地面积概率分布

图5 出租汽车蓄车场占地面积概率分布　　图6 人行广场占地面积概率分布

经调研26个铁路枢纽人行广场面积服从正态分布,均值约为3万m²(长、宽尺寸约为200m×150m)。广场尺度过大、空间品质不高、功能空间单一、缺乏整体设计等问题在高速铁路车站前广场设计中普遍存在[4],导致旅客换乘不便、步行距离增加,同时造成土地资源的浪费。例如惠山站、无锡东站,前者北广场拥有约10万m²的人行广场,后者人行广场总面积达到了约8.5万m²;而过小的人行广场会导致紧急事件发生时旅客疏散安置不便,例如义乌站、嘉兴南站,两站的人行广场面积分别约为3000m²与6000m²。

各类配套交通场站建筑面积(含人行广场)比例如图7所示。

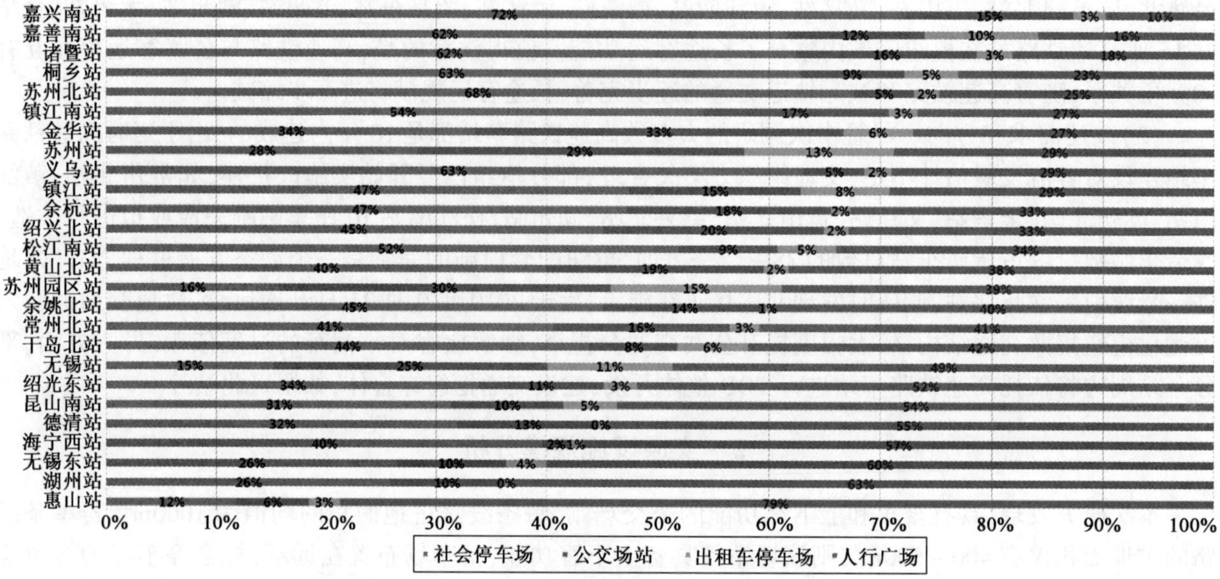

图7 各类配套交通场站建筑面积比例(含人行广场)

3 换乘时间分布规律

高速铁路旅客至各接驳交通方式的换乘时间直接体现了枢纽的运行效率,这个指标能够很好地反映枢纽设施空间布局的合理性。本文采用实地调查的方法,由调查员手持秒表记录从铁路出站口到各类枢纽配套交通设施上客区的步行时间,进而折算成换乘距离,统计结果如图8所示。

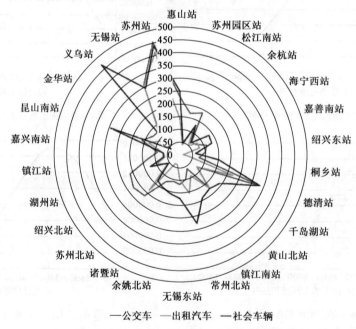

图8 高速铁路站出口至主要交通设施上客区换乘距离(单位:m)

统计发现,90%的高速铁路站出口至主要交通设施上客区的换乘距离均控制在300m以内,对应的换乘时间控制在5min左右;约10%的高速铁路站出口至主要交通设施上客区的换乘距离超过300m但小于500m,对应的换乘时间为5~10min。对于中型高速铁路枢纽而言,步行超过5min的换乘是应该尽量避免的。如无锡站、德清站、苏州站公交场站换乘距离较远,无锡站、苏州站出租汽车换乘距离较远,常州北站、昆山南站、无锡站、德清站、苏州站、义乌站社会停车场距离较远。

不同高速铁路车站出站口至公交上客区、出租汽车上客区、社会停车场的换乘时间分别如图9~图11所示。

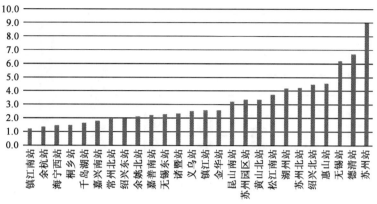

图9 高速铁路站出站口至公交上客区换乘时间(单位:min)

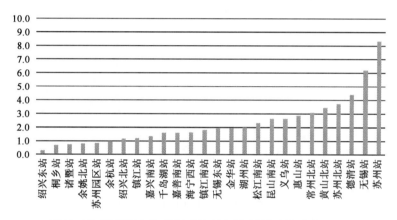

图10 高速铁路站出站口至出租汽车上客区换乘时间(单位:min)

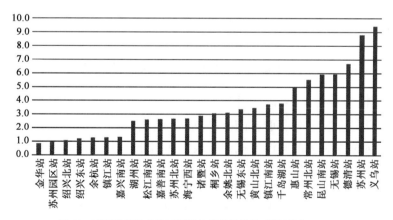

图11 高速铁路站出站口至社会停车场换乘时间(单位:min)

值得注意的是，苏州站、无锡站、义乌站、昆山南站等车站现状高峰小时发送量排名靠前，车站规模及配套设施规模较大，应注意控制因规模扩大造成换乘时间变长的问题；德清站、常州北站客流相对较小，但换乘时间却较长，设施布局相对分散。

在26座调研车站中，有轨道交通配套的车站仅6座，有长途客运站配套的有11座。下面是对这两类交通设施与高铁之间的换乘时间分别进行的统计分析。其中：轨道交通车站与高速铁路站的换乘相对比较方便，多数车站的换乘时间可控制在3min以内；由于长途客运站占地面积较大，新建高速铁路枢纽也只能将其布置在相邻地块上，导致换乘距离普遍较远[5]，换乘时间超过5mins(对应距离约360m)的车站有6座，分别是镇江站、绍兴东站、苏州站、湖州站、无锡站、金华站，这样的换乘距离会给携带行李较多的长途旅客造成不便。

不同车站出站口轨道交通、长途客运的换乘时间分别如图12、图13所示。

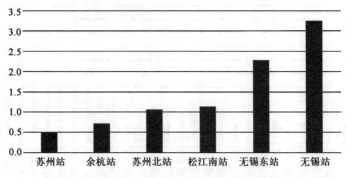

图12 高速铁路站出站口至轨道交通换乘时间

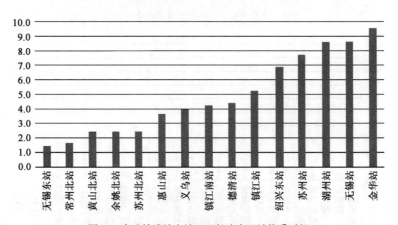

图13 高速铁路站出站口至长途客运站换乘时间

综上分析,应将"换乘时间5min"(换乘距离300m)作为设施布局换乘指标的上限要求,并争取通过立体、垂直等紧凑布局手段,将换乘时间控制在3min以内,对应换乘距离为150~200m,以此作为设计方案的原则性要求。

4 铁路客运量与设施总体规模及换乘时间的关系

4.1 设施总规模与换乘时间的关系

铁路枢纽站的接驳交通总换乘时间与配套设施总面积(含人行广场)成正相关关系。将配套设施总面积(含人行广场)设为x,总换乘时间设为y,进行线性回归分析,得到回归方程$y=0.0018x+179.78$,拟合优度$R^2=0.4099$,拟合效果较好(图14)。

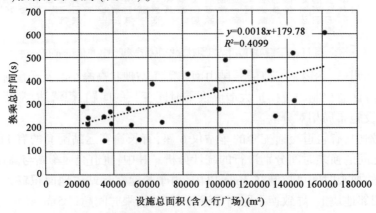

图14 设施规模(含人行广场)与换乘时间关系曲线

假设某高速铁路枢纽站设施总面积为10万 m^2,则乘客的平均换乘时间(各类交通方式换乘时间总和)会达到6min以上,换乘效率与服务水平较低。若要将换乘时间控制在6min之内,则需建设立体枢纽以减少设施占地面积,从而减少换乘时间。

4.2 高峰小时发送量与配套设施规模及换乘时间的关系

铁路枢纽站的高峰小时旅客发送量和配套设施总面积(不含人行广场)成正相关。将高峰小时旅客发送量设为 x;配套设施总面积设为 y,进行线性回归得到回归方程式 $y = 22.853x + 22127$,拟合优度 $R^2 = 0.4405$,拟合效果较好。含人行广场的配套设施总面积与高峰小时发送量相关性较差,$R^2 = 0.2776$ 表示布置多大规模的人行广场更多是从景观效果和空间尺度考虑,与铁路客流关系不大(图15)。

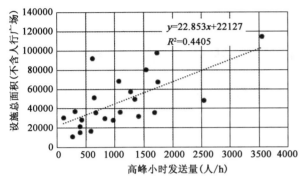 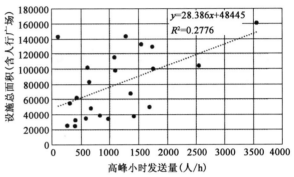

图15 配套设施总面积(不含/含人行广场)与高峰小时旅客发送量关系曲线

铁路枢纽站的高峰小时旅客发送量和接驳交通总换乘时间成正相关关系。将高峰小时旅客发送量设为 x,接驳交通总换乘时间设为 y,进行线性回归,可得到回归方程式:$y = 0.1091x + 206.23$,拟合优度 $R^2 = 0.7148$,拟合效果较好(图16)。

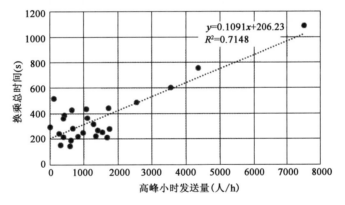

图16 接驳交通总换乘时间与高峰小时旅客发送量关系曲线

5 结 语

综合上述对上海及周边26座中小型高速铁路枢纽配套交通设施的分析,归纳了此类枢纽规划设计的共性问题和需求差异,总结了相关设施规模和换乘时间控制的指标参数,提出应通过立体、紧凑布局手段,实现将换乘时间控制在3min以内,对应换乘距离控制在150~200m的目标,同时应注意控制因设施规模扩大、客流规模增加造成的换乘时间变长问题,为枢纽配套交通设施综合评估提供参考。

本研究的不足之处在于调研样本均位于长三角地区,缺少对其他地区、不同自然地理、气候条件的高速铁路枢纽设施布局和客流特征的对比分析;中小型高速铁路枢纽通常缺少分方式的集散交通量数据,受人力、时间资源投入限制,未对调查车站各类集散交通量做长期的数据监测,对集散模式的总结更多关注的是现有设施的规模,这也是将来需要继续探讨的问题。

参考文献

[1] 国家发展和改革委员会.关于推进高铁站周边区域合理开发建设的指导意见(发改基础[2018]514号)[EB/OL].[2018-05-08].

[2] 张红星.近年来中国中小型铁路旅客车站设计若干问题的研究[D].北京:清华大学,2015.

[3] 周洁.中小城市高铁枢纽交通设施规划研究[D].南京:东南大学,2019.

[4] 杨圆圆.中小型高铁站站前广场设计研究[D].南京:重庆大学,2017.

[5] 李传成,杨依林,周希霖,等.高速铁路客运枢纽关键用地指标研究[J].规划师,2015,31(09):97-103.

An Improved Multi-valued Cellular Automaton Approach for Non-motorized Traffic Flow Considering Counterflow

Yifan Dong　Haipeng Shao　Miaoran Zhang

(College of Transportation Engineering, Chang'an University)

Abstract　Non-motorized traffic mode (e.g., regular bicycles and electric bicycles) is an important component of urban transportation. However, the study for dynamic characteristics of mixed bicycle traffic flow is limited. A series of unsafe behaviours emerge in an endless stream, for example, driving in a reverse direction. In this paper, an improved extended Burgers cellular automata (EBCA) model for heterogeneous bicycle traffic flow is proposed based on the study of driving characteristics of non-motorized vehicles. Also, the existence of counterflow is considered within this model, which is common in reality. Simulation results show that with the consideration of speed separation for regular bicycles and electric bicycles, improved model covers a broader range of flow-density, especially when bicycles with lower speed take a large proportion. Moreover, it is found that the existence of counterflow can not only affect the traffic efficiency of normal bicycle flow, its disturbance to fast bicycles is greater than slow ones which are moving in a normal direction. The improved model studies the performance of dynamic characteristics of heterogeneous bicycle traffic flow under the conditions of different traffic compositions, different path widths and the existence of counterflow, which can guide the construction of bicycle lanes and solve the problems caused by counterflow pertinently.

Keywords　Regular bicycles　Electric bicycles　Counterflow　Multi-valued cellular automaton　Fundamental diagram

0　Introduction

The traditional car-oriented transportation strategy has brought cities a sharp increasing in the number of motor vehicles, both traffic congestion and air pollution become serious issues (Li & Han, 2016) (Sultan et al., 2016). Being aware of these problems, the U.S and some European countries first began to build bicycle systems and introduced a lot of policies to support bicycle traffic, so that bicycles were able to revived (Buehler et al., 2017, Pucher & Buehler, 2017). In recent years, bicycle sharing rate in other Asian countries, such as Tokyo, most cities of India, has become higher and higher (Suzuki & Nakamura, 2017, Tiwari et al., 2016). In China, the share of bicycles in urban transportation is only 5.5 percent before the emergence of bike-sharing companies, after then, this figure has doubled to 11.6 percent (Anonymous, 2017). Different from other counties, with the rapid development of Delivery and Takeaway Market in the same period, the number of electric bicycles has increased dramatically (Feng, 2018). Consequently, as the big differences in speed and flexibility of regular bicycles and electric bicycles, it is common to see the phenomena of counterflow, lane changing and overtaking frequently of e-bikes when they running in the same lane. Due to the increase in both regular bicycles and electric bicycles, it is necessary to study the new patterns heterogeneous bicycle traffic flow presents and give constructive suggestions for the design, operation and control of bicycle facilities.

Since the 1990s, many traffic flow models (such as the car-following models, cellular automata (CA) models, gas-kinetic models and hydrodynamic models) have been proposed and studied to understand the behaviour of the traffic flow (Bando et al., 1995, Nagel & Schreckenberg, 1992, Barlovic et al., 1998, Helbing et al., 2001, Axel, & Raimund, 2000 and Jiang et al., 2002). As an approach to study the microscopic model of traffic flow, CA model is an ideal physical system with discrete time and space and each interacting unit can only have a finite number of discrete states (Schadschneider et al., 2010). CA184 (Wolfram, 1994) is the most basic model to describe the movement of vehicles, where maximum velocity of vehicles maintaining 1. The multi-valued cellular automaton which Nishinari and Takahsshi (1998) first derived from the ultradiscretization of the Burger equation, is an extension form of CA184. Subsequently, Nishinari and Takahsshi (2000) proposed the EBCA1 and EBCA2 models, in which the maximum velocity of vehicles increased to 2 comparing with the Burger Cellular Automaton (BCA) model. However, the multi-valued cellular automaton model is not suitable to study the high-speed traffic flow because when the speed-span becomes larger, the number of neighbour cells becomes larger, the movement of vehicles will become too complicated to describe. Nevertheless, non-motorized vehicles, in contrast, move slower than motorized vehicles. And their lane-changing behaviour is more flexible. In addition, bicycle lanes are not so distinctly partitioned as motorized vehicle lanes, and it is improper to set lane-changing rules to let them move accordingly.

Research on non-motorized traffic flow starts with bicycles. Jiang et al. (2004) introduced the stochastic randomization to EBCA1 and EBCA2 models by considering the interference from pedestrians, other cyclers and some unexpected cases in real life, stipulating that the number of bicycles that can move two cells decreases by 1 with probability p. Jia et al. (2007) proposed a mixed bicycle flow model considering two types of bicycles with different maximum speeds in the view of speed difference of bicycles. Based on EBCA1 model, Xue et al. (2017) considered the velocity effects of the preceding bicycles and divided one step of the movement of bicycles into two sub-steps, the initial movement and the following movement. The modified model enables bicycles to move smoothly and increases the critical density to a more rational level than the original model. As for electric bicycles, Jin et al. (2015a) regarded electric bicycles as bicycles with higher velocity and relevant fundamental diagrams under different model parameters (stochastic randomization probability, the proportion of electric bicycles and the number of lanes) are analyzed and discussed (Jin et al., 2019). It could be found that the mentioned studies focused mainly on bicycles, and when it came to mixed non-motorized traffic flow, the speed difference was considered only between regular bicycles and electric bicycles. While in real life, regular bicycles themselves do not have the same maximum velocity due to different characteristics of their own and proficiency levels of cyclists, so do the electric bicycles. Therefore, this paper expands the maximum velocity of both regular and electric bicycles according to the data investigated in Xi'an City, and proposes an improved model based on the EBCA1 model to analyze the characteristics of mixed non-motorized traffic flow. Also, according to our daily observation, there exist some bicycles moving in a reverse direction and it is necessary to analyze the causes and impacts of this phenomenon. Therefore, the movement of counterflow is another improvement in this model.

The rest of the paper is organized as follows. In section 2, the speed characteristics of non-motorized vehicles via surveying data and is analyzed firstly. Then, EBCA1 is briefly reviewed and an improved multi-valued cellular automaton model based on EBCA1 is introduced to study the mixed non-motorized traffic flow with the consideration of counterflow. In section 3, the simulation results of the improved model are presented and analyzed. Conclusions and proposals are given in section 4.

1 Materials and Methods

1.1 Speed Characteristics of Non-motorized Vehicles

Surveys were conducted in the urban area of Xian, China. Xi'an has greatly developed non-motor system these years and non-motorized vehicles are popular in residents' trips.

We chose four segments named Tangyan Road, Youyi East Road, Taiyi Road, and Taibai South Road to record videos during early peaks (7:00—9:00) and late peaks (17:30—19:00) between October 14 and October 17, 2016 and the weather was cloudy or sunny. Then the team detected and recorded moving time with the application of After Effect software. Geometric designs and samples situation of every road segments are shown in Tab.1. More than half of travelers traveling by non-motorized vehicles observed chose electric bicycles rather than regular bicycles according to the statistics. The average speed of one single bicycle was calculated from the measured road length and its running time on the study segments. The histogram of the speed distribution of regular bicycles and electric bicycles in each section is shown in Fig.1. It can be found that the speed for the most regular bicycles traveling on the road is 2 ~ 6m/s, and 4 ~ 8m/s for the most electric bicycle. The range of speed distribution is wide and some regular bicycles even run faster than electric bicycles. The analyzing results of field data was then used to define the improved multi-valued cellular automaton.

Geometric designs and samples situation of road segments Tab.1

Survey site	Length(m)	Width(m)	Sample size	Ratio of RBs(%)	Ratio of EBs(%)	Volume(bikes/h/m)
Tangyan Road	27	4.5	1737	34	66	1295
Youyi East Road	25	2.5	1643	41	59	1017
Taiyi Road	25	3.5	1557	45	55	985
Taibai South Road	25	3	1730	38	62	1188

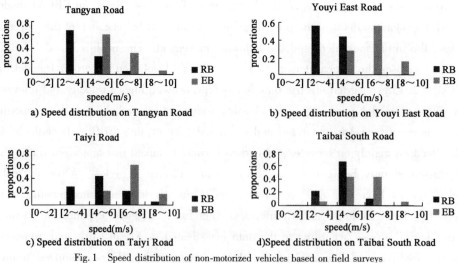

Fig.1 Speed distribution of non-motorized vehicles based on field surveys

Note: RB = regular bicycles; EB = electric bicycles.

1.2 Methodology

In this sub-section, the basic EBCA1 model was described first, then the improved model was proposed for modeling mixed non-motorized traffic flow with the consideration of counterflow.

1.2.1 EBCA1 Model

There are two successive procedures when vehicles move forward from t to $t+1$ in the EBCA1 model:

(1) Vehicles can move to their next site if the site is not fully occupied;

(2) Only those vehicles that have moved in procedure (1) can move further one site if their next site is not fully occupied after procedure (2).

And the evolution equation of EBCA1 is given by:

$$U_j(t+1) = U_j(t) + b_{j-1}(t) - b_j(t) + c_{j-2}(t) - c_{j-1}(t) \tag{1}$$

Where: $b_j(t) = \min[U_j(t), M - U_{j+1}(t)]$ ——the number of moving vehicles at site j and time t in procedure (1);

$c_j(t) = \min[b_j(t), M - U_{j+2}(t) - b_{j+1}(t) + b_{j+2}(t)]$ ——the number of vehicles that can move in procedure (2);

$U_j(t)$ ——the number of vehicles at site j and time t;

M —— the maximum number of vehicles that can be accommodated in each site.

The Fig. 2 shows an illustration of moving process of vehicles in EBCA1 model.

Fig. 2 An illustration of moving process of vehicles in EBCA1 model. The yellow thick arrow represents the vehicles which can move in procedure (1), and the green thin one represents the vehicles which can go on moving another site in procedure (2)

1.2.2 The Improved Multi-valued Cellular Automaton Model

This sub-subsection consists of two parts: the determination of cell size and maximum speed of non-motorized vehicles, as well as the updating rules for the improved model.

1) Cell size and maximum speed of non-motorized vehicles

In a cellular automaton model, each cell is a discrete, specified representation of one section of the bicycle lanes in real life. The determination of cell size is the foundation for establishing model. According to a field survey of 522 non-motorized vehicles in Hangzhou, China by Jin et al. (2015b), the width of regular bicycle is (0.572 ± 0.061) m, the length is (1.710 ± 0.100) m, the width of electric bicycle is (0.685 ± 0.077) m, and the length is (1.820 ± 0.110) m. Although there are some differences in the size of these two types of non-motorized vehicles, the spatial disparity they occupy when moving is not very large. The trajectory of non-motorized vehicle moving on the paths is in the shape of a snake, swing 0.2m to the left and right, thus the width of one cell takes 1m in this model. Also, non-motorized vehicles need a certain longitudinal distance to keep safe, thus the length of one cell takes 2m. Given all that, the size of one cell is identified as 2m × 1m in this paper, which is also used in many other cell automaton models.

Based on the field data in section 2 and the speed limit of traffic regulations, set 1 cell/s and 2 cells/s (equivalent to 2m/s and 4m/s) as the maximum speed of slow bicycles and fast bicycles, 2 cells/s and 3 cells/s (equivalent to 4m/s and 6m/s) as the maximum speed of slow electric bicycles and fast electric bicycles.

2) Updating rules for the improved model

Because of the higher speed, stability and flexibility of electric bicycles, we assume that the electric bicycles have priority to pass forward in the model and of course, vehicles with higher speed also have priority comparing with slow one. The parallel updating rules are as follows:

(1) All non-motorized vehicles move to their next cell if the cell is not fully occupied. During this movement, fast electric bicycles have the first priority, slow electric bicycles have the second priority, followed by fast bicycles, and the last is slow bicycles;

(2) All electric bicycles and fast bicycles that move in step (1) can continue to move to their next cell if the cell is still not fully occupied. While moving, fast electric bicycles have the first priority, followed by slow electric bicycles, and the last is fast bicycles;

(3) The fast electric bicycles that move in step (2) can continue to move one further cell forward if the cell is still not fully occupied.

If there are non-motorized vehicles moving in a reverse direction on the current cell, considering their common nervous psychology and the intention to avoid collisions with normal moving vehicles, set 1 cell/s (equivalent to 2m/s) as their speed and Fig. 3 shows an illustration of moving process of non-motorized vehicles in this improved multi-valued cellular automaton model.

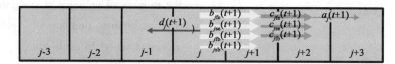

Fig. 3 An illustration of moving process of non-motorized vehicles in the improved multi-valued cellular automaton model. The yellow thick arrows represent the vehicles which can move in procedure (1), the green thinner arrows represent the vehicles which can move another site in procedure (2), the red thinnest arrow represents the electric bicycles which can go on moving one further sitein procedure (3), and the blue arrow represents the vehicles moving against normal traffic flow.

Where: M —— the maximum number of non-motorized vehicles that can be accommodated in the cell;

$U_j(t)$ —— the number of non-motorized vehicles in cell j at time t;

$U_j^{fe}(t)$ —— the number of fast electric bicycles in cell j at time t;

$U_j^{se}(t)$ —— the number of slow electric bicycles in cell j at time t;

$U_j^{fb}(t)$ —— the number of fast bicycles in cell j at time t;

$U_j^{sb}(t)$ —— the number of slow bicycles in cell j at time t;

$N_j(t)$ —— the number of retrograde vehicles in cell j at time t;

$b_j^{fe}(t)$ —— the number of fast electric bicycles that move from cell j at time t in step(1);

$b_j^{se}(t)$ —— the number of slow electric bicycles that move from cell j at time t in step(1);

$b_j^{fb}(t)$ —— the number of fast bicycles that move from cell j at time t in step(1);

$b_j^{sb}(t)$ —— the number of slow bicycles that move from cell j at time t in step(1);

$c_j^{fe}(t)$ —— the number of fast electric bicycles that move from cell j at time t in step(2);

$c_j^{se}(t)$ —— the number of slow electric bicycles that move from cell j at time t in step(2);

$c_j^{fb}(t)$ —— the number of fast bicycles that move from cell j at time t in step(2);

$a_j(t)$ —— the number of fast electric bicycles that move from cell j at time t in step(3);

$d_j(t)$ —— the number of retrograde vehicles that move from cell j at time t.

Relevant evolution formulas for this model are as follows:

Step1: Calculate $b_j^{fe}(t+1)$, $b_j^{se}(t+1)$, $b_j^{fb}(t+1)$ and $b_j^{sb}(t+1)$ $(j=1,2,\cdots,K)$;

$$b_j^{fe}(t+1) = \min[U_j^{fe}(t), M - U_{j+1}(t)] \tag{2}$$

$$b_j^{se}(t+1) = \min[U_j^{se}(t), M - U_{j+1}(t) - b_j^{fe}(t+1)] \tag{3}$$

$$b_j^{fb}(t+1) = \min[U_j^{fb}(t), M - U_{j+1}(t) - b_j^{fe}(t+1) - b_j^{se}(t+1)] \tag{4}$$

$$b_j^{sb}(t+1) = \min[U_j^{sb}(t), M - U_{j+1}(t) - b_j^{fe}(t+1) - b_j^{se}(t+1) - b_j^{fb}(t+1)] \tag{5}$$

$$b_j(t+1) = b_j^{fe}(t+1) + b_j^{se}(t+1) + b_j^{fb}(t+1) + b_j^{sb}(t+1) \tag{6}$$

Step2: Calculate $c_j^{fe}(t+1)$, $c_j^{se}(t+1)$ and $c_j^{fb}(t+1)$ $(j=1,2,\cdots,K)$;

$$c_j^{fe}(t+1) = \min[b_j^{fe}(t+1), M - U_{j+2}(t) - b_{j+1}(t+1) + b_{j+2}(t+1)] \tag{7}$$

$$c_j^{se}(t+1) = \min[b_j^{se}(t+1), M - U_{j+2}(t) - b_{j+1}(t+1) + b_{j+2}(t+1) - c_j^{fe}(t+1)] \tag{8}$$

$$c_j^{fb}(t+1) = \min[b_j^{fb}(t+1), M - U_{j+2}(t) - b_{j+1}(t+1) + b_{j+2}(t+1) - c_j^{fe}(t+1) - c_j^{se}(t+1)] \tag{9}$$

$$c_j(t+1) = c_j^{fe}(t+1) + c_j^{se}(t+1) + c_j^{fb}(t+1) \tag{10}$$

Step3: Calculate $a_j(t+1)$ $(j=1,2,\cdots,K)$;

$$a_j(t+1) = \min[c_j^{fe}(t+1), M - U_{j+3}(t) - b_{j+2}(t+1) + b_{j+3}(t+1) - c_{j+1}(t+1) + c_{j+2}(t+1)] \tag{11}$$

Step4: Calculate $d_j(t+1)$ $(j=1,2,\cdots,K)$;

$$d_j(t+1) = \min[N_j(t), M - U_{j-1}(t) - b_{j-2}(t+1) + b_{j-1}(t+1) - c_{j-3}(t+1) + c_{j-2}(t+1) - a_{j-4}(t+1) + a_{j-3}(t+1)] \tag{12}$$

Step5: Update $U_j^{fe}(t+1)$, $U_j^{se}(t+1)$, $U_j^{fb}(t+1)$, $U_j^{sb}(t+1)$, $N_j(t+1)$ and $U_j(t+1)$ $(j=1,2,\cdots,K)$.

$$U_j^{fe}(t+1) = U_j^{fe}(t) - b_j^{fe}(t+1) + b_{j-1}^{fe}(t+1) - c_{j-1}^{fe}(t+1) + c_{j-2}^{fe}(t+1) - a_{j-2}(t+1) + a_{j-3}(t+1) \tag{13}$$

$$U_j^{se}(t+1) = U_j^{se}(t) - b_j^{se}(t+1) + b_{j-1}^{se}(t+1) - c_{j-1}^{se}(t+1) + c_{j-2}^{se}(t+1) \tag{14}$$

$$U_j^{fb}(t+1) = U_j^{fb}(t) - b_j^{fb}(t+1) + b_{j-1}^{fb}(t+1) - c_{j-1}^{fb}(t+1) + c_{j-2}^{fb}(t+1) \tag{15}$$

$$U_j^{sb}(t+1) = U_j^{sb}(t) - b_j^{sb}(t+1) + b_{j-1}^{sb}(t+1) \tag{16}$$

$$N_j(t+1) = N_j(t) - d_j(t+1) + d_{j+1}(t+1) \tag{17}$$

$$U_j(t+1) = U_j^{fe}(t+1) + U_j^{se}(t+1) + U_j^{fb}(t+1) + U_j^{sb}(t+1) + N_j(t+1) \tag{18}$$

2 Results

The simulation of the improved multi-valued cellular automaton model is realized by MATLAB2019a. The updating time step is 1 second. Besides, they are randomly distributed on the lane with a length of $K = 100$ cells (equivalent to 200 meters) and the maximum number of vehicles that can be accommodated in one cell is 3 ($M = 3$). The model updates in parallel under periodic conditions. The ratio of bicycles to electric bicycles is R, the ratio of fast bicycles to slow bicycles is $r1$, the ratio of fast electrical bicycles to slow electric bicycles is $r2$, and the ratio of retrograde non-motorized vehicles to the total non-motorized vehicles is $r3$. The density and flow per lane are calculated by:

$$\rho(t) = \frac{1}{KM} \sum_{j=1}^{K} U_j(t) \tag{19}$$

$$q(t) = \frac{1}{KM} \sum_{j=1}^{K} [b_{j-1}(t) + c_{j-2}(t) + a_{j-3}(t)] \tag{20}$$

Where $\rho(t)$ and $q(t)$ are the density and flow per lane of the simulated bicycle path system at time t, respectively.

2.1 Effect of different traffic compositions

Fig. 4 shows the fundamental diagrams of non-motorized vehicle flow under different traffic compositions. Fig. 4a) considers the case where $R = 4$, $r1 = 1$, $r2 = 1$, Fig. 4b) considers the case where $R = 1$, $r1 = 1$, $r2 = 1$, and Fig. 4c) considers the case where $R = 1/4$, $r1 = 1$, $r2 = 1$. It could be found that when the proportion of bicycles is 80 percent or 50 percent ($R = 4$ or $R = 1$), the multiple states effect doesn't occur neither in the free flow region nor in the congested flow region except a branch which represents $q = \rho$, and the diagram only displays a state of chaos. The reason for the lowest branch is that when the number of bicycles is large, it is more likely for the lane to be occupied by 3 slow bicycles simultaneously and they will form a stable moving bottleneck by moving side by side, so that fast bicycles cannot overtake them and have to follow behind them. However, the mechanism to form other stable moving bottleneck does not show up in any one of the systems because of the complication of composition of vehicle velocity. In addition, when the proportion of bicycles is higher, more state points appear above the branch $q = \rho$ with no obvious branches forming, meaning that with more slow non-motorized vehicles existing in the system, more unstable the traffic flow will be. The critical density in all cases is between 0.3 and 0.4, and when the electric bicycles accounts for 80 percent ($R = 1/4$), the maximum flow in the system increase, indicating that with an increase in the electric bicycles' percentage, the capacity of bicycle path increases.

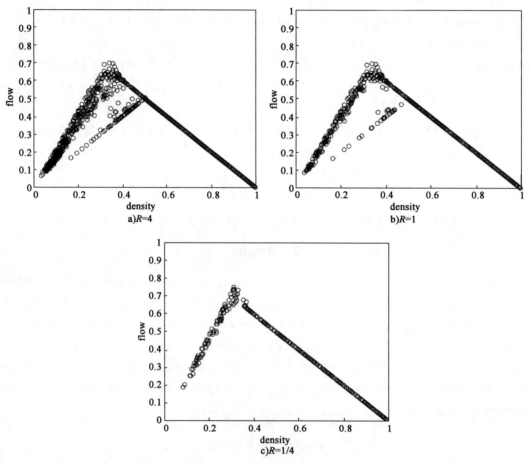

Fig. 4 Fundamental diagram under different traffic compositions where $r1 = 1$, $r2 = 1$

2.2 Effect of different path widths

Simulations of $M = 2$, $M = 3$, and $M = 4$ were conducted and Fig. 5 shows the fundamental diagrams of non-motorized traffic flow under the condition of $r1 = r2 = 1$ and $R = 2/3$. It can be seen that with an increase in the path width, the maximum flow also increases. This can be explained by the fact that when path width increases, lane changing becomes easier, and electric bicycles have more opportunities to overtake bicycles. In addition, when the width is narrow ($M = 2$), the branch $q = \rho$ appears again. It is because when a path can only hold two vehicles, the possibility for it to be occupied by two slow bicycles also increased, and a stable moving bottleneck will come into being again. When the path becomes wider ($M = 4$), a shape of inverse λ can be seen in the figure. Because when the critical density is not reached, the number of vehicles entering the system continues to increase, wider lanes make it easier for non-motorized vehicles to change lanes, and the flow comes up to its maximum. At the same time, if the number of vehicles entering the system continues to increase, it is difficult for the electric bicycle to keep on moving at its maximum speed, resulting in a sudden decrease in the speed of the system and congestion occurs.

2.3 Effect of counterflow on capacity of bicycle paths

The proportion of cyclists driving reversely is much lower than that driving in a normal way. Therefore, simulation was conducted under the case when $r3 = 0, 0.02, 0.05, 0.08$, and 0.10, respectively. Non-motorized vehicles driving normally maintain a fixed proportion of $R = 2/3, r1 = r2 = 1$, and M is equal to 4, the simulation results is presented in Fig. 6. It can be seen from the figure that with an increase of the retrograde ratio, the capacity of the lane decreases. Moreover, the effect of counterflow on the region of free flow is not as remarkable as on the congested flow. When $r3 = 0.02$, three branches appear in the congested flow, and when $r3 = 0.05$, the pattern coincides with the lowest branch of the case when $r3 = 0.02$. It all comes down to the same result that counterflow does seriously affect the stability of non-motorized traffic flow of normal driving, especially for the flow in the congested region. When $r3$ exceeds 0.05, the flow in the congested flow region is 0. The reason is that when the retrograde vehicles occupy a cross section of the bicycle path in the model, the normal driving non-motorized vehicles are completely blocked and cannot go on moving forward.

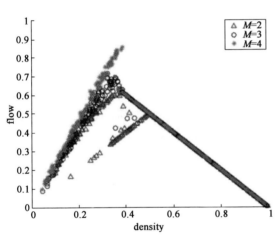
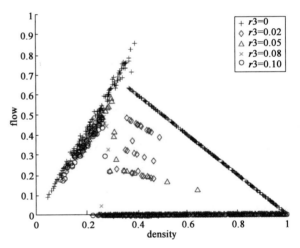

Fig. 5 Fundamental diagram under different path widths ($R = 2/3, r1 = 2 = 1$)

Fig. 6 Fundamental diagram under different retrograde ratios ($R = 2/3, r1 = r2 = 1$)

2.4 Effect of counterflow on normal driving non-motorized vehicles

Assuming that all normal driving vehicles on the path are slow (maximum velocity = 1) ones or fast (maximum velocity = 3) ones. Simulation is conducted under situation of $r3 = 0.1, 0.2, 0.3$, and 0.4, and simulation result is presented in Fig. 7. It can be seen from the figure that when the density is equal to 0.4 in the slow-speed system, bidirectional non-motorized vehicles will be blocked face to face so that the flow is equal to 0. While In the fast-speed system, this phenomenon already comes in being when the density is close to 0.2. Although the system is more stable when there more fast vehicles existing, the ability for them to resist disturbance is lower than that of slow vehicles, so that the probability for them to be blocked by reverse vehicles is larger than the slow ones. Moreover, the speed of fast vehicles itself is relatively fast, so when the proportion of retrogrades increases by the same rate, the decrease in traffic flow is more obvious than that of slow vehicles. In summary, when retrograde non-motorized vehicles exist in the system, the impact on fast vehicles is greater than on slow ones.

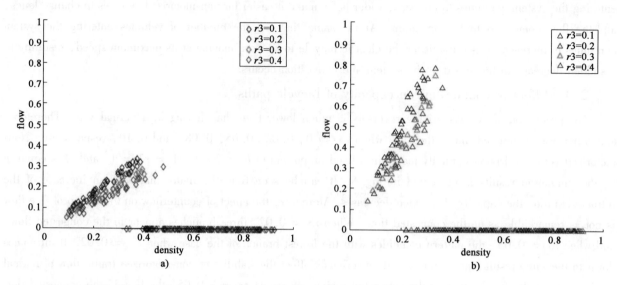

Fig. 7 Fundamental diagram for the system with different maximum velocities under different retrograde ratio

3 Conclusions and Future Study

This paper established an improved multi-valued cellular automaton model considering a hybrid condition of non-motorized vehicles moving on the path with different maximum velocities. The features of fundamental diagrams under different model parameters were analyzed with the simulation model. The study also evaluated the traffic flow features with counterflow in an ideal system, for example, only consisting of regular bicycles or electric bicycles. The results showed that more complicated the speed distribution was, more complicated the system would be. Besides, due to the fact that bicycle paths and motorized vehicle lanes are always physically separated with each other, which reducing the risk of collision with motorized vehicles, some cyclists prefer to ride reversely on bicycle paths in order to reach their destination as soon as possible. Although retrograde non-motorized vehicles only account for a small proportion, it does hinder the moving of normal non-motorized vehicles, and the simulation results showed that impact on fast vehicles is more serious. The simulation results suggest that if the proportion of retrograde bicycles is high, it is essential for traffic management departments to implement countermeasures.

However, there are several limitations.

(1) Research in this paper is a theoretical exploration, and further numerical validation is needed.

(2) The model proposed in this paper based on the assumption of fast vehicles will overtake slow ones if possible. In future work, an overtaking probability should be introduced for model calibration.

References

[1] Anonymous. White papers on bike-sharing and urban development[J]. Urban and Rural Development, 2017(8):5.

[2] Axel Klar, Raimund Wegener. Kinetic Derivation of Macroscopic Anticipation Models for Vehicular Traffic [J]. Society for Industrial and Applied Mathematics, 2000.

[3] Bando M, Hasebe K, Nakayama, A, et al. Dynamical model of traffic congestion and numerical simulation[J]. Physical Review E, 1995, 51(2):1035-1042.

[4] Barlovic R, Santen L, Schadschneider A et al. Metastable states in cellular automata for traffic flow[J]. The European Physical Journal B-Condensed Matter and Complex Systems, 1998, 5(3):793-800.

[5] Buehler R, Pucher J, Gerike R, et al. Reducing car dependence in the heart of Europe: lessons from

Germany, Austria, and Switzerland[J]. Transport reviews,2017,37(1):4-28.

[6] Feng Y. Investigation and Research on User Demand for Electric Vehicles Used in Takeout Food Delivery in China[J]. 2018 znd International Conference on Social Scierce,Arts and Humanities,2018.

[7] Helbing D, Hennecke A, Shvetsov V,et al. Master: macroscopic traffic simulation based on a gas-kinetic, non-local traffic model[J]. Transportation Research Part B,2001,35(2):0-211.

[8] Jia B, Li X G, Jiang R, et al. Multi-value cellular automata model for mixed bicycle flow[J]. The European Physical Journal B,2007,56(3):247-252.

[9] Jiang R, Jia B, Wu Q S. Stochastic multi-value cellular automata models for bicycle flow[J]. Journal of Physics A: Mathematical and General,2004,37(6):2063.

[10] Jiang R, Wu Q S., Zhu Z J. A new continuum model for traffic flow and numerical tests[J]. Transportation Research, Part B (Methodological),2002,36(5):0-419.

[11] Jin S, Qu X, Xu C, et al. An improved multi-value cellular automata model for heterogeneous bicycle traffic flow[J]. Physics Letters A,2015,379(39):2409-2416.

[12] Jin S, Qu X, Zhou D,et al. Estimating cycleway capacity and bicycle equivalent unit for electric bicycles [J]. Transportation Research Part A: Policy and Practice,2015(77):225-248.

[13] Jin S, Xu L, Xu C, Ma D. Lane width - based cellular automata model for mixed bicycle traffic flow [J]. Computer-Aided Civil and Infrastructure Engineering,2019.

[14] Li Han-ru. Study on green transportation system of international metropolises[J]. Procedia Engineering, 2016(137):762-771.

[15] Nagel K, Schreckenberg M. A cellular automaton model for freeway traffic[J]. Journal de physique I, 1992,2(12):2221-2229.

[16] Nishinari K, Takahashi D. Analytical properties of ultradiscrete Burgers equation and rule-184 cellular automaton. Journal of Physics A: Mathematical and General,1998,31(24):5439.

[17] Nishinari K, Takahashi, D. Multi-value cellular automaton models and metastable states in a congested phase[J]. Journal of Physics A: Mathematical and general,2000,33(43):7709.

[18] Pucher J, Buehler, R. Cycling towards a more sustainable transport future. Transport Reviews,2017,37 (6):689-694.

[19] Schadschneider A, Chowdhury D,Nishinari K. Stochastic transport in complex systems: from molecules to vehicles[J]. Elsevier,2010.

[20] Sultan Z, Tini N. H,Moeinaddini M. Exploring the Implementation and Success of Green Urban Mobility in Asian Cities[J]. PLANNING MALAYSIA JOURNAL,2016,14(4).

[21] Suzuki M,Nakamura H. Bike share deployment and strategies in Japan[J]. ITF Discussion Paper,2017.

[22] Tiwari G, Jain D, Rao K R. Impact of public transport and non-motorized transport infrastructure on travel mode shares, energy, emissions and safety: Case of Indian cities[J]. Transportation research part D: transport and environment,2016(44):277-291.

[23] Wolfram S. Cellular Automata and Complexity Addison-Wesley[J]. Reading,1994.

[24] Xue S, Jia B, Jiang R, Li X,Shan, J. An improved Burgers cellular automaton model for bicycle flow [J]. Physica A: Statistical Mechanics and its Applications,2017(487):164-177.

Research of Car-following Models Based on Deep Learning in Different Traffic Scenarios

Xing Guo[1]　Cheng Wei[1]　Wenwei Wang[2]

(1. University of Chang'an, Department of Computer Science and Technology;
2. Zhejiang Tianxingjian Intelligent Technology Co., Ltd)

Abstract　In the modern traffic flow dynamics research, the car-following model is necessary as a crucial tool. Even though many car-following models have been proposed and widely used in many studies, the accuracy and robustness of existing car-following models are still not enough. In this research, two new car-following models based on deep learning (including BiLSTM and combination of IDM and BiLSTM) are proposed, and the two different traffic scenarios which from NGSIM dataset are built to test and validate the efficiency of two proposed car-following models. The simulation experiment results indicate that two new car-following models outperform IDM car-following models in two traffic scenarios.

Keywords　Car-following model　Traffic Flow　Deep Learning　Bi-directional Long Short-Term Memory (BiLSTM)

0　Introduction

Car-following model is a basic method to simulate the micro traffic flow dynamics and describes the interaction between the continuous vehicles in the same lane when the vehicles are moving. The car-following models could be divided into two types according to the modelling methods: theory driven and data driven. The theory driven car-following model is modelled by kinematics formulation and traffic flow theory, and the parameters of it has clearly physical meanings. The theory driven car-following models originated from Pipes, since then many representative and widely applied theory driven car-following models were proposed. Such as Gazis-Herman-Rothery car-following model, Newell car-following model, Wiedemann car-following model, Gipps car-following model, Optimal Velocity (OV) car-following model, and Intelligent Driver Model car-following model. However, these car-following models cannot reflect the actual traffic flow well, many researches wanted to improve them. Jiang et al. proposed the full velocity difference (FVD) car-following model, it considered the influence of velocity difference for car-following behavior. Tang et al., developed a car-following model with consideration of road condition, the experiment indicated that the proposed method was better than other models. Tang et al., proposed a car-following model with inter-vehicle communication, however the model has not been tested with actual experimental data. Jiang et al., extended car-following model with consideration of platoon, but the model was not validated in different traffic density. Zhang et al., accounted for the impact of preceding car's taillight and improved the car-following model. Yu et al., proposed relative velocity difference car-following model and validated the performance of model under ACC strategy. Sun et al., combined the driver's memory and average speed effect of preceding vehicle, proposed the new car-following model based on the OV model.

With the development of Machine Learning (ML) technology, the ML car-following model is based on the big data, and it takes the ML technology to predict the car-following behavior at the next time step. Compared with theory car-following models, the ML car-following does not need mathematical formulation or model parameters calibration. The ML methods can be divided into three categories: support vector regression (SVR), nonparametric regression and neural network, respectively. Wei and Liu proposed a car-following model based SVR to investigate the feature of car-following behavior of the following vehicle. The neural network as the significant branch of the ML, has been used in many car-following model studies. Jia et al. proposed a car-following model that is based on the back propagation (BP) neural network. The simulation experiment indicates that it can simulate the acceleration of the following vehicle. Sakda and Dia proposed a car-following model that used neural network to predict the action of following vehicle. The proposed model was evaluated from micro and macro perspectives. Chong et al. used the agent-based neural network to build the car-following model. The results showed that agent-based model outperformed the GHR model and has a higher accuracy. Khodayari et al. built a neural network car-following model and added the impact of the driver behavior. Zhou et al. proposed a new car-following model with RNN (Recurrent Neural Network) model, and analyzed the influence of different driving behaviors to the car-following behavior. Ma and Qu used the LSTM (Long Short-Term Memory) model to establish a new car-following model, and studied the performance of the proposed model under the vehicle platoon scenario. Compared with IDM model, the simulation experiments indicated that the LSTM model is more precisely.

From above literature review, it can be seen that notwithstanding some new car-following methods (theory driven or data driven) have been proposed, the robustness of existing car-following model is still not good. These studies only use single dataset or simple traffic flow to test the proposed model and actual experiments are not insufficient, which is not convincing. In this research, a new car-following model based on BiLSTM is proposed firstly, and then IDM and BiLSTM car-following model are combined with optimal weighting method as a new hybrid car-following model. The new models are trained by different dataset, which includes urban data and highway data. The aim of the research is to improve the robustness and accuracy of the model.

1 Data Preparatien and Preprocessing

The NGSIM (Web-1) data includes three sub datasets, and they are I-80 freeway dataset, Lankershim Boulevard dataset, and 101 highway dataset, respectively. In this research, the 101 dataset that represents the highway data and Lankershim dataset that represents the urban data are used to train and test the proposed method. The velocity and trajectory example of lane 2 are shown in Fig. 1.

In order to exclude the negative influence on the neural network, the moving-average filter algorithm was used to process the data. In this research, the following requirements need to be satisfied:

(1) Filtered data less than one hundred sample points.
(2) Filtered the vehicles which are in lane-change behavior.
(3) Filtered suddenly jump/ fake collision data sample.

After filtering, 1586325 sample points were extracted from the two datasets, and randomly select 80% (1269060) of them for training, and the rest 20% (317265) for validating.

2 Methodology

In this research, the BiLSTM and IDM car following models are used to build the new hybrid car-following model. The change of the later data is influenced by the basis of the earlier data, and the BiLSTM model can better capture the two-way dependence of car-following behavior on the time series. Besides, the addition of IDM also can ensure both influence of velocity difference and space headway are considered. The input of the model has four labels, and they are velocity, velocity difference, space headway, and acceleration of following vehicle at the current timestep, respectively. The output of the model is the velocity of following vehicle at the next timestep.

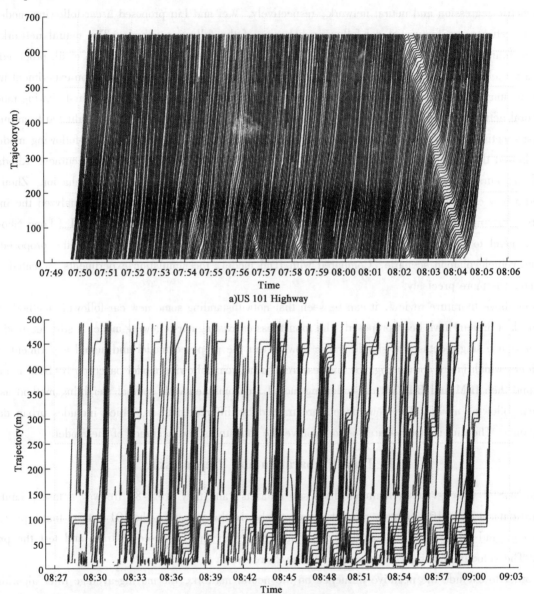

Fig. 1 Illustration of vehicle trajectories of 101 highway and Lankershim.

2.1 Parameters Calibration of IDM Car-following Model

The IDM car-following model is an excellent classic car-following model, and it is used in many research of micro flow, such as the longitude control of vehicle platoon. Compared with other car following models, both velocity and space headway of vehicle are considered in IDM. The formulation of IDM is given below:

$$a_n = \alpha \left[1 - \left(\frac{v_n(t)}{v_0} \right)^\delta - \left(\frac{s_n^*(t)}{s_n(t)} \right)^2 \right] \qquad (1)$$

where a_n, α, $v_n(t)$, v_0, δ, $s_n^*(t)$ and $s_n(t)$ represents the acceleration of vehicle n, max acceleration, velocity of vehicle n at time t, desired velocity, acceleration exponent, desired space headway, and actual space headway of vehicle n at time t. The definition of desired space headway is as follows:

$$s_n^*(t) = s_0 + \max\left(0, T v_n + \frac{v_n(t) \Delta v_n(t)}{2\sqrt{\alpha\beta}} \right) \qquad (2)$$

where s_0, T and β represents the minimum distance, reaction time and comfort deceleration, respectively.

Parameters calibration means the parameters setting of classic car-following model need to be revised depend on different traffic environment, and target is to find a set of parameters whichminimize the error between the simulation values and actual values. For example, the desired space headway would be longer when vehicle runs on the highway instead of on the urban roads. In order to more precisely simulate the motion of the vehicle, it is necessary to calibrate parameters in micro traffic flow study. In the IDM car-following model, six parameters are need to be calibrated. They are max acceleration, desired velocity, acceleration exponent, desired space headway, reaction time, and comfort deceleration, respectively.

Once the dataset required for parameters calibration is extracted, the method of calibration is vital. There are many widely use parameter optimization algorithm, the most representative of them are simulated annealing algorithm and genetic algorithm (GA). The simulated annealing algorithm is used in this research due to the simple and lower computational cost.

The result of the model calibration is shown in Tab. 1. After calibration, the calibrated parameters can more accurately simulate the following behavior of the vehicle. The acceleration and deceleration are larger than the original parameters, which indicates that many rapid acceleration and deceleration behaviors exist in the urban data are added into training dataset.

Calibration of IDM parameters Tab. 1

Parameters	Description	Bounds	Originate	Calibrated
α(m/s^2)	Max acceleration	[0.1,5]	1.0	2.43
v_0(km/h)	Desired velocity of FV	[1,252]	54	56.59
δ	Acceleration exponent	[1,40]	4	3.85
β(m/s^2)	Deceleration of FV	[0.1,5]	1.5	3.61
s_0(m)	Minimum distance	[0.1,10]	2	4.30
T(s)	Time gap	[0.1,5]	1	4.99

2.2 BiLSTM Car-following Model

In 1997, the LSTM was proposed by Hochreiter et al., and now it has been one of the mostly applied models in many areas. The LSTM also have the advantages that RNN processes time series and solves the problems of gradient vanishing and explosion. The BiLSTM combines forward and back ward LSTM and easily to get data features from the two different directions. The model which is used is based on a layer of BiLSTM neural network and a layer of fully connected network. The input of the model is state of following vehicle, and the result is used as the input of the fully connected neural network to predict the velocity of following at the next timestep.

Fig. 2 shows the internal structure of LSTM cell. Where I_t is input data; c_t and h_t are the memory cell state and output of LSTM cell at time t. f_t, x_t, and o_t are the gating vectors. σ and $tanh$ are activation function, as defined in Eq. 1 and Eq. 2.

$$\sigma(x) = \frac{1}{1+e^x} \quad (3)$$

$$\tan h(x) = \frac{e^x - e^{-x}}{e^x + e^{-x}} \quad (4)$$

The definition of three controlling gates are given below, where w_{fh}, w_{fi}, w_{xh}, w_{xi}, w_{ch}, w_{ci}, w_{oh}, and w_{oi} are weighted matrices, and b_f, b_i, b_c, and b_o are the bias in gates.

Forget gate:

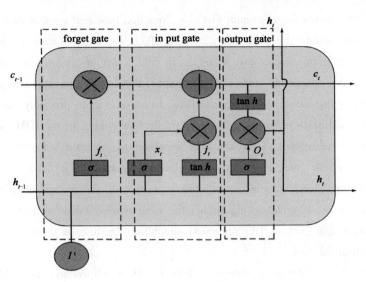

Fig. 2 Internal structure of LSTM cell

$$f_t = \sigma(w_{fh}h_{t-1} + w_{fi}I_t + b_f) \quad (5)$$

Input gate:

$$x_t = \sigma(w_{xh}h_{t-1} + w_{xi}I_t + b_i) \quad (6)$$

$$j_t = \tanh(w_{ch}h_{t-1} + w_{ci}I_t + b_c) \quad (7)$$

$$c_t = f_t c_{t-1} + x_t j_t \quad (8)$$

Output gate:

$$o_t = \sigma(w_{oh}h_{t-1} + w_{oi}I_t + b_o) \quad (9)$$

$$y_t = h_t = o_t \tanh(c_t) \quad (10)$$

BiLSTM has forward and backward two layers. Each training sequence is composed of an LSTM, and both of them are connected to an output layer. This structure can provide complete past and future time series data for each point in the input sequence of the output layer. That is, the data in the clockwise and counterclockwise time directions will be saved by the hidden layer.

2.3 Construction of Hybrid Car-following Model

In the construction of the car-following model, different prediction approaches provide different parameter dimensions of the vehicle motion state due to different modeling mechanisms and starting points. Therefore, the prediction biases of each model are not the same. In order to make full use of the physical information provided by various car-following models, it is more efficient to combine different models to form the combined model to improve the accuracy of the established model. The current research on hybrid models can be divided into two categories: variable weight combination method and constant weight combination method. In order to integrate the advantages of the above two car-following models and make the prediction results fully reflect the safety and comfort of car-following behavior, this paper uses the optimal weighting method of combination prediction theory to build the IDM-BiLSTM hybrid car-following model.

The key of hybrid prediction is to determine the value of weighting coefficients $\lambda 1$ and $\lambda 2$. The total error function is defined as Eq. 11:

$$f = \sum_{i=1}^{n} \alpha_i (y_i - f_i) \quad (11)$$

where y_i is the actual observed value, f_i is the prediction value, α_i is the coefficient of the $i-th$ method. The prediction error vector of the $i-th$ prediction models is as follows:

$$\mathbf{E}_i = [e_{i1}, e_{i2}, \cdots, e_{in}]^T \quad (12)$$

Error matrix:
$$e = [E_1, E_2] \quad (13)$$

Error information matrix:
$$E_r = e^T e = \begin{bmatrix} E_{11} & E_{12} \\ E_{22} & E_{22} \end{bmatrix} \quad (14)$$

Then the sum of square errors of the hybrid model:
$$S = \sum_{t=1}^{n} e2_t = \sum_{t=1}^{n} (\sum_{i=1}^{2} w_i e_{it})2 = W^T E_r W \quad (15)$$

The optimal value:
$$W = \frac{E_r^{-1} R_r}{R_r^T E_r^{-1} R_r} \quad (16)$$

3 Experiment

In the experiment section, two different simulation experiments are tested. One is from the US101 highway dataset and the other is from the Lankershim dataset. The velocity and trajectory of IDM, BiLSTM, and IDM-BiLSTM are given. In addition, the RMSE of every model is also calculated.

3.1 US101 Highway Experiment

US101 Highway (Web-2) dataset is collected at the US 101 highway, in Los Angeles, CA, on June 15th, 2005. A car-following behavior pair without idling was extracted from dataset to test the performance of different car-following models.

Fig. 3a) shows the velocity of car-following models. Notwithstanding the IDM car-following can simulate the car-following behavior of the following vehicle, it cannot simulate more details. On the contrary, BiLSTM and IDM-BiLSTM have better prediction ability and can capture more details even there are some small oscillations. Figure 3b) shows the trajectory of car-following models. The simulation experiment result is the same as the velocity, and the trajectory of LSTM and BiLSTM models almost coincides with the raw trajectory. However, even if the model parameters have been calibrated by training dataset, IDM car-following performs worst.

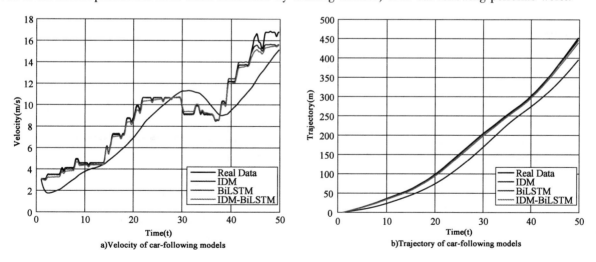

Fig. 3 Performance of car-following models at US101 highway

In addition, for the purpose of distinguishing which model is better between IDM model and BiLSTM model, the Root Mean Square Error (RMSE) is used. The RMSE calculation formula is given below:
$$\text{RMSE} = \sqrt{[\sum_{I=1}^{m}(x_i - y_i)2]/m} \quad (17)$$

where m represents the volume of sample; x represents the actual value; y represents the prediction value.

Tab. 2 shows the results of RMSE of velocity and trajectory of car following models at US101 highway. Compared with IDM and other models, the RMSE of velocity and trajectory of IDM is significantly larger than other models. For BiLSTM and IDM-BiLSTM models, the BiLSTM is better. The reason is that the IDM will affect the performance of IDM-BiLSTM. However, this conclusion is not absolute. If the accuracy of IDM car-following models is improved, the performance of IDM-BiLSTM car-following model will perform better. It indicates the proposed BiLSTM model performs best on the US101 highway.

RMSE of velocity and trajectory of car-following models　　Tab. 2

Models	IDM	BiLSTM	IDM-BiLSTM
RMSE of Velocity	1.8684	0.3371	0.4505
RMSE of Trajectory	28.9202	1.6107	5.2063

3.2 Lankershim Experiment

Lankershim dataset (Web-3) is collected at the Lankershim Boulevard in the Universal City neighborhood of Los Angeles, CA, On June 16, 2005. The preceding vehicle ID is 76, and the following vehicle ID is 85. In order to reflect the marked feature of the urban roads, the car-following pair which includes the stop-go behavior is extracted from the dataset.

Fig. 4a) shows the velocity of car-following models at Lankershim Boulevard. The IDM model can simulate the stop-go behavior of the following vehicle at the intersection, but the accuracy is lower. It can be seen from the figure that the following vehicle stops at 10s. However, the velocity simulated by IDM is approximately 0 at 22s, which is untruthfulness. Besides, the actual velocity of following vehicle is larger than the velocity simulated by IDM. On the contrary, the LSTM and BiLSTM car-following models can more precisely simulate the stop-go behavior of following vehicle and many little oscillations are included. Fig. 4b) shows the trajectory of car-following models at Lankershim Boulevard. The performance of IDM is also lower than other models because the trajectory is integrated by velocity, and the error of velocity is amplified.

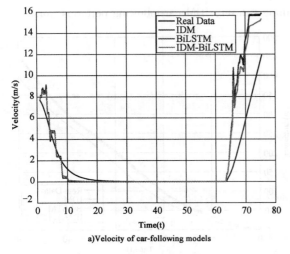
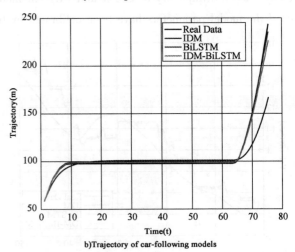

a) Velocity of car-following models　　　　　　　　b) Trajectory of car-following models

Fig. 4　Performance of car-following models at Lankershim Boulevard

Tab. 3 shows the RMSE of velocity and trajectory of car-following models at the Lankershim Boulevard. The RMSE of IDM is larger than the other two models greatly. Compared with BiLSTM model, the RMSE of velocity of IDM-BiLSTM is higher but the RMSE of trajectory is lower. Here are some possible reasons. For velocity simulation experiment, it may be because the IDM has a negative influence to velocity simulation. For trajectory simulation experiment, the IDM model considers the influence of velocity difference and space headway, and it helps the IDM-BiLSTM outperform the BiLSTM.

RMSE of velocity and trajectory of car-following models Tab. 3

	IDM	BiLSTM	IDM-BiLSTM
RMSE of Velocity	2.0821	0.1262	0.2931
RMSE of Trajectory	14.9578	3.3774	3.2047

4 Conclusions

In this research, a new hybrid car-following model based on IDM and BiLSTM was proposed. The US101 highway and Lankershim Boulevard dataset are used to test and validate the different models. We firstly calibrate the IDM car-following model parameters with simulated annealing algorithm, and then build a car-following model based BiLSTM method. Finally, optimal weighting algorithm is used to combine two models. The contributions of this research can be concluded:

(1) Calibrated the IDM car-following models.
(2) Proposed a new car-following model based on BiLSTM neural network.
(3) Combined IDM with BiLSTM as a new car-following model.

The results indicate that the BiLSTM car-following model has the strongest performance and theIDM-BiLSTM car-following model also perform better than the IDM. However, this research still has some limitations. The performance of ANN depends on the training dataset heavily, so how to improve the robustness of ANN models is significant. In addition, the reaction delay also has an important effect on car-following behavior. These are future work directions.

References

[1] Bando M, Hasebe K, Nakayama A, Shibata A, Sugiyama Y. Dynamical model of traffic congestion and numerical simulation[J]. Physical review E,1995,51(2), 1035.

[2] Chong L, Abbas M M, Medina A. Simulation of driver behavior with agent-based back-propagation neural network[J]. Transportation Research Record, 2011,2249(1), 44-51.

[3] Gazis D. C, Herman R, Rothery R W. Nonlinear follow-the-leader models of traffic flow[J]. Operations research,1961,9(4), 545-567.

[4] Gipps P G. Abehavioural car-following model for computer simulation[J]. Transportation Research Part B: Methodological,1981,15(2), 105-111.

[5] Hochreiter S, Schmidhuber J. Long short-term memory[J]. Neural computation,1997,9(8), 1735-1780.

[6] Hongfei J, Zhicai J, Anning N. Develop a car-following model using data collected by" five-wheel system" [C]. In Proceedings of the 2003 IEEE International Conference on Intelligent Transportation Systems (Vol. 1, pp. 346-351). IEEE,2003.

[7] Jiang R, Wu Q, Zhu Z. Full velocity difference model for a car-following theory[J]. Physical Review E, 2001,64(1), 017101.

[8] Jiang R, Hu M B., Zhang H M., Gao Z Y., Jia B, Wu Q S. On some experimental features of car-following behavior and how to model them[J]. Transportation Research Part B: Methodological,2015(80):338-354.

[9] Khodayari A, Ghaffari A, Kazemi R, Braunstingl R. A modified car-following model based on a neural network model of the human driver effects[C]. IEEE Transactions on Systems, Man, and Cybernetics-Part A: Systems and Humans, 2012,42(6), 1440-1449.

[10] Kirkpatrick S, Gelatt C D., Vecchi M P. Optimization by simulated annealing[J]. science,1983,220 (4598), 671-680.

[11] Ma L, Qu S. A sequence to sequence learning based car-following model for multi-step predictions considering reaction delay[J]. Transportation research part C: emerging technologies, 2020(120):102785.

[12] Newell G F. Nonlinear effects in the dynamics of car following[J]. Operations research, 1961, 9(2), 209-229.

[13] Panwai S, Dia H. Neural agent car-following models[C]. IEEE Transactions on Intelligent Transportation Systems, 2007, 8(1), 60-70.

[14] Pipes L A. An operational analysis of traffic dynamics[J]. Journal of applied physics, 1953, 24(3), 274-281.

[15] Schuster M, Paliwal, K. K. Bidirectional recurrent neural networks[C]. IEEE transactions on Signal Processing, 1997, 45(11), 2673-2681.

[16] Sun Y, Ge H, Cheng, R. An extended car-following model considering driver's memory and average speed of preceding vehicles with control strategy[J]. Physica A: Statistical Mechanics and Its Applications, 2019(521):752-761.

[17] Tang T, Wang Y, Yang X, Wu Y. A new car-following model accounting for varying road condition[J]. Nonlinear Dynamics, 2012, 70(2), 1397-1405.

[18] Tang T, Shi W, Shang H, Wang Y. A new car-following model with consideration of inter-vehicle communication[J]. Nonlinear dynamics, 2014, 76(4), 2017-2023.

[19] Treiber M, Hennecke A, Helbing D. Congested traffic states in empirical observations and microscopic simulations[J]. Physical review E, 2000, 62(2), 1805.

[20] Wei D, Liu H. Analysis of asymmetric driving behavior using a self-learning approach[J]. Transportation Research Part B: Methodological, 2013(47):1-14.

[21] Whitley D. A genetic algorithm tutorial[J]. Statistics and computing, 1994, 4(2), 65-85.

[23] Yu S, Tang J, Xin, Q. Relative velocity difference model for the car-following theory[J]. Nonlinear Dynamics, 2018, 91(3), 1415-1428.

[24] Zhang J, Tang T Q, Yu S W. An improved car-following model accounting for the preceding car's taillight[J]. Physica A: Statistical Mechanics and Its Applications, 2018(492):1831-1837.

[25] Zhou M, Qu X, Li X. A recurrent neural network based microscopic car following model to predict traffic oscillation[J]. Transportation research part C: emerging technologies, 2017(84):245-264.

基于交通波参数的排队长度估计方法

白孜帅[1] 张伟斌[1] 张峻屹[2]

(1.南京理工大学电子工程与光电技术学院；2.广岛大学)

摘 要 排队长度作为衡量交叉口运行状态的重要指标之一，其长度估计具有重要意义。本文通过分析交叉口信号控制下所产生的交通波，分析启动波与停止波的空间性关系，推导了交叉口排队长度的计算公式。采用轨迹数据作为研究数据，通过最小二乘法对交叉口启动及停止波波速进行了参数估计，并且通过临近周期聚合的方法解决了交叉口GPS车辆渗透率低的问题。选用现实路口数据作为仿真原型，在渗透率为10%的情况下仿真验证本文了所提方法，仿真结果显示各相位估算平均误差约为10.13%，估算精度较高，为现阶段基于轨迹数据的交叉口交通状态估计提供了条件。

关键词 交通状态估计 排队长度 最小二乘法 轨迹数据 交通波理论

0 引言

交叉口排队长度作为衡量交叉口运行状态的重要指标,一直是交通状态估计的研究重点。轨迹数据[1]、视频数据[2]及多种数据源融合数据[3]均被用于排队长度的估计,本文选取轨迹数据作为理论研究的数据源,推导基于轨迹数据的交通波参数估计及排队长度估计方法。

基于轨迹数据的排队长度估计方法主要有基于概率论和基于交通波理论两个方向。从概率论的角度来说,文献[4]分析了渗透率与交叉口排队长度的分布关系,得出了仅依靠交叉口排队最后一辆车的位置来计算交叉口排队长度的公式。文献[5]则考虑了车辆到达排队队列的时间,将排队长度的估计研究扩展到了时间及空间纬度。文献[6]则将排队长度的动态变化转化为状态转移过程,利用卡尔曼滤波对交叉口排队长度进行逐周期的估算求解。文献[7]则从贝叶斯定理及排队分布角度对交叉口排队长度估算方法进行了总结和创新。文献[8]通过车辆在交叉口的旅行时间建立了车辆队列延时模型来对交叉口排队长度的最大值及最小值进行估计。交通波理论在排队长度估计中也大放异彩,文献[9]提出了将分散的 GPS 车辆轨迹数据的集体效应与交通流冲击波分析及数据挖掘相结合的交叉口队列排队长度估计方法,并验证了其方法在过饱和及队列溢出场景下的有效性。文献[10]将冲击波理论与排队长度估计联系起来,利用轨迹数据内速度位置变化的拐点来估计冲击波速,进而对排队长度及交叉口信号配时进行估计。文献[11]则提出了基于冲击波的临界阈值算法对冲击波速进行计算继而对交叉口排队长度进行估计。文献[12]则提出了基于交通波的饱和与过饱和情况下都适用的交叉口排队长度估算方法。文献[13]提出了一种在较低的渗透率场景下使用采样车辆轨迹数据的基于交通波的排队重点估计方法。文献[14]则结合交通波理论提出了一种在较低渗透率下的排队长度最大似然估计方法。此外,交通波理论还被应用于交通事故分析[15]、交通信号控制优化[16]等领域。

本文在总结前文的基础上,利用轨迹数据提出了基于交通波参数估计的排队长度实时估计算法。采用周期聚合的方法解决了现阶段道路渗透率较低的问题,并且利用轨迹数据中车辆的停车点及启动点为交通波参数提供了估计方法。仿真研究表明,本方法精度较高切实有效。

1 基于交通波的排队长度估计

1.1 交通波理论基础

交通波理论是基于流体力学的原理发展而来,用以描述车流的连续性模型。当道路交通流状态发生变化时,就会生成交通波。其计算公式如下:

$$v_w = \frac{\Delta q}{\Delta k} = \frac{q_2 - q_1}{k_2 - k_1} \quad (1)$$

式中:v_w——波阵面速度即交通波波速;

q_1, q_2——车流量;

k_1, k_2——车流密度。

其中车道流量车流密度关系如图 1 所示。

由图 1 可知,初始时,随着车流密度的增加车道流量也在逐渐增加。当车流密度不断增大并超过一个阈值 k_m 后,车道上过高的车流密度限制了车辆的移动速度,车道流量开始呈下降趋势。其中车道流量、车流速度与车辆密度关系如下:

$$q = ku \quad (2)$$

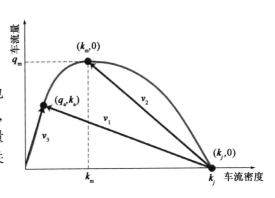

图 1 流量与车流密度关系图

式中：q——平均流量；
  k——车流密度；
  u——车流平均速度。

1.2 交叉口排队长度估计

由交通波理论可知当车辆到达交叉口时，由于信号灯的控制，车流状态在交叉口发生变化，交通波产生。其中由于红灯车辆停车产生的交通波称为停止波，而绿灯放行时产生的交通波称为启动波。交叉口信号周期内的交通波示意图如图2、图3所示。v_1为停车波波速，v_2为启动波波速，v_3为当前车流情况下车辆自由移动速度，v_4表示二次排队情况下的二次停车累计波速度。X_Q是启动波与停止波交汇处距交叉口中心的距离；X_P为选用GPS轨迹的停车点距交叉口中心距离；T_A为车辆停止时间；T_g为绿灯开始时间；T_{max}为排队长度最大的时间。X_R为上一周期未放行二次排队车辆的最大距离；T_{min}为其对应的时间；T_r为红灯开始时间。

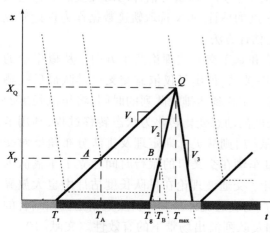

图2 非饱和状态下交叉口交通波示意图

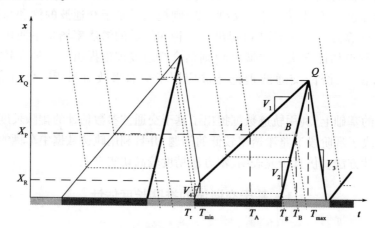

图3 饱和状态下交叉口交通波示意图

图2与图3分别显示了非饱和与饱和状态下的交叉口交通波示意图。根据式(1)可得交叉口交通波的计算公式分别如下：

$$v_1 = \left| \frac{0 - q_a}{k_j - k_a} \right| \tag{3}$$

$$v_2 = \left| \frac{q_m - 0}{k_m - k_j} \right| \tag{4}$$

$$v_3 = \left| \frac{q_a}{k_a} \right| \tag{5}$$

$$v_4 = \left| \frac{0 - q_m}{k_j - k_m} \right| \tag{6}$$

式中：q_a——当前方向车流的平均流量；
  q_m——当前方向车流的最大流量；
  k_a——当前方向车流的平均车流密度；
  k_m——当前方向车流的最大车流密度；

k_j——车道车辆阻塞密度。

由上述四个交通波的计算,并根据图 3 中的几何关系可得以下公式:

$$X_Q - X_P = v_1(T_{\max} - T_A) \tag{7}$$

$$X_Q = v_2(T_{\max} - T_g) \tag{8}$$

联合两式即可求解最大排队长度 X_Q 与最大排队长度时间 $T_{\max}$ 分别为:

$$T_{\max} = \frac{1}{v_2 - v_1}(X_P + v_2 T_g - v_1 T_A) \tag{9}$$

$$X_Q = \frac{1}{v_2 - v_1}[v_2 X_P + v_1 v_2(T_g - T_A)] \tag{10}$$

因此可根据停车波与启动波波速及 GPS 车辆轨迹对交叉口最大排队长度 X_Q 进行求解。同时,根据 A 点位置及红灯开始时间,可获得关系式如下:

$$X_Q - X_R = v_1(T_A - T_{\min}) \tag{11}$$

$$X_R = v_4(T_{\min} - T_r) \tag{12}$$

联合式(11)和式(12)可以求解 $T_{\min}$ 与 X_R 为:

$$T_{\min} = \frac{1}{v_2 - v_1}(X_P + v_2 T_r - v_1 T_A) \tag{13}$$

$$X_R = \frac{1}{v_2 - v_1}[v_2 X_P - v_1 v_2(T_A - T_r)] \tag{14}$$

因此根据式(13)和式(14)即可求取上一周期未能及时放行的二次排队车辆的最大长度,当信号周期内没有二次排队车辆时,即 $X_R = 0$,图 3 所展示的图像转化图 2。

由上述推理可知,需要求解几种波的波速才可对交叉口排队长度进行估计,现场测量交叉口在流量及车辆密度信息费时费力,因此下文提出基于轨迹数据的交通波波速计算方法,使用 GPS 轨迹数据和交叉口信号配时信息对交通波波速进行估计。

2 交通波参数估计方法

轨迹数据可以提供车辆的位置、速度及方向信息,可以从车辆的角度为我们提供交通状态的分析数据。本小节利用轨迹数据对交叉口启动波及停止波波速进行估计,为交叉口排队长度估计提供参数依据。

由启动波物理意义可知,启动波 v_2 是由交叉口相位排队放行所产生的。由于各个周期的绿灯放行初始状态相同,故各周期启动波速度应该相同,其大小应为常量。这一点由 v_2 的计算公式也可以看出。因此在已知交叉口信号配时的情况下,可以将几个周期的车辆轨迹平移到同一相位周期,使得我们总能找到两辆在交叉口停车且不重合的 GPS 车辆轨迹,轨迹聚合示意如图 4 所示。X_{A2}, X_{A1} 分别为轨迹点 A_2 与 A_1 距离交叉口的距离,其与 B_2, B_1 点在空间上处于同一位置距离;B_2, B_1 分别为轨迹的启动点;T_{B2} 与 T_{B1} 分别为其对应的车辆启动时间。

如图 4 所示,经过点 A_1 与 A_2 的两条轨迹是经周期聚合的不同周期的采样轨迹。A_1, A_2 与 B_1, B_2 分别对应其时空坐标系上的停止点及启动点。因此,根据两辆车的启动时间及位置可以计算启动波 v_2 的准确数值,计算公式如下:

$$v_2 = \frac{X_{A2} - X_{A1}}{T_{B2} - T_{B1}} \tag{15}$$

由此 v_4 的值也计算出来,式(15)中由于可以将几个周期的车辆轨迹平移到一个周期内,故在交叉口 GPS 车辆渗透率较低的情况下也是适用的。

式(5)中 v_3 表示车辆启动波与停止波相遇消散后车辆自由移动的速度,其穿过红绿灯的时间即为相位应有的最小相位绿灯时长,由计算可知其等于车流移动速度,可以从轨迹数据的车辆速度进行获取。

v_1 为车辆的停止波,因为各周期车辆到达会有细微波动,因此在低 GPS 车辆渗透率情况下,难以直接在一个周期内找到两辆 GPS 车辆轨迹。但是在相邻的几个周期内,可以合理的假设车辆的到达情况近似不变,因此在相邻的几个周期内,交叉口的停止波速度相似,表现在图表上为各周期轨迹停止点相连组成的直线的斜率大小相近,其示意如图 5 所示。

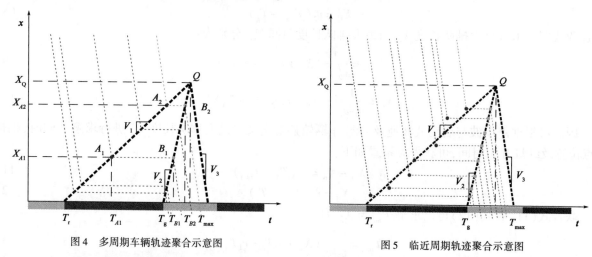

图 4　多周期车辆轨迹聚合示意图　　　　　　图 5　临近周期轨迹聚合示意图

如图 5 所示,当临近周期的车辆到达相似时,各周期轨迹数据的停止点都分布在过 T_r 的停止波附近。因此可以将邻近几个周期的 GPS 车辆轨迹聚集到一个周期内,对经过停止点的直线斜率进行拟合,当所有停止点到达直线的距离最小时即可求取这几个周期的平均停止波速度 v_1。其中停止波速的计算公式如下:

$$k = \mathrm{argmin}(\sum_{i=1}^{N_{GPS}} d_i) \tag{16}$$

式中:k——直线斜率即待求取的停止波速度 v_1;

d_i——停止点 $A_i \in \{A_1, A_2, \ldots, A_N\}$ 距离直线的距离;

N_{GPS}——GPS 轨迹车辆总数目。其中 d_i 的计算公式如下:

$$d_i = \frac{|kt_{A_i} - x_{A_i} + t_0|}{\sqrt{k^2 + 1}} \tag{17}$$

式中:t_{A_i}——停车点 A_i 的修正后停车时间;

x_{A_i}——车辆停止位置;

t_0——常量。

由于是求解满足等式的最小值,t_0 处于分母位置对求解没有影响,因此可设置 $t_0 = 0$,式(17)可转化为下式:

$$d_i = \frac{|kt_{A_i} - x_{A_i}|}{\sqrt{k^2 + 1}} \tag{18}$$

联合式(16)与(18)求解 k,即可得启动波速 $v_1 = k$。在对 k 求解时,由于求解公式(18)内含有绝对值,将(18)式平方去除绝对值再代入式(16)即可获得等价求解公式如下:

$$k = \mathrm{argmin}(\sum_{i=1}^{N_{GPS}} d_i^2)$$
$$= \mathrm{argmin}(\sum_{i=1}^{N_{GPS}} \frac{-2kt_{A_i}x_{A_i} + x_{A_i}^2 - t_{A_i}^2}{k^2 + 1} + \sum_{i=1}^{N_{GPS}} t_{A_i}^2) \tag{19}$$

由公式可知所求解 k 值出现在待求解函数的极小值点。对 $\sum_{i=1}^{N_{GPS}} d_i^2$ 求导可得

$$\frac{\partial \sum_{i=1}^{N_{GPS}} d_i^2}{\partial k} = \frac{1}{(k^2+1)^2}\left[(2\sum_{i=1}^{N_{GPS}} t_{A_i}x_{A_i})k^2 - 2\sum_{i=1}^{N_{GPS}}(x_{A_i}^2 - t_{A_i}^2)k - 2\sum_{i=1}^{N_{GPS}} t_{A_i}x_{A_i}\right] \tag{20}$$

令式(12)导数等于零即可得:

$$k = \frac{1}{2\sum_{i=1}^{N_{GPS}} t_{A_i} x_{A_i}} \left\{ \sum_{i=1}^{N_{GPS}} (x_{A_i}^2 - t_{A_i}^2) \pm \sqrt{\left[\sum_{i=1}^{N_{GPS}} (x_{A_i}^2 - t_{A_i}^2) \right]^2 + 4\left(\sum_{i=1}^{N_{GPS}} t_{A_i} x_{A_i} \right)^2} \right\} \qquad (21)$$

由于 $\sum_{i=1}^{N_{GPS}} d_i^2$ 的倒数的分母是关于 k 的开口向上的二次函数,且其等于零有解,故 $\sum_{i=1}^{N_{GPS}} d_i^2$ 关于 k 的函数在 $k>0$ 的范围内先减后增,在 $k>0$ 的范围内其最小值点在极值点处取得,故可以得到 k 取导数值等于零的右侧零点,即

$$k = \frac{1}{2\sum_{i=1}^{N_{GPS}} t_{A_i} x_{A_i}} \left\{ \sum_{i=1}^{N_{GPS}} (x_{A_i}^2 - t_{A_i}^2) + \sqrt{\left[\sum_{i=1}^{N_{GPS}} (x_{A_i}^2 - t_{A_i}^2) \right]^2 + 4\left(\sum_{i=1}^{N_{GPS}} t_{A_i} x_{A_i} \right)^2} \right\} \qquad (22)$$

由上述计算即可获得交叉口的平均停止波速度 v_1,联合式(15)与式(10)即可对交叉口周期内最大排队长度进行求取。

3 仿真验证

3.1 路口搭建

本论文选用南京江宁区爱涛路与天元西路交叉口作为仿真路口原型,根据视频识别各相位车流量数据作为交叉口的流量数据并根据实际交叉口路口渠化图建立仿真。仿真路口卫星地图如图6。

采用视频识别的方法对各相位的流量进行统计,获得了交叉口的流量及信号配时信息。本仿真统计了选取交叉口2018年12月27日13:00~15:00流量数据作为仿真流量输入。交叉口各向流量统计表如表1所示,交叉口信号配时方案如表2所示。

图6 爱涛路与天元西路交叉口卫星图

交叉口各向流量统计表(单位:辆) 表1

方向	西方向左转	西方向直行	北方向左转	北方向直行	东方向直行	东方向左转	南方向左转	南方向直行	南方向右转
流量	122	1450	567	85	980	85	315	76	104

表1为各向流量统计表,由于东西北三个方向均有右转专用道且基本没有排队累计,故在此表格中没有将其数值列举出来。在仿真时,未考虑东西方向右转车辆对交叉口运行的影响。

由表2可知,交叉口信号方案的相序依次为东西方向直行、东西方向左转、北进道口全部放行、南进道口全部放行。

交叉口信号配时方案表(单位:s) 表2

相 位	绿灯时长	黄灯时长	红灯时长	零点相位差
东西直行	57	3	90	0
东西左转	21	3	126	60
北进道口放行	30	3	117	84
南进道口放行	30	3	117	117

根据上述采集到的信息,我们可以使用城市交通仿真软件(Simulation of Urban Mobility,SUMO)对交叉口路网进行仿真搭建。交叉口渠化及运行图如图7所示。

3.2 排队估计分析

根据上文的方法阐述,可以将不同周期内的车辆轨迹聚合到同一周期内对交叉口启动波及停止波波速进行估计。本文中将车辆停止、启动的时间及其所在位置取出来,对交叉口启动及停止波速度进行估计进而估计排队长度。交叉口各相位车辆启动、停止及交通波速度的关系如图8所示。

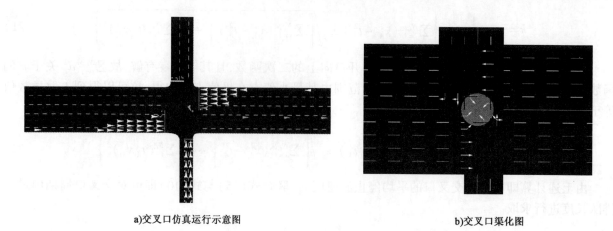

a) 交叉口仿真运行示意图   b) 交叉口渠化图

图7 交叉口仿真图

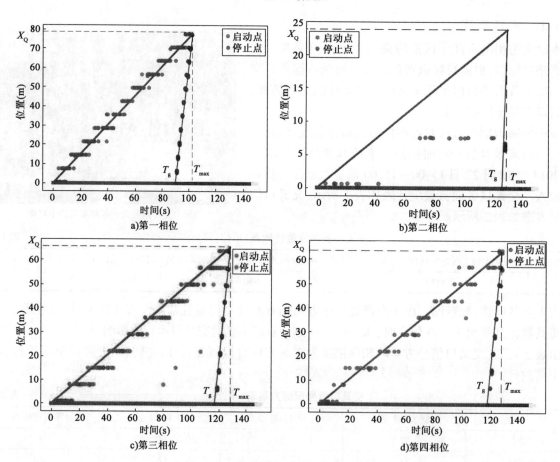

a) 第一相位   b) 第二相位

c) 第三相位   d) 第四相位

图8 各相位启动与停止时间-位置关系图

图中红色和绿色的散点分别对应轨迹数据的停止点及启动点。由各点的数据,可根据式(22)及式(15)对停止波及启动波波速进行计算。图8中绿色及红色的直线分别代表相位的启动及停止波,直线斜率即是计算出的启动波及停止波速度。由此,依据式(9)及(10)可以计算周期的最大队列长度及队列消散时间,分别对应上图中两波交汇点(Q点)的纵坐标X_Q及横坐标T_{max}。本文选用平均绝对百分误差(Mean Absolute Percentage Error,MAPE)作为估计精度的衡量标准,其计算公式如下:

$$\text{MAPE} = \frac{1}{N}\sum_{i=1}^{N}\frac{|\bar{L}-L_i|}{L_i}\times 100\% \tag{23}$$

交通波波速及排队长度估算结果见表3。

交通波波速及排队长度估计表　　　表3

相　位	启动波速 （m/s）	停止波速 （m/s）	排队消散时长 （s）	实际排队长度 （辆）	估计排队长度	MAPE(%) 10.13#
东西直行	6.54	0.76	9.67	9.38	10.14	8.06
东西左转	7.54	0.08	2.42	2.98	2.42	18.66
北进道口	7.03	0.52	7.36	8.51	7.39	13.48
南进道口	7.16	0.50	8.78	8.97	8.90	0.32

注意：10.13#表示各相位排队估计MAPE的均值。

由表可知，各相位的启动波速度在7m/s附近波动，各相位启动波速度相差不大，符合前文启动波速度为常量的公式结论。而各相位的停止波速度均不相同，其中流量大的相位单位时间内到达的车辆较多，其停止波速度相对较大，而流量小的相位其停止波速就小，呈现一个近似的线性关系，也符合公式规律。

由表3后3列可知，各相位的排队长度估算误差都在20%以下。其中，南进道口的排队长度估算精度最高，MAPE值仅为0.32%。而东西左转相位的排队长度估算精度最低，MAPE值达18.66%。原因在于东西左转相位的车流量较小，相位排队平均长度仅为2.98，故造成了其MAPE值偏高，整个方法的相位平均MAPE值约为10.13%。仿真结果证明了本文方法的有效性。

4　结　　语

对交叉口排队长度的估计方法有很多，基于概率论及基于交通波的方法均有研究。本文选取轨迹数据作为研究对象，通过分析交叉口的交通波的产生情况，给出了一个周期内各个交通波的计算公式，并且通过对启动及停止波的空间性分析，推导出了交叉口排队长度的计算方法。然后通过对相邻周期内车辆轨迹的聚合，解决了交叉口联网车辆渗透率较低带来的精度问题，采用最小二乘法拟合实现了对交叉口交通波波速的估计，实现了基于轨迹数据的交叉口各相位排队长度的估计。仿真实验证明，本方法的估算误差约为10.13%，方法切实有效，在现阶段具有较高的实用价值。

虽然本方法已经实现了较高的精度，但仍无法解决交通变化较快情况下的排队长度估计问题，如何将相邻周期车流的差异性考虑到交叉口的排队长度估计中以扩大方法的适用范围是作者下一步的研究点。

参考文献

[1] Mei Y, Gu W H, Edward C S, et al. A Bayesian Approach for Estimating Vehicle Queue Lengths at Signalized Intersections Using Probe Vehicle Data[J]. Transportation Research Part C, 2019: 109.

[2] Wang H, Ju J M, Wu Z X, et al. Estimation of Queue Length at Signalized Intersections based on Electronic Police Data[J]. Journal of Physics: Conference Series, 2020, 1549(4).

[3] Tan C P, Liu L, Hao W, et al. Fuzing license Plate recognition Data and Vehicle Trajectory Data for Lane-based Queue Length Estimation at Signalized Intersections[J]. Journal of Intelligent Transportation Systems, 2020, 24(5).

[4] Comert G, Cetin M. Queue Length Estimation from Probe Vehicle Location and the Impacts of Sample Size[J]. European Journal of Operational Research, 2009, 197(1): 196-202.

[5] Comert G, Cetin M. Analytical Evaluation of the Error in Queue Length Estimation at Traffic Signals From Probe Vehicle Data[J]. IEEE Transactions on Intelligent Transportation Systems, 2011, 12(2): 563-573.

[6] Li J Q, Zhou K, Shladover S E, et al. Estimating Queue Length under Connected Vehicle Technology: Using Probe Vehicle, Loop Detector, and Fused Data[J]. Transportation research record, 2013, 2356

(1): 17-22.

[7] Zhao Y, Zheng J, Wong W, et al. Various Methods for Queue Length and Traffic Volume Estimation Using Probe Vehicle Trajectories[J]. Transportation Research Part C: Emerging Technologies, 2019, 107: 70-91.

[8] Ban X J, Hao P, Sun Z. Real Time Queue Length Estimation for Signalized Intersections Using Travel Times from Mobile Sensors[J]. Transportation Research Part C: Emerging Technologies, 2011, 19(6): 1133-1156.

[9] Ramezani M, Geroliminis N. Queue Profile Estimation in Congested Urban Networks with Probe Data[J]. Computer-Aided Civil and Infrastructure Engineering, 2015, 30(6): 414-432.

[10] Li F, Tang K, Yao J, et al. Real-time Queue Length Estimation for Signalized Intersections Using Vehicle Trajectory Data[J]. Transportation Research Record, 2017, 2623(1): 49-59.

[11] Cheng Y, Qin X, Jin J, et al. An Exploratory Shockwave Approach to Estimating Queue Length Using Probe Trajectories[J]. Journal of intelligent transportation systems, 2012, 16(1): 12-23.

[12] Wang Z, Cai Q, Wu B, et al. Shockwave-based Queue Estimation Approach for Undersaturated and Oversaturated Signalized Intersections Using Multi-source Detection data [J]. Journal of Intelligent Transportation Systems, 2017, 21(3): 167-178.

[13] Zhang H, Liu H X, Chen P, et al. Cycle-based End of Queue Estimation at Signalized Intersections Ising Low-penetration-rate Vehicle Trajectories[J]. IEEE Transactions on Intelligent Transportation Systems, 2019.

[14] Tan C, Yao J, Tang K, et al. Cycle-Based Queue Length Estimation for Signalized Intersections Using Sparse Vehicle Trajectory Data[J]. IEEE Transactions on Intelligent Transportation Systems, 2019.

[15] 余贵珍,刘玉敏,金茂菁,王云鹏.基于交通波的高速公路事故的交通影响分析[J].北京航空航天大学学报,2012,38(10):1420-1424.

[16] 曲大义,万孟飞,李娟,王进展,许翔华.基于交通波理论的干线相位差优化及其控制方法[J].吉林大学学报(工学版),2017,47(02):429-437.

Time-space Trajectory Similarity-based Performance Evaluation of Signal Coordination Via Smartphones

Zhenlong Li[1]　Jingsi Zhang[1]　Lei Yang[2]

(1. College of Metropolitan Transportation, Beijing University of Technology;

2. Beijing Key Laboratory of Traffic Engineering College of Metropolitan Transportation,

Beijing University of Technology)

Abstract　Measures of effectiveness must be selected to evaluate the performance of signal coordination. The evaluation based on the traditional measures is an outcome evaluation and lacks a holistic assessment of the vehicle traveling process. The study proposed a novel measure by combining both the process and outcome evaluations. The basic idea was to compare the vehicle's actual trajectory with the ideal trajectory. First, traffic information was collected using smartphones, and time space trajectories of the vehicles were obtained. The trajectory was segmented using a series important point algorithm. Second, turning function-based distance between two trajectories was proposed to measure the similarity of location. The fluctuation of the speed along the trajectory was characterized by the similarity of the speed. The similarity of location and the similarity of the speed were integrated to form the entire trajectory similarity. The bigger the entire trajectory similarity, the more similar to the ideal trajectory, and the better the performance of signal coordination. Finally, a before-and-after evaluation of a case site in Beijing was studied to illustrate the measure and method. The results show that the entire trajectory similarity considers not only the outcome, but also the detail of the vehicle traveling process. The evaluation based on the entire trajectory similarity focuses on the degree to which the actual trajectory is similar to the ideal trajectory.

Keywords Trajectory similarity Turning function-based distance The fluctuation of the speed Arterial signal coordination

0 Introduction

The metropolitan regions of China have experienced increased traffic congestion problems over the past several years. Studies indicated that the daily congestion time was about 55 minutes for commuting travel in Beijing in 2018. Congestion can cause several issues. The study of Mao indicated that traffic congestion costs, including time delays, extra oil combustion, vehicle loss, traffic accident direct economic loss, environment pollutants, etc., was approximately 58 billion Yuan RMB (4.22% of GDP) in Beijing in 2010. Furthermore, traffic congestion has become a problem for second- and third-tier cities.

Minimizing congestion is one of the objectives of traffic signal control systems. Among traffic signal control systems, the signal coordination system is the most widely used system. A common objective of coordinating traffic signals is to provide a smooth movement of traffic along an arterial in order to reduce stops, travel times, and delay. The signal coordination is to establish relationships between adjacent signalized intersections using offsets. Fig. 1 illustrates offsets and ideal vehicle trajectories through a series of intersections using a time-space diagram. Generally, the methods used for

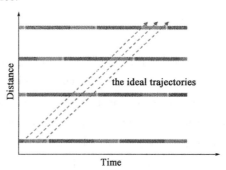

Fig. 1 Time-Space Diagram

evaluating the performance of signal coordination can be classified into the following two types: diagram-based method and measures of effectiveness-based method. A diagram-based method is to compare before-and-after time-space diagrams of vehicles along the arterial. It highlights the stops and travel times under the before and after conditions. However, only qualitative analysis can be performed using the time-space diagram unless the measures are extracted from it. Measures of effectiveness (MOE) include travel time, stops, delay, fuel consumption, and emission data. Many studies used travel time, stops, and delay to evaluate the performance of signal coordination. Some studies used "smoothness of the flow of traffic" and the variety of performance measures to evaluate the performance. The evaluation based on the above measures is an outcome evaluation, which measures a strategy or an algorithm's results and examines whether the intended outcomes are achieved. Outcome evaluations have many values to offer to traffic engineers. However, outcome evaluations have some limitations. First, outcome evaluations cannot contain the detailed information about how a signal coordination strategy or an algorithm operates. Outcome evaluations lacks a holistic assessment of the vehicle traveling process. For example, three tests or trips were conducted to evaluate traffic signal performance. All three tests have the same outcomes, which are travel time of 70 s, number of stops of 1, and stop time of 10 s as shown in Fig. 2a). The outcomes cannot contain the detailed information of the vehicle traveling. The spatial-temporal processes of the vehicle traveling are clearly different. The first test (blue line) was running at a speed of 9 m/s for 50 s, parking for 10 s, and running at 5m/s for 10s. The second test (red line) was running at a speed of

8.33 m/s for 30 s, parking for 10 s, and running at 8.33 m/s for 30 s. The third test (yellow line) was running at a speed of 10 m/s for 10 s, parking for 10 s, and running at 8 m/s for 50 s. This limitation of outcome evaluations is further exemplified in another example shown in Fig. 2b). All three tests have the same outcomes, which are travel time of 70 s and number of stops of 0. However, the holistic processes of the vehicle traveling are clearly different. Second, outcome evaluations are analyzing the measured MOEs to determine whether the intended outcomes were achieved. They cannot examine whether the process or program was performed as desired or designed. It is a one-sided evaluation.

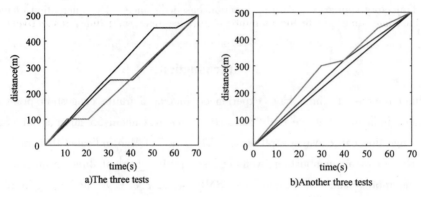

Fig. 2 Examples of trips

To overcome these limitations, a paradigm shift in performance evaluation is needed. Process perspectives and holistic assessment of the process need to be introduced. Process evaluations help traffic engineers develop a comprehensive picture of how a strategy or an algorithm operates. It can tell whether the strategy or algorithm is operating as desired or designed, which is known as "fidelity." This paper proposes a new comprehensive measure by combining both the process and outcome evaluations. The basic idea is to compare the vehicle's actual trajectory with the ideal or designed trajectory. Therefore, a key issue is how to evaluate the similarity between two trajectories. The similarity is a measure of the resemblance between curves, shapes, data sets, or trajectories. The similarity is an active research field in applied mathematics, computational geometry, and computer science. To measure the similarity, a wide variety of distance functions or metrics have been proposed, such as the Euclidean distance, cosine distance, Jaccard coefficient, the dynamic time warping distance (DTW), longest common subsequence (LCSS), derivative DTW (DDTW), the angular metric for shape similarity (AMSS), edit distance with real penalty (ERP), Hausdorff distance, Frechet distance, and turning function. Inspired by turning function and depending on the context in the process of the vehicle running, we proposed the adjusted turning function-based distance (ATF distance) to measure the similarity between two trajectories based on a shape feature.

The primary goal of this paper is to propose a novel measure (ATF distance) to evaluate the performance of arterial signal coordination. An auxiliary goal is to develop an evaluation method based on the new measure. The remainder of the paper is organized as follows: Section 1 presents the methodology, which includes definitions and remarks. Section 2 presents a case study and results. Section 3 presents the discussions. Lastly, section 4 summarizes the conclusions and proposes future work.

1 Methodology

Recently, GPS-Enabled smartphones have increasingly been used for collecting traffic data. Using GPS-Enabled smartphones to evaluate the performance of arterial signal coordination includes five steps: data preprocessing, extracting the traditional performance measures, segmenting the trajectory into sub-trajectories, proposing the novel performance measure (ATF distance) and evaluating the performance of arterial signal coordination. The related methods are presented below.

1.1 Data Preprocessing

To ensure the reliability and accuracy of the data, it is necessary to preprocess the mobile data, which was updated at a frequency of 1Hz in this study. There are several methods for identifying the abnormal data. After preprocessing, the data can be formulated as follows:

Definition 1. GPS point: a GPS point can be set as follows:

$$P^G = \{Lng, Lat, date, time\} \quad (1)$$

where, Lng, Lat, date, time denote the longitude, latitude, date, and time, respectively.

Definition 2. Time space point: a time space point can be set as follows:

$$P^{TS} = \{D, t\} \quad (2)$$

where, D and t denote the distance and the timestamp, respectively. D can be obtained using GPS points.

Definition 3. Time space trajectory: a time space trajectory can be defined as a series of time space points ordered by time as follows:

$$T = \{P_1^{TS}, P_2^{TS}, \cdots, P_i^{TS}, \cdots, P_n^{TS}\} = \{(D_1, t_1), (D_2, t_2), \cdots, (D_i, t_i), \cdots, (D_n, t_n)\} \quad (3)$$

where, $t_1 < t_2 \cdots < t_i \cdots < t_n$. Generally, a time space trajectory consists of time space points, which are collected in one performance test of the arterial signal coordination system.

1.2 Trajectory Segmentation and Representation

The goal of the segmentation is to find the boundaries. There are numerous segmentation algorithms, such as the bottom-up algorithm, top-down algorithm and sliding window algorithm. A series important point (SIP) segmentation algorithm was used in the paper. The set of important points obtained using the SIP algorithm is:

$$X_{IP} = \{(D_{IP1}, t_{IP1}), (D_{IP2}, t_{IP2}), \cdots, (D_{IPm}, t_{IPm})\} \quad (4)$$

where, $(D_{IP1}, t_{IP1}) = (D_1, t_1), (D_{IPm}, t_{IPm}) = (D_n, t_n), m < n$.

Piecewise linear representation indicates the approximation of a trajectory T of length n with m-1 ordered connective straight lines (38). Piecewise linear representation of the trajectory was constructed based on the series important points.

Definition4. Piecewise linear representation of the trajectory: a PLR of trajectory T is as follows,

$$T^L = \{f_1((D_{IP1}, t_{IP1}), (D_{IP2}, t_{IP2})), f_2((D_{IP2}, t_{IP2}), (D_{IP3}, t_{IP3})), \cdots f_{m-1}((D_{IPm-1}, t_{IPm-1}), (D_{IPm}, t_{IPm}))\} \quad (5)$$

where, the function $f_i(\ )$ denotes the linear function at the interval $[(D_{IPi}, t_{IPi}), (D_{IPi+1}, t_{IPi+1})]$.

Fig. 3 illustrates the segmentation results and representation. The comparison of PLR and the original trajectory is shown in Fig. 4.

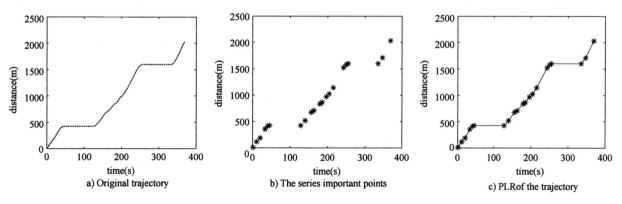

Fig. 3 The Segmentation and Representation of the Trajectory

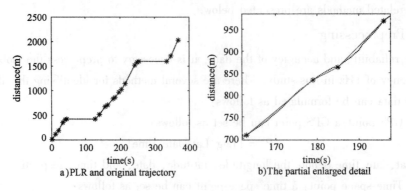

Fig. 4　The Comparison of PLR and Original Trajectory

1.3　New Performance Measure: The Adjusted Turning Function-Based Distance (ATF Distance)

Generally, the optimal vehicle trajectories were designed to achieve traffic signal coordination strategies, such as green-wave oriented control strategies and Eco-driving-oriented control strategies. The basic idea of the evaluation is to compare the vehicle's actual trajectory with the ideal or designed trajectory. If the actual trajectories of all vehicles are the same as the ideal trajectory, the process of vehicles traveling would be excellent. Accordingly, stops and stop time would be 0, and the average speed would be the same as the ideal speed, that is to say, the outcome would also be excellent. In this case, the performance of traffic signal coordination is best. However, it is impractical or difficult to achieve this goal. In reality, vehicles travel as similar to ideal trajectory as possible. A natural problem is to what extent is the actual trajectory similar to the ideal trajectory. How to measure the similarity between two trajectories. As stated in the previous section, we proposed turning function-based distance to measure the similarity between two trajectories.

Turning function is a cumulative measure of the angles through which a trajectory or curve turns. Turning function is easy to characterize a trajectory or curve. It has been used to measure the similarity in many different fields. Turning function $\phi(s)$ describes the change of the angle φ along the polygonal curve. It is independent of translation and scaling.

The curves are re-scaled so that the total length is 1. Define the L_p distance between two polylines or polygons A and B as.

$$\delta_p(A,B) = \| \phi_A(s) - \phi_B(s) \|_p = \left(\int_0^1 | \phi_A(s) - \phi_B(s) |^p ds \right)^{\frac{1}{p}} \tag{6}$$

where, $\| \ \|_p$ denotes the L_p norm.

Inspirited by turning function and dependent on the context in the process of the vehicle running, we proposed turning function-based distance to measure the similarity between two trajectories. T_A^L is an ideal/designed time space trajectory and T_B^L is an actual time space multi-segment trajectory as shown in Fig. 5. $V(t)$ (in m/s) measures the change of the speed along the trajectory as a function of the time t (in seconds) as shown in Fig. 6. Without loss of generality, we assume that the speed curves of the trajectories are rescaled so that the total time is the time required to travel 1000 meters at the desired/designed speed (in m/s). In other words, the speed curves are rescaled so that the total time is equal to the distance of 1000 meters divided by the ideal/designed speed, as shown in Fig. 7.

Definition 5.　Turning function-based distance: turning function-based distance is the L_1 norm between the speeds of the two trajectories, which can be given as follows:

$$D = \int_0^{1000/v_d} [\hat{V}_A(t) - \hat{V}_B(t)] dt \tag{7}$$

where, v_d is the desired/designed speed (in m/s). $\hat{V}_A(t)$ and $\hat{V}_B(t)$ are the rescaled speed of trajectory T_A^L and T_B^L, respectively. Turning function-based distance describes the similarity of the location.

To make the difference between trajectories become more relative, the similarity of the changes of the speed was introduced.

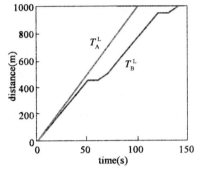 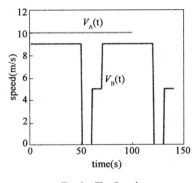 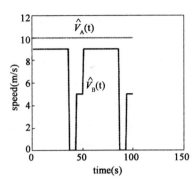

Fig. 5 Two Trajectories   Fig. 6 The Speed   Fig. 7 The Rescaled Speed

Definition 6. Speed growth rate between segments: speed growth rate between segments is the percentage change of the speed of two adjacent segments.

Speed growth rate between segments is equal to the absolute value of the difference between the speeds of two adjacent segments divided by the speed of the previous segment, which can be denoted as follows:

$$C_i = \begin{cases} \dfrac{|v(i+1) - v(i)|}{v(i)} & v(i) \neq 0 \\ \gamma & v(i) = 0 \end{cases} \tag{8}$$

where, $v(i)$ is the speed of segment I of the trajectory. γ is used to denote the percentage change of the speed when the vehicle is starting. Speed growth rate describes the complexity of two adjacent segments of a trajectory.

Definition 7. The similarity of the changes of the speed: the similarity of the changes of the speed C is the sum of the complexity of every two adjacent segments of a trajectory divided by traveling distance, which can be given as follows:

$$C = \dfrac{\sum_{i=1}^{n-1} C_i}{L} \times 1000 \tag{9}$$

where, L is traveling distance (in meters). n is the number of segments of a trajectory.

Definition 8. The adjusted turning function-based distance: the adjusted turning function-based distance is as follows.

$$sim = \alpha \widetilde{D} + \beta \widetilde{C} \tag{10}$$

where, α and β are weights. $\widetilde{D}$ and $\widetilde{C}$ denotes the normalized D and C.

The adjusted turning function-based distance measure the entire similarity between the vehicle's actual trajectory and the designed or desired trajectory.

To illustrate the definitions, an example constructed by the simulation was given below. Four trajectories/trips were collected as shown in Fig. 10. The first is to travel for 40s at a constant speed of 8m/s, the next 30s at a speed of 6m/s, the next 40s at a speed of 8m/s and the final 30s at a speed of 6m/s. The second is the uniform motion at a speed of 7.14m/s for 140s. The third is to travel for 20s at a constant speed of 10m/s, stop for 40s and then travel 800m in the next 80s. The fourth is to travel for 20s at a constant speed of 10m/s, stop for 20s, travel for 40s at a constant speed of 10m/s, stop again for 20s and then travel for 40s at a constant speed of 10m/s. The fifth is the uniform motion at a speed of 8.33m/s for 120s. Turning function-based distance D, the complexity C and the adjusted turning function-based distance were calculated as shown in Tab. 1. γ was set to the maximum of speed growth rates of all drivers. α and β were set to 0.5. γ can be set a larger value if the effect of the number of stops was highlighted. The characteristics of the ATF distance (the entire similarity) are as follows.

(1) The holistic. The ATF distance contains the detail of the traveling process of vehicles and assesses the quality of the entire trip. The traditional MOEs of case 1 and case 2 are the same. According to the results, the performance of case 1 and case 2 are the same. However, the spatial-temporal processes of the vehicle traveling of case 1 and case 2 are clearly different. The ATF distance of case 1 and case 2 is 0.753 and 0.857, respectively. The ATF distance provides a holistic assessment of the vehicle traveling process. Case 2, which is the uniform motion, has a bigger than case 1. In fact, the overall performance (traffic efficiency and ride comfort) of case 2 is better than that of case 1.

(2) The concise. It is difficult to determine which performance is better based only on the average speed. It is necessary to further evaluate using other measures, such as total stop time and number of stops. However, we can easily determine the performance based on the sim, as shown in Tab. 1. The gap between the actual trajectory and the ideal trajectory is embodied by the sim, and hence it can directly tell us how far the actual performance is from the ideal instead of conducting a comprehensive gap analysis of the multiple measures. The sim is the measure to show meaningful changes in the process of the vehicle running.

The MOEs of Four Trips Tab. 1

	average speed (m/s)	total stop time (s)	number of stops	D	C	sim
case 1	7.14	0	0	285.71	0.83	0.753
case 2	7.14	0	0	285.71	0.00	0.857
case 3	7.14	40	1	285.71	2.00	0.607
case 4	7.14	40	2	285.71	4.00	0.357
case 5	8.33	0	0	166.67	0.00	0.917

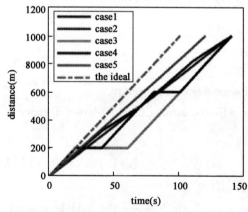

Fig. 8 the trajectory of four trips

It should be noted that only qualitative analysis can be performed using the time-space diagram as shown in Fig. 8. The degree of the actual trajectory similar to the ideal trajectory cannot be accurately measured through figure. A quantitative measure is necessary to accurately measure the similarity between two trajectories. It is one of motivations of proposing the ATF distance.

Here, we explain the physical meaning of ATF distance. Turning function-based distance is based on the L_p distance as shown in Eq(6). In general, L_1 norm is used to calculate the distance. Taking case 1, 2 and 3 as the examples, L_1 norm is the area between $\hat{V}_{ideal}(t)$ and $\hat{V}_B(t)$ (the rescaled speed), as shown in Fig. 9a) and Eq. (11). The physical meaning of L_1 norm is the sum of the difference the actual speed and the ideal speed multiplied by the time when the actual speed is not equal to the ideal speed. In other words, L_1 norm describes the difference between the actual traveling distance and the ideal traveling distance, as shown in Fig. 9b). L_1 norm describes the similarity of location. The similarity of the changes of the speed describes the similarity of shape of speeds between the actual speed and the ideal speed, as shown in Fig. 9c). γ describes the effect of the number of stops on the performance. Accordingly, the ATF distance (the entire similarity) integrates the travel distance, the details of speed, and stops.

$$\| V \|_{L1} = | \hat{V}_{ideal}(t) - \hat{V}_B(t) | \Delta t = \Delta V \Delta t = \Delta L \tag{11}$$

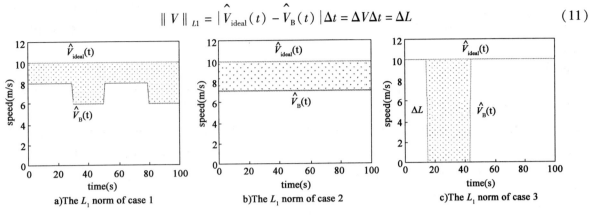

Fig. 9 The L_1 norm of case 1, 2, and 3

1.4 Evaluating the Effectiveness of Arterial Signal Coordination

As mentioned in Section 1.4, the ATF distance considers not only the outcome, but also the detail of the vehicle traveling process. It characterizes the traveling process in more detail. Therefore, the performance of arterial signal coordination can be evaluated based on the entire similarity.

The following remarks can be made regarding the entire similarity.

Remark 1 The bigger similarity distant, the more similar. As the entire similarity becomes bigger, the similarity between two trajectories becomes bigger.

Remark 2 As the *sim* becomes bigger, the similarity between two trajectories becomes bigger. If the *sim* is equal to 1, two trajectories are the same.

Remark 3 The *sim* of uniform motion is maximum when traveling the same distance in the same amount of time.

Remark 4 The more similar to the designed or desired trajectory the vehicle's actual trajectory is, the better the performance of a signal coordination algorithm will be.

2 Case Study

To illustrate the proposed performance measure, a case study was performed in Beijing (China). Guanganmen Inner Street was selected for before-and-after the implementation of signal coordination control, as shown in Fig. 10. The road is a four-lane major arterial road in Beijing. The road is approximately 1.2 kilometers in length with 3 signalized intersections. One-way (westbound) traffic signal coordination control (Green Wave Coordinate Control) was implemented. The coordinated timing plan is shown in Fig. 11a). The ideal speed was 40 km/h. The ideal/designed trajectory was a straight line whose slope is 11.11m/s, as shown in Fig. 11b). GPS-Enabled smartphones combine the advantages of GPS and mobile sensors, and hence are able to provide accurate location information. Test vehicles equipped with smartphones (Samsung Galaxy Note 4) were used to collect the data in this study. With smartphones, time, latitude, and longitude were recorded at a sampling frequency of 1Hz. The data were collected during off-peak period (09:00 AM-05:00 PM) on weekdays.

The data were collocatedbefore and after the implementation of signal coordination control. The similarity measure, i.e. the adjusted turning function-based distance *sim* was calculated using the proposed method. A total of 55 travel runs were obtained under the before condition and 55 travel runs under the after condition. Time-space diagram of vehicles along Guanganmen Inner Street under the before and after conditions are shown in Fig. 12. Before-and-after trajectories of vehicles highlight the locations that experience the stops. However, only qualitative comparison between before and after study was conducted using the time-space diagram. To further quantify the performance, it is necessary to calculate MOEs. It can be seen from Tab. 2 that signal coordination control improves all measures. The similarity measure sim increased from 0.454 to 0.501, an increase of 11.73%. It means that the average similarity between the vehicle traveling trajectories and the ideal trajectory is increased by 11.73%. In other words, the performance of signal coordination is increased by 11.73%. The result also shows that it still has a distance of 0.499 to reach the ideal performance. From the sample mean shown in Tab. 2, the conclusions of the evaluation based on the traditional measures and the evaluation based on the ATF distance are the same, i.e., the performance is improved by implementing signal coordination. It is proved that the proposed method is valid and accurate. From individual before-after data, the individual test results of the two evaluation methods are not necessarily consistent. The reason is that the mechanisms of two evaluation methods are different. The evaluation based on the speed, number of stops, and stop time is an outcome evaluation, from which only the results of the vehicle traveling can be evaluated, lacking the assessment of the vehicle traveling process. The ATF distance assesses the entire trip quality and combines both the process and outcome. The ATF distance is a good indicator to describe meaningful changes between before and after the implementation of signal coordination control. See the discussions in Section 4 and the example given in Section 2.3 for more detail.

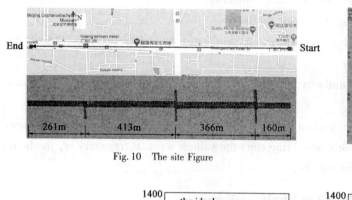

Fig. 10　The site Figure　　　　　　　　　　　Fig. 11　The coordinated timing plan

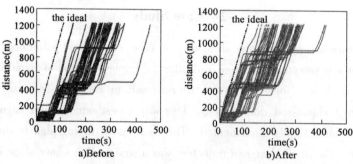

Fig. 12　Time Space Diagram (Before-and-After)

Moes of Before-And-After Study　　　　　　　　　　　　　　　　　　　　Tab. 2

Item	Averagespeed(km/h)		the number of stops		total stop time(s)		sim	
	mean	std	mean	std	mean	std	mean	std.
Before	16.58	3.42	2.80	0.97	131	43.35	0.454	0.113
After	17.69	3.82	2.25	1.04	114	54.48	0.501	0.108
Percent change	6.72%		-19.48%		-3.16%		11.73%	

3 Discussions

The similarity-based evaluation not only contains the outcomes but also examines whether the process was carried out as designed. Similarity judgments will thus become a key problem. There are many distance functions or metrics proposed to measure the similarity. The adjusted turning function-based distance between two trajectories was proposed to measure the similarity in this paper. The case study shows that the adjusted turning function-based distance can be used to suitably measure the similarity. The further studies are worth and needed to examine if other distance metrics suitably measure the similarity between two trajectories for the evaluation of the performance of the traffic signal coordination strategies.

The evaluation based on the three traditional measures is an outcome evaluation, which lacks a holistic assessment of the vehicle traveling process. The evaluation based on the ATF distance assesses the quality of the entire trip and focuses on the degree to which the actual trajectory is similar to the ideal trajectory. The difference between the actual trajectory and the ideal trajectory was embodied by the ATF distance. Several individual travel runs (trajectories) were taken as examples to further illustrate the rationality and accuracy of the similarity measure. In the cases shown in Fig. 13 and Fig. 14, the evaluation result based on the ATF distance is the same as the result of the three traditional measures. To fully and accurately evaluate the performance of arterial signal coordination, it is necessary to comprehensively consider the average speed, total stop time, and stops. The similarity measure evaluates objectively the whole process of

	—Before traiectory 1	—After traiectory 2
average speed(km/h)	15.50	14.06
total stop time(s)	154	154
number of stops	3	3
The *sim*	0.442	0.382

Fig.13 the trajectory of case 1

driving. The ATF distance is a good indicator to measure meaningful changes between before and after study. Compared with the three traditional measures, the ATF distance is more concise and objective. The ATF distance can be used to suitably evaluate the performance of arterial signal coordination.

It can be seen that the ATF distance-based result is basically consistent with the three traditional measures-based result. However, there are some minor differences in results between the two methods. For example, in the case shown in Fig.15, the performance of trajectory 6 is better than that of trajectory 5 based on the three measures. However, the ATF distance of trajectory 5 and trajectory 6 is 0.548 and 0.547, respectively. It means that the performance of trajectory 5 is better than that of trajectory 6. The evaluation result based on the ATF distance is different from the result of the three traditional measures. The reason is that the similarity measure assesses objectively the overall travel quality. The complexity of trajectory 5 and trajectory 6 is 20.86 and 21.69, respectively. In other words, the change or fluctuation of the speed of trajectory 6 is larger than that of trajectory 5. Compared with trajectory 5, the complexity of trajectory 6 is increased by 3.95%, which makes the *sim* of trajectory 6 smaller. Accordingly, the inherent similarity between trajectory 5 and the ideal trajectory is greater than that between trajectory 6 and the ideal trajectory. The ATF distance-based result is inconsistent with the three traditional measures-based result. It's hard to answer which one is right or reasonable, but at least one thing is certain that the result of the ATF distance-based evaluation is to combine the outcomes with the process. The similarity measure contains the detail of the vehicle traveling process and examines whether the process was carried out as designed. It provides a better description of the nature of the trip than the point-to-point average speed. Compared to the traditional MOEs, the similarity measure is a more comprehensive and meaningful measure. In fact, the signal evaluation itself is an art, and different people have different opinions. The similarity-based evaluation provides a new perspective and method to evaluate signal coordination.

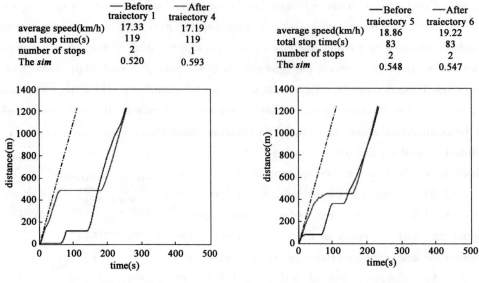

Fig. 14　the trajectory of case 2　　　　Fig. 15　the trajectory of case 3

It should be noted that γ is used to denote the changes of the speed when the vehicle is starting. It describes the effect of stops on the overall operation. The larger it is, the greater the effect is. γ was set to the maximum of speed growth rate of all drivers in the paper. γ can be set a larger value if the effect of the number of stops was highlighted. In addition, the entire trajectory similarity was characterized by the weight α and β. The further study on the value of weight is needed. Even so, the similarity-based evaluation is feasible and reasonable. It would be very meaningful to find or propose a similarity measure that reasonably integrates the complexity (speed fluctuations) rather than regards it as a weight.

4　Conclusions

To analyze the performance of a signal coordination system, traffic measures of effectiveness (MOE) are needed. Traditionally, common measures are travel time, delay time, number of stops, fuel consumption, emission data, etc. These measures describe different aspects of the system's performance. However, the traditional measures-based evaluation is an outcome evaluation which has some limitations. To overcome these limitations, this paper proposed a novel measure: the adjusted turning function-based distance, namely, the entire similarity (integrating the similarity of location and the similarity of the changes of the speed). To illustrate the proposed performance measure, the case site in Beijing was studied.

The primary conclusion from this study is that the ATF distance can be used to suitably evaluate the performance of arterial signal coordination. Compared with the traditional measures, the ATF distance has two advantages: (1) The holistic. The ATF distance contains the detail of the traveling process of vehicles and assesses the quality of the entire trip. (2) The concise. The ATF distance is a good indicator to measure meaningful change in the vehicle traveling process. Now, it has become easy to acquire trajectory data. The increasing presence of smartphones and mobile computing devices do offer the potential for dramatically more data to obtain the new measure - the ATF distance. The ATF distance will provide some new ideas and methods for the evaluation of traffic congestion, the objective function of traffic signal control and traffic assignment problem, and the performance evaluation of trajectory tracking of manned driving or autonomous driving. One limitation of this study is that speed fluctuations were regarded as a weight. The further study is needed to propose a similarity measure which reasonably integrates the complexity (speed fluctuations).

5 Acknowledgments

This work was partly supported by the Science and Technology Plan Project of Beijing Municipal Commission of Transport and the program of China Scholarship Council (201806545020).

References

[1] Mao L Z, Zhu H G, Duan L R. The Social Cost of Traffic Congestion and Countermeasures in Beijing. 2012.

[2] Mahmood, mahmoodi nesheli, che puan Othman, and moradkhani roshandeh Arash. Optimization of Traffic Signal Coordination System on Congestion: A Case Study. WSEAS Transaction on Advance in Engineering Education, 2009.

[3] Park B. (Brian), J. Won, I. Yun. Application of Microscopic Simulation Model Calibration and Validation Procedure: A Case Study of Coordinated Actuated Signal System. Transportation Research Record: Journal of the Transportation Research Board, No. 1978, 2006, pp. 113-122.

[4] Martin P T, J. Perrin, B R Chilukuri, C Jhaveri, Y Feng. Adaptive Signal Control II. 2003.

[5] Park B. (Brian), Y. Chen. Quantifying the Benefits of Coordinated Actuated Traffic Signal Systems: A Case Study[J]. Vtrc 11-Cr2, 2010, p. 27.

[6] Samadi S, A P Rad, F M K H Jafarian. Performance Evaluation of Intelligent Adaptive Traffic Control Systems: A Case Study[J]. Journal of Transportation Technologies, No. 2, 2012, pp. 248-259.

[7] Day C M, R Haseman, H Premachandra, T M Brennan, Jr, J S Wasson J R. Sturdevant, D M. Bullock. Evaluation of Arterial Signal Coordination: Methodologies for Visualizing High-Resolution Event Data and Measuring Travel Time [J]. Transportation Research Record: Journal of the Transportation Research Board, No. 2192, 2010, pp. 37-49.

[8] So J J, A Stevanovic, P Koonce. Estimating Performance of Traffic Signals Based on Link Travel Times [J]. Journal of Advanced Transportation, Vol. 50, No. 5, 2016, pp. 786 – 801. https://doi.org/10.1002/atr.1375.

[9] Dutta Utpal McAvoy D S. Comparative Performance Evaluation of SCATS and Pre-Timed Control Systems, 2010.

[10] Tian Z, F Ohene, P FengHua. Arterial Performance Evaluation on an Adaptive Traffic Signal Control System. Procedia Social and Behavioral Sciences, No. 16, 2011, pp. 230-239.

[11] Liu D, R Cheu. Comparative Evaluation of Dynamic TRANSYT and SCATS-Based Signal Control Logic Using Microscopic Traffic Simulations, 2004.

[12] Abdel-Rahim A, W C Taylor. Potential Travel Time and Delay Benefits of Using Adaptive Signals, 2000.

[13] Al-Mudhaffar A, K L Bang. Impacts of Coordinated Traffic Signal Control Strategies and Bus Priority. 2006.

[14] Wolshon B, W C Taylor. Impact of Adaptive Signal Control on Major and Minor Approach Delay. Journal of Transportation Engineering, Vol. 125, No. 1, 1999, pp. 30-38.

[15] Park B Brian, M. Chang. Realizing Benefits of Adaptive Signal Control at an Isolated Intersection. 2002.

[16] Byungho B, H, K Larry, K Shayan. Systematic analysis of traffic signal coordination using connected-vehicle technology. Proceedings, Transportation Research Board Annual Meeting, 2017.

[17] Day CM E, A M Tahsin. Trajectory-Based Performance Measures for Interrupted-Flow Facilities.

Proceedings, Mobil. TUM 2018.

[18] Berndt D J, J Clifford. Finding Patterns in Time Series: A Dynamic Programming Approach. InAdvances in Knowledge Discovery and Data Mining, pp. 229-248.

[19] Das G, D Gunopulos, H Mannila. Finding Similar Time Series. 1997.

[20] Keogh E J, M J Pazzani. Derivative Dynamic Time Warping. 2001.

[21] Nakamura T, K Taki H Nomiya, K Seki, K. Uehara. A Shape-Based Similarity Measure for Time Series Data with Ensemble Learning. Pattern Analysis and Applications, 2013. https://doi.org/10.1007/s10044-011-0262-6.

[22] Chen L, R Ng. On The Marriage of Lp-Norms and Edit Distance. InProceedings 2004 VLDB Conference.

[23] Chakmakov D, Celakoska E. Estimation of Curve Similarity Using Turning Functions. International Journal of Applied Mathematics, Vol. 15, No. 4, 2004, pp. 403-416.

[24] Arkin E M, L P Chew, D P Huttenlocher, K Kedem, J S B Mitchell, L P Chewt, K Kedemt. An Efficiently Computable Metric for Comparing Polygonal Shapes I Rj (R1Ot SATEM ~ ENT A. An Efficiently Computable Metric for Comparing Polygonal Shapes. IEEE Transactions on Pattern Analysis and Machine Intelligence, Vol. 13, No. 3, 1989, pp. 209-216.

[25] Zhang H, X Song Y, Long T Xia K Fang, J Zheng, D Huang, R Shibasaki, Y. Liang. Mobile Phone GPS Data in Urban Bicycle-Sharing: Layout Optimization and Emissions Reduction Analysis. Applied Energy, 2019. https://doi.org/10.1016/j.apenergy.2019.03.119.

[26] Gang H, L Fu, C Liu, Z Shen. Using Massive Mobile Signaling to Monitor the Highway Traffic. No. 494, 2019, pp. 221-228.

[27] Demissie M G, S Phithakkitnukoon. L Kattan. Trip Distribution Modeling Using Mobile Phone Data: Emphasis on Intra-Zonal Trips. IEEE Transactions on Intelligent Transportation Systems, 2019. https://doi.org/10.1109/TITS.2018.2868468.

[28] Montero L, X Ros-Roca, R Herranz, J Barceló. Fusing Mobile Phone Data with Other Data Sources to Generate Input OD Matrices for Transport Models. 2019.

[29] Yim Y. The State of Cellular Probes. 2003.

[30] Amin S, et al. Mobile Century Using GPS Mobile Phones as Traffic Sensors: A Field Experiment. h World Congress on Intelligent Transportation Systems, 2008. https://doi.org/10.1.1.152.8548.

[31] Yoon H, C Shahabi. Robust Time-Referenced Segmentation of Moving Object Trajectories. 2008.

[32] Pratt K B, E Fink. Search for Patterns in Compressed Time Series. International Journal of Image and Graphics, Vol. 02, No. 01, 2002, pp. 89-106. https://doi.org/10.1142/s0219467802000482.

[33] Zhou D, M Li. Time Series Segmentation Based on Series Importance Point. Computer Engineering, Vol. 34, No. 23, 2008, pp. 14-16.

[34] Bankó Z, J Abonyi. Correlation Based Dynamic Time Warping of Multivariate Time Series. Expert Systems with Applications, 2012. https://doi.org/10.1016/j.eswa.2012.05.012.

[35] i, C., S. Liu, C. Yang, L. Wu, L. Pan, and X. Meng. A Piecewise Linear Representation Method Based on Importance Data Points for Time Series Data. 2016.

[36] Yan C, J Fang, L Wu, S Ma. An Approach of Time Series Piecewise Linear Representation Based on Local Maximum Minimum and Extremum[J]. Journal of Information and Computational Science, Vol. 10, No. 9, 2013, pp. 2747-2756. https://doi.org/10.12733/jics20101797.

[37] Herrera J C. Assessment of GPS-Enabled Smartphone Data and Its Use in Traffic State Estimation for Highways. 2009.

普通信号交叉口行人早开先退相位设置研究

宋 杰 王永岗 郑少娅

（长安大学）

摘 要 如何处理交叉口人车冲突，保障交叉口人车通行效率和安全性一直是一个热点问题。本文针对这一问题，以行人早开相位为出发点，考虑了行人流与车流的冲突情况，提出了行人早开先退相位的概念。在对临界冲突点进行详细分析的基础上，对相位的早开时间和先退时间阈值进行了量化。通过VISSIM仿真对普通四相位交叉口设置行人过街早开先退相位前后的车流延误和人流通行能力进行对比，认为设置行人早开先退相位能够在保障行人过街通行能力的情况下，有效缓解人车冲突，减少车辆延误。

关键词 交通控制 信号设置 冲突分析 行人早开先退相位 交通仿真

0 引 言

城市信号交叉口作为城市交通的重要组成部分，其疏导各种形式交通流的能力影响着城市总体路网交通的运行效率。在我国，很多交叉口处，大量的车流常常伴随着大量的行人流，车流和行人流的冲突严重制约了交叉口的通行能力，也对行人的过街安全造成威胁。此外，我国的行人过街"绿闪"信号缺乏法律定义，导致行人将"绿闪"信号也视为过街信号，一定程度上加重了交叉口的危险性[1]。

现有许多研究针对行人过街模式进行了分析，主要集中在行人过街特性及模型、行人过街信号优化、行人过街专用相位、行人早开相位等方面。

目前针对行人过街行为、清空时长等方面的行人过街特性及模型研究有了诸多研究成果[2,3]。针对行人过街信号优化的研究，也有了包括遗传算法在内的许多计算模型[4]。行人过街专用相位近年来受到更多关注，相关研究逐渐深入[5]。

相较于国内，国外对行人早开相位的研究起步更早，研究也更为丰富。Dittberner等[6]认为实施行人信号提前可以显著提升行人过街的安全性和舒适度。P. Sangjun[7]利用VISSIM仿真和SSAM模型研究了行人信号提前的效果，认为提前7s是最为理想的。虞笑晨等[8]在对上海市不同类型交叉口进行调查分析的基础上，提出我国让行情境下更应设置行人先动信号的观点。曲昭伟等[9]以行人到达分布模型为基础，利用交通波模型对行人早开相位模型进行了参数标定，为我国行人早开相位的设计提供了参考。

综上所述，目前国内关于行人早开相位的研究相对较少。实际上，早开相位的初期和末期都存在与交叉口左转相位的重叠和交替。本文以早开相位和左转相位的可能冲突分析为基础，提出了行人早开先退相位的概念，通过模型建立和仿真模拟，对行人早开先退相位的设置进行了研究。

1 行人早开相位冲突分析

1.1 普通行人早开相位交叉口概况

选取普通四相位交叉口进行分析，交叉口基本情况满足如下条件：
(1)各进出口道满足左转直行右转各有至少一条专用车道。
(2)相位转换顺序依次为南北方向直行右转，南北方向左转，东西方向直行右转，东西方向左转，如图1所示。
(3)交叉口南北向和东西向行人过街信号较同相位直行右转车辆提前若干秒释放，如图2所示。

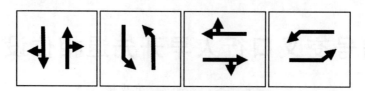

图1 普通四相位交叉口相位转换示意图

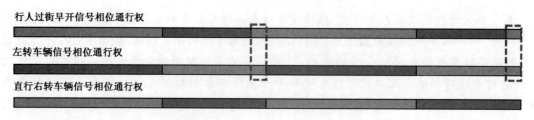

图2 行人过街早开相位与其他相位关系图

1.2 冲突点分析

由图2可知,在行人早开相位的绿灯初期和末期,分别存在与上一相位左转绿灯末期车流和下一相位左转绿灯初期车流的重叠和接替。以交叉口西侧的进出口道为例进行冲突分析,冲突可能发生点如图3中的A点和B点。

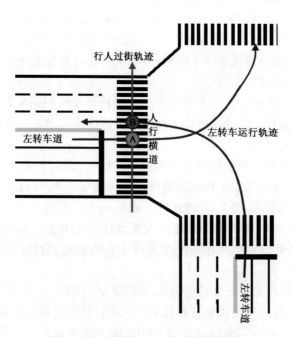

图3 交叉口西侧行人过街人车冲突示意图

2 行人早开先退相位设置研究

2.1 行人早开先退相位概念的提出

行人早开先退即通过充分利用行人早开的"附加时间",在保证行人过街有效绿灯时间不变的情况下,针对国内"绿闪"信号警示性不强的问题,对"绿闪"信号设置模型进行分析。结合早开时间,设置行人信号早退,将"绿闪"融入早退信号,解决行人"绿闪"期间依然进入交叉口带来的交通问题。行人过街早开先退相位与其他相位关系如图4所示。

图4　行人过街早开先退相位与其他相位关系图

2.2 早开先退相位初期阈值设置研究

在建立模型前,作出如下假定:

(1)所有机动车均遵守交通规则,在交叉口范围内有序通过。

(2)行人行走至某条车道中心线时,该条车道和其位于行人前进方向上的相邻车道上的车辆会受到影响而采取减速或停车等行为,其他车道内的车辆正常通行。

2.2.1 行人临界早开时间的提出

将行人临界早开时间定义为在不干扰可能与早开时段所重叠相位车流运行的条件下,行人过街信号可以最多比同相位直行右转车流提前发出的时间阈值。

2.2.2 行人临界早开时间 T_1 的计算

行人早开相位的早开时间应满足其不能影响与其相重叠的上一相位左转车流,而可以充分利用与其不相冲突的相位车流的车道空间来使行人提前过街。考虑行人过街的人流双向性,行人分别会从出口道处和进口道处过街。

对于出口道过街,行人至少需要通过一条车道才能减少冲突,剩余的出口道均不涉及冲突。由假定(2),行人流头部行人到达出口道最内侧车道中心线时,到达时间上的冲突临界点A1。

同理,对于进口道过街,除进口道左转车道,其余进口道均不影响行人通过,行人流头部行人到达进口道最内侧直行车道中心线时,到达时间上的冲突临界点A2。出口道过街临界冲突点A1和进口道过街临界冲突点A2位置如图5所示。

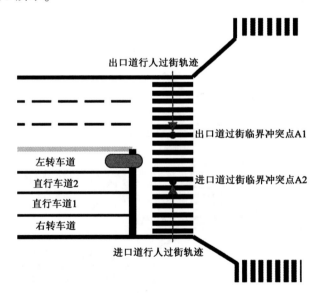

图5　行人过街临界冲突点(相位初期)

由上述分析,可得出口道过街临界早开时间 T_{EX} 表达式如下:

$$T_{EX} = T_p + \frac{(n-0.5)L_E}{V_p} \tag{1}$$

式中:T_{EX}——出口道过街临界早开时间,s;

T_p——行人反应时间,s。一般平均取值为3s;
n——交叉口出口道车道数;
L_E——交叉口出口道车道宽度,m;
V_p——行人步行速度,m/s,一般为1.1~1.5m/s。

同理,可得进口道过街临界早开时间T_{EN}表达式如下:

$$T_{EN} = T_p + \frac{0.5L_{s_m} + \sum_{i=1}^{m-1}L_{s_i} + \sum_{j=1}^{q}L_{r_j}}{V_p} \tag{2}$$

式中:T_{EN}——进口道过街临界早开时间,s;
　　m——交叉口进口道直行车道数,编号由人行道往道路中心线方向依次为1,2,…,m;
　　L_{s_m}——紧靠进口道左转车道的直行车道宽度,m;
　　L_{s_i}——编号为i的直行车道宽度,m;
　　q——交叉口进口道右转车道数,编号由人行道往道路中心线方向依次为1,2,…,q;
　　L_{r_j}——编号为j的右转车道宽度,m。

综合以上两种行人过街情形,为保障行人过街安全,避免人车冲突,最终的早开时间不应大于各临界早开时间的理论取值,即:

$$J_1 = \text{INT}[\min(T_{EX}, T_{EN})] \tag{3}$$

式中:T_1——行人临界早开时间,s。

2.3 早开先退相位末期阈值设定研究

依据上文对于先退信号的定义,可认为先退时间等于早开相位的清空时间,设早开相位清空时间为T_2,则有$T_q = T_2$。

2.3.1 早开相位清空时间的定义

在设有行人早开相位的交叉口,在确保单一周期内行人流量不发生变化的同时,可以将早开时间考虑在内,结合交叉口几何性质和人车冲突情况确定一个最佳的清空时间。

2.3.2 早开相位清空时间T_2的计算

在计算T_2前,有必要对于冲突点B进行进一步分析,如图6所示。

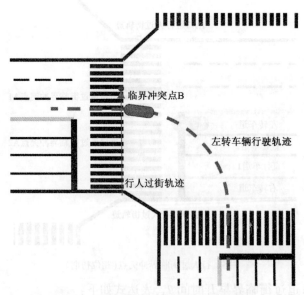

图6 行人过街临界冲突点(相位末期)

在临界冲突状态下,左转车队头部车辆能够恰好避免与信号末期的过街行人发生冲突。此时,首先需要计算行人和车辆到达临界冲突状态点的行程时间TT_p和TT_c。

1)左转车辆行程时间TT_P的计算

车辆左转的轨迹可大体分为3个阶段。这三个阶段可大致简化为直线—圆曲线—直线的轨迹模型[10]。本文简化为直线—圆曲线—直线模型,故TT_P的表达式为:

$$TT_P = T_{RC} + \frac{L_B + L_{CR} + k\sqrt{W_{NS}^2 + W_{EW}^2} - L_C}{\overline{V}_C} \tag{4}$$

式中:TT_P——左转车辆行程时间,s;

T_{RC}——左转驾驶员的反应时间,s,一般取0.6s;

L_B——停车线后撤距离,m;

L_{CR}——人行横道宽度,m;

k——转换系数,表示起终点相同的圆弧与直线的长度比;

W_{NS}——交叉口南北向几何尺寸,m;

W_{EW}——交叉口东西向几何尺寸,m;

L_C——车辆长度,m;

$\overline{V}_C$——车辆左转平均行程速度,m/s。

2)行人行程时间TT_C的计算

由临界冲突点的位置可确定TT_C的表达式为:

$$TT_C = T_1 + \frac{L_1 + 0.5L_{S_m} + 1.5L_E}{V_P} \tag{5}$$

式中:TT_C——行人行程时间,s;

L_1——交叉口进口道左转车道宽度,m。

考虑到行人过街到达冲突点和左转车辆到达冲突点所需的行驶时间,在不考虑信号早开的情况下,清空时间T_{gf}一般可以确定为:

$$T_{gf} = |TT_C - TT_P| \tag{6}$$

式中:T_{gf}——清空时间,s。

2.3.3 早退信号阈值T_q的确定

在本文分析的行人早开相位情境下,由于行人信号已经先于一般情况下若干秒开启,如清空时间按照一般情况处理,行人过街的实际绿灯时间T_g可表示如下:

$$T_g = T_1 + G \tag{7}$$

式中:T_g——行人过街的实际绿灯时间,s;

G——非早开相位行人过街绿灯时间,s。

由此,将早开时间运用到清空时间中,则行人早开相位的清空时间至少可以达到T_1,同时考虑固有清空时间T_{gf},得到早开相位清空时间T_2的表达式如下:

$$T_2 = \max\{T_1, T_{gf}\} = T_q$$

3 仿真模型构造及结果分析

3.1 仿真模型构建

模型以上海市浦东新区某四相位交叉口为例进行仿真分析,仿真软件采用VISSIM软件。根据实地考察,得到交叉口基本信息,见表1、表2。

交叉口信号控制方案(单位:s) 表1

南北直行右转	南北左转	东西直行右转	东西左转	绿灯间隔	周期
40	20	30	18	3×4	120

交叉口高峰小时机动车流量(单位:pcu/高峰小时)　　　　　表2

进口道	左	直	右	小计	合计
东进口	20	165	40	225	855
南进口	20	155	10	185	
西进口	20	255	0	275	
北进口	20	130	20	170	

考虑该交叉口未来发展,以扩大一倍的车流量进行仿真。设置左右转车辆比例为1:1,通过调整转弯车辆数与直行车辆数的比例来观察该交叉口设置行人早开先退相位前后左右转车辆和行人的延误情况。

3.1.1 仿真基本参数确定

仿真基本参数见表3。

仿真基本参数　　　　　表3

进口道车道数及尺寸(东西南北相同)(m)	4×3.0
出口道车道数及尺寸(东西南北相同)(m)	3×3.5
机动车信号灯控制方案	如表1
人行道宽度(m)	5
机动车运行速度(km/h)	服从正态分布,均值40,上下限分别45,50
行人行走速度(km/h)	服从正态分布,均值5,上下限分别4,6
交叉口各人行横道行人过街流量(pcu/h)	1400

3.1.2 仿真基本原理

仿真中行人早开先退相位的实现主要依靠设置三组信号控制机来完成。由本模型中计算出的行人早开先退时间阈值约为 $T_1 = T_q = 5s$。三组控制机的设置情况分别见表4、表5。

机动车信号控制方案(控制机1)(单位:s)　　　　　表4

相位	绿灯开始时间	绿灯结束时间	黄灯时间	周期
↕	2	42	3×4	120
↰↱	45	65		
↔	68	98		
⇆	101	119		

行人信号控制方案(控制机2,3)(单位:s)　　　　　表5

相位		绿灯开始时间		绿灯结束时间	周期
↰↱	常规	2	常规	42	120
	早开先退	117	早开先退	37	
⇆	常规	68	常规	98	
	早开先退	63	早开先退	93	

3.2 仿真结果分析

针对交叉口设置行人早开先退相位的有无和转弯车流比例的调整,进行两组仿真对比实验,相关数据输出结果如下。

(1) 当左右转车流较大时(比例为3:4:3):

设置行人早开先退相位前后各转弯车道车辆运行延误结果见表6。

转向车辆占比较大时机动车交叉口延误(单位:s) 表6

项 目		西进口	东进口	北进口	南进口	平均值
左转车道	设置前	3.1	2.9	2.6	2.0	2.7
	设置后	0.6	0.6	0.8	0.9	0.7
右转车道	设置前	28	32	25.1	27.4	28.1
	设置后	23.1	30.2	24.0	23.2	25.1

设置行人早开先退相位前后通过交叉口西侧人行道的单向人流量结果见表7(每10个周期统计一次)。

转向车辆占比较大时西侧人行横道单向人流量情况(单位:pcu/h) 表7

项 目	1200s(10个周期)	2400s(20个周期)	3600s(30个周期)
设置前	225	462	703
设置后	224	462	701

(2) 当左右转车流不大时(比例为1:4:1):

同样进行车流延误和行人流量数据输出,结果见表8、表9。

转向车辆占比较小时机动车交叉口延误(单位:s) 表8

项 目		西进口	东进口	北进口	南进口	平均值
左转车道	设置前	3.5	3.2	2.3	2.2	2.8
	设置后	0.9	0.9	1.1	1.3	1.1
右转车道	设置前	23.5	25.1	23.2	20.9	23.2
	设置后	17.7	20.6	22.6	17.7	19.7

转向车辆占比较小时西侧人行横道单向人流量情况(单位:pcu/h) 表9

项 目	1200s(10个周期)	2400s(20个周期)	3600s(30个周期)
设置前	225	462	703
设置后	224	462	701

结合输出数据进行分析可知,设置行人早开先退相位下左转延误降低了61%~72%(设置前为3s左右,设置后为1s左右),右转延误降低了11%~15%(设置前为23s左右,设置后为20s左右)。因此,此举对于减少交叉口人车冲突有着积极的影响。

在转向车流占比不同的情况下,延误的减少情况差异不大。由于过街人流量为确定值,可初步分析得出人流量对于交叉口的影响更为显著。

在行人过街方面,本案例中交叉口早开时间恰好等于先退时间,行人过街流量能够保持稳定,设置早开先退相位没有对行人过街通行能力造成影响,且仿真输出中行人延误在设置早开先退相位前后未发生明显变化。实际上大部分普通交叉口早开和先退时间相差并不大,这也能保证行人过街的有效绿灯时间。综上所述,设置行人过街早开先退相位有一定的价值和可行性。

4 结 语

行人过街早开先退相位的设置对于交叉口左右转车辆和行人间的人车冲突有着一定的缓解。本文对于普通四相位交叉口进行了分析和模拟,发现设置行人早开先退相位后,可在一定程度上减少交叉口转弯车辆延误,减轻交叉口人车冲突严重程度,保障人车过街安全。

对于早开先退的可行性分析,模型主要针对交通冲突临界点来建立,对于行人流和行人过街的行为考虑较少。同时,模型对于减少右转车辆延误的有效性也有待进一步提升,需要充分考虑人行横道双向人流的影响,早开时间有进一步优化的必要。对于不同类型的交叉口,例如含有行人二次过街设施的大型交叉口,如何设置早开早退信号以及是否可以设置,也需要后续的研究。

参考文献

[1] 李克平,倪颖. 科学设置行人清空信号 破解行人"过街难"问题[J]. 汽车与安全,2018(09):86-88.

[2] 韩婷. 信号交叉口行人过街交通行为和速度特性研究[J]. 汽车实用技术, 2018(23):300-303.

[3] 陈鹏,潘汉中. 城市交叉口行人过街信号清空时间设置研究[J]. 公路与汽运,2011(06):65-68.

[4] 马庚华,何瑞,郑长江,等. 考虑行人过街因素的环形交叉口配时优化方法研究[J]. 华东交通大学学报,2019,36(01):59-65.

[5] 董洁霜,卞春,王嘉文,等. 数据驱动的两相位信号控制交叉口行人专用相位动态设置方法[J]. 公路交通科技,2020,37(01):85-95.

[6] Dittberner R, Vu N. How Long Is Your LPI? Balancing Pedestrian Comfort and Traffic Impacts with an Elongated Leading Pedestrian Interval[J]. ITE journal, 2017, 87(12):44-49.

[7] Kim D, Park S. The Impact Analysis of Leading Pedestrian Interval Using Surrogate Safety Assesment Model[J]. Korean Society of Transportation, 2019(37):232-244.

[8] 虞笑晨,陈怡立,邵丹. 机动车礼让行人背景下的交叉口交通分析——以上海市为例[J]. 城市交通,2020,18(01):65-74.

[9] 曲昭伟,曹宁博,陈永恒,等. 信号交叉口的行人信号提前建模[J]. 浙江大学学报(工学版),2017,51(03):538-544.

[10] 南春丽,张生瑞,严宝杰. 基于停车线位置的左转车辆行驶轨迹仿真模型[J]. 计算机工程与应用,2009,45(09):24-27.

流量不对称干线信号协调相位设计研究

李丙烨[1]　张　敏[1]　向宇杰[2]　彭恩鹏[2]　李超同[2]
(1.长安大学运输工程学院;2.长安大学公路学院)

摘　要　为解决流量不对称造成的道路资源浪费和交通拥堵问题,提出了流量不对称干线信号协调相位方案。应用 Synchro 软件仿真,以最大公共周期、相位差、绿信比为变量,干线最小延误为优化目标,比较不同流量比例情况下各种相位方案的适用性。试验设计三种相位方案、两种车道功能方案,将方案进行组合,设置不同流量比例对方案仿真,并就仿真结果进行对比分析,确定不同流量比例下信号控制方案适用性,结果显示在不对称系数较小的情况下,三种相位控制方案在造成的车辆平均延误上差异较小,随着不对称系数的增大,两相位方案中设置专用左转车道和设置直行左转混行车道会优于搭接相位设置,在搭接相位和单进口道放行上,搭接相位放行会比单进口道放行上造成的车辆平均延误更小。以兰州市某条道路为实例对上述方案进行应用,使用两相位干线协调控制方案对其优化,得出车辆平均延误减少 26%,车辆停车次数减少 13%,每公里燃油量减少了 12%,优化后的各项指标相对于现状都有一定提升。

关键词　交通控制　相位设计　交通仿真　不对称系数

0　引　言

潮汐交通是目前常见的交通现象,其浪费了道路资源,造成了在早晚高峰时间段交通供给与交通需求不匹配问题,其具有周期性、单向性、规律性的特点[1]。目前解决交通潮汐现象而造成的交通拥堵问题多从交通管理与控制入手,代磊磊等[2]针对北京潮汐交通明显的路段,通过交通调查分析了设置潮汐车道的可行性,并提出了潮汐车道设置方案,通过 Vissim 仿真对潮汐车道设置效果前后进行评价,结果表明潮汐车道对提高路段主要交通流向通行能力和降低延误有重要作用;姜涛[3]分析了常规可变车道普适性较差的局限性,提出了借道通行和组合式可变车道,并设置预信号进行协调,有效解决了普通潮汐车道利用率不高、视线诱导不足的问题;曹俊业等[4]以青岛市滨海大道为例,考虑信号因素,采用分段绿波控制方式,通过设置瓶颈控制适当缓解下游交通压力,实现了车辆连续快速通过交叉口;张亮[5]分析了流量不对称情况下对称流向放行相位方案的局限性,运用传统的信号配时方法和延误模型确定了十字交叉口在不同交通需求情况下应选取的相位设计方案。过往对于解决流量不对称问题大多是以某一条路为例,普适性较差,与此同时对关于设置可变车道的研究较多,从信号优化控制方面研究较少,对于信号控制也停留在某个交叉口层面,缺少对流量不对称情况下线控的研究。关于干线信号协调,在研究初期设定线控通常是基于车辆运行状态下的时间-距离图,用图解法或数解法计算相邻交叉口的相位差,以最大绿波带宽度为目标,确定干线信号控制方案。相邻交叉口的相位差是影响线控的重要因素,曹交交[6]等在分析城市干线系统控制方式的基础上,建立了以干线双向绿波到达交叉口的时刻差值最小为目标的交通干线信号动态优化控制模型,并采用遗传算法对模型进行求解,得出结果获得较大带宽,但考虑交叉口数目较少,不能满足干线要求;高云峰等[7]考虑交叉口群,采用多目标优化方法以公共周期长度、相位差、绿信比为优化自变量,以机动车在交叉口处的平均延误、停车次数、排队长度和流量为优化目标建立多目标优化模型,其考虑了交叉口群的影响,但是关于流量不对称的特点未展开研究;卢凯等[8]利用速度变换和相位结合的方法,给出了非对称通行条件下的双向绿波协调控制数解算法,对公共信号周期、交叉口信号相位组合和各交叉口相位差进行整体优化设计。林晓辉[9]比较单口放行方式和对称放行方式两种相位设计方法的特性,分析了不同交通需求下两种相位设计方法的平均延误时间、排队长度、停车次数等交通信号控制性能指标优劣。

从研究现状来看,对于流量不对称情况,研究主要集中在设置潮汐车道和单个交叉口信号优化上,干线信号协调集中在参数的优化上,缺少考虑流量不对称情况的交通流情况以及对各个相位设置的相关研究。本文以四个连续交叉口为研究对象,通过 Synchro 仿真确定在两方向不同流量比例情况下相位方案的适用性研究,并以兰州市建宁路为例进行实例应用。

1 流量不对称干线信号协调设计

1.1 研究对象

流量不对称取决于该相位交通流不对称系数是否超过了阈值[10]。在进行流量不对称分析时,需要选择合适的交通模型,本文的研究对象为由四个连续交叉口组成的干线,在主干路上的交叉口进口道数目较多,与之相交的交叉口多为次干路或支路,进口道数目有限。在本文研究中,将与干线相交的进口道数目设置为两车道,主干路为三车道。为了更清晰了解流量不对称比例对控制方案的影响,在控制支路的流量的基础上改变双向直行的车流量及主干路的渠化类型来进行研究。

1.2 方案设计

1.2.1 相位方案

单进口道放行是指在各个进口道都设相位,即在普通的十字交叉口设置四个相位,在该相位内该进口道全部转向的车辆,满足了各个流向之间的饱和度均衡的要求。在主干路进行控制时,单进口放行信号控制下可以进行一定的改进,在主干路方向上的两个交叉口进行单进口放行,次干路的两个方向在一个相位上放行,可以相对减少整个交叉口的延误,相位控制方案如图1a)所示,此图以东西方向为主干路。

对称方向放行由于右转车流与交叉口内部其他车流均无冲突,所以在两相位设置中,不需对右转车流加以管控。其相位方案设计如图1b)所示。

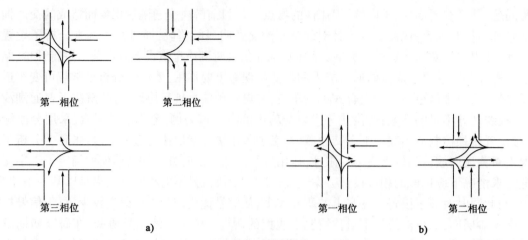

图 1 相位方案图

由于在交叉口车辆 16 处冲突中有 12 处冲突是左转车辆产生的,为了防止东西干线中直行车辆受到左转车辆的冲突,所以在干线上设置专用左转相位,与此同时搭接相位是解决流量不对称情况下常用的相位设置方案,故在两个基本相位之间设置搭接相位。

1.2.2 车道方案

对于单进口道放行,因为在某个相位上全部车辆一同放行,所以在进口道功能设计上,一般情况下都会将原有的专用左转车道改为直行左转车道。增加了干线直行的车道数目,扩大了对于直行车辆的供给,减少了道路资源浪费,同时也使每个进口道的各个车道的饱和度均衡,避免了单方向上直行车辆过多然而左转车道车辆较少的情况。主干路的单进口道放行设置的一般渠化如图 2a) 所示,支路的单进口道放行条件下的一般渠化如图 2b) 所示。

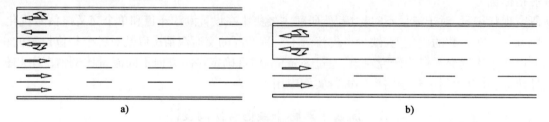

图 2 车道功能图

1.2.3 流量方案

次干路上的左转、右转车流量设置为每小时 100 辆,直行车流量设置为每小时 150 辆,主干路上的左转、右转车流量设置为每小时 100 辆;交叉口的信号配时方面,假设车流量的高峰小时系数(Peak Hour Factor)设置为 0.92,大车与小车之比为 2∶8。

由西向东的直行设置为 800veh/h,由东向西的直行设置为 800~1800veh/h,在仿真过程中由东向西的车辆以 100 为变化值来逐一增加车辆数目,具体流量不对称指标以及各个方向直行交通量见表 1。通过改变增加车辆数目来对三种仿真方案进行仿真并总结仿真结果,以车辆平均延误为指标,对干线协调控制方案进行比较。

主干路仿真流量设置情况　　　　　　　　　　　　　　　　　表 1

由西向东直行车辆数	由东向西直行车辆数	流量不对称比值
800	800	1
800	900	1.125
800	1000	1.25
800	1100	1.375
800	1200	1.5

续上表

由西向东直行车辆数	由东向西直行车辆数	流量不对称比值
800	1300	1.625
800	1400	1.75
800	1500	1.875
800	1600	2
800	1700	2.125
800	1800	2.25

1.3 仿真实验

通过修改不同进口道功能以及不同相位设置,将仿真方案设置为五种,各种方案的进口道功能以及相位设置见表2。

控制方案设置情况　　　　表2

项　目	车道设置	相位设置
方案一	专用左转、直行、直行右转	两相位
方案二	直行左转、直行、专用右转	两相位
方案三	直行左转、直行、直行右转	两相位
方案四	直行左转、直行、直行右转	单进口道放行
方案五	专用左转、直行、直行右转	搭接相位

通过 Synchro 对各方案进行仿真,对仿真结果进行总结,如图3所示。

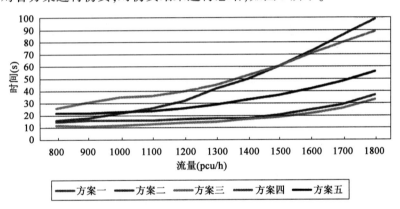

图3　不同控制方案不同流量下的车辆平均延误

从仿真结果来看,在此种支路数目、车流量及此种主干路转弯车流量情况下,相同相位方案不同进口道功能的仿真结果显示,相同相位不同进口功能设置专用右转车道会因不能分担直行车流,同时给左转车流带来一定压力而导致车辆平均延误,无论在何种流量比的情况下,都比其他两个方案大;设置专用左转车道与设置直行左转混行车道在两相位设置情况下差距不明显;直行、左转、右转混行的方案三在任何流量比的情况下,都优于其他方案。

相同进口道功能不同相位设置的比较:两相位中设置专用左转车道与搭接相位方案相比,在不对称系数较小的情况下,两者造成的车辆平均延误差距较小,随着不对称系数的增大,两相位方案中设置专用左转车道优于搭接相位方案。对于搭接相位方案,由仿真结果分析可得,搭接相位方案优于单进口道放行方案。

综上所述,在相同车道功能的前提下,无论何种流量比,两相位方案优于搭接相位方案,而搭接相位方案优于单进口道放行方案;车道功能影响车辆平均延误,在两相位控制方案中,车道数目较少的情况下不建议设置专用右转车道。

2　实例分析

选取兰州市安宁区的建宁路为主干路进行分析,以与其交叉的宝石花路、学府路、万新南路、银滩路为次干路或支路进行实例分析。

通过交通调查来搜集交通量资料,通过对交通量资料的分析得出交通量随着时间以及其他因素的变化规律,并且分析现状及优化设计。交通调查时间在早高峰阶段7:30—9:30、午高峰阶段11:30—13:30、晚高峰阶段17:30—19:30。在调查过程中,车辆分别按照左转车辆、直行车辆、右转车辆计数,其中以小型客车为基本单位1计算,大型客车的换算系数1.5,之后按照换算系数来确定交通量的大小。

除了调查交通量之外,还需调查目前的交通相位、信号配时、各个进口道功能,在交叉口附近是否有学校、停车场等较大交通量产生区域,以及交叉口的断面形式,是否存在人行天桥、地下通道等行人交通设施。在调查完成之后,整理分析调查数据,通过对数据的整理得出在早高峰由于上班、上学等原因导致东西方向直行流量不对称系数为1.3。早高峰各进口道的数据见表3。

早高峰各交叉口车流量(单位:pcu/h)　　　　　　　　　表3

方位	方向	不同方向车流量			
		宝石花路	学府路	万新南路	银滩路
北	左	142	149	220	156
	直	234	0	224	120
	右	122	160	160	127
南	左	372	0	108	120
	直	222	0	190	204
	右	236	0	192	299
东	左	198	0	347	150
	直	1176	477	492	407
	右	150	147	84	172
西	左	136	126	116	120
	直	926	384	304	314
	右	332	0	76	270

现状交通信号相位如图4所示。

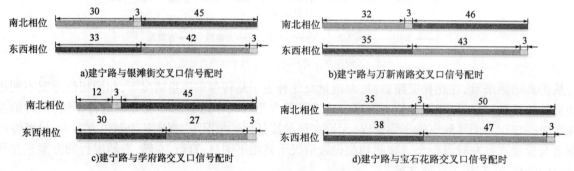

图4　交叉口信号配时情况

将上述交通信号以及交通流量数据导入仿真软件中进行仿真,并通过Synchro软件进行优化,总结仿真结果见表4。

仿真结果　　　　　　　　　表4

评价指标	银滩街交叉口		万新南路交叉口		学府路交叉口		宝石花路交叉口		现状方案	两相位方案	单进口道放行	搭接相位
	优化前	优化后	优化前	优化后	优化前	优化后	优化前	优化后				
行车延误(s)	10	7	17	12	12	4	27	23	19	14	21	40
停车次数(次)	0.41	0.4	0.56	0.5	0.55	0.28	0.76	0.68	0.6	0.52	0.61	0.62
燃油消耗(L/km)	0.15	0.14	0.15	0.14	0.13	0.11	0.22	0.2	0.17	0.15	0.17	0.21

由表4得出在优化前后建宁东路的各个交叉口由于拥堵而产生的行车延误、行车时间、停车次数都有一定程度的降低。在通过交叉口处的车辆数没有变化的前提下,建宁东路与银滩街交叉口的行车延误由原来的10s降低至7s,平均停车次数及燃油消耗没有较大变化。与此同时,建宁东路与万新南路交叉口的行车延误由原来的17s降低至12s,平均停车次数由原来的0.56次降低至0.5次。建宁东路与学府路交叉口的行车延误由原来的12s降低至4s,平均停车次数由原来的0.55次降低至0.28次,燃油消耗减少了0.02L/km。建宁东路与宝石花路交叉口的行车延误由原来的27s降低至23s,停车次数由0.76次降低至0.68次。综上所述,若对建宁路实施干线协调控制相比于现状的交通情况,交通拥堵问题会得到有效解决,相应的运行速度也会提高,交叉口的服务水平会有所提高。

不同相位方案之间对比:两相位控制方案优于其他控制方案,平均行车延误为14s,相对于现状方案平均延误减少了26%,实施两相位控制方案后,行车效率明显提升;停车次数由现状0.6次缩减至0.52次,行车减少了13%的停车次数,行车舒适性有所提升;燃油消耗方面,每公里燃油由现状0.17L减少至0.15L,减少了12%。路段的通行时间变短,运行速度变大,从仿真结果来看,两相位信号协调控制方案总体优于其他信号控制方案。优化后的方案相比现有方案大大提高了道路通行能力、提升了运行速度、减少了通行延误,从而可以将上述干线协调控制方案作为对建宁路的改进方案。

3 结　语

(1)本文通过设计不同相位控制不同进口道功能改变流量比例的方案,比较了在不同流量比下干线信号协调控制相位的适用性。仿真实验结果说明在不对称系数较小的情况下,几种方案造成的车辆平均延误差距不明显,随着不对称系数的增大,双相位方案中设置专用左转车道以及直行左转混行车道优于搭接相位方案。搭接相位方案造成的平均延误比单进口放行方案造成的延误小;两相位控制方案优于搭接相位控制方案,而搭接相位方案优于单进口放行方案。

(2)本文通过实例前后方案指标对比,发现两相位干线信号协调控制方案在平均行车延误、停车次数、燃油消耗指标上优于现有控制方案,论证了试验结果的有效性。

参考文献

[1] 戴昕. 城市主干线潮汐车道交通流特性及设置方法研究[D]. 西安:长安大学,2018.
[2] 代磊磊,顾金刚,俞春俊,等. 潮汐车道交通流特性与设置方案仿真研究[J]. 交通信息与安全,2012,30(1):15-19.
[3] 姜涛. 信控平交口可变车道设置方法研究[D]. 西安:长安大学,2019.
[4] 曹俊业,李涛,陈秀锋,等. 面向潮汐交通流的信号控制策略优化[J]. 青岛理工大学学报,2015,36(2):87-94.
[5] 张亮,张存保. 流量不对称"十"字交叉口信号相位设计方法研究[J]. 交通信息与安全,2009,27(2):77-80,84.
[6] 曹交交,韩印,姚佼. 城市交通干线动态双向绿波优化控制模型[J]. 公路交通科技,2015,32(9):115-120.
[7] 高云峰,胡华,韩皓,等. 城市道路交叉口群信号协调控制多目标优化与仿真[J]. 中国公路学报,2012,25(6):129-135.
[8] 卢凯,刘永洋,吴焕,等. 非对称通行条件下的双向绿波协调控制数解算法[J]. 中国公路学报,2015,28(6):95-103.
[9] 林晓辉. 十字交叉口的单口放行与对称放行相位设计方法对比研究[J]. 交通信息与安全,2014,32(3):69-72.
[10] 蒋贤才,于晨. 信号交叉口不对称交通流的优化控制方法[J]. 交通运输系统工程与信息,2018,18(6):48-54.

基于通行需求的绿灯时间计算模型

董栩鑫[1]　张伟斌[1]　张峻屹[2]　姜影[3]

(1.南京理工大学电子工程与光电技术学院;2.广岛大学;3.大连理工大学)

摘　要　传统信号控制优化的目标主要是周期和绿信比,相位绿灯时长较依赖周期时长和分配到的绿信比,因此如果周期设置不满足通行需求,就会影响交叉口运行效果。为了满足各相位所需的绿灯时长,同时完善对绿灯时长的约束和计算方法,本文对车辆的到达以及驶离情况进行建模分析,计算得到了满足各相位通行需求的绿灯时长。结合实际案例分别对两个不同时段使用 VISSIM 进行仿真,选择平均延误时间和平均排队长度作为评价指标,对比原配时方案,Webster 模型和本文提出的模型后发现,本文的模型在两个时段的仿真中,相比于 Webster 模型,平均延误时间分别下降了 6.8% 和 4.1%,提高了绿灯的利用效率,验证了本文模型在信号控制方面的有效性。

关键词　交通信号控制　绿灯时间　建模分析　交叉口信号配时　单交叉口

0 引　言

随着城市化的推进,交通拥堵问题日益严重,评价一个交叉口的信号控制是否合理主要有两个方面,一个是在平峰时期是否会有相位绿灯信号的浪费情况("空放"现象),"空放"会增加其余相位的等待时长,造成不必要的浪费;另一个是高峰时期是否会有相位因为车流量较大,在相位绿灯时间内无法清空而产生的二次排队现象,二次排队会导致车辆在停车线后不断堆积,甚至造成车队"溢流"到上游路口,严重的会导致交通进入"死锁"状态,需要人工协调才能完成车辆的清空工作。因此,如何提高绿灯的利用率以及如何保证不产生二次排队成为本文的主要研究方向。

目前,常用的交叉口信号配时方法有 Webster 模型、ARRB 模型等,然而这些方法只适用于饱和度较低的情况下,当饱和度趋于1时,Webster 模型的分母会趋于0,因此得到的周期会趋于无穷大。当饱和度大于1时,即路口处于过饱和状态下时,Webster 模型得到的周期会变为负数,因此,该模型在现有交通状态下并不适用。

针对过饱和状态的研究方面,Xiang 通过静态反馈控制来研究过饱和交叉口实时信号控制问题;Liu 创建了过饱和交叉口信号控制的反向因果模型,提出最大化驶离率来优化过饱和情况下的通行能力;曹倩霞通过建模分析,在多个周期中寻找总延误最小的最佳信号周期;Wu 在对能耗问题的研究中提出了过饱和信号交叉口的能耗分析方法;Eriskin 使用消除配对系统对过饱和交通状态下的信号控制策略进行优化;卢凯提出了过饱和交通状态下的停车延误协调控制模型,对车辆的到达和驶离情况通过图形化建模的方式得到了停车延误模型的表达式;徐建闽在交叉口车辆延误模型的基础上,基于平均延误时间最小为优化目标,计算得到了最佳信号周期公式;裴玉龙研究了饱和交通状态下的绿信比优化方法。通过最佳周期以及绿信比得到的绿灯时长在未饱和状态下往往可以发挥不错的效果,但是不一定能满足过饱和情况下的交通需求。

绿灯时长需要根据流量或者排队长度来进行确定,因此,基于排队最远点约束的最大周期时长优化方法和以排队长度最短为优化目标的信号交叉口最大周期时长优化方法被提出;Tong 提出了过饱和交叉口信号配时的随机规划模型,给出了过饱和状态下的绿信比和绿灯时长的约束条件,通过排队长度等参数来调整相位绿灯时长;凌墨通过对交通流的预测,提出了交通流不确定情况下的单交叉口信号配时

基金项目:国家自然科学基金项目(编号:71971116)。

方法。钱红波分析了绿灯间隔时间对交通安全的影响。乔健使用模糊控制算法,基于通行需求提出了一种新的信号控制策略。

本文在上述研究的基础上,考虑将车辆到达和驶离的过程进一步细化,通过最小化滞留车辆数来计算得到相位不产生二次排队所需满足的最小绿灯时长。根据相位的流量需求来调整绿灯时长,在平峰状态下,可以有效降低绿灯的浪费现象,同时在高峰状态下可以保证相位等待车辆的及时驶离,不会因为二次排队导致某相位出现"溢流"现象。

1 绿灯时间计算模型

绿灯时间计算模型的优化目标是使待放行的流量小于或等于当前信号控制下可以驶离的流量。具体计算步骤如图1所示。

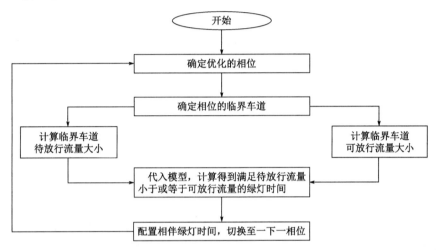

图1 绿灯时间计算模型流程图

首先选择相位中流量最大的车道作为临界车道,临界车道能否顺利将待放行车辆清空作为衡量模型有效与否的标准。其次将临界车道的参数代入待放行流量模型以及可驶离流量模型,计算得到临界车道的待放行流量大小和当前信号控制下可驶离的流量大小,通过使待放行的流量小于等于可驶离的流量,即可保证临界车道不会产生二次排队的现象。假设某交叉口相位集合为 μ,设相位 i 包含 t 个车道,假设车道 k 为相位 i 的临界车道,则可以得到优化模型如下:

$$\min_{i \subset \mu}(A_i^k - D_i^k) \tag{1}$$

式中:A_i^k——相位 i 中车道 k 的待放行流量;

D_i^k——相位 i 中车道 k 的可驶离流量。

1.1 待放行流量

公式(1)中 A_i^k 主要包括3部分,分别为前一周期绿灯时间结束时滞留的车辆数,前一周期中红灯期间到达的车辆数,当前绿灯时间内到达的车辆数。因此将 A_i^k 表示如下:

$$\begin{aligned}
A_i^k &= \mathrm{vol}_0^k + \mathrm{vol}_r^k + \mathrm{vol}_g^k \\
&= \mathrm{vol}_0^k + \frac{q_i^k(C' - g_i')}{3600} + \frac{q_i^k g_i}{3600} \\
&= \mathrm{vol}_0^k + \frac{q_i^k(C' - g_i' + g_i)}{3600}
\end{aligned} \tag{2}$$

式中:vol_0^k——前一周期车道 k 滞留的车辆数;

vol_r^k——红灯期间车道 k 到达的车辆数;

vol_g^k——当前绿灯时间内车道 k 到达的车辆数;

q_i^k——车道 k 的平均车辆到达率,pcu/h;
C'——前一周期的周期时长,s;
g_i'——前一周期相位 i 的绿灯时长,s;
g_i——当前周期相位 i 的绿灯时长,s。

1.2 可驶离流量

公式(1)中,D_i^k 主要由启动延误时长、相位的绿灯间隔时长以及平均车头时距来确定。因此将 D_i^k 表示如下:

$$D_i^k = \frac{(g_i - L + \Delta_i)}{d} + 1 \tag{3}$$

式中:g_i——相位所需绿灯时长,s;
L——首车启动延误时长,s;
Δ_i——相位 i 的绿灯间隔时长,s,包括黄灯时长和清空交叉口车流的全红时长;
d——平均车头时距,s。

1.3 绿灯时长

根据优化目标,令 $A_i^k - D_i^k$ 小于或等于 0,可以得到相位 i 的绿灯时长 g_i 的表达式如下:

$$g_i \geq \frac{3600 \times d(\text{vol}_0^k - 1) + q_i^k \times d(C' - g_i') + 3600(L - \Delta_i)}{3600 - q_i^k d} \tag{4}$$

同时相位 i 的绿灯时长应满足行人最短通行时长要求,行人最短通行时长 $g_{\min}$ 需要根据具体路口实际情况确定。

综上,将各相位的绿灯时长相加,即可得到满足不产生二次排队的最小周期时长。将上述约束条件整理后得到的模型如下:

$$g_i = \max\left\{g_{\min}, \frac{3600 \times d(\text{vol}_0^k - 1) + q_i^k \times d(C' - g_i') + 3600(L - \Delta_i)}{3600 - q_i^k d}\right\} \tag{5}$$

2 案例分析

本文以某市某拥堵严重的交叉口为例,该路口西面为城市快速路,东面为过江大桥,因此东西两面流量较大。北面为学校,南面为商铺,因此南北两面在平峰和高峰时段有明显的流量变化,是该市典型的易发生拥堵的路口之一。交叉口渠化图如图2所示,由于南北方向直行和左转车道并道,如果设计南北双向放行会阻碍南北左转方向车流行驶,因此设计相位 A 为南直行加南左转;相位 B 为北直行加北左转;东西方向无左转车道,因此相位 C 为东西方向直行。综上,考虑设计交叉口为三相位,具体如表1所示。

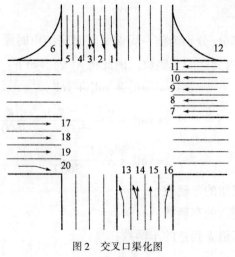

图2 交叉口渠化图

本文选择该路口两个时段的流量数据在 VISSIM 上进行仿真验证,各时段对应的临界车道平均车辆到达率如表 1 所示。

相位临界车道平均车辆到达率(单位:pcu/h) 表1

时 段	相 位		
	A	B	C
时段1	271	253	552
时段2	363	337	501

参数设置方面,g_{min} 设定为 20s;首车启动延误 L 设为 2s;绿灯间隔时长 Δ_i 设定为黄灯时长 3s,全红时长 2s,因此 Δ_i 为 5s;平均车头时距 d 根据路口实际情况设定为 2.5s;滞留车辆数 vol_0^k 需要根据实际情况获取,本文均假设滞留车辆为 0;初始周期的配时信息,本文假定为周期为 90s,各相位绿灯时长均为 30s。

根据上文提供的数据和参数,使用 Webster 模型和本论文的模型分别进行配时后得到如表 2 所示配时方案。

配时方案(单位:s) 表2

时 段	方 案	
	Webster 模型(相位:A-B-C)	本论文模型(相位:A-B-C)
时段1	16-15-34(周期:65)	25-24-53(周期:102)
时段2	31-29-42(周期:102)	33-31-46(周期:110)

从配时结果中可以发现,时段 2 与时段 1 相比,相位 A 和 B 的流量有所增加,而相位 C 的流量有所降低,然而由于 Webster 模型依据流量比分配绿灯时长,因此时段 2 的周期增大后,给予相位 C 的时长也明显增大,然而相位 C 的实际绿灯需求时长却不明确,且 Webster 模型依赖于流量比的大小,当流量比之和接近 1 时,计算得到的周期就会趋于无穷大,而当流量适中时,计算得到的周期又会偏小,因此在实际应用中难以根据实际需要给予相位所需的绿灯时长。本文提出的模型综合考虑了车辆通行的需求时间,因此绿灯时长可以根据具体流量大小的变化而变化。

3 仿 真 验 证

将上述案例中表 1 的两个时段的平均车辆到达率和表 2 的配时方案分别在 VISSIM 软件中进行仿真,为了避免一次仿真带来的随机性对结果的影响,本文进行了 10 次仿真,仿真种子从 42 增加到 51,仿真评价参数方面选择平均延误时间和平均排队长度两个指标,结果取平均值,如表 3 所示。

仿 真 结 果 表3

时 段	评价指标	本文模型	与原始方案对比		与 Webster 模型对比	
			原始方案	优化率	Webster 模型	优化率
时段1	延误时间(s)	67.3	77.4	13.0%	72.2	6.8%
	排队长度(m)	49.7	52.4	5.1%	47.8	−4.0%
时段2	延误时间(s)	73.3	83.6	12.3%	76.4	4.1%
	排队长度(m)	50.8	57.3	11.3%	51.3	2.0%

仿真结果如图 3 和图 4 所示。在时段 1 中,本文的模型在延误时长和排队长度方面相比于 Webster 模型,延误时间优化了 6.8%,然而在排队长度降低了 4.0%。经过分析,本文的模型在应对流量较大的情况下,会优先保证当前相位不产生由于二次排队造成的车辆延误,因此会增加其余相位的等待时间,其余相位到达车辆增加,因此排队长度会有所增大,但是整体的车辆延误会由于绿灯利用率的提升而降低。

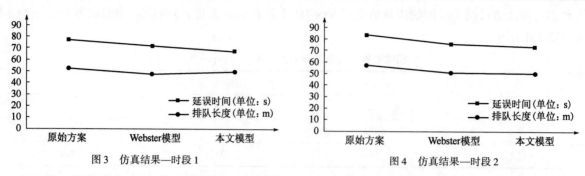

图3 仿真结果—时段1　　　　　　　　　图4 仿真结果—时段2

在时段2的仿真中,本文模型的延误时间和排队长度相比Webster算法均有一定的优化,其中延误时间优化了4.1%,排队长度优化了2.0%。由于时段2中各相位流量值较接近,因此本文模型计算得到的配时方案与Webster模型得到的配时方案也比较接近。

4 结　语

传统信号控制策略大多基于给定周期的情况下,对各相位进行合理的绿信比分配,然而如果周期的大小设定与车辆通行需求不符,则会导致在平峰时段容易产生浪费绿灯时间的现象,平峰时段的绿灯时长浪费会增加其余相位的等待时间,同时增加了交叉口车辆延误的时间。而在高峰时段容易产生绿灯时间不足导致的车辆二次排队现象,一旦某一相位出现车辆二次排队现象,则排队长度会随着交叉口在高峰期的车辆到达率不断增加,容易造成相位堵塞甚至"溢流"到上游交叉口。

因此本文通过对车辆的到达和驶离情况进行建模分析,提出了满足车辆通行需求的绿灯时间计算模型,该模型通过优先考虑各相位所需的绿灯时长来调整信号控制方案,可以有效地保证车辆所需的通行时间。通过仿真验证表明,该模型相比于Webster模型,在延误时间方面有一定的改善。在排队长度方面,由于各相位流量均较大时,满足某一相位的通行需求会导致其余相位排队长度的增加,但是整体的延误时间会有所下降。由此证明,本文提出的模型在信号控制方面对交叉口绿灯利用率有一定的优化作用。

在实际应用中,考虑到交叉口的特殊性,尤其是过饱和情况下,可以结合交叉口整体的延误情况,对交叉口绿灯时间的最大值有一定的约束,该方面本研究尚未考虑,后续方向可以寻找使得交叉口整体通行能力最大,平均延误达到最小的信号控制策略。

参考文献

[1] Webster F V. Traffic Signal Setting[R]. Road Research Technical Paper No.39, Department of Transport, HMSO, London, 1958.

[2] Akcelik R. Traffic Signals: Capacity and Timing Analysis[M]. Australia: Australian Road Research Board, 1981.

[3] Xiang W, Xiao J, Jiang Y. Real-time Signalization for An Oversaturated Intersection Via Static State Feedback Control: A Switched System Approach[J]. Journal of the Franklin Institute, 2015, 352(8): 3304-3324.

[4] Liu H, Balke K N, Lin W H. A Reverse Causal-effect Modeling Approach for Signal Control of An Oversaturated Intersection[J]. Transportation Research Part C Emerging Technologies, 2008, 16(6): 742-754.

[5] 曹倩霞,王修江,龙科军.饱和状态交叉口信号配时优化[J].系统工程,2010(07):123-126.

[6] Wu L, Ci Y, Wang Y, et al. Fuel Consumption at the Oversaturated Signalized Intersection Considering Queue Effects: A Case Study in Harbin, China[J]. Energy, 2020, 192(Feb.1): 116654.1-116654.9.

[7] Eriskin E, Karahancer S, Terzi S, et al. Optimization of Traffic Signal Timing at Oversaturated Intersections Using Elimination Pairing System[J]. Procedia Engineering, 2017, 187: 295-300.

[8] 卢凯,徐建闽,李林.过饱和交通状态下的停车延误协调控制模型[C]//第21届中国过程控制会议.
[9] 徐建闽,荆彬彬,卢凯.过饱和状态下的单交叉口最小延误信号周期模型[J].控制理论与应用,2015(04):521-526.
[10] 裴玉龙,蒋贤才.饱和交通状态下的绿信比优化及其应用研究[J].哈尔滨工业大学学报,2005(11):1499-1502.
[11] 王殿海,付凤杰,蔡正义,等.基于排队最远点约束的最大周期时长优化方法[J].华南理工大学学报(自然科学版),2014,42(05):67-74.
[12] 王殿海,别一鸣,宋现敏,等.信号交叉口最大周期时长优化方法[J].吉林大学学报(工学版),2010,40(增刊).
[13] Tong Y, Zhao L, Li L, et al. Stochastic Programming Model for Oversaturated Intersection Signal Timing[J]. Transportation Research Part C: Emerging Technologies, 2015, 58(SEP. PT. C):474-486.
[14] 凌墨,吴桢,郭建华.考虑交通流不确定性的单交叉口信号配时方法[J].南通大学学报(自然科学版),2020,019(001):33-41.
[15] 钱红波,李克平.绿灯间隔时间对交叉口交通安全的影响研究[J].中国安全科学学报,2008(06):166.
[16] 乔健,宣慧玉.一种基于通行需求度的单交叉口模糊控制算法[J].系统工程(10):59-64.

Simulation Analysis of Applicable Conditions of Two-Way Left-Turn Lane under the Condition of Multi Factor Combination

Junjie Cai   Binghong Pan   Zhenjiang Xie   Lin Zong

(School of Highway, Chang'an University)

Abstract At present, the research on Two-way left-turn lane in China is still in its infancy, and there is no targeted research on its applicable conditions. In order to study the appropriate traffic volume range of Two-way left-turn lane under different influence factors, this paper used VISSIM simulation software, and chose average delay, average queue length and conflict times as evaluation indexes to study the change law of each evaluation index of the three-lane road with Two-way left-turn lane, considering the influence of the main road hourly traffic volume, branch road traffic volume, the proportion of left turning vehicles on the main road and the distance between branches under different levels. Therefore, the applicable conditions of Two-way left-turn lane under the condition of multi factor combination were studied.

Keywords Traffic engineering   Two-way left-turn lane   Traffic simulation   Grey relational grade

0 Introduction

By the end of 2019, China's car ownership has reached 260 million, an increase of 21.22 million over that of 2018, an increase of 8.83%. National highway mileage was 5.0125 million kilometers, an increase of 166 thousand kilometers or 3.42 percent over the previous year. There are more and more contradictions between the slow increase of transportation supply and the rapid increase of transportation demand. Some cities have serious road congestion, heavy traffic pressure and frequent traffic accidents. However, due to the restrictions on land use and other conditions, the traffic pressure of some roads can not be alleviated by adding more lanes. Transforming the road into Two-way left-turn lane is an effective way to relieve traffic pressure and reduce traffic accidents.

Two-way left-turn lane(hereinafter referred to as "LTL") is a special kind of median, which is set in the middle of the road for vehicles to turn left or turn around, as shown in Fig. 1. It has the advantages of reducing conflict, improving driving safety and purifying traffic (Zhang, 2018). The results showed that TLT can significantly reduce the accident rate and has little impact on the delay(Knapp et al., 2001), and the driver's driving behavior has been improved after the TLT was set on the road(Garcia et al., 2019). In addition, the technology of transforming a four lane urban roads into a three lanes one with TLT("Four-to-three") is often used. Relevant studies have shown that "Four-to-three" can improve traffic safety due to the reduction of conflict points and the improvement of sight distance(Welch et al., 2000), and "Four-to-three" can basically meet the requirements of improving road safety on the basis of maintaining a certain level of road service(PENG et al., 2008).

Therefore, TLT has significant advantages. For urban roads with more branches on the roadside, TLT can reduce the accident rate without increasing traffic delay. It is also necessary to study TLT. However, the application conditions of TLT in foreign countries are based on the average daily traffic volume. The survey and research results of different states are very different, which can not be used as a unified standard directly. At present, there is no specific research on the applicable conditions of TLT in China, and there is no actual project case. Only a small number of literatures are still on the level of using foreign research results to popularize the concept. Moreover, there is no relevant technical specification to guide the setting of TLT, and the relevant designers can not find the design basis, and can not make clear under what traffic conditions TLT can be set. As a result, TLT has not been effectively promoted in China. Therefore, it is necessary to study the appropriate traffic volume range of TLT under the influence of multiple factors according to the actual situation in China.

The purpose of this paper is to study the applicable conditions of Two-way left-turn lane, the core of which is to find the traffic volume range suitable for urban road reconstruction from the aspects of traffic efficiency and driving safety. Therefore, we used VISSIM simulation software and selected the average delay, average queue length and conflict time as evaluation indexes to study the applicable conditions of TLT under the condition of a variety of influencing factors. Finally, the influence degree of each factor was analyzed through the grey correlation theory.

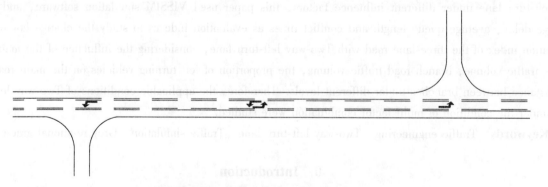

Fig. 1　Schematic Diagram of Two-Way Left-Turn Lane

1　VISSIM Simulation Experiment

There are many factors that affect the setting of TLT. The traffic volume of primary and secondary roads, the spacing between intersections of TLT, the density of access points, the proportion of left turn traffic, sight distance factors, the number of lanes, pedestrian crossing requirements, the form of branch access to the main road, road land conditions and future traffic volume are all factors affecting the setting of bidirectional TLT(YU, 2019). From the above factors, this paper selected the main road hourly traffic volume, branch hourly traffic volume, the proportion of left turning vehicles on the main road and the distance between branches to analyze.

VISSIM software was used to establish the two-way three-lane road model with TLT. The average delay, the average queue length and the number of conflicts were selected as the evaluation indexes(SHAO, 2019a,b), and change rules of each evaluation index of two-way three-lane road with TLT were studied under different influence factors. Therefore, the applicable conditions of TLT under the condition of multi factor combination were studied.

1.1 Calibration of Simulation Parameters and Division of Influencing Factors

The TLT simulation model was established in VISSIM. According to the research results(YU, 2019; HOU, 2008) of the values of road geometric parameters in the simulation model are shown in Tab. 1.

In order to study the influence of the main road of hourly traffic volume, branch hourly traffic volume, proportion of left turning vehicles on the main road and branch spacing on TLT Lane setting, different levels of influencing factors were selected.

The Value of Geometric Parameters of the Simulation Model   Tab. 1

Road Form	Design Speed (km/h)	Length of Main Road Section(m)	Length of Branch Road Section(m)	Branch Spacing (m)	Number of Lanes	Lane Width (m)
Main Road	50	600	100	100	2	3.5
Branch Road	30	600	100	100	2	3.5
LTL	/	600	100	100	1	4

(1) The main road hourly traffic volume calculation base of the simulation model was based on two-way four lanes. Representative traffic volume of 1700 veh/h was selected as the basic capacity of each lane on the main road, and different V/C levels were selected for simulation experiments.

(2) Three levels of 100, 200 and 300 veh/h were selected as the one-way hourly traffic volume of the branch road(HOU, 2008).

(3) The proportion of left turn traffic volume was taken as 10%, 20% and 30% based on the actual observation data. In order to reduce the impact of right turn traffic and simplify the experiment, the right turn traffic ratio was taken as 10%.

According to the above parameters, the simulation model was established in VISSIM. The road network was constructed by a three-way intersection without signal control, without considering the influence of non motor vehicles on both sides of the road, turning left and turning right twice. Four three way intersections were set up, as shown in Fig. 2. Through the experiment, it was found that when the V/C was more than 0.4, the simulation environment would be destroyed. This is because the two-way three-lane road bears the traffic pressure of the two-way four lane road. When the V/C exceeds 0.4, the traffic volume of the one-way through lane has reached 1360 veh/h, which is close to the basic capacity of 1700 veh/h of the lane. The left turning vehicles on the road can not find the inscrutable gap, and the queue length and delay increase sharply. Therefore, seven V/C levels of 0.1, 0.15, 0.2, 0.25, 0.3, 0.35 and 0.4 were selected for the study. Combined with the proportion of left turn traffic volume and branch traffic volume under different levels, a total of 63 traffic conditions were selected, as shown in Tab. 2.

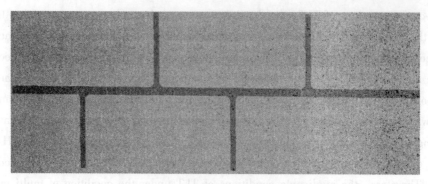

Fig. 2 TLT Model Simulation Diagram

Traffic Volume Composition under TLT model Tab. 2

V/C	One Way Total Traffic Volume (veh/h)	Left Turn Traffic Ratio	Left Turn Traffic Volume (veh/h)	Right Turn Traffic Volume (veh/h)	One Way Through Traffic Volume	Traffic Volume of Branch Road (veh/h)
0.1	340	0.1	34	34	272	100,200,300
		0.2	68	34	238	100,200,300
		0.3	102	34	204	100,200,300
0.15	510	0.1	51	51	408	100,200,300
		0.2	102	51	357	100,200,300
		0.3	153	51	306	100,200,300
0.2	680	0.1	68	68	544	100,200,300
		0.2	136	68	476	100,200,300
		0.3	204	68	408	100,200,300
0.25	850	0.1	85	85	680	100,200,300
		0.2	170	85	595	100,200,300
		0.3	255	85	510	100,200,300
0.3	1020	0.1	102	102	816	100,200,300
		0.2	204	102	714	100,200,300
		0.3	306	102	612	100,200,300
0.35	1190	0.1	119	119	952	100,200,300
		0.2	238	119	833	100,200,300
		0.3	357	119	714	100,200,300
0.4	1360	0.1	136	136	1088	100,200,300
		0.2	272	136	952	100,200,300
		0.3	408	136	816	100,200,300

1.2 Analysis on the Influence of Traffic Volume of the Branch Road and Left Turn Vehicle Proportion of Main Road

The simulation experiment was carried out in VISSIM, and each condition was simulated 10 times under the above traffic conditions (WANG, 2008). Finally, the average delay, average queue length and conflict time corresponding to the branch traffic volume and the proportion of left turning vehicles on the main road under different V/C were obtained, and the curve showed in Fig. 3 was drawn.

The average delay and average queue length reflect the traffic efficiency of the road model, and the number of conflicts reflects the traffic safety of the road model. Therefore, this paper analyzes the simulation data of two-way three-lane models from two aspects of traffic efficiency and driving safety.

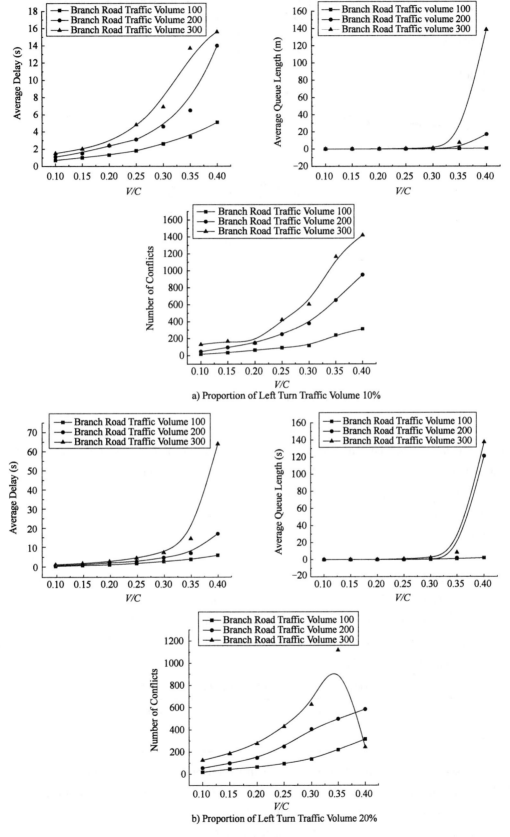

Fig. 3

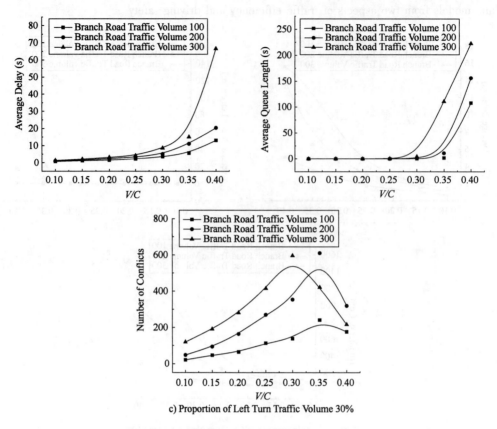

Fig. 3 Two-Way Three-Lane Model Simulation Data Diagram

(1) Traffic Efficiency Analysis of Three Lane Model

The average delay and queue length increase with the increase of V/C and the initial increase is slow. Under the same V/C condition, the average delay and the average queue length increase with the increase of the branch traffic volume when the proportion of left turn traffic volume is fixed.

The Los of unsignalized intersections is divided in HCM2010, as shown in Tab. 3. When the proportion of left turn traffic volume is 10%, the service level of three lane model can maintain A, B and C levels under different levels of branch traffic volume, and the road traffic efficiency is higher; When the proportion of left turn traffic volume is 20%, 30%, and the branch traffic level is 100, 200 veh/h, the service level of three lane model can be maintained at A, B, C level. However, when the V/C reaches 0.35, the average delay increases sharply and the service level changes from C to E or even F under the condition of 300 veh/h branch traffic volumes, resulting in serious vehicle congestion and worse traffic environment. The variation of average queue length is similar to that of average delay.

Service Levels Under Different Delays in HCM2010 Tab. 3

Delay(s)	≤5	5~10	10~20	20~30	30~45	≥45
Service Level	A	B	C	D	E	F

The analysis shows that the suitable V/C of the main road decreases with the increase of the ratio of branch traffic volume to left turn traffic volume. Moreover, suitable V/C of the main road is less affected by the left turn traffic volume and more affected by the branch traffic volume. Since the average delay and the average queue length are almost the same, the average delay which can reflect the service level is taken for analysis. The change rule is shown in Fig. 4.

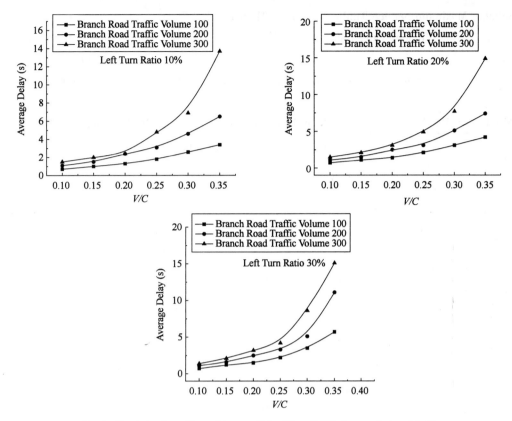

Fig. 4 Simulation Data Chart of Average Delay When V/C is between 0.1 and 0.35

Combined with the analysis in Fig. 3 and Fig. 4, the simulation section can maintain A-level service level as the standard, and the left turn traffic volume proportion is 10% as an example: When the traffic volume of the branch road is less than 100 veh/h, the V/C of the main road should not exceed 0.4; When the traffic volume of a branch road is between 100 ~ 200 veh/h, suitable V/C of main road should not exceed 0.35; When the traffic volume of the branch road is between 200 ~ 300 veh/h, the V/C of the main road should not exceed 0.25. When the proportion of left turn traffic is 20% or 30%, the law is similar. This is because when the traffic volume of the main road is too large, there are too many vehicles on the main road, so that the main road can not provide the insertable gap, so that there is enough space for left turn and branch road vehicles to turn. Therefore, the V/C of the main road should not be too large.

(2) Traffic Safety Analysis of Three Lane Model

By analyzing the conflict frequency curve in Fig. 2, it can be found that under the condition of specific left turn traffic volume ratio and branch traffic volume, the conflict frequency increases with the increase of V/C of the main road. However, when the proportion of left turn traffic is between 20% and 30%, when V/C exceeds 0.3, the number of conflicts in the section with branch traffic between 200 and 300 veh/h begins to show a downward trend. This is because the road congestion is serious, and the simulation environment is destroyed. Thus the road vehicles can not move, resulting in fewer conflicts.

Regardless of the destruction of the simulation environment, when the branch traffic volume is within 100veh/h, the number of conflicts increases with the increase of V/C. However, the growth is relatively flat, and the numerical difference is small. When the branch traffic volume is 200 ~ 300 veh/h, the number of conflicts increases sharply after V/C exceeds 0.3, and it is 2-3 times of that when the branch traffic volume is 100 veh/h. Therefore, from the perspective of traffic safety, when the traffic volume exceeds 200 veh/h, the V/C of the main road should not exceed 0.3.

(3) Suitable Maximum Service Traffic Volume of Main Road

Considering traffic efficiency and traffic safety, in order to maintain high service level and traffic safety of two-way three lane road, this paper summarizes the maximum service traffic volume of main road with appropriate proportion of traffic volume of different branch roads and left turning vehicles of main road, as shown in Tab. 4.

One Way Hourly Traffic Volume Applicable to the Main Road with Branch Road Spacing of 100 m　　Tab. 4

Left Turn Traffic Ratio	One way hourly traffic volume of Branch Road (veh/h)					
	100		200		300	
	V/C	Traffic (veh/h)	V/C	Traffic (veh/h)	V/C	Traffic (veh/h)
10%	0.4	1360	0.33	1122	0.25	850
20%	0.37	1258	0.3	1020	0.24	816
30%	0.35	1190	0.27	918	0.22	748

1.3 Influence Analysis of Branch Spacing

The above simulation model was established based on the relevant theoretical research under the condition of branch spacing of 100 m. In order to study the influence of branch road spacing on traffic efficiency and traffic safety, combined with the conclusions of the above study, a comparison model with branch road spacing of 50 m and 200 m was established by selecting the proportion of branch road traffic volume and left turning vehicles on the main road as 200 veh/h and 20%. The simulation experiment was carried out in the range of V/C 0.1-0.4, and the simulation data are obtained and plotted, as shown in Fig. 5.

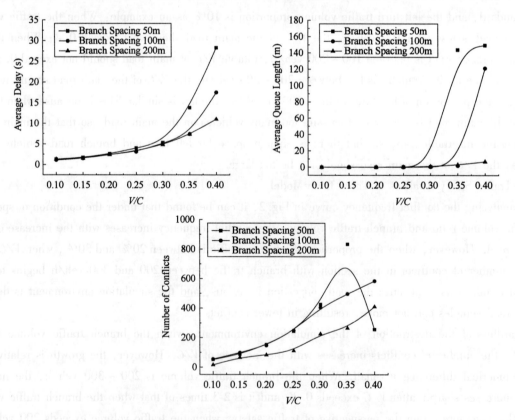

Fig. 5　Simulation Data Graph under Different Branch Spacing

(1) Traffic Efficiency Analysis of Three Lane Model

It can be found from the figure that the larger the average queue length is, the faster the average queue length increases. When V/C is greater than 0.3, the change trend is more obvious. Especially when V/C reaches 0.4, the simulation road model with 50 m branch spacing can not be input by vehicles, and the simulation environment is destroyed. However, the simulation road model vehicles with branch spacing of 100 and 200 m can still keep normal operation. This shows that the larger the distance between the branches, the more traffic the two-way three car road section can serve.

(2) Traffic Safety Analysis of Three Lane Model

When V/C is less than 0.3, the increasing trend in the number of conflicts between 50 m and 100 m is basically consistent. When V/C exceeds 0.3, the number of conflicts increases sharply at 50 m interval. When V/C reaches 0.35, the number of conflicts is two times of that at 100 m and four times of that at 200 m. When V/C reaches 0.4, the two-way three lane model with 50 m spacing has serious road congestion and the simulation environment is destroyed. The number of conflicts increases slowly with the increase of V/C at 200 m spacing, which is less than that at 50 m spacing and 100 m spacing.

(3) Suitable Maximum Service Traffic Volume of Main Road

Considering the traffic efficiency and traffic safety, under the condition that the ratio of branch road traffic volume to left turning vehicles on the main road is 200veh/h and 20%, the suitable maximum service traffic volume of the main road for two-way three lane road with different branch road spacing is shown in Tab. 5.

One Way Maximum Traffic Volume of Main Road Under Different Branch Spacing Tab. 5

Branch Spacing (m)	50		100		200	
	V/C	Traffic	V/C	Traffic	V/C	Traffic
Maximum one way traffic volume (veh/h)	0.3	1020	0.35	1190	0.4	1360

2 Analysis of Influence Degree of Various Factors Based on Grey Correlation Degree

In order to quantitatively study the influence of the main road hour traffic volume, branch road hour traffic volume, the proportion of left turn vehicles on the main road and the distance between intersections on the average delay, the average queue length and the number of conflicts, this paper used the grey correlation theory to study.

The basic idea of grey correlation analysis is to judge whether the sequence curves are closely related according to the similarity of their geometric shapes. The analysis step is to initialize the original data sequence. Then calculate the correlation coefficient to get the correlation matrix and the correlation degree. Finally, the sequence of related factors is sorted according to the value of the correlation degree.

2.1 Analysis Steps and Calculation Results

(1) Selecting dependent variable and independent variable. In this paper, the average delay, the average queue length and the number of conflicts were taken as dependent variables, and the main road hour traffic volume, branch traffic volume, the proportion of left turn traffic volume and branch distance were taken as independent variables.

(2) Establish the original data matrix $X_i = \{x_i(k), k=1,2,\cdots,n\}$, Where $i=1,2,3,4$. $x_i(k)$ denotes a certain level under the i-th influencing factor.

(3) Data normalization. In order to prevent the data from eating decimals in the process of operation, Eq. (1) was used to normalize the data.

$$x'_i(k) = \frac{x_i(k) - \min x_i(k)}{\max x_i(k) - \min x_i(k)} \quad (1)$$

where $x'_i(k)$ denotes normalized value. $x_i(k)$ denotes original value. $\min x_i(k)$ denotes the minimum value of the original value. $\max x_i(k)$ denotes the maximum value of the original value.

(4) Difference sequence. The expression is as follows:

$$\Delta_{0i}(k) = |x'_0(k) - x'_i(k)|, \Delta_{0i}(k) = \{\Delta_{0i}(1), \Delta_{0i}(2), \cdots, \Delta_{0i}(n)\}, i = 1,2,3,4 \quad (2)$$

(5) The maximum and minimum values in the difference sequence were recorded as M and N respectively.

$$M = \max_i \max_k \Delta_{0i}(k), \quad N = \min_i \min_k \Delta_{0i}(k) \quad (3)$$

(6) Find the correlation coefficient.

$$\gamma_{0i}(k) = \frac{N + \zeta M}{\Delta_{0i}(k) + \zeta M}, \zeta \in (0,1), k = 1,2,\cdots,n; i = 1,2,3,4 \quad (4)$$

where ζ denotes resolution coefficient, its function is to improve the significance of correlation coefficient. When $\zeta \leq 0.5463$, the resolution is the best, usually $\zeta = 0.5$ (LIU,2015).

(7) Calculation of correlation degree:

$$\gamma_{0i} = \frac{1}{n-1} \sum_{k=1}^{n} \gamma_{0i}(k) \quad (5)$$

Using Python Programming for auxiliary calculation, finally get the correlation degree of each factor in the average delay, average queue length and the number of conflicts, as shown in Tab. 6.

Correlation Degree of Various Factors under Different Indicators Tab. 6

Influence Factor	Hourly Traffic Volume of Main Road	Left Turn Traffic Ratio	Branch Road Traffic Volume	Branch Spacing
Average Delay Correlation	0.6406	0.6169	0.6389	0.6070
Average Queue Length Correlation Degree	0.6449	0.6117	0.6417	0.6065
Correlation Degree of Conflict Times	0.6704	0.6527	0.6584	0.5866

2.2 Conclusion Analysis

Generally, the closer the correlation value is to 1, the better the correlation between the factor and the main direction of system development, that is, the greater the impact on the evaluation index. If the correlation degree ⩾ 0.8, the correlation is the best. If the correlation degree is 0.6-0.8, the correlation is better. If the correlation degree is 0.5-0.6, the correlation is general. If the correlation degree is less than 0.5, there is almost no correlation. The correlation degree values obtained in the table are almost all above 0.6, indicating that the correlation of the four influencing factors is good. In the aspect of the influence degree, the influence of each influencing factor on the three evaluation indexes is similar. That is: hour traffic volume of main road > traffic volume of branch road > proportion of left turn traffic volume > distance of branch road.

Obviously, the increase in traffic volume on the main road is the root cause of queue congestion and conflict growth. And because the main road vehicles have the highest priority, the growth of its traffic volume also leads to the reduction of its insertable gap, which also has a great impact on the capacity of the branch road.

The influence degree of branch road traffic volume is second only to the hour traffic volume of main road. The reason may be that there are many branches and the length of the road section is short (relative to the main road). When the traffic volume of the branch road increases slightly, and the influence of the main road leading, the queue length will rise rapidly to fill the whole road section, and the phenomenon of vehicle queue jumping in the branch road at the intersection will also increase correspondingly, which will greatly affect the whole road network.

The influence of left turn traffic proportion is less than that of traffic volume of branch road. This is due to the separation of left turn traffic and through traffic on the main road after setting LTL, and the increase of left turn proportion has little impact on other vehicles on the main road. And when the left turn proportion is large and the LTL is full, the rear left turn vehicles can only turn left by way of far lead U-turn, which avoids the delay and conflict caused by the left turn lane occupying the through lane waiting to enter the LTL. To a certain extent, it also shows that after setting LTL, the adverse effect of left turn is reduced.

3 Conclusions

In this paper, VISSIM software was used to establish a two-way three lane simulation models, and the average delay, average queue length and conflict time were selected as evaluation indexes. Under the combination of different influencing factors, such as hour traffic volume of main road, left turn traffic volume proportion, branch traffic volume and branch distance, the gray correlation degree is used to analyze the influence degree of each factor on the evaluation indexes, and the two-way traffic flow model with TLT is proposed The three lane road can meet the requirements of traffic volume. However, the influence of non motor vehicles on both sides of the road is not considered in the simulation process, and its traffic characteristics are more complex, which needs further research.

References

[1] CJJ 37—2012, Code For Design of Urban Road Engineering[S]. Beijing: CC Press, 2012.
[2] Garcia R N, Valdes D, Figueroamedina A M, et al. Evaluation of the Effectiveness on the Implementation of a Two-Way Left-Turn Lane with Educational Material in Highway PR-107 using a Driving Simulator[J]. Transportation Research Record, 2019, 2673(9): 287-296.
[3] HOU Jia, ZHOU Guang, DU Xiao-chuan, et al. Simulation Study on Left-Turn Traffic Organization of Urban Arterial Road Entrances[C]//National Intelligent Transportation System Coordination Guidance Group, Ministry of Transportation Research Institute of Highway. 2008 Fourth China Proceedings of the Intelligent Transportation Annual Conference. Beijing: CC Press, 2008: 1-5.
[4] Knapp K K, Giese K. Guidelines for the Conversion of Urban Four-Lane Undivided Roadways to Three-Lane Two-Way Left-Turn Lane Facilities. Iowa: Center for Transportation Research and Education Iowa State University, 2001.
[5] LIU Xiangyun. Research on combination forecasting method of road traffic accidents based on grey correlation degree[J]. Beijing: Beijing Jiaotong University, 2015.
[6] PENG Yonghui, CHENG Jianchuan. A Study on the Transformation of Four Lanes into Three Lanes on Urban Roads[J]. Sino-Foreign Highway, 2008, 28(1): 190-193.
[7] SHAO, Yang, et al. (2019). Evaluating the sustainable traffic flow operational features of an exclusive spur dike U-turn lane design. PLoS one, 14.4: e0214759.
[8] SHAO Yang, et al. Evaluating Signalization and Channelization Selections at Intersections Based on an Entropy Method[J]. Entropy, 2019, 21(8):808.
[9] Welch T M. The Conversion of Four Lane Undivided Urban Roadways to Three Lane Facilities[J].

Transportation Research Circular,2000:28-30.
[10] WANG Ning. Simulation Research on reasonable distance between entrances and exits of urban trunk road[D]. Xi'an:Chang'an University,2008.
[11] YU Yingjie. Research on the Technical Indicators of Traffic Organization and Design for Two-Way Left-Turn Traffic on Urban Roads[D]. Xi'an:Chang'an University,2019.
[12] Zhang Xingjie. Study on geometric elements design of two-way left turn lane [J]. Fujian quality management,2018(22):275.

基于虚幻4引擎的道路交通场景逼真化建模

雷凯婷　杜志刚
(武汉理工大学)

摘　要　本文介绍了一种基于虚幻4引擎,结合3D stucto MAX(以下简称"3ds MAX")建模软件和TransModeler交通仿真软件的道路交通场景逼真化建模的方法。将3ds MAX建模软件搭建的模型导入虚幻4进行光照渲染增加场景的真实度,将TransModeler导出的行车轨迹数据与虚幻4蓝图功能结合,实现了第一、第三人称视角驾驶的动态模拟应用。以期达到丰富道路交通建模方法,提高情境模拟驾驶用户的视觉体验,进而提高道路交通安全的效果。

关键词　交通建模　逼真化建模　虚幻4引擎　道路交通场景　蓝图

0　引　言

随着我国社会快速发展,交通建设行业蒸蒸日上,提高道路交通安全一直是我国高度重视的问题,人与道路交通环境复杂多变的特点,决定了事故原因的多种多样,为了节约成本和确保安全性,研究复杂道路交通场景下驾驶人的驾驶决策和行为,多采用对驾驶视景仿真建模的方法。

通过对文献的梳理整合发现,目前道路交通场景仿真建模基本上是基于SUMO仿真平台和MultiGen Creator系列软件、OpenSceneGraph三维平台等,并用OpenGL作为辅助,建立不同环境下的道路或建筑模型。例如王贤隆[1]基于SUMO仿真平台和OpenSceneGraph三维平台引擎,提出了自动构建大规模三维城市交通场景的算法,研究不仅基于真实的道路数据自动构建出大规模的三维交通场景,还提供了三维交通仿真和几何场景交互的接口。夏萍[2]则运用了三维城市建模工具MultiGen Creator对城市道路交通环境进行仿真建模,再用OpenGVS对场景进行实时渲染和驱动;在文献[3]中,罗元则研究了虚拟现实三维建模方法,运用OpenGL实现了不同格式的三维模型的转换,建立了不同环境下的城市道路和建筑模型。总的来说,各个平台的难易程度、可实施性有所差异,但基本都存在着画面粗糙、视觉体验差、用户沉浸感不强的缺点。

虚幻4引擎(以下简称"UE4")是国内外公认的目前最先进、最强大的商业引擎,其强大的光影渲染、深度展现的材质和基于现实的刚体碰撞给用户带来强劲的视觉冲击,而且,其蓝图功能,只需用户将各种"节点"排列连接就能以可视化的形式创建复杂的互动性功能,为不会编程的人员提供方便。目前研究人员主要应用UE4进行一些自然场景[4]、建筑可视化设计[5-7]、校园漫游系统等[8]制作。本文将UE4引入交通工程领域,综合考虑行车特性和UE4灯光计算能力及蓝图功能,以期制作出复杂逼真的道路交通场景,提高模拟驾驶用户的视觉体验,令其有身临其境的感觉,具体建模逻辑图如图1所示。每年全球由于交通事故的损失高达数千亿元,利用UE4进行逼真化建模以提高道路交通安全无疑是一个零风险、低投入、高效率的解决办法。

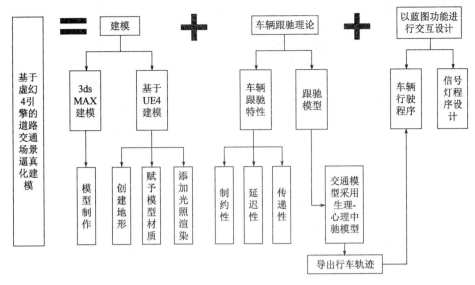

图 1　建模逻辑图

1　基于 UE4 的道路交通场景建模

1.1　创建地形

地形是场景的基础部分,其他模型都是在地形上创建的。地形的创建有两种方式:一种是设置参数直接创建(图2),然后运用引擎工具(例如雕刻、平滑、平整、斜坡……)修饰地形细节;第二种是通过一张高度贴图来导入地形。在本文中,为减小工作量,地形不设起伏,需要细致雕刻的工作量也较小,故选择第一种方法。

参数设置完毕后,赋予地形材质。创建项目时选择设置"具有初学者内容",文件夹下有材质球(图3)可供使用。这类材质球比自行设置的方法更简便,视觉效果也更逼真。材质赋予完毕后,直接点击创建即可在视图窗口里看到创建的地形。

图 2　设置地形参数

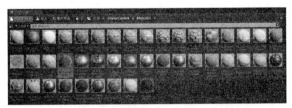

图 3　"具有初学者内容"下的材质球文件

1.2　基于 3ds MAX 的模型制作过程

建筑、植被、车辆、红绿灯等模型的制作大部分都是应用 3ds MAX 建模软件制作,本文采用多边形建模的方法完成模型的搭建,各类模型制作完毕后,导入 UE4 并赋予材质。然后将模型摆放至地形上,调整各模型位置,搭建出合理的道路交通场景。

1.3　调节光照渲染

基本道路交通场景搭建完毕后,利用灯光渲染使模型效果逼真。UE4 具有强大的图形灯光计算功能,在此基础上,对模型进行细致的渲染,不仅可以表现出模型在各类灯光下的真实效果,也能将想象的虚拟场景真实的表达。本文模型的光效采用动态光,添加天光、光照、雾效、后处理等效果,使得区域内的光照可以二次反射,极大提高了场景的真实度和逼真效果。添加光照渲染前后对比如图4所示。

a)添加光照渲染前

b)添加光照渲染后

图4 光照渲染前后对比

2 车辆跟驰理论及交通模型仿真模拟

2.1 车辆跟驰理论

车辆跟驰理论是运用动力学方法研究在限制超车的单车道上,行驶车队中前车速度的变化引起的后车反应。在道路上行驶的车队通常分为自由行驶状态下的车队和非自由行驶状态下的车队,跟驰理论只研究非自由行驶状态下车队的特性。非自由行驶状态下的车队有3个特性:制约性、延迟性、传递性。

2.2 交通模型仿真模拟

基于UE4的初始车辆模型的运动是匀速的、无意识的机械运动,为了准确地把握和模拟道路上的交通流,本文对车辆模型的运动添加跟驰行驶进行了研究。交通模型采用生理—心理跟驰模型和基于规则的换道模型、间距接受模型,本文利用交通模型导出车辆行驶轨迹,根据轨迹模拟车辆的运动。

得到车辆行驶轨迹(图5)难度较小,但导入UE4里却涉及坐标变换。交通模型输出的行车轨迹由经纬度来表示,UE4里却是空间直角坐标系,且为左手坐标系统,x轴向后,y轴向右,z轴向上。由于前期创建地形没有设计地形的起伏,故设置z轴坐标为0,只转换成x、y轴坐标即可。本文实验中使用商业软件ArcMap中的投影定义工具,设定投影参数,使用兰伯特投影(等角投影),车辆运动方向不因投影转换而发生偏移误差。转换完成后的结果示例如表1所示。

ID	Class	Time	Segment	Dir	Lane	Offset	Distance	Speed	Acceleration	Mileage	Heading	Longitude	Latitude
1232	SU Truck	28800.5	2061	0	1	0	224.50665	25	0	0.001389	101	114261186	30567441
10162	Car Mid MPR	28800.5	1042	0	1	0	33	25	0	0.001028	101	114261488	30569172
9700	SU Truck	28800.5	2329	0	1	0	33.320908	25	0	0.002778	85	114260120	30571668
10009	Car Mid MPR	28800.5	984	0	2	0	234.08991	30	0	0.003333	60	114260272	30577768
1751	Pickup/SUV	28800.5	2083	0	1	0	635.36395	30	0	0.000833	110	114258809	30581802
1527	Motorcycle	28800.5	2117	0	2	2.717065	626.27576	30	0	0.001667	68	114258839	30581831
1655	Car Mid MPR	28800.5	2117	0	2	0	627.74243	25	0	0.001389	68	114258817	30581867
684	Car Mid MPR	28800.5	2122	0	2	0	99.991905	24.75	-3.666667	0.001385	161	114260685	30583262
238	Car Mid MPR	28800.5	2122	0	2	0	102.9069	30	0	0.000833	161	114260718	30583279
4287	Car Mid MPR	28800.5	2181	0	1	0	813.24738	25	0	0.003472	316	114279018	30565777
3374	Car High MPR	28800.5	964	0	1	0	513.27264	25	0	0.000694	75	114278316	30574275
6384	Trailer Truck	28800.5	1059	0	3	0	201.72534	35	0	0.001944	118	114276978	30589776
4620	SU Truck	28800.5	1030	0	1	0	48.400002	30	-0.002665	27	114290621	30580172
9091	Car Mid MPR	28800.5	1469	0	1	0	322.55377	25	0	0.001389	127	114290738	30578783
3853	Motorcycle	28800.5	145	0	2	0	676.27374	25	0	0.003472	143	114285353	30589973
11622	Car Mid MPR	28800.5	835	0	4	0	325.57474	25	0	0.001389	128	114281674	30593394
3899	Car Mid MPR	28800.5	365	0	1	0	141.97969	37.51336	0	0.001042	173	114285316	30599001
11075	Pickup/SUV	28800.5	1188	0	1	0	97.92621	25	-3.666667	0.000694	141	114286291	30599393
7577	Pickup/SUV	28800.5	654	0	3	0	2914.676	30	0	0.004167	307	114317950	30606530

图5 行车轨迹数据示例

坐标转换结果示例　　　　　　　　　表1

序号	ID	Class	时间(s)	x	y
1	1232	SU Truck	28800.5	884120.0775	3822455.897
2	10162	Car Mid MPR	28800.5	884126.261	3822649.377
3	9700	SU Truck	28800.5	883963.8158	3822908.065
4	10009	Car Mid MPR	28800.5	883898.9346	3823579.598
5	1751	Pickup/SUV	28800.5	883707.4893	3824006.091
6	1527	Motorcycle	28800.5	883709.9623	3824009.613
7	1655	Car Mid MPR	28800.5	883707.4042	3824013.319
8	684	Car Mid MPR	28800.5	883866.7283	3824187.509

3　模型交互设计

3.1　行车轨迹数据在UE4蓝图中的使用

本文实验全部用UE4的蓝图功能实现,行车轨迹数据文件利用结构体导入,设置变量类型,导入即可。

导入的数据存放到Game Mode中,然后通过Game Mode来获取(图6)。由此,当要获得行车轨迹时,只需要设置每隔一定的时间重新读取数据,获得车辆的坐标,更新车辆位置,再配合使用车辆行驶程序,车辆在UE4里就可以实现符合车辆行为模型的行驶。

图6　Game Mode

3.2　车辆行驶程序

车辆行驶程序制作包括了第一、第三人称视角。为了实现不同视角的切换,采用玩家生成不同的默认角色,虽使用同一城市街景地图,但每种模式地图唯一,游戏模式是每个地图的运行模式。

在第三人称视角中,使用Construction Script节点,车辆蓝图的模型即随机产生,定义模型对象的生成点(SpawnVehicle)、继续点(Continue)、移除点(RemoveVehicle)、目标点(NextNode),并定义各自显示颜色样式等属性。当生成点与行车起始点坐标对应,使用AI Move To节点(图7)使其移动到下一点的位置,到达目标点后获取下一目标点,如此循环。

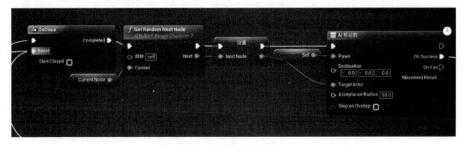

图7　AI Move To节点

第一人称驾驶视角(图8)使用的车辆模型具有车辆内部细节设计的,然后把UE4的摄像机放到车内部朝前,使之呈现道路场景。

使用Open Level函数实现用键盘按钮tab切换两个视角,便于观察。

图8 第一人称驾驶视角

3.3 信号灯程序设计

信号灯程序的设定不仅仅是简单的灯色改变,还要区分交叉口不同方向的信号灯以及明确信号灯与过交叉口的车辆间的联系。

如表2所示使用变量Off set来区分南北/东西信号灯,当变量值为0时是南北信号灯,变量值为1时是东西信号灯。使用变量Lights Num区分当前是红灯还是绿灯。当变量值为0时是红灯,变量值为1时是绿灯。通过更换信号灯材质球变换红/绿灯,通过时间Delay控制红灯绿灯的切换。

表2 区分交叉口信号灯

变量	变量值	
	0	1
变量Offset	南北信号灯	东西信号灯
变量Lights Num	红灯	绿灯

使用布尔型变量Tick建立信号灯程序与车辆行驶程序之间的联系。布尔变量Tick为真时,检测到信号灯的LightsNum值为1即为绿灯,把值传给车辆行驶程序,车辆继续移动并将布尔变量Tick置为假,关闭信号灯程序的Tick事件;布尔变量Tick置为假时,检测到信号灯的LightsNum值为0即为红灯,把该值传给车辆行驶程序,停车线前车辆停止移动并将布尔变量Tick置为真,开启信号灯程序的Tick事件。

4 结 语

本文利用UE4尝试了一种逼真化的道路交通场景建模方法,实现了模拟驾驶第一、第三人称视角的仿真。依托UE4的光影渲染能力和蓝图功能,达到道路交通场景的逼真效果,为后续VR智能技术提供了准备,也为情境模拟驾驶提供新的方法。但仍存在着一些不足:①实验过程运用到UE4蓝图、3Ds MAX、TransModeler、ArcMap软件,对计算机硬件配置有较高要求;②实验中未设置地形起伏,复杂地形及道路线形的场景建模未来还有待研究;③TransModeler和UE4中路网不对应,导致行车轨迹数据不能一一对应,增加了工作量。随着虚拟现实技术的日益成熟与完善,解决以上不足,在不影响场景的逼真效果下尽可能简化步骤,并通过驾驶人实际体验验证建模逼真效果,是未来的努力方向。

参考文献

[1] 王贤隆.交通场景的自动三维建模技术研究[D].西安:长安大学,2017.
[2] 夏萍.基于虚拟现实技术的复杂城市道路交通仿真平台研究[D].武汉:湖北工业大学,2011.
[3] 罗元.城市道路交通流智能化模拟虚拟现实系统研究[D].北京:清华大学,2012.

[4] 符清芳,张茹.基于虚幻4的自然场景制作[J].电脑知识与技术,2016,12(31):188-189.
[5] 姜寿晖.基于交互式三维动态视景的虚拟现实模型技术[J].电子技术与软件工程,2018(02):72.
[6] 张俊,李骁,方强,等.利用HTC VIVE制作城市规划浸入式虚拟现实展示平台[J].城市勘测,2018(04):8-12.
[7] 陈骅.三维古建筑场景仿真研究[D].西安:西安科技大学,2017.
[8] 屈宇轩,王俊洁.基于虚幻引擎的3D虚拟校园漫游系统建设[J].电子技术与软件工程,2018(12):142-143.
[9] 王殿海.交通系统分析[M].北京:人民交通出版社,2007:85-86.
[10] Andrew S. An introduction to unreal engine 4[M]. London: Taylor and Francis,2016.

快速路高峰期激励诱导出行——以苏州为例

赵 坡[1] 施庆华[2] 王 翔[3] 吴 戈[1]

(1.苏州大学轨道交通学院;2.苏州市城市道路交通委员会办公室知行项目组;
3.苏州大学轨道交通学院知行项目组)

摘 要 为了改善苏州市快速路高峰时段交通状态,本文提出了快速路高峰期激励诱导出行方案,在缓解高峰拥堵的同时缩短出行者行程时间。首先,基于高德路况数据识别拥堵路段与拥堵发生源路段,并计算高峰期需诱导交通量,以及各时段可接受诱导交通量;其次,利用快速路卡口过车数据分析高峰期出行者的出行强度与出发时刻离散度,运用K-means++算法识别高峰期快速路重点诱导对象;最后,根据出行特征形成个性化错峰、绕行出行方案,并通过积分奖励来提高用户参与度。通过单个出行者的案例分析,错峰出行后行程时间减少27%,论文所提出的方案能够有效减少高峰期行程时间。

关键词 交通网络管理与控制 诱导出行方案 聚类分析 出行者 快速路

0 引 言

交通需求在时空维度上的不均衡分布,是导致快速路高峰时段交通拥堵的主要原因之一。缓解快速路高峰时段拥堵状态,不仅能够缩短出行者行程时间,同时还能有效节约能耗、减少排放污染。交通需求管理(Travel Demand Management)是缓解拥堵的有效手段之一,并已有大量研究。然而,有学者指出单纯依靠设置拥堵收费区、车辆限行等"惩罚式"交通管理政策存在一定弊端。交通拥堵治理并不仅采用"惩罚"的方法,基于"激励"的策略也越来越受到人们的重视,如Li Ruimin等人提出的拼车出行方案,Xie Yifei等人建立诱导系统激励出行者选择更可持续的出行方式等。Kacperski, Celina和Kutzner, Florian发现在象征激励和经济激励条件下,超过20%的参与者选择了绿色路线。

结合已有研究,本研究提出面向城市快速路高峰激励诱导出行方案制订方法,诱导车辆错峰出行和绕行地面道路,来分散原本时空高度集聚的交通需求。

1 数据说明及质量控制

1.1 卡口过车数据

卡口过车数据用于分析车辆出行特征,记录的信息包括车辆的车牌号与经过时刻等。本文研究范围包括苏州内环快速路及其延伸线,里程共计205km(双向),共有快速路卡口133个,地面道路卡口约6100个。

基金项目:国家自然科学基金项目(52002262)。

分析时段为 2020 年 3 月 15 日至 2020 年 4 月 14 日,每日数据量约为 5000 万条。数据存在的问题包括字段缺失、车牌长度和车牌前两位信息有误、数据重复等。经数据质量控制后,有效数据占比 80%。

1.2 高德路况数据

高德路况数据用于分析路段时变拥堵情况,识别拥堵源路段。数据包含快速路各路段的时变平均速度,时间粒度是 4min,快速路每日数据量约为 27 万条。个别路段在某些时段的数据有缺失,处理办法是将其前一时段的数据作为当前时段的数据,缺失比例为 0.7%。

2 激励诱导分流方案设计要素

2.1 确定拟诱导分流路段与需求交通量

基于高德历史路况数据计算快速路各路段的时变车速。定义车速低于 40km/h 时为拥堵状态,各类型快速路早晚高峰小时平均车速见表 1。

表 1 快速路路段类型统计结果

类 型	路段数(个)	早高峰小时平均车速(km/h)	晚高峰小时平均车速(km/h)
1	122	62	63
2	27	52	31
3	37	28	53
4	30	30	31
合计	216	50	53

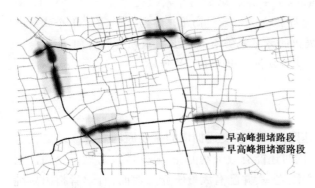

图 1 快速路早高峰拥堵路段与拥堵源路段分布

在识别出拥堵路段(早高峰为类型 3 与 4,晚高峰为类型 2 与 4)的基础上,识别拥堵源路段。拥堵源路段的显著特点是,同一时刻拥堵源路段速度小,下游路段速度较大。基于上述特点,利用高德路况数据识别出拥堵路段与拥堵源路段,如图 1 所示。

在识别出重点诱导分流路段后,需根据路段时变交通状态确定需要诱导分流的交通量。采用 Greenshields 模型拟合路段交通流特征。路段诱导分流需求量的计算如下:

$$Q_{\text{need}} = (K_{\text{peak}} - K_{v=40}) \times 40 \tag{1}$$

式中:Q_{need}——诱导需求量;

K_{peak}——高峰时段密度;

$K_{v=40}$——路段车速为 40km/h 对应的密度(K_{peak} 与 $K_{v=40}$ 通过标定后的 Greenshields 模型计算得到);

V_{peak}——高峰期路段平均车速。

2.2 确定可诱导分流交通量

可诱导分流交通量包括快速路错时可诱导交通量和地面道路绕行可诱导交通量。给定早高峰最早诱导出发时刻(6:00),计算 6:00 到拥堵时段开始时刻间的冗余通行能力,即为快速路错时可诱导交通量。

最终诱导交通量为需要诱导分流交通量与可诱导分流交通量中的较小值。

2.3 确定拟诱导对象车辆

利用历史卡口过车数据分析车辆出行特征,包括出行强度和出行时刻离散度。

出行强度,指车辆在分析时段内使用快速路的天数。通过快速路卡口过车数据进行统计。出行离散度,指车辆各天经过快速路时刻的标准差。若同一天的早高峰经过快速路多个卡口,则以第一次的经过时刻为准。将卡口记录的时间按 10min 划分时间单元,然后计算检测时间单元的标准差。

根据上述指标,利用 K-means++ 算法对快速路车辆出行特征分类,结果见表2。

早高峰快速路使用车辆各类出行特征　　表2

类　型	车　辆　数	出行强度	出行离散度
1	644370(60%)	1	0.09
2	174528(16%)	5	1.99
3	129609(12)	5	4.35
4	122575(11%)	17	1.79
合计	1071082(100%)	4	1.11

早高峰期间,类型1车辆数多,但使用强度低,诱导收益低;类型2车辆数较少,出发时刻弹性小;类型3出发时刻弹性大,易被诱导错峰出行;类型4车辆数少,但出行次数占比高,主要为通勤出行,诱导收益大。因此,优先考虑类型4和类型3,然后考虑类型2,预算充足的话考虑类型1。

2.4 确定差异化诱导分流方案

根据出行者预约信息中的起讫点与出发时刻,利用百度 API 实现不同出发时段的行程时间估计,并生成快速路错时诱导、地面道路绕行诱导方案。若出行者的出发时刻离散度较大(如类型3出行者),且在计划出发时段内存在错时可诱导交通量,则推荐错时方案。若出行者的出发强度高(如类型4出行者),且地面道路绕行路径的行程时间在可接受范围内,则推荐绕行方案,具体绕行路径和行程时间根据百度 API 获得。

2.5 确定诱导方案奖励值与发放条件

错时方案奖励根据不同出发时段的冗余通行能力,并考虑用户出发时刻的改变程度来确定错时方案奖励值。冗余通行能力越大、改变程度越高,则奖励值越高。绕行方案奖励采取单次奖励方式,每次奖励值相同。

用户需要在出发前与到达目的地后分别进行一次打卡,同时获取两次打卡的位置与时间。若用户选择错时出行方案,则根据快速路卡口是否在打卡时间区间有该辆车的数据记录来判断用户是否遵循诱导方案。若用户选择绕行方案,则通过判断地面卡口是否在打卡时间区间有该辆车的数据记录来判断遵循诱导方案。

3 激励诱导分流实施案例分析

3.1 案制订范围

以西环快速路南向北的早高峰拥堵主线路段为例,包含5段早高峰拥堵路段,位置如图2a)所示。早高峰时变流量与速度情况如图2b)所示。可以发现,早高峰期间的交通量大,但车速低,高峰期之前(6:00-7:00)交通状态较好,能够承受一定的车流量。

3.2 确定诱导需求与供给量

根据诱导需求量的确定方法,计算得到各拥堵路段的诱导需求量,结果见表3。

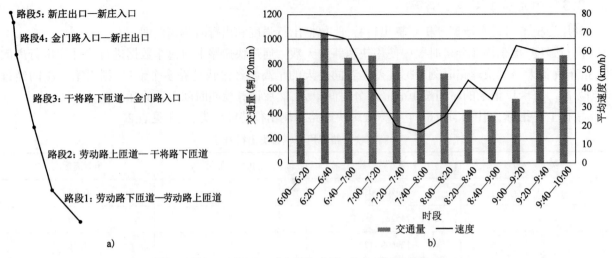

图 2　西环快速路南向北早高峰拥堵路段分布和时变交通量与速度

各拥堵路段的拥堵时段与诱导需求量　　　　　　　　　　　　　　　　　　　　　　　　表 3

路段	拥堵时段	诱导需求量
1	7:48—10:12	440
2	6:44—10:12	2602
3	6:56—9:24	2761
4	7:04—9:02	1404
5	7:08—8:58	1805

计算非拥堵状态下各时段冗余通行能力作为错时供给量。错峰时段及错时供给量分配见表4。

错峰时段的交通量与错时诱导供给量　　　　　　　　　　　　　　　　　　　　　　　　表 4

路段	错峰时段	错时供给量	错时供给量分配
1	6:40—7:40	659	248(6:40—7:00),142(7:00—7:20),269(7:20—7:40)
2	6:00—6:40	754	390(6:00—6:20),364(6:20—6:40)
3	6:00—6:40	936	472(6:00—6:20),464(6:20—6:40)
4	6:00—7:00	1305	463(6:00—6:20),450(6:20—6:40),393(6:40—7:00)
5	6:00—7:00	1319	461(6:00—6:20),445(6:20—6:40),412(6:40—7:00)

3.3　实际使用效果

假定某位用户(属于类型3)参与预约,输入的起讫点为友新新村—苏州市新庄小学,出发时间为7:00,在快速路上行程时间为15min,如图3所示,可绕行方案如图4所示。

后端自动识别此次出行将要经过快速路拥堵路段的高峰时段(6:44—10:12),同时判断目前参与激励诱导出行人数是否达到诱导需求上限。若已达到上限人数,则不需要诱导。当尚未达到诱导需求上限时,后端查询是否存在错时供给量(表4)。

根据后端处理结果,前端返回信息包括错时与绕行的诱导方案、各方案下的行程时间、剩余可预约人数和奖励积分。后端查询到该用户属于类型3(出发时刻离散度高),同时绕行出行的行程时间(百度API预估20min)多于快速路的行程时间,因此将与早高峰开始时刻间隔时间最短的方案(6:20—6:40出行)作为推荐方案返回到前端。用户根据自身情况选择其中一种推荐方案,用户完成预约后,系统后端自动更新诱导需求量与诱导供给量。

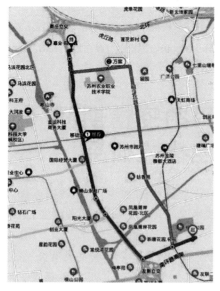
图3　出行起讫点及快速路路线

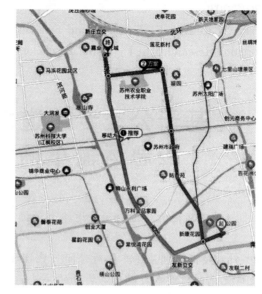
图4　绕行方案路线

假定用户选择出发时间在6:20—6:40的错时方案。用户在出发与到达时需打卡,以便于后端验证用户是否按照选择方案出行。后端结合预约出发时段与打卡时间来判断用户是否按照所选方案出行。若满足奖励方法条件,小程序中返回此次诱导出行行为有效,同时后端的个人积分数据库中加上这次出行的奖励积分。

4　结　语

本研究以苏州快速路为分析对象,提出了高峰期激励诱导分流方案,在缓解路段拥堵的同时减少出行者的行程时间。论文所提出的方案已部署在"苏周到"App中,目前已上线运行。最后通过案例分析,错峰出行行程时间减少4min(27%)。由此可见,诱导出行能够有效缓解快速路高峰期的拥堵状况。

该诱导方案还存在不足,主要问题在于部分快速路卡口覆盖率较低,导致对车辆行为的监测不全面,对诱导出行行为判断有负面影响。后期会逐步完善卡口设施建设,同时考虑在出行诱导方案中增加公共交通出行方式。

5　致　谢

研究用到的部分样本数据来自苏州市交通大数据研究的知行项目团队,在此表示感谢。

参考文献

[1] 陈艾卉. 秦皇岛市智慧交通发展研究[D]. 天津:天津工业大学, 2015.
[2] 姜桂艳,郑祖舵,白竹,等. 拥挤条件下可变信息板交通诱导信息对驾驶行为的影响[J]. 吉林大学学报(工学版), 2006, 36(2):183-187.
[3] Wang X, Qiu T Z, Niu L, et al. A Micro-simulation Study on Proactive Coordinated Ramp Metering for Relieving Freeway Congestion[J]. Canadian Journal of Civil Engineering, 2016, 43(7):599-608.
[4] 戴晶辰,李瑞敏. 基于微观仿真的北京市拥堵收费研究[J]. 系统仿真学报, 2019, 31(11):2458-2470.
[5] 刘水林. 车辆限行规制的法经济学分析[J]. 学术月刊, 2016, 48(6):76-84.
[6] Li R, Liu Z, Zhang R. Studying the Benefits of Carpooling in An Urban Area Using Automatic Vehicle Identification Data[J]. Transportation Research Part C:Emerging Technologies, 2018, 93:367-380.
[7] Xie Y, Danaf M, Lima Azevedo C, et al. Behavioral Modeling of On-demand Mobility Services:General Framework and Application to Sustainable Travel Incentives[J]. Transportation(Dordrecht), 2019, 46

(6): 2017-2039.
[8] Kacperski C, Kutzner F. Financial and Symbolic Incentives Promote 'Green' Charging Choices[J]. Transportation Research Part F: Traffic Psychology and Behaviour, 2020, 69: 151-158.

基于公交专用道复用的疫情期间应急运输车辆管控模式研究

蒋瑶 赵智 李泓辰 王江锋

(北京交通大学综合交通运输大数据应用技术交通运输行业重点实验室)

摘要 针对疫情期间应急车辆对时间可靠性要求较高的特点，让其对城市现有公交专用道进行复用，通过交叉口优先控制策略实现应急物资的快速运输。建立公交专用道复用效益模型，分别针对应急车辆到达交叉口时间区间，应用绿灯延时、红灯早断和速度调节三种信号优先控制策略，实现其不停车通行。基于所设计的优先控制策略，将应急车辆到达信息融入交叉口配时中，代替传统Dijkstra算法中的无延误节点，提出一种考虑交叉口动态配时信息的负责路网中路径选择的算法。本文以武汉市路网为例，对所提出的算法模型进行实证分析。分析结果显示，对公交专用道进行复用可有效提高应急运输车辆的运行效率。所提出的路径选择算法可实现与交叉口优先控制策略的协同，应急运输车辆复用效益最高可提升17.7%。本文所研究的基于公交专用道复用的疫情期间应急运输车辆管控模式，可为类似场景的应急车辆的物资运输提供路径选择参考。

关键词 道路交通 交通工程 路网信号动态调控 Dijkstra 标签法 公交优先 车路协同

0 引言

医疗物资是保证患者康复，以及进一步阻止疫情扩散的关键。在突发公共卫生事件情况下，如何将稀缺的应急物资尽快运输到最需要的地方尤为重要[1]。应急运输车辆在城市内部的优先通行权总是碍于各种各样的交通问题不能完全得到保障[2]。

公交专用道存在时段性的闲置现象，造成道路资源浪费[3]。因此，本文提出一种让疫情期间的应急运输车辆对现有城市公交专用道进行复用的策略，可使应急运输车辆享受与公交车等同或者更高的路口优先通行权。

关于公交优先理论的基础研究在很多场景下得到了应用，但都基于微观层面，没有一种在宏观路网层面控制路网所有交叉口动态配时的解决方案。针对本问题，应使应急运输车辆从城市路网中的某点到另一点，尽可能无延误地通过路网中的交叉口，同时兼顾其经过的每一个交叉口其他车辆的实际流量，充分保障其时效性和安全性。本文在交叉口效益指标评价的基本框架下，研究出在车路协同场景下基于感应的特殊车辆信号优先控制策略，将其应用于应急运输车辆，评价方案带来的影响和效益。

1 公交专用道复用效益模型

本研究以效益评价指标PI来决定信号的调整策略[4,5]。信号优先权的交付需要一个控制判断标准，用于判断是否给予应急运输车辆优先通行权，在普遍的公交优先问题中，PI是交叉口所有乘客的延误总和，单位为秒(s)。

基金项目：国家重点研发计划项目(2018YFB1600703)；国家自然科学基金项目(61973028)；"车联网"教育部-中国移动联合实验室开放基金项目(ICV-KF2019-01)。

用 ΔPI 表征执行优先前和执行优先后的交叉口效益变化值,它实际上代表的是交叉口的所有乘客等待时间之和的变化量。当 $\Delta PI < 0$ 时,信号调节后交叉口整体效益提高;当 $\Delta PI > 0$ 时,信号调节后交叉口整体效益降低。本文以 $\Delta PI = 0$ 为界限划分是否执行信号调节。

如果执行优先给交叉口带来了整体效率的下降,则不应该调节原有的信号[6]。因此,对于绿灯延时和红灯早断,其存在调节时间的最大值。这两者的最大值均可通过 $\Delta PI = 0$ 计算出来。绿灯延时和红灯早断的区间限值如图1所示。

红灯区间可以按到达点不同分为3种:绿灯延时区间、红灯早断区间和速度调节区间,如图2所示。

图1 绿灯延时区间和红灯早断的区间限值　　图2 红灯区间按到达点不同分类

由图2可知,绿灯延时区间和红灯早断区间均由满足 $\Delta PI = 0$ 的临界 ΔT 给出,而剩余的红灯区间则为速度调节区间。当到达时间点在绿灯延时区间时,执行绿灯延时;当到达时间点在红灯早断区间时,执行红灯早断;当到达时间点既不在绿灯延时区间又不在红灯早断区间时,执行速度调节[7,8]。

2 基于复用效益的路径选择算法

2.1 基本思路

本文在 Dijkstra 算法[9]的框架上,提出一种基于复用效益的路径选择算法[10]:采取标签剪枝[11]的办法来确定路网中每个点的标签,以标签比较的方法来确定每一步生成的路径[12]。具体过程为:以起始点为中心向外层层扩展,每扩展到一个点都生成一个新的标签,每个标签都代表了一条从起始点开始到当前节点结束的局部路径。标签的构成见表1。

标签构成　　　　　　　　　　　　　　　　　　　　　　　　表1

last_last_node	前溯点的前溯点	now_node	当前节点
last_node	前溯点	t	总时间

2.2 算法伪代码

本文给出的算法伪代码见表2。

算法伪代码　　　　　　　　　　　　　　　　　　　　　　　　表2

标签法
1:输入路网图 $G(V,A)$
2:在起始点生成初始标签
3:将初始标签放入标签库 U 中
4:$k = 1$ % 当前标签位置
5:$count = 1$ % 记录标签总数
6:if i 点为设置了公交专用道的路口
7:　　$delay_i = 0$
8:else
9:　　根据路口的相位情况和应急运输车辆的方向确定 $delay_i$

标签法
10：end
11：while $k \leq count$
12：　for each $(i,j) \in A$ %i 为当前节点
13：　　if 存在可行路径
14：　　　生成新标签
15：　　　if 标签未被支配
16：　　　　将该标签加入标签库 U 中
17：　　　　$count = count + 1$
18：　　　end
19：　　end
20：　end
21：　$k = k + 1$ %转到下一标签
22：end

2.3 标签的生成

当路径从当前节点 i 拓展到下一节点 j 时进行路径可行性判断，如果路径可行，则按如下规则生成一个新标签：

(1) $last\_last\_node_l = last\_node_k$

(2) $last\_node_l = now\_node_k = i$

(3) $now\_node_l = j$

(4) $t_l = t_k + delay_i + t_{ij}$

其中，当前节点是 i，当前标签是 k，即将扩展到的节点是 j，新生成的标签是 l。

2.4 标签剪枝规则

在决定标签是否扩展时，需要检查它是否被同一节点上的现有标签所支配。这种情况在设置了公交专用道和未设置公交专用道的路口时是不同的。本文也针对这两种不同的情况提出了相应的标签剪枝规则。

i 点为设置了公交专用道的路口 $now\_node_k = now\_node_l$
$t_k < t_l$
$label_l$ 被 $label_k$ 支配，剪去 $label_l$，保留 $label_k$
i 点为未设置公交专用道的路口 $now\_node_k = now\_node_l$ $last\_node_k = last\_node_l$
$t_k < t_l$
$label_l$ 被 $label_k$ 支配，剪去 $label_l$，保留 $label_k$

3 案例分析

考虑如下场景：从武汉市内的金银潭医院运送一批应急物资到武汉市内的火神山医院，如图3所示。

在如图4所示的路网中，有①~⑭交叉路口，其中③、⑦、⑩、⑪和⑬为设置了公交专用道的路口，可以通过对其信号调节来实现优先。

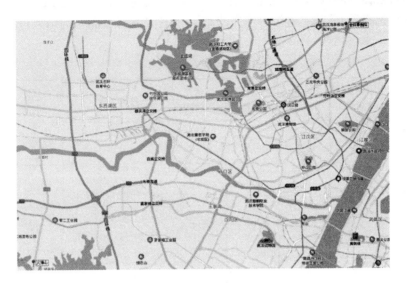

图 3　金银潭医院与火神山医院位置

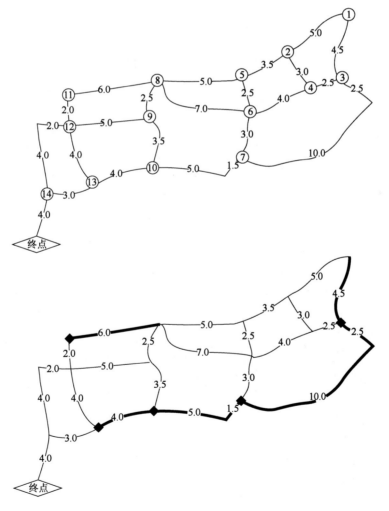

图 4　编号和标记后的路网

利用实际网络对所设计的算法进行验证,分别改变信号周期、相位分布和信号初始时间。基于所提出的控制策略和路径选择算法,将实施信号优先的结果和不实施信号优先的结果进行对比,实验结果见表3。

实 验 结 果(单位:s)   表3

实验编号	南北直行结束时间	南北左转结束时间	东西直行结束时间	信号周期	初始时间是否相同	无优先总时间	路 线	有优先总时间	路 线
1	20	30	50	60	否	334	1→3→7→10→13→14	275	1→3→4→6→7→10→13→14
2	20	30	50	60	否	305	1→3→4→6→7→10→13→14	265	1→3→4→6→7→10→13→14
3	20	30	50	60	否	305	1→3→7→10→13→14	275	1→3→4→6→7→10→13→14
4	30	40	50	60	否	329	1→2→5→6→3→7→10→13→14	279	1→3→4→6→7→10→13→14
5	30	40	50	60	否	319	1→2→5→6→7→10→13→14	304	1→2→5→8→9→10→13→14
6	10	20	50	60	否	324	1→3→7→10→13→14	324	1→3→7→10→13→14
7	10	20	50	60	否	305	1→2→5→8→11→12→14	295	1→2→5→8→9→10→13→14
8	30	60	90	120	是	364	1→3→4→6→7→10→13→14	354	1→2→9→8→10→13→14
9	40	60	100	120	是	349	1→3→4→6→7→10→13→14	319	1→3→4→6→7→10→13→14
10	40	80	100	120	是	325	1→3→7→10→13→14	275	1→3→4→6→7→10→13→14

在实验1、2、3中,保持信号周期、各信号相位时长不变,仅改变信号初始时间即应急运输车辆进入路网的时间。比较3组实验结果可知:实验1提升了17.7%的时间效益,实验2提升了13.1%的时间效益,实验3提升了9.8%的时间效益。在实验4、5中,信号周期不变,变更信号相位时长,2组实验为信号初始时间不同的对比实验。比较2组实验结果可知:实验4提升了15.2%的时间效益,实验5提升了4.7%的时间效益。在实验6、7中,信号周期不变,再一次变更信号相位时长,两组实验也为信号初始时间不同的对比实验。比较2组实验结果可知:实验6为特殊情况,没有带来时间效益的增长,实验7提升了3.3%的时间效益。在实验8、9、10中,将信号周期为60s更改120s,仅改变各信号相位时长,让应急运输车辆在路网信号启动后的相同时间进入路网。比较3组实验结果可知:实验8提升了2.7%的时间效益,实验9提升了8.6%的时间效益,实验10提升了15.4%的时间效益。

经过科学分析,可得出如下结论:

(1)让应急运输车辆利用路网中设置了公交专用道的路口必然会带来运输过程中时间效益的增长,而这个增长值是动态的,取决于车辆在信号运转的哪一个时间点进入路网。

(2)周期越长,信号优先带来的效果越明显。

(3)有公交专用道路口的分布会影响车辆的路径。在路径选择上,如果走远路经过有公交专用道的路口所花费的时间比走近路但需在无公交专用道的路口等待所花费的时间要短,则车辆会做出选择前者的决策。

4 结 语

本文在道路资源未充分利用的情况下,提出了一种创新的道路使用方法:疫情期间让应急运输车辆使用城市中现有的公交专用道,同时使其经过的交叉口对其实行信号优先。在重大突发公共卫生事件下从整体到局部研究如何对公交专用道复用从而提升应急运输车辆的时效性和安全性。如果城内对应急车辆采取一直放行的措施,会带来诸多交通安全问题和交通效率问题,本文从交叉口信号调节以及道路资源复用的现实角度来解决特殊车辆延误问题。

同时,本文提供的是一种有现实意义的交通管控措施——在动态信号配时的框架中,智能、高效地解决问题,这不论在理论设计层面还是实验验证层面均取得了较好的效果。

参考文献

[1] 胡晓伟,宋浪,杨滨毓,等.重大突发公共卫生事件下城市应急医疗物资优化调度研究[J/OL].中国公路学报:1-11[2020-10-29].

[2] 朱晔.突发公共卫生事件下应急物资运输保障对策[J].城市交通,2020,18(05):102-109.

[3] 宋娟,杨兴宇,崔梓钰,等.基于车路协同和车车通信的公交专用道时分复用体系研究[J].信息记录材料,2019,20(07):195-198.

[5] Li Zhou, Yizhe Wang, Yangdong Liu. Active signal priority control method for bus rapid transit based on Vehicle Infrastructure Integration. 2017, 6(2):99-109.

[6] Peter G. Furth, Theo H. J. Muller. Conditional Bus Priority at Signalized Intersections: Better Service with Less Traffic Disruption. 2000, 1731(1):23-30.

[7] 张宇.基于延误的单个交叉口公交优先信号控制方法研究[D].长春:吉林大学,2008.

[8] 李鹏凯,杨晓光,吴伟,等.车路协同环境下信号交叉口车速引导建模与仿真[J].交通信息与安全,2012,30(03):136-140,156.

[9] 马万经,吴明敏,韩宝新,等.考虑可变速度调节的单点交叉口公交信号优先控制方法[J].中国公路学报,2013,26(02):127-133.

[10] 包渊秋,严凌.面向交通规划的交叉口延误函数的研究和应用[J].上海理工大学学报,2005(03):253-258.

[11] 王琪.车路协同环境下基于公交优先的交叉口配时优化[D].重庆:重庆交通大学,2019.

[12] 盛新,陈沛帅.最短路算法(dijkstra算法)的研究[J].科技信息,2008(26):82-84,44.

疫情持续期间城市公共交通的设施改善及运营优化研究

张焕炯

(浙江交通科学研究院)

摘 要 城市公共交通抗疫是整个抗疫的重要组成部分。在抗疫和复工复产的特殊时期,确保城市公共交通抗疫效果的同时,较好地展现城市的活力,促进经济和社会的发展,是需要重点解决的难题。本文通过对病毒传播机理的分析,归纳了病毒和疾病传播的具体影响因素,在此基础上,针对性地提出了城市公共交通的运营优化和交通工具的设施改善相关建议,它们能阻断病毒的传播链,可有效提高城市公共交通抗疫效果。

关键词 疫情 城市公共交通 设施改善 运营优化

0 引言

COVID-19病毒所致的新冠肺炎具有较强的传染性,由此所引起的重大公共卫生事件,对城市公交的运行带来极大的挑战。一方面,城市公交是维护城市活力的重要保障,是城市居民出行的一种重要选择,它承担着城市中大量人员的日常流动。但无论是公交汽车,还是地铁和轻轨,它们都具有空间相对封闭和狭小等共同的特点,尤其在公共交通运营的高峰期,车厢内人员的拥挤程度,甚至可用"摩肩接踵"来形容。但另一方面为了有效抗疫,要避免人员互相之间的密集接触,以防止病毒的传染,从而阻断疾病的传播、遏制疫情的扩散。2020年初疫情暴发之际,为有效切断COVID-19病毒的传播链,武汉采用了"封城"的方式,其他城市则采用停止运营公共交通等举措,这种"一刀切"的方法,虽在有效阻断病毒传染方面,能起到切实的效果,但它以牺牲城市的活力为前提,只能算作是一种危难时期的极端手段,不能作为常态化的处理手段进行长时间和高频度的使用。所以,在疫情持续期间,需要有既能实现有效抗疫的目标,又能保持较高的城市交通分担率的公共交通运营的新方案来代替这种极端化的处理方法。尤其在疫情与复工复产并存的特殊时期,对城市公共交通进行必要的优化,使之既满足于维护城市的常态和活力,展现城市应该有的"烟火气",又能有效抗疫,确保疫情不扩散、不蔓延、不暴发,成了一个需要深入研究的重要课题。

迄今,针对疫情持续时期的城市公共交通抗疫的文献相对较少,文献[1]以疫情暴发期的厦门市公交为例进行了分析,文献[2]分析了疫情暴发期间的交通应急,但它更多地以供应疫区的物资应急和人员求援为重点加以分析的。而在疫情虽已得到有效控制,但尚未完全消失,以输入性病例为主的较长时间内,城市在一定程度上已经实现了较好的复工复产,城市公共交通就为市民上下班等的交通出行,提供了重要支撑的同时,更因它具有公共性的特点,客源相对复杂及交通工具重复使用频度高等原因,易于病毒和疾病的传播,尤其在外有输入性病例的前提下,一旦输入性病源在公共交通中扩散,那后果就严重到不堪设想的地步,且随着2020年秋冬季的来临,疫情进入了反弹和反复的特殊时期,注重城市公共交通的抗疫,通过对公共交通的设施改善和运营优化,避免病源通过公共交通的途径传染,它更是一个十分重要而亟待解决的课题,但针对这个领域,尚未出现有关针对性的文献。因此,非常有必要对它进行深入的研究。

本文就在疫情控制相对平稳,城市具有良好的复工复产状况,但外有输入病例风险的条件下的城市公共交通的设施改善和运营策略优化展开研究。首先,根据传染病学的相关理论,分析在相对狭小的封闭空间中的病毒传播机理,由此得到影响疾病传播的影响因素。在此基础上,结合城市公共交通设施及具体运营的特点,针对性地提出了具体建议,希望这些建议能用到实际之中,在城市公共交通抗疫的过程中发挥积极的作用。

1 病毒传播机理分析

医学研究业已表明,COVID-19病毒具有较强的传染性,且具有人传人的特点。有文献(3-5)指出,$5\mu m$以下的飞沫核在空气中的沉降速度大约为0.15mm/s,如一旦病毒携带者呼出含有病毒的飞沫核,它将长时间地漂浮(或悬浮)在空气中,并随着气流的流动而散布,它们一旦被健康人吸入体内,就有可能由此滋生(复制)大量病毒,进而感染健康人而产生新的病例。除此外,活性的病毒黏附在诸如包装盒、电梯按钮等物品上,人一旦接触,就有可能感染病毒,可能产生新的病例。所以,空气、相关接触物等都是病毒传染的媒介物。

在传染病学中,感染率是定量反映人们被感染病毒后最终致病的可能性的一个变量,它具体受病原体(病毒)的毒性、数量、传播途径以及宿主(被感染者)的易感程度等多个客观条件的综合影响。在这些具体条件中,病毒的数量显得尤其重要,通常用quanta来表示,它被定义为使得一个人致病时,所需要的最少的病原体数目,由于被感染而致病的人所承受最低的病原体的数目因人而异,所以quanta是一个统计意义上的概念,致使一个人生病的概率为$P = 1 - e^{-1} \approx 0.632$。进一步,随着传染病学研究的不断深入[6],已出现了相关的针对空气传播疾病的感染概率的具体模型,比较重要的有 MA(mass action)模型和 Wells-Riley 模型等。

对于公共交通的车厢(公交车和地铁车厢等)来说,虽然空间相对封闭和狭小,但可以辅助通风设备,实现不间断换气。由此,对 Wells-Riley 模型[7-8]进行必要的修正,得到车厢内病毒的传播模型:

$$P = \frac{C}{S} = 1 - \exp\left(-\frac{Iqpt/V}{Vn_v + n_f + n_d}\right) \tag{1}$$

$$C = rIS \tag{2}$$

$$r = \frac{qpt}{Q} \tag{3}$$

式中:C——一次爆发中心所产生的被感染的人数;

S——总的易感人数;

I——感染人数;

r——有效接触率;

q——感染者的 quanta 产生率;

p——呼吸通风量;

t——暴露的时间,也就是在车厢内共处,有可能接触和被感染病毒的时间,可理解为乘车时间;

V——城市公共交通的车厢箱体的体积;

n_v——换气次数,$n_v = \frac{Q}{V}$;

n_f——回风量和过滤器过滤效率的乘积;

n_d——飞沫核沉降在车厢内设施表面上的数量;

Q——车厢的通风量。

由式(1)不难看出,公共交通的车厢内病毒传播致病的可能性,也就是传染概率受到了车厢内的感染人数(变量 I)、quanta 量(变量 q)、通风量(变量 p)、时间(变量 t)、换气次数(变量 n_v)、车厢空间(变量 V)、过滤器(变量 n_f)及带病毒的飞沫沉降在车厢内设施表面上的数量(变量 n_d)等的影响,它们成为传染率具体的影响因素(factors)。

进一步分析这些影响病毒传播的因素,其中感染人数,quanta 量等来自病毒本身,当 quanta 值相当大时,就易产生超级传播者(Super-spreader);而通风量、换气次数和过滤器等可以通过在车厢中的空调和换气设备等的使用来实现,时间也是影响病毒传播的一个重要因素,与传染概率成正相关的关系。实际上,所谓的隔离,本质上就是在时空维度上的分开,在空间上表现为距离远,在时间上则表现为共处的时间为零;而车厢的空间体积在一般情况下是固定的,但也可通过对车体内的设施的处理等方式来改变空间的大小,带病毒的飞沫数量,既与病毒数量有关,也与病毒的接触性传播有关,这可用对车厢内的设施进行严格的消毒、乘客通过不直接接触车厢内的设施等方式来消除影响。

3 城市公共交通的设施改善及运营优化

在抗疫和城市复工复产并重的特殊时期,城市公共交通的抗疫不仅是整个抗疫战役中不可或缺的组成部分,更是城市恢复活力和"烟火气"的重要保障,它是一个多种因素互相关联的综合性的系统工程,需要多方面的协调配合。它更需要依据传染病学的基本原理,梳理影响病毒传播的具体要素,通过对这些要素的相关处理,以达到切断病毒传播链的目的,进而实现有效的防疫和抗疫。

城市公共交通系统的正常运行需要 3 个基本要素的共同支撑,一是驾驶员和乘客组成的驾乘人员,二是交通工具,三是公共交通运行公司的线路规划和班次的调度。由此,针对性的抗疫措施也需从这 3 个方面加以具体考虑:对司乘人员来说,需加强自身的安全防护,具体如佩戴口罩等进行必要的防备;而对交通工具及交通班次的运行调度等来说,它相应的优化举措应该有:

（1）对乘客采用准入制度，通过一定的条件设置，杜绝病毒携带者、病人以及与确诊病人的密集接触者（包括疑似病人等）乘坐公共交通。这方面需要有具体而又切实可行的举措来实施，如出示相关证明健康的证件等方式不失为一种简单可行的方法，但相关证件必须以严谨的医学科学为基础，需要具有高度的科学性、权威性等特性，能真实地反映持有者的健康状况。而对于地铁，则建议在地铁站的每一个入口处，增加测温设备等，以便更好地落实相应的准入制度。

（2）在相对狭小的车厢内，除了对具体设施进行消毒外，还需对车厢内的乘客数进行必要的控制，以确保乘客之间有较大的距离间隔，避免密切接触等情况的发生。此外，因一般的交通工具装备了空调和换气设备，因此，增加通风量和换气次数也是一个易于实施的举措，通过对车厢内外空气的流通和交换，有效降低病毒的感染概率。

（3）针对公共交通班次的调度等，不是简单地减少运营班次甚至是停止运营，这些举措在某些时间点上能发挥积极作用，但仅是一种极端情况下的非常之举，在疫情和复工复产并存期间，它是不适用的。在此期间，较好的调度方案就是尽可能缩短公共交通班次之间的间隔时间，增加公共交通工具的数量，这可在两个方面有效影响病毒的传染概率，一是缩短时间间隔，从而减小了时间变量值，二是增加了交通工具，就增加了车辆空间变量 V，从而由式（1）得到，它们就能有效较低病毒的传染概率。

公共交通的班次调度，实际上是一种在给定多种条件下的具体算法的设计，一种针对性的算法实现的基本原理可描述为，在确定的公交线路上，假定在某一个时刻发出一个班次，则通过对它的行程、具体时间及车厢内的乘客数的多少来判断下一个班次的发车时刻，当车厢内的乘客数接近额定数的规定值时，或时间间隔达到预定值时就发出下一个班次。这种动态式的班次调度，就能较好地达到降低病毒传染概率的目的。而且这样的调度方式，不仅适合于一般的公交，也适合于地铁班次等的调度。

（4）地面上的城市道路的好坏也直接影响到公共交通行驶的时间，尤其那些施工路段，成为道路拥堵点，它们直接影响到公交车线路的行驶时间，进而也影响到病毒的传染概率。因此，在疫情期间，消除道路上的拥堵点，借助城市管理平台，在同一时段，对城市区域内的车辆总数进行一定的限制，更采用错峰出行等手段，保持道路的通畅，适度提高公交车的行驶速度，这些也是公共交通班次调度的一种重要的辅助手段。

4 结　语

必须指出，在疫情面前，有效抗疫是一盘棋式的具有高度整体性的一件事情，它的任何一个环节或部分出现纰漏，则可能是全盘皆输。城市公共交通作为城市交通的重要分担者，是展现城市活力、体现城市"烟火气"的重要保障。城市公共交通因客源广杂，涉及面多，中间环节和过程复杂等因素，更在抗疫和复工复产的双重要求下，它的抗疫难度则更大。借助病毒传播机理的分析，针对城市公共交通的设施及运营条件和策略的改善和优化进行研究，并根据实际情况，为城市公共交通的运营及应急管理的相关举措提供科学依据，进而提出能有效促进运营优化等的具体建议，对提高城市公共交通抗疫效果有直接的促进作用。

包括公共交通工具在内的交通场景是病毒传播的一种重要途径，面向交通的流行病学将成为一个交叉性的学术分支，传染病学的相关理论与包括城市公共交通在内的交通理论和技术进行深度融合，将成为研究的热点。

参考文献

[1] 李健,陈田,张懿木.面向传染病疫情防控的公共交通运行管理决策支持研究[J].中国公路学报, 2020(7).

[2] 张改平,李红昌,萧赓,等.新冠肺炎疫情下对我国应急交通运输体系的思考和建议[J].交通运输研究(抗疫专刊),2020,6(1):81-88.

[3] 钱华,郑晓红,张学军.呼吸道传染病空气传播的感染概率的预测模型[J].东南大学学报,2012,3(42):468-472.

[4] 舒瞳. 气流组织对空气中病毒传播的影响评估[J]. 铁道勘测与设计,2018(1):99-102.
[5] J K Gupta, C-H Lin, Q Chen. Risk Assessment of Airborne Infectious Disease in Aircraft Cabins[J]. Indoor Air,2012.
[6] Dong Yunchun. Study on Ventilation Efficiency and Infection Risk of Negative Pressure Differential Isolation Rooms[D]. 中国台北:台北科技大学,2008.
[7] G N Sze To, C Y H Chao. Review and Comparison Between the Wells-Riley and Dose Response Approaches to Risk Assessment of Infectious Respiratory Diseases[J]. Indoor Air,2010(1):2-16.
[8] Bradley G Wagner, Brian J Coburn Sally Blower. Calculating the Potential for Within-flight Transmission of Influenza A(H1N1)[J]. BMC Medicine,2009(7).

中小城市公交优先发展策略研究
——以浙江省天台县为例

陈坤杰 杜璇 朱雨晴 朱力颖 刘歆余
(浙江数智交院科技股份有限公司)

摘 要 中小城市经济社会的快速发展对公共交通提出了更高的要求。本文结合浙江省天台县实际,分析天台县公交发展中存在的主要问题,包括场站用地缺口较大、运力配置不足、公交线网覆盖不足、公交对青壮年群体吸引力不足等,从推动场站综合开发、厘清线网层次、完善票价体系、建立补贴考核机制等方面提出公交优先发展策略。

关键词 交通工程 公共交通 数据分析 中小城市 线网优化 场站规划

0 引 言

随着城乡一体化进程的加快和经济社会的进一步发展,城市与乡村之间的联系日益密切,统筹城乡公交发展是打破城乡二元结构、实现公共服务均等化的必然要求。另外,中小城市的高速铁路车站建设、新城区以及商业中心的快速推进都扩大了公共交通的需求。但是,目前大多数中小城市公交基础设施并不完善、服务水平低下、运行环境较差,公交总体发展比较落后,导致了中小城市的公交发展现状不能满足居民公交出行的需求。本文结合浙江省天台县公交规划实践,从场站用地、线网布局等角度探讨中小城市城乡公交一体化的发展策略。

1 天台县城市和公交发展概况

天台县位于浙江省东中部,以境内天台山得名,东连宁海、三门,西接天台,南邻仙居、临海,北接新昌,天台以佛宗道源、山水神秀著称,是佛教天台宗发祥地、道教南宗创立地,是国家AAAAA级旅游景区、国家级生态县、国家生态旅游区。截至2019年底,全县常住人口约40.6万人,城镇化率58.6%。

2019年1月,天台县完成了城乡公交一体化改造,县域内实现了从挂靠式经营到公车公营的转变。现状天台县共有公交车辆211辆(折合196标台),其中城区公交82辆(84标台),城乡公交129辆(112标台);实际运营公交线路65条,其中城区公交线路11条,城乡公交线路54条。

2 天台县公交发展主要问题

2.1 用地保障不足,公交场站缺口较大

天台县在大型居民小区、商业区、工业园区规划建设时,并未预留公交场站及配套设施,公交基础设

施建设的重要性并未得到充分认识。现状中心城区仅有 5 处永久公交场站,其中仅客运中心和客运北站为永久用地,城乡仅有白鹤镇、平桥镇 2 处公交场站。县域公交场站总面积约 1.9 万 m^2,车均场站面积 99m^2/标台,相比浙江省平均值 123m^2/标台有一定差距。

受土地资源制约,天台县公交无法形成科学合理的枢纽站、首末站体系,降低了线网运行效率,造成了线路绕行多、车辆空驶率高、新线路难以开辟等问题。场站面积严重不足也导致了车辆进场率低,公交车不得不在马路上"安家落户"。充电桩更无立足之地,无法保证新能源车的正常运行。

2.2 运力配置不足,发班频率无法保证

如图 1 所示,天台县公交车辆数量在浙江省处中下游位置。

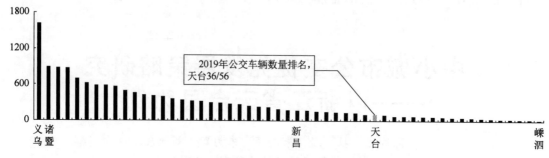

图 1 浙江省各区县公交车辆数量排名

车辆配置不足导致发车间隔较大。城区公交仅 6 条线路发车间隔在 15min 以内,其余线路都在 18~30min 不等;城乡公交除天街线、平桥线、天洪线以及泳溪线 4 条城乡主干线外,其余线路发车间隔都超过 1h。对比邻近的新昌县,城区公交线路发车间隔都在 10~20min,城乡公交均在 1h 内。发车间隔过大,导致乘客候车时间过长,公交乘车体验较差。

2.3 线网覆盖不足,整体可达性不高

由于公交出行需求总量相对较小,加之空间结构简单、走廊相对集中,线路大多汇集在主要客流走廊上,城区公交线路重复率较高,其中经过赤城路的重复线路达到了 9 条,线路重复情况如图 2 所示。而在其他区域,为保证线路运营效益,客流集聚程度有限,城区公交站点 300m 覆盖率仅为 42%,500m 覆盖率仅为 75%,覆盖情况如图 3 所示。

图 2 城区公交线路重复情况示意图

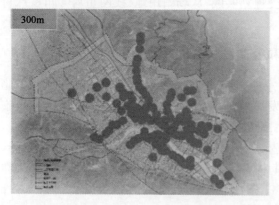 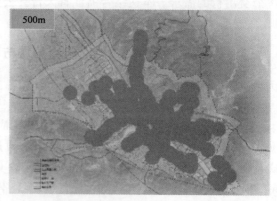

图 3 城区公交站点 300m 和 500m 覆盖情况示意图

在城乡公交方面,由于缺乏系统规划,行业管理部门为满足个别区域诉求,盲目追求行政村"直达城区",导致线网层次不清、线路功能模糊。以发往坦头镇、泳溪乡方向的线路为例,开设的所有 14 条城乡公交线路均经过坦头镇,其中有 8 条线路从中心城区直达行政村(表 1)。城乡公交线路数量虽多,但大

多重复运营,"换乘"概念缺失,导致"只有首末站,没有换乘站",运输组织效率低下。

坦头镇、泳溪乡方向城乡公交线路一览表　　　　　　　　　　　　　　　　　　表1

公交线路	途经站点				
线路1	客运中心	客运北站	坦头	洋头	洪畴
线路2		客运北站	坦头		
线路3		客运北站	坦头	洋头	洪畴
线路4		客运北站	坦头	泳溪	
线路5		客运北站	坦头	泳溪	岩下蒋
线路6			坦头	欢西	欢山
线路7			坦头		欢东
线路8			坦头		大山
线路9			坦头	泳溪	横山
线路10			坦头	泳溪	苍华
线路11			坦头	泳溪	山里周
线路12			坦头	泳溪	紫云山
线路13			坦头		外溪
线路14			坦头	尖山	苍华

2.4　乘客以老年人为主,对青壮年群体缺乏吸引力

中小城市空间尺度小,布局紧凑,居民出行距离短,特别是城区内部,出行一般不会超过10km。在这样的空间尺度下,电动车、自行车等灵活性较好的点对点出行方式优势明显。而天台县公交线网布局不合理、运力配置不足等问题引发的候车时间过长、绕行耗时过长,进一步降低了公交吸引力,尤其是对出行时间更加敏感的青壮年群体不愿意乘坐公交。分析天台县公交刷卡数据,老年群体(60周岁以上)虽然乘坐公交的人数不多,约占30%,但乘车频率更高,多为每月乘车16次以上的忠实乘客,所占公交客流比例超过88%,如图4所示。

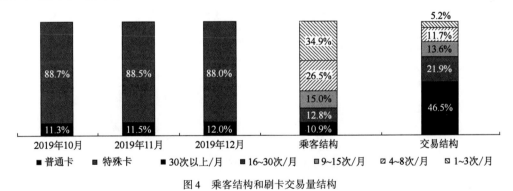

图4　乘客结构和刷卡交易量结构

3　天台县公交优先发展的策略

3.1　保障公交设施用地,探索场站综合开发新模式

针对新建产业集聚区、开发区等加强公交设施用地的规划、审批及监管力度。在设施规划层面应具有足够的前瞻性,确保合理公交设施用地面积,合理划分区域内公交设施用地区位。

位于城市核心区域的公交用地,其区位条件较好,途经线路数较多,场站规模需求也较大,因此此类

公交用地的公益性成本最高,土地的市场利益与公益性的矛盾最大。针对此类用地,要在满足交通功能的基础上,积极推动公交系统与商业、居住、便民服务等业态有机融合,从平面式独立建设的"城市用地上的公交场站"向立体式综合开发的"城市建筑里的公交场站"转变,化解土地的市场利益与公益性的矛盾。公交场站的综合开发也有利于引导公交出行、改善地区的交通条件、美化城镇形象、提升土地价值、拉动地区经济。

3.2 "功能分级,服务分区",提高线网运行效率

"功能分级"指根据公交线路的走向、沿途客流、服务区域等特点,明确线路的功能等级,构建层级清晰的"三级"网络布局模式。

一级线网为中心城区的城市公交网络,包括快线、干线和支线三类。快线是一级线网的主骨架,沿主要客流走廊布设,提供快速、大容量的公交服务。干线在一级线网中处于基础地位,旨在提高公交的覆盖深度和广度。支线主要满足微观层面短途公交出行,主要服务乘客出行"开始一公里"和"最后一公里",补充一级线网服务空白区。

二级线网为中心城区到各乡镇的城乡干线,以城区与重点乡镇,以及重点乡镇之间的公交联系为主,依托县域主要交通走廊,承担中长距离的城乡居民出行服务。二级线网以城市公交枢纽、重要乡镇换乘站为依托,发挥衔接城区、城乡公交网络的重要作用。

三级线网为各重点乡镇至各行政村的城乡公交支线网络,以乡镇换乘枢纽为起点,保证线网纵深。三级网络是实现"村村通公交"基石,对于填补县域公交空白,提高城乡公交吸引力有重要作用。由于公交支线运行的道路等级较低,客流较少,应灵活选择车型。

"服务分区"指依据不同区域居民公交出行需求特征的差异,将县域分为若干个服务区,以便针对不同区域提供适宜的公交服务,集约利用运输资源,提高网络整体效率。结合天台县特点,划分6个城乡公交服务片区,并设置相应城乡公交枢纽,用以锚固城乡支线毛细网络,服务区域公交出行。

天台县公交网络服务分区示意图如图5所示。

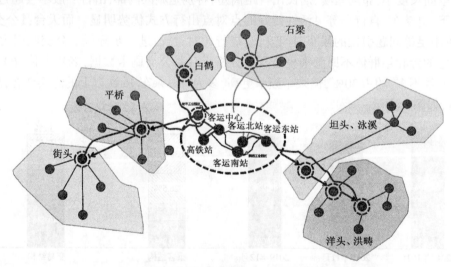

图5 天台县公交网络服务分区示意图

3.3 建立动态调价机制,完善票价优惠政策

综合考虑各种车型、运输成本、供求关系、道路运输行业平均利润率、社会承受能力等因素,平衡好公共交通与私人交通工具的比价关系,遵循政府、企业和乘客合理分担原则、运价调整与经济发展水平基本一致的原则,测算能够反映公共交通运营成本变化的合理调价幅度,制定科学的票价调整办法,形成动态的票价调节机制,充分体现市场经济规则,并兼顾城市公共交通企业的发展与公众的承受力,更好地发挥价格的导向和杠杆作用,积极引导公众采取公交出行。

打破城区、城乡二元分割局面,积极推行城乡公交票制票价一体化,扩大票价优惠政策惠及范围至全

县域,确保县域基本公共服务均等化。尽快研究出台换乘优惠政策,引导居民采用公共交通换乘形式出行,改变居民普遍存在的无论出行距离长短均要求直达出行的习惯。合理分配公共交通资源,研究实行错峰差异票价政策,在工作早晚高峰将公交资源向青壮年群体倾斜,引导老年人群体错峰出行。

3.4 加强财政资源要素保障,突出制度体系建设

国内中小城市普遍没有形成制度化、系统化的公交运营补贴保障机制,由于缺乏有效的资金保障,公交企业难以推进长期性、连续性的发展战略,影响企业的可持续发展。以天台县为例,在电动自行车、私家车等其他方式竞争的情况下,公交客运量提升难度较大,企业运营压力较大,运营亏损逐年上升。为了保证公交线路运营效益,往往采取线路大量绕行以尽可能增加客流,同时减少配车并增大发车间隔以减少运营成本,这些手段无异于饮鸩止渴,使得公交竞争劣势更加明显。如果解决不好公交财政补贴到位率问题,公交就不能恰当发挥其公共职能。

加强公交财政要素资源保障应当突出强化机制建设。建立科学的补贴核算方法及考核指标体系,实现对公交企业服务质量的监督和财政补贴资金使用效率的考核有据可依,保证公交补贴资金提供的科学性和使用的有效性,强化政府管理抓手。同时,积极拓宽公交补贴资金来源,采取征收中心城区停车费、拥堵费等方式适度提高私家车使用成本补贴于公交。

4 结 语

公共交通在中小城市城镇化、现代化进程中发挥着不可替代的作用,是实现经济社会可持续发展你的必然要求。相比大城市为解决交通拥堵问题"被动式"提倡公交优先发展,中小城市应提前谋划,"引导式"发展公共交通,积极探索契合自身特征的公交发展模式。本文以浙江省天台县为例分析中小城市公交发展存在的主要问题,并提出公交优先发展的策略,即应当加强公交用地保障,推动场站综合开发,厘清线网层次,打造三级线网结构,建立动态调价机制,完善票价优惠政策,强化财政资源倾斜,突出补贴考核机制建设。

参考文献

[1] 陈程,俞一杰. 城市公交场站综合开发模式研究[A]. 中国城市规划学会、贵阳市人民政府. 新常态:传承与变革——2015 中国城市规划年会论文集(05 城市交通规划)[C]. 中国城市规划学会、贵阳市人民政府,2015:10.

[2] 于鹏,姚伟奇. 中小城市公共交通发展的思考[A]. 中国城市规划学会城市交通规划学术委员会. 创新驱动与智慧发展——2018 年中国城市交通规划年会论文集[C]. 中国城市规划学会城市交通规划学术委员会,2018:10.

[3] 程龙,陈学武,王利斌,等. 中小城市公共交通优先发展的策略研究——以浙江省长兴县为例[J]. 交通运输工程与信息学报,2015(01):26-32.

[4] 向楠,葛华,邵源,聂丹伟. 中小城市公交场站发展对策及实施保障研究[J]. 江苏城市规划,2015(01):19-21,28.

[5] 严文利. 中小城市公交发展策略研究——以淮安市为例[J]. 淮阴工学院学报,2016(05):54-59.

[6] 瞿飞,韩宝睿. 中小城市公交规划发展探索[J]. 森林工程,2014(03):124-127.

[7] 张帅,韩宝睿,张冰洁. 中小城市公交发展问题分析与实践研究[J]. 交通科技与经济,2014(03):8-12.

[8] 卓健,尉闻,李云娜. 城乡公交一体化建设的实施困境与应对策略[J]. 规划师,2019(15):19-25.

[9] 缪雯婷. 完善扬州市公交票价管理机制研究[D]. 扬州:扬州大学,2017.

[10] 刘敏,赵磊,刘祥锋,等. 中小城市公交票价体系改革策略[J]. 交通与运输,2020,36(01):79-83.

[11] 许飒,张玉清,杜云柯. 城市公交票价调节机制设计研究[J]. 交通运输研究,2016,2(03):23-29,35.

Electric Bus Scheduling Optimization Based on Charging Strategy

Guo Linfeng　Xue Yongzhe　Liang Jingxin　Ji Hao　Han Yan

(University of Beijing University of Technology, Department of Transportation)

Abstract　Designinga better charging strategy and optimizing bus scheduling scheme is an urgent problem should be solved to improve the operational efficiency of pure electric bus. Taking pure electric bus as the research object, charging strategy are made based on IC card data. The interval of line and other operational characteristics were found and the limited of charging station, charging mode, charging rate, battery status, departure strategy and other comprehensive factors were considered. Aiming at minimizing the cost, study built a pure electric bus scheduling optimization model were established based on the charging strategy of "fast charging is the main part, slow charging is supplement". An algorithm was designed and a pure electric bus line in Beijing was taken as an example to verify the model effectiveness. The results showed that in electric bus scheduling, the number of operating electric bus can reduce 33% and company's operating costs can be reduced based on the combined fast-slow charging strategy and electric bus scheduling optimization, which optimize the operating environment of pure electric and can provide a new scheme for the sustainable development of city.

Keywords　Urban transportation　Pure electric bus　Charging strategy　Bus scheduling optimization　IC card data

0　Introduction

In the near future, an increased deployment of electric bus vehicles(EBVs) is envisioned due to the rapid development of battery charging technologies, lower transportation costs and environment conservation benefits. Using green electricity, we have the chance to overcome more than 200 years of burning fossil fuels since the development of the first steam locomotives and steamboats. Especially in urban traffic with a lot of accelerating and braking, electric vehicles are very energy efficient and they make an important contribution to air pollution control. Hence, the electric bus vehicles are used in public transport, because they have obvious advantages than fuel buses in terms of energy efficiency and emission reduction[1]. When considering driving range limitation, the EBVs need to be charged once or more times a day. Consequently, many new navigational questions arise. Instead of asking for a shortest path by means of time or distance, we should ask for the route with the least energy consumption. There is a growing transportation demand that calls for finding a solution for the optimal charging stations placement. However, since such a charging station has a limited capacity itself, planning is needed to charge all these batteries in time. This directly leads to the corresponding network flow problem of routing with limited charging capacity.

Different charging strategies were prompted. It can be found that charging strategies have a direct impact on the bus configuration, road planning and operating costs of electric bus lines. Furthermore, it does not have to charge the battery completely, which could be a waste of time, since the charge rate typically decreases at higher charge levels. On the other hand, unreasonable charging strategies can lead to higher bus acquisition and operating costs, thus further aggravated the operating losses of bus enterprises[2]. Therefore, it is necessary for the transport transit company to plan consecutive routes at once and plan the recharging of the battery such that it coincides with the operation activities.

Charging strategies are mainly divided into slow charging, fast charging and battery replacement. Domestic and foreign experts have carried out a large number of traffic scheduling optimization research based on different electric bus charging strategy[3]. From the perspective of fast charging strategy, Zhou D set up a double-layer optimization model, in which charging cost and battery loss cost are minimized[4]. Zhang X M used IC card and GPS to collect passenger flow information, and obtained pure electric bus departure time based on battery replacement strategy[5]. Li established a pure electric bus battery charging model with fast charging strategy with the actual operation data of charging station,[6]. In general, recent studies are mainly focused on those charging strategies such as fast charging and battery replacement. The charging strategy is relatively single. In order to save charging costs, the bus charging time is usually arranged and concentrated at night for the lower electricity price. The relationship among electricity price in the different period, charging time, efficiency, cost, the bus number and bus scheduling are rarely considered. Furthermore, it does not have to charge the battery completely, which could be a waste of time, since the charge rate typically decreases at higher charge levels. The electric bus vehicle scheduling optimization under multiple charging strategy has not been studied.

Li excavated the travel chain through the IC card data of fuel bus, and optimized the bus scheduling considering the passengers' interests[7]. Based on the historical IC card data of fuel bus, Zhao obtained the bus peak curve through clustering analysis, established a scheduling optimization model and obtained an optimal route departure interval with immune algorithms[8]. In summary, based on this data, domestic and foreign experts carried out the optimization studies on the scheduling of fuel buses and new energy buses. However, only a few studies have discussed the excavation of electric bus charging data and how charging strategy affects electric bus scheduling. In reality, charging strategy is a critical factor that may significantly influence and constrain the scheduling and the total operation cost, and the scheduling optimization also has significant effects on charging strategy at the same time. Therefore, understanding their two-way relationship will help to provide an effective and reasonable charging strategy to optimize the electric bus scheduling.

The rest of the paper is organized as follows. Section 2 briefly reviewed the operating characteristics and charging strategy analysis of pure electric bus. It showed the function of data analysis and the advantages and disadvantages of three different charging strategies were analyzed. In section 3, we established an optimization model to minimize the total cost and solved the model. In the section 4, a case study was given to verified the effectiveness of electric bus scheduling optimization model. The pure electric bus operation scheduling scheme and the non-operating time of the bus were optimized, which reduced the operating cost and improved the service level of the bus line.

1 Operation Characteristics and Charging Strategy Analysis of Pure Electric Bus

1.1 Operating Characteristics Analysis of Pure Electric Bus Based on IC Card Data

It is necessary for the formulation of charging strategy and scheduling optimization of pure electric bus to obtain the operating datum, such as the departure interval and load rate of bus line, the bus number chain, the power load pure electric bus needs to consume in per plan execution, the charging time of the bus, etc. and analyze and accurately grasp the operating characteristics of the pure electric bus line. The popularization and utilization of IC card make the above-mentioned goals become possible. Domestic and foreign experts have studied the operation characteristics of public transport based on IC card data. Based on the bus IC card data, passengers on and off time, boarding time, travel time, etc. can be obtained and the line section passenger flow, full load rate and so on can be calculated. As shown in Fig. 1, based on the actual operational data, the bus operation status can be distinguished and then can be divided into four kinds: waiting to departure, operating, charging, and non-operational. Based on IC card data, the charging status of pure electric bus and the passenger flow characteristics will be excavated. Considering the capacity of the charging station and the limit of charging time, the non-operating time and pure electric bus scheduling will be optimized to improve the operational efficiency.

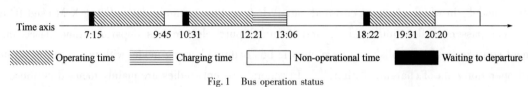

Fig. 1 Bus operation status

1.2 Charging Strategy Analysis

Charging is the main energy supply mode of pure electric buses, if the charging is disorderly, not only affect the normal operation of the shift, but also affect the safe operation of the distribution network. In the traditional mode, there are three main charging strategies[9], namely slow charging, fast charging and battery replacement. Combined with domestic and foreign research on pure electric bus charging[10-11], the summary of three different energy supplement methods are shown in Tab. 1.

(1) Slow charging, it is a mode which operation during the day time and charging at night. The charging cost is lower at night, but it needs more buses, which resulting in high bus acquisition costs. And it is necessary to consider whether the charging pile can fully charge the bus during non-operational time, hence, the charging station requirements are higher.

(2) Fast charging, the charging rate is faster and charging can be completed in the bus operating gap. Because the charging time is during electricity price peak period, electric charge is higher and fast charging has a high demand for the battery pack.

(3) Battery replacement, this mode is more flexible. The bus battery can be replaced in a short period of time, but the power station construction and maintenance costs are higher, and a large number of additional battery packs are needed to be purchased.

Tab. 1 Comparison of three charging methods

Type of charge	Slow charging	Fast charging	Battery replacement
Charging current	About 15 A	150-400 A	10-40 A
Charging time	7-8 hours	15-30 minutes	About 10 minutes
Charging cost	Lower	Higher	Higher
Construction cost of charging facility	Lower	Higher	Lower
Site requirements	Larger	Smaller	Smaller
Impact on the power grid	Lower, can be charged with valley electricity	Higher, difficult to use valley electricity to charge	Lower, can be charged with valley electricity
Difficulties of maintenance management	More demand for charging piles, management and maintenance is difficult	Less demand for charging piles, better for management maintenance	Battery management, easy to maintain recycling

Comparing the advantages and disadvantages of those three charging methods, the charging strategy of "fast charging during the daytime, slow charging at night" is selected. Considering the purchase cost of pure electric buses, battery consumption and charging cost, the charging steps are as follows:

(1) During the daytime bus operation, the intermittent charging strategy is taken, after each bus completes a task, it is necessary to judge and choose whether to enter the charging station to use fast charging for recharge;

(2) During intermittent recharge period, the remaining battery capacity of the charging bus shall not be lower than the amount of battery capacity required to complete a mission;

(3) During the non-operational period at night, all buses can be arranged to be charged slowly until all buses are fully charged.

At night, as the buses are in non-operational status, the bus are arranged to line up and fill up in turn and quickly recharge can be arranged during the day time. As shown in Fig. 2, when a bus completes an operation and drive back to the charging station, there will be a judgment whether its remaining power can support the next operation. If remaining power can support the next operation, the bus will be arranged to return to the charging station, waiting for the next operation. If remaining power can support the next operation, the bus will be arranged to enter the charging station and charge the bus to ensure that the battery still has minimum limit power SOC_{min} after a round of operation. Once the charge is complete, the bus immediately returns to the station to prepare for the next operation.

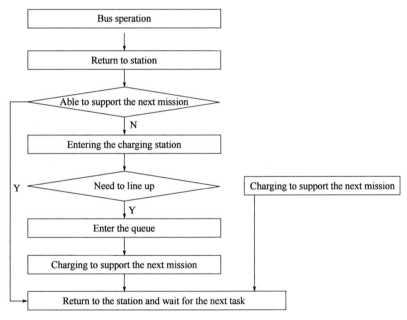

Fig. 2 Charging strategy flow chart

Considering that queuing occurs as shown in fig. 3. Based on the queuing theory, the in turn charging model of buses is constructed, and the operation stage is divided into four states: ① The first bus to be charged arrives at the state; ② Dynamic operation state, in which there are buses waiting to charge, and buses can queue to charge in turn; ③ Stop arriving state; ④ End the queuing and service stop state, charge mode can be switched to slow charging after the operation is over.

2 Pure Electric Bus Scheduling Optimization Model

Some assumptions are given about the experimental environment to simplify the problem: ① Bus information such as route, bus station, timetable, charging station and etc. is known; ② The road usually does not appear traffic jams; ③ The buses are arranged to immediately drive to the charging station after the operation closing-time; ④ The battery is full charged before the start of the vehicle's daily task; ⑤ Weather effects are ignored when considering the battery function.

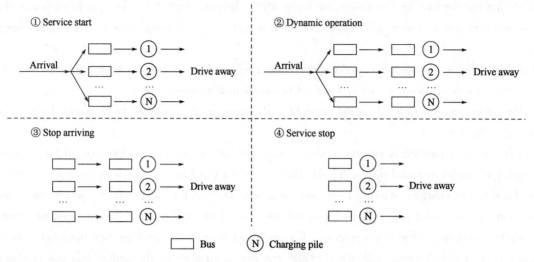

Fig. 3 Bus charging queuing model

2.1 Model established

The model variables are shown in Tab. 2.

Model variable table　　　　　　　　　　　　　　　　Tab. 2

Variable	The meaning of the variable	Variable	The meaning of the variable
V	Collection of buses	c	Charging rate
v	Number of buses	t_w	Waiting time
N	Number of charging piles	SOC_x	Electricity consumed by the bus to complete a single task
T	A collection of moments	T_r	A moment within the scope of the collection T
i	Bus number	$T_i(A_{ij})$	The arrival time of bus ij
j	The task number	$T_i(S_{ij})$	The launch time of bus ij
t	The interval	$SOC_i(A_{ij})$	The power of bus ij
t_t	Bus transfer time		

The operating time of the whole day is divided into some moments by the unit of 1 minute and these moments set are defined as T.

This paper considers the goal of minimizing the operating cost of single-pure electric buses and an optimization model was established.

The objective function:

the goal is to minimize the daily operation cost of vehicle C_{min}.

$$c_{min} = C_V + C_c + C_o \qquad (1)$$

In the formula, C_V is the vehicle cost; C_c is charging cost; C_o is the other charge.

Vehicle cost
$$C_V = v \times C_M \qquad (2)$$

C_M is the price of each vehicle (YUAN/vehicle)

Charging cost
$$C_c = [v_c N(t+t_1)] \times C_1 \qquad (3)$$

C_1 is the unit price of electricity [YUAN/(kW·h)]

Constraints:

Before the vehicle begins to operate, it must be guaranteed that its remaining power is not lower than the minimum electric quantity limit SOC_{min} after one lap of the operation. Shown as equation (4):

$$\text{SOC}_i(A_{ij}) + c(t + t_t) - \text{SOC}_x \geq \text{SOC}_{\min} \tag{4}$$

When a vehicle completes its operation, it will take the bus t_t driving from the station to the charging station for charging. Assuming that the vehicle is the i th vehicle, when the i + N vehicle arrives at the charging station, the vehicle i leaves the charging station. It also will take the bus t_t returning to the station.

If the electric quantity of vehicle i does not meet equation(4), the vehicle i + N waiting time t_w is set, namely the equation(5).

$$\text{SOC}_i(A_{ij}) + c(t + t_t) + ct_w - \text{SOC}_x \geq \text{SOC}_{\min} \tag{5}$$

The interval time between the vehicle's previous arrival time $T_i(A_{ij})$ and the next departure time $T_i[S_{i(j+1)}]$ must be greater than the sum of the vehicle's charging time $N(t + t_t)$ and the possible queuing time t_w, as shown in equation(6).

$$T_i(A_{ij}) + N(t + t_t) + t_w < T_i(S_{i(j+1)}) \tag{6}$$

Set upper and lower limits for the battery state $\text{SOC}_{\min}$ and $\text{SOC}_{\max}$ of all vehicles as shown in equation(7).

$$\text{SOC}_{\min} > 0, \text{SOC}_{\max} < 1 \tag{7}$$

2.2 Solution of Vehicle Departure Plan

Taking 24 hours(1440 min) a day as the research cycle, the pure electric bus is charged by fast charging method during the operation period. Assuming that the time of the first and last bus and the total number of departures are known, the process is as follows:

Step 1: analyse the characteristics of bus operation. Through the analysis of pure electric bus IC card data, the daily section passenger flow is obtained. The time of day is divided into morning peak, flat peak and evening peak, and the departure plan is discussed respectively.

Step 2: Determine the minimum number of vehicles. Starting from the departure number $j = 1$, calculate the arrival time $T_i(A_{ij})$ of each vehicle and the charged state $\text{SOC}_i(A_{ij})$ when the vehicle arrives at the station. The number of starts is increasing $j = j + 1$, the start time $T_i(S_{ij}) = T_i(S_{ij-1}) + t$, if the departure time is earlier than the arrival time of the previous vehicle $T_i(A_{ij})$, the next vehicle v = v + 1 will be arranged, otherwise, the previous vehicle can arrive in time and can be arranged for the following operation. Finally, we can obtain is the minimum number of vehicles for one route v.

Step 3: Judge whether the remaining electric quantity of the vehicle meets the requirements. It starts from the starting number $j = 1$, record the remaining electric quantity $\text{SOC}_i(A_{ij})$ after the vehicle arrives, and judge its electric quantity after power supplement: $\text{SOC}_i(A_{ij}) + c(t - t_t - t_w) > \text{SOC}_x$. If the requirements are met, judge the next bus. If the requirements are not met, rerun the step 2.

3 Case Study

3.1 The Basic Condition of The Line

To verify the scheduling optimization model in this paper, a line in Beijing is selected as an example. The specific station information and lines are shown in Fig. 4. The line runs for 38 km and passes through 36 stations including Shawodian, Fengheying, Zhanggezhuang, Nijiacun and Dalizhuang. The standard journey time is 80 minutes, with 48 departures per day and an interval of 15 – 30 minutes between departures. The first and last buses depart at 5:30 and 20:30 respectively. There are 18 buses equipped on this segmented pricing route and three charging piles were settled at the first station, Shawodian.

3.2 Line Operation Characteristics Analysis Based on IC Card Data

We obtained IC card data from March 1, 2018 to March 7, 2018, with a total of 16552 data. Pure electric bus operation characteristics were analysed based on datum. Datum include the time of passengers' swiping

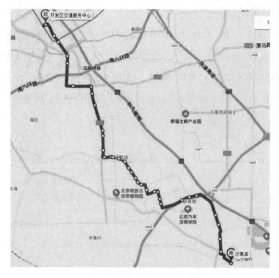

Fig. 4 Route information

card while getting on bus, boarding station, getting off station and transaction time while getting off.

3.2.1 Bus operation diagram

In order to intuitively indicate the actual situation of bus operation, a bus operation diagram is drawn, as shown in Fig. 5, in which the abscissa is the time of one day and the ordinate is vehicle number. It can be seen from Fig. 5 that there exist some buses such as number (1)(6)(12) and their interval time between two tasks is 6 hours. Buses such as number (5)(9)(15) even be cancelled the subsequent departure tasks, and some shuttle buses were temporarily assigned to carry passengers. The current situation is not ideal, and which leads to the low bus utilization rate and a lot of waste of resources.

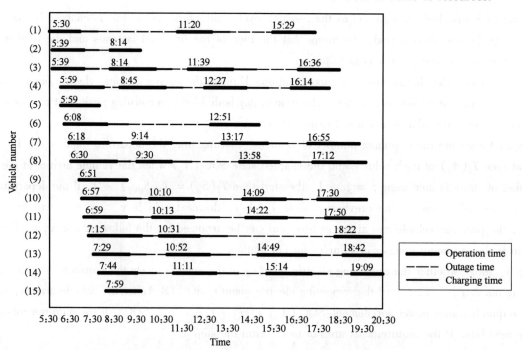

Fig. 5 Real situation diagram of bus operation

3.2.2 Sectional passenger flow distribution

The passenger flow distribution of line section is shown in Fig. 6. The maximum passenger flow is 401 persons/hour, and the morning and evening peak hours of passenger flow are: 6:00 to 8:00, 17:00 to 18:00.

3.2.3 The daily average bus utilization rate

Daily average bus utilization rate is the ratio of average operating time of all buses on one day to the total service time of the line. From 7-day statistical data, it is found that the daily average bus utilization rate of this route is only 45.47%, which indicated that for each vehicle, less than half of the time in operation, the actual utilization rate is too low (Fig. 7).

It can be concluded that due to the intermittent power supply of pure electric buses, the actual departure interval of buses does not meet specified departure time (15 minutes to 30 minutes), resulting in departure

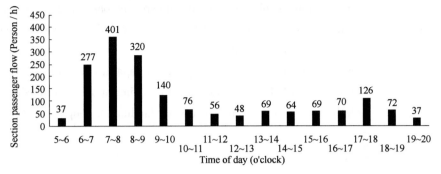

Fig. 6 Section passenger flow

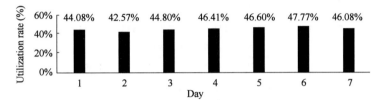

Fig. 7 Average bus utilization

intervals ranging from 5 minutes to 40 minutes, which is chaotic. The low bus utilization rate and the serious waste of bus resources increased the company's additional operating cost. In addition, the actual average operation time per shift reached 114 minutes, which caused the number of passengers in lots of buses far exceeded the carrying capacity, leading to a decline in the service level of pure electric buses.

3.3 Model Results

Based on the above model, this paper proposed an optimized charging model and a departure timetable for this line as shown in Fig. 8. In the figure, the abscissa is the time of one day, and the ordinate is the vehicle number.

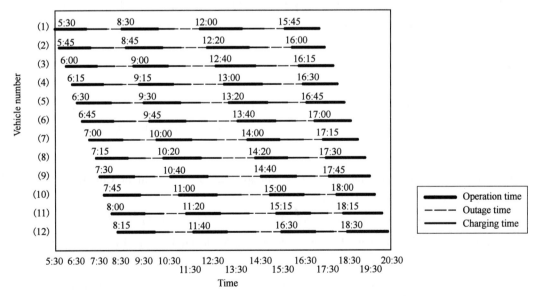

Fig. 8 Optimization of charging model and bus departure schedule

The departure interval is set to 15 minutes and 20 minutes in the optimized schedule the 15-minute interval is used for peak hours and the 20-minute interval is used for normal hours. To a certain extent, the departure sequence of buses will become more reasonable, which improves the original low bus utilization rate, the number of buses is reduced from 18 to 12 and greatly reduces operation cost. In addition, the optimized schedule can effectively alleviate the problem of the excessive number of passengers at a specific time. The standardized departure interval can make the distribution of the number of daily passengers even and reasonable and improve the service level of pure electric buses at the same time.

The comparison between before departure intervals and optimized departure intervals is shown in Fig. 9, the results show that: compared with the chaos before optimization, the optimization of the model clearly made the shift time interval stable and orderly, and save time and cost while facilitating people to ride.

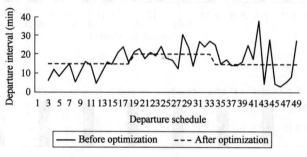

Fig. 9 The comparison of departure interval

4 Conclusions

First, the dual limitations of bus driving range and charging time are considered in the model of this paper. By adopting the charging strategy of "fast charging is the main part, slow charging is supplement", buses will be recharged during the shift interval and the battery power will be controlled within a standard range, which meets the power requirement for normal operation. Hence, the goal of minimizing total cost can be achieved.

Secondly, this research result can improve the current unreasonable operating conditions for the line in case, including reducing the number and cost of buses, optimizing the departure interval and schedule during peak and normal periods and improving the utilization rate of buses, etc.

Finally, the results of this study are also applicable to other similar pure electric bus routes to the line in case, and this study made a targeted and concrete analysis for specific problems of different routes in terms of the number of buses, departure interval, and scheduling order. The corresponding optimization measures will improve the service level of pure electric buses.

In practice, the consumption of vehicle battery is often closely related to the natural environment, passenger weight and road conditions, thus increase the instability of model operation. For the further research, it is necessary to consider the effect of the consumption law of battery which will make the model more realistic.

References

[1] HAN L. Analysis on the Development of New Energy Bus[J]. Journal of Chifeng University Natural Science Edition, 2017, 33(22): 102-103.

[2] DING W B. Analysis and Development of Pure Electric Bus[J]. Auto Time, 2018(02): 31-32.

[3] ZHANG T, HU J, BIAN Dun-xin. Review of Charging Mode on Electric Bus[J]. Chinese Journal of Power Sources, 2015(12): 2796-2798.

[4] ZHOU D, REN Z W, SUN K, et al. Optimal Charging Strategy of Fast Charging Bus in Complex Operation Environment[J]. Energy Storage Science and Technology, 2020, 9(01): 195-203.

[5] ZHANG X M. The Research on Urban Dispatching Optimization Problem of Qingdao Pure Electric Bus [D]. Qingdao: Qingdao University, 2019.

[6] LI C L. Research on Optimal Charging Strategy of Electric Bus Charging Station[D]. Beijing: Beijing Jiaotong University, 2018.

[7] LI S. Research on Bus Intelligent Dispatching Based on the Data of Bus IC Card[D]. Chengdu: Southwest Jiaotong University, 2016.
[8] ZHAO Q. Research on Bus Dispatching Optimization Based on Survey Data of Bus IC Card[D]. Dalian: Dalian University of Technology, 2007.
[9] LI J, TANG X Y, ZHAO C X. Dispatch Optimization of Pure Electric Buses Based on Charging Strategy [J]. Journal of Chongqing Jiaotong University(Natural Science), 2015, 34(04):107-112.
[10] XU G. Research on Optimization of Battery Electric City Bus Scheduling[D]. Nanjing: Nanjing University of Science & Technology, 2017.
[11] HE J L. Study on Pure Electric Bus Scheduling Based on Different Charge-Discharge Process[D]. Guangzhou: South China University of Technology, 2017.

城市机动化与公共交通运输需求关联分析研究

秦选龙[1] 杨琦[1] 魏娜[2]

(1.长安大学;2.西安旅游集团)

摘 要 城市化带来机动化,也带来了交通拥堵等问题,由此提出"优先发展城市公共交通"。为验证城市机动车数量激增对公共交通需求的影响,以中国城市统计年鉴中各地级市的万人公交车数量为衡量,通过聚类分析将284个地级市分为4类,其中第一类城市人均公交车数量最少,第四类人均公交车最多,运用2005—2018年统计数据,以公共交通客运量为因变量,滞后一期的公共交通客运量、当期和滞后一期的民用汽车保有量作为自变量建立计量经济模型。分析得出:第一、第二和第三类城市短期内,城市机动车数量的激增对公共交通需求影响显著,第一和第三类城市为促进影响,且第三类城市影响作用远大于第一类;第二类城市表现为抑制作用;第四类城市则表现长期的促进作用。将四类城市视为城市公共交通发展的四个阶段,随着人均公交车数量的增长,机动化进程对公共交通运输需求的促进作用由短期逐渐转变为长期。

关键词 公共交通需求 城市机动化水平 聚类分析 混合数据

0 引 言

随着改革开放的不断深入,我国经济保持稳速发展,经济总量不断增加,城市化进程也在不断加快,除直辖市外的地级市个数由1978年的98个上升到2018年底的293个,城市规模日益扩大。而城市经济快速发展带来的空间集聚和人口聚集效应,城市机动化问题日益突出。随着城市化水平越来越高,城市规模及城市交通基础设施在不断完善,居民出行方式也发生了重大变化。在出行方面,居民对高效、便捷、舒适的等方面有了明确要求,进而居民普遍通过购买家用汽车来实现出行需求。据2018年国家经济和社会发展统计公报显示,截至2018年底全国汽车保有量达24028万辆,其中私人汽车保有量20730万辆,民用客车保有量13451万辆,其中私人客车12589万辆,机动车出行已成为人们出行的主要方式。但随着汽车保有量不断增加,交通拥堵、环境污染等问题成了城市发展中无法治愈的顽疾。虽然各地方政府不断出台限号、限购等抑制机动车增长速度的相关政策,提倡绿色环保、公交出行,但城市机动化表现出高速度增长、高密度集聚的特点。公共交通的建设具有周期性和基础性,居民在公共交通需求方面

基金项目:陕西省社会科学基金项目"关中平原城市群综合交通运输体系构建及优化策略研究"(2019S032);陕西省社科界重大理论与现实问题研究重点项目"陕西省科技产业集群高质量发展路径及对策研究"(2020Z361);陕西省科技厅软科学研究计划一般项目"陕西经济高质量发展与综合交通运输体系协同发展研究"(2021KRM054)。

表现为具有复杂性和多变性,本文通过研究城市机动化水平与公共交通需求之间的内在联系,发现全国各地级城市机动化与公共交通需求的特点,从而充分发挥城市公共交通系统保障城市高速运转和活力,努力使公交出行成为城市居民出行的首选和重要方式,减少自驾出行,从而实现绿色、环保、节能、高效、可持续的交通运行模式。

1 现状研究

随着国民经济、社会的不断发展,我国开启全面建成小康社会的新时期。城镇规模急剧扩张,城市人口快速增长,汽车保有量的不断增加给城市发展带来了各式各样的问题。陈明星、陆大道等从城市化内涵的人口、经济、社会、土地4个方面,构建中国城市化水平的综合评价指标体系。基于熵值法,对1981—2006年的中国城市化进行综合测度,结果表明中国城市化综合水平持续提高,以经济增长和机动车保有量的快速演进为主要特征[1]。徐骅,金凤君总结国际经验和中国机动化发展进程,引入了机动化经济增长弹性系数,定量分析机动化与经济发展的关系,对45个国家1928年以来各个年代的机动化经济弹性系数进行了计算,发现机动化的发展虽然有时快于经济的发展,有时慢于经济的发展,但是机动化率大致上随着人均国内生产总值的增长而增长[2]。随着中国经济的飞速发展,机动化程度越来越高,机动化对城市发展的负外部性也日益显现。一是碳排放带来的环境污染;二是城市交通的日益拥挤,抵消许多由机动化带来的好处,降低城市的生活质量和舒适性。

刘爽等探讨了城市机动化的发展趋势及影响因素。分析了城市经济发展水平、人口密度、道路设施和公共交通发展对机动化发展的影响,据此判断城市机动车保有量仍将保持高速增长态势。城市应根据自身特点发展公共交通并采取相应的交通管理措施引导小汽车合理使用,不断优化交通结构[3]。潘海啸提出在小汽车到来之前推行"全域公交"优先,建立与大公共交通相互耦合的都市区发展模式[4]的观点;若公共交通发展滞后,将促进机动车尤其是私人小汽车的增加;若公共交通得到优先发展,乘坐公共交通可满足居民对出行时间、费用、便捷、舒适等各方面的需求,则可在一定程度上抑制或延缓机动车的发展。中国大城市交通正处于高速发展、结构优化阶段,大部分城市在大力发展公共交通的同时并没有强力遏制机动车的发展,机动车保有量与公共交通设施几乎同步增长[5]。李林波等提出大公共交通系统以及体系构架[6],赵云毅等通过分析首尔通过路中央公交专用道改革和运营线路优化等改革措施,分析北京地面交通客运量快速下降的趋势,对提高北京地面公交的运营速度、准点率和换乘的便利性进行研究,从而提高地面公共交通的乘坐率,增加人们对地面公交的满意度[7]。

黄新民等提出大中城市建设以轨道交通系统为主干的区域性综合公共交通体系[8]。汪新凡等提出了属性数学识别模型评价城市公共交通发展水平以及其评价指标体系与分级标准[9]。城市道路客运量的增长是交通需求增加的最直接表现,为了满足需求,必然需要增加供给。吴玲玲,黄正东考虑不同群体的需求差异,提出既考虑距离衰减和公共交通吸引力,融合多样性的幂函数测度方法,并基于空间分析单元计算测度指数,为"公交都市"建立多层次、多速度、多换乘和多覆盖的多模式公共交通体系提供重要参考[10]。李朝阳等从香港公共交通系统发展历程、规划设计和运营管理等视角,归纳总结其经验和发展趋势[11]等。

大量学者对机动化进程和公共交通发展及建设等方面做了长期研究,但对城市机动化水平对公共交通需求影响的研究却极为少见。虽然学者们都提出大力发展公共交通来应对城市机动化的快速发展,但却忽视了城市机动化对公共交通需求产生的影响,通过研究两者的关系有助于更加有效地发展公共交通,本文试图探索两者间的关联,厘清公共交通需求与城市机动化之间的关系,为城市健康发展提供参考意见。

2 城市公共交通发展的聚类分析

由于4个直辖市特点较为突出,本文统计了我国2005—2018年293个地级市的公共交通信息,综合选取统计年鉴中的每万人拥有公共汽车(辆)衡量区域间差异,每万人拥有的公共交通车辆数的计算公式为:每万人拥有公共交通车辆数(标台) = 全市公共交通车辆标台数 ÷ 城市总人口(万人)。其中公共交通车辆标台数是指不同类型的运营车辆按统一的标准当量折合成的运营车数,标准运营车辆数 = ∑(每类型车辆数)×相应换算系数)——具体以建设部《城市建设统计指标解释》(建综〔2001〕255 号)为准。通过聚类分析进行分类,在不考虑因等待时间过长而放弃选择公共交通出行的损失情况下,假设公共交通供给与需求相等,以公共交通客运量反映公共交通需求,以民用汽车保有量反映城市机动化,探索不同地级市机动车增长及公共交通需求间的规律。

2.1 聚类分析原理及步骤

聚类分析是将某个对象集合分为若干组的过程,使同一个组内的数据对象具有较高的相似度,而不同组中的数据对象是不相似的,是通过数据建模简化数据的一种方法[12]。具体分析步骤为:①选取样本;②数据标准化;③相似性计算;④确定类数;⑤结果的分析和阐述。

2.2 聚类分析度量方法

距离是衡量不同类别之间差异的度量,本文选取欧氏距离衡量该指标。欧氏距离两个样本 m 个指标值差平方和的平方根为:

$$d_{ij} = \left[\sum_{r=1}^{m} (x_{ia} - x_{ja})^2 \right]^{\frac{1}{2}} \tag{1}$$

度量分析中,i 和 j 代替样本,用 d_{ij} 表示两个样本间的距离,设 c_a,c_b 为两个类,分别有 m_a 和 m_b 个样本。如果类 c_a 中有样本 $x_1, x_2 \cdots x_n$,则均值为:

$$\overline{x_e} = \frac{1}{m_e} \sum_{i=1}^{m_a} x_i \tag{2}$$

该均值为类 c_a 的重心。假设类 c_a,c_b 的距离记为 d_{ab},计算类间的度量采用 Ward 提出的离差平方和法(Ward 法):

$$D_{ab}^2 = \frac{m_a m_b}{m_a + m_b} (\overline{x_a} - \overline{x_b})^T (\overline{x_a} - \overline{x_b}) \tag{3}$$

2.3 聚类结果分析

运用统计软件 SPSS19.0 中的系统聚类分析法时,发现哈密、儋州、林芝、日喀则、昌都、三沙、海东、山南、桂平 9 个城市的数据异常,故将这 9 个城市剔除后对全国 284 个地级及以上城市作为样本进行聚类分析,结果如表 1 所示。

2018 年我国城市万人公交车数量聚类结果　　　　表 1

聚类	聚类中心	聚类中案例数	城市(部分)
1	2.948	88	陇南,广安,亳州,安康,贺州,贵港,崇左,莆田,遂宁,商洛,六安,忻州,眉山,玉林等
2	6.398	96	新余,邵阳,泸州,驻马店,咸宁,漳州,防城港,佳木斯,淮南,宝鸡,永州,濮阳,嘉峪关等
3	10.671	70	东莞,抚顺,衡阳,河源,攀枝花,柳州,舟山,郴州,松原,镇江,六盘水,芜湖等
4	16.610	30	武汉,西宁,佛山,中山,青岛,邢台,邯郸,鄂尔多斯,温州,大连,合肥,杭州,石家庄,昆明,厦门,成都等

根据聚类分析将 284 个城市的每万人人均公交车数量分为 4 类,进一步利用 ARCGIS10.0 软件将各地市的数据以空间可视化表达,分别用蓝、绿、橙和红色表示第一、第二、第三和第四类,为进一步检验城市机动化水平与公共交通运输需求间的关联,再通过构建模型进行实证检验。

3 民用汽车保有量与公共交通运输需求实证检验

3.1 建立模型

为了研究时间和截面单元两个方向上每一聚类的变化规律及不同时间、不同单元的个体特征,本研究选取面板数据分析中混合回归模型的固定效应变截距模型进行分析。通过对《中国城市统计年鉴》2005—2018年各期数据的整理，以城市公共交通客运总量(pas)为因变量，以民用汽车保有量(veh)为自变量建立计量模型。考虑到公共交通需求受到诸多因素影响，故在自变量中加入滞后一期的客运量，体现其他因素对客运量增长的影响。同时模型中加入了滞后一期的民用汽车保有量作为自变量，研究中长期对客运量增长造成的影响。建立模型如下：

$$\text{pas} = \alpha_{it} + \beta_1 \text{pas}_{it-1} + \beta_2 \text{veh}_{it} + \beta_3 \text{veh}_{it-1} + \mu_{it} \tag{4}$$

式中：i——284个城市；

t——年份；

α_{it}——个体特征项；

$\beta_1 、\beta_2 、\beta_3$——模型的待估参数；

μ_{it}——随机干扰项。

3.2 实证结果

通过利用Eviews7对4个聚类分别建立多元回归模型，建立模型过程中参照回归系数的t检验值及其双侧显著性水平(P值)确定最终的自变量。

3.2.1 第一类城市公共交通客运需求与民用汽车保有量的实证检验

利用第一类城市的相关数据对模型进行回归，结果见表2。滞后一期的民用汽车数量t统计量不显著，删去该项影响因素建立的模型样本决定系数R^2和F统计量以及$\beta_1 、\beta_2$(10%的显著性水平下)均显著，拟合优度较高，模型具有较好的说服力，β_2系数为正(0.00163)，说明第一类城市中当期民用汽车保有量对公共交通运输需求呈现正相关关系。

第一类城市实证检验结果 表2

变量	变量名称	回归系数	标准差	t统计量	P值
β_1	2017年公交客运总量	1.04016	0.010	104.88	0.000
β_2	2018年民用汽车保有量	0.00163	0.001	1.795	0.077
固定效应	常数项	固定效应	常数项	固定效应	常数项	固定效应	常数项
菏泽市	639.4036	茂名市	630.3891	日照市	881.609	陇南市	94.77364
昭通市	972.9378	南充市	2658.091	汕头市	1136.745	娄底市	1159.761
临沧市	730.0852	平凉市	303.1614	遂宁市	408.9669	天水市	324.1067
临汾市	1565.602	宜春市	444.0661	台州市	1282.841	…	…
模型检验结果
R^2	0.99591	因变量均值	6476.9
调整R^2	0.99580	F检验统计量	9366.951
回归标准误差	1259.674	相伴概率	0.000
DW统计量	2.067		

注：考虑到篇幅限制没有列出全部城市，仅列出代表性城市。

3.2.2 第二类城市公共交通客运需求与民用汽车保有量的实证检验

使用第二类城市的相关数据对模型进行回归结果如表3所示。结果显示滞后一期的民用汽车数量t统计量不显著，删去该项影响因素建立的模型样本的决定系数R^2和F统计量以及$\beta_1 、\beta_2$(5%的显著性水平下)均显著，拟合优度较高，模型具有较好的说服力，β_2系数为负(-0.00153)，说明第二类城市聚类中当期民用汽车保有量对公共交通运输需求呈现负相关关系。

第二类城市实证检验结果 表3

变量	变量名称	回归系数	标准差	t统计量	P值
β_1	2017年公交客运总量	1.110608	0.035464	104.88	0.000
β_2	2018年民用汽车保有量	-0.001529	0.001110	1.795	0.017
固定效应	常数项	固定效应	常数项	固定效应	常数项	固定效应	常数项
丽水市	199.4353	南通市	629.5423	阜新市	1136.712	荆州市	3658.932
安庆市	248.2663	通化市	702.3109	咸阳市	1235.675	淮南市	4124.5
延安市	415.3527	淮北市	930.6375	岳阳市	3248.704	本溪市	9186.556
曲靖市	422.2748	咸宁市	1014.741	泰州市	3256.11	…	…

模型检验结果			
R^2	0.925784	因变量均值	6476.9
调整R^2	0.924077	F检验统计量	546.623
回归标准误差	1259.674	相伴概率	0.000
DW统计量	2.000		

注:考虑到篇幅限制没有列出全部城市,仅列出代表性城市。

3.2.3 第三类城市公共交通客运需求与民用汽车保有量的实证检验

使用第三聚类城市的相关数据对模型进行回归结果如表4所示。结果显示滞后一期的民用汽车数量t统计量不显著,删去该项影响因素建立模型样本的决定系数R^2和F统计量以及β_1、β_2(10%的显著性水平下)均显著,拟合优度较高,模型具有较好的说服力,β_2的系数均为正(0.0133),说明第三类城市当期民用汽车保有量与公共交通运输需求呈现正相关关系。

第三类城市实证检验结果 表4

变量	变量名称	回归系数	标准差	t统计量	P值
β_1	2017年公交客运总量	0.690378	0.029447	23.444	0.000
β_2	2018年民用汽车保有量	0.013311	0.007203	1.848	0.070
固定效应	常数项	固定效应	常数项	固定效应	常数项	固定效应	常数项
许昌市	637.3154	随州市	3454.885	镇江市	5797.1	新乡市	8402.289
泉州市	875.6063	松原市	3958.388	郴州市	5852.83	衡阳市	8696.731
嘉兴市	3313.814	铜陵市	4996.893	秦皇岛	8243.714	攀枝花	11823.53
绍兴市	3436.214	龙岩市	5085.759	鸡西市	8296.435	…	…

模型检验结果			
R^2	0.910463	因变量均值	
调整R^2	0.907376	F检验统计量	294.890
回归标准误差		相伴概率	0.000
DW统计量	1.853		

注:考虑到篇幅限制没有列出全部城市,仅列出代表性城市。

3.2.4 第四类城市公共交通客运需求与民用汽车保有量的实证检验

使用第四类城市的相关数据对模型进行回归结果如表5所示。结果显示当期的民用汽车数量t统计量不显著,删去该项影响因素建立的模型样本的决定系数R^2和F统计量以及β_1、β_3(5%的显著性水平下)均显著,拟合优度较高,模型具有较好的说服力,β_3的系数均为正(0.0084),说明第四聚类中滞后一期民用汽车保有量对公共交通运输需求呈现正相关关系。

第四类城市实证检验结果 表5

变量	变量名称	回归系数	标准差	t统计量	P值
β_1	2017年公交客运总量	0.931404	0.034580	26.935	0.000
β_3	2017年民用汽车保有量	0.008408	0.003859	2.178	0.039
固定效应	常数项	固定效应	常数项	固定效应	常数项	固定效应	常数项
株洲市	-804.166	珠海市	6148.042	武汉市	13026.59	广州市	33256.28
晋城市	2557.378	滨州市	7502.702	合肥市	16156.35	厦门市	37190.96
十堰市	3309.842	中山市	8878.006	青岛市	18413.48	成都市	70855.92
邢台市	3990.073	宁波市	8935.063	杭州市	18435.94	大连市	20426.32
模型检验结果							
R^2		0.993729		因变量均值			
调整R^2		0.993246		F检验统计量		2060.146	
回归标准误差		8151.466		相伴概率		0.000	
DW统计量		2.002					

注:考虑到篇幅限制没有列出全部城市,仅列出代表性城市。

3.3 结果分析

通过对4类城市的数据进行对比分析表明,民用汽车保有量与城市公共交通客运量之间确实存在影响但又各有差异:第四类城市中的滞后一期民用汽车保有量对城市公共交通客运量具有明显的促进作用,即城市机动化程度对公共交通需求的长期促进作用要大于其短期的影响;第一类、第二类和第三类城市中,当期的民用汽车保有量对城市公共交通客运量的需求作用明显,说明城市机动化水平对公共交通需求增长的短期影响较大,其中第二类城市呈现出抑制作用,即随着城市民用汽车保有量的增加,公共出行量反而下降;第一和第三类城市呈现促进作用,但第三类城市的作用较第一类城市更加强烈。具体表现如下:

第一,城市机动车数量的激增短期内就能促进第一类(人均公交车数量最少的一类城市)和第三类城市中的居民出行更倾向于公共交通,这可能是因为这类城市或者说处于这一阶段的城市,机动车增长的数量不足以满足大多数居民的出行,反而由于道路拥挤等交通问题刺激了人们选择公共交通出行。第三类城市的促进作用要高于第一类城市,两类城市并不同质。第二类城市呈现相反的规律,短期内,城市机动车数量的增加,对公共交通客运量的起到抑制作用。

第二,第四类城市(人均公交车数量最多的一类)表明当人均公交车数量达到一定程度,公共交通发展到一定阶段,城市机动化进程的推进对人们选择公共交通出行具有长期的促进作用,相比其他三类城市,短期影响将不再明显,这可能是由于公共交通发展到一定阶段,城市公共交通供给发达,机动车数量的增长所带来的影响不能在短期内迅速改变人们的出行选择。

4 结 语

本文首先采用聚类分析以城市每万人拥有公共汽车数量(辆)为统计量将全国284个城市分为4类(其中第一类城市人均公交车数量最少),进一步选取2005—2018年中国统计年鉴中的混合面板数据进行分析,以公共交通客运量作为因变量,并以滞后一期的公共交通客运量和当期和滞后一期的民用汽车保有量为自变量,分别对这4类城市建立计量经济模型进行回归,进而得出城市机动化水平的增长对城市公共交通的需求具有十分重要的影响。当人均公共交通数量较低时,机动车数量的增长带来公共交通出行需求的大幅增长,实际可以理解城市机动化水平的增长反映了社会经济水平的提高,进而政府会加大对公共交通的投入,公共交通的投入最直接的表现就是公共交通车辆的增加、交通线路的增加,公交的出行便捷程度就会促进公共出行需求的迅速提升；而随着公共交通车辆投放的不断增加，城市机动化水平的迅速增长会带来城市拥堵、空气污染等城市问题，进而抑制公共交通客运量的增长；当公交车数量继续按照人口比重增加时，低碳环保、绿色出行的社会需求又成为促进公共交通运输需求的因素；因此，城市发展过程中必须充分考虑机动化与公共交通需求之间的关系，考虑不同地区和不同阶段机动车水平发展带来的公共出行需求，进而在规划、建设、管理和服务等各个环节为实现"公共交通优先发展"提供条件。

参考文献

[1] 陈明星,陆大道,刘慧.中国城市化与经济发展水平关系的省际格局[J].地理学报,2010,65(12)：1443-1453.
[2] 徐骅,金凤君.国际经验与我国机动化发展研究[J].软科学,2006,(04):24-28
[3] 刘爽,赵明亮,包婠娜,等.基于交通结构发展情景分析的城市交通碳排放测算研究[J].交通运输系统工程与信息,2015,15(03):222-227.
[4] 潘海啸.多模式城市交通体系与方式间的转换[J].城市规划学刊,2013,(06):84-88.
[5] 张廷侠.大城市机动化发展态势分析及对策研究[D].北京:清华大学,2017.
[6] 李林波,吕颖钊,吉锴,等.基于差距模型的公交服务质量评价[J].交通工程,2017,17(01):22-26.
[7] 赵云毅,赵坚.首尔公交改革对北京优化地面交通的启示[J].北京交通大学学报(社会科学版),2019(03):1-9.
[8] 黄新民,吴晓,黄芳.公共交通建设与城市可持续发展[J].城市问题.2007(08):37-41.
[9] 汪新凡.城市公共交通发展水平的属性数学识别模型[J].交通运输工程学报,2007(05)：118-122.
[10] 吴玲玲,黄正东.基于多样性的大城市公共交通服务水平研究[J].交通运输系统工程与信息,2019,19(01):222-227.
[11] 李朝阳,华智.新时期大都市公共交通发展策略研究——香港公交发展启示[J].人文地理.2011(01):105-108.
[12] 武旭,杜奕,贾传峻.基于全距离完全度量聚类的交通运输能耗区域划分[J]交通运输系统工程与信息,2019,8(04):23-30.

基于 RBF 神经网络 PID 的四轮转向汽车循迹控制仿真研究

刘 强 杨蔡进 张卫华 张众华
(西南交通大学牵引动力国家重点实验室)

摘 要 为解决四轮转向汽车在循迹过程中所面临的道路曲率变化和外界干扰等非线性问题,提高循迹控制精度,本文结合 RBF 神经网络优良的自学习性能和非线性拟合能力以及 PID 控制的简单、可靠等优势,设计了一种基于 RBF 神经网络 PID 控制的转向控制器,利用 RBF 神经网络实时调节 PID 控制器的3个参数,保证循迹过程始终在最优的控制参数下进行。搭建了 CarSim-Matlab/Simulink 联合仿真试验平台,设计了一条涵盖多种车辆运行工况的目标轨迹和一条包含强侧向风的直线目标轨迹,并分别与传统的 PID 控制方法一起进行了对比仿真试验。仿真结果表明：相同参数下,本文所设计的基于 RBF 神经网络 PID 理论的控制算法相比于传统的 PID 控制算法,循迹误差更小,调节速度更快；以 34km/h 极限速度经过半径 15m 的曲线道路时,最大误差可控制在 5cm 以内,而传统的 PID 最大误差接近 8.2cm；以 90km/h 的行驶速度经过风速 90km/h 的强侧向风路段时,稳定后的偏移量在 2cm 左右,而传统的 PID 控制偏移量达到2.7cm。

关键词 交通工程　循迹控制　RBF神经网络　PID控制　四轮转向　无人驾驶

0　引　言

四轮转向汽车要实现循迹功能,必须依赖于良好的循迹控制模型和算法。国内外现有的无人驾驶汽车循迹控制模型包括几何学模型、运动学模型、动力学模型[1],所用到的基本控制方法有PID控制[2]、模型预测控制(MPC)[3]、模糊控制[4]、神经网络控制[5]、鲁棒控制[6]以及滑模控制[7]等。其中,神经网络由于具有强大的自适应性和非线性拟合能力,在无人驾驶领域受到了越来越多的关注和应用。杨文忠[8]等提出了车辆换道时间预测的BP神经网络模型,用来提高车辆换道的安全性。HAMID等[9]提出了一种基于指数样滑模模糊两型神经网络的控制方法来提高道路自动驾驶车辆的路径跟踪性能。高琳琳[10]等设计了四轮转向车辆的径向基神经网络复合控制器,可改善不同速度工况下四轮转向车辆的操作稳定性。张琨[11]等提出了一种基于模糊神经网络控制和神经网络预测的智能循迹控制策略,实现了对车辆的速度和转向控制。

本文考虑到四轮转向汽车的循迹过程存在着诸如道路弯道曲率变化、车辆速度变化以及前后轮同时转向相互干涉等诸多的非线性问题,而传统的PID控制是一种线性控制,面对复杂的非线性问题时存在控制精度低、调节时间长等问题,又考虑到BP神经网络收敛速度慢且容易出现局部最优解问题,故选用逼近精度更高、收敛速度更快的RBF神经网络,提出了一种基于RBF神经网络PID的四轮转向汽车循迹控制策略,利用RBF神经网络的自学习、自适应性和非线性拟合能力实时在线调节PID控制器的参数,再通过PID控制器快速调节被控参数,从而保证车辆能够高效地自主循迹。

1　车辆建模

1.1　创建车辆模型

本文仿真实验选用CarSim动力学仿真软件提供的一款B级车作为研究对象,并将前后轴均设置为转向轴,车辆模型具体参数如表1所示。

车辆参数表　　　　表1

参数名称	数　值	参数名称	数　值
轴距	2600mm	簧载质量	1111kg
第一轴轮距	1481mm	发动机功率	125kW
第二轴轮距	1486mm	轮胎型号	185/65R15
整车高度	1535mm	x轴转动惯量	288.0kg·m²
整车宽度	1695mm	y轴转动惯量	2031.4kg·m²
质心至前轴距离	1040mm	z轴转动惯量	2031.4kg·m²

1.2　预设目标轨迹

本文在CarSim中创建了一条用于动力学仿真的目标轨迹,其形状如图1所示。

该目标轨迹包含3条直线段和5条圆弧段:一条长30m的直线段,两条半径25m的圆弧段,一条半径20m的圆弧段,一条长20m的直线段,一条半径60m的圆弧,一条半径15m的圆弧段以及一条长30m的直线段。

1.3　定义预瞄偏差

本文的控制模型建立在单点预瞄控制的基础上。预瞄偏差的定义如下:车辆在直线道路运行时,选取侧向偏差作为预瞄偏差;在曲线道路运行时,选取径向偏差作为预瞄偏差。预瞄原理如图2所示。A点为当前时刻控制点(x_1,y_1),B点为预瞄点(x_2,y_2),C点为目标点(x_3,y_3),设纵向速度为v,采样时间为

Δt,预瞄距离为 l,车辆航向角为 θ,预瞄偏差为 Δs,曲线段圆心为 (x_0,y_0)、曲线段半径为 r,则有如下公式:

$$l = v \times \Delta t \tag{1}$$

$$x_2 = x_1 + l \times \cos\theta \tag{2}$$

$$y_2 = y_1 + l \times \sin\theta \tag{3}$$

$$\Delta s = \sqrt{(x_2-x_0)^2+(y_2-y_0)^2} - r \quad (\text{圆弧段}) \tag{4}$$

$$\Delta s = y_2 - y_3 \quad (\text{直线段}) \tag{5}$$

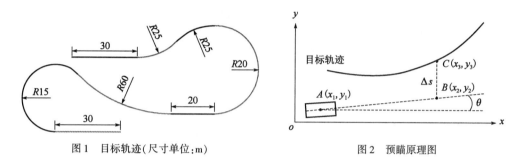

图 1　目标轨迹(尺寸单位:m)　　　　　图 2　预瞄原理图

2　控制器的设计

2.1　RBF 神经网络

RBF(径向基函数)神经网络是一种高效的前馈式神经网络,其结构如图 3 所示,由一个输入层、一个中间层和一个输出层构成。其最显著的特点就是隐含层采用输入量与中心节点的距离作为激活函数的自变量,并使用径向基函数作为激活函数。RBF 网络能够以较高的精度逼近任意的非线性函数,具有较快的学习、收敛速度,且不存在局部最优的问题,这些优点使得 RBF 神经网络在非线性时间序列预测中得到广泛应用。

2.2　RBF 神经网络 PID 控制器的设计

本文所设计的转向控制器系统结构如图 4 所示。控制系统的输入为目标轨迹(r),输出为车辆控制点的实际轨迹(y)。RBF 神经网络的输入层包含 3 个节点,对应输入分别为目标轨迹、实际轨迹以及被控参数(u)。RBF 神经网络接收到 3 个输入量之后经过内部运算输出被控参数的 Jacobian 信息,经过算法整定之后输给 PID 控制器所需的 3 个参数(k_p,k_i,k_d),PID 控制器再结合接收到的轨迹偏差(e),经过运算后输出车辆的被控参数,并作用于被控车辆,最后被控车辆再输出实际轨迹,并反作用于转向控制器。

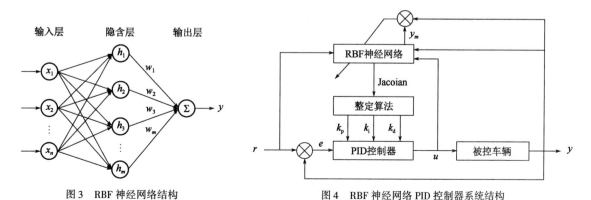

图 3　RBF 神经网络结构　　　　　图 4　RBF 神经网络 PID 控制器系统结构

本文所用 RBF 神经网络选用高斯函数作为径向基函数，结合图 3 的 RBF 神经网络结构与图 4 的控制器系统结构，开始计算并更新系统各个参数的值。设输入层共有 n 个节点，则输入层输入为 $x = [x_1, x_2, \cdots, x_n]^T$，$x_i$ 为输入层第 i 个节点的输入；设隐含层共有 m 个节点，则隐含层输出为 $h = [h_1, h_2, \cdots, h_m]^T$，$h_j$ 为隐含层第 j 个节点的输出，其计算方式如下：

$$h_j = \exp\left(-\frac{\|x - c_j\|}{2b_j^2}\right) \tag{6}$$

其中，$c = [c_1, c_2, \cdots, c_m]$，$c_j = [c_{1j}, c_{2j}, \cdots, c_{nj}]^T$，$c_{ij}$ 为输入层第 i 个节点所对应的隐含层第 j 个节点的中心，$b = [b_1, b_2, \cdots, b_m]^T$，$b_j$ 为隐含层第 j 个节点的基宽。

RBF 神经网络隐含层输出权值为：

$$w = [w_1, w_2, \cdots, w_m] \tag{7}$$

RBF 神经网络的系统输出为：

$$y_m = h_1 w_1 + h_2 w_2 + \cdots + h_m w_m \tag{8}$$

RBF 神经网络辨识的性能指标为：

$$J(t) = \frac{1}{2}[y(t) - y_m(t)]^2 \tag{9}$$

采用梯度下降法，计算更新隐含层的输出权值、节点中心和基宽：

$$\Delta w_j(t) = -\eta \frac{\partial J}{\partial w_j} = \eta[y(t) - y_m(t)]h_j \tag{10}$$

$$w_j(t) = w_j(t-1) + \Delta w_j(t) + \alpha[w_j(t-1) - w_j(t-2)] \tag{11}$$

$$\Delta c_{ij}(t) = -\eta \frac{\partial J}{\partial c_{ij}} = \eta[y(t) - y_m(t)]w_j h_j \frac{x_i - c_{ij}}{b_j^2} \tag{12}$$

$$c_{ij} = c_{ij}(t-1) + \Delta c_{ij}(t) + \alpha[c_{ij}(t-1) - c_{ij}(t-2)] \tag{13}$$

$$\Delta b_j(t) = -\eta \frac{\partial J}{\partial b_j} = \eta[y(t) - y_m(t)]w_j h_j \frac{\|x - c_j\|^2}{b_j^3} \tag{14}$$

$$b_j(t) = b_j(t-1) + \Delta b_j(t) + \alpha[b_j(t-1) - b_j(t-2)] \tag{15}$$

式中：η——学习速率，$0 < \eta < 1$；
α——动量因子，$0 < \alpha < 1$。

接下来进行 PID 控制器参数的计算更新，本文采取增量式 PID 控制器，其控制误差为：

$$e(t) = r(t) - y(t) \tag{16}$$

增量式 PID 控制器的 3 个输入为：

$$e_p(t) = e(t) - e(t-1) \tag{17}$$

$$e_i(t) = e(t) \tag{18}$$

$$e_d(t) = e(t) - 2e(t-1) + e(t-2) \tag{19}$$

RBF 神经网络 PID 控制器整定的性能指标为：

$$E(t) = \frac{1}{2}[r(t) - y(t)]^2 \tag{20}$$

同样采用梯度下降法计算更新增量式 PID 控制器的参数：

$$\Delta k_p(t) = -\eta_p \frac{\partial E}{\partial k_p} = -\eta_p \frac{\partial E}{\partial y}\frac{\partial y}{\partial u}\frac{\partial u}{\partial k_p} = \eta_p e(t)\frac{\partial y}{\partial u}e_p(t) \tag{21}$$

$$k_{\mathrm{p}}(t) = k_{\mathrm{p}}(t-1) + \Delta k_{\mathrm{p}}(t) \tag{22}$$

$$\Delta k_{\mathrm{i}}(t) = -\eta_{\mathrm{p}} \frac{\partial E}{\partial k_{\mathrm{i}}} = -\eta_{\mathrm{p}} \frac{\partial E}{\partial y} \frac{\partial y}{\partial u} \frac{\partial u}{\partial k_{\mathrm{i}}} = \eta_{\mathrm{p}} e(t) \frac{\partial y}{\partial u} e_{\mathrm{i}}(t) \tag{23}$$

$$k_{\mathrm{i}}(t) = k_{\mathrm{i}}(t-1) + \Delta k_{\mathrm{i}}(t) \tag{24}$$

$$\Delta k_{\mathrm{d}}(t) = -\eta_{\mathrm{p}} \frac{\partial E}{\partial k_{\mathrm{d}}} = -\eta_{\mathrm{p}} \frac{\partial E}{\partial y} \frac{\partial y}{\partial u} \frac{\partial u}{\partial k_{\mathrm{d}}} = \eta_{\mathrm{p}} e(t) \frac{\partial y}{\partial u} e_{\mathrm{d}}(t) \tag{25}$$

$$k_{\mathrm{d}}(t) = k_{\mathrm{d}}(t-1) + \Delta k_{\mathrm{d}}(t) \tag{26}$$

式中：η_{p}——学习速率，$0 < \eta_{\mathrm{p}} < 1$；

$\frac{\partial y}{\partial u}$——Jacobian 信息，反映了被控车辆的输出 y 对被控参数 u 变化的灵敏程度，其值由 RBF 神经网络辨识得到：

$$\frac{\partial y}{\partial u} \approx \frac{\partial y_m}{\partial u} = \sum_{j=1}^{m} \frac{\partial w_j h_j}{\partial u} = \sum_{j=1}^{m} w_j h_j \frac{c_{1j} - x_1}{b_j^2} \tag{27}$$

综合上述信息，可计算出被控参数 u：

$$u(t) = u(t-1) + \Delta u(t) = u(t-1) + k_{\mathrm{p}}(t)e_{\mathrm{p}}(t) + k_{\mathrm{i}}(t)e_{\mathrm{i}}(t) + k_{\mathrm{d}}(t)e_{\mathrm{d}}(t) \tag{28}$$

3 仿真分析

本文将在 CarSim 与 Matlab/Simulink 联合仿真平台上，分别用传统的 PID 控制策略与基于 RBF 神经网络 PID 的控制策略，对车辆在极限速度工况下及强侧向风干扰工况下的循迹控制进行联合仿真试验，以验证所设计的 RBF 神经网络 PID 控制算法的优越性。

3.1 极限速度下的循迹仿真试验

本次仿真试验所预设的目标轨迹的路面附着系数为 $\mu = 0.8$，目标轨迹如图 1 所示。由于车辆转弯时所需的侧向力 F 由轮胎与地面之间的摩擦力 f 提供，假设车辆转弯时所受的地面摩擦力全部用于提供侧向力，则通过以下公式可计算出车辆转弯时的极限速度：

$$f = \mu m g \tag{29}$$

$$F = \frac{mv^2}{r} \tag{30}$$

$$F = f \tag{31}$$

式中：r——目标轨迹的最小曲线半径，$r = 15\mathrm{m}$；

m——车辆总质量；

g——重力加速度，取 $g = 9.8\mathrm{m/s}^2$。

联立式(29)~式(31)，可求得车辆转弯时极限工况下的极限速度为：$v = 39\mathrm{km/h}$。考虑到车辆纵向速度需要摩擦力提供纵向力以及轮胎为柔性体，其横向扭曲变形会消耗部分摩擦力等因素，故本次仿真试验取其近似的极限速度为 $v = 34\mathrm{km/h}$，最大横向加速度为 $a = 5.95\mathrm{m/s}^2$。在循迹仿真过程中，车辆行驶速度从 0 逐步加速至极限速度并保持该速度继续行驶，直到仿真结束，其循迹仿真结果如图 5 所示。

根据图 5 仿真结果分析可知，在车辆起动过程中，面对速度的快速提升，基于 RBF 神经网络的 PID 控制方法能够更快的保持稳定，且调节过程中出现的最大偏差也小于传统的 PID 控制。在道路曲率变化处及过渡处，传统的 PID 控制为保持控制精度会出现持续的小范围内的振荡，收敛速度慢；而 RBF 神经网络 PID 控制不仅能够快速调节、恢复稳定，且循迹偏差更小。在以极限速度通过最小半径曲线道路时，本文所设计的控制方法其控制效果明显优于传统的 PID 控制，能够快速调节并收敛，不会出现长时间的衰减振荡，也不会出现较大的超调量，且循迹偏差能够保持在 5cm 以内，而传统的 PID 控制在调节过程中的最大误差达到了 8.2cm，稳定后的循迹误差也接近 6.8cm。

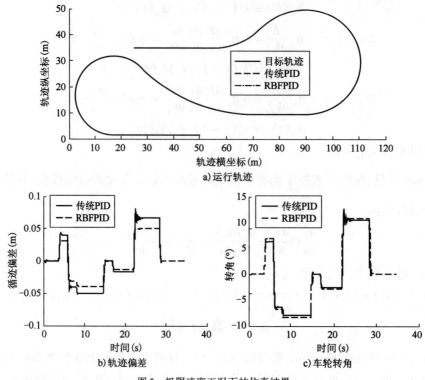

图5 极限速度工况下的仿真结果

3.2 强侧向风干扰下的循迹仿真试验

为了验证在外界持续干扰情况下RBF神经网络PID控制方法调节的稳定性,本次仿真试验将进行加入强侧向风干扰的直线循迹控制研究,侧向风速为90km/h。首先预设一条500m长的直线路段作为目标轨迹,并将路面附着系数设为$\mu=0.8$。本次试验设定车辆在整个循迹仿真过程中的行驶速度为90km/h,车辆沿直线稳定行驶3s后进入强侧向风路段,其仿真结果如图6所示。

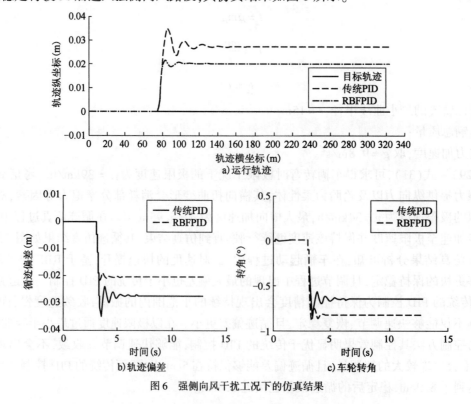

图6 强侧向风干扰工况下的仿真结果

根据图6结果可知,从第3s进入强侧向风路段后,基于RBF神经网络的PID控制经过1.6s的调节之后,已基本达到了稳定状态,调节快速,偏差超调较小,稳定之后的偏移量可控制在2cm左右,而传统的PID控制在第6.5s之后才逐渐进入到稳定状态,调节速度较慢,偏差超调较大,且稳定之后的实际运行轨迹偏离目标轨迹2.7cm左右。相比之下,面对外界的持续干扰,RBF神经网络PID控制能够在较短的时间调节回到稳定状态,且偏差更小,控制精度更高,具有较为优越的控制稳定性和抗干扰能力。

4 结 语

(1)本文设计了一种基于RBF神经网络PID的转向控制器,结合了RBF神经网络和PID控制器的优点来解决四轮转向汽车在循迹过程中所面临的非线性问题,并设计了两种包含特殊工况的目标轨迹,与传统PID控制一起进行了仿真对比试验。

(2)极限速度工况下的仿真试验表明,基于RBF神经网络PID的控制方法面对速度突变、道路曲率突变等非线性问题,能够较快地进行调节,并将循迹误差控制在较小的范围以内,且以极限速度通过最小半径曲线段时,控制效果明显优于传统的PID控制,不会出现超调量过大、调节时间过长等问题。

(3)强侧向风干扰工况下的仿真试验表明,基于RBF神经网络PID的控制方法面对外界的持续干扰,依旧能通过较快的调节恢复到稳定运行状态,并保持较高的控制精度,具有较强的鲁棒性和抗干扰能力。

(4)后续将以非线性问题更为复杂的车辆模型——铰接式客车为研究对象,研究基于RBF神经网络PID的控制方法处理铰接式客车车间干涉和协同转向等非线性问题的能力和效果,使铰接式客车在无人驾驶领域有进一步的应用和发展。

参考文献

[1] 熊璐,杨兴,卓桂荣,等.无人驾驶车辆的运动控制发展现状综述[J].机械工程学报,2020,56(10):127-143.

[2] 任肖红,王琪.分阶数PID控制的四轮转向系统研究[J].机械设计与制造,2020,(2):134-137.

[3] YIBo-liang, BENDER P, BONARENS F, et al. Model predictive trajectory planning for automated driving[J]. IEEE Transactions on Intelligent Vehicles, 2019, 4(1): 24-38.

[4] GHAFFARI S, HOMAEINEZHAD M R. Autonomous path following by fuzzy adaptive curvature-based point selection algorithm for four-wheel-steering car-like mobile robot[J]. Proceedings of the Institution of Mechanical Engineers, Part C: Journal of Mechanical Engineering Science, 2018, 232(15): 2655-2665.

[5] CHEN Ming-zhi, ZHU Da-qi. Real-time path planning for a robot to track a fast moving target based on improved Glasius bio-inspired neural networks[J]. International Journal of Intelligent Robotics and Applications, 2019, 3(2): 186-195.

[6] LI Ming-xing, JIA Ying-min, MATSUNO F. Attenuating diagonal decoupling with robustness for velocity-varying 4WS vehicles[J]. Control Engineering Practice, 2016(56): 49-59.

[7] 张庭芳,张超敏,刘明春,等.基于改进型滑模控制的4WS汽车控制策略研究[J].北京理工大学学报,2017,37(11):1129-1136.

[8] 杨文忠,梁凡,李东昊,等.基于BP神经网络的车辆换道时间预测[J].现代电子技术,2020,43(21):85-88.

[9] HAMID T, SUBHASH R. Path-tracking of autonomous vehicles using a novel adaptive robust exponential-like-sliding-mode fuzzy type-2 neural network controller[J]. Mechanical Systems and Signal Processing, 2019(130): 41-55.

[10] 高琳琳,金立生,郑义,等.四轮转向车辆的径向基函数神经网络复合控制器设计[J].吉林大学学报,2016,46(2):366-372.

[11] 张琨,崔胜民,王剑锋.基于模糊神经网络的智能车辆循迹控制[J].汽车工程,2015,37(1):38-42.

无人驾驶货车编队控制方法综述

鲁果亚[1]　吴问涛[2]　孙怡平[3]　董海霞[4]　文子卿[5]　晏秋[2,6]

(1.西南交通大学茅以升学院；2.西南交通大学交通运输与物流学院；
3.西南交通大学信息科学与技术学院；4.西南交通大学力学与工程学院；
5.西南交通大学数学学院；6.综合交通大数据应用技术国家工程实验室)

摘　要　随着智慧交通系统的发展,无人驾驶货车的编队控制方法成为研究热点。目前,最主要的研究方法有领航者-跟随者法、基于行为法、虚拟结构法、人工势场法等,此外,信息一致性理论和人工鱼群算法的应用也正处于探索阶段。本文分析了几种编队控制方法的主要思想及其在无人驾驶货车领域的应用,并对编队方法的优缺点进行对比分析。在此基础上,提出了无人驾驶货车编队控制理论与应用有待进一步研究的主要问题。

关键词　智慧交通系统　编队控制　无人驾驶货车　人工鱼群算法

0 引　言

随着现代信息技术的飞速发展,智慧交通系统应运而生。2019年9月,中共中央、国务院印发《交通强国建设纲要》,明确要大力发展智慧交通,推动大数据、互联网、人工智能等新技术与交通行业深度融合。2020年8月,《关于开展2020年网络安全技术应用试点示范工作的通知》发布,以满足智能驾驶系统、车联网平台、复杂环境感知、等网络安全需求。

车辆控制系统作为智慧交通系统的子系统,是保障行车安全、扩充道路容量的关键性环节。车辆控制策略是指在运动过程中,各智能车既要保持队形稳定,又要适应环境约束的车路协同控制技术[1]。合适的控制策略可以提高道路车辆密度以及车辆列队的柔性与灵活性,从而大大提高货车列队行驶的效率。

无人驾驶货车编队问题源于机器人领域的多智能体编队问题。围绕该问题,国内外众多学者展开了研究,比较成熟的研究方法有领航者-跟随者法、基于行为法、虚拟结构法、人工势场法等,此外,信息一致性理论和人工鱼群算法也可应用于货车编队,但目前研究尚在探索阶段。本文在我国建设智慧交通系统的背景下,对现有的编队控制方法进行分析,为货车编队控制系统的改进提供思路。

1 主要编队控制方法的分析

1.1 领航者-跟随者法

领航者-跟随者的概念最早由Cruz提出,其后有研究者将其应用于机器人的编队控制,Kumar教授及其团队通过大量的理论和实验研究,提出了控制相对距离不变的l-l编队跟随方式和控制相对距离和偏航角不变的l-φ编队跟随方式,构建了领航者-跟随者法的基本模型。该模型的基本思想是,在整个货车车队中挑选一个或几个领航者,其余车辆作为跟随者。领航车控制整个编队的前进路线,跟随车依据其相对于领航车的距离及方位信息跟随领航车前进,实现编队控制。

记$G_l(x_l,y_l)$为领航车的位置坐标,$G_f(x_f,y_f)$为跟随车的位置坐标,l_x和l_y分别为跟随车与领航车在水平方向和垂直方向上的相对距离,v_{fx}和v_{fy}分别为跟随车在水平方向和垂直方向上的速度。如图1所示,曲线代表车辆行驶轨迹[2]。

四川省交通运输科技项目经费资助(2020-D-03)。

则 t 时刻领航车的位置可表示为：

$$\begin{cases} x_l(t) = v_{x0}t \\ y_l(t) = v_{y0}t \end{cases} \quad (1)$$

式中：v_{x0}、v_{y0}——领航车在水平方向、垂直方向上的初始速度。

理想情况下，跟随车不受任何影响，在水平和垂直两个方向上始终与领航车保持初始距离 l_{x0} 和 l_{y0}，则跟随车位置可以表示为：

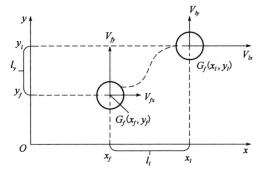

图1 领航者-跟随者法示意图

$$\begin{cases} x_f(t) = v_{x0}t - l_{x0} \\ y_f(t) = v_{y0}t - l_{y0} \end{cases} \quad (2)$$

实际行驶过程中的路面并非理想状态，跟随车的速度会受到随机扰动。用 a_x 和 a_y 分别表示跟随车受到扰动后在水平方向和垂直方向上的加速度，则跟随车的位置重新表示为：

$$\begin{cases} x'_f(t) = x_f(t) + v_{fx}(t)\Delta t + \frac{1}{2}a_x\Delta t^2 \\ y'_f(t) = y_f(t) + v_{fy}(t)\Delta t + \frac{1}{2}a_y\Delta t^2 \end{cases} \quad (3)$$

式中：Δt——扰动加速度维持的时长。

此时跟随车与领航车的相对距离可表示为：

$$\begin{cases} l_x(t) = x_l(t) - x'_f(t) \\ l_y(t) = y_l(t) - y'_f(t) \end{cases} \quad (4)$$

将式（1）和式（3）代入式（4），可得：

$$\begin{cases} l_x(t) = v_{x0}t - x_f(t) - v_{fx}(t)\Delta t - \frac{1}{2}a_x\Delta t^2 \\ l_y(t) = v_{y0}t - y_f(t) - v_{fy}(t)\Delta t - \frac{1}{2}a_y\Delta t^2 \end{cases} \quad (5)$$

由式（5）可知，在受到扰动后，跟随车通过分别控制水平和垂直两个方向上的加速度，可以在一定时间内恢复并保持与领航车的相对距离。

领航者-跟随者法将各车间的追随关系简化成单一两车关系，将控制车队整体简化为控制领航车，在静态环境中，该方法可以较好地保持队形的稳定性。但系统过于依赖领航车，一旦领航车出现故障，就可能引起编队系统的瘫痪，适应能力较弱。针对这个问题，Wei W[3]引入了虚拟领航者的概念。虚拟领航者的存在能够很好地消除真实领航者故障导致系统失控的隐患，大大提高了系统的稳定性。

1.2 基于行为法

基于行为的编队控制策略最早由 Balch 和 Arkin 提出，其核心思想是将整个车队的宏观行为分解成简单的基本行为，再通过局部规则设计以控制车辆的基本子行为，从而实现对车队整体行驶行为的控制。实际编队控制中，每辆车有各自的运动目标，但这些运动目标都由基本的行为方式组成。本文设定的简单基本行为包括：奔向目标行为、保持队形行为、躲避静态障碍物行为以及躲避智能车行为[4]。

（1）奔向目标行为：

$$V_{\text{move-to-goal}} = \frac{1}{\sqrt{(x_g - x_c)^2 + (y_g - y_c)^2}} \begin{bmatrix} x_g - x_c \\ y_g - y_c \end{bmatrix} \quad (6)$$

式中：$[x_g, y_g]^T$——目标点坐标；

$[x_c, y_c]^T$——货车当前位置坐标。

(2) 保持队形行为：

$$V_{\text{keep-formational}} = \frac{1}{\sqrt{(x_{fg} - x_c)^2 + (y_{fg} - y_c)^2}} \begin{bmatrix} x_{fg} - x_c \\ y_{fg} - y_c \end{bmatrix} \tag{7}$$

式中：$[x_{fg}, y_{fg}]^T$——每辆跟随车基于领航车发送的下步位置信息计算出的各自理想目标点坐标。

(3) 躲避静态障碍物行为：

$$V_{\text{avoid-stastic-obstacle-behavior}} = \begin{bmatrix} \cos(\pm(\beta+\alpha)) & -\sin(\pm(\beta+\alpha)) \\ \sin(\pm(\beta+\alpha)) & \cos(\pm(\beta+\alpha)) \end{bmatrix} \begin{bmatrix} x_d \\ y_d \end{bmatrix} \tag{8}$$

式中：$[x_d, y_d]^T$——货车当前运动方向；其中，"±"为根据货车当前运动方向与障碍物的相对关系确定，取 + 表示货车躲避方向为向左转；取 – 表示货车躲避方向为向右转；

β——货车当前运动方向与货车和障碍物连线间的角度；

α——角度裕量。

(4) 躲避智能车行为：

$$V_{\text{avoid-robot}} = \begin{bmatrix} \cos(-\phi) & -\sin(-\phi) \\ \sin(-\phi) & \cos(-\phi) \end{bmatrix} \begin{bmatrix} x_d \\ y_d \end{bmatrix} \tag{9}$$

式中：ϕ——货车偏转角度。

基于行为法的队形反馈比较精确，个体货车的行驶只需接收来自相邻货车的信息，不受智能车数量和规模的限制。但其缺点是很难定义群体行为，无法用数学模型进行精准分析，因此队形保持不够稳定。针对此问题，高强[5]提出可以采用双向虚拟参照点法代替单项法对此控制方法进行改进，并在子行为设计中引入阶梯控制区法，这种方法可以把因货车对自身位置误报而产生的影响降到最小，从而提高队形控制的容错性。

1.3 虚拟结构法

虚拟结构法由 Lewis, M Anthony 等人于 1997 年提出，该方法能够实现高精度的容错运动。此后，Brett J Young 等人将虚拟结构法应用于移动机器人，并提高了编队系统的稳定性。而虚拟车辆的概念最早由 J. Shao 等人提出，并建立了多 Pioneer 3Dx 车辆的编队误差模型。虚拟结构法的基本思想是将编队系统看作是刚性的虚拟结构，而固定在结构上的单个个体可以以一定的自由度改变其方向。队形改变时，系统中的个体直接跟踪虚拟结构上的固定坐标点就可以完成设定好的编队行驶巡检路线。

虚拟结构模型的控制算法是通过货车间的相互通信配合，让所有车辆的行驶状态趋于一致。目标货车 i 的虚拟结构动力学模型如下所示[6]：

$$\begin{pmatrix} \dot{r}_i \\ \dot{v}_i \\ \dot{\theta}_i \\ \dot{\omega}_i \end{pmatrix} = \begin{pmatrix} v_i \\ 0 \\ \omega_i \\ 0 \end{pmatrix} + \begin{pmatrix} 0 & 0 \\ \frac{1}{m_i} & 0 \\ 0 & 0 \\ 0 & \frac{1}{J_i} \end{pmatrix} \begin{pmatrix} f_i \\ \tau_i \end{pmatrix} \tag{10}$$

式中：r_i——目标货车 i 的位置，$r_i \in R^2$；

v_i——其速度，$v_i \in R^2$；

θ_i——其偏转角度，$\theta_i \in R^1$；

ω_i——角速度，$\omega_i \in R^1$；

m_i——虚拟转动质量；

J_i——虚拟转动惯量；

f_i——施加在目标货车 i 上的虚拟力，$f_i \in R^2$；

τ_i——施加在目标货车 i 上的虚拟力矩，$\tau_i \in R^1$。

令 $X_i = [r_i^T, v_i^T, \theta_i, \omega_i]^T$，该式表示目标货车 i 的局部虚拟结构的状态向量，则整个编队的期望状态可定义为 $X^d = [r^{dT}, v^{dT}, \theta^{dT}, \omega^{dT}]^T$。

虚拟结构法能够容易地指定货车群体的行为，降低任务分配的难度，保持编队系统队形整齐，并能实现一些特定的几何队形。同时，各货车之间没有明确的功能划分和相互作用关系，不涉及复杂的通信协议和算法约束，对通信条件要求较低。但它要求编队货车始终保持固定的位置及同步运动关系，缺乏灵活性和适应性。针对此问题，王睿烽[7]等人结合领航者-跟随者法，提出了动态虚拟领航跟随的队形控制方法，提高了跟随车对虚拟领航车跟随行为的灵活性。

1.4 人工势场法

人工势场法由 Khatib 于 1986 年提出。其基本思想是根据使用目的及使用环境构建一个人工虚拟势场，由目标点对车辆产生的引力场和障碍物对车辆产生的斥力场共同组成，运动目标在此人工虚拟势场中受力的作用而运动[8]。

处于位置 q 的目标货车所受引力函数 $U_{\text{att}}(q)$ 为：

$$U_{\text{att}}(q) = \frac{1}{2} \xi \rho_g^2(q) \tag{11}$$

式中：ξ——引力场系数；

ρ_g——目标货车距目标点距离。

位于位置 q 的目标货车所受斥力函数 $U_{\text{rep}}(q)$ 为：

$$U_{\text{rep}}(q) = \begin{cases} \frac{1}{2} \eta \left(\frac{1}{\rho(q)} - \frac{1}{\rho_0} \right)^2 & \rho(q) \leq \rho_0 \\ 0 & \rho(q) > \rho_0 \end{cases} \tag{12}$$

式中：η——斥力场系数；

ρ——目标货车距障碍物距离；

ρ_0——障碍物会对目标货车产生影响的距离。

此时，位于位置 q 的目标货车所受势函数 $U(q)$ 为：

$$U(q) = U_{\text{att}}(q) + U_{\text{rep}}(q) \tag{13}$$

人工势场法是一种反馈控制策略，对传感和控制误差有一定的鲁棒性，有利于编队货车适应周围环境的变化，避障实时性高。在货车编队中，可以运用其局部控制方面的优势简化规划。而其缺点在于，每次队形变化都需要对势场函数重新进行配置，不够灵活。此外，人工势场法还有易陷入局部最优值、零势能点的存在将导致车辆停止运动等缺点。针对此类问题，郜辉等人提出通过增加子目标点的方式，可以使智能体成功逃脱局部极小点，抵达目标点。该方法不仅可以解决局部极小点问题，还可以更快的规划出路径，且规划出的路径更加平滑[9]。

1.5 信息一致性

近年来,信息一致性理论已逐渐开始应用于编队控制、集群运动、姿态同步等领域,仅依靠局部信息交互的一致性算法逐渐成熟。Olfati-Sabe[10]提出了利用信息一致性理论的多智能体编队控制策略框架,给出了拓扑结构为平衡图的平均一致的充要条件。在此基础上,对于具有固定拓扑与切换拓扑的有向加权网络的一致性问题,Ren 和 Beard 指出,当系统拓扑结构中包含有向生成树时,系统才能够达到一致。

一致性是多智能体协同控制中的一个基本问题,其基本思想是借助图论等代数工具,将各智能体的通信数据构成信息流,得到各智能体相对于其他智能体的误差,通过控制此误差来保持所有智能体状态一致。下面尝试介绍一种基于信息一致性的货车编队控制算法[12]。

考虑一个货车编队 N,含有 n 辆无人驾驶货车,控制输入量为 $u_i(t)$。不考虑编队内其他货车,目标货车 i 的控制率修正量 $u(t)_{i1}$ 可表示为:

$$u_{i1}(t) = K_1[\delta_i(t) - h_i(t)] \tag{14}$$

式中:K_1——该情况下的描述函数矩阵;
δ_i——目标货车 i 的状态控制向量;
h_i——目标货车 i 的目标队形在状态空间中的描述。

为了保证队形的稳定性,需要考虑其邻接无人车的状态空间误差和本车状态空间误差之间的差。因此,其中控制率修正量 $u_{i2}(t)$ 可表示为:

$$u_{i2}(t) = K_2 \sum_{j \in N} a_{ij} \{[\delta_j(t) - h_j(t)] - [\delta_i(t) - h_i(t)]\} \tag{15}$$

式中:K_2——该情况下的描述函数矩阵;
a_{ij}——平衡图的加权邻接矩阵的元素;
δ_j——邻接货车 j 的状态控制向量;
h_j——邻接货车 j 的目标队形在状态空间中的描述。

综上,控制率 $u_i'(t)$ 可以表示为:

$$u_i'(t) = u_i(t) + K_1[\delta_i(t) - h_i(t)] + K_2 \sum_{j \in N} a_{ij} \{[\delta_j(t) - h_j(t)] - [\delta_i(t) - h_i(t)]\} \tag{16}$$

此方程即为无人驾驶货车编队行驶的控制协议。

信息一致性理论具有更低的运算成本、更高的智能性等优点,为编队控制提供了一条新思路。在智能交通研究中,通过货车编队缩短车头时距以提高路网效率已经成为共识,但采用信息一致性理论编队时会出现"抖振"问题,货车汇入编队时易发生碰撞。因此,文献[13]提出逐渐压缩队形几何约束来减少间距,实现从松编队到紧编队的过渡,避免碰撞。

1.6 人工鱼群算法

鱼群的避障行为、集群行为、觅食行为等与货车车队的行驶具有一定相似性,因此,一些学者开始考虑将人工鱼群算法引入到货车编队控制算法的设计中。来磊和曲仕茹首先将人工鱼群算法应用到车辆编队控制中,他们采用邻域平均法和改进的人工势场函数构造鱼群模型,提出了一种可实现行驶、避障、队形变换等行为的协同控制对策。人工鱼群算法的主要思想是鱼在运动时,其下一时间的行为受上一时间自身行为、附近鱼的行为以及所处环境影响,且自身行为也反过来影响整体的行进。

假设道路上有 n 辆无人驾驶货车,在鱼群自组织行为模型基础上,结合货车编队的具体受力建模[15]。作用在目标货车 i 上的力可表示如下:

$$m_i a_i = F_{i1}(t) + F_{i2}(t) \tag{17}$$

式中:m_i——目标货车 i 的质量;
a_i——目标货车 i 的加速度;

$F_{i1}(t)$——对齐控制分量；
$F_{i2}(t)$——避障控制分量。

为了保持车队的统一性，行驶过程中，每辆货车需保持与相邻货车一致的方向，即目标货车 i 在 t 时刻的加速度 $a_i(t)$ 是其所有相邻货车 j 在 $t-1$ 时刻的平均加速度，如下式所示：

$$a_i(t) = \frac{1}{n_i(t-1)} \sum_{j \in N_i(t-1)} a_j(t-1) \quad (18)$$

于是，可以得到对齐控制分量 $F_{i1}(t)$：

$$F_{i1}(t) = m_i a_i(i) \quad (19)$$

基于货车的动力学性能方程，目标货车 i 与其相邻货车 j 保证不发生碰撞的极限距离 $R_{ij}(t)$ 为：

$$R_j(t) = \frac{[v_i(t)]^2 - [v_j(t)]^2}{2\mu g} \quad (20)$$

式中：v_i、v_j——目标货车 i 与相邻货车 j 的速度；
　　　μ——摩擦力系数；
　　　g——重力系数。

当 $r_{ij}(t) > R_{ij}(t)$ 时，目标货车 i 受到吸引力 F_{xy}，且 F_{xy} 随着 R_{ij} 的增大而增大；而当 $r_{ij}(t) < R_{ij}(t)$ 时，目标货车 i 受到排斥力 F_{pc}，且 F_{pc} 随着 $R_{ij}(t)$ 减小而增大。

则目标货车 i 与其它货车之间的引力 F_{xy2} 为：

$$F_{xy2}(t) = \frac{r_j(t) - r_i(t)}{\| r_j(t) - r_i(t) \|} m_i A_0 e^{-\frac{s_{ij}(t)}{R_{ij}(t)}} \quad (21)$$

目标货车 i 与其他货车之间的斥力 $F_{pc2}(t)$ 为：

$$F_{pc2}(t) = \frac{r_i(t) - r_j(t)}{\| r_i(t) - r_j(t) \|} m_i A_1 e^{-\frac{s_{ij}(t)}{R_{ij}(t)}} \quad (22)$$

式中：A_0、A_1——引力、斥力的吸引力系数。

避障控制分量 $F_{i2}(t)$ 为：

$$F_{i2}(t) = F_{xy2}(t) + F_{pc2}(t) \quad (23)$$

人工鱼群算法解决无人驾驶货车的编队问题不需要严格的机理模型，只需比较目标函数值，对目标函数性质、参数设定、初值的要求不高，鲁棒性强，且具备并行处理能力和较好的全局寻优能力，能快速跳出局部最优点，对于一些精度要求不高的场合，可以用它快速得到一个可行解。人工鱼群算法的缺点是后期收敛速度慢且受鱼群规模大小的影响。为了改善后期收敛速度慢的问题，Li Guangqiang 等人提出将群体分为两个具有相同大小的子群，对两个子群分别应用不同的适应策略，使一个子群集中在全局搜索上，另一个子群集中在局部搜索上，这种方法能够显著提高算法的收敛效率和优化精度；而对于鱼群规模大小对算法产生的影响，张毅[17]等人提出了一种混合 A*算法和改进人工鱼群算法的新型算法，通过 A*算法得到的次优路径确定人工鱼群的规模，改善人工鱼群规模对算法的影响，提高算法解的质量，并提出基于非线性惯性权重因子 ω 的自适应行为，平衡算法全局优化和局部优化能力，以提高算法的收敛速度和精度。

2 控制方法的优缺点对比

无人驾驶货车编队控制方法对比与分析见表 1。

无人驾驶货车编队控制方法优缺点对比表　　表 1

货车编队控制方法	优　点	缺　点
领航者-跟随者法	(1) 只需控制领航者； (2) 静态环境中的队形稳定； (3) 路径规划明确	(1) 领航者运动过快时，跟随者难以及时跟踪，队形不稳定； (2) 系统过于依赖领航者，鲁棒性较差

续上表

货车编队控制方法	优　点	缺　点
基于行为法	(1) 不受智能车数量的限制； (2) 货车行驶仅需相邻货车的信息	(1) 无法明确定义群体行为，难以用成熟的控制理论对其稳定性、收敛速度等进行分析； (2) 难以保证队形的稳定性
虚拟结构法	(1) 便于队形的保持； (2) 对通信条件要求低	缺乏灵活性和适应性
人工势场法	(1) 局部处理能力强； (2) 实时性高； (3) 对控制和传感误差有一定的鲁棒性	(1) 队形变化时需重新配置势场函数，不够灵活； (2) 易陷入局部最优值； (3) 零势能点的存在将导致车辆停止运动
信息一致性理论	运算代价更低	避障能力差
人工鱼群算法	(1) 对问题的机理模型要求不高； (2) 鲁棒性强； (3) 具备并行处理能力和较好的全局寻优能力	(1) 后期收敛速度慢； (2) 受鱼群规模大小的影响

通过对以上编队控制方法的分析，可得出以下结论：

(1) 目前，对于各种编队控制方法的具体适用场景还没有形成固定的方案，且对于不同的环境，这些方法各有其优劣之处，不具有普适性。因此，在实际应用中，往往不是某种控制方法独立出现，很多情况下是几种方法结合使用，以此改善某方法的特定缺陷。比如，遇障碍时队形的拆分、重建、保持、切换问题，往往是采用基于行为法，但这种方法不能很好地保障编队的稳定性，因此往往结合人工势场法以保障车队运行的安全平稳。

(2) 稳定性与灵活性难以共存。稳定性是行驶安全的保障，而灵活性又是实现各种编队行为的基础，二者缺一不可，而有些控制方法从理论上很难得到保证。例如，领航者-跟随者法、基于行为法具有较强的灵活性但较难保证稳定性，虚拟结构法与人工势场法较为稳定但缺乏灵活性与适应性。对于车路协同系统来说，它的控制策略比单个货车的控制要复杂得多，这不仅仅由于货车数量的增多，更重要的是货车之间还需要协调和协作。如何使二者产生有机结合，有待进一步的研究和探索。

(3) 多数算法对车队的形态默认为一条纵向直线，而在某些特殊情况下，需要智能车实现特定的几何队形，如正方形、菱形或者三角形，此类需求尚未得到满足。例如人工势场法中的车队形状取决于于目标点以及使用环境，领航者-跟随者法则只能实现直线的车队控制，如何满足特殊的队形控制需求，满足柔性编队，需要进一步的研究。

(4) 对无人驾驶货车的编队控制方法多来自机器人编队控制方法的延伸，将货车理想化地视为一个质点，未结合货车的动力学模型，即将系统的速度作为控制输入但忽视了货车的动态模型的不确定性，同时货车间隙的计算公式所得到的间隙与真正的间隙存在偏差，存在一定的局限性。

(5) 货车实际行驶过程中，需要受到交通规则的约束，这里既包括交通标线的静态约束也包括合理避障的动态约束，这些约束给控制器的设计带来了困难。对于满足具体交通规则约束方面的研究，还相对较少。

(6) 在货车实际行驶过程中，会遇到各种各样的特殊情况，使得模型参数发生变化。对于此类不确定性情况，货车既需要及时识别，保持一定的灵敏度，又需要抵抗干扰，保持自身系统的鲁棒性。由于编队控制问题较为复杂，不确定性较大，很少有文献对此类不确定性问题进行处理，但二者之间的关系的处理方式，对于控制器的设计十分重要。

(7) 实际运动中，货车接受的信息量十分巨大，如何对这些信息进行筛选排除将直接影响控制器作出决策的速度,因此,我们需要的不仅仅是快速收敛的算法,计算速度快的硬件保障以及信息排查都是不可忽视的环节。

(8)编队过程中的信息传递、通信保障也十分重要,我们期望用尽量少的信息量完成设定的编队任务。因此,不同通信协议、信息传递方式将对编队行为产生何种影响,也是未来研究的方向。

3 结 语

货车编队控制技术作为智慧交通系统中的一个重要技术热点,其应用可以在很大程度上提高货车车队韧性,从而达到保障行驶安全,提高运输效率的目的,因此研究其编队控制方法具有重要意义。本文对主流编队控制方法进行了对比与分析,特别是将正处于探索阶段的信息一致性理论和人工鱼群算法在编队领域的应用性纳入总结范围,在此基础上提出有待进一步研究的问题与研究方向。相信在将来的研究中,通过理论和实践相结合,无人驾驶货车编队控制方法的研究将获得更大的突破,为智慧交通系统建设提供技术支撑。

参考文献

[1] 曹伟,孙明. 基于迭代学习的部分非正则多智能体编队控制[J]. 控制与决策,2018,33(9):1619-1624.
[2] 张浪,牛彦杰,刘正男. 基于领航—跟随法的无人车编队控制研究[C]// 第八届中国指挥控制大会论文集,2020.
[3] Wei W. A new formation control strategy based on the virtual-leader-follower and artificial potential field [C]// 2019 34rd Youth Academic Annual Conference of Chinese Association of Automation(YAC). IEEE, 2019.
[4] 雷艳敏,冯志彬,宋继红. 基于行为的多机器人编队控制的仿真研究[J]. 长春大学学报,2008,18(8):40-44.
[5] 高强,庞毅,吕东灏. 基于行为的多机器人队形控制仿真研究[J]. 自动化与仪表,2012,27(8):14-17.
[6] 何真,陆宇平,刘燕斌. 基于虚拟结构的分布式编队控制方法[J]. 应用科学学报,2007,25(4):387-391.
[7] 王睿烽. 复杂环境下的多无人直驱纯电动汽车编队控制研究[D]. 南京:东南大学,2017.
[8] 姚远. 基于改进人工势场的多无人机三维避障研究法[J]. 电子世界,2020(14):99-103.
[9] 郜辉,吕志刚. 人工势场法目标不可达的研究[J]. 国外电子测量技术,2018,37(1):29-33.
[10] Olfati-Saber R, Murray R M. Consensus problems in networks of agents with switching topology and time-delays[J]. IEEE Transactions on Automatic Control, 2004, 49(9):1520-1533.
[11] Ren W, Beard R W. Consensus seeking in multiagent systems under dynamically changing interaction topologies[J]. IEEE Transactions on Automatic Control, 2005, 50(5):655-661.
[12] 王超瑞. 基于信息一致性理论的无人机编队控制算法研究[D]. 哈尔滨:哈尔滨工业大学,2017.
[13] 朱旭,张逊逊,尤谨语等. 基于信息一致性的无人机紧密编队集结控制[J]. 航空学报,2015,36(12):3919-3929.
[14] 来磊,曲仕茹. 基于鱼群效应的多车协同行驶控制方法[J]. 西北工业大学学报,2012,30(03):373-377.
[15] 田大新,康璐. 基于鱼群效应的无人驾驶车辆编队算法研究[J]. 无人系统技术,2018,1(4):62-67.
[16] Li G Q, Yang Y W. Zhao F Q, et al. Parallel Adaptive Artificial Fish Swarm Algorithm Based on Differential Evolution[J]. Proceedings2016 9th International Symposium on Computational Intelligence and Design, 2016,(1):269-273.
[17] 张毅,杨光辉,花远红. 基于改进人工鱼群算法的机器人路径规划[J]. 控制工程,2020,27(7):1157-1163.

A Model with Time Windows for Share-A-Ride Problems

Min Zhang[1]　Jing Xue[2]　Kaijun Zhou[2]　Shuguang Hou[1]

(1. Nanjing Tech University, College of Transportation Science & Engineering;
2. Nanjing University of Posts and Telecommunications, School of Computer Science)

Abstract　This paper introduces a new model of a public transportation system in cities that allows sharing a taxi between one passenger and parcels with speed windows consideration. The model contains many real-life case features and is presented by a mathematical formulation. Different speed windows induce the dynamic graph model for road networks and make the problem much more difficult to solve. There are 2 steps to solve the problem. Step 1 is to handle parcels requests and planning and scheduling for parcels. Step 2 starts from a given route for handling parcels requests and inserts a unique passenger request into this route. We propose an Improved Ant Colony Optimization algorithm(IACO) and a greedy solution to resolve the Share-a-Ride Problem (SARP). The obtained numerical results provide valuable insights into successfully implementing a taxi sharing service.

Keywords　Passengers and parcels sharing　Share-a-ride　Improved ant colony Optimization algorithm　Time windows

0　Introduction

In common transportation systems, passengers and parcels requests are served separately because of their different characteristics. This significantly increases the operation costs and causes many social problems such as traffic jams and the environmental pollution. In most cities, parcels usually have small dimensions and low weights so that they can be transferred along with passengers without significantly affecting the private space and the comfortability. One of the biggest challenges while considering the share-a-ride problem between passengers is the privacy, comfortability and the security of passengers. Usually, passengers have different requirements and objectives such as the traveling time, the private space, etc. These induce the model of sharing between different passengers inapplicable in the real-life situation. Therefore, we propose an applicable share-a-ride model between a unique passenger and parcels. In respect of setting the highest priority for the passenger and lower priorities for parcels, the passenger is delivered directly without any interruption for other pickup or delivery stops.

In step1, we develop model 1, considering difference to due date, split loads, speed windows and time window constraints. We consider the trade-off between two objective functions. In step 2, we develop model 2, which starts from a given route for handling parcels requests and inserts a unique passenger request into this route. To resolve the SARP, we propose IACO.

From a city perspective, this system has a potential to alleviate urban congestion and environmental pollution. From the perspective of a taxi company, new benefits from the parcel delivery service can be obtained.

In the research community, our problem is classified as a SARP which is a generalization of the Taxi Routing Problem family. A reduced problem based on the SARP is proposed(Baoxiang Li et al., 2014), and the work is extended on a people and parcel share-a-ride taxis transportation model (Nguyen Van Son et al., 2017).

Some algorithms are proposed to solve SARP, e.g. an adaptive large neighborhood search heuristic (Baoxiang Li et al., 2015 & 2016, Nguyen Van Son et al., 2019, Zixuan Peng et al., 2021), a simulated annealing (SA) algorithm (Vincent F. Yu et al., 2018), a novel dynamic programming (DP) algorithm (Yongxin Tong et al., 2018), and a greedy algorithm (Yongxin Tong et al., 2018, Phan-Thuan Do et al., 2018).

Although a larger fleet size reduces waiting time, it also intensifies congestion, which, in turn, prolongs the total travel time. Such congestion effect is so significant that it is nearly insensitive to passengers' willingness to share and flexible supply (Caio Vitor Beojone & Nikolas Geroliminis., 2021).

1 Model 1

1.1 Constants

Q_i: the demand/supply of node i for parcels

V: Set of taxis

D: Set of delivery nodes of parcels

S: Set of pickup nodes of parcels

$N = S \cup D$

$O = \{0\}$: The virtual node

C^V: Carrying capacity of taxi v

E_s^v: The earliest possible time to start loading at node $s(s \in S)$ on the first visit by taxi v

H^v: Set of numbers of possible speed of taxi v

$l^{v,h}$: The h^{-th} possible speed of taxi v

$l_{\min}^v$: The minimal speed of taxi v, $l_{\min}^v = \min\{l^{v,h}\}$

G_{ij}: Distance between nodes i and j

t_1: Loading time per unit

t_2: Unloading time per unit

$u_{\max}^v$: Maximum possible number of visits by taxi v

U^v: Set of possible visits by taxi v

Y_i: Set of days during which loading/unloading is available at node i

$[a_{i,r}, b_{i,r}]$: Time window of node i on the r^{-th} day

$q_{i,r}$: Accumulated time it is not available for loading/unloading before the earliest possible time to start on the r^{-th} day at node i

B: A large positive number

λ: A parameter that represents required load factor, with $0 \leq \lambda \leq 1$

T: Predetermined planning horizon, for instance, 10 days

1.2 Variables

$t_i^{u,v}$: Start time for loading/unloading at node i by taxi v on its u^{-th} visit

$w_i^{u,v}$: Number of parcels unloaded at node i by taxi v on its u^{-th} visit

$x_i^{u,v}$: Number of parcels transported by taxi v to destinations before reaching the node i or returning to the virtual node during its u^{-th} visit

$x_s^{u,v}$: Number of parcels loaded by taxi v at node s on its u^{-th} visit

$$I_{i,r}^{1,u,v} = \begin{cases} 1 & \text{if vehicle } v \text{ starts loading/unloading at node } i \text{ on the } r^{-th} \text{ day on its } u^{-th} \text{ visit} \\ 0 & \text{otherwise} \end{cases}$$

$$I_{i,r}^{1,u,v} = \begin{cases} 1 & \text{if vehicle } v \text{ finishes loading/unlaoding at node } i \text{ on the } s^{-th} \text{ day on its } u^{-th} \text{ visit} \\ 0 & \text{otherwise} \end{cases}$$

$$y_{ij}^{u,v,h} = \begin{cases} 1 & \text{if taxi } v \text{ visits node } j \text{ directly from node } i \text{ at the } h^{-th} \text{ speed on its } u^{-th} \text{ visit} \\ 0 & \text{otherwise} \end{cases}$$

Model 1 is set up to determine routes and schedules for parcels transportation during the planning horizon, for instance, 10 days, in which all parcels requests must be served. Carrying capacity of taxis can be different. Some taxis may be not available at the beginning of the planning horizon. Split delivery, changeable speeds, and waiting time are considered to satisfy time windows of nodes. Loading/Unloading time and load factor are calculated to ensure efficiency.

1.3 Objective Functions

Generally, minimization of differences to due date is considered inscheduling and routing problem. Therefore, we set an objective function to minimize the total difference to due date.

$$F_1 = \sum_{v \in V} \sum_{u \in U^v} \sum_{i \in D} t_i^{u,v} - \sum_{v \in V} \sum_{u \in U^v} \sum_{i \in D} \sum_{r \in Y_i} a_{i,r} I_{i,r}^{1,u,v} \quad (1)$$

Lately, speed reduction has become a very popular operational measure to reduce fuel consumption and can obviously to be used to curb CO_2 emissions. Therefore, we propose an objective function to minimize speeds for transportation.

$$F_2 = \sum_{v \in V} \sum_{u \in U^v} \sum_{h \in H^v} \sum_{i \in NO} \sum_{j \in NO-\{i\}} y_{ij}^{u,v,h} (l^{v,h} - l_{\min}^v) \quad (2)$$

$l^{v,h}$ and $l_{\min}^v$ are constants. For instance, there are 3 possible speeds of taxi 1. $l^{1,1}=50, l^{1,2}=45, l^{1,3}=40$, $l_{\min}^v = \min\{50,45,40\} = 40$. This objective function is a variant of speed penalty. For all taxis, if the minimal speeds are always used on all visits, the value of F_2 will become zero. Otherwise, the value of F_2 will be positive.

1.4 Constraints

(1) Constraints with respect to taxi scheduling:

$$\sum_{h \in H^v} \sum_{j \in D} y_{ij}^{u,v,h} = \sum_{r \in Y_i} I_{i,r}^{1,u,v} \quad (v \in V, u \in U^v, i \in S) \quad (3)$$

$$\sum_{h \in H^v} \sum_{j \in DO-\{i\}} y_{ij}^{u,v,h} = \sum_{r \in Y_i} I_{i,r}^{1,u,v} \quad (v \in V, u \in U^v, i \in D) \quad (4)$$

$$\sum_{i \in S} \sum_{r \in Y_i} I_{i,r}^{1,u+1,v} \leq \sum_{i \in S} \sum_{r \in Y_i} I_{i,r}^{1,u,v} \quad (v \in V, u \in U^v - \{u_{\max}^v\}) \quad (5)$$

$$\sum_{r \in Y_i} I_{i,r}^{1,u,v} = \sum_{p \in Y_i} I_{i,p}^{2,u,v} \quad (v \in V, u \in U^v, i \in N) \quad (6)$$

$$t_j^{u,v} + T(1 - \sum_{i \in S} \sum_{h \in H^v} y_{ij}^{u,v,h}) \geq \sum_{i \in S} t_i^{u,v} + \sum_{j \in D} w_j^{u,v} t_1 + \sum_{i \in S} \sum_{p \in Y_{i,p}} q_{i,p} I_{i,p}^{2,u,v} - \sum_{i \in S} \sum_{r \in Y_i} q_{i,r} I_{i,r}^{1,u,v} + \sum_{i \in S} \sum_{h \in H^v} (G_{ij} y_{ij}^{u,v,h}/l^{v,h})$$

$$(v \in V, u \in U^v, j \in D) \quad (7)$$

$$t_i^{u+1,v} + B(1 - \sum_{r \in Y_i} I_{i,r}^{1,u+1,v}) \geq t_j^{u,v} + w_j^{u,v} t_2 + \sum_{p \in Y_j} q_{j,p} I_{j,p}^{2,u,v} - \sum_{r \in Y_j} q_{j,r} I_{j,r}^{1,u,v} + \sum_{h \in H^v} (G_{ji} y_{ji}^{u,v,h}/l^{v,h})$$

$$(v \in V, u \in U^v - \{u_{\max}^v\}, i \in S, j \in D) \quad (8)$$

$$t_j^{u,v} + T(1 - \sum_{h \in H^v} y_{ij}^{u,v,h}) \geq t_i^{u,v} + w_i^{u,v} t_2 + \sum_{p \in Y_i} q_{i,p} I_{i,p}^{2,u,v} - \sum_{r \in Y_i} q_{i,r} I_{i,r}^{1,u,v} + \sum_{h \in H^v} (G_{ij} y_{ij}^{u,v,h} / l^{v,h})$$
$$(v \in V, u \in U^v, i \in D, j \in D - \{i\}) \quad (9)$$

Constraints (3) ~ (6) fix the original and destination nodes of taxis. For example, if the first visit of taxi 2 doesn't exist, the second visit will not exist. If taxi 2 arrives at node 4, it must leave too. Constraints (7) ~ (9) compute the travel times and loads of taxis, with time windows, loading/unloading time and changeable speeds under consideration.

(2) Constraints with respect to time windows:

$$t_i^{1,v} \geq \sum_{h \in H^v} \sum_{j \in D} E_i^v y_{ij}^{1,v,h} \quad (v \in V, i \in S) \quad (10)$$

$$t_i^{u,v} \geq \sum_{r \in Y_i} a_{i,r} I_{i,r}^{1,u,v} \quad (v \in V, u \in U^v, i \in N) \quad (11)$$

$$t_i^{u,v} \leq \sum_{r \in Y_i} b_{i,r} I_{i,r}^{1,u,v} \quad (v \in V, u \in U^v, i \in N) \quad (12)$$

$$\sum_{i \in S} t_i^{u,v} + \sum_{j \in D} w_j^{u,v} t_1 + \sum_{i \in S} \sum_{p \in Y_i} q_{i,p} I_{i,p}^{2,u,v} - \sum_{i \in S} \sum_{r \in Y_i} q_{i,r} I_{i,r}^{1,u,v} \geq \sum_{i \in S} \sum_{p \in Y_i} a_{i,p} I_{i,p}^{2,u,v} \quad (v \in V, u \in U^v) \quad (13)$$

$$\sum_{i \in S} t_i^{u,v} + \sum_{j \in D} w_j^{u,v} t_1 + \sum_{i \in S} \sum_{p \in Y_i} q_{i,p} I_{i,p}^{2,u,v} - \sum_{i \in S} \sum_{r \in Y_i} q_{i,r} I_{i,r}^{1,u,v} \leq \sum_{i \in S} \sum_{p \in Y_i} b_{i,p} I_{i,p}^{2,u,v} \quad (v \in V, u \in U^v) \quad (14)$$

$$t_j^{u,v} + w_j^{u,v} t_2 + \sum_{p \in Y_j} q_{j,p} I_{j,p}^{2,u,v} - \sum_{r \in Y_j} q_{j,r} I_{j,r}^{1,u,v} \geq \sum_{p \in Y_j} a_{j,p} I_{j,p}^{2,u,v} \quad (v \in V, u \in U^v, j \in D) \quad (15)$$

$$t_j^{u,v} + w_j^{u,v} t_2 + \sum_{p \in Y_j} q_{j,p} I_{j,p}^{2,u,v} - \sum_{r \in Y_j} q_{j,r} I_{j,r}^{1,u,v} \leq \sum_{s \in Y_j} b_{j,s} I_{j,s}^{2,u,v} \quad (v \in V, u \in U^v, j \in D) \quad (16)$$

Some taxis may be not available at the beginning of the planning horizon as defined in constraints (10). Some taxis still carry out tasks of the last planning horizon when the current planning horizon starts. Constraints (11) and (12) ensure that each node has a time window within which it must be served. For instance, loading at node 1 is available between 8 a.m. and 8 p.m. from Monday to Friday, between 8 a.m. and 2 p.m. on Saturday, and not available on Sunday. Waiting time and loading/unloading times are accounted for when taxis start services at nodes are calculated in constraints (13) ~ (16). Loading/Unloading time can't be ignored in many real-life situations. Waiting time exists because of time windows of nodes.

(3) Constraints with respect to taxi route and capacity:

$$\sum_{h \in H^v} \sum_{j \in D} y_{ij}^{u,v,h} = \sum_{h \in H^v} y_{0i}^{u,v,h} \quad (v \in V, u \in U^v, i \in S) \quad (17)$$

$$\sum_{h \in H^v} \sum_{i \in N - \{j\}} y_{ij}^{u,v,h} = \sum_{h \in H^v} \sum_{m \in DO - \{j\}} y_{jm}^{u,v,h} \quad (v \in V, u \in U^v, j \in D) \quad (18)$$

$$B \sum_{h \in H^v} \sum_{i \in S} y_{ij}^{u,v,h} \geq \sum_{h \in H^v} \sum_{m \in D - \{j\}} y_{jm}^{u,v,h} \quad (v \in V, u \in U^v, j \in D) \quad (19)$$

$$\sum_{s \in Y_i} I_{i,s}^{2,u,v} \leq 1 \quad (v \in V, u \in U^v, i \in NO) \quad (20)$$

$$\sum_{v \in V} \sum_{u \in U^v} w_i^{u,v} = Q_i \quad (i \in D) \quad (21)$$

$$\sum_{i \in D} Q_i = \sum_{j \in S} Q_j \quad (22)$$

$$x_0^{u,v} = \sum_{i \in D} w_i^{u,v} \quad (v \in V, u \in U^v) \quad (23)$$

$$\sum_{v \in V} \sum_{u \in U^v} x_j^{u,v} = Q_j \quad (j \in S) \quad (24)$$

$$x_0^{u,v} \geq \sum_{i \in S} \sum_{r \in Y_i} \lambda C^v I_{i,r}^{1,u,v} \quad (v \in V, u \in U^v) \quad (25)$$

$$x_j^{u,v} + C^v(1 - \sum_{h \in H^v} y_{0j}^{u,v,h}) \geq x_0^{u,v} \quad (v \in V, u \in U^v, j \in S) \tag{26}$$

$$x_j^{u,v} + C^v(1 - \sum_{h \in H^v} y_{ij}^{u,v,h}) \geq x_i^{u,v} + w_i^{u,v} \quad (v \in V, u \in U^v, i \in D, j \in DO - \{i\}) \tag{27}$$

$$x_0^{u,v} + C^v(1 - \sum_{h \in H^v} y_{0j}^{u,v,h}) \geq x_i^{u,v} \quad (v \in V, u \in U^v, j \in S) \tag{28}$$

$$x_j^{u,v} \leq \sum_{h \in H^v} C^v y_{0j}^{u,v,h} \quad (v \in V, u \in U^v, j \in S) \tag{29}$$

$$x_j^{u,v} \leq C^v(1 - \sum_{h \in H^v} \sum_{i \in S} y_{ij}^{u,v,h}) \quad (v \in V, u \in U^v, j \in D) \tag{30}$$

Constraints (17) ~ (20) ensure that each node can be visited more than once if necessary. That is to say, split delivery can be allowed. All parcels must be transported as defined in constraints (21) ~ (24). We suppose that the fleet of taxis can satisfy all requests of parcels. Constraints (25) ~ (30) ensure that one taxi can begin its transportation from the nodes more than once if necessary. In reality, taxis often cruise, taking more than one visit.

(4) Binary and non-negative constraints:

$$I_{i,r}^{1,u,v}, I_{i,r}^{2,u,v}, y_{ij}^{u,v,h}: 0-1 \ variables \tag{31}$$

$$t_i^{u,v}, w_i^{u,v}, x_i^{u,v} \geq 0 \tag{32}$$

2 Model 2

We set up model 1, considering split delivery, changeable speeds, load factor, time windows and etc. All parcels must make a reservation in advance, and the decision system make routes and schedules for the planning horizon. Different from parcels, each passenger must make an actual time order and be served immediately. Then we set up model 2, in which all passenger requests must be served. We insert passengers into the predetermined routes and schedules in model 1.

We propose an applicable share-a-ride model between a unique passenger and parcels. In respect of setting the highest priority for the passenger and lower priorities for parcels, in model 2, the passenger is always delivered directly without any interruption for other pickup or delivery stops. Thereby, for a scheduled parcel, the following scenarios are permitted: (1) collected and dropped before picking the passenger up; (2) collected and dropped after delivering the passenger; (3) collected before picking the passenger up and dropped after delivering the passenger.

2.1 Objective Function

Extra benefits of passenger transportation are usually considered when we insert one passenger into predetermined routes and schedules. Therefore, we propose an objective function to maximize extra benefits for passenger transportation in model 2.

$$F_3 = \delta_1 \sum_{z \in Z} G_{z^p z^d} - \delta_2 \sum_{v \in V} \sum_{u \in U^v} \sum_{h \in H^v} \sum_{z \in Z} \sum_{j \in NO} \sum_{m \in N-\{j\}} (y_{jz^p}^{u,v,h} G_{jz^p} + G_{z^p z^d} + y_{z^d m}^{u,v,h} G_{z^d m} - G^{u,v}) \tag{33}$$

Z is the set of passengers.

z^p is the pickup node of passenger z, and z^d means the delivery node of passenger z.

δ_1 represents the extra transportation revenue per km for each taxi.

δ_2 represents the extra transportation cost per km for each taxi.

$G^{u,v}$ is the total route length of taxi v on its u^{-th} visit, calculated by model 1.

2.2 Constraints

In model 2, when the decision system received an actual time reservation from a passenger, it must decide which taxi to carry the passenger. Then the designed taxi must serve the passenger immediately. Pre-process function is needed, in which we make sure that the values of objective functions F_1 and F_2 will not change no matter we insert one passenger into one visit of a taxi or not. Therefore, if we receive an actual time order from a passenger, we must make sure that extra transportation time of passengers is less than $\rho_{jm}^{u,v}$ (spare time before leaving node j for node m on the designed taxi v's u^{-th} visit, calculated by model 1). i.e.,

$$\sum_{h \in H^v} \sum_{z \in Z} [y_{jz^p}^{u,v,h} G_{jz^p}/l^{v,h} + y_{z^p z^d}^{u,v,h} G_{z^p z^d}/l^{v,h} + y_{z^d m}^{u,v,h} G_{z^d m}/l^{v,h}] \leq \rho_{jm}^{u,v} \quad (v \in V, u \in U^v, j \in NO, m \in N - \{j\}) \quad (34)$$

$$\sum_{h \in H^v} \sum_{m \in D} y_{z^d m}^{u,v,h} = \sum_{h \in H^v} \sum_{j \in D - \{m\}} y_{jz^p}^{u,v,h} \quad (v \in V, u \in U^v, z \in Z) \quad (35)$$

$$\sum_{h \in H^v} \sum_{m \in S} y_{z^d m}^{u,v,h} = \sum_{h \in H^v} y_{0z^p}^{u,v,h} \quad (v \in V, u \in U^v, z \in Z) \quad (36)$$

$$\sum_{h \in H^v} \sum_{m \in D} y_{z^d m}^{u,v,h} = \sum_{h \in H^v} \sum_{j \in S} y_{jz^p}^{u,v,h} \quad (v \in V, u \in U^v, z \in Z) \quad (37)$$

$$\sum_{h \in H^v} \sum_{m \in N} y_{z^d m}^{u,v,h} = \sum_{h \in H^v} y_{z^p z^d}^{u,v,h} \quad (v \in V, u \in U^v, z \in Z) \quad (38)$$

$$\sum_{v \in V} \sum_{u \in U^v} \sum_{z \in Z} \sum_{h \in H^v} y_{z^p z^d}^{u,v,h} = 1 \quad (39)$$

Constraints(34) ensure that inserting a passenger into one visit of a taxi still satisfy time windows of nodes. For a scheduled parcel, the following scenarios are permitted: ① collected and dropped before picking the passenger up, shown in constraints(35); ② collected and dropped after delivering the passenger, shown in constraints(36); ③ collected before picking the passenger up and dropped after delivering the passenger, shown in constraints(37). Constraints(38)(39) make sure that all passengers must be served. We suppose that the fleet of taxis can satisfy all requests of passengers.

3 Algorithm 1

We propose IACO to obtain some Pareto-optimal solutions for the multi-objective model 1.

3.1 Selection Mechanism

There are many groups of ants. Each group only includes one kind of taxi. For instance, in group $K = \{1, 2, \cdots, k, \cdots\}$, all ants share the same pheromone.

To select the next ant k, we use the following equation.

$$p_k = \frac{(\omega_k)^\sigma \times \max[(\tau_{i,j,k})^\alpha]}{\sum_{c=1}^{m} \{(\omega_c)^\sigma \times \max[(\tau_{i,j,c})^\alpha]\}} \quad (k \in K) \quad (40)$$

Where m means the number of ants. ω_k is the capacity of ant k, and parameter $\sigma(\sigma>0)$ establishes the importance of carrying capacity.

Where $\tau_{i,j,k}$ is defined as pheromone which is shared by ant k on the arc between node i and j. Parameter α ($\alpha>0$) establishes the importance of the pheromone.

To select the next node j, ant k uses the following equation.

$$\begin{cases} \arg\max[(\tau_{i,u,k})^\alpha \times (\eta_{i,u})^\beta \times (\sigma_{i,u})^\xi] (u \notin Tabu) & q < q_0 \\ p_{i,u} & q \geq q_0 \end{cases} \quad (41)$$

q is a uniform random number in the range $[0,1]$, and q_0 is a constant. $\eta_{i,u}$ is defined as the inverse of the waiting time between node i and u. $\sigma_{i,u}$ is defined as the inverse of the speed penalty. Parameter $\beta(\beta>1)$ establishes the importance of the waiting time. Parameter $\xi(\xi>0)$ establishes the importance of the speed penalty.

Where

$$p_{i,u} = \begin{cases} \dfrac{(\tau_{i,u,k})^\alpha \times (\eta_{i,u})^\beta \times (\sigma_{i,u})^\xi}{\sum_{j \notin tabu}[(\tau_{i,j,k})^\alpha \times (\eta_{i,j})^\beta \times (\sigma_{i,u})^\xi]} & u \notin tabu \\ 0 & \text{otherwise} \end{cases} \quad (42)$$

To select the speed, we use the mechanism to select the speed.

$$P_h = \frac{\psi_{h,k}}{\sum_{h=1}^{H}[(\psi_{h,k})^\alpha]} \quad (k \in K) \quad (43)$$

$\psi_{h,k}$ is defined as another pheromone which is shared by ant k.

3.2 Updating Information

When ant k visits an arc with a speed, the pheromone on the arc and the pheromone of the speed is updated with the following equation.

$$\tau_{i,j,k} = (1-\mu)\tau_{i,j,k} + \mu\tau_0 \quad (44)$$

Where $\mu(0<\mu<1)$ is a parameter that decides the speed of evaporation, τ_0 is defined as an initial pheromone value assigned to all arcs and ψ_0 is defined as an initial pheromone value assigned to all speeds.

Considering time windows, we update the pheromone on the arc (i,j) and the pheromone of the speed that are deleted due to time windows as follows:

$$\tau_{i,j,k} = (1-\mu)\tau_{i,j,k} \quad (45)$$

After a predetermined number of ants construct a feasible route, global trail updating is performed by adding pheromone to the best visit.

$$\tau_{i,j,k} = (1-\gamma)\tau_{i,j,k} + \gamma L^{-1} \quad (46)$$

$\psi_{h,k}$ is updated in the same way as $\tau_{i,j,k}$.

Where $\gamma(0<\gamma<1)$ is a parameter that controls the speed of evaporation. L is equal to the value of objective function F_1 or F_2.

4 Algorithm 2

As shown in model 2, when the decision system receives an actual time reservation from a passenger, it must decide which taxi to carry the passenger. Then the designed taxi must serve the passenger immediately. Pre-process function is needed, in which we make sure that the values of objective function (1) and (2) will not change no matter we insert one passenger into one visit of a taxi or not. Therefore, if we receive an actual time order from a passenger on day r, we must make sure that extra transportation time of passengers is less than the spare time.

For example, suppose that taxi2 is leaving delivery node 5 for delivery node 3 at its first speed $l^{2,1}$ on its first visit when the decision system receives an actual-time reservation from passenger $z(z \in Z)$. And unloading at node 3 and 5 starts and finishes on the same day without waiting.

Then the spare time $\rho_{jm}^{u,v} = \rho_{53}^{1,2} = t_3^{1,2} - t_5^{1,2} - w_5^{1,2} t_2$, which can be calculated directly from output data in model 1. Considering the spare time of each taxi, we list all usable taxis for choosing. Then we use a greedy solution to choose an appropriate taxi, which always maximize extra benefits according to F_3.

5 Numerical Example

5.1 Input Data

In this case, there are 4 pickup nodes and 20 delivery nodes of parcels, 10 pickup/delivery nodes of passengers, and 5 taxis.

A location on Fig. 1 is represented by a pair of numbers in range of $[-500, 500]$. For the simplicity, we converted geometry nodes (longitude, latitude) into Cartesian coordinate nodes. We use Haversine formula to calculate the distance of each edge of geometry nodes (longitude, latitude).

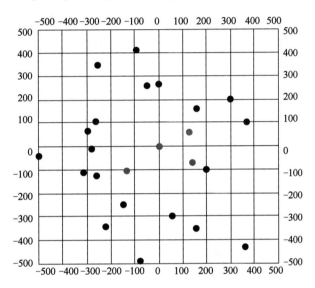

Fig. 1 Coordinates of the locations (km)

In real road map, roads are represented by some continuous straight lights. Hence, a node on a road is considered as a connecting node if it is neither a stop nor an intersection. We consider only connecting nodes to reduce the map. For each 2-degree node that are not pick-up or delivery nodes, we remove this node and then connect its two neighbor nodes by a new edge with the same distance. This step helps to reduce the redundancy nodes without affection to the technique of routing finding in Fig. 1. The planning horizon lasts for 10 days, starting from Monday.

Loading at node 1 is available between 8 a.m. and 8 p.m. from Monday to Friday, between 8 a.m. and 2 p.m. on Saturday, and not available on Sunday. In this paper, we can set working times and days off by assigning time windows. The time window of node 2, 3, 4 is the same as that of node 1.

Unloading is available at each node for two days. The required parcels will be accepted and unloaded within the two-day specified time window of the node. If a taxi arrives at the node ahead of its schedule, it will wait until the node is ready to unload it.

5.2 Output Data

We can obtain the following Pareto-optimal solutions using IACO. We implement the algorithm and greedy solution on a personal computer with Intel Core is i5-5200U CPU @ 2.20GHz 2.19GHz and Windows 10 operating system.

However, as shown in Tab. 1, average time of calculation increases too fast by Lingo. We propose IACO to make schedules and routes for parcels before the planning horizon starts. We can obtain Pareto-optimal solutions for the above SARP problem within a reasonable time frame, while no feasible solution has been found for this problem after using Lingo for 120 hours.

Sensitivity Analysis with Different Nodes and Taxis   Tab. 1

Pickup/Delivery nodes of parcels	Taxis	Pickup/Delivery nodes of passengers	Average time of calculation (hr) by Lingo	Average time of calculation (sec) by IACO
1,3	1	2	1.6	2.5
2,7	3	3	4.3	10.7
3,14	4	6	21.7	35.1
4,20	5	10,10	>120	<120

The efficiency of our algorithm and solution proposed to determine the transport routes and schedules of transportation with time windows and split delivery in changeable speeds considering multi-objective functions is shown in Tab. 2.

The Characteristics of Solutions   Tab. 2

Algorithm	The total difference to due date (F_1)	The speed penalty (F_2)	The extra benefits (F_3)	SD	CS	Time of calculation (sec)
IACO + Greedy solution	35.3 (minimal)	340	159.3	○	○	114.2
	406.8	50 (minimal)	860.5	○	○	103.5
	219.3	80	570.4	○	○	104.6
	171.9	200	391.2	○	○	104.7

○: Indicates that it happened in the solution.

In Tab. 2, we can see the trade-off between three objective functions. With higher value of the total difference to due date, which results in lower customer satisfaction, taxis trend to reduce speed to avoid speed penalty, such as more fuel consumption, more CO_2 emissions. In this situation, the extra benefits trend to be higher because we can list more taxis for choosing to carry passengers. Split delivery and changeable speeds happen in all solutions, showing the importance of considering them.

6 Conclusions

We set up 0-1 integer programming model 1 and 2 to solve the SARP problem. Model 1 contain many real-life case features, such as split delivery, changeable speed, load ratio, and time windows. However, as shown in Tab. 1, time of calculation increases too fast by Lingo. We propose IACO to make schedules and routes for parcels before the planning horizon starts.

In model 2, when the decision system received an actual time reservation from a passenger, it must decide which taxi to carry the passenger. Then the designed taxi must serve the passenger immediately. Considering the spare time of each taxi, we list all usable taxis for choosing. Then we use a greedy solution to choose an appropriate taxi, which always maximize extra benefits at the moment. The time for calculations in Tab. 2 demonstrates that we can make enough Pareto-optimal solutions to make decisions on schedules and routes for all parcels and passengers.

In Tab. 2, we can see the trade-off between three objective function. With higher value of the total difference to due date, which results in lower customer satisfaction, taxis trend to reduce speed to avoid speed penalty, such as more fuel consumption, more CO_2 emissions. In this case, the extra benefits trend to be higher because we can list more taxis for choosing to carry passengers.

Knowledge about split delivery, multi pickup and delivery, changeable speed, load ratio, and time windows can be utilized in SARP and other related problems. There has been no research to set up a multi-objective 0-1 mixed-integer programming model for SARP, and propose IACO and greedy solution to resolve it. Further research is still needed to solve the largescale scheduling and routing problem more efficiently.

References

[1] Li B Krushinsky, Dmitry Reijers, Hajo Van Woensel et al. The Share-a-Ride Problem: People and Parcels Sharing Taxis[J]. European Journal of Operational Research, 2015, 238(1). 31-40.

[2] Son Nguyen Babaki, Behrouz Dries, Anton Pham, et al. Prediction-based optimization for online People and Parcels share a ride taxis[J]. 2017:42-47.

[3] Li B Krushinsky, Dmitry Van Woensel, Tom Reijers, et al. The Share-a-Ride problem with stochastic travel times and stochastic delivery locations [J]. Transportation Research Part C: Emerging Technologies, 2016(67):95-108.

[4] Demir Emrah Bektaş, Tolga Laporte, Gilbert. An adaptive large neighborhood search heuristic for the Pollution-Routing Problem[J]. European Journal of Operational Research. 2012(223), 346-359.

[5] NGUYEN, Van Pham, Dung Anh Tu, et al. An Adaptive Large Neighborhood Search Solving Large People and Parcel Share-a-Ride Problem[C]. 6th NAFOSTED Conference on Information and Computer Science(NICS), 2019:303-308.

[6] Peng Zixuan Feng, Rui Wang, Chenyu Jiang, et al. Online bus-pooling service at the railway station for passengers and parcels sharing buses: A case in Dalian[J]. Expert Systems with Applications, 2021(169):114354.

[7] Yu, Vincent Purwanti, Sesya Redi, Perwira Lu, et al. Simulated annealing heuristic for the general share-a-ride problem[J]. Engineering Optimization, 2018, 50(2): 1-20.

[8] Tong Yongxin Zeng, Yuxiang Zhou, Zimu Chen, et al. A unified approach to route planning for shared mobility[J]. Proceedings of the VLDB Endowment, 2018(11):1633-1646.

[9] DO Phan-Thuan NGHIEM, Nguyen-Viet-Dung NGUYEN, Ngoc-Quang PHAM, et al. A time-dependent model with speed windows for share-a-ride problems: A case study for Tokyo transportation[J]. Data & Knowledge Engineering, 2017(114): 67-85.

[10] Beojone Caio Geroliminis, Nikolas. On the inefficiency of ride-sourcing services towards urban congestion [J]. Transportation Research Part C: Emerging Technologies, 2021(124): 102890.

V2X 与边缘计算相结合的交叉口高精度地图信息服务系统架构及其应用

周轶[1] 魏俊生[1] 安康[2] 韩慧[1] 刘靖馨[1]

(1. 上海淞泓智能汽车科技有限公司;2. 上海国际汽车城(集团)有限公司)

摘 要 本文旨在将V2X与边缘计算技术引入车路协同场景下高精度地图信息服务系统架构及其应用问题。基于"云-边-端"服务生态,通过梳理高精度地图信息服务的需求等级、服务主体和实施流程,构建了一个应用于边缘计算节点的 V2X 高精度地图信息服务系统架构模型。通过在上海市某开放测试道路的一个应用实例来说明本文提出的高精地图系统架构的正确性和有效性。所获结果表明：本文提出的服务系统架构，在提升地图数据的准确性和时效性等方面表现出较为明显的特征，在实际应用中具有较强的可操作性和拓展性。

关键词 智能交通 高精度地图 信息服务系统架构 柯拉斯尼地图信息传输模型 V2X 边缘计算

0 引言

近几年,服务于自动驾驶和网联车辆的高精度地图逐步从理论走向应用,典型案例如上海市嘉定区智能网联车开放测试道路,先后在智能网联汽车 C-V2X"四跨""新四跨"活动中向参与车辆提供厘米级高精度定位地图,为交叉口闯红灯预警、左转通行辅助等应用提供精确的信息参考和辅助。国内城市道路的智慧化等级也在不断升级,5G-V2X、边缘计算等新的通信和计算手段正被不断引入路侧智能设备中,为优化高精度地图服务框架和数据内容创造了工程基础。

许多学者从不同层面对这一领域开展了广泛而又深入的研究。张进明等指出了高精度地图对智能网联汽车的重要意义[1],王冕从自动驾驶角度分析不同级别自动驾驶需要高精度地图具备的特征[2]。申泽邦指出高精度地图语法标注信息有助于自动驾驶车路理解静态道路语义[3]。特别是刘经南等人针对自动驾驶的高精度地图基本特征,提出了图层结构丰富、分类更加精细的一种标准化划分体系[4],从地图学理论上提出智能高精地图信息传输模型。此外,周桥立等研究了开放道路应用场景中与高精度地图强相关重要因素[6],李秀知指出车路协同融合系统中的高精度地图与传统导航地图区别和联系[7]。杨明珠则提出了一种利用深度学习和同步建图及定位来实现基于边缘计算的高精地图建图方法[8];余卓渊等还提出了一种融合多源数据的高精度地图建图框架,并指出地图中应包含道路动、静态信息[9]。

虽然相关研究卓有成效,但目前将边缘计算、高精度地图、V2X 车路协同三者有机融合的工作还相对较少。问题主要源于两个层面:其一,面向 V2X 车路协同的高精度地图其服务流程和数据内容尚不明确;其二,车端高精度地图通常基于单车的传感器,受限于车辆单视角,难以实时检测了解道路实时动态。因此,迫切需要在"云-边-端"生态下,对 V2X 车路协同场景下高精度地图在物理和逻辑上信息的交互方式、体系结构和服务方法等进行系统而又深入的研究,这正是本文研究背景及意义。

1 高精度地图信息服务的系统架构

本节旨在介绍如何将 V2X 通信与边缘计算技术相结合,引入车路协同场景下高精度地图信息服务系统架构及其应用问题,以下将逐一介绍高精度地图信息服务的需求等级、服务主体、实施流程、系统架构。

1.1 需求等级

L3~L5 级的自动驾驶车辆随着自动化程度的提高,越来越需要高精度地图提供感知、决策和规划的依据[12],相应的地图需求等级见表1。

高精度地图需求等级　　表1

自动驾驶等级	地图名称	精度(m)	形态	协同模式	目的
L3	半动态地图	0.2~0.5	静态+动态	车+路	导航+安全
L4	动态地图	0.05~0.2	静态+动态/事件	车+路	导航+主动安全

基金项目:国家重点研发计划项目,科技部"自动驾驶电动汽车集成与示范"项目子课题"测试示范区协同创新的环境创建、运行组织与管理技术研究"(2018YFB0105201)资助。

续上表

自动驾驶等级	地图名称	精度(m)	形态	协同模式	目的
L5	智能地图	0.05~0.2	静态+动态/事件+服务	车+路+云	自动寻路+主动安全+服务

1.2 服务主体

针对V2X的车-路-云协同场景下高精度地图的生态环境,参考刘经南提出的高精度地图信息传播模式[4],在路端边缘计算设备引入改进的柯拉斯尼地图信息传输模型:

$$HT = (P_1, P_2, U'_1, U'_2, C, M, F)$$

式中:P_1——制图者,包括MEC、云端、车辆;

P_2——用图者,应用生态下以车辆为主;

U'_1——制图者对空间环境的认识,为边缘计算设备对周边动静态环境元素的特征提取和抽象认知;

U'_2——用图者对空间环境的认识,为车辆对相应驾驶场景空间地理元素的关联和分析;

C——设备检测范围内的时空环境;

M——C-V2X网联环境下提供信息服务的智能高精度地图;

F——用户认知特征及需求,为车辆针对不同的驾驶场景对地图数据服务内容的侧重性需求。

数据交互依赖于C-V2X通信手段,U'_1、U'_2受到标准《合作式智能运输系统车用通信系统应用层及应用数据交互标准》的限制。

1.3 实施流程

基于上述地图信息传输模型的认知,提出如下实施流程。

步骤1:地图需求认知阶段:通过V2X通信手段,获取车辆个性化的地图需求F。

步骤2:地图信息获取阶段:基于路侧和车载传感器获取的环境信息,结合车辆的地图需求F,形成边缘计算节点对空间的认识U'_1[9]。

步骤3:地图信息加工阶段:将边缘节点对空间的认识,基于相应V2X信息交互标准,进行相应的信息加工,形成高精度地图M,通过5G/LTE-V2X将相关消息传递给使用者[7]。

步骤4:地图信息解译阶段:车辆等用图者通过C-V2X通信设备接收地图消息,基于合作式协议等相应V2X信息交互标准进行消息解码工作。

步骤5:地图信息反馈和更新阶段:车辆对边缘计算节点提供的地图服务做出评价,中心云则对地图信息进行整体规划和引导[8]。

1.4 系统架构

梳理高精度地图信息服务的需求等级,服务主体和实施流程后,建立如图1所示的系统架构模型。

本文构建的模型综合考虑了V2X网联环境与边缘计算"下沉式计算"的影响,相对于参考的信息传播模型[4],在以下几个方面做了改进:

(1)明确制图者为边缘计算节点,用图者为智能网联车辆,认知的主要对象为边缘计算检测节点内的地理时空环境。

(2)进一步优化地理时空环境C,包含的基本要素为静态的路网拓扑信息、半动态的交通事件和交通流信息、动态的交通目标运动信息以及其他道路交通环境信息。

(3)完善了V2X信息交互网络,用图者的认知特征和用途需求可以实时传递给制图者,辅助制图者构建当前的用户地图需求模型。

(4)进一步规范了地图格式和内容受到的约束,需符合V2X信息交互标准规定的语义。

(5)用图者基于自身传感器的环境认知与高精度地图提供的环境认知相互比对,对地图数据质量做出评价和反馈,促使制图者不断优化地图信息服务内容。

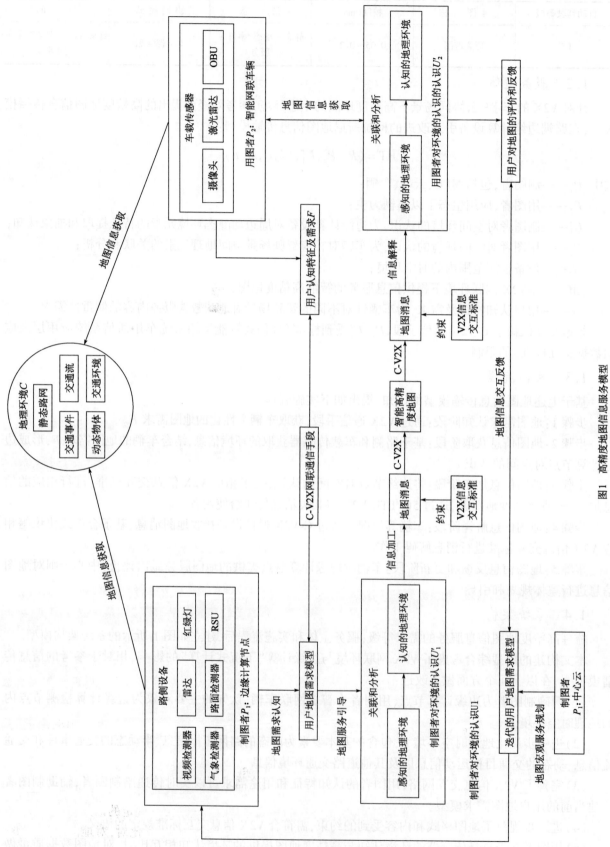

图1 高精度地图信息服务模型

2 地图信息服务方法应用实例

2.1 实例背景和应用

上海市某智能网联车开放测试道路交叉口,以边缘计算节点为核心,集成了激光雷达、行人检测器、RSU 等路侧传感通信设备,参照本文提出的高精度地图传输模型,按如下步骤提供应用服务。

步骤 1:获取车辆发出的地图服务请求。

步骤 2:将传感器采集数据统一到同一时空坐标轴下,采用与余卓渊等研究方法类似的多源数据融合算法,将融合后的环境数据分别归类进静态地图数据、动态地图数据,对不同层次的地图数据进一步做时间和空间上的索引和关联,建立起交通目标、事件、信号与地图的时空关联。

步骤 3:将地图信息整理包装成符合车辆 V2X 认知语义的动静态地图消息。

步骤 1~3 如图 2 所示。

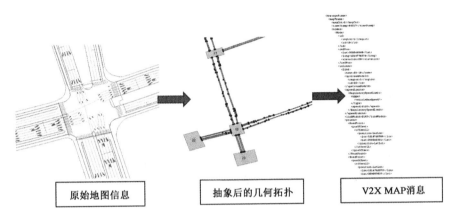

图 2 节点地图信息处理过程

步骤 4:车辆解码地图消息及应用。车辆解码边缘计算节点提供的 MAP、SPAT、RSM 等 V2X 地图消息,在接近路口时成功触发闯红灯预警提示,如图 3 所示。

图 3 基于地图消息的车载安全提醒

2.2 对比测试

以车路协同场景中常用的交叉口碰撞预警(ICW)为基础设计了一个对比实验,测试对象为一辆搭载 V2X 和自动驾驶系统的测试车 RV-1、一辆只具备自动驾驶系统的测试车 RV-2,检测目标为安全员控制的一辆普通车辆 HV。

测试流程为 RV-2、RV-1、HV 在距交叉口中心点同一距离起步,RV-1、RV-2 在同一车道共同行驶,RV-2 更靠近车道右侧,防止被 RV-1 挡住视线,HV 所在车道与 RV-1、RV-2 所在车道垂直。边缘计算节点不断通过 V2X 设备向 RV-1 更新周边的高精度地图信息,RV-2 则纯粹依赖自身传感和预存静态数据完成构图。测试场景示意如图 4 所示。

测试指标为 RV-1 和 RV-2 初次检测到 HV 时,HV 距离交叉口中心点的垂直距离以及检测坐标与 HV 实际坐标间的误差。改变 HV 在测试场景下的一些起始条件,测试结果如表 2 所示。

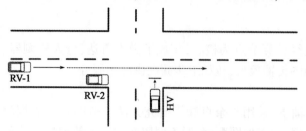

图 4 基于 ICW 的地图数据服务方法对比测试

对比测试试验结果 表 2

测试编号	HV 初始距离(m)	HV 行驶速度(km/h)	RV-1 发现 HV 时 HV 距离(m)	RV-1 定位 HV 偏差(m)	RV-2 发现 HV 时 HV 距离(m)	RV-2 定位 HV 偏差(m)
1	150	40	130.17	0.83	66.15	1.89
2	150	60	133.34	0.94	53.82	1.62
3	200	40	136.70	1.32	64.78	2.53
4	200	60	131.89	1.21	50.32	1.64
5	300	40	133.28	1.27	57.65	2.37

2.3 实例结论

从上述对比测试实例可知,边缘计算节点能为 RV-1 提供更长距离、更精确的地图信息服务,能够更早地提示检测盲区信息,方便后续的控制决策。证明本文提出的系统模型能够为提升智能网联车开放道路应用测试环境中发挥重要作用。

3 结 语

本文对 V2X 与边缘计算相结合的高精度地图信息服务架构与应用方法展开了研究,构建了一种改进的高精度地图信息服务系统架构。并在上海市某开放道路测试示范区进行了应用实践,证明本文的研究成果具备相当的指导和实践价值。本文的研究成果对国内智能化城市道路开展车路协同地图信息服务提供了理论和应用参考。

参考文献

[1] 张进明,孙灿,刘兆丹,等. 智能网联汽车高精地图技术指标及标准化需求研究[J]. 中国汽车,2019(10).

[2] 王冕. 面向自动驾驶的高精度地图及其应用方法[J]. 地理信息世界,2020,27,142(04):115-120.

[3] 申泽邦. 面向自动驾驶的高精度地图优化和定位技术研究[D].

[4] 刘经南,吴杭彬,郭迟,等. 高精度道路导航地图的进展与思考[J]. 中国工程科学,2018,v.20(02):107-113.

[5] 刘经南,詹骄,郭迟,等. 智能高精地图数据逻辑结构与关键技术[J]. 测绘学报,2019(8).

[6] 周桥立,李睿硕. 基于车路协同的开放道路应用场景落地研究[J]. 信息通信,2020,206(02):34-36.

[7] 李秀知. 一种基于多维时空融合的车路协同系统[J]. 信息通信,2019,000(012):44-46.

[8] 杨明珠. 基于边缘计算的自动驾驶高精地图建图与定位方法[J]. 自动化博览,2019,036(009):30-33.

[9] 余卓渊,闾国年,张夕宁,等. 全息高精度导航地图:概念及理论模型[J]. 地球信息科学学报,2020,022(004):760-771.

借非机动车道右转交通组织在城市道路交叉口中的实践与探索

廖诗琪 谢和杰 尤 彬 刘长清

(四川省德阳市公安局交通警察支队)

摘 要 本文通过分析在道路资源有限的情况下右转交通的现状及问题,结合实际情况,提出了借非机动车道右转的思路,并概括阐述了借非机动车道右转交通组织的适用条件和设置方法,通过合理设置交通安全设施,充分利用现有非机动车空间资源,有效组织非机动车交通,减少路口借非机动车道右转机动车与非机动车之间的交通冲突。最后,将借非机动车道右转交通组织应用于实际路口,最终发现借非机动车道右转能充分利用现有空间资源,提升路口通行效率。对国内其他城市治理交叉口交通拥堵具有借鉴和指导意义。

关键词 借非机动车道右转 交通组织 交通安全设施 空间资源 通行效率 城市道路交叉口

0 引 言

交叉口是城市道路交通系统的重要组成部分,也是城市道路交通系统的关键节点和瓶颈,交叉口的畅通直接影响着整个城市系统的运行效率。在城市道路空间限界的限制下交叉口进口道难以无限拓宽[1],因此,有效利用现有空间资源,优化交通组织方式,尽可能挖掘交叉口潜在通行能力,成为缓解城市交通拥堵的重要手段。

目前,针对交叉口拥堵问题,各大城市通过设置直行待行区、借道左转等多种交通组织模式来解决左转和直行交通问题。但对交叉口右转交通组织研究较少,基本上通过提前分离右转车辆(如在设置有机非分隔带且非机动车道较宽的道路上,提前借用非机动车道分离右转车辆等)、设置右转专用车道等方式解决;若道路资源受限,无条件提前分离右转车、设置专用右转车道,则通常较难寻找到能有效解决右转车流的交通组织方法。本文将以我国四川省德阳市具体路口为例,结合交通现状及实际,在有限的道路资源条件下,对借非机动车道右转交通组织方式进行研究。

1 现状交叉口右转交通组织方式

交叉口交通组织优化通常采用车道划分、交通信号灯控制等方式,明确不同交通流的时间和空间路权,在交叉口内将不同类型、不同方向的交通流从时间和空间上进行分离,减少各种交通流之间的相互冲突,保障交叉口交通有序、畅通[2]。

交叉口路权的时间分配主要依据路口交通信号灯绿灯相位时间,空间分配则主要依据交通标线,两者的优化是提升交叉口通行率的主要决定性因素。以德阳市长江路—龙泉山路交叉口为例,该交叉口为主干道路与次干道相交,南北进口道为1条左转车道+1条直行车道+1条直右车道+1条非机动车道;东进口道为1条左转车道+3条直行车道+1条右转和公交共用车道+1条非机动车道;西进口道为2条左转车道+2条直行车道+1条右转和公交共用车道+1条非机动车道(图1)。

南北进口道受道路条件、交通流量的影响,最外侧机动车道设置为直右车道,该车道在实际运行中存在以下问题,影响通行效率:

(1)当最外侧车道出现直行车排队等候时,后方右转车辆必须跟车排队。

(2)当南北向为绿灯放行时,右转车辆需让行南北向直行非机动车、行人,影响右转车后方直行车辆。

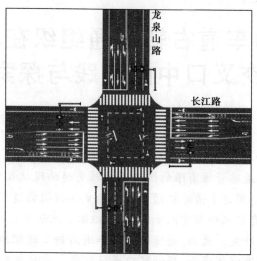

图 1 长江路—龙泉山路交叉口改善前示意图

2 借非机动车道右转通行适用条件

借非机动车道右转交通组织是指:在确保非机动车安全的情况下,路口右转车辆可借用非机动车专用车道,实现右转。设置借非机动车道右转的目的是缓解直右车道排队长度及绿灯时期右转车辆对直行车辆的影响,以提高路口通行效率。但借非机动车道右转的交通组织需要结合道路实际情况,在一定条件下采用借非机动车道右转的交通组织,才是科学合理的。具体条件如下:

2.1 车道条件

(1)交叉口进口道未设置右转专用车道,该交叉口已进行过渠化,但仍无条件设置右转专用车道。主要原因包括:①交叉口空间不足,不能通过压缩渠化等方式设置 1 条右转专用车道或提前分离;②直行需求大,1 条或 2 条车道无法满足;③左转需求大,无法设置直左车道。

(2)进口道设置有非机动车专用车道,一般非机动车道宽度不小于 2.5 m,机动车道与非机动车道之间未设置机非隔离设施。

2.2 交通组织条件

(1)为消除左转非机动车与借非机动车道右转机动车之间的干扰,左转非机动车通过二次过街完成左转(图 2)。

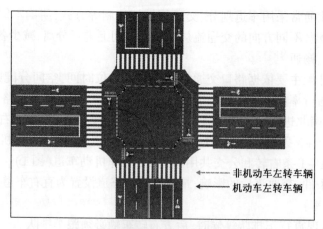

图 2 左转非机动车二次过街流线示意图

(2)机动车信号灯采用"机动车信号灯"或"左转方向指示灯"+"机动车信号灯"组合方式,右转机动车在确保安全的情况下不受信号灯控制;非机动车可根据"机动车信号灯"通行。

2.3 交通流量条件

(1)右转交通流量可参考《城市道路交叉口规划规范》(GB 5047—2011)的规定:当高峰15min内每信号周期右转车平均达到量达4辆时,宜设置右转专用车道。

(2)高峰小时每信号周期直行、左转车流量明显大于右转流量。

(3)高峰时期,非机动车排队长度尽量不超过机动车停止线。

(4)一般考虑城市内道路交叉口,仅限于小汽车,禁止载货汽车通行。

3 借非机动车道右转的设置方法

3.1 借道起点位置

右转车辆借道起点距离位置距离停止线过近,若直行车排队较长,则会影响右转借道通行,导致右转车无法完成借道;右转借道起点距离停止线过远,则非机动车道变成了机非混行车道,影响非机动在路段上的正常通行。因此,借非机动车道右转的起点位置一般考虑设置进口道于渐变段起点位置(若路口未进行渠化,则考虑设置于导向车道线后方 10 ~ 15m);若直行车排队过长,则借非机动车道右转起点可考虑后退 10 ~ 15m。

3.2 借非机动车道右转非机动车交通组织

非机动车等候区前移至人行横道前方,并保证不影响另一侧非机动车通行,为借非机动车道右转机动车预留借道通行空间,通常有两种模式:

(1)交叉口空间充足(一般为干道与干道相交),有条件设置非机动车等候隔离护栏,如图 3 所示。

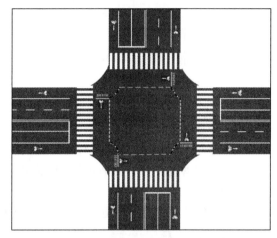

图 3 交叉口设置非机动车等候区护栏示意图

(2)交叉口空间有限,无条件设置非机动车等候隔离护栏,如图 4 所示。

3.3 交通标志、标线设计

(1)进口道机动车与非机动车之间的白实线调整为虚线,如图 5 所示。

(2)在进口道来车方向路侧适当位置设置借非机动车道右转提示标志(可考虑2套),如图 5 所示。

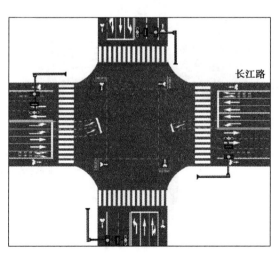

图 4 交叉口无条件设置非机动车等候区护栏示意图

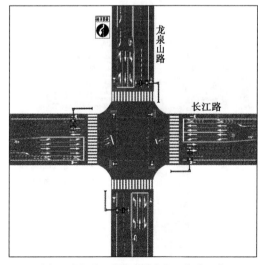

图 5 长江路—龙泉山路交叉口北进口道借非机动车道右转交通组织示意图

4 借非机动车道右转的实践与应用

将借非机动车道右转实践应用于德阳市长江路—龙泉山路交叉口北进口道,如图5所示。在信号配时方案不变的情况下,对改善前和改善后交通情况进行对比分析(表1)可知:实施借非机动车道右转后,交叉口北进口道高峰小时内总交通流量提升23.5%。其中右转交通流提升最为明显,增加了49.1%;借非机动车道右转后对左转、直行交通流也产生了一定程度的积极影响,高峰小时内通过的左转、直行机动车分别增加了9.1%、14.4%。

龙泉山路—长江路交叉口北进口借非机动车道右转前后对比表   表1

交叉口	进口道	高峰小时交通流量情况							
		借道前高峰流量(pcu/h)			借道后高峰流量(pcu/h)			借道后提高比例		
		左转	直行	右转	左转	直行	右转	左转	直行	右转
龙泉山路—长江路口	北	132	724	334	144	828	498	9.1%	14.4%	49.1%
总计			1190			1437			23.5%	

注:信号配时方案未发生变化。

实践表明,借非机动车道右转可一定程度缓解交叉口交通压力,提高通行效率,但其对非机动车通行安全及通行效率也产生一定程度影响,根据实践应用与分析,总结借非机动车道右转交通的优缺点。

主要优点:

(1)充分利用非机动车道路空间资源(图6),提高了交叉口机动车通行效率。

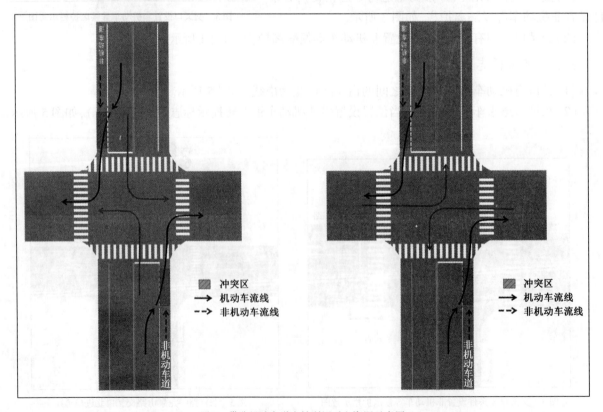

图6 借非机动车道右转利用时空资源示意图

(2)充分利用交叉口左转信号相位时间资源,既消除了右转机动车与过街非机动车、行人之间交通冲突,又提高了交叉口机动车通行效率。

主要缺点:

①借道右转机动车与同向直行非机动车之间交通冲突增加(图9),影响非机动通行效率,影响交通安全。

(2)借道右转机动车与过街直行非机动车、行人之间交通冲突增加(图8),在等候非机动车、行人过街时影响后方非机动车通行。

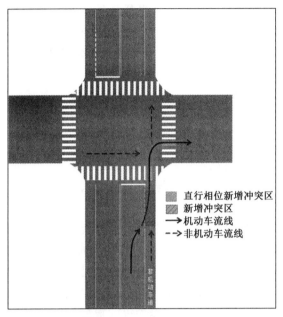
图7 借非机动车道右转新增交通冲突示意图

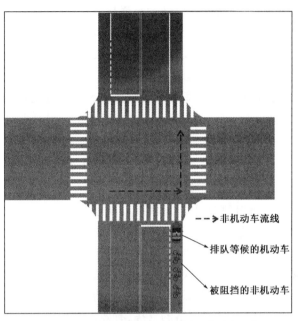
图8 借非机动车道右转影响非机动车通行效率示意图

5 结 语

本文分析了现城市道路交叉口右转交通的常用交通组织方式,以及在道路资源有限的情况下,现有右转交通存在的问题。结合现有问题及实际情况,提出了借非机动车道右转的交通组织方式。阐述了借非机动车道的设置条件及设置方法,通过充分利用现有道路空间资源,交叉口合理组织非机动车交通流,配套设置借非机动车道右转交通安全设施,能有效提升路口通行效率。对国内其他城市治理交叉口交通拥堵具有借鉴和指导意义。

本文在研究过程中未对交叉口使用借非机动车道右转时具体的非机动车流量(含等候区交通流量)阈值做出定量分析,后期为进一步深入推广应用,应对上述问题做进一步分析研究。

参考文献

[1] 刘洋,顾金刚,卢健,等.借道左转交通组织使用条件及管理设施设计研究[J]中国公共安全(学术版),2018(4):80-86.

[2] 苏文鹏.交叉口右转机动车不礼让行人致因分析及改善方法[J].安全管理.

[3] 李克平,倪颖.城市道路交叉口精细化规划设计与控制管理[J].城市交通,2014(12-5):54-59.

[4] 李爱增,王炜,李文权.城市道路交叉口借非机动车道右转车道设置方法[J].公路交通科技,2010,27(3):125-129.

对"超级高速公路"的几点深度思考

张焕炯

(浙江交通科学研究院)

摘　要　新出现的"超级高速公路"不仅为高速公路、智慧公路等的未来发展提供了充分的想象,它更成了相关先进技术实际应用所追求的新标杆。本文针对"超级高速公路"的概念内涵和关键性的支撑技术的应用进行深入辨析,力图从根本上揭示"超级高速公路"的实质,以便为有关高速公路建设的进一步发展提供有益的启示。

关键词　超级高速公路　技术支撑　智能控制　光伏充电

0　引　言

我国在近30、40年间,高速公路从无到有。截至2018年底,高速公路里程总数已突破14万km,已形成了相对完备的陆上交通骨干网络。随着科技的进步和高速公路运营管养的日益深入,如何有效解决高速公路出现的问题,切实提升高速公路的各项性能,实现高速公路整体性的升级换代等越来越成了一个重要课题。尤其在"互联网+"、新一代人工智能、大数据技术、云计算技术等迅猛发展的当下,在交通强国战略实施的背景下,高速公路作为高新技术的集成应用的重要领域,是时候通过革命性的变革来实现高速公路的升级换代,使得现有高速公路的各项性能有根本性的提高[1-3]。由此,人们提出了智慧高速公路的概念,希望通过完备的交通信息化基础建设,形成强大的信息化网络,实现交通网与信息网的深度融合,并通过信息网络的支撑,有效提升高速公路系统的决策、管理、运营和养护等的智慧化,实现高速公路品级的全面提升。在此背景下,不仅出现了"超级高速公路"这个新名词,更出现了着手建设"超级高速公路"的新情况。

"超级高速公路"似乎已进入了具体的建设和试验运营的阶段,能本质地表征超级高速公路特性的核心技术和性能指标,已不再是仅仅满足于相关概念的描述,而是成了需要具体落实的工程实现。因此,需要对它们进行正确而又精准的认识,也就是说,需要对"超级高速公路"的那些带有根本属性的技术、性能指标等进行系统的梳理,不仅要考察它们在理论上的正确性,更要考虑它们在应用中的可实现性。

本文以"超级高速公路"为研究对象,分析其概念内涵的同时,对其关键性的支撑技术及核心功能等的具体实现进行分析和评估,以揭示概念的本质特性的同时,形成相应的结论。希望这些工作,不仅对正确认识"超级高速公路"这个新概念有所帮助,更为我国高速公路的务实、科学、有序地发展提供有益的启迪。

1　"超级高速公路"支撑性技术

"超级高速公路"是目前高速公路发展的前沿,理所当然地需要一些相对独到的关键技术和指标来支撑,或者说,需要一些独特的理论和技术来综合性地表征它的基本性能特征。根据该新名词最先出现时的描述,"超级高速公路"在"智能""快速""绿色"和"安全"4个方面将有重大的突破,它将在交通的有效性、安全性和节能环保等方面有非常靓丽的性能表现,"超级高速公路"具有不可替代的性能特征,主要包括如下4个方面:

(1)智能控制

首先,要求通过构建人车路协同综合感知体系和构建路网综合运行监测与预警系统。以最大限度地实现控制的智能化。

(2) 安全快速

其次,实现快速,打破现有高速公路对最高速度 120km/h 的限制,从而有效提升高速公路的交通效率。超级高速公路将为无人驾驶提供安全的驾驶环境,针对安全性问题,超级高速公路通过智能化和容错设计,将把事故的危害程度降到最低,实现全天快速通行车辆、零死亡。

(3) 光伏路面

第三,实现绿色,汽车未来的发展方向是电动化,近期的发展目标是通过太阳能发电、路面光伏发电,插电式充电桩电量的补充,为电动车提供充电服务。在光伏路面设计方面,把道路分为三层:最表层为透光混凝土路面层,具有强度大、透光率高两大特点;中间层为光伏面板,光电转化,利用路面空闲时间吸收阳光发电;第三层为绝缘层,既有对光伏面板的物理保护作用,又防水防潮等。

(4) 无线充电

最后,超级高速公路可实现无线充电,以实现电动车在此路段行驶过程中,边行驶边充电,从而避免了车辆在缺电的时候,到处找充电桩的"囧事"发生。

以上四点作为超级高速公路的支撑性要素,具有表征性意义。也就是说,它们是判别超级公路的最基本的条件,即只有当这四个条件同时成立时,才能把高速公路称为超级高速公路。

2 "超级高速公路"概念的支撑性技术实现

根据"超级高速公路"的内涵的基本特征表述,为其实现智能、快速、绿色和安全的目标,需要先进技术的支撑,由此分别从理论依据、可实现性和相应的性能指标、预期表现等具体的维度加以具体辨析,从而可更深入地揭示"超级高速公路"的本质。

"超级高速公路"的第一个基本特征是智能控制,尤其需要实现人、车、路的高度协同,这样不仅可解决交通效率,还可实现交通安全。但是必须看到,人车路作为协同体系中的三个要素,它们既互相独立,又互相联系和影响。在整个协同体系中,彼此的信息感知、交互等,不仅受"路"这一方面的影响和制约,还受到"车"和"人"这些要素的深刻影响,单纯地从"路"这个方面来构建人车路协同的综合感知体系、网络综合运行检查和预警系统,而忽略其他两个要素的影响,这样的智能控制体系的架构,是否能完全胜任在复杂交通环境下的智能控制还有待进一步研究和分析。而且,从技术和体系的理论依据来看,它们尚未从根本上突破控制理论(Cybernetics)、信息理论和网路理论等的理论体系,从具体的实施和工程实现的角度来看,迄今所出现的各种感知技术,它们都既有各自的长处的同时,也或多或少都存在各种缺陷和不足。如以视频技术为基础的充分感知系统,在夜间环境下就很难发挥卓越的功能,而有关以 GPS 等为基础的感知技术,遇到长隧道时就会失去优势,等等。由此,真正的以人、车、路协同为基础的具有全天候、无死角的充分感知的系统的技术本身还未完全成熟,离实际的应用尚有很长的距离。同样的,以道路为中心的智能监控系统,不仅在理论依据和技术支撑上存在不足,更在具体产品化的过程中,尚未充分验证系统和设备的稳健性、可靠性等性能,它们离在实际的道路上的安装和使用,进而发挥积极作用,中间还有很多难题需要逐一解决。所以,无论是信号和信息的采集、信号的传输和智能化的处理,还是具体的控制和反馈等,让它们在复杂的道路交通环境下,都能实现全天候、全方位、高精准度、安全可靠的智能控制,至少在现阶段,还不能完全实现。

关于安全快速方面的性能,从已能查阅到的关资料来看,存在如下几点问题。一是,如何定量地描述和界定快速,对现行的高速公路来说,它的速度要求介于 60km/h 与 120km/h 之间,在速度方面体现了"高速"字,那么为要在速度上体现"超速度",具体界定为 200km/h、300km/h,还是其他所设想的速度,这需要有一个定量的界限。二是要达到"超高速",在路方面,具体需要具备什么要求?在车方面,还需要另外的哪一些具体要求?如汽车发动机、制动、材质等方面的具体要求;三是在人方面,如何确保在交通工具上的驾乘人员在这样的速度下的安全性、舒适性等,这实际上也是一个需要解决的难题。

在能源方面,"超级高速公路"强调用绿色能源,并提出了光伏路面的概念,试图利用太阳能的转换,以期获得源源不断的能量供应;在能量续存方面,除强调用充电桩外,还重点提出了应用无线充电技术的方法来解决连续性的能源补给问题,这些相对靓丽的创新思路,似乎从根本上解决了能源问题,体现了能源的绿色环保。但实际上,姑且不论这些创新思维是否具有坚实的理论依据的支撑,单就它们具体应用这一点来看,还存在很多有待解决的难题。首先,对于光伏路面来说,道路仅在白天太阳光充足的条件下才有可能获得能源,晚上或雨雪天,尤其是冬季的雨雪天,路面难以吸收太阳能,路面就无法获得能源补给,这是否意味着在晚间和雨雪天时道路关闭?其次,路面作为吸收太阳光的主要区域,道路的横竖布置,周边环境等对采光有直接的影响,更严重的是,由于车辆在路面行驶,这意味着太阳光照射到的路面区域是不固定的,而且它们光照时间与车流量的大小有直接的关系,一个路面区域,在间断性地接收太阳光的前提下,它如何实现稳定的能源转化和能源输出?这同样是一个难题。其三,在路面的三层设计中,如何保证所设计的路面在竖直方向上的完好无损?因为路面承受着不同车载的负荷,严格意义上来讲,路面在竖直方向上的不平整是绝对的,所以路面的损坏一定会发生,光伏路面的完好性就受到极大挑战;此外,路面一旦损坏,在确保正常的交通流和光伏设置中的电线回路等不受影响的前提下,实现快速地修复,这不是一件容易的事,尤其保障光伏系统的正常运行,是关乎整条超级高速公路的能源供给,是关系到整条道路是否关闭的大问题,所以它的安全性和可靠性的要求是非常高的,这也是一个难点。第四,在采用无线充电方面,现今,支撑无线充电的技术主要有电磁感应、无线电波和共振作用等,利用电磁感应技术的无线充电技术相对成熟,但它也有较高的要求,如充电物之间的距离要非常近,而且磁场的分布区域相对集中且磁场强度需要较强等,而现今所大多以相对静止状态的充电方式出现,这些情况,实际上并不适合于给行驶在道路上的车辆实施无线充电,究其原因,车辆与道路之间因车轮的支撑就不可能相距太近,此外,车辆动态的状态也不利于获得相对稳定的充电环境等等。另外,"大功率无线电能充电传输"等的充电方式,需要能量的两次转换(电能转化成磁能,再由磁能转化电能)才能实现,而这技术的具体应用,除了需建构相对较强的磁场以外,还需考虑较大的能耗,以及无线充电传输距离(一般不超过5m)较短等实际问题。相对较强的磁场不仅需要很高的建设成本的投入,它们还可能直接损害车辆上的驾乘人员的身心健康,这种充电方式是否适合于超级公路的建设,还需要多方面的具体论证等等。

3 建议

通过对"超级高速公路"的核心指标关联技术的原理、具体实现等的分析,除了对这个概念有更本质的认识外,还针对性地形成了富有建设性的几点建议:

(1)公路交通是以路、车、人要素所构成的系统,在这个系统中,路和车之间的关联程度更大,所有的技术进步,交通模式的更替,都是路和车(道路及其他基础设施和交通工具)两者协同进步的前提下才能成为现实。所以,在考虑"超级高速公路"的过程中,一定需要以系统的整体性的进步为前提。

(2)要分清"超级高速公路"的研究试验和实际使用的分际,"超级高速公路"作为线性的一段线路,对它进行单独的测试分析,未尝不可,但不能把它接入到实际的高速公路网中,使之成为运营的公路网的一部分。因为一旦把它接入到实际运行的高速公路网中,因在公路网中行驶车辆的性能尚未达到与"超级高速公路"相适配的要求,它们在其他路段可正常行驶,但行驶到"超级高速公路"时,因为车辆不能协同于"超级高速公路",这一段路段至多只能发挥一般高速公路的性能,有的时候甚至连一般高速公路的性能都发挥不了,那么它的价值就不能体现出来。

(3)相关的新技术,虽然就其单一的性能来说都很有优势,但多种技术如何进行有效的组合集成,集成后的技术优势是否是各种技术优势简单的相加,这些都是需要细致入微地考虑的问题,只要中间有一个环节出现问题,那么整个体系就是有问题的,所以在具体研究和实施过程中,这方面也要引起高度的重视。

此外,新概念的提出,要有科学的严格论证,更需要有具体数量的界定及定量分析,以体现概念的清晰、明确和科学。

4 结语

通过对"超级高速公路"的概念及核心指标的技术和性能的深度辨析,可以得到如下的结论:"超级高速公路"迄今还只是一个新名词,一个新概念,它离投入使用尚有很长的距离。在路的方面,尚有很多技术壁垒、工程壁垒等需要克服外;在车的方面,要形成与路的性能相适配的性能的车辆,也绝非短时间内一蹴而就,还需不断地积累。此外,在车、路、人等为要素的交通体系中,交通性能的提升,总是以各要素协同的进步为前提的,这一条基本规律也需要遵守。

"超级高速公路"实际上是"高速公路将有怎样的发展"这一问题的一种回答,更是高速公路发展到一定阶段后,面临具体发展瓶颈的背景下的一种"响应"。它为高速公路的发展提供了一种远景式的思路,能较多地顾及当前科技的发展态势,具有一定的前瞻性。通过对其深入分析研究,辩证思考,吸收合理的成分,扬弃不合理的,推动高速公路的下一步发展。

参考文献

[1] 张焕炯.智能交通的若干新进展[M].北京:人民交通出版社股份有限公司,2015.
[2] 张焕炯.智能交通技术在高速公路网中的应用[M].北京:人民交通出版社股份有限公司,2019.
[3] 张焕炯.智慧高速云平台构建及关键技术研究[C].重庆:第十一届智能交通年会,2016.

中国国际航空航天博览会交通运输保障方案研究

陈 叶 周 越

(珠海市规划设计研究院)

摘 要 中国国际航空航天博览会已跻身世界五大航展之列,为保障其观展交通协调有序,本文基于展会场地容量、周边路网容量等实际情况,提出"总量控制,需求管理;分区引导,严格控制;公交优先,航展专线;外围停车,接驳换乘;合理布局,高效组织"的组织策略,并针对航展核心区域关键性节点构建微观仿真模型,确保了航展期间市域道路交通安全、有序、顺畅。

关键词 交通组织 保障方案 需求管控 区域分级 瞬时客流

0 引 言

如何合理利用有限的城市交通基础设施资源,应对大量瞬时客流是举办大型会展活动最大的挑战。本文分析了珠海市金湾机场片区周边实际交通条件,针对瞬时大量且逐年增长的客流,提出了总量管控的总体策略,并针对性地提出了分区管控(三级分区)、公交优先(分担率超过90%)的管控措施。

1 中国国际航展交通问题

1.1 机场地理位置特殊

珠海航展馆处于路网末端,停车场集中在场馆两侧,场馆地区只能通过机场路进出。外地观展车辆分别经广澳高速公路、广珠西线高速公路、江珠高速公路、西部沿海高速公路进入珠海机场高速公路后,由展馆西侧的机场西路排队等候通过驶往展馆。珠海本地观展车辆经珠海大道、湖心路往展区的车辆合流,由展馆东侧的机场路前往展馆,最后东西两侧的巨大车流形成对冲和交织,无法得到有效快速地疏散。

1.2 航展客流巨大,规模逐年增长

航展观展人数逐年递增,从2006年(第六届)的29.3万人次增长至2014年(第十届)的41万人次,增长了39.93%。[1]因未设置票务总量管理且采用通票形式,市民可以在公众日中任意一天前往观展,无法准确预测市民观展出行需求,这往往导致观展市民在公众日某天集中出行,人车流给航展馆和主要道

路造成巨大压力。

1.3 自驾观展占比大,公交出行比例低

前十届航展交通方式极端化现象突出,航展交通量(机动车约5.5万车次)中,绝大部分为小汽车(91.81%)。[2]且由于航展小汽车出行时间高度集中,出行集中在上午9:00—10:00入场和下午离场15:00—16:00两个时段,由此引发出行高峰时段主要道路交通节点、近展区路段以及停车场出入口路段的交通严重拥堵。

1.4 公共交通薄弱

珠海市内尚未开通城市轨道,航展期间公共交通运输主要以常规公交、摆渡巴士以及航展专线三种形式为主。但由于航展专线站点设置较少、航展专线数量不足,导致无法应对集中高峰时期产生的客流需求,据统计,高峰时期,航展专线的排队等候时间超过30分钟,整体服务质量偏低,乘客乘坐舒适感较差。此外,公交专用道管理不力、常规公交及航展专线周转率地下等等因素,也导致选择常规公交、摆渡巴士及航展专线出行的观展人数不足20%。

1.5 小结

(1)航展展区位于城市最南端,路网呈多条道路汇聚末端的漏斗式状态,航展车流从北、东、西方向汇聚至机场路,成为航展交通拥堵的根源。

(2)随着中国国际航展知名度及规模的逐年上升,航展观展人数也随之增多,巨大的客流压力加剧了航展交通拥堵。

(3)相对于城市有限的道路供给,以小汽车为主导的航展出行方式进一步加剧了航展展区周边的交通拥堵。

(4)航展观展出行结构中公交出行比重不足20%,专线乘车点不足,航展专用道设施管控不力,导致乘客乘坐舒适感较差,使得观众更倾向于采用小汽车出行。

2 交通组织策略

从航展博览会的大型会展交通的特点出发,提出了金湾机场地区的交通组织策略:"总量控制,需求管理;分区引导,严格控制;公交优先,航展专线;外围停车,接驳换乘;合理布局,高效组织",确保金湾机场地区交通通道顺畅。具体策略如下:

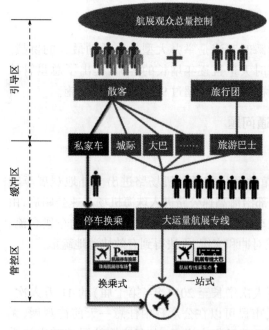

图1 中国国际航展交通运输保障策略

2.1 总量控制,需求管理

主要包括票务管理和非票务观众管理两个方案。票务管理是针对观众总量进行控制,并进行票务分类管理,优先销售团体票。非票务观众管理主要是严禁无票客流进入核心区。

2.2 分区引导,严格控制

主要是实施三级管控,将珠海市市域范围分为核心区、管控区和引导区。

2.3 公交优先,航展专线

主要包括航展专用道设置、市内乘车点布设、市外航展专线设置以及核心区航展专线停车场布设。

2.4 外围停车,接驳换乘

结合三级管控措施,在管控区和引导区合理设置外围换乘点和应急停车场,引导小汽车出行的观众进行停车换乘,保障核心区内交通秩序(图1)。

2.5 合理布局，高效组织

主要针对不同车辆(航展专线、摆渡巴士、参展商车辆等)合理引导至核心区对应停车场，保证核心区内交通组织流线顺畅。另一方面是在航展前夕进行适当的宣传引导工作，将交通组织方案融入综合宣传方案中。

3 交通保障方案

结合上述交通组织策略，提出本次航展的具体交通保障方案：从根源控制，采用票务总量管理措施；在珠海市市域内进行三级管控区域划分；采用P+R停车换乘及布设航展专用道；基于仿真模型的航展核心区关键节点交通保障等。具体保障方案如下：

3.1 票务总量管理

针对逐年增长的观展客流，考虑到航展馆的实际容量及市域内交通基础设施的承载能力，同时结合上两届航展分日限额票务政策的成功经验，十三届航展仍采用分日售票，并结合交通承载能力分析，建议每日售票限额数量不超过10万人。

3.2 航展交通分区管控

将珠海市全市划分为管控区、缓冲区和引导区三类(图2)。管控区主要以限制小汽车出行及满足安保为目的，重点强化边界管理，保障安全，实现有序的设施布局与交通组织的管理目标；缓冲区主要为保障航展集约化交通快速、顺畅抵达航展地区，规划设置航展保障通道，为航展专线、团体巴士、常规公交等大运量集约化车辆提供专属路权空间；引导区重点在于明确的信息发布和交通指引，对于自驾车辆，在进入市区高速公路后，发布停车换乘诱导信息，引导行车方向及路线；主城区设置航展专线乘车点，引导观众采用大运量公共交通出行。

3.3 P+R停车换乘及航展专线

3.3.1 P+R停车换乘

金湾机场地区在停车泊位和道路资源极其紧缺的条件下，应结合交通管控分区范围，并考虑以上选址因素以及现有用地落实情况，结合珠海市对外高速公路、西部沿海高速公路、机场高速公路、机场北路等沿线，最终确定4处停车场，构建航展P+R停车换乘体系，即P7定家湾停车场、P8银隆停车场、P9乾务镇停车场、P10金台寺停车场[3]，如图3和表1所示。

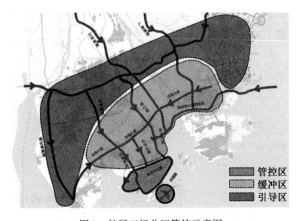

图2 航展三级分区管控示意图

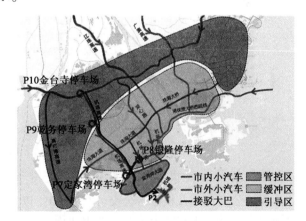

图3 第十三届航展停车换乘点布局及组织方案

第十三届航展停车场布局及规模　　　　表1

类　型	停车场编号	用地面积(m²)	小车车位(个)	接驳泊位	责任部门
缓冲区停车场（换乘公交）	P7 定家湾	8万	2000	50	金湾区
	P8 银隆	30万	8000	160	

续上表

类　型	停车场编号	用地面积(m²)	小车车位(个)	接驳泊位	责任部门
引导区停车场 (应急接驳巴士)	P9 乾务	1.5万	370	10	斗门区
	P10 金台寺	8万	2000	50	
总计 (社会车辆停车场)	—	47.5万	12370万	270	—

3.3.2 航展专用道

为贯彻公交优先的保障策略,本届航展在港珠澳大桥西延线－洪鹤大桥－机场东路－机场路等道路设置航展专用路。并将上届航展专用道(珠海大道—机场东路)作为航展专线应急专用道使用,其中南湾互通立交－珠海大桥段辅道整体作为航展专用道,其他路段沿用现有公交专用道(双向最右侧车道)作为航展专用道,保证大运量交通和应急交通顺畅通过,做到大运量、集约化出行方式的优先通行。

此外,航展期间,主城区内人民西路、九洲大道、迎宾路现有公交专用道,需要加强交通监管措施,提高航展专线交通组织效率(图4)[4]。

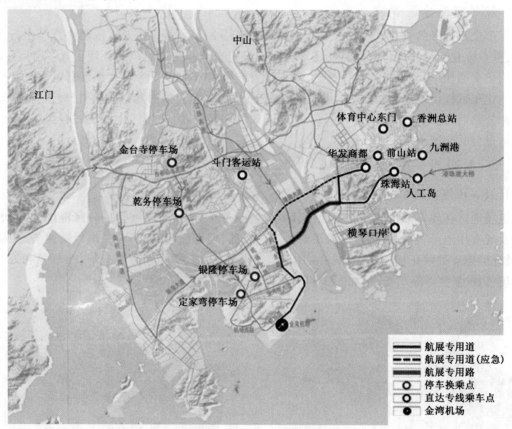

图4　第十三届航展专用路方案

3.4　基于仿真模型的航展核心区关键节点交通保障

为保证公交优先及核心区公交分担率90%以上的目标,本次研究采用Vissim微观交通仿真软件对场馆周边车辆及行人在两个公共交通枢纽周边的道路及相应配套的行人交通设施上的交通组织和运动过程进行了仿真模拟,重点分析在一定的公共交通场站规模条件下,公交枢纽的设计和公交调度组织方式的设计和优化(图5)。

(1)公交枢纽的仿真模型

本次公交专线运行服务水平评价采用公交专线车辆在枢纽各出入口的平均停车次数、平均车辆延误及出入口通行能力等指标对整体交通组织和循环系统进行优化。

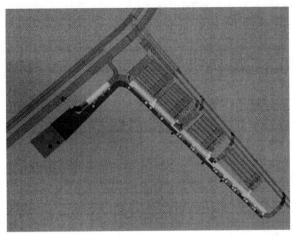
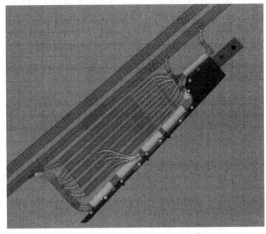

图 5 P1 枢纽(左)及 P2 枢纽(右)仿真平面模型构建

(2) 观众活动的仿真模型

本次观展观众服务水平评价采用平均排队时间、平均排队长度、高峰人流密度等指标来描述。通过对往届航展调查数据分析及国内各类大型活动期间行人交通流特性参数的调查,对行人步行速度、行人面域、行人路径、公交站台及等候区等进行了构建和标定。通过观众散场的仿真得到观众散场后到达各站点的规律。

(3) 改善措施及仿真评价

由仿真输出结果可以发现,在散场高峰时段 P1 枢纽周边主要节点机场路-海滩路东进口会出现公交车辆左转排队进入枢纽的情况,其原因是交叉口左转通行能力不足、公交车辆排队较长,造成进入枢纽车辆行驶速度下降、观众等待时间增加,需针对该情况提出改善措施并进行仿真测试。两个枢纽仿真情况见图 6。

a) P1 枢纽　　　　　　　　　　　　　　b) P2 枢纽

图 6 仿真情况示意

本次研究针对 P1 停车场公交专线运作情况提出改进措施,对机场路-海滩路东进口进行改造,增加 1 个左转车道。改善措施在仿真软件中修改后进行测试,交叉口左转的公交专线车辆等候队列较改善前下降约 30%,对车辆进出枢纽的干扰减少,公交车辆的行程车速较改善前提高约 10%,同时观展观众平均候车时间较改善前下降约 15%,枢纽载客能力有一定程度的提升。

4 结 语

本文在基于十三届航展现实挑战及总结历届航展交通组织的经验基础上,提出了第十三届航展交通组织策略与措施,即通过单日票务需求控制、区域分级管控、构建三级停车换乘 P+R 体系、停运分离、设置航展专线及专用道等多种交通管理措施,来保障航展交通组织的安全、有序和通畅。

参考文献

[1] 中国国际航空航天博览会[EB/OL]. http://www.airshow.com.cn.

[2] 珠海市规划设计研究院. 第十二届珠海航展交通保障方案效果评估报告[R]. 2018.
[3] 田野, 欧阳陈海. 中国(珠海)航展交通组织策略及实践[J]. 道路交通科学技术, 2018, (5).
[4] 珠海市规划设计研究院. 第十三届中国航展交通运输保障总体方案研究[R]. 2020.
[5] 陈桂龙. 大数据助力第十一届航展交通安保[J]. 中国建设信息化, 2017, (7).

Literature Review of HOV Lane and HSR Control on Freeway

Yao Xu[1] Huachun Tan[2]

(1. Southeast University, Southeast University-Monash University Joint Graduate School;
2. Southeast University, School of Transportation)

Abstract Dynamic lane management is an efficient and intensive way to improve road utilization under resource constraints, in which HOV lane and HSR control are two feasible approaches. This paper sorts out the literatures of HOV lane and HSR control from different countries, combined with the theoretical research and practical experience. The common planning model and dynamic traffic flow model are summarized, the characteristics of bi-level programming model and cell transmission model are compared with their applicability in the transportation system, the limitations of HOV lane and HSR control are discussed, the necessity of constructing complete lane management system is clarified, and the development direction of dynamic lane management in the future is considered.

Keywords Active traffic management Dynamic lane management HOV lane HSR control

0 Introduction

With the rapid growth of traffic demand, the phenomenon of traffic congestion is becoming more and more frequent, especially the freeway congestion during holidays. Due to the constraints of land utilization, environment and finance, it is not realistic to continuously expand lane and build sufficient infrastructures. Therefore, how to make the most of the benefits under the condition of limited resources has become the key to solve the problem of freeway congestion.

ATM(Active Traffic Management) originated from European and American countries, including a series of complete and coherent traffic management measures. It can dynamically manage frequent and occasional traffic congestion, so as to give full play to the maximum benefit of existing traffic facilities(Hu and Zhou, 2014). Active traffic management measures mainly include the application of HOV lane, HSR control, Variable Speed Limits(VSLs), Variable Message Signs(VMS), Toll Management(TM), etc. HOV and HSR mainly give play to the benefits of existing traffic infrastructure from lane level, while the other active traffic management measures above mainly intervene vehicles from the aspects of speed, information and economy. Different management measures are defined as follows:

(1) HOV lane: High occupancy lane is a high-load lane which gives priority on freeways, expressways, or urban roads for vehicles carrying two or more people.

(2) HSR: Hard shoulder running refers to the opening of hard shoulder as temporary lane during peak hours or bottleneck sections of freeway to expand the road capacity.

(3) VSLs: Speed in the area is adjusted in real time to achieve the uniformity of traffic flow to reduce the

impact of congestion and reduce the possibility of secondary accidents.

(4) VMS: The variable information board and traffic control center provide drivers with various travel information to achieve path guidance, so as to reduce the traffic pressure in the congested area.

(5) TM: By monitoring the traffic flow of toll lane in real time, passing vehicles are charged dynamically to control the size of section flow.

This paper is divided into four parts. Section 2 describes the application status of HOV lane, compares the commonly used models in the development process, then puts forward thoughts on its future development direction. Based on HSR control application cases in Europe, America and other countries, section 3 is the part to explain the basic principle of HSR control. The problems in cell transmission model and application process of basic road sections are reviewed, and the coordinated application of multi-active traffic management measures is emphasized. Section 4 is the final part to summarize this whole paper.

1 Literature Review on HOV Lane

This section mainly compares the development history of HOV lane in different countries, and summarizes relevant algorithm models with application cases.

1.1 HOV Lane Application Status

HOV lane first appeared in the United States and have been encouraged elsewhere since the first bus lane was built on Shirley Street with great success. Meanwhile, in Europe, where land use is more intensive, the public transport system is relatively developed, and the average number of passengers per vehicle in most countries is 1.3. Therefore, the carpooling mode has been well implemented (Bi, 1997). While the development of HOV lane in China starts relatively late. Then in 2010, based on relevant experience and Chinese current situation, Wang firstly proposed the planning content of carpool priority. Later, China began to plan the setting of HOV lane, and the first HOV lane was operated in Wuxi. Specific relevant cases are shown in Tab. 1 and Tab. 2.

HOV lane construction schedule in Occident (Wei et al., 2017)　　　　Tab. 1

Country	Lane Access	Time	Site	Comment
America	4 +	1973	Shirley Street	First bus lane in 1969
Canada	—	1990	Vancouver, Toronto	—
Australia	2 +	1992	Melbourne	—
Netherlands	3 +	1993	—	Low utilization, cancelled in 1994

HOV lane construction schedule in China (Zeng, 2019)　　　　Tab. 2

City	Lane Access	Time	Site	Implementation period
Wuxi	3 +	2014	Xingyuan Road Lihu Avenue	7:30—9:30; 17:30—19:30
Jinan	2 +	2015	Lvyou Road	7:00—9:00; 17:00—19:00
Shenzhen	2 +	2016	Binhai Avenue Meiguan Freeway	7:30—9:30; 17:30—19:30
Chengdu	2 +	2017	Kehua Road	7:30—9:00; 17:00—19:00
Dalian	2 +	2017	Northeast Expressway	6:30—8:30; 16:30—19:00

1.2 Application and Selection Conditions of HOV Lane

Research on HOV lane mainly includes two aspects: managers need to determine under what circumstances the road needs to set HOV lane, that is, the conditions that HOV lane should be applied. While road users' value under what circumstances they need to choose to use HOV lane which represents their travel choice.

1.2.1 Threshold for Introducing HOV Lane

Generally, the conditions for setting HOV lane lie in the basic parameters of traffic flow, that is, the comparison of section flow and capacity, and the average speed of section. In addition, there are indicators such as road occupancy and lane saturation (Hu 2013). Zhou et al. in 2020 defined a new metric based on the travel time, that is, per capita delay index (d') which could be calculated by the following equation:

$$d' = \frac{q_b \times n_b \times d_b + q_c \times n_c \times d_c}{q_b \times n_b + q_c \times n_c} \quad (1)$$

Where q_b and q_c refer to the traffic volume of high occupancy vehicles and single occupancy vehicles, n_b and n_c refer to the number of people in each high occupancy vehicles and single occupancy vehicles, d_b and d_c refer to the delay for each high occupancy vehicles and single occupancy vehicles, respectively. Therefore, this index not only considers the passenger load and traffic volume of each vehicle on the road section, but also introduces the delay index. By setting a threshold for this index, it can be determined whether or not to apply a HOV lane under any circumstances.

1.2.2 Travel Selection Model

Despite the fact that the HOV lane is available, how likely are drivers to use the HOV lane. The common model is the Logit model of multiple travel choices (Chen et al., 2010). The model generally assumes that the total number of road trips required is constant; except for cars, the passenger capacity of other vehicles is constant. The model can be represented as follows:

$$P'_i = \frac{P_i \times e^{\Delta V_i}}{\sum_{i=1}^{k}(P_i \times e^{\Delta V_i})} \quad (2)$$

Where P_i is the probability using basic travel mode i, P'_i is the probability using mode i after introducing HOV lane, ΔV_i is the change in travel mode i which can be calculated as follows:

$$\Delta V_i = \alpha \times \Delta IVTT_i + \beta \times \Delta OVTT_i + \gamma \times \Delta COST_i \quad (3)$$

Where $\Delta IVTT_i$ refers to changes in vehicle travel time for mode i, $\Delta OVTT_i$ refers to changes out of vehicle travel time for mode i, $\Delta COST_i$ refers to changes in travel cost for mode i.

Based on this model, Wang et al. in 2019 studied the setting of HOV lane on Hexing Road in Harbin. Model prediction shows that after adding HOV lane, the number of single occupancy vehicles decreases significantly, while the number of other different types of HOV 2 + vehicles increases to different degrees. To some extent, it achieves the purpose of setting HOV lane. Similarly, Wei et al. in 2017 conducted an analysis of HOV lane setting on Xuefu road in Chongqing during peak hours, and predicted the change of travel choice mode after the introduction of HOV lane through Logit model. The results showed that the number of single occupancy vehicle decreased from 32.23% to 24.16%, and the proportion of high occupancy vehicles increased from 35.89% to 42.48%. Converting a general lane on Xuefu road into a HOV lane is feasible to relieve traffic pressure.

1.2.3 Bi-level Programming Model

When both take planners making the best benefit of the road network and the decision of traveler selection into consideration, the two-layer programming model comes into being (Huang, 2016).

The upper planning model generally considers the generalized cost (T), including the construction cost of HOV lane (B), energy consumption cost of transportation system (P) and pollution emission cost of road network system(H). The specific model expression can be expressed as follows:

$$\min T = B + P + H \tag{4}$$

$$B = h \times L_a \tag{5}$$

$$P = \varphi \times t_a \times q_a \tag{6}$$

$$H = \mu \times t_a \times q_a \tag{7}$$

$$\text{s.t.} \begin{cases} B \leqslant B_{\max} \\ P \leqslant P_{\max} \\ H \leqslant H_{\max} \end{cases} \tag{8}$$

Where a is the road, L_a is the length of the road, t_a is the travel time on the road, q_a is the traffic flow on the road, h is the cost of setting a HOV lane per unit length, φ and μ are the cost of energy consumed per unit of time and the cost of pollution discharged per unit of time a vehicle is operating, respectively. Eq. (7) is the constraint condition of the upper planning model and represents the limited cost of the system.

The lower level planning model is to shorten the travel time of road network users by choosing their own travel strategies on the premise that the road network layout has been determined. UE equilibrium of Wardrop principle is usually used to represent the lower level planning model. UE equilibrium not only considers the traffic impedance of the road network, but also emphasizes that travel costs can be minimized only if all road users have chance to change routes, which is exactly what all road users expect.

Xue in 2018 considered the mutual influence between the planning layout of HOV lane and the traveler's travel path selection behavior. Taking the classical Sioux Falls network and the real road network of Zhongguancun district in Beijing as examples, the genetic algorithm is applied to solve the optimal solution of the model. The result of the case shows that the bi-level programming model can not only ensure the maximum traffic efficiency of the road network, but also control the energy consumption at a low level. Fan has done similar research, except that he focuses on HOT lane (High Occupancy Toll lane-HOV lane that are paid for by single occupancy vehicles) and models the pricing strategy based on the traditional bi-level programming model. The upper-level model is the operator's pricing strategy, while the lower-level model is still the UE equilibrium model, which simulates the traveler's behavior of making choices according to traffic state and charging level.

1.3 Expansion Thinking of HOV Lane

The evaluation of HOV lane is not always positive, and some scholars have raised doubts about the application of HOV lane. Through collecting and analyzing the data of HOV lane in California for several months, it is found that the capacity of HOV lane is about 20% lower than that of general lane. In addition, HOV lane utilization is not high, 81% of HOV lane have a traffic flow below 1400 vehicles per hour during peak hours, which means that the promotion of HOV lane in California has not produced significant incentive effect on local carpools (Kwon and Varaiya, 2008).

In this context, more and more scholars begin to pay attention to the expansion of the research direction of HOV lane, that is, HOT lane. Burris et al. in 2014 investigated the impact of HOT lane on carpools, finding that the transition from HOV lane to HOT lane would cause some carpools break up and become SOVs, which will add traffic flow and emissions on the road. SOVs with different values of time (VOTs) affect their willingness to switch from the GP lane to HOT lane, thus affecting the efficiency of the HOT lane. However, VOTs are generally unknown to the operator, so dynamic charging measures for HOT lane appear. Fees paid by different SOVs using HOT lane are independent and unrelated. Based on this idea, Jin et al. in 2020 proposed stable

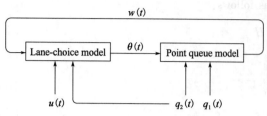

Fig. 1　Block diagram of the HOT lane charging strategy

dynamic charging scheme independent of the lane-choice models for HOT lane. Specifically, there are logit model, vehicle-based user equilibrium model with heterogeneous values of time and general lane-choice model. Then the output of the lane-choice model is taken as the input of the point queue model to obtain the differences in the queueing times on the GP and HOT lane. By adjusting fees on HOT lane in the lane-choice model, the average lane delay is minimized. The specific process is shown in Fig. 1 below.

At time t, $q_1(t)$ and $q_2(t)$ are arrival rates of HOVs and SOVs, respectively. $u(t)$ is the fee driving on the HOT lane, $w(t)$ is the difference in the queueing times on the GP and HOT lane, $\theta(t)$ is the residual capacity of the HOT lane.

2　Literature Review on HSR Control

The HSR control has been in operation in the United States and European countries. This section mainly explains the basic principle of HSR control, summarizes the commonly used models, and compares the application cases in different countries.

2.1　The Basic Principle of HSR Control

The idea of HSR control is to increase the capacity of the road by providing an additional lane. Germany is the first country to apply HSR control. When applying HSR control, speed coordination is carried out with the speed limit of 100 km/h. Such a design increases the capacity of the A5 freeway during peak hours by about 20% (Geistefeldt, 2012). The application of HSR control in other European and American countries is shown in Tab. 3.

HSR operation schedule in Occident (Ye, 2016)　　Tab. 3

Country	Time	Site	Speed Limit(km/h)	Performance
America	1992	Minnesota	56	Average travel time is reduced by 5 – 15 minutes
Netherlands	2004	—	70	—
England	2006	Birmingham M42 Freeway	—	Average travel time reduced by 9% ~ 26%

The impact of HSR control is illustrated on the fundamental diagram as shown in Fig. 2 below. The solid and dashed lines respectively represent the fundamental diagram between traffic flow and density when HSR control is not applied and when HSR control is applied. Where Q is the capacity flow without HSR control, ρ_{cri} is the critical density without HSR control, $\bar{\rho}$ is the jam density without HSR control. On the contrary, the other marks on the figure are the traffic flow parameters corresponding to HSR control.

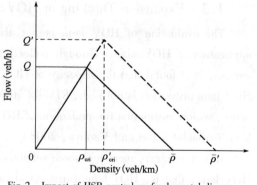

Fig. 2　Impact of HSR control on fundamental diagram

2.2　Dynamic Traffic Modelling and HSR Control Problem

The research on HSR control mainly focuses on the dynamic traffic flow model and some problems in the application. Among them, traffic flow model refers to cell transmission model, while the application problems mainly refer to the upstream and downstream problems of congestion points.

2.2.1 Cell Transmission Model

Cell Transmission Model (CTM) was first proposed byDaganzo in 1994 which could simulate traffic dynamics and network performances, as shown in Fig. 3.

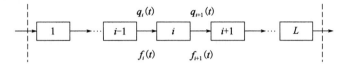

Fig. 3 Schematic diagram of basic module cells in CTM model

The basic idea of this model is to discretize time and space, divide the road section into continuous cells, and the flow continuity between cells is conserved. In Fig. 3, the road section is divided into continuous L cells, $q_i(t)$ is the maximum traffic flow allowed into cell i from cell $i-1$ within the time interval t, and $f_i(t)$ is the real traffic flow into cell i within the time interval t. Certainly, the number of vehicles flowing into cell i at the time interval t is determined by the transmitting capacity of upstream cell $i-1$ and the receiving capacity of current cell i.

Li et al. in 2014 focused on the active traffic management strategy and used the cell transmission model aiming at minimizing vehicle delay. The model was represented by linear programming and mixed integer programming, and was solved by Cplex software. Since the use of hard shoulder occupies the buffer area of emergency, the scholars also strengthened the need to balance the relationship between hard shoulder running time and speed coordination. Based on a deeper understanding of the cell transmission model, Li et al. in 2019 established a METANET model aiming at minimizing the total travel time of road network, and presented a solution algorithm based on genetic algorithm. Finally, taking I-80E highway in California as an example, the traffic flow data is simulated and analyzed. The analysis results show that if the traffic volume in each lane is greater than 1600 veh/h, the application of HSR can reduce the total travel time by 14.39%. But if the traffic volume in any one lane is more than 1600 veh/h, the application of HSR operation will increase the travel time of the road network.

2.2.2 Problems in HSR Control

The temporary application of HSR control in congested or accident sections can bring some benefits, but there are still some problems in the implementation process. According to traffic state parameters such as flow and density, freeway control center analyzes road condition and applies the HSR control, which may lead to congestion in downstream sections.

Aron et al. in 2013 researched the measure of applying one 3 meters wide hard shoulder as an auxiliary lane during the peak periods of the A4 and A86 freeway in the east of Paris. They proposed that although the congestion relief effect was relatively obvious, the accident rate in the downstream section increased, that is, the possibility of accident migration was higher due to the displacement of the traffic bottleneck. Based on the car following model, Li in 2018 researched the minimum safety distance of freeway under lane change behavior when the hard shoulder control was applied, and conducted simulation evaluation on G24 Shanghai-Nanjing freeway. The result shows that the average delay time decreases from 10 – 15 min to less than 5 min, and the traffic efficiency of the whole section increases. However, it does not consider the traffic conditions downstream of the congestion point, that is, it does not take full account of the impact that the spatiotemporal migration of the traffic bottleneck on the downstream brings.

2.3 Expansion thinking of HSR control

The setting of the freeway hard shoulder is aimed at guaranteeing the rapidity of the channel for breakdown vans, but the application of HSR control will take up the emergency channel. So how does not affect the breakdown vans when accident happens, at the same time greatly reduce the degree of the congestion will need to consider. In this context, Bhouri et al. in 2016 researched reliability indicators for road traffic.

Additionally, it is not limited to the coordination of HSR and variable speed limit control, other active traffic management measures can also be integrated in many aspects. Liao et al. designed seven hybrid active traffic management schemes including ramp control, HSR operation and variable message signs. By evaluating and comparing the average queue length, average density and average travel speed under each scheme, the possibility of coordinated optimization is realized. Details are shown in Tab. 4.

Overview of HSR operation development　　Tab. 4

Author	Research Site	Research Object	Method or Model
Bhouri et al.	Paris A86 Freeway	Travel time reliability index	Compare the travel time standard deviation, skewness, and probability of exceeding the threshold
Liao et al.	Hsueh-Shan Tunnel	Hybrid application of ATM measures	Dyna TAIWAN simulation
Khattak and Fontaine	I-66 in Virginia	Injury severities from ATM deployment	Full Bayesian framework

3　Conclusions

HOV lane and HSR control have been applied in occident earlier, covering the willingness of travelers, traffic economy, traffic emissions, road network efficiency and other aspects. However, China starts late. European and American countries are different from China in terms of driving mode and road network density, which makes different countries have different abilities to mitigate the degree of congestion in the road network. In spite of this, researches on dynamic lane management from occident countries still can be used for reference in solving traffic congestion problems in China.

Under the condition of limited road resources, dynamic lane management plays an important role as a part of active traffic management. Its application practices in different countries have shown significant advantages in eliminating congestion. The travel selection model takes the users' benefit as the optimization object, and the bi-level programming model takes global variables into consideration to achieve the optimal balance between the interests of planners and users; the cell transmission model reflects the dynamic changes of traffic flow based on different capacity. However, the current research on the optimal combination of multiple management measures is relatively few, and lane-level management lacks an overall strategy in the road network layout. These aspects need to be further deepened.

References

[1] Aron M, Seidowsky R, Cohen S. Safety impact of using the hard shoulder during congested traffic. The case of a managed lane operation on a French urban motorway[J]. Transportation Research Part C, 2013, 28:168-180.

[2] Bhouri N, Aron M, Scemama G. Travel time reliability with and without the dynamic use of hard shoulder: Field assessment from a French motorway [J]. Journal of Traffic and Transportation Engineering, 2016,3(6): 520-530.

[3] Bi R. Current situation and development trend of HOV lanes in foreign countries[J]. Highway, 1997, 16-18.

[4] Burris M, Alemazkoor N, Benz R, et al. The impact of HOT lanes on carpools[J]. Research in Transportation Economics, 2014,44(1): 43-51.

[5] Chen S, Zhang, X, Ding J. Feasibility on HOV Lanes Based on Multinomial Logit Model[C]. 2010 2nd IEEE International Conference on Information and Financial Engineering Information and Financial Engineering(ICIFE), IEEE, 2010, 135-138.

[6] Daganzo C F. The cell transmission model: A dynamic representation of highway traffic consistent with the hydrodynamic theory[J]. Transportation Research Part B, 1994,28(4): 269-287.

[7] Fan W. Modeling High-occupancy/toll Lanes in US[J]. Journal of Transportation Systems Engineering and Information Technology, 2015,15(3): 204-213.

[8] Geistefeldt J. Operational experience with temporary hard shoulder running in Germany[J]. Transportation Research Record, 2012,(2278): 67-73.

[9] Hu S, Zhou Y. Foreign active traffic management technology and its application prospect in China[J]. Transportation management, 2014: 51-55.

[10] Hu Y. Design and evaluation of HOV lane scheme[D]. 2013.

[11] Huang J. Multi-mode traffic network flow distribution model and system optimization including carpool[D]. 2016.

[12] Jin W, Wang X, Lou Y. Stable dynamic pricing scheme independent of lane-choice models for high-occupancy-toll lanes[J]. Transportation Research Part B, 2020,140: 64-78.

[13] Khattak Z H, Fontaine M D. A Bayesian modeling framework for crash severity effects of active traffic management systems[J]. Accident Analysis and Prevention, 2019, 145, 105544.

[14] Kwon J, Varaiya P. Effectiveness of California's High Occupancy Vehicle(HOV)system. Transportation Research Part C: Emerging Technologies, 2008,16(1): 98-115.

[15] Li B. Research on the comprehensive utilization of hard shoulder of expressway. Sichuan Building Materials, 2018,44(7): 149-152.

[16] Li R, Ye Z, Li B. Speed coordination with temporary use of shoulder integrated simulation optimization[J]. Journal of System Simulation, 2019,31(3): 468-475.

[17] Li Y, Chow A H F, Cassel D L. Optimal control of motorways by ramp metering, variable speed limits, and hard-shoulder running[J]. Transportation Research Record, 2014,2470: 122-130.

[18] Liao T, Hu T, Ho W. Simulation studies of traffic management strategies for a long tunnel[J]. Tunnelling and Underground Space Technology, 2012,27(1): 123-132.

[19] Wang L, Li Y, Wang Y. Research on HOV Lane setting scheme of Hexing Road in Harbin[D]. 2019: 1-10.

[20] Wang W. Carpool Priority Planning Methods in Central Area of Large Cities[J]. Journal of Chongqing Jiaotong University, 2010,29(2): 2-7.

[21] Wei Y, Tang Q, Chen R. Study on application Effect of HOV Lane Design—Taking Xuefu Avenue in Chongqing as an example[J]. Technology & Economy in Areas of Communications, 2017, 19(6): 12-16.

[22] Xue H. Study on the Optimization of Urban HOV Lane Setting based on two-layer Programming Model[D]. 2018.

[23] Ye Z. Study on optimization of highway Shoulder for temporary Use[D]. 2016.

[24] Zeng Y. Research on effect Evaluation System of HOV Lane implementation — Taking Shenzhen as an example[J]. Technology & Economy in Areas of Communications, 2019,21(5).

[25] Zhou G, Mao L, Hu P, et al. Research on HOV Lane Priority Dynamic Control under Connected Vehicle Environment[J]. Journal of Advanced Transportation, 2020.

Intelligent Scheduling Algorithm of Bus Priority Control Strategy in the Internet of Vehicles Environment

Yao Jiang   Zhi Zhao   Hongchen Li   Jiangfeng Wang

(MOT Key Laboratory of Transport Industry of Big Data Application Technologies for Comprehensive Transport, Beijing Jiaotong University)

Abstract   Aiming at the problems of delays of BRT operation in road network and green light loss based on the current priority strategies, this paper designed an algorithm that by the real-time detection of vehicles arriving at the intersection under the environment of Internet of Vehicles, taking the total delay of passengers as the benefit function, the BRT priority was implemented in the case of nonreduction of the total delay, so as to realize BRT driving through the road network without stopping. Based on the predicted BRT travel time, the algorithm determines different time windows within a cycle of BRT's arriving point, and then chooses corresponding priority strategies: green extension, red truncation and speed regulation. Taking the BRT 4 in Beijing as the research object, the simulation experiments were carried out through VISSIM modelling, and the proposed algorithm model was empirically analyzed. The results show that compared with the previous signal control scheme, this algorithm can reduce BRT's stops by more than 90%, BRT's delay by about 16%-18%, the total delay of all passengers in the road network by 8.95%, and improve BRT's speed by about 22.41%.

Keywords   Internet of vehicles   Bus rapid transit   Bus priority   Traffic engineering   Intelligent transportation system   VISSIM

0 Introduction

International Association of Public Transport proposed the PTx2 strategy (2009), which aimed to double the passenger volume of global public transport by 2025. A new campaign called Growing With Public Transport was launched in support of the PTx2 strategy to help global policymakers improve their understanding of public transport and recognize the advantages of more and better public and sustainable transport. The Chinese government issued *Guidelines on Priority Development of Public Transport in Cities* (2012). The National Public Transport City Demonstration Project initiated by the Ministry of Transport was started (2011). By 2020, 87 cities have been selected as pilot cities of the National City Demonstration Project. These pilot cities have further implemented the concept of giving priority to the development of public transport, increased investment in urban public transport, and provided higher-quality infrastructure and higher-level services. As one of the effective measures in Public Transport City, BRT can provide higher quality service. It is of great practical significance to improve the service quality of BRT with advanced technology.

The two key technologies of BRT are the layout of bus-only lanes and the setting of bus signal priority. Without bus signal priority, the efficiency of bus-only lanes will be greatly reduced. The current problem is that it is difficult to obtain the priority of bus time. The reality is that no city in China has fully implemented the principle of signal priority. In general, BRT routes are located in the main road with heavy traffic, and the waiting time for traffic lights will be longer accordingly. If the waiting time exceeds 60 s, BRT cannot run quickly.

The technology to realize bus priority currently mainly uses GPS technology, but on the one hand, for signal adjustments that take only a few seconds, accuracy cannot be guaranteed. On the other hand, because the signal adjustment cannot be connected with the bus, the loss of green light will cause signal phase instability, and lead to unstable shock wave. On this issue, Internet of Vehicles has a broad application prospect. Compared with the intelligent transportation system which is widely used in the field of road transportation, Internet of Vehicles can realize a more comprehensive perception of various interconnections and intelligent information processing and application integration. Through wireless communication between electronic devices mounted on vehicles, it can extract and effectively utilize the static and dynamic information of all vehicles on the information network platform, connect vehicles with vehicles and roadside infrastructure, realize real-time information exchange, and serve people's transportation. In this kind of environment, with the support of communication infrastructure, intersection control unit can obtain more accurate data, can be more flexible to control the vehicle to move. The V2X technology of vehicle-road cooperation has developed rapidly in recent years. Real-time communication between vehicle-road-cloud can solve the disadvantages of traditional traffic detection methods in information exchange. The vehicle-road collaboration V2X technology can effectively improve urban traffic safety and operational efficiency through the rapid and stable information transmission between different transportation equipment and transportation infrastructure, combined with intelligent optimization algorithms. Using advanced communication technology, real-time traffic information can be transmitted to BRT to ensure that BRT makes full use of the adjusted signal time and avoid the loss of green light.

Aiming at the problems of delays of BRT operation in road network and instability in traffic flow based on the current priority strategies, this paper designed an algorithm for signalized intersections based on the total delay PI of intersections in the environment of Internet of Vehicles using real-time information, for a variety of bus priority signal timing scheme. And it took BRT 4 in Beijing as the research object to conduct empirical analysis with the data of investigation.

1　Literature Review

BRT has to wait for the red light at the signalized intersection, which will lead to the reduction of the overall level of service of BRT. This problem has become a hotspot in related fields. BRT has gained international popularity following the opening of the world's first BRT line in Curitiba, Brazil. The first city to study bus signal priority is Los Angeles in the United States. It is found that signal priority can improve bus efficiency, level of service of BRT and reach the destination more conveniently.

Firstly, it is the literature review of bus priority algorithm. Richardson A. J. et al. (2019) introduced two new evaluation methods for perceived delay and predicted delay. It was verified that the evaluation model is of great significance to signal priority and public transportation management, and verified the rationality of active public transportation priority. Hongchao Liu et al. (2004). Proposed a theoretical model to determine the relationship between the position of the bus detector and the validity of the final result in the bus signal priority. The theoretical model and the simulation results are very consistent. They believe that this conclusion can better serve the bus signal priority system. On the basis of signal control, Chen Jun(2009) studied the control flow of the model, analyzed the signal control parameters from multiple angles, established the model with goal of reducing the total passenger delay, and optimized the overall structure of the model and the control strategy. Andy-An-Kai Jeng et al. (2013). proposed an adaptive traffic signal control method for bus priority, which determined non-fixed phase sequence and length based on collaborative information to improve the performance of the bus system. The simulation results showed that this method could effectively reduce the waiting time of the bus and ensure operation of the bus according to the schedule. Xiaosi Zeng et al. (2014). proposed a random mixed integer nonlinear model and applied the model to signal priority for comparison. The results showed that under the background of low and medium traffic volumes, the total delay at intersections increased. And under the background of high volume, the model can effectively reduce the overall delay.

Secondly, it is the literature review of bus priority schemes. N. B. Hounsell et al. (2007). applied the global positioning system to the signal priority system through the virtual configuration and the vehicle's own induction, to provide more accurate location positioning, and provide more accurate location for the signal controller. Guojiang Shen et al. (2009). proposed a networked traffic intelligent coordinated control technology, which set up a network of bus lines passing through areas. The entire road network was considered a large system, and each subsystem was each intersection. The multi-phase intelligent traffic signal controller was installed in each intersection, and cooperate with adjacent intersections. Through the exchange the information from community vehicle detector and the positioning collecting device, and cooperate with adjacent signal controller, they realized the entire road network of vehicles coordination and public transport priority in order to improve the robustness of the system. Additionally, the fuzzy rule base system was also added in the each module. Yinsong Wang et al. (2014). established a collaborative bus priority system in Internet of Vehicles. The system was deployed and verified at an intersection with two adjacent bus stations in Taicang. The results showed that the system can travel time and the number of stations. Bo Haijian et al. (2018). proposed a bus signal priority model based on a networked environment, which prioritizes vehicles based on the vehicle travel time and the vehicle's predicted arriving point at the parking line. The results showed that under the background of increasing a small amount of community vehicle delays, the punctuality and average speed of vehicles had been greatly improved.

It can be seen form the literature review that many researches still focus on the priority strategies of single intersection. And many experiments are also based on numerical simulation rather than real-time detection by detectors along the roadside. At the same time, various studies lack implementation technology or corresponding scenarios, so it is impossible to verify the application of BRT priority to the actual situation. In addition, researches on the balance between public transportation and community vehicles are still very imperfect.

2 Methodology

In the environment of Internet of Vehicles, the control of signals at each intersection needs to consider the real-time position of BRT, which is realized through the communication technology of Internet of Vehicles. The algorithm model proposed in this paper performs signal adjustment under the condition that the total delay of the intersection is not reduced with a constant cycle, and at the same time, the shortened green time of phases that are conflicted with the BRT's phase should be allocated in proportion to the flow rate of each phase. Based on the micro bus priority strategies of single intersection, the benefits of the macro bus priority in road network (including multiple intersections where bus priority can be implemented) were studied in this paper.

The applicable conditions of this algorithm are as follows:

(1) Bus-only lanes are set at the aimed intersections.

(2) The original cycle-length and signal timing plan is fixed at the aimed intersection.

(3) The signal operation of the aimed intersection is independent of other intersections.

(4) The speed of BRT and community vehicles can be obtained.

(5) Real-time location of BRT can be obtained.

(6) Real-time ridership of BRT and community vehicles can be obtained.

(7) The queue of vehicles at each intersection can be obtained.

2.1　Scenario Description

This section introduces the working principle and simulation scenarios of implementing bus priority at multiple intersections of the main line in the Internet of Vehicles environment.

Under the technology of vehicle-road collaboration or V2X, it is necessary to network BRT and traffic lights. When the BRT enters the area near the intersection, it sends a priority request to the RSU through the OBU. The RSU's built-in bus priority algorithm (that is, the intelligent priority algorithm proposed in this article) adjusts the phase time and phase sequence according to the time point when the vehicle is expected to arrive at the stop line and the current signal light state, so that the BRT can pass the intersection first. The real-time scenario is shown in Fig. 1.

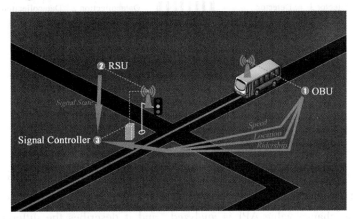

Fig. 1　The real-time scenarios under V2X technology

In short, the system architecture of the above scenario applies the smart travel configuration of public transportation under V2X technology, as shown in Fig. 2.

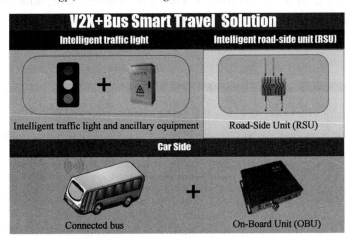

Fig. 2　The system architecture of V2X technology

The following is the layout and working mode of the detectors at single intersection: set Detectors to detect the arrival of BRT at suitable positions upstream of the intersection, and set Datacollections to count the amount of community vehicles at other suitable positions upstream of the intersection. The positions of Detectors and Datacollections are shown in Fig. 3.

In Fig. 3, on the main road, Detector 1 and Detector 2 are detectors closer to the intersection, and Detector 3 and Detector 4 are Detectors farther from the intersection. At the same time, on both the main road and the branch road, two Datacollections are set at each entrance to count the community vehicles.

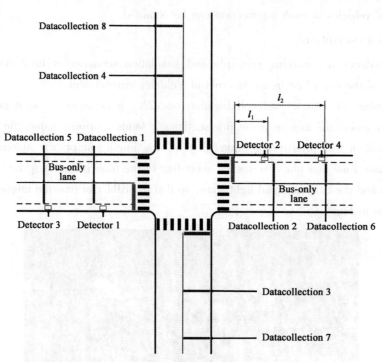

Fig. 3 The layout of Detectors and Datacollections

In this paper, the benefit function PI based on the total delay of the intersection is adopted. Taking every person at the intersection as the measurement object, PI represents the total delay of the intersection in a cycle, measured in seconds. The change value ΔPI is analyzed, and it describes the difference between the overall operation benefit of the intersection after the implementation of signal adjustment and that before the implementation of signal adjustment. When ΔPI < 0, the overall benefit of the intersection will be improved. While ΔPI > 0, the overall benefit of the intersection will be decreased. Here, with ΔPI = 0 as the boundary, whether to adjust the signal is divided.

When the Detectors detects BRT, it calculates the arriving point (arriving at the intersection), and its arriving modes can be divided into 3 types, as shown in Fig. 4.

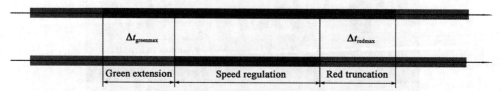

Fig. 4 The intervals of the priority control strategies

2.2 BRT Priority Plans Modelling

(1) The positions of Detectors and the maximum green extension time (the maximum red truncation time)

Each phase of the intersection is divided: set the phase that allows BRT to pass as set i while set the phase that does not allow BRT to pass as set j. Take a two-phase intersection as an example. If BRT goes straight from west to east when passing through the intersection, $i = \{\text{the first phase}\}$, $j = \{\text{the second phase}\}$, as shown in Fig. 5.

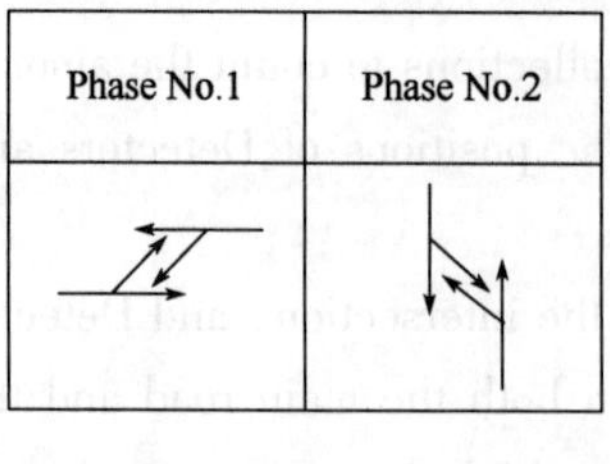

This paper adopts a dual detector method to detect the arrival of BRT. The detectors closer to the intersection can be more accurate to predict the arrival of BRT, so that the predicted ΔPI is closer to the actual value. And the farther detectors are to detect the following situation: when the arriving point predicted

Fig. 5 The directions of each phase

is in the interval of speed regulation, to ensure that BRT has enough acceleration distance, it is necessary to detect the BRT in advance. When the speed regulation needs to be implemented, the acceleration instruction will be sent to BRT so that BRT can arrive at the point in the interval of green extension.

The distance between the detector closer to the intersection and the intersection l_1:

$$l_1 \geqslant v_{bus} \cdot \Delta t_{green\ max} \tag{1}$$

where

v_{bus} ——the current speed of the bus;

$\Delta t_{green\ max}$ ——the maximum green extension time.

The algorithm is to adjust the signal under the condition of the same cycle. Once the green light of BRT phase becomes longer, the green light of other phases will be shortened. In principle, it is necessary to ensure that vehicles in other phases waiting at the intersection due to red light can leave within a green light release. In this way, the calculation of the maximum green extension time $\Delta t_{green\ max}$ and the maximum red truncation time $\Delta t_{red\ max}$ are the same. The maximum green extension $\Delta t_{green\ max}$ can be calculated by Eq. (2).

$$\Delta t_{green\ max} = \sum_{r \in j} \left(\frac{s^r - q^r}{s^r} T - t_{red}^r \right) \tag{2}$$

where

s^r ——the sum of vehicle departure speeds in each lane of phase r;

q^r ——the sum of vehicle arrival speeds in each lane of phase r;

T ——cycle-length;

t_{red}^r ——the red light time of phase r.

The distance between the detector farther from the intersection and the intersection l_2:

$$l_2 \geqslant l_1 + \frac{v_{bus\ max} \cdot v_{bus}}{v_{bus\ max} - v_{bus}} (t_{red}^i - \Delta t_{red\ max} - \Delta t_{green\ max}) \tag{3}$$

where

$v_{bus\ max}$ ——the maximum speed for safe BRT driving;

v_{bus} ——the current speed of the bus;

t_{red}^i ——the red light time of phase i;

$\Delta t_{red\ max}$ ——the maximum red truncation time.

(2) The total delay at the intersection

In order to calculate ΔPI quantitatively, it is assumed that the traffic flow on the road network reaches the signal intersection at a constant speed. Fig. 6 shows the amount of the community vehicles affected by the green extension of the phases that are conflicted with BRT, namely Q_1 and Q_2. Fig. 7 shows the amount of the community vehicles affected by the green extension of the same BRT's phase, namely Q_3.

ΔPI of green extension is shown in Eq. (4).

$$\Delta PI = n \cdot \left(Q_1 + \frac{1}{2} Q_2 \right) \cdot \Delta t_{green} - \left(M + \frac{1}{2} n \cdot Q_3 \right) \cdot (t_{red}^{bus} - \Delta t_{green}) \tag{4}$$

where

n ——the average amount of passengers in a community vehicle;

M ——the amount of passenger in BRT;

t_{red}^{bus} ——the red light time of BRT's phase;

Δt_{green} ——the green extension time;

Q_1——the current amount of waiting community vehicles of the phase j;
Q_2——the amount of community vehicles arriving within Δt_{green} of the phase j;
Q_3——the amount of community vehicles arriving within Δt_{green} of the phase i.

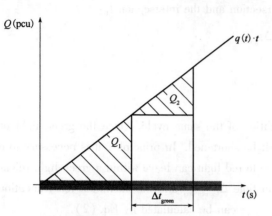

Fig. 6　The phases that are conflicted with BRT's phase and Q_1 & Q_2

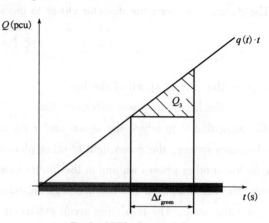

Fig. 7　BRT's phase and Q_3

Similar to green extension, it is assumed that the traffic flow on the road network reaches the signal intersection at a constant speed. Fig. 8 shows the amount of the community vehicles affected by the red truncation of the phases that are conflicted with BRT, namely Q_4 and Q_5. Fig. 9 shows the amount of the community vehicles affected by the red truncation of the same BRT's phase, namely Q_6.

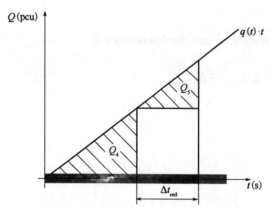

Fig. 8　The phases that are conflicted with BRT's phase and Q_4 & Q_5

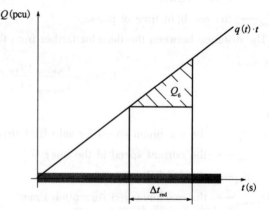

Fig. 9　BRT's phase and Q_6

ΔPI of red truncation is shown in Eq. (5).

$$\Delta \text{PI} = n \cdot Q_6 \cdot (t_{red}^{bus} + \Delta t_{red}) - \left(M + n \cdot Q_4 + \frac{1}{2} n \cdot Q_5\right) \cdot \Delta t_{red} \tag{5}$$

where

n——the average amount of passengers in a community vehicle;
M——the amount of passenger in BRT;
t_{red}^{bus}——the red light time of BRT's phase;
Δt_{red}——the red truncation time;
Q_4——the current amount of waiting community vehicles of the phase i;
Q_5——the amount of community vehicles arriving within Δt_{red} of the phase i;

Q_6——the amount of community vehicles arriving within Δt_{red} of the phase j.

The calculation of ΔPI of speed regulation is the same as green extension, which is shown in Eq. (6).

$$\Delta PI = n \cdot \left(Q_1 + \frac{1}{2}Q_2\right) \cdot \Delta t_{green} - \left(M + \frac{1}{2}n \cdot Q_3\right) \cdot (t_{red}^{bus} - \Delta t_{green}) \qquad (6)$$

The algorithm flow includes three parts: the judgement of speed regulation, the judgement of signal adjustment and signal control. The flow chart is shown in Fig. 10.

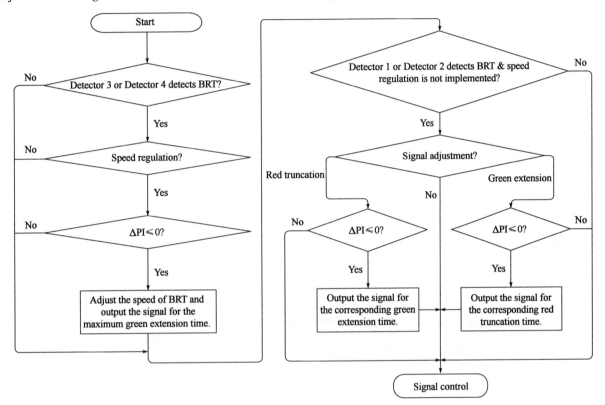

Fig. 10 The process of signal priority control of BRT at a single intersection

When the farther detector detects BRT, according to the speed of BRT and the distance from BRT to the intersection, predict the arriving point of BRT, and then judge whether the arriving point is in the interval of speed regulation according to the current phase state. If speed regulation is needed, calculate ΔPI and make corresponding decision.

When the closer detector detects BRT, in order to get a more accurate result, according to the speed of BRT and the distance from BRT to the intersection, predict the arriving point of BRT again, and then judge whether the arriving point is in the interval of signal adjustment (green extension, red truncation) according to the current phase state. If signal adjustment is needed, calculate ΔPI and make corresponding decision.

According to the fixed cycle-length and the result of adjustment, the signal controllers control the signal changes to minimize the total delay at the intersection.

3 Case Validation

3.1 Simulation Parameters Setting

This paper conducted an empirical analysis of BRT 4 in Beijing. The objects were five consecutive signal intersections, namely the intersections of Nanlishi Road-Beilishi Road and Fucheng Road, Zhanlanguan Road-

Sanlihe East Road and Fucheng Road, Sanlihe Road and Fucheng Road, Capital Stadium South Road and Fucheng Road, and Fucheng North Second Street-Fucheng South Second Street and Fucheng Road, which are shown in Fig. 11. And the total length is 1.5 kilometers. The investigation time is the morning rush hour and noon off-peak in workday and holiday. The data collection form is shown in Tab. 1.

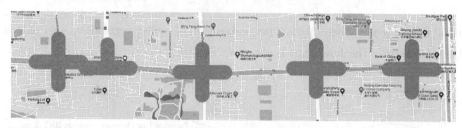

Fig. 11　Five Intersections on the Map

Data collection form　　　　　　　　　　　　　　　　　Tab. 1

The Morning Rush Hour in Workday of Nanlishi Road-Beilishi Road and Fucheng Road (pcu/h)											
WBL	WBT	WBR	EBL	EBT	EBR	SBL	SBT	SBR	NBL	NBT	NBR
213	821	422	245	1092	194	324	156	143	303	174	270

The signal timing of the five signalized intersections is shown in Fig. 12.

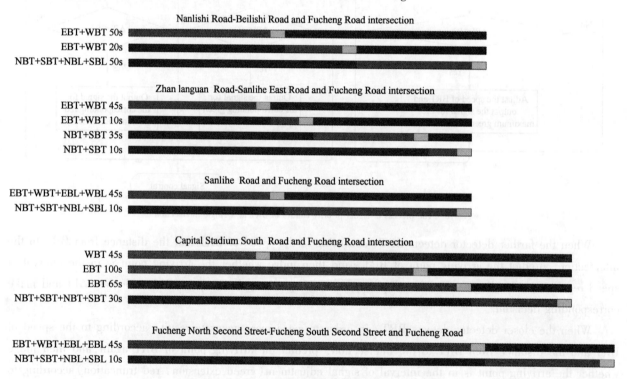

Fig. 12　The signal timing of the five signalized intersections

As shown in Fig. 13, this paper implemented the proposed algorithm through the secondary development of C# and the algorithm was tested in simulation experiments on VISSIM 4.3 after integrated through COM interface. This simulation includes four sets of experiments, which are respectively carried out under the data corresponding to the morning rush hour and the noon off-peak in workday and holiday (Fig. 14).

3.2　Result Analysis

We have conducted 254 effective experiments, and the experimental results are shown in Tab. 2 and Fig. 15 to Fig. 18.

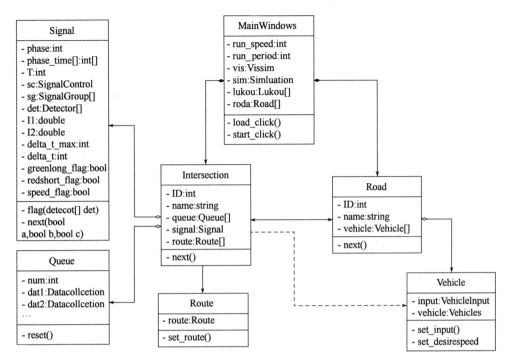

Fig. 13 Class diagram of Simulation System

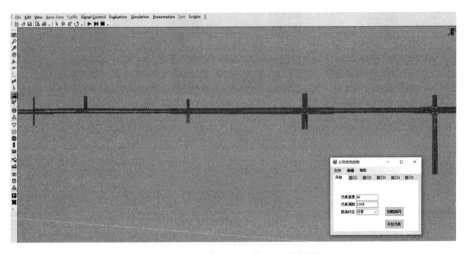

Fig. 14 Simulation interface on VISSIM

The data of the results   Tab. 2

		The Morning Rush Hour in Workday	The Noon Off-peak in Workday	The Morning Rush Hour in Holiday	The Noon Off-peak in Holiday
Stops of BRT	Without Priority	2.2966	2.2966	2.2966	2.2966
	With Priority	0.3349	0.2706	0.2614	0.1649
Average delay of BRT	Without Priority	74.7297	72.8179	69.0355	66.4468
	With Priority	13.3543	12.4701	12.1446	11.0169
Average speed of BRT	Without Priority	25.5730	26.4892	26.9422	25.7398
	With Priority	32.8095	32.9460	32.9655	33.1730
Total delay of all passengers (Only count the cycles that BRT goes through)	Without Priority	10.3985	7.1247	8.5041	6.3789
	With Priority	9.4681	6.1943	7.5736	5.4485

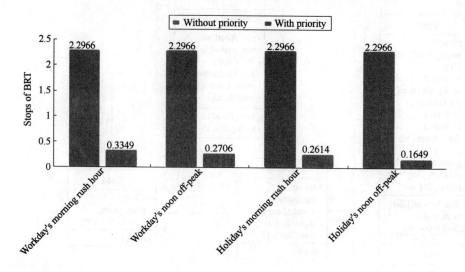

Fig. 15 Stops of BRT

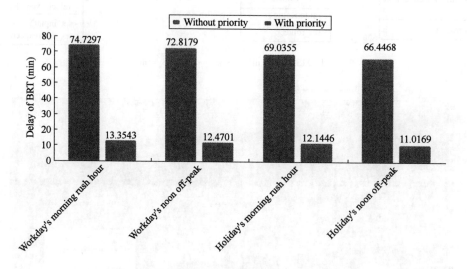

Fig. 16 Delay of BRT

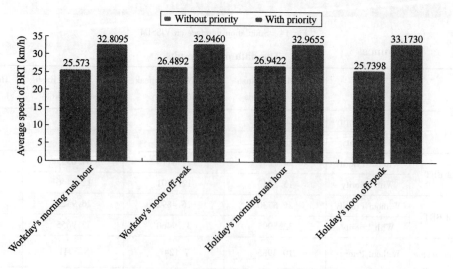

Fig. 17 Average speed of BRT

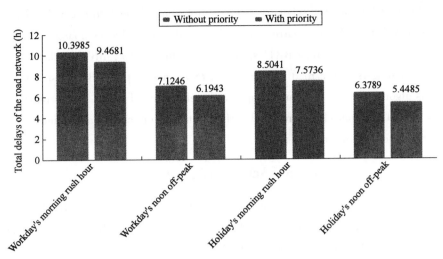

Fig. 18 Total delays of the road network

(1) The stops of BRT decreased significantly in the four cases, among which, the decrease of 92.91% in the noon off-peak in holiday ranked the first. The result is shown in Fig. 15.

(2) The average delay of BRT was reduced in the four cases, among which, the decrease of 82.19% in the morning rush hour in workday ranked the first. The result is shown in Fig. 16.

(3) The average speed of BRT increased in the four cases, among which, the increase of 22.41% in the noon off-peak in holiday ranked the first. The result is shown in Fig. 17.

(4) The total delay of all passengers in road network (only count the cycles that BRT goes through) decreased in the four cases, among which, the decrease of 8.95% in the morning rush hour in workday ranked first. The result is shown in Fig. 18.

The situation of BRT driving without stopping was further analyzed. According to the experimental data, 74.41% of the 254 times of simulation experiments could realize BRT driving without stopping, as shown in Fig. 19.

For intersections with shorter cycles, the strategies of green extension and red truncation account for more. For intersections with longer cycles, the strategy of speed regulation becomes obviously more, but is still less than green extension and red truncation.

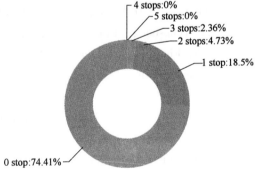

Fig. 19 Proportion of the stops of BRT

This case simulates the peak and flat peak of BRT 4. BRT priority is more likely to be implemented during peak periods. This is because the traffic flow on the main road is greater than usual at this time, and the implementation of priority will reduce the total delay of the road network. During the flat peak periods, the traffic flow on the main road is at a normal level. Once the traffic flow of the secondary road increases, the possibility of implementing BRT priority will be reduced.

To sum up, the simulation results show that the algorithm proposed has brought some positive effects, including the reduction of the stops of BRT, the delay of BRT, the total delay of all passengers in road network, and the improvement of the speed of BRT, all of which indicate that the algorithm has a broad application prospect.

4 Conclusions

The establishment of the strategies of bus priority is of great significance to the implementation of public transport priority. Different bus priority schemes in theenvironment of the Internet of Vehicles are proposed in this paper, and the empirical analysis is carried out. The results show that compared with the previous signal control scheme, this algorithm can reduce BRT′ stops by more than 90%, BRT′s delay by about 16%-18%, the total delay of all passengers in the road network by 8.95%, and improve BRT′s speed by about 22.41%, which mean that this algorithm can significantly improve the efficiency of BRT. In this paper, multi-intersection control and precise real-time control are realized. Multi-intersection coordination and BRT parking priority control are the further research area of this paper.

5 Acknowledgement

This research was supported by grants from National Key R&D Project (2018YFB1600703), National Natural Science Foundation of China(61973028), "Internet of Vehicles" Ministry of Education-China Mobile Joint Laboratory Opening Fund Project(ICV-KF2019-01).

References

[1] State Council. Guiding Opinions of the State Council on Priority Development of Public Transportation in Cities(Guo Fa[2012]No.64). Beijing: State Council, 2012.

[2] Ministry of Transport. Notice of The Ministry of Transport on relevant Matters concerning the Implementation of National Public Transport Urban Construction Demonstration Project (Jiao Yun Fa [2011]No.635). Beijing: Ministry of Transport, 2011.

[3] Yang Kai. The contribution and existing problems of BRT in urban development[J]. Traffic World, 2018, 17: 20-22.

[4] Sun Xiaohong. Research on Key Technologies and Applications of Internet of Vehicles [J]. Communication Technology, 2013,46(04): 47-50.

[5] Wang Yongsheng, Tan Guozhen, Liu Mingjian, et al. Bus Adaptive Priority Method in Internet of Vehicles Environment. Computer Application, 2016,36(08): 2181-2186.

[6] Zhao Jie, Ye Min, Zhao Yixin. Overview of foreign BRT development[J]. Urban Planning International, 2006,3: 32-37.

[7] Richardson A J, Ogden K W. EVALUATION OF ACTIVE BUS-PRIORITY SIGNALS[J]. Transportation Research Record, 1979,718: 5-12.

[8] Hongchao Liu, Alexander Skabardonis, Weibin Zhang, et al. Optimal Detector Location for Bus Signal Priority. Transportation Research Record: Journal of the Transportation Research Board, 2004,1867: 144-150.

[9] Chen Jun. Bus Signal Priority Control and Its Application in BRT[J]. Journal of Central South University, 2009.

[10] Andy An-Kai Jeng, Rong-Hong Jan, Chien Chen, et al. Adaptive Urban Traffic Signal Control System with Bus Priority. Vehicular Technology Conferrence. IEEE,2013.

[11] Xiaosi Zeng, Yunlong Zhang, Kevin N Balke,et al. A Real-Time Transit Signal Priority Control Model Considering Stochastic Bus Arrival Time. Transaction on Intelligent Transportation Systems. IEEE,2014.

[12] N B Hounsell, B P Shrestha, F N Mcleod et al. Using Global Positioning System for Bus Priority in London: Traffic Signals Close to Bus Stops[J]. IET Intelligent Transportation System, 1, (2). 131-137.

[13] Guojiang Shen, Xiangjie Kong. Study on Road Network Traffic Coordination Control Technique With Bus Priority[J]. IEEE Transactions on Systems Man and Cybernetics Part C (Applications and Reviews), 2009,39(3): 343-351.

[14] Yinsong Wang, Wanjing Ma, Wei Yin et al. Implementation and Testing of Cooperative Bus Priority System in Connected VehicleEnvironment: Case Study in Taicang City, China[J]. Res. Rec. J. Transp. Res. Board,2014, 2424:48-57.
[15] Bo Haijian, Ren Guixiang, Dong Ruijuan. Bus Signal Priority Method Based on Station Schedule in Network[J]. Journal of Chongqing Jiaotong University(Natural Science Edition), 2018, 37(07): 85-91.

进口单独放行交叉口非机动车组织仿真分析

杨 震[1] 马健霄[1] 王宝杰[2] 董可可[1]

(1. 南京林业大学汽车与交通工程学院;2. 长安大学运输工程学院)

摘 要 为解决进口单独放行交叉口左转非机动车与直行机动车的冲突问题,首先提出了非机动车钩形左转的组织方式,改进了非机动车停车线提前的组织方法,并分析了各种相序条件下非机动车组织策略;然后分析了进口单独放行交叉口的信号配时设计方法;最后考虑各种相序和非机动车组织方式的组合,运用VISSIM软件构建了实例交叉口的16个仿真模型,并进行了仿真评价。结果表明:当交叉口采用东南西北(顺时针)相序时,四个进口都应实行停车线提前的策略;采用东北西南(逆时针)相序时,四个进口都应实行钩形左转的策略;采用除顺时针、逆时针以外的其他四种相序时,应实行钩形左转与停车线提前相结合的策略。

关键词 交通组织与运营管理 钩形左转 停车线提前 进口单独放行 非机动车 VISSIM仿真

0 引 言

交叉口是城市道路网络的节点和瓶颈,其运行效率关系到整个路网的通行能力。与交叉口交通控制及运行组织相关的一系列问题,包括渠化改进、相位设计、信号配时、行人及非机动车交通组织等,一直是国内外交通工程师们关注的热点。国外早在20世纪50年代起就由Webster和Akcelik等发起了对交叉口交通控制的研究。近年来,Wong等[1]提出了交叉口车道功能和信号配时的组合优化模型。Jovanović等[2]提出了用于求解低饱和以及过饱和交叉口信号配时方案的蜂群优化算法。

交叉口通用的相位方案是美国国家电气制造商协会(National Electronic Manufacturers Association, NEMA)提出的ring-barrier八相位[3],我国普遍采用的对称四相位实际上是它的特例。另一种相位是各进口单独放行相位,即每个进口道上所有流向的车流都在同一相位放行[4]。依据进口放行顺序的不同,进口单独放行相位共包含东南西北、东北西南、东西南北、东西北南、东南北西和东北南西这六种相序。采用进口单独放行的交叉口可设置直左合用车道来平衡直行、左转的交通需求,提高通行效率[5]。国内学者[6-8]也将进口单独放行相位运用于双向绿波协调的线控系统中,达到了比对称四相位更好的效果。同时,与对称四相位相比,驾驶人对进口单独放行相位的相序变化不敏感,因此进口单独放行相位适用于信号协调系统中的交叉口。

尽管进口单独放行相位有这些优势,但其存在的最大问题是各进口的左转非机动车会与直行机动车形成冲突,显著影响交叉口的通行效率及安全性。已有文献对这一问题缺乏深入的讨论,因此有必要系统性地研究进口单独放行条件下非机动车交通的组织问题。

基金项目:国家自然科学基金青年科学基金项目(No. 51908060),江苏省自然科学基金资助项目(No. BK20170932),南京林业大学青年科技创新基金(No. CX2017011)。

1 非机动车组织方式及适应性分析

针对进口单独放行交叉口存在的问题,笔者在已有文献的基础上,提出非机动车钩形左转的组织方式,并改进非机动车停车线提前方法,将两种组织方式应用于进口单独放行交叉口的非机动车交通组织中,并分析两种方式对于不同相序的适应性。

1.1 非机动车钩形左转

钩形转弯(hook-turn)起源于澳大利亚墨尔本(交通规则为左行),最初是为了解决右转机动车与直行有轨电车冲突而发明的[9],其工作方式为(图2):右转车在红灯期间进入最左侧车道与左转车一起在停车线后排队等待;待本向绿灯启亮后,进入贴近本向直行斑马线的待行区停车等待;等到相交道路绿灯启亮后,待行区内的右转车完成转弯并驶离交叉口。因右转车的转弯轨迹近似于钩子,故将这种交通组织方式取名为"hook-turn"。成卫等[10]将钩形转弯沿用到我国右行规则的交通环境中,此时左转车以钩形转弯的方式通过交叉口。

考虑到非机动车的行驶灵活性明显高于机动车,这种钩形转弯方式完全可以应用于非机动车,如图2所示。以南进口为例,左转非机动车在南进口绿灯启亮时进入东进口前方的待行区,在东进口绿灯启亮时完成转弯并驶离交叉口。因此,当左转非机动车采用钩形转弯后,可消除与本向直行车的冲突。

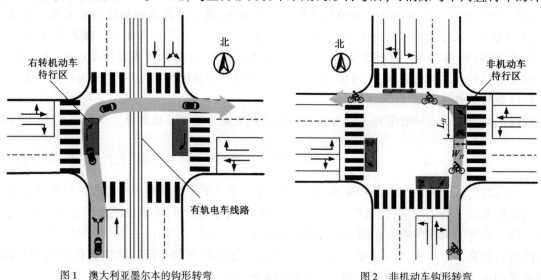

图1 澳大利亚墨尔本的钩形转弯　　　　　图2 非机动车钩形转弯

为避免待行区内等候的左转非机动车阻挡本向直行非机动车的通行,待行区和本向非机动车道不宜在同一直线上,应朝斑马线位置右移。为方便非机动车左转,待行区的停车线可与相交道路远端边线相距一个非机动车道的距离。此外,为避免待行区内的非机动车与对向左转机动车的流线产生冲突,待行区的最大长度不宜超过相交道路所有机动车进口道和中央分隔带的总宽度。钩形转弯待行区内所能容纳的非机动车数可按式(1)计算:

$$N_B = L_H \cdot W_H / \rho_B \tag{1}$$

式中,N_B 为钩形转弯待行区内所能容纳的最大自行车数;L_H 和 W_H 分别为钩形转弯待行区的长度(m)和宽度(m);ρ_B 为平均每辆非机动车的停放面积(m^2),一辆非机动车的停放长度按文献[11]取为 1.8 ~ 2.0m,停放宽度可取为 1.0m,则 ρ_B 可取为 1.8 ~ 2.0m^2。

1.2 非机动车停车线提前

非机动车停车线提前(advanced stop line)是将进口道上原本重合的机非停车线分离,使之错开一定的距离。两条停车线之间的区域供各流向的非机动车等候通行,当本向绿灯启亮后,非机动车将先于机动车通过交叉口,从而消除了机非冲突。设机非停车线之间的距离为 L_A(m),本文参照文献[12]和英国

的标志标线设计规范[13],将L_A的最小值和最大值分别规定为4.0m和7.5m,提出了L_A的计算公式:

$$L_A = \min(\max(q_B \cdot \rho_B/B + \Delta L, 4.0), 7.5) \tag{2}$$

式(2)中q_B为一个信号周期内到达的各流向非机动车数;B为进口车道的总宽度(m);ΔL为考虑自行车穿行的宽度(m),一般可取1m。利用式(2)计算的L_A既能给予非机动车足够停放空间,又不会显著影响机动车的绿灯间隔时间。此外,为避免左转和直行非机动车的冲突,可在人行横道上方增设专供左转非机动车等候的区域(图3),以提前分流左转非机动车。该区域的宽度可设为本向机动车道的宽度总和,长度以不与相邻进口的直行机动车流线冲突为宜。改进后的非机动车停车线提前渠化方案如图3所示。

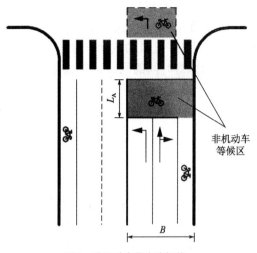

图3 非机动车停车线提前

1.3 适应性分析

从最大化行车效率考虑,若进口单独放行交叉口采用东南西北(顺时针)相序,则交叉口适合于实行非机动车停车线提前策略;若采用东北西南(逆时针)相序,则适合于实行非机动车钩形左转;若采用东西南北、东西北南、东南北西和东北南西这四种相序,可分别在东进口、北进口、南进口和西进口实行非机动车停车线提前策略,而在其余进口实行钩形左转(也就是钩形左转与停车线提前相结合)。下文将结合具体的交叉口来验证该组织方案的合理性。

2 进口单独放行交叉口信号配时设计

进口单独放行交叉口的信号配时设计以进口为基本单位。以典型的十字交叉口为例,当进口i上只设有左转、右转专用道,而无直左、直右等合用车道时,该进口的关键车道流量比采用式(3)计算:

$$y_{ic} = \max_j \left(\frac{Q_{ij}}{n_{ij}S_{ij}} \right), i \in A, j \in D \tag{3}$$

式中,y_{ic}为进口i(或相位i)的关键车道流量比;Q_{ij}、S_{ij}和n_{ij}分别为进口i流向j交通流量(pcu/h)、饱和流量(pcu/h)和车道数;A为交叉口进口方向的集合,D为交叉口流向的集合且$D=\{l,t,r\}$,其中l、t和r分别为左转、直行和右转流向的索引。当进口i上设有直左合用车道,而右转采用专用道时,该进口的关键车道流量比采用式(4)计算:

$$y_{ic} = \max\left(\frac{1}{n_{il}+n_{it}} \cdot \left(\frac{Q_{il}}{S_{il}}+\frac{Q_{it}}{S_{it}}\right), \frac{Q_{ir}}{n_{ir}S_{ir}}\right), i \in A \tag{4}$$

当进口i上设有直右合用车道,而左转采用专用道时,该进口的关键车道流量比采用式(5)计算:

$$y_{ic} = \max\left(\frac{1}{n_{it}+n_{ir}} \cdot \left(\frac{Q_{it}}{S_{it}}+\frac{Q_{ir}}{S_{ir}}\right), \frac{Q_{il}}{n_{il}S_{il}}\right), i \in A \tag{5}$$

当进口i上同时设有直左、直右合用车道时,该进口的关键车道流量比采用式(6)计算:

$$y_{ic} = \frac{1}{n_{il}+n_{it}+n_{ir}} \cdot \left(\frac{Q_{il}}{S_{il}}+\frac{Q_{it}}{S_{it}}+\frac{Q_{ir}}{S_{ir}}\right), i \in A \tag{6}$$

在确定了各进口的关键车道流量比后,即可按Webster信号配时法对交叉口进行配时设计[14]。为保证行人过街安全,规定当某一进口机动车放行时,仅允许进口右侧人行横道上的行人过街,行人过街所需绿灯时间按式(7)计算[15]:

$$G_{pi} = 7 + \frac{L_{pi}}{v_p} - I_i, i \in A \tag{7}$$

式中,G_{pi} 为进口 i 的行人过街所需要的绿灯时间(s),同时也是该进口的最小显示绿灯时间;L_{pi} 为进口 i 右侧的人行横道长度(m);v_p 为行人第 15 百分位步行速度,可取为 1.2 m/s;I_i 为进口 i 的绿灯间隔时间(s)。当某一进口的机动车绿灯时间不足以让行人顺利过街时,按照文献[15]的方法,在满足该进口最小显示绿灯时间的同时,等比例扩大其他进口的绿灯时间,如式(8)所示:

$$G_i' = G_{pk} \cdot \frac{y_{ic}}{y_{kc}}, i \in A \cap i \neq k \tag{8}$$

式中,G_i' 为进口 i 调整以后的显示绿灯时间(s);k 为不满足最小显示绿灯时间的进口索引;其他符号含义同上。

3 实例应用

以上分析了进口单独交叉口非机动车组织方式及信号配时设计方法,本节将其应用于南京市南林东路－花园路交叉口,运用 VISSIM 仿真软件分析进口单独放行的六种相序对机动车及非机动车延误的影响。

3.1 交叉口基础数据

南林东路—花园路交叉口是一个位于南京市中心城区的交叉口,其现状渠化及几何尺寸信息如图 4 所示。经实地观测,该交叉口晚高峰时期的机动车(已换算成标准小客车)、非机动车(包括自行车和电动车)、行人交通流量如表 1 所示。

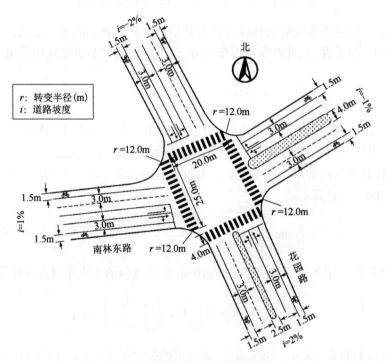

图 4 实例交叉口现状渠化图

实例交叉口晚高峰交通流量   表 1

进口道名称	机动车流量/(pcu·h^{-1})			非机动车流量/(veh·h^{-1})			行人流量/(ped·h^{-1})
	左转	直行	右转	左转	直行	右转	
东进口	74	17	218	27	14	24	181
南进口	15	315	43	14	161	50	38

续上表

进口道名称	机动车流量/(pcu·h⁻¹)			非机动车流量/(veh·h⁻¹)			行人流量/(ped·h⁻¹)
	左转	直行	右转	左转	直行	右转	
西进口	46	16	29	52	9	37	38
北进口	109	413	68	40	190	38	59

3.2 交叉口渠化和信号配时设计

根据该交叉口的基础数据,结合式(1)和式(2),可计算得到各进口分别实行非机动车钩形左转和停车线提前的渠化参数。与此同时,将交叉口相位设置为进口单独放行,并运用第2节所述方法对该交叉口进行信号配时设计。配时过程中左转、直行和右转进口道的基本饱和流量分别取为1550pcu/h、1650pcu/h和1550pcu/h,同时考虑车道宽度、坡度、转弯半径、行人非机动车、合用车道等因素对基本饱和流量进行校正,具体方法见文献[14];各相位起动停车损失时间取为3s;绿灯间隔时间取为4s,包括黄灯时间3s和全红时间1s。最终得到交叉口各项渠化参数和信号配时参数,如表2所示。

实例交叉口渠化及配时参数　　　　表2

参数类型	进口方向	东进口	南进口	西进口	北进口
钩形左转渠化参数	待转区长度 L_H(m)	10.0	8.5	6.0	6.0
	待转区宽度 W_H(m)	1.5	2.0	1.5	1.5
	最大容纳非机动车数 N_B	8	9	5	5
非机动车停车线提前渠化参数	进口车道的总宽度 B(m)	7.5	7.5	7.5	7.5
	机非停车线距离 L_A(m)	4	4	4	4
信号配时参数	绿灯时长(s)	36	24	20	38
	信号周期(s)	134			

3.3 非机动车交通组织方法评价

为评价进口单独放行交叉口非机动车交通组织方法的适应性,本文使用德国PTV公司的VISSIM交通仿真软件,根据进口单独放行的相序种类以及各进口非机动车组织方式,建立南林东路—花园路交叉口的16个仿真模型(表3)。模型中非机动车钩形左转待行区的尺寸以及停车线提前策略中机非停车线之间的距离均按表2进行设定,另外还设置了冲突区域,以保证钩形左转待行区内以及双停车线之间的非机动车相对于同向机动车具有优先通行权。在现实中,可设置非机动车信号灯并提前启亮,以达到和仿真模型中相同的效果。

仿真模型建立后,选取各进口左转非机动车的平均延误、直行机动车的平均延误以及两者的总平均延误作为评价非机动车交通组织方案运行效果的依据。运行各仿真模型,最终结果如表3所示。

实例交叉口仿真运行结果　　　　表3

相序	仿真模型数量	延误类型	非机动车交通组织方式		
			四进口都为钩形左转	四进口都为停车线提前	钩形左转与停车线提前相结合
东南西北(顺时针)	2	左转非机动车平均延误(s)	130.5	40.6	—
		直行机动车平均延误(s)	37.9	46.6	—
		总平均延误(s)	51.7	45.7	—
东北西南(逆时针)	2	左转非机动车平均延误(s)	56.8	36.0	
		直行机动车平均延误(s)	38.9	51.9	
		总平均延误(s)	41.6	49.5	

续上表

相　序	仿真模型数量	延误类型	非机动车交通组织方式		
			四进口都为钩形左转	四进口都为停车线提前	钩形左转与停车线提前相结合
东西南北	3	左转非机动车平均延误(s)	90.6	40.9	72.9
		直行机动车平均延误(s)	37.5	40.6	37.5
		总平均延误(s)	45.4	44.2	42.8
东西北南	3	左转非机动车平均延误(s)	107.0	40.6	73.1
		直行机动车平均延误(s)	38.1	46.9	36.7
		总平均延误(s)	48.4	46.0	42.1
东南北西	3	左转非机动车平均延误(s)	87.4	37.7	83.3
		直行机动车平均延误(s)	37.7	45.7	37.4
		总平均延误(s)	45.1	44.5	44.2
东北南西	3	左转非机动车平均延误(s)	99.2	35.8	63.0
		直行机动车平均延误(s)	38.3	48.2	38.4
		总平均延误(s)	47.4	46.4	42.1

从表3中可以看出,不论在何种相序条件下,当各进口均采用钩形左转时,左转非机动车的平均延误要高于各进口均采用停车线提前的方式,而直行机动车的平均延误则反之。这是因为采用钩形左转时,左转非机动车一般要经过两次停车(进口道上一次,待行区内一次)才可通过交叉口,导致了其延误的增加;而采用停车线提前方式时,非机动车先于机动车通过交叉口,导致了机动车延误的增加。

当交叉口采用东南西北(顺时针)相序时,各进口均实行停车线提前策略的总平均延误(45.7s)要低于钩形左转(51.7s),说明在该相序条件下,四个进口应实行非机动车停车线提前;当交叉口采用东北西南(逆时针)相序时,四个进口均实行钩形左转的总平均延误(41.6s)要低于停车线提前(49.5s),说明在该相序条件下,四个进口应实行钩形左转。

当交叉口采用除顺时针、逆时针相序以外的其他四种相序时,从表3中可以看出,不论采用何种相序,总平均延误的变化趋势是:钩形左转>停车线提前>钩形左转与停车线提前相结合。说明在这四种相序条件下,交叉口应实行1.3节所述的钩形左转与停车线提前相结合的非机动车组织策略。确定了各种相序的最优非机动车组织方式后,各相序的左转非机动车交通组织设计如图6所示。

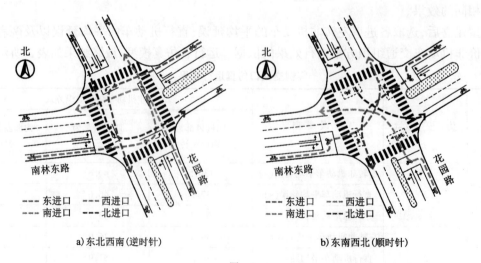

a) 东北西南(逆时针)　　　b) 东南西北(顺时针)

图　5

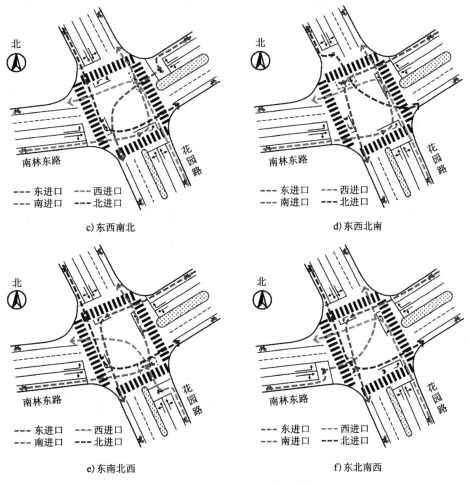

图 5 左转非机动车交通组织设计

4 结 语

本文针对进口单独放行交叉口左转非机动车与直行机动车的冲突问题,首先提出非机动车钩形左转的组织方式,改进了非机动车停车线提前方法;然后选取南京市南林东路—花园路交叉口,运用VISSIM仿真软件,针对各种不同的相序及非机动车组织策略构建了16个仿真模型,对每一种情形进行了仿真评价。结果显示当交叉口采用东南西北(顺时针)相序时,四个进口都应实行停车线提前策略;当交叉口采用东北西南(逆时针)相序时,四个进口都应实行钩形左转方式;当交叉口采用其他相序,即东西南北、东西北南、东南北西和东北南西相序时,应分别在东进口、北进口、南进口和西进口实行非机动车停车线提前策略,而在其余进口实行钩形左转。本文局限在于当左转非机动车流量较大时,非机动车待行区的清空时间较长,会显著增加直行机动车的延误,因此不适合于左转非机动车流量过大的交叉口。

参考文献

[1] WONG C K, WONG S C. Lane-based optimization of signal timings for isolated junctions [J]. Transportation Research Part B: Methodological, 2003, 37(1): 63-84.

[2] JOVANOVIĆ A, TEODOROVIĆ D. Pre-timed control for an under-saturated and over-saturated isolated intersection: a bee colony optimization approach[J]. Transportation Planning and Technology, 2017, 40(5): 556-576.

[3] National Electrical Manufacturers Association (NEMA). NEMA TS 2-2016 Traffic Controller Assemblies with NTCIP Requirements [S]. NEMA, Rosslyn, Virginia, 2016.

[4] 张小宁,邓静媛.交叉口单口放行方法相位设计设置研究[J].公路交通科技,2010,27(8):87-90,95.
[5] 林晓辉.十字交叉口的单口放行与对称放行相位设计方法对比研究[J].交通信息与安全,2014,32(3):69-72.
[6] 林晓辉,徐建闽,卢凯,等.各进口单独放行条件下的双向绿波设计方法研究[J].交通与计算机,2007,25(5):8-12,16.
[7] 李林,徐建闽,卢凯.进口单独放行的改进绿波数解法[J].交通信息与安全,2009,27(3):64-67,73.
[8] 卢凯,徐建闽,李轶舜.进口单独放行方式下的干道双向绿波协调控制数解算法[J].中国公路学报,2010,23(3):95-101.
[9] HOUNSELL N B, YAP Y H. Hook turns as a solution to the right-turning traffic problem [J]. TransportationScience, 2013, 49(1): 1-12.
[10] 成卫,别一鸣,刘志远.基于机动车延误的Hook-turn交叉口信号控制方案优化方法[J].中国公路学报,2015,28(3):94-101.
[11] GB 51038—2015,城市道路交通标志和标线设置规范[S].北京:中国计划出版社,2015.
[12] 杨晓光.城市道路交通设计指南[M].北京:人民交通出版社,2003:64-67.
[13] INSTRUMENTS S. The Traffic Signs Regulations and General Directions 2016 [S]. UK: The Stationery Office Limited, 2016.
[14] 吴兵,李晔.交通管理与控制[M].北京:人民交通出版社,2009:154-160.
[15] ROESS R P, PRASSAS E S, MCSHANE W R. TrafficEngineering [M]. Bergen County: Pearson/Prentice Hall, 2004: 489-522.

城市轨道交通地下行人设施评价方法

郝鑫桐 杨帅 武方涛 史伟伟 黄旭

(1.长安大学;2.北京交通大学)

摘要 利用层次分析法确定影响城市轨道交通地下行人服务设施的服务效率影响因素的比重,利用软件VISSIM进行行人仿真,分别研究2000人/h,4000人/h,6000人/h三种情况下中的哪些因素对服务等级的影响较大。研究结果表明在影响地下设施服务水平方面,楼扶梯的影响偏多一些。客流量为2000人/h和4000人/h的时候,经营者需要注意在客流速度方面提高地下行人设施的服务水平。然而在客流量为6000人/h的时候,经营者需要注意在设施利用率方面提高地下行人设施的服务水平。当客流量达到6000人/h的时候,楼扶梯的影响比重稍微大一些。

关键词 车站服务水平 层次分析法 计算机仿真 地下行人设施

0 引言

城市轨道运输交通地下轨道车站的建设造价相对较高,同时管理地位也非常重要,是一个规模巨大的地下车站工程。由于地下公交车站建设具有一些特殊性,所以它必须是我国城市轨道网络交通建设需要重点深入研究的一个对象。国内二十多条近期已经竣工的地下轨道交通车站造价成本决算系统数据分析表明,对于所有的我国城市轨道运输交通地下轨道线路,车站的建筑造价成本可以直接达到所有土建建筑成本的50%左右,达到建筑总成本20%的左右,是我国城市轨道运输交通总建筑成本的重要不可组成的一部分。同时,轨道交通换乘车站也认为是方便乘客随时感受城市轨道交通公共服务的最直接到达界面,地位重要,因此,本文用层次分析法和仿真度的方法针对闸机和楼扶梯两样地下设施进行分析,分别研究 2000 人/h,4000 人/h,6000 人/h 三种情况下中的哪些因素对服务等级的影响较大。

1 研究内容和方法

本文以常用方法来作为评价层次定性分析指标的一种层次定性分析法为例来对其进行层次分析。层次分析法(AHP)[1]:它是一种完全可以将客体定性和主观定量相互地结合的评价方法、它不仅可以将其对人的主观评价判断通过一种数量化的形式进行表达和综合处理,不但不仅可以使人充分体现主观评价判断指标和主观评价判断过程的模糊性,而且它还能尽量多地消除人对个人主观评价判断的各种片面性,从而可以使人的评价结果更加客观、令人信服。层次分析法最初被美国用于运筹学理论的 T. L. Saaty 教授在 20 世纪 70 年代中期提出,层次分析法的一个基本原理主要是:通过对系统内所可能包含的关键因素及其他相关比率关系要素进行层次分析,将每个问题进行条理化、层次化的进行表达,从而重新构造一个客观的相对多层次的比率分析系统结构理论模型;对每一个关键层次内的各个关键要素分别进行两两级的比较,通过计算引入一个比率标度的算法从而构造并得出一个判断矩阵;然后通过计算各个判断向量矩阵从而分别得到最大权重特征向量值及最小特征向量,再根据以上分析结论排序得到各层次各个要素后再对上一百个层次某部分要素的各个重要性进行排序,从而重新建立权重特征向量;最终对问题进行综合判断。之后再根据仿真方法[2]分析影响地下设施服务水平的因素。

2 评价方法

2.1 指标体系

为了针对我国轨道交通地下地铁车站的庞大客流及车站功能评价特征,本文选择了"目标——准则——指标"层次结构的评价模式应用来研究建立一个轨道交通地下地铁车站的功能评价质量指标体系,形成有序的等级层次结构,提出了一种多目标、多层次的综合评价与分析方法。评价的标准体系共可被分为 3 层,分别被称为评价目标规定层(A 层)、准则规定层(B 层)、指标规定层(C 层),如图 1 所示。

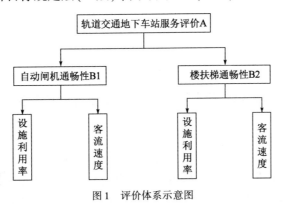

图 1 评价体系示意图

2.2 权重分配

确定了 2 个准则层指标和 4 个方案层指标来评价车站服务水平,因此综合评价集 B = {B1,B2},二级指标集 U1 = {C1,C2},U2 = {C3,C4},构建判断矩阵。

(1)准则层

	B1	B2
B1	1	1/3
B2	3	1

最大特征值 $\lambda =2$;特征向量 $w_1 =(1,3)$。
进行一致性检查：

$$\text{CI} = \frac{\lambda - n}{n-1} = \frac{2-2}{2-1} = 0 \tag{1}$$

$$\text{CR} = \frac{\text{CI}}{\text{RI}} = \frac{0}{0.25} = 0 < 0.1 \tag{2}$$

RI 值如表 1 所示，通过一致性检查。

随机一致性指标 RI 的数值   表1

n	1	2	3	4	5	6	7	8	9	10
RI	0	0	0.58	0.90	1.12	1.24	1.32	1.41	1.45	1.49

对特征向量进行归一化整理得：

$$w_1 = (0.25, 0.75) \tag{3}$$

(2)方案层

	C1	C2
C1	1	1/4
C2	4	1

此阵为完全一致阵了，满足一致性检查
$w_2 = (1,4)$ 进行归一化处理：

$$w_2 = (0.20, 0.80) \tag{4}$$

	C3	C4
C3	1	1/4
C4	4	1

此阵为完全一致阵，满足一致性检查。
$w_2 = (1,4)$ 进行归一化处理得：

$$w_3 = (0.20, 0.80) \tag{5}$$

3 基于行人仿真地下车站服务等级与设计参数的选定

3.1 分值确定方法

城市轨道公共交通沿线车站的每次到达的客流量和到达的特点主要是随着旅客列车的每次到达而呈现一种脉冲式的客流分布，并非连续的、均衡的，车站内的行人设施在短时间内受到人流的影响。在客流高峰时段时，大量行人进出车站使得检票设施、楼扶梯设施等通过类设施得到很大的冲击，这种巨大冲击影响作用也是对交通设施疏散能力的最大限度考验，检票通过设施、楼梯、通道等通过设施往往是直接无法承受这种巨大冲击影响作用的主要交通设施，是容易出现形成客流瓶颈的重要限制也是车站区间整体交通疏散客流能力的关键。设施利用能力通过利用效率就是反映设施客流量的规模大小与整个设施最大程度通过利用能力的一个协调利用程度，通过设施高峰小时的最大通过客流量与整个设施的最大通过利用能力的一个比值可以表示。

$$\theta = \frac{Q_h}{C} \tag{6}$$

式中：Q_h——小时通过量；
C——设施最大通过能力；

经过反复仿真试验,得知闸机的最大通过能力是9000人/h,楼扶梯最大的通过能力是6000人/h。

城市轨道交通地下车站服务水平标准　　　　　　　　　　　　　　　　　　表2

设 施	单 位	A	B	C	D	E	F
检票闸机	(人/m·min)	≤10	10~14.7	14.7~17.3	17.3~22	22~30	>30
通道	(人/m·min)	≤24.8	24.8~32.1	32.1~47.3	47.3~66.2	61.2~68.2	>68.2
通道	(人/m²)	≤0.31	0.31~0.42	0.42~0.70	0.70~1.08	1.08~2.10	>2.10
楼梯	(人/m·min)	≤25.6	25.6~32.8	32.8~36.8	36.8~44.9	44.9~53.9	>53.9
楼梯	(人/m²)	≤0.60	0.60~0.90	0.90~1.10	1.10~1.60	1.60~2.40	>2.40
站台	(人/m²)	≤0.72	0.72~0.95	0.95~1.33	1.33~3.28	3.28~4.87	>4.87

客流速度分指表　　　　　　　　　　　　　　　　　　表3

等级	A	B	C	D	E	F
分值	100~90	90~80	80~70	70~60	60~50	50~40

设施利用率分值表　　　　　　　　　　　　　　　　　　表4

θ	>90%	90%~80%	80%~70%	70%~60%	60%~50%	50%~40%
分值	100~90	90~80	80~70	70~60	60~50	50~40

将楼梯服务等级按照客流密度人,分为六个等级,如下所示:

■ 代表区域密度为 D 级(1.1人/m² ~1.6人/m²);
■ 代表区域密度为 E 级(1.6人/m² ~2.4人/m²);
■ 代表区域密度为 F 级(>2.4人/m²);
■ 代表区域密度为 A 级(≤0.60人/m²);
■ 代表区域密度为 B 级(0.6人/m² ~0.9人/m²);
■ 代表区域密度为 C 级(0.9人/m² ~1.1人/m²)。

3.2　2000人/h 的仿真

分别对闸机和楼扶梯进行行人仿真模拟,模拟效果图如图2所示,结果如表5~表7所示。

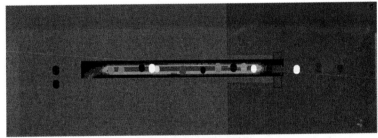

图2　2000人/h 仿真图

闸机结果　　　　　　　　　　　　　　　　　　表5

评价指标	输出结果	单 位
检测面域行人数	57.90	(人)
检测面域行人密度	10.78	(人/m²)
行人流量	5.79(A级)	(人/m·min)

楼扶梯结果　　　　　　　　　　　　　　　　　　表6

评价指标	输出结果	单 位
行人数	17.00	(人)
密度等级	D	

闸机—楼扶梯综合结果　　　　　　　　　　　　　　　　　　　表 7

设施		指标	设施权重	指标权重	权重乘积	指标分值	总分值
2000 人/h	闸机	设施利用率	0.25	0.20	0.05	42	21.3
		客流速度		0.80	0.20	95	
	楼扶梯	设施利用率	0.75	0.20	0.15	44	43.8
		客流速度		0.80	0.60	62	

楼扶梯的分值比闸机的分值高,闸机的客流速度的分值比设施利用率的分值大,说明在影响闸机的服务效率方面,客流速度这个因素对闸机的影响偏大,楼扶梯的客流速度的分值比设施利用率的分值大,说明在影响楼扶梯的服务效率方面,客流速度这个因素对楼扶梯的影响偏大,相对于楼扶梯,闸机在客流量方面对地下交通行人设施的影响更大一些。

3.3　4000 人/h 的仿真

模拟效果图如图 3 所示,结果如表 8 ~ 表 10 所示。

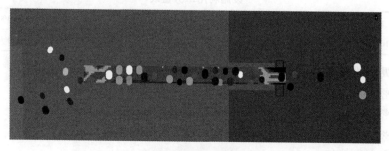

图 3　4000 人/h 仿真图

闸机结果　　　　　　　　　　　　　　　　　　　表 8

评价指标	输出结果	单位
检测面域行人数	118.60	(人)
检测面域行人密度	22.10	(人/m²)
行人流量	11.86(B 级)	(人/m·min)

楼扶梯结果　　　　　　　　　　　　　　　　　　　表 9

评价指标	输出结果	单位
行人数	41.80	人
密度等级	E	

闸机—楼扶梯综合结果　　　　　　　　　　　　　　　　　　　表 10

设施		指标	设施权重	指标权重	权重乘积	指标分值	总分值
4000 人/h	闸机	设施利用率	0.25	0.20	0.05	45	19.45
		客流速度		0.80	0.20	86	
	楼扶梯	设施利用率	0.75	0.20	0.15	67	43.05
		客流速度		0.80	0.60	55	

楼扶梯的分值比闸机的分值高,闸机的客流速度的分值比设施利用率的分值大,说明在影响闸机的服务效率方面,客流速度这个因素对闸机的影响偏大,楼扶梯的客流速度的分值比设施利用率的分值小,说明在影响楼扶梯的服务效率方面,设施利用率这个因素对了楼扶梯的影响偏大,相对于楼扶梯,闸机在客流量方面对地下交通行人设施的影响更大一些。

3.4 6000 人/h 的仿真

模拟效果图如图 4 所示,结果如表 11~表 13 所示。

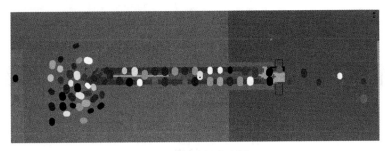

图 4　6000 人/h 仿真图

闸 机 结 果　　　　　　　　　　　　　　　　　　　表 11

评价指标	输出结果	单位
检测面域行人数	248.10	（人）
检测面域行人密度	46.23	（人/m^2）
行人流量	24.81（E 级）	（人/m·min）

楼扶梯结果　　　　　　　　　　　　　　　　　　　表 12

评价指标	输出结果	单位
行人数	52.60	（人）
密度等级	F	

闸机—楼扶梯综合结果　　　　　　　　　　　　　　表 13

	设施	指标	设施权重	指标权重	权重乘积	指标分值	总分值
6000 人/h	闸机	设施利用率	0.25	0.20	0.05	65	14.05
		客流速度		0.80	0.20	54	
	楼扶梯	设施利用率	0.75	0.20	0.15	92	39
		客流速度		0.80	0.60	42	

　　楼扶梯的分值比闸机的分值高,闸机的客流速度的分值比设施利用率的分值小,说明在影响闸机的服务效率方面,设施利用率这个因素对闸机的影响偏大,楼扶梯的客流速度的分值比设施利用率的分值小,说明在影响楼扶梯的服务效率方面,设施利用率这个因素对了楼扶梯的影响偏大,相对于闸机,楼扶梯在设施利用率方面对地下交通行人设施的影响更大一些。

4　结　　语

　　论文利用层次分析法和 VISSIM 软件进行影响城市轨道交通地下行人服务设施的服务效率影响因素的对比和分析,研究结果表明:①在影响地下设施服务水平方面,楼扶梯的影响偏多一些。②客流量为 2000 人/h 和 4000 人/h 的时候,经营者需要注意在客流速度方面提高地下行人设施的服务水平。然而在客流量为 6000 人/h 的时候,经营者需要注意在设施利用率方面提高地下行人设施的服务水平。③当客流量达到 6000 人/h 的时候,楼扶梯的影响比重稍微大一些。

　　本文虽然根据调研数据对计算机行人仿真参数进行了标定,但仿真的结果与实际情况仍然具有一定的差异。怎样开展更多关于计算机行人仿真方面的研究,从而使仿真更加贴近实际情况,值得进一步探讨。

参考文献

[1]　李雯,陈晓荣,王红斌,等. 基于 AHP 方法的制造企业数字化供应链成熟度评估[J]. 上海管理科学,

2020,5:74-80.
[2] 赖艺欢,张星臣,陈军华,等.基于多层次行人行为模型的地铁大客流仿真[J].大连交通大学学报,2019,3:1-6.

城市相邻景区内部路径优化分析及交通组织优化
——以西安市大唐不夜城为例

陈桂珍

(长安大学运输工程学院)

摘 要 为研究相邻景区内部最佳游览路径,优化游客出行链条,本文通过SP调查数据分析游客游览特征,确定出行者游览路径的影响因素,并据此建立费用公式、标定路阻函数,通过最短路算法确定相邻景区内部的游览路线。应用所提出的方法,以西安市大唐不夜城步行街同相邻景区大雁塔、大唐芙蓉园为例,对三个相邻景区内部游览路径进行优化,为游客出行提供建议。

关键词 交通组织优化 路径优化 SP调查 最短路算法 大唐不夜城

0 引 言

城市内部旅游景区的发展对城市周边交通产生的影响不可忽视。为增强相邻景区之前的联动性,分析城市相邻景区游客出行特性,优化游客出行路径,制定合理的交通组织优化方案,对增强城市内部相邻景区的流动性,方便游客出行具有重要意义。

现有对城市旅游的研究多为公共交通[1]、高铁[2]、航空[3]等出行方式对旅游景区的影响程度和促进关系,城市旅游的时空特征[4]等,这些研究内容将城市内部旅游同交通发展相联系,对旅游交通理论具有重要贡献。但是,现有对城市内部相邻景区交通运行特征的研究较少。

对于路径优化,现有研究已经有很多。从路径优化方法来看,既有经典的Floyd算法[5]、Dijkstra算法[6],也有现在的蚁群算法[7]、遗传算法[8]等;从路径优化的对象来看,既有公交路径优化[9],也有轨道[10]、非机动车[11]等。然而,现有研究对于城市相邻景区内部路径优化较少。

景区交通系统在运行特征、接驳方式和交通组织等方面有其特殊性,特别是城市内部旅游的出行目的、时间等与居民存在显著差异[12]。因此,应有目的地分析城市内部旅游景区游客"时-空"出行特性及与相关周边区域客流交换特征,提升改善步行街内部道路,为游客提供更加便捷的交通接驳服务及舒适的步行空间。

西安市大唐不夜城步行街、大雁塔和大唐芙蓉园是曲江新区的重要景点,同时三个景区紧密相连,交通相互影响程度高。本文以大唐不夜城及其相邻景区大雁塔、大唐芙蓉园为例,通过对相邻景区游客运行特性进行分析,确定相邻景区游客出行费用函数,通过调查数据进行参数标定,利用Dijkstra算法确定最短路径。同时对游客出行费用影响因素进行分析,并据此系统优化交通组织,对城市相邻旅游景区内部交通组织系统化提供建议。

1 模 型

1.1 影响因素分析

游客出行具有个体差异性,不同的游客受出行目的、时间、距离等因素的影响,在相邻景区会有不同的路径选择。建立合适的出行路径选择模型,需要对游客选择出行路径时所考虑的因素进行调查分析。

对西安市大唐不夜城、大雁塔和大唐芙蓉园的游客进行问卷调查,调查问卷共 2850 份,有效问卷为 2156 份,调查结果显示:游客出行选择看重因素中时间占比为 45%,花费占比为 28%,路程占比为 17%,拥挤程度占比为 10%,由于景区拥挤程度很难找到合适的判别程度规则,因此将时间、费用和距离作为游客选择最短游览路线的量化指标。

1.2 模型构建

1.2.1 费用函数

为统一量化游客在相邻景区路径选择特征,本文提出游客路径选择费用函数。游客出行选择不同的接驳方式,其时间、费用和距离有不同的指标,最短路径的选择也不同。而旅游景区因其特殊出行目的,接驳方式的选择需要根据当地景区交通规划规范。因此,费用函数首先确定相邻景区可选择的接驳方式,根据不同接驳方式确定不同的出行费用,即路段阻抗。出行费用函数如式(1)所示。

$$C_i = a_{ij} x_i \tag{1}$$

式中:i——接驳方式;

j——影响因素;

a_{ij}——i 接驳方式 j 因素的影响系数;

x_i——选择第 i 种接驳方式。

1.2.2 最短路算法

常用的最短路算法有 Floyd 算法、Dijkstra 算法、Bellman-Ford 算法和 SPAF 算法,其中 Dijkstra 算法是典型的单源最短路径算法,以起始点为中心向外层层扩展,用于计算一个节点到其他所有节点的最短路径。Dijkstra 算法求解步骤如下:

(1)对路网进行网格化处理,将所有的目的地点进行标号,集合 P 表示已知最短路径的顶点,Q 表示未知的顶点集合,向量 $d[i]$ 代表源点到点 i 的最短路径长度。

(2)进行初始化,起始点 s 的路径权重被赋为 $0(d[s]=0)$。设置起始点到其他顶点的路径值,放置于 d 中。

(3)找出点集 Q 中 $d[i] i \in Q$ 最小的点,这个点为进入点集 P 的候选节点,然后通过该点松弛点集 Q 中其他的点,更新向量 d。

(4)重复上一步,直到 Q 为空,此时 d 数组中就是源点到各个顶点的最短路径。

本文通过费用函数得出路段阻抗,利用 Dijkstra 算法进行求解,研究路线如图 1 所示,模型求解步骤如图 2 所示。

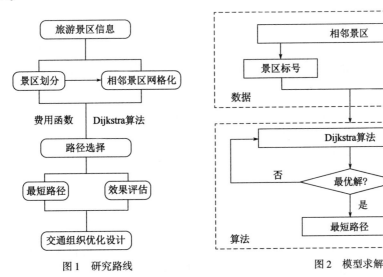

图 1　研究路线　　　　　　　　　　图 2　模型求解

2 西安大唐不夜城案例分析

2.1 大唐不夜城空间分布及影响范围

大唐不夜城是西安市著名的旅游景区,地理位置如图3所示,旅游经济发展导致周边区域道路网功能结构及交通流运行发生着较大的变化。如图4所示,步行街与大雁塔、大唐芙蓉园之间联系紧密,客流交换频繁。问卷调查结果显示,到达步行街的游客中,47%为大雁塔与步行街景区组合游玩,22%为大雁塔、步行街与大唐芙蓉园组合游玩,20%为步行街与大唐芙蓉园组合游玩,仅11%为只游步行街。

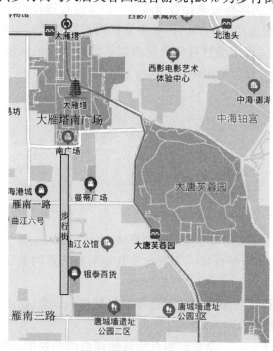

图3 大唐不夜城空间分布

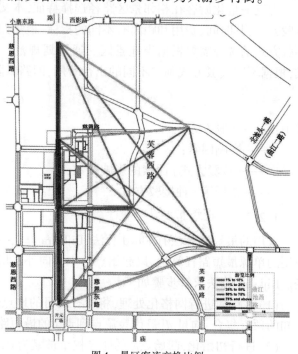

图4 景区客流交换比例

2.2 大唐不夜城客流出行特性

2.2.1 游客年龄构成分析

根据调查结果分析,步行街吸引的主要游客群体为青年人(18~35岁)和中年人(35~55岁),其中青年人所占比例最大,为46%;其次为中年人,占比为32%。老年人(55岁以上)和儿童、少年(0~18岁)所占比例近似,均为10%左右。

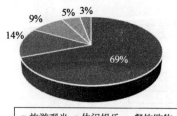

图5 步行街及其邻近景区游客出行目的构成

2.2.2 游客出行目的分析

如图5所示,游客主要出行目的为旅游观光,约占69%;其次为休闲娱乐、餐饮购物、酒店会议和其他,分别占比14%、9%、5%和3%。

2.2.3 游客来源分析

普通节假日期间主城区游客为主要客流来源,占比78%,特殊节假日期间主城区游客占比48%。说明特殊节假日游客的平均出行距离变长,跨省、跨区域出行比例上升。

调查显示,市内游客86.21%来源于明城墙及以北区域、电子城及以西区域、曲江新区,其中,明城墙及以北区域占比43.84%。境外游客主要来源于中心市区。

2.3 模型求解

调查显示,游客在步行街及其相邻景区内部接驳方式主要为步行、公交和自行车。因此本文根据费用公式,比较不同交通方式的时间、费用、路程,将其作为评价指标,以不同交通方式基础设施供给情况和调查数据为基础确定不同交通方式的系数,选取最少费用作为最优的交通方式。将最小费用设为路段阻抗,利用 python 代码通过 Dijkstra 算法对最短路径求解。

SP 调查结果显示,大唐不夜城步行街、大雁塔和大唐芙蓉园是紧密联系的相邻景区,对这三个景区进行网格化处理,如图 6 所示。

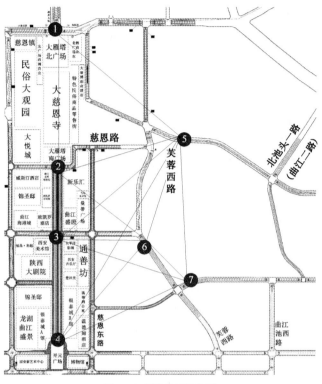

图 6 相邻景区网格化图

根据不同的起终点可以得出不同的结果,本文以起始点为大雁塔北广场,终点为大唐芙蓉园,得出最优游览路径为 1→2→3→4→6→5→7,这一计算结果和调查显示情况相符。

3 交通组织优化分析

结合调查数据和模型求解,对大唐不夜城交通组织优化提出如下建议:

(1)完善现有接驳方式,根据游客接驳点和分布情况,重新规划公交站点、路线。同时考虑到景区面积范围,可进一步分析乘客对景区内部接驳车和观光游览车价格接受程度,适当规划接驳车和观光游览车的放置和价格。

(2)完善非机动车系统,打造便捷连续的非机动车网络,充分发挥非机动车系统在旅游景区内部的便捷特性,以使整个交通系统的效率达到最优。

(3)根据客流分布,进行行人出行诱导,减少冲突。

4 结 语

(1)本文通过 SP 调查数据得出西安市大唐不夜城步行街及其相邻景区游客出行特征,结合费用模型和最短路算法,得出三个景区内部游览最优路径,为景区路径规划提供参考。

(2)步行街旅游景区作为一种尊重和关怀人的城市空间,其设计要坚持"以人为本"的原则,通过各类交通方式为游客抵达、离去提供有效的交通路径。

(3)不同时间段游客出行有不同的特性,在进一步研究中,将会考虑不同时间段最优路径选择和交通组织优化方法。

参考文献

[1] 黄红良,赵航,龙立美,等. 基于城市公共交通的贵阳市旅游景点可达性分析[J]. 贵州师范大学学报(自然科学版),2018,036(006):68-77.

[2] Albalate D, Fageda X. High speed rail and tourism: Empirical evidence from Spain[J]. Transportation Research Part A, 2016, 85(Mar.):174-185.

[3] Maxim C. Sustainable tourism implementation in urban areas: a case study of London[J]. Journal of Sustainable Tourism, 2016(7).

[4] 张鲜鲜,李婧晗,左颖,等. 基于数字足迹的游客时空行为特征分析——以南京市为例[J]. 经济地理,2018,38(012):226-233.

[5] 潘福全,邢英,魏金丽,等. 基于开放街区的车辆行驶最优路径设计[J]. 深圳大学学报(理工版),2020,v.37;No.160(02):37-44.

[6] 王亚、任燕、夏林元. 交通运输网络的二叉堆索引及路径算法优化[J]. 应用科学学报,2020,v.38(06):117-127.

[7] 吴耕锐,郭三学,吴虎胜,等. 改进多目标蚁群算法在动态路径优化中的应用[J]. 计算机应用与软件,2019,036(005):249-254,288.

[8] Abdallah A M F M, Essam D L, Sarker R A. On solving periodic re-optimization dynamic vehicle routing problems[J]. Applied Soft Computing, 2017, 55:1-12.

[9] Lang G. A summary of research on customized bus route optimization for commuter needs[J]. IOP Conference Series: Earth and Environmental Science, 2020, 546(5):052037(5pp).

[10] B A Y A, C B W B, C J H B, et al. Service replanning in urban rail transit networks: Cross-line express trains for reducing the number of passenger transfers and travel time[J]. Transportation Research Part C: Emerging Technologies, 115.

[11] 李岩,汪帆,陈宽民. 历史城区自行车绿道系统规划与设计的实证研究[J]. 长安大学学报(社会科学版),2020,022(002):62-70.

[12] 周静,俞秋田. 旅游景区交通集散枢纽供给能力研究——以苏州阳山地区为例[J]. 交通与运输,2016(z2).

基于区块链的超限超载运输治理应用研究

张炜[1] 施展[1] 赵彩娥[2]

(1.华设设计集团股份有限公司;2.南京信息工程大学)

摘要 在分析当前超限超载运输造成的各类事故隐患以及在超限治理中省、市管理部门存在的问题时,提出超限治理区块链系统设计思路,明确了运输环节信息上链、执法处理业务上链的业务流程,提出了基于区块链超限治理平台技术框架,并明确了区块链在落地实践中需注意的事项。

关键词 公路运输 区块链 超限 超载 超限超载治理

0 引 言

货车超限超载运输不仅严重破坏公路基础设施,给公路和桥梁带来严重危害,降低公路使用寿命,而且威胁交通安全,极易引发交通事故[1]。因超限超载引起的交通事故频频发生,近年来多地也发生了多起因为超限超载运输引发的车辆制动失灵及操作问题而造成道路损毁、桥梁断裂甚至垮塌等恶性事件,直接导致大量的财产损失及人员伤亡。

同时,因超限运输导致的路面损坏、大幅度缩短公路使用年限等道路资产损失也极为巨大。据测算,如果行驶公路的车辆超限超载50%左右,以一般等级沥青路面设计使用年限12~15年为例,实际使用寿命仅为2~3年,养护费用大幅增加,造成国家经济损失[1]。

国务院、交通运输部相继出台相关管理办法加强对超限超载违法运输行为的治理,保障公路设施和人民生命财产安全。2018年6月,交通运输部印发了《全国治超联网管理信息系统省级工程建设指南》,提出省级治超工程的建设思路及总体框架,要求"加强超限运输监管和服务,减少违法超限运输行为,保护公路基础设施和人民生命财产安全,推进治超领域的治理体系和治理能力现代化"[2]。力图近期全面掌控超限超载违法车辆并提高处罚精准度,远期大幅度降低超限超载违法现象。

1 超限治理及信息系统现状

1.1 超限治理及信息系统情况

随着各省市"联合治超"工作全面开展,治超工作重心不断前移。以江苏省为例,当前主要采用现场治超与非现场治超相结合的方式进行治理,超限检测站采取固定、流动及非现场相结合的治超方式。

1.1.1 现场治超

现场治超由交警现场筛查疑似超限车辆,前方引导至超限检测站,经精检认定是否超载。该模式检测效率低,投入资源大,易发生冲突,检测成果不易巩固,同时易引发交通堵塞。如图1所示。

图1 现场治超

1.1.2 非现场治超

非现场治超通过高精度动态称重检测设备自动获取车辆称重数据,并明确动态称重系统设备所使用的计量软件应满足以下要求:应对计量软件进行印封,如无法实现印封,则该软件的任何改变都应留有相应日志[3]。如图2所示。

图2 非现场治超

目前省级治超信息系统主要包括以下系统:

(1)公路超限管理系统。

公路超限管理实现公路超限案件执法管理、超限检测站点运行监管、超限管理基本信息查询、超限信息抄告、超限信息统计、超限台账报表、黑名单管理、联合执法等功能。

(2) 运政在线系统。

运政在线系统包括运政业务子系统、日常监管子系统和执法管理子系统,涵盖道路运输、公交、出租车、驾培、维修、检测站等业务,实现人、车、户数据的统一与关联。

(3) 大件运输许可管理系统。

目前大件运输许可系统实现与跨省大件运输许可系统部级平台的对接和协同,满足跨省大件运输并联许可企业注册、申请受理、跨省协调、审查决定等业务需求。

(4) 重点营运车辆日常运营规范性监测系统。

重点营运车辆日常运营规范性监测系统主要针对省内两客一危、重载普货实时位置监控,并根据交通运输部的考核办法出具相应考核报表。

(5) 动态检测点动态称重系统。

动态检测的超限数据实时上传至省执法局。对通过公路主线车道的车辆,系统能够自动检测出该车辆的总量、轴重、连轴信息、连轴重量、车速等信息,并将称重数据上传。

1.2 超限治理中存在的主要问题

现有业务系统在过去很长时间,很好地支撑了省级各项超限治理工作的有效开展。但随着治超形势的变化及治超工作的新要求,目前系统也存在以下不足。

1.2.1 省级治超主管部门

(1) 数据接入不全面。

超限数据来源虽广泛,包括固定治超站、动态检测点、源头治超点、高速公路收费站、普通公路收费站等,但较零散未进行统一的数据接入处理。

(2) 缺乏超限预警机制。

原超限管理相关系统只进行了数据采集,未对超限车辆以及严重超限违法行为进行预警,省级治超主管部门无法第一时间掌握现场实际情况,防控较为被动。

(3) 缺乏关联数据检索能力。

一线治超人员无法通过信息系统获取执法所需的车辆基本信息、所属货运企业信息、历史违法超限记录和案件相关信息,且原超限管理系统未与运政在线等相关系统对接。

(4) 公众信息服务能力待加强。

省执法局在公众信息服务方面渠道较少,治超相关的政策法规与实时动态无法与货运从业者进行宣贯和交流,超限违法记录和案件处理信息未对公众公开。

1.2.2 市级治超主管部门

各地市辖区内固定治超站和动态检测点的实时数据均直接传输至省级,市级部门缺乏对辖区内超限信息的实时监测,无法有针对性地开展治超工作;原系统在省市、市际间缺乏联动机制,无法有效地衔接省级与市级之间业务的流转,相邻市之间也缺乏协调联动手段。

1.2.3 治超执法业务

非现场执法取证难度较大。对高速公路和普通公路违法超限行为取证时,需协调公路运营等单位,以人工方式获取,取证周期长;非现场超限违法案件确认后,目前为人工协调获取违法车辆所属企业的联系方式,数据也较为滞后,函告成功率相对较低。

根据对多个省市治理超限工作的调研,除各地管理体制造成的差异,对技术而言,上述问题及执法过程中的新需求可归为信息有孤岛无法及时互通;部门间信息无法信任无法充分共享;关键信息如称重等有被篡改风险,信息可追溯性较差等。

2 超限治理区块链系统设计

区块链技术是一种技术集成创新,为不同组织机构提供在非可信环境下建立信任的可能性,降低了电子数据取证成本,带来了建立可信范式的转变,为破解政务环境中可信数据共享交互、业务协同及权利人可信授权示证等难题提供了有效的技术解决手段[4]。该技术近几年在金融、征信管理等领域已经广泛应用,其技术特点也能解决超限治理所面临的不少问题。

2.1 区块链技术及特点[5]

区块链(Blockchain)是一种由多方共同维护,使用密码学保证传输和访问安全,能够实现数据一致存储、难以篡改、防止抵赖的记账技术,也称为分布式账本技术(Distributed Ledger Technology)。

按照系统是否具有节点准入机制,区块链可分类为许可链和非许可链。许可链中节点的加入退出需要区块链系统的许可,根据拥有控制权限的主体是否集中可分为联盟链和私有链;非许可链则是完全开放的,亦可称为公有链,节点可以随时自由加入和退出。区块链的适用场景可以总结为"新型数据库、多业务主体、彼此不互信、业务强相关"。

2.2 超限治理区块链系统架构

区块链的技术特点可在超限治理方面解决传统管理模式及信息系统面临的多个顽疾,实现以下目标:建立治超管理各政府主管部门的统一服务体系,防止运输过程中称重数据、车辆、人员以及货运企业等信息人为篡改;为交通执法、工商及税务管理等部门等提供便利的跨区域、跨部门信息互信共享;降低货场、运输企业及货物买卖双方等多方参与人员的信息共享难度,减少各类纸质单据、单证的使用、降低使用成本,提高运输效率。

2.2.1 技术思路

根据区块链技术特点、超限治理的实际业务特点及难点,可采用区块链进行省级平台的构建,从而既能保证系统具备多中心、可授权管理以及较高效率的特点,同时还能应用区块链的数据可信、防篡改及可追溯等特点在超限治理上。

以江苏省为例,可建立全省1+13个节点构成的区块链。其中的1为省级执法管理节点,由其进行授权、认证、管理及调用功能;13个地市级分节点,负责各地市超限治理的数据管理、证书管理及数据服务等。地市级分节点与各地市交通执法、工商及税务管理、应急管理等部门进行数据对接,并为货场、运输企业、买卖双方等提供单据、交易核验服务。

2.2.2 主要业务流程

货物买卖双方通过线下或线上平台交易成功后,将货物相关信息(包括货种、质量、货物外廓、首末场站等)及交易凭证信息上链;买方选定运输企业,运输企业将车辆、驾驶员等信息上链;货场管理方根据链上可信数据核对后由运输企业起运货物,并同时将车牌、称重数据、运输时间、相关照片等信息上链。运输环节业务流程如图3所示。

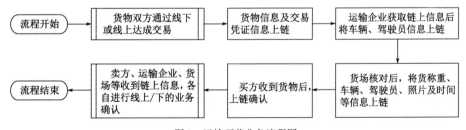

图3 运输环节业务流程图

根据表1,货物交易 HASH 为:365190D740BEAF1C6F607C6FA47A815CD8841E1F。

货物交易信息表 表1

货物种类	货物总质量(t)	货物外廓长、宽、高(m)	货物发出地	货物目的地	交易凭证
板式建材	32.5	6×3×2.5	南京货场1	武汉货场2	交易凭证1.jpg

根据表 2 中选择的运输企业分配的车辆、驾驶员信息及货物交易 HASH 码,获得运输信息 HASH 为:5C5592DF1036AA4D1EF917DCAFFB8F47387D87E5。

运输信息表　　　　　　　　　　　　　　　　表 2

运输企业	驾驶员	运输车辆	货物交易 HASH
都市快运	张三	苏 A99999	365190D740BEAF1C6F607C6FA47A815CD8841E1F

超限执法管理部门根据链上数据及高速预检(快速称重)、高清视频(货物体积超限检测)等技术手段核对车辆及货物信息;如涉嫌超限则发出指令,协同交警等对车辆进行精检确认。对于确定超限违章的,在确认货主、货场、运输企业等责任后,按规则进行黑/灰名单的评分处理,并将数据上链,供社会公众等查询,增加超限治理的社会影响力,减少侥幸超限运输的可能性。业务流程如图 4 所示。

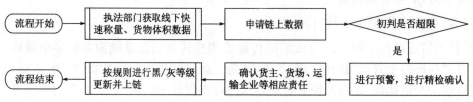

图 4　执法处理业务流程图

通过链上链下技术对接,在链下运行原有登记业务系统,在链上节点汇聚生成的电子证照版式文件和电子数据,上链记录电子证照指纹(HASH 值)信息和共享信息[6],实现流程的可追溯、可信发布和共享。链式结构如图 5 所示。

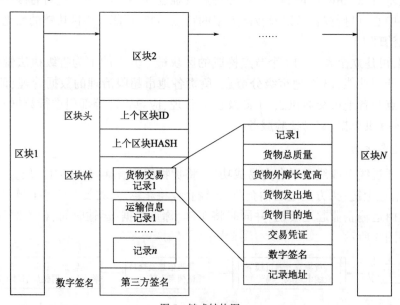

图 5　链式结构图

所有的监管机构、利益相关方均可通过公钥私钥及签发的数字签名进行相关信息的获取和校验,即解密相关信息后,将记录原始息进行 HASH 后与块链中记录 HASH 相比较,验证是否为块链中声明的记录信息[7]。

2.2.3　技术架构

根据图 6 技术架构图,省级主节点可对各地市分支节点进行授权管理并实现信息共享服务的管理;地市节点根据货物交易系统、运输服务系统、各类第三方管理服务系统的特点进行线下或者线上交易,将关键信息及结果信息上链即可保证信息的可靠、可控及可信的共享。

对省级管理部门而言,可实现固定、动态、源头场站、各类收费站数据的全面接入,进行超限违法行为的快速预警,打通数据链路极大提升了数据关联检索能力,并可及时向公众提供案件及黑灰名单信用情

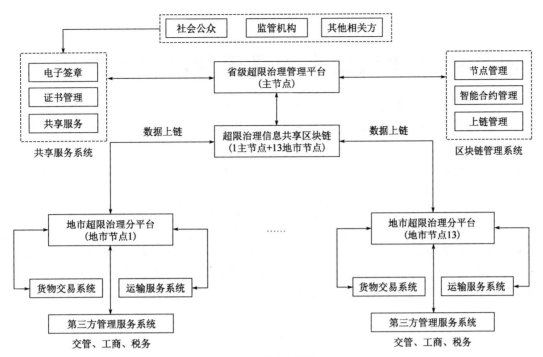

图6 技术架构图

况;对各地市而言,能快速监测辖区及邻区的信息并实现联动。

综上,对于各地超限执法中存在的共性需求,包括打破信息孤岛,实现信息的充分共享;关键称重信息的可信追溯,都能通过引入区块链技术较好地解决。

3 结 语

当前,各省市正快速推进全国治超联网管理信息系统省级工程建设,部分省份已初见成效。但据前期调研,尚未有省级超限治理平台利用区块链进行数据可信、共享等应用。在这个阶段,引入区块链构建省级乃至国家级超限治理超级链,可快速打通超限治理的各环节,形成超限治理可信大数据,为后续信息追溯、信用联网及对接金融体系打下良好的基础。

同时也应看到,尚有不少问题需在实践中不断完善。一方面,区块链作为一项新技术,还需各项政策及制度的约束,以便更好地在相关场景推广;另一方面,区块链可以保障链上数据的可信、可控和可追溯,但对于称重源头数据如对接来的各货场地磅数据的真实和有效性尚无法保障,这些都需后续进一步完善。也期待相关省市能先行先试,率先进行项目实践,发扬区块链优点,取得应用效果。

参考文献

[1] 交通运输部.把准脉搏 精准发力 全面加强超限超载治理—交通运输部公路局局长解读《关于进一步做好货车非法改装和超限超载治理工作的意见》[EB/OL].(2016-08-22). http://xxgk.mot.gov.cn/2020/jigou/glj/202006/t20200623_3312535.html.

[2] 中华人民共和国交通运输部.交通运输部办公厅关于印发全国治超联网管理信息系统省级工程建设指南的通知[Z].2018.

[3] DB32/T 3314—2017.公路运输车辆动态称重系统技术规范[S].

[4] 杨东.区块链+监管=法链(RegChain)[M].北京:人民出版社股份有限公司,2018.

[5] 中国信息通讯研究院可信区块链推进计划[C]//区块链白皮书,2018:1-6.

[6] 贾文珏,张菲菲.基于区块链的全国不动产登记信息共享服务思路初探[J].国土资源信息化,2020(2):3-8.

[7] 杨茂江.基于密码和区块链技术的数据交易平台设计[J].信息通信技术,2016(04):24-31.

基于科学知识图谱的汽车智能化发展研究

张奕骏[1,2]，张 晖[1,2]，肖逸影[1,2]，张 琦[1,2]

(1.武汉理工大学智能交通系统研究中心；2.国家水运安全工程技术研究中心)

摘 要 通过Web of Science核心合集数据库筛选出4645篇在2000—2020年(截止到2020年6月30日)间出版的汽车智能化研究领域的英文文献，使用VOS viewer和Excel软件进行全球文献年度分布趋势图、国家及机构合作网络图、核心作者群、文献共被引聚类图的分析。结果表明，国际汽车智能化研究由稳步增长趋势转为快速增长趋势，美国和中国的发文量位居前列；中国、美国、加拿大的研究机构与其他机构的合作较多；但目前未形成普莱斯定律中所定义的核心作者群；目前领域研究热点方向包括车辆各子系统基础研究、自动驾驶相关问卷调查、整车算法融合研究、微观仿真建模与分析。

关键词 交通工程 文献综述 科学知识图谱 汽车智能化 VOSviewer 可视化

0 引 言

由于现在技术尚未完全成熟，法律法规框架不够完整，大众对自动驾驶汽车的接受度不一，信息安全保障也存在问题，都给汽车智能化领域研究带来了挑战[1]。国内外该领域的学者从不同角度进行了大量研究，但目前还缺乏对汽车智能化领域全面系统的分析。

本文将采用文献计量学的分析方法，利用科学知识图谱分析工具VOSviewer1.6.15软件，分析近二十年(2000—2020年)收录在Web of Science核心合集数据库的汽车智能化领域的4645篇英文文献。利用可视化方式对该研究领域的时间、国家/地区、研究机构、作者、高频被引文献等方面进行分析，为今后的研究提供参考。

1 数据来源及研究方法

本文数据均来自WOS(Web of Science)核心合集数据库，由于汽车智能化研究主要为智能汽车[2]，因此，针对关键词"autonomous car/vehicle""self-driving car/vehicle""unmanned car/vehicle"进行检索，检索时间选取2000—2020年，最终检索时间为2020年6月30日，排除与汽车智能化无关的文献，最终筛选出4645篇英文文献。

将文献数据导入Microsoft Excel 2016软件和VOSviewer1.6.15软件中，使用VOSviewer和Excel软件进行全球文献年度分布趋势图、国家及机构合作网络图、核心作者群、文献共被引聚类图的分析。

2 汽车智能化研究领域文献特征分析

2.1 全球文献年度分布及趋势

根据Web of Science提供的检索分析，有关汽车智能化领域文献年度分布及趋势如图1所示。2000—2011年，全球范围内研究都处于初级起步阶段，论文年平均在100篇左右；2012—2015年，处于稳步增长阶段；2016—2019年，呈快速增长阶段，且2019年达到峰值809篇。汽车智能化研究领域近二十年文献产出数量前10名的国家/地区见表1，其中，美国文献产出第一，达1360篇，占成果总数的29.28%，且篇均被引频次为13.62次，明显高于其他国家/地区。

基金项目：国家重点研发计划/National Key Research and Development Program of China(2019YFB1600803)、中央高校基本科研业务费专项资金/Fundamental Research Funds for the Central Universities of Ministry of Education of China(2020-zy-092)。

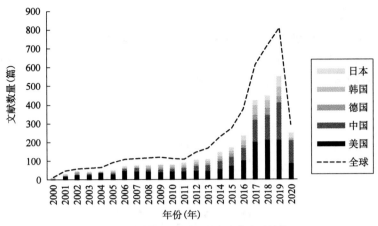

图 1　汽车智能化领域文献年度分布及趋势

近二十年文献产出数量前 10 名的国家/地区　　　　　　　　　　　　　　表 1

序号	国家/地区	文献数量(篇)	百分比(%)	总被引频次	排名	篇均被引频次	排名
1	美国	1360	29.28	18527	1	13.62	1
2	中国	894	19.35	6005	2	6.72	9
3	德国	303	6.52	2612	3	8.62	4
4	韩国	274	5.90	1910	5	6.97	8
5	日本	228	4.91	1324	9	5.81	10
6	法国	224	4.82	2456	4	10.96	2
7	英国	201	4.33	1504	7	7.48	7
8	加拿大	188	4.05	1453	8	7.73	6
9	西班牙	166	3.57	1315	10	7.92	5
10	澳大利亚	163	3.51	1588	6	9.74	3

文献共涉及 91 个国家和地区,筛选出相关研究成果 5 篇及以上的国家/地区共有 62 个。图 2 为文献所属国家在时间维度上的分布,其中颜色由深到浅对应研究时间从早到晚。结合图 1 和图 2 分析得出,研究早期以美国、日本、意大利、西班牙等为主,其中美国为研究主力,拥有较多的研究成果,随后在新加坡、澳大利亚、中国等迅速发展,中国赶超德国,成为发文量第二的国家。

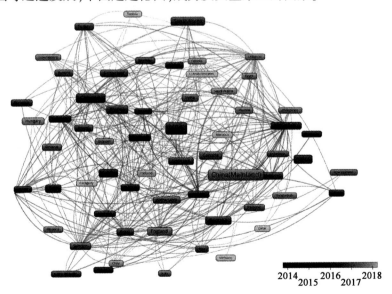

图 2　文献所属国家/地区

2.2 发文机构分布及合作情况

经统计,一共有 2911 个研究机构,通过 VOSviewer 得到最大子合作网络,如图 3 所示,共包含了 823 个研究机构、1754 对合作关系,图中节点大小表示机构在汽车智能化领域发表论文的多少,连线表示机构间的合作关系。各机构参与该领域研究的时间越早,颜色越浅。

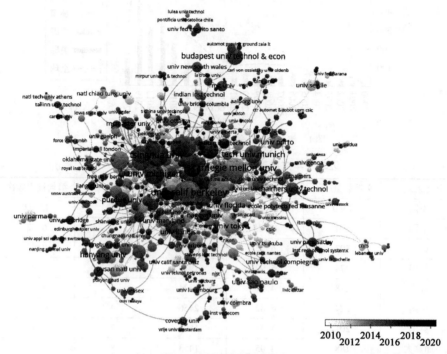

图 3 研究机构合作网络图

将 VOSviewer 生成的合作网络图数据导入 Excel 处理,得到与其他机构合作度排名前 10 的研究机构,如表 2 所示。中国、美国、加拿大的研究机构与其他机构的合作较多。其中,清华大学、加州大学伯克利分校、中国科学院、麻省理工学院在汽车智能化领域表现活跃,合作机构数量及合作度排名都位居前列。在论文发表量方面,加州大学伯克利分校位列第一,清华大学和麻省理工学院并列第二。得克萨斯大学奥斯汀分校论文总引用频次排名第一,其次是麻省理工学院、加州大学伯克利分校,这三个机构都隶属于美国,与前文结论一致,美国在汽车智能化领域影响力较大。

与其他机构合作度排名前 10 的研究机构   表 2

序号	机构	合作机构数量	排名	论文总发表量	排名	论文总被引频次	排名
1	中国清华大学	47	1	61	2	513	5
2	美国加州大学伯克利分校	44	2	68	1	1147	3
3	中国科学院	39	3	43	7	427	7
4	美国麻省理工学院	37	4	61	3	1867	2
5	美国卡内基·梅隆大学	29	6	56	4	802	4
6	美国密歇根大学	23	8	53	5	355	8
7	中国东南大学	23	9	42	8	431	6
8	美国得克萨斯大学奥斯汀分校	26	7	49	6	1943	1
9	加拿大滑铁卢大学	32	5	38	9	328	10
10	美国乔治亚理工学院	22	10	38	10	340	9

2.3 核心作者群分析

核心作者群指论文发表量大且影响力较大的作者集合[3],根据普莱斯定律和洛卡特定律,有:

$$m = 0.749\sqrt[2]{n_{max}}$$

式中:m——某一领域核心作者最少发文量;

n_{max}——某一领域核心作者最大发文量。

以第一作者(含独立作者)搜索,厦门大学郭景华的论文发表量最多为13篇。最高引论文为2016年发表的论文《Nonlinear Coordinated Steering and Braking Control of Vision-Based Autonomous Vehicles in Emergency Obstacle Avoidance》,研究基于非线性反步控制理论和自适应模糊滑模控制技术,提出了一种新颖的协调转向和制动控制策略,并利用李雅普诺夫理论证明了该协调控制系统的渐近收敛性。选取13篇作为最高产作者论文发表量,根据公式计算后向上取整得到3,即论文发表量大于或等于3篇的作者为核心作者,近二十年来,共计有148名作者,总发文量为555篇,占总文献的11.94%,远低于50%,说明国际汽车智能化领域还未形成普莱斯定律中所定义的核心作者群。

发文量超过14篇的高产作者　　　　表3

作　者	机　构	论文发表量	总被引频次	首次发表论文时间
胡川	中国东南大学/加拿大麦克马斯特大学/美国得克萨斯大学奥斯汀分校	18	455	2015年
Borrelli, Francesco	美国加州大学伯克利分校	16	1007	2006年
Althoff, Matthias	美国卡内基·梅隆大学/德国慕尼黑工业大学	15	169	2007年
Kockelman, Kara M.	美国得克萨斯大学奥斯汀分校	15	963	2014年
郭景华	中国厦门大学	14	178	2015年
Levin, Michael W.	美国得克萨斯大学奥斯汀分校/美国明尼苏达大学	14	288	2015年
李克强	中国清华大学	14	171	2015年

筛选出文章署名作者发文量超过14篇的有8名,所属机构、总被引频次、首次发表论文时间相关信息汇总如表3所示。其中单篇文献引用频次最高的是美国加州大学伯克利分校Borrelli等在2007年发表的论文《Predictive active steering control for autonomous vehicle systems》,研究提出了一种模型预测控制(Model Predictive Control, MPC)方法,用于控制自动驾驶汽车的主动前转向系统。结合上文可得出结论,汽车智能化领域的高产作者一开始是聚焦于车辆本身架构研究开发,后续研究扩展至自动驾驶所面临的机遇和挑战、算法融合研等更多维度,这也与汽车智能化发展进程相一致。

2.4 文献共被引分析

共被引反映的是两篇被引证论文之间的关系,即如果有2篇文献被第3篇文献同时引用,则前2篇文献构成"共被引"关系,文献共被引分析常用于探究科学文献的内在联系以及描绘科学发展的动态结构[4]。利用VOSviewer筛选出最小被引频次不小于20篇的论文有173篇,共被引聚类网络图如图4所示,由173个网络节点和4153条连接线组成。图中节点大小表示论文被引总频次大小,节点不同灰度表示论文所属的聚类。

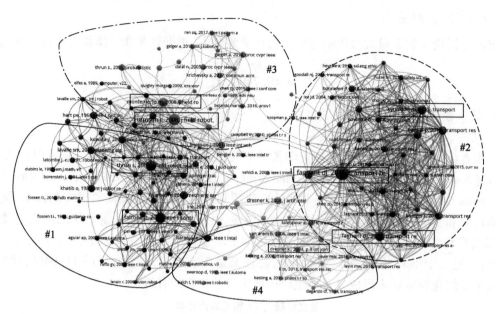

图 4 文献共被引聚类网络图

(1)群集1:车辆各子系统基础研究。

群集1是4个聚类中最大的簇。早期研究多数采用模拟的手段,从车辆的主动安全性角度出发,针对制动防抱死系统、牵引力控制系统、车身稳定控制系统等车辆自身系统进行研究,提高汽车安全性。

(2)群集2:自动驾驶相关问卷调查。

群集2是4个聚类中第二大的簇,是该网络中与群集1相邻最远的簇。该部分的研究主要是汽车智能化未来的机遇与挑战,以及人们对自动驾驶的看法。该部分研究大多采用问卷的方法,被调查者来自中国、美国、法国、挪威、新加坡、丹麦等不同的国家。

(3)群集3:整车算法融合研究。

群集2是与群集1相邻最近的簇,说明该群集与群集1的研究内容具有较高相关性。该部分的研究主要是整车各系统算法优化及融合的研究。近几年研究运用的算法包括基于采样的最大熵逆增强学习算法、机器学习算法、深度强化学习算法等。

(4)群集4:微观仿真建模与分析。

群集4是4个聚类中最小的簇,该部分研究主要侧重于自动驾驶车辆在高速公路上的微观仿真建模与分析。多数学者从自动驾驶车辆对高速公路交通状况影响情况(稳定性、流量等)进行研究,采用微观仿真的方法进行建模分析。

3 结 语

(1)从2012年开始,国际汽车智能化研究处于稳步增长趋势,研究主力为美国、日本等国家,在2015年转变为快速增长趋势,在澳大利亚、中国等国迅速发展。美国文献产出第一,达1360篇,且篇均被引频次为13.62次,明显高于其他国家/地区,中国发文量达894篇,超越德国,位居第二。

(2)2000—2020年间共有2911个研究机构,其中中国、美国、加拿大的研究机构与其他机构的合作较多。在合作机构数量及合作度排名方面,清华大学、加州大学伯克利分校、中国科学院、麻省理工学院位居前列。在论文发表量方面,加州大学伯克利分校排名第一,清华大学和麻省理工学院并列第二。在论文总引用频次方面,得克萨斯大学奥斯汀分校排名第一,其次是麻省理工学院、加州大学伯克利分校。但是,据统计,国际汽车智能化领域还未形成普莱斯定律中所定义的核心作者群。

(3)通过对文献共被引网络进行分析,汽车智能化领域的早期研究多数采用模拟的手段,从车辆的主动安全性角度出发,针对车辆各子系统进行研究。随着汽车智能化知识的普及,研究同时关注了自动驾驶所面临的机遇和挑战以及大众对其的看法,在车辆子系统研究的基础上,研究重点开始向整车算法融合研究和微观仿真建模与分析这两个方面倾斜。未来汽车智能化领域研究会继续与车联网和大数据技术紧密结合,升级自动驾驶汽车技术,加快汽车高自动化程度的进程。

参考文献

[1] 冼毅瑶. 自动驾驶汽车发展现状与形态预测[J]. 中阿科技论坛(中英阿文), 2019(01):1-4, 105-109.

[2] Brummelen J V, O'Brien M, Gruyer D, et al. Autonomous vehicle perception: The technology of today and tomorrow[J]. Transportation Research Part C Emerging Technologies, 2018.

[3] 任贤强. 基于CSSCI的新能源研究的文献计量分析[J]. 科学与管理, 2019, 39(06):80-88.

[4] 张旭欣, 王雪松, 马勇, 等. 驾驶行为与驾驶风险国际研究进展[J]. 中国公路学报, 2020, 33(06):1-17.

[5] Morando A, Victor T, Dozza M. A Reference Model for Driver Attention in Automation: Glance Behavior Changes During Lateral and Longitudinal Assistance[J]. IEEE Transactions on Intelligent Transportation Systems, 2018:1-11.

台辉高速公路铁路并行段铁路行驶眩光对高速行车安全影响分析及解决对策研究

刘 昊 钱 威 明小梅 陈 杰

(华设设计集团股份有限公司)

摘 要 铁路列车照射用光源导致高速公路交通标志和周边环境的对比度大幅度下降,增大了夜晚高速公路道路环境的复杂性,使得驾驶员对交通标志的视认能力受到影响。本文首先分析眩光的产生机理及其对视觉功能的影响,然后从铁路列车光源入手研究铁路列车光源特性,分析评价了台辉高速公路公铁并行段铁路列车光源对高速公路驾驶员造成的眩光影响程度,并提出了相应解决措施。

关键词 公铁并行 光源 防眩光 高速行车安全

0 引 言

眩光是影响高速公路通行安全的一个重要因素,很多学者均对高速公路防眩进行过研究。张明浩[1]开展高速公路视觉景观对行车安全的影响研究,对于优化高速公路景观设计、降低交通事故发生概率有重要意义。张振东[2]等对在高速公路中央分隔带设置防眩设施进行了研究,主要包括植树防眩以及防眩板防眩。

本文针对台辉高速公铁并行段的特殊情况[3],首先分析眩光的产生机理,然后从列车光源入手研究铁路列车光源特性,分析评价了公铁并行段铁路列车光源对高速公路驾驶员造成的眩光影响程度,并提出了方案对策。

1 台辉高速现场条件

台辉高速是连接豫北、鲁西的一条东西向高速通道,其豫鲁界至范县段存在汤台铁路并行段,具体如图1所示。

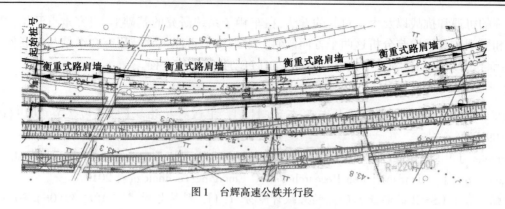

图 1 台辉高速公铁并行段

2 眩光的产生和影响

2.1 眩光的产生

眩光是一种视觉条件,是由于亮度分布不适当或变化的幅度太大,或空间、时间上存在着极端对比,以致引起观察者不舒适或降低观察重要物体的能力,或同时产生这两种现象。眩光的产生会降低人眼对目标对象的视认效果,延长视认时间,进而干扰到驾驶人员对车辆、路况信息的获取和处置,极易诱发公路交通事故。

眩光可以分为不舒适眩光和失能眩光[4]。本文涉及铁路光源对高速公路驾驶人员形成的眩光是失能眩光,其由于眩光源的散射光线在视网膜上产生了视感,与目标物成像产生了重叠,导致成像的对比度下降,从而降低了视觉效能和视觉的清晰度。

2.2 失能眩光评价

要定量研究有关失能眩光对人眼视觉的影响[5],首先需要分析眩光源在人眼内叠加的等效光幕亮度。眩光之所以会降低视功能,是因为无眩光时的障碍物和背景路面的亮度对比 C,在有眩光时则产生等效光幕亮度 L_v,而变为 C',而 $C \geq C'$,从而造成障碍物的对比度降低,故对失能眩光评价方法总结为以下步骤:

步骤一:计算等效光幕亮度值。在公路照明中当视线与眩光源光线入射方向的夹角在 1.5°~60° 范围内时,等效光幕亮度可通过下面经验公式计算得到:

$$L_v = K \frac{E_{CI}}{\theta^2}$$

式中:L_v——等效光幕亮度(cd/m²);

K——常数,取决于 θ 的单位,当 θ 用角度表示时,$K = 10$,用弧度表示时,$K = 3 \times 10^{-3}$;

E_{CI}——眩光源在观察者眼中,位于垂直于视线的平面上产生的照度(lx);

θ——视线与眩光源光线入射方向的夹角。

步骤二:计算多个眩光源 L_{vi} 叠加形成的总的等效光幕亮度值。在道路上对人眼视觉工作造成影响的眩光源往往不止一个。因此应计算各个眩光源 L_{vi} 叠加形成的总的等效光幕亮度。其计算公式如下:

$$L_v = \sum_{i=1}^{n} L_{vi}$$

步骤三:基于眩光限制阈值确定影响效果。增量国际照明委员会(CIE)提出了用眩光限制阈值增量来考核、控制眩光源的影响效果。等效光幕亮度的产生提高了视场内的背景亮度,一方面会提高对比灵敏度,另一方面亮度对比度会有所下降,其结果就是处于阈值对比条件下的目标物体在眩光条件下将无法被正常识别。而阈值增量 TI 即定义为在有眩光存在的条件下,能够再次刚刚看到目标物体所需要增加的额外对比与原对比的比值。因此,要限制眩光对人眼视认效果的干扰,需要对允许的阈值增量范围予以限定。在背景亮度范围为 0.05cd/m² < Lav < 5cd/m² 时,阈值增量 TI 的计算公式可近似为:

$$TI = 65 \times \frac{L_v}{L_{av}^{0.8}}\%$$

式中：TI——相对阈值增量(%)；

L_v——等效光幕亮度(cd/m^2)，假定观察者总是以与水平线成1°角注视与路轴平行的正前方(即注视正前方90m处路面上的一点)；

L_{av}——路面平均亮度(cd/m^2)，平均亮度为路面亮度的总体水平。公路照明条件下，路面的平均亮度一般均处于 $0.05cd/m^2 \sim 5cd/m^2$ 的范围内，可采用上式直接进行计算。

3 铁路列车干扰光源对高速行车安全影响分析研究

3.1 研究方法

本章运用眩光评价理论对眩光评价点进行眩光程度计算，根据铁路与高速公路的相对平面和立面位置，选取以最短路肩平距点的路肩平距值和铁路与高速公路高程值组合即"最不利条件"来评价整个路段受到的眩光影响。

3.2 铁路光源特征提炼

3.2.1 光源确认及参数

铁路列车主要影响光源为前照灯，前照灯主要使用的光源有卤钨光源、气体放电光源两种，相关特征参数参考《机车、动车组前照灯、辅助照明灯和标志灯》(TB/T 2325.1—2013)定义。

3.2.2 光源特征

根据前照灯光源参数，目前使用的铁路前照灯光源中光强度最高的为气体放电光源，其基准轴上的光强度可达200万cd，照射距离可达800m。这种前照灯灯锥体与母线的夹角为4°，由于它的聚光性很好，向外围发散的光束强度不高，在水平方向4°的灯锥体母线上，其相对光强度仅为基准轴上光强度的3%。

另外一种卤钨灯光源其基准轴上的光强度为90万cd，照射距离为600m。这种前照灯灯锥体与母线的夹角为4°，它的聚光性比气体放电光源差，有较多的光束分布在外围，在水平方向4°的灯锥体母线上，其相对光强度为基准轴上光强度的8%。

两种光源都需要进行考虑。

3.3 光源强度预估

3.3.1 评价位置选取

由图1和表1可知，并行段内铁路与高速公路的相对空间关系不同，铁路光源对高速公路的影响也有所不同。故在公路段选取7个主要评价位置来进行评价。保守起见，针对每一个评价点都假设为最不利的条件。

公路铁路空间参数表(单位：m) 表1

桩 号	铁路枕木高程	靠近铁路一边的高速路肩设计高程	公铁土路肩间距
K117+300.493	47.231	49.283	23.38
K117+350.850	47.374	49.019	19.73
K117+400.436	47.49	48.635	15.42
K117+450.126	47.572	48.167	14.5
K117+500.376	47.628	47.697	16.5
K117+550.404	47.698	47.266	18.5
K117+600.597	47.694	47.24	19.5
K117+650.513	47.332	46.919	26.8

3.3.2 前照灯光源强度预估

当前照灯离眩光评价计算点的纵向距离越近，眩光评价点相对于铁路轨道上的垂足点接受到的光强度越大,但是前照灯与眩光评价点的夹角也就越大,而角度越大,相对光强度百分比也就越小,分析时需综合考虑。

(1) 气体放电光源光强度预估

对于以气体放电光源为前照灯的铁路列车,照射距离可达800m。本文以100m为步长,设置8种情况,气体放电光源的计算结果如表2所示(仅列举了一处)。

K117+300处气体放电光源光强度预估　　　　表2

前照灯离该点纵向距离(m)	与前照灯水平夹角 α	与前照灯垂直夹角 β	相对光强度百分比	与前照灯距离(m)	照度值(lx)
100	16.28	0.11	—	104.18	—
200	8.31	0.10	—	202.12	—
300	5.56	0.10	—	301.42	—
400	4.18	0.10	—	401.07	—
500	3.34	0.09	4.47	500.85	0.36
600	2.79	0.09	6.04	600.71	0.34
700	2.39	0.09	8.04	700.61	0.33
800	2.09	0.09	10.34	800.53	0.32

(2) 卤钨灯光源光强度预估

对于以卤钨灯光源为前照灯的铁路列车,照射距离为600m。本文以100m为步长,设置6种情况进行计算,结果如下表3所示。

K117+300处卤钨灯光源光强度预估　　　　表3

前照灯离该点纵向距离(m)	与前照灯水平夹角 α	与前照灯垂直夹角 β	相对光强度百分比	与前照灯距离(m)	照度值(lx)
100	16.28	0.11	—	104.18	—
200	8.31	0.10	—	202.12	—
300	5.56	0.10	—	301.42	—
400	4.18	0.10	—	401.07	—
500	3.34	0.09	11.07	500.85	0.40
600	2.79	0.09	15.07	600.71	0.38

3.3.3 预估结果综合评价

由表2、表3可知本文中铁路和高速横向距离小,同时眩光源视线夹角小,在铁路前照灯的扩散角范围内,铁路列车的基准轴上的光源在其扩散范围内会对高速公路产生显著的眩光影响。

3.4 眩光评价

根据第二节失能眩光评价方法可得到如下结果,如图2所示。

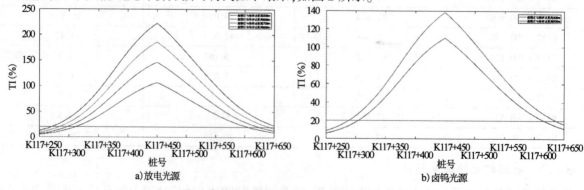

图2　气体放电光源和卤钨光源照射下的眩光影响

由结果可知,k117+450处眩光程度最强。k117+150至k117+700路段内路段眩光评价计算点的眩光阈值增量都超过了规定允许的20%。因此,该路段都会受到眩光影响,须采取措施对眩光进行控制。

4 铁路并行段高速公路的防眩对策研究

4.1 防眩设施选取

目前高速公路上使用比较普遍的防眩设施[6-8]为:植树防眩、防眩网和防眩板。本项目中公铁并行路段,植树受限于空间,不适用;而防眩网景观效果及防眩效果均较差,因此选取防眩板。

4.2 防眩板布设研究

前照灯的干扰光可以采用几何图形计算方法,利用线性关系进行光束遮挡。其防眩板的高度参数可根据如下计算结果进行选取。

设防眩板高度为$x(m)$。防眩板高度需要满足两个条件,一是保证眩光板能将铁路眩光"挡"到公路离铁路较远一侧路肩边缘外,二是保证沿直线传播的眩光光线至少不能影响离铁路最远一侧车道上驾驶员的视线。按相对于铁路的最不利位置处附近数值进行计算。

保证通过眩光板的眩光至少射到高速公路离铁路较远一侧的路肩边缘。

根据相似三角形比例得:

$$\frac{L_2}{\Delta L + L_2} = \frac{x}{h_0 + \Delta h}$$

式中:L_2——高速公路宽度;

ΔL——铁路与高速公路路肩平距(最不利位置);

h_0——铁路机车前照灯高度,取4m;

Δh——铁路与高速公路高程差(最不利位置),为方程中的参数赋值,代入求解得:$x_m = 2.64m$

因此建议前照灯对应的防眩设施高度至少为3m。设计样图如图3所示。

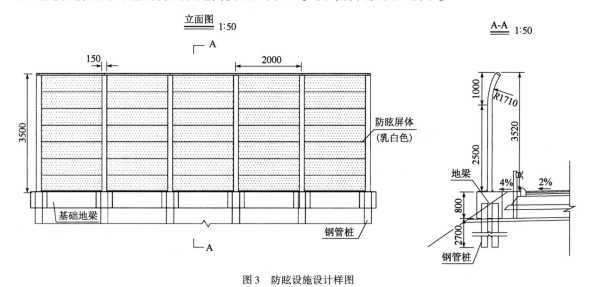

图3 防眩设施设计样图

5 结语

本文针对台辉高速公铁并行段列车夜间行驶对高速公路驾驶员产生眩光的问题进行了分析和研究,提出了合理的防眩措施,并在台辉高速正式通车后有效保障了行车安全。

参考文献

[1] 张明浩. 高速公路视觉景观对行车安全的影响研究[D]. 重庆:重庆交通大学,2016.
[2] 张振东,杨国辉. 高速公路中央分隔带防眩实效分析[J]. 科技创新导报,2015(24):106-107.
[3] 韩国倩,董长坤,韦刚. 公铁并行路段安全性分析及防护对策研究[J]. 公路,2020,65(03):197-200.
[4] 冯鹏,薛晓光. 眩光污染对高速公路行车安全的危害及对策分析[C]. 2018.
[5] 张鸣杰,杨静华,孙超等. 道路照明眩光的计算和测量[J]. 中国照明电器,2016(04):34-37.
[6] 冯茂,赖伟清. 浅谈高速公路防眩设施及其应用[J]. 四川水利,2017(02):77-78.
[7] 蒙晓新. 高速公路防眩设施设置与效果评价[J]. 科技经济导刊,2015,22(01):181-182.
[8] 路旭. 高速公路防眩设施优化设计与综合评价研究[D]. 天津:河北工业大学,2018.

京港澳高速公路河南省路网段运营风险评估与事故预防措施研究

赵建有 张振东 李 斌 董贝贝 刘清云

(长安大学汽车学院)

摘 要 对高速公路运营风险进行评估能更加科学地认识交通安全系统的各个影响因素,从道路基础设施提供的平均交通运行安全水平角度量化测评路网各组成部分交通事故发生及损失的可能程度,对风险水平进行分级,并基于评估结果制定最优化的安全完善策略,以结合实际采取合理的事故预防措施,降低事故风险及发生率。本文以河南运营高速公路网京港澳高速公路(K597+526~K690+400段)路网段为研究对象,对全线路段的基础设施、车流量、车型、事故发生情况等进行调研分析、数据收集,通过风险数值的量化计算,得到该路段不同区间的风险等级,最后提出降低和预防交通事故的具体措施。

关键词 交通安全 事故预防 风险评估 高速公路

0 引 言

近年来,随着河南省经济又好又快的发展,人们出行越来越方便快捷,高速公路等基础设施的建设也取得了丰硕的成就。截至2020年,河南全省高速公路通车里程达到7100km。但在高速公路快速发展的同时,交通安全问题仍然是不容忽视的重要问题。2017年河南省高速公路发生事故305起,占全国总数的3.63%;死亡人数253人,全国占总数的4.40%;受伤人数381,占总数的3.53%,经济损失高达1583.47万元[1]。由于河南省高速公路(网)重要的地理位置,交通组成复杂,加之管理系统尚不完善,造成河南省高速公路交通事故时有发生。

此次针对河南运营高速公路网京港澳高速公路K597+526~K690+400段风险评估借鉴了国际道路风险评估组织iRAP相关技术,包括风险评估原理、模型框架、风险系数、对策等,参照了交通运输部《公路安全生命防护工程实施技术指南(试行)》,并吸收了部分科研项目的研究成果、综合考虑河南省高速公路的道路和交通特点。研究成果以期能有效改进河南省高速公路安全设计技术,提高河南省高速公路安全管理与控制水平,提升河南省高速公路运行安全性,进一步推动河南省高速公路交通发展水平。该项目研究具有重要的社会经济意义和现实必要性。

基金项目:《基于交通行为安全性的河南省高速公路运行控制技术研究》,项目编号:2019G-2-11。

1 事故特征分析

此研究在把握京港澳高速公路交通量、交通组成、运行车速等交通特征的基础上,利用从公安交通管理部门获取的事故数据,从交通事故的时间特性和形态特征、天气特征等角度,系统分析京港澳高速公路的交通安全现状,并进一步对交通事故进行量化分析,提取安全水平相对较低路段,为管理单位实施安全改善工作提供参考。

研究根据京港澳高速公路交通管理部门提供的2015年1月—2018年9月交通事故数据,统计分析京港澳高速公路的交通安全现状。

1.1 事故分布形态特征

2015年—2018年9月京港澳高速公路 K597+526~K690+400 段交通事故形态分布如图1所示。

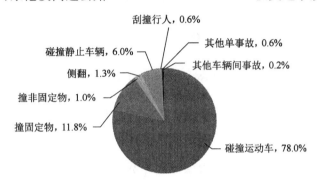

图1 京港澳高速公路 K597+526~K690+400 段交通事故形态分布图

该期间以车辆间事故为主,占总数的84.2%;事故的具体形式以碰撞运动车辆为主,占总事故数的78%,其中以追尾事故为主;其次是撞击固定物,占总数的11.8%;碰撞静止车辆占6%。另外,针对事故车型分布的统计显示,事故以小型车为主,占比76%,大型车仅占24%。

1.2 事故分布气候特征

京港澳高速公路 K597+526~K690+400 段交通事故气候分布及事故率分布情况如图2所示。

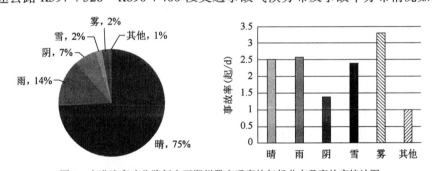

图2 京港澳高速公路新乡至郑州段交通事故气候分布及事故率统计图

晴天发生的事故占总数的75%,不良天气(雨、阴、雪、雾)发生的事故占总数的25%。虽然雾天发生的事故仅占总数的2%,但是事故率最高,可见视野受限会显著影响交通流状态进而影响交通安全[2]。

1.3 事故分布驾驶行为分布特征

京港澳高速公路 K597+526~K690+400 段交通事故驾驶行为分布如图3所示,根据交通事故数据分析,交通事故发生的主要原因是人操作不当或存在违法行为。如图3所示,主要违法行为包括未保持安全距离、变更车道影响正常车辆行驶、疲劳驾驶和其他影响安全行为。

另外,在时间分布上,首先2015年—2018年9月京港澳高速公路 K597+526~K690+400 段交通事故发生的数量逐年增加,由2015年的70起左右上升至2018年的近900起,并且上升速率也逐年增加。其次,4年期间在8月、9月发生的事故数量达到528起。8月、9月天气炎热,人容易疲劳,同时中秋节、国庆节即将来临,出行人员增多,交通量增长幅度较大,部分驾驶人员对路况不熟,容易发生交通事故,导致事故率明显高于其他月份。

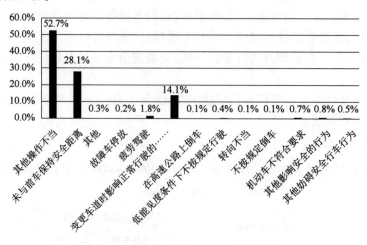

图3 京港澳高速公路 K597+526～K690+400 段交通事故驾驶行为分布特征图

2 事故影响因素分析

2.1 道路基础设施因素

通过现场调查和数据标准化处理,得到京港澳高速公路 K597+526～K690+400 段道路基础信息,包括公路和交通等条件,通过基础设施的信息来了解高速公路的总体情况,进而分析其事故影响因素。

(1)从京港澳高速公路 K597+526～K690+400 段的路域总体环境条件来看,其有如下特点:从行驶过程中的路侧条件来看,驾驶员一侧(行驶方向左侧)100.00%的路段为中央分隔带护栏,左侧净空均小于1m(0.75m);副驾驶员一侧(行驶方向右侧)100%设置有护栏,但是部分出入口三角端防护能力欠佳,右路侧净空范围为 1~5m(实为右侧硬路肩宽度,3.25m)。

(2)护栏防撞能力或导向能力欠佳。在京港澳高速公路 K597+526～K690+400 段沿途防护栏中,其中 75.25% 为波形梁护栏,24.75% 为混凝土护栏。设有中分带开口42处,占全路段的2.26%,其中多数中央分隔带开口的活动护栏防撞能力或导向能力欠佳。另外,路基波形梁护栏和桥梁混凝土护栏未进行有效过渡。

(3)全线诱导类标志标线设置基本齐全,特别是在团雾多发路段设置有雾灯诱导设施;但是护栏上的附着轮廓标夜间视认性不良。另外,评估路网中,存在标志遮挡的情况。

(4)照明路段不足,经统计,京港澳高速公路 K597+526～K690+400 段中约 29.06% 的路段设置有照明,主要集中在刘江黄河大桥和城区路段,照明条件较差。

2.2 车辆运行速度因素

由于车速会对车辆行驶安全产生较大影响,本研究实地测量了小轿车和大货车的际运行车速,其运行速度标准差如图4所示。

早在1964年,美国学者 Solomon 研究了交通事故和速度两者之间的关系。在研究中,他将事故诱因归结为速度的变化,认为车速分布得越离散,事故率越高,而后来 Reimer B. 对高速公路和乡村公路白天、夜晚的事故情况进行了类似的调查[4],验证了 Solomon 的结论。国内专家对中国部分高速公路的速度标准差和亿车公里事故率进行了回归分析,研究认为事故率随着速度标准差的增大而增大,即车速分布得越离散,事故率越高[5],

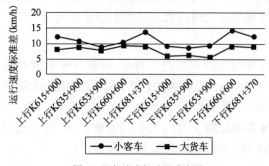

图4 运行速度标准差分布图

这与国外的研究结果是一致的。

因此,速度的离散性可以反映出车辆之间的速差,离散性越大,车辆之间的速差越大,车辆超车的可能性和频率都会增加,发生事故的概率也会增加。离散性可以用标准差来衡量。另外,小客车的运行速度明显高于大货车,小客车的车速标准差相对较大,容易产生超车行为,更容易发生事故[6]。

3 公路运营风险评估

公路风险评估作为客观地衡量交通安全水平的分级评估工具,其风险评估结果反映公路基础设施可为道路使用者提供安全行车条件的程度。风险评估技术是实现路网安全管理的基础,也是当前道路交通安全研究领域的热点,该项技术目前在美国、欧洲、澳大利亚等发达国家有较多的研究和应用,中国从2008年开始系统性研究和应用。

得到京港澳高速公路 K597+526~K690+400 段风险总体评估结果见表1。

京港澳高速公路 K597+526~K690+400 段风险总体评估结果　　表1

公路风险等级	长度(km)	百分比(%)	合　　计
Ⅰ	0	0.00	98.39%
Ⅱ	17.6	9.47	
Ⅲ	165	88.92	
Ⅳ	3	1.61	1.61%
Ⅴ	0	0.00	
合计	185.8	100%	

通常情况下,认为Ⅳ级和Ⅴ级公路风险相对较高是安全改善中需要重点关注的路段。从表1中可以看出,京港澳高速公路 K597+526~K690+400 段风险为Ⅳ级的里程长度为3km,占总评估里程的1.61%;公路风险为Ⅴ级的里程长度为0km,占总评估里程的0.00%;公路风险为Ⅳ级和Ⅴ级的里程长度为3km,占总评估里程的1.61%。

通过风险成因分析,发现交通风险主要体现在交通负荷、主线出入口、主线互通立交、公路线形、标志标线、团雾多发、路侧安全、路侧植被等方面。

(1)交通负荷:高速公路存在交通量大、货车比例高、交通组成复杂、速差大等问题,远超出现状车道数所能适应的交通量范围,难以满足正常运营需求。

(2)主线出入口:出入口处是车辆车道变换、加减速比较集中的区域,各类设施应能满足车辆的换道指引和防护,目前出入口处主要的问题有出口指路标志信息过载或信息选取不合理,路侧和匝道口双柱结构指路标志容易被大车遮挡,三角端区域视距受限、三角端防护欠佳等。

(3)主线互通立交、收费站、服务区、部分主线收费站、服务区距离互通立交过近,减少了有关标志标线的布设空间,加重了收费站前后的交通交织度,部分互通立交(刘江枢纽)、收费站(新乡收费站)匝道布置复杂,加之标志指示欠佳,影响驾驶员判断等。

(4)公路线形:恶劣天气及夜间条件下,不良的线形组合容易发生事故,如相邻曲线半径比较大、较大纵坡等。

(5)团雾多发:全线存在团雾多发路段,是事故发生的集中点,易发生重大事故。目前,如 K599~K616 为团雾多发路段,发生事故较多。

4 交通安全保障措施

根据存在的各类公路致险因素,按照"消除、减弱、隔离、警告"的原则有针对性地给出相应的可选处置对策,具体措施总体上可以分为工程性措施、养护性措施和管理性措施等。

工程性措施,包括设置避险车道、设置爬坡车道、设置/升级护栏、增强路面抗滑性、设置路侧振动标线、设置突起路标、设置雨夜反光标线等工程性安全设施等。

养护性措施,如修剪树木开拓视野、局部路面改造、改善标志标线等诱导设施等。

管理性措施,如综合速度控制和管理措施、接入管理(如路宅分家)等。对于非高风险路段,也要通过加强日常的安全养护、安全管理等来进一步提升安全水平,并且避免由于路面损坏、标线磨损等转化为高风险路段。

另外,基于风险评估结果,主要有如下建议:

(1)针对提取出的高风险路段和一般风险路段(总计35.048km),作为重点路段开展安全性评价工作。

(2)本次风险评估主要从基础设施条件方面提出需安全完善的重点路段,完善的高速公路基础设施条件是保障路网安全性的必要前提,但在系统的安全管理中,仍需要着力提升交通参与者的安全意识和加强车辆的安全整治。为提升交通参与者的安全意识,应强化针对交通参与者的安全教育,切实提高驾驶人的培训及考试发证质量,严格监管驾驶人培训机构,严把客货运驾驶人从业资格准入等。加强车辆的安全整治方面,应严格排查取缔非法车辆,强化监管报废汽车回收企业,定期巡查车辆改装维修企业和安检机构,加强大中型营运车辆监管等。在车辆本身的安全性能提升方面,应注重加强大型车辆的车头缓冲吸能设计,提升重型货车的制动性能。

5 结　语

本文通过收集近几年京港澳高速公路 K597+526~K690+400 段的道路状况、交通条件、交通流数据以及事故特征,利用《高速公路基础设施数据标准化系统》(包含高速公路数据预处理工具研究标准化系统及质量控制系统的准备),对该段高速公路进行事故风险评估与分级,找出该段道路的主要致险因素并对此提出降低事故风险的具体措施,从而提高道路的安全水平。研究结果可进行推广,从而进一步推动河南省甚至全国高速公路网的交通发展水平。

本文的创新点在于:

(1)建立适合河南省区位特征的高速公路交通行为与安全性的关系模型;

(2)从车辆运行、道路情况、天气条件以及事故分布四个主要方面对道路安全进行评估;

(3)通过对不同路段进行风险评估分析来采取不同形式不同程度的改善措施。

参考文献

[1] 中华人民共和国道路交通事故统计年报[R].公安部交通管理局.

[2] 张存保,彭汉辉,张珊,等.雾天高速公路实时交通安全状态评价方法[J].中国安全科学学报,201727(4):110-115.

[3] Laugier C, Paromtchik I E, Perrollaz M, et al. Probabilistic analysis of dynamic scenes and collision risksassessment to improve driving safety [J]. IEEE Intelligent Transportation Systems Magazine, 2011,3(4):4-19.

[4] Reimer B. Impact of cognitive task complexity on drivers' visual tunneling [J]. Transportation Research Record Journal of the Transportation Research Board, 2010, 2138(138):13-19.

[5] 杜博英.道路交通事故与车速建模[J].公路交通科技,2002,19(6):116-118.

[6] 刘志强,王兆华,钱卫东.基于速度的交通事故分析[J].中国安全科学学报,2005,15(11):35-38.

[7] 裴玉龙,马骥.道路交通事故道路条件成因分析及预防对策研究[J].中国公路学报,2003,16(4):77-82.

基于博弈论的高速公路合流区汇入决策分析

景云超[1,2] 朱彤[1,2] 王兴隆[2] 李青[1,2] 朱秭硕[1,2]

(1. 长安大学汽车运输安全保障技术交通行业重点实验室；2. 长安大学运输工程学院)

摘 要 为研究高速公路合流区驾驶人的汇入决策，分析合流区加速车道车辆的换道特点，根据博弈论相关方法，对换道决策阶段加速车道汇入车与目标车道跟随车博弈过程进行分析，建立非合作混合策略博弈模型。结果表明：合流区汇入车辆的换道行为受到自由换道和强制换道的共同作用；在合流区汇入博弈过程中，博弈双方的策略选择主要取决于对方驾驶人的时间系数和安全系数。本研究可以为规范合流区驾驶人的安全驾驶行为、提高加速车道车辆汇入目标车道的成功率提供理论参考。

关键词 合流区 自由换道 强制换道 博弈论

0 引 言

研究表明，高速公路合流区发生交通事故的频率和严重程度远高于高速公路系统中的其他组成部分[1]，研究合流区车辆的汇入行为十分必要。

目前，学者主要采用元胞自动机仿真、多智能体建模等方法研究交织区换道行为。王百里等根据道路合流区的实际数据，建立基于跟车和换道规则的元胞自动机模型[2]。Shen等提出一种基于碰撞时间(TTC)的小时综合风险指数(HCRI)评价高速公路合流区交通安全[3]。Gu X等根据无人机采集的车辆数据提出一个多级随机参数逻辑回归模型[4]。这些研究主要集中在车辆进入交织区后对路段上其他交通因素的影响上，对车辆本身的换道决策研究较少。

从博弈论角度，换道本质是准备换道的车辆驾驶人与目标车道驾驶人之间的博弈过程。Kita等将博弈论观点应用到高速公路入口匝道上，建立驾驶人换道概率模型[5]。杨晓芳等建立了考虑速度、安全间距、邻道车辆、时间演化等因素的驾驶人换道行为模型[6]。王晓原等建立了混合模糊多人多目标的车道选择模型，通过微观交通流仿真验证模型的实用性。巴兴强等基于非合作混合战略博弈理论，根据公交车和站点之间位置建立车辆换道概率模型，描述公交车驾驶人换道意愿[8]。以上研究将博弈论观点应用到换道领域，但对高速公路合流区的换道决策缺乏深度研究。因此，本文基于博弈理论建立加速车道汇入车与目标车道跟随车之间的交互博弈模型，从而分析高速公路合流区车辆汇入的最优策略。

1 换道概率模型

根据换道动机，换道行为可分为自由换道和强制换道，由于高速公路合流区驶入车辆必须在加速车道末端完成换道，因此有学者将其归为强制换道[4]，但大多数汇入车辆有充裕的换道空间，强制换道只是其中一部分。为更好描述合流区驾驶人的换道行为，本文综合考虑自由换道和强制换道。

如图1所示，加速车道汇入车A_1在驶入初期，即s_1阶段，A_1有充裕的时间换道，此时自由换道动机起主导作用，设其自由换道概率为θ_f。当接近加速车道末端时，即s_2阶段，A_1为了成功汇入目标车道，必须采取强制换道策略，此时强制换道动机起主导作用，设其强制换道概率为θ_d。

综上，建立合流区车辆综合换道概率模型：

$$\theta = \theta_f + (1 - \theta_f)\theta_d \tag{1}$$

基金项目：国家重点研发计划(2019YFE0108000)。

式中,θ是合流区车辆综合换道概率;自由换道概率θ_f取0.55,强制换道概率θ_d取$Q(L-x)/(1+\exp(\gamma x))$,其中$Q$、$\gamma$为常数,可根据加速车道实际行驶数据拟合,$L$为加速车道长度,$x$为当前车辆位置距加速车道末端的距离。

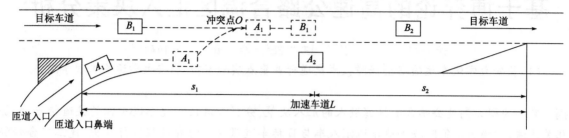

图1 合流区车辆汇入示意图

2 换道博弈模型

2.1 博弈理论

博弈论是研究参与方在对局中基于交叉效应意识行为互动的理论,一般由6个基本要素组成:局中人或参与者、规则、策略、行动、支付和策略均衡。从整体角度而言,博弈论可分为合作博弈与非合作博弈。前者表示博弈方的行为受到具有强制性协议的制约;后者表示协议没有强制力,个体参与者可根据其利益采取行动。

2.2 换道博弈特性分析

如图2所示,A_1为加速车道待汇入车辆,A_2为A_1前导车,B_1为目标车道跟随车,B_2为B_1前导车,当A_1与A_2的间隙较小或A_1已经临近加速车道末端必须汇入目标车道时,就会产生换道意图。O为A_1执行换道操作而B_1保持当前行驶状态时目标车道上可能发生碰撞的冲突点。A_1换道受A_2、B_1及B_2的共同作用,但A_1与B_1之间的交互占主导地位,因此只考虑这两辆车采取的策略对汇入行为的影响。

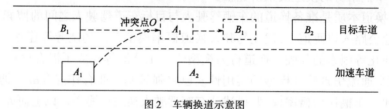

图2 车辆换道示意图

2.3 假设及模型建立

为建立高速公路合流区汇入车辆换道策略模型,引入如下假设:

(1)驾驶人换道决策过程中,具备完全理性,即能够根据收益做出对自己最有利的决策。

(2)驾驶人在行车过程中只考虑时间和安全两大因素,因此引入时间收益期望T和安全收益期望S,其中T、S值可根据大样本调查的方法,剔除不合格数据后取均值确定。

(3)A_1驾驶人策略集(换道,不换道);B_1驾驶人策略集(让行,不让行)。

(4)为准确描述不同类型驾驶人决策行为的影响因素,同时统一量化收益,引入时间系数p_i(i取1、2)、安全系数q_i(i取1、2)分别表示时间及安全收益对A_1及B_1的权重,$p_i+q_i=1$(i取1、2)。

基于以上假设,建立表1所示的收益矩阵。

博弈双方收益矩阵　　　　表1

目标车道跟随车驾驶人 B_1	加速车道汇入车辆 A_1	
	换道	不换道
让行	$(-p_2T+q_2S, p_1T)$	$(-p_2T, -p_1T)$
不让行	$(p_2T-q_2S, -q_1S)$	$(p_2T, -p_1T)$

3 纳什均衡求解及最优策略选择

3.1 纳什均衡求解

设 A_1 的混合策略为 $\delta_1 = (\theta, 1-\theta)$,即 A_1 在加速车道某处换道概率为 θ,不换道概率为 $1-\theta$;设 B_1 的混合策略为 $\delta_2 = (\lambda, 1-\lambda)$,即其以概率 λ 选择让行,以概率 $1-\lambda$ 选择不让行。

则 A_1 期望效用函数:

$$u_1(\delta_1,\delta_2) = \theta\lambda p_1 T - \theta(1-\lambda)q_1 S - (1-\theta)\lambda p_1 T - (1-\theta)(1-\lambda)p_1 T \tag{2}$$

B_1 期望效用函数:

$$u_2(\delta_1,\delta_2) = \lambda\theta(-p_2 T + q_2 S) - \lambda(1-\theta)p_2 T + (1-\lambda)\theta(p_2 T - q_2 S) + (1-\lambda)(1-\theta)p_2 T \tag{3}$$

为确定此博弈的混合策略纳什均衡点,对 u_1 和 u_2 采用偏导数求极值法,以确定 θ 和 λ 的最优值。选择对 A_1 期望效用最大的 θ,结合式(2),令:

$$\frac{\partial u_1}{\partial \theta} = \lambda p_1 T - (1-\lambda)q_1 S - \lambda p_1 T - (1-\lambda)p_1 T = 0 \tag{4}$$

解得:

$$\lambda^* = (q_1 S - p_1 T)/(q_1 S + p_1 T) \tag{5}$$

当 B_1 采取让行策略的概率 $\lambda > \lambda^*$ 时,A_1 换道会获得更大收益;当 $\lambda < \lambda^*$ 时,A_1 不换道会获得更大的收益;当 $\lambda = \lambda^*$ 时,A_1 选择两种策略所获得的收益没有差异。

选择对 B_1 期望效用最大的 λ,结合式(3),令:

$$\frac{\partial u_2}{\partial \lambda} = \theta(-p_2 T + q_2 S) - (1-\theta)p_2 T - \theta(p_2 T - q_2 S) - (1-\theta)p_2 T = 0 \tag{6}$$

解得:

$$\theta^* = p_2 T / q_2 S \tag{7}$$

当 A_1 采取换道策略的概率 $\theta > \theta^*$ 时,B_1 让行会获得更大收益;当 $\theta < \theta^*$,B_1 不让行会获得更大收益;当 $\theta = \theta^*$,B_1 选择两种策略所获得的收益没有差异。

因此,高速公路合流区车辆汇入博弈唯一的混合策略纳什均衡解为:

$$\lambda^* = (q_1 S - p_1 T)/(q_1 S + p_1 T), \theta^* = p_2 T / q_2 S \tag{8}$$

3.2 基于纳什均衡解的汇入行为分析

对于 A_1,若 B_1 倾向于加速冲过冲突点 O,由于 $p_i + q_i = 1$(i 取 1、2),相应的 q_2 就会降低,由式(7)可知 θ^* 增大,A_1 更有可能提前选择强行换道策略。反之,若 B_1 倾向于减速让行,让 A_1 率先通过冲突点,由式(7)可知 θ^* 减小,表明 A_1 选择换道的纳什均衡点减小,即 A_1 更有可能等待合适的时机换道。同理,对于 B_1,若 A_1 倾向于提前通过冲突点 O,由式(5)可知 λ^* 减小,B_1 更有可能选择不避让策略。反之,若 A_1 倾向于选择暂不换道,由式(5)可知 λ^* 增大,B_1 更有可能选择让行策略。

综上所述,在高速公路合流区汇入博弈过程中,博弈双方的策略选择主要取决于对方驾驶人的时间系数和安全系数,若对方更注重速度满意度,则驾驶人更倾向于选择冒险性策略,若对方更注重行车安全,则驾驶人更倾向于选择保守策略,这与实际行车状况基本相符[8]。

3.3 加速车道车辆最优汇入策略

基于以上分析,合流区加速车道车辆的汇入决策主要由距加速车道末端的距离以及目标车道跟随车

驾驶人的行为特征两种因素决定,因此将驾驶人综合换道概率式(1)与纳什均衡解式(7)联立:

$$\begin{cases} \theta = \theta_f + (1-\theta_f)\theta_d = 0.55 + 0.45Q(L-x)/(1+\exp(\gamma x)) \\ \theta^* = p_2T/q_2S \end{cases} \tag{9}$$

由式(9)可知,若令 $\theta = \theta^*$,即可用纳什均衡解表示加速车道驾驶人换道位置,可以通过大样本调查取均值的方法,得到目标车道上保守型、普通型、激进型驾驶人相对应的时间系数 p_2 和安全系数 q_2,计算出目标车道不同类型驾驶人时加速车道汇入车的最佳换道位置。

4 算例分析

根据西安市绕城高速公路长安路收费站入口调研结果(图3)标定 $L=250\text{m}$, $Q=0.019$, $r=0.033$。经问卷调查与处理,标定 $T=8$, $S=10$,目标车道保守型驾驶人时间系数0.55,安全系数0.45,普通型驾驶人时间系数0.4,安全系数0.6,激进型驾驶人时间系数0.2,安全系数0.8。代入式(9),得到各类驾驶人最优汇入策略。

图3 西安市绕城高速公路长安路收费站入口

保守型:

$$\begin{cases} \theta_1 = 0.55 + 0.45 \times 0.019 \times (250-x)/[1+\exp(0.033x)] \\ \theta_1^* = p_2T/q_2S = 0.55 \times 8/0.45 \times 10 \\ \theta_1^* = 0.9777, x = 14.6310 \end{cases} \tag{10}$$

普通型:

$$\begin{cases} \theta_1 = 0.55 + 0.45 \times 0.019 \times (250-x)/[1+\exp(0.033x)] \\ \theta_1^* = p_2T/q_2S = 0.4 \times 8/0.6 \times 10 \\ \theta_1^* = 0.5333, x = 37.4299 \end{cases} \tag{11}$$

激进型:

$$\begin{cases} \theta_1 = 0.55 + 0.45 \times 0.019 \times (250-x)/[1+\exp(0.033x)] \\ \theta_1^* = p_2T/q_2S = 0.2 \times 8/0.8 \times 10 \\ \theta_1^* = 0.2000, x = 68.2800 \end{cases} \tag{12}$$

以上结果表明,保守型驾驶人以97.77%在距加速车道末端14.63m处换道最佳;普通型驾驶人在距离加速车道末端37.43m处以53.33%换道最佳;激进型驾驶员在距离加速车道末端68.28m处以20.00%换道最佳。结果表明,激进型驾驶人更易在距离加速车道末端较远的位置强制换道,计算结果与实际基本相符,验证了本文建立的换道概率模型的准确性。

4 结 语

(1)本文根据高速公路合流区交通流特征建立综合换道概率模型,在描述加速车道末端车辆必须强制换道这一特征的同时,将行驶过程中存在的自由换道行为综合考虑,更加符合道路实际情况。

(2)结果表明,增大驾驶人的安全系数,减少其时间系数可以提高道路安全性。综合考虑换道概率模型和换道博弈模型,可以求出目标车道驾驶人类型不同时加速车道驾驶人不同的最优换道位置。

(3)本文提出的博弈模型假设驾驶人的时间收益期望和安全收益期望都是定值,但实际驾驶环境中行车效益不应统一定量,后续研究可以对模型参数做出改进。此外,本文仅考虑了加速车道末端单车汇入情况,实际情况可能有多辆车同时汇入,可就此展开进一步研究。

参考文献

[1] Ahammed M A, Hassan Y, Sayed T A. Modeling Driver Behavior and Safety on Freeway Merging Areas [J]. Journal of Transportation Engineering, 2008, 134(9):370-377.

[2] 王百里,杨晓芳,刘红杏.道路交通合流区换道行为仿真研究[J].计算机仿真,2016,033(002):211-215,238.

[3] Shen L, Qiaojun X, Yongfeng M, et al. Crash Risk Prediction Modeling Based on the Traffic Conflict Technique and a Microscopic Simulation for Freeway Interchange Merging Areas[J]. International Journal of Environmental Research & Public Health, 2016, 13(11):1157-1171.

[4] Gu X, Abdelaty M, Xiang Q, et al. Utilizing UAV video data for in-depth analysis of drivers' crash risk at interchange merging areas[J]. Accident Analysis & Prevention, 2019: 159-169.

[5] Kita H. A merging-giveway interaction model of cars in a merging section: a game theoretic analysis[J]. Transportation Research Part A, 1999, 33(3-4):300-312.

[6] 杨晓芳,张盛,付强.基于博弈论的完全信息下的驾驶行为研究[J].公路交通科技,2015,32(7):105-111.

[7] 王晓原,张敬磊,刘振雪,等.基于混合模糊多人多目标非合作博弈的车道选择模型[J].自动化学报,2017(11):168-178.

[8] 巴兴强,刘娇娇.基于博弈论的公交进站换道决策行为研究[J].重庆理工大学学报(自然科学),2019,033(002):P.111-116.

[9] 刘有军,曹珊.基于元胞自动机的强制换道模型研究[J].交通信息与安全,2009,027(003):78-80.

礼让行人背景下无信号控制人行横道交通冲突研究

郑少娅 王永岗 宋杰

(长安大学)

摘 要 为了改善礼让行人的新交通环境下行人过街交通安全状况,本文对该背景下无信号控制人行横道处交通冲突进行了调查研究。首先,使用无人机拍摄视频采集相关基础数据,利用 Tracker 软件对车辆、行人轨迹数据进行提取,并分别以距离碰撞时间(TTC)、后侵占时间(PET)作为车车冲突、人车冲突度量指标对非信控人行横道交通冲突进行判别,进而分析其交通冲突特性。在此基础上,采用 K-means 聚类分析法对交通冲突严重程度进行等级划分。研究结果表明:中间车道机动车未礼让率最高,而外侧车道未礼让率最低;车道分布、交通量、未礼让行人次数对交通冲突数量均有显著影响;礼让行人可能导致车辆追尾冲突,但人车冲突比车车冲突频率更高;车辆间严重冲突等级阈值为2s,人车间严重冲突等级阈值为2.4s。

关键词 交通安全 交通冲突 K-means 聚类分析 无信号控制人行横道 礼让行人

0 引言

根据 2017 年公安部交通管理局统计数据显示,2014—2017 年全国在斑马线上发生机动车与行人的交通事故 1.4 万起,其中机动车未按规定让行导致的事故占了全国事故的 90%[1]。此后,虽然全国各地开始实行"礼让行人"规定,但对于无信号控制人行横道,机动车未礼让行人的现象依然广泛存在,且礼让行人易导致车辆追尾冲突,无信号控制人行横道处交通安全水平仍有待提高[2-3]。

传统的交通安全分析方法多以大量历史事故数据为基础,但高精度、完整的数据往往难以获取。交通冲突技术作为一种非事故的交通安全研究手段,具有快速、可靠、需要事故数据少等优点。已有研究表明,交通冲突与交通事故之间存在密切关系,交通冲突发展到一定程度则会演变为交通事故[4-6]。近年来,国内外学者利用交通冲突技术开展了许多相关研究,不仅验证了交通冲突技术的有效性,更将其应用在道路交叉口、分合流区等处的交通安全评价与风险预测中[7-10]。但是,目前的相关研究中,以无信号控制人行横道为研究对象的研究较少,且很少考虑新交通环境下机动车礼让行人行为对交通冲突的影响。鉴于此,本文利用图像识别技术从视频中提取交通参与者轨迹数据,对礼让行人背景下无信号控制人行横道处的交通冲突类型与特征进行了分析,然后采用 K-means 聚类算法对交通冲突严重程度进行划分,并基于交通冲突分析结果提出相应的无信号控制人行横道交通安全改善措施。

1 机动车礼让行人行为调查分析

1.1 机动车礼让行人规则

礼让行人规定从本质上给予了行人优先通行权,行人通过无信号控制人行横道时无须等待,机动车必须主动停车或减速让行,其具体规则如图 1、表 1 所示[11]。

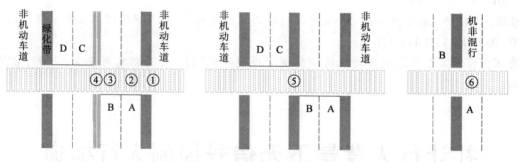

图 1　行人位置与车辆位置示意图

机动车礼让行人规则　　　　表 1

序 号	行人位置	礼让行人规则
1	①	A、B 车辆减速通行
2	②	A、B 车辆停车让行
3	③	B 车辆停车让行,A 车辆减速通行
4	④	C、D 车辆停车让行
5	⑤	C、D 车辆减速通行
6	⑥	A 车辆停车让行,B 车辆减速通行

1.2 数据采集与提取

本文选取西安市长安北路某无信号控制人行横道为研究对象,对其交通流参数及机动车礼让行人行为进行调查研究。首先,采用无人机高空录像的方式获取该路段人行横道由南至北单方向的相关数据。

基金项目:陕西省自然科学基础研究计划面上项目(2020JM-252)。

无人机高空摄像时,将其分辨率调至 720P,帧速率设定为 30 帧/s,且尽量避开树木及其他障碍物遮挡。通过反复观察拍摄所得视频,初步筛选出 348 个可能存在交通冲突的视频片段,将其导入至 Tracker 软件中,以人行横道和道路边界线交点为坐标原点建立坐标系,以道路宽度为标尺,将处理步骤大小设置为 3 帧,具体步骤如图 2 所示,即可得到时间间隔为 0.1s 的车辆轨迹数据,用于后续交通冲突判断与严重程度等级划分研究中。

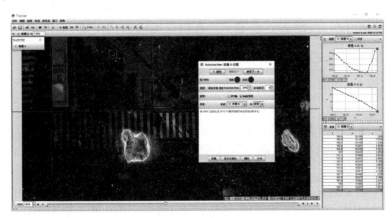

图 2　Tracker 软件提取数据示意图

1.3　数据统计分析

为体现路段车道分布和机动车流量对机动车礼让行人行为的影响,定义机动车未礼让率为该车道机动车未礼让行人次数与该车道当量交通量比值。将四个车道由外侧(公交车专用道)至内侧分别记为 1 车道、2 车道、3 车道、4 车道,则未礼让率计算公式如下:

$$P_i = \frac{N_i}{Q_i}, i=1,2,3,4$$

式中:P_i——i 车道机动车未礼让率;
　　　N_i——i 车道每小时机动车未礼让行人次数;
　　　Q_i——i 车道当量小时交通量。

通过对视频数据统计分析,得到各车道机动车礼让行人情况,如表 2 所示。

机动车未礼让行人行为统计　　　　　　　　　表 2

车　道	Q_i	N_i	P_i
1	335	8	2.39%
2	408	61	14.95%
3	621	108	17.39%
4	663	87	13.12%
总计	2027	264	13.02%

根据表 2 统计结果可知,整体上,随交通量的增大,机动车未礼让行人次数呈增大趋势。机动车未礼让率总体为 13.02%,3 车道未礼让率最高达 17.39%,1 车道未礼让率最低,仅为 2.39%。3 车道未礼让次数与未礼让率都较高,而 1 车道均较低,原因可能有三点:一是车道交通量的影响;二是 1 车道距离路侧最近,便于驾驶员观察和判断行人过街意图,而 3 车道处于中间靠内侧位置,可能由于其他车道车辆或障碍物的遮挡影响驾驶员视线;三是 1 车道为公交专用道,西安公交推行"5321"礼让标准,并将其纳入驾驶员奖惩体系中,因此公交车驾驶员安全意识和礼让意识都较强。

2 无信号控制人行横道交通冲突特性

2.1 交通冲突判别

2.1.1 交通冲突度量指标

目前,TTC 与 PET 是最常用的时间距离法度量指标。TTC 指如果冲突双方都不改变当前的运动状态,两车到碰撞点的预期时间,因此其更适用于具有相似运动轨迹车辆,如追尾冲突情况,其计算公式如下[9]:

$$TTC = \frac{X_2(t) - X_1(t) - L_1}{V_2(t) - V_1(t)}$$

式中:TTC 表示车辆1与车辆2发生交通冲突的距离碰撞时间;$X_2(t)$ 表示 t 时刻后车位置坐标;$X_1(t)$ 表示 t 时刻前车位置坐标;L_1 表示前车车身长度;$V_2(t)$ 表示 t 时刻后车速度,$V_1(t)$ 表示 t 时刻前车速度,且 $V_2(t) > V_1(t)$。

PET 是指交通参与者通过某个潜在交通冲突面或点的时间差,更适用于具有相交运动轨迹车辆,如道路交叉口。且 PET 的计算需要的参数更少,运用较为方便,其计算公式如下[9]:

$$PET = t_b - t_a$$

式中,PET 表示交通参与者 a 与交通参与者 b 后侵占时间;t_a 表示前一交通参与者 a 离开冲突面或点的时刻;t_b 表示后一交通参与者 b 到达冲突面或点的时刻。

2.1.2 交通冲突类型

对于礼让行人背景下的无信号控制人行横道,产生的交通冲突主要有人车冲突与车车冲突两种。

(1)人车冲突。

由于过街行人与直行通过的车辆之间存在轨迹交叉,若两者到达某一潜在冲突面或点的时间距离过小,则会导致侧向冲突,因此选取 PET 作为衡量无信号控制人行横道人车冲突指标。根据已有研究结果,将 PET≤5s 视为一次侧向冲突。

(2)车车冲突。

机动车驾驶员在无信号控制人行横道前礼让行人时,通常需要采取明显的制动或减速措施。前车由于礼让行人速度突然减小,而后车驾驶员仍保持相对高速,则易产生追尾冲突。本文选取 TTC 作为衡量追尾冲突指标。根据已有研究成果,取 TTC≤5s 为一次车车冲突。

2.2 交通冲突分析

基于从 348 个可能存在交通冲突视频中提取得到的人车轨迹数据,采用 MATLAB 计算其 TTC、PET 值,得到判定有效的交通冲突共 310 次,其中人车冲突 258 次,车车冲突 52 次。考虑到交通量、未礼让行人次数等变量间可能存在相关关系,采用因子分析法来分析各变量之间相关性,具体情况如表3、表4所示。

交通冲突判别结果　　　　表3

车道	车车冲突(次)	人车冲突(次)	总计
1	0	36	36
2	15	75	90
3	16	68	84
4	21	79	100
总计	52	258	310

相关性矩阵　　　　　　　　　　　表4

	交通量	未礼让次数	交通冲突数
交通量	1	0.952	0.851
未礼让次数	0.952	1	0.837
交通冲突数	0.851	0.837	1

根据以上计算统计结果显示,4车道上产生的车车冲突与人车冲突均最多,原因可能是该车道机动车流量较大,且机动车未礼让行人次数也较多。同一时间段内,人车冲突发生频率大于车车冲突频率。通过对变量进行相关性分析,可见交通量与未礼让次数之间存在强相关关系,且两者均对交通冲突数量均有较显著的影响。而机动车交通量是随时间一直变化的,说明要想减少交通冲突数量,需要严格执行礼让行人规定,提高机动车礼让率。

3 无信号控制人行横道交通冲突严重程度等级划分

由于K-means聚类算法适用于任何维度数据,且迭代次数少、分类精度高,因此本文采用K-means聚类算法对礼让行人背景下无信号控制人行横道交通冲突进行严重程度划分。将所得310个有效交通冲突样本数据按人车冲突、车车冲突分别导入SPSS软件中进行分析,设置分类数量为3,将无信号控制人行横道交通冲突分为严重冲突、一般冲突、轻微冲突三个等级,得到交通冲突严重程度分级结果,见表5。

交通冲突严重程度等级划分结果　　　　　　　　　　　表5

冲突等级	车车冲突		人车冲突	
	TTC(s)	聚类中心(s)	PET(s)	聚类中心(s)
严重冲突	(0,2]	1.34	(0,2.4]	1.87
一般冲突	(2,3.6]	2.82	(2.4,3.6]	3.03
轻微冲突	(3.6,5]	4.21	(3.6,5]	4.31

以上结果表明,无信号控制人行横道两种交通冲突严重程度等级划分结果及严重冲突等级阈值差异较大,且同等级严重程度中,车车冲突聚类中心均大于人车冲突聚类中心值,说明交通参与者速度对交通冲突严重程度有一定影响。

最后,对聚类变量进行单因素方差分析,以对分类结果的合理性进行检验。由表6结果可知,自变量TTC与PET的P值均为0.000,显著水平小于0.05,说明此次分析具有统计学意义,将礼让行人背景下的无信号控制人行横道处人车冲突、车车冲突划分为三个等级是比较科学、合理的。

单因素方差分析结果　　　　　　　　　　　表6

	聚类		误差		F	显著性
	均值	df	均值	df		
TTC/s	235.030	2	0.198	365	1186.621	0.000
PET/s	115.274	2	0.144	255	803.173	0.000

4 结　语

本文通过采集无信号控制人行横道处行人、车辆运动轨迹数据及交通流数据,分析了礼让行人背景下车道分布、交通量、礼让行人行为等因素对交通冲突的影响,并对无信号控制人行横道交通冲突严重程度进行了等级划分。研究结果表明:

(1)中间车道未礼让行人行为频率更高,达17.39%,而最外侧车道未礼让率最低,仅2.39%。交通环境、驾驶员本身素质对礼让行人行为有较大影响。

(2)在礼让行人背景下,人车冲突比车车冲突更容易发生,且随着交通量和未礼让行人次数增加,交通冲突数量呈明显上升趋势,说明严格实行礼让行人规定有助于减少交通冲突数量,提高行人过街安全性。

(3)当TTC≤2s时,由于礼让行人而导致的车车之间冲突处于严重追尾冲突状态;当PET≤2.4s时,过街行人与直行机动车之间处于严重冲突状态。

(4)机动车驾驶员礼让行人意识有待于进一步提高,建议从加强驾驶员和行人素质教育、推广使用人行横道禁停区和让行线、出台礼让行人细则等方面采取措施,减少无信号控制人行横道交通冲突。

参考文献

[1] 周云月,李红伟,刘海平,等."礼让斑马线"对无信号控制人行横道处通行能力影响研究[J].贵州大学学报(自然科学版),2020,37(02):113-118.

[2] 雷爱国,胡启洲,李慧慧,等. 无信号交叉口过街行人与司机演化博弈行为研究[J].南京理工大学学报,2020,44(06):705-714.

[3] 李慧慧,胡启洲,雷爱国,等. 基于计划行为理论的驾驶员未礼让行为研究[J]. 交通运输工程与信息学报,2020,18(04):110-119.

[4] 刘小明,段海林. 平面交叉口交通冲突技术标准化研究[J]. 公路交通科技,1997(03):31-36.

[5] Hauer E, Garder P. Research Into the Validity of the Traffic Conflicts Technique[J]. Accident Analysis & Prevention, 1986, 18(6): 471-481.

[6] Salman NK, Al-Maita KJ. Safety Evaluation at Three-leg Unsignalized Intersections by Traffic Conflict Technique[J]. Transportation Research Record, 1995, 1485: 177-185.

[7] Essa M, Sayed T. Traffic Conflict Models to Evaluate the Safety of Signalized Intersections at the Cycle Level[J]. Transportation Research Part C: Emerging Technologies, 2018, 89(APR.): 289-302.

[8] Apronti D T, Saha P, Moomen M, et al. Truck Safety Evaluation on Wyoming Mountain Passes[J]. Accident Analysis & Prevention, 2017, 122(JAN.): 342-349.

[9] 林兰平. 高速公路合流区交通冲突预测与安全评价研究[D].哈尔滨:哈尔滨工业大学,2017.

[10] 丁柏群,宋子龙. 基于交通冲突的城市交叉口风险影响因素分析[J]. 森林工程,2019,35(05):98-105.

[11] 华夏经纬网. 公安交管部门细化车辆礼让"斑马线"行人规则[N/OL]. (2017-06-27)[2019-01-15]. http://www.huaxia.com/mlcq/zqsy/bysk/2017/06/5372794.html.

[12] Guo Y, Essa M, Sayed T, et al. A Comparison Between Simulated and Field-measured Conflicts for Safety Assessment of Signalized Intersections in Australia[J]. Transportation Research Part C: Emerging Technologies, 2019, 101(APR.): 96-110.

附:参数解释表

序 号	参 数	含 义
1	P_i	i车道机动车未礼让率
2	N_i	i车道每小时机动车未礼让行人次数,
3	Q_i	i车道当量小时交通量
4	TTC	前后两车的距离碰撞时间
5	$X_2(t)$	t时刻后车位置坐标
6	$X_1(t)$	t时刻前车位置坐标
7	L_1	L_1表示前车车身长度
8	$V_2(t)$	t时刻后车速度
9	$V_1(t)$	t时刻前车速度,$V_2(t) > V_1(t)$
10	PET	交通参与者a与交通参与者b之间的后侵占时间
11	t_a	前一交通参与者a离开冲突面或点的时刻
12	t_b	后一交通参与者b到达冲突面或点的时刻

基于动态PET算法的互通立交合流区交通冲突研究

宋 杰 王永岗 郑少娅

(长安大学)

摘 要 针对高速公路互通立交合流区交通事故高发，车辆行驶安全性较低的问题，本文结合车辆运行数据和区域几何特性构建了合流区侧向冲突后侵入时间PET(Post Encroachment Time)动态判别模型，选取典型路段采集相关数据确定严重冲突和一般冲突的PET阈值分别为1.7s和4.4s。依据数据和判别结果对侧向冲突特性进行了研究，认为合流区主线外侧车道是侧向冲突发生的主要地点，且严重冲突动态PET值的变化相较一般冲突更不稳定。基于此，对合流区减少侧向冲突发生概率，缓解冲突严重程度提出了相应的改善措施。

关键词 交通安全 冲突判别 动态PET算法 合流区 冲突特性

0 引 言

高速公路互通立交合流区作为连接城市道路与高速公路的桥梁，涉及繁杂的车辆交织。不同行驶方向的车流由于可穿越间隙不足，车速差异较大等因素而极易引发交通事故[1]。交通冲突分析作为研究交通事故的有效手段，对交通安全研究具有重大意义。

交通冲突分析主要包括数据采集和冲突判别两部分内容。数据采集以人工观测、录像观测和仪器检测等方式为主。赵欢[2]采用背景差分法对车辆目标进行了提取，实现了对运动车辆目标的实时跟踪。Nicolas等[3]开发了一种基于视频传感器的道路安全分析方法，通过对获取到的车辆轨迹数据进行聚类，达到判别交通冲突的目的。

在冲突判别及分析方面，现有研究采用时间距离指标较为普遍。Minderhoud等[4]依据车辆轨迹数据，提出了衡量冲突碰撞时间的两个新指标TET和TIT。张诗雯等运用交通仿真软件VISSIM提取了车辆运行轨迹和车速等关键因素，选取交通冲突碰撞时间TTC、后侵入时间PET两大指标建立了交通冲突判别模型。Charly[6]等基于车辆精确位置及车辆宽度参数，运用改进的TTC模型对交通冲突进行了识别。张志召[7]依据立交合流区交通流基本参数数据，运用TTC模型判别追尾冲突，PET模型判别变道冲突。马艳丽等[8]结合车辆运动信息，在充分考虑车辆尺寸对交通冲突点影响的基础上，建立了基于PET算法的立交匝道合流区交通冲突识别模型。Huimin Ge等[9]提出了一种改进的碰撞时间模型，结合车辆减速率实现了高速公路限速条件下的追尾冲突预测识别。Ye Li等[10]提出了一种新的评价指标TTCD(TTC的导数，即碰撞时间变化率)，以此确定了追尾冲突中的主要车辆的组合形式及其对应的冲突指标特性。

本文从高速公路互通立交合流区这一研究背景出发，通过对合流区几何特性及交通流特性进行分析，建立合流区侧向交通冲突识别模型，利用实测数据实现冲突的动态判别与更新，最终确定冲突严重程度阈值。最后，对冲突发生位置和冲突过程进行研究，为如何减少冲突、减轻冲突严重程度提出相应的改善措施。

1 冲突机理及判别模型选择

1.1 立交合流区交通冲突形成机理

本次研究主要针对直接式加速车道合流区进行分析。如图1所示，经由匝道加速车道合流进入高速公路主线的车流会与主线原有行驶车辆间发生侧向冲突。

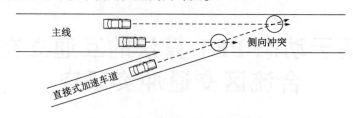

图1 直接式加速车道合流区交通冲突

1.2 侧向冲突判别模型选择

（1）TTC模型：假定冲突双方保持原有运动状态，到达理论碰撞时间所需时间长度为冲突的TTC值。该模型适用于车辆行驶速度变化较为稳定的路段，如高速公路基本路段，且模型计算较为简单，实用性更好。

（2）PET模型：模型研究冲突双方到达潜在冲突点的时间差值并将其作为冲突的PET值。

相较于TTC模型来说，PET模型适用范围更为广泛，可综合考虑冲突参与者的运动变化情况，但需提前确定潜在冲突点，且模型构建较为复杂。

高速公路互通立交合流区内侧向冲突主要发生于汇入车流和主线车流之间，主线车流一般速度较高，汇入车流则相较主线速度较低。由此可见，合流区内车辆行驶特性存在较大差异，使用PET模型更优。综上所述，确定PET模型为侧向冲突判别模型。

2 冲突判别模型构建

2.1 PET基本模型建立

2.1.1 潜在冲突点及侵入面的确定

本文将潜在冲突点所在的道路断面定义为冲突侵入面。在建模前，有必要确定侵入面的位置。

如图2所示，假定主线车辆为A，合流车辆为B，综合考虑A、B分别作为冲突先导车辆和冲突跟随车辆的两种组合情况进行分析。

先导车辆为主线车辆A：在此情况下，合流车辆B尚未进入主线，但其必须在合流车道结束前完成汇入。此外，在高速公路合流区域内，存在主路优先通行规则，当冲突即将发生时，汇入车辆B需要让行主路车辆A，导致冲突点一般更为靠近合流区域末端。对于直接式加速车道而言，合流冲突范围较小，故可将合流车道末端点确定为潜在冲突点，其所在断面为侵入面。

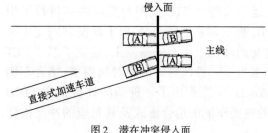

图2 潜在冲突侵入面

先导车辆为合流车辆B：在此情况下，合流车辆B已经驶入主线，其与跟随车辆主路车辆A的潜在冲突侵入面即为合流区域终点所在断面。综上所述，可将合流区域终点确定为潜在冲突点，其所在断面确定为侵入面。

2.1.2 后侵入时间的确定

（1）主线车辆到达侵入面时间 T_1 的计算。

主线车辆在合流区域内行驶时，由于驾驶员驾驶特性的差异，存在不同的行驶状况。为实现侧向冲突的动态判别更新，本文针对微观时间段进行分析。而在极为短暂的时间段内，可将车辆的运动视为匀变速运动，即在 $[t, t+\Delta t]$ 时间段内，车辆保持当前的行驶状态，Δt 为时间间隔。若车辆以该微观时间段的行驶状态行驶直至潜在冲突点，依据运动学方程，车辆在 T_1 时间段内行驶过的距离为：

$$X_1 = V_A T_1 + \frac{1}{2} a_A T_1^2 \tag{1}$$

式中:X_1——主线车辆行驶至潜在冲突点的距离,m;
V_A——主线车辆实时速度,m/s;
a_A——主线车辆实时加速度,m/s²。

可得 T_1 为:

$$T_1 = \frac{\sqrt{4V_A^2 + 8a_A X_1} - 2V_A}{2a_A} \tag{2}$$

(2)合流车辆到达侵入面时间 T_2 的计算。

合流车辆在到达侵入点时与主线车辆同样具有不同的运行状态,可得 T_2 为:

$$T_2 = \frac{\sqrt{4V_B^2 + 8a_B X_2} - 2V_B}{2a_B} \tag{3}$$

式中:X_2——合流车辆行驶至潜在冲突点的距离(m);
V_B——合流车辆实时速度,m/s;
a_B——合流车辆实时加速度,m/s²。

则该微观时间段内侧向冲突的 PET 值为:

$$\text{PET}_{[t,t+\Delta t]} = |T_2 - T_1| \tag{4}$$

2.2 数据采集与分析

2.2.1 数据采集

选取福银高速公路陕西段某互通立交直接式合流区进行数据采集,采集仪器为德尔福 Delphi ESR 毫米波雷达,通过相关卫星地图资料收集分析,确定雷达布设位置位于侵入面上游210m处的合流三角区域内。雷达覆盖区域半径最远为250m,数据采集间隔为0.1s。在天气晴朗的条件下,选取9:00~10:00时间段收集该合流区一小时内的行车数据。采集内容包括车辆实时速度、实时位置以及加速度等基本参数。

2.2.2 模型实例化

考虑检测雷达布设的位置及合流区相关几何参数、雷达工作原理等因素,对2.1节中的PET基本模型进行实例分析,雷达检测示意如图3所示。

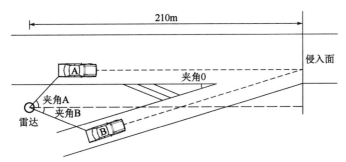

图3 雷达检测示意

由图3得:

$$X_1 = 210 - D_A \cos\theta_A \tag{5}$$

$$X_2 = \frac{210 - D_B \cos\theta_B}{\cos\theta_0} \tag{6}$$

式中:D_A、D_B——主线车辆 A、合流车辆 B 尾部与雷达直线距离,m;

θ_A——车辆 A 与雷达之间的角度(°,逆时针为负值);

θ_B——车辆 B 与雷达之间的角度(°,顺时针为正值);

θ_0——合流区主线和加速车道之间的夹角(°)。

模型参数中,X_1、X_2 可通过雷达获取的距离、角度参数由式(7)、式(8)得到,a_A、a_B、V_A、V_B 可通过雷达数据直接获取。由于数据采集的间隔为 0.1s,故 Δt 取 0.1。

2.3 PET 模型动态判别实现

2.3.1 PET 动态判别原理

运用 MATLAB 对采集到的数据依据所建立的动态判别模型进行分析,对同一时刻可能发生冲突的车辆进行识别。对于可能发生冲突的车辆之间,生成一组随时间变化的序列数据 $L_{PET_{AB}} = \{PET_t, PET_{t+\Delta t}, PET_{t+2\Delta t}, \cdots, PET_{t+n\Delta t}\}$,$\Delta t = 0.1s$。该序列数据反映了冲突车辆之间的 PET 值随着冲突持续时间的变化情况。将各组冲突数据序列中所计算的 PET 最小值确定为该冲突的最终 PET 值,即:

$$PET_{AB} = \min(L_{PET_{AB}}) \tag{7}$$

2.3.2 侧向冲突严重程度阈值确定

由 MATLAB 计算结果,在剔除异常值后,发现识别到有效冲突的 PET 序列数据值基本处于 0~5.6s 这一区间内。侧向冲突 PET 值累积频率曲线如图 4 所示。

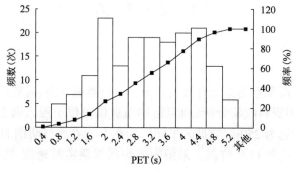

图 4 侧向冲突 PET 值累积频率曲线

由图可得 15% 和 85% 分位值分别为 1.7s 和 4.3s,并将其作为严重冲突和一般冲突的阈值。故将该合流区的侧向冲突 PET 值范围划分为三个模块,对应三种不同严重程度等级,划分结果如表 1 所示。

侧向冲突严重程度划分　　　　　表 1

PET 值(s)	冲突严重程度	PET 值(s)	冲突严重程度
0 < PET ≤ 1.7	严重冲突	PET > 4.4	潜在冲突
1.7 < PET ≤ 4.4	一般冲突		

3 冲突特性研究

3.1 冲突位置分析

3.1.1 车辆运行情况

通过对主线车辆和合流车辆的速度分析,发现主线车辆车速较合流车辆明显偏大。如图 5a)所示,主线车辆速度分布于 20~35m/s 区间内,合流车辆分布于 14~25m/s 区间内。

如图 5b)所示,主线车辆与合流车辆的加速度大小集中于 0~1m/s² 区间内,但其分布存在差异。位于图像左半边的主线车辆中,大部分车辆选取加速方式通过合流区,且角度越大的车辆(内侧车道车辆)加速度选取越大;也有部分主线车辆选择减速通过,以外侧车辆占比尤为明显,采取减速通过的车辆占到一半比例。

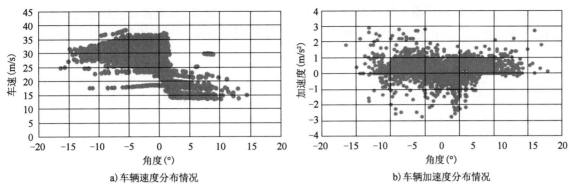

a) 车辆速度分布情况 b) 车辆加速度分布情况

图 5　车辆运行状况

合流车辆中,几乎所有车辆都选择加速通过合流区,这与驾驶人试图尽快进入快速车道行驶的意愿相一致;少部分车辆在接近合流冲突点时采取减速措施。

3.1.2　冲突车道分布

依据加速度分布,内侧车道相较外侧车道而言车辆更加倾向于选择快速通过的方式,也表明内侧车道行车相对更为顺畅,发生侧向冲突的可能性不大。外侧车道采取减速通过的比例明显上升,尤其是靠近冲突点附近,表明外侧车道是侧向冲突发生的主要位置。

3.2　冲突过程研究

针对侧向冲突阈值划分结果,选取严重冲突和一般冲突研究不同冲突严重性的侧向冲突 PET 值变化情况。

依据采集到的冲突数据及其分析结果,综合考虑冲突有效时长等因素,选择 PET 值为 1.68s 的严重冲突和 PET 值为 3.31s 的一般冲突,对二者冲突过程中 PET 值的动态变化情况进行分析,如图 6 所示。

对于所选严重冲突而言,在冲突过程中,其 PET 值的动态变化相对稳定,各采样时刻更新的 PET 序列值在最终值周围上下浮动,可视为一种相对稳定的冲突过程;对所选严重冲突而言,其 PET 值的变化趋势有较为明显的起伏。

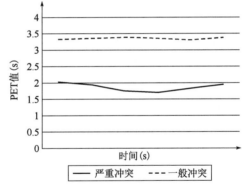

图 6　所选严重冲突与一般冲突 PET 值动态变化过程

选取可能影响侧向冲突 PET 值动态变化的因素,如速度差、加速度差等对冲突过程进行研究。定义速度差 $\Delta V(m/s)$ 为冲突中跟随车辆与先导车辆间的车速差值,$\Delta a(m/s^2)$ 为冲突中跟随车辆与先导车辆间的加速度差值。所选的严重冲突与一般冲突动态 PET 值及相关影响因素随时间变化情况如表 2 所示。

所选严重冲突与一般冲突动态 PET 值及相关影响因素随时间变化情况　　表 2

时间	严重冲突			一般冲突		
	PET 值	ΔV	Δa	PET 值	ΔV	Δa
0.1	2.10	5.44	-0.6	3.36	1.32	0.7
0.2	2.02	5.38	-0.3	3.34	1.39	0.8
0.3	1.94	5.35	0.1	3.36	1.47	0.7
0.4	1.76	5.36	0.3	3.39	1.54	0.3
0.5	1.68	5.39	0.4	3.36	1.57	0.5
0.6	1.85	5.43	0.1	3.31	1.62	0.9
0.7	1.95	5.44	0	3.39	1.71	0.3

由表2可知,所选取的严重冲突中车辆速度差明显大于一般冲突,而两者车辆加速度差差异不大,但严重冲突的PET值动态变化更不稳定。可初步判断速度差相对加速度差来说对冲突严重程度的影响更为显著。

3.3 冲突改善措施

就车辆运行状况、冲突发生位置、冲突过程研究的结果来看,减少高速公路立交合流区侧向冲突发生概率,减轻冲突严重程度可从以下几点入手:

(1)加强合流区域主线车辆限速管理,可尝试设置分车道限速措施,减小主线车辆和合流车辆的车速差。

(2)科学设置导流区域,引导车辆各行其道,使车辆在合流区域减少变道、超车等危险驾驶行为,避免导致车辆间车速差的突然变化。

(3)进一步优化合流区预告信息布设方案,分离需要快速通过合流区的车辆并引导其提前进入内侧车道,缓解外侧车道车流特性差异大的情况。

4 结 语

本文在分析高速公路立交合流区侧向冲突形成机理的基础上,建立了综合考虑车辆运行数据及合流区几何性质的侧向冲突PET动态判别模型,并运用冲突判别结果对侧向冲突严重程度阈值进行了划分;结合车辆运动信息和PET动态变化过程对侧向冲突特性进行了研究。结果表明:

(1)合流区侧向冲突中严重冲突和一般冲突的阈值分别为1.7s和4.4s。

(2)侧向冲突主要发生在合流区主线外侧车道上,该车道主线车流采用减速通过的概率大大增加。

(3)严重冲突的PET值动态变化有明显的起伏,而一般冲突更趋向稳定。

研究冲突中相关指标的动态变化对于揭示交通冲突的演化过程和冲突特性有着重要的作用,本文运用动态PET判别模型对侧向冲突进行了研究,但缺少对于冲突中车辆型号的考虑,后续的研究中将进一步优化判别模型,使之具有更广泛的适用性;在冲突特性研究方面,将进一步研究更多冲突组合,提炼更为可靠的冲突特性信息。

参考文献

[1] WANG YP, E W J, TANG W Z. Automated on-ramp merging control algorithm based on internet-connected vehicles[J]. IET Intelligent Transport Systems, 2013, 7(4): 371-379.

[2] 赵欢. 基于视频的交通冲突自动判别技术研究[D]. 长春:吉林大学,2014.

[3] Saunier N, Sayed T. Automated road safety analysis using video data[J]. Transportation Research Record: Journal of the Transportation Research Board, 2007, 2019(57): 9-10.

[4] Michiel M Minderhoud, Piet HLB. Extended time-to-collision measures for road traffic safety assessment[J]. Accident Analysis & Prevention, 2001(33): 89-97.

[5] 张诗雯,邢莹莹,陆键,等. 基于交通冲突技术的货车比例对交通安全影响[J/OL]. 西南交通大学学报,20204-09-05/2021-01-18.

[6] Charly A, Mathew TV. Estimation of traffic conflicts using precise lateral position and width of vehicles for safety assessment[J]. Accident Analysis & Prevention, 2019, 132, 105264.

[7] 张志召. 高速公路立交分合流区和收费站交通冲突研究[D]. 哈尔滨:哈尔滨工业大学,2014.

[8] 马艳丽,祁首铭,吴昊天,等. 基于PET算法的匝道合流区交通冲突识别模型[J]. 交通运输系统工程与信息,2018,18(02):142-148.

[9] Ge H, Xia R, Sun H, et al. Construction and Simulation of Rear-End Conflicts Recognition Model Based on Improved TTC Algorithm[J]. IEEE Access, 2019, 7:134763-134771.

[10] Li Y, Wu D, Lee J, et al. Analysis of the transition condition of rear-end collisions using time-to-collision index and vehicle trajectory data[J]. Accident Analysis & Prevention, 2020, 144:105676.

基于天气状况和光照条件共同影响的交叉口多车事故影响因素分析

吴建清[1,2,3] 吕 琛[1,2,3] 江健宏[4] 皮任东[1,2,3] 宋修广[1,2] 张 朔[5] 何海东[1,2] 王 冰[3,6]

(1. 山东大学齐鲁交通学院;2. 山东大学苏州研究院;3. 山东省智慧交通重点实验室(筹);
4. 山东省交通规划设计院有限公司;5. 长安大学运输工程学院;6. 山东旗帜信息有限公司)

摘要 本研究旨在辨识不同光照条件和天气状况共同影响下交叉口多车事故严重程度影响因素。以美国华盛顿州 2015—2018 年交叉口多车事故数据为基础,本文选取道路、事故、天气和乘客 4 个特征共计 26 个解释变量,采用随机参数 logit 模型分别建立良好天气+白天、良好天气+黑夜、恶劣天气+白天和恶劣天气+黑夜四种组合情况下的事故严重程度(未受伤、受伤和死亡)估计模型。模型估计结果表明:当考虑天气状况和光照条件共同影响时,乘客年龄、乘客性别、事故发生时间、乘客落座位置(如第二排或第三排)、道路路面类型、道路表面状态等多个影响因素与事故严重程度显著相关。并且,乘客落座在第二排和第三排、沥青路面等影响因素在各种情况下对事故严重程度的影响是一致的,而曲线路面条件等影响因素只在一些特定组合情况下与事故严重程度显著相关。本研究成果为特定条件下的主动交通安全管控提供了科学依据,同时为恶劣条件下驾驶员驾驶行为安全决策提供了参考。

关键词 交通安全 事故严重程度 天气状况 光照条件 随机参数 Logit 模型 交叉口多车事故

0 引 言

作为机动车、非机动车以及行人混行最为严重的区域,道路交叉口由于其交通状况的特殊性极易发生交通事故[1]。仅在 2017 年,我国交叉口发生的交通事故数就已高达 43838 起,占当年事故总数的 21.5%。其中,死亡人数超过 1.1 万人,占全年事故死亡总人数的 17.7%[2]。此外,鉴于交叉口环境复杂易发生多车事故、相较于单车事故会造成更大的人员财产损失等特性,本研究以交叉口多车事故数据为基础,分析选定因素对交叉口事故严重程度的影响。(注:本研究所述多车事故是指涉及车辆不低于 2 辆的事故)。

目前,国内外对于交叉口交通事故的研究主要集中在影响事故严重程度的各类因素。赵丹[3]通过建立双变量 Probit 模型,系统研究了农村公路交叉口事故的影响因素。研究结果表明:光照、天气等因素对事故严重程度有显著影响;交叉口的道路线形、控制设备等越完善,事故严重程度越低;涉事车辆车型越大,事故严重程度越高。杨硕等[2]通过建立基于支持向量机的交叉口交通事故影响因素分析模型,发现天气、时段、道路能见度等因素对交叉口事故严重程度有着显著影响,其中不良天气会加剧事故严重程度。Zhenning Li 等[4]采用聚类分析和层次贝叶斯模型相结合的方法系统研究了新墨西哥州两年内交叉口发生的交通事故数据,研究结果表明天气、光照、道路坡度等因素对司机受伤严重程度有显著影响。Zhuanglin Ma 等[5]以发生在交叉口且涉及行人的交通事故为研究对象,通过建立有序 Probit 模型发现行人年龄、天气情况等因素对此类交通事故中行人受伤严重程度具有显著影响。

从上述研究结果中不难发现,光照或天气条件对事故严重程度有显著影响,并且不良天气状况和光照条件共同作用会加剧交通事故严重程度,这足以看出光照和天气两种因素在进行交通事故影响因素分析时的必要性。为探究光照条件或天气状况对交通事故严重程度的影响机理,国内外相关研究人员对此进行了一些研究。

刘志强等[6]以济南市雾霾天气下的交通事故数据为研究对象,通过建立贝叶斯模型发现当事故影响因素中其他条件不变,车速和雾霾等级同时增加时,发生交通事故的概率将会显著提高。温惠英和薛刚[7]先后通过构建脆弱性模型和风险要素分析模型,系统分析了山区公路在雨雾综合作用下的交通事故死亡风险概率。Mohammad Saad Shaheed 等[8]将事故分为与天气状况相关和与天气状况无关,通过构建分层贝叶斯多项式 logit 模型发现,交通事故严重程度影响因素在这两种条件下具备一定的差异性。Majbah Uddin 和 Nathan Huymh[9]研究了发生在农村和城镇道路与载货汽车相关的交通事故在不同光照条件下影响因素的显著性,研究结果表明不同的光照条件下,显著影响交通事故严重程度的因素不尽相同。Zhenning Li 等人[10]以发生在低能见度下的交通事故为研究对象,通过建立随机参数模型发现,路面潮湿、黑夜等因素对驾驶员受伤严重程度有显著影响。但上述研究仅针对天气状况或光照条件,单一方面对交通事故严重程度的影响,并未考虑两者共同作用产生的影响。

事实上,在不同的光照条件下(白天或黑夜),驾驶员的视野范围和反应时间有着较大差异。当驾驶员在黑夜中行车时,其视野受限且驾驶员本身更易处于疲劳状态,这会导致驾驶员注意力无法高度集中,驾驶员在行车环境中对事物的感知能力有所下降,相较于白天行车更易发生交通事故。除此之外,恶劣天气(雨雪雾霾)也会降低驾驶员的行车视距并分散其注意力,这将增加驾驶员行驶过程中出现不当驾驶行为的可能性[11-12],这些不当行为将直接影响行车安全。当不良天气状况与不同光照条件共同作用时,其对驾驶员驾驶行为、反应时间以及行车视野造成严重的不良影响,很大程度上增加了事故发生的可能性及事故的严重程度。

鉴于目前针对天气状况或光照条件的交通事故影响因素的相关研究较少,且缺乏对天气状况和光照条件同时作用下的交通事故影响因素的研究,本文充分考虑天气状况和光照条件的影响,对交叉口交通事故影响因素进行了深入分析。本研究通过分析美国华盛顿州 2015—2018 年交叉口交通事故相关数据,在保证样本数量的前提下,设定两种天气状况:良好天气(晴天或多云)和恶劣天气(雨、雪、雾、霾、大风等),并设定两种光照条件:白天(包括黄昏和黎明)和黑夜,将全体事故数据分为良好天气 + 白天、良好天气 + 黑夜、恶劣天气 + 白天和恶劣天气 + 黑夜四种类型,分别建立模型对事故严重程度影响因素进行分析,旨在探究光照条件和天气状况共同作用下交通事故发生的机理。

2 研究数据概述

本文选取了美国华盛顿州 2015—2018 年的交叉口交通事故数据,共 35581 起(已剔除不合理值及缺失值),在保证每个分组样本量的条件下,将初始的七种事故严重程度(未受伤、可能受伤、无致残伤、有致残伤、于医院中死亡、于途中死亡、当场死亡)合并为三种:未受伤、受伤和死亡。考虑天气状况和光照条件共同作用,将其分为四种组合情况,组合一:良好天气 + 白天;组合二:良好天气 + 黑夜;组合三:恶劣天气 + 白天;组合四:恶劣天气 + 黑夜。四组数据分布情况如图 1 所示。

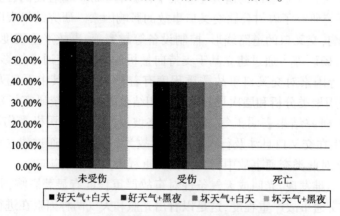

图 1 不同天气和光照条件组合数据分布图

由图 1 可以发现,各组数据均包含未受伤、受伤和死亡三种事故严重程度类型的数据,且其分布较为相似。每组数据均包含表征交通事故相关信息的四种数据类型:事故特征数据(事故发生时间、事故发生类型等)、环境特征数据(天气、光照等)、乘客特征数据(乘客年龄、乘客性别等)以及道路特征数据(道路路面类型、道路路面状况等）。构建各组数据模型所涉及的解释变量,如表1~表4所示。

组合一交通事故影响因素交叉统计表 表1

变量名称	未受伤	受伤	死亡
乘客年龄小于25岁*[良好天气+白天]	6965	4597	27
乘客年龄25~60岁[良好天气+白天]	3378	2289	13
乘客年龄大于60岁[良好天气+白天]	1097	920	6
男性乘客*[良好天气+白天]	4854	3119	19
女性乘客[良好天气+白天]	6128	4386	25
乘客落座在第一排*[良好天气+白天]	5454	3745	22
乘客落座在第二排[良好天气+白天]	1886	1316	11
乘客落在在第三排[良好天气+白天]	4100	2745	13
乘客留在车内*[良好天气+白天]	11425	7790	43
乘客完全甩出车外[良好天气+白天]	2	4	3
乘客部分甩出车外[良好天气+白天]	5	3	0
乘客没有佩戴安全装置*[良好天气+白天]	120	121	6
乘客佩戴安全装置[良好天气+白天]	8708	6090	29
儿童乘客佩戴安全装置[良好天气+白天]	2612	1595	11
道路路面为混凝土路面*[良好天气+白天]	1310	861	6
道路路面为沥青路[良好天气+白天]	10099	6926	39
道路路面为碎石路[良好天气+白天]	13	5	1
农村道路*[良好天气+白天]	1151	1138	19
城镇道路[良好天气+白天]	10285	6667	27
事故发生在工作日*[良好天气+白天]	7768	5182	31
事故发生在周末[良好天气+白天]	3672	2624	15
事故发生道路为直线线形*[良好天气+白天]	9667	6755	44
事故发生道路为曲线线形[良好天气+白天]	1105	643	2
道路路面为干燥*[良好天气+白天]	10949	7472	41
道路表面潮湿\有积雪\有冰[良好天气+白天]	482	327	5
道路路面为其他状态[良好天气+白天]	8	7	0

注:*为基准变量。

组合二交通事故影响因素交叉统计表 表2

变量名称	未受伤	受伤	死亡
乘客年龄小于25岁*[良好天气+黑夜]	1592	1106	17
乘客年龄25~60岁[良好天气+黑夜]	839	580	9
乘客年龄大于60岁[良好天气+黑夜]	135	115	1
男性乘客*[良好天气+黑夜]	1113	732	11
女性乘客[良好天气+黑夜]	1351	1015	16
乘客落座在第一排*[良好天气+黑夜]	1260	919	11
乘客落座在第二排[良好天气+黑夜]	331	244	3
乘客落在在第三排[良好天气+黑夜]	975	638	13
乘客留在车内*[良好天气+黑夜]	2557	1788	26
乘客完全甩出车外[良好天气+黑夜]	0	4	1

续上表

变量名称	未受伤	受伤	死亡
乘客部分甩出车外[良好天气+黑夜]	3	3	0
乘客没有佩戴安全装置*[良好天气+黑夜]	25	40	2
乘客佩戴安全装置[良好天气+黑夜]	2111	1508	20
儿童乘客佩戴安全装置[良好天气+黑夜]	430	253	5
道路路面为混凝土路面*[良好天气+黑夜]	362	219	2
道路路面为沥青路[良好天气+黑夜]	2196	1579	25
道路路面为碎石路[良好天气+黑夜]	3	0	0
农村道路*[良好天气+黑夜]	191	160	7
城镇道路[良好天气+黑夜]	2375	1641	20
事故发生在工作日[良好天气+黑夜]	1706	1142	14
事故发生在周末[良好天气+黑夜]	860	659	13
事故发生道路为直线线形*[良好天气+黑夜]	2187	1572	26
事故发生道路为曲线线形[良好天气+黑夜]	205	109	0
道路路面为干燥*[良好天气+黑夜]	2300	1626	27
道路表面潮湿\有积雪\有冰[良好天气+黑夜]	261	169	0
道路路面为其他状态[良好天气+黑夜]	5	6	0

注：*为基准变量。

组合三交通事故影响因素交叉统计表　　　　表3

变量名称	未受伤	受伤	死亡
乘客年龄小于25岁*[恶劣天气+白天]	2924	1686	16
乘客年龄25~60岁[恶劣天气+白天]	1394	909	2
乘客年龄大于60岁[恶劣天气+白天]	468	306	5
男性乘客*[恶劣天气+白天]	2055	1179	7
女性乘客[恶劣天气+白天]	2550	1639	11
乘客落座在第一排[恶劣天气+白天]	2259	1455	7
乘客落座在第二排[恶劣天气+白天]	820	458	8
乘客落在在第三排[恶劣天气+白天]	1707	988	8
乘客留在车内*[恶劣天气+白天]	4776	2895	23
乘客完全甩出车外[恶劣天气+白天]	0	0	0
乘客部分甩出车外[恶劣天气+白天]	2	3	0
乘客没有佩戴安全装置*[恶劣天气+白天]	42	59	0
乘客佩戴安全装置[恶劣天气+白天]	3613	2288	17
儿童乘客佩戴安全装置[恶劣天气+白天]	1131	554	0
道路路面为混凝土路面*[恶劣天气+白天]	580	333	3
道路路面为沥青路[恶劣天气+白天]	4199	2556	20
道路路面为碎石路[恶劣天气+白天]	4	2	0
农村道路*[恶劣天气+白天]	517	310	5
城镇道路[恶劣天气+白天]	4267	2591	18
事故发生在工作日*[恶劣天气+白天]	3061	1834	17
事故发生在周末[恶劣天气+白天]	1725	1067	6

续上表

变量名称	未受伤	受伤	死亡
事故发生道路为直线线形*[恶劣天气+白天]	4059	2495	19
事故发生道路为曲线线形[恶劣天气+白天]	461	263	2
道路路面为干燥*[恶劣天气+白天]	1479	897	12
道路表面潮湿\有积雪\有冰[恶劣天气+白天]	3281	1972	11
道路路面为其他状态[恶劣天气+白天]	26	32	0

注：*为基准变量。

组合四交通事故影响因素交叉统计表 表4

变量名称	未受伤	受伤	死亡
乘客年龄小于25岁*[恶劣天气+黑夜]	1513	991	8
乘客年龄25~60岁[恶劣天气+黑夜]	787	597	2
乘客年龄大于60岁[恶劣天气+黑夜]	169	112	0
男性乘客*[恶劣天气+黑夜]	1080	687	1
女性乘客[恶劣天气+黑夜]	1301	959	8
乘客落座在第一排*[恶劣天气+黑夜]	1250	872	5
乘客落座在第二排[恶劣天气+黑夜]	353	238	0
乘客落在在第三排[恶劣天气+黑夜]	866	590	5
乘客留在车内*[恶劣天气+黑夜]	2458	1693	8
乘客完全甩出车外[恶劣天气+黑夜]	0	1	2
乘客部分甩出车外[恶劣天气+黑夜]	3	2	0
乘客没有佩戴安全装置*[恶劣天气+黑夜]	21	32	4
乘客佩戴安全装置[恶劣天气+黑夜]	2073	1423	5
儿童乘客佩戴安全装置[恶劣天气+黑夜]	375	245	1
道路路面为混凝土路面*[恶劣天气+黑夜]	351	238	0
道路路面为沥青路[恶劣天气+黑夜]	2109	1460	10
道路路面为碎石路[恶劣天气+黑夜]	4	1	0
农村道路*[恶劣天气+黑夜]	189	130	4
城镇道路[恶劣天气+黑夜]	2280	1569	6
事故发生在工作日*[恶劣天气+黑夜]	1581	1067	6
事故发生在周末[恶劣天气+黑夜]	888	633	4
事故发生道路为直线线形*[恶劣天气+黑夜]	2078	1438	9
事故发生道路为曲线线形[恶劣天气+黑夜]	216	171	1
道路路面为干燥*[恶劣天气+黑夜]	388	304	0
道路表面潮湿\有积雪\有冰[恶劣天气+黑夜]	2074	1375	10
道路路面为其他状态[恶劣天气+黑夜]	7	11	0

注：*为基准变量。

3 研究方法

在进行事故严重程度影响因素分析时需考虑交通事故数据异质性对分析结果带来的影响，数据异质性即为同一影响因素在不同交通事故中造成的影响具有明显的差异性[13]。截至目前，随机参数logit模型[14-18]、考虑随机参数均值异质性的logit模型[19]以及考虑随机参数均值和方差异质性的logit模型[20-21]

均已用于研究交通事故严重程度的影响因素,并定性分析了数据异质性对事故严重程度的影响。故本研究将采用随机参数 logit 模型对事故严重程度影响因素进行分析。

本研究将交通事故严重程度类型分为三种:未受伤、受伤、死亡,为构建四组数据的随机参数模型,设 S_{kn} 为事故 n 严重程度为 k 的可能性,X_{kn} 为事故严重程度的解释变量,β_k 为模型待估计的参数,ε_{kn} 为误差项服从极值分布,决定事故严重程度的效用函数如式(1)所示:

$$S_{kn} = \beta_k X_{kn} + \varepsilon_{kn} \tag{1}$$

当式(1)中的待估计参数 β_k 服从某一分布(正态分布、均匀分布和正态分布)时,即 $\beta_k \sim f(\beta_i|\theta)$(其中 θ 表示 β_k 所服从分布的参数),则式(1)可表示为:

$$P_n(k) = \int \frac{\text{EXP}(\beta_k X_{kn})}{\sum_{\forall k} \text{Exp}(\beta_k X_{kn})} f(\beta_i|\theta) \mathrm{d}\beta \tag{2}$$

式(2)中,$P_n(k)$ 表示事故 n 严重程度为 k 的可能性,其他变量表示意义与式(1)一致。

之前的一些研究表明随机参数服从正态分布时,估计模型表现出较好的拟合结果。在本文中将采用 Halton 模拟技术进行参数估计,相应的 Halton 点集大小为 300[22-25]。

4 结果分析

4.1 参数估计

本研究通过极大似然估计法进行模型参数估计,通过 0.1、0.05 和 0.01 表示的三种显著性水平对解释变量的显著性进行判别,各模型参数估计的结果如表5、表6所示。

表5 在良好天气+白天和良好天气+黑夜条件下的事故严重程度模型参数估计结果

变量名称	良好天气+白天			良好天气+黑夜		
	未受伤	受伤	死亡	未受伤	受伤	死亡
常数	0.473	—	—	0.854	—	—
乘客年龄 25~60 岁	0.995	—	—	2.037	—	—
乘客性别为女性	1.486	1.692	—	—	1.603	—
乘客落座在第二排	—	—	−1.821	—	—	−1.577
乘客落在在第三排	—	—	−2.369	—	—	−1.002
乘客佩戴安全装置	—	0.348	—	—	0.414	—
道路路面为沥青路	−0.132	—	−2.863	−0.416	—	−2.333
事故发生在城镇道路	—	—	—	0.414	—	—
事故发生时间为周末	1.236	1.331	—	—	0.272	—
事故发生道路为曲线线形	—	−0.204	—	—	−0.181	—
随机参数	—	—	—	—	—	—
事故发生在城镇道路	0.851	—	—	—	—	—
事故发生在城镇道路的标准差	2.563	—	—	—	—	—
乘客年龄 25~60 岁	—	1.804	—	—	1.067	—
乘客年龄 25~60 岁的标准差	—	1.445	—	—	4.949	—
乘客性别为女性	—	—	—	1.616	—	—
乘客性别为女性的标准差	—	—	—	3.043	—	—

由表5可知,考虑到乘客特征方面,在良好天气条件下,乘客年龄为 25~60 岁时会显著增加未受伤事故发生的可能性,乘客为女性时将会增加受伤事故发生的可能性,并且当乘客座落在第二排或者第三排时会显著降低死亡事故发生的可能性。在恶劣天气+白天条件下时,女性乘客与发生未受伤事故显著相关。

考虑到道路特征方面,在良好天气条件下,道路类型为沥青路时会显著降低未受伤事故和死亡事故发生的可能性;与直线路段相比,车辆行驶在曲线路段时会显著降低受伤事故发生的可能性。上述结果的出现可能是由于在良好天气条件下,驾驶员具备更好的行车视野,相较于直线路段,驾驶员行驶至曲线路段时注意力会更加集中。因此,良好天气条件下曲线路段发生交通事故的可能性较低。在良好天气+白天的条件下,事故发生时间为周末与未受伤事故的发生显著相关;在良好天气+黑夜的条件下,事故发生在城镇道路与事故严重程度为"未受伤"显著相关。

考虑搭配事故特征方面,在良好天气条件下,相较于混凝土路面,当路面类型为沥青路面时,会显著降低未受伤和死亡事故发生的可能性;当事故发生在周末时,易发生严重程度为"受伤"的事故。

由表6可知,考虑到乘客特征方面,在恶劣天气条件下,乘客落座在第三排会显著降低死亡事故发生的可能性,且乘客佩戴安全保护装置与受伤事故的发生显著相关。这些结果均与在良好天气条件下的数据分析结果一致。在恶劣天气+白天的条件下,乘客落座在第二排时能够显著降低死亡事故发生的可能性。该结果的出现可能是由于当车辆发生碰撞时,相较于前排位置,乘客落座在后排受到的冲击更小。在恶劣天气+黑夜的条件下,乘客为女性时能够显著降低死亡事故发生的可能性;

在恶劣天气+白天和恶劣天气+黑夜条件下的事故严重程度模型参数估计结果　　　表6

变量名称	恶劣天气+白天			恶劣天气+黑夜		
	未受伤	受伤	死亡	未受伤	受伤	死亡
常数	1.305	—	—	2.089	—	—
乘客性别为女性	—	—	—	—	—	−1.557
乘客落座在第二排	—	—	−3.237	—	—	—
乘客落在在第三排	—	—	−1.699	—	—	−0.894
乘客佩戴安全装置	—	0.361	—	—	0.405	—
道路路面为沥青路	−0.224	—	−3.740	−0.3253	—	−2.790
城镇道路	—	0.315	—	—	1.059	—
事故发生时间为周末	—	1.968	—	40.533	—	—
道路路面为其他状态	−0.713	—	—	−32.922	—	—
随机参数	—	—	—	—	—	—
乘客性别为女性	—	—	—	4.027	—	—
乘客性别为女性的标准差	—	—	—	23.596	—	—
事故发生时间为周末	1.976	—	—	—	31.036	—
事故发生时间为周末的标准差	0.913	—	—	—	64.290	—

考虑到道路特征方面,在恶劣天气条件下,相较于混凝土路面,当车辆行驶在沥青路面时,会显著降低未受伤和死亡事故发生的可能性;相较于农村道路,在城镇道路上行车更易发生受伤事故,这与城镇道路行车环境复杂、车流量较大有关;当道路表面处于泥泞等其他状态时,无论在黑夜还是白天条件下,都会显著降低未受伤事故发生的可能性。因此,当路表状态不佳时,驾驶员驾驶车辆行驶时应更加小心谨慎。

考虑到事故特征方面,在恶劣天气条件下,当事故发生在周末白天时,会显著增加受伤事故发生的可能性;当事故发生在周末黑夜时,会显著增加未受伤事故的发生可能性。上述结果的出现可能是由于周末车流量及私家车出行占比较大,易发生交通事故。

从表5、表6的参数估计结果可以发现,无论在何种天气及光照条件下,乘客落座在后排均会显著降低死亡事故发生的可能性。相较于混凝土路面,当车辆行驶在沥青路面时能够显著降低严重程度为"未受伤"和"死亡"事故发生的可能性。当事故发生时间在周末时能够显著增加各类严重程度事故发生的可能性。除此之外,其他一些影响因素只在特定的天气状况和光照条件下对事故严重程度表现出显著影响,例如:在良好天气驾车行驶时,相较于直线路段,曲线路段不易发生受伤事故;相较于行驶在干燥路面,当车辆行驶在其他状态(泥泞、积水)的路面时会显著降低"未受伤"事故发生的可能性。

4.2 随机参数分析

本文建立了四个随机参数 logit 模型,共识别出七个变量作为随机参数,分别为良好天气+白天:事故发生在城镇道路,乘客年龄25～60岁;良好天气+黑夜:乘客年龄25～60岁,女性乘客;恶劣天气+白天:事故发生时间为周末[NI];恶劣天气+黑夜:女性乘客,事故发生时间为周末。

为进一步探索事故数据异质性对交通事故严重程度的影响,以在良好天气+白天组合模型下识别出的随机参数:事故发生时间为周末和乘客年龄25～60岁为例做进一步分析(图2)。

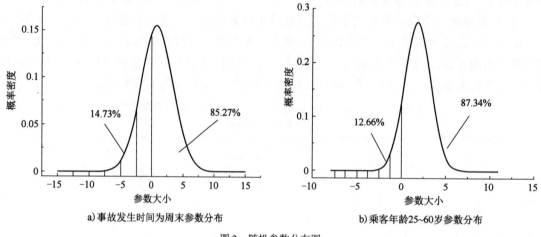

a) 事故发生时间为周末参数分布　　　　b) 乘客年龄25~60岁参数分布

图2　随机参数分布图

事故发生时间为周末,这一参数服从均值为0.851,方差为2.563的正态分布。也就是说,对于85.27%发生在周末的事故来说,发生未受伤事故的可能性要大于其他受伤严重程度事故发生的可能性。而对于14.73%发生在周末的事故来说,其他两种受伤严重程度事故发生的可能性要高于未受伤事故发生的可能性。

乘客年龄25～60岁,这一参数服从均值为1.804,方差为1.445的正态分布。也就是说,当乘客年龄为25～60岁,对于87.34%发生的事故来说,发生受伤事故的可能性要大于其他受伤严重程度事故发生的可能性,而对于12.66%的发生的事故来说,乘客年龄为25～60岁时,其他两种受伤严重程度事故发生的可能性要高于受伤事故发生的可能性。

4　结　语

本研究以三种事故严重程度(未受伤、受伤和死亡)作为因变量,选取乘客特征、事故特征、道路特征四个方面共计26个解释变量,通过可捕捉事故数据异质性影响的随机参数 logit 模型,对天气状况和光照条件对应组合的4组数据分别建立数学模型,进行事故严重程度影响因素的定性分析。

(1)四种随机参数 logit 模型的参数估计结果表明:在不同的天气状况和光照条件下,交通事故的显著影响因素有明显异同。在良好天气和恶劣天气的条件下,乘客落座在第二排、乘客落座在第三排,道路路面为沥青路以及事故发生时间为周末这些影响因素对事故严重程度影响的趋势是一致的;事故发生道路为曲线线形这一影响因素只在"良好天气"条件下与事故严重程度显著相关;当处在"恶劣天气"条件下时,道路路面为其他状态(泥泞、积水)时与事故严重程度显著相关。

(2)四个估计模型识别出的七个随机参数表明:同一影响因素在不同天气状况和光照条件下对交通事故严重程度的影响并不一致。例如,乘客年龄25～60岁在"良好天气+白天"和"良好天气+黑夜"这两种条件下,以及事故发生在周末在"恶劣天气+白天"和"恶劣天气+黑夜"这两种条件下对交通事故严重程度的影响均不相同。

(3) 本研究在不同光照条件和天气状况下分析得到的事故严重程度显著影响因素,对于在不同天气、不同光照条件下制定主动交通管控措施具有重要的意义。例如,在恶劣天气条件下,可通过激光雷达、摄像头等路侧设施实时监测路面状态,进行车辆行驶预警,以保障车辆安全行驶。

本研究还存在以下不足:

(1) 由于数据样本量的限制,本文只考虑到部分影响交通事故严重程度的因素,考虑因素不够全面;

(2) 未进行更加详细的天气状况与光照条件组合划分,以便更加细致地分析每种组合的显著影响因素;

(3) 只建立了随机参数 logit 模型,对于其他可考虑数据异质性影响的模型如马尔科夫链模型未进行研究。以上几方面将是未来一段时间研究工作的重点。

5 致 谢

本研究获得国家自然科学基金项目(52002224)、江苏省自然科学基金项目(BK20200226)、苏州市科技发展计划(SYG202033)和山东省重点研发计划(2019GSF109045)资助。

参考文献

[1] 孟祥海,马亿鑫,孙佳豪.城市道路平面信号交叉口交通事故成因分析[J].交通工程,2020,20(03):1-6,13.

[2] 杨硕,孙晨,高纯.基于支持向量机的交叉口交通事故分析方法[J].交通工程,2019,No.141(04):183-187.

[3] 赵丹,马社强,张雨萌,等.农村公路交叉口交通事故特征关联性与风险因素分析[J].中国安全科学学报,2020,v.30(07):150-155.

[4] Zhenning L, Cong C, Qiong W, et al. Exploring driver injury severity patterns and causes in low visibility related single-vehicle crashes using a finite mixture random parameters model[J]. Analytic Methods in Accident Research, 2018, 20:1-14.

[5] Ma Z, Lu X, Chien I J, et al. Investigating factors influencing pedestrian injury severity at intersections[J]. Traffic Injury Prevention, 2017.

[6] 刘志强,王玲,张爱红,等.基于贝叶斯模型的雾霾天高速公路交通事故发生机理研究[J].重庆理工大学学报(自然科学版),2018,032(001):43-49.

[7] 温惠英,薛刚.山区公路交通事故多要素风险综合分析方法:以山区雨雾天气为例[J].中国安全科学学报,2019,v.29(09):165-170.

[8] Shaheed M S, Gkritza K, Carriquiry A L, et al. Analysis of occupant injury severity in winter weather crashes: A fully Bayesian multivariate approach[J]. Analytic Methods in Accident Research, 2016, 11:33-47.

[9] Uddin M, Huynh N. Truck-involved crashes injury severity analysis for different lighting conditions on rural and urban roadways[J]. Accident Analysis & Prevention, 2017, 108C(nov.):44-55.

[10] Zhenning L, Cong C, Qiong W, et al. Exploring driver injury severity patterns and causes in low visibility related single-vehicle crashes using a finite mixture random parameters model[J]. Analytic Methods in Accident Research, 2018, 20:1-14.

[11] Yichuan, Peng, Yuming, et al. Examining the effect of adverse weather on road transportation using weather and traffic sensors.[J]. PloS one, 2018.

[12] Alnawmasi N, Mannering F. A statistical assessment of temporal instability in the factors determining motorcyclist injury severities[J]. Analytic Methods in Accident Research, 2019, 22.

[13] Mannering F L, Shankar V, Bhat C R. Unobserved heterogeneity and the statistical analysis of highway accident data[J]. Analytic Methods in Accident Research, 2016, 11:1-16.

[14] Behnood A, Mannering F L. The temporal stability of factors affecting driver-injury severities in single-vehicle crashes: Some empirical evidence[J]. Analytic Methods in Accident Research, 2015, 8:7-32.

[15] Behnood A, Mannering F L. An empirical assessment of the effects of economic recessions on pedestrian-injury crashes using mixed and latent-class models[J]. Analytic Methods in Accident Research, 2016, 12:1-17.

[16] Chang F, Xu P, Zhou H, et al. Investigating injury severities of motorcycle riders: A two-step method integrating latent class cluster analysis and random parameters logit model[J]. Accident Analysis & Prevention, 2019, 131(OCT.):316-326.

[17] 陈昭明,徐文远,曲悠扬,等.基于混合Logit模型的高速公路交通事故严重程度分析[J].交通信息与安全,2019,37(03):42-50.

[18] 刘建荣,郝小妮.基于随机系数Logit模型的地铁拥挤度影响参数研究[J].华南理工大学学报(自然科学版),2019,47(04):61-66,75.

[19] Behnood A, Mannering F. The effect of passengers on driver-injury severities in single-vehicle crashes: A random parameters heterogeneity-in-means approach[J]. Analytic Methods in Accident Research, 2017, 14:41-53.

[20] Muhammad, Waseem, Anwaar, et al. Factors affecting motorcyclists' injury severities: An empirical assessment using random parameters logit model with heterogeneity in means and variances[J]. Accident Analysis & Prevention, 2018.

[21] Behnood A, Mannering F. Determinants of bicyclist injury severities in bicycle-vehicle crashes: A random parameters approach with heterogeneity in means and variances[J]. Analytic Methods in Accident Research, 2017, 16:35-47.

[22] Anastasopoulos P C, Labi S, Bhargava A, et al. Empirical Assessment of the Likelihood and Duration of Highway Project Time Delays[J]. Journal of Construction Engineering & Management, 2011, 138(3):390-398.

[23] Anastasopoulos P C, Mannering F L. The effect of speed limits on drivers' choice of speed: A random parameters seemingly unrelated equations approach[J]. Analytic Methods in Accident Research, 2016, 10:1-11.

[24] John, C, Milton, et al. Highway accident severities and the mixed logit model: An exploratory empirical analysis[J]. Accident Analysis & Prevention, 2008, 40(1):260-266.

Injury Severity Analysis of Electric Bicycles-Involved-Crashes during Peak Traffic Periods

Zishuo Zhu   Tong Zhu   Pei Xie

(Chang'an University)

Abstract　This paper investigated electric bicycles involved crashes to determine the statistically significant factors during peak traffic periods, which include morning peak and evening peak. The study utilized 2142 single-vehicle-single-electric bicycle crashes of a city, including 61 no injury crashes, 1469 minor injury crashes, 367 severe injury crashes and 244 fatal crashes. Multinomial logistics models are estimated for influences of variables among different severity levels (no injury, severe injury and fatal injury) in terms of Chinese traditional peak traffic periods. The model estimation results show that in terms of traffic peak periods, electric bicyclist injury severity affected by driver, vehicle and road characteristics. The research suggests: (1) male electric bicyclist and adult electric bicyclist experienced more safe driving circumstance, providing additional driving training or safety courses for specific groups; (2) oversize vehicle should be pass-limited during traffic peak periods; (3) relative automobile driving behavior should be limited or punished during traffic peak periods, as well as traffic control; (4) supervision of road segments like elevated road, tunnel and narrowed line should be noticed during traffic peak periods, like alternate peak open right of way. The study could provide more ideas of traffic optimizing under traffic peak periods.

Keywords Electric Bicycle-Involved Crash   Injury Severity   Traffic Peak Period   Multinomial Logistics Model   Traffic Safety

0 Introduction

According to the China Traffic Management Bureau, the number of e-bikes was 250 million in 2017. Meanwhile, from 2013 to 2017, e-bike related crashes have resulted in about 56200 injuries and 8,431 fatalities in China. The traffic safety of e-bikes cannot be ignored (Wu, 2020). Among the fatal crashes involved electric bicycles, the automobile accounted for 71.01% (Yang et al., 2020), which indicated that crashes involved electric bicycles and automobile deserved more study.

The study investigates the relationship between electric bicycles crash factors and injury severity levels during traffic peak periods. In terms of traffic peak periods, previous studies mainly concentrated on driver injury severity with analysis of crashes involving oversize vehicle like trucks and buses (Chen and Chen, 2011; Khorashadi et al., 2005; Pahukula et al., 2015). However, there is no studies have been done on electric vehicle accidents during peak periods, so the direction needs to be more investigated.

With regard to methodology, most of the previous studies of electric bicycle crashes, utilized accident simulation like MADYMO, LS-DYNA to simulate the crash situations to study exact injury parts, especially head injury (Gao et al., 2020; Han et al., 2020; Huang et al., 2020). On the other hand, previous studies of electric bicycle crashes also considered analytic approaches to investigate. The previous studies also did retrospective studies to investigate the electric bicycles crashes (King et al., 2020). Besides, in terms of studies of traffic peak periods, they utilized multinomial logit to make an exploratory analysis (Khorashadi et al., 2005). The aim of the present study is investigated electric bicycles involved crashes to determine the statistically significant factors during peak traffic periods, which include morning peak and evening peak. In this study, we utilized multinomial logit models to study electric bicycles driver injury severity with different dependent variables. The electric bicycles driver injury severity was divided into four types: no injury, minor injury, severe injury and fatal injury. From the model's estimations, the study could provide valuable insight into the nature of electric bicycle driver injury severities in different injury types during traffic peak periods.

2 Data Description

The data used in the present study are local traffic control department collected automobile and electric bicycle involved crashes of a city from 2006 to 2017. For integrity and availability of data, the study extracted the single-automobile-single-electric bicycle crashes happened in morning traffic periods and evening traffic periods (2142), which contained no injury (61), minor injury (1469), severe injury (367) and fatal injury (244). Each observation of the data set contained electric bicycle injury severity and driver characteristics, vehicle characteristics and road characteristics influenced the crashes. Tab. 1 presents the injury severity level frequency and percentage distribution by traffic periods and variable descriptions and summary statistics by traffic peak periods. It should be noted that the data set did not only include all of the possible factors that counted for electric bicycle driver injury.

Summary Statistics of Dependent Variables　　　　　Tab. 1

Variable	Percentage(%)
Crash Severity	
No Injury/Minor Injury/Severe Injury/Fatal Injury	2.9/68.6/17.1/11.4
Driver and Bicyclist Characteristics	
Female Vehicle Driver/Male Vehicle Driver	91.0/9.0
Female Electric Bicyclist/Male Electric Bicyclist	71.1/28.9
Electric Bicyclist Age: <18yrs, 18–30 yrs, 31–40 yrs, 41–50 yrs, over 50 yrs	1.3/18.4/20.2/23.6/36.5
Vehicle Driver Age: 18–30yrs, 31–40 yrs, 41–50 yrs, over 50 yrs	35.9/33.1/24.1/6.9
Vehicle Driving Experience: 1–5 years, 6–10 years, 11–15 years, over 15 years	21.5/26.1/41.2/11.2
Vehicle Characteristics	
Vehicle Insurance: Insured/not Insured	99.0/1.0
Sedan/Passenger Car/Truck/Motorcycle	73.8/6.0/17.9/2.2
Vehicle Safety: Normal/Abnormal	98.9/1.1
Overloaded/Not Overloaded	1.6/98.4
Pre-crash vehicle movement Characteristics	
Go Straight/Turning around/Turning Left/Turning Right	76.4/2.5/9.9/11.2
Roadway and Environmental Characteristics	
Time of Accident: Weekday/Weekend	73.1/26.9
Traffic Signals/No Traffic Signals	18.2/81.8
Roadside Protection: No Roadside Protection/Trees/Green Belts/Fences/Truck Escape Ramps	60.2/13.9/13.4/7.4/5.1
Road Surface Condition: Good/Rough	98.7/1.3
Road Dryness: Dry/Wet	89.4/10.6
Pavement Structure: Bituminous/Others	91.8/8.2
Road Segments/Road Entrances	79.4/20.6
Road Alignment: Flat and Straight/Others	89.6/10.4
Road Type: General Urban Road/Classified Highway/Urban Expressway or other Urban Road	57.9/28.4/13.7
Weather Conditions: Sunny/Cloudy/Rainy/Snowy or Hail Weather	78.4/13.3/7.1/1.3
Visibility: >200 m, 50–100 m, 100–200 m, <50 m	48.9/19.7/22.7/8.8
Landform: Plain Road/Others	97.0/3.0
Lighting Condition: Daytime/Street Lamps at Night/No Lamps at Night/Dawn or Dusk	70.1/19.8/7.2/2.3
Location of Accident: Downtown/Suburb	44.6/55.4

2　Methods

In statistics, multinomial logistic model could generate an indifferent regression to at least two different categories, which is a model used to predict the probability of different possible outcomes for a dependent variable with a category distribution. For the dependent variable, which maintains M categories, requires $M-1$ equations. Each category refers to a reference category, which contributes to describe the interrelation between the studied dependent variable and each independent variable.

The adoption of multinomial logistic models for the present examine is related to division of dependent variable(electric bicycles driver injury severity)into four types: minor injury($y=1$), no injury($y=2$), severe injury($y=3$)and fatal injury($y=4$). As possessing the largest part data number, minor injury was selected as the reference category to be compared with the last three different categories. The slope coefficients show how each predictor affects the possibility of categorizing the electric bicycles driver injury severity as no injury, severe injury and fatal injury, relative to minor injury.

For the probability of no injury(reference category):

$$P(Y=1) = \frac{1}{1 + \sum_{h=2}^{M} \exp(Z_h)} \tag{1}$$

For the probability of severe injury:

$$P(Y=2) = \frac{\exp(Z_2)}{1 + \sum_{h=2}^{M} \exp(Z_h)} \tag{2}$$

For the probability of fatal injury:

$$P(Y=3) = \frac{\exp(Z_3)}{1 + \sum_{h=2}^{M} \exp(Z_h)} \tag{3}$$

3 Results

The statistical software STATA was utilized to perform the tests for model estimation. Tab. 2 shows the multinomial estimation results and marginal effects for crashes during morning and evening traffic periods. The study retained explanatory variables that passed the test of 10%, 5% and 1% confidence levels. The study will explain in terms of driver characteristics, vehicle characteristics and road characteristics.

Model Estimation Results   Tab. 2

Type	Variable	Coefficient	Z-Statistic	Marginal Effects		
				Fatal Injury	Severe Injury	No Injury
Fatal Injury	Vehicle Equal Liability	1.792***	8.85	0.142	-0.009	0.004
	Passenger Car	1.402***	4.75	0.104	0.048	-0.013
	Truck	1.763***	9.46	0.122	0.101	-0.001
	Vehicle Turning around	-1.774*	-1.69	-0.107	-0.183	-0.008
	Vehicle Turning Left	-1.217**	-3.10	-0.063	-0.207	0.023
	Roadside Protection Trees	-0.468*	-1.92	-0.023	-0.077	-0.003
	Type of Road Segments	0.361*	1.71	0.010	0.082	0.027
Severe Injury	Passenger Car	0.636**	2.29	0.104	0.048	-0.013
	Truck	1.177***	6.95	0.122	0.101	-0.001
	Vehicle Turning around	-1.902**	-2.53	-0.107	-0.183	-0.008
	Vehicle Turning Left	-1.963***	-4.88	-0.063	-0.207	0.023
	Vehicle Turning Right	-1.565***	-5.18	-0.003	-0.176	0.017
	Traffic Control	-0.352**	-1.73	0.0137	-0.046	0.018
	Roadside Protection Trees	-0.750***	-3.27	-0.023	-0.077	-0.003
	Roadside Protection Fences	-0.992***	-2.96	-0.003	-0.106	-0.017
	Type of Road Segments	0.812***	3.82	0.010	0.082	0.027
	Strait Road	1.302***	3.18	-0.002	0.143	0.007

Continue

Type	Variable	Coefficient	Z-Statistic	Marginal Effects		
				Fatal Injury	Severe Injury	No Injury
No Injury	Electric Bicyclist Gender	1.461 ***	3.37	−0.003	0.014	0.037
	Electric Bicyclist 18 – 30 Years old	−1.501 **	−2.35	−0.011	0.059	−0.041
	Electric Bicyclist 31 – 40 Years old	−1.471 **	−2.34	0.017	0.070	−0.042
	Electric Bicyclist 41 – 50 Years old	−2.359 ***	−3.47	0.018	0.065	−0.064
	Electric Bicyclist >50 Years old	−2.043 ***	−3.28	0.058	0.027	−0.056
	Vehicle Primary Liability	0.518 *	1.68	0.018	0.001	0.012
	Motorcycle	1.864 ***	2.95	−0.044	0.058	0.047
	Traffic Control	0.642 *	1.85	0.0137	−0.046	0.018

*, **, *** represent the significance levels are 10%, 5% and 1%.
'a' represents the marginal effect value doesn't equal to zero but with correcting to three decimal places.

According to Tab. 2, when automobile was determined as the equal liability, electric bicycle drivers would refer to suffer fatal injuries (1.792 ***). Conversely, electric drivers would suffer safely if automobile undertook the primary liabilities (0.518 ***). Electric bicycle driver gender (1.461 ***) also have positive impact on contributing to safety electric bicycle driver situation, which indicates that male electric bicycle driver would suffer less vulnerable to harm. Besides, compared with underage electric bicycle drivers, other electric bicycle driver age groups would be prone to keep dangerous situations (−1.501 **, −1.471 **, −2.359 *** and −2.043 ***).

In terms of vehicle type, when the automobile type is passenger car or truck, the electric bicycle drivers will refer to suffer bad injury, i.e. fatal injury (1.402 *** and 1.763 ***) and severe injury (0.636 ** and 1.177 ***), which also can reply to the moment when the automobile drivers choose to turn around (−1.774 * and −1.902 **) or turn left (−1.217 ** and −1.963 ***). Especially, when automobile driver turn right just leads to electric bicycle driver severe injury rather than fatal injury (−1.565 ***). Besides, when the crash involved motorcycle and electric bicycle, the latter driver could suffer less dangerous situation (1.864 ***).

Traffic control under would contribute to decrease the probability of electric bicycle drivers suffering severe injury (−0.352 **) and increase the probability of electric bicycle suffering no injury (0.642 *), which illustrates with the control by policemen and traffic lights, the electric bicyclists will experience more stable and safer situation. Road protection includes trees and fences which influence studied drivers' injury significantly. Trees will have a positive effect on decreasing possibility of having electric bicyclist fatal injury (−0.468 *) and severe injury (−0.0750 ***). Fences like protective pier just show their positive impact on declining electric bicycle driver severe injury (−0.992 ***), regardless of fatal injury. Occurred on segments like elevated roads, major bridges, narrowed lanes and tunnels will contribute to surge possibilities of suffering fatal (0.361 *) and severe injury (0.812 *) of electric bicyclists. Possibility of electric bicyclists driving on the strait roads suffering severe will rise (1.302 ***). When driving in the night, the electric bicyclists will suffer dangerous situation, no matter there's light or not (with lamp: 0.332 **, without lamp: 0.623 **).

4 Discussion

Separate models of injury severity levels by traffic periods provide precious insights about contributing factors affecting electric bicyclist injury severity in vehicle-electric bicycle crashes. The multinomial models manifest different factors will make various impacts on different injury severity levels. Forexample, when electric bicyclist crashing with motorcycle can electric bicyclist suffer safely with possibility of no injury surging. However, motorcycle do not make any difference in other injury severity. The study also observes that some factors are proved to be different significance in different injury severities. For instance, if crash happens before automobile driver turn left, the electric bicyclist will more likely suffer fatal injury, according to the marginal effect results, shown in marginal effects in Tab. 2.

4.1 Driver Characteristics

Not only electric bicyclists' own characteristics but automobile drivers' performance would have influences on e-bicyclists involved crash injury severity. The present study shows male e-bicyclist prefer to suffer no injury, which is in accord with the gender differences survey of Norway in accident risk with e – bikes(Fyhri et al., 2019). That is probably because male riders maintain lower rate of wrong – way travel(Qian et al., 2020), and relative proper riding way could contribute to better travel performance. Electric bicyclist age also makes some contributions, compared with underage drivers, the study observed that other electric bicyclists are prone to access harder injuries. The phenomenon could be explained by electric bicycle usually occupied by older drivers, so the young drivers account for less portion(Mohamed and Bigazzi, 2019).

4.2 Vehicle Characteristics

As for vehicle aspect, the study manifests that vehicle liability could reflect the electric bicyclist injury severity in a way, when the vehicle overtakes equal or secondary liability, then electric bicyclists will suffer more serious injuries. Vehicle type also affects e-bicyclist injury severity: when the automobile is passenger car or truck, the probability of occurring serious injury, which could be also manifested under different weather conditions(Uddin and Huynh, 2020). During driving, while turning left will cause electric bicyclist experience severe injury, even fatal injury; when vehicle turning right will cause electric bicyclist just experience severe injury. The phenomenon can also be illustrated in fatal factors in two-wheels analysis, which indicates that turning left is the most likely to cause accidents, accounting for 29.19%. Conversely, turning right only accounts for 2.96% (Yang et al., 2020).

4.3 Road Characteristics

Road characteristics include road hardware settings and road performances. Under control of traffic lights and policemen, the possibility of electric bicyclist suffering severe injury will decline. On contrary, running red light is a major cause of conflict for e-bikes(Bai et al., 2013). Turning without signaling is identified as an important risk factor for e-bike traffic accidents(Qian et al., 2020). The proportion of electric bikes running red lights is higher than that of traditional bikes, and when participants turn right, they run red lights more than 40 percent of the time(Schleinitz et al., 2019). Electric bicyclist injury severity also depends on roadside protection. Among the protection, guardrails or fences were designed to deter vehicle access to off-road areas and consequently prevent hitting rigid fixed objects alongside the road(e. g. trees, utility poles, traffic barriers, etc.)(Meng and Untaroiu, 2020). With the settlement of trees and fences, the electric bicyclist could reduce the possibility of suffering fatal and severe injury, which is in line with Meng and Untaroiu(2020). Occurring crash on the segments like tunnels, elevated route or narrowed line could also increase the possibility of electric bicyclist fatal and severe injury. The rate of red light traffic is highest at T-shaped intersections, and the rate of red light running is lower at four-arm intersections. It is found that traffic light violation rate is relatively high on roads without intersections(Schleinitz et al., 2019). Importantly, driving on the strait road could also happen severe injury. The study suggests that the strait road maintains unchanged eyesight and driving behaviours, which could lead to driving fatigue and distraction(Bin et al.,2021;Nosseir and EI-Sayed,2021).

5 Conclusions

The paper investigated electric bicycle driver injury severity under traffic peak periods using local traffic control department collected automobile and electric bicycle involved crashes of a city from 2006 to 2017. A quantity of significant variables were found in different electric bicyclist injury severity models. Specifically, it was found that 7 significant variables under electric bicyclist fatal injury (vehicle equal liability, passenger car or truck, vehicle turning around, turning left or right, etc.); 12 significant variables under electric bicyclist severe injury (passenger car or truck, vehicle turning around, turning left or right, roadside protection, etc.) and 8 significant variables introducing to no injury (male electric bicyclist, motorcycle, etc.).

The results obtained from this examine maintain a number of implications. Electric bicyclist injury severity affected by driver, vehicle and road characteristics. Firstly, male electric bicyclist and adult electric bicyclist experienced more safe driving circumstance, providing additional driving training or safety courses for specific groups. Secondly, while driving passenger car or truck would more likely to cause serious injury. Conversely, when the vehicle type turns to be motorcycle, electric bicyclist would prefer to stay safe, without injury occurring. This findings suggests that oversize vehicle should be pass-limited during traffic peak periods. Besides, when vehicle driver choose to turn around, turn left or right, the movements will have a positive influence on causing serious injury. It manifested that relative automobile driving behavior should be limited or punished during traffic peak periods, as well as traffic control. Finally, supervision of road segments like elevated road, tunnel and narrowed line should be noticed during traffic peak periods, like alternate peak open right of way.

However, the study has limitation of using inadequate electric bicyclist and vehicle driver characteristics. The model could be optimized according to interrelation among the quantities of variables and their influences on electric bicyclist injury severity, which deserves more detailed research.

6 Acknowledgements

This study is supported by Science and Technology Cooperation Program: In-Depth Accident Study for Improved Injury Assessment Tool and its Coupling with Driver Behaviours for Precise Injury Prevention (No. YS2019YFE010338).

References

[1] Arvin R, Khattak A J. Driving impairments and duration of distractions: Assessing crash risk by harnessing microscopic naturalistic driving data[J]. Accident Analysis and Prevention, 146. doi:10.1016/j.aap.2020.105733.

[2] Bai L, Liu P, Chen Y, et al. Comparative analysis of the safety effects of electric bikes at signalized intersections[J]. Transportation Research Part D-Transport And Environment, 2013, 20: 48-54. doi:10.1016/j.trd.2013.02.001.

[3] Bin H, Renwen C, Wang X, et al. Improved Fatigue Detection Using Eye State Recognition with HOG-LBP. Proceedings of the 9th International Conference on Computer Engineering and Networks[J]. Advances in Intelligent Systems and Computing, 2021(1143): 365-374. doi:10.1007/978-981-15-3753-0_35.

[4] Chen F, Chen S. Injury severities of truck drivers in single- and multi-vehicle accidents on rural highways[J]. Accident Analysis & Prevention, 2011, 43(5): 1677-1688.

[5] Fyhri A, Johansson O, Bjornskau T. Gender differences in accident risk with e-bikes-Survey data from Norway[J]. Accident Analysis and Prevention, 2019, 132. doi:10.1016/j.aap.2019.07.024.

[6] Gao W, Bai Z, Li H, et al. A study on cyclist head injuries based on an electric-bicycle to car accident

reconstruction[J]. Traffic Injury Prevention, 2020. doi:10.1080/15389588.2020.1821882.

[7] Han Y, He W, Shi L, et al. Helmet protective performance via reconstruction of electric two-wheeler rider's head-to-ground impact accidents[J]. International Journal Of Crashworthiness, 2020, 25(5): 493-504. doi:10.1080/13588265.2019.1616886.

[8] Huang Y, Zhou Q, Koelper C, et al. Are riders of electric two-wheelers safer than bicyclists in collisions with motor vehicles[J]. Accident Analysis and Prevention, 2020, 134. doi:10.1016/j.aap.2019.105336.

[9] Khorashadi A, Niemeier D, Shankar V, et al. Differences in rural and urban driver-injury severities in accidents involving large-trucks: An exploratory analysis[J]. Accident Analysis & Prevention, 2005, 37(5): 910-921.

[10] King C C S, Liu M, Patel S, et al. Injury patterns associated with personal mobility devices and electric bicycles: an analysis from an acute general hospital in Singapore[J]. Singapore Medical Journal, 2020, 61(2): 96-101. doi:10.11622/smedj.2019084.

[11] Meng Y, Untaroiu C. Numerical investigation of occupant injury risks in car-to-end terminal crashes using dummy-based injury criteria and vehicle-based crash severity metrics[J]. Accident Analysis and Prevention, 2020, 145. doi:10.1016/j.aap.2020.105700.

[12] Mohamed A, Bigazzi A. Speed and road grade dynamics of urban trips on electric and conventional bicycles[J]. Transportmetrica B-Transport Dynamics, 2019, 7(1): 1467-1480. doi:10.1080/21680566.2019.1630691

[13] Nosseir A, El-sayed M E. Detecting Cues of Driver Fatigue on Facial Appearance, 2021.

[14] Pahukula J, Hernandez S, Unnikrishnan A. A time of day analysis of crashes involving large trucks in urban areas[J]. Accident Analysis & Prevention, 2015, 75(5): 155-163.

[15] Qian Y, Sun Q, Fei G, et al. Riding behavior and electric bike traffic crashes: A Chinese case-control study[J]. Traffic Injury Prevention, 2021, 21(1): 24-28. doi:10.1080/15389588.2019.1696963.

[16] Schleinitz K, Petzoldt T, Kroeling S, et al. (E-)Cyclists running the red light - The influence of bicycle type and infrastructure characteristics on red light violations[J]. Accident Analysis and Prevention, 2019, 122: 99-107. doi:10.1016/j.aap.2018.10.002.

[17] Uddin M, Huynh N. Injury severity analysis of truck-involved crashes under different weather conditions[J]. Accident Analysis and Prevention, 2020, 141. doi:10.1016/j.aap.2020.105529.

[18] Wu Z, Zeng X, Wang L. A New Traffic Conflict Measure for Electric Bicycles at Intersections[J]. Promet -Traffic&Transportation, 2020, 32(3): 320.

[19] Yang N, Li Y, Liu T, et al. Analysis of fatal factors influencing accidents involving two-wheel electric vehicle drivers at intersections[J]. Legal Medicine, 2020, 45. doi:10.1016/j.legalmed.2020.101696.

分心行为对驾驶员视觉的影响研究

米 奇[1] 吉 柯[2]

(1.长沙理工大学交通运输工程学院;2.中南大学交通运输工程学院)

摘 要 在驾驶过程中,各种导致驾驶员漏掉信息或信息获取不足的分心行为,都极易导致交通事故的发生。因此,研究分心行为对驾驶员的视觉行为影响,具有重要意义。本文设计了分心驾驶模拟实验,共设置四种交通场景。在此基础上,基于聚类分析对视觉区域进行了划分,并对注视扫描路径、注视时间进行了对比。得出的结论可以为道路安全、驾驶员培训、交通设施设计等提供参考及理论依据。

关键词 眼动行为 聚类分析 注视区域 视觉特性

0 引 言

据国家数据网统计,我国2017年机动车交通事故总计182343起,交通事故死亡人数总计63772人,直接财产损失121311万元[1]。交管部门对交通事故的原因进行分析,发现与人相关的因素占96.4%,其中由驾驶人违法导致的交通事故占74%[2]。而在行车过程中,视觉提供了80%的交通信息[3],各种导致驾驶员漏掉信息或信息获取不足的分心行为,都极易导致交通事故的发生,因此,有必要对分心行为对驾驶员视觉行为的影响展开研究。

国内外学者对驾驶员的分心行为进行了诸多的研究,邢伟伦和王雪松利用自然驾驶观察法调查中国驾驶人使用手机的情况,发现驾驶人使用手机发送短信、通话和阅读三种情况最易造成驾驶员分心驾驶[4]。彭丹丹等人研究发现使用车载设备设置导航、车载手机拨号等任务时,无论是语音控制还是手动控制,都会影响驾驶人对车辆的操控能力[5]。马勇等人研究发现分心驾驶对眼跳行为也会产生一定的影响[6]。肖遥分析了使用手机软件、喝水、接听电话三种分心行为对交通安全和效率的影响[7]。马艳丽等人认为如果音乐节奏选择恰当、音量大小控制得当,将有利于驾驶人缓解疲劳[8]。Carney等针对青少年分心驾驶现象进行研究,在追尾事故中,发现超过75%的驾驶人发生分心驾驶行为,最频繁的分心驾驶行为是使用手机、向车外观看和与乘客交谈[9]。

目前大多数学者的研究是单一道路场景下的分心现象,对不同交通流条件下驾驶员视觉分心行为的研究较少。因此,本文分别设置了两个不同的交通流状态下的驾驶场景,对获得的实验数据进行对比分析,从而探究分心行为对驾驶员视觉行为特征的影响,以探究分心驾驶行为规律、指导驾驶员安全驾驶。

1 实验设计

1.1 实验场景

模拟场景为双向四车道城市快速路,车道宽度3.5m,道路全长17km,限速80km/h。分别设置自由流和跟驰流两种情况下的正常驾驶和分心驾驶四个实验场景进行对比。实验人员共10名(8名男性和2名女性),年龄在30岁到60岁之间,身体状况良好,驾驶里程均在5000km以上。如图1所示,实验中,视景仿真系统显示道路场景,实验人员驾驶模拟驾驶器、佩戴眼动仪。对实验人员进行两位数加减法的提问,从而模拟驾驶过程中的分心行为。共进行10次加减法的提问,每次设置5s的回答时间。

a) 驾驶模拟器　　　　　　　　　　b) 眼动仪

图1　试验环境

1.2 实验数据与指标选取

综合考虑各视觉行为特征,本实验选取注视时间作为特征数据。将数据值明显偏离其他数据值的数据作为异常数据。采用拉依达准则进行筛选[10]。拉依达准则的公式如下：

$$|x_i - \bar{x}| > 3\sigma \tag{1}$$

其中，x_i 为某具体数据值，$\bar{x}$ 为样本均值，σ 为样本方差。当某一数据 x_i 与其算术平均值 $\bar{x}$ 之差大于其三倍标准差时，该数据将被剔除。

2 注视区域划分

通过 Matlab 对实验数据运用 K-Means 聚类分析法进行聚类分析，分别选取 K 值为 4、5、6，得出最适合的注视区域划分方法。

2.1 自由流状态

2.1.1 不分心状态

比较三种结果发现：在自由流不分心驾驶状态下，注视区域分为四类较为合理，聚类结果如表1和图2所示。

自由流不分心状态下的聚类中心及样本数　　　　表1

类　别	聚类中心点坐标	样本数量
1	(215.39,95.46)	193
2	(323.71,243.17)	17
3	(448.07,255.23)	394
4	(499.72,318.23)	53

2.1.2 分心状态

根据对不分心状态进行聚类分析的结果，将分心状态下的数据按照 $K=4$ 进行聚类，聚类结果如表2、图3所示。

自由流分心状态下的聚类中心及样本数　　　　表2

类　别	聚类中心点坐标	样本数量
1	(347.22,195.77)	45
2	(412.04,232.26)	32
3	(307.29,234.97)	73
4	(208.11,161.29)	32

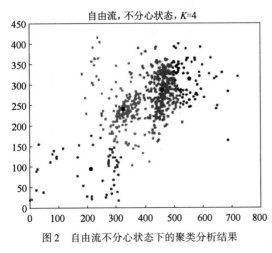

图2　自由流不分心状态下的聚类分析结果

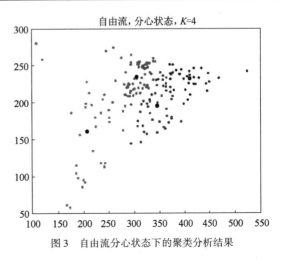

图3　自由流分心状态下的聚类分析结果

比较结果发现：在自由流分心状态下，驾驶员注视位置更加分散，且右上角注视位置明显增多。

2.2 跟驰流状态

2.2.1 不分心状态

比较三种结果发现:跟驰流不分心状态下分为六类较为合理。聚类分析结果如表3、图4所示。

表3 跟驰流不分心状态下的聚类中心及样本数

类 别	聚类中心点坐标	样 本 数 量
1	(333.70,231.13)	179
2	(576.81,300.72)	51
3	(240.80,331.71)	20
4	(470.47,323.61)	196
5	(209.01,93.69)	50
6	(454.50,247.91)	161

2.2.2 分心状态

根据对不分心状态进行聚类分析的结果,将分心状态下的数据按照 $K=6$ 进行聚类,聚类结果如表4和图5所示。

表4 跟驰流分心状态下的聚类中心及样本数

类 别	聚类中心点坐标	样 本 数 量
1	(233.59,263.81)	21
2	(135.08,205.72)	14
3	(173.52,219.60)	14
4	(283.39,265.92)	26
5	(316.14,237.81)	18
6	(244.77,204.48)	16

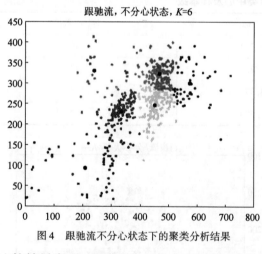

图4 跟驰流不分心状态下的聚类分析结果

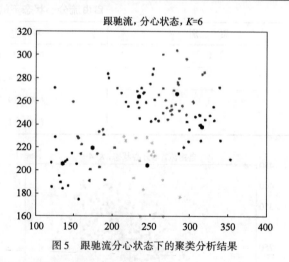

图5 跟驰流分心状态下的聚类分析结果

比较结果发现:跟驰流分心状态下注视点区域更广,且注视位置更加偏上。

3 不同驾驶环境下眼动行为的研究

3.1 注视扫描路径分析

扫描路径图由大小不一的圆及各个圆心的连线组成,可以显示注视点位置及各个注视点的注视时间等信息。圆心代表注视点位置,大小反映驾驶员在该点注视时间的长短。通过BeGaze3.7分别对四个场景下10s内的注视扫描路径图进行分析比较。得出如图6所示结果。

a) 自由流不分心状态　　　　　　　　b) 自由流分心状态

c) 跟驰流不分心状态　　　　　　　　d) 跟驰流分心状态

图 6　不同状态下的注视扫描路径

图 6a)中,驾驶员注视位置较为集中,基本集中在前方道路和引导车上。图 6b)中,驾驶员注视位置较为分散,且注视点位置偏上。图 6c)中,驾驶员注视位置较多,主要落在左右车道两个区域,且大多落在自身车道。图 6d)中,驾驶员注视位置偏上,且注视位置较远。

综合上述分析可知,对不同交通流状态的注视扫描路径来说,跟驰流状态下注视位置更为分散。对同一状态下不同驾驶行为的注视扫描路径来说,分心行为会导致驾驶员注视位置更加分散且位置偏上。

3.2　注视时间分析

3.2.1　注视持续时间分布分析

分别针对上述四种状态下的注视时间按 100ms 为时间间隔进行分区段统计,结果如图 7 所示。

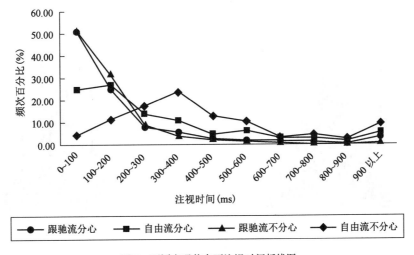

图 7　不同交通状态下注视时间折线图

由图 7 可知,四种交通状态下,注视时间大多皆集中在 0~400ms。驾驶时的分心行为会使得注视时间频次百分比明显增大,且在分心情况下,跟驰流明显大于自由流的时间频次百分比。

3.3.2 注视时间概率分布拟合

采用 Matlab 对实验数据进行正态分布拟合。图 8 种不同情况下注视时间正态分布拟合图。

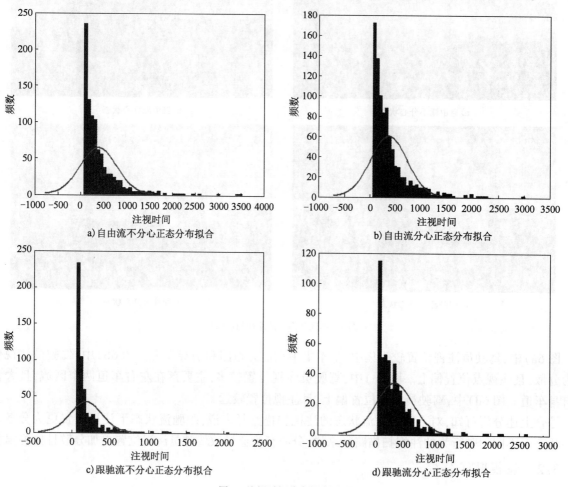

图 8　注视时间分布拟合图

从图 8 可以看出:正态分布拟合曲线与实验数据均有不同程度的偏差,因此认为,注视时间分布不服从正态分布。对实验数据取对数,再次运用 Matlab 进行数据拟合。如图 9 所示。

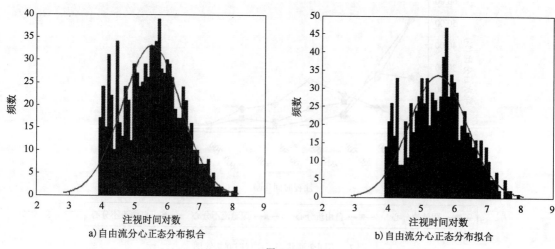

图 9

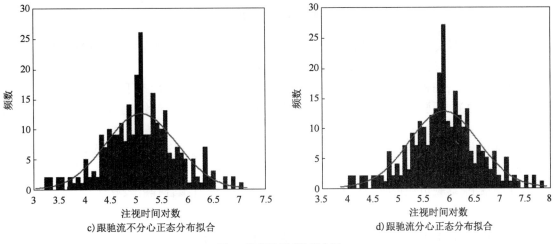

图 9 注视时间对数拟合图

与图 8 相比：对数据取对数再拟合更符合正态分布。因此认为：四种情况下驾驶员注视时间大体服从于对数正态分布。对注视时间取对数进行拟合优度检验，运用 Matlab 绘制 Probability Plot 图。如图 10 所示。

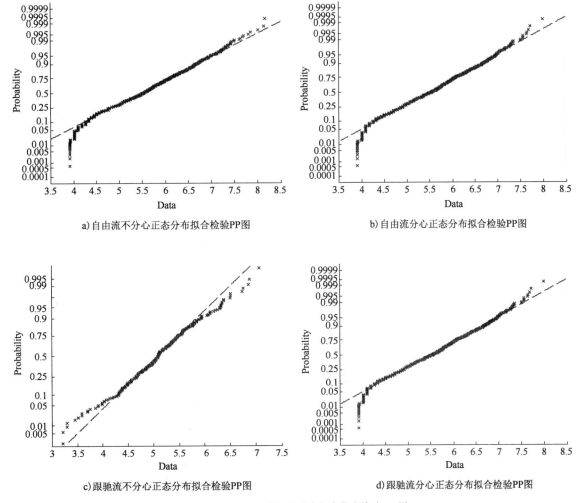

图 10 注视时间对数正态分布拟合优度检验 PP 图

图 10 中的倾斜直线为实际数据的平均值和标准差得出的参考线，蓝色曲线为实际实验数据。因此，可以得出：四种不同情况下的驾驶员注视时间符合对数正态分布。

4 结语

本文通过驾驶模拟实验,利用眼动仪收集驾驶员在驾驶过程中的眼动数据,使用 Matlab、BeGaze 等工具,对不同交通状态下驾驶员的眼动数据进行了分析对比,具体结论如下:

(1)自由流状态下,注视区域划分为四类较符合实际情况,而跟驰流状态下划分为六类更为合适。

(2)相较于自由流,跟驰流状态下注视位置更为分散,分心行为会导致驾驶员注视位置更加分散且位置偏上。

(3)注视时间大多皆集中在 0～400ms。驾驶时的分心行为会使得注视时间频次百分比明显增大,且跟驰流的分心行为导致注视时间频次百分比明显大于自由流状态。

(4)四种场景下,驾驶员注视时间均近似服从对数正态分布,且拟合程度较好。

参考文献

[1] 国家统计局. 中国统计年鉴[M]. 北京:中国统计出版社,2018.
[2] 毕建彬. 道路交通事故的人因分析与驾驶员可靠性研究[D]. 北京:北京交通大学,2012.
[3] 冀炳魁. 基于驾驶员视觉特性的驾驶行为预测方法研究[D]. 吉林:吉林大学,2014.
[4] 邢祎伦,王雪松. 基于自然驾驶的中国驾驶员驾驶使用手机行为研究[J]. 汽车与安全,2017(07):114-123.
[5] 彭丹丹,田伟,石京. 手机导航方式对驾驶行为的影响研究[J]. 中国安全科学学报,2017,27(09):39-44.
[6] 马勇,付锐,王畅,等. 视觉分心时驾驶人注视行为特性分析[J]. 中国安全科学学报,2013,23(05):10-14.
[7] 肖遥. 分心行为对交通安全和交通效率的影响分析与建模[D]. 北京:清华大学,2016.
[8] 马艳丽,高月娥,史惠敏. 车内音频娱乐系统操作对驾驶绩效的影响研究[J]. 武汉理工大学学报(交通科学与工程版),2017,41(3):454-457.
[9] Carney C, Harland KK, Mcgehee D V. Using event-triggered naturalistic data to examine the prevalence of teen driver distractions in rear-end crashes[J]. Journal of Safety Research, 2016,57:47-52.
[10] 陈建珍,潘勇制,李任波. 基于 Matlab 的二维实验数据粗差检测[J]. 误差与数据处理,2007(5):61-63.

交叉口未按规定让行的车辆驾驶行为研究

陶 锋[1]　邵海鹏[1]　苏松茂[2]

(1. 长安大学;2. 通号(郑州)电气化局)

摘　要　为研究交叉口机动车之间的让行行为特征及其影响因素,使用调查问卷的方法,对机动车驾驶员在交叉口的让行数据进行收集,利用 SPSS 统计软件对收集到的样本数据进行统计分析,研究了驾驶员个体特征和五种未按规定让行行为之间的关系,找出对驾驶员让行行为影响较为显著的因素,并对驾驶员违规驾驶的原因进行分析。研究表明,性别、驾照类型和对让行规定的了解程度与让行行为之间有显著的影响关系,对未按规定让行行为及其后果的认识不足是导致驾驶员违规行驶的主要原因。

关键词　驾驶行为　未按规定让行　方差分析　相关性分析　机动车让行

0 引言

据统计,不按规定让行违法行为所引起的交通事故死亡人数位居所有机动车交通违法行为之首[1]。

马明发现,在7种常见的机动车违法行为中,不按规定让行所造成的机动车与行人、自行车、机动车碰撞的事故分别占事故总数的60.95%、40.63%、17.13%[2]。

相关学者对未按规定让行的原因进行研究发现,未按规定让行多与驾驶员缺乏安全意识、赶时间有关。Kotikalapudi 和 Dissanayake 研究发现,与驾驶员个人特征相关的变量是造成大型卡车撞车事故的最重要因素[3-4]。Sun 等发现,大约90%的交通事故都是由驾驶员的失误导致,其中,不按规定让行是年轻驾驶员引起交通事故最主要的因素之一[5]。丁新国等发现不按规定让行与驾驶员缺乏道路交通法律意识及安全意识有关[6]。文进发现驾驶员的不良驾驶行为与其经济利益驱动或抢时间而挣道抢行、存在侥幸心理以及贪图方便等因素密切相关[7]。谭勉发现在无信号路口或支路路段,驾驶员不按规定让行的主要原因有:性格因素、驾驶习惯、经验不足、抢时间、相交道路无车辆或行人通过以及驾驶员过于自信等[8]。白云等发现相比于人口统计信息、骑车经历等因素,驾驶者的态度和驾驶技术对"抢行"行为更具影响[9-12]。艾冠韬等发现年龄较大的驾驶员和受教育程度高的驾驶员更倾向于在人行横道处让行[13]。

目前,对交叉口机动车之间未按规定让行行为的研究较少,因此,本文在现有文献研究的基础上,进一步对交叉口机动车之间的未按规定让行行为进行深入研究。

1 交叉口让行规则

机动车在无信号控制交叉口和无方向指示控制的信号控制交叉口的让行主要有以下三大原则:右侧先行、右转让左转、转弯让直行。环岛交叉口内,环岛外侧车辆需要让行环岛内侧车辆。具体如图1所示,图中的黄色车辆需要让行浅蓝色车辆。

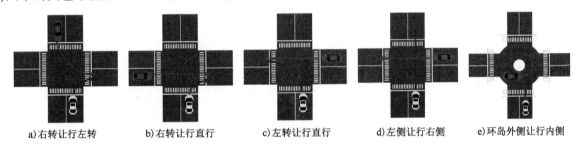

a) 右转让行左转　　b) 右转让行直行　　c) 左转让行直行　　d) 左侧让行右侧　　e) 环岛外侧让行内侧

图1　交叉口让行规则示意图

2 研究方法

本研究采用问卷调查法。问卷调查分为四部分:第一部分是驾驶员的基本信息;第二部分是驾驶员"未按规定让行"行为调查,调查驾驶员过去一段时间内发生"未按规定让行"行为的频率,选项按照 Likert 量表测量方法,频率顺序为:1-从不,2-很少,3-有时,4-经常,5-总是;第三部分是驾驶员的驾驶技术,Lajune 等[14]的驾驶技术调查表得到了较为广泛的应用,本研究驾驶技术量表借鉴了其中的一部分;第四部分是驾驶员抢行原因。

本次问卷调查共发放问卷500份,最终获得有效问卷465份,被调查者的个人属性与背景信息见表1。

个人属性与背景信息统计　　表1

个人信息变量	类　别	人　数	百分比(%)
性别	男	305	65.67
	女	160	34.33
年龄	25岁以下	216	46.33
	26~35岁	133	28.67
	36~45岁	68	14.67
	45岁以上	48	10.33

续上表

个人信息变量	类 别	人 数	百分比(%)
最高学历	高中/中专及以下	106	22.67
	大专	71	15.33
	本科	240	51.67
	硕士及以上	48	10.33
驾龄	1 年以内	172	37
	1～3 年	108	23.33
	4～6 年	87	18.67
	7～9 年	42	9
	10 年以上	56	12

3 数据统计与分析

3.1 驾驶员让行情况

在调查问卷中设立 5 种最为常见的让行情景：右转车让行左转车、右转车让行直行车、左转车让行直行车、左侧车道车辆让行右侧车道车辆、环岛外车辆让行环岛内车辆，来调查驾驶员的让行情况。图 2 为五种情景下的让行情况统计数据。

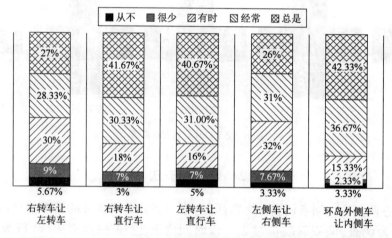

图 2 让行情况统计数据

从统计图中可以看出，右转车让行直行车、左转车让行直行车和环岛外侧车让行内侧车的让行情况大致相近，车辆的让行情况较好，70%的驾驶员能够做到经常和总是让行。右转车让行左转车和左侧车让行右侧车的让行情况大致相近，车辆的让行情况较差，55%的驾驶员可以做到经常和总是让行。

3.2 驾驶员个人属性对让行情况的影响分析

本部分是研究驾驶员的人属性与背景信息对其驾驶行为的影响。通过方差分析检验多组样本均值是否具有统计意义上的差异，研究性别、年龄、学历、驾龄、驾照类型、对让行规定的了解程度、驾驶技术这七个方面对其让行情况影响的显著性，结果见表 2。满分为 5 分，分值越高，让行表现越好。

从表中可以发现，性别对右转让直行、左转让直行和环岛外侧让内侧车辆表现出显著性影响，驾龄对环岛外侧车辆让行内侧车辆表现出显著性差异，驾照类型对五种让行行为均表现出显著性影响，对让行规定的了解程度对右转让行左转和左转让行直行表现出显著性影响，年龄、学历和驾驶技术对五种让行行为均没有表现出显著性差异。

个人信息与让行行为的方差分析 表2

个人属性		右转让行左转		右转让行直行		左转让行直行		左侧车辆让行右侧车辆		环岛外侧车辆让行内侧车辆	
		均值	P	均值	P	均值	P	均值	P	均值	P
性别	(1)男	3.67	0.294	4.12	0.010**	4.09	0.005**	3.72	0.435	4.21	0.038*
	(2)女	3.52		3.79		3.70		3.62		3.96	
年龄	(1)25岁以下	3.67	0.909	4.09	0.497	3.99	0.224	3.71	0.461	4.20	0.071
	(2)26~35岁	3.56		3.86		3.83		3.59		3.95	
	(3)36~45岁	3.61		4.02		3.84		3.64		4.00	
	(4)45岁以上	3.58		4.03		4.29		3.94		4.42	
学历	(1)高中、中专及以下	3.72	0.195	4.00	0.463	4.09	0.059	3.76	0.293	4.19	0.124
	(2)大专	3.89		4.17		4.24		3.89		4.39	
	(3)本科	3.52		3.93		3.79		3.63		4.01	
	(4)硕士及以上	3.48		4.16		4.06		3.48		4.13	
驾龄	(1)1年以内	3.77	0.280	4.03	0.461	3.91	0.850	3.86	0.120	4.32	0.005**
	(2)1~3年	3.57		4.07		3.99		3.50		4.10	
	(3)4~6年	3.41		3.80		3.89		3.64		3.75	
	(4)7~9年	3.60		4.08		4.05		3.62		4.14	
	(5)10年以上	3.77		4.03		3.91		3.86		4.32	
驾照类型	(1)C2	3.25	0.026*	3.26	0.017*	3.19	0.023*	3.26	0.032*	3.27	0.019*
	(2)C1	3		3.16		3.15		3.14		3.26	
	(3)B2	3.23		3.41		3.51		3.43		3.53	
	(4)B1	3.46		3.76		3.64		3.67		3.64	
	(5)A3	3.91		4.04		4.11		4.18		4.11	
	(6)A2	3.74		4.01		3.84		3.86		4.02	
	(7)A1	4		4.1		4.18		4.27		4.18	
驾驶技术	(1)很差	3.50	0.890	4.38	0.646	4.00	0.553	4.00	0.723	4.00	0.760
	(2)较差	3.40		4.00		3.85		3.80		4.25	
	(3)一般	3.65		3.97		3.86		3.70		4.08	
	(4)良好	3.66		4.08		4.09		3.70		4.19	
	(5)优秀	3.57		3.86		3.86		3.53		4.02	
对让行规定的了解程度	(1)完全不了解	2.88	0.015*	3.81	0.249	3.50	0.013*	3.44	0.487	3.81	0.299
	(2)了解一点	3.60		3.85		3.71		3.61		4.03	
	(3)比较了解	3.59		4.12		4.15		3.70		4.17	
	(4)非常了解	3.87		4.06		4.04		3.81		4.24	

注：*在0.05级别（双尾），相关性显著；**在0.01级别（双尾），相关性显著。

从均值可以看出，不同个人属性的驾驶员在让行行为方面表现出的差异性。男性在五种让行行为方面的均值全高于女性，说明男性的让行表现更好。45岁以上的驾驶员比其他年龄段的驾驶员让行情况更好，能够做到经常和总是让行，26~35岁的驾驶员让行表现最差，呈现出"中间低、两头高"的趋势。学历方面，大专学历的让行表现最好，本科学历的让行表现最差。驾龄在1年以内和10年以上的驾驶员让行表现较好，和年龄一样，呈现出"中间低、两头高"的趋势。C类驾驶证的让行表现最差，A类驾驶证的让行表现最好，总体而言，驾照类型等级越高，让行表现越好。驾驶技术方面，技术最差的让行表现最好。

对让行规定的掌握程度方面,驾驶员对让行规定越了解,让行表现越好。

3.3 相关性分析

相关性分析用于分析两个变量之间的相关程度,下面通过相关性分析研究个人属性和让行行为之间的相关程度。结果见表3。

个人信息与让行行为的相关性分析　　　　　表3

皮尔逊相关性	右转让行左转	右转让行直行	左转让行直行	左侧车辆让行右侧车辆	环岛外侧让行内侧
性别	−0.061	−0.149**	−0.161**	−0.045	−0.120*
年龄	−0.028	−0.027	0.030	0.034	0.007
学历	−0.093	−0.007	−0.086	−0.088	−0.076
驾龄	−0.061	0.000	0.038	−0.075	−0.088
驾照类型	0.114*	0.228**	0.152**	0.211**	0.243**
驾驶技术	0.020	−0.041	0.027	−0.071	−0.008
对让行规定的了解程度	0.148*	0.089	0.149**	0.089	0.107

注:*在0.05级别(双尾),相关性显著;**在0.01级别(双尾),相关性显著。

性别和右转让行直行、左转让直行、环岛外侧让行内侧车辆有显著的负相关关系。驾照类型和五种让行行为均表现出明显的正相关关系,可能是因为驾驶证类型等级越高,驾驶人的职业性越高,驾驶人承担的安全责任和风险越高,所以驾驶证类型等级越高,驾驶员的让行表现更好。对让行规定的了解程度和右转让行左转、左转让直行表现出明显的正相关关系,说明驾驶员不按规定让行可能和驾驶员对让行规定的不了解有关。年龄、学历、驾龄、驾驶技术和五种让行行为表现出一定的相关关系,但不具有统计学意义。

3.4 致因分析

为了分析驾驶员未按规定让行的原因,从以下四个方面做了相关调查:对未按规定让行行为及其后果的认识、跟随抢行的频率、特殊情况下的抢行频率、未注意到让行标志、标线。结果见表4。

未按规定让行行为的原因调查　　　　　表4

	您认为哪种行为最危险?	
	(1)分心驾驶	6.00%
	(2)疲劳驾驶	10.00%
	(3)饮酒驾驶	61.30%
	(4)超速驾驶	13%
	(5)不按规定让行	9.70%
	您认为哪种行为最不危险?	
对未按规定让行行为及其后果的认识	(1)分心驾驶	21.00%
	(2)疲劳驾驶	10.00%
	(3)饮酒驾驶	6.70%
	(4)超速驾驶	15.00%
	(5)不按规定让行	47.30%
	您认为哪种行为造成的后果最严重?	
	(1)分心驾驶	3.00%
	(2)疲劳驾驶	8.00%
	(3)饮酒驾驶	47.70%

续上表

对未按规定让行行为及其后果的认识	(4)超速驾驶	33.70%
	(5)不按规定让行	7.70%
	根据调查:未按规定让行占据"十大机动车死亡事故肇事原因"的首位,超过了违反交通信号、酒后驾驶和无证驾驶三种交通违法行为之和,您对这一调查结果是否感到惊讶?	
	(1)和我了解的情况基本一致	30.30%
	(2)有点意外	46.70%
	(3)十分意外	23.00%
跟随抢行	前方车辆没有遵循让行规定,发生"抢行"行为,您会?	
	(1)跟随前车一起通过	12%
	(2)遵循让行规定,停车让行	88%
特殊情况下的抢行行为	您在什么情况下会出现"抢行"的行为?	
	(1)上班	8.1%
	(2)急事	53.81%
	(3)看情况	23.81%
	(4)其他	14.29%
未注意到让行标志、标线	您是否有过没注意到"停车让行"或者"减速让行"标志的情况?	
	(1)总是	19%
	(2)经常	26.3%
	(3)有时	27.3%
	(4)很少	19.7%
	(5)从不	7.7%

4 结 语

本次研究通过调查问卷对"未按规定让行"这一驾驶行为进行研究,分析得出以下主要结论:

(1)右转让行直行、左转让行直行、环岛外侧让行内侧的让行情况分布基本一致,让行表现良好。右转车让行左转车和左侧车让行右侧车的让行情况分布基本一致,让行表现较差。

(2)通过方差分析和相关性分析,性别、驾驶证类型、对让行规定的了解程度对未按规定让行行为具有显著影响。交管部门和驾培部门可以从以上三个方面着手制定相应的管理政策和方法,以减少违规情况的发生。

(3)通过对未按规定让行行为的原因分析,发现大多数驾驶员尚未正确认识未按规定让行行为及其后果,很多驾驶员是因为没有注意到让行标志标线而违规。今后,需要加强对驾驶员的安全教育,在设计交通标志标线时要从驾驶员视角出发,考虑驾驶人员对标志标线的视认情况。

参考文献

[1] 公安部道路交通安全研究中心.中国大城市道路交通发展研究报告之四[M].北京:中国建筑工业出版社,2018.

[2] 马明.基于多元统计方法的城市道路交通事故分析研究[D].武汉:武汉理工大学,2010.

[3] Kotikalapudi S, Dissanayake S. Study of characteristics and evaluation of severity affecting factors associated with large-truck crashes[J]. Advances in Transportation Studies, 2013, 108(29):19-34.

[4] Kotikalapudi S, Dissanayake S. Characteristics and Contributory Causes Associated with Large-Truck Crashes and Countermeasures for Mitigation[C]. Transportation Research Board Meeting, 2013.

[5] Sun D, Benekohal R F, Estrada H. Comparative analysis of the attitude and behavior of young drivers' use

of two-way two-lane highways[J]. Advances in Transportation Studies, 2008, 15(15):75-84.

[6] 丁新国,赵云胜,陈瑞晶.区域道路交通事故驾驶员原因的灰色关联分析[J].中国安全生产科学技术,2008(05):96-99.

[7] 文进.道路交通伤害的病例交叉研究[D].成都:四川大学,2005.

[8] 谭勉.运营驾驶员不安全驾驶行为检测方法研究[D].西安:长安大学,2016.

[9] 白云.北京市小型机动车驾驶者"抢行"行为及其影响因素研究[D].北京:清华大学,2009.

[10] 石京,陶立,白云.北京市机动车驾驶员"抢行"行为及影响因素分析[J].中国安全科学学报,2010,20(08):30-39.

[11] 石京,陶立,芦杰.基于介入型实验的机动车驾驶员"抢行"行为研究[J].交通信息与安全,2011,29(3):69-73.

[12] 陶立.机动车驾驶员不当驾驶行为特征与判别指标分析[D].北京:清华大学,2012.

[13] 艾冠韬,邓院昌,舒凡.广州市机动车人行横道让行行为及影响因素分析[J].中国安全生产科学技术,2016,12(12):133-137.

[14] Timo Lajunen, Heikki Summala. Driving experience, personality, and skill and safety-motive dimensions in drivers' self-assessments[J]. Personality and Individual Differences,1995,19(3).

Research on Management of Traffic Anomie Behavior Based on Theory of Reasoned Action

Guohua Liang Chenchen Dong Yanwen Han

(University of Chang'an, College of transportation engineering)

Abstract According to behavioral intentions, a modified reasoned action model is proposed for two anomie behaviors of non-motor vehicles mixed into the motorway and forced lane changing, replace the subjective normative variables in the reasonable behavior model with two variables that can affect typical traffic anomie behaviors, psychological factors and normative identity. Logit model is used to analyze the variables of typical traffic anomie behaviors, from behavior attitudes, psychological factors, and normative identity. Analysis of the impact on typical traffic anomie behaviors. For non-motor vehicles mixed into the motorway, the factors that have the greatest impact on behavioral intentions are psychological factors and normative identity; for forced lane changes, the factors that have the greatest impact on behavioral intentions are behavior attitudes. From the two aspects of subjective regulation and publicity and education countermeasures to regulate traffic behavior are proposed to provide a basis for effectively stopping typical traffic anomie behaviors.

Keywords Traffic anomie behavior Theory of reasoned action Traffic management Traffic safety

0 Introduction

The road traffic participants expect to reduce the delay of traveling and get to the destination quickly. The habits of thinking and the behaviour is varying from people to people, and the travel need of residents which is diversified and personalized contribute to traffic loading miserably. These problems continue to cause intense competition among road traffic participants for limited traffic resources. When the contradiction between traffic supplied and demand is difficult to alleviate or the road facilities are not perfect, phenomena such as illegal lane change, non-motor vehicles mixed into the motorway, and competition between people and vehicles frequently appear. Motor vehicles forcibly change lanes in the intersection control area, and non-motor vehicles invade the motor vehicle lanes in the road section, which are regarded as two typical traffic anomie behaviours, have an important impact on the safety and efficiency of the intersection operation, and are a major traffic safety hazard in road traffic operations. The forced lane change of a motor vehicle in the intersection control area refers to the traffic behavior that the motor vehicle enters the solid line area of the intersection entrance lane and compacts the line due to various reasons to achieve the demand for lane change. The intrusion of non-motorized vehicles into the motor vehicle lane on the road sections to refer to the traffic behavior of non-motorized vehicles actively invading the motor vehicle lane in order to pursue higher driving efficiency when the non-motor vehicle lane is not occupied and blocked.

Foreign research on anomie behavior is earlier, but for traffic anomie behavior, there are more studies related to traffic safety, and there is less research on traffic efficiency. Some scholars have predicted and intervened in the study of illegal driving behavior through the theory of planned behavior. The results show that young and skilled drivers are particularly prone to traffic violations as shown by Sonja E. Forward (2009). Singh Karandeep and Li Baibing (2012) used the information provided by the loop detector to consider the time-varying nature of the driver's lane change operation, and used many discrete choice models to model the lane change probability. Guangnan Zhang et al. (2014) found that several factors are significantly related to the possibility of speeding and drunk driving, especially male drivers, private cars, lack of street lights at night, and poor visibility. Afghari Amir Pooyan et al. (2019) found that drivers tend to commit minor speed limit violations, regardless of causal factors. Through questionnaire surveys and logit model research, Ma Changxi et al. (2020) revealed the potential relationship between the personal characteristics of electric bike riders and illegal occupation of motor lanes.

The research on anomie behavior in our country started late. At first, there were more discussions on the fields of sociology and psychology. Shu Xiaobing (2000) discussed the causes of anomie behavior from a sociological perspective, and believed that traffic laws, psychological factors, management, infrastructure, and economic factors are the five main reasons that affect anomie behavior in urban traffic. Based on the improved planning behavior theory, Zou Qingru (2011) conducted research and analysis on pedestrians' traffic anomie behaviors, and found that pedestrians often have one or more of the psychological behaviors, and she believes that strengthening subjective norms can reduce pedestrians' intention to violate the rules, but the influence is weak. Wang Lin (2015) studied the characteristics of the lane-changing behavior of urban road vehicles, and the results showed that the influence between the frequency of lane-changing and the density of traffic flow is mutual. He Lei (2017) conducted a research on the illegal lane change behavior at signal-controlled intersections, described the characteristics of illegal lane change behavior in the intersection guide lane line area. Li Xing et al. (2019) conducted research and analysis on the behavior characteristics and influencing factors of pedestrians and non-motorized crossing violations during the traffic signal light transition period, and studied the behavior characteristics and influencing factors of anomie behaviors in different periods. Shi Ningning (2018) analyzes the key influencing factors by studying the frequency distribution of driver accidents and based on the zero inflation model.

In summary, most scholars' research on anomie behavior is the analysis of its influencing factors and traffic safety, and certain results have been achieved. However, there are many factors that affect drivers' traffic anomie behavior. Relatively speaking, the existing research cannot provide more explanations for the changes in driver behavior decisions. The reasoned action model has been widely used in various fields of sociology, and its research results also show the predictive effectiveness of the model. Therefore, the driver is selected as the survey object, based on the theory of reasoned action, and the theory of reasoned action is expanded according to the actual situation. Through the method of questionnaire, regression analysis is used to conduct research from the psychological level, to explore the influencing factors of forced lane changing and mixed traffic between vehicles and non-motor vehicles, and propose corresponding traffic management countermeasures.

1 Methodology

1.1 Theory of Reasoned Action

Reasoned action theory was first proposed by AJZEN and FISH-BEIN. This theory assumes that most behaviors in psychology are within the control range, and that under certain circumstances, the specific behavioral intentions formed by individuals will affect their behavior. The theory of reasoned action studies the specific behavior intention, which is controlled by will. Under certain circumstances, a person's specific behavior intention affects the subsequent behavior. According to the reasonable behavior model, personal factors and social norms are the main factors that determine the specific behavior intention, which can be expressed by Eq. (1):

$$\text{TB} \sim \text{TBI} = [A_{\text{act}}]w_0 + [\text{SN}]w_1 \qquad (1)$$

Among them, TB represents typical traffic anomie behavior, TBI represents typical traffic anomie behavior intention, An act represents behavior attitude towards forced lane changing and mixed traffic between vehicles and non-motor vehicles behavior, and SN represents subjective norm. w_0 and w_1 are the weights of typical traffic anomie behaviors and subjective norms, respectively. Behavioral attitude A_{act} refers to the positive or negative evaluation of typical traffic anomie behaviors when an individual travels in a certain traffic environment. Subjective norms are the pressure from society or other groups when an individual performs the behavior of forced lane changing or mixed traffic between vehicles and non-motor vehicles, generally from the evaluation made by relatives and friends.

1.2 Establishment of Model

According to the attribution analysis of typical traffic anomie behavior, this paper replaces the subjective norm variables in the reasonable behavior model with two variables: psychological factors that can affect typical traffic anomie behavior and normative identity. In fact, whether travelers will make typical traffic anomie behavior has a great relationship with the individual's risk perception of traffic anomie behavior and the traffic environment at that time. The traffic environment is mainly the actual traffic conditions, and the first external traffic information that travelers receive is the traffic environment. If the traffic environment meets the driver's psychological expectations, it is not easy for drivers to make anomie behavior. If the traffic environment at that time does not meet the driver's psychological expectations, the possibility of drivers' anomie behavior will inevitably increase. Traffic anomie behavior is closely related to traffic environment from decision-making to implementation, so this paper adds variable traffic environment to describe the research object of this paper more accurately and meticulously, thus forming a reasonable behavior correction model for typical traffic anomie behavior [Eq. (2)]:

$$\text{TB} \sim \text{TBI} = [A_{\text{act}}]w_0 + [\text{SNI}]w_1 + [M]w_2 \qquad (2)$$

In the formula, SNI represents normative identity, M represents psychological factors, and w_2 is the weight of M.

2 Analysis of Typical Traffic Anomie Behavior Variables Based on Reasoned Action Modification Model

2.1 Survey Design and Data Collection

This study uses questionnaire survey as the main measurement method. The main content of the questionnaire is the corresponding indicators of the typical traffic anomie behavior intention, a total of 10, the questionnaire uses an online survey, and a total of 806 valid questionnaires were collected. The sample situation is shown in Tab. 1.

Basic Characteristics of the Sample   Tab. 1

Statistical variables	group	frequency	percentage
age	Under the age of 18	73	9.06%
	18-30 years old	410	50.87%
	31-45 years old	214	26.55%
	46-60 years old	105	13.03%
	Over 60 years old	4	0.5%
gender	male	474	58.81%
	female	332	41.19%
Education level	Junior high school and below	42	5.21%
	High school diploma	110	13.65%
	Bachelor degree/junior college degree	373	46.28%
	Master degree or above	281	34.86%
porfession	student	349	43.3%
	Government and public institution staff	166	20.6%
	Corporate staff	174	21.59%
	Freelancers	57	7.07%
	others	60	7.44%
way to travel	Bicycle	131	16.25%
	Electric bicycle	465	57.69%
	Car(as a driver)	210	26.05%

2.2 Variable Analysis and Design

According to the questionnaire data, the dependent variables are two typical traffic anomie behaviors, namely, non-mixed traffic and forced lane change. In order to study this kind of traffic anomie behavior more accurately, the dependent variables are classified, and the frequency of traffic anomie behavior is divided into three categories, which are rare, frequent and always occurring. Behavioral attitude, psychological factors and normative identity are the main independent variables of the reasonable behavior modification model, but they can not be observed directly, and need to be measured by explicit variables in the questionnaire. Independent variables are divided into three dimensions. The first dimension examines the frequency of typical traffic anomie behaviors and the traffic conditions under which such traffic anomie behaviors occur, that is, the influence of behavior and attitude on traffic anomie behaviors. The second dimension is mainly Q12, which examines the influence of psychological factors on typical traffic anomie behaviors. The third dimension includes Q9 and Q10, the social and personal evaluation of traffic anomie behaviors, which also regulates the influence of identity on typical traffic anomie behaviors.

In this paper, Logit model is selected to analyze the variables of typical traffic anomie behavior, and its expression is:

$$\text{Logit}(P\tfrac{i}{j}) = \alpha_0 + \beta X \tag{3}$$

In the formula, P_i represents typical traffic anomie behavior, and takes the rare cases as reference, α_0 is intercept, β represents regression coefficient, and X is independent variable in three aspects: behavior attitude, psychological factors and normative identity.

Variable Definition Tab. 2

Variable name		Questionnaire options
Typical traffic anomie behavior	Frequency of non-motor vehicles mixed into the motorway	Q6
	Frequency of forced lane changes	Q7
Behavior attitude	Endure time	Q8
	The impact of mixed	Q9
	The attitude of forcibly changing lanes	Q10
	Risk perception of forced lane change	Q11
Psychological factors	Herd mentality	Q12
	habit	Q13
Code of conduct identity	Public opinion	Q14
	The impact of traffic order	Q15

2.3 Variable Analysis of Anomie Behavior

The frequency of motor vehicle and non-motor vehicle mixed and the frequency of forced lane change are classified as "rarely", "frequently" and "always". The questionnaire selection frequency of 0–2 is "rarely" and recorded as Grade Ⅰ, the questionnaire selection frequency of 3–6 is "frequently" and recorded as Grade Ⅱ, and the questionnaire selection frequency of 7-10 is "always" and recorded as Grade Ⅲ. Using multiple Logistic regression method, the frequency of motor vehicle and non-motor vehicle mixed behavior and the frequency of forced lane change behavior are classified as dependent variable, and the influence of patience time, motor vehicle and non-motor vehicle mixed behavior, forced lane change behavior, herd mentality, habit, public opinion and traffic order are taken as independent variables, and the questionnaire data about machine-non-mixed traffic anomie behavior is imported into SPSS26.0 for multiple logistic regression, taking Grade Ⅰ as a reference, that is, "rarely occurring" as a reference class, and the following conclusions are drawn in Tab. 3 and Tab. 4.

Multi-classification Logistic Regression Results of Non-motor Vehicles Mixed into the Motorway Tab. 3

	Independent variable	Model 1 (Grade Ⅱ)			Model 2 (Grade Ⅲ)		
		Regression coefficients	Standard error	Exp(B)	Regression coefficients	Standard error	Exp(B)
Psychological factors	Herd mentality	0.529	0.294	1.696	1.313	1.094	1.573
	habit	1.592	0.430	4.913	1.021	1.290	3.396
Behavior attitude	Endure time	−0.173	0.145	0.841	2.343	0.885	0.540
	The impact of mixed	−0.471	0.245	0.625	−1.373	1.001	0.254
Code of conduct identity	The impact of traffic order	0.272	0.246	1.312	0.937	0.940	1.166
	Public opinion	0.418	0.369	0.658	−.540	1.142	0.404

Multi-classification Logistic Regression Results of Forced Lane Change Anomie Behavior Tab. 4

	Independent variable	Model 1 (Grade Ⅱ)			Model 2 (Grade Ⅲ)		
		Regression coefficients	Standard error	Exp(B)	Regression coefficients	Standard error	Exp(B)
Psychological factors	Herd mentality	1.644	0.601	5.175	0.453	0.443	3.717
	habit	0.758	0.780	2.134	1.223	0.538	2.776

	Independent variable	Model 1 (Grade II)			Model 2 (Grade III)		
		Regression coefficients	Standard error	Exp(B)	Regression coefficients	Standard error	Exp(B)
Behavior attitude	Endure time	0.873	0.347	2.394	−0.616	0.204	10.407
	The impact of mixed	−0.296	0.687	0.744	−1.371	0.370	0.253
Code of conduct identity	The impact of traffic order	−0.404	0.377	0.667	0.154	0.482	2.551
	Public opinion	0.276	0.569	1.318	−0.907	0.557	0.583

3 Results and Discussion

Through analysis, it can be seen that the influence of behavioral intention on the non-motor vehicles mixed into the motorway behavior is tested by the significance test, and The behavior of cyclists who choose non-motorized vehicles to drive into the motorway is mainly affected by behavioral intention. In terms of psychological factors, the regression coefficient of herd mentality is 0.529, but it is not significant ($z = 1.728$, $p = 0.072 > 0.05$), which means that herd mentality does not have a significant impact on the traffic anomie behavior of non-motor vehicles mixed into the motorway; The regression coefficient of habit is 1.592, and it is significant at 0.01 level ($z = 2.811$, $p = 0.000 < 0.01$), which means that habit will have a significant positive influence on the traffic anomie. In terms of behavior and attitude, the effects of endurance time and non-motorized vehicles entering motor lanes significantly negatively affect the behavior of mixed traffic, and the coefficients are −0.173 and −0.471. In terms of normative identity, the influence of traffic order has a significant impact on people's choice of machine-out-of-mixed behavior, with coefficients of 0.272. From this, it can be concluded that psychological factors and subjective norms have the greatest influence on behavior intention for mixed traffic between vehicles and non-motor vehicles. When studying countermeasures, we can put forward more effective measures for these two aspects.

Through the analysis, it can be seen that the behavioral intention has a significant influence on the anomie behavior of forcibly changing lanes, while public opinion, herd mentality and habits are all non-significant influencing factors. In terms of psychological factors, the regression coefficients of herd mentality and habit are large, but they are not significant, which means that herd mentality will not have a significant impact on the anomie behavior of mixed traffic; In terms of behavior attitude, forced lane change attitude and risk perception both significantly affect the behavior of non-mixed traffic. In terms of normative identity, traffic order and public opinion have no significant influence on the anomie behavior of forced lane change. From this, it can be concluded that the behavioral attitude is the most influential factor on behavioral intention for the anomie behavior of forcibly changing lanes. When studying countermeasures, we can put forward more effective measures in this respect.

4 Conclusions

Through the revised reasoned action model, two variables that can affect typical traffic anomie behaviors are used to replace the subjective normative variables in the reasoned action model, and the behavior intention has a significant impact on typical traffic anomie behaviors. For non-motor vehicles mixed into the motorway, the factors that have the greatest impact on behavioral intentions are psychological factors and normative identity; for forced lane changes and anomie behaviors, the most influential factors on behavioral intentions are attitudes.

According to the revised model, the management countermeasures for typical traffic anomie behaviors are proposed from two aspects: subjective norms and publicity and education to provide a basis for effectively stopping typical traffic anomie behaviors.

(1) Improve self-quality and construct individual subjective norms.

Demand can affect behavior. Psychological needs and needs stimulate people's proactiveness and continue to move forward. Maslow's hierarchy of needs theory is introduced in regulating traffic behaviors to provide a theoretical basis and ideas for traffic education and publicity. The construction of traffic publicity and education goals should pay full attention to the goal structure, transform rigid legal provisions into the improvement of people's moral quality, build subjective norms, and effectively prevent people from choosing traffic anomie behaviors.

The abundance of traffic education and publicity, the clarity of pertinence, and whether it can increase the participation of travelers will all affect the effect of improving people's sense of standardization. For students, they mainly focus on class lectures, so that the concept of choosing to regulate traffic behavior is deep-rooted, and psychologically abandon traffic anomie behavior; for staff, it is unrealistic for them to receive instruction in class, so they should be taught in the usual way. During the period of time, attention is paid to publicity, and when people choose traffic anomie behaviors such as mixed traffic or forced lane changes, both punishment and education are emphasized to build people's subjective norms. In addition, people of different ages and different levels of education should receive different education content. In the face of different groups of people, pay attention to teach students in accordance with their aptitude.

(2) Develop education and publicity to create a good social atmosphere.

Propaganda and education to regulate traffic behaviors, through different communication methods, use communication skills to improve the effect of traffic propaganda and education, and use relevant theories of communication to subtly infiltrate correct traffic behaviors and positive attitudes into people's lives to create a norm The social atmosphere of traffic behavior.

Through propaganda to arouse the empathy of the public, we can create story-line public service advertisements, through the dim lens effect and sad background music to set off a heavy atmosphere, conveying that anomie traffic behavior will cause serious consequences, and then produce common Emotional psychology arouses the driver's sense of responsibility. In the era of new media, the Internet has become one of the important channels for the public to obtain information. Therefore, it is possible to establish different levels of traffic official Weibo, official WeChat public account and other Internet platforms with frequent contact with netizens, and publish traffic-related new information on such platforms. Promulgated regulations, short publicity videos, public service advertisements, animations related to traffic safety and management, real-time traffic-related information, events, and opinions, infiltrate correct traffic behaviors and positive public opinion attitudes into people's lives. Let people unknowingly get the correct information about traffic while surfing the Internet.

References

[1] Forward Sonja E. The theory of planned behaviour: The role of descriptive norms and past behaviour in the prediction of drivers' intentions to violate[J]. Transportation Research Part F: traffic psychology and behaviour, 2009, 12(3):198-207.

[2] Singh Karandeep, Li Baibing. Discrete Choice Modelling for Traffic Densities with Lane-Change Behaviour[J]. Procedia-Social and Behavioral Sciences, 2012, 43:367-374.

[3] Zhang Guangnan, Kelvin K W Yau, Gong Xiangpu. Traffic violations in Guangdong Province of China: Speeding and drunk driving[J]. Accident Analysis and Prevention, 2014,64:30-40.

[4] Afghari Amir Pooyan, Haque Md Mazharul, Washington Simon. Applying fractional split model to examine

the effects of roadway geometric and traffic characteristics on speeding behavior[J]. Traffic injury prevention, 2019: 1-7.

[5] MaChangxi, Zhou Jibiao, Yang Dong, et al. Personal Characteristics of e-Bike Riders and Illegal Lane Occupation Behavior[J]. Journal of Advanced Transportation, 2020,1840975.

[6] Shu Xiaobing. Analysis on the Reasons of Anomie Behavior in Urban Traffic[J]. Urban Planning, 2000, 24(3),21-25.

[7] Zou Qingru. Traffic behavior analysis based on improved planning behavior theory[D]. Beijing: Beijing Jiaotong University,2011.

[8] Wang Lin. Research on the characteristics of lane-changing behavior of urban road vehicles[D]. Beijing: Beijing Jiaotong University,2015.

[9] He Lei. Research on the impact of illegal lane changes at signalized intersections on traffic efficiency[D]. Xi'an: Chang'an University,2017.

[10] Li Xing, Yang Xiaobao, Zheng Tianyu. Analysis of illegal crossing behavior and its influencing factors during the transition of traffic signal lights[J]. Comprehensive Transportation, 2019, 41(01):63-68.

[11] Shi Ningning. Analysis of the frequency distribution of driver accidents and its influencing factors[D]. Beijing: Beijing Jiaotong University,2018.

三对应原理之实施8——三三归一续消除

黄剑飞

（浙江杭州市公安局）

摘　要　本文对道路交通安全的三对应原理实施的真法理，"三三归一"的运用进行继续论述。首先回顾原理与"三三归一"的概况。其次运用四种基本鉴定方法中的两种，继续进行对应的事故原因鉴定（而继续消除不对应的鉴定）。再次用事故原因鉴定的结论，为消除其他不对应继续提供依据。

关键词　原理实施　三三归一　不对应

0　引　言

笔者已经提出了道路交通安全的三对应原理（以下简称原理），即原理的含义（含解释与解释的补充）、推论、推论的解释；也提出了原理实施的"三三归一"真法理（以下简称"三三归一"），即"三三归一"的含义、原则；也已对"三三归一"的运用进行了论述，即以全体用路人选举出来的"事故原因（含当事人责任）鉴定（以下均称原因鉴定）委员会"为鉴定主体、按由下而上的顺序鉴定，以迹证分析法、违章分析法、让行分析法、因果分析法四种基本方法进行的鉴定。这些在此不再一一重复了。由于不对应的原因鉴定较多，因此笔者运用让行分析法、因果分析法，继续进行对应的原因鉴定（而继续消除不对应的鉴定），并为消除其他不对应继续提供依据。

1　让行分析法进行对应的鉴定（继续消除不对应）

（1）例1：在南北、东西路宽均为25m的四岔路口，甲驾轿车由西向东直行、乙驾轿车由北向南直行，两车在路口西南侧相撞，造成车损人伤，事后甲、乙均称当时来不及反应与措施了；现场上两车相撞部位为甲车左前侧与乙车右前侧，相撞后两车旋转程度相当，相撞位置到路口北侧进口的距离大于到路口西侧进口的距离。按照"三三归一"的含义、原则，由于两车碰撞后旋转程度相当，故两车车速相当，则可判断当甲车到达路口西侧进口时,乙车已经过路口北侧进口,后又在路口内行驶了一半以上的距离,此时相撞位置到甲车的距离与到乙车的距离相当,故两车措施距离的余地也相当;但由于此时乙车的位置只能看到路口内的小部分,而甲车的位置能看到路口内的大部分,并且此时乙车在路口内甲车的前方,而甲车在路口外乙车的右侧,这使甲车容易反应到乙车,而乙车难反应到甲车,故反应时间的余地甲车大于乙车;再往回推,当乙车到达路口北侧进口时,甲车还未到达路口西侧进口,此时双方措施距离的余地也相当,反应时间的余地也是甲车大于乙车。根据原理推论的解释三"当用路双方发生时空冲突时双方都要谦让、反应时间与措施距离大的更要谦让于小的,是用路上的让行注意义务的参照",在甲车到达路口西侧进口时,由于反应时间余地大的甲没有让行小的乙,从而导致事故的发生,因此事故的主要原因是甲未履行驾驶上的让行注意义务(安全注意义务的简称,下同),甲负主要的当事人责任;由于乙在还有反应时间余地的情况下没有尽力反应,因此事故的次要原因是乙履行驾驶上的反应注意义务不够,乙负次要的当事人责任。

(2)如果例1中两车碰撞后旋转程度是乙车大于甲车,即两车车速是甲车高于乙车,则甲车到达路口西侧进口时,乙车已经过路口北侧进口,后又行驶了一半以上的距离(比例1更长),此时相撞位置到甲车的距离大于到乙车的距离,故双方措施距离的余地是甲车大于乙车;由于此时乙车的位置只能看到路口内的小部分(比例1更小),而甲车的位置能看到路口内的大部分,并且此时乙车在路口内甲车的前方,而甲车在路口外乙车的右侧(比例1更右),这使甲车容易反应到乙车,而乙车难反应到甲车(比例1更难),故反应时间的余地甲车大于乙车(比例1更大);再往回推,当乙车到达路口北侧进口时,甲车还未到达路口西侧进口(比例1更未),此时双方措施距离的余地也是甲车大于乙车,反应时间的余地也是甲车大于乙车(比例1更大)。根据原理推论的解释三,在甲到达路口西侧进口时,反应时间与措施距离余地都大的甲应当让行乙(比例1更应当)。此其一。其二,如果例1中两车碰撞后旋转程度是甲车大于乙车,即两车车速是乙车高于甲车,则当甲车到达路口西侧进口时,乙车也差不多到达路口北侧进口,此时相撞位置到乙车的距离大于到甲车的距离,故双方措施距离的余地是乙车大于甲车;此时虽然两车的位置都能看到路口内的大部分,但由于甲车在乙车的前方,而乙车在甲车的左侧,这使乙车容易反应到甲车,而甲车难反应到乙车,故反应时间的余地是乙车大于甲车;再往回推,则双方都还未到达路口进口,但在临近路口进口时,双方措施距离的余地也是乙车大于甲车,反应时间的余地也是乙车大于甲车。根据原理推论的解释三,在双方同时到达路口进口时,反应时间与措施距离余地都大的乙应当让行甲。

(3)以上是例1这类事故相撞的三种基本状况。另外情况中,与之程度相近的可归类于其中,(比如)在乙车车速高于甲车,甲车到达路口进口时乙车略先(或略后)到达路口进口的情况,就可归类于前面的第三种状况;与之程度相远的就是不能相撞的情况了,(比如)在甲车车速高于乙车,甲车又比乙车先(或同时)到达路口进口的情况,则是乙车到达路口南侧时,甲车早已到达路口东侧了。因此,要根据现场、以三种状况为参照进行鉴定。此其一。其二,车辆直行是跨过整个路口才完成的,故鉴定时应以整个路口作为让行区域,而不是路口内的某一段。其三,由上可知,反应时间余地大小的表现是,后到达路口进口车辆的反应时间大于先到达的;措施距离余地大小的表现是,同时到达路口进口时,左侧车辆的措施距离大于右侧车辆(右行系统中)。因此,"余地大的"应当让行"余地小的"。

2 因果分析法进行对应的鉴定(继续消除不对应)

(1)由于"三三归一"是以原理对应状态下的客观注意义务(而不是以现有法规)为准绳进行鉴定的,因此如果当事人的被鉴定责任是现有法规造成的,而当事人没有提出指控,那也是他自己"甘愿受罚","三三归一"难以继续鉴定;但如果被鉴定责任的当事人提出指控,那就需要重新鉴定。(比如)例1中甲指控"法规规定左侧车辆须让行右侧车辆(右行系统中),所以不管任何情况,他都得让我",乙则指控"我已在路口内了,怎么让他?我将要到路口了,他撞上来还有理?法规的这个规定不对"。而法律("道路交通法"或"道路交通安全法")(下同)、规章("道路交通安全规则"或"安全法实施条例的通行规定",下同)中也的确只有这样的规定,那就需要重新鉴定。按照"三三归一",根据原理,由于法规中只有"左侧车辆须让行右侧车辆(右行系统中)"的规定,而没有"左侧车辆须让行右侧车辆,但左侧车辆已到中心位置则右侧车辆须让行左侧车辆(右行系统中)"的让行注意义务要求,属于规定片面、让行注意义务残缺,是立法规中的不对应。因此,由于这个立法规中的不对应,造成甲乙认识不清,而没有履行真正的让行注意义务,从而导致了事故的发生,因此事故原因的原因是立法规的人没有履行正确(即对应)的立法规注意义务,其负全部的当事人责任。

(2)(例2)某东西方向的城市快速路,北侧一条小路并排,由东向西并入快速路,小路在并入口呈左转与上坡状。也就是说,车辆要开上快速路,须先由东向西直行,左转90°(此时路面成40°上坡),再垂直于快速路路边进入快速路。于是由东向西进入快速路骑行二轮电动自行车的乙,与由东向西甲驾驶的轿车在快速路上相撞,造成车损人伤。事后甲称"他一下子穿出来,我来不及反应了",乙称"这里既要左转又要上坡,我只有加速才不至于翻车,所以一上快速路就看见他,但来不及采取措施了"。按照"三三归一",根据原理,由于供路人提供的道路造成乙"加速进入快速路",而使甲乙没有反应时间与措施距离,从而导致了事故的发生,因此事故原因是供路人(即建造人、许可人)没有履行正确(即对应)的供路注意义务,其负全部的当事人责任。

(例2)的供路人这么做很可能是"为了逼迫电动车骑车人下车推行,以此保证安全",如果供路人这么解释,那就需要补充鉴定,但是补充鉴定的结论仍是维持前面的鉴定结论。理由是:一,根据原理,保证用路人有反应时间与措施距离是供路人"安全上的注意义务",保证用路人骑行而不推行是供路人"交通上的注意义务",两者都要兼顾,不能以牺牲骑行来保证安全,否则违背了道路交通的宗旨,也违背了原理,因为原理的推论之一是"只有安全权利优先之下往运用车辆能量的方向去控制,才能达到三对应";二,这样的供路的确使骑行人容易翻车,但这不代表骑行人就会下车推行,因为决定骑行人是否下车推行还有两个重要因素,即骑行任务与骑行能力,因此多数骑行人是选择加速而不是下车推行,这就使电动车进入快速路时用路各方的反应时间与措施距离严重减少,从而产生不安全,因此以逼迫推行来保证安全是行不通的;三,笔者以前论述"根据原理,提供必须去适应用路的反应时间与措施距离,而不是反过来,否则就是必须消除的不对应",因此必须是供路人去适应乙而不是反过来,如果以这样的路要求乙去适应,那就是例2的事故。当然,如果供路人没有作如此解释,那就到前面鉴定结论为止。

3 为消除其他不对应继续提供依据

"三三归一"的运用不仅消除了不对应的鉴定结论,也能为消除其他不对应继续提供依据。(比如)例2的鉴定结论(包括补充鉴定),能为执法规中取缔(即消除)供路中的类似情况(即不对应),提供依据。(比如)如果将例1中的甲车变成由西向南右转弯,乙车变成由东向南左转弯,或者将乙车变成由东向南左转弯,甲车不变,则结论与前面的一样,因为依据都是原理推论的解释三。所以前面的鉴定结论能为立法规(包括修正法规)后的新法规中,必须具有:交通流量小的道路上的车让行大的,但小的已到中心位置则大的让行小的;左侧车让行右侧车,但左侧车已到中心位置则右侧车让行左侧车(右行系统中);转弯车让行直行车,但转弯车已到中心位置则直行车让行转弯车;转弯半径大的车让行小的,但大的已到中心位置则小的让行大的之要求(即驾驶上的让行注意义务),提供依据。此其一。其二,因为已到中心位置的车也就是先进入路口的车,所以"其一"的说法与笔者以前"同时(或先后)进入路口"的说法是同一回事的不同说法,因为它们的依据都是原理推论的解释三。

4 结 语

(1)笔者以前所说的"三三归一"的运用原则,已在本文中直接使用了,如根据原理进行鉴定、就是"客观义务为准绳"原则的运用,让行分析中的鉴定就是"先到先行"原则的运用,因果分析中的鉴定就是"多方竞合"原则的运用,此处不再一一注明了。此其一。其二,三对应原理是道路交通安全的基本原理,"三三归一"是原理引导出来道路交通安全肯定的真法理;由于道路交通中具体的不对应很多,因此

"三三归一"必须不断地消除原因鉴定中的不对应(而进行对应的鉴定),不断地为消除其他不对应继续提供依据,才能消除道路交通中的所有不对应,从而实现交通安全。

(2)本文是笔者"三对应原理之实施"系列论文的第8篇,故根据排列而命名本文为《三对应原理之实施8》。

参考文献

[1] Jianfei Huang. The Three Corresponding Principles of Road Traffic Safety and Their Supplements[C]// Proceeding of the 15th International Forum of Automotive Traffic Safety,2018:41-46.

低速提示音对电动汽车车内噪声影响的测试分析

马 可[1] 陈 煜[1] 匡成效[2] 仄伟杰[3]

(1.河海大学机电工程学院;2.江苏常荣电器股份有限公司;
3.永安行科技股份有限公司)

摘 要 以某型电动汽车低速提示音为研究对象,依据相关标准对其进行车辆初始状态的测试,得到试验车辆在低速行驶并且开启低速提示音时的车内有关数据,数据包括计权声压级和响度两个参量。然后依据声音传递路径有关理论进行噪声控制试验,得到试验结果并与车辆初始状态的数据进行对比分析,试验结果表明音源置于不同位置时,低速提示音对车内驾乘人员的影响无明显区别,而对车辆的孔洞和缝隙部位进行封堵,则可以显著降低低速提示音对车内驾乘人员的影响。研究结果对电动汽车噪声污染的防治以及驾乘舒适度的提升具有积极意义。

关键词 交通污染 低速提示音 车内噪声 电动汽车 汽车噪声检测

0 引 言

纯电动汽车以低于20km/h的车速行驶时,平均车外噪声比传统内燃机汽车低10dB左右,使得道路的其他使用者不容易察觉到车辆的接近,容易导致发生交通事故。为解决此问题,国际上近年来的研究一致倾向于在安静行驶的车辆上配备一种能够在低速时发出提示音的系统AVAS(Acoustic Vehicle Alerting Systems)[2],旨在提醒前方行人正有车辆向他们靠近,做好避让准备,以此来减小与行人发生交通事故的概率。

2009年日本某机构研究表明,车辆的提示音系统对于帮助行人或者有视力障碍的人士辨识出低速行驶的电动汽车或混合动力汽车有着重要作用[3]。2011年美国颁布法案,对纯电动汽车和混合动力汽车安装低速提示音有了明确规定[4]。2016年联合国在瑞士日内瓦欧洲总部举行会议,明确规定电动汽车需要安装低速提示音装置[5]。国内的研究,主要涉及提示音工作时的车速范围、声级限值、频率要求、声音类型要求和试验方法等[6],如中国汽车技术研究中心有限公司的陆春等人分析了电动汽车低速提示音的声学特性和技术要求[7]。在建立标准方面[8],《纯电动乘用车 技术条件》(GB/T 28382—2012)中明确规定了电动汽车在低速行驶时必须配备能够发出提示音的装置。

电动汽车开启低速提示音时虽然能够对车外行人起到提示作用,但同时也会对车内人员产生噪声困扰。从现有的研究现状可以看出,国内外鲜有人员研究电动汽车低速提示音在工作时对车内驾乘人员的影响。因此,本文从声音的传递路径角度出发,针对国内某型自主生产的纯电动汽车,研究其提示音对车内驾乘人员的影响,并通过改变声音传递路径的方法来对车内噪声进行优化。

基金项目:江苏省重点研发计划(BE2018004-01),常州市科技计划项目(CE20205044)。

1 主要测试参数

在汽车NVH(噪声、振动与声振粗糙度,Noise,Vibration,Harshness)领域中常用车内声品质(Sound Quality)来衡量噪声对驾乘人员的影响状况。声品质是指在特定的技术目标或者任务内涵中研究声音的适宜性,声品质中的"声"是人耳的听觉感知,"品质"则是指人耳对声音传递的听觉感知过程,并最终做出的主观判断,因此,通俗来说,声品质就是人们对声音的主观感受[9]。由于人是声品质最终的获取者和最直接的评价者,所以声品质受到诸多因素的影响,包括人的心理和生理上的差异、声音本身的特性等。为了对声品质进行定量描述,引入声学中的计权声压级(Weight Sound Pressure Level)、响度(Loudness)这两个参数。

1.1 计权声压级

声压级对声音的特征的反映较为狭隘,它并没有考虑频率这个因素[11]。而人耳对声音的感受,与声压有关的同时也和频率相关。因此,为了能更加客观而又真实地反映人耳对声音的主观感受,一般采用计权声压级,其包括了A级、B级和C级三种,其中A级计权声压级(A-weight Sound Pressure Level)是最接近人耳的主观感受,因此有关研究中较为常用。

1.2 响度

响度(Loudness)是汽车NVH领域最常见、最重要的声品质参数之一,它不仅可以反映出人耳对声音强弱的主观感受程度,而且能够较为准确地反映声音的响亮程度;响度的单位是sone(宋),一般规定1kHz、40dB时纯音的响度为1sone(采用ISO 532B diffuse field标准得到的)[12]。一般来说,随着声音响度的减小,其声品质越好,但声音响度并不是衡量声品质的唯一标准。

2 车辆初始状态测试

本测试的目的是收集试验车辆(初始状态)在低速行驶情况下并且开启低速提示音时的车内噪声有关参数,包括车内包括声压级、粗糙度、语言清晰度和尖锐度。

2.1 测试方法

2.1.1 测试设备及测试环境

本测试作为一种声学试验,用到的设备主要有测试用传声器(麦克风)和多通道数据采集系统(包括多通道数据采集前端和测试软件),测试环境为整车四驱转毂半消声室。

2.1.2 测试工况及测点

(1)D挡(前进挡):在整车四驱转毂半消声室的四驱转毂上,测试车辆分别以10km/h和20km/h的恒定车速行驶。

(2)R挡(倒车挡):在整车四驱转毂实验室的四驱转毂上,测试车辆以6km/h的车速恒定行驶。

(3)测点:主驾驶位和后排中间位置各布置一个测点,其具体位置示意图如图1所示。

2.1.3 测试步骤

(1)将试验车辆置于整车半消声室的四驱转毂上并将传声器布置到相应的测点上。

(2)利用信号传输线连接好传声器、多通道数据采集前端和计算机,在计算机上对测试软件进行相关设置。

(3)利用测试软件LMS Test.Lab进行数据采集。

2.2 测试结果

图2是试验车辆在前进挡20km/h时车内测点的车内各项与声品质有关的评价指标的测试结果的原始信号。图中,AutoPower表示的是自功率谱,它可以显示信号中含有哪些频率成分;Zwicher表示为响度

计算的一种方法;FRLE 表示主驾内侧测点,RERI 表示后排中间测点。后文该类图中英文含义相同,将不再赘述。

a) 主驾驶位

b) 后排中间

图 1 车内测点位置

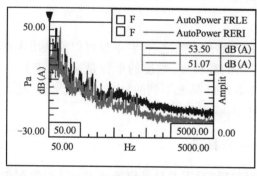
a) 计权声压级

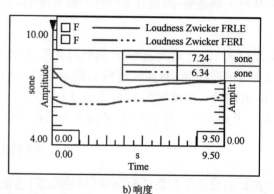
b) 响度

图 2 车速为 D 挡 20km/h 时车内各指标测试结果

完成各挡位测试并将数据汇总,结果见表 1。随着测试车辆速度的增加,计权声压级和响度这两个指标的数值整体上保持增大的趋势,且主驾内侧测点位置的计权声压级和响度的数值均大于后排中间测点位置。对上述结果进行分析可知,由于车辆速度的增加会导致轮胎与路面间噪声增大,且存在一定的风噪,因此在车辆自身状态不变的情况下,车内声品质会有所下降,计权声压级和响度在数值上随着声品质的下降而增大。且由于主驾位置相比于后排座位更接近车辆的前舱,因此会接收到更多的低速提示音的能量,导致其计权声压级和响度在数值上要大于后排位置。

表 1 初始状态下车内各项指标数据汇总

工况	指标			
	计权声压级[dB(A)]		响度(sone)	
测点位置	主驾(FRLE)	后排(RERI)	主驾(FRLE)	后排(RERI)
R 挡 6km/h	47.82	44.43	4.78	4.33
D 挡 10km/h	48.13	46.60	5.43	4.86
D 挡 20km/h	53.50	51.07	7.24	6.34

3 车内噪声控制试验

前文对车辆初始状态的测试表明低速提示音对车内驾乘人员的舒适度(声品质)有一定的影响,因此有必要通过采取一定改进措施,达到优化车内声品质有关指标,提高车内人员舒适性的目的。

3.1 更改音源位置试验

3.1.1 试验原理

从能量的角度来分析,声音在介质中的传递时,其声能会逐渐减小,该过程被称为声能衰减。造成声能衰减的因素有很多,比如由于声音传递范围的增大而导致的几何扩散衰减、空气吸收而导致的吸收衰减以及壁面或构筑物等因素而导致的其他衰减。根据声学有关理论,半自由声场中距离声源的位置不同,其声压级也会不同,且距离越远,其声压级下降的越明显[13-14]。对于本研究,由于是在半消声室环境中进行,可以认为是半自由声场,因此考虑到与声源的距离不同,此时低速提示音对车外行人的影响可能会发生改变,所以想到进行更改音源位置的试验,以探求不同位置下其发出的声音对车内外人员的影响。

3.1.2 位置方案

从声音的传播路径来看,音源越靠近前保险杠,其传递到车外的路径上的阻碍越少,传递到车内的路径上的阻碍越多,这样可以尽可能保证对车外影响大,对车内影响小。因此,音源放置的位置尽可能靠近前保险杠,本文所用试验车辆在初始状态下的音源位于前舱保险杠右端车灯下方部位,如图3所示。现将音源置于左端并与右端对称的位置进行测试。

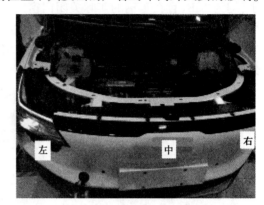

图3 音源位置方案

3.1.3 测试结果分析

除改变音源位置为前保险杠左端之外,其他测试工况与车辆初始状态相同,所得测试结果见表2。为了更直观地将音源放在左端时车内各指标的结果与音源放在右端时(即音源初始状态测得的车内结果与表1的结果作对比,现将音源放在左端测得的数据与音源放在右端时的数据做差,其结果见表3。

音源置于左端时车内各项指标数据汇总 表2

工况	指标			
	计权声压级[dB(A)]		响度(sone)	
测点位置	主驾(FRLE)	后排(RERI)	主驾(FRLE)	后排(RERI)
R挡6km/h	49.15	43.31	4.63	4.39
D挡10km/h	49.16	44.55	4.80	4.85
D挡20km/h	53.89	52.48	7.48	6.49

音源置于两端时车内各参数差值 表3

工况	指标			
	计权声压级[dB(A)]		响度(sone)	
测点位置	主驾(FRLE)	后排(RERI)	主驾(FRLE)	后排(RERI)
R挡6km/h	+1.33	-1.12	-0.15	+0.06
D挡10km/h	+1.03	-2.05	-0.63	-0.01
D挡20km/h	+0.39	+1.41	+0.24	+0.15

由表3可以看出,从整体上来看,音源放置在左端与放置在右端时车内各指标参数的变化量并不大。除了主驾内侧的计权声压级在数值上保持增大的情况之外,其他各工况下各指标的数值既存在增大,也存在减小现象,因此可以认为音源置于右端与音源置于左端对车内驾乘人员的舒适度影响并不明显。

3.2 封堵试验

3.2.1 试验原理

车辆在出厂后车身会存在一些不可避免的孔洞和缝隙,如汽车的前围上会存在工艺开孔,包括空调冷管和热管进口、内外循环口、真空助力口和转向机口等,同时汽车门窗、门把手以及前风窗玻璃与车架接合处也可能存在密封性能不够好的问题,会产生一定的缝隙,低速提示音发出后总会有一部分声音通过这些前孔洞和缝隙传递到车内,从而影响车内驾乘人员的舒适感。

孔洞和缝隙会显著降低车辆的隔声量[15],因此,为了减小低速提示音传递到车内的能量,考虑在其传递路径上进行一定的隔绝,即对存在的这些孔隙进行封堵,以提高车辆对外部的隔声量。

3.2.2 封堵方案

过声泄露测试确定了试验车辆隔声量较薄弱的位置,下面考虑对其进行一定的封堵措施,以提高车辆关键部位对低速提示音传递至车内过程的隔声量,减小声音对车内的影响。

试验使用的主要封堵材料是阻尼材料,在进行封堵操作时,由于车门缝隙和车窗缝隙的声泄露量较小,均为1dB,且在车辆的实际关闭门窗的情形下,车门和车窗的缝隙的存在是不可避免的,不可能从外部将其完全封闭,而且车门和车窗涉及的缝隙较多,会消耗大量的阻尼材料,因此车门和车窗部位并不需要和其他部位一样使用橡胶阻尼板进行封堵,本研究选择试验用黄色胶带对其粘贴以代替橡胶阻尼板的封堵效果。各个部位的封堵示意图如图4所示。

a) 空调冷暖管进口　　　b) 封堵内外循环口　　　c) 封堵门把手缝隙

d) 封堵车窗缝隙　　　e) 封堵前风窗玻璃接合处

图4 车辆各个泄露位置封堵示意图

3.2.3 测试结果分析

除采取以上封堵措施之外,其他测试工况及测试方法与车辆初始状态相同,所得测试结果见表4。为了更直观地将封堵试验车内各指标的结果与车辆初始状态测得的车内结果(表1)作对比,现将封堵试验测得的数据与车辆初始状态时的测得数据做差,其结果见表5。相比于车辆初始状态,封堵试验在各工况下车内各测点的计权声压级和响度在数值上均呈现较大幅度的减小(计权声压级减小幅度3dB以上,响度减小幅度1sone以上,这在声学中属于较明显的变化情况)。由于计权声压级和响度越小说明车内声品质越好,即驾乘人员的舒适度越高。因此,可以认为在对车辆存在声泄露的部位进行封堵后的情况下可以在较大程度上降低低速提示音对车内驾乘人员的影响。

表4　封堵后车内各项指标数据汇总

工况	指标			
	计权声压级[dB(A)]		响度(sone)	
测点位置	主驾(FRLE)	后排(RERI)	主驾(FRLE)	后排(RERI)
R挡6km/h	43.44	41.11	3.17	2.56
D挡10km/h	44.90	43.25	4.40	3.69
D挡20km/h	49.37	46.69	5.23	4.39

封堵后与初始状态车内各指标差值 表5

工况	指标			
	计权声压级[dB(A)]		响度(sone)	
测点位置	主驾(FRLE)	后排(RERI)	主驾(FRLE)	后排(RERI)
R挡6km/h	-4.38	-3.32	-1.61	-1.77
D挡10km/h	-3.23	-3.35	-1.03	-1.17
D挡20km/h	-4.13	-4.38	-2.01	-1.95

4 结 语

(1)确定试验工况以及测点,在整车四驱转毂半消声室中对实验车辆进行初始状态的测试,获取车内的有关参数的数据。

(2)设计了更改音源位置试验和封堵试验。对于更改音源位置实验,将音源由右端改为置于左端。对于封堵实验,考虑车身的孔洞或者缝隙会削弱车辆的隔声效果,这会使得其传递到车内时声音能量有所增强,因此用阻尼板对孔洞和缝隙进行封堵操作。

(3)试验结果分析表明音源放置于左端时的车内噪声相对于音源置于右端时并无明显变化,因此可认为音源位置的影响效果并不明显。而对于封堵试验,各工况下车内各测点的声品质指标在数值上有较大幅度的优化,说明对存在泄露的部位进行封堵能够较明显地使得试验车辆的低速提示音对车内驾乘人员的影响更小,即舒适度更高。

参考文献

[1] 郝鹏.行驶车辆主要噪声源的车外声场识别[D].北京:清华大学,2012.
[2] 曹蕴涛,汤乐超,刘英杰.电动汽车低速提示音系统的法规适应性研究[J].汽车工程,2020,42(8):1110-1116,1138.
[3] Japanese Automobile Standards International Centre. A study on approaching warning systems for hybrid vehicle in motor mode[R]. Informal document No GRB-49-10, 2009.
[4] Lawrence Rosenblum. Hybrid Cars Are Harder to Hear[R]. University of California, Riverside, 2008.
[5] Emar Vegt. Designing Sound for Quiet Cars[C]//9th International Styrian Noise, Vibration and Harshness Congress: The European Automotive Noise Conference. Graz, 2016, 1.
[6] 胡爱军,王朝晖.汽车主动安全技术[J].机械设计与制造,2010(07):97-99.
[7] 陆春,谢东明,徐金国,等.电动汽车低速提示音标准与试验研究[J].中国汽车,2018(12):49-53.
[8] 全国汽车标准化技术委员会.纯电动乘用车 技术条件:GB/T 28382—2012[S].北京:中国标准出版社,2012.
[9] 葛林鹤.AVAS行人警示音系统设计方法研究[D].长春:吉林大学,2018.
[10] 郭栋,石晓辉,胡纬庆,等.基于语义细分法的某汽车传动系声品质评价[J].中国公路学报,2017,30(6):307-314.
[11] 陈剑,王开明,刘策,等.汽车加速通过噪声室内预测方法研究[J].噪声与振动控制,2019,39(2):81-84,127.
[12] 陈卓.钢轨波磨对地铁车内噪声影响及其控制试验研究[J].铁道标准设计,2019,63(8):169-176.
[13] 周明刚,董琦飞,刘阳,等.Zwicker时变响度的一种计算方法[J].中国机械工程,2014,25(22):3073-3076.
[14] 岳舒,侯宏,王谦.线阵波束形成声强缩放方法估算声源的辐射声功率[J].声学学报,2020,45(2):169-175.
[15] 李泽宇,邢海英,周伟旭,等.城际动车组噪声控制技术研究[J].大连交通大学学报,2020,41(4):78-81.

基于用户调研的换电式出租车满意度与技术需求分析

李晓菲[1,2] 李 成[1,2] 吴忠宜[1,2]

(1. 交通运输部科学研究院;2. 城市公共交通智能化交通运输行业重点实验室)

摘 要 充电时间过长是电动出租车推广应用相对滞后的主要原因之一,换电式出租车能够快速完成能源补给,在北京、厦门等城市试点应用后受到广泛关注。为客观了解换电式出租车使用情况和用户诉求,本文在全面整理换电式出租车发展环境的基础上,基于北京、厦门市开展的针对368位出租车驾驶员的问卷调研,分析了用户对换电式出租车的满意程度、接受意愿、技术需求和使用特征。结果显示,出租车驾驶员对换电式出租车总体上较为满意,具有电动汽车驾驶经验的驾驶员更容易接受换电式出租车,北京和厦门两地因车辆使用强度不同,驾驶员对车辆技术指标和使用特征的需求有明显差异。建议进一步提升换电式出租车的技术性能,提高换电效率,完善政策标准环境,加强产业链合作。

关键词 电动出租车 换电模式 用户满意度 技术需求 问卷调研

0 引 言

2020年我国提出"二氧化碳排放力争于2030年前达到峰值,努力争取2060年前实现碳中和"的目标,对交通运输行业电动化转型提出了长远要求。交通运输行业一直是我国推广应用新能源汽车的主阵地。截至2019年底,全国新能源公交车、新能源出租车总量分别约为41万辆、7.7万辆[1],在各自领域内占比分别约为59%、6%,相比城市公交领域,出租车领域的新能源汽车推广速度明显滞后。主要原因是纯电动车续驶里程短、充电时间长,导致出租汽车驾驶员有效运营时间缩短,收入下降,驾驶员使用意愿不足。换电模式作为电动汽车电能补充的技术路线之一,相较于充电模式,能够极大缩减电能补充所需的时间,避免出租汽车充电带来的工作时间浪费、里程焦虑下驾驶员不敢承接长距离订单等问题,在北京、厦门、广州等多地出租车领域已开展试点使用。在全国多个城市都在加快推动出租车电动化的背景下,换电式出租车的试点应用效果受到广泛关注。

针对电动出租车相关的研究,国内学者有一些探索。2013年,才艺欣等[2]对充电式出租车和换电式出租车的盈利能力分析得出,受限于当时的政策、技术,换电式出租车的盈利能力较差。2017年,何晔巍等[3]对上海市出租车驾驶员开展纯电动出租车使用意愿调查分析,通过20份问卷的数据分析,得出了使用纯电动出租车使用意愿的主要影响因素。赵转转等[4]对西安市比亚迪纯电动出租车运营半年的运营情况进行了调研分析,提出了改善运营效果的对策和建议。2019年,涂彦平[5]对北京市几位燃油出租车驾驶员进行过随访调查,了解了北京市出租车驾驶员更换电动出租车的忧虑和想法。既往调查研究集中在充电式出租车方面,针对换电式出租车的研究较少,且调查覆盖的对象群体较少。

为了客观认识换电式出租车使用现状,为行业决策提供参考,本文在换电式出租车具有一定规模的北京市、厦门市开展较大规模的问卷调研分析,了解驾驶员群体对换电式出租车的满意程度和接受程度,掌握行业对换电式出租车技术性能的实际诉求,进而提出对换电式出租车可持续发展的保障措施建议。

1 换电式出租车发展环境

近年来的新能源汽车发展相关政策对换电模式电动汽车在出租行业的推广应用给予了充分的支持。

基金项目:交通运输部科学研究院结余资金资助项目,换电模式电动汽车在出租汽车行业适用性研究。

2019年,国家发展和改革委员会等3部门联合发布了《推动重点消费品更新升级畅通资源循环利用实施方案(2019—2020年)》,提出"鼓励企业研制充换电结合、电池配置灵活、续驶里程长短兼顾的新能源汽车产品"。2020年,国务院办公厅正式发布了《新能源汽车产业发展规划(2021—2035年)》,明确提出要大力推动充换电网络建设,鼓励开展换电模式应用。

在相关政策扶持下,2018年以来,换电式出租车取得较快发展。据不完全统计,截至2020年3月底,全国投入运营的换电站144座,换电式电动出租车共8556辆。其中,北京市、厦门市的换电模式出租车推广数量较多,出台的扶持政策也较为完善。北京市选定充换电兼容模式作为车辆主要技术路线,给予每辆车奖励上限为7.38万元的资金奖励,并给予额外出租车运营指标奖励,截至2020年3月底,投入运营的换电出租车已有4410辆,全市已建成换电站92处,已投入运营33处。厦门市也出台了推动换电式出租车推广应用的一系列便利优惠政策,包括换电站建设缩减建站审批的程序和时间、电动汽车充电电费低于当地大工业目录电价的一半等,截至2020年3月底,厦门市换电出租车已有1213辆投入运营,已建成换电站16处。

2 换电式出租车用户满意度和用户需求分析

(1)问卷调研说明

为全面了解换电式出租车在北京和厦门等地的试点应用情况和行业需求,本研究于2019年底针对北京市、厦门市的出租车驾驶员开展了大范围问卷调研。调研对象范围涵盖换电式出租车、传统燃油燃气车、充电式出租车、插电式混合动力出租车等全部类型出租车的驾驶员。问卷的题目类别包括打分、单项选择、多项选择、问答填空以及开放式提问等多种形式。

针对换电式出租车驾驶员,本次调研共计收集有效问卷284份,包括北京市190份、厦门市94份。针对传统燃油燃气车、充电式出租车、插电式混合动力出租车驾驶员共计收集有效问卷有效问卷84份。

(2)出租车驾驶员使用换电式出租车的满意度评价

为评价具有换电式出租车驾乘经验的出租车驾驶员对换电式出租车的满意程度,问卷中设计了经济性、效率性、舒适性、安全性、便捷性五个类别共计14项指标。采用李克特量表方法,每一项指标均设置了"非常满意""满意""一般""不满意""非常不满意"五种回答,分别记分为5、4、3、2、1。以各指标打分均值记为该指标的最后得分,如图1所示。北京市3.40分,厦门市3.45分,均高于一般的满意度水平2.5分,说明换电式出租车驾驶员总体上对换电式出租车较为满意。其中,对于换电操作时间、换电站开放时间、操控稳定性和舒适性四项指标满意度均较高。通过座谈交流了解到,目前,换电式出租车的换电操作时间约3分钟,能源补给时间已与加油、加气时间相当,相对于快充式出租车充电一次需要1.5小时,优势明显。大部分换电站的营业时间均为24小时不间断营业,提供全天候服务。电动汽车噪声低、无离合器等特点提升了车辆操控性和舒适性,降低了驾驶疲劳感。问卷中还设置了若有重新选择机会,是否选择换电式车辆的问题,北京市和厦门市分别有84%和83%的出租车驾驶员表示仍会选择换电式车辆,进一步说明了换电式出租车的用户满意度较高。

此外,针对经济性和效率性指标,北京市和厦门市有显著差异。厦门市驾驶员在车辆承包费、换电费用、维修保养费用、月收入等经济性指标上的满意度均高于北京市。原因主要是厦门市用电费用较低,换电场站运营商提供包干制的支付模式,换电费用与用电量无关,统一采用每天110元计费,按照厦门市出租车日均行驶里程550公里计算,驾驶员每公里的电价支出仅0.2元。北京市驾驶员对换电操作时间、换电等待时间等效率性指标的满意度高于厦门市,由于北京市一般为单班制,日均运营时间为12小时左右,日均运营里程220千米,换电次数少,而换电站较多;厦门市则以双班制为主,全天运营,日均运营里程550千米,相较北京市有更高的换电需求,由于换电站数量较少,换电站经常出现排队的现象,在高峰期甚至需要等候20~30分钟。由此可见,更好地推广使用换电式出租车,需要提前布局换电站,保证换电设施充足,提升换电效率。

(3)出租车驾驶员对换电式出租车的接受度分析

针对未曾接触过换电式出租车的驾驶员群体对于换电式出租车的接受度的调研结果如图2所示,根据目前驾驶员使用的车辆动力类型对其进行了分类。

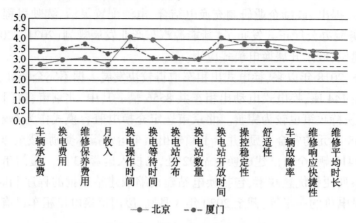

图1 换电式出租车驾驶员的满意度调研结果

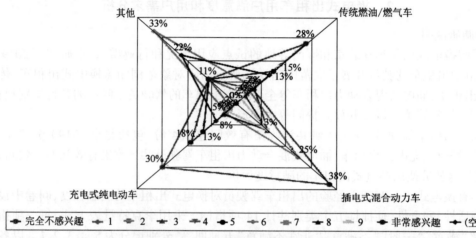

图2 各出租车驾驶员群体对于换电式的兴趣程度

由图可知,28%的燃油燃气车型的出租车驾驶员对换电式出租车完全不感兴趣,而新能源出租车(包括充电模式纯电动车和插电式混合动力车)驾驶员中至少30%以上对于换电式出租车非常感兴趣。说明新能源车驾驶员群体由于具有电动汽车的驾乘经验,对电动汽车舒适性、经济性等方面的优点有了切身感受,更容易接受电动汽车,对能够解决电动汽车充电时间长这一短板的换电模式也更加期待。由于目前新能源出租车车龄较新,暂时不会报废更新,下一步换电式出租车的推广对象主要是燃油燃气车,而燃油燃气车驾驶员对换电式出租车的兴趣低,更需要相关部门在加大政策宣传引导,丰富宣传方式方法等方面做出更大努力。

(4) 出租车驾驶员对换电式出租车辆及换电技术性能需求研究

问卷中还对出租车驾驶员对换电式出租车的技术需求进行了调查。本部分问卷题目使用开放性较强的填空题形式,经过归纳整理,出租车驾驶员的需求主要包括对车辆技术性能的需求和对换电技术的需求两大部分,具体包括续航里程、百公里电耗、故障率水平、换电效率、补电方式等,见表1。

出租车驾驶员对换电式出租车辆和换电技术的性能需求 表1

序号	需求类别	北京市	厦门市
1	续航里程	每天换电1次即能满足一天运营需要	
2	百公里电耗	百公里耗电量≤10kWh	百公里耗电量≤15kWh
3	故障率水平	降低故障率,维保费用≤2540元/年	降低故障率,维保费用≤1000元/年
4	换电效率	保证每次更换的备用电池是满电量状态换电站布局合理	
5	补电方式	补电时可自由选择充电或换电方式	

在车辆续航里程方面,出租车驾驶员期待能够一天换电一次即能满足全天的运营需要。目前北京市和厦门市的主流车型的标称续驶里程为300km,按照SOC(剩余电量)25%时必须充电的用户习惯进行测算,在动力电池电量不衰减、工况环境的理想情况下,可供运营使用续驶里程约为225km,勉强满足北京市日均运营里程220km的要求,与厦门市等双班制日均500公里的需求差距较大。建议车辆生产企业一方面提高换电车型的续航里程,另一方面提高换电便利性,降低驾驶员对换电的抵触。

在车辆百公里电耗方面,出租车驾驶员提出了较高的要求。由于厦门市实行换电费用包干制,百公里耗电量对出租车驾驶员的支出无直接影响,故厦门市出租车驾驶员提出的指标较宽容,希望百公里耗电量保证在15kW·h以下,而北京市出租车驾驶员的换电费用依据行驶里程或者电量计费,其对提升车辆百公里耗电量的诉求更为迫切,希望百公里耗电量在10kW·h以下。目前主流车型的NEDC工况条件下百公里耗电量约为15kW·h,在实际路况下将会更高,距离驾驶员的希望仍有差距。

由于车辆故障维修将占用出租车驾驶员的运营时间,影响驾驶员收入,所以驾驶员对于车辆故障水平较为敏感。厦门市的换电式出租车目前由出租车公司统一进行维修保养,驾驶员不承担相关维保费用,驾驶员对维保支出的心里预期为1000元以下。而北京市换电式出租车的维保费用由驾驶员承担,年维保费用约为4000元,而北京市的出租车驾驶员对维保费用的心里预期为每年2540元以下,维保费用和车辆故障水平仍需进一步降低。

在换电效率方面,驾驶员对目前3分钟左右完成换电的技术水平已经较为满意,但也提出优化换电站布局和提升备用电池电量的要求。在补电方式方面,出租车驾驶员希望自由选择换电和充电两种方式。换电方式的优势是换电时间短、节约出租车的运营时间,但充电方式也在一些场景下具有优势,例如深夜车辆处于休息时,如有充电条件,充电方式能够降低用电成本,或者在附近无换电站时应急补电。

3 换电式出租车的使用特征分析

本研究在了解驾驶员需求的基础上,进一步对换电式出租车驾驶员的换电行为特征开展了问卷调查,如换电时剩余电量、换电时间点选择、换电所需时长[①]等(图3),调研结果有利于提出更具针对性的组织效率优化的举措。

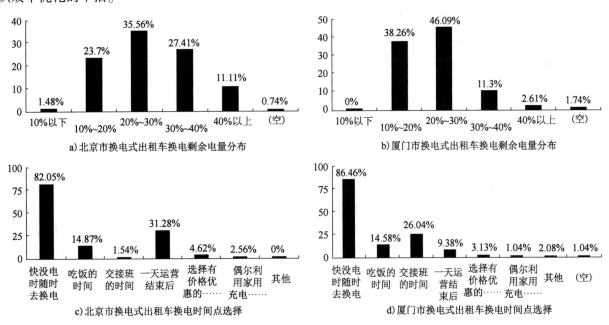

图 3

---

① 换电所需时长包括换电时间(机器操作时间)、换电等待、准备换电和收款等的时长。

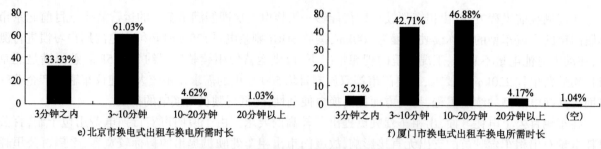

图3 换电式出租车驾驶员的换电行为特征

在换电时的剩余电量方面，出租车驾驶员均在剩余电量为20%～30% SOC 时进行换电。在换电时间点选择方面，大部分驾驶员均选择"随用随换"的策略，即快没电的情况下随时就近充电，部分驾驶员会选择在一天运营结束后、交接班的时间（厦门市）或者吃饭的时间进行换电，充分利用非营运时段。在换电所需时长方面，北京市换电站较为充足，一般在10分钟之内完成换电，而厦门市换电场站较少，往往需要10～20分钟才可以完成换电，这也导致厦门市出租车驾驶员在需要换电时会在 App 中搜索排队较少的站点。

4 换电式出租车可持续发展保障措施建议

通过对出租车驾驶员问卷调查结果的分析，对换电式出租车的使用效果和用户诉求有了更清晰的认识，为了更好满足用户需求，推动换电式出租车可持续发展，对车辆生产企业、换电站运营企业、政府行业管理部门、出租车运营企业等各相关方提出以下建议。

（1）进一步提升换电式出租车技术水平

车辆生产企业作为产业链最前端的产品供应商，需要确保产品质量满足行业需求，并做好配套保障服务工作。在车型设计方面，首先，根据城市运营特征提升车辆续航里程，尽力减少换电次数，在单班运营的城市做到一日一换；其次，持续降低耗电量，巩固换电式车辆的经济性优势；同时，降低车辆故障率，进一步降低驾驶员的维保费用支出；此外，建议积极推出网约车等其他领域的适用车型，与巡游出租车统一换电标准，形成规模效应，降低换电价格。

（2）完善换电站布局，优化换电站运营

在换电站建设方面，坚持换电设施先行，提前规划，保证换电站数量和布局的合理性，稳定行业预期；在保证换电时间不变的条件下，进一步提升换电效率，通过为驾驶员智能规划换电站点、辅以优惠激励等手段，引导驾驶员合理有序地选择换电时间点和地点，充分保证备用电池数量，保证系统运转效率；丰富驾驶员补电方式和换电收费模式，根据城市特点和发展阶段特征，探索采用"换电为主，充电为辅"的补电方式，丰富包干制、按里程计费、按用电量计费等收费模式，提高换电式出租车对驾驶员的吸引力。

（3）完善扶持政策和标准规范

在政策保障方面，建议各级政府部门统筹制定购车补贴、电价优惠、指标奖励等扶持政策，有效发挥政策合力；加强各部门协调沟通，优化换电站建设流程，鼓励商业模式创新。在标准规范方面，由于换电的通用性技术高度依赖于标准化，建议加快相关标准制修订，对于暂不适合制定国家标准和行业标准的，可探索制定团体标准和地方标准，同时，及时制定换电站运营服务和安全保障类的标准，提升换电站服务水平和安全水平。

（4）强化产业链合作和宣传引导

建议出租车运营公司主动作为，以保障出租车驾驶员权益为出发点，协调车辆生产企业、换电站运营企业和金融机构，做好换电式出租车的维修保障和商业保险服务等工作，解决驾驶员的后顾之忧。各方共同加大对传统出租车驾驶员的宣传引导，创新采取换电式出租车试驾、驾驶员经验分享会、网络答疑等方式，帮助潜在用户更好地了解换电式出租车，促进换电式出租车的推广使用。

5 结语

本文对换电式出租车的发展环境进行了系统的梳理,根据368份针对换电式出租车、燃油燃气出租车、充电时出租车、插电式混合动力出租车司机的问卷调研结果,系统分析了用户对换电式出租车的满意程度、接受意愿、技术需求和使用特征,以推动换电式出租车可持续发展为目标,对相关各方提出了建议,可为生产企业有效提升车辆性能、换电企业提高换电效率、政府管理部门精准优化扶持政策、出租车公司加速换电式出租车推广提供决策参考。鉴于本文调研数据处理方式较为简单,统计分析方法也存在改进的空间,研究结论具有一定的局限性,后续研究中可以通过与实际运行监测数据结合,扩大样本范围,进一步提升分析结论的准确度和适用性,提出针对性更强的措施和建议。

6 致谢

感谢北京市交通委员会、厦门市交通运输局、北京新能源汽车股份有限公司、奥动新能源汽车科技有限公司、厦门海峡出租汽车股份有限公司等机构对本研究在实地调研、问卷调查等方面提供的大力支持。

参考文献

[1] 中华人民共和国交通运输部. 中国城市客运发展年度报告(2019)[M]. 北京:人民交通出版社股份有限公司, 2020.
[2] 才艺欣,王贺武,叶强,等. 深圳和杭州电动出租车充电或换电池服务的商业模式[J]. 汽车安全与节能学报,2013,4(1):54-60.
[3] 何晔巍,干宏程,刘凯强. 纯电动出租车使用意愿分析[J]. 上海理工大学学报,2017,39(1).
[4] 赵转转,张磊. 西安市纯电动出租车运营现状调查[J]. 汽车实用技术, 2017(15):87-89.
[5] 涂彦平. 北京出租车油改电调查[J]. 经营者(汽车商业评论), 2019.

基于景观格局的生态旅游公路最优路径模型

陈帅铭　邵海鹏

(长安大学)

摘　要　随着旅游业的不断发展,旅游公路作为一种新兴的旅游方式开始逐渐被人们所接受。但大多数旅游公路只体现出了旅游公路的交通廊道的特性,而没有将旅游公路的特色表现出来。本文针对旅游公路没有与区域景观有效结合起来的问题,通过遥感技术,对区域景观要素进行提取,研究区域内景观空间格局特征。依据景观空间格局特征,提出确定生态旅游公路景观主题的方法,构建景观格局场,将景观特征对旅游公路最优路径的影响抽象成景观格局场的影响,提出了基于景观格局场的旅游公路最优路径模型。选取南阳市淅川县为具体研究区域,利用2019年4月的Landsat 8 OLI遥感影像,选择低山灌木作为生态旅游公路的景观主题,可穿插辅以阔叶林、草甸及水域的景观,模型给出的最优路径可以很好地利用当地已有的优势景观,从而最大限度地开发利用生态旅游资源,表明此模型给出的路线选择能够很好地契合当地的景观特点,能将生态旅游公路有效地与区域景观结合起来。

关键词　交通工程　生态旅游公路　景观格局　路径规划

0 引言

大多数关于旅游公路的概念是从旅游公路的"交通功能"的角度进行理解和阐述的。通常认为旅游公路是通往旅游区的公路和风景区内的道路。薛明等人[1]在此基础上将旅游公路的概念扩展为专门为沟通景点而专门建设的道路。秦晓春等人[2]则提出了一个较为广泛的定义,认为旅游公路是连接重要旅游区或旅游圈内连接各景区的以旅游交通为主要功能的公路。近年来,旅游公路的概念也越来越注重道路旁的景观特点。旅游公路被认为是能够满足游客的审美要求并且能够为其提供符合生理、心理需求的整体安全、美观的公路[3,4]。

目前旅游公路存在缺乏特色,没有完全挖掘出区域旅游资源的问题[5]。旅游公路在规划时要考虑区域旅游资源的分布[5-6],要将沿途区域的人文风景特点融合在一起,其要义是要体现公路的个性[7],而这种个性通常是在公路与周围景观相融合的时候确定的[8]。景观格局常涉及土地利用、生态系统、空间格局、道路系统。通常采用景观格局指数来对景观格局的特征进行定量分析[9]。若能利用区域内景观格局的特征,以最大限度契合景观格局的方法来进行旅游公路的规划,则能够最大限度地开发利用生态旅游公路周围的自然景观。

1 生态旅游公路景观格局

旅游公路是以旅游交通通行为主,同时又能够连接旅游景点或路侧具有旅游价值的带状公路走廊,是由公路主体及附属设施、服务设施、慢行设施、信息解说设施、景观设施共同构成的综合系统,并具有交通、生态、游憩、文化、教育等复合功能。旅游公路按照旅游交通功能分类可分为干线旅游公路和支线旅游公路[10]。本文研究的旅游公路是指狭义上路侧具有生态旅游价值的公路,也称生态旅游公路。

景观格局在形成过程中,不同的因素在景观格局形成与演化的过程中,其重要性是与空间尺度密切相关的。一般而言,气候和地形因素是大尺度范围内空间异质性的决定性因素,生物学过程则在小尺度范围内决定斑块的空间分布。

2 生态旅游公路景观格局分析

2.1 区域生态景观特征提取

引入景观类型占比 PLAND,计算公式为:

$$\text{PLAND} = P_i = \frac{\sum_{j=1}^{n} \alpha_{ij}}{A}$$

式中:α_{ij}——景观类型 i 中斑块 ij 的面积;
p_i——景观类型 i 占总景观的比例;
A——景观总面积。

定义相散布毗邻指数 IJI 如下:

$$\text{IJI} = \frac{-\sum_{k=1}^{m}\left[\left(\frac{e_{ik}}{\sum_{j=1}^{m}e_{ij}}\right)\ln\left(\frac{e_{ik}}{\sum_{j=1}^{m}e_{ij}}\right)\right]}{\ln(m-1)}$$

式中:e_{ik}——斑块类型 i 与 k 之间总的边缘长度;
m——斑块类型总数。
$0 < \text{IJI} \leq 1$。

定义聚集度 AI 如下:

$$AI = \frac{g_{ij}}{\max(g_{ij})}$$

式中:g_{ij}——基于双计数方法的景观类型 i 的栅格之间的相似邻接的数量;
$\max(g_{ij})$——基于双计数方法的景观类型 i 的栅格之间的相似邻接的最大数量。

引入信息论中的 SHDI 和 SHEI 指标:

$$\text{SHDI} = -\sum_{i=1}^{m} p_i \ln(p_i)$$

$$\mathrm{SHEI} = \frac{-\sum_{i=1}^{m} p_i \ln(p_i)}{\ln(m)}$$

式中：p_i——景观类型 i 的占比；

m——景观中所有景观类型总数。

对于斑块层面，引入斑块面积 PA 来度量其空间大小。

$$\mathrm{PA} = \sum_{j=1}^{n} a_{ij}$$

式中：a_{ij}——斑块 ij 的面积（$1000\mathrm{m}^2$）。

相应的，定义邻近指数 CONTIG（$0 \leq \mathrm{CONTIG} \leq 1$）：

$$\mathrm{CONTIG} = \frac{\left(\frac{\sum_{r=1}^{z} c_{ijr}}{a_{ij}}\right) - 1}{v - 1}$$

式中：c_{ijr}——斑块 ij 中栅格 r 的邻近数；

v——3×3 单元格模板中值的和；

a_{ij}——斑块 ij 的面积。

2.2 景观特征综合分析

引入信息论中熵的概念，对各个指标的熵权重进行计算。其具体步骤如下：

(1) 数据标准化。假定有 k 个指标 $X_1, X_2, \cdots, X_k$，其中 $X_i = \{x_{i1}, x_{i2}, \cdots, x_{in}\}$，则标准化处理后的值为 $Y_1, Y_2, \cdots, Y_k$，其中 $Y_i = \{y_{i1}, y_{i2}, \cdots, y_{in}\}$，$y_{ij} = \frac{x_{ij} - \min(x_{ij})}{\max(x_{ij}) - \min(x_{ij})}$。

(2) 求各指标的信息熵。

$$E_i = -\ln(n)^{-1} \sum_{i=1}^{n} p_{ij} \ln(p_{ij})$$

其中 $p_{ij} = \frac{y_{ij}}{\sum_{i=1}^{n} y_{ij}}$，如果 $p_{ij} = 0$，则定义 $\lim_{p_{ij} \to 0} p_{ij} \ln(p_{ij}) = 0$。

(3) 计算各指标的熵权重。计算出各个指标的信息熵为 $E_1, E_2, \cdots, E_k$，则各个指标的熵权重为 $W_i = \frac{1 - E_i}{k - \sum_{i=1}^{k} E_i}$。得到综合评价指标 $F = \sum_{i=1}^{k} W_i y_{ij}$。

3 景观格局场模型

3.1 景观格局场的构建

整个空间的势场可看作三种子势场的叠加，即：

$$\vec{U} = \vec{U}_{\mathrm{attp}} + \vec{U}_{\mathrm{attl}} + \vec{U}_{\mathrm{rep}}$$

式中：$\vec{U}_{\mathrm{attp}}$——目标点产生的引力势场，具有负势能；

$\vec{U}_{\mathrm{attl}}$——空间中景观吸引点产生的引力势场，具有负势能；

$\vec{U}_{\mathrm{rep}}$——空间中景观排斥点产生的斥力势场，具有正势能。

目标点引力势场 $\vec{U}_{\mathrm{attp}}$ 的一般形式为：

$$\vec{U}_{\mathrm{attp}} \vec{X} = \frac{1}{2} k_{\mathrm{attp}} \rho^{m_p}(\vec{X}, \vec{X}_\mathrm{p})$$

式中：k_{attp}——目标点引力势场的修正系数；
$\vec{X}$——移动点当前的位置坐标；
$\vec{X}_p$——目标点的位置坐标；
m_p——目标点引力势场因子；
$\rho(\vec{X},\vec{X}_p)$——移动点与目标点之间的欧式距离，$= \|\vec{X}-\vec{X}_p\|$。

吸引点引力势场 $\vec{U}_{attl}$ 的一般形式为：

$$\overrightarrow{U_{attl}(X)} = \frac{1}{2}k_{attl}\rho^{m_1}(\vec{X},\vec{X}_1)$$

式中：k_{attl}——吸引点引力势场的修正系数；
$\vec{X}_1$——吸引点的位置坐标；
m_1——吸引点引力势场因子；
$\rho(\vec{X},\vec{X}_1)$——移动点与吸引点之间的欧式距离，$= \|\vec{X}-\vec{X}_1\|$。

本文取 $m_p = 2, m_1 = 1$。引力是引力势场的负梯度作用力：

$$\overrightarrow{F_{attp}(X)} = -\overrightarrow{\nabla U_{attp}(X)} = -\frac{1}{2}k_{attp}\nabla\rho^2(\vec{X},\vec{X}_p) = -k_{attp}\rho(\vec{X},\vec{X}_p)$$

不难看出，引力函数 $\overrightarrow{F_{attp}(X)}$ 是距离的一次函数，其值的大小随着 $\rho(\vec{X},\vec{X}_p)$ 的增加而线性增加。

$$\overrightarrow{F\ attl(X)} = -\overrightarrow{\nabla U_{attl}(X)} = -\frac{1}{2}k_{attl}\nabla\rho(\vec{X},\vec{X}_1) = -\frac{1}{2}k_{attl}$$

引力函数 $\overrightarrow{F_{attl}(X)}$ 为常数，其值的大小与距离无关，仅与 k_{attl} 有关，可令 $k_{attl} = F$。同时取 $k_{attp} = \text{Max}(F)$。

定义排斥点所产生的斥力势场函数 $\overrightarrow{U_{rep}(X)}$ 为：

$$\overrightarrow{U_{rep}(X)} = \begin{cases} \frac{1}{2}k_{rep}\left(\frac{1}{\rho(\vec{X},\vec{X}_o)} - \frac{1}{\rho_o}\right)^2 & \rho(\vec{X},\vec{X}_o) \leq \rho_o \\ 0 & \rho(\vec{X},\vec{X}_o) > \rho_o \end{cases}$$

式中：k_{rep}——斥力势场正比例因子；
X_o——排斥点的位置坐标；
$\rho(\vec{X},\vec{X}_o) = \|\vec{X}-\vec{X}_o\|$——移动点与排斥点之间的欧式距离；
ρ_o——排斥点斥力势场最大影响距离。

排斥力函数 $\overrightarrow{F_{rep}(X)}$ 为：

$$\overrightarrow{F_{rep}(X)} = -\overrightarrow{\nabla U_{rep}(X)} = \begin{cases} k_{rep}\left(\frac{1}{\rho(\vec{X},\vec{X}_o)} - \frac{1}{\rho_o}\right)\frac{1}{\rho(\vec{X},\vec{X}_o)^2}\frac{\partial(\vec{X},\vec{X}_o)}{\partial\vec{X}} & \rho(\vec{X},\vec{X}_o) \leq \rho_o \\ 0 & \rho(\vec{X},\vec{X}_o) > \rho_o \end{cases}$$

3.2 最优路径算法

将三种势场进行叠加，得到总的景观格局场，其势场函数 $\overrightarrow{U(X)}$ 为：

$$\overrightarrow{U(X)} = \overrightarrow{U(X)}_{attp} + \overrightarrow{U(X)}_{attl} + \overrightarrow{U(X)}_{rep}$$

移动点在合势场力的作用下从起始点一直移动到最终点，该点的运动轨迹就是规划的路径。其算法实现流程如下：

(1) 载入栅格地图。
(2) 移动点开始移动之前，检测环境中的目标点以及吸引点是否能达到，如果存在无法到达的情况，则直接结束算法。

(3) 在每一次移动点开始移动之间,检测是否到达目标点,如果到达目标点,则结束算法,如果没有到达目标点,则继续下一步算法。

(4) 判断是否已经进入排斥力势场的作用范围,如果已经进入,则计算排斥力和吸引力,如果没有进入,则计算吸引力。

(5) 计算合成力的大小与方向,并根据合成力的大小方向计算出移动点下一步的前进方向与前进距离。

(6) 检测是否到达目标点,没有则循环规划,直至抵达目标点。

4 实例分析

选取河南省南阳市淅川县区域 2019 年 4 月的 Landsat 8 OLI 遥感影像,并对影像进行辐射标定和大气校正(图1)。将地物划分为五类:阔叶林、低山灌丛、草甸、农作物、水域。分类结果如图2所示。

图1 误差校正后影像

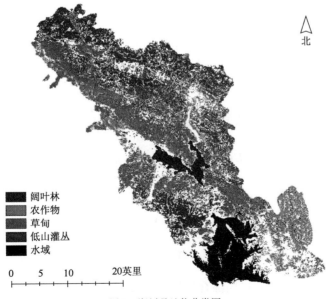

图2 淅川县地物分类图

利用 FRAGSTATS3.0 软件,对整个区域的景观格局指数进行计算,见表 1 和图 3。

表 1 景观水平指数

指标	SHEI	AI	SHDI
数值	0.9207	88.8230	1.4818

区域内主要景观类型为阔叶林以及低山灌木,可以确定生态旅游公路的景观主题为阔叶林景观及低山灌木景观。

根据图 4 容易发现,研究区域内的五种景观类型的聚集度均高,反映出各景观类型多数呈团状分布,聚集在一起。其中草甸景观的散布毗邻指数仅为 0.0603,表明草甸景观类型分布极为分散,呈零星的团簇状分布,只能将其作为辅助景观。

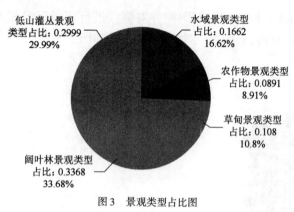

图 3 景观类型占比图

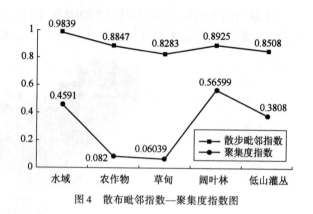

图 4 散布毗邻指数—聚集度指数图

指标权重见表 2。

表 2 指标权重

指标	PA	CONTIG
权重	0.9731	0.0269

通过加权计算,得到总的斑块水平指数得分,记为:

$$Score = 0.9731 \times PA + 0.0269 \times CONTIG$$

取 $k_{attp} = \text{Max}(Score) = 22199.18$,$k_{attl} = Score$,$k_{rep} = Score_o$,其中,$Score_o$ 为排斥点景观对应的 Score 值。

考虑到划分研究区域内的景观为五大种类:阔叶林、低山灌丛、草甸、农作物、水域,阔叶林景观、低山灌丛、草甸为环境中的吸引点景观,农作物和水域设置为排斥点景观,构建出的景观格局场的势场函数如下:

$$\overrightarrow{U(X)}_{attp} = 11099.59\rho^2(\vec{X}, \vec{X}_p)$$

$$\overrightarrow{U(X)}_{attl} = \frac{1}{2} Score_i \rho(\vec{X}, \vec{X}_l)$$

$$\overrightarrow{U_{rep}(X)} = \begin{cases} \frac{1}{2} Score_o \left(\frac{1}{\rho(\vec{X}, \vec{X}_o)} - \frac{1}{\rho_o} \right) & \rho(\vec{X}, \vec{X}_o) \leq \rho_o \\ 0 & \rho(\vec{X}, \vec{X}_o) > \rho_o \end{cases}$$

其中,$Score_l$ 为吸引点 l 处的景观格局综合指标,ρ_o 可取 500m,$Score_o$ 为排斥点 o 处的景观格局综合指标。

计算出势能函数以及势能力函数之后,可以计算出在给定规划起终点之后的最优路径。计算结果通过 ArcGIS10.8 软件进行可视化,如图 5 所示。

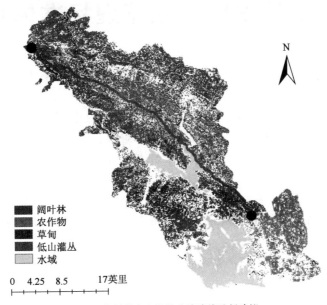

图 5　淅川县生态旅游公路路线选择建议

选择的道路穿越区域基本上为低山灌丛景观区域,同时,有一路段邻近水域景观区域,其余沿线均穿插阔叶林景观与草甸景观。可以很好地利用当地已有的优势景观,从而最大限度地开发利用生态旅游资源。

5　总结与展望

本文针对现有的关于道路与景观的交叉研究存在的问题,给出了一种在景观格局特征指标的基础上延伸而出的景观格局场,并通过物体在场中的受力情况推算出其位移参数,从而完成道路规划的方法。景观的生态旅游开发价值是受到多种因素共同影响,本文仅用了景观的空间格局来对其开发价值进行衡量,研究具有局限性,后续的研究中应增加影响因子的数量。

参考文献

[1] 薛明,马忠英,叶奋,等.青海省高原旅游道路的景观与环境设计[J].中国公路学报,2001(S1):41-45.
[2] 秦晓春,张肖宁.旅游公路景观设计及美学研究[J].公路,2007(10):212-217.
[3] 孟强.关于我国旅游公路发展的思考与探索[J].公路交通科技(应用技术版),2009,5(08):196-198.
[4] 安振华.旅游公路景观评价研究[D].西安:长安大学,2009.
[5] 巴可伟,李永晟.大众旅游时代我国旅游公路规划要点分析[J].交通世界,2019(08):3-5.
[6] 刘毅,彭铁军.旅游公路线形设计研究[J].公路交通科技(应用技术版),2018,14(12):100-102.
[7] 彭归来.旅游公路景观设计探讨——以溧阳1号公路为例[J].绿色科技,2019(11):66-70.
[8] 王俊帅,王云.溧阳南山片区乡村旅游公路选线适宜性评价[J].上海交通大学学报(农业科学版),2018,36(06):74-82,91.
[9] 张安琪,夏畅,林坚,等.景观演化特征指数及其应用[J].地理科学进展,2018,37(06):811-822.
[10] 王萌萌,孔亚平,陈兵,等.旅游公路概念、属性及分类[J].公路,2019,64(03):176-181.

跨海大桥建设期应急管理标准体系构建

王冀[1]　吴忠广[1]　张宇[1]　孙晓军[2]　潘硕[1]　陈巍峰[3]

(1.交通运输部科学研究院；2.浙江省交通工程管理中心；3.浙江交工集团股份有限公司大桥分公司)

摘　要　针对当前跨海大桥建设期应急管理标准体系尚未构建，应急管理关键环节标准存在空缺等行业普遍存在的问题，运用三维结构空间分析法及平行分解法，首先分析了跨海大桥建设期应急管理主要内容与特点，其次研究提出跨海大桥建设期应急管理标准体系的建设思路。第三，分析了跨海大桥建设期应急管理标准实施现状及问题需求。在此基础上构建了包括安全生产影响因素、标准种类、应急管理内容三个维度的应急管理标准体系结构。最后，运用平行分解法，以应急管理工作主要内容为划分，研究提出跨海大桥建设期应急管理标准体系框架为提升跨海大桥建设期应急管理标准化水平提供技术支撑。

关键词　跨海大桥　工程施工　应急管理　标准体系

0　引　言

近年来，我国沿海地区桥梁建设工程逐渐增多，跨海大桥因其独特的地理位置及施工特点，对建设期应急管理提出了更高的要求。然而，当前跨海大桥建设期应急管理尚未形成一套成体系、可推广的标准体系，从交通运输行业层面探索预防、准备、响应、恢复全过程构建标准体系，对于提升新时期跨海大桥施工安全应急管理能力，具有重要的现实意义。

国外对跨海桥隧工程应急管理十分重视，美国、欧盟、日本等发达国家和地区都逐步建立了完备的应急管理体系，涉及法律法规、监管机构、应急指挥体系等方面[1]，随着应急管理的逐步发展，信息化和通信技术的应用在现代应急管理中发挥着越来越大的作用[2-3]。交通运输部2016年印发了《交通运输安全应急标准体系(2016年)》，支撑行业交通运输安全监督与应急管理职责[4]。针对桥梁工程建设期安全应急管理，尤捷[5]、薛天兵[6]分别对大型土木工程施工安全突发事件应急管理系统构建、大型桥梁灾害性天气应急资源调配决策进行研究；胡敏涛[7]、单琳[8]、段国钦[9]、梁勋[10]、欧阳瑰琳[11]等分别以港珠澳大桥为对象，对工程建设中应急管控措施、安全应急管理手段与措施等问题进行研究。

综合现有研究成果，针对于跨海大桥建设期应急管理各阶段和主要环节的技术方法相对较少，缺乏对应急管理工作的技术支撑。本文针对跨海大桥建设期应急管理工作特点，通过对跨海大桥施工期应急管理标准实施现状及问题需求进行分析梳理，从预防、准备、响应、恢复阶段构建应急管理标准体系，提升海上桥梁建设应急管理水平。

1　跨海大桥建设期应急管理主要内容与特点

跨海大桥建设期应急管理主要包括跨海大桥主体工程施工过程中的工程结构安全、施工人员安全、防台及其他典型气候灾害、海上交通安全等内容。

跨海大桥交通工程施工作业区通常跨越多条重要航道，易发生施工期海上交通安全事故；台风、暴雨、雷电等自然恶劣天气对施工安全构成较大危险；吊装作业坍塌、特种大型机械设备使用安全事故、海上交通运输量增大导致的安全事故等风险源较多；长距离封闭桥面，主体工程远离陆地，应急救援难度大；陆上及海底施工环境复杂带来的风险因素等，使沿海大型桥梁建设工程在应急管理主要阶段和关键环节仍然存在一定不足，应急管理工作面临较大的挑战。

基金项目：浙江省交通质监行业科技计划项目(ZJ202003)。

2 标准体系建设基本思路

2.1 体系内涵及范围

标准体系是一定范围内的标准按其内在联系形成的科学有机整体。跨海大桥建设期应急管理标准体系,则是以跨海大桥建设期为对象,围绕交通运输行业应急管理管理职责范围,研究梳理跨海大桥建设期应急管理实施现状及相关需求,按照跨海大桥建设期应急管理特点进行有机梳理形成的完整体系。

结合跨海大桥施工建设安全生产影响因素,将纳入本体系标准的范围界定为:针对跨海大桥建设期作业人员、设施设备、施工技术与工艺、管理制度、自然环境等安全生产影响要素,在应急管理各阶段工作中涉及的相关标准,适用于跨海大桥建设期陆域工程部分及水上施工部分,大体分为基础标准、管理标准、技术标准、产品标准等。

2.2 构建依据

以国家、行业针对生产安全与应急管理相关法律法规与制度文件要求为总体指导,对照《交通运输标准化体系》与《交通运输安全应急标准体系(2016年)》中应急管理相关标准,针对跨海大桥项目建设应急管理自身特点与要求,按照《标准体系表编制原则和要求》(GB/T 13016—2009)研究构建跨海大桥建设期应急管理标准体系。

2.3 构建原则

(1)系统性。标准体系应覆盖应急管理各阶段,在内容上包含基础、管理、技术、方法等方面的应急管理相关标准,确保标准体系内容完整。

(2)针对性。标准体系需体现跨海大桥工程应急管理特点,突出事前预防,提升事故应急处置,加强事后总结恢复,增强标准体系对跨海大桥应急管理工作的指导作用。

(3)协调性。标准体系的制定要求与国家、行业应急管理相关法律法规、政策制度、应急指挥体系相协调的同时,还应与《交通运输安全应急标准体系》中应急管理相关标准互相协调衔接。

3 跨海大桥建设期应急管理标准实施现状及问题需求

3.1 跨海大桥施工建设标准现状

通过对当前现行国家标准、相关行业标准进行梳理,跨海大桥施工建设共有标准51项,其中国家标准33项,交通运输行业标准17项,住建部门行业标准1项。目前现行标准侧重于设计施工、产品材料、工艺工法、检测等标准类型(图1),针对建设期安全应急管理相关标准未涉及。

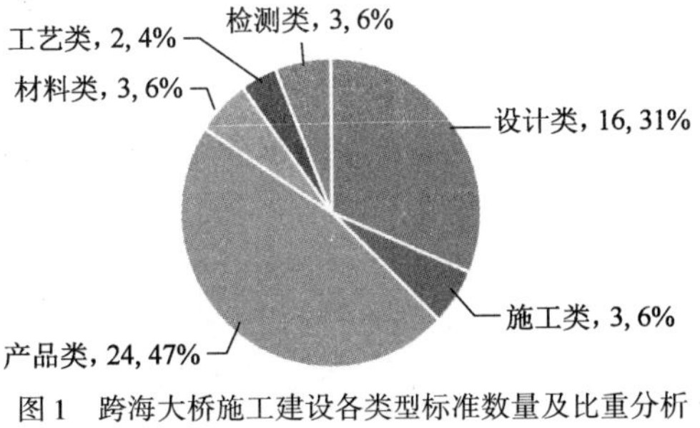

3.2 交通运输行业工程建设应急管理标准现状

目前交通运输应急管理类现行标准主要指向道路运输、货物运输或运营期应急管理等方向,工程建设施工应急管理类标准较少。目前与工程建设应急管理直接相关的标准为2项,为公路水运工程生产安全事故应急预案编制、公路隧道工程施工应急抢险救援相关标准,均为纳入计划正在研究制定的标准。由此可见,当前尚无与交通运输工程施工建设应急管理直接相关标准,正在研究制定标准远不能满足应急管理工作需要,标准的支撑引导作用没有得到充分发挥。

图1 跨海大桥施工建设各类型标准数量及比重分析

3.3 跨海大桥建设期应急管理标准需求

通过梳理分析,跨海大桥建设应急管理在各阶段标准制定存在较大需求。具体表现在:应急预防阶段,应急组织机构和责任体系、应急预案体系、应急监控体系、事故隐患排查治理等工作亟需标准进行规范。应急准备阶段,各类应急资源配置需求、内容、调配与管理方面需要统一规范指导。应急响应阶段,应急响应联动、外部救援力量协调利用需要进一步完善。应急恢复阶段,相关经验未能及时总结并转化为技术标准。

4 跨海大桥建设期应急管理标准体系构建

4.1 跨海大桥建设期应急管理标准体系三维空间结构分析

标准体系的对象范围维度、标准类型维度及水平维度构成标准体系目标分析的三维关系,即在目标三维空间中寻找定位[12],其主要思想对全面系统构建标准体系具有一定借鉴作用。结合跨海大桥建设期应急管理要求及主要特点,提出跨海大桥建设期应急管理标准体系的三维空间架构,包括安全生产影响因素、标准种类以及应急管理内容(图2)。

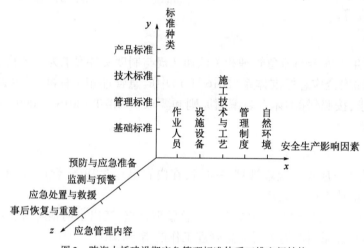

图 2　跨海大桥建设期应急管理标准体系三维空间结构

4.2 跨海大桥建设期应急管理标准体系结构框架分析

基于三维空间结构分析,借鉴相关经验,进一步运用平行分解法进行跨海大桥建设期应急管理标准体系的构建。以应急管理各阶段工作为主要划分,将标准体系主要结构分为100应急准备、200监测预警、300处置救援、400恢复重建、500支撑保障五个部分(图3)。

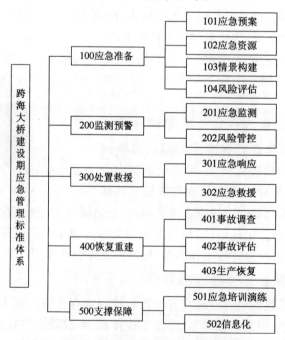

图 3　跨海大桥建设期应急管理标准体系结构框架

5 结语

本文从问题导向、需求导向的角度出发,通过分析跨海大桥建设期应急管理标准实施现状及标准制定需求,提出跨海大桥建设期应急管理标准体系的内涵与范围,运用平行分解法构建了应急管理标准体系框架,对于支撑跨海大桥建设期应急管理工作,提高应急管理标准化水平起到一定借鉴作用。

鉴于当前针对跨海大桥建设期应急管理标准空缺现状,建议进一步推动标准体系构建机制,强化部省联动,提高行业与地方应急管理标准规范的协调性。进一步推动跨海大桥各类从业单位履行各自职责,结合自身工程建设实际,制定严于国家、行业标准的企业标准或相关规范性技术文件,推动跨海大桥建设项目应急管理先进经验快速向标准转化,推动构建协调统一、要素完备的应急管理标准体系。

参考文献

[1] Rhodes N. Road Tunnels: Operational Strategies for Emergency Ventilation[J]. Strategic Planning, 2011(03): 22-25.
[2] Amy K Donahue, Philip G Joyee. A Framework for Analyzing Emergency Management with an Application to Federal Budgeting[J]. Public Administration Review, 2001, 61(6):728-740.
[3] Eliot Jennings, Sudha Arlikatti, Simon Andrew. Determinants of Emergency Management Decision Support Software Technology: An Empirical Analysis of Social Influence in Technology. Adoption[J]. Journal of Homeland Security & Emergency Management 2015, 12(3): 603-626.
[4] 张宇,王伟,史砚磊.交通运输安全应急标准体系构建研究[J].标准科学,2017(3):44-47.
[5] 尤捷.大型土木工程施工安全突发事件应急管理研究[D].南京:南京林业大学,2017.
[6] 薛天兵.大型桥梁灾害性天气应急资源存储方式选择和应急调配研究[D].上海:上海交通大学,2013.
[7] 胡敏涛.港珠澳大桥主体工程建设期应急管理技术探讨[J].公路交通科技(应用技术版),2013(6):147-149.
[8] 单琳.港珠澳大桥交通工程施工项目安全管理与实践研究[J].公路交通科技,2017,34(12):103-105.
[9] 段国钦,陈伟,余烈,等.跨海大桥建设中的通航安全[J].中国公路,2015(21):92-95.
[10] 梁勋.台风区跨海桥连续梁挂篮施工防台安全管控[J].低温建筑技术,2020(8):148-151.
[11] 欧阳瑰琳,刘刚军,聂荣,等.海上桥梁施工安全管理[J].公路.2006(03):133-138.
[12] 麦绿波.标准体系方法论中程序模块的理论和方法[J].标准科学,2011(11):13-19.

基于驾驶安全舒适性的公路隧道分类研究

胡江碧 王 旭

(北京工业大学城市建设学部)

摘 要 不同长度的公路隧道运行环境对驾驶员驾驶行为特性和信息需求产生不同影响,研究满足驾驶安全舒适性需求的隧道长度分类,对提升隧道影响区域驾驶员运行安全舒适性和运营安全管理水平具有现实意义。基于驾驶安全舒适性理论和驾驶工作负荷度的测量方法,分别在54~12330m不同长度、运行速度60km/h的单向双车道高速公路隧道影响区域,对18名驾驶员进行了典型车型实车驾驶试验,采集了驾驶员在不同长度隧道运行速度、驾驶工作负荷度指标;通过数据分析,研究得出不同长度隧道内驾驶员驾驶工作负荷度的变化规律及交通环境对驾驶员驾驶安全舒适性的影响差异,结果表明,驾驶员驾驶的安全舒适性随不同隧道长度类型的增加呈逐渐降低的规律性变化,并最终得出运行速度为60km/h时单向双车道高速公路隧道的安全舒适性分类:长隧道$L>4000\text{m}$、一般隧道$450 \leq L \leq 4000\text{m}$、短隧道$L<450\text{m}$。

关键词 公路隧道 隧道分类 驾驶安全舒适性 驾驶工作负荷 隧道长度

0 引言

公路隧道是与外界隔绝的管状道路构造物,驾驶员驾驶视野受到隧道封闭空间的阻碍。随着公路隧道长度的增加,驾驶员紧张压抑感愈加明显,运行的风险越高,引发交通事故的数量越多,交通安全问题突出[1]。隧道长度不同,洞口断面内外光环境条件、中间段的道路线形条件、交通安全设施的设置类型及数量不同,导致驾驶员在不同长度类型公路隧道的驾驶行为特性和安全行车需求不同。理解驾驶员在不同长度类型隧道驾驶的安全舒适性和驾驶行为特性机理,研究满足隧道运营安全管理分类,对提高隧道运行的安全舒适性,改善隧道影响区域道路线形条件、横断面及交通安全设施的设置具有现实意义。

目前国内外对公路隧道分类研究方面,美国消防协会为保障隧道消防安全和人员生命安全的最低标准,根据隧道长度进行规定并分5类[2];日本根据交通性质和使用条件、建设地址、施工方法、道路构造令将隧道分4类[3];我国现行《公路工程技术标准》(JTG B01—2014)、《公路隧道设计规范 第一册 土建工程》(JTG 3370.1—2018)根据公路隧道长度分4类[4-5],《公路隧道设计规范 第二册 交通工程与附属设施》(JTG D70/2—2014)综合考虑隧道单洞长度和设计交通量将隧道分5类[6]。陈晓利以隧道长度和交通量为基本分类指标,建立隧道管理分类判别函数,将隧道分3类[7]。王少飞参考隧道设计规范,根据隧道发展现状及趋势,将公路隧道按长度分6[8]类。

在驾驶安全舒适性评价指标和方法方面,国内外学者采用驾驶员心率[9]、脑电[10]、瞳孔面积[11]、肌电[12]和反应时间[13]等生心理指标评价驾驶的安全舒适性;赵亮采用心率变化率和瞳孔面积变化率指标表征驾驶员的紧张程度,研究了驾驶员紧张程度与道路线形安全的关系[14];杜志刚采用瞳孔面积变化速度和持续时间变化为视觉舒适度评价指标,用于评价隧道出入口行车的安全性[15];袁伟采用驾驶员心率增长率、心率变异性时域指标和心率变异性频域指标表征驾驶员工作负荷,分析驾驶员在城市道路不同路段类型的安全性[16]。

综上,目前对公路隧道的分类主要基于隧道建设规模、工程建设难度进行,缺乏对运营管理阶段公路使用者——驾驶员的动态认知过程和生心理特性的考虑,导致对隧道的运营管理难以满足驾驶员安全舒适驾驶的要求。因此,本文在课题组对驾驶员驾驶工作负荷度有效表达驾驶安全舒适性研究成果的基础上,采用驾驶工作负荷度指标,定量分析不同长度类型公路隧道对驾驶安全舒适性的影响,从而为不同长度类型公路隧道进行精细化安全舒适性管理奠定基础。

1 驾驶安全舒适性评价方法及标准

课题组在驾驶员驾驶安全舒适性评价体系方面,提出了表征驾驶员驾驶安全舒适性评价标准——基于驾驶员生心理的驾驶工作负荷理论和方法,以驾驶工作负荷度指标计量公路运行的安全舒适性[17]。驾驶工作负荷是指驾驶员在道路上驾驶车辆时,需要不断重复道路交通环境信息的采集、加工处理、决策和反应操纵的过程,在道路交通环境条件对驾驶员施加的工作任务和信息频率而产生的精神压力,在此压力下,驾驶员支撑工作的信息道能力[18]。采用驾驶员心率变异性(HRV)与车辆运行速度(V)共同作为评价驾驶员驾驶工作负荷度(K)的指标,可以有效地消除驾驶员生心理存在的个体差异,同时考虑运行速度对驾驶员生心理的影响,驾驶工作负荷度计算模型如式(1)所示[19]。

$$K_{ij} = \left[\left(\frac{\text{LF}}{\text{HF}}\right)_{ij} - A_i\right] / V_{ij} \tag{1}$$

式中:K_{ij}——驾驶员i在道路上j位置的驾驶工作负荷度;

基金项目:国家自然科学基金资助项目(61531005)。

$\left(\dfrac{\mathrm{LF}}{\mathrm{HF}}\right)_{ij}$——驾驶员 i 在道路上 j 位置的 HRV 值,HRV 指驾驶员心率变异性;LF 指心率变异性低频段 $(0.04 \sim 0.15\mathrm{Hz})$ 的功率,ms^2;HF 指心率变异性高频段 $(0.15 \sim 0.4\mathrm{Hz})$ 的功率,ms^2;

A_i——驾驶员 i 正常驾驶时 HRV 值,以驾驶过程中 HRV 值的众数为表征值;

V_{ij}——驾驶员 i 在道路上 j 位置的运行速度,m/s。

根据驾驶员在不同道路交通环境条件下产生的驾驶工作负荷度水平差异,得到驾驶工作负荷度分级阈值,分为高驾驶工作负荷度、较高驾驶工作负荷度、标准驾驶工作负荷度、较低驾驶工作负荷度和低驾驶工作负荷度等五级,不同驾驶工作负荷度阈值范围内驾驶安全舒适性等级见表1[20]。

驾驶工作负荷度和安全舒适性分类阈值　　　　　表1

驾驶工作负荷度种类	指标变化阈值	驾驶安全舒适性	量表陈述
高	$K > 0.060$	安全舒适性差	模糊、松懈,感觉无聊,开始丧失保持清醒的兴趣,驾驶操纵行为缓慢;对道路状况不能完全适应,驾驶操纵忙乱,十分紧张,担心
低	$K \leqslant -0.012$		
较高	$0.030 < K \leqslant 0.060$	安全舒适性较好	清醒、松弛,有响应,没有完全处于警觉状态,能够较低处理突发状况
较低	$-0.012 < K \leqslant -0.001$		
标准	$-0.001 < K \leqslant 0.030$	安全舒适性好	处于顶峰状态:感觉有活力、清醒、警觉、驾驶操纵自如、反应快速;处于非顶峰状态:能够集中注意力,有警觉,反应及时

通过现场试验,分析隧道影响区域驾驶员驾驶工作负荷度变化与隧道长度的相关性,并研究公路隧道的安全舒适性分类方法。

2　公路隧道驾驶试验方案设计

试验欲采集天气晴朗的白天,自由流交通下,驾驶员在不同长度公路隧道影响区域的驾驶工作负荷度指标及车辆的运行速度数据,研究驾驶员在公路隧道影响区域驾驶工作负荷度特征及变化规律。

2.1　试验隧道

为消除隧道的线形、照明、路面等因素对驾驶员安全舒适性的影响,选取隧道线形为直线段、路面平整坚实、视距良好满足《公路隧道设计规范　第一册　土建工程》(JTG 3370.1—2018)要求,公路隧道照明条件满足《公路隧道照明设计细则》(JTG/T D70/2-01—2014)要求的罗富高速公路、西汉高速公路和宝天高速公路隧道开展自然驾驶试验,试验隧道基本情况见表2。

试验隧道情况　　　　　表2

试验路段	运行速度(km/h)	车道数	隧道数量(座)	隧道长度范围(m)
罗富高速公路 K0+000~K49+647	60	单向两车道	10	237~902
西汉高速公路 K33+000~K118+000	60	单向两车道	52	54~6100
宝天高速公路 K1289+010~K1304+340	60	单向两车道	1	12330

2.2　试验车辆和驾驶员

根据最不利视认原则,选取试验路段上交通比例较高的典型小客车作为试验车辆,每辆车配备1名试验员记录驾驶员驾驶行为和路况条件;采用现场随机抽样方法选取身体健康、视力正常、驾驶技术熟练且休息良好、遵纪守法的驾驶员,不同试验路段及相应被试驾驶员数量见表3。

试验样本量　　　　　表3

试验路段	试验驾驶员样本量(个)	试验路段	试验驾驶员样本量(个)
罗富高速	6	宝天高速	6
西汉高速	6		

2.3 试验设备

2.3.1 动态眼动仪

iViewX 1.05 build 49 HED 型动态眼动仪如图 1 所示,用于动态记录试验过程中驾驶员前方的试验场景、驾驶员注视点分布位置,在后期数据处理过程中,剔除因超车、被超车和打电话等事件对驾驶员驾驶行为产生影响的异常数据。

2.3.2 动态生理检测仪

KF-2 型动态生理检测仪如图 2 所示,用于采集驾驶员驾驶过程中的心率、呼吸、体位(体动)以及体表温度等生心理信号。

图 1 iViewX 1.05 build 49 HED 型动态眼动仪

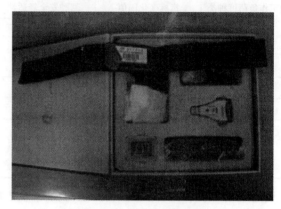

图 2 KF-2 型动态生理检测仪

图 3 非接触式多功能速度仪

2.3.3 非接触式多功能速度仪

CTM-8C 系列非接触式多功能速度仪如图 3 所示,用于采集汽车实时运行速度、行车距离等参数,真实反映车辆的行驶状态和驾驶员的驾驶行为。

2.4 试验方法

试验采用现场动态试验方法,采集不同隧道长度类型条件下驾驶员驾驶工作负荷度及车辆的运行速度数据,进行定量分析。首先校正试验设备时间为统一的北京时间,然后为驾驶员佩戴动态眼动仪、动态生理检测仪,分别采集被试驾驶员在行车过程中视野内道路场景、驾驶员生心理参数指标;在试验车辆上安装非接触式多功能速度仪,采集车辆的运行速度变化,最后被试驾驶员驾驶试验车辆依次通过试验隧道。试验过程中,随车试验员负责记录车辆行驶起终点时间、车辆驶过隧道入口和出口的时间、试验车沿途超车或被超车时间及在驾驶过程中的其他可能引起驾驶员生心理指标、车辆运行状态变化的异常行为。

3 不同长度公路隧道驾驶试验结果分析

将动态生理检测仪和非接触式多功能速度仪采集的数据按照时间进行匹配,通过对动态眼动仪采集的注视点信息和试验员记录的异常行为信息进行分析,剔除受非自由流及外界干扰事件影响的异常数据,对驾驶员驾驶工作负荷度进行统计、分析和归纳,最终得到小客车驾驶员驾驶工作负荷度有效试验数据 247 组。

3.1 驾驶员在不同类型隧道的驾驶安全舒适差异特性分析

对罗富高速公路、西汉高速公路和宝天高速公路试验路段的 6 名小客车驾驶员驾驶工作负荷度数据做均值处理,绘制驾驶员驾驶工作负荷度分布图,如图4所示。横坐标表示以隧道入口为基点,驾驶员距隧道入口的距离,纵轴表示驾驶员在某一隧道位置的驾驶工作负荷度。

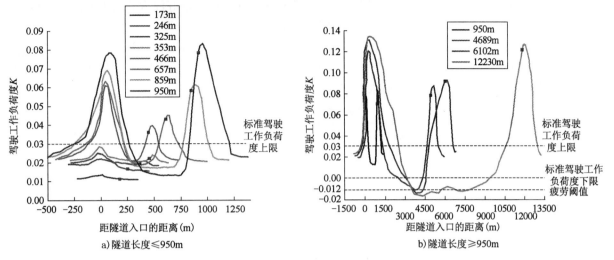

图4 试验路段驾驶员驾驶工作负荷度
注:横坐标零点表示隧道入口,■标注点表示隧道出口。

驾驶员在隧道运行影响区域行驶时,驾驶工作负荷度水平的差异主要受隧道运行环境条件的影响,进而表现为驾驶安全舒适性不同。从图4a)、b)曲线变化趋势可见:当隧道长度为173m、246m、325m和353m时,驾驶员驾驶通过公路隧道运行影响区域的驾驶工作负荷度保持在较低水平且趋于平稳,驾驶工作负荷度均一直处于标准驾驶工作负荷度范围($-0.001 < K \leq 0.030$);当隧道长度为466m、657m、859m、950m、4689m、6102m和12330m时,驾驶员从隧道外普通路段到隧道入口段驾驶工作负荷度明显增加,行驶到隧道中间段驾驶工作负荷降低且逐渐趋于稳定,直至行驶至出口段时驾驶工作负荷度又有明显升高,最后行驶到隧道外普通路段驾驶工作负荷降低至正常水平。驾驶员在隧道出入口段驾驶工作负荷度高于隧道外普通路段和隧道中间段,超出标准驾驶工作负荷度范围($-0.001 < K \leq 0.030$)。根据驾驶员在不同长度公路隧道的驾驶工作负荷度变化趋势,得出以下规律:①当隧道长度小于466m时,驾驶员驾驶工作负荷度较低且呈现平稳变化趋势;②当隧道长度大于466m时,驾驶员驾驶工作负荷度呈"高-低-高-低"大幅变化趋势。由此得出隧道长度大于一定值(466m)时,隧道长度是影响驾驶员在公路隧道运行影响区域驾驶安全舒适性变化的重要指标。

不同长度公路隧道的洞口处断面内外光环境、中间段的道路线形条件、标志的版面信息及设置位置、隧道出入口处标线和护栏设置的过渡方式不同,形成了具有差异性的公路隧道运行环境。当隧道长度较小时,隧道出入口段与隧道洞外普通路段的亮度差异小于一定范围,驾驶员受隧道"明暗"适应的影响不明显,隧道内光环境与隧道外光环境的差异对驾驶员安全视认能力无影响,标志标线设置方式较为简单,不受中间段运行环境的影响,驾驶工作负荷度较低且平稳变化,驾驶员的驾驶安全舒适性好。随着隧道长度的增加,隧道内外光环境明暗差异大,隧道洞口处急剧的光环境变化会使驾驶员产生视觉"明暗"适应问题,出现视觉滞后现象;标志和标线密集布置、信息繁多,驾驶员需要理解和接受的信息量增加,驾驶员难以在安全视觉需求时间内适应运行环境变化,增加了驾驶员视认困难和紧张程度,驾驶工作负荷度大幅变化,不利于驾驶员的驾驶安全舒适性。隧道长度越长,相对封闭、稳定、单调的隧道中间段距离越长,驾驶员若长时间在隧道中间段运行环境行驶,需要理解和接受的信息量少,会产生紧张、压抑、烦躁等不良的生心理反应,容易产生驾驶疲劳,不利于行车的安全舒适性。

当驾驶员驾驶工作负荷度低于标准驾驶工作负荷度且低于疲劳阈值($K = -0.012$)时,意识开始模糊、松懈,感觉无聊,开始丧失保持清醒的兴趣,驾驶操纵行为缓慢,即驾驶员开始产生驾驶疲劳,驾驶员的驾驶安全舒适性差。由图4知,驾驶员在长度为4689m、6102m和12330m的隧道驾驶时均出现驾驶疲劳。根据最小极限距离,假定驾驶员驾驶到隧道某一位置时产生疲劳,此位置距离隧道出口的距离恰好等于注视距离,则产生驾驶疲劳的隧道最小长度 L_0 等于驾驶员进入隧道产生疲劳的时间段内行驶距离 L_1 与驾驶员注视距离 L_2 之和。这是由于驾驶员产生驾驶疲劳和压抑时恰好注视到前方隧道出口的条件下,隧道出口的运行环境会对驾驶员生心理产生影响,驾驶工作负荷增加,驾驶员自身进行心理暗示,压抑和疲劳得到缓解。通过分析驾驶员在长度为12330m、运行速度为60km/h的隧道内驾驶时驾驶工作负荷度变化规律得到,驾驶员在隧道内产生了驾驶疲劳,从进入隧道开始至产生疲劳的时间由动态眼动仪和动态生理检测仪记录的数据耦合分析求得,见表4。

被试驾驶员疲劳时间 表4

被试驾驶员	驾驶员 i 从进入隧道开始至产生疲劳的时间 $t(s)$	被试驾驶员	驾驶员 i 从进入隧道开始至产生疲劳的时间 $t(s)$
1	211	5	223
2	221	6	226
3	230	平均值 $\bar{t}$	225
4	239		

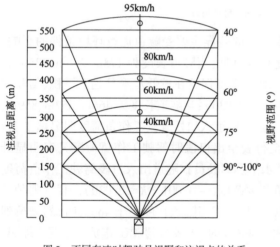

图5 不同车速时驾驶员视野和注视点的关系

将6名驾驶员在长度为12330m的隧道内产生驾驶疲劳时间的平均值 $\bar{t}$ 作为一般驾驶员在隧道内产生疲劳的表征值,即驾驶员在隧道内行驶到 $L_1 = 225 \times 60/3.6 = 3750(m)$ 处开始产生疲劳。根据不同车速驾驶员视野和注视点的关系,当运行速度为60km/h时,驾驶员注视点距离 L_2 约为300m,如图5所示。因此,驾驶员在隧道内驾驶产生驾驶疲劳的最小隧道长度 $L_0 = L_1 + L_2 = 4050m$。

3.2 基于驾驶安全舒适性的公路隧道分类

通过分析驾驶员在不同长度公路隧道驾驶工作负荷度变化规律,得到基于驾驶员安全舒适性的公路隧道类型划分阈值,见表5。

公路隧道划分阈值 表5

隧道运行速度(km/h)	隧道长度(m)	公路隧道类型
60	$L \leq 450$	短隧道
	$450 < L < 4000$	一般隧道
	$L \geq 4000$	长隧道

短隧道:隧道长度 $L \leq 450m$ 时,隧道运行环境对驾驶员驾驶安全舒适性无明显影响,驾驶工作负荷较低且平稳变化,驾驶安全舒适性好。

一般隧道:隧道长度 $450m < L < 4000m$ 时,驾驶员受隧道内外光环境的光源特性、中间段道路线形条件、标志标线、出入口段断面的变化影响,引起较大的生心理变化和认知活动的改变。驾驶员在隧道洞口处产生"明适应"或"暗适应",在驾驶过程中处理信息量过大会造成精神紧张,导致驾驶员对有效行车信息的视认能力降低,使其产生不舒适,行车不稳定,驾驶工作负荷增高。

长隧道:隧道长度 $L \geq 4000m$ 时,驾驶员不仅会在隧道洞口产生"明适应"和"暗适应",同时还会受到隧道内单调的线形、压抑枯燥的环境、标志标线设置不合理、汽车排放尾气和噪声的影响,导致紧张、焦虑和心理压抑,产生驾驶疲劳,驾驶工作负荷过低,驾驶工作效率降低,不利于驾驶员的稳定、舒适行车,增加交通运行风险。

4 结 语

基于驾驶工作负荷理论、量化方法和驾驶安全舒适性标准阈值,通过在公路隧道运行影响区域现场试验,研究驾驶员在不同长度公路隧道的驾驶工作负荷度变化规律,得到高速公路隧道安全舒适性分类标准及结论:

(1)当隧道长度小于466m时,驾驶员驾驶工作负荷度较低且平稳变化;当隧道长度大于466m时,驾驶工作负荷度呈"高－低－高－低"大幅变化趋势。

(2)当隧道长度大于466m时,驾驶员在4689m、6102m和12330m的隧道内驾驶时均出现驾驶疲劳,产生驾驶疲劳的最小隧道长度L_0为4050m。

(3)隧道长度是影响驾驶员驾驶工作负荷度变化的重要指标,通过运行速度为60km/h时的驾驶安全舒适性隧道分类阈值(450m和4000m),将公路隧道划分为长隧道$L \geq 4000m$、一般隧道$450m < L < 4000m$和短隧道$L \leq 450m$。

(4)当隧道运行速度为60km/h时,不同长度类型的公路隧道运行环境对驾驶员驾驶安全舒适性影响不同,短隧道的运行环境对驾驶员驾驶安全舒适性的影响程度最小,其次是一般隧道,长隧道最为严重。

本文是仅在高速公路隧道运行速度为60km/h时的分类研究,不同运行速度对隧道分类的影响可在本研究方法的基础上进行拓展研究。

参考文献

[1] 赖金星,张鹏,周慧,等. 高速公路隧道交通事故规律研究[J]. 隧道建设,2017,37(01):37-42.
[2] 李国辉. 美国隧道分类[J]. 消防科学与技术,2016,35(05):671.
[3] 徐文勤. 日本道路隧道的分类[J]. 隧道建设,1988(04):48-50.
[4] 中华人民共和国交通运输部. 公路工程技术标准:JTG B01—2014[S]. 北京:人民交通出版社股份有限公司,2014.
[5] 中华人民共和国交通运输部. 公路隧道设计规范 第一册 土建工程:JTG 3370.1—2018[S]. 北京:人民交通出版社股份有限公司,2018.
[6] 中华人民共和国交通运输部. 公路隧道设计规范 第二册 交通工程与附属设施:JTG D70/2—2014[S]. 北京:人民交通出版社股份有限公司,2014.
[7] 陈晓利,郭兴隆. 公路隧道运营管理分类方法研究[J]. 公路交通技术,2010(05):121-123,128.
[8] 王少飞. 公路隧道分类及公路隧道群概念探讨[J]. 公路隧道,2009(02):10-14.
[9] FENG Z X,YANG M M,KUMFER W,et al. Effect of Longitudinal Slope of Urban Underpass Tunnels on Drivers'heart Rate and Speed:A Study Based on a Real Vehicle Experiment[J]. Tunnelling and Underground Space Technology,2018,81:525-533.
[10] 闵建亮,蔡铭. 基于前额脑电多尺度小波对数能量熵的驾驶疲劳检测分析[J]. 中国公路学报,2020,33(06):182-189.
[11] 焦方通,杜志刚,王首硕,等. 城市水下特长隧道出入口视觉及舒适性研究[J]. 中国公路学报,2020,33(06):147-156.
[12] 胡宏宇,周晓宇,张慧珺,等. 考虑肌电信号的驾驶人弯道操纵行为分析[J]. 中国公路学报,2020,33(06):77-83.
[13] 郭梦竹,李世武. 基于驾驶员反应时间的驾驶疲劳量化[J]. 吉林大学学报(工学版),2020,50(03):951-955.
[14] 赵亮. 基于驾驶员心生理反应的双车道公路线形研究[D]. 北京:北京工业大学,2008.
[15] 杜志刚,潘晓东,杨轸,等. 高速公路隧道进出口视觉震荡与行车安全研究[J]. 中国公路学报,2007(05):101-105.

[16] 袁伟,郭应时,付锐,等.城市道路类型对驾驶人工作负荷的影响[J].长安大学学报(自然科学版),2014,34(05):95-100.
[17] 胡江碧.基于驾驶员驾驶工作负荷的路线安全评价理论与方法[D].北京:北京工业大学,2009.
[18] 胡江碧.事故多发地点形成机理及分析方法的研究[D].北京:北京工业大学,2004.
[19] 胡江碧,李安,龙伟峰.汽车驾驶员驾驶工作负荷计算方法:中国,200910093545.0[P].2010-04-07.
[20] 刘建蓓,郭忠印,胡江碧,等.公路路线设计安全性评价方法与标准[J].中国公路学报,2010,23(S1):28-35.

Accessibility of Integrated Transportation Systems Against Debris Flow Hazards

Junhao Jiang   Liu Hong

(School of Artificial Intelligence and Automation, Huazhong University of Science and Technology)

Abstract Transportation systems are the lifeline for the normal operation of society. They are sensitive to natural hazards (such as earthquake, flood, debris flow) because they are widely distributed and have passed many different, natural geographical units. It is essential to implement disaster management actions for transportation systems, such as pre-disaster investment, to mitigate the physical damages and socio-economic impacts on transportation systems. This paper proposes a framework to obtain the optimal pre-disaster investment strategies to improve the accessibility of the transportation system under debris flow hazards. The framework includes: (1) transportation system model which models the highway, railway and aviation systems as an integrated system because they mainly provide long distance traveling services for people; (2) natural disaster model which describes the physical and functional impact on road sections; (3) a two-stage stochastic optimization model to obtain the optimal accessibility enhancement strategy under cost constraints. This framework is applied to a case of debris flow hazards on the integrated system of the Southwest of China. The results can supply decision support for regional accessibility enhancement actions. Beyond the assessment and enhancement of the accessibility of integrated transportation system under debris flow hazards, the framework can be applied to other natural hazards (such as flooding, waterlogging) or other transportation systems (such as bus system, metro system).

Keywords Transportation systems   Debris flow   Accessibility   Pre-disaster investment

0 Introduction

The highway, railway and aviation systems, mainly provide long distance traveling services for people. In China, most people's travel choices are related to these three types of transportation. Based on this background, this paper regards these three systems as a whole, called integrated transportation systems. Integrated transportation systems are a key component of a nation's critical infrastructures. These systems are widely distributed and have passed many different, natural geographical units, so they are sensitive to natural disasters, such as earthquake(Kiremidjian et al., 2007), flood(Wang et al., 2019) and hurricane(Ma et al., 2013). Among these disasters, rainstorms and consequent secondary disasters (including landslide, debris flow, flooding) are the main threatens to the transportation systems(Liang et al., 2017). Especially, debris flow is the most significant geological disaster due to its characteristics of sudden outbreak, great destructiveness, and periodic impact on transportation infrastructures near disaster-prone points(Masiro et al., 2017). There are more than 6000 typical debris flow gullies along highway of China(Cui et al., 2004), and the direct economic loss of Chinese roads caused by debris flows is more than billions of yuan per year. Hence, the problem of how to reduce the impact of debris flow on traffic system is attracting more and more attention(Lam et al., 2018).

Some researches study the transportation systems' vulnerability under debris flow hazards. Most of these work discuss how the debris flow damage the transportation infrastructures(component level), others focus on system functionality decreasing under debris flows(system level)(Fell et al., 2005). The component level work mainly studies the vulnerability or fragility of various infrastructure components under debris flow disaster, the components' fragility is usually represented by fragility curve or fragility matrix. The methods can be divided into three categories: (1) Judgemental/heuristic methods, (2) Data-driven methods, (3) Analytical/physical model-based methods. Considering that the physical destruction of components will extend to all areas and activities related to it in the system(Merz et al., 2010), more and more scholars are studying how to describe and quantify the impact of disasters on transportation network. Various metrics, such as realistic network flows, travel time and accessibility, are chosen to measure the systematic vulnerability. Among these metrics, accessibility is most frequently used to evaluate the performance of transportation system. Postance et al. (2017) used a network model to simulate realistic network flow and define network flow as accessibility, coupled with landslide susceptibility data to calculate system vulnerability in terms of total travel time delay. Utasse et al. (2016)proposed a best travel time model of accessibility to calculate functional vulnerability of roads in the French Alps.

These studies involve different debris flow models and transportation system models, and they are related through the fragility curve. Debris flow hazards models in the literature emphasize different perspectives of the disaster. From the perspective of the natural process, some models describe the whole process of debris flow from the beginning to the deposition. Others focus on the correlation between rainfall and debris flow, and use probability to express the uncertainty. Varne et al. (1984)defined a debris flow hazard as "the probability of a potentially destructive phenomenon occurring within a specific time and a specific area.", time occurrence of debris flow be divided into heuristic methods(Wong et al., 2005), rational methods(Haneberg et al., 2004), empirical probability(Crovelli et al., 2000) and indirect approaches(Guzzetti et al., 2008). The use of the model depends on the scope of the study area and the input data.

To model the transportation network, a few literature use traffic models to simulate realistic network flows (Dotoli et al., 2005, Sullivan et al., 2010). This method is computationally complex and has data requirements. Some other literature use network-based methods to represent transportation networks with graphs and adjacency matrices (Ferber et al., 2009). This method models a transportation system through the definition of nodes and edges. To study the coupling of different kinds of transportation systems, scholars have introduced the concept of interdependent edge. Therefore, different types of transportation system can be modeled by network-based model, such as train and air systems, bus and subway systems.

The above researches significantly improve people's understanding on how debris flows affect transportation systems, but there are still some problems that have not been fully explored. First, most of the related literature only consider the impact of debris flow on a single transportation system(Meyer et al., 2015, Postance et al., 2017). Second, most of the related literature discuss this problem on urban scale or sit-specific scale, there are few studies on regional or national scale.

This paper considers the integrated transport networks including road, railway and aviation systems, and models them using network-based method. Then the susceptibility map is used to obtain the probability of damage to the large-scale transportation system under debris flow. Finally, the improved Dijkstra algorithm is applied to calculate the accessibility and a two-stage stochastic model is proposed to obtain the accessibility optimal set of preparedness actions.

1 Model Description

This section first introduces the modeling of integrated transportation system and then describes the debris flow susceptibility map to relate it with integrated transportation system. Finally, the calculation method of the accessibility to evaluate the performance of the integrated transportation system against debris flow hazards is introduced.

1.1 Network-based Description of Integrated Transportation System

This paper uses a network-based method to represent integrated transportation networks. An integrated system, composed of highway systems, railway systems and aviation systems can be modeled by a network $G = \{G_{road}, G_{train}, G_{air}, G_{integrated}\}$, where three subsets $G_{road/train/air}$ represents the corresponding subsystem with node set V and are set E. For each node in the study area, node in road network is a virtual point representing the center coordinates of a city. Train node and aviation node represent train station and airport, respectively. If two nodes are connected by road, train, air or they are in the same city, there is an arc e between them. Fig. 1 is a depiction of the integrated transportation system network. Nodes in different sub-networks but interconnected are in the same city, such as city A (inside the green ellipse). For a given nodes pair, which are yellow nodes in figure, the shortest path in the figure is given by the red arrow. Based on network model, shortest travel routes can be obtained using graph algorithms. This paper focuses on the time-based minimum travel time between cities via the integrated transportation system. The main algorithm to calculate the minimum travel time is based on Dijkstra algorithm.

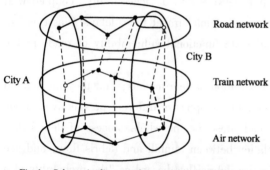

Fig. 1 Schematic diagram of a trip from city A from city B via the integrated transportation system

The road network data for this paper comes from PUGDP (see Web-1). For each road, this paper assumes the speed that across the road is 80 km/h. Railway and airline timetables are crawled using python (see Web-2 and Web-3). After data processing, we obtained an integrated transportation network with 68 road nodes, 126 rail nodes and 44 air nodes.

1.2 Debris Flow Susceptibility and Road Network Fragility

In China, fatal landslides are most often distributed in the southwest region. This paper chooses southwest region (Yunnan, Sichuan, Xizang, Guizhou and Chongqing) in China as the study area to analyze the susceptibility of debris flow.

The historical data of debris flow used in this paper comes from the RESDC (see Web-4). There are 11260 recorded debris flow events in the Southwest region. The watershed data used in this paper is based on a research of Xu et al. (2004). This data divides the study area into 97 catchment areas. Combined with the spatial distribution of debris flow historical data, each catchment area is divided into 5 debris flow susceptibility levels (within a year) and using probability to quantify it. The result is shown in Fig. 2. It can be seen that the susceptibility level is clearly higher in areas with large mountain ranges, due to the fact that debris flow is more likely to form in such areas.

We use risk to describe the impact of debris flow on links. Risk can be defined as $R = H \times V$. Here H stands for the probability of debris flow, in Section 2.2, we describe the calculation of H. V, vulnerability (or fragility), indicating the expected loss caused by disasters. In this paper, for simplifying the calculation, the fragility is set as a unified value. With this method, we can obtain R, the probability that each road was damaged by debris flow.

In section 2.2, the study area is divided into 97 catchment areas with 5 debris flow susceptibility levels. The fragility of roads is uniformly set to 0.5. It represents the resistance of the road to debris flow, depending on factors such as material strength. After calculating the probability of damage for all roads, the results are shown in Fig. 3. Although studies have shown that debris flows can damage railroads (Totscnig et al., 2011), the physical distribution of railroads in the study area is characterized by an overall sparse, high density within a small area, which is not in a debris flow prone area. Therefore, the impact of debris flows on railroads is not considered in this paper.

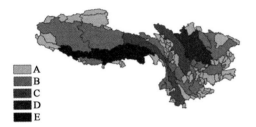

Fig. 2 A debris flow susceptibility map of SW region

Fig. 3 A map of southwest region showing the road segments which are susceptible to debris flow

1.3 Accessibility Metric

In this paper, travel time is selected as the accessibility metric because it is easy to understand and can feasibly be generated at large scales. Travel time based accessibility (TTA) TTA_{od}^t from node O in city a to node D in city b at departure time t is calculated as section 2.2. If there is no path between O and D, $\text{TTA}_{od}^t = M$, where M is a large value. For a node a at the departure time t, the accessibility is calculated as follows:

$$\text{TTA}_a^t = \sum_{b \neq a} q_{ab} \cdot \text{TTA}_{ab}^t \tag{1}$$

where q_{ab} is the weighted coefficient for the trip from node a to node b. In this paper, q_{ab} is set as a unified value. We think that the assumption is reasonable because big cities usually have more nodes. The accessibility of all OD pairs at departure time t via integrated transportation system is quantified as follows:

$$\text{TTA}^t = \sum_{i \in V} \text{TTA}_i^t \tag{2}$$

Since the schedule of trains and airplanes takes 24 hours as the cycle, we define the integral of TTA^t within 24 hours as the accessibility of the integrated transportation system.

2 Mathematical Model

In this section, we formulate the pre-disaster investment program as a two-stage stochastic program, and then we give the algorithm for solving the problem.

2.1 Two-stage Stochastic Program

To obtain the optimal investment strategy for accessibility, this paper formulates the problem as a two-stage stochastic program. In order not to lose the generality, we give a general description of the model. We are given a network $G = \{G_{\text{road}}, G_{\text{train}}, G_{\text{air}}, G_{\text{integrated}}\}$, it can also be expressed as $G = \{V, E\}$. Let $p_e (0 < p_e < 1)$ be the damage probability of link e, it can change to q_e by preparedness actions with a cost c_e. Since it is unrealistic to strengthen all links, a budget B is given here. We use a binary variable y_e to indicate whether to strengthen the link e. After the occurrence of a debris flow, each link has two states: operational, non-operational. This uncertainty is usually reflected in probability, that is, the set of all possible situations $\tilde{\xi}$ after the disaster is fixed, but the occurrence probability of each situation p_ξ is different. For each possible situation ξ, calculate the minimum travel time for a given OD pair. If there is no path connecting O to D, a fixed penalty cost M is incurred.

The two-stage stochastic program P is given as follow:

First stage:

$$Z = \min_y E_{\tilde{\xi}|y}[F(\xi)] \tag{3}$$

subject to:

$$y_e = 0 \text{ or } 1 \quad \forall e \in E \tag{4}$$

$$\sum_e c_e y_e \leq B \quad \forall e \in E \tag{5}$$

Second stage:

$$F(\xi) = \min \int_0^t \sum_{i \in V} \sum_{b \neq a} \text{TTA}_{ab}^t(\xi) dt \tag{6}$$

subject to:

$$t_k^1 = t \quad \forall k \in K_W \tag{7}$$

$$t_k^i > t_k^{i-1} \quad \forall i \subset k, k \in K_W \tag{8}$$

$$t_k^i = \begin{cases} t_k^{\text{iend}} + 1440 \cdot \left(\left| \dfrac{t_k^{i-1}}{1440} \right| \right) & \text{if } i, i-1 \in V_{\text{air}}, V_{\text{train}} \\ t_k^{i-1} + t_k^e & \text{if } i \notin V_{\text{air}}, V_{\text{train}} \text{ or } i-1 \notin V_{\text{air}}, V_{\text{train}} \\ t_k & \text{if } i+1 \notin k \end{cases} \quad \forall i \in k, k \in K_W \tag{9}$$

$$\text{TTA}_{ab}^t \geq (t_k - t_d) \quad \forall k \in K_W, w \in W \tag{10}$$

where $F(\xi)$ is the second stage objective function, and it is the minimum accessibility between OD pairs. If there is no path between OD pairs, $F(\xi) = M$. The first stage, gives a strengthen strategy y. In second stage, there is a set K_W to store set of shortest path k connecting OD pair W. For every $k \in K_W$, it presents a unit flow from O to D in the network. t_k^i describe the arrive time along route k. For a given situation ξ, second stage calculate the optimal accessibility of the integrated transportation system.

However, this problem is difficult to solve because: (1) there are many options for retrofit strategy w, it grows exponentially with the changes of the system scale; (2) for a given retrofit strategy w, there are 2^E possible component damage scenarios, and their probability distribution varies with w; (3) the model includes integer variables.

2.2 Solution Algorithm

This paper aims to select a set of damage scenarios to represent all damage scenarios for a given retrofit strategy y, with less scenarios than Monte Carlo simulation. The method uses the optimization model introduced by Brown et al. (2011). To generate a finite number of component damage scenarios and their occurrence probability that make the error between each component's estimated brittleness based on these finite component damage scenarios and its "true" brittleness. The sum of the differences is minimized, as demonstrated in detail by Brown. This method can be divided to 2 steps. In the first step, this method first randomly generates a large number of damage scenarios by Monte Carlo simulation. In the second step, this method chooses a set of damage scenarios with a predefined size L to minimize the error, in this paper L is set as 160.

This method can reduce the difficulty of solving the model effectively. Based on this method, this paper proposes a genetic algorithm to solve the model. The process of the genetic algorithm is shown in Fig. 4.

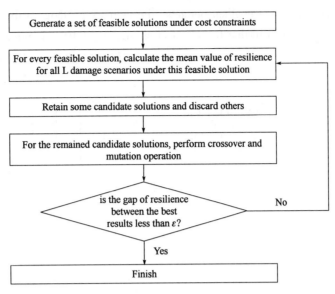

Fig. 4 The process of the genetic algorithm

In this paper, the number of generations NGA is set as 20 and the number of populations pop is set as 100, the crossover probability is 0.6 and the mutation probability is 0.001.

3 Case Study

Applying southwest region as the study area, we compare the accessibility difference between strengthened and not strengthened strategies after debris flow. For the convenience of display, we take the reciprocal of accessibility and normalize it. As shown in Fig. 5, result shows that for the integrated transportation networks, the strengthen measures can increase the accessibility of transportation system. And the increase range is 40% ~ 60%, especially in the period of 6:00 to 18:00 in the daytime, which is the time when most people travel. This result implies that the strengthen for road network can effectively enhance the accessibility of the integrated transportation system.

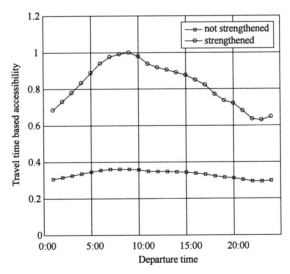

Fig. 5 The accessibility difference between strengthened and not strengthened strategies

Since it is unrealistic tostreng then all links, a budget B is given to calculate the optimal strategy of accessibility. All strengthen costs c_e are set a uniform value here. We explore the impact of different budget on the optimal strategy and the corresponding accessibility. The result is normalized and shown as Fig. 6a). We study the accessibility under different strengthen budgets, the increase of budget will lead to the improvement of accessibility. It can be found in Fig. 6b) that the effect of strengthen of 10% is remarkable, while the effect of strengthen of 20% ~ 80% is not so remarkable. If we want 80% accessibility after debris flow, strengthening the 90% edge will be a better choice.

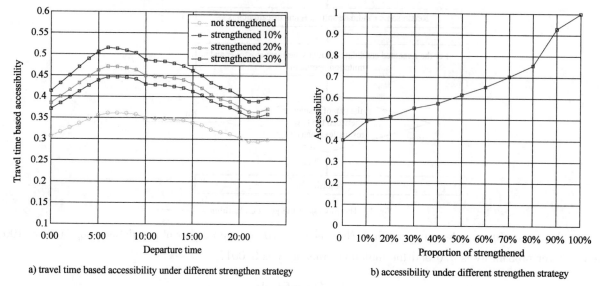

a) travel time based accessibility under different strengthen strategy

b) accessibility under different strengthen strategy

Fig. 6

The impact of city size and distance between cities on travel time is shown in Fig. 7. Fig. 7a) is two travel time curves from Chengdu to Kunming. The red one is travel time via road networks, and the blue one is travel time via integrated transportation system, obviously, the timeliness of integrated transportation system is better than that of road network. Another conclusion is that even if we randomly destroy 90% of the edges in the road network, the blue curve will not be affected. This is because the train network and air network between big cities provide a good complementary for the road network. For two big cities with close geographical location, such as Chengdu and Chongqing, the result is shown as Fig. 7b), the destruction of the road network only affects the travel time from 0:00 to 7:00. For small cities, the results are quite different, we choose travel time from Meishan to Anshun, it can be seen in Fig. 7c) that there is a difference in travel time when 20% of the road network is damaged randomly. When 60% of the road network is damaged, the two cities are hardly connected.

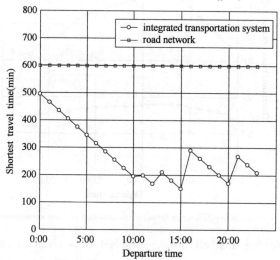

a) travel time from Chengdu to Kunming via integrated transportation system and road network

Fig. 7

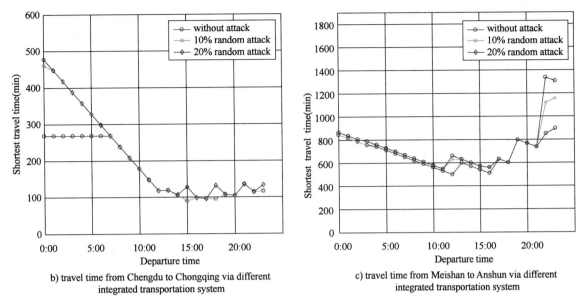

b) travel time from Chengdu to Chongqing via different integrated transportation system

c) travel time from Meishan to Anshun via different integrated transportation system

Fig. 7

4 Conclusion

This paper proposes a general framework to strengthen the accessibility of the integrated transportation system under debris flow hazards. Based on the network-based model, an improved shortest path algorithm can be used to calculate the minimum travel time. After combining the debris flow model with the fragility of the road to obtain the probability of road damage, this paper proposes a two-stage stochastic programming model to select an optimum set of edges for investment to minimize the expected accessibility with the consideration of limited budget. To solve this model, this paper uses a limited component damage scenarios based method, and then proposes a genetic algorithm that integrate with this method. Then the numerical analyses of SW region in China show that strengthen for road network can effectively enhance the accessibility of the integrated transportation system. Considering the budget constraint, when making strengthen decision, the cost and corresponding effect should be considered comprehensively. Only consider the accessibility between two cities, the scale of cities and the distance between them will affect the accessibility.

Compared with the previous research of accessibility of transportation against debris flow, this paper chooses the integrated transportation system of large scale area as the research object. In reality, when the highway is interrupted by debris flow, people can choose other transportation mode, such as air or rail as an alternative way. And the long-distance transportation systems always are distributed in large-scale areas. This paper analyzes the accessibility of large-scale areas under debris flow, provide reference for future research on regional accessibility.

There are still some limitations in this paper. First, this paper assumes that after the road network is damaged, the traveler immediately knows this information and adjusts the shortest path. The impact of road condition information on system accessibility can be the direction of future work. Second, this paper uses a data-driven approach to divide the study area for debris flow susceptibility and assumes consistent fragility of road segments. In future, more accurate debris flow models and fragility curves will make the framework more complete. Finally, this paper does not consider the problem of post disaster recovery, how to increase the resilience of transportation systems is another direction for future research.

References

[1] Brown N J. Optimizing the Selection of Scenarios for Loss Estimation in Transportation Networks[J].

Sandia National Lab. (SNL-NM), Albuquerque, NM(United States).

[2] Crovelli R A. Probabilistic models for estimation of number and cost of landslides. Open file report 00-249. US Geological Survey, Reston, 2000, 23.

[3] Cui P. Debris flow disaster and disaster mitigation countermeasures in western mountainous traffic[J]. Journal of Mountain Science, 2004, 3: 326-331.

[4] Dotoli. Validation of an Urban Traffic Network Model using Colored Timed Petri Nets[J]. IEEE International Conference on Systems, 2005.

[5] Fell R. A framework for landslide risk assessment and management[C] in Landslide risk management, London, 2005, 3-26.

[6] Ferber C V. Public transport networks: empirical analysis and modeling[J]. The European Physical Journal B, 2009, 68(2): 261-275.

[7] Guzzetti F. The rainfall intensity-duration control of shallow landslides and debris flows: an update[J]. Landslides, 2008, 5: 3-17.

[8] Haneberg W C. A rational probabilistic method for spatially distributed landslide hazard assessment[J]. Environ Eng Geosci, 2004, 10: 27-43.

[9] Kiremidjian A. Seismic Risk Assessment of Transportation Network Systems[J]. Journal of Earthquake Engineering, 2007, 11(3): 371-382.

[10] Lam J C. Stress tests for a road network using fragility functions and functional capacity loss functions [J]. Reliability Engineering & System Safety, 2018, 173: 78-93.

[11] Liang Pa, Ding Y. The Long-term Variation of Extreme Heavy Precipitation and Its Link to Urbanization Effects in Shanghai during 1916-2014[J]. Advances in Atmospheric Sciences, 2017.

[12] Ma S. Strong Hurricane Risk Assessment and Zoning Methods of High-Speed Rail[J]. Transportation Standardization, 2013, 06: 94-96.

[13] Marchi L. Characterisation of selected extreme flash floods in Europe and implications for flood risk management[J]. Journal of Hydrology, 2010, 394(1): 118-133.

[14] Masiro L, Maggi R. Estimation of indirect cost and evaluation of protective measures for infrastructure vulnerability: A case study on the transalpine transport corridor[J]. Transport Policy, 2012, 20: 13-21.

[15] Merz B. Assessment of economic flood damage[J]. Natural Hazards & Earth System Science, 2010, 10 (8): 1697-1724.

[16] Meyer N K. Roads at risk: traffic detours from debris flows in southern Norway[J]. Natural Hazards and Earth System Sciences, 2015, 15(5): 985-995.

[17] Postance B. Extending natural hazard impacts: an assessment of landslide disruptions on a national road transportation network[J]. Environmental Research Letters, 2017, 12(1). 14010-14010.

[18] Sullivan J L. Identifying critical road segments and measuring system-wide robustness in transportation networks with isolating links: A link-based capacity-reduction approach[J]. Transportation Research Part A Policy & Practice, 2010, 44(5): 323-336.

[19] Totscnig R. A quantitative vulnerability function for fluvial sediment transport[J]. Natural Hazards, 2011, 58(2): 681-703.

[20] Utasse M. Territorial Accessibility and Decision-Making Structure Related to Debris Flow Impacts on Roads in the French Alps[J]. International Journal of Disaster Risk Science, 2016, 7(2): 186-197.

[21] Varnes D J. Landslide Hazard Zonation: a Review of Principles and Practice[J]. Natural Hazards, 1984, 3.

[22] Wang W. Local floods induce large-scale abrupt failures of road networks[J]. Nature Communications,

2019,10(1).
[23] Wong H. Landslide risk assessment for individual facilities-state of the art report[A]. In Proceedings of the International Conference on Landslide Risk Management[C]. London, 2013, 237-296.
[24] Xu X. Automated extraction of drain ages in China based on dem in gis environment[J]. Resources and Environment in the Yangtze Basin, 2004,13: 343-348.